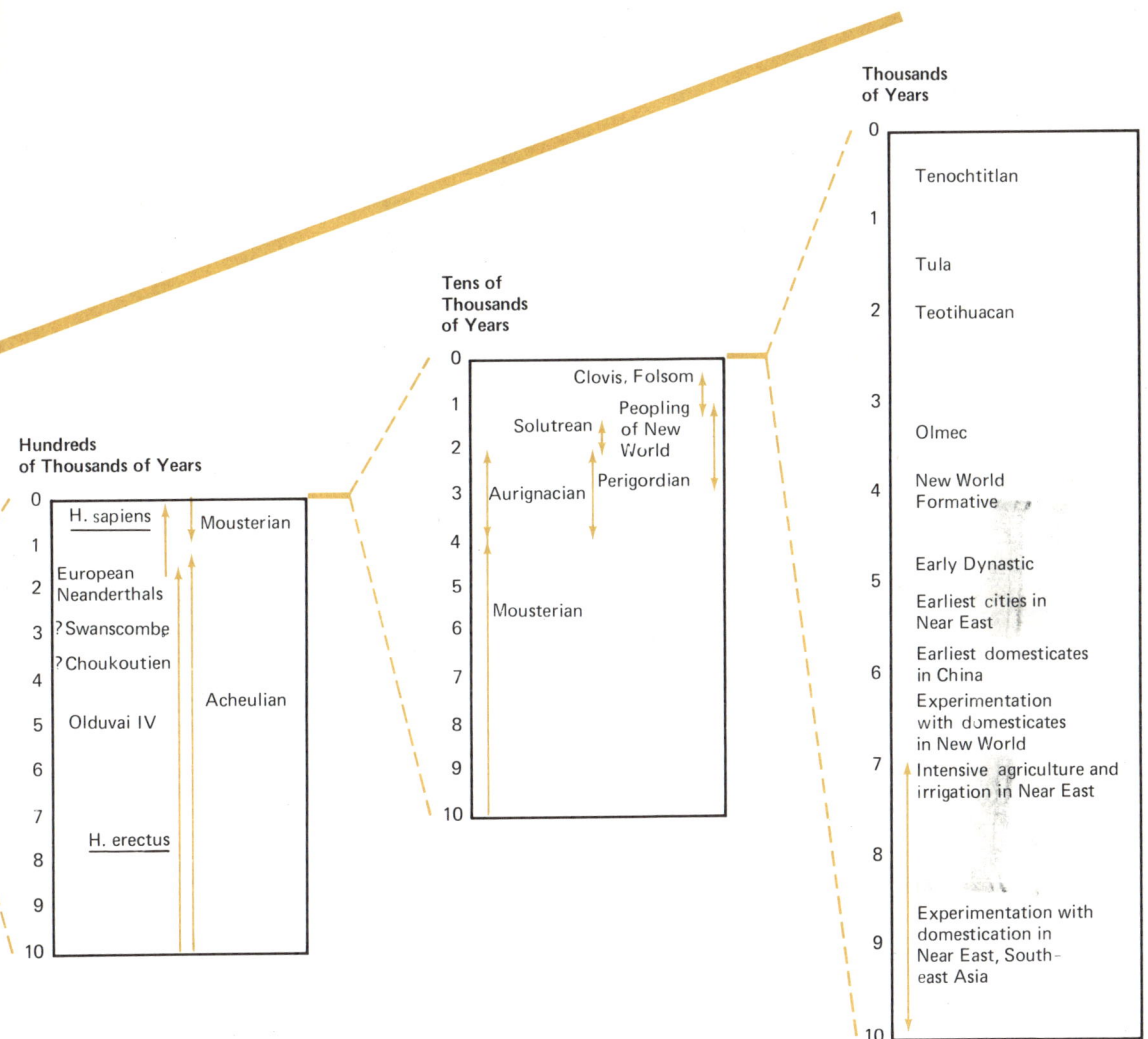

If the entire history of earth were compressed into a single year, the appearance of human life would occur at 8:00 P.M. on New Year's Eve. (Baur, 1975:29)

Anthropology

Fred Plog
Arizona State University

Clifford J. Jolly
New York University

Daniel G. Bates
Hunter College
University of the City of New York

Anthropology
Decisions, Adaptation, and Evolution

ALFRED A. KNOPF   New York

First Edition

9 8 7 6 5 4 3 2 1

Copyright © 1976 by Alfred A. Knopf, Inc.

All rights reserved under International and Pan-American Copyright Conventions. No part of this book may be reproduced in any form or by any means, electronic or mechanical, including photocopying, without permission in writing from the publisher. All inquiries should be addressed to Alfred A. Knopf, Inc., 201 East 50th Street, New York, N.Y. 10022. Published in the United States by Alfred A. Knopf, Inc., New York, and simultaneously in Canada by Random House of Canada Limited, Toronto.
Distributed by Random House, Inc., New York.

Library of Congress Cataloging in Publication Data

Plog, Fred.
   Anthropology: decisions, adaptation, and evolution.

   Bibliography: p.
   Includes index.
   1. Anthropology. I. Jolly, Clifford J., 1939– joint author. II. Bates, Daniel, G., joint author. III. Title.
GN25.P47   301.2   75-43825
ISBN 0-394-31893-5

Manufactured in the United States of America

Cover and text design: James M. Wall

Photo Research: Frances Orkin and Lynn Goldberg

Line art: Biruta Akerbergs

Charts and graphs/maps: Vantage Art Inc.

Endpaper map: Jean Paul Tremblay

Photo credits for cover: *(desert)* George Holton/Photo Researchers; *(bowl)* Leningrad, Hermitage/Metropolitan Museum of Art; *(girls)* Victor Engelbert/Photo Researchers; *(primate)* Pierre Dupont/Jacana.

Photo credits for part openers: (3) George Rodger/Magnum; (19) The American Museum of Natural History; (189) George Rodger/Magnum; (245) Werner Bischof/Magnum; (481) Marc Riboud/Magnum

ACKNOWLEDGMENTS:
P. 48: Figure, (a) modified from F. A. Jenkins, ed., *Primate Locomotion.* Reprinted by permission of Academic Press, Inc.; (b) courtesy of Animal Talent Scouts, Inc. from a photograph by Ralph Morse, *Life Magazine,* © Time, Inc.; (c) modified from J. R. Napier and A. C. Walker, "Vertical Clinging and Leaping: A Newly Recognized Category of Locomotor Behavior Among Primates," *Folia Primatologica* 6 (1967). Permission granted by S. Karger AG, Basel; (d) modified from M. Hildebrand, "Symmetrical Gaits of Primates," *American Journal of Physical Anthropology* 26 (1968). Permission granted by The Wistar Press. P. 70: Figure, (a) from I. Tattersall, *Man's Ancestors: An Introduction to Primate and Human Evolution,* Transatlantic Arts, Inc. Permission granted by the author; (b) from W. K. Gregory, "On the Structure and Relations of *Northarctus,* an American Eocene Primate," *American Museum of Natural History Memoirs* (1920). Reprinted by permission of the American Museum of Natural History. P. 115: Figure,
(continued on page 588)

Contents

1 introduction   2

one   Decisions, Adaptation, and Evolution   5
The Anthropological Perspective   5
Humans as Biological and Cultural Beings   7
Subdisciplines of Anthropology   10

2 human physical and cultural evolution   18

two   The Processes and Patterns of Evolution   21
Genes and the Individual   21
Genes in Populations   23
The Major Patterns of Evolution   26
Unraveling Evolutionary Relationships   32

three   The Living Primates   39
Primate Realms and Habitats   39
Themes of Primate Adaptation   42
Primate Diversity   43
Primate Adaptations   47

four   Primate Evolution   65
The Fossil Record   65
Mesozoic Mammals and Primate Adaptations   69
Paleocene Primates   70
The New Primates of the Eocene: The First Prosimians   71
Oligocene Primates: The Anthropoid Transition   71
Miocene Primates   72
The Earliest Undoubted Hominids   74

five   The Emergence of Cultural Essentials   87
The Emergence of Toolmaking Traditions   88
The Emergence of the Division of Labor   94
The Emergence of Specialized Behavior Patterns   98
Trends in Evolution   103

six   The Emergence of Cultural Diversity   107
The Advanced Hunters of Europe   107
The Advanced Hunters of the New World   114
Mesolithic and Archaic Stages   120
Trends in Evolution   123

seven The Emergence of Food Production — 127
- The Origins of Agriculture: Speculation and Theory — 128
- Changes in Plants and Animals — 129
- Adaptive Value of Agriculture — 133
- The Adoption of Agriculture — 134
- Agricultural Technologies — 143
- Trends in Sociocultural Organization — 145

eight The Emergence of the State and Urban Society — 151
- Civilization, City, and State — 151
- Why Did the State Evolve? — 153
- State Formation in the New and Old Worlds — 157
- Trends in Evolution — 165

nine Physical Variation in Modern Homo Sapiens — 169
- Interpreting Patterns of Human Variation — 169
- Variation in Blood Proteins — 170
- More Complex Characters — 177
- Human Variation and the Concept of Race — 181

3 studying contemporary peoples — 188

ten History of Anthropological Theory — 191
- Why Do Societies Differ? — 191
- How Do Societies Differ? — 198
- What Is the Relationship Between the Individual and Society? — 202

eleven Methods of Cultural Anthropology — 211
- Preparing for the Field — 211
- Field Techniques — 212
- Being in the Field — 221
- Interpreting the Data — 225

twelve Ethics of Cultural Anthropology — 233
- The Issues — 234
- The Anthropologist Between Two Governments — 237
- A Code of Ethics — 240
- Four Positions — 241

4 cultural diversity and adaptive strategies — 244

thirteen Language and Communication — 247
- Animal Communication — 247
- Animal vs. Human Communication: Similarities and Differences — 250
- The Evolution of Language — 253
- Language and Physiology — 256
- Language and Culture — 257
- The Evolution of Communications Media — 261

fourteen	**Linguistic Variation**	**267**
	Variations in the Structure of Language	268
	Variations in Meaning and Linguistic Classification	273
	The Nature of Linguistic Variation	274
	Linguistic Variation and Change	276
	The Ecology of Language	280
fifteen	**Culture and the Individual**	**287**
	The Influence of Biology on Human Behavior	287
	The Influence of Culture and Social Learning on Behavior	290
	The Influence of Situations on Human Behavior	301
	The End Product: People as Decision Makers and Manipulators	304
sixteen	**Resources, Environment, and Procurement Strategies**	**309**
	Obtaining Resources: Variations in Procurement Systems	309
	Procurement Systems and Adaptation to Environmental Conditions	317
	Major Procurement Patterns	323
	The Evolution of Procurement Patterns	325
seventeen	**Economics: Ownership, Production, Distribution, and Exchange**	**329**
	Regulating Access to Resources	329
	Production	333
	Economic Equality and Inequality: The Final Distribution of Products	338
	Exchanging Resources and Products	343
	Economic Experimentation and Change	346
eighteen	**Social Structure and Social Behavior**	**351**
	Networks, Groups, and Social Categories	351
	Kinship and Kin-Based Groups	354
	Age and Age-Based Groups	371
	Sex and Sex-Based Groups	372
	Ethnicity and Ethnic Groups	374
nineteen	**Marriage, Families, and the Organization of Domestic Groups**	**379**
	Marriage	380
	Families	391
	Domestic Groups	394
twenty	**Religious Belief and Ritual**	**399**
	Defining Religion	399
	Variations in Religious Belief Systems	400
	Variation in Religious Ritual	402
	The Organization of Religion	405
	Evolution of Religious Practices	407
	Adaptive Aspects of Religious Belief and Ritual	408

twenty-one	**Politics: Power, Authority, and Conflict**	**419**
	The Nature of Political Processes	419
	Variations in Political Organization	424
	The Evolution of Political Organization	430
	Political Relations Between Societies	432
twenty-two	**Social Conflict and Social Control**	**439**
	Rules, Deviance, and Social Control	439
	Informal Means of Social Control	441
	Formal Means of Social Control	446
twenty-three	**Culture Change and Applied Anthropology**	**457**
	What Is Change?	457
	Studying Culture Change	458
	Patterns of General Evolution	461
	Specific Evolution	465
	Culture Change and Adaptation	468
	Problems Caused by Change in Today's World	472
	Applied Anthropology	474

5 adaptive patterns   480

twenty-four	**Hunters and Gatherers**	**483**
	The Hunting and Gathering Adaptation	483
	The !Kung Bushmen	485
	The Eskimo	491
	The Miskito	496
twenty-five	**Horticulturalists**	**501**
	Horticultural Adaptations	501
	The Yanomamö	503
	The Tsembaga	508
	The Pueblo Indians	513
twenty-six	**Pastoralists**	**521**
	The Pastoralist Adaptation	521
	The Karimojong	525
	The Yörük of Southeastern Turkey	529
	The Navajo	533
twenty-seven	**Intensive Agriculturalists**	**539**
	Agricultural Intensification	539
	Two Chinese Villages	542
	Oaxaca Valley	546
	The Rise of Islam	550
twenty-eight	**Industrialism in a Global Society**	**557**
	Agro-Industry: The Second Agricultural Revolution	560
	Beyond Industrialism	566

twenty-nine	**Humans in Evolutionary Perspective**	**575**
	The New Synthesis	575
	The Concept of the Ecosystem	576
	Success in Evolution	578
	Culture as Learned Behavior	580
	Persistence as Success	581
glossary		589
references		607
index		623

Preface

Our object in this book is to introduce the study of general anthropology to students with little previous background in the subject. This is an important time in the development of anthropology. The last ten years have seen many changes in theory and practice in all of the subfields of the discipline. While these changes are often regarded as brand new and highly innovative, in fact most "new" developments in anthropology have pasts much longer than a single decade. Our current understanding of the human species has grown out of the findings and insights of previous generations of researchers. This book attempts to bring together the best of the "old" and the "new" in anthropology—to combine some of the ideas anthropologists have developed over the long history of their discipline with some of the ideas that are currently in the forefront of anthropological research. We wish to provide the student with a knowledge of what our discipline can and does contribute to the scientific understanding of people. In doing so, we hope that we will also convey some of the excitement and controversy that are part of the ongoing, developing science of anthropology.

Part I of the book surveys some of the most important perspectives, concepts, and goals of anthropology. It also presents the major themes—decisions, adaptations, and evolution—which serve to unify this text. In Part II, we focus on the human past, emphasizing that human biological and cultural evolution are not separate threads in our history, but inextricably interwoven aspects of ongoing processes. Part III turns to the study of contemporary peoples and to anthropology as a field of scientific inquiry. Here we explore the history of anthropological theory, the research methods anthropologists use, and the important question of ethics in anthropological research. Part IV discusses cultural diversity and adaptive strategies while focusing on the many topic areas of anthropology—language, economics, kinship and marriage, religion, politics, and culture change. Finally, in Part V, we look at the adaptive patterns of societies as wholes, taking up some of the problems faced by different hunting and gathering, horticultural, pastoral, intensive agricultural, and industrial societies. The book concludes with a chapter on humans in evolutionary perspective.

While all the authors commented on and contributed to one another's work, each had major responsibility for certain chapters. Part I, the archeological material in Part II, and Parts III and IV, are primarily the work of Fred Plog; the physical anthropology in Part II, the work of Clifford Jolly; and Part V, the work of Daniel Bates.

Producing a clear, readable text that does not gloss over up-to-date research and advanced ideas is a difficult undertaking, requiring the collective efforts of a team of professionals—writers, editors, reviewers, and illustrators—all of whom invested more time in this book than would normally be the case. In particular, we would like to credit our editors, Virginia Hoitsma, Mary Schieck, and Helen Litton, who directed and coordinated the entire project. Ann Levine, Carol Doerflinger, and Karen Reixach all contributed to the text's clear and readable style. Biruta Akerbergs provided drawings that reflect both the structure and beauty of her subjects. Our sincere thanks are due to colleagues who read and commented on various parts of the text: Edward Bendix, Francis Conant, Glenn Conray, Robert Eckhart, John Fischer, Brian Foster, Daniel Gross, Neville Dyson-Hudson, Susan Lees, Michael Little, June Nash, Burton Pasternak,

David Pilbeam, Charles Redman, Michael Rose, Abe Rosman, Eugene Sterud, Stephen Straight, Fred Szalay, and Charles Weitz. We are especially grateful to Philip Salzman for his contribution at an early stage of the project. Graduate students Ronald Anzalone, David Brooks, Bruce Donaldson, Margie Green, Bruce Harley, John Knoerl, Lucy Lavin, Frank McManamon, Judy Rasson, Michael Rothman, Lisa Slater Spotnitz, and Walter Wait provided valuable assistance. Catherine Anzalone deserves special thanks for her extensive help in developing Chapters 13 and 14 on anthropological linguistics, and for her thorough criticism of the various drafts of this material.

F. P. *Tempe, Arizona*
C. J. *New York City, N.Y.*
D. B. *New York City, N.Y.*

Anthropology

1 introduction

one
Decisions, Adaptation, and Evolution

When the pioneers of anthropology embarked for the South Seas and other exotic places, the world was not the "global village" it is today. By the middle of the nineteenth century, only a few Europeans had penetrated the heart of the "dark continent," as Africa was then called. Indian tribes still held vast stretches of the American West, resisting the expansion of white settlers. The barren arctic, home of the Eskimo, had yet to be fully explored by Europeans. And virtually nothing systematic was known about the peoples who inhabited the jungles of South America or the wilds of New Guinea. Nevertheless, scattered reports from missionaries, explorers, and traders suggested amazing diversity in the ways people throughout the world lived—the customs they practiced as well as the values and beliefs they held.

It was in such a world that the earliest anthropologists began to travel to remote parts of the earth, collecting firsthand information on the human populations that lived there. Their efforts were inspired by a desire to learn more about the fascinating species, *Homo sapiens*, to which they themselves belonged. Over the years, succeeding generations of anthropologists systematically accumulated an enormous amount of data on human diversity. Some have explored the biological variations in contemporary human populations, from body build and structure to blood types and internal chemical processes, while others have searched the earth for fossil clues to our origin and evolution as a species. Still others have also probed the past, but their primary concern is not with human biological evolution but with the evolution of human ways of life—that is, the study of now-extinct cultures, how they developed, and the light they can shed on our understanding of cultural variation today. And finally, some anthropologists have turned their attention to the thoughts and behaviors of contemporary peoples, their modes of communication, their belief systems, their ways of viewing the world, the great diversity of customs they practice. Thus the goal of anthropology is indeed ambitious: no less than the comprehensive and scientific study of humankind in all its diversity.

The Anthropological Perspective

What is to be gained from an approach so broad in scope? In a world increasingly dominated by specialists, isn't a discipline as comprehensive as anthropology anachronistic? The answer is that it is anthropology's very breadth that places it in a unique position to contribute to our understanding of humankind. Anthropology is concerned with all peoples everywhere, both those alive today and those who lived in the remote past. And it is concerned with every aspect of human ways of life, from people's physiological makeup to the tools, customs, or cosmologies they have devised. The anthropological perspective, then, is *holistic;* its very goal is to cross some of the boundaries that other disciplines concerned with particular aspects of humanity have helped to create.

Every society, past or present, offers a unique way of looking at the world and of adapting to its environment. Through an understanding of why people in different societies behave as they do, we can enrich our understanding of ourselves. (Cornell Capa/Magnum)

The Holistic Viewpoint

By focusing on humankind in all its diversity, anthropologists are able to break down some of the academic walls that separate, for example, the study of human biology from the study of human social behavior, or that divide the social sciences into distinct disciplines such as sociology, psychology, political science, or history. Although such a division of labor is absolutely necessary if researchers are to obtain in-depth understandings of diverse aspects of human life, specialization also has its dangers. Foremost among these is a tendency to view a particular problem or issue from a narrow range of vision and in the process to overlook inadvertently some of the many influences at work. This can be seen in the study of the present environmental crises. Biologists are concerned with the effects of environmental change on all the many plant and animal species that make up an ecosystem. Political scientists take a different view, emphasizing the political processes surrounding the initial development of an environmental crisis, as well as the political processes involved in any current effort to combat it. Thus we have diverse perspectives, offered by diverse disciplines. Yet we realize today that it is impossible to really understand the problem of environmental degradation without considering every aspect of it and how these aspects interrelate. This is one of the important goals of anthropology: to integrate diverse perspectives on humankind through the holistic point of view.

Cultural Relativism

By focusing its attention as broadly as it does, anthropology makes another important contribution to the study of human life: it makes us aware that to take patterns of human behavior out of context, labeling one "modern" and another "backward," one "good," and another "bad," is to have only a very limited perspective. If anthropology has taught us anything, it is that we have much to learn from any human society, no matter how technologically simple or complex. We have learned, for example, that the Bushmen of the Kalahari Desert obtain a good, nutritious diet with only a few hours of work a day, while we live in a society where deaths occur from the stresses related to overwork. We have learned that the elderly in many societies are highly respected for their experience and are often accorded roles of authority, while many older people in our own society lead lonely and isolated lives. We have also learned that complex political systems, such as the Ashanti kingdom, flourished in Africa long before white men arrived on the continent, while some of our children's history texts still suggest that Europeans brought civilization to the "dark continent." And the more we learn, the more we see that it is impossible to gain a full perspective on humankind without examining societies other than our own.

The tendency to evaluate other peoples' customs in terms of one's own conceptions is universal. We are all *ethnocentric* (culturally self-centered) to some degree. However, in studying anthropology we discover that we share numerous problems with both living and extinct societies that at first glance appear quite different from our own. Some have devised better solutions to these problems than we have; others have tried solutions that failed completely. The point is that we are not alone. We can learn a great deal about ourselves from the study of other cultures — if we develop an appreciation of human diversity. *Cultural relativism* (an openness to cultural variety) is perhaps the most important humanistic "message" of anthropology.

Cultural relativism involves learning not to judge other peoples' customs without first seeking to understand why they behave differently than we do. For example, by our standards, infanticide is cruel and unnatural. It is difficult to imagine a society in which people consider it acceptable for someone to kill or neglect a newborn baby. However, if we examine those societies in which infanticide is practiced, we find that many people are often faced with a very difficult choice: allowing a newborn infant to die, or watching both the newborn and its older brother or sister grow weak and sick from hunger. The only way a small child can obtain enough protein is by nursing, and a woman cannot nurse two children at once. In advocating cultural relativism, anthropologists are not suggesting that we can or even should condone everything people in other societies do. But we should be aware that there is customary behavior in our own society that other peoples would find deplorable. For example, although we have strong sanctions against the practice of infanticide, we are frequently complacent when faced with persistent malnutrition in large segments of our population. Thus if we jump to moral conclusions about any society's customs, we deny ourselves the opportunity to understand why they behave as they do. In this way, the humanistic message of anthropology greatly contributes to the discipline's central scientific objective — understanding human behavior.

Humans as Biological and Cultural Beings

All science is an effort to describe and explain certain natural or social phenomena. The aim of the discipline of anthropology is to describe and explain the nature of a particular part of the world, the human species. Like other social scientists, anthropologists are concerned with people, the varied ways in which they organize and carry out their lives, and how they came to be what they are today. But anthropologists approach this question from the holistic viewpoint, which encompasses humans as both biological organisms and cultural beings. Psychologists, sociologists, political scientists, economists, and historians, in contrast, tend to emphasize the distinctiveness of human beings, to *oppose* man and nature. All study relations among human beings and human groups, but most stop short of investigating the relations between humans and other species. This is where anthropology begins: with the place of the human species in nature and its relations to the rest of the living world.

Our Place in Nature

When viewed as biological organisms, humans are part of nature, not separate from it, and kin to everything that lives. We are related to frogs and snails, dogs, parrots, goats, rhinoceroses, monkeys, and chimpanzees — not just in a metaphorical sense, but in the sense that two siblings are related through common parents. Ultimately, all living things are descended from minute organisms that lived billions of years ago in a world we would not recognize. Although we are kin to all living things, we are more closely related to some species than to others. In terms of molecular structure, anatomy, development, and behavior, humans have more in common with a chimpanzee (our nearest living relative) than a monkey, a monkey than a dog, a dog than a frog, a frog than a bacterium.

Like any species, we humans have certain physical and behavioral peculiarities that set us apart from the rest of the animal kingdom. We walk upright on two feet, use our hands extensively for grasping and manipulating objects, live in social groups, fashion and use many kinds of tools to aid us in survival, are capable of learning abstract theories and complex ideas, and have developed language, a complex form of symbolic communication. Yet most of these characteristics, when broadly interpreted, are not ours exclusively. We are not the only animal that walks on two feet (consider the birds) or uses its hands (all apes and monkeys do). We are not the only creature that lives in societies (insects, for example, have evolved complex forms of social organization). Like humans, chimpanzees, baboons, even sea otters and some birds use natural objects as tools. Nor are we the only species that is capable of learning and transmitting behaviors to new generations. Researchers have observed macaque monkeys inventing new ways to prepare food and then teaching these innovations to other members of their bands. Recent experiments suggest that chimpanzees may have a rudimentary capacity for using symbols and thus an undeveloped potential for language. However, humans are the only species that *depends* on language, learning, tools, and flexible forms of social organization—the only species for which culture is the essence of survival.

Humans as Creators and Creations of Culture

Much of anthropological inquiry focuses on the diversity of human customs and practices that are collectively called culture. Economic and political systems, sexual restrictions, marriage customs, and family organization, the ways in which groups and organizations of every kind are formed, a society's religious beliefs, its folk tales, art, and mythology are all cultural creations. It is the extent to which they have developed culture that sets the human species apart from all others. To the anthropologist, people everywhere have culture in that all have customary ways of thinking and of dealing with the world around them. Yet specific cultural patterns vary widely from society to society.

It is through their culture that people learn to attach meaning to particular behaviors. Consequently, identical behavior can be interpreted in very different ways in different cultures. For example, in any society a man might have more than one wife. If he lives in a society with a cultural preference for this practice (known as polygyny), he may well be one of the most respected members of the community and the envy of other men with only one wife. If, on the other hand, monogamy is the cultural rule, a man with more than one wife would be labeled a bigamist and ostracized or even jailed if the fact were discovered. By the same token, very different behaviors can be interpreted in the same way in different cultures. When a small child continually cries, for example, verbally comforting him, beating him, ignoring him, or even masturbating him are all considered appropriate responses in different cultures. Culture, therefore, enables the members of a society to interpret and give meaning to human actions.

Anthropologists have come to regard culture as a key concept in understanding human similarities and differences. Although the meanings people read into their activities and creations vary, the process of ordering the world in meaningful patterns and configurations is universal. People everywhere depend on culture—on the system of shared meanings they learn from their society to use in interacting with their surroundings, communicating with others, and coping with their world. Let us look, in more detail, at what anthropologists mean by culture.

Culture Is Learned No other animal is as dependent on learning as humans are. Although all animals have some capacity to learn, and learning is important to the survival of members of most species, human behavior is based to an enormous extent on learning rather than instinct. In a sense, human beings are born incomplete. We require years of "coaching," as well as adequate nutrition, to reach maturity. Who does the coaching and how it is done have a decisive influence on who we become. An American child transplanted into a Chinese family at an early age will grow up thinking and acting like a person born in China, whereas a puppy raised among cats will grow up barking and wagging its tail, not meowing and purring. We inherit the *capacity* for culture biologically, and all human populations have an equal capacity for cultural development. But we do not inherit genes for speaking English (as opposed to French), eating three times a day (as opposed to once), adopting a particular religion or political ideology, or believing a person should only have one spouse at a time. We learn these skills, habits, and attitudes in the course of growing up.

The term *socialization* refers to this process of acquiring culturally appropriate patterns of behavior through interaction with adults and peers. To a substantial degree, childhood training makes conformity to our society's ideas of appropriate behavior seem "only natural"; most people grow up wanting to do what they are expected to do. Of course, socialization is never perfect in the sense that each new generation is a carbon copy of the last. But the universal experience of being dependent on adults who have the power to give or withhold sensitizes most people to social pressure to think and act in approved ways. Ceremonies, formal training, public and private confrontations, gossip and praise can all act to reinforce childhood socialization.

Culture Is Transmitted via Symbols Language is basic to the transmission of culture from generation to generation, person to person. And it is one of the things that sets humans apart from other species. Of course, animals communicate with all kinds of cries, calls, gestures, and chemical emissions. But when a bird screeches "danger," it is responding reflexively to the immediate situation with a genetically predetermined sound. The meaning of the sound is fixed, and its use is limited. Animals do not combine calls in new ways to communicate complex data, novel perceptions, or abstract ideas, as do humans. This is because human language, unlike forms of animal communication, is symbolic. Words are arbitrary representations of ideas, things, and activities. They are invented symbols, and as such are highly flexible. Language enables people to communicate what they *would* do if such and such happened, to categorize their surroundings and order their experiences, and to express thoughts never spoken before. Thus we have developed customary solutions to persistent problems, created economic, political, and social systems—we have become cultural animals.

Culture Is Differentially Shared Culture establishes a common ground of understandings, a set of shared notions about how the world is ordered and how people ought, ideally, to behave. We know without asking, for example, that the proper way to greet an acquaintance is to smile and say hello or to shake hands, not to buffet him on the head or shoulders, stroke him affectionately, or scratch his palm, although these are all appropriate greetings in other societies. Similarly, we also know without asking that most of our neighbors will attribute a thunderstorm to meteorological activities, not to a fight among the gods, angry ancestors, or a rain ceremony performed the night before. Shared understandings give human relations order and a degree of predictability. In general terms, we know how people will act in a given situation and what they expect from us.

Of course, there is cultural variation within as well as between societies—that is to say, culture is differentially shared within every human group. Membership in different ethnic, professional, or age categories, for example, gives people a particular slant on life. This is not to say that Christians and Jews, construction workers and physicians, teenagers and people over forty constitute separate and distinct "tribes." But the numerous situations in which members of these different classifications of people interact and cooperate enable them to exchange information, attitudes, strategies for coping, even ways of dressing and talking. To some extent, therefore, they come to view the world in a particular way. For example, if we asked young and middle-aged people to rate their attitudes toward premarital sex on a scale of 1 (for strongly approve) to 10 (for strongly disapprove), we would probably find young people clustered at one end of the scale, middle-aged people at the other. But we would also find a number of middle-aged people who sided with the young, and young people whose attitudes were like those of the middle-aged, and many people between the two extremes. Thus when we speak of the "youth culture" we are not describing a watertight compartment into which all young people fit, but a *tendency* among the young to see things in certain ways and act on those perceptions.

Culture as a Tool There is some debate within anthropology about the degree to which the culture in which people are raised influences the ways they think and act. Much of the older anthropological literature describes culture as a set of rules for behavior that individuals obey more or less automatically, like puppets on a string. From this point of view, culture becomes an independent, self-perpetuating force that serves to maintain stability, continuity, and conformity. People are simply culture's unwitting servants.

Today, however, most anthropologists agree that this is a gross overstatement of the influence of culture on human behavior. We know that people everywhere have ideas about what is appropriate to do in a given situation, but they do not always act accordingly. And when we look at the ways in which people break the rules they espouse, an interesting pattern emerges. Most of us "sin" in more or less the same way that our neighbors sin: we deviate in packs. A simple example of this is speeding. When the legal limit is 50 mph, most people drive at about 60 or 65 mph, not 45 or 80 mph. Perhaps even more revealing, most of us consider people who obey rules to the letter deviants. The rigid bureaucrat who plods through every inch of red tape, refusing to cut corners, is highly exasperating to everyone who must deal with him. People glare at drivers who delay everyone else by driving at the legal speed. Many of us are a little surprised when we hear of individuals who refuse to pad their income tax deductions a little. And although few Americans would openly condone lying, all would agree that there are many social circumstances in which telling the complete truth would be offensive. This is true in all societies. People everywhere establish rules for acceptable behavior, and then proceed to break the rules in more or less regular ways. The question is why.

Most individuals have a need to feel good or proper. Why else would we go to such lengths explaining and attempting to justify our actions? Culture provides definitions of the "good," blessed by age and tradition, for people to fall back on, and to provide continuity with the past. But survival depends on being able to cope, to solve problems in the immediate environment and *adapt* to changing circumstances. And adaptation depends on smartness not propriety, "ingenuity not piety, . . . resourcefulness, not goodness" (Freilich, 1971:286). People spend much of their time looking for a "smart" solution to their problems. Having found one, they invariably begin to argue that the "smart" is also "good"; the expedient, proper.

In rationalizing what at first seemed a questionable way of solving a problem, people are actively *manufacturing* culture. This is why we say culture is a tool. It is a system of meanings people create by modifying and rearranging strategies they inherit from the past to solve immediate problems they encounter in interacting with the environment and with people of their own and other groups. Like all other tools, particular cultural practices can be altered or discarded when they begin to lose their usefulness. But although culture is the creation of people, to some extent people are also the creations of culture. Our behavior in many ways is guided by the cultural norms we are taught and come to accept as our ideals. This paradox—that humans create culture, yet in some sense are created by culture—underlies all anthropological inquiry.

Subdisciplines of Anthropology

Although all anthropologists are engaged in the study of human beings, the discipline as a whole is generally divided into physical anthropology (the study of the evolution of *Homo sapiens* and of physical variations in contemporary human populations), archeology (the study of now-extinct cultures and the processes of cultural evolution), cultural anthropology (the study of variations in contemporary human cultures or in cultures of the recent past), and anthropological linguistics (the study of how the many languages human beings speak are structured and how they have developed historically). With the rapidly increasing accumulation of anthropological knowledge, some kind of specialization and division of labor is essential for research purposes. No longer is it possible for a single person to master all of the many areas with which the discipline is concerned. But in many ways, viewing anthropology in terms of the four traditional subfields creates artificial separations. Much of the most interesting recent research in anthropology is occurring when the former boundaries of the subdisciplines are crossed. Therefore, a more meaningful way of looking at the anthropological division of labor is to focus on some of the tasks with which anthropologists in general are concerned. In the following sections, we will consider three: describing similarities and differences among people, understanding biological and cultural evolution, and attempting to explain cultural diversity.

Describing Human Similarities and Differences

The description of human similarities and differences begins with the human organism, the human species as part of the animal kingdom. This job falls to physical anthropologists, who are essentially biologists specializing in the human species (and whose training and methods are therefore rather different from those of other anthropologists). These anthropologists study both the mechanism of biological inheritance (genetics) and resulting biological variations among human populations. In the early part of this century, physical anthropologists (like many other scientists and nonscientists) were primarily concerned with defining races and analyzing the differences among them in terms of observable characteristics, such as skin color, hair texture, eye shape, body build, and so on. But this attempt ultimately proved futile. For the majority of biological characteristics, variations within "races" were found to be as great or greater than those between them, making it impossible to draw lines between one race and another. Today, physical anthropologists describe biological variation in terms of slight and gradual differences in specific characteristics between human populations. The popular term "race" refers to a social rather than a biological phenomenon, and most physical anthropologists are content to leave the subject to socio-cultural anthropologists. Contemporary physical anthropologists concerned with biological variation search for the *adaptive* significance of such variations (for example, of differences in the capacity to adjust to climates, susceptibility to diseases, and the like).

Ethnography (which means, literally, writing about people) is the branch of cultural anthropology that focuses on describing variations in behavior patterns and the meanings people ascribe to their experiences and activities. Ethnographers collect data on personality development; the strategies different groups employ to satisfy their material needs (technology); economic behavior (the distribution of goods and services); social organization (including different ways of reckoning kinship, contracting marriage, and organizing families); political behavior (customary patterns for making decisions that affect the community, settling disputes, and relating to outside groups); and religious, magical, and scientific strategies for explaining the world around them. Ethnographers collect such data firsthand, through participant observation and related techniques. For many who study nonindustrial societies, this has amounted to a race against time, because such groups are fast disappearing. However, in recent years ethnographers have begun to apply their curiosity to the industrial world and to urban communities.

Describing the diverse cultures of extinct societies, most of which left no written records, is one of the archeologist's goals. Because there is no direct evidence of prehistoric lifeways and much of what past societies left behind is buried in the earth, this requires painstaking training and labor. An archeologist must learn to locate sites; to recognize the broken remains of artifacts and clues as to the date, climate, environment, diet, and the like; to dig without destroying evidence; to piece together what he or she finds; to discover and interpret patterns. All this requires a special combination of scientific precision and imagination—as well as frequent consultation with geologists, ecologists, and other specialists.

Anthropological linguists concerned with describing human languages do not simply compile dictionaries of previously unwritten

Careers for Anthropology Majors

Many students taking an introductory course in anthropology will consider majoring in the field, but some will hesitate because they do not know what they can "do" with a BA in anthropology. For what careers does an undergraduate degree in anthropology help to prepare a person? In the past, some professors of anthropology would have been inclined to answer, not many. Granted, a BA has always been the first step toward an advanced degree (MA or PhD) which qualifies a person for research, teaching, or museum positions. But a BA alone is not a professional certificate; it does not establish a person as an anthropologist.

Today, however, it is widely recognized that traditional jobs for those with advanced degrees in anthropology are becoming more and more limited relative to the number of qualified candidates. In response to this situation, the American Anthropological Association has begun to study the kinds of positions available for persons holding undergraduate degrees in the field. H. Russell Bernard and Willis E. Sibley (1975) have prepared a booklet entitled "Jobs and Anthropology" which summarizes some of the occupations relevant to people with backgrounds in anthropology. Particularly relevant are jobs requiring an understanding of cultural and subcultural differences. Take, for example, positions in local agencies that provide counseling services to deal with such problems as mental illness, alcoholism, drug addiction, child abuse, or aging. The ability to understand the cultural bases of these and other social problems is an important skill that students of anthropology can offer. For somewhat similar reasons, training in anthropology is also useful for careers in such areas of business as advertising, market research, public relations, sales, and personnel management. Many positions in these fields are open to people with BA degrees only and no other special training.

The opportunites for those with advanced degrees in anthropology are becoming more diversified. A variety of new laws have created jobs for anthropologists to evaluate the impact and effectiveness of federal government programs on past and contemporary cultural resources. Also, there are job opportunities for qualified people in the area of applied anthropological work. Organizations such as the Agency for International Development, for example, employ anthropologists with special expertise in social and economic modernization. These are careers that anthropology majors who have decided to continue their educations may well want to consider.

languages, although this is part of their work. "Descriptive linguistics" involves the systematic study of the ways people combine sounds into words, and words into meaningful statements. It is also concerned with the ways people use words to categorize their experiences and order their social relations, as well as with the ways speech varies depending upon the social and situational context. Given the importance of language to the transmission of culture, this knowledge is essential to anthropological inquiry. Little more than ethnographers' assistants in the early days, linguists now constitute a coequal branch of anthropology.

Understanding Biological and Cultural Evolution

Physical anthropologists carry on the search for human origins in two ways: first, by collecting and analyzing fossils of prehumans and early humans; and second, by studying the structure, movements, and adaptations of our closest living relatives, the primates. "Comparative morphology" enables physical anthropologists to interpret fossilized teeth, fragmentary skulls, jaws, and limb bones, which in most cases are all the evidence we have.

Archeologists use the remains of extinct societies to reconstruct prehistory—that is, to describe the major events that took place before people began keeping written records of their activities. Much as physical anthropologists interpret fossils by reference to living species, archeologists interpret the remains of past societies by reference to contemporary societies. By analyzing clues to population, settlement patterns, subsistence strategies, technology, and so on, archeologists attempt to identify the periods during which early human groups began to diversify and specialize in their activities, to produce (rather than hunt and gather) food, to build cities — "events" that shaped cultural evolution.

One of the events in human history that was key to the evolution of people's capacity for culture was the development of language. For this reason, anthropological linguists are interested in the origins of language—how our complex, symbolic form of communication had its beginnings. In addition, anthropological linguists are concerned with the development of the many different languages spoken today. Tracing the history of languages back to long-forgotten ancestral tongues is a well-developed scientific technique. Linguists identify families of languages (those that share a common ancestral tongue) by analyzing cognates, or words that are so similar they suggest a single prototype. The number of cognates describing climate, plants, animals, and the like in a family of languages provide clues to the place a language originated and the migrations of people who spoke the ancient tongue—thus supplementing the data archeologists gather.

Cultural anthropologists who specialize in ethnohistory piece together the more recent past of groups that do not keep written records. This involves analyzing official records and documents; reading explorers' and missionaries' journals; collecting oral histories, myths, and folk tales; and interviewing people who remember the "old days" and their parents' and grandparents' stories.

Explaining Cultural Diversity

All science is concerned not only with description but also with explanation. Anthropologists agree that the attempt to ultimately explain human diversity is the central goal of their discipline. But especially in the area of cultural anthropology, there is substantial disagreement about what those explanations are. In Chapter 10, we will discuss some of the theories cultural anthropologists have developed in an effort to explain why societies differ. At this point, however, we want to describe the position taken in this book.

Our approach to understanding cultural diversity focuses on ecology (the study of people's adaptation to their natural and social environment) and evolution. Interestingly, the concept of evolution—that change reflects a continuing process of adaptation to the environment—originated in the humanities and social sciences, not in the physical sciences with Charles Darwin's *The Origin of Species*, as many people believe. The poet Goethe; social philosopher Herbert Spencer (whose phrase "the survival of the fittest" Darwin borrowed); indeed, Darwin's grandfather, Erasmus Darwin, a physician and man of letters who speculated about evolution in verse—all were preoccupied with this notion. But it was Charles Darwin who demonstrated how the mechanism of natural selection operated as a cause of evolutionary change, carefully documenting his ideas with data he had collected in his years on the *HMS Beagle* and some twenty years wandering the British countryside.

Darwin observed that all species of plants and animals produce more offspring than the environment can support, leading to intense competition for living space, resources, and mates. Only a favored few survive to reproduce. In addition, Darwin noted that individual members of species vary in ways that may enhance or diminish their chances of winning the struggle for survival. Whether these variations prove advantageous or disadvantageous depends on the environment. Those individuals whose deviations give them a competitive edge in a particular environment produce more offspring, offspring that inherit the parent's deviation and in turn survive longer and produce more offspring. The "advantaged" branch of a population increases at the expense of less favored individuals, so that in time the species as a whole becomes better adapted to the environment. Adaptation to different environments (when part of a population migrates) and to changes in the environment explains the emergence of new and distinct species and the great variety we find in nature. This is the essence of Darwin's theory of natural selection. "The process is similar to a game in which a population is one player and the environment another. The organisms produce variation and the natural environment selects (favors) certain moves [variations] over others" (Alland and McCay, 1973:171).

What Darwin could not explain was how "favored" individuals passed advantageous characteristics on to their offspring. The answer was supplied by an obscure Augustinian monk, Gregor Mendel, whose pioneering experiments in genetics were rediscovered at the turn of the century—posthumously saving Darwin from his critics in the scientific community.

But genetic deviations and the transmission of *biological* advantages do not directly explain patterns of *cultural* evolution and the diversity of lifeways among human groups. For this reason, nineteenth-century anthropologists attempted to create a separate but parallel theory of cultural evolution based on progress from simple to complex social institutions. However, these early theorists failed to appreciate behavioral variability, and assumed that all societies passed more or less uniformly through the same evolutionary stages. They did not understand that because human beings, like all life forms, have an overriding urge toward survival, we respond by changing our behavior in opportunistic, not simply in progressive, ways. Thus, the early cultural evolutionists and their immediate successors tended to ignore the role that environment plays as a source of selective pressure acting on behavioral and cultural diversity—or in some cases to overstress environmental factors in deterministic theories that ignored the extent to which human beings alter and interact with their environments. Consequently, the effort to explain cultural change and diversity in the evolutionary terms of variation and selection was largely abandoned for a time. But by the middle of this century, American anthropologists increasingly came to believe that evolutionary models were central to understanding cultural variability, change, and regularities of behavior. And in recent years, cultural anthropologists and archeologists have begun to focus explicitly on variation *within* cultures.

Differences in biological endowment, skills, personality, desire to conform, and so on, and the search for "smart" solutions to problems produce variety in all human groups. Those variations that prove adaptive are translated into the "good" and passed on to new generations through learning. Those that do not are abandoned (or the groups who adopt or cling to unsuccessful strategies fall into marginal positions or extinction). The environment acts to stimulate as well as limit change, creating situations to which people must adapt and setting limits to possible solutions.

Alexander Alland and Bonnie McCay (1973) have related the natural selection of cultural traits to operant conditioning (based on B. F. Skinner's theory of learning). Using techniques of operant conditioning, an experimenter allows an organism (usually a laboratory animal) to explore its environment at will, in random moves. When, by chance, it performs the act the experimenter wants to encourage (for example, pressing a bar), it receives a reward (usually food). By rewarding the animal each time it happens to do what the experimenter wants, the desired behavior pattern can be gradually strengthened. Alland and McCay suggest that feedback (rewards) from the environment shapes human behavior in much the same way that conditioning shapes animal behavior. "In [cultural] evolution the environment plays the role of experimenter shaping the responses of the organism" (pp. 171–172)—with one qualification: human beings are capable of thinking about environmental problems and of evolving theories which enable them to modify their environment to a far greater extent than other animal species. However, in culture as in biology, evolution involves setbacks as well as progress, overspecialization and extinction as well as the emergence of successful, better adapted groups and lifeways. To the extent that people cannot foresee the long-term effects of changing their behavior, innovations are random events and the environment is restored to the role of "natural selector."

The return to an evolutionary view of social change in the last decade or two has brought ecology to the forefront of anthropological inquiry. The emphasis in most current research is on the place (or econiche) different human groups occupy in their natural and social environment, their use of resources, and their relations with competitors.

In this text we seek to expand the evolutionary and ecological approach to anthropology. Most evolutionary and ecological theories of cultural diversity have focused on the material aspects of life, to the exclusion of all else. As a result, anthropologists studying political and religious ideologies, kinship systems, and so on have often found the ecological approach, when narrowly defined, inadequate. However, we will attempt to show that religious and political beliefs and practices and even kinship systems are as much a factor in human adaptations as are subsistence strategies and economic practices.

Second, many anthropologists assume that evolutionary theories of cultural diversity contradict other theories of social organization or stability. We believe that studies of change and stability are only incompatible if (1) theories of stability ignore the contradictions and dynamics inherent in all organizations, and (2) evolutionary theories focus only on major patterns of long-term change and not on the short-term variations and fluctuations that produce them.

Finally, evolutionary theories tend to focus on large social aggregates, thereby contributing to a sharp distinction between the individual and society. We will attempt to show that the ways in which individuals (acting alone and in groups of varying size and membership) use culture is essential to both stability and change. When we take both smart and the proper behavior into account, the dichotomy between individual actions and social patterns as well as between stability and change begins to evaporate.

In short, while our approach is essentially an evolutionary and ecological one, we feel that much of the material anthropologists have excluded from this perspective may now be incorporated. Thus, *decisions* arrived at by individuals, the *adaptive strategies* of people and societies, and the *evolutionary processes* of which these are a part are central topics on which we will focus throughout this book.

summary

Curiosity about the diversity of the human species engendered the discipline of anthropology, and the scientific study and understanding of humanity have remained its dominant concerns. Anthropologists maintain a *holistic* perspective—all cultures concern them, whether extinct or vital, as do all aspects of human life, past or present. The *holistic* viewpoint encompasses humans as both biological organisms and as cultural beings.

This breadth of intellectual concern teaches us the value of *cultural relativism,* that it is senseless to try to take patterns of human behavior out of context by imposing our values on unfamiliar societies. Although everyone is somewhat *ethnocentric,* regarding the world from his or her particular cultural vantage point, anthropology underscores the common problems that all humans share. We do not have to accept the behaviors of people in different cultures, but we are obligated to seek to understand why people act as they do.

Where other social sciences emphasize the opposition between human beings and the natural world, anthropology seeks instead to understand our place in nature and to clarify our relationship to the other animal species. Nonetheless, we are the only species whose survival depends on our ability to use language, tools, learning, and adaptable social organizations. It is these collective necessities, which we call culture, that provide the focus of anthropological inquiry. And it is our ability to create culture that ultimately sets us apart from all other animal species.

Anthropologists understand all human beings as possessing culture—the beliefs, customs, and practices that enable them to communicate with others and to deal with their social and physical environment. Of course, patterns of culture are extremely variable, but the process of ordering the world into significant and coherent configurations is universal, and it provides a key to understanding human similarities and differences. Although all human beings inherit a biological capacity for culture, the particular cultural patterns we adopt are learned through the childhood process of *socialization.* Language aids in this process of cultural transmission. Through language, we have been able to improve our survival strategies and create the complex political, economic, and social systems that mark us as cultural animals.

Culture tends to clarify the expectations people have of each other and gives human relations order and a degree of predictability. However, it is not an absolute influence on human behavior. Culture provides guidelines as to what is appropriate, but in fact deviation from the norm is expected. In our need to adapt to change in order to survive, resourceful behavior is often more valuable than proper behavior, and serves as a tool for formulating the most efficient survival strategy.

The separation of anthropology into the subdisciplines of *physical anthropology, archeology, cultural anthropology,* and *anthropological linguistics* has been necessitated by the growing complexity of the field, but it unfortunately tends to create artificial distinctions. Anthropologists in all disciplines share several areas of concern, for example, tracing the similarities and differences among people. The physical anthropologists approach this task by studying genetics and the resultant biological variations in human populations. The cultural anthropologists known as *ethnographers* describe variations in the patterns of people's beliefs and behavior by going into the field and collecting firsthand data on all aspects of life in a particular society. Archeologists, on the other hand, seek to describe the cultures of extinct societies. Finally, anthropological linguists, besides studying how people combine sounds into words and then combine words into meaningful utterances, have recently begun to investigate how language is used to order the human experience and how speech varies depending upon the social context.

Anthropologists are also concerned with the biological and cultural evolution of the human species. Physical anthropologists have attempted to trace our ancestry through study of prehuman and early human fossil remains and the primates, our closest living relatives. Archeologists attempt to reconstruct prehistory through analysis of remains left by extinct cultures. Anthropological linguists have contributed to this effort by tracing the development of today's languages from ancestral tongues.

But the ultimate goal of anthropology is to explain as well as describe human diversity, a goal complicated by the many possible theoretical approaches to the problem. The approach of this book emphasizes ecology and evolution, stressing the inextricable link between people and their environment. Nineteenth-century attempts to apply Darwin's theory of natural selection to the area of cultural evolution failed, but lately cultural anthropologists have begun to specifically focus on individual variation within cultures.

Variations within human groups are due to differences in biological endowment, intellect, and personality among individuals in the population. Those variations that are successful are viewed as good by the culture and are passed on to other generations through the socialization process. The environment acts as an additional stimulus, by creating problems to which humans must adapt and by limiting the solutions to these problems. Human behavior is thus shaped to a degree by feedback from the environment. The environment acts as "natural selector," with the qualifications that human beings are more capable of modifying their environment than any other animal species.

The evolutionary and ecological approach to anthropology was criticized in the past for its exclusive emphasis on the material aspects of life, which was found inadequate to explain such nonmaterial phenomena as religious and political beliefs and practices. It is our intention to show that these aspects of human life are as important in human adaptation as economic practices and subsistence strategies. Our book hopes to illustrate the breadth of the evolutionary approach through attention to decisions made by individuals; by dealing with the adaptive strategies of both individuals and societies; and by discussing the evolutionary processes of which these adaptive strategies are a part.

suggested readings

APPLEMAN, P., ed.
1970 *Darwin.* New York: Norton. A comprehensive collection of extracts, not only from Darwin himself, but also from contemporary critics and supporters and from workers who built upon Darwinian foundations.

FAGAN, B.
1975 *In the Beginning.* Boston: Little, Brown. A highly readable introduction to the theory, method, and practice of archeology.

FRIED, M.
1972 *The Study of Anthropology.* New York: Crowell. Describes anthropology as a profession and as a career; focuses on some of the decisions that will be faced by an undergraduate student considering a career in anthropology.

HYMES, D., ed.
1972 *Reinventing Anthropology.* New York: Vintage Books. A series of essays addressed to the uses of anthropology and to anthropological analyses of specific issues in today's world.

KROEBER, A. L.
1963 *Culture: A Critical Review of Concepts and Definitions.* New York: Vintage Books. A comprehensive review and synthesis of the many definitions of culture that anthropologists have developed.

● Anthropology is a most ambitious science. Its subject is the human species in all its complexity: biology and evolution, culture and adaptation. Because the human species is a part of nature, subject to the same natural laws that apply to all living things, we begin by exploring human biology, the place of *Homo sapiens* in the living world.

In recent years, two broad principles have emerged as the central themes of biological and anthropological science. The first of these is that all sustained adaptive changes have their origin in the process of *evolution through natural selection*. The second, closely related to the first, is that of the *ecosystem* — the principle that every species in a natural community is linked to all the others in a web of delicately balanced relationships. Our initial purpose is to examine the evolutionary changes that have brought our species to its present position of dominance in the world ecosystem. We first examine in Chapter 2 the basic processes and patterns of all evolution, including that of humans, and then in Chapters 3 and 4 take a look at the characteristics and evolution of our closest relatives, the primates.

For physical anthropologists, a main reason for studying the primates is to understand the relationship between structure and function, anatomy and behavior. How do the bones of quadrupeds, arm swingers, knuckle walkers, and bipeds differ? What do teeth tell us about diet — and lifestyle? The answers to these questions and others like them enable us to interpret the fossil record and thus to piece together the story of human evolution.

The biological evolutionary events resulting in *Homo sapiens* have been revealed in the skeletal morphology of ancient primates. Human evolution, however, involves culture as well as biology. As we turn to the study of cultural evolution and its processes in Chapters 5 through 8, we are still dealing with skeletons — the skeletons of past societies that archeologists recover in the form of artifacts. From these artifacts emerges a picture of the major evolutionary episodes up to the historic period: the emergence of cultural essentials, division of labor, specialized behavior patterns, cultural diversity, food production, and the state and urban society. In explaining the evolution of cultural diversity among human groups we emphasize three main areas: *technological change* (the diversity of toolmaking traditions, changes in raw materials, manufacturing techniques, the efficiency of tools, and specificity of function); *changes in subsistence strategies* (changes in the resources that groups acquire and their means for acquiring them); and *changes in social organization* (changes in the form and size of human groups, the degree of specialization and distribution of wealth within groups, and the relations between groups).

With their unspecialized structure and technological advances, human beings are capable of existing in a wide range of environments. In expanding their geographical boundaries, they have been exposed to many different climates, terrains, food resources, and diseases. In Chapter 9 we consider all these factors in discussing the physical variations present in humans today. Although we know that these human variations are the result of a long chain of genetic and environmental interactions, our ability to explain variations found within and among human populations is limited. Much more research has to be done before we will gain any real idea of their meaning in terms of the evolution of the species *Homo sapiens*.

human physical and cultural evolution

2

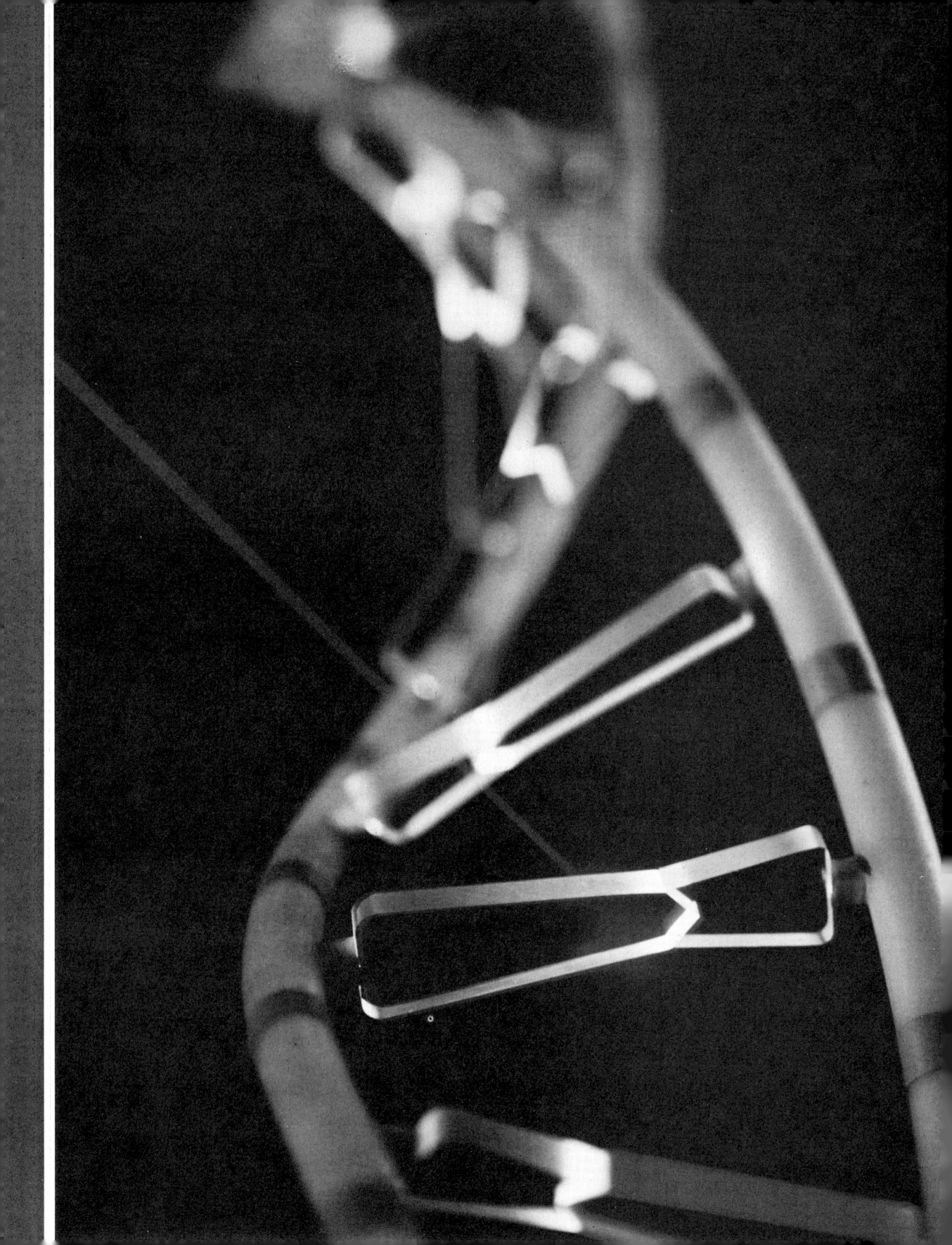

two
The Processes and Patterns of Evolution

In the next few chapters, we shall trace steps in the evolution of the human species. We shall be telling a story that is pieced together from many kinds of evidence: the structure of protein molecules, the behavior of living primates, the shape of fossil bones, and the artifacts recovered by archeologists. This evidence, however, does not speak for itself. To interpret its message, we employ a body of evolutionary theory that has itself evolved over the past two hundred years. In this chapter, we shall review this *synthetic theory* of evolution.

Genes and the Individual

Like all organisms that reproduce sexually, we develop from a single cell—a fertilized egg, or *zygote*. The zygote is not a human being, but it has the potential to develop into one, using material from its environment—first in the womb, then in the world. This potential depends upon a set of genetic instructions derived from the nuclei of the two cells—the *gametes*, the mother's ovum and the father's sperm—that fused to produce the zygote. These instructions will be carefully duplicated and passed on to the nucleus of each of the millions upon millions of body cells derived from the zygote.

The Chromosome Set

At some stages of cell division, the cell's genetic material is visible under the microscope as a series of *chromosomes*. The chromosomes are the bearers of thousands of *genes*—the individual units of heredity that determine characters such as hair color, eye color, blood group, and so on. If this is a human cell, there will be 46 chromosomes, consisting of two matching sets of 23. Therefore, every gene in the set has a twin, or *allele,* on the matching chromosome. In females, there are 23 matching pairs; in males, 22 pairs match, but the other two chromosomes are "odd." One (X) matches one of the female's pairs (XX). The other (Y) is found only in males. The male received his Y chromosome from his father and will pass it on to his sons. His X chromosome came from his mother; he will pass it on to his daughters.

The place of a particular gene on the chromosome pair is called its *locus* (plural, *loci*). Together, the allele pair constitutes the individual's *genotype*. If the two alleles are exactly alike, the individual is said to be *homozygous* at this locus. If they are slightly different, the individual is said to be *heterozygous* at this locus.

Genes and Proteins

The genetic material is a double chain of nucleotides—*deoxyribonucleic acid (DNA)*—and the function of DNA is to convey the information necessary to construct proteins. Because its double strand can unzip to form a pattern for another strand, DNA has two remarkable properties that permit it to store genetic information: (1) it carries the information necessary for self-copying so that each cell can receive an identical set of genetic instructions; (2) the structure of a particular DNA strand can be translated into the structure of a protein. Each gene corresponds to

The long double-strands of the DNA molecule, sometimes called the "master molecule," are the carriers of the genetic codes necessary for reproduction.

the DNA section that carries the information necessary to make a particular protein or part of a protein. Different alleles provide slightly different plans, thus coding for variants of the same protein.

The active proteins carry out essential roles in the body. Some are transporters, carrying nutrients from the sites where they are taken into the body to the tissues where they are to be used. Other proteins are enzymes, biological catalysts that control chemical reactions in the cell. Each active protein carries out only one very precise role. Thousands of different proteins are needed to keep the machinery of the body functioning.

Proteins are also believed to play an essential role in embryological development. The enormously complex process of cell division, differentiation, and formation into tissues and organs is controlled by enzymes and other active proteins, which in turn are coded by the DNA of the genes. Thus, provided that the environment is suitable, growth and development follow the plan laid down in the zygote's genetic blueprint. Cells continue to replicate under genetic guidance throughout the individual's life, for being alive means maintaining a constantly self-renewing system through which materials and energy flow along pathways controlled by enzymes and other active proteins. By influencing the processes of development and metabolism in different ways, variations in proteins, and hence in genes, are expressed as observable differences among individuals.

Environmental Interaction with the Genotype

Genes and the proteins they produce are not the only factors involved in individual development. The observable characters, or traits—the *phenotype*—develop under genetic guidance, but are also influenced by the environment in which the genes and proteins work. For example, some people put on fat easily and lose it with difficulty; others eat heartily yet remain slim. Since such tendencies run in families, it is very likely that genes are involved, but it would be an oversimplification to say that there are genes that "make you fat" or "keep you slim." A person with a tendency to obesity who diets carefully may well carry less fat than a "naturally" thin person who consistently overeats. In other words, the genotype may predispose the development of a particular character, but it does not dictate the phenotype independently of environmental influences.

Genetic Variation

Every individual is unique because he or she carries a unique "mix" of genes derived from his or her two parents. When sex cells, or gametes, are formed, the number of chromosomes in each cell is reduced from the double set to a single set. Chromosomes are distributed without regard to their origin from either sperm or egg in the previous generation. Thus, if we consider only chromosomes 1 and 2, a man who inherited 1F and 2F from his father and 1M and 2M from his mother will form four kinds of sperm cells: 1F 2F, 1F 2M, 1M 2F, 1M 2M. Each of these kinds will be formed in approximately equal numbers. Alleles are assorted independently of one another, and the more loci we consider, the more different combinations will appear.

Assortment of whole chromosomes in this way obviously provides very considerable variety among gametes. Even more variation is produced by the process of *crossing over,* whereby chromosomes exchange parts of their length before being drawn into different gametic cells. Thus, even genes whose loci lie on the same chromosome (linked loci) stand a chance of being reshuffled during gamete formation.

To appreciate the degree of variation to be found among human gametes, remember that each normal human being carries 46 chromosomes, from which 2^{23} or over 8 million possible combinations can be formed in the gametes. The chromosomes have from 1,000 to 100,000 separate loci, which are further reassorted by crossing over during gamete formation. It is believed about 16 percent of these loci will be heterozygous in the average animal. It is evident that no two gametes, even if formed by the same person, are likely to carry precisely the same genetic information.

Genes in Populations

Individuals, pairs of mates, and sets of offspring are not units within which evolutionary trends can be seen. Evolutionary geneticists work with a wider unit known as the *Mendelian population*. In a Mendelian population, each member is more likely to mate with another member than with an outsider. It is thus a group within which a body of genes is usually transmitted. The combined genes of the population can be imagined as a *gene pool,* from which the genotype of each individual and each new generation is drawn.

Barriers between populations may be geographical or social. Among humans, ethnic, religious, class, kin, and political allegiances affect the choice of a mate. A human is likely to belong to a series of crosscutting groups, each of which conforms to the definition of a Mendelian population.

The most inclusive Mendelian population is the biological *species,* which may be defined as a group of interbreeding populations that is reproductively isolated from other such groups. Although the populations within a species are capable of exchanging genes by interbreeding at their boundaries, populations belonging to different species do not exchange genes.

Gene Frequency and Evolutionary Change

In order to describe the gene pool of a population and to measure the evolutionary changes that can occur in its constitution, geneticists use the concept of *gene frequency*. The frequency of a particular gene in a population is simply its abundance in that population relative to that of its alleles. From a genetic viewpoint, *evolution* is change in gene frequencies. We shall now consider the forces that can cause such change and that, between periods of change, can stabilize the gene pool of the population. Such factors can be considered under four headings: mutation, gene flow, natural selection, and non-Darwinian evolution.

Mutation *Mutation*—the raw material of evolution—is the source of new genes. The process by which DNA copies itself millions upon millions of times during the lifetime of an organism is highly efficient, but not entirely foolproof. Every so often a mistake is made, and a "new" allele, producing a new phenotypic effect, appears. There is still much to be learned about genetic mutation and its causes. It seems that there is a natural rate of mutation for each gene and each organism, which can, however, be dramatically increased by exposure to radiation or chemical mutagens.

Mutation is totally random with respect to the needs of the organism. For instance, bombarding a population of fruit flies with x-rays increases the mutation rate, but will probably not produce any mutation-carrying resistance to radiation sickness. If such advantageous mutants do occur, it is quite by chance.

Many geneticists believe that the majority of mutations are neutral—that is, they have no significant effect on the phenotype of the organism and do not affect its survival. Of the mutations that are not neutral, most are harmful. This is inevitable, since the genetic makeup of a species has evolved into a state of balance over many hundreds of generations. Any random change in such a system is likely to be deleterious.

Gene Flow Mutation supplies new genetic variation to the species as a whole. However, most biological species consist of more than one population. Individuals move from one population to another, or mate with individuals across the boundary, thus introducing new alleles into its gene pool. This process is called *gene flow*. Through gene flow, one population may acquire alleles from another. If the immigrants are very different from their hosts, even a low rate of immigration can cause a large amount of evolution in the gene pool. Thus gene flow supplements mutation as a source of genetic variability in any specific population.

However, from the viewpoint of the species as a whole, gene flow is a process that promotes homogeneity. It counteracts the tendency of populations to diverge from one another in gene frequencies. Such divergence is due to the evolutionary forces of natural selection and non-Darwinian evolution.

Natural Selection *Natural selection* is said to occur when one or more genotypes in a population are regularly less successful than other genotypes in transmitting their genes to the next generation. The reproductive success of a particular group within a population compared to that of other groups is called its *fitness*. An example of natural selection in action is the genetically caused abnormality of hemoglobin (the oxygen-carrying protein of the blood) called sickle cell anemia. For every ten children produced by normal individuals or by heterozygote "carriers" of the abnormal gene, sickle cell anemics produce only one. Since the death of sickle cell anemics removes the Hb^s (sickle cell) gene selectively from the population, it will lead to a change in gene frequency, other things being equal. In each generation there will be fewer Hb^s genes in the gene pool. This is an example of *directional selection*.

Genetic Load However, natural selection does not always lead to the complete elimination of one allele and the *fixation* (100 percent frequency) of another. Even very deleterious genes can persist at low frequencies if their effect is only manifested in homozygotes. Most of the genes will persist undetected in normal heterozygotes. These hidden, deleterious genes comprise the *genetic load* of a population.

Balanced Polymorphism Another circumstance where more than one allele persists in the population is called *balanced polymorphism*. A polymorphic population is one in which more than one genetically determined physical type is found. The peppered moth populations of industrial England were polymorphic during the nineteenth century; they included both gray and black individuals. This was a *transient* polymorphism. As soot blackened the surroundings, the gene for the darker color was favored by selection, and gradually ousted the gene for gray coloration. But other polymorphisms persist over long periods of time; they are not transient but instead are *balanced* by opposing selective forces.

A classic case is provided again by sickle cell anemia in humans. As we discussed earlier, homozygotes ($Hb^s Hb^s$) have a very low fitness. Yet the Hb^s gene persists in some populations, notably in parts of equatorial Africa, at frequencies up to 0.2. This apparent anomaly seems to be due to the selective effects of tropical malaria. Malarial infection is more frequent and serious in normal individuals ($Hb^A Hb^A$) than in heterozygotes who carry one Hb^s gene. Selection by malaria removes Hb^A genes selectively from the population, balancing the loss of Hb^s genes from sickle cell anemia. When heterozygotes are the most fit genotype—as in this case, neither allele ousts the other—they both persist at frequencies determined by the balance between the two selective forces—in this case, malaria and anemia. Such examples show us that natural selection is an agent of stability as well as change. Once the population has attained gene frequencies that are most advantageous in a given environment, natural selection will act as a normative agent maintaining these frequencies so long as the environment remains stable.

Polymorphism is very common in animal species. It is believed that many of these polymorphisms, like sickle cell, are maintained because of balancing selective forces. However, in most cases, the selective forces involved are unknown, and some geneticists suspect that a good deal of polymorphism may be transient and due to the random effects of non-Darwinian evolution (see p. 25). Whatever the cause, polymorphisms are an enormously important part of the genetic makeup of a species. They provide the variability upon which natural selection can work to achieve new adaptations. Without such variability, the population would have no means of responding adaptively to new selective challenges in the changing environment and would lose its potential for adaptive evolutionary change.

The Evolution of Gene Complexes A final point should be made about directional selection. The adaptation of a population to its environment depends not only upon a single gene, but also upon combinations of genes. Since all gene products interact, an evolving change in gene frequency at one locus is likely to change the fitness conferred by other genes and so set off a "chain reaction" of genetic readjustment.

Non-Darwinian Evolution Natural selection preserves some genes and eliminates others, just as a careful gardener culls his stock, weeding out undesirable specimens. Non-Darwinian evolution determines the fate of genes by random processes, like a gambler throwing dice.

The Establishment of a Neutral Mutation Consider first a new neutral mutation appearing in a single individual. Its chances of becoming established are very low indeed. Its bearer is, of course, of heterozygote. Only half his genotype will be transmitted to his offspring, and it is as likely as not that the part transmitted will not include the new gene. Each generation of the new gene runs the risk of elimination. Very few such mutants persist for more than a generation or two. But evolutionary time is long, and mutation produces a steady supply of new genes. A very low, but predictable proportion will, against all the odds, eventually become established as polymorphisms in the population.

Genetic Drift Under what circumstances can one neutral allele (that is, one with no apparent adaptive effect) totally displace another in a population? Mathematical geneticists have shown that population size is the important factor. The smaller the population, the less the gene frequencies of the offspring are likely to reflect those of the parental generation. Gene frequencies will fluctuate from generation to generation, and the smaller the population, the wider the fluctuations (Figure 2–1). Eventually, the effect of such fluctuation is inevitably the fixation of one gene and the elimination of its allele. On the average, the smaller the population, the more rapidly such fixation will occur, so that small populations will tend to lose variability by *genetic drift* and become highly homozygous. However, given enough time, fixation will occur even in large populations. Note that although we can predict that one of the alleles will inevitably be fixed, we cannot predict which one it will be in any given population.

The Founder Effect Closely related to genetic drift, the *founder effect* is liable to occur when a new population is established by a few settlers, colonists, or survivors of a catastrophe. The founders constitute a sample of the population from which they are derived, and carry only a small fraction of its gene pool. Gene frequencies among the founders are likely to differ from those of the parent population—an example of sampling error. The population derived from the founders will reflect the gene frequencies of the founders, not those of the parent population. Once again, variation is likely to be lost in this way.

The Effects of Non-Darwinian Evolution Unlike natural selection, non-Darwinian evolution is not directed by the demands of adaptation. Its direction is controlled only by available mutation, and its results are predictable only in a statistical sense. Apart from very exceptional cases (as when a founder population is extremely small), it cannot work against natural selection and is thus effective only with respect to neutral or near-neutral genes. Nevertheless, its evolutionary importance should not be underestimated.

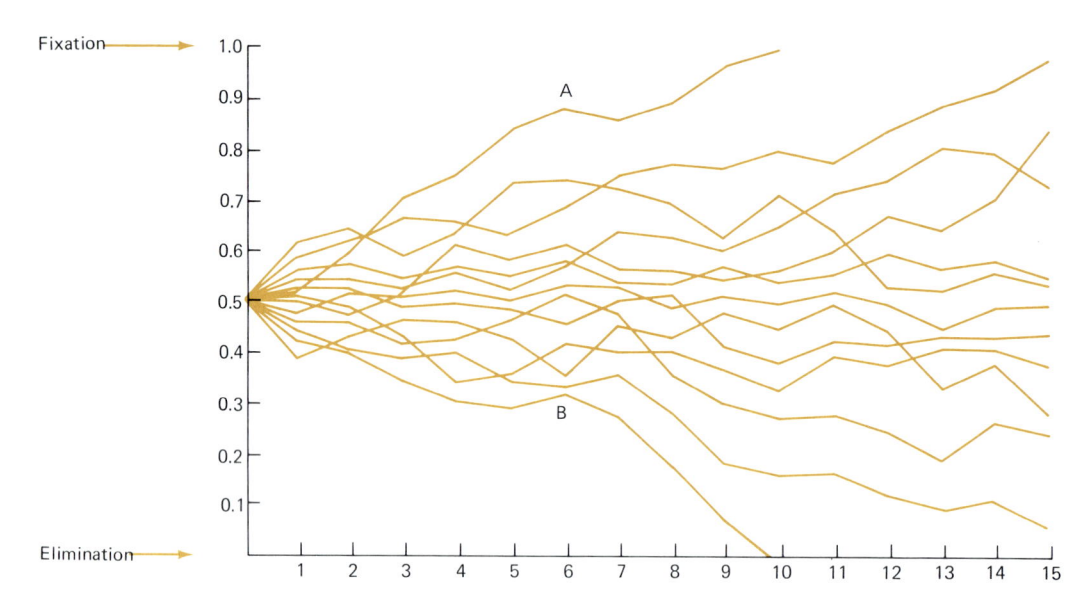

Figure 2–1. Change in gene frequencies under the action of genetic drift in a series of populations. Each line represents the frequency of an allele in a particular population over fifteen generations. At the beginning, all populations show a frequency 0.5. After fifteen generations, the allele has been fixed in one population (A), eliminated for another (B), and varies widely in frequency among the others.

population size.[1] This is a discovery of some importance, for it provides a theoretical justification for using differences in protein structure as good indicators of evolutionary relationship. However, since geneticists are still divided on the question of how much protein evolution can in fact be attributed to non-Darwinian factors rather than to classical natural selection, most evolutionary biologists still regard such interpretations with caution.

One effect is to enhance diversity among the semi-isolated populations of a species. Together with local selective effects, genetic drift causes such populations to diverge from one another, producing a *polytypic species*—that is, one whose constituent populations differ in their gene frequencies and phenotypic characters. Furthermore, "neutral" characters established by drift in a population may take on selective significance if environmental conditions change or if they come to be used by the organisms themselves as signals in social communication.

Another effect of non-Darwinian evolution is the accumulation of selectively neutral changes in proteins. It has been shown that the rate of accumulation is proportional only to the mutation rate and is independent of

The Major Patterns of Evolution

In the previous section, we focused on the details of the evolutionary process. We saw how the process of reproduction merges the genetic endowment of the individual with the gene pool of the population, and how that gene pool can change from generation to generation, evolving under the influence of natural selection and of non-Darwinian factors. In this section, we look at evolution from a longer perspective. We trace the patterns that emerge as the gene pools of populations move through spans of time encompassing hundreds of thousands of generations and

---

[1] For details see King and Jukes (1970).

millions of years. From this perspective, generation merges with generation, and populations of organisms are seen as lines of descent, *lineages.* The lineages gradually change under the influence of evolutionary forces, flourishing, splitting, dwindling, or becoming extinct.

Each living species, including *Homo sapiens,* has its own complex evolutionary history, and the evolutionary place of each species in the living world is defined by the events of its past. In spite of their complexity, these long-term evolutionary changes are the result of the conceptually simple forces of mutation, natural selection, gene flow, and genetic drift. Moreover, the complexity is more manageable if we realize that there are patterns in long-term evolutionary change, phenomena that tend to occur again and again even in unrelated groups of plants and animals.

Rates of Evolutionary Change

Evolutionary change, under the influence of natural selection, does not occur at a steady pace over long periods of time. A species that is firmly ensconced in a stable econiche will change rather little, remaining phenotypically stable over very long spans of time. For instance, the common North American opossum is very close in structure and general appearance to early mammals of about 100 million years ago. During the same period, other mammals have become as diverse as elephants, bats, kangaroos, and whales. Extreme evolutionary conservativism, such as that shown by the opossum, does not mean that natural selection has ceased to work in such a lineage, but merely that in such a lineage most selection is normative, weeding out deleterious mutations but producing little or no change. Nor is there any reason to think that such a lineage has run out of evolutionary potential. Given new ecological opportunities, it could respond as effectively as any other population—provided that it has retained the necessary variability in its gene pool.

In contrast to the conservative species, others have evolved rapidly. Changing environmental circumstances or a radical shift in the animal's way of life brings strong directional selective pressures to bear upon the population's gene pool. The elephant family provides good examples of rapid evolutionary change over the past few million years. Several distinct lineages can be traced in the fossil record as the ancestral elephants shifted from browsing (feeding upon the tender leaves of trees and bushes) to grazing (feeding upon grasses and other tough herbage). Under the selective pressure of the new way of life, the jaws of the elephants gradually

The common North American opossum, a species similar in structure and general appearance to mammals living 100 million years ago, is a conservative species in evolutionary terms.
(Molly Adams/Photo Researchers)

become modified into efficient grinders. The entire orientation of the chewing muscles was altered. The lower tusks disappeared, and the chewing teeth finally developed into massive, high-crowned grindstones that were well adapted to tough, abrasive vegetation. The snout became a mobile trunk used to gather bundles of herbage and stuff them into the mouth. Each change in the chewing and food-gathering apparatus was an adaptation that fitted the elephants more comfortably into their new econiche—grazing in open grassland.

Note the chain of causation in such an evolutionary change. First, the *environment* changed, opening a new opportunity to be exploited (grass eating in open country). Second, the proto-elephants responded to the environmental challenge with a *behavioral* shift (more grazing, less browsing), altering the selective forces acting on their jaws and teeth. And finally, their *anatomy* was modified by the directional selection imposed by the new selective forces. Of course, proto-elephants adapted for browsing did not move suddenly and directly into open grassland. More likely, a cycle of *positive feedback* was established between habitat, behavior, and structure. Each structural modification produced by new feeding habits allowed the animals to become more dependent upon grazing, to move further into open country, and hence to be subjected to further selective pressures toward grass-eating adaptations.

When, using the fossil record, we trace evolving lineages through time, we usually find that the course of such evolutionary change did not proceed smoothly. Periods of rapid change typically alternate with long periods of *stasis* when little or no evolutionary change is observable and the animal is occupying a stable adaptive plateau. Each burst of evolutionary change represents a response to a further step in behavioral specialization, itself triggered by new environmental opportunities. We shall see many comparable cases as we trace the course of human and primate evolution in the fossil record.

Anthropologists attempt to interpret the structural changes that they see occurring in the human lineage by posing the questions:

1. What behavior shift could have caused this structural change?
2. What environmental factors might have triggered this change in behavior?

The Opportunism of Darwinian Evolution

This unevenness of evolutionary change, slowing and accelerating under the influence of fluctuating selectional forces, is one aspect of what has been called the opportunism of evolution. Another aspect of the same phenomenon is that new adaptations are always built upon existing structures. Natural selection can work only upon the variation that exists within the population, favoring certain genotypes while discriminating against others. Natural selection cannot "invent" genes or phenotypic characters no matter how advantageous they might be to the population. Evolution by selection results in the modification of *existing* structures. New adaptations are built upon old ones, and traces of the old adaptations can often be perceived in the animal's anatomy. Thus the structure of a particular animal includes both *heritage* (or ancestral) characters, which reflect the adaptations of its ancestors and which it has inherited from them, and *habitus* (or derived) characters, which are the result of its own more recent adaptation. One result of this is that even animals that have taken to very similar ways of life never come to resemble each other in all respects.

The Irreversibility of Evolution

Because of the way in which heritage characters are retained, some biologists have proposed a so-called law of the irreversibility of evolution. It is true that once structures and their genetic bases have totally disappeared from a population, natural selection cannot "call them back." Evolutionary reversals that result in the reappearance of such lost features are indeed extremely rare. But the "law" must not be too rigidly interpreted. Evolutionary trends involving changes in the size and proportion of parts of the organism, which depend upon simple changes in the frequency of genes in the population, can be and often are reversed. Overemphasis upon this "law" of irreversibility can lead to fruitless searches for hypothetical, totally unspecialized ancestral forms that never in fact existed.

Specialization and Generalization

Increasing specialization is the usual consequence of evolutionary trends directed by natural selection. Some animals, however, become adapted to econiches where they are not heavily committed to the exploitation of a particular narrow set of resources. These generalized forms forgo the benefits of extreme specialization, the advantages of being the sole occupant of a narrow econiche, but from their broader ecological base they retain a flexibility that enables them to survive in the face of changing circumstances. On the whole, primates — members of the order Primates, the subgroup of the mammalian class to which the human species belongs — have tended to remain more generalized than other mammals. The order is called Primates (pronounced Pry-máy-tees); members of the order are called primates (pronounced pry-mayts).

Diversification and Speciation

So far we have discussed evolution as though each species comprised a single homogeneous population. More often, as we saw, species comprise a number of geographical populations, each with its own semiisolated gene pool. Genetic drift and adaptation to the local environment inevitably cause the gene pools of such populations to evolve in different directions. But as long as genetic communication is still possible between them, these disruptive effects will be counteracted by gene flow. The result is a polytypic species.

Given the right circumstances, however, the process of *diversification* may proceed further, leading ultimately to the appearance of a new species. *Speciation* is the process by which the gene pool of a species splits permanently and irreversibly, producing "daughter" species separate from the "parent." The two separate species, parent and daughter, then pursue separate evolutionary paths. Their gene pools are independent of each other, no longer subject to the effects of gene flow between them. Speciation, repeated time upon time, has produced the multiplicity of animals and plants that have succeeded each other through evolutionary time. Speciation and adaptation are the two most fundamental evolutionary processes.

Modern biologists agree that, at least in animals,[2] speciation always involves each of the stages shown in Figure 2–2. The first step is the isolation of a subpopulation from the rest of the species by a geographical barrier. The barrier may be an uncrossable river, a rising mountain chain, or a stretch of desert between the remnants of shrinking forest; its nature is unimportant. Freed from the homogenizing effect of gene flow, the gene pools of the two isolated subpopulations diverge under the influence of genetic drift and natural selection. The crucial test for speciation arises if and when the two populations, parent and isolate, again become *sympatric* — that is, occupy overlapping ranges. If the members of the two populations recognize each other as potential mates, breed, and produce fully fit offspring, full speciation has not occurred; within a few generations their gene pools will merge again. If, on the other hand, genetic divergence during isolation has reached the point where members of the two populations are no longer able or inclined to mate, they will now behave as members of separate species.[3]

---

[2] Many new *plant* species are produced "instantly" from a single individual that undergoes a radical genetic change and then reproduces by self-fertilization.

[3] Sometimes the outcome of isolation is less clear-cut. Members of the two populations may still mate, but their offspring are less fit. In such cases, behaviors will almost certainly evolve to eliminate such wasteful, infertile matings and thus complete the process of speciation.

Human Physical and Cultural Evolution

(a) Temporary isolation of subpopulations No speciation

(b) Temporary isolation, semi-speciation completed after barrier removed

(c) Speciation followed by extinction of one branch

(d) Speciation followed by divergence

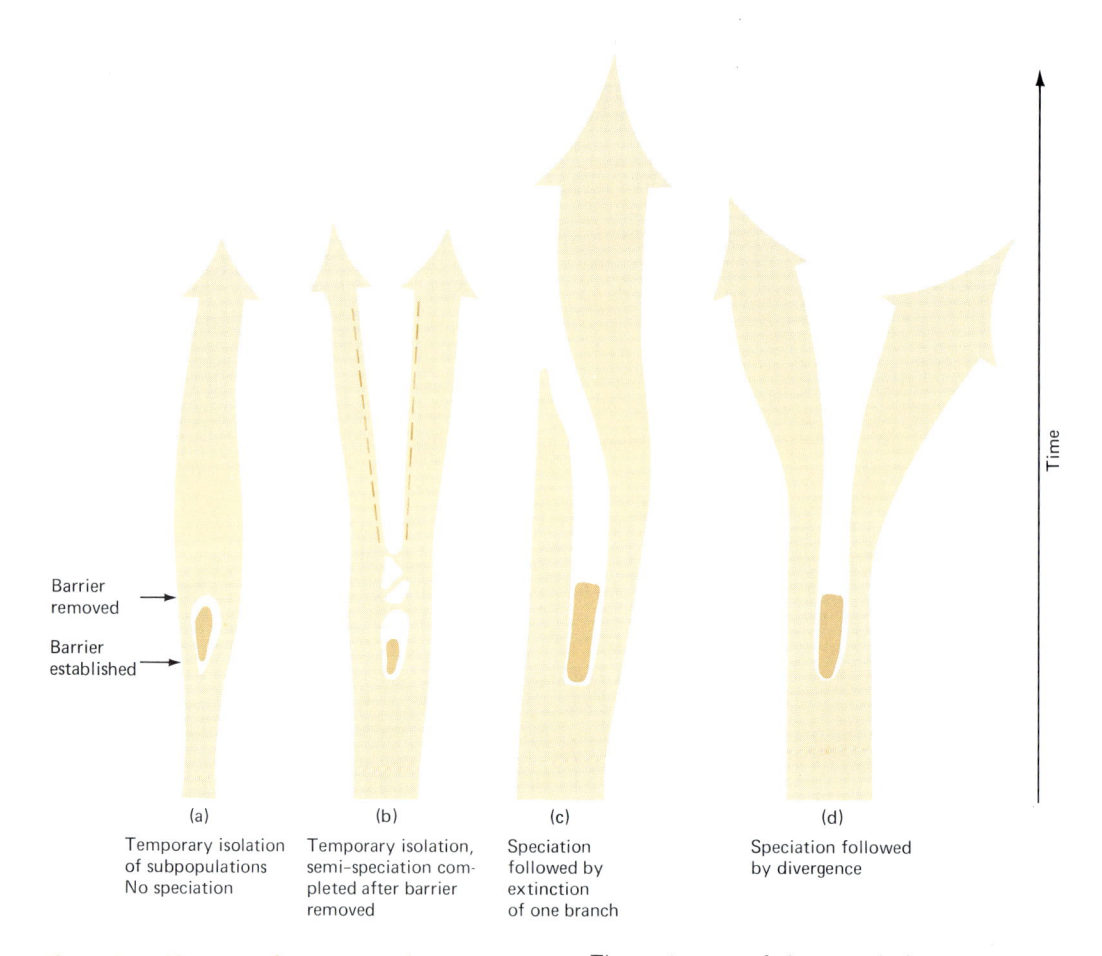

Figure 2–2. Diagrammatic representation of alternative evolutionary patterns resulting from temporary geographical isolation of populations. (a) Two populations are temporarily isolated, but do not speciate. After removal of the barrier, they merge again. (b) Two populations are temporarily isolated and partially speciate. After the barrier is removed, some interbreeding takes place, but the hybrids are relatively unfit so that gene flow is restricted. Eventually, speciation is completed as behavioral isolating mechanisms evolve to prevent cross-breeding. The two new species then diverge. (c) Two populations are isolated and speciate. After removal of the barrier, they compete and one becomes extinct. (d) Two populations are isolated and speciate. After the removal of the barrier they diverge.

The outcome of the speciation process is that two closely related species now compete for the same resources and living space. According to circumstances, one of two things may now happen. One of the species may be slightly better adapted to the particular environment and may be capable of displacing the other species, which eventually becomes extinct. In this case, the end result of the speciation process is once again a single species occupying much the same econiche as before. However, the successful species is likely to have undergone evolutionary change during the period of intense competition. Some biologists argue that most spurts of evolutionary change have been associated with speciation, although the fossil record is usually too incomplete to document the relatively brief period when the two species existed side by side.

The second possible outcome of speciation is *divergence*. If the circumstances permit it, the two related species may continue to coexist by dividing the habitat between them, either geographically or ecologically. In this case, the selective influence of slightly different econiches will encourage further physical and behavioral divergence on the part of each species. As a result, with the passage of time, each will become more and more distinct from the other in behavior and structure. The result of speciation and displacement is the appearance of two new species, each more specialized than the one from which both are descended, exploiting different econiches in the same general habitat.

Adaptive Radiation Repeated speciation from a single ancestral stock, with the survival of the derived branches, gives rise to an *adaptive radiation*. Radiations typically occur when a group of animals colonizes a new geographical area that offers numerous "open" econiches.

The marsupials of Australia provide an example of adaptive radiation. When the ancestors of the present marsupials reached Australia, the absence of competing placental mammals allowed them to diversify in innumerable ways. Some have become tree dwellers; others live on the ground or burrow beneath it. Some are herbivores, others carnivores, still others anteaters or insectivores.

Occasionally, adaptive radiations occur when a particular animal stock, hitherto insignificant in the fauna, evolves adaptations that fortuitously open up previously unusable habitats. For example, between 375 and 350 million years ago a group of fishes, members of the superorder Crossopterygii, modified the swim bladder, an organ that in most fish provides buoyancy in swimming, into a lung. They thus acquired the ability to take oxygen directly from the atmosphere. At the same time, their fins became stumpy but muscular lobes that enabled them to move about, in a limited fashion, out of the water. These crossopterygians (lobe-fins) probably lived in shallow pools in a hot and seasonably variable climate. Their unique specializations enabled them to survive seasons when the water in their pools became foul and deoxygenated or dried up altogether. As we saw, all specialization is a gamble, with the odds heavily in favor of extinction. The lobe-fins' ability to breathe air, however, is an example of a rare kind of specialization—one that turns out to be a *preadaptation*. It formed the basis for the successive adaptive radiations of land vertebrates (amphibians, reptiles, mammals, birds), all of which have inherited their lungs and basic limb structure from their crossopterygian ancestor.

As we shall see, successive stages of evolution in the human ancestry seem to have been based upon such fortuitous breakthroughs, specializations that were originally narrow, but that opened up wide new opportunities. For instance, mammals probably perfected the control of their internal temperature as a specialization for active insect-hunting in the cool of the night. Primates probably acquired their grasping hands and keen vision as specialized hunters in the forest canopy. And the human family may even have originated when a marginal population of small apes specialized in exploiting a particular set of food resources.

The successive radiations of the amphibians, reptiles, and mammals illustrate another recurrent pattern in large-scale evolution. Each time a single generalized stock makes a significant adaptive breakthrough such as breathing air or achieving a constant body temperature, an extensive adaptive radiation arises from this stock. After a period of flourishing and diversification, the radiation typically "collapses." Most of its branches become extinct, and a new radiation, often derived from an obscure side branch of the previous one, springs up in its place.

Convergence and Parallelism Independent adaptive radiations tend to produce evolutionary lines that adopt the same general mode of life and hence develop similar special adaptations. These adaptations are, however, superimposed on different basic body plans. When dissimilar unrelated lineages evolve superficially similar forms in this way, the phenomenon is called *convergence.* For instance, the reptile radiation of 200 million years ago included sea-living forms, the ichthyosaurs—animals that resembled fish in outward appearance, although an examination of their structure clearly indicates that they were reptiles. Subsequently, the mammalian radiation produced a similar group, the whales and dolphins, also fishlike in outward appearance, but fully mammalian in their physiology and anatomy.

A related phenomenon is called *parallelism.* This is said to occur when related species with similar general adaptations independently take up similar ways of life, and consequently come to resemble each other in special adaptations more than either resembles the ancestral form. We shall see many examples of parallel evolution in the order Primates. The resemblances between animals that are due to parallelism and convergence are known as *analogies.* They are conceptually opposed to *homologies,* which are resemblances retained from a common ancestor.

The outcome of the evolutionary processes of speciation, radiation, and extinction is a great array of species, some still extant, others extinct and known (if at all) only from their fossil remains. Evolutionary theory tells us that all these species are ultimately related to each other. Each species can be considered as the tip of a branch of an imaginary *phyletic tree,* whose forks represent events of speciation and subsequent divergence.

It is one thing, however, to comprehend in a theoretical way that all species are interrelated by descent and quite another to be able to say just how one particular group is related to another. Theoretically, only one phyletic tree can represent what "really happened" in evolutionary history—the true pattern of evolutionary relationships among species. How do we go about reconstructing these ancient evolutionary events from the information available to us in the present?

Unraveling Evolutionary Relationships

A phyletic tree is a branching diagram representing ideas about the evolutionary relationships of a group of species. Comparisons between the species concerned provide the basic raw materials used to reconstruct such trees. Structures such as limbs, teeth, and even protein molecules, as well as elements of social behavior, can serve as the basis for such comparisons. (See the box on p. 34 for a discussion of biological classification.)

If we compare enough morphological (relating to structure) and physiological (relating to function) characters, we can eventually arrive at a reasonable estimate of overall resemblance or *phenetic distance* among species. We can say, "Species A resembles Species B in twenty characters, but Species C in only five. A is phenetically closer to B than it is to C." Because of the basic conservatism of the evolutionary process, phenetic distance provides quite a good indication of phyletic relationship. We can state, then, as a general principle, that *animals that share detailed resemblances are usually closely related to each other.* This general principle provides a useful guide for sorting species into broad groups of relatives.

If this first general principle were universally true, our task as evolutionary biologists would be simple. Phyletic relationships could be directly inferred from phenetic distance. The more two animals resemble each other, the more recent their common ancestry. However, not all resemblances are of equal weight in indicating phyletic relationships. Some resemblances are due to heritage from an ancient common ancestor and do not reflect a recent common ancestry. These are the so-called *primitive characters.* The opossum, for example, shares with humans the characteristic of having five fingers and five toes, and both species differ from the horse, which has only one toe on each foot. (See Figure 2–3.) Does this indicate that opossums and humans are the more closely related pair of this trio of species? It does not, because the five-digited condition represents the primitive, or ancestral, condition for all land vertebrates. Frogs, salamanders, crocodiles, lizards, and turtles all have five digits, and so did the common ancestor of all mammals including humans, opossums, and horses. Thus the fact that opossums and humans share this character tells us only that these two species belong to the broad group that includes all land vertebrates; it reveals nothing at all about the exact relationship of either to the horse.

On the other hand, the fact that the zebra resembles the horse in having only one functional toe *is* of phyletic significance. Reduction of the number of toes to one is a relatively new or *derived character* among mammals. It is shared by the zebra and horse but not by other mammals. It probably first appeared in an animal that was the common ancestor of the horse and the zebra, but was not in the ancestry of humans or opossums. If zebras and horses shared such an ancestor, they are closer to each other than to the other mam-

Figure 2–3. The interpretation of ancestral and derived characters in reconstructing phylogeny. Here, the problem is to deduce the phyletic relationships among the zebra, horse, human, and opossum. In practice, we would use many characters to make the decision; here, for simplicity, we consider only one character, the number of fingers. Humans are like opossums in having five fingers, but this resemblance is due to retention of the ancestral condition, seen also in many reptiles. It has no phyletic significance. Zebras are like horses in having only one functional finger. This is a derived condition and indicates that they share a relatively recent common ancestor.

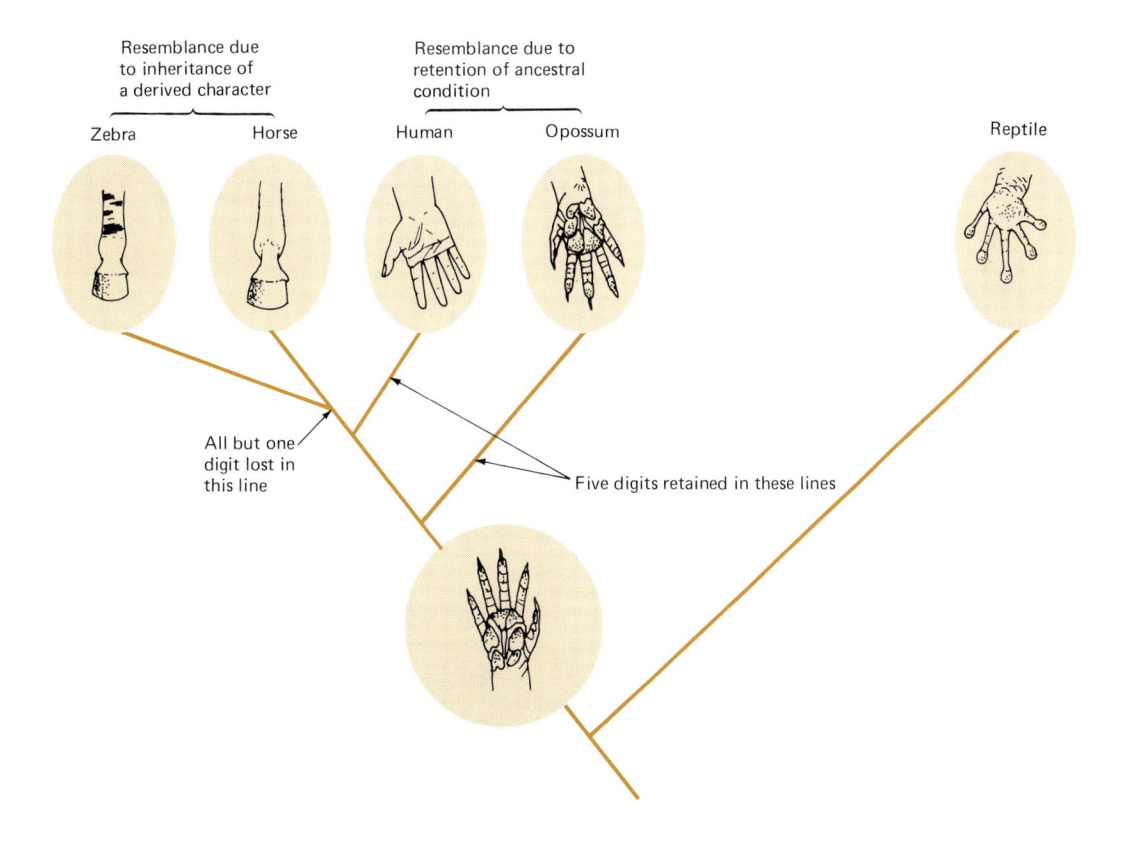

Elements of Biological Classification

Like all scientists, biologists classify the objects they study. Such classifications, however, are not an end in themselves; they are simply ways of grouping and labeling categories or objects that are frequently discussed as a group, and for which a collective term is needed. The essential quality of a good classification is *usefulness*; categories that are rarely used are not worth naming—or remembering. Biologists use various classificatory schemes, based on different criteria. Some are ecologically based ("forest animals"); others use geographical or chronological criteria ("Australian marsupials," "Cretaceous mammals"). But "classification" in biology generally means the all-purpose *neo-Linnaean* classification of plants and animals (sometimes called the *natural* or *scientific* classification). This system is based on usages established over 200 years ago by the great Swedish naturalist, Karl von Linné (Carolus Linnaeus).

Linnaeus established an unambiguous way of naming species and a formal hierarchical scheme for establishing higher categories that consist of groups of species. To Linnaeus, species were fixed and immutable, the building blocks of a system that reflected the orderliness of the Divine Creator's plan. Linnaeus labeled each species with a *binominal* (double) name. The domestic dog, for instance, is *Canis familiaris*. This name tells us that the species belongs to the genus *Canis,* as does the related wolf, *Canis lupus*. Every species belongs to a genus (plural, genera) that may also include other, related species. Genera are grouped into families, families into orders, and so on (see Figure 3–2). Each category, or *taxon* (plural, taxa), includes one or more taxa of the next rank down. The names of some categories have standard endings. The reader should take care to distinguish these, for words differing only in their ending may refer to very different groups of organisms.

Two related conventions govern the allocation of names, especially to species. One is that the earliest name validly used for a group, but no earlier than the 1758 edition of Linnaeus' classification, is the valid name for that group. For instance, *Equus caballus* is the valid name of the domestic horse. The other rule is that the earliest use of a name is the only valid one. *Equus caballus* cannot be used as a name for any animal but the horse, nor can the horse be called anything but *Equus caballus*.

Given the basic structure of the Linnaean system, how does one decide which species to group in a single genus, which genera in a family, and so on? Post-Darwinian biologists have retained the form of the Linnaean classification, but base their categories on the modern biological philosophy centered upon the fact of evolution. Most biologists believe that taxa should be defined *phyletically*. That is, a genus should be a group of species all descended from a single ancestral species, a family should include similarly related genera, and so on. Because species retain many heritage characters, such groups of relatives will share many characters, and so will be the most useful grouping for a variety of purposes. But most biologists also make some concession to phenetic distance in their classifications. For instance, in Figure 3–2 the genera *Pan* (chimpanzees) and *Gorilla* (gorilla) are obviously phyletically closer to *Homo* (humans) than to *Pongo* (orangutan). Yet chimpanzees and gorillas are commonly classified not with humans in the family Hominidae, but with orangutans in the family Pongidae. Most anthropologists retain this classification because of the radically new *derived* characters that evolved in the human lineage after it diverged from the African apes, and because they find it convenient to have a category (Pongidae) that includes all apes but excludes *Homo*. Other biologists insist on a more strictly phyletic classification, and put chimpanzees and gorillas in Hominidae. The merits of the two schemes cannot be discussed here; the important point is that both are compatible with the phyletic tree shown in Figure 3–2. One's choice between them depends upon preference, not upon interpretation of the evolutionary evidence.

A final problem concerns the definition of taxa. A biological species, as we saw, has an unambiguous definition; it is the maximum Mendelian population. But other taxa have no such firm definition; they are merely clusters of related species, genera, and so on. How wide a group of species, then, should be included in a genus? How many families comprise an order? There is no clear-cut answer to these questions. Genera, families, and orders are as widely defined as is useful; their breadth is a matter of taste, not proof. The only constraint is that taxa should be roughly equivalent in diversity throughout a major group; each family in the order Primates, for instance, should be about as diverse as families of rodents or carnivores.

mals. Thus we can state a second general principle for determining evolutionary relationships: *Phyletically related groups are to be recognized by the derived characters that they share.*

However, this second principle also requires modification, for as we have seen, not all resemblances, even in derived characters, necessarily indicate a recent common ancestry. Similar characteristics can also be acquired independently through parallel and convergent evolution. Superficial convergence, such as that between dolphins and ichthyosaurs, is generally easy to recognize, because other derived characters indicate that true relationships of the animals (the large, complex brain, "warm" blood, mammary glands, and a host of other derived features indicate the dolphin's relationship to other mammals). For instance, paleontologists have discovered the remains of extinct South American grazing mammals called Litopterns. Among these are some forms which, like the horse and zebra, have reduced the number of functional toes to one. This is a derived character for the Litopterns and it is shared with horses, but it was acquired independently, as is clearly shown when other parts of the body, such as teeth and skulls, are examined. We can see that such characters tell us little about common ancestry. They are so closely tied to the function of fast running that they are likely to be evolved by any herbivore taking to a grazing life in open country.

This case exemplifies a third general principle that modifies the other two: *Shared derived characters that are simple correlates of function are likely to be due to parallelism or convergence and thus are weak indicators of phyletic relationship.*

Figure 3–2 in the next chapter is an example of a phyletic tree reconstructed using these principles. It represents our concept of the evolutionary relationships in one small section of the living world—the part that includes the lemurs, monkeys, apes, and humans. These animals together constitute the living members of the order Primates and are the subject of the next several chapters of this book. Although we hope that they agree with its overall shape, many of our colleagues will certainly disagree with this or that detail of our construct. This is to be expected. There is no simple, foolproof formula for determining phyletic relationships. Applying general principles to particular cases requires judgment on the part of the biologist. It poses questions such as: Which characters are primitive, which are derived, for this particular group? How much similarity can reasonably be attributed to parallelism in this case? If traditional anatomy and biochemistry tell different evolutionary stories, which does one believe? Competent authorities often disagree in their interpretations of the facts, and hence come up with slightly different phyletic trees. But considering the immense diversity of the living world, the amount of agreement is impressive testimony to the consistency of the synthetic theory of evolution.

summary

The basic processes of evolution—as they are understood in the modern, *synthetic* theory of evolution—are based largely on the principles of genetics. In species that reproduce sexually, an individual develops from a fertilized egg according to a pattern determined by instructions that are encoded in the *genes*—the individual units of heredity—located on paired *chromosomes* in the nucleus of each cell. Each of the 46 chromosomes in the human cell is an immensely long molecule of *deoxyribonucleic acid (DNA)*. The DNA molecule carries instructions for the construction of *proteins,* organic molecules that are central to the structure and functioning of all living organisms. The particular characters of each individual are thus determined, in large part, by its inherited complement of DNA.

Genes are normally found in pairs in the individual, one member of each pair inherited from each parent. With respect to any one gene, an individual may be *homozygous* or *heterozygous;* that is, he may carry, respectively, identical or different *alleles* of the gene—its variant forms—on both chromosomes. The unique combination of genes carried by an individual—the *genotype*—determines one's physical character, or *phenotype.* The individual's genetic makeup, which is transmitted to his or her progeny, may be altered by *mutations* of various kinds; mutation is the source of genetic variability in both individuals and groups.

In the process of reproduction, genes are assorted in each generation. Inheritance rearranges the genetic material in each generation. In studying evolution, geneticists focus on the *Mendelian population:* this is a group within which genetic material is usually transmitted. The largest possible population is the biological *species,* a group of interbreeding populations that is reproductively isolated from other such groups. *Evolution* may be defined as any significant change in the gene frequencies in a species' *gene pool.*

Four factors are the most important forces operating to influence gene frequencies in a population: *mutation, gene flow, natural selection,* and *non-Darwinian evolution.* Of these, natural selection is usually the most significant, causing adaptive changes in gene frequencies, and stabilizing the gene pool in a well-adapted species by eliminating deleterious mutant genes. When natural selection is altering gene frequencies in response to environmental pressure, it is *directional;* the elimination of deleterious genes serves to adapt the species more efficiently to the demands of its habitat. Some recessive deleterious genes remain in the pool, forming the species' *genetic load.* Most populations are highly *polymorphic,* carrying several different alleles at many loci. Non-Darwinian evolution is observed most easily in small populations, where *genetic drift* may serve to fix certain genes in the population. However, in the long run, non-Darwinian evolution is independent of population size and may have played an important role in evolution, especially that of protein structure.

For millions of years, organisms and populations have evolved through mutation, natural selection, gene flow, and genetic drift. Seen in this long-term perspective, organisms and populations merge into evolutionary continua called lines of descent, or *lineages.*

Two factors determine a species' propensity for evolutionary change. First, the rate of change depends upon the relationship between an organism, its mode of life, and its habitat. For an organism that is secure in its econiche, there may be very little evolutionary change for long periods of time. On the other hand, changes in environment, or radical shifts in a population's mode of life, may subject the population's gene pool to powerful directional selective pressures, thereby causing rapid evolutionary change. Second, evolutionary adaptation resulting from natural selection can only be modifications of or variations upon genotypes already existing within the population.

Isolated segments of a population may evolve in different directions, due to genetic drift and adaptation to local environments. This process is called *diversification.* If this tendency is carried further and the gene pool of a species splits permanently and irreversibly from the "parent" species to produce a "daughter" species that follows a separate evolutionary path, the process is called *speciation.* Speciation and adaptation are the most fundamental evolutionary processes. Speciation in a population can lead to one of two consequences: (1) The species better adapted to a particular environment displaces the other species, which eventually becomes extinct. This results in a single species occupying the econiche as before. (2) The two related species will coexist by dividing the habitat between them either geographically or ecologically. They then coexist as separate species, each more specialized than the one from which both are descended, and each exploiting a different econiche in the same habitat. This outcome of speciation is called *divergence.*

Repeated speciation and divergence from a single ancestral stock, with the survival of the derived branches, is called *adaptive radiation.* This is a recurrent pattern in large-scale evolution. Often, extensive adaptive radiations arise when a single stock makes a significant adaptive breakthrough. Most radiations eventually "collapse."

Convergence is the evolution of superficially similar forms in different lineages. *Parallelism* occurs when related species with similar general adaptations independently come to resemble one another more than either resembles their common ancestral form. Resemblances among species due to parallelism and convergence are called *analogies*. Resemblances among species retained from a common ancestor are called *homologies*.

In their attempts to depict evolutionary history, biologists construct *phyletic trees,* branching diagrams that represent ideas about evolutionary relationships among groups of species. Comparisons among species are based on physical structures and elements of social behavior. The judgments about phyletic relationships are founded upon the following principles: (1) Animals that share detailed resemblances are usually closely related to each other. (2) Phyletically related groups are to be recognized by the *derived* characteristics that they share. (3) Shared derived characteristics that are simple correlates of function are likely to be due to parallelism or convergence and thus are weak indicators of phyletic relationships.

suggested readings

CAVALLI-SFORZA, L. L., AND BODMER, W. F.
  1971 *The Genetics of Human Populations*. San Francisco: W. H Freeman. A full and readable account of population genetics that does not avoid mathematical formulations, but makes them as palatable as possible for the nonmathematically inclined reader.

DOBZHANSKY, T.
  1962 *Mankind Evolving*. New Haven: Yale University Press. A leading geneticist reviews human heredity and evolution, and considers their ethical and historical applications.

McKUSICK, V. A.
  1969 *Human Genetics*. 2d ed. Englewood Cliffs, N.J.: Prentice-Hall. A succinct and authoritative coverage of all major aspects of human genetics.

SIMPSON, G. G.
  1967 *The Meaning of Evolution: A Study of the History of Life and of Its Significance for Man*. Rev. ed. New Haven: Yale University Press. A review of the major phenomena of large-scale evolution, especially from the point of view of the paleontologist.

  1961 *Principles of Animal Taxonomy*. New York: Columbia University Press. An exposition of the principles of classification still accepted by the majority of animal taxonomists.

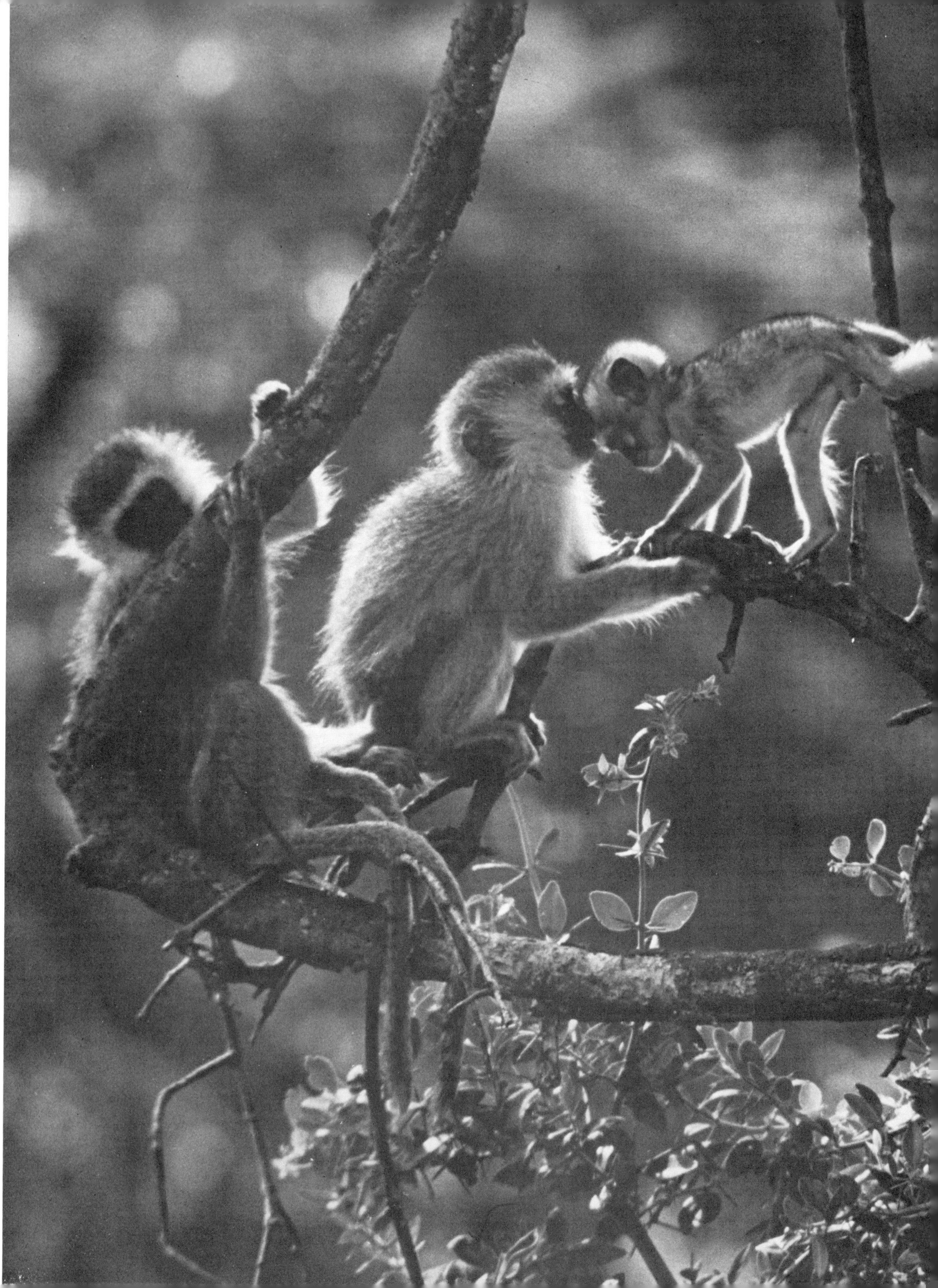

three
The Living Primates

Primatology as a distinct branch of science has burgeoned since World War II. It combines the earlier disciplines of comparative anatomy and physiology with data derived from behavioral research (much of it collected during field research on wild primates) and information on molecular structure gleaned from the most recent findings of biochemistry.

Anthropologists use the data of primatology for three major purposes. The first is to define the peculiarities of the human species. For example, until the 1960s, humanity was often defined by its capacity for toolmaking, but research showed that chimpanzees use tools also. This knowledge led anthropologists to reconsider tool use as an important stimulus to the development of hominid traits and to define more carefully the distinctiveness of the use of tools by humans.

Second, primatology helps the anthropologist to reconstruct the hypothetical forms ancestral to humans. Because living primates often conserve ancestral characteristics in their behavior and structure, we can use them to reconstruct ancestral stages in primate evolution. Since all living primate species have evolved through time, and specializations and adaptations have taken place in each line just as they have in ours, we cannot assume that any extant primate is a living fossil that resembles an ancestral form in all ways.

Third, primatological data helps the anthropologist to interpret by analogy the characteristics of forms known only as fossils. These analogies enable the researcher to compare similarities that have been acquired independently by separate lines. If two evolving animal species independently acquire a certain physical characteristic, we can assume that they also share the behaviors that can be functionally linked to that characteristic, however distantly related and generally dissimilar in overall structure the two may be. If one of them is living and the other is extinct, we can use our knowledge of the former's behavior to reconstruct that of the latter. In tracing the course of human evolution, we shall come across several cases in which it is helpful to make use of living animals to interpret the structure of fossils through analogies of this kind.

Primate Realms and Habitats

According to evolutionary theory, the diversity of a group such as the primates reflects to a large extent the adaptive responses the members of the group have made to varied environmental opportunities. Thus in order to understand primate diversity, one must first understand something of the nature of the habitats in which primates live. The great majority of living primates are to be found in the belt between the northern and southern tropics. Within this broad zone, however, is a variety of habitats with distinctive climates and different types of vegetation. (See Figure 3–1.) Each of these habitats makes different demands upon its inhabitants. The evolutionary line leading to man apparently went through several stages in which it was adapted first to one and then to another of these major zones; this has had a profound influence upon the direction its evolution has taken.

A young ververt monkey (Cercopithecus aethiops) "mothers" an infant. (Donald Paterson/Photo Researchers)

A wild chimpanzee and her daughter use simple tools to "fish" for termites in the Gombe Stream National Park, Tanzania. This group was observed for many years by Jane Goodall; the old female, named Flo, was the center of a kin group, and became a grandmother shortly before she died. (Jane van Lawick-Goodall, © National Geographic Society)

(For an account of some interesting primate field research, see the box on pages 58–59 for the discussion of a study of baboons in the Awash National Park.)

Tropical Rain Forests

Tropical evergreen rain forests are the primate heartland. There, primate faunas are richest in diversity of species, and this is the only zone in which primates often dominate the total mammalian fauna in numbers and in biomass (that is, the total mass of living substance constituting a species). Many of the peculiarities of the order seem to be related to the rain forest habitat, indicating that it was probably the region in which the primates first emerged and which profoundly influenced the early evolution of all its major branches.

The climate of the equatorial rain forest belt is more or less continuously hot and humid. Some rain falls every month, providing sufficient moisture for plant growth throughout the year. Trees are the dominant form of life, and the crowns of the mature trees form a continuous closed canopy of leaves through which very little sunlight can penetrate to the lower layers. Because so little light reaches the ground, the ground cover of vegetation in a mature forest is characteristically very sparse. The best living in a tropical rain forest, therefore, is to be made by climbing animals that can reach the canopy and its food supplies. Many forest primates spend their whole lives in the swaying world of the canopy. Others prefer the tangled growth of shrubs that spring up when the canopy is broken by the fall of a giant tree. Still others specialize in the resources offered by the swamp forest or travel on the ground.

In the stable climate of the rain forest, insects continue to be active and trees continue to produce fruit and new leaves throughout the year. This combination of factors means that the forest provides a particularly large number of distinct but rather narrow and specialized econiches for primates and other animals.

The comparative lack of seasonal variation

in the rain forest environment affects the reproductive strategy of its inhabitants. In the rain forest, there is no pronounced lean season similar to winter in a northern woodland, when food supplies decrease dramatically and animal populations are drastically reduced. Nor is there a spring, when resources burgeon and populations are rapidly swollen by a new crop of young animals. In such a habitat, the most advantageous strategy is to rear few offspring, but to do so carefully, so that a high percentage survives to maturity, with each individual animal well prepared to step into a "vacancy" when an adult of the species dies. The fact that the early primates evidently adopted this strategy rather than the alternative "shotgun" approach typical of mammals such as rodents is another indication of the rain-forest origin of the order and the profound effect that this environment had on the establishment of its characteristic features.

Tropical Woodlands and Savannas

The tropical rain forest zone is flanked north and south by a belt of tropical woodlands and savannas. In these regions there is adequate rainfall for vigorous plant growth, but the precipitation is more seasonally distributed than in the forest, occurring almost entirely within one or two comparatively short rainy seasons. During the dry season, most of the trees lose their leaves, and the herbaceous plants die back. The first rains stimulate a flush of vigorous growth, with trees and shrubs putting out new leaves, and new green shoots coming up from the seeds or dormant underground parts of grasses and herbaceous plants. Depending on local conditions, the tree cover may vary from an almost continuous canopy to nearly none at all in areas of almost pure grassland. Because the canopy is thin and bare of leaves for part of the year, light can penetrate to the ground, permitting the growth of the vigorous ground cover characteristic of the zone.

Figure 3–1. Diagrammic profile of major habitats of nonhuman primates: (a) tropical rain forest—several major layers, little ground cover; (b) swamp forest—dense growth on waterlogged ground within rain forest; (c) woodland—deciduous, low-canopy trees, lush ground cover; (d) gallery forest—taller, evergreen trees along a waterway in woodland or steppe; (e) dry savannas or steppe—scattered trees and shrubs, short grass. (Biruta Akerbergs)

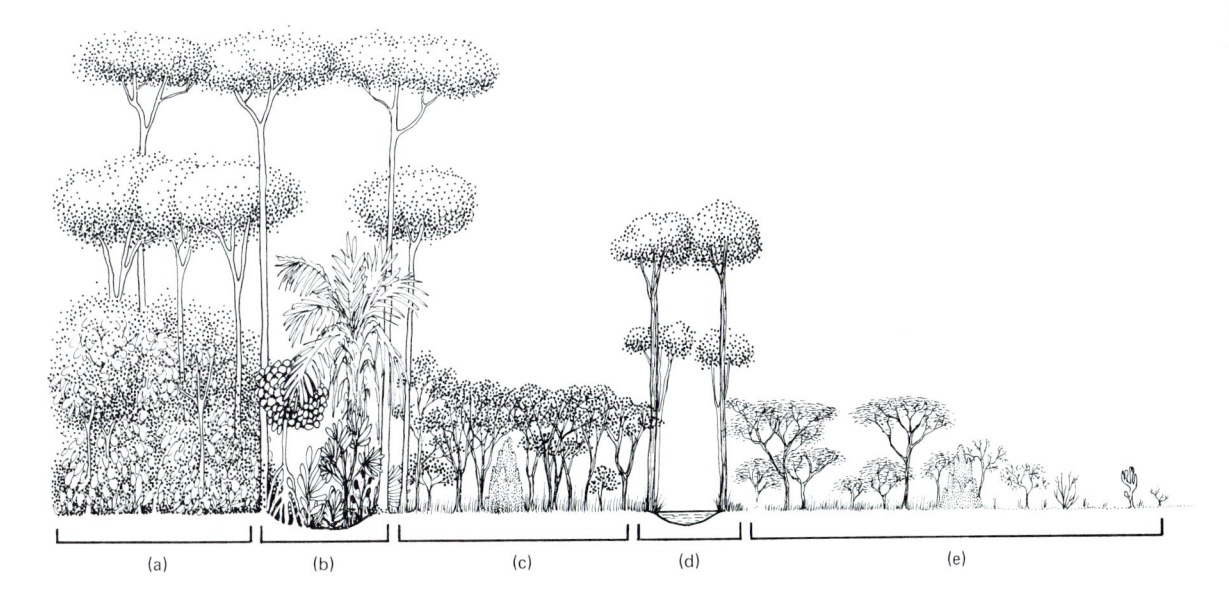

Compared to the tropical rain forest, the woodlands and savannas pose new problems for their primate inhabitants and call for somewhat different strategies of survival. Each food resource becomes available in its season and then disappears, so savanna primates must be more adaptable and able to exploit a wider spectrum of resources than their relatives in the rain forest need to do. They must be able to move on the ground between food resources and should also be adapted to feeding on the ground during at least part of the year.

Moisture can also be a problem in the grasslands. Foods that grow in the savanna are generally less juicy than those in the rain forest, and surface water is relatively scarce. Thus, in periods other than the rainy season, primates must often trek to water holes or riverbanks to drink; at these sites they have to compete with other animals for water, and they run the risk of meeting lurking predators. As we shall see, the move from the comparatively stable ecological situation of the rain forest to the new challenges of the savanna probably had an important influence on the evolution of the human family.

Themes of Primate Adaptation

The living members of the order Primates, which we can define as the mammalian order to which *Homo sapiens* belongs, usually show certain characteristics in their structure and behavior. Not all of these characteristics have been retained by all primates in the course of their evolution, and some of the characteristics are also seen in members of other orders. On the whole, however, they give the members of the order a "family resemblance" that enables one to recognize them. Some are characters retained from the primitive nonprimate ancestry of the order; others are features that had probably developed in the ancestral primate stock from which all living primates are descended.

The primitive characteristics of primates include (1) a five-digited, or pendactyl, hand and foot (the primates have not modified their limbs into flippers, wings, or hooves, as have mammals of other orders), and (2) a rather unspecialized dentition (set of teeth) suitable for processing a wide variety of foods.

The specialized trends distinctive of primates include adaptations for arboreal existence: (1) the development of grasping hands and feet with fingers and toes capable of encircling the branch of a tree and gripping it with nails rather than claws, and a big toe (hallux) that is abductible; (2) a tendency for vision to become the dominant sense to the exclusion of the others, especially smell, with a concomitant enlargement of the visual association areas of the brain; and (3) a tendency toward use of the hand as an exploratory organ rather than simply for locomotion. Primates reach for things and grab them with their hands, rather than literally poking their noses into them and grabbing them with their muzzles and teeth. Recently, Matt Cartmill (in Tuttle, 1972) has shown that these characters are best explained as adaptations to life among the small branches of the forest canopy; animals in this econiche could best hunt insects by stalking and grabbing them. He suggests that the ancestor of all living primates was such an animal and that this way of life established these characteristics as basic attributes of the order. The theory is an appealing one, though it is as yet unproven.

A second set of characters is related to reproductive strategy. There have been tendencies toward: (1) a reduction in the number of young in a litter and an increase in the time of dependency of the young upon the mother, the period during which learning takes place; an increase in the relative size of the brain, especially those parts of the brain associated with "higher functions"—namely, learning and association; an increase in the length of the individual's life span; and finally, a tendency toward life in permanent groups consisting of individuals of all ages and both sexes. These four characters also form a functionally linked group. As an order, primates have specialized in rearing rather few offspring but rearing them very carefully. During the long period of immaturity, the offspring learns from its parents and other group members, acquiring both social skills and techniques for dealing with its environment. These features seem to have been acquired not so much for life in the trees as for life in the unique ecosystem of the tropical rain forest. This suggests, then, that the ancestor of all living primates lived in the tropical rain forest and established in that habitat the adaptive trends that were inherited and developed by all its descendants, including man.

The broad range of the primate order is divided by deep water barriers into three distinct realms: South America; Madagascar; and Africa and Asia. Each of these has a distinctive primate fauna: in South America, the platyrrhines, or New World monkeys; in Africa-Asia, the lorises, tarsiers, Old World monkeys, and anthropoid apes; and in Madagascar, the lemurs. Man is the only primate common to all three, and his arrival in South America and Madagascar is comparatively recent. Many of the ecological opportunities are similar in the three regions, and this has resulted in a good deal of parallel evolution among their primate faunas. Each realm, for instance, houses species of tree-living, leaf-eating primates as well as insect eaters and fruit eaters. And both Africa-Asia and Madagascar are, or were, the home of primates that independently forsook the trees for life on the ground. In the next section we will take a closer look at these diverse forms, their phyletic relationships, and the parallels between them.

Primate Diversity

There are some thirty or so living genera of primates and well over a hundred species, each with its own unique range, habitat, and way of life. For a variety of reasons, it is convenient to treat the living primates by starting with humans and their closest relatives, and moving outward on the phyletic tree to the more distant and less familiar members of the order.

Humans are the only living member of the family Hominidae. They are really the fifth great ape, whose closest relatives—chimpanzee, pygmy chimp, gorilla, and orangutan—belong to the family Pongidae. (See Figure 3–2.)

The hominids and pongids, together with a third family, the Hylobatidae—to which the long-armed, tree-swinging gibbons belong—form the superfamily Hominoidea. All hominoids lack an external tail, and in spite of variations in the length of their arms and legs, share the basic shape of the trunk that is seen in humans: broad-chested, with the rib cage flattened from front to back.

By contrast, the monkeys of Asia and Africa, who belong to the superfamily Cercopithecoidea, have tails and a more conventional mammalian trunk shape—long and narrow from side to side, but deep from front to back. When they move on all fours, which is their usual gait both in the trees and on the ground, the monkeys rest upon the palms of their hands or on their finger pads, not on their knuckles as the apes do. While they are nearly all agile climbers, they are much less inclined when in the trees to swing beneath the branches by their arms (to brachiate) than the apes are. Genetic and protein studies show that the cercopithecoids are all rather closely related to one another, indicating that their adaptive radiation was a relatively recent one.

The Old World monkeys, apes, and man belong to a single infraorder, the Catarrhini. The two families of South American monkeys are allocated to a separate infraorder, Platyrrhini, expressing their phyletic distinctness from the Old World group. Although many of the platyrrhines look superficially like Old World monkeys, various anatomical features set them apart from all catarrhines. The way in which the ear region of the skull is constructed, for instance, is different; and they have three rather than two premolar teeth in each jaw. In both these respects, they are more primitive than the catarrhines. Some—though by no means all—have a prehensile tail used mainly as a "fifth hand" to support the animal as it hangs to feed in the canopy. No catarrhine has this. Studies of blood proteins support the idea that the platyrrhines

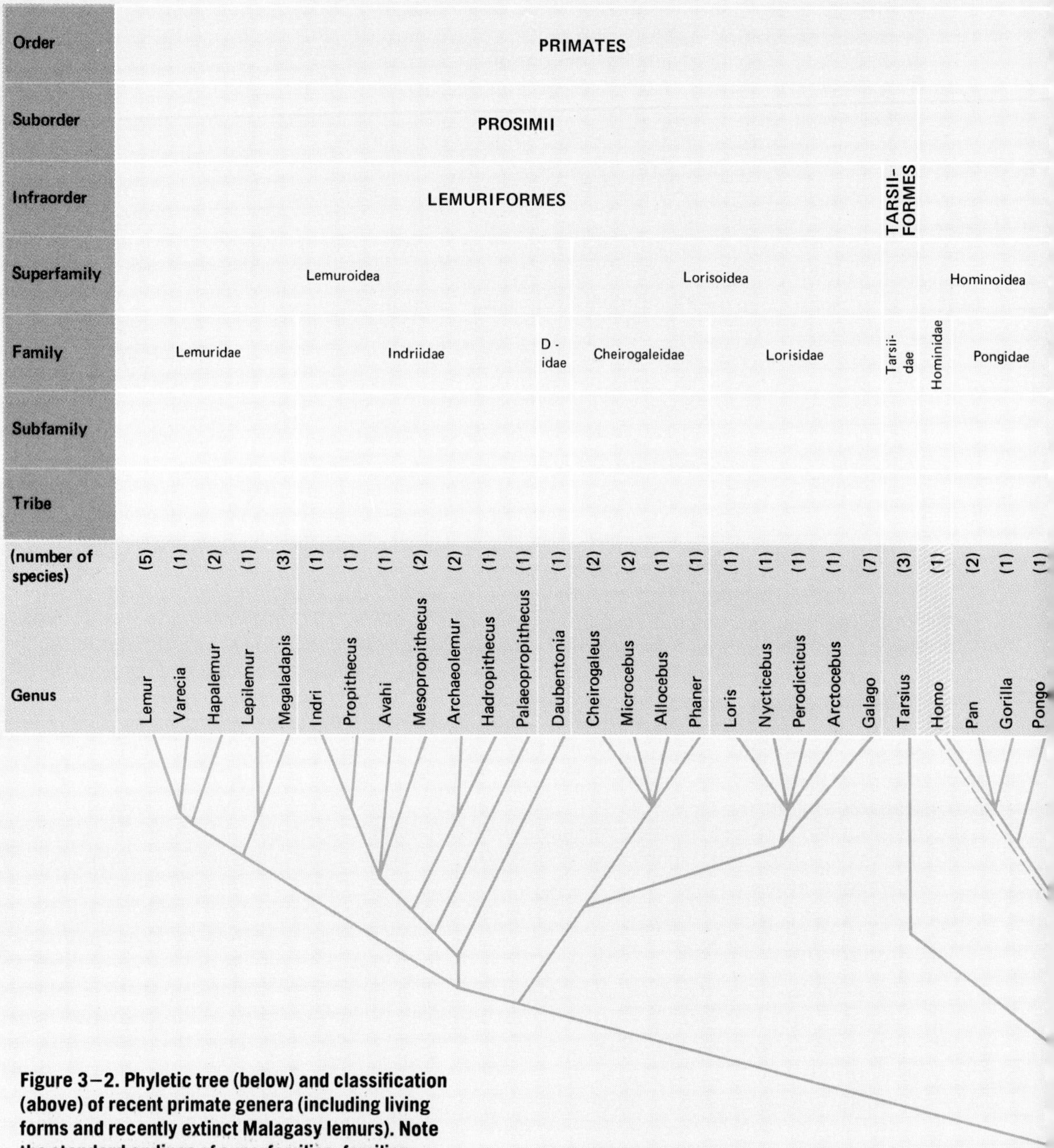

Figure 3–2. Phyletic tree (below) and classification (above) of recent primate genera (including living forms and recently extinct Malagasy lemurs). Note the standard endings of superfamilies, families, subfamilies, and tribes, and how they are formed from generic names. Classification conforms closely to phylogeny, but there are some deviations, notably the classification of Pan and Gorilla in Pongidae rather than Hominidae.

PRIMATES

ANTHROPOIDEA

CATARRHINI · PLATYRRHINI

Cercopithecoidea

Hylobatidae · Cercopithecidae · Cebidae · Callitrichidae

Cercopithecinae · Colobinae · Cebinae · Alouattinae · Aotinae · Atelinae · Pitheciinae · C-inae · Callitrichinae

Cercopithecini · Papionini

(6) Hylobates
(17) Cercopithecus
(1) Erythrocebus
(11) Macaca
(5) Cercocebus
(2) Papio
(1) Theropithecus
(2) Mandrillus
(12) Presbytis
(3) Rhinopithecus
(2) Nasalis
(4) Colobus
(1) Procolobus
(4) Cebus
(2) Saimiri
(5) Alouatta
(1) Aotus
(3) Callicebus
(4) Ateles
(1) Brachyteles
(2) Lagothrix
(2) Pithecia
(3) Cacajao
(2) Chiropotes
(1) Callimico
(8) Callithrix
(3) Leontideus
(1) Cebuella
(22) Saguinus

Other placental mammals

CLASSIFICATION

PHYLETIC RELATIONSHIP

Tarsier (Tarsius). Both the adult and young tarsier show the long ankle (tarsus) that gives the animal its name. Its long legs are flexed, ready to hop. Its huge eyes reflect its nocturnal habits. (San Diego Zoo)

Ring-tailed lemur (Lemur catta). Like all lemuriform prosimians, this ring-tailed lemur has a moist rhinarium ("dog's nose"), long, slender fingers for climbing, and nails on its fingers and toes. This species is diurnal in its habits, and quite frequently comes to the ground to forage. (Jen and Des Bartlett/Photo Researchers)

are only distant relatives of the catarrhine group. To the student of human evolution, their major significance is that their radiation has in some respects paralleled that of the catarrhines. Often their behavior helps us to reconstruct by analogy stages through which catarrhines passed long ago, but which are now represented only by fossils.

In spite of their diversity, all the primates we have described so far are readily recognized as relatives of humans. Their large, rounded braincase with close-set eyes that face directly forward from above the nose; their immobile rounded ears, set close to the side of the head; and their mobile, expressive faces give them a humanlike appearance that is unmistakable. This similarity, and the phyletic relationship that underlies it, is expressed by grouping catarrhines and platyrrhines together into the suborder Anthropoidea.

The members of the remaining families of living primates, comprising the suborder Prosimii, are much less obviously humanlike. Most have smaller, flatter braincases, above which project pointed mobile ears. A pointed muzzle usually projects from between the eyes and in most cases is tipped by a wet, naked patch of skin (like a dog's nose) called a rhinarium. The whole set of the face is more reminiscent of small cats or foxes than of a human. Below the neck, however, the prosimians clearly betray their primate affinities, with mobile limbs and hands and feet adapted for climbing by grasping.

On the whole, the prosimians have departed less from the primitive mammalian form and from the early primates of 50 million years ago than have the Anthropoidea. Having said this, however, we must also stress that the prosimian level of organization has proved remarkably adaptable and has given rise to such a variety of specially adapted types that generalization about the group as a whole is difficult. This is especially true of the lemurs of Madagascar, which, with virtually an empty ecosystem to populate, produced an amazing array of adaptive types.

The lemurs, along with the lorises and bush babies of Africa and Asia, belong to the infraorder Lemuriformes. While these animals are best classified in the primate order, there is little doubt that the lemuriforms have an independent evolutionary history going back to the earliest days of the primates. The second infraorder, the Tarsiiformes, has anatomical features—notably the absence of a rhinarium and the structure of the placenta—that strongly suggest that it is more closely related to the monkeys and apes than to lorises and lemurs. However, the relationship is a very distant one, and most primatologists still prefer to classify the tarsiers with other prosimians.

Primate Adaptations

To speak of "the ape," "the monkey," or "the lemur" is a gross distortion. Each of these groups represents one or more major adaptive radiations that have produced an array of special adaptive types. These separate radiations have produced many instances of parallel evolution, enabling us to speak of adaptive types such as "leaf eater," "brachiator," and so on, that cut across taxonomic boundaries. Some of these adaptive types are of particular relevance to the interpretation of the evolutionary stages that led to the human species. If we can establish consistent and convincing connections in living primates between anatomical features on the one hand and behavior on the other, then we have a firm foundation for interpreting fossils. In this section, we will describe these connections for four areas especially crucial for survival—locomotion, feeding, senses and the brain, and social organization.

The Locomotor System

The locomotor system includes the behaviors and structures concerned with posture and movement of the body. The structures most concerned in these activities are the bones, joints, and muscles of the limbs and trunk. Clearly, postural and locomotor habits are a fundamental aspect of the ecological strategy of any animal group. But among the primates such adaptations in locomotor habits are especially important. It has been remarked that almost every major primate adaptive radiation has involved changes in locomotor patterns that opened a new array of econiches.

Repertoires and Profiles of Locomotor Activity
Primates have a very wide repertoire of locomotor activities in comparison to most other mammals. If you watch a group of monkeys for any length of time, the chances are that within an hour or so you will see them stand, walk, and run on all fours (quadrupedally); stand bipedally (on two feet); climb vertical trunks and branches; hang by one, two, three, or four limbs; swing by one or two arms; jump, hop, and leap. This wide locomotor repertoire is directly related, of course, to living in trees, especially in the tangled openwork of the canopy. Although most primates share this locomotor versatility, primate species vary widely in the degree to which they use and depend upon the different movements of which they are capable. Some species specialize in bipedal leaping, others specialize in arm swinging, and still other species move mostly in the quadrupedal position. Thus we can say that although locomotor repertoires of primates are uniformly wide and rather similar to one another, their locomotor *profiles* are quite different.

Locomotion and Natural Selection Field studies suggest that many wild primates operate on a very tight "energy budget," at least at some times of the year. That is to say, the amount of energy in the form of food that can be gathered and processed only just balances the amount of energy expended in traveling to find it, collecting it, and digesting it. The animal that expends the least energy in such maintenance activities will have the most left over to burn in producing milk for young and competing for mates, or simply to store in the form of fat against future shortages. Locomotor efficiency will directly enhance fitness, and natural selection favors structural modifications that make economical use of energy in locomotion.

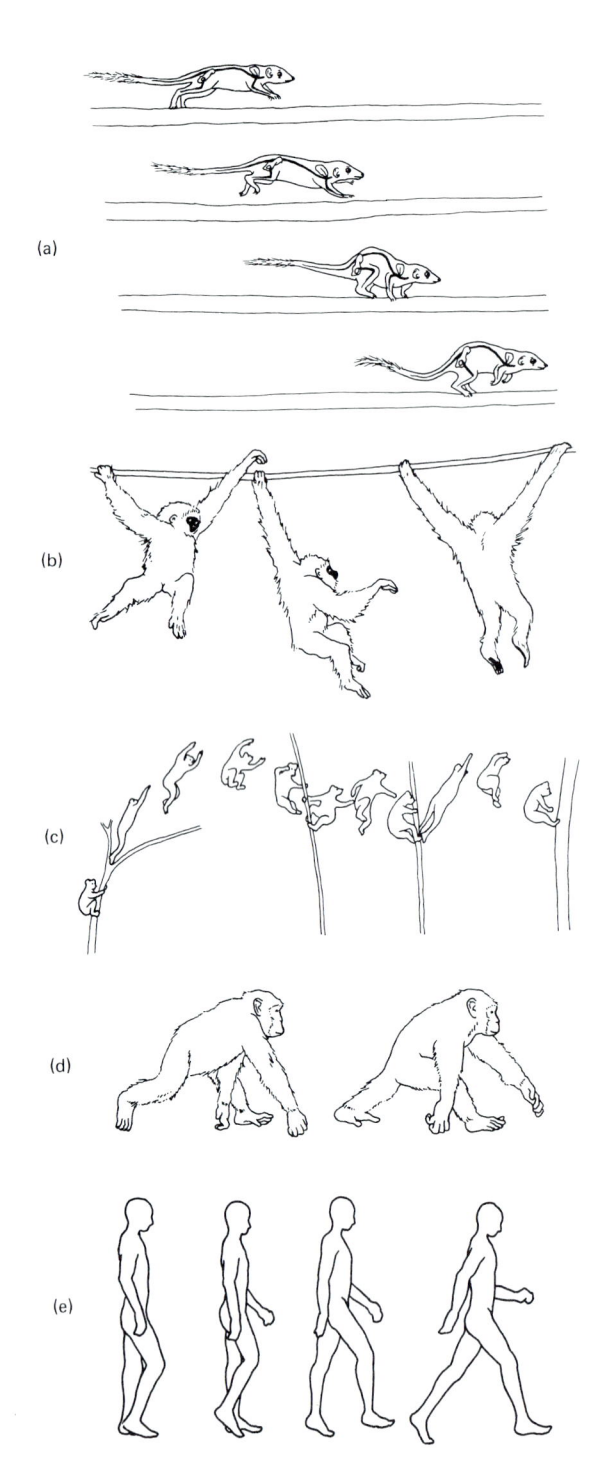

As we might expect, then, natural selection adapts the limb structure of a species to fit its locomotor and postural profile. However, it should be emphasized again that evolution is an opportunistic phenomenon, with natural selection working on the variation at hand, not designing new structures from scratch. Any structure that has undergone evolutionary change will reflect "old" adaptations as well as new ones.

Locomotor Profiles Fortunately, the living primates preserve a variety of locomotor adaptations, some more primitive and others more highly derived. The primates can be arranged in a series such that each represents a stage built on the adaptations of the preceding one. (See Figure 3–3.) This arrangement does not represent an evolutionary tree. There is no time scale. All the animals included are modern. Each modern form is only standing in a general way for the ancestor of another; it will not be like the true ancestor in all respects.

The pen-tailed tree shrew is believed to retain the primitive mammalian form from which the primates are derived. It is a small, agile arboreal mammal that climbs, leaps, and scampers quadrupedally among the branches of the forest canopy.

In many mammalian lineages, the basic body plan has been greatly modified; some limb bones have been lost or fused together, entailing a sacrifice of locomotor flexibility for the sake of efficiency in a few locomotor activities. Among primates as a group, much of the primitive flexibility has been retained and enhanced. The primitive primate form is illus-

Figure 3–3. Some locomotor activities of primates: (a) branch-running (arboreal quadrupedalism) — tree shrew (an insectivore); (b) brachiation — gibbon; (c) leaping from one vertical support to another — **Indri**; (d) knuckle-walking quadrupedalism — chimpanzee; (e) bipedalism — man. [Biruta Akerbergs after (a) F. A. Jenkins, 1974; (b) courtesy of Ralph Morse and Animal Talent Scouts, Inc.; (c) J. R. Napier and A. C. Walker, 1967; (d) M. Hildebrand, 1968]

trated by the dwarf lemur of Madagascar. The hands and feet show the basic primate adaptation to climbing by grasping.

The spider monkey differs from the more generalized arboreal quadrupeds in making greater use of suspension by the arms in its locomotion and posture. It hangs from its arms while feeding and often moves by brachiation, swinging hand over hand through the branches. Brachiation allows quite large-bodied animals to move and feed safely among branches too small for them to balance upon. In this way, they are able to feed in the outer twigs of the canopy where much fruit and new leaf growth occurs. However, extreme adaptation for brachiation, such as in the case of the gibbon, has its disadvantages. It eliminates conventional quadrupedal locomotion because the animal's back is too short, its arms too long, and its joints too highly adapted to hanging.

The chimpanzee represents a brachiator with secondary modifications for moving on the ground. The brachiator structure of the trunk and limbs is retained, and the animal often uses suspensory locomotion when climbing in the trees to feed. On the ground, it usually walks on all fours, supporting its body weight on its knuckles. Because of its long arms and rather short legs, the back is sloping rather than horizontal. As adaptations to knuckle walking, the bones and ligaments of the wrist are modified in structure and arrangement so as to strengthen it, and the knuckles are surfaced with tough, hairless friction pads.

Bipedalism *Homo sapiens* is the only living primate to use bipedalism as its habitual posture and gait, although many primates occasionally stand or even walk a few steps on their hind legs. Although there is some disagreement as to what locomotor type immediately preceded the bipedal hominid type—a semi-brachiator, such as *Ateles;* an advanced brachiator, such as the orangutan or gibbon; or an ex-brachiator (knuckle walker), such as the chimpanzee—there is little doubt that hominids passed through some kind of brachiating stage. The human trunk and forelimb are very similar in general shape and proportions to those of the brachiators, though with shoulders that are less hunched and a hand modified for manipulatory ability.

A gibbon (<u>Hylobates lar</u>) feeds from a small twig while hanging by one arm. The gibbon's apparatus for hanging in this way enables it to exploit food resources in the outer canopy of the forest that are not easily accessible to other primates. (Courtesy, D. J. Chivers)

The major modifications associated with bipedalism in humans involve the hindlimb, the pelvis, and the lumbar vertebrae. The hindlimb of *Homo sapiens* is one of his most specialized features. Whereas other primates have hindlimbs capable of supporting their body weight for a few upright steps, humans have specializations of the pelvis, thigh, leg, and foot that virtually rule out any other use of the hindlimb in locomotion. In all quadrupedal locomotion, including knuckle walking, the body weight is distributed between forelimbs and hindlimbs. The spine is more or less horizontal, and the weight line falls well in front of the leg. In bipedal gaits, the body weight is transmitted more or less directly down through the nearly vertical spinal column, the pelvis, thigh, knee, ankle, and foot. Most of the modifications of these structures as seen in humans (detailed in Figure 3–4), can be regarded as simple adaptations to increased weight bearing in bipedalism.

Adaptation to bipedalism as a habitual gait and posture is unique to *Homo sapiens* among living primates. Unlike any other primate, humans, while walking, have both hands free to carry, throw, gather, or signal. This has been a profound factor in the elaboration of human culture.

Figure 3–4. Comparison of Homo sapiens and Pan troglodytes: (a) skeleton of chimpanzee in bipedal position; (b) skeleton of modern human; (c) chimpanzee and human "bisected" and drawn to the same trunk length for comparison of limb proportions. It is the contrast in leg length that is largely responsible for the proportional difference between man and ape. Note also the hunched shoulders of the chimpanzee. (Biruta Akerbergs)

The Feeding System

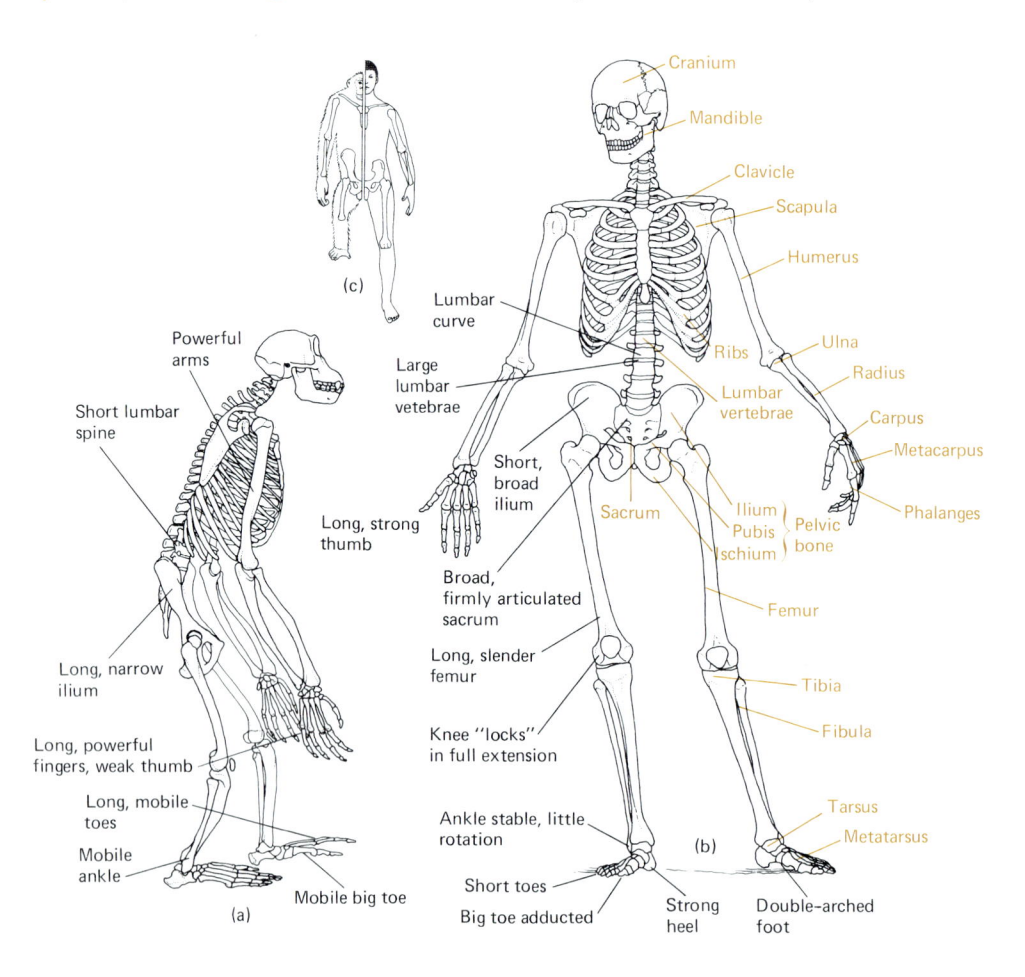

An animal's feeding habits are a most basic part of its adaptive strategy. What it eats to a large extent determines its position in the ecosystem of which it is a part. The behavioral side of the feeding system, in turn, determines the selective effects that act upon the structures used in gathering food and utilizing its nutrients in the body. In primates, the structures whose variation in form predominantly reflects the demands of feeding habits include the lips, tongue, cheeks, teeth, jaws, jaw muscles, stomach, and intestines. Of these, we shall concentrate upon the teeth and jaws, which are often found as fossils, and the jaw muscles, which leave recognizable marks on bones and can thus be reconstructed from fossil evidence. The hand reflects the demands of both feeding and locomotion.

Primate Feeding Habits Most primates are omnivores, eating a mixed diet of fruit, leaves, and animal food, generally insects. Adaptability in feeding habits is one of the distinctive features of the order. But all primate diets are not the same. Just as locomotor profiles vary, so do dietary profiles. There are specialized insect eaters, specialized leaf eaters, and those that favor a mixed diet based mainly on fruit. Forest-dwelling fruit eaters feed largely on tough-skinned but juicy fruits. Species living in savannas—as, for example, baboons—must eat a higher proportion of hard, dry fruits, like the seeds of the acacia tree. One primate species, the gelada baboon, has specialized in feeding on grass blades or shoots. Each of these foods makes different demands on the food-processing apparatus (fruit, for example, must be peeled; grass must be finely ground), and these demands will, through the action of natural selection, ultimately be reflected in the structure of the teeth, jaws, and the rest of the digestive system.

However, we must remember that primate diets always include a wide variety of foods, and only the most demanding and dominant of such foods will be reflected in tooth and jaw structure. Also, we must bear in mind that in the teeth, even more than in the locomotor system, new adaptations can be superimposed on existing plans. Each major group of primates shows common features of the dentition that tell us more about their phyletic relationship than about their diet. Only when close relatives are compared can contrasts in the dentition confidently be attributed to functional differences.

The Dentition and Masticatory Muscles The teeth can be divided into four major groups: incisors, canines, premolars, and molars. The incisors are generally used to seize food and, along with the hands, are employed in its initial preparation. The canines primitively functioned as part of the seizing-holding apparatus, and in some primates they have retained that function, but in many others they have been elaborated for fighting and display. We shall discuss canine size and structure in the context of social interaction. The premolars and molars are generally used in chewing, grinding, and shearing to break food down for swallowing.

In food processing, the lower teeth, set in the mandible, work against the upper set, set in the maxilla and premaxilla. These mandibular movements are produced by the muscles of mastication, which run from the skull to the mandible. In incisal biting, the jaw is pulled up and backward. In chewing, it is swung up and down and from side to side as upper and lower molars grind across each other. (The reader can check these movements and the contrasting functions of incisors and cheek teeth by eating an apple.) The muscle attachments therefore give further evidence of eating habits.

Feeding Profiles Typical insect eaters have sharp, pointed incisors to seize their prey. Their molars have sharp crests that, shearing past each other in chewing, slice the tough skins of insects into digestible pieces.

Fruit eating involves less shearing but more crushing than insect eating. The upper molars retain the primitive triangular crown of insect-eating forebears, but a fourth cusp or point has been added, providing a greater surface area and a flatter platform for crushing. Fruit eating also requires a mechanism in the front of the mouth to bite through thick rinds. Among the monkeys and apes, habitual fruit eaters have broad, chisel-like incisors and strong, backward-sloping temple muscles for a powerful bite.

The adaptations of the grass-eating gelada baboon are of some interest, since some of them are paralleled in the earliest hominids. The incisors are quite small, since grass is plucked by hand, but the molars and premolars are large and high-crowned. The crowns have many complex folds of enamel. As they wear, fresh enamel edges are exposed and form a self-renewing set of tiny mincing blades. The jaw muscles lend more crushing and grinding power to the cheek teeth at the expense of incisal biting.

A gorilla (Gorilla gorilla) in a zoo relieves his boredom by fiddling with a piece of straw. This shows the delicate precision grip between index finger and thumb characteristic of the catarrhine primates' anatomical specializations of the hand and their fine coordination between hand and eye. (Ron Garrison/San Diego Zoo)

Humans Although human teeth are much like those of apes in structure, our whole masticatory apparatus is reduced. Compared to the size of the body they nourish, the teeth and jaw muscles are generally small and weakened, and the third molars (wisdom teeth) often fail to erupt. This trend has been attributed to human use of cutting tools, grindstones, cooking, and other technology to replace the food-preparing functions of the teeth. According to this plausible theory, the masticatory apparatus is simply degenerating, the usual evolutionary fate of redundant structures.

The Hand Although treated here as part of the feeding system, primate hands are used for all kinds of manipulation—grooming, digging, and picking things apart, as well as picking up food. In other mammals, many of these tasks are performed by snouts and teeth. The primate trend has been to rely more on the hand and less on the teeth and the snout for investigation and manipulation.

The grasping hand, originally part of the small-branch-climbing complex, made this trend possible. In prosimians, the hand grasp is a simple grab, with the fingers and thumb pressing the object to be held against the palm. This *power grip* is retained in monkeys and apes, but they and we also have a *precision grip* of thumb against index finger, used for finer manipulation. This grip is made possible by modifications of the muscles and ligaments of the hand that allow the pad of the thumb to be rotated so as to oppose it to the index finger, but it also depends upon the brain. The finely tuned motor control of the hand in higher primates permits even the clumsy-looking hands of the gorilla to perform fine manipulatory tasks. The precision grip is used by higher primates in a variety of situations requiring fine manipulation. Monkeys use it to pick apart leaf buds and bark as they search for insects. The chimpanzee uses it to shape and handle its "termiting" twig. But the most regular and consistent use of the precision grip in nonhuman primates is in small-object feeding—picking up morsels such as seeds or grass blades one by one from the ground. All baboons are adept at this, and the gelada, the specialized small-object feeder, shows special adaptations for it.

Senses and the Brain

Primates, like other animals, rely on a constant flow of information from their environment. This information is gathered through the special senses of vision, olfaction (smell), taste, hearing, and touch, and transmitted by the nervous system to the brain, where it is processed, stored, and used as a basis for further action on the part of the animal. As we have mentioned, primates as a group are characterized by elaboration of the sense of sight, largely at the expense of olfaction; by localization of the tactile sense in the hands rather than in the muzzle; and by the possession of a brain that is both larger and functionally more sophisticated than that of most other mammals. Variation among living primates mainly concerns the degree to which these trends have been emphasized.

The Brain Compared to other mammals, primates have brains that are large in proportion to their bodies, and their brains are characterized by an extensive development of the cerebral cortex, the seat of the so-called higher functions of the brain. In addition, the brain's proportions reflect the importance of visual information, in comparison to other forms of sensory input.

Variation among primates in brain structure reflects the degree to which these trends are expressed. Among lemuroids, for instance, the parts of the brain receiving and processing olfactory information are still comparatively large. In anthropoids, the areas receiving visual stimuli and information from tactile receptors in the hand are comparatively larger and more elaborate.

More significant are the differences in development of the cortical areas that do not have an immediate simple relationship to sensory input. These are the so-called association and quiet areas of the brain. These are concerned with functions such as memory, storage of information, comparison of new experiences with those of the past, and integration of information and memories from different sensory channels. When we observe that brain expansion is a primate trend, it is largely these areas that are involved in the increase.

The living primates represent four major grades of cortical expansion. Most primitive, as usual, are the prosimians. The monkeys, platyrrhine and catarrhine, represent the next grade. The apes, especially the Pongidae, are more advanced still, and finally, the human species stands quite alone in the highest grade.

Two major areas of cortical expansion are especially distinctive of modern humans: the frontal lobes and the parietal association area (Figure 3–5). In humans, the function of the frontal lobes seems to be related to the ability to direct sustained attention to a long-term task or goal, to screen out distracting stimuli, and to inhibit conflicting impulses. Without such control, some of the most characteristic activities of humans would be impossible—spending days in pursuit of a wounded game animal, for instance, or devoting years to planning an advantageous commerical deal, or subordinating the impulse to eat gathered food to the higher goal of filling the communal pot. The parietal association area seems to be concerned primarily with integrating information already "digested" by the primary association areas. Information received by one sensory pathway, such as hearing, may stimulate memories gathered by other channels. Both speech and the capacity for abstraction depend upon such features.

It is possible that primates initially embarked on a trend toward dominance of the visual sense as part of a rather narrow adaptive pattern—stalking insects in the canopy. Similarly, the long period of immaturity, which is correlated with a brain capable of absorbing and integrating complex patterns of experience, was probably initially an adaptation to life in the rain forest. Be this as it may, it proved to be preadaptive to many other life-

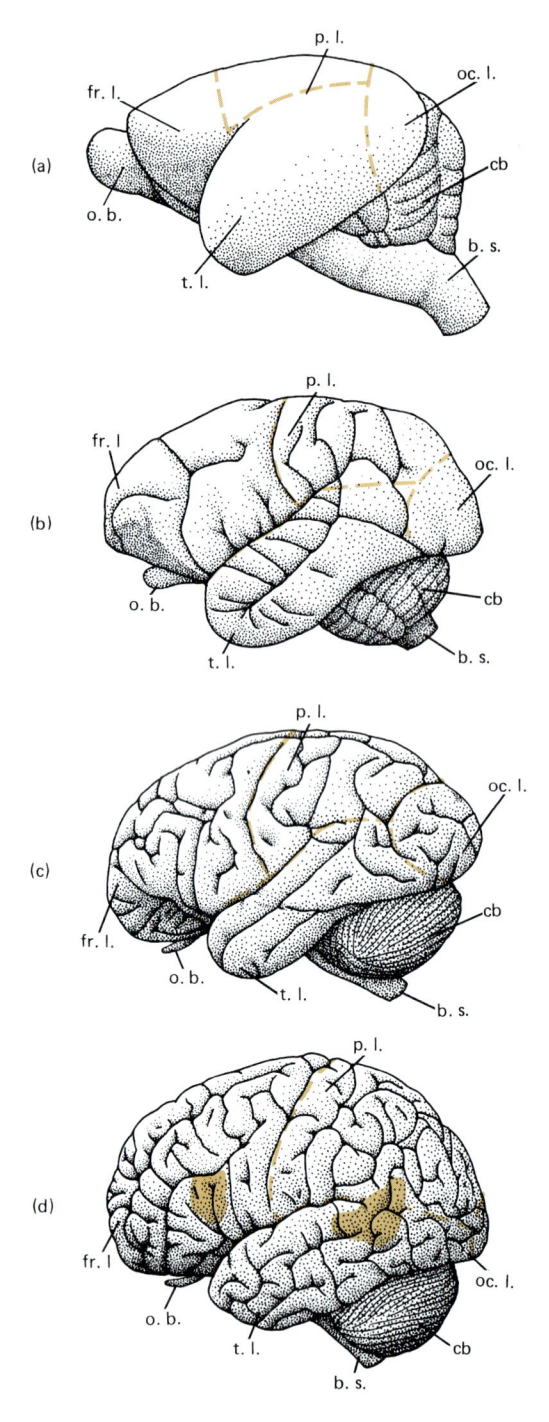

Figure 3–5. Brains of some primates (from the left side): (a) Microcebus, rather primitive prosimian; (b) Cebus, platyrrhine monkey; (c) Pan troglodytes, chimpanzee; (d) Homo sapiens. Note the relative expansion of the temporal, parietal, and frontal lobes in the human brain. Some of the areas believed important for the production of speech and language in humans are situated in the left cerebral hemisphere and are shown in (d). (Biruta Akerbergs)

Key:
p. l.   parietal lobe
oc. l. occipital lobe
cb   cerebellum
b. s.   brain stem
t. l.   temporal lobe
fr. l. frontal lobe
o. b.   olfactory bulbs

styles. Primates have used their sharp eyes, quick wits, and adept hands to good effect on the ground and in the savannas as well as in the trees of the forest. Ultimately, the same combination provided the major foundation upon which human culture was built.

Social Organization

As much as its feeding behavior or the structure of its teeth, the social behavior and parts of the body used in social signaling are elements of an animal's phenotype, subject to evolution by natural selection. The processes of reproduction prescribe a minimum level of social interaction in mammals—contact between adults of the opposite sex for mating and a period during which the infant is nursed and protected by its mother. In many mammals, more elaborate social structures have been evolved from this simple base. Social groupings have become more permanent and have often taken on functions beyond the regulation of reproductive behavior. In some cases, social behavior has opened up new feeding strategies (social carnivores, such as wolves, are a good example of this). In others, specialized, cooperative defensive behaviors used against predators have enabled the species to extend its range into new habitats.

As social behavior evolves, so do the structures used in social interaction—manes and colored hair tufts, canine teeth that can be bared in threat or used in fighting, facial muscles used to convey by expression more subtle changes of mood.

Primate Social Organization Among the primates, these kinds of adaptations have appeared in one group or another. As an order, primates are among the most sociable of mammals—many species living in permanent groups that include all ages and both sexes. But the expression of this sociability varies among members of the order. At one extreme, some prosimian species restrict face-to-face contact to the very minimum consistent with mating and raising young. Olfactory communication plays a major role in social interaction, the animal leaving a "calling card" of scent to mark its territory and to warn off its neighbors.

At the other extreme, some monkeys spend their entire lives within sight, sound, and often touch of other group members, immersed in a constant stream of social communication. Although scent still provides important social cues (signaling, for instance, a female's readiness to mate), in the Catarrhini the visual communication channel is dominant, with complex facial muscles permitting varied and subtle gestures, conveying shades of meaning from one animal to another.

In its social behavior, as in other aspects of its biology, the human species is like other primates and unique at the same time. In the context of human evolution, we ask the following questions about the social organization of living primates:
1. How does natural selection act upon social organization?
2. How do modern primates vary among themselves in their type of social organization?
3. Can we relate features of social organization to habitat and phyletic groupings so that we can reconstruct the social organization of human ancestors at various stages?

Selection and Society As much as its dietary preferences, its locomotor profile, or the shape of its skull, social responses appropriate to its age and sex are phenotypic traits that will appear in any normal member of the species growing and developing in its social environment. Carefully controlled laboratory experiments indicate that the social repertoire typical of a species is neither totally genetically determined (instinctive) nor totally determined by social experiences (learned). It develops through the interaction between genetic makeup and social environment.

Having a genetic basis, social behaviors typical of a species can evolve under the influence of natural selection. This selection operates on two levels—through the competition of the population with others of the same species for living space and resources, and through the competition among individuals in finding mates and raising offspring.

Social Organization as Ecological Strategy As with feeding and locomotion, natural selection will favor those social behaviors that result in safe and economical exploitation of the particular environment in which the group lives. For instance, if food resources are concentrated in small and scattered patches, foraging in herds hundreds strong would be a most uneconomical way of exploiting them. At any given time, most of the animals in the group would be sitting around waiting for a chance to feed. On the other hand, if food resources are relatively plentiful and predators constitute a threat, it may be more advantageous to seek safety in numbers and live in larger groups.

Social Organization as Reproductive Strategy As we saw in the chapter on genetics and evolution, Darwinian fitness is defined in terms of the number of offspring produced and reared to maturity. In large part, fitness is determined by the strategies that the animal uses to exploit its environment. But fitness will also be determined by the individual's success in social behavior that is directly related to reproduction—activities such as finding a mate, mating at the most fertile point in the reproductive cycle, and caring for the young.

Female Reproductive Strategy Reproductive physiology, to some extent, dictates the strategies that each sex can use to increase its reproductive success. For the female, the number of offspring produced in a lifetime is limited by the time taken up by gestation and lactation. Female primates spend most of their adult lives either pregnant or nursing (with short intervals between, during which mating takes place), but even so, they can produce a maximum of fifteen to twenty weaned offspring in a lifetime. Since she can produce only a limited number of offspring in her lifetime, her most effective strategy is to take great care of each of them, even risking injury to herself in their defense.

It is advantageous for the female to be mated by the strongest and most vigorous male. Not only will he pass on these qualities to his offspring, which are also hers, but also in species that live in permanent groups, the consort of the most dominant male and her offspring share preferential access to scarce food resources and a position in the physical center of the troop, less exposed to an attack by predators. Thus it is advantageous for the female to develop behaviors and structures that signal her readiness to mate, thereby stimulating competition among males.[1]

Male Reproductive Strategy In the case of males, reproductive strategy is not physiologically limited in the way it is for females. A male can father a virtually unlimited number of offspring, *provided* that he can compete successfully with other males in attracting and holding females. In some species, this aspect of reproductive behavior becomes hugely exaggerated. Adapting for bluff, display, and shows of strength, the male becomes much larger than the female and evolves special structures that, like a peacock's tail, make him appear even bigger and more intimidating to his rivals and more impressive to potential mates.

Although this strategy, which we may call "competitive begetting," is a common reproductive pattern among mammals, an alternative is possible, which we may call "nurturing." In this pattern (which is more common among birds than mammals), the male concentrates upon finding and establishing a bond with a single mate and then devotes his energy to helping to protect and raise their offspring. Often he feeds the mother while she is nursing the small and helpless young. This pattern characterizes some social carnivores, as, for example, the wolf. Among primate males, both "begettors" and "nurturers" are to be found, but most species compromise by using both strategies without being highly specialized for either. The "choice" of reproductive strategy adopted by a species seems to depend, as we shall see, at least partly upon its ecological relationships.

Primate Social Bonds: Agonistic and Hedonic
Although reproductive strategies are important to primate social organization, it is a mistake to imagine primate societies linked by bonds of continuous sexual desire. Another common misapprehension is imagining primate social organization maintained by constant fighting and violence. These notions, current a generation ago, were based upon studies of animals crowded artificially into zoo enclosures, which is rather like describing human social behavior on the basis of a coed penal colony. Field studies of wild primates have helped to correct the picture. It was found, for instance, that females spend most of their lives in a sexually nonreceptive state, so that sexual attraction could hardly be a major social bond. Moreover, breeding is often seasonal, and the mating season, far from being a time of social cohesiveness, is when

---

[1]On the other hand, it is not advantageous for the male to respond to such signals by fighting so fiercely as to cause exhaustion, injury, or death. The best strategy for him is to appear to fight fiercely, with great show and display, while in fact he is pulling his punches and deciding the contest without injury.

the social order tends to break down under the strain of competition among males. Similarly, violent interactions are relatively rare among wild primates, who, unlike caged animals, have little time or energy to spare for such unproductive pursuits.

Social relationships among primates are expressed in more subtle ways. Chance (1970) has suggested a useful twofold classification of primates' social interactions into an agonistic mode and a hedonic mode. Both types of behavior are used by all individuals of most primate species, but they are used in different contexts. *Agonistic* behavior implies a power relationship between the actors. One animal attacks or threatens another, who responds by fighting, fleeing, or "submitting"—making a gesture acknowledging subordinate status. Although the ultimate sanction of violence lies behind agonistic encounters, very few involve actual fighting. Relationships of dominance and submissiveness are generally expressed by subtle body language—a lowered tail, a raised eyebrow, or a curl of the lip.

Hedonic interactions involve reciprocity rather than power relationships, reassurance rather than threat. They cement society together with bonds of relaxed friendliness, rather than the tense, hostile interactions of the agonistic mode. In many primate species, mutual grooming—picking through the fur with fingers or combing it with the teeth—plays an important part in hedonic interactions, but assurance of friendliness and support may be expressed through a variety of gestures, sounds, and postures.

Diversity in Primate Social Organization The following series of primate social organizations implies a general sequence of increasing complexity, but it is not meant to represent an irreversible evolutionary sequence.

The One-Male Group In primitive primate forms, individuals defend their own territory. In a few species, a mated pair fends off intruders. But a more common form of primate society is typified by the savanna-dwelling patas monkey. A group of six or so female patas forms the core of the group. Adult males compete with one another for the role of "resident male" in such a troop. "Bachelor" males form troops of their own or wander independently, awaiting their chance to challenge a group male. This behavior selects for structures in the male that enhance his fighting prowess. However, in spite of his impressive size and weapons, the patas male plays little part in the life of the troop. His main interest lies outside—looking out for, and fighting off, challenges from "bachelors."

The Multimale Troop Many primates live in groups that include more than one adult male. As our example we may take the macaques and baboons, species that have been quite thoroughly studied. Troops, which may consist of as many as one hundred or more animals, include several large males as well as many females and young. The relationships among males are governed largely by relationships of respect and subservience. One or more "dominant" animals form the core of the group. Priority in mating is largely

A male hamadryas baboon yawns in threat, showing his canine teeth. Broken teeth like these are quite common among wild baboons. (Toni Angermayer/Photo Researchers)

The Awash Baboon Project:
A Multidisciplinary Approach to a Primatological Problem

The baboons that live along the Awash River, 60 miles northeast of Addis Ababa, Ethiopia, are one of the most thoroughly studied primate populations, and their ecological strategies and social organization are well known. In addition, a large proportion of the population has been tabulated in a computerized record that includes, for each individual, a tooth cast, a set of fingerprints, photographs, and a detailed genetic profile. The story of why and how this material was collected exemplifies a new trend in primate fieldwork—the multidisciplinary approach that draws no hard-and-fast lines between "biological" and "behavioral" studies.

Hans Kummer, a Swiss primatologist, first drew scientific attention to the Awash baboons in the early 1960s. During a survey of Ethiopian baboons, he discovered that along the Awash the range of the large, gray-brown anubis baboon adjoined that of the smaller, light grey hamadryas. And, at the junction of their ranges, he found baboons that seemed to be hybrids of anubis and hamadryas, although they were generally thought to be separate species who theoretically should not interbreed. Since hamadryas baboons have a "one-male group" social system, whereas Anubis baboons live in multimale troops, Kummer theorized that hamadryas males sometimes "kidnapped" anubis females and adopted them into their harems, where they produced hybrid offspring. He showed in field experiments that hamadryas males will adopt anubis females released in their range. During 1967 and 1968, Kummer's student, Ueli Nagel, mapped the intergrade zone and closely observed the abnormal social behavior of the hybrids.

The case of the Awash hybrids posed an interesting theoretical issue. Speciation is a key evolutionary process (p. 29), but very rarely do we see it in progress in real animal populations. Were the Awash hybrids fully fertile? And if they were, did they transmit genes across anubis and hamadryas populations? If so, was the gene flow approximately equal in either direction? Such questions could be tackled only by examining genetic markers in the animals' blood factors and proteins. Such studies could also throw light on behavioral problems of theoretical interest to anthropology—questions such as how often nonhuman primates change troops. Such questions could only be tackled by years of intensive, uninterrupted study.

Accordingly, in consultation with Kummer, a research plan was formulated for live trapping and taking blood samples from the Awash baboons. A team was assembled under the general direction of Clifford J. Jolly. Frederick L. Brett planned and led the field expedition, and Ronald Cauble, an experienced baboon trapper, organized the capture of the animals. For nearly a year, the field team built cages, cleared tracks through the thornbush, charted the baboons' movements, and hauled traps to the trapsites. A major apprehension proved groundless as the baboons eagerly fed on the corn scattered as bait, and confidently entered the traps, undeterred by the sight and sound of fellow troop members already caught. Each trapping day, about 40 animals would be trapped, tranquilized, and taken back to the improvised field laboratory.

Here the team took blood, saliva, and hair samples; weighed, measured, photographed, and fingerprinted each animal; and made a cast of its upper teeth. Each animal was also marked for future identification. When the whole troop had been captured and processed, the "prisoners" were released at the trapsites. They did not seem to mind the experience; in fact, some were retrapped when they returned for another free corn ration.

In all, twelve troops, comprising 534 anubis, hamadryas, and hybrid baboons, were processed. Data and materials were shipped to laboratories in New York and London for examination. Analysis of the data is still in progress, but some findings are emerging. One is that each troop of baboons is rather distinctive genetically from its neighbors. Gene frequencies differ considerably, suggesting that the exchange of members is probably infrequent. Certain genetic markers are characteristic of anubis baboons, others of hamadryas. Tentatively, it is thought that, as Kummer theorized, genes are flowing from anubis to hamadryas, but very few if any in the other direction. Whether this makes them two species or one is an issue best left to theorists to argue. The demographic profiles of the troops—based upon size, weight, and the eruption and wear of the teeth—are also interesting. Many of the animals are quite old, suggesting a long potential life span. But there are few very young animals, far fewer than theoretically necessary to maintain the population. It is suggested that the catastrophic drought of 1972 to 1974 took its toll of the baboons as it did of humans.

Much more information remains to be extracted from the data; analysis will take years. A return trip to Ethiopia is planned, where, armed with fingerprints and genetic profiles, an attempt will be made to renew old acquaintances and decipher the latest chapter in the microevolutionary story of the Awash baboons.

determined by the dominance hierarchy—the dominant males mating the females at their most fertile time. The structure of a large multimale group may be quite complex, with alliances, friendships, juvenile play groups, and other subgroupings.

The multimale troop seems to be a more evolved form than the simple one-male group seen in patas, and probably arose by a modification of the agonistic behavior of males.

In a one-male species like patas, the outcome of an encounter between adult males, if females are present, is always the defeat and flight of one of the contenders. Among macaques and baboons, submissive behaviors have evolved that enable the loser effectively to switch off the aggression of the victor. Thus the loser can continue to live in the troop so long as he expresses his subservience. Ultimately, he may become strong enough to challenge the dominant animal again and reverse their statuses. What adaptive advantage, then, does such behavior confer over the more rough-and-ready patas system? A clue may be found in the habitat of multimale species.

Many multimale species live in richer savannas and woodlands, areas where resources are plentiful enough to permit large troops of animals to forage together, but where movement on the ground is essential and predators are common. The multimale group may be considered a strategy to use the brawny bodies and powerful fighting teeth of the males that originally evolved for competing among themselves in cooperative defense against predators. Groups of macaques or baboons with several large males are able to frighten and ward off all but the largest predators and stand a much better chance of survival than small groups or isolated individuals. But the penalty for retaining many males in the group may be energy lost in maintaining the dominance hierarchy—chasing, threatening, strutting, occasionally fighting, and building up large muscular bodies. The hamadryas and gelada baboons, who live in habitats where the living is harder, seem to have modified the multimale system to minimize these drawbacks.

One-Male Groups Within a Troop   Hamadryas baboons of the Ethiopian desert country live in multimale troops, but their troop structure differs from that seen in the troops of their relatives of the savanna. Every adult female belongs to the "harem" of an adult male (some of these "harems" include as many as ten—or as few as one—female). The group male, unlike the patas male, is the center and focus of his group. The male has evolved a handsome cape of fur around the neck and shoulders, which probably makes him appear larger and more impressive and at the same time delightfully groomable to his "wives."

This reproductive strategy may be less costly in energy than that of savanna baboons and hence adaptive to life in a semidesert. And because it also permits more effective exploitation of the scattered food resources to be found there, it is particularly interesting to the anthropologist, since the earliest hominids probably occupied such a habitat.

Chimpanzee Social Organization   Formally, chimpanzee "local population" is a multimale

An adult female hamadryas baboon grooms the fur of her mate. Note the short, strong fingers of this ground-dwelling monkey. (Toni Angermayer/Photo Researchers)

troop, although its members, unlike the baboon troops, rarely assemble at one spot. There are no exclusive mating partnerships, no "harems." Males recognize a rank order among themselves and are dominant to females and young. Rank is achieved, and occasionally expressed, by violent display. But chimpanzee organization is most noteworthy for its deemphasis of the agonistic mode and the richness of its friendly, hedonic interactions. More than any other primate, chimpanzees embrace, touch, pat, greet, groom, and reassure one another. And with the chimpanzee, we see the only hint among nonhuman primates of cooperation and reciprocity extended to the food quest—the males scouting fruit trees and then calling the rest of the group, sharing meat in response to a begging gesture, and cooperating to capture a colobus monkey. These are all foretastes of the economic relationship distinctive to humans.

Human Social Organization It is clearly impossible to summarize, in a brief section, the immense variety of forms of social organization among humans. This variety itself points to a human peculiarity: namely, the flexibility of our social organization. Without (so we believe) any significant variation in its genetic basis, human social organization has taken on many forms as part of the diversity of human culture. This variety has been an important part of the human adaptive strategy, permitting our species to occupy many different econiches. But within this diversity, some aspects of human social organization are so nearly universal that we can perhaps assume them to be basic attributes of the species. In form, human society, like that of the hamadryas baboon, might be described as consisting of multimale troops formed of aggregates of one-male groups. But the functions and activities of these groups are quite different from those seen in other species.

Division of Labor Perhaps the most basic feature of human social organization, as we have mentioned, is the extension of mutuality and reciprocity beyond friendship and grooming into the economic sphere.[2] In the simplest modern human societies, men hunt and women gather. Husband, wife or wives, and children pool the spoils of the day in the evening meal. Hunters are expected to support one another in the hunt; and if one hunter is luckier than the others, he is expected to share his kill with other families with the expectation of return when he is among the less fortunate. As society becomes more complex, as we shall see, so does the division of labor and the network of exchange of goods and services. Some men become specialist craftsmen; others, specialist politicians and leaders. Eventually, in some societies, both sexes begin to take on such roles, finally breaking down and crosscutting the ancient division between women's work and men's work.

Marriage For most of history, marriage has been primarily an economic and political institution, regulating the exchange of daughters for wives among groups of men. Often the exchange is regulated through elaborate systems of kinship terminology and customs specifying the behavior appropriate to various categories of kin. This is an entirely human institution, presumably growing out of the general human emphasis upon reciprocity and exchange of valuables as a social bond. The ancient primate "You scratch my back and I'll scratch yours" has become the human "I'll give you my daughter now, if you'll give your granddaughter to my son in fifteen years' time." This institution is made possible by the rules of *exogamy,* which stipulate marriage outside the immediate kin group. Its function was originally probably twofold. First, like the grooming relationship in simpler nonhuman societies, it cemented alliance and friendship between groups that were widely scattered. Second, it insured that for every hunter, there was a gatherer, and for every new mother-infant cluster, a hunter to provide.

---

[2] Significantly, the chimpanzee is the only nonhuman primate species in which mothers have been observed giving solid food to their infants.

summary

There are more than two hundred living species of the order Primates. Despite the great diversity of primate species, the order is distinctive for its members' lack of specialization and wide adaptability. Two characteristics are found in most primates: the five-digited, or pendactyl, hand and foot; and a rather unspecialized dentition suitable for processing a wide variety of foods. Several specialized trends, which are adaptations for an arboreal existence, are distinctive of primates: (1) the development of grasping hands and feet; (2) a tendency for vision to become the dominant sense, and the concomitant enlargement of the visual association areas of the brain; (3) a tendency toward use of the hand as an exploratory organ as well as for locomotion. The following trends reflect a distinctive primate reproductive strategy: (4) a tendency toward a reduction in the number of young in a litter and an increase in the dependency of the young upon the mother; (5) a tendency toward an increase in the relative size of the brain, especially those areas concerned with learning and association; (6) a tendency toward an increase in the length of the individual's life span; (7) a tendency toward life in permanent groups.

This primate reproductive strategy, in addition to the arboreal adaptations, suggests that the ancestors of extant primates lived at first in tropical rain forests, where they established these adaptive trends that were inherited and developed by their descendants. Their lack of specialization and their adaptability enabled the primates to venture into different vegetational and climatic zones and thereby further increased the opportunities for a wide range of primate evolution.

In the family Pongidae, we find our closest living primate relatives, the great apes: the gorilla, the orangutan, the chimpanzee, and the pygmy chimp. Although chimpanzees are primarily rain forest dwellers, some groups have become savanna foragers. Chimpanzees display occasional rather than habitual bipedalism; the formation of a community with other chimps of an area; the manipulation of leaves, twigs, and bits of grass as tools; and occasional hunting and meat sharing.

Before trying to infer the behavior of extinct primates on the basis of fossil remains and geological evidence, we have to determine the relationship between anatomy and habitat and between anatomy and behavior in living primates.

Primate locomotor systems show clearly the correlation between structure and behavior. By studying this correlation in a number of primates, we can make educated guesses about the successive locomotor adaptations involved in the development of the human species. An arboreal quadruped, retaining its primitive mammalian locomotor flexibility, probably gave rise to a primitive primate form, adapted to quadrupedalism and climbing by grasping. From this form were derived others more adapted to suspensory locomotion. Structural adaptations to suspension may be seen not only in extant brachiators but also in humans, who almost certainly passed through a brachiator stage.

Homo sapiens is the only living primate that is habitually bipedal. Structural adaptations to bipedalism involve mainly the modification of the hindlimb, pelvis, and lumbar vertebrae to carry the whole body weight in the upright position. Bipedalism, by allowing humans to use their hands for other functions, has greatly facilitated the development of human culture.

Primate feeding habits are reflected in structural adaptations, too—in this case in the teeth, jaws, and digestive system. Primates are omnivorous, but show different emphases in their diet. Insect eaters, fruit eaters, and leaf eaters all have teeth adapted to the demands of their diet. The human masticatory structure is much like that of apes, but smaller and weaker, and it may be regarded as having degenerated from a larger ancestral condition.

four
Primate Evolution

The study of the behavior and structure of living primates can carry us a long way in reconstructing human evolutionary history, but there is some information that only the hard evidence of fossils can provide. Sometimes fossils disprove hypotheses based only on living animals. Compared to modern apes, humans have relatively small, lightly built jaws; given this, one would never suspect that the distinguishing features of the earliest hominids included massive jaws and large molars. Yet this proved to be the case when fossils of early hominids came to light.

In addition, fossils provide vital information about the context in which new adaptations emerged. The Darwinian theory of evolution holds that changes in the environment bring about changes in structure and function through the action of natural selection. Applying this theory to human evolution, paleontologists speculate that hominids emerged as a distinct lineage when forests shrank and savannas expanded because of climatic changes. Indeed, some of the earliest hominid fossils are associated with grassland animals, and geological evidence for a relatively dry seasonal climate supports this idea.

Finally, only fossils inform us about many species that became extinct, and so give us some sense of the full breadth of the successive adaptive radiations that have arisen and declined in the course of mammalian evolution.

The Fossil Record

Behind the public galleries of our great museums, with their careful displays of a few choice fossil specimens, are row upon row of drawers and cabinets packed with more fragmentary fossils, the raw material of the science of paleontology. *Fossils* are the remains of plants and animals that have been preserved and mineralized through geological accident. In relation to the countless plants and animals that have lived, this is a very rare occurrence, and it depends upon a series of highly unlikely events.

The Unevenness of the Record

At death most animals are rapidly "recycled" into the ecosystem. Fortunately for us, this process of dissolution is occasionally interrupted at some point, and some parts of the animals are preserved as fossils. The chances of fossilization depend on local geological conditions. To be protected from the effects of weathering, the remains must be buried. If decay is delayed long enough for the material surrounding the bone to solidify, this can become a natural mold, and the decaying organic matter may be replaced by fine-grained material, forming a natural cast. Such fossils preserve the external form of bone. Under other conditions, minerals from the surrounding rock replace both the internal and external structure of a bone, molecule for molecule, producing a complete and finely detailed specimen.

The discovery of fossils is as unlikely as their preservation. A map of fossil primate sites of a given era tells us more about the distribution of suitable sediments, the distribution of erosion sites and engineering sites in modern times, and the distribution of paleon-

---

Oreopithecus, a fossil primate of 13 to 14 million years ago. Although it is not a direct hominid ancestor, it may have been bipedal. (Johannes Hurzeler/Natur-Historiches Museum)

Geological Processes

Paleoanthropologists use the techniques and concepts of geology to find, extract, date, and interpret fossils and artifacts.

In recent years, a major revolution has occurred in geological theory. *Plate tectonics* now provide a framework to accommodate various geological phenomena such as mountain building, earthquakes, and volcanism. According to current ideas, the earth's crust consists of a series of semirigid plates. Along one margin of each plate, new crust is formed as molten rock wells up from below and hardens. On the plate's opposite side, crust is consumed, plunging into the deeper, molten layers of the mantle. Infinitely slowly, crust travels across the plate's surface. The continents, consisting of less dense rock, float along on this moving layer. When a continent reaches the edge of a plate, it may buckle, thereby forming a mountain range, or it may collide and fuse with another continental block, thrusting up mountains as it does so. New crust welling up below a continent will split it apart, first forming a deep crack, the precursor of a new ocean. Molten material, formed in the crust under the stress of plate movements, often erupts as volcanic ash, lava, and cinders. Strings of volcanos girdle the earth, tracing the margins of moving crustal plates.

These tectonic processes constantly renew the *relief* of the continental surface, creating new mountains, rifts, and trenches. *Erosion* attacks this relief even as it forms. Rain, frost, and plant roots detach particles from the rock surface. Propelled by wind, water, or ice, the particles scour the rock surface, eroding it further. *Glaciers* are particularly effective erosional agents. Inching their way down mountainsides, glaciers pluck rock from the surface beneath them, crush it to an abrasive gravel, and gouge deep, U-shaped valleys.

Gradually, loose material from mountain peaks and hillsides finds its way into low-lying areas. Here, it accumulates *sediments* in orderly, horizontal layers, or *strata* (singular, *stratum*). These often contain fossils. In volcanic areas, sediments often contain ash, and may alternate with layers of lava or pumice. Such layers permit the paleontologist to use K-A dating. Hardened sedimentary rocks become subject to uplift, contortion, and erosion in future tectonic episodes, exposing the fossils they contain, while disturbing the orderly arrangement of strata. *Stratigraphy* is concerned with disentangling these processes, and deciphering the correct chronological relationships of strata—and the fossils and artifacts they contain.

tologists than it does about the range of primates in ancient times.

Most fossils are damaged before discovery, gnawed by scavengers, distorted under the weight of overlying sediment, or broken in excavation. It is important that the anthropologist recognize the effects of damage when he interprets fossil bones. Crushed skulls and bones can be misinterpreted as evidence of aggressive attacks, and bones gnawed by animals can look remarkably like human artifacts. Moreover, it is extremely rare to find a complete skeleton, and there are only a few known instances of skin and soft tissues becoming fossilized. An incomplete or damaged specimen inevitably challenges the imagination of the paleontologist to fill in the gaps. If one is using a plaster replica of a reconstructed fossil, one should be careful to distinguish the parts that are reconstructed from the parts that represent the hard facts of the fossil evidence. To interpret fossils, one must appreciate that their shape and structure is the product not only of biological forces that affected the animal during its lifetime, but also of the geological factors that have acted upon it since death, and the artificial devices used to excavate, preserve, and reconstruct it. (See the box on geological processes for a more detailed discussion of these phenomena.)

Interpreting Fossils

Once a fossil specimen is discovered, collected, cleaned, and catalogued, the next task is identification. Does it belong to a known taxonomic category? Or is it so different from the existing specimens that it must be assigned to a "new" species or genus? How many different species are represented in an assortment of fossils from a particular site? This preliminary sorting requires judgment, attention to detail, and most important, an appreciation of the degree of variability to be expected within living populations. Every individual is unique, the product of a unique genotype and a personal life history. It is important to be able to distinguish such normal intrapopulational variations from the kinds of differences that indicate membership in different species.

Determining Phyletic Relationships This preliminary sorting is only the first stage in the analysis of fossils. The next is to fit the fossil species we have defined into its place in the natural order, to determine its evolutionary relationships with other species living and extinct, and to reconstruct, as far as possible, its place in the ecosystem of which it was a part. Determining the phyletic relationships of a fossil species is a matter of comparative anatomy, just as it is with living species; the paleontologist, however, has less to go on, for the viscera, proteins, and other "soft" parts that are helpful in sorting living species have long since disappeared. Fortunately, the crowns of teeth are often preserved as fossils and are normally good indicators of phyletic relationship. The paleontologist relies heavily upon dental evidence to construct his phyletic trees.

Usually, we are not content to determine the phyletic relationships of a fossil species; we are also interested in its way of life, its locomotor profile, its habitat, and its diet. We can never reconstruct full dietary repertoires or complete locomotor profiles of extinct animals. We can often deduce their salient features by interpreting structural features in functional terms, using our knowledge of living primates to provide comparisons and analogies. But the fossil is not our only source of information.

Evidence of the Context The rock matrix in which a fossil is embedded, the cracks and splits in its surface, and even its orientation in the ground can provide us with as much information as the fossil's anatomical structure. Fossilized pollens buried with it may also give some clues about the environment of the period.

Fossils of other animal species found in the same stratum help to complete the picture. The study of "death assemblages" (*taphonomy*, from the Greek *taphos*, tomb) begins with the list of the species found in a given locality. But this is only the beginning, for animals that are buried together did not necessarily live together. It is very rare for land animals to be buried and fossilized where they died. Most death assemblages are a motley collection of remains with different histories of transport and dismemberment. The taphonomist's job is to disentangle such mixtures by reconstructing the processes that brought each specimen to the burial point.

Such taphonomic detective work helps the paleontologist to piece together the ecology of the extinct animal. For instance, if it is associated mainly with grazing animals, this indicates that the animal lived in open grasslands; a predominance of browsing animals or arboreally adapted apes suggests that it lived in bush or forest. Information of this kind enables us to test hypotheses about the circumstances surrounding particular evolutionary events, particularly those relating to the emergence of separate evolving lineages.

The Geological Time Scale

One of the major roles of paleontology is to give evolution a time depth—to tie particular evolutionary trees to a universal timetable of the earth's history, the geological time scale. This scale is based primarily upon the stratigraphic relationships of rock units (that is, the layers of rocks) and the fossils they contain. From the basic principle of dating, that rocks of similar age contain similar fossils, correlations can be derived for fossil deposits throughout the world. However, this system only allows us to assign life forms a position in the geological time scale. Other techniques, such as radiometric dating methods, are used to derive an age in years. (See the box on radiometric dating techniques, pp. 68–69.)

The geological time scale is divided into three major eras, each dominated by a particular vertebrate group: the Paleozoic era, dominated by ancient fish, amphibians, and primitive reptiles; the Mesozoic era, dominated by reptiles; and the Cenozoic era, dominated by

Radiometric Dating

Traditionally, physical anthropologists dated fossils by relating them to the standard sequence of rocks in the geological timescale. In recent decades, however, researchers have developed new techniques that relate fossils not to geological timescales but to scales based on the constant rate of decay of radioactive isotopes. For calibrating human evolution, the two most useful of these *radiometric* methods are radiocarbon dating and potassium-argon dating.

Radiocarbon dating is based on the premise that the radioisotope ^{14}C exists in the atmosphere in a more or less constant proportion. Living organisms take up ^{14}C just as they do the common nonradioactive isotope ^{12}C (plants do this by utilizing atmospheric CO_2, and animals by eating plants). Because living organisms are constantly exchanging carbon with the atmospheric reservoir of CO_2, the proportion of ^{14}C they contain remains similar to that found in the atmosphere. When the organism dies, however, the radioisotope begins to decay, leading to a decline in the proportion of ^{14}C to ^{12}C.

Like other radioactive isotopes, ^{14}C decays at a constant rate: one-half of a given amount decays into nitrogen in 5,730 years. This period is called the *half-life* of the isotope. By measuring the proportion of ^{14}C remaining in a sample of organic material, and then comparing this measurement with the constant rate of decay, we can establish with some accuracy the time that has elapsed since the organism's death.

In taking these measurements, researchers must be extremely careful to determine that the sample has not been contaminated by later carbon. Such contamination, which can occur through weathering or handling, or from rootlets or humic acid seeping from higher levels in the soil, can be the source of appreciable error.

The margin of error is also affected by the age of the sample. Because too little ^{14}C remains after about 70,000 years of radioactive decay, radiocarbon dating is effective only with materials of late Pleistocene and recent age. Within this range of time, the greatest probability of error exists in the older dates. This difference in accuracy results from the fact that although the radiocarbon method depends on ^{14}C existing in the atmosphere in a constant proportion, data suggest that there have been fluctuations. By determining the radiocarbon age of the annual growth rings of long-lived trees, archeologists have been able to correct the ^{14}C scale for the last few thousand years; however, this correction cannot be applied to older remains.

The *potassium-argon (K-A)* dating method also depends on the constant rate of decay of a radioactive isotope. It differs from the radiocarbon method in two major ways, however: it is used with much more ancient material (the *youngest* material than can be dated is about 500,000 years old), and the substances dated are not fossils or organic material but minerals found in volcanic rock.

Potassium (including ^{39}K, ^{41}K, and the radioisotope ^{40}K) is found in many rocks. Radioactive ^{40}K has an extremely long half-life: every 1.3 billion years, half the ^{40}K in a mineral decays into ^{40}A, an isotope of the inert gas argon. If the mineral is sufficiently dense in structure, the gas is trapped in the crystal lattice and cannot escape. If the rock is strongly heated, however (for instance, if it is reduced to a molten lava or white-hot ash in a volcanic eruption), all the accumulated argon is driven off; when the rock cools, argon begins again to accumulate. By determining the ratio of argon to potassium in such a volcanic rock, and then comparing this ratio with the disintegration rate of ^{40}K, we can determine the time that has elapsed since the rock cooled. Paleontologists and archeologists can then use such determinations to date whatever fossils and artifacts are related stratigraphically to the dated layer. The East African *Ramapithecus* fossils discussed in this chapter, for instance, were dated by ^{40}K-^{40}A analysis of volcanic rocks overlying the Fort Ternan site.

Although simple in principle, the K-A dating method requires scrupulous laboratory techniques. Such care is especially important when dealing with the relatively young rocks, less than 70 million years old, of the Cenozoic period. These rocks are so young compared with the half-life of ^{40}K that they have accumulated comparatively little argon, making them very difficult to date. Stringent precautions must also be observed against contamination by atmospheric argon. Furthermore, the geological history of the rock may be less straightfoward than the ideal case described above. If a sample contains particles of material from an earlier eruption, for instance, its age may be overestimated. Conversely, if argon has diffused out of the rock, or if a subsequent volcanic episode has reheated the rock and driven out some of its argon, it will appear to be younger than it actually is. Researchers must be aware of the existence of such possible distortions so that they may correct for them when necessary.

Together, K-A and radiocarbon dating can calibrate most of primate and human evolution. Neither method can be employed, for the period between .50 and .07 million years, however, which is a crucial time in hominid evolution. Thus, the search continues for a reliable radiometric-dating technique to fill this gap.

mammals and birds. Each era is further demarcated into periods and epochs by geological and evolutionary changes.

Mesozoic Mammals and Primate Adaptations

In the last period of the Mesozoic era, the Cretaceous, an important floral revolution—the expansion of the *angiosperms* (flowering plants, grasses, herbs, shrubs, and trees) at the expense of the *gymnosperms* (ferns, mosses, cycads, and conifers)—created a novel evolutionary environment. This floral revolution seems to have set off a chain reaction of adaptive changes among animals, which all ultimately depend upon plants. Many angiosperms need insects to pollinate their flowers. They advertise for this service with showy petals and pay for it in nectar. As angiosperms spread, insects multiplied in numbers and diversity, and insect-eating animals in turn also thrived. In addition, many angiosperms produced edible nuts, berries, and fruits as a bribe to enterprising animals who helped to disperse their seeds. In short, the new vegetation of the Cretaceous offered unique evolutionary opportunities for small, agile, and adaptable creatures. Among the vertebrates, two groups responded to the challenge. One was the feathered branch of the dinosaur clan that became the birds. The other was the mammals, descendants of a group of reptiles that had flourished in the early Mesozoic.

By the late Cretaceous, two major groups of mammals had emerged. The *multituberculates*, whose rodentlike teeth suggest they lived on a vegetarian diet, flourished for some tens of millions of years and became extinct in the Eocene. The *Theria* included the ancestors of living placentals and marsupials, virtually all of today's mammals. Judging by their teeth (and we have little else to go on), these early *Theria* were small animals that fed on insects and small vertebrates, supplementing their diets with soft fruits. They had an all-purpose dentition which included the basic three-cusped molar that was to prove so infinitely adaptable in mammalian evolution. In general appearance, they probably resembled such modern, but very primitive, therians as the opossum or the tree shrew.

Paleocene Primates

At the end of the Cretaceous, about 69 million years ago, dinosaurs, which had dominated the earth for nearly 150 million years, died out, and the surviving reptiles slipped into the marginal ecological roles they occupy today. The mammals multiplied into the vacant ecospaces.

Primate fossils of the Paleocene epoch are common and have been found in North America and western Europe. These primates were quite small, ranging from the size of a tiny mouse to that of a cat. The limb bones that survive indicate that many Paleocene primates had the mobile ankles and forearms that are needed for climbing. Unlike contemporary insectivores, they had evidently taken to the trees. However, they show no signs of the typical primate features associated with climbing by grasping. The skull structure is primitive, lacking such distinctive primate

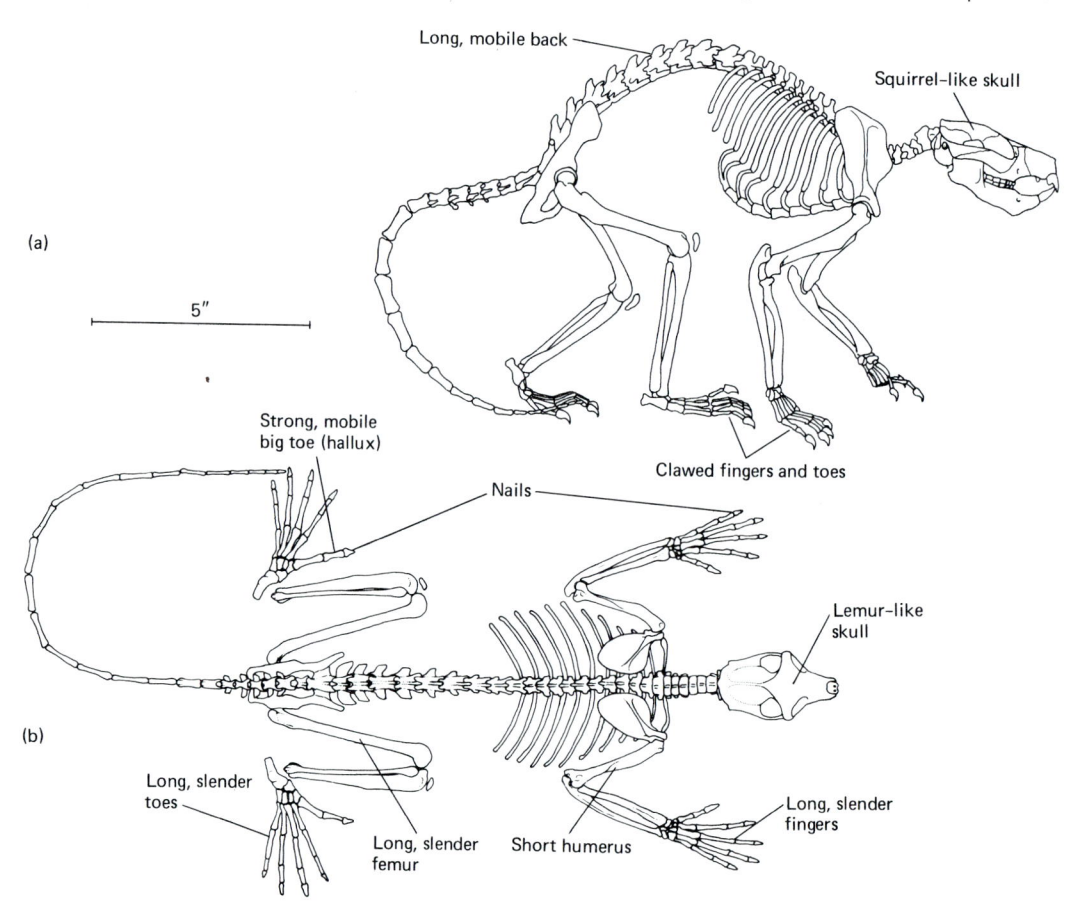

Figure 4–1. (a) Reconstruction of the skeleton of Plesiadapis, from the Paleocene of France and Colorado; (b) skeleton of Northarctus, an Eocene lemuriform primate of North America. (Biruta Akerbergs, after (a) I. Tattersall, 1970, and (b) W. K. Gregory, 1920)

traits as increased braincase size, sharper vision, or reduced olfactory apparatus. (See Figure 4–1.)

Judging by the abundance and variety of the fossil remains, this first known radiation of primates was immensely successful. They were the equivalent, in their day, of our tree rats, mice, and squirrels. However, with the radiation of true rodents in the Eocene, they disappeared completely. Their specializations rule them out of the direct ancestry of later primates, and they show no evidence of trends distinctive of later primates. But the details of their molar teeth and the construction of the bony capsule that encloses the middle ear are so like those of other primates and unlike those of other mammalian groups that most primatologists unhesitatingly class them in the primate order.

The New Primates of the Eocene: The First Prosimians

As in the Paleocene, most of our evidence of primates comes from North America and western Europe, although it is likely that primates lived in Africa throughout the Eocene and reached South America by its close. Some Eocene primates are the last survivors of the Paleocene radiation. The remainder are quite different. They show typical primate traits in limbs, skull, and teeth.

There is no doubt that these creatures are true primates. Though their brains were small and simple by the standards of modern primates, they are relatively large compared to other Eocene mammals. They were beginning to depend at least as much on eyesight as on smell to locate food, detect danger, and keep track of one another. They had small, unspecialized incisors, from which we can infer that they did not need ratlike teeth to manipulate fruits, seeds, and leaves, perhaps because they were able to use their hands for these tasks. A well-preserved skeleton, *Northarctus,* from North America and fragments of other forms show mobile, elongated digits that were clearly adapted for grasping; nails rather than claws; and the long hindlimbs and powerful mobile large toe of a habitual vertical clinger and leaper. (See Figure 4–1.)

These characteristics of the "new" primates of the Eocene leave no doubt of their primate status, but this is not their main significance. More importantly, they are clear evidence of a behavioral breakthrough. It is at this time that the adoption of a distinctively primate survival strategy emerged, based upon the fine coordination of sharp wits, keen eyes, and skillful manipulatory hands, and also the slow, careful rearing of the young, one or two at a time. The limb skeleton of the Eocene primates implies a thoroughgoing commitment to life in the trees, beyond that seen in the more generalized Paleocene forms. The Eocene primates, then, had clearly attained the prosimian grade of organization and established the fundamental adaptive trends of the primate order. The later stages of primate evolution, even the emergence of the human species itself, are largely due to the elaboration of these basic factors.

Oligocene Primates: The Anthropoid Transition

The earth's climate began to cool significantly during the early Oligocene, and latitudinal variations were intensified. The Tethys Sea, which had separated Europe from Africa, and the epicontinental sea, which had covered much of North America and which separated Europe from Asia, were shrinking. Grasslands began to encroach upon the tropical and subtropical forests, and the climate of the mid-latitudes became less mild and more seasonal. Although a few stragglers lingered on into the Miocene, most mid-latitude primates disappeared with the warm forests. In the earliest Oligocene, the ancestors of the platyrrhines appear for the first time in South America, presumably as immigrants from Central America. The focus of our study, however—the origins of the human lineage—lies in the Old World.

Fortunately, just as primates disappear from the fossil faunas of Europe, a fresh time window opens onto North Africa. The most important fossil deposit is in the Fayum, a wind-scoured depression in the Egyptian desert fifty-six miles (90 km) southwest of Cairo. During the Oligocene, the Fayum was in the delta of a large river flowing from the interior of Africa to the Mediterranean. The area supported a rich mammalian fauna, quite unlike that of the northern continents.

The primates of the Fayum were very different from the Eocene prosimians of Europe or North America. None is a prosimian. All belong to the Catarrhini, or Old World branch of the Anthropoidea (higher primates), and there is little doubt that from their ranks sprang the cercopithecoid monkeys, the apes, and ultimately the human stock. Various features indicate that the primate trend toward precedence of the sense of sight over smell had been carried beyond the prosimian level. The snout was quite small, especially in the smaller forms, and the nasal cavity was reduced. As the olfactory apparatus shrank, the orbits moved further forward onto the face, and each was protected behind by a complete postorbital plate, not a simple postorbital bar. Another feature of Fayum primates—the two halves of the lower jaw being firmly fused at the chin—is of uncertain functional significance, but strongly suggests anthropoid status.

All the Fayum primates were small. All had unspecialized dentitions, which suggests they were omnivorous and lived on fruits, leaves, and some insects. And all seem to have been arboreal quadrupeds. There is no evidence that the Fayum primates were adapted for brachiation, like the apes, or for quadrupedal running on the ground, like cercopithecoids. This is not to say that all Fayum primates were alike; a number of distinct genera have been identified. Indeed, several authorities have argued that the cercopithecoid and hominoid lineages had already diverged by the Oligocene. Whether this is true or not, the Fayum primates are important because they bridge the gap between the basic primate traits of the Eocene prosimians and the advanced apes and monkeys that first appear in the Miocene.

Miocene Primates

The surface of the earth changed dramatically during the Miocene (22.5 to 5 million B.P.). In the last half of the Miocene, as the climate became drier, open savannalike grasslands spread through southern Europe and replaced moist, temperate forests. Compared to Europe and Asia, Africa was a relatively stable mosaic of forest and savannas as it is today. A primatologist familiar with modern Africa visiting a forest in the early Miocene of Kenya about 20 million years ago would have found its fauna far more familiar than that of the Fayum.

The anthropoid primates are much larger than their Oligocene forebears. The smallest are about the size of a vervet monkey, the largest as big as a large chimpanzee. The few skulls that we have of Miocene monkeys and apes no longer show the primitive proportions seen in Oligocene forms. The olfactory apparatus is as reduced, and the braincase as full and rounded, as those of modern apes and monkeys. Presumably, this means that they were also as behaviorally advanced as living Anthropoidea, as flexible in their response to environmental challenges, as sophisticated in their social interactions, and as dependent upon socially mediated learning as a gibbon or a macaque if not a chimpanzee.

Yet monkeys (Cercopithecidae) were comparatively rare in Miocene forests; the ecospace they presently fill was occupied by a variety of apes (Hominoidea). Most Miocene hominoids fall into one of two main groups: the small, gibbonlike *Dendropithecus* and *Pliopithecus,* and *Dryopithecus,* which is closer to a gorilla or chimpanzee. Its limb structure indicates that, unlike modern apes, *Dendropithecus* was adapted principally for arboreal, quadrupedal locomotion.

Dryopithecus

With the apes of the genus *Dryopithecus,* we approach the critical problem of the origin of our own family, for most paleontologists agree that it is among this group that the common ancestor of hominids and modern pongids is to be found. Dryopiths evidently originated in Africa, where they first appeared nearly 20 million years ago. Crossing the land bridge to Eurasia, they flourished in the warm, temperate forests of the Tethys basin and spread into Asia, where their remains have been found in Turkey, Pakistan, and India.

Because of the controversy surrounding the locomotor stages preceding hominid bipedalism, it would be of great interest to know whether dryopiths were quadrupedal "prebrachiators," habitual arm swingers, or brachiators secondarily modified for knuckle walking. The postcranial remains we have are insufficient to tell us for certain, but the small *D. africanus* (the best known) seems to have been rather monkeylike in limb proportions. However, some anatomists interpret the structure of its wrist bones as evidence that it had passed through a brachiating stage and was a semiterrestrial knuckle walker, like a miniature version of the modern chimpanzee.

Dental structure provides other clues to dryopith behavior. Their dentition was balanced in proportion, with back teeth large enough to deal with leafy vegetation and tough stems, as well as incisors adequate for slicing and peeling fruits. They did not have the very large incisors of modern chimpanzees and orangutans, which are used principally for fruit peeling. In this feature, they were both less specialized and more humanlike than modern apes.

Other details can be filled in by informed guesswork based on the behavior of living apes. If dryopiths were like chimpanzees, they probably spent most of their time in the trees, searching for food, building nests, and socializing. Perhaps they also used simple tools occasionally, ate the meat of small mammals when they could catch them, and made the Miocene Riviera ring with shouts of discovery in the season when figs ripened. Like chimpanzees, they were adaptable animals, evidently as much at home in the subtropical oak woods of southern Europe as in the forests and woodlands of equatorial Africa.

Adaptable as they were, however, the dryopiths seem to have been dependent upon the trees and their products. About 10 million years ago, dryopiths disappear from the fossil record of Europe, Pakistan, and India as savannas advanced to replace the moist forests. In Africa, the latest dryopith is about 14 million years old. Presumably, as the forests shrank, the dryopiths retreated with them into the Congo Basin and Southeast Asia, where their descendants—the chimpanzee, gorilla, and orangutan—are still to be found. But together with the remains of dryopiths, we find a few fossils whose structure indicates that an offshoot of the dryopith group was beginning to pursue a new way of life—one that would make it independent of the forest and perhaps ultimately give rise to the human species. These remains belong to *Ramapithecus*.

Ramapithecus

Ramapithecus shows a number of adaptive characteristics that suggest it had adopted a way of life rather different from that of its dryopith ancestors and cousins; these features include

1. Large, broad cheek teeth with thick enamel, but small, rather slender incisors.
2. Palate, face, and mandible heavily buttressed with bone.
3. Jaw muscles set well forward and oriented for maximum crushing power between the molars, rather than for incisal slicing.

No one of these characters alone represents a major departure from *Dryopithecus*. However, taken together they add up to a coherent adaptive pattern: more powerful chewing with the back teeth and less food preparation with the incisors. This could mean that *Ramapithecus* depended less on the juicy fruits of the forest and more on the harder, drier food objects found on the ground in savanna woodlands and bush—the kind of food that savanna-dwelling chimpanzees eat during the dry season.

Is Ramapithecus a Hominid? As we shall see, open-country adaptations, along with heavily built jaws and big back teeth for heavy grinding, characterized the first indubitable hominids—the australopiths of the Pliocene. This is the major reason for also assigning *Ramapithecus* to an ancestral position within the hominid family itself.

Bipedalism and small canines in males, associated with the use of such artifacts as tools and weapons, are striking features of later hominids, as we shall see. But many anthropologists are beginning to suspect that these features were not necessarily present in the earliest hominids, and that the first stages of hominid evolution may have been based upon a new habitat and a different feeding strategy—with bipedalism and tool use coming later in the story. Regardless of whether *Ramapithecus* was a biped, a quadruped, or a knuckle walker, and whether the canines of males were large or small, it is the derived features of his chewing appartus that make him a good candidate for hominid status.

We still have a lot to learn about *Ramapithecus*. Given the present state of knowledge, it is probably wiser not to attempt to fit every fragmentary fossil into a particular pongid or hominid lineage, but to take a wider view—namely, that in the middle Miocene various hominoid populations scattered across the Old World were experimenting with life outside the closed canopy forest, and consequently were adapting to the food resources of the grassy steppes and savannas. One of these, not necessarily one represented in our present museum collections, was the founder of the family Hominidae, to which we belong.

The Earliest Undoubted Hominids

In the time period stretching from the latest Miocene, about 5.5 million years ago, to the early Pleistocene, about 1 million years ago, there is no question that the remains we are dealing with belong to hominids. The question now becomes how many different kinds of hominids there were, how they are related to each other and to *Homo sapiens,* and how far each had advanced along the path toward humanity. We have literally hundreds of undoubted hominid fossils dating from this period. They are spread from South Africa to Java and are diverse in size and structure. Certainly, not all our colleagues will agree with our interpretation of this diversity, and we would not claim that it is the last word on the subject. New material has led to revisions in the past, and undoubtedly will do so in the future.

We believe that two genera of hominids can be distinguished in the fossil record of the past 5 million years. One of these, *Homo,* first appears about 2.7 million years ago and probably forms a single, unbranched, evolving lineage. The members of this evolving lineage become progressively more human in their structure and behavior. From the start, they are dependent upon stone toolmaking. As they evolve, and their material culture becomes more elaborate, their physical structure reflects more and more strongly their dependence upon the use and transmission of culture. This lineage, of course, culminates in modern populations of *Homo sapiens*. The remaining Pliocene and Pleistocene fossils are, according to our view, best put into another genus, *Australopithecus*.

Although there are many questions still to be answered, we now have a reasonable outline picture of the australopiths, as members of this genus may be called. They were bipedal, upright-walking creatures, small-brained and heavy-jawed by human standards, but with features of limb and tooth structure that clearly demonstrate their hominid status. They represent the culmination of the first phase of hominid evolution—the move from forest to open country, and an adaptive plateau from which the true humans of the genus *Homo* sprang.

On our reading of the evidence, australopiths first appear about 5.5 million years ago.[1]

---

[1] If *Ramapithecus* is indeed a hominid, then we may expect that as intervening deposits become better known, the complete series of hominids linking him with *Australopithecus* will be discovered. At the moment, we have only a scatter of indeterminate hominoid molars from East Africa to span the gap.

Some populations of *Australopithecus* probably gave rise to *Homo;* others persisted alongside the evolving human species until about 1 million years ago, when the last australopiths became extinct. Although the group may have been spread throughout the Old World tropics, all known specimens come from sub-Saharan Africa. This section offers an interpretation of the australopith group. We trace the evolutionary story of the genus *Homo* in following chapters.

The Hominid Status of Australopiths

The first major issue posed by the australopiths was whether they were hominids or pongids. Although the issue is no longer a live one, it is worthwhile considering the justification for their attribution to Hominidae. First, we should recall that modern taxonomy is based upon phylogeny, not upon resemblance. In other words, australopiths are not classified in Hominidae just because in some respects they look like humans. This would be a weak argument anyway, because in other ways they look like apes, and in still others they resemble neither. Rather, they are classified as Hominidae because they share certain *derived* characters with *Homo sapiens* that indicate relationship to humans through an ancestor that is not shared by any ape.

These characteristics fall into two complexes: (1) modifications of the hindlimb, especially the pelvis and foot, which can be plausibly related to bipedal stance and gait; and (2) modification of the shape and size of the canine tooth so that it no longer projects as a point or blade beyond the crowns of the neighboring premolars and molars, even in males.

Although it is just conceivable that this combination of features could have evolved twice, in parallel, it seems more likely that it evolved only once among hominoids, in an ancestral hominid from which both *Australopithecus* and *Homo sapiens* are descended. On the other hand, australopiths share none of the derived features of modern apes, such as very broad incisor teeth and very short lumbar region of the spinal column.

Those characters in which they resemble apes, such as their small cranial capacity, are primitive traits inherited from the ancestral hominoid stock.

The features that *Australopithecus* shares with *Homo sapiens* are phyletically important. They show us that australopiths are hominids, close phyletic relatives of *Homo sapiens*. But they are important from another perspective. They are part of the total adaptive complex of *Australopithecus:* the ways in which it differed from ancestral apes and the ways in which its lifestyle had come to differ from the pongid pattern.

The Australopith Pattern

How far is it legitimate to talk of a single pattern of adaptation that is characteristic of all australopiths? Even omitting, as we do, the specimens attributed to the genus *Homo,* there is considerable variation among australopiths in size and structure. Some anthropologists regard this variation as evidence for the existence of two or more adaptive types within the australopith group.

One of the more popular of these schemes proposes dividing the australopiths into two groups corresponding to two supposed adaptive types. The *robust* australopith, with its relatively large cheek teeth and smaller incisors, was considered a rather specialized vegetarian. The *gracile* one, with more balanced dental proportions, was considered a more omnivorous creature, an active hunter who included considerable quantities of meat in its diet. Unfortunately, the dietary hypothesis was seized upon and exaggerated in the popular literature, with journalists sparing no superlative in contrasting the poor, stupid, peaceable, clumsy, specialized robust australopiths with their wily, bloodthirsty, nimble cousins who eventually did them in.

We believe that a less dramatic story is closer to the truth. When the full range of variation among australopiths is taken into account, the line between gracile and robust begins to blur. These differences seem to us to represent variations on a theme, the sort of differences to be expected among individuals and populations of a lineage widely dispersed in space and time. They represent evolutionary variation within a single adaptive zone rather than the result of divergent evolutionary trends.

Disconcerting as it may be to those who seek cut-and-dried answers, it is likely that we shall never know how many species and subspecies of australopiths are really represented in our fossil samples, or how many local populations became temporarily or permanently isolated from the main stem, fated to become extinct or to again merge their genes in the common pool of the species. We believe that common adaptive themes run through the whole group and can best be shown by describing three rather arbitrarily separated forms that are generally given the rank of species.

1. *Australopithecus africanus:* small-sized primitive forms that are differentiated least from the ancestral pongid condition and in general seem to be earliest in time.
2. *A. robustus:* medium-sized, more evolved forms from South Africa, probably derived from *Australopithecus africanus*.
3. *A. boisei:* large, evolved australopiths from East Africa, presumably derived from an East African form resembling *A. africanus*.

Australopithecus africanus

On present evidence, *A. africanus* was the earliest australopith to appear and, more important, the most *primitive*—that is, the least differentiated from the presumed ancestral pongid condition. It therefore offers the most direct clues to the way in which australopiths as a group originated.

Habitat *A. africanus* did not live in forests and woodlands, as did most Miocene apes and modern pongids. At all sites it is associated with geological evidence for a rather arid seasonal climate, not unlike that of the South African veldt and East African savannas today, and with typical nonforest animals such as grazing antelopes and horses. Its primate associates are baboons, not apes or arboreal monkeys. Prehistoric savannas should not be imagined as treeless prairies; they were undoubtedly varied by strips of riverine forest, wooded parkland, and bush. But *A. africanus* clearly lived in a habitat where locomotion on the ground was essential, and the trees served, at most, as night refuges and an occasional source of food. Since we do not have rain forest faunas among the fossils of this period, we cannot be sure whether leaving the forest and becoming adapted to savannas was in itself a primary factor in the origin of hominids, or whether *A. africanus* had merely extended its range from a forest base. However, as we shall see, some australopith features seem best explained as adaptations to exploiting open country and the resources to be found there.

Brain Size and Structure The endocranial volume and estimated brain size of five adult specimens ranges between 435 and 485 cc, with an overall range of about 400 cc.

These are ape-sized brains. However, for the size of the animal, they are proportionately larger than any modern ape's. They exceed the average for chimpanzees and approach that of gorillas, although the latter are much larger animals. We know very little about the cranial capacity of the Miocene apes, but it is unlikely to have been greater than that of modern chimpanzees and gorillas. Accordingly, we can be fairly sure that an increase in relative brain size was a derived feature of the australopiths. Moreover, Holloway's (1972) careful studies of the structure of endocranial casts indicates that size increase was not a matter of simple expansion. It seems to have involved differential expansion of the cerebral cortex in general, and particularly the parietal lobe, increasing its association areas. We really know too little as yet about the functioning of the brain, especially of the cerebral cortex, to be able to interpret this feature in more than the vaguest terms. However, in humans, parts of the parietal association cortex seem to be concerned with language production.

This may mean that the australopiths had advanced further than the apes in the development of a symbolic communication system based upon a sound code.

Teeth, Jaws, and Feeding Adaptations By human standards, the jaws of *A. africanus* appear disproportionately large next to the braincase. They are not, however, the jaws and teeth of an ape. They show distinct deviation away from the presumed ancestral condition that is seen in Miocene and modern pongids.

Back Tooth Dominance The back teeth dominate the dentition of *A. africanus*. The molars are very large, and the premolars broad and molarized—that is, their crowns have become somewhat more complex, with extra cusps to increase the grinding area. The incisors, on the other hand, are quite small.

Most paleoanthropologists have explained the proportions of the australopith dentition in terms of tool use. Supposedly, cutting tools took over the function of the front teeth, leading to their reduction. But this explanation misses the main point. When body size is taken into account, the dental proportions of *A. africanus* are obviously due to *expansion* of the back teeth rather than to *reduction* of the incisors. In fact, a fifty-pound *A. africanus*, has back teeth that far exceed the norm for chimpanzees and are closer to those of a two-hundred-pound female gorilla. Its incisors are not especially reduced; they are scarcely smaller than the primitive condition seen in *Dryopithecus,* although they are indeed smaller than those of the fruit-eating chimpanzee. (See Figure 4–2.)

The shape of the jaw and the position of the muscular attachments also reflect "back tooth dominance." The muscles of mastication (the masseter and temporalis), which close the jaw and produce grinding movements, are set further forward than those of the chimpanzee. This means that the full force of the muscles can be exerted in crushing food and grinding it between the teeth—the kind of movement you use to eat peanuts or sunflower seeds. The arrangement is less well suited to pulling the jaw back and upward, as you do when taking a hearty bite from an apple.

As in the case of *Ramapithecus,* we can relate these adaptive traits to the demands of open-country vegetarianism, feeding more upon tough rhizomes and hard, dry seeds of savanna trees, shrubs, and bushes, and less upon the kind of juicy fruit to be found in the forests. A back-tooth-dominant dentition is ideal for foods that require plenty of hard grinding but relatively little incisal preparation. This is, of course, not to say that australopiths ate only small, hard foods like seeds. They certainly ate a great variety of other foods to be picked up in the savanna, including, no doubt, small game. The australopiths may well have gone in for some systematic cooperative hunting, as chimpanzees do. They could certainly have chewed meat with their powerful jaws. However, specialized meat eaters have bladelike slicing cheek teeth for chopping meat into chunks for swallowing, so we can be fairly sure that it was not meat eating that provided the selectional force behind the development of the broad, flat molar crowns of *A. africanus*. The jaws and teeth of *A. africanus* are not an ape's, but neither are they those of a meat eater. There is no anatomical evidence that australopiths were more carnivorous than living chimpanzees. The analogy of the chimpanzees suggests that their meat eating would be confined to small game caught when the opportunity arose.

Nonprojecting Canine Teeth One of the distinctively nonpongid features of all australopiths is that both sexes have nonprojecting canine teeth. This observation has several implications. First, and most obviously, it presumably means that when australopiths fought and threatened, either among themselves or against prowling predators, they probably brandished sticks and threw stones rather than biting or displaying their canines. Since such behavior is seen in savanna chimpanzees, it need not be considered a great

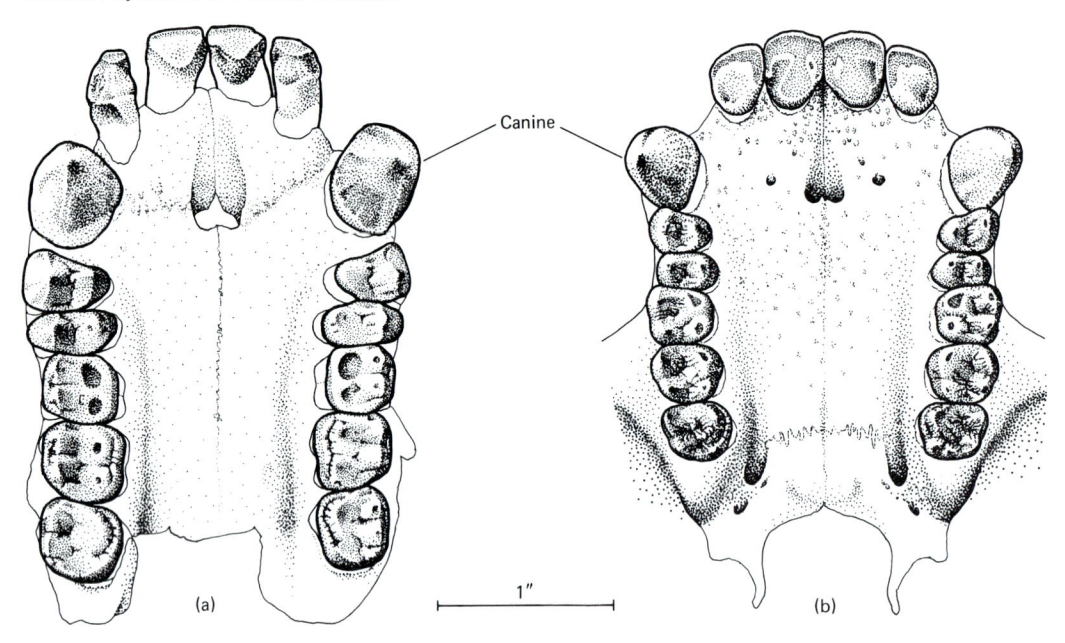

Figure 4–2. Upper dentitions of Pongidae and Hominidae. (a) Dryopithecus major (from Moroto, Uganda, c. 20 m.y., probably male) — probably primitive dental proportions, with moderate-sized incisors and molars; (b) Pan troglodytes (male) — compared to primitive condition, incisors are larger, molars smaller; (c) Australopithecus boisei (Olduvai Hominid 5, believed to be male) — compared to primitive condition, molars are larger, incisors smaller; (d) Homo sapiens (modern African, male). Note small canines in (c) and (d). (Biruta Akerbergs)

departure from the primitive condition.

Since chimpanzees use artifacts in display and defense, yet retain large male canines as a backup system, why did hominids lose their fighting canines and come to depend on artificial weapons? Perhaps, once again, this is part of the back-tooth-dominance complex associated with small-object feeding. A large male canine may be a useful weapon, but it reduces chewing efficiency. Smaller canines could be of considerable adaptive significance to a hard chewer, particularly one with a long potential life span. Females, already enjoying the benefits of low-crown canines, would not be subjected to this selective pressure, although they too were hard chewers. The result would be the reduction of male canines until they were no more projecting than a female's.

Posture and Locomotion Some of the most distinctive features of a modern human in the pelvis, femur, leg bones, and foot can be interpreted as adaptations to a habitual upright posture and bipedal locomotion. The lumbar vertebrae of *A. africanus* form a distinct lumbar curve and the complex of features of the pelvis concerned with transmitting weight from the trunk via the vertebral column is closely similar to the human. Thus the habitual posture of *A. africanus* was probably one in which the trunk was balanced upright upon the pelvic girdle, with the forelimbs playing little or no part in bearing the body weight — in other words, some form of bipedalism.

Another set of relationships in proportions, however, shows a less human condition. The *acetabula,* sockets for the femoral heads, face more directly sideways; the iliac blade, though broad as in humans, is oriented less anteriorly, so that the support of the lesser gluteus muscles during the swing phase of walking may have been less efficient. Perhaps *A. africanus* waddled as he walked. The ischium, that part of the pelvis projecting behind and

(c)

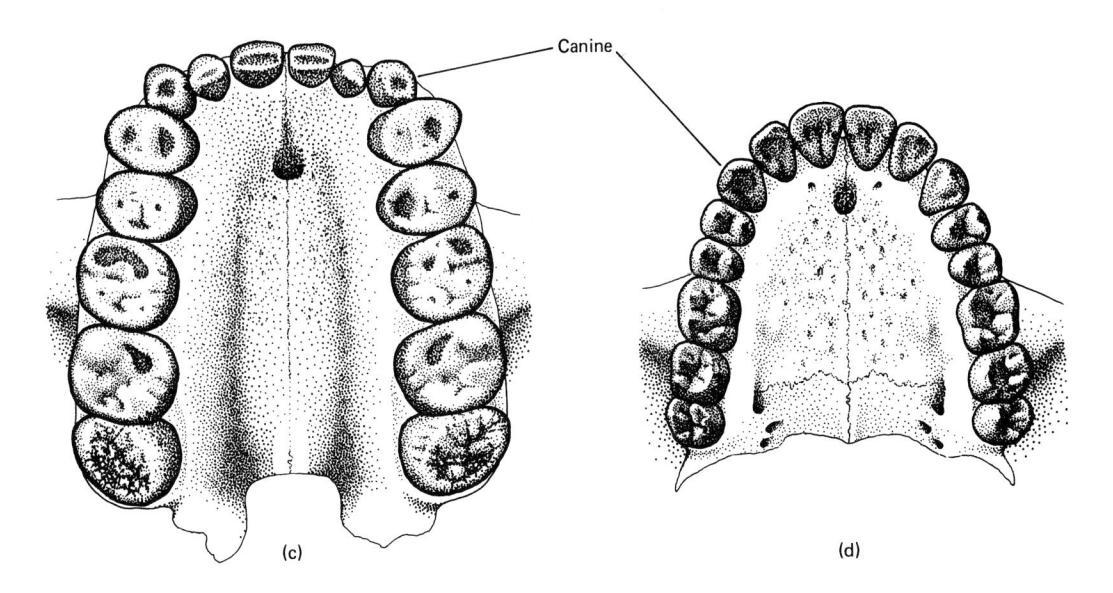

(d) Canine

below the hip joint, is comparatively long like a human's. (See Figure 4–3.) In spite of these features, however, the overall shape of the pelvis in *A. africanus* is much closer to that of a human than to that of an ape, and there can be little doubt that it was habitually bipedal in posture and locomotion.

The Adaptive Value of Bipedalism Apart from hominids, all primates that regularly move on the ground do so quadrupedally, either by knuckle walking or in a baboonlike way. The appearance of bipedalism in the hominids, therefore, demands some explanation. Part of the answer might be a preadaptation in their arboreal ancestor. As we saw, some primates, especially the gibbon, have arms that are so highly adapted for suspension that when placed on the ground these primates often walk bipedally rather than subject their arms to the compressive forces of quadrupedalism. It is possible that the prehominid may have been such a creature. A very fragmentary scapula from Sterkfontein shows features said to be reminiscent of an orangutan's. But this explanation supposes that the prehominid was a very highly arboreal animal, almost certainly living in a rain forest. Such an animal would be unlikely to move directly into open savanna or grassland. It seems more likely that the prehominid was a woodland animal, perhaps a knuckle walker when on the ground, but, like the chimpanzee, capable of bipedal stance and locomotion when circumstances called for it. The question then arises, why did the australopiths (or hominids ancestral to them) become habitual rather than occasional bipeds?

It is difficult for us to focus clearly on this problem. Dependent as we are upon habitual bipedalism, we tend to see only its advantages—carrying food, tools, and babies; peering over tall grass and bushes; using the hands in gesturing; and so forth. But an ape would view bipedalism rather differently. An animal adapted to knuckle-walking quadrupedalism is a master of a highly efficient locomotor pattern that is economical in energy. The animal, which can move fast when necessary, is securely balanced on a broad base with weight evenly distributed over four limbs and along the vertebral column, which permits easy movement over rough and steep surfaces, through underbrush, and beneath branches. Becoming a habitual biped means losing some of these advantages, and clearly this will happen only if there is some overriding necessity to become upright.

Human Physical and Cultural Evolution

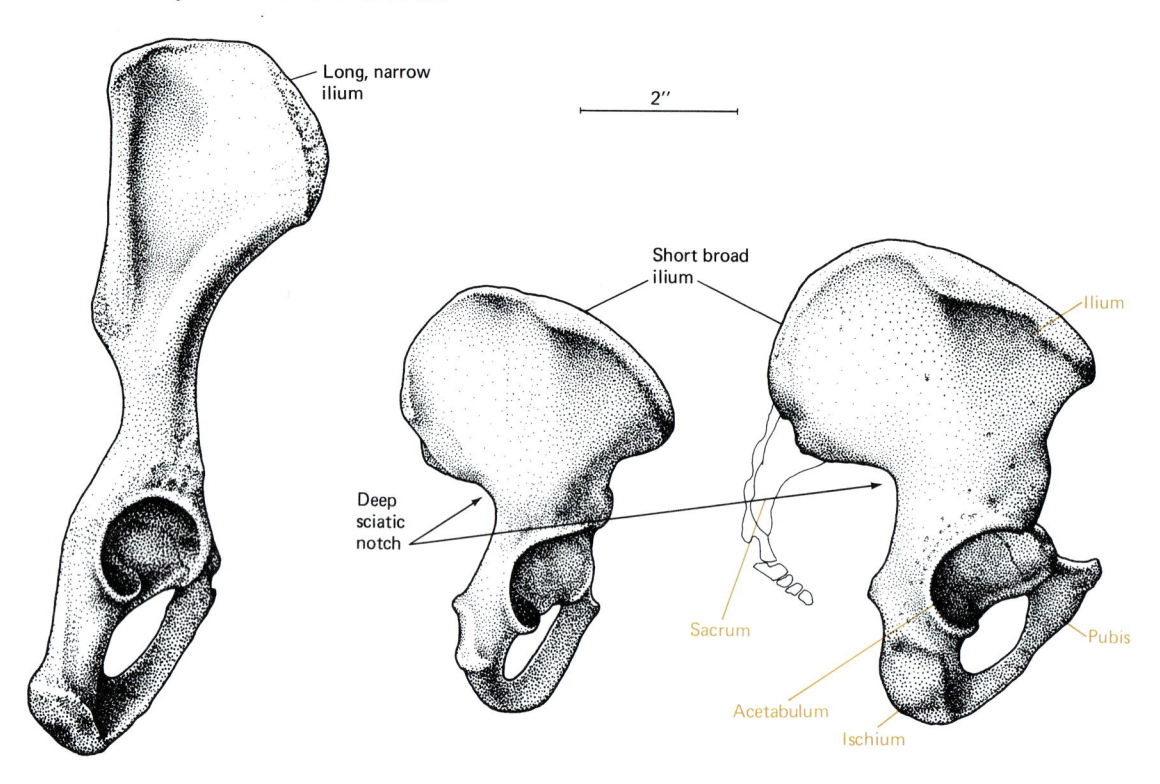

Figure 4–3. Pelvic bones (innominates) from the side view. (a) **Homo sapiens**; (b) **Australopithecus africanus** (based on a specimen from Sterkfontein); (c) **Pan troglodytes**. The sacral vertebrae (base of the spine) and the three bones comprising the innominate have been indicated in the human specimen. (Biruta Akerbergs)

A clue can be gained from situations in which quadrupedal monkeys and apes do and do not use bipedal stance and locomotion on the ground. First, it is clear that you do not need to be bipedal to carry a helpless infant, a stick, or a large piece of food; to feed from the ground or from a shrub; or to use a stick as a prodder or a tool. All these things are done sitting or in a tripedal stance, with both feet and one hand on the ground. Peering over tall grass, beating the chest in display, or brandishing a branch require occasional but not habitual bipedalism, for they are activities that occupy only a tiny fraction of each day. Since nonhuman primates spend the greater part of each day gathering and eating food, we should perhaps examine the foraging behavior of living primates for a situation in which the animal, needing both its hands free, is forced to hold its trunk erect unsupported by its forelimbs. Bipedal walking has been seen in wild chimpanzees, for instance, when they are presented with a heap of food such as bananas or papayas. Picking up armfuls of fruit, they make off with it into the bush to feed at leisure.

Although carrying food back to a home base undoubtedly became important later in human evolution, it is doubtful that it was a primary factor in the early appearance of bipedalism. For one thing, nonhuman primates hardly ever carry food around. There is no advantage in doing so, and most is eaten where it is found. Carrying certainly became more important in the genus *Homo* as people developed a distinctively human foraging pattern. This involved fanning out over the countryside around the base camp and bringing foodstuffs, particularly meat, back to camp to share. However, the earliest evidence we have for this kind of behavior is associated with hominids more advanced than the australopiths, and there is no reason to suppose that it was part of the initial hominid pattern.

One feeding situation will regularly elicit a kind of bipedalism in monkeys and apes. In this situation, the animal is faced with a scatter of food objects like peanuts or grains of corn, with other members of the group competing for the food. Each animal will squat or crouch in a bent-knee position, using both hands to pick up food and pass it to the mouth as rapidly as possible. Having both hands free for use means effectively doubling the possible rate of feeding. (This is quite unlike the situation of feeding on fruits and other large food objects, where the rate of feeding is controlled not by the speed at which the hands work but by the speed at which each object can be prepared by the incisor teeth, and where the whole operation can be economically carried out in a tripedal stance using one hand only.) If the food objects are not only small, but rather evenly scattered, such as seeding heads of grasses and other plants in a meadow, the rate of feeding is increased still further if the animal not only sits with the trunk erect but also moves bipedally. The hands are thus kept free, and the need to drop on all fours to shift position is avoided. Among all living primates, the gelada baboon is the expert at small-object feeding. Its diet requires it to spend most of the day in a trunk-erect squatting position. As it feeds, it shuffles "bipedally" forward on its haunches, using both of its extremely nimble hands to pluck grass and stems.

Of course, not only is two-handed feeding advantageous when feeding from the ground, but it is equally useful in gathering small nuts, berries, or seeds from low bushes or from tall grasses. It is the *size* of the food object that is critical. All this would be of little consequence but for the fact that the kinds of foods that demand two-handed gathering — seeds, nuts and berries, shoots, and rhizomes — are also those that the australopith chewing apparatus was adapted to process, and those, moreover, that appear in the diet of savanna chimpanzees. Taken together, all this seems to add up to quite a strong, if circumstantial, case for small-object feeding having played an important role in the appearance of habitual bipedalism in early hominids, and also, incidentally, in the evolution of the nimble, precision-gripping hominid hand.

Bipedalism and Toolmaking   Even if hominid bipedalism started as a feeding adaptation, it obviously had implications that reached far beyond this. Hands liberated from locomotor functions — their dexterity enhanced by generations of selection for nimble food gathering, and combined with the inventiveness and mental flexibility of a chimpanzeelike ape — would certainly be turned to all kinds of manipulative tasks, including, quite probably, the making of tools more refined and complex than any produced by a chimpanzee. It is quite likely that *A. africanus* used digging sticks, clubs, and perhaps stone flakes as cutting or scraping tools, but it must be recognized that archeological evidence for such activities is very meager indeed.

Raymond Dart and others have claimed that many of the bone fragments found at South African sites were tools made and used by australopiths. Recent studies, however, have shown that when carnivores crunch bones, they often produce fragments that can look extraordinarily like artifacts and that exactly match the types that Dart believed to be the most characteristic tools and weapons of *Australopithecus*.

What, then, are we to make of *A. africanus*? It is a hominid, certainly, quite distinct from any ape in structure and behavior. About the size of a small chimpanzee and living in open country, it shows physical adaptations that seem mostly to have been concerned with exploiting the kind of vegetable resources to be found there. It probably used artifacts as tools and weapons at least as much as living chimpanzees do, and perhaps more. It would certainly have supplemented its diet with animal food, and although the evidence for this is very slim, it may well have been a more efficient and habitual hunter and carnivore than modern apes and monkeys are. It may have lived longer and matured more slowly than modern apes do, and processed more information in its expanded cerebral cortex.

A. robustus and A. boisei: Evolved Forms of Australopiths

Several sites in Africa have yielded evidence of more and less primitive forms of australopiths, *A. robustus* and *A. boisei*. For a number of years the geological evidence was thought to indicate that the robust australopiths lived in a wetter, more densely vegetated habitat than *A. africanus*. This is not now generally accepted. Like *A. africanus*, they seem to have been animals of dry grasslands, woodlands, and savannas.

A. robustus, from South Africa, and *A. boisei*, from East Africa, were somewhat larger in size, with larger brains (though not proportionately larger) than *A. africanus*. Back tooth dominance was even more developed, with their very large molars adapted to heavy chewing. Like the smaller species, they were adapted for bipedalism; the foot, for instance, had well-developed arches, and the big toe was not a mobile grasping organ. These later australopiths seem also to have been principally vegetarian, adapted to foraging on low vegetation rather than striding long distances in pursuit of game.

Toolmaking Stone tools have now been found at several sites that have also yielded the remains of evolved robust australopiths. A skull of *A. boisei*, for instance, was found on a "living floor" at Olduvai with tools of the Oldowan culture. For some authorities, such associations are sufficient proof that evolved australopiths made these artifacts. Others have always doubted this interpretation and such doubts have been strengthened by the discovery of members of the genus *Homo* at each of the sites. If two or more hominid species are found with stone tools at a particular site, archeology is no help in deciding which of them, if either, was the toolmaker. Most paleoanthropologists faced with such a situation assume, reasonably enough, that the species which is the more human in appearance is likely to be the more technologically accomplished. However, even if the robust australopiths did not make the comparatively sophisticated tools of the Oldowan industry, it does not follow that they did not make and use simpler tools. In fact, just as we have suggested about *A. africanus*, it would be very surprising if they did not use simple digging sticks, clubs, pounders, and cutting tools.

The Extinction of the Australopiths

Contrary to a view that was widely held for some years, the australopiths clearly do not represent a short-lived transitional stage between apes and man. *A. boisei* alone survived through a time span ten times as long as that of *Homo sapiens*. They represent a stable, widespread, and successful adaptation to life on tropical savannas. Yet, a little over a million years ago, they disappeared from the scene. In Africa, the disappearance seems to follow soon after the appearance of a new stone-tool culture, the Acheulean.

It seems possible (and the reader is warned that this is pure speculation) that the Acheulean industry was part of a general technological advance that also included ways of preparing tough vegetable foods with pounders or grindstones rather than by chewing, as well as using containers for gathering such vegetable foods more efficiently. If this were so, it would enable early humans, members of the genus *Homo*, to expand their econiche to the detriment of the australopiths by using technology to exploit the same resources to which australopiths were physically adapted. Of course, australopith extinction may have had nothing to do with competition from early humans. We may never know what caused it, nor does this greatly matter.

The important point is that extinction is a commonplace of mammalian history, and there is no reason to imagine that hominids were immune from it, especially early in their history when physical adaptation and specialization were as important as culturally determined behavioral responses. Not all anthropologists would accept this view. Proponents of the *single species hypothesis* believe that the specimens we call *Homo habilis* are in fact australopiths, that all australopiths made Oldowan tools, that the Acheuleans evolved from the late australopiths, and that no extinction took place. We find this a possible but less plausible interpretation, partly because *A. boisei* and *A. robustus* show specializations that make them unlikely ancestors of true humans, but mostly because we think that there is now reasonably clear evidence for the existence of primitive members of the genus *Homo* distinct from, but contemporary with, late australopiths. If these early *Homo* were not directly ancestral to the makers of the Acheulean culture and to still later humans, they at least seem to have been considerably closer to that ancestry than was any australopith. We shall follow their story in the next chapter.

summary

Fossils are the remains of plants and animals that have been preserved and mineralized through geological accident. They provide hard evidence of extinct animal forms and information beyond that which can be obtained by the study of the behavior and structure of living species. They also can provide data about the prehistoric environment in which new adaptations emerged. Through careful examination of fossils, the anthropologist can interpret structural features in functional terms; and using our knowledge of living primates to provide analogies and comparisons, we can often make cautious inferences about a species' econiche, locomotor patterns, habitat, and diet.

The geological time scale is based primarily upon the stratigraphic relationships of rock units and the fossils they contain. It is divided into three major eras, each dominated by a particular vertebrate group. Each era is further demarcated into periods and epochs by geological and evolutionary changes.

In the last period of the Mesozoic era, the Cretaceous, an important floral revolution—the expansion of the *angiosperms* at the expense of the *gymnosperms*—created a novel evolutionary environment, which led to the proliferation of insects and consequently of small, agile vertebrates. Two lines of mammals that developed at this time were a rodentlike group, the multituberculates, and the ancestors of virtually all of today's mammals, the *Theria.*

Fossil evidence suggests that Paleocene primates were a highly diversified group with many specialized adaptations. Analysis of fossil limb bones indicates that they were tree climbers; anatomical details of their teeth and middle ear place them in the order Primates.

It is in the Eocene primates that we first find the prosimian level of organization and the first signs of the distinctive characteristics of living primates: relatively larger brains, dependence upon eyesight, unspecialized dentition, elongated digits for grasping, and nails rather than claws.

The African Oligocene primates were quite unlike the prosimians of Europe and North Africa. They belong to the Catarrhini, or Old World branch of the higher primates, and there is little doubt that from their ranks sprang the cercopithecoid monkeys, the apes, and ultimately the human lineage. The Fayum primates bridge the gap between the Eocene primates and the advanced apes and monkeys that first appear in the Miocene.

Fossil Miocene monkeys and apes no longer show the primitive characters observed in Oligocene forms. For the most part, Miocene hominoids form two main groups: the small, gibbonlike *Dendropithecus* and *Pliopithecus,* and the apelike *Dryopithecus.*

Most paleontologists agree that the genus *Dryopithecus* included the common ancestor of hominids and pongids. Dental remains indicate that dryopith dentition was more humanlike than that of modern apes. *Dryopithecus* appears to have been adaptable, but dependent upon a forest environment. As savannas replaced the moist forests, we assume that dryopiths followed the shrinking forests into central Africa and Southeast Asia, where their descendants, the great apes, survive.

Fossils found among dryopith remains suggest that an offshoot of the dryopith group, *Ramapithecus,* was beginning to pursue a new way of life independent of the forest. *Ramapithecus* fossils display an innovative adaptive pattern: more powerful chewing with the back teeth and less food preparation with the incisors, which may indicate that *Ramapithecus* had abandoned the fruits of the forest to become a forager for the harder, drier food objects of the savanna woodlands and bush. These dental adaptations are also characteristic of the first undoubted hominid, *Australopithecus* of the Pliocene. The first stages of hominid evolution were perhaps based upon a new habitat and feeding strategy.

"Apelike" in some respects, australopiths share certain derived features with humans (notably, adaptation for bipedalism and modifications of the canine tooth) that warrant their classification as early hominids. Although there is considerable variation among fossil australopiths in size and structure, we believe that this variation falls within the expected range for populations so widely dispersed in time and space, and that all belong to the genus *Australopithecus.*

A. africanus, the smaller species and the first to appear, lived in a rather arid savanna habitat, where locomotion on the ground was mandatory. Its brain capacity was proportionately larger than that of any modern ape. There is some evidence of differential expansion of the parietal lobe, which may be associated with language.

The back teeth dominated this species' dentition: it had very large molars, modestly sized incisors, and jaw muscles adapted for crushing and grinding. This suggests that *A. africanus* ate more seeds, roots, and nuts than fruits, and was not adapted for meat-eating.

Postcranial remains indicate that *A. africanus* shared with modern humans many of the derived features associated with habitual bipedalism (although some anatomists believe it may not have been an efficient biped). The selective pressures acting to make this hominid a habitual biped most likely resulted from the one situation in which squatting upright and using both hands is clearly advantageous for primates—when they are competing to gather small items of food, such as nuts or grain. In addition, two-handed gathering favors the nimble precision grasp of the hominid hand. This dexterity, plus mental flexibility, laid the biological foundation for making more complex and refined tools than chimpanzees produce.

A. robustus, from South Africa, and *A. boisei,* from East Africa, were somewhat larger in size, with larger brains (but not proportionately larger) than *A. africanus.* The back tooth dominance was even more developed; they, too, were adapted for bipedalism.

As a group, then, australopiths were quite distinct in structure and behavior from any ancient or modern ape. They lived in open country, probably used sticks and stones as tools and weapons, and perhaps supplemented their diet with occasional game. We can also infer that they lived longer and matured more slowly than apes do, and stored more learned information in the expanded cerebral cortex. They survived more than 4 million years (considerably longer than *Homo sapiens* has to date).

suggested readings

BISHOP, W. W., AND MILLER, J. A., EDS.
1972 *Calibration of Hominoid Evolution.* Toronto: University of Toronto Press. Papers describing methods of dating and their application to primate-bearing deposits of the late Cenozoic.

BRACE, C. L.
1967 *The Stages of Human Evolution: Human and Cultural Origins.* Englewood Cliffs, N.J.: Prentice-Hall. An account of hominid evolution as seen by one of the leading protagonists of the single-species hypothesis.

CLARK, W. E. LE GROS
1966 *History of the Primates.* 5th ed. Chicago: University of Chicago Press. An elementary but authoritative introduction to the study of primate evolution.

JOLLY, C. J., ED.
1975 *Early African Hominids.* London: Duckworth. A collection of papers presenting new data and interpretations of the hominids of this crucial period.

SIMONS, E. L.
1972 *Primate Evolution: An Introduction to Man's Place in Nature.* New York: Macmillan. A leading primate paleontologist's account of fossil primates.

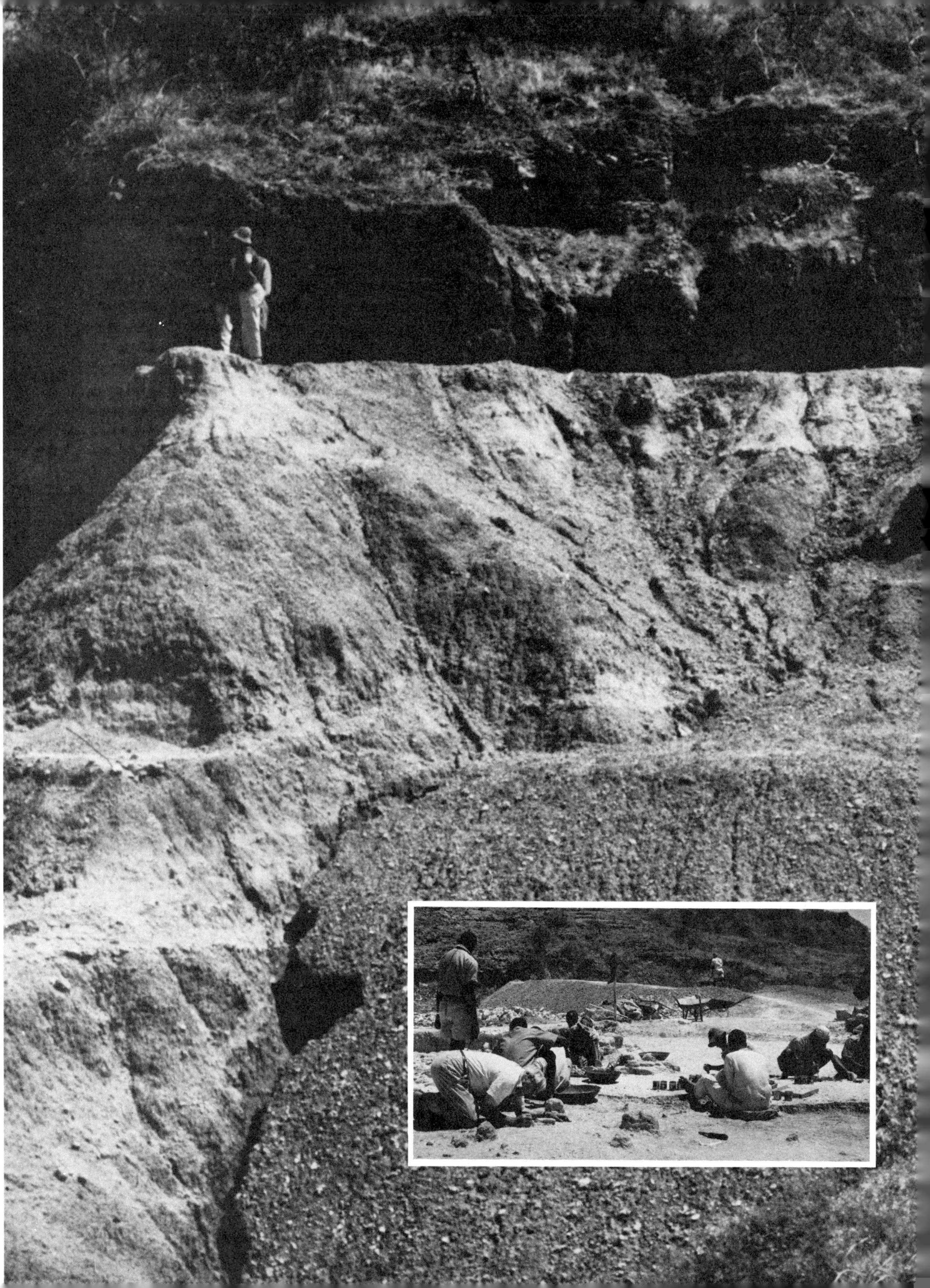

five
The Emergence of Cultural Essentials

This is the beginning of a new phase in the human evolutionary story. So far we have been tracing the evolution of nonhuman primates, relating their adaptive strategies to their physical adaptation through successive stages. We have had to infer behavior indirectly from anatomical adaptations. In this phase, for the first time, we have direct evidence of behavior in the form of *artifacts,* things such as tools and shelters that are made by human hands, and *living floors,* sites preserving the traces of human activities that were carried on there. The interpretation of behavior from these remains is the business of archeology. (See the box on p. 89 for a more detailed discussion of what archeologists do.) Such evidence, combined with that of the fossil remains, discloses a new phase of evolution, one that is distinctly human.

What does it mean to be human? We now know that our nearest primate relatives, the chimpanzees, hunt, use tools, have some ability to learn a language, and respect the ties of kinship. However, there are still enormous gaps in all these respects between our closest nonhuman relatives and the simplest modern human societies.

First, humans use a variety of artifacts, and they depend upon these artifacts for survival. Artifacts are made to a pattern that is shared by a group of people and is transmitted from one generation to another. This is one aspect of human culture.

Second, all humans have an economic division of labor, while in nonhuman primate groups roles are differentiated only in the defense of the group or in the care of the young. Tasks are shared, and each member makes a contribution to the economic well-being of the whole family. Among human hunter-gatherers, men generally hunt, women and children gather. Much food is carried back to the base camp, where it is shared with other members of the family. The existence of a base camp allows group members who are young, sick, or temporarily disabled to stay at home and be fed by the other members of the group until they become stronger. Furthermore, in more complex human groups, such as our own, this division of labor encompasses a wide range of social, political, and economic specialization.

Next, humans organize the world: they tame the nonhuman world outside society by categorizing it. Myths, rituals, and other systems of organizing nature and aligning it with society are also specific to groups of human beings. This is another aspect of culture that is passed on by learning. This chapter, then, is the story of the development of these specifically human behaviors.

Archeologists find it useful to distinguish a succession of stages in human technology and cultural development, and paleoanthropologists identify successive species in the fossil record. In this chapter, we will divide the development of culture into three such stages: the emergence of cultural essentials, the emergence of a division of labor, and the emergence of specialized behavior.

Olduvai Gorge in Tanzania is part of a rift valley composed of eroded canyons and lake beds. The skeletal remains of australopiths and other early hominids discussed in this chapter have been discovered here, along with tools from the earliest toolmaking traditions. Most of these finds were excavated by the late Louis B. Leakey (shown kneeling in the left-hand corner of the insert photo) and his wife, Mary. (DeVore/Anthro-Photo; *insert,* Mohamed Amin/Nancy Palmer)

Similarly, we divide the evolving *Homo* lineage somewhat arbitrarily into three successive species: *Homo habilis, Homo erectus,* and *Homo sapiens.* Archeological interpretation of the cultures of early humans depends largely on the changes in stone tools and the behavior that can be inferred from them. We divide this continuously evolving cultural sequence into three technological stages.

The Emergence of Toolmaking Traditions

Early humans are known to a large extent by the tools they made. As has been mentioned, chimpanzees use and modify natural objects to employ them as tools, and there is little doubt that australopiths were at least as skillful. But for at least 2½ million and for perhaps more than 3½ million years, hominids have been modifying natural objects to make tools to a set and regular pattern. For most of that time, the commonest tools were simple choppers made of pebbles and flakes with a naturally sharp cutting edge. These tools belong to what archeologists call the Oldowan tradition.

Oldowan Technology

The name *Oldowan* is taken from Olduvai Gorge, Tanzania, where artifacts up to 1.8 million years old have been unearthed, along with the remains of hominids. Not only have stone tools been found, but also flakes and other raw materials from which tools were made, indicating that tool manufacture was carried on there. The presence of a large variety of animal bones, especially those of mammals, provides clear evidence of butchering, and by inference, hunting or scavenging and food sharing. There is even evidence for a crude windbreak, or shelter. These remains imply that the area was used over and over for base camps. Overlying these layers are more recent cultural levels and human fossils, providing glimpses of successive stages of human evolution in the area over hundreds of thousands of years.

The earliest known tools, however, come not from Olduvai, but from East Rudolf in Kenya; they were used more than 2.6 million years ago, perhaps to butcher kills (Isaac, 1972: 407). Exploration and analysis of the East Rudolf finds is continuing. Because of the richness of the material already uncovered and that which undoubtedly remains to be unearthed, it may be many years before the whole story of its human inhabitants is known.

In the deposits in the Omo Valley of Ethiopia, a scattering of tools that may reach back 3 million years has been found. Outside East Africa, there are many sites in South Africa, a few in North Africa and the Middle East, and even one in southern France that seem to be contemporaneous with Olduvai. This concentration of sites in Africa currently seems to indicate that toolmaking evolved there, but only further explorations in other parts of the world will confirm this guess.

Many Oldowan tools are slightly modified pieces of stone, often hard to distinguish from rocks battered by natural wear and tear. The toolmakers shaped the pebbles by *percussion flaking,* in which a stone was used as a hammer to chip off some flakes on one or two sides of another stone. When a core was modified by removing flakes from one side, we say that the core was *unifacially* worked; when flakes were removed from both sides, we say it was *bifacially* worked. (See Figure 5–1.) From a pound of stone, using the Oldowan technique, the stone worker could produce a cutting edge only about two inches (5 cm) long (Butzer, 1971:475), but the resulting edge is surprisingly sharp, far superior to nails or teeth in cutting through the skin or sinew of an animal or in shaping a piece of wood.

Crude as they were, these tools represent an enormous step forward in our ancestors' control of their environment. And at a very early stage, they realized that not all raw materials were equally appropriate for tools. In the lower levels of Olduvai Gorge, archeologists have found tools made of stone not native to the area. People brought appropriate raw materials from some distance to the work site.

The number of different kinds of tools was limited. Unifacial tools, known as *choppers,* are the most frequent form. Sometimes flakes

The Archeologist's Task: Tracing Human Prehistory

Archeology is the anthropological study of extinct societies. Accordingly, its raw materials are the things of the past: the remnants of prehistoric hunts, bits and pieces of early tools, the remains of ancient temples. Although such artifacts are but a pale reflection of the family life, tribal councils, markets, ceremonies, and other events for which they were used, they provide sufficient information to enable the archeologist to reconstruct the most important evolutionary episodes of the past and even to know some ancient societies in great detail. With this knowledge, the archeologist seeks to trace the paths of human prehistory and understand the processes of cultural evolution.

For many people, the word "archeologist" conjures up an image of a person on hands and knees with eyes focused on the ground and hands busy searching for tools, pieces of pottery, and other remains of the past. Because the primary means by which archeologists collect their data are *surveys* and *excavations,* this image is at least partially correct.

Recovering Evidence: Surveys and Excavations. The decision to work in a particular location can be determined in a number of ways. Typically, archeologists employ survey techniques to discover a site, although historical documents, explorers' journals, and even legends about ancient dwelling places and migrations also may play a role.

A survey is a systematic examination of the surface of a designated area. Sites are usually marked by artifacts or house rubble. To a trained eye, however, there are other indications that a site was inhabited; certain variations in soil and overgrowth may, for example, suggest buried buildings, irrigation canals that have filled with silt, and the like. Because the original territorial boundaries are often unknown, archeologists generally define surveys around a geographical unit such as an island or valley that they believe may contain the answers to some important questions.

Surveys are extremely useful to archeologists who are interested in previously unstudied areas. A thorough inventory gathered by a survey enables the researcher to choose the site or sites that are most likely to yield valuable information through excavation.

In the last decade or two, archeologists have also begun to consider the survey as a primary research tool, not just as a precedent or supplement to excavation. Surveys are the only way to establish the boundaries of prehistoric cultures; they can tell us where one subsistence and toolmaking tradition stops and another begins, for example. And they are the only way to gather data on the distribution of populations and ecological strategies in prehistoric times and on the relationship between them.

Once the survey has been completed, the archeologist may begin to excavate. The process of excavating a site, or digging to recover artifacts and other buried evidence of human activity, is far more complex than it may initially sound. As with fossils, artifacts are not always easy to recognize: often they are broken into hundreds of fragments, and some artifacts, such as very early stone tools, are barely distinguishable from natural (as opposed to manmade) objects. Artifacts may also be accidentally destroyed or simply overlooked. Furthermore, once an artifact has been identified, the archeologist must take care to note precisely where it was found, for the location of artifacts is as important to understanding the past as the objects themselves.

The first step in the actual excavation is mapping the site and its surroundings and establishing a datum, or reference, point. This point may be the corner of a building, a large rock, a cement post, or a metal rod—indeed, it can be anything, as long as it is visible and permanent enough to serve as a point of reference. Usually, the crew then digs one or more test pits, from which they collect data on the natural layering of the soil, the depth of cultural deposits, and the presence of architecture or other features. This information can then be used to make certain strategic decisions. (1) What percentage of the site will be excavated? Large units are generally preferable, for they enhance the possibility of significant finds and minimize the danger of cave-ins. If the site is large or the crew small, however, the archeologist may decide on a sample of small (3 to 5 foot [1 to 1.5 m]) pits scattered over the area. (2) What shape pits will be dug? Sometimes, architectural features such as rooms dictate the dimensions of excavation units. More often, however, archeologists impose a structure on the site by dividing it into squares, rectangles, or trenches. (3) Can natural stratification be used to segregate finds from different levels in the pit? If so, the site is ideal, for stratification marks different chronological levels. If there is no visible layering in the soil, or if the layers are too thick to be useful, the excavator must decide on arbitrary levels—usually 3 or 6 inches (7.5 to 15 cm). (4)

What kinds of materials are to be collected? In addition to artifacts, the excavator may want to collect charcoal or other material for dating, or seeds, pollen, and animal bones for ecological data. Each kind of material requires its own special handling.

These decisions made, the crew lays a grid of squares on the site (using the datum point as a reference) so that they will be able to record the exact location of every find. They can now dig—square by square, layer by layer. Working with anything from power machinery to bent screwdrivers and small brushes (depending on the site), they begin. Artifacts are bagged and labeled according to their location in the grid and the natural or arbitrarily determined layer in which it is found. Usually, the crew makes a photographic record of each phase of the excavation process and each find so that others can see what they have done and can retrace their steps. Excavation may take a few days, months, or years, most of the work being done in the summer. (The record for time spent at a single site is probably Susa, Iran, where successive teams of archeologists have been digging more or less continuously for some 90 years.) But excavation is only a beginning. The task of interpreting the finds still remains.

Reconstructing Past Societies. To someone trained in archeological detective work, the motley assortment of broken and jumbled remains found at a site—known collectively as an *assemblage*—contains numerous clues about the people who used them. In interpreting these clues, the archeologist relies on a number of techniques. To take a relatively simple example, an archeologist was excavating a site at the bottom of a cliff in Colorado when he found a large assemblage of dismembered bison skeleta and a number of ancient flint points. From the remains, he hypothesized that a group of prehistoric men had driven the animals over the cliff and butchered them on the site. A team of researchers then calculated the size of the hunting group by counting the butchered animals and estimating the size of prehistoric bison, how long it would take one man to butcher one animal, the amount of meat that men, women, and children might eat in a day, the length of time bison meat keeps, and so on. To give precision to their calculations and interpretations, they referred to first hand accounts of similar hunts conducted by Plains Indians in the last century (Wheat, 1967).

Making inferences about past behavior on the basis of observed behavior is also a technique used in the interpretation of prehistoric tools. Often an archeologist will seek to learn how a tool was made and what it was used for by looking for analogues in the tool kits of technologically primitive people who have been observed firsthand. In a slightly different vein, a number of archeologists have attempted to make the tools themselves, using the appropriate raw materials and replicating prehistoric technology. In their efforts to understand prehistoric artifacts, archeologists are helped by the recent development of techniques for analyzing wear patterns on tools that tell them whether the tools were used to work wood, hides, or some other material.

In order to understand the place of any artifact in cultural evolution, the archeologist must know how old it is. To establish a relative date, the archeologist can employ the techniques of stratigraphy (observing soil layers) and seriation (observing the gradual increase and decrease in popularity of various styles). For absolute dates, the procedures of examining tree rings and measuring radiocarbon and potassium-argon decay are available.

Understanding an artifact in its full context often entails the coordinated efforts of a number of scientists in different fields. Thus, the archeologist may at times turn to a geologist, whose soil analysis can tell how a deposit was formed and what the environment was like at the time the site was inhabited. Similarly, a paleontologist may be called in to fill in details about the faunal contemporaries of the human subjects in question. Chemists, through their analysis of stone, metal, and pottery, can further provide the archeologist with data on the technique of the manufacture of artifacts and the origins of raw materials. Indirectly, chemical analysis can also tell us something of social organization and relations with other groups. For example, the fact that the huge (4 to 36 ton [3,628 to 32,652 Kg]) statues found in La Venta, Mexico, were made from stone obtained 90 miles [144 Km] away indicates not only that the Olmecs had advanced engineering skills but also that they were sufficiently sophisticated to organize large numbers of people (Heizer, 1966).

Using the kinds and relative quantities of artifacts, the archeologist can begin to reconstruct the ways in which a prehistoric people lived. From these reconstructions, *cultures* (a collection of artifacts made by the same technique and found over great distances) and *traditions* (a collection of artifacts made by the same techniques found in sites covering a large span of time) can be inferred. After that, the archeologist goes on to identify *stages* in cultural evolution (periods of time during which techniques for making and using tools and patterns of adaptation remained more or less the same) and thus lay the foundation for prehistory.

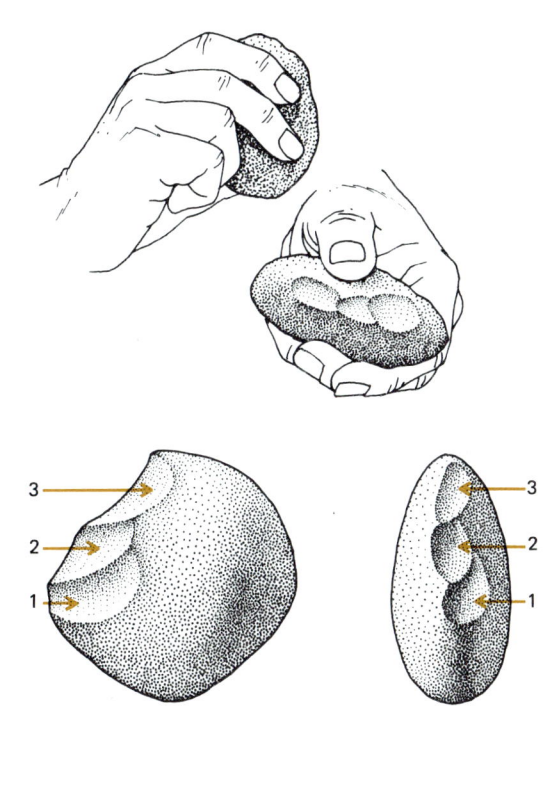

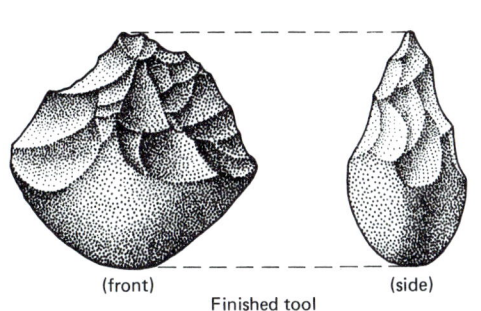

The Emergence of Cultural Essentials

Figure 5–1. Percussion flaking is the oldest and simplest technique for making stone artifacts. It does not permit a great deal of precision in shaping a tool as indicated by the crude and very generalized characteristics of Oldowan tools. Front and side views of tool are shown. (Biruta Akerbergs)

last for a million years, and these ancient wooden tools must have rotted and disintegrated long ago.

An Oldowan chopper could have been used for a variety of tasks: cutting skins, meat, or wood; crushing seeds and nuts; abrading bone or wood; slicing meat; and so on. But the chopper would not have been especially effective at any one of these tasks. Its value was as an all-purpose tool. Apart from food processing, chopping tools were probably used in working hides and wood and in making other tools and shelters, such as the windbreak found at Olduvai.

Subsistence and Social Organization

The early humans of the Oldowan tradition seem to have lived in the same areas as the australopiths (described in Chapter 4)—along rivers and lakes in tropical savannas. In addition to hunting or scavenging meat and gathering seeds, grains, and insects, as the australopiths did, we believe that early humans more systematically supplemented their diet with meat. The savannas offered a plentiful supply of large grazing animals like antelope, that came to drink and feed on the banks of the river or lake. The tropical savanna, then, offered another source of food for hominids besides the vegetable foods and small game exploited by the australopiths.

From the bones at the sites, it is clear that humans did not subsist solely on large kills. They apparently also ate a wide variety of animals, including rodents, porcupines, pigs, birds, fish, tortoises, and snakes. Whether the disarticulated skeletons at Oldowan sites were the product of an organized hunt or not is a matter of controversy. Some of the

(front) (side)
Finished tool

that were removed in the process of making a chopper were themselves sharpened and modified to form tools. Some specialized stone tools are found in very late Oldowan assemblages. Ground or polished stone and bone that may have been used as tools have also been found. We must assume that wooden tools were also plentiful, since wood is easier to work than either bone or stone, and among modern hunters sharpened sticks are the most common tools. But wood does not

larger animals might have died naturally, or been killed by other predators, and the carcasses scavenged by meat-eating hominids.

The archeological record probably overemphasizes meat eating, because bones are preserved far better than vegetable matter, and stone tools far better than baskets or skin bags that may have been used for collecting foods. Fossilized plant material, which would provide the evidence of gathering activities, is harder to detect, and it has only recently been sought by sifting sites for fossilized pollen or larger vegetable remains. From the example of modern hunter-gatherers, however, we can guess that early humans ate a variety of plant and animal foods.

The Band One way of getting around the problems of the archeological record is to use, as models, modern peoples who still pursue a simple way of life. Hunter-gatherers, such as the Bushmen of the Kalahari or the Aborigines of Australia, provide some insight into the subsistence strategies of early humans. From them and from traces in the archeological record, we believe that early humans probably lived in bands totaling less than a hundred people—most frequently about twenty-five. During a day of food seeking, individuals or small groups from the band may have dispersed and walked in different directions to exploit the food resources of several square miles. Since the community could have procured a two- or three-day supply of food in one day, the band could establish a base camp for periods longer than a single night. Permanent settlements were out of the question, however, because the food within range of the camp would eventually be exhausted, forcing the group to move its base.

Simple division of labor between the sexes is characteristic of modern hunters and probably began with early humans. Food was shared among members of the band. As a result of this sharing, differences in wealth among families, such as developed in later human societies, were nonexistent. Leadership roles were determined primarily by sex, age, and especially personal ability, but were not formalized in such a way that some members of the band held permanent control over others. (We discuss the band form of social organization in more detail in Chapter 21.)

People of the Oldowan Tradition: The Physical Evidence

According to our interpretation, hominid fossils contemporary with Oldowan artifacts include both australopiths and early members of the genus *Homo*. It might be tempting to state dogmatically that Oldowan tools were made only by the early human, *Homo habilis*. However, when trying to relate cultural remains to hominid fossils, we can never be sure that we are looking at the bones of the toolmakers themselves, even when those bones are found on the living floors.

Where two species are present at a site that also yields archeological evidence of such

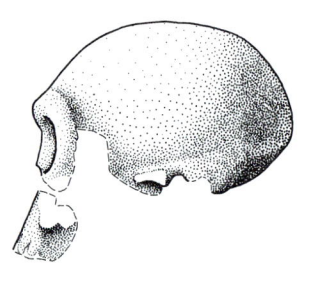

(a) *Homo habilis*

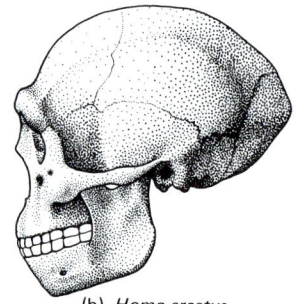

(b) *Homo erectus*

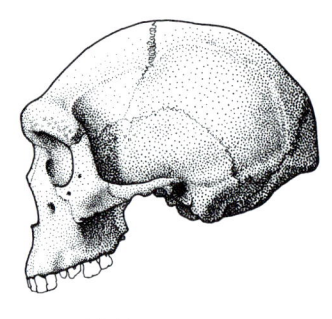

(c) *Homo erectus–Homo sapiens*

activity, we can logically suppose that the one (*H. habilis*) that is structurally most advanced in the direction of *H. sapiens* is likely to be the hunter and the maker of stone tools. Because the transition to the human way of life represented a new departure for evolution, reflected in physical structure as well as in culture, it deserves taxonomic recognition. We therefore allocate the Plio-Pleistocene hominids into separate genera, *Australopithecus* and *Homo*, and regard *H. habilis* as an early form of the distinctly human line. (See Figure 5–2.)

Not all anthropologists believe that this hominid represents a new lineage separate from the australopith line. Those who prefer a single line of hominid evolution regard the fossils we classify as *H. habilis* as part of the lineage linking the later australopiths with the later and larger-brained *H. erectus*. As we indicated in Chapter 4, we take the view that the later australopiths represent a separate lineage living contemporaneously with early humans. They remained general foragers and eventually died out. Meanwhile, the *Homo* lineage engaged in systematic meat eating, hunting, systematic toolmaking, and other complex behavior that we have seen in the Oldowan stage.

The period during which the tools of Oldowan type were the only distinctive stone industry was very long—longer than all the rest of human history taken together. Having only one name to cover human populations from the beginning to the end of the period may well prove inadequate after more fossils have been discovered and described. But for now, there is insufficient evidence to subdivide the group of fossil humans we call *H. habilis*.

Human Adaptations This group of fossils reveals a hominid whose physical structure is consistent with dependence upon tools and upon a hunting and gathering way of life, and one who has physically adapted to dependence upon culture. The anatomical-functional areas that are crucial in these changes are those that were important in the Australo-

Figure 5–2. Skulls of the genus Homo. (a) Homo habilis (East Rudolph ER 1470, assembled but not reconstructed). More than 2.8 m.y. old. This early form retains australopith features, especially a long and heavy face. Its main progressive feature is its large cranial capacity. (b) Homo erectus. Reconstruction of a small individual from Choukoutien. The braincase and mandible are known, the face is reconstructed. Middle Pleistocene. (c) Homo erectus-Homo sapiens transition. The skull of "Rhodesian Man," Zambia. Entire cranium known, mandible reconstructed. Middle Pleistocene. (d) Archaic Homo sapiens ("neandertal" variety). The La Chapelle aux Saintes skull, France. Cranium and mandible known, some parts reconstructed. Late-Middle or early-Upper Pleistocene. (e) Late Archaic Homo sapiens. The Skhul 5 skull, Mount Carmel. Cranium and mandible partly reconstructed. Upper Pleistocene. (f) Modern Homo sapiens (African). (Biruta Akerbergs)

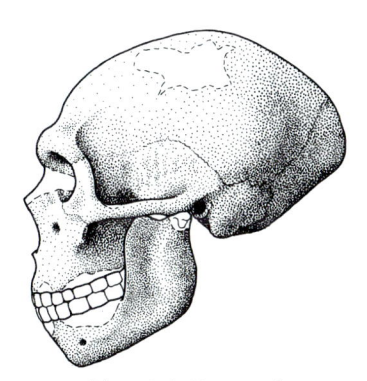

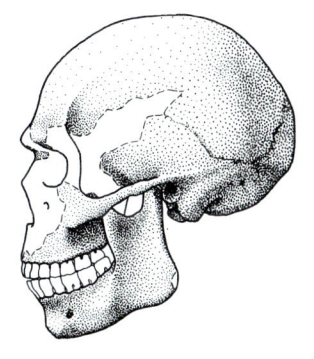

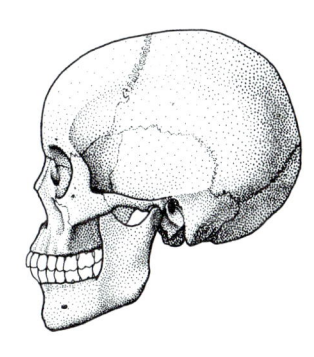

(d) Archaic *Homo sapiens*   (e) Late Archaic *Homo sapiens*   (f) Modern *Homo sapiens*

pithecine adapatation too: the braincase, the face and teeth, and the hindlimb.

From the description of the remains, we have already seen an increase in cranial capacity, and presumably in brain size and complexity, over *Australopithecus*. (See Figure 5-2.) This larger, more complex brain is consistent with the need to store and manipulate the large amount of information necessary to maintain a relatively complex technological culture. Whether this culture included language or speech, we cannot tell from the physical remains, but the sophistication of culture would have been hard to maintain with the simple communication systems used by apes.

The teeth and jaws of *H. habilis* are much the same in size and proportions as those of *A. africanus:* the back teeth are large and the incisors are not disproportionately smaller (compared with the huge molars and premolars and quite small front teeth in the late robust australopiths). The molars are somewhat narrower than is typical for *A. africanus,* and later individuals tend to have smaller molars. Since *H. habilis* probably processed more and more food with tools rather than relying on teeth, this might account for the reduction in molar size. The retention of large incisors suggests that these had an important function, perhaps meat eating. Since humans of this time had no fires for cooking their food, they needed the large incisors for gnawing and tearing raw meat.

The hindlimb skeleton is known from isolated femora (thigh bones) found at East Rudolf. These femora do not differ from those of modern humans in characteristics important to locomotion and posture.

Conclusions The development of culture and the changes in the physical structure of hominids are interrelated. Brain, hand, and artifacts evolved together. Larger, more complex brains and physical dexterity led to even better tools. Because these better tools were more efficient in subsistence tasks, they "selected" for improvements in the brain, hand, and coordination to enhance dexterity. Culture became part of the adaptive system, an increasingly important part as time went by.

The Emergence of the Division of Labor

About 1½ million years ago, a new cultural phase began. The most important characteristic of this stage is solid evidence of societies in which the division of labor between adults of the same sex was a basic organizational principle. Archeologically, this stage is defined by the appearance of new and different kinds of tools in Africa. Produced with a new stone-working technique that allowed greater precision in shaping the stone, the tools of this tradition—the *Acheulean*—are more standardized and more specialized. Some of the crudely shaped all-purpose pebble tools of the Oldowan tradition might be mistaken for natural stones, but Archeulean tools are unmistakably man-made to standard patterns. The variety of Oldowan tool shapes results in large part from the variety in the original shapes of the stones. The variety in the Acheulean state is intentional, for each tool had its own uses.

By 500,000 B.P. humans had moved northward from the tropics into the cooler temperate climates of Europe and Asia, a significant expansion of geographical distribution and ecological range made possible by technological innovations. Better tools are only part of this story. Fire was domesticated and used to evict hyenas and bears from their cave dens, which were then occupied by humans. Shelters were built. Australia, isolated by water, was still uninhabited, and the frigid steppes of central Asia and the wastes of the arctic and antarctic are barren of sites, but most of the mainland of the Old World was populated by this time.

The technological advances were accompanied by an increase in brain size and reduction in teeth and jaws, as cultural pressures continued to interact with physical characteristics. The australopiths finally died out, perhaps outcompeted by the hunting bands of these advanced toolmakers. As humans spread throughout the far reaches of Asia, geographical differences in biological and cultural characteristics appeared.

Chipped Stone Technology

Two chipped stone tool traditions are present at this stage: the chopper-chopping tool tradition and the Acheulean tradition of hand axes. A much larger number of flakes were removed from the core to form tools of the Acheulean tradition.

The characteristic tool of the Acheulean tradition, the hand axe, is a pear-shaped implement 4 to 16 inches (10 to 15 cm) long with a cutting edge and picklike point. The combination of cutting edge and pick made this a versatile tool. Flake tools are common in the Acheulean. In some instances, the flakes were not mere by-products of core tool manufacture, but were clearly intentionally removed from the core and then retouched. At some European sites, more than three-quarters of the tools are made from flakes.

The appearance of tools of the Acheulean tradition reflects a number of evolutionary changes. First, the manual dexterity of the people who make the tools probably increased to some extent. Second, there was a greater selectivity in the choice of raw materials for making tools. A few flakes can be removed to form a sharp edge on many kinds of naturally occurring stone, but relatively few rocks have a crystalline structure sufficiently fine to permit enough flakes to be struck off to form a fine tool without the stone being shattered. The more finely worked tools of the Acheulean tradition indicate knowledge of the kinds of raw materials that could be used. This precision in stone working was possible because of a new method of flaking, the *soft percussion,* or *soft hammer,* technique. (See Figure 5–3.) Instead of detaching a flake from a cobble or core by striking it with a rock, a flake was detached by striking the core with a wooden, bone, or antler hammer. The use of these softer materials as hammers allowed a great deal more control over the length, width, and thickness of the flake that was removed.

These three changes—in dexterity, in selec-

Typology

Archeologists are interested in similarities among artifacts. To study such similarities, they set up *typologies*. Quite simply, a *type* is a group of artifacts that share characteristics or attributes, which suggests they were made in the same way and used for the same purpose. Given the apparently unintelligible assortments of broken artifacts that excavators unearth, classification is essential to archeological detective work.

Establishing typologies is arduous work. For one thing, visible attributes can be misleading. Suppose, for example, an archeologist finds hundreds of fragments of pottery, some red or reddish, some brown. He might conclude that these represent two types of pottery. However, if he arranged the pieces along a continuum, he might discover that most of the pottery was red-brown, with a few clear red and brown pieces at the extremes.

Of course, all artifacts have hundreds of attributes (some of which can be discerned only through chemical analysis). A researcher might not discover a pattern until he has examined many different combinations of attributes. Suppose he has 200 pot sherds—some of which are red, some gray, some painted, and some incised. (*Potsherds* are broken pottery fragments.) Sorting them by color and design suggests there is no relationship between the two attributes.

Potsherd	Painted	Incised
Red	50	50
Gray	50	50

However, if he also considers form (whether the potsherds are from bowls or jars), a clear pattern emerges:

	Bowls		Jars	
Potsherd	Painted	Incised	Painted	Incised
Red	50	0	0	50
Gray	0	50	50	0

Through the use of computers, archeologists have been able to analyze dozens of attributes and the numerous potential relationships between them with relative ease.

Why are archeologists so concerned with the similarities among artifacts? Artifact types describe how people in a particular culture at a particular time made and used their tools. If we find different types of artifacts at nearby sites, we may assume we have discovered the boundary between two cultures; if we find different types of artifacts at the same site, we may infer that we are dealing with different stages in cultural evolution. Typologies thus assist archeologists in establishing patterns of human prehistory.

Figure 5–3. The use of a bone or wood hammer, which was softer than stone, enabled toolmakers to be more precise in sizing and shaping the flakes removed in making an artifact. This technique resulted in the creation of more refined and diverse forms of tools. (Biruta Akerbergs)

(front) (side)
Finished tool

tion of raw materials, and in the use of the technique of percussion—resulted in a far more efficient set of tools. Tools of the Acheulean tradition generally have much sharper edges than Oldowan tools. Also, more specialized tools could more easily be made by using the soft hammer technique. Oldowan choppers are general-purpose tools—they can be used for a variety of cutting, scraping, and pounding tasks—and specialized tools are rare in the Oldowan. But in Acheulean assemblages, we regularly find tools made to a variety of patterns. This suggests that specialized tools were being made for specific tasks: cutting, scraping, pounding, and so forth. This emerging technological specialization can be related to important changes in social organization.

Shelters

Not all the tools were used for food preparation. People of the Middle Pleistocene built more elaborate shelters than the simple Oldowan windbreak. At several sites, circular arrangements of stones suggest that people built simple stone structures, but at one location—Terra Amata on the Mediterranean coast of France—imprints of stakes driven into the ground reveal the walls of oval shelters as large as 26 by 50 feet (8 by 15 cm). The settlement was not a permanent village. Shelters were occupied seasonally for brief periods over at least a decade. Such huts provided the occupants with protection from the weather, which was colder than today's. Fire and shelters were part of the technology that permitted the expansion of the human species into such relatively inhospitable climates.

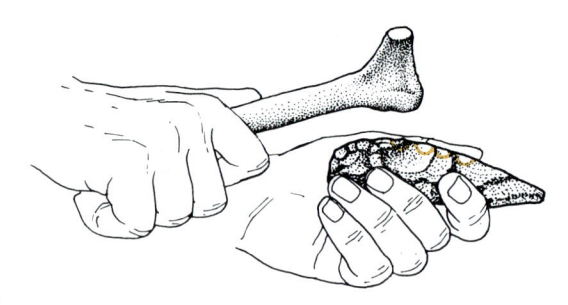

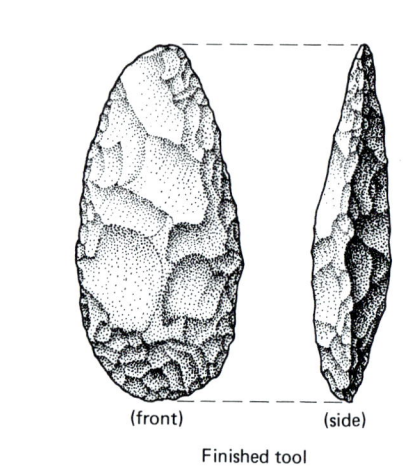

Subsistence In this stage, technology and social organization solved many of the problems of survival, but did not yet permit humans to dominate their surroundings. Humans lived as one predator among many.

The presence of disarticulated and splintered bones in Oldowan sites indicates only that meat was eaten, not whether it was obtained by scavenging or hunting. But Acheulean sites provide convincing evidence that big game was hunted and killed. The Acheulean's quarry included the huge forest elephant, the largest land mammal of its time. Cooperative hunting was certainly necessary for such undertakings.

But although big-game hunting was a spectacular advance in the economy of Middle Pleistocene humans, it was certainly not the whole story. Hunters also ate birds, reptiles, and some seafood, as well as gathering vegetables, grains, seeds, and fruits. At

Choukoutien in China, hackberry seeds survive as scanty evidence of the vegetable part of the prehistoric diet. At Kalambo Falls in Malawi, there are large collections of vegetable matter, including some fruits.

Social Organization

Hunting and gathering is not simply a form of subsistence. It is a way of life. As we saw, it affects social organization in a number of ways. One important aspect is the division of labor. Language may have been a factor in this development, since it could enable populations to split up into small task-specific groups and reassemble at a time and place in the future. As the basis for wide-reaching kinship ties, it would also provide bonds between separate bands that would enable them to take part in cooperative ventures such as an elephant hunt, which demanded more manpower than could be mustered by a single band. At Oldowan sites, there is little direct evidence of such behavior. In the Acheulean sites, the evidence is clearer.

Howell and Clark (1963) have analyzed artifacts from a number of levels at three sites in Africa. They were able to define at least four tool kits in the different levels of the sites. These different tool kits are probably not the work of separate human groups but were produced by the same people performing different tasks at different times.

In addition, we know of living sites like Choukoutien and butchering sites such as Torralba in Spain. Different kinds of activities were being carried out at different sites, occupied at different times. Clearly, a great deal more coordination of social activity was occurring.

A second major change in the complexity of social organization associated with the emergence of a division of labor is the apparent coexistence of two cultural traditions. The hand axe, or Acheulean proper, predominates in Africa, parts of Europe, and India; and the chopper-chopping tool tradition, lacking hand axes, predominates in eastern Asia.

What we are probably witnessing are two very different but contemporaneous technological traditions. This pattern of coexistence has two important implications. First, although there is no evidence of any formal organization above the level of the band, sufficient contact must have occurred among members of different bands to produce these relatively homogeneous traditions over very large expanses of territory. Intergroup communication had begun to be substantial. Exogamy provides one mechanism for such contact. Isaac argues that this form of cultural transmission, in which males remain within the band of their birth while females marry outside their native band, would have set up "a vast web of contacts that extended over large areas" (1972:400). This system was highly stable and explains the persistence of the two traditions over thousands of years. Second, two culturally distinct traditions were probably existing side by side, at least in some boundary areas such as Europe and India. Geographical barriers can account for some of the distribution, but social barriers must also have existed—conflict, avoidance, language differences, and so on—to maintain the boundary between groups. As we shall see in the next stage, this important evolutionary development was to become even more significant.

Peoples of the Acheulean and Contemporary Cultures: The Physical Evidence

Most of the human remains from the time in which these two traditions flourished are generally assigned to the species *Homo erectus*. Like *H. habilis* and *H. sapiens,* this species name is merely a convenient label for an arbitrarily defined section of a complex, evolving lineage. It should be noted, too, that the equation "*H. erectus* equals Acheulean man" is only very broadly correct. Early *H. erectus* was contemporary with the developed Oldowan tradition as well as the early Acheulean in Africa, and at the other end of the span, humans contemporary with the late Acheulean include specimens that are generally classified as *H. sapiens*.

Human Adaptations Arranging the *H. erectus* fossils in a rough chronological sequence and comparing them with *H. habilis,* we can see general trends that can be related to a continuing "adaptation for culture." In the general shape of the skull, the expanding braincase comes to dominate the shrinking face. (Refer to Figure 5-2.) The teeth, especially the postcanine chewing teeth, are reduced in size and in fact come within the modern human range. Supporting structures of teeth and jaw musculature (for example, the zygomatic arch and the maxilla) become smaller and more delicate. The smaller back teeth probably indicate that food was processed more with tools. Among late *H. erectus* populations, it was probably cooked. The incisors remained large and were still used for biting and slicing tough foods like meat.

Increasing brain size has been an important trend in hominid evolution, and this trend continued in *H. erectus.* The earliest *H. erectus* skulls, such as "Pithecanthropus IV" from the Djetis level at Java, are as small-brained as some examples of *H. habilis,* but later populations (for instance, that at Choukoutien) have relatively larger, more filled out braincases. This trend is carried further in the late European representatives of the lineage—Petralona, Steinheim, and Swanscombe.

As the brain gets larger, the skull fills out, becoming more convex in contour, especially in the frontal region, as the forehead becomes wider and higher. This trend presumably reflects increasing "intelligence" and the further evolution of the distinctively human mental traits of abstraction and concentration.

The thick bones and large brow ridges of the skull are a specialization of *H. erectus.* This massiveness, although subsequently lost in *H. sapiens,* is not a primitive characteristic for the genus *Homo.* Its significance is obscure. Overall, the postcranial skeleton was probably modern in function and the gait of *H. erectus* was entirely like that of *H. sapiens.* (Ironically, there is a chance that the Trinil femur, which is entirely like that of modern man and first gave the name "erectus" to this group, may actually be a modern bone.)

In overall body size, *H. erectus* was perhaps rather larger than *H. habilis* on average, although the evidence for this is inconclusive because postcranial skeletal material is relatively scarce. The difference between the sexes is much greater than that generally seen in modern humans. There is also evidence for geographical variation in size. But these local differences could be an indication of local variation or simply an accident of the small sample.

The Question of Geographical Variation Despite their broad similarities, the known *H. erectus* populations seem to show geographical variations. Do these represent real geographical differences; if so, are they the origin of racial differences in modern humans?

There do seem to be some indications of genetic continuity between *H. erectus* populations and modern populations living in the same areas. For example, the Lantian jaw from China has no third molar. The absence of this tooth occurs with varying frequency in modern populations, and it is notably common among modern Asians. Similarly, the Choukoutien people had so-called shovel-shaped incisors, another characteristic of modern Asiatics.

On the other hand, the resemblances between *H. erectus* populations are more striking than their differences. Similarities in tooth size and other details of structure strongly suggest that human evolution proceeded more or less concurrently over a broad area of the Old World from Africa to the East Indies. This interpretation of Middle Pleistocene evolution suggests a network of contacts between human bands that permitted gene flow as well as cultural continuity between populations.

The Emergence of Specialized Behavior Patterns

About 100,000 years ago, new techniques of stone working began to appear in Europe and Africa. Like the Acheulean before it, this tradition, known as *Mousterian* in its European form, gradually replaced earlier techniques. By 40,000 to 30,000 B.P., the Mousterian tradition had been supplanted.

Because people occupied very diverse habitats during this phase, the ways in which the technology changed vary widely. In Africa, for example, the tentative incursions into equatorial forests, deserts, and semiarid lands begun in the time when Acheulean traditions flourished were succeeded by continuous occupation of virtually every ecological zone; this diversity was reflected in African stone-working traditions. The tools of North Africa resembled European Mousterian, but south of the Sahara one tool tradition, the Sangoan, seems to be that of forest dwellers; it contains large picks and a distinctive tool that may be a plane for woodworking. The Fauresmith tradition of South Africa, which included tools made by the Mousterian technique, was adapted to semiarid grasslands. What we see in Africa is true elsewhere: an expansion of the human species into new habitats and a concomitant increase in cultural diversity and cultural specialization.

The occupation of new territories was in part a product of the climatic changes during the Upper Pleistocene, but the exploitation of many of these newly occupied territories required technological innovations and adaptations. Northern Europe, for example, was much colder than it is today, and was a productive hunting ground only for people with a technology advanced enough to exploit it by concentrating upon the specialized hunting of big-game animals (Butzer, 1971:463). In this period, we see the beginnings of a trend toward concentration on a few prey species, which will be fully elaborated only in the next stage of cultural development.

By the time that this new stage began 100,000 years ago, archaic forms of our own species were widespread over Europe, Africa, and Asia. Their way of life, however, had a long way to go before fully modern technological and organizational forms were to appear. There are important changes in social organization and technology that separate the Mousterian and contemporary cultures from the Acheulean stage. Earlier trends are modified, setting the stage for a burst of innovations in the following phases of cultural development. The essence of this modification is *specialization:* in tool forms, in subsistence, in site activity, and in cultural identity. It is for that reason that we see the Mousterian and Mousterian-like traditions as indicators of the emergence of specialized behavior patterns. There are two specialized behavior patterns that are of particular importance. First, sedentism becomes more evident, and we see increasing evidence for human activities that are not completely utilitarian. Humans begin to treat objects in ritual ways, reflecting a mind that is now dealing with death, afterlife, and the control of natural forces. We will limit our coverage of these emerging trends to their expression in Europe, where their interpretation has gone furthest.

Chipped Stone Technology

The changes in chipped stone toolmaking associated with the Mousterian stage are primarily in the processes and patterns of tool manufacture. The first of these changes was the development of a new method of making tools, which enabled Mousterian toolmakers to strike off thin, fine flakes of predetermined size and shape with greater precision. This *Levallois technique* involves preparing a core by removing a large number of flakes from it to produce a desired shape. Once the core has been shaped in this manner, a large flake struck from it will have a precise and predetermined shape, with a relatively longer and sharper cutting edge. (See Figure 5–4.) Not all Mousterian implements were of Levallois construction, but it is sufficiently common that it is used as a marker of this stage.

Using the Levallois technique, along with other increases in the skill of tool manufacture, Mousterian knappers were able to produce about forty inches (100 cm) of cutting edge from a pound of stone (Butzer 1971: 475). Acheulean techniques were four times more productive than those of Oldowan knappers, and the Mousterian techniques were five

Figure 5–4. The tools of the Mousterian traditions show a substantial increase in the degree of their specialization. This variability enables archeologists to more accurately reconstruct the exploitative activities and organization of the groups which produced these tools. The steps involved in the Levallois technique are shown here. The color portions preview the next step. (Biruta Akerbergs)

times more productive than those of the Acheulean.

A second important characteristic of Mousterian assemblages is the number of different types of tools. Recall that an important difference between the Oldowan and Acheulean traditions was in the replacement of very generalized tools with ones made for more specific activities. In the case of the Mousterian, there were at least a dozen kinds of special-purpose tools (Binford and Binford, 1968), and Bordes (1968) has defined sixty different tool types. In comparison with the Acheulean, the purposes for which these tools were being made had become even more narrowly defined. Not only can we observe that some tools were being made for cutting and others for scraping, but we can also see that Mousterian peoples were, for example, using a number of different kinds of scrapers, each suited to some small step in an activity that involved scraping. People were learning to make tools with characteristics more and more precisely suited to the activities in which they were being employed.

Mousterian Traditions Perhaps the most important change in material culture associated with the change from the Acheulean to the Mousterian stage is the increase in the number of traditions. Five Mousterian traditions, based on varying percentages of chipped stone artifacts, have been identified in Europe alone.

The question is, of course, what these variants signify. Why do some assemblages include a much heavier use of the Levallois technique than others? Why are scraping tools found in much greater abundance in some assemblages than in others? Three very different answers have been proposed for such questions.

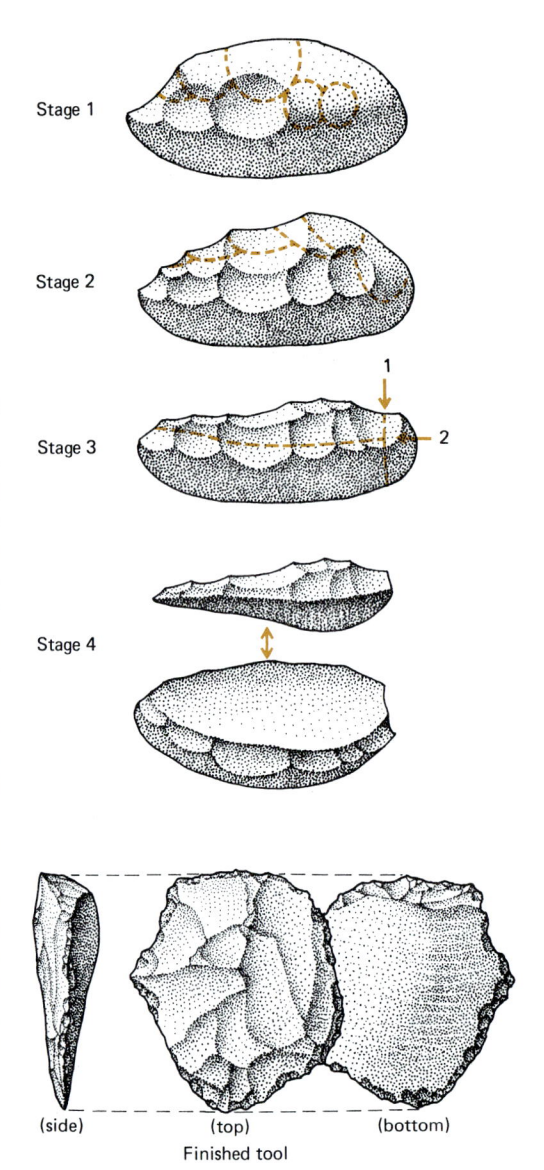

First, a number of archeologists argue that the traditions belong to different time periods during the Mousterian stage. According to this view, the traditions reflect an evolution of technology through separate stages. Second, it is argued that each represents the work of a distinctive ethnic group, which was contemporaneous with other groups that produced different traditions (Bordes, 1968). Each group moved through an area, leaving its cultural remains above those of some other group and below those of later groups. Third, the Binfords (1968) have argued that the five traditions reflect different activity systems in which the tools were used.

Clearly, this last answer need not exclude the other explanations. Populations living at different periods of time might have engaged in very different activities, which would have produced functionally different assemblages, as might populations in different territories.

Each of the answers suggests an important conclusion about the Mousterian stage. If each tradition in fact reflects a different period of time, then clearly the rate of change in the processes of tool manufacture and use was accelerating during the stage. If each represents the work of a different ethnic or cultural group, then we have the first good evidence of relatively tightly bonded social groupings above the level of a single band, occupying a relatively restricted geographical area. If each represents a different way of structuring activities within a population, then we are seeing the evolution of groups that adapted their activities to resource-exploitation tasks in very specialized ways and that persisted in their distinctive strategies for many, many generations.

In any case, we see a pattern that contrasts strongly with that of the previous stage. Then only two traditions existed, and tools from sites 100,000 miles apart were very similar. Now tools and tool kits from nearby sites show marked differences, and most areas from which we have detailed data are characterized by a number of traditions. Here, then, is the beginning of patterns of specialization that involved both "ethnic" and economic dimensions.

Subsistence and Social Organization

There are other indications of changes in subsistence and social organization based on more clear-cut evidence. First, there is direct evidence of increasingly specialized subsistence practices. Archaic *H. sapiens* had a sufficiently advanced culture to survive and even thrive in the colder middle latitudes of Europe. Aided by fire and shelters, they had colonized these areas earlier and adapted as the climate grew even colder. They were big-game hunters, subsisting on a diet of meat supplemented with fowl, fish, fruits, and seeds. Reindeer, wild horse, and mammoth were among the important sources of food. At several sites, the proportion of reindeer (or, in some cases, red deer) bones outnumber by far those of other animals, indicating that at least seasonally, the groups occupying the sites were specializing in hunting this game animal (Mellars, 1973:263). Hunting such large creatures as mammoths, and such fleet creatures as horses and birds, required courage, skill, and the cooperation found in the band. We have already mentioned alternative patterns of specialization in Africa.

Second, it is in this period that humans began to settle down. Some of the cave sites in southwestern France show signs of year-round occupation, which may indicate that sedentary patterns of existence had begun among populations in temperate forest-tundra zones, with more reliable animal food resources at their disposal. Several sites show efforts to improve on the cave by covering the entrance with a screen of branches or hides. At the mouth of the cave or inside were hearths for keeping warm or cooking meat. But open-air sites and the evidence of sites with seasonally specialized tool kits seem to show the persistence of a more nomadic way of life. Seasonal migration certainly remained the lifestyle of those in the colder tundra regions, where people had to depend on the migrating herds.

Ritual and Religion

At this stage, we find direct evidence of human activities with symbolic as opposed to utilitarian intent. Humans had begun to consider powers outside themselves, to propitiate them, and to structure specialized activities around these concerns. Prehistoric cave dwellers did not litter bear skulls around the caves in the same offhand manner as the other bones but seemed to have arranged them with some care. At one site, more than twenty bear skulls were collected in a rectangular pit sealed by a large slab. These seem to be evidence of a bear cult, but its purposes and rituals cannot be reconstructed.

As people began to think about death and an afterlife, burial became ritualized. At the Shanidar Cave in Iraq the body of a thirty-year-old man had been buried with flowers cushioning his body and completely covering it, a beautiful farewell from people who obviously cared about their fellows and were capable of marking this in symbolic fashion. At other sites, people have been buried with tools or with food.

From France, Italy, Iraq, and the other archeological sites comes a picture of human populations capable not only of feats of hunting, toolmaking, and shelter construction but of complex symbolic behavior as well.

Archaic *Homo sapiens*

The changes from *H. erectus* to early forms of our own species, *H. sapiens*, are gradual. As with the habilis/erectus transition, we cannot draw a sharp line between the species. As a species, *H. erectus* evolved over time, the most obvious trends being an increase in brain size, with expansion of the frontal and parietal lobes, and a moderate decrease in back tooth size. By the later Acheulean, we have evidence of people, such as Swanscombe and Steinheim, who in their skull structure retained features of *H. erectus* but at the same time have brains of essentially modern size. By the time of the Mousterian and contemporary cultures, the same trends had given rise to populations that may be classified as primitive or archaic members of *H. sapiens*. In general, these people had a brain at least as large as that of modern humans, though of different proportions, combined with a robust face, larger teeth, and a flat, low braincase with heavy brow ridges. Despite this overall resemblance, there is evidence for considerable geographical variation among peoples of this period, perhaps paralleling the cultural diversity that was developing.

The Problem of the Neandertals From Europe and the Near East, we have a large sample of distinctive skulls and limb bones, dating from the last interglacial and the first part of the last glacial period—about 120,000 to 35,000 years ago—which are generally lumped together as "neandertals." The neandertals were generally short, stocky, and barrel-chested.

Their specialized characteristics are most strikingly seen in the face, with its broad but high-bridged and prominent nose, high, rounded orbits, and swept-back cheekbones. The braincase was large but low, bulged at the sides, and was long from front to back. Set well forward on a thick neck, the skull was flat on top. The cranial capacity in some instances was even greater than that of most modern skulls, reaching 1,600 and 1,800 cc. However, its shape was not fully modern, with apparently less expansion of the frontal lobes. (Refer again to Figure 5-2.)

Between 30,000 and 40,000 years ago, humans of essentially modern form appeared in Europe. Their skull was high, its sides flat, its top rounded. The face was no longer so prominent, although the chin was more distinct. Heavy brow ridges had been replaced by a high, rounded forehead. The earliest "modern" humans had more rugged skulls and larger teeth than we have, but that is about the extent of the difference. The apparently rather sudden appearance of structurally modern people in Europe poses problems of interpretation. Where did they come from, and what happened to the neandertals they replaced?

Of human remains dating from the last interglacial and early last glacial periods, those specimens that look most "modern" in general appearance seem to be clustered in North Africa and southwest Asia. Some authorities have interpreted this as evidence that humans of modern type evolved in a relatively restricted region, centered upon this area, perhaps while classic neandertals were still living in Europe and other more typically archaic populations occupied the rest of the Old World. From this homeland, modern types spread quite quickly, displacing or absorbing other populations. This is actually a revival of an old idea that fell into disrepute in favor of the view that archaic populations everywhere evolved modern traits. If this view is correct, then some significant advance must have been achieved among the early modern populations to permit their rapid expansion.

The change in cranial shape may give us a clue as to the nature of this advantage. The high forehead reflecting expanded frontal lobes may indicate that the human quality of long-range persistence and planning ability was more fully developed among the moderns. It has also been suggested that the change in shape of the skull with the face shortening and the cranial base bending may have altered the relative positions of mouth and larynx. It is argued that the new position made possible more rapid and precise articulation of sounds, so language could convey more information faster than among earlier peoples.

Anthropologists are currently divided as to whether this ingenious theory explains the explosive expansion of early modern *H. sapiens* from their area of origin, and indeed, even as to whether such an expansion did ever in fact occur. Many still adhere to the view that evolutionary change itself altered the neandertals and that later populations of Europe were their direct descendants. A problem is that the European neandertals were a particularly aberrant race of archaic humans. Their structure seems too distinctive to have evolved so rapidly into that of the Upper Paleolithic Europeans who are supposed to be descended from them.

It is important to distinguish the fate of the neandertals of Europe from the evolutionary history and position of archaic *H. sapiens* as a whole. Although the extreme European type may have been replaced by a combination of hybridization and extinction, there is no reason to doubt that in a general sense, archaic *H. sapiens* were the direct ancestor of more modern forms of *H. sapiens*.

Trends in Evolution

This chapter nearly concludes the story of the physical evolution of humans by describing what is known of the earliest members of the genus *Homo* (of which modern humans are but the latest form) and begins a new phase, that of cultural evolution, and in particular the advent of systematic toolmaking, regular meat eating, hunting, broader and systematic food sharing, a more distinct division of labor, and recognizable symbolic behavior. These, rather than strictly physical structures, define the border between human and nonhuman.

This is not to say that processes of biological evolution came to an end, for as we shall see later, they are still operating today. Rather, we have simply begun to investigate a period of time when changes in material culture, subsistence practices, and the organization of society were of increasingly greater importance and formed what Isaac has called a "joint brain-culture system" (1972:403).

This new phase began slowly. For more than a million years after their advent, the tools that humans made changed little. In fact, the art of toolmaking was probably gained and lost hundreds of thousands of times. Equally slow were the changes in manual dexterity and conceptual ability that facilitated advances in tool manufacture. But early humans learned to select appropriate raw materials and to treat those materials in increasingly different ways so that various tools fashioned from diverse materials were made and used. Tools did not, however, simply increase in numbers. Underlying this quantitative trend was an evolution toward specific kinds of tools adapted to increasingly specific tasks, and also toward regional specialization of tools.

This improvement in tools, combined with the growth of the brain and perhaps increasingly sophisticated language skills, changed the way in which humans lived by improving their users' ability to obtain and process food, to build shelters, and subsequently to live under a variety of different environmental conditions. With such successes came expansion in the range of territory occupied by our human ancestors, increases in their numbers, and as the process of adaptation to particular regions continued, more and more culturally distinct groupings.

The changes in subsistence practices, first seen in the eclectic diet of *H. habilis,* also gathered momentum slowly. When humans actually began regular big-game hunting is hard to tell; but by the time of archaic *H. sapiens,* humans were tackling large game and beginning to concentrate on a few species.

The importance of hunting lay not only in its effect upon subsistence but upon social organization as well. Division of labor, sharing, and coordination became part of band behavior. These were probably enhanced by the development of language and ritual systems.

The stages through which humans passed should not be seen simply as stops on the way to full humanity. These were extremely successful adaptations that persisted for periods longer than that of modern *H. sapiens.* The dynamic element that created pressures for change was the need for cooperation and coordination that produced selective pressures for brain reorganization and expansion. By the end of the period we have just examined, the brain had reached fully modern proportions, and the dynamic element in changing human behavior became the cultural system itself. It is to this that we now turn in Chapters 6 through 8.

summary

The first humans we know of appeared about 2½ to 3 million years ago in East Africa. They were little different from their australopith relatives in physique, but their behavior was significantly different. What separated the two was the emergence of cultural essentials: toolmaking, language, and band organization based on language. The first recognizable tradition, the Oldowan, had largely crude choppers formed by percussion flaking (chipping a few flakes off the edge of a stone to make a tool slightly sharper than naturally chipped rocks). These tools were useful for a variety of tasks associated with the hunting and gathering way of life. Subsistence practices in early bands consisted of roving over a large area in search of plant and animal foods that could be brought back to a central camp for sharing with other members of the band. The band was held together by language, mutual obligation, and kinship ties. Social cohesion, planning of subsistence strategies, and transmission of toolmaking skills were probably promoted by language of some sort.

The evolution of such behavior depended upon a brain capable of processing more complex kinds of information. *H. habilis* is this larger-brained creature, the first member of the human genus. His smaller back teeth and jaws suggest that this creature relied on tools to process food. Some anthropologists see *H. habilis* as a direct descendant of later australopiths, but our interpretation is that the later australopiths, who were general foragers, died out as another branch, who were systematic meat eaters as well as foragers, became more successful in terms of cultural adaptations.

In the next stage, a more complex pattern in the division of labor emerged. By about 1½ million years ago, tools became more specialized. The appearance of these tools of the Acheulean tradition reflect not only greater manual and mental dexterity on the part of their makers, greater selectivity of raw materials, and better stone-working techniques based on soft percussion, but, most important, increased differentiation of tasks. Part of this may be attributed to the growing importance of hunting, which requires greater social coordination and division of labor. People began to perform different tasks at different sites; and at some camps, there are even remnants of semipermanent shelters. These shelters and the use of fire permitted humans to expand into colder climates of Europe and Asia. With this expansion of range, two identifiable traditions appear—those using the chopper-chopping tools and those using the hand axes. Physical differentiation may also have begun at this stage. The adaptation to culture evidenced by smaller back tooth size and enlarged cranial capacity continued, even though *H. erectus* shows certain specializations that are neither primitive carry-overs nor transitional to modern forms.

As humans expanded into new habitats, they adopted behavior patterns specialized to their particular surroundings. By about 100,000 years ago, specialization is seen not only in tool forms but in subsistence practices, site activities, and ritual. In Europe alone, there are five traditions associated with the Mousterian stage. Group identity was undoubtedly reinforced by the rituals that were practiced by these early humans.

Regional variations in physique are an important part of the physical story during this stage. The European form, the neandertals, were quite distinctive, posing the question of how fully modern humans appeared in this area. It is likely that in most regions of the world, archaic humans evolved directly into modern forms. In Europe, the process perhaps involved the movement of more modern populations into the area and the disappearance of the neandertals through extinction and hybridization with the newcomer populations. This transition marks the last major physical change in humans, although certainly physical evolution is still continuing. From this point on, however, changes in social organization, technology, and subsistence practices form the central themes of the account of human evolution.

suggested readings

BORDAZ, J.
1970 *Tools of the Old and New Stone Age.* Garden City, N.Y.: Natural History Press. A thorough discussion of the variety of tools used by early humans and changes in techniques of manufacture.

BORDES, F.
1968 *The Old Stone Age.* New York: McGraw-Hill. A discussion of cultural evolution through the Upper Paleolithic, with particular emphasis on tool traditions.

BUTZER, K. W.
1971 *Environment and Archeology: An Ecological Approach to Prehistory.* 2d ed. Chicago: Aldine. A comprehensive review of the aims, methods, and findings of human paleogeography.

HOWELL, F. C., AND EDITORS OF TIME-LIFE BOOKS.
1973 *Early Man.* New York: Time-Life Books. A readable, beautifully illustrated treatment of primate and human evolution.

HOWELLS, W. W.
1973 *The Evolution of the Genus Homo.* Reading, Mass.: Addison-Wesley. A concise and very readable account of human paleontology.

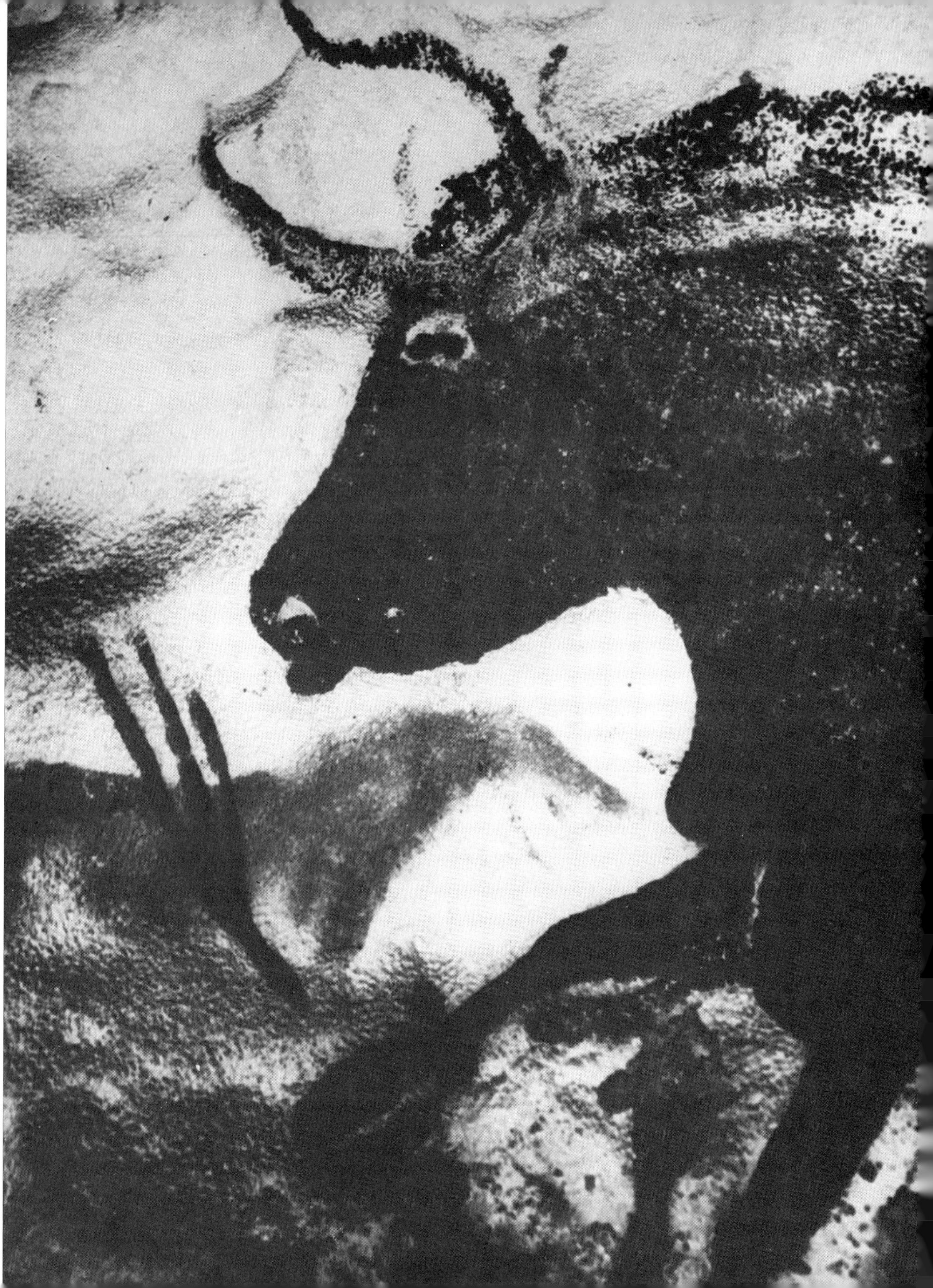

six
The Emergence of Cultural Diversity

In the last chapter, we considered the emergence of the cultural essentials: tools, language, and band organization based on these two elements, as well as full division of labor and specialized behavior patterns. In this chapter, we will discuss a period of time, basically between about 40,000 and 10,000 years ago, during which a continuation of these trends began to produce dramatically different results. Successful adaptations led to human populations' exploiting an increasing number of diverse environments, and employing practices increasingly specialized to the exploitation of particular resources and resource zones. Specialized hunting of big-game animals seems to have been the most common subsistence practice, although the particular animals that were most important for different groups varied widely. Specialization in harvesting, fishing, and hunting small-game animals also occurred.

Looking at any one group, the change was toward greater *specialization;* looking at many groups, the change was toward *diversification*. In addition, the number of successful subsistence strategies that could be employed in one location increased, as groups exploited nearby areas, and perhaps even different niches in the same area, in different ways. Reliance on a broad range of resources provided a more stable mode of existence. With specialized groups occupying proximate territories, we also see the use of symbolic forms to mark the beginnings of a permanent organizational pattern above the level of the band, particularly for trade.

These patterns—increasing specialization, diversification, and their consequences—seem to characterize most if not all areas of the world, although the specific resources, artistic traditions, and so on varied considerably. We will focus our discussion on Europe and North America because the greater amount of research done in these areas increases the potential for interpretation.

We will first consider the stages referred to as the Upper Paleolithic by European archeologists and the Paleo-Indian by North American archeologists. We will then turn to the Mesolithic stage of Europe and the Archaic stage of North America to see the emergence of diversity from specialization.

The Advanced Hunters of Europe

When we left off our account of cultural evolution in Chapter 5, humans had spread into Europe and were beginning to specialize in the big game that was abundant there. In the Upper Paleolithic, the peoples of Europe became skilled big-game hunters, which had cultural consequences far beyond subsistence practices. The advanced hunters of Europe had highly specialized economies and depended upon large herd animals most abundant in the region where they lived, a factor that began to reinforce the cultural diversity that we saw developing in the Mousterian stage. Let us turn, then, to these groups and see how and why this diversity occurred.

Subsistence and Settlement: Regional Diversity

The hunting of big game rested upon both a few new tactics and many new tools. Craft was

---

In this chapter, we discuss the emergence of art in the Upper Paleolithic. This cave painting from Lascaux, France, is representative of an early artistic tradition dating from the first half of this period (35,000 to 17,000 B.P.). (Monkmeyer Press Photo)

The "jump" technique is a group hunting strategy in which part of the hunting group stampedes a herd of animals over a cliff and the rest of the group kills and butchers the wounded and dying animals. Killsites at the bases of cliffs containing hundreds of skeletons of butchered bison, horses, and reindeer demonstrate that this technique was common among both New World and Old World Upper Paleolithic groups. (American Museum of Natural History)

the hunter's best weapon. Group hunting methods such as the "jump" or the "surround" were of great importance. The hunting group would stampede large herds over cliffs to their death or into box canyons, where the animals would easily be slaughtered. At Solutré, France, over 100,000 horse skeletons were found at the bases of cliffs, a demonstration of the efficacy of such methods. Later, the hunting tools were greatly improved. The *atlatl,* or spear thrower—a hooked rod containing a groove in which the butt of the spear shaft rests—revolutionized the art of spear throwing. The atlatl increased the range of the spear and the force of its impact by enabling the thrower to have a more powerful thrust. Even more important was the invention of the bow and arrow, which further increased the range and force of early weaponry.

The Upper Paleolithic developments in Europe occurred during the last part of the Würm glaciation, beginning about 40,000 years ago and ending about 11,000 years ago with the onset of the postglacial climatic changes. Great herds of large herbivores, including wild horses, bison, mammoth, and reindeer, roamed over most of the unglaciated plains regions, with fallow deer, ibex, wild ox, and wild boar abundant in forest areas of southwestern Europe. In eastern Europe, the hunters tended to concentrate on mammoth; in western Europe, on reindeer. These provided an ample subsistence base for the peoples of Europe (Butzer, 1971).

Technology

Specialization in the subsistence base seems to have reinforced the growth in the number of tool traditions. The Upper Paleolithic stage in Europe was characterized by at least as many traditions as the Mousterian, but the variations among assemblages are far more marked. This wider variety resulted from a combination of advances in technology and an increase in the kinds of raw materials used. Before outlining the traditions, it may help to examine the important innovations.

The basis of many of the Upper Paleolithic tool forms is the *blade,* a thin, parallel-sided flake whose length is usually more than twice its width. By the use of new techniques, blades of an almost standard size and shape could be struck, allowing virtual mass production of tools. *Percussion flaking* was used to produce blades from a core prepared as a cylinder or pyramid, with the apex removed to form a striking platform. More commonly, a new, indirect percussion technique called *punch flaking* was used. (See Figure 6–1.) The knapper placed an intermediate tool— the punch—between the hammer and the

Understanding Past Environments

If we are to understand the context in which the cultural processes and changes in a given society are imbedded, we must be able to reconstruct the environmental conditions under which that society existed. For example, knowledge of the paleoclimate, botany, and zoology of a region is important. Archeologists use several interesting techniques to help them to learn about these factors.

Soil analysis is one method used by archeologists. Various characteristics of modern soils, like buried or paleosoils, can be associated with particular climatic conditions such as temperature, rainfall, and radiation. Since we know the climatic conditions under which modern soils have been formed, we can infer what conditions were like when the paleosoil was formed by matching its characteristics to those of modern soils. Soil analysis will offer some clues about the vegetation cover of a region, too, which helps archeologists further understand what the environment was like and what resources were available at a particular time. In fact, almost everything we know about the environment for the time periods discussed in Chapters 5 and 6 is derived from soil analysis.

Palynology, the study of pollen, has proved another valuable technique for archeologists. Most wind-pollinated trees and grasses produce large amounts of pollen, and pollen grains have a waxy outer coating that makes them almost indestructible. If oxidation is slow, grains will be preserved as fossil pollen for long periods of time. Furthermore, pollen grains differ greatly in size and shape, and they are usually easy to identify by genus. Also, most trees can be identified specifically. Thus, an analysis of the prehistoric pollen grains found within or near a site gives archeologists information about the type of vegetation prevailing at the time the site was inhabited. Because vegetation is strongly influenced by climatic conditions, the vegetation type should also tell us something about some of the more general climatic variables that prevailed. This technique has been useful in understanding the Mesolithic-Archaic period (Chapter 6) and the Neolithic period (Chapter 7).

Of course, some pollens are transported long distances by wind or streams, so that pollen grains may end up in an assemblage miles away from where they were produced. Sometimes these anomalous grains constitute only a minute portion of the total assemblage and can be properly identified. However, transport may have been massive, giving a misleading picture of local climate. In addition, studies indicate over- and under-representations of certain species in pollen assemblages because of (1) excessive pollen production by some species; (2) small production of pollen by other species; (3) different resistance to decay among pollen types; and (4) different preservation of pollen because of environmental conditions. When we look at pollen assemblages, we must take into account all these possibilities.

Dendroclimatology is the study of past environmental conditions by tree-ring analysis. In it, archeologists use the same techniques used in dendrochronology (see the box "Dating Techniques," on page 117). Here, however, the tree rings are used to help understand the climatic conditions at a given point in time, as well as changes in climatic conditions.

From an analysis of *floral and faunal remains,* archeologists can determine which plant and animal species were part of the subsistence pattern of the inhabitants of a particular site. This gives us an idea of the vegetal and animal populations of the region during the time the site was inhabited. In turn, species of flora can yield information about the climatic conditions that prevailed at that time. Certain fauna are equally sensitive indicators of paleoclimate. Two examples are the barren-ground caribou and the musk-ox, which today are found only in tundra and other zones with very cold climates. Thus, when archeologists find caribou or musk-ox remains in sites far from the present locations of these species, they infer that at the time of habitation the area had a cold climate and was covered with tundra or spruce woodland vegetation.

There are some limitations to this analysis. For one thing, if a site is located in a mountain and valley region where vertical ecological zones may be markedly different, data are difficult to rely on. Another is that the analysis assumes that the ecological adaptations of the various species have remained constant throughout history and prehistory, a premise that is certainly open to question. A final limitation on the analysis of the remains of flora and fauna is that such remains may reflect only the specialization of the group that used the site rather than the total number of species present in the region or, for that matter, their relative abundance. Despite these limitations, analysis of these remains has aided our understanding of the environment of almost every site we discuss in every time period.

Overall, these various kinds of analyses have aided archeologists in their attempts to understand the conditions under which prehistoric societies lived.

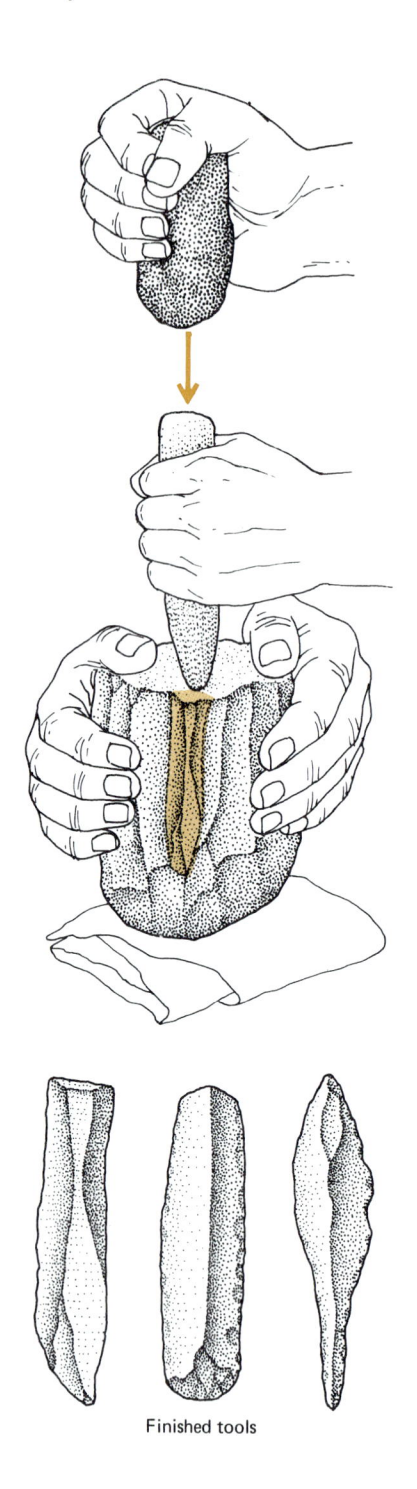

Figure 6-1. The manufacture of chipped stone tools using the blade technique increased both the efficiency and specificity of tool manufacture. On the one hand, more tools could be made from a single core. On the other, the standardized blade form permitted many different kinds of tools to be made with minimal modification. (Biruta Akerbergs)

Finished tools

prepared core. The punch directed the force of the blow precisely. Blades were also produced by attaching a punch to a length of wood and leaning on it, a version of a technique called *pressure flaking*. In all cases, blades were struck off around the core.

The variety of tools produced from blades was increased by refinements in the art of retouching through pressure flaking. The tool was further shaped not by striking off chips but by pushing them off with the tip of a punch. The knapper placed the tip of the punch near the edge of the tool, pressed forward and down, and removed flakes to leave a very smooth, flat, tool surface and a sharp edge.

The blade technique was more efficient than previous modes of stone working. The knapper could produce as much as 40 feet (1,200 cm) of cutting edge from a single pound of stone, compared with about three and a half feet (100 cm) using techniques characteristic of the Mousterian stage. Thus the rate of change accelerated enormously. Over the course of 2 million years, ending with the Mousterian traditions, the efficiency of tool-manufacturing techniques had increased 20 times, but during a few thousand years of the Upper Paleolithic, a 12-fold increase occurred (Butzer, 1971).

Traditions Although the techniques, materials, and principles associated with Upper Paleolithic tools permitted greater diversity, the traditions of this stage do not represent a complete departure from the Mousterian. The two earliest traditions of the Upper Paleolithic in Europe—the *Aurignacian* and the *Perigordian*—contain Mousterian-like tools, suggesting a partially shared tradition or parallel technological evolution.

The next tradition, the *Solutrean,* was rather short-lived for reasons that are not yet known. It occurred at sites dated from 21,000 to 17,000 B.P., and was limited to southwestern France and Spain. Despite its limitations in time and distribution, this tradition is distinguished by the laurel-leaf blades that represent the zenith of stone-working techniques.

Contemporaneous with the Solutrean and late Aurignacian and Perigordian traditions was the *Gravettian,* which dates from about 27,000 to 17,000 B.P. This tradition seems to be limited primarily to eastern Europe. The major economic activity was mammoth hunting, which may explain the highly developed bone- and ivory-working technologies.

The *Magdelenian* tradition is the last Upper Paleolithic tradition to develop, dating from about 17,000 to 10,000 B.P. Sites are found throughout Europe, and the tool kits are the most diverse of any Upper Paleolithic tradition. Bone and antler harpoons, the atlatl, and the first *microliths*—small bladelets an inch or less in length used alone or with handles—define this tradition. Reindeer were the specialty of this group of toolmakers. The Magdelenian tradition ceased once the climate of Europe warmed up, the tundra gave way to forest, and the reindeer upon which the hunters depended grew scarce.

While we have tried to identify the most typical dates, regions, and tools associated with each of these traditions, it is important to understand that there are many traditions. The same possible explanations for diversity in the Mousterian may apply to the Upper Paleolithic, but at the later stage, we have more diversity within smaller territories for shorter time periods than ever before.

The Appearance of Art

The people of Upper Paleolithic Europe were not just hunters and toolmakers; they decorated their tools, sculpted small pieces of stone and bone, and engraved, carved, and painted on the walls of caves. These are the first concrete symbols of man's inner life, the effort to record thoughts, feelings, and events in forms in which they could be seen, pondered, and understood by other humans whom the artist might never know. We have hints of an aesthetic impulse earlier; ritual, song, and story were probably part of the cults in the Mousterian stage, and the scatterings of ochers at some Mousterian sites imply that people had begun decorating hides or painting their bodies. But the first unequivocal evidence of artistic traditions appears in the Upper Paleolithic stage, and like the tools, the artistic styles belong to different traditions.

Explaining Paleolithic Art These ancient objects and paintings stir the imagination, tantalizing the contemporary viewer with the promise of understanding people dead tens of thousands of years if only the imagery and intentions of the artists could be determined. Viewing a single work will not give the necessary insight, and when the entire 30,000-year span of art is examined, its variety is bewildering.

Paleolithic man was extraordinarily varied in his choice of where to camp, the use he appears to have made of caves, in the selectivity of subjects which he chose to decorate, in the techniques he used and in the combinations of subjects which he favored. . . . Within any one cave . . . it is possible to imagine that many . . . possibilities apply: that some representations were the work of children . . . , that some were used in acts of sympathetic magic . . . , that some were placed in particular situations in order to please . . . , that some were illustrations of myths and traditions. . . . It is very possible, however, that some and perhaps many Paleolithic representations were made for reasons which still totally escape the modern observer. (Ucko and Rosenfeld, 1967:238–239)

Magic If a universal explanation is impossible, there are nonetheless some striking features that suggest partial interpretations. For instance, why are so many of the middle Upper Paleolithic works of art found deep inside caves that seem to have been otherwise uninhabited? What brought people into these areas, sometimes through passageways barely big enough for a person holding a torch to squirm through? It seems plausible that these areas were sacred and that the art there was inspired by religious motives. The majority of the figures are animals, some of which appear to be wounded. The artists may have been working hunting magic, killing an effigy of an animal in hopes that later they would be able to kill the animal itself. This may explain the curious "superpositioning," or drawing over and over, in a single area. If hunting magic were involved, the act of drawing the animal would be important, but the final image would not, and it could be drawn over by later artist-supplicants.

If this is so, however, why would artists go to the trouble to make some animals realistic, selecting stone formations that echoed the shape of the animal or rendering it in some detail? Ethnographic studies of modern peoples who invoke hunting magic have found that a bare sketch of the animal may suffice.

Some of the animals are not prey but predators—cave bears, lions, and other animals feared by the hunters. Drawing them may have been a way of obtaining protection from them or even a way of taking on their ferociousness to increase hunting success.

Perhaps we should regard the Magdelenian cave pictures as the final phase of a development that began as simple killing magic at a time when big game was plentiful but shifted its meaning when the animals became scarce. . . . The main purpose may no longer have been to "kill" but to "make" animals—to increase their supply. Could it be that the Magdelenians felt they had to practice their fertility magic in the bowels of the earth because they thought of the earth itself as a living thing from whose womb all other life springs? (Janson, 1969: 20)

Ideology The most systematic attempt to explain Paleolithic art was made by André

These sculptures and engravings are examples of the late Upper Paleolithic artistic traditions. Like cave paintings, they are thought to have had both aesthetic and magico-religious functions. The sculpture in the bottom center, for example, is often referred to as a "Venus" or "mother-goddess" figure and is thought to have been used in fertility rites. (American Museum of Natural History)

Leroi-Gourhan (1968). From a quantitative analysis of the distributions of various types of human, animal, and geometric figures in the caves, he concluded that cave art is not a random accumulation of religious symbols created by artists over many centuries, but a highly organized system representing a world view based on the opposition of masculine and feminine forces. The mysterious geometric markings on cave walls, he believes, are either phallic or vulvar. They are consistently associated with different animal species and are located in different parts of the cave: the entrance and rear of the cave are devoted to male signs associated with horses, ibex, and deer; the central panels are devoted to female signs associated with bison and oxen. The many figures that overlay each other are simply one means of association. In effect, the caves are like the medieval cathedrals, whose symbolic decorations and layouts were built up according to a system that persisted for centuries.

The foundations of Leroi-Gourhan's interpretation are the spatial organization of the cave and the association of images, both of which have been questioned (Ucko and Rosenfeld, 1967). Many caves do not have the discrete areas that Leroi-Gourhan identifies. And in others the panels blend into one another. Furthermore, Leroi-Gourhan does not take number into account when identifying animals; 12 bison in a panel count as one occurrence of bison. He also ignores the fact that many animals are incompletely drawn while others are fully depicted; that some dominate the panels while others are quite small; and that not all animals are the same color. These differences might be as significant as the ones he concentrates on.

Calendrics One explanation for some markings on certain walls and pieces of bone is that they were strictly utilitarian. Alexander Marshack (1964) believes that such markings may have been the first calendars. Although new evidence suggests ever earlier dates for the appearance of calendars, the Upper Paleolithic is the first period of abundance.

Explaining the Diversity

Clearly, in the art as well as the technology, we are seeing the reinforcement of the cultural diversity that began with the Mousterian stage—that is, the use of symbols to aid in scheduling activities and to mark cultural boundaries. Many of the interpretations of Upper Paleolithic traditions are plagued with the same problems that we encountered in the previous stage—namely, determining whether they reflect spatial, temporal, or functional differences. But whatever the explanation for a particular tradition, there are general forces at work that account for the overall diversity. Of particular importance is that subsistence strategies reinforced the diversity of traditions we saw beginning with the Mousterians. On the one hand, specialization led to sedentism, territoriality, and stronger patterns of sharing above the band affinities. On the other hand, it led to instability and the rapid replacement of one tradition by another. Let us look at each of these.

Specialization, Instability, and Diversity A good deal of cultural diversity is likely among specialized groups, because instability is inherent in predatory populations dependent on hunting large game for subsistence. The size and range of the game fluctuate as a result of the predator-prey relationship and environmental changes; the human population dependent on the game varies accordingly. As segments of a community die off because of declines in game—which takes place perhaps only every 1,000 or so years—the culture will be drastically changed by the smaller remaining population, who carry a random selection of the special patterns of tool manufacture and use (as well as other cultural traditions) from the larger society. Furthermore, "innovations, even if they did not occur more often under conditions of stress, might spread more readily in a small population and thus become conspicuous in the archeological records" (David, 1973). Thus, the founder effect (which we discussed in Chapter 3 in terms of biological evolution, and which can also be used with regard to cultural evolution) speeds cultural change and diversity.

One way of adapting to the loss of game is to exploit a variety of resources more intensively—that is, to diversify subsistence strategies. Traces of bird and fish bones indicate that fishing and fowling were becoming more important sources of food. Unlike earlier tool assemblages, Upper Paleolithic ones have elaborate implements for fishing. And the sites of Magdalenian settlements were often beside rivers. With only the faunal remains to go by, we might doubt the extent to which this was an innovation, since bird and fish remains are extremely fragile and simply may not have survived from the much older Mousterian and Acheulean sites. But the cultural evidence seems conclusive. Greater exploitation of a variety of resources in an area was occurring in the Upper Paleolithic stage. Such adaptations reinforced local differences and also may have led to a less nomadic life, since people could depend on local resources to meet their needs.

Specialization, Sedentism, and Diversity The primary determinant of sedentism (that is, living in one place) at this stage, however, was the distribution of the game in which groups specialized. Groups who relied on seasonally migrant species, such as reindeer, had seasonally nomadic settlement systems, consisting of fall and winter cave habitations and summer open-air camps. Hunters who concentrated on animals abundant locally year-round, such as the Gravettian mammoth hunters, dwelt in more permanent open-air settlements.[1]

Many of the open-air sites contain the remains of dwellings whose forms vary from region to region. These were local specializations, adaptations and styles of life that set one group apart from the others. Sedentism reinforced these, for with them came a stable territory and a spatially well-defined tradition.

The culture of advanced hunters of Europe in the late Pleistocene represents not only an impressive elaboration of behavioral alternatives but also a highly successful adaptation to conditions of that period. We cannot help but be impressed by these hunters, who were able to dispatch gigantic mammoth or fleet-footed wild horses. Their weapons and tools are finely wrought and sometimes bear decorations that reveal the cultural sophistication of these people. Because of the reliance on big game, the population of given groups was not stable, but this should not be confused with the success of the adaptation. Overall, population was growing, to judge by the increased number and density of habitation sites as well as the large number of tools. The late Pleistocene populations in Europe may have been up to ten times greater than those in the middle Pleistocene (Isaac, 1972).

The Advanced Hunters of the New World

The ultimate measure of the rapidity in growth of population during the late Pleistocene is the scale of territorial expansion associated with it. The entire New World was populated during this period; and from Southeast Asia, peoples crossed a strait into Australia. To understand how the expansion to the New World took place, we must imagine the changing geography of the late Pleistocene epoch.

The Route to the New World

During the Pleistocene epoch, extensive glaciation locked up large amounts of water, which lowered sea levels and reexposed the land mass across the Bering Strait from northeastern Siberia to northwestern Alaska. The Bering Plain, or Beringia, was definitely not a narrow bridge or isthmus as was once thought, but rather a very extensive land area which supported large herds of mammoth, reindeer, musk oxen, horses, bison, and other cold-steppe and tundra animals. Even during the warm periods, when the straits were covered by sea, they were probably navigable

---

[1] Our discussion of the differences between Mousterian and Upper Paleolithic subsistence and settlement patterns is based largely on Mellars (1973).

The Emergence of Cultural Diversity 115

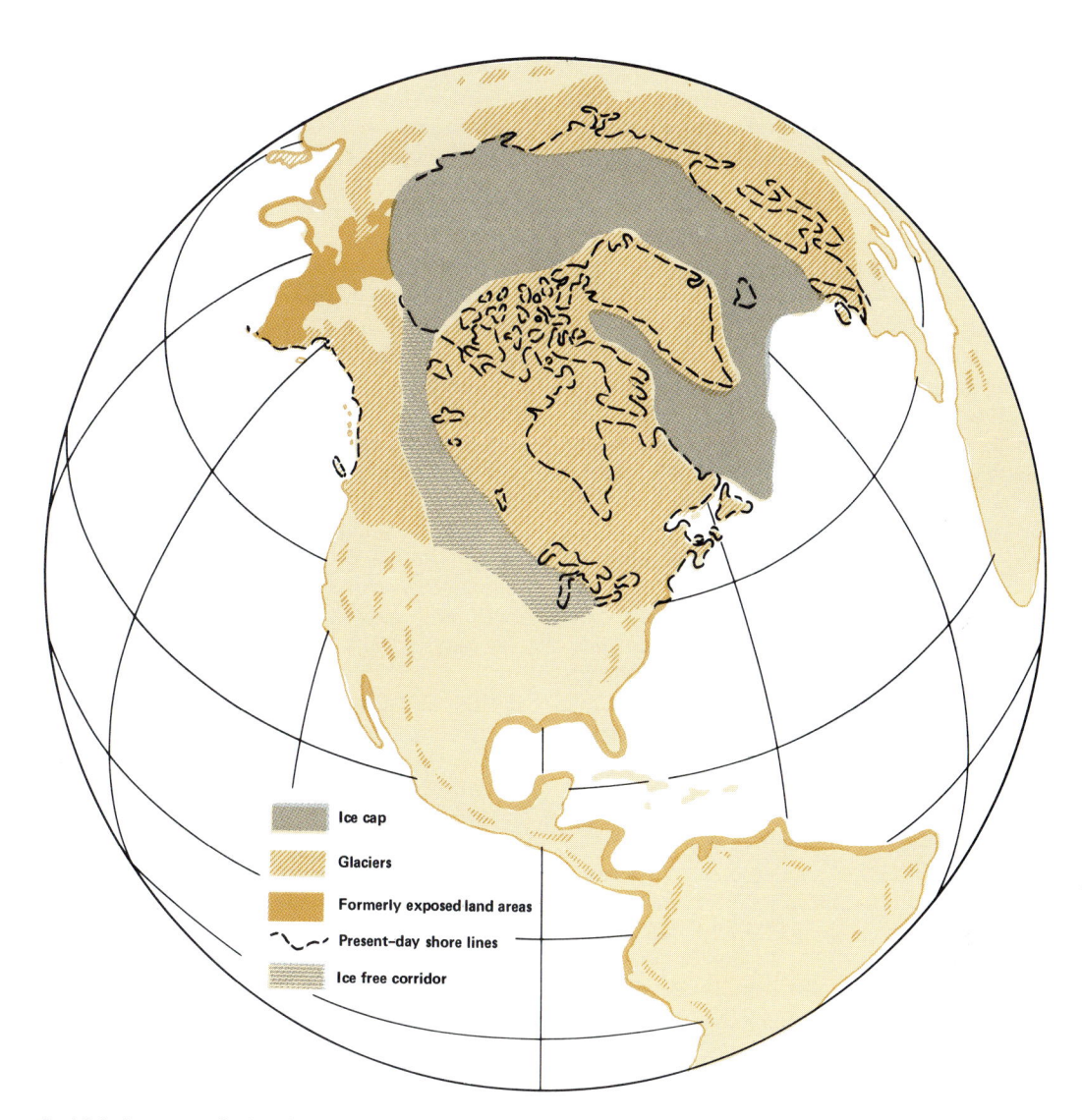

- Ice cap
- Glaciers
- Formerly exposed land areas
- Present-day shore lines
- Ice free corridor

in hide boats, to judge by the ease with which modern hunter-gatherers in this region cross this stretch of water.

But how did the groups disperse from Beringia into the rest of the New World, when southern Alaska, British Columbia, the Yukon, and the northwestern United States were covered by the Cordilleran ice sheets and eastward lay the Laurentide sheet? Dispersal from Beringia through the rest of North America could have been accomplished only via an ice-free corridor between the two sheets

Figure 6–2. During the last glaciation, much of the northern part of this continent was covered with ice sheets. The human populations that crossed the Bering Plain connecting Siberia and Alaska found access via an ice-free corridor. (After J. D. Jennings, 1974 and C. V. Haynes Jr., 1973)

through the eastern foothill region of the Rocky Mountains. (See Figure 6–2.) Most of the time the corridor was covered with forest-tundra and grassland that supported large herds of game upon which the late Pleistocene groups were economically dependent.

Unfortunately, the sites in Siberia and Alaska are few, and the evidence of early peoples' passage lies beneath the waters of the Bering Sea, under tons of sediment deposited by the melting of the glaciers at the end of the Pleistocene epoch. Archeological data do suggest that the earliest human groups in the New World were descendants of Upper Paleolithic Siberian populations.

Dating the Arrival The precise date people began to arrive in the New World still stirs great debate. Archeologists have traditionally assumed that migrants did not come before about 12,000 B.P. But some archeologists now argue for a relatively early date—as much as half a million years ago—on the basis of evidence from a few sites. One of these is Calico Hills, near Yermo, California, which contained objects identified as crude scrapers, flakes, and bifaces in a stratum dated to between 500,000 and 250,000 years ago. But there is some controversy about interpreting these finds.

There is some convincing evidence of early occupation of the New World, especially from Central and South America. In the Valsequillo region near Puebla, Mexico, artifacts associated with extinct animal remains have been radiocarbon-dated to 22,000 and 24,000 B.P. (Irwin-Williams, 1968a). Caves near Ayacucho, Peru, have yielded a stratified cultural sequence spanning from 22,000 to 450 B.P. (MacNeish, 1973:96–97). The lowest level contains a chopper scraper complex and the bones of extinct ground sloths. If people had reached Central and South America by 24,000 B.P., they must have crossed the Bering Strait at an even earlier date.

Migration or Expansion? How long did the occupation of the New World take, from the time of crossing to the time when South America was settled? Migration was difficult for small hunter-gatherer bands who had no horses or wagons, who could accumulate little surplus food, and who survived by exploiting to the fullest what they had at hand. Assuming an initial group as small as 25 people (it could easily have been larger), estimating the density necessary for their survival in a region to which they were not specifically adapted and the amount of territory to be occupied in the New World, Martin Wobst (1974) calculates that it would take only 3,000 years for the Pleistocene population to attain the initial carrying capacity of the land and spread throughout the New World. Although these specific calculations should not be taken literally, the general picture is accurate. Groups simply ranged a bit farther in search of food than they had before, and mile by mile made their way across the land bridge connecting Asia with North America, down a corridor between two glacier systems of North America, and into a whole new continent, where they developed their own specialized subsistence strategies and toolmaking traditions over millennia.

North America in Paleolithic Times The environments into which people moved through the ice-free corridor were very different from those found in North America today. The upper Great Plains and the Great Lakes region were dominated by spruce, while the Northeast and Northwest were covered by spruce and pine. Mean annual temperatures probably were well below freezing—about 21.6°F (12°C) colder than they are today. The Midwest was probably a mixture of forest with meadows and grassland. The southwestern United States, which today is desert and scrub, was covered with parklands or closed forests dominated by pine, with spruce at higher elevations. Pollen profiles suggest that southern California had an extensive cover of juniper. Throughout the West, there were very large lakes. These woods and lakes indicate that the Southwest was moister than it is today and was able to support a large animal population. The Southeast was a mixed coniferous forest. Across these regions roamed reindeer, elk, musk ox, mammoth, mastodon, bison, and antelope. About 11,000 years ago, the glaciers began to recede, and climatic conditions became more and more like they

Dating Techniques

In addition to radiocarbon and potassium-argon dating (described in Chapter 6), there are several other interesting methods of dating artifacts. One ingenious technique is *dendrochronology,* an absolute dating method based upon the patterns of tree-ring growth. Some types of trees put on one ring a year. The size of the ring will depend upon climatic conditions affecting the tree during the course of that year. If rainfall was plentiful, the ring will be thick; if it was not, the ring will be narrow. By comparing the tree rings of extant trees with a series of increasingly older specimens found at archeological sites, dendrochronologists in the American Southwest have formulated a "master log" of tree-ring patterns extending from the present to 5,000 B.P. If archeologists compare the tree-ring patterns of wood from prehistoric shelters, hearths, roofs, or other artifacts with the master log, they can determine the precise date at which the tree had been cut down to make an object. It is desirable to obtain the entire section of the ring from the birth to the death of the tree. Partial cross sections of wood are difficult to date because we do not know if they contain the last ring added prior to the tree's death. At present, dendrochronology is workable only in such arid regions as the American Southwest, where appropriate climatic conditions and vegetation are found.

Archeomagnetism is another absolute dating method. This technique is based upon a study of the characteristics of and changes in the earth's magnetic intensity over several hundred years—in essence, the movement in the precise location of the magnetic North Pole. Such changes can also be determined by studies of hearths, wattle and daub fragments, kilns, and other baked clay objects containing ferromagnetic minerals. Interestingly, when a clay object is heated, the iron particles in the clay become aligned with the earth's magnetic field at the time the clay is fired. If the exact position of the object during heating is known, then the direction of the earth's magnetic field can also be determined. These clay objects can then be compared to baked clay objects dated by other methods. Analysts have begun to formulate archeomagnetic curves representing the changes in magnetic field.

A relatively new dating method is *obsidian hydration.* Obsidian is a volcanic glass produced by the rapid cooling of molten lava; it absorbs atmospheric or soil moisture at a constant rate, creating a hydration layer beginning at its surface. By measuring the thickness of the hydration layer of an obsidian artifact, archeologists can, in theory at least, date the time of its use. Hydration rates are influenced by such variables as atmospheric or soil temperature, chemical and mineralogical composition, soil chemistry, and solar radiation. Because these factors vary geographically, hydration rates must be determined for each specific geographical region. Since physical decomposition of an obsidian hydration layer does not occur for at least 100,000 years after the creation of its fresh surface, the hydration method should allow us to date objects up to 100,000 years old.

Seriation is an imaginative relative dating method that makes use of the popularity cycle of objects in trying to date them. Usually, when a particular object is created and introduced to the public, only a few people use it at first. Gradually more and more people accept it, and its popularity peaks, after which fewer and fewer people utilize it. Eventually, it becomes obsolete and disappears from use. Seriation has been used particularly for dating pottery.

Creating seriations of archeological assemblages is a three-step process. The archeologist first divides the artifacts into various types. Next he calculates the relative popularity of each type within each assemblage. He then arranges the assemblages so that the frequencies of each type form a popularity curve. Since the popularity process is a gradual one, sites closest in time most closely resemble each other. Thus, the assemblages are now arranged in chronological order. Unfortunately, the seriation method does not enable the archeologist to determine which end of the curve represents the oldest or youngest assemblage.

Despite the individual variations of these methods, they are all based on a common principle. Essentially, they can help us to determine the age of a specific site or object by correlating it with some physical or cultural process that changes at a given rate. And even though each technique has certain limitations, they can often be used to complement one another.

are today. Most of our evidence of occupation dates from after the glacial recession, when the climate and environment were changing.

Paleo-Indian Traditions of North America

Although the earliest known Paleo-Indian tradition consists of choppers and scrapers, we know little of the people of this preprojectile period. Instead, we must begin later in the occupation of North America, with the hunters of the *Clovis,* or *Llano,* tradition. Sites of this tradition was found from the Southwest to Nova Scotia and date from 11,500 to 9,500 B.P. The *Folsom* tradition appeared in the West between 11,000 and 9,000 B.P. Sites of both traditions are identified by fluted points, distinctive blades flaked from the base along the center to form a flute or groove for attaching the point to a shaft. These blades seem to be a strictly American form. They were used for hunting the large game that roamed the grasslands of the Great Plains and Southwest. Clovis-tradition peoples seemed to specialize in mammoth, whereas peoples of the Folsom tradition hunted bison, probably because of changing environmental conditions, including a growing scarcity of mammoth.

Overlapping these and continuing later is the *Plano* tradition, 10,000 to 7,000 B.P., which is found from the Rockies to the Atlantic and Mexico to Canada. Plano points are not fluted, but instead have a fine patterning of parallel pressure-flaked scars. Clusters of hearths and artifacts at sites predating this tradition may mark the location of flimsy windbreaks or tents, but the oldest housing remains are known from three Plano occupations.

Hunting In comparison with the Old World Upper Paleolithic cultures, the subsistence practices of the New World traditions are relatively well known. In some cases, the evidence is so unmistakable that even the direction of the wind on the day of the hunt can be reconstructed (Wheat, 1973:80).

Sites of Clovis-tradition hunters are usually located near bogs or marshes; they contain artifacts made of materials whose source was as much as 100 to 200 miles (167 to 334 km) away, suggesting either exchange or a large territorial range. Both site location and territorial size appear to be adaptations to the behavior of these hunters' favorite prey, the mammoth.

The most feasible hunting strategy would have been to ambush the herd along the route to one of its favored feeding areas but far from a water source. After the initial attack, the wounded mammoth would have fled to the nearest water source, where the hunters could easily have dispatched the animal as it stood exhausted and trapped within the bog.

Folsom hunters specialized in the now extinct long-horned bison, which probably behaved much like modern bison. Modern bison have poor eyesight, but a very good sense of smell, so hunters may easily close in on a herd as long as the hunters remain downwind. When frightened, the herd closes ranks and blindly flees, or stampedes. Folsom groups took advantage of this behavioral trait by introducing two new techniques into the Paleo-Indian hunting repertoire—the *jump* and the *surround kill.* In the jump technique, hunters stationed downwind behind a herd frighten the animals into a stampede. Other hunters stationed along the herd's flanks then set up a great noise to direct the stampede toward a high cliff, over which all the animals in the entire herd would run to their deaths. Many of the Folsom killsites are located at the bases of such cliffs. The surround kill follows a similar procedure, except that instead of going over a cliff, the herd charges into a box canyon, arroyo, or corral, where they can easily be slaughtered without danger to the hunters. The Folsom-type site in New Mexico is one such killsite.

Like the Folsom groups, Plano tradition hunters utilized both the jump and surround techniques. By the time Plano peoples appeared, the big game available consisted of modern species, mainly bison. At the Plainview site in Texas, hundreds of modern bison skeletons associated with Plano tools were excavated from the base of a cliff over which they had apparently been stampeded. At the Olsen-Chubbuck site in eastern Colorado, about two hundred modern bison had been stampeded into an arroyo trap.

Gathering The description of hunting strategies may convey the idea that the Paleo-Indian economy depended completely on big-game hunting, but this does not seem to be the case. Two early types of sites are found in the Arizona region: (1) Paleo-Indian killsites where large animals were butchered, and (2) sites with ground stone tools for woodworking and plant processing, such as milling stones, manos, heavy choppers, and scraper planes. The two contemporary site complexes were probably seasonal settlement types within a single Paleo-Indian subsistence-settlement system. This cultural system probably does not represent the first Paleolithic gathering economy, but to date, southern Arizona is the only area providing clear evidence of an association of both big-game and extensive gathering activities, although big-game specialization had the most important effect on society.

Settlement Patterns and Social Organization

A similar pattern seems to emerge when one examines the different kinds of Paleo-Indian sites known at present. The account of Paleo-Indian groups so far suggests that they had rather complex subsistence-settlement systems and social organization. Settlements seem to be of different types. In some, activities were specialized. Besides the killsites and plant-processing stations, there were quarry workshops where lithic materials were gathered and manufactured into rough or finished tools. At the central camp, which was a semipermanent location, many domestic activities were carried out.

The activities at different sites involved successively larger numbers of people, integrated into more complex structural units (Wilmsen, 1968:38). The band segment—a task-oriented group or a small group of related band members—settled briefly at a site for a particular purpose (such as harvesting a plant in season), often returning year after year to the same spot. At times, all the band segments gathered together, and these sites reflect a wider range of activities. Finally, several bands might have met in the course of ranging about for food and have cooperated in a wide variety of activities, including hunting, arranging marriages, and perhaps carrying on rituals.

The Problem of Extinctions At the end of the Pleistocene epoch, many animals became extinct, especially in North America. Although the fossil record is full of species no longer in existence, the rapidity with which a large group of animals simply disappeared makes this period unique. One explanation offered for this catastrophe is the advent of humans in the New World. According to the "overkill" theory, humans were no longer one predator among many but a dominant force in the environment; and moving into regions where the prey were not adapted to human hunting, they were responsible for killing off the animal groups.

The overkill theory has several flaws, however. First, a number of extinctions seem to have occurred before humans arrived. Furthermore, Paleo-Indians seem to have been too few in number and too little dependent on big-game hunting to have finished off the herds. Third, if the species were not initially adapted to human predators, the extinctions should have become less frequent in later periods as species adapted to the new danger. Instead, the evidence indicates fewer extinctions in the early part of the period than in the later part.

Perhaps, then, climatic changes were to blame, since the extinctions occurred during the changeover from glacial to postglacial conditions. One theory is that the shift from colder to warmer and from moister to drier conditions produced increasing desiccation, shrinking habitats, and mass starvation of many animals. There are several problems with this theory, and a second group of environmental theorists believe that the fatal element was greater variation in mean temperatures over the year, or the decrease in *equabil-*

ity. About 10,000 B.P., seasonal contrasts in both Europe and the New World became more pronounced. Since the young are more vulnerable to extremes, mammals with long gestation periods, small litters, and a fixed birth season would have been most likely to have lost entire generations (which they could not rapidly replace) and to have become extinct. Larger mammals today have such characteristics, and the larger mammals of the late Pleistocene were the ones that became extinct (Bruiuer, 1970). In short, the available evidence suggests that decreased equability was the key factor in the late Pleistocene mammalian extinctions.

But equability was not the sole factor. In order to understand the extinction process, we should consider it in terms of a feedback situation in which environment and hunting practices interacted to reduce and finally eradicate certain animal populations unable to adapt to the changing surroundings. Perhaps if the depredations of the hunters had not coincided with increased environmental stress, many of the extinct genera might have survived.

Mesolithic and Archaic Stages

About 10,000 years ago, adaptations that archeologists define as the *Mesolithic* stage in Europe and the *Archaic* stages in North America began. During these stages, particular groups combined specialized subsistence strategies to form more diversified strategies. In this sense, they are a logical consequence of processes that had been operating for thousands of years. Climatic factors, too, played an important role in the changes that occurred.

The disappearance of the mammoth and bison, along with the changes in climate and landscape in the areas we have been concentrating on, could not have left human groups unaffected. Imagine the impact on our society if cattle and pigs gradually disappeared and the grain belt turned into forest. This would probably be enough to plunge us into a new Dark Age. But band societies are more resilient. Cave art did disappear and camp sizes shrank, but cultural collapse never occurred and new cultural features appeared: an even greater diversity of tools, more intensive foraging, and later on, more sedentary settlements and the development of trade networks. In fact, the focus of cultural evolution shifted from primarily technological advances to changes in subsistence, settlement, and social organization.

The Impact on Population

Although the known Mesolithic-Archaic sites are of small size, they greatly outnumber those of the Upper Paleolithic stage. This suggests that the impact of post-Pleistocene extinctions may not have been as drastic as site size suggests. Moreover, the Mesolithic peoples occupied open-air sites, which were more likely to be destroyed and are more difficult to find than Upper Paleolithic sites, many of which are in caves and rock shelters. The smaller size of the Mesolithic sites, some of which contain only a few artifacts, makes their discovery more difficult. So the known number of Mesolithic sites probably represents a much smaller percentage of the total than do the known Upper Paleolithic sites. For these reasons, it seems safer to assume that the Mesolithic-Archaic population did not shrink and might even have grown, despite the environmental crises of the postglacial period (McManamon, 1974).

Subsistence and Settlement

To see the important features and development of the Mesolithic-Archaic way of life, let us look at the lower Illinois River valley, where one Archaic population has been exceptionally well studied (Struever, 1968). The subsistence and settlement systems of this 75-mile-long (125 km) area of the Illinois River belong to two periods, the Early and Middle Woodland. During this time, the lower Illinois River valley and adjacent areas were a fertile area for both plant and animal life, containing four main zones of vegetation: the shoreline and flood plain of the river, an oak-hickory forest along the valley margin, an upland forest above a gravelly bluff, and beyond, the grassland prairie.[2]

The *Early Woodland* groups, who inhabited the region from 2,500 to 2,200 B.P., subsisted by foraging in the river valley and surrounding hills. Excavation and site surveys indicate only two main settlement types located in the two most productive zones of the region: one on the riverbank for gathering animals and plants from the river bottom, and a few other sites close to the bluffs that may have been nut-gathering centers. The small number of artifacts and the absence of storage pits and housing indicate that the Early Woodland groups occupied the sites only temporarily and that they were seasonally nomadic, stopping where food was most plentiful at that time of year. Burial sites were rudimentary, with no indication of status differences among those interred.

By *Middle Woodland* times—2,200 B.P. to 1,500 B.P.—all this had changed. The number of settlements had increased enormously and were of four types: fairly permanent base camps, flood-plain summer agricultural camps, mortuary camps for preparation and burial of the dead, and a regional exchange center. The base camps were located at the foot of the bluffs, midway between three zones, where groups could wander forth and take advantage of the abundant foods in the area—fish, fowl, deer, nuts, and seeds. The few sites in the flood plain suggest that the groups might have begun to experiment with cultivated crops on the rich soil brought by the annual river floods. Such a harvesting economy required substantial division of labor and the coordination that entails.

Together, these four site types reveal an elaborate culture based on intensive gathering, with differential access to goods and therefore some kind of stratification system supported by wide-scale trade with other groups in the region. The contrast between the Early and Middle Woodland groups reveals the main features of cultural development: more specialized and seasonal subsistence strategies, more permanent settlements with surrounding specialized sites, and more complex social structures. Because the Mesolithic-Archaic populations were so acutely sensitive to local environments, these general features were expressed in different ways in different regions.

Seasonality Groups in the Mesolithic-Archaic period tended to have even more specialized sites than those of Upper Paleolithic groups. Such specialization was part of the adaptation to the new conditions of the postglacial period. Since the climate had become less equable, people could not count on an even seasonal distribution of a diverse group of plants and animals, but instead faced a marked change in resource availability from season to season and locale to locale. Groups survived by concentrating on intensive foraging of seasonal foods, and tended—at least in the early Mesolithic-Archaic—to be more nomadic than Upper Paleolithic groups.

In subsistence, then, Mesolithic-Archaic strategies seem to involve adaptation to a locality by exploiting the range of resources available there, shifting the diet from season to season. We have seen this strategy of specialization through diversification in the Upper Paleolithic, but not to this extent. The intimate acquaintance with the properties of local plants and animals necessary for survival using this subsistence strategy laid the foundations for experimentation with local resources that ultimately led to domestication and the beginnings of agriculture.

Sedentism Intensive foraging of seasonal foods seems to have slowed the development of permanent settlements. The paucity of houses and the diffuse artifact assemblages at early Mesolithic-Archaic sites indicate fairly temporary settlements and a more nomadic existence than in the preceding period. Certainly, the Early Woodland sites confirm this.

---

[2]Because Woodland groups reflect a preagricultural lifestyle, we group them with the archaic adaptations.

However, by the late Mesolithic-Archaic stage, the base camp with satellite camps had reemerged, as we saw in the Middle Woodland settlements. Why this should occur is a matter of debate.

Archeologists once attributed the appearance of sedentism to the introduction of agriculture. In some areas, fully sedentary villages do appear within early agricultural economies, but in others they precede agriculture and occur within late Mesolithic-Archaic foraging economies. Agriculture can hardly be the full explanation.

One important factor was population growth. As the population grows, the strain on local resources is avoided either by resorting to birth control or by exporting excess population into any uninhabited surrounding areas. Since the New World had vast open areas, the migration of groups was more likely. When the process of expansion involved large numbers of distinct groups, the entire area may eventually have been filled with people. As groups were confined to more restricted areas, mobility was limited, and settling down may have been desirable to defend a territory. In this way, population growth and a subsequent emphasis on territoriality may have fostered sedentism among Mesolithic-Archaic groups.

Resource distribution was also important in the process. The most favorable areas for intensive foraging are often ones with a variety of zones of vegetation and animal life. Groups in that area no longer needed to travel in seasonal rounds, since the variety of nearby resources was sufficient to support a centrally located sedentary camp.

Whatever its origins, sedentism was not ultimately incompatible with intensive foraging of seasonal resources. Nonetheless, there remained the need for groups to disperse from the central base and then meet again, sometimes days or even weeks later.

Trade and Social Organization

This pattern of dispersal and coalescence in subsistence strategies may also explain the origins of trade. In Upper Paleolithic times, bands joined for large hunts, particularly before the onset of winter. At these times they may have swapped articles, as well as shared food and conducted rituals. As large-scale hunting decreased in importance and sedentism and more tightly defined territories became more characteristic, such casual swapping would have become more difficult. The need for exchange would not have abated, however, because as the territories of groups became more restricted, the diversity of resources encountered in a seasonal round would have decreased.

By Mesolithic-Archaic times, the evidence of regularized trade is unmistakable. Trade was occurring not simply between neighboring groups but over long distances. At the Indian Knoll sites in Kentucky, there are sea shells from central Florida, shells that had somehow been transported over 600 miles inland. Likewise, copper from the Lake Superior region appears at these Kentucky sites (Winters, 1968). This is placed at 4,500 to 4,000 years ago, when transportation was entirely by foot and groups did not roam far from their accustomed territory.

Trade is a form of social organization (Wilmsen, 1972). It evolves as groups schedule contacts that have previously been informal and create institutions for regulating these relationships. Band-level organization becomes a part of a larger system and may be altered (or reinforced) by it. The full impact of trade on social organization will be left to Chapter 7, with its account of the refinement of the Archaic regional exchange system into a hierarchy of specialized sites within the Hopewell Interaction Sphere. What is important at this stage is that trade has become institutionalized and involves peoples over a wide territory.

Technology

The higher levels of social organization implied by trade systems were not so strong that they unified material culture. Regional diversity and specificity of use are the hallmarks of the technology of the Mesolithic-Archaic stage.[3]

The technique of tool manufacture was flexible enough to permit such diversity. No longer were knappers turning out elaborately formed stone shapes. Instead, they refined the microlith or small blade, which first appeared in the Upper Paleolithic stage. Formed either by the blade technique from small cores or by the fracturing of a larger blade into smaller pieces, microliths were no more than 2 inches (5 cm) long and often no longer than a fingertip. A dozen or so microliths could be made by breaking a blade. A bladelet is one-tenth to one-hundredth the size of a normal blade. Thus microliths afforded at least a tenfold increase in cutting edge per pound of stone. These blades were used alone or mounted on wood as arrows, sickles, and a myriad of other tools that reflected the particular needs of that community. In many areas of the world, small, thin, but irregularly shaped flakes were simply struck from a core, picked up and used without major modifications. Thus if in making microliths, Mesolithic-Archaic populations had learned to obtain the maximum number of tools from a core, they had also learned that there were circumstances under which such precision was unnecessary.

Another technique produced ground stone tools, better suited to the plant processing and woodworking important in this period. Occasional ground tools are found in assemblages from the Oldowan stage on. Now they become important. Formed by flaking, the edges of these tools were finished by abrasion, much as we sharpen knives or polish stones today. These ground stone tools became abundant during this period in the Old World, where post-Pleistocene forests covered many areas that had once been tundra, and the sharp axes and planes were excellent for shaping wood. Grinding tools such as the mortar and pestle were probably made of wood in these areas, but in the New World such stone tools were plentiful in the Archaic stage, providing further evidence of increasing dependence upon plant resources. Ground stone tools assumed an even greater importance in the next stage of cultural development, when plants were finally domesticated and agriculture became the basis of subsistence.

Trends in Evolution

If the Upper Paleolithic and Mesolithic-Archaic stages are short in comparison with the Oldowan, Acheulean, and Mousterian stages, this brevity is not reflected in the knowledge people gained and the skills they mastered. In these two stages, we see both the final mastery of particular technological and organizational forms and the beginning of evolution along new and very different routes.

The control of lithic technology that Upper Paleolithic and Mesolithic-Archaic toolmakers demonstrate has never been surpassed. These tools were shaped to extremely precise forms, forms appropriate to highly specialized tasks. During these two stages humans also began to extensively use a new range of raw materials—bone and ivory in particular—and to shape rock by a technique other than knapping, namely grinding.

The innovations of these stages, then, stem from growing knowledge and experience in the knapper's craft. Some tools directly aided in the quest for food; others allowed new tools to be made that increased the survival potential of the groups possessing them, and still others simply increased the time available for the subsistence quest.

A similar story can be told of the evolution of social organization. For millions of years people had lived in bands. During the Upper Paleolithic, these bands began to adopt a more sedentary way of life. Another trend was the growing links between groups; big-game hunting required cooperation between bands, and sedentism required resource exchange between bands. Trade and other forms of organization above the level of the band developed, and it is these forms that will become

---

[3]For a fuller account of the regional diversity during the Archaic period, see Jennings (1974), Chapter 4.

important in the succeeding chapters.

Both the achievements in technology and the changes in social organization directly reflect the growing success of subsistence skills: the ability to bring down large game, the ability to make use of more diverse resources from a local environment, and the ability to schedule activities so that the resources of different seasons could be exploited. Here again, the increasing knowledge of the environment laid the foundation of a new stage in evolution, a stage in which humans control and even create their environment through technology, through social organization, and to an increasingly greater extent, through symbolic expression.

summary

Were we to select a symbol for this chapter, the most fitting one might be the Tower of Babel, that mythical symbol of the origin of human cultural diversity. Archeological explanations attribute this diversity to two processes: specialization, and the combination of specialized practices to exploit a diverse range of resources within a limited locality. The Upper Paleolithic stage represents the final development of specialization based on big-game hunting, whereas the Mesolithic-Archaic stage involves a shift to diversification based on local specialization.

About 40,000 B.P., while the last glaciation was still gripping parts of Europe as far south as France and of North America as far south as New York, new traditions appear in Europe. Their bearers lived in bands just as hominids had done millions of years before, but they were far more numerous and their ability to exploit the environment was more specialized. These were the advanced hunter-gatherers of the Upper Paleolithic stage.

To improve their hunting chances these people had spear throwers (and later, bows and arrows). Their tools were made in an even greater variety of ways than Mousterian tools had been. The stone technology was based on the blade, which could be produced in almost standard forms and shapes by percussion flaking, punch flaking, or pressure flaking. For the first time, bone, antler, and ivory were used systematically as raw materials. The bone tools were sometimes decorated, as were the walls of some caves. Personal adornments and small sculptures also survive. This is the first art tradition we know of.

Population density of these advanced hunters increased, but this did not bring greater cultural unity. In Europe, five distinct traditions have been identified: the Aurignacian, Perigordian, Solutrean, Gravettian, and Magdalenian. They are set apart not only by characteristic tool types but by artistic styles as well.

Reliance on big game was responsible for diversification. The instability of the herds made for unstable human populations in which rapid cultural change was likely. Where game was plentiful and populations sedentary, human groups developed carefully defined territories and cultural barriers that set them apart from groups beyond their areas.

The growth in population resulted in an expansion into new continents—the Americas and Australia. Groups ranged a little farther in search of food and gradually moved across the land bridge exposed between Asia and Alaska, down a corridor between two glacier systems in North America, and from there into North, Central, and South America. In North America, Paleo-Indian cultures were based on big-game hunting, but there is some evidence that plants were an important seasonal resource. Such subsistence practices required more complex social organization, involving task groups who worked at specialized sites and macrobands who formed to hunt and perhaps to perform rituals that integrated the groups.

At the end of the last glaciation, the climate changed relatively rapidly, as did the flora, the fauna—and the culture of humans. Since big-game animals were either becoming extinct—

victims of decreasing climatic equability and the predations of humans—or changing territory, peoples placed greater reliance on a variety of foods available in a locality at different seasons. Sedentism increased. Ground stone tools used in plant processing gained in importance; and smaller flakes, called microliths, were combined with bone or wood to make compound tools with even greater specificity of use than before.

For highly specialized groups, exploiting relatively limited territories, trade afforded access to other resources; and in the Mesolithic-Archaic stage, extensive and systematic trade began. Such broad networks meant that the band was no longer self-sufficient nor the only unit of social organization. The advent of trade marked the beginning of a change in social organization.

The Upper Paleolithic and Mesolithic-Archaic stages represent relatively rapid advances in technology, subsistence practices, and social organization—measured in millennia rather than in hundreds of thousands or millions of years. The adaptations of the Mesolithic-Archaic stage provided a transition to the even more intensive exploitation of the environment during the early farming stage.

suggested readings

BORDAZ, J
1970 *Tools of the Old and New Stone Age.* Garden City, N.Y.: Natural History Press. A thorough discussion of the variety of tools used by early people and changes in techniques of manufacture.

BORDES, F.
1968 *The Old Stone Age.* New York: McGraw-Hill. A discussion of cultural evolution through the Upper Paleolithic, with particular emphasis on tool traditions.

KLEIN, R. G.
1973 *Ice-Age Hunters of the Ukraine.* Chicago: University of Chicago Press. A well-written discussion of archeological sites from which important evidence of Upper Paleolithic house forms has been obtained.

WILMSEN, E. N.
1974 *Lindenmeier: A Pleistocene Hunting Society.* New York: Harper & Row. Reconstruction of Paleo-Indian lifeways based on evidence from a site in Colorado.

MACNEISH, R. S., ED.
1973 *Early Man in America: Readings From Scientific American.* San Francisco: Freeman. Articles from *Scientific American* reporting the results of the excavations from which some of our most important information on the New World's earliest inhabitants has been obtained.

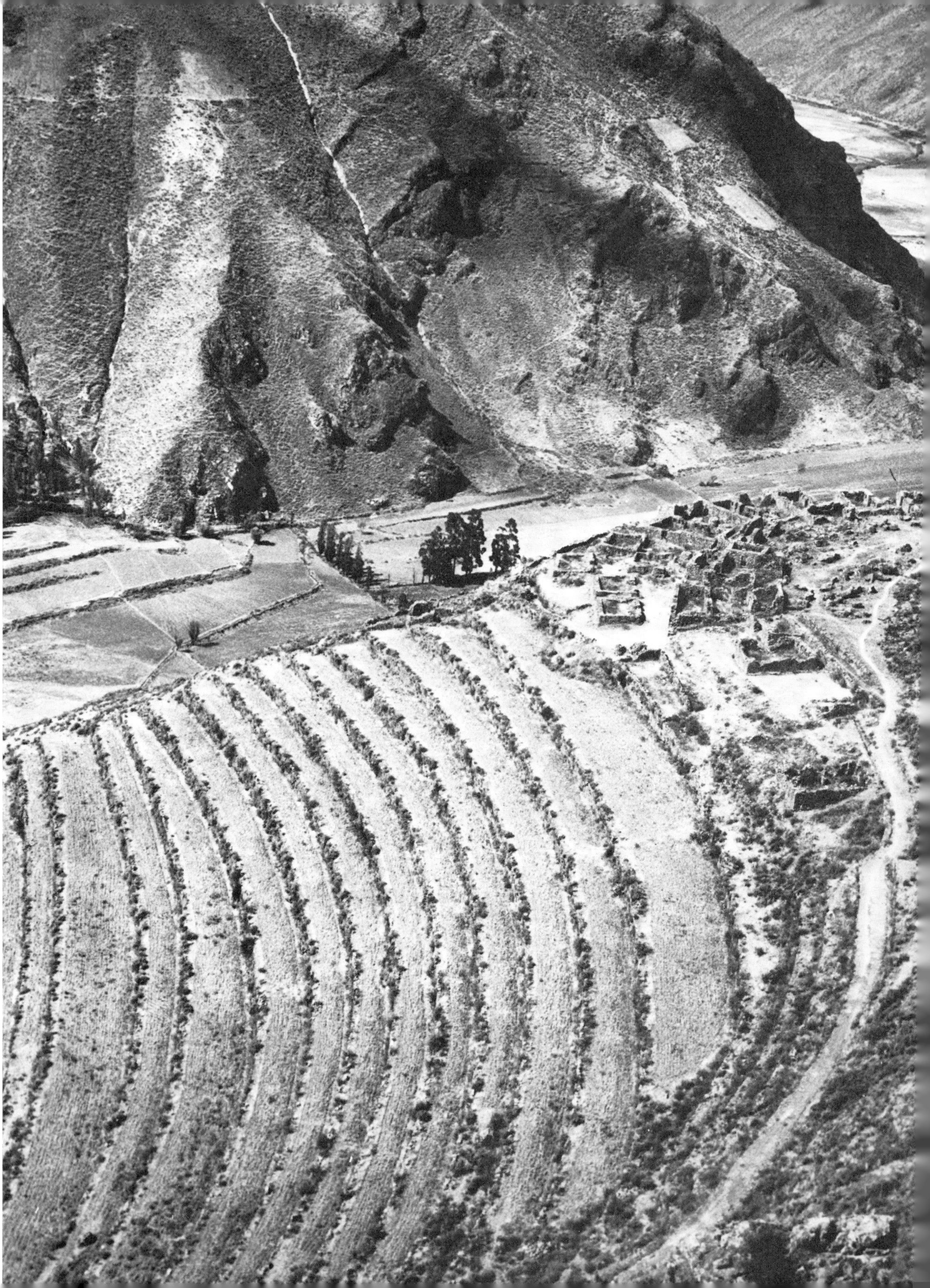

seven
The Emergence of Food Production

For more than 99 percent of the time humans have spent on earth, people have lived by hunting and gathering. Even today a few groups of people throughout the world continue to live much as their foraging ancestors did thousands of years ago. The Bushmen of the Kalahari Desert, the Pygmies of the Ituri Forest, the Eskimo, aboriginal Australians, and a few Indian groups in North and South America still survive by hunting and collecting assorted wild plants as they become available seasonally. In most areas of the world, however, life has not continued in this fashion. About 10,000 years ago, people in some areas began to produce food. Rather than relying solely on available game or wild plants, they began to plant and harvest crops systematically and to bring various animal species under human control—a process called *domestication*. We refer to the stage during which these events occurred as "the emergence of food production."

During the past two decades archeologists have given more attention to the emergence of food production than to any other period of the human past. Archeologists in the Near East, China, Thailand, Mexico, Peru, and elsewhere have unearthed the remains of early plants and animals domesticated by humans—wheat, barley, millet, and corn; goats, sheep, and cattle. Why has all this attention been lavished on one aspect of prehistory? Over the years, we have come to realize that this stage was a complex and revolutionary period, that culture began to change at a rapidly increasing rate and human beings began adapting to change itself as a way of life. More technological and social innovations blossomed during this stage than in all the preceding millions of years. Humans learned how to spin and weave, to fire clay and produce pottery, to construct bricks and arched masonry, to smelt and cast metals. The first formal villages appeared, providing a new social environment; egalitarian social organization began to give way to stratification; resources unavailable in one region were obtained through intricate systems of exchange.

Many of these trends, of course, were evident in the preceding stage of specialized foraging—manipulation of local resources, sedentism, and trade, in particular. Nevertheless, the basic way of life still consisted of hunting and gathering. Not until the end of the food-production stage did people begin to *purposefully* reshape their environment on a large scale: moving and manipulating plant and animal species to suit their own needs and preferences; controlling the supply of space, water, and other natural resources; remodeling the land to increase productivity. Once across the threshold to full agricultural production, people rapidly developed full-scale cities with markets, streets, temples, and palaces; an impressive array of sculpture and mural art; systems of writing, weights and measures, and mathematics; and new forms of political and social organization, which we shall discuss in Chapter 8. The food-producing revolution altered human life and the relationship of human beings to the rest of the natural world in the most fundamental sense.

In this chapter, we discuss the origins of food production and its effects on sociocultural organization. In the ancient Peruvian community of Pisac (the ruins of which can be seen in the center right), terrace farming was practiced. The terraced fields at the bottom left demonstrate that the modern descendants of Pisac use the same agricultural technology as their predecessors. (Black Star)

The Origins of Agriculture: Speculation and Theory

Exactly how did people first begin to domesticate plants and animals? Why did they give up hunting and gathering in favor of cultivation and herding? And where did these events first take place? Early theorists assumed that agriculture was a discovery that was made only once or twice, either gradually or in a brilliant flash of insight, and that it caught on and spread as more and more people recognized the benefits of domestication. But today we know that it is not ignorance that keeps people from becoming agriculturalists. Every human group has some knowledge of this phenomenon, and Paleolithic people undoubtedly understood it as well. Why, then, didn't agriculture develop earlier, and why didn't all foraging populations become agriculturalists? Archeologists began to wonder what unique set of social and environmental pressures encouraged some foraging groups to put their knowledge to work and change their subsistence strategies.

The Ecological Setting

British archeologist V. Gordon Childe (1951) attributed the change to pressures from increasing aridity in the Near East at the end of the last glaciation. Robert J. Braidwood (1967) was one of the first archeologists to test Childe's ideas by investigating specific environmental zones where food production might have originated. Braidwood maintained that these "nuclear zones" were not situated in the arid lowland plains of the Near East, as Childe believed, but in the surrounding upland areas, or hilly flanks, where the wild ancestors of today's domesticates were once abundant and where dense stands of wild wheat and barley grow even today.

Ecology and Culture: Our Most Recent Perspective Critics have pointed out that few societies accept change for its own sake—especially when it concerns subsistence. A new practice or technology must satisfy some need. People living in an area of abundant natural resources have little need to begin exploiting new resources and not much reason to modify their already proven and productive subsistence strategies. Moreover, before a plant or animal can be domesticated, certain genetic changes must take place. Although some initial changes may occur within a species' natural environment, the econiche to which it has become adapted, *major* changes are more likely to occur when the plant or animal has been taken to a new environment with different selective pressures. Under these new conditions, it is more apt to undergo the transformation from a wild species into a domesticate.

Kent Flannery (1973) believes it more likely that domestication experiments began among populations living in less bountiful marginal areas, where human populations would have been motivated to increase productivity and where wild plant forms indigenous to nuclear zones would have changed genetically in adaptation to the new environment. Some recent archaeological finds support this conclusion, indicating that domestication in fact began not *in* but *adjacent to* the nuclear zones.

Domestication, then, was not simply a matter of planting seeds and reaping the benefits. It involved two separate but interacting processes: changes in plants and animals, and changes in human subsistence strategies. New genetic and phenotypic characteristics were selected for in certain plants and animals. The changes differentiated these strains from their wild ancestors and ultimately made them dependent on humans for survival. As these genetic transformations occurred, the newly modified resources became an important part of the human diet and were utilized in new ways by humans.

To understand these processes of change, we need to look at three separate issues:

1. What genetically based phenotypic changes are involved in domestication, and how did they come about?

2. What adaptive advantages does the subsistence strategy of domestication confer? Why has it persisted and become fundamental to human survival?
3. What leads to the adoption of agriculture by a particular group?

Changes in Plants and Animals

Wherever domestication occurs, plants and animals are modified. A domesticate almost by definition is different from its wild relative. We can see this contrast by examining one of the earliest and most important domesticated plants in the New World—corn.

The evolution of Tehuacan corn is shown here. The earliest examples of domesticated maize (left-hand side of photo) contained many of the characteristics of their wild ancestor. This maize was a pod corn with small cobs containing only a few rows of kernels enclosed in tough husks. With years of hybridization and cultivation, the maize plant gradually became larger and sturdier. More and longer cobs and rows of kernels developed, and a single soft husk covered the entire cob rather than each kernel. The ear of Nal-tel corn at the extreme right of the photograph is an example of the maize commonly grown today. (Courtesy, R. S. Peabody Foundation for Archaeology. Photo by R. S. MacNeish and Paul Mangelsdorf)

The Changes in Corn

Unlike wheat or other food plants, corn has never been found growing in its wild state. Consequently, archeologists and botanists are not sure what the wild ancestor actually looked like. Some maintain that Indian corn—or, more properly, maize—is descended from a form of wild pod-popcorn, now extinct (Mangelsdorf, MacNeish, and Galinat, 1964). Others believe it developed from a tall, coarse grass such as teosinte, the nearest relative of modern corn. Today teosinte grows wild throughout the semiarid and subtropical zones of Mexico and Guatemala, and some Indian groups use it as "starvation food." At first glance, teosinte looks almost exactly like corn. It bears seeds on the side of the stalk, as corn does; but unlike corn, it has only 7 to 12 seeds enclosed in very hard cases situated on a brittle stalk (Flannery, 1973).

Our first clue to the origins of domesticated maize comes from the Tehuacan Valley in Mexico, where archeologists found tiny, one-inch-long cobs dated to about 7,000 B.P. We do not know for sure whether these specimens represent a type of wild maize or a transitional, semidomesticated descendant of teosinte. Whatever the case, these early forms differ greatly from corn as we know it. The short cobs were soft, with no more than eight rows of tiny kernels, each sheathed in a separate protective husk, or glume. The whole ear was only partially enclosed in a few light husks that allowed the seeds to disperse at maturity.

Modern corncobs, by way of contrast, are about ten times larger and have many more rows of kernels. The glumes are much smaller, and the husk system has developed to enclose and protect the entire ear. The cob is the grain-bearing axis of the corn plant, and like the rachis of domesticated wheat and barley, it has become tough and nonshattering. The structure of the cob makes corn extremely useful, since it is easy to harvest, store, and shell. Unlike wheat, corn is open to cross-fertilization and hybridizes easily with other closely related grasses. As a result, it has developed into an unusually vigorous plant, adaptable to a wide variety of growing conditions and different purposes. Today, corn has the widest geographical range of any major crop plant.

Recognizing Plant Domesticates

This example shows that reconstructing the domestication process is often a precarious undertaking, based on deductions from both circumstantial and primary evidence, and sometimes open to several interpretations.

Despite the problems of distinguishing wild and domesticated specimens, botanists have been able to specify a number of identifying characteristics. Typically, the seeds and sometimes the entire plant of a domesticated species are larger than the wild form. Larger seeds or plants mean greater productivity: crops that produce a higher yield per unit area. Domesticated plants, then, are often more productive than wild ancestral forms.

In addition to size differences, wild and domesticated species often vary in terms of their *morphology,* or shape and structure. One of the most prominent changes in cultivated vegetables and grains is the loss of natural seed-dispersal mechanisms. In wheat, barley, and corn, domesticated forms have a tougher rachis (the connective tissues holding the seed pods to the stem). The result is a crop plant that can be harvested more successfully but cannot release its seeds without human help. This characteristic is a sure sign of domestication, since without a dispersal mechanism the plants could not survive unless tended by people.

The Changes in Goats

Like plants, wild and domesticated animal species also differ in terms of size and morphology. Goats provide one of the most striking examples. About 11,000 years ago, Near Easterners began to keep flocks of goats as a food reserve. The evidence for this comes from relatively large numbers of animal bones found in refuse heaps. Under human protection and care, modifications began to occur in the anatomy of goats. One of the most obvious and strangest changes affected the shape of their horns. Ancient wild goats had smooth, scimitar-shaped horns that appear four-sided in cross-section. Gradually an almond-shaped horn core evolved, as one side became flattened and the other side formed a crescent. After several more centuries of domestication, goat horns became kidney-shaped and developed a slight corkscrew twist.

We do not fully understand why such radical changes in horn shapes occurred. They do not seem adaptive, and there is no apparent reason why early breeders would have consciously selected for new horn shapes. Probably the transformations were genetically linked to some other desirable characteristic, such as high milk yield. Whatever the cause, the new forms spread rapidly to populations throughout the foothills and mountains of Iraq and Iran.

Recognizing Animal Domesticates

The archeologist investigating animal domestication faces the same problems as in the case of plants. First, there is the question of identification. For instance, is the specimen a goat or a sheep? Often it is difficult to tell, since the two are closely related to each other, and in the earliest stages of domestication, their bones look much alike.

Another problem is determining whether the specimens represent wild or domesticated populations. One method is to analyze the dentition and bone fragments to determine the age and sex ratios of these herds. If there is a high proportion of butchered immature or young male animals, there is a good chance that the herd was on its way to being domesticated. At least it suggests that some sort of selection process was going on.

Another criterion for differentiating between wild and domesticated animals is bone size. Although a few domesticated species (the horse, the rabbit, and various fowl) are normally larger than their wild counterparts, in general, small bone size is associated with domestication. This development may simply reflect the fact that under human protection and care, more smaller and weaker animals survived. Early herders may also have purposefully selected smaller, more docile animals because they were easier to handle. Bone size, however, does not always provide clear-cut evidence. There is a great range in size among both domesticated and wild species, and small bone structure may reflect other variables — as for example, inadequate nutrition — that have nothing to do with domestication.

Humans as Selective Agents for Change

These, then, are some of the changes that we associate with domestication. We must now ask how they interacted with human behavior.

The changes that made plants and animals easier to cultivate or to herd were in part a product of the natural random variations inherent in all populations. Mutations occur in all species; new variations are always appearing in a few individuals. Most of these are not advantageous to the plant or animal, and die out. But a few provide survival value, and individuals with these traits form a greater and greater proportion of the species as time goes by. Human beings, as domesticators, changed the environment for certain plants and animals, and by their intervention, created new selective pressures that favored certain mutations. Selection is the important phenomenon — and human beings were the selecting agents.

Selection occurs as a result of both conscious and unconscious behavior. Given a range of alternative food plants, the more productive resources will be used more frequently. Some of this selectivity is conscious and purposeful, but much of it is not. If a seed stalk shatters when touched, for instance, people will not be able to harvest seeds from plants with that genotype. They may try — they are not consciously selecting against this characteristic — but not as many of these seeds can be collected. The seeds that will be carried to new environments will be the more

Estimating Prehistoric Populations

Many of the theories presented in Chapters 7 and 8 postulate fluctuations in population, in human numbers, as a major cause of certain economic and organizational changes in prehistoric groups. But how does an archeologist know how many people lived at a particular site or within a particular region? Obviously, he or she has no way of making a direct count of that population, as a modern census taker would. However, over the years a number of techniques have been developed that enable archeologists to discuss not only how many people lived in a particular area but also how their numbers were distributed throughout a region. Their population estimates are based on several sources of data; and because of the limitations of each method, an archeologist may use more than one method at a site.

The Environment   Usable food resources are unevenly distributed among the earth's different environments; grasslands, deserts, and forests, for example, have varying potentials for supporting humans. Archeologists estimate this potential, referred to as the *carrying capacity* of the environment, by carefully studying the kinds and quantities of resources available in a given environment. Although resource availability is sometimes the only data source for making inferences about the prehistoric population of a region, archeologists prefer not to estimate population by this method, for, at best, the carrying capacity can only suggest a certain level of population. The number of people living in a region may, in fact, have exceeded or fallen below the estimated carrying capacity.

Number of Artifacts   Usually, the density of artifacts left at a site will reflect the number of occupants. Thus, estimates of the relative population of two different sites are sometimes based on relative artifact densities: a greater density of artifacts means a larger population. However, artifact density also reflects the length of time a site was occupied and the organization of work in a society; so that artifact density alone does not give a clear indication of population

Floor Space and Number of Rooms   Living conditions are also used to estimate population. Using cross-cultural data, Raoul Naroll (1962) estimated that for the average society there is one person for every 107 square feet (10 m^2) of enclosed floor space. Thus, an archeologist can try to estimate a particular population by measuring the area of enclosed space at a site.

Often the archeologist can locate a nearby group that currently lives in sites similar to those he is excavating. By finding the ratio of people to rooms in such a society, he formulates a model for reconstructing population. In the American Southwest, for example, the usual figure is five or six persons per room. In this region, prehistoric populations are estimated by multiplying the number of rooms at a site by five or six.

Burial Data   The number of burials found at a site is also sometimes used to estimate the number of individuals who lived there. In many societies, formal interment in a cemetery is not so common as in our own, and some burials may therefore be missing from a burial ground. Despite this handicap, a careful study of the ages of the individuals who were buried and a comparison of these with models of the normal age distribution among known groups can lead archeologists to make a relatively precise estimate of population.

These methods are used to compare sites in different regions. Of course, in making comparisons such as these, the archeologist must be sure that apparent differences between two regions do not reflect merely the thoroughness with which they were surveyed. If examined with care, however, the relative density of sites throughout a region can provide valuable information concerning the importance of different resources and resource zones. In addition, the relative sizes and populations of sites are important clues to the degree to which organization is centralized or decentralized in a region.

harvestable varieties with a genotype resulting in a tougher rachis that does not shatter on contact. In other cases, the choice is conscious. It was no accident that wild barley and wheat were the first domesticates in the Near East. Both of these cereal grasses are extremely productive in the wild. In certain fertile areas even today, they grow in natural stands that are nearly as dense as a cultivated field. Undoubtedly, foraging groups deliberately chose these productive plants rather than plants that yielded less for the same amount of work. The high-yield resources were the ones they carried with them to new habitats. Thus humans act as selective agents in both conscious and unconscious ways.

While early cultivators were deliberately concentrating on more productive resources, they were also unconsciously selecting against alternative food sources. As maize and beans became more and more productive, early Mesoamerican cultivators neglected other plants—cactus fruits, for example—that were usually collected at the same time that corn and beans had to be planted or harvested. The result was a change in diet—fewer wild foods and more corn and beans. The extra time and effort spent on these resources meant that the more productive varieties of corn and beans were selected for, and their usefulness increased still further. In this way, the cycle of human selection and dependence on that selection continued. Of course, none of these changes occurred rapidly, and the process of plant domestication was therefore a matter of several millennia. Gradually, over this long period of time, human behavior, both conscious and unconscious, led to certain changes in food resources. The question is, why did people's behavior change?

Adaptive Value of Agriculture

The development of food production involved more than changes in plants and animals. Human populations had to adopt new economic strategies based on domesticated resources. To understand the persistence and growth of this subsistence pattern, we must know what makes it advantageous or adaptive. What is it about the practice of food production that led to its expansion within the populations that took it up, and later induced new populations to adopt it?

It might seem reasonable that food production began because domesticated resources provided a more nutritious or better-balanced diet. Perhaps early food producers had a better chance of survival than groups who relied solely on wild resources. Plausible as the argument sounds, there is no evidence to suggest that early cultivators were any better nourished than their foraging ancestors. Because they relied on a narrower range of products, early agriculturalists may in fact have been *less* healthy than their food-collecting ancestors. Cavities and various other health problems, relatively rare among earlier human populations, appear more frequently after the development of food production. Early cultivation, then, did not necessarily bring an improvement in people's diet and health. It must have proved adaptive in some other way.

Cultivation and herding modify the energy flow in the environment, so that the amount of resources increases relative to the amount of energy expended to obtain them. In both the Near East and Mesoamerica, one sees evidence of gradually increasing yields per acre, as more and more sophisticated, albeit time-consuming, techniques are employed. Deliberate selection of the sites where crops are grown, year after year, could partially overcome variations in yield. Planting in very wet locations, for example, serves as a hedge against a dry year. Planting in a variety of locations insures some crop, whatever the climatic conditions of a growing season. Finally, tending a crop reduces competition from other plants and the ill effects of insect and mammalian pests. The net result of these changes is a larger and more stable food base at a given level of labor input. Thus the group that adopts these practices grows. Later, as these advantages become clear to other groups, they begin to imitate the successful practices.

The Adoption of Agriculture

There was no single pathway leading to the adoption of this subsistence strategy, however. Rather, it was a complex series of events involving long periods of experimentation with various food crops, agricultural technologies, and forms of social organization. The process took place in many diverse localities, beginning for different reasons and following a distinct course in each case. (See Figure 7-2.)

Centers of Local Innovation

In some regions, domestication began locally, essentially independent of any outside developments. These primary centers include the Near East, Mesoamerica, South America, and Southeast Asia and China. Probably in the years ahead we will find evidence of still other primary regions.

The Near East The earliest evidence of cultivation and herding comes from the Near East. Domestication began toward the end of a cool, dry climatic period among people who had learned to extract an unusually varied fare by exploiting resources in a number of closely juxtaposed environmental zones. According to the season, they hunted herd animals—sheep, goats, and deer; collected a wide variety of small animal species—land snails, turtles, fish, crabs, and mussels; and harvested nuts, wild legumes, and cereal grasses.

Late in the hunting and foraging period, two important patterns emerged that ultimately shaped the development of food production in the Near East. First, as foragers traveled from one zone to another in their seasonal wanderings, they began *moving key plant and animal resources* out of their native habitats into new areas, subjecting them to new selective pressures. These early cultivators and herders began to select, both consciously and unconsciously, for characteristics that were more favorable to their own needs and environmental situations. Second, we suspect there was a gradual movement of population from more favorable environmental zones into marginal areas. After 10,000 B.P., population density became greater than ever before within the hilly, fertile regions richest in plant and animal resources, and Flannery (1973) speculates that the overflow spilled into adjacent regions such as the Assyrian steppe, where resources were more limited. In response to the need for additional food, the emigrants began to experiment more intensively with wild cereal grains, deliberately trying to create strands as dense as those that grew wild in the nuclear zones.

Few specimens of carbonized grain have been found from the early stages of domestication, but two developments suggest that various groups were beginning to focus on intensive collection of wild grains. After 12,000 B.P. the storage bins, cooking facilities, and grinding implements that we would ex-

Figure 7-1. In the Near East, early cultivators and herders exploited resources in a number of closely juxtaposed ecological zones. The high plateau is a rocky and for the most part infertile region. But as the snows melt during the summer, a few pockets of grassland appear. These areas probably served early herders as grazing grounds during the months when pastures at lower altitudes had dried up. Rich in mineral deposits, the high plateau was a major source of copper and turquoise for prehistoric peoples. The oak-pistachio woodland belt is the zone richest in plant and animal resources. Dense stands of wild wheat and barley grow there even today. Sometimes referred to as the "hilly flanks" or "nuclear zone," this fertile area probably supported large numbers of preagricultural foragers who ultimately spilled over into adjacent regions. The Assyrian steppe, hot and dry during the summer, is transformed by winter rains into a natural grassland area. Sections too salty for effective agriculture are still used for winter grazing. Other parts of the steppe—the fertile flood plains of the area's larger rivers—are well suited to certain cereal crops. Wheat and barley have been harvested in this region probably since 9000 B.P. The lowland alluvium or piedmont is an extremely arid region that supported few wild plant or animal resources. Food production did not come to this area until relatively late—after the development of irrigation made cultivation possible. (After K. V. Flannery, 1965)

The Emergence of Food Production

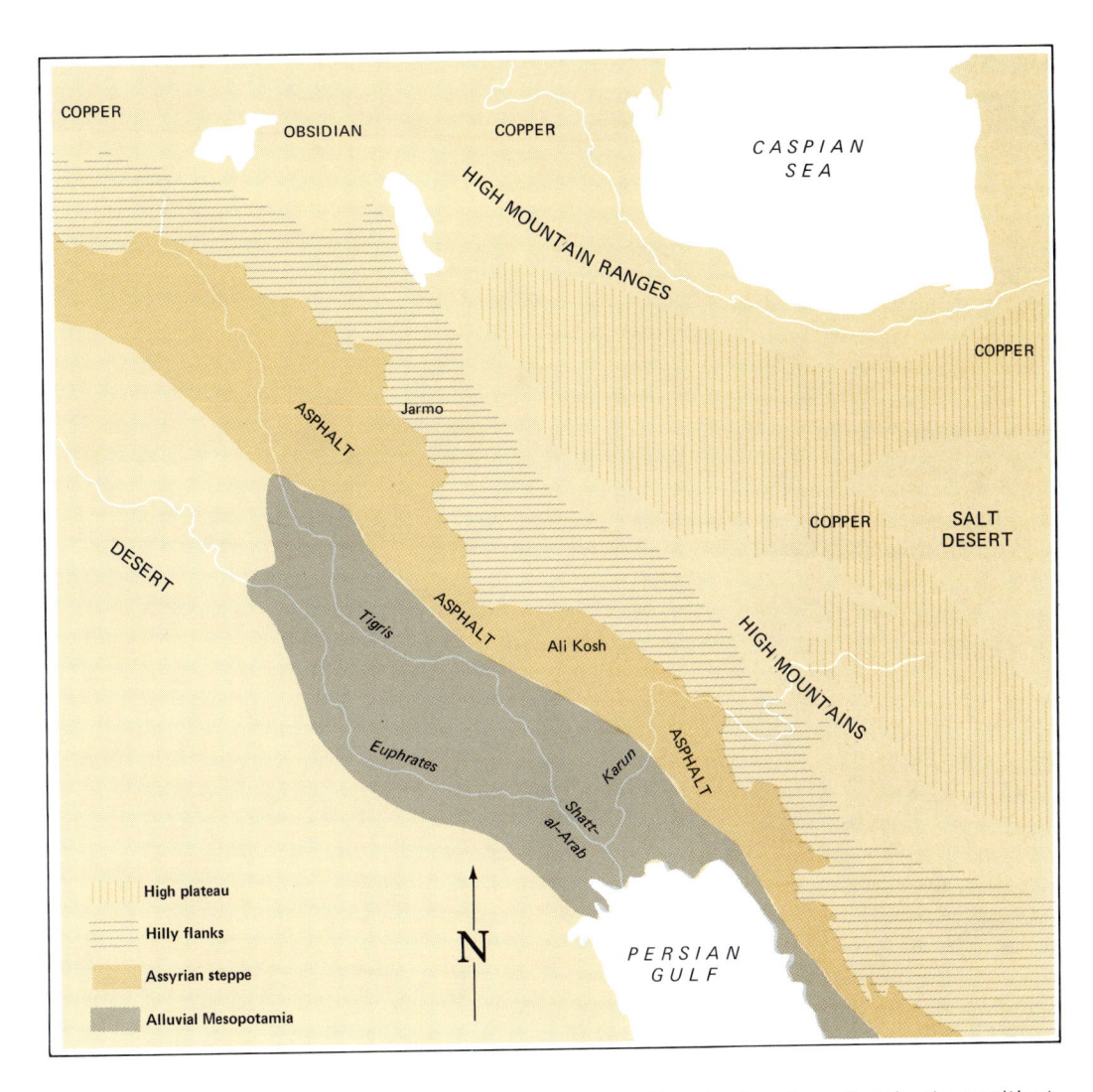

pect to find associated with heavy reliance on wild cereals began to increase rapidly. About this same time there was a shift to more permanent settlements. Some groups developed an organizational base that was more appropriate to harvesting and storing large quantities of wild cereals. Among other groups, social arrangements seem to have been adapted to more intensive herding practices (Redman, 1975).

Between 10,000 and 7,500 B.P. experimentation with domesticates became widespread throughout the Near East. Many groups began to practice dry farming—that is, they cultivated emmer wheat and barley without irrigation. Some also began to herd sheep and goats. In 9,000 B.P. the residents of Ali Kosh, a village in the Assyrian steppe, were intensively collecting wild alfalfa and tiny-seed wild legumes. And goat herders, wandering over the arid piedmont, were harvesting emmer wheat during the late winter and early spring (Hole, Flannery, and Neely, 1969). Previously archeologists had assumed that intensive plant collecting was practiced only in favorable environmental zones such as the hilly woodland

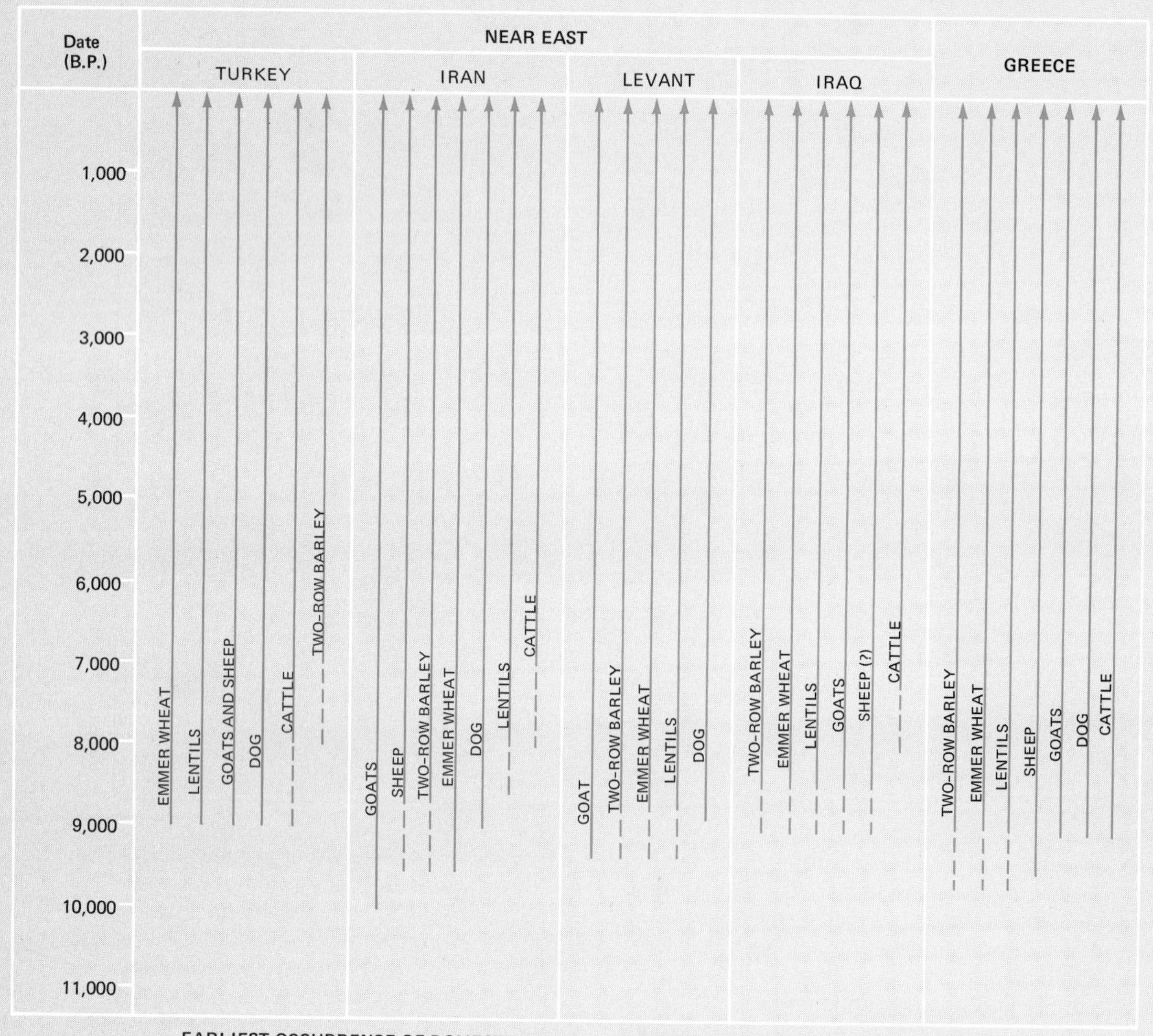

Figure 7-2. EARLIEST OCCURRENCE OF DOMESTICATES AT ARCHEOLOGICAL SITES: THE OLD WORLD

EARLIEST OCCURRENCE OF DOMESTICATES AT
ARCHEOLOGICAL SITES: THE NEW WORLD

areas. But the Ali Kosh data suggest that the practice may have been common throughout all regions. Collectors from the arid lowland and the steppe regions could easily have harvested one crop of local plants during the spring and then moved north to higher areas where these plants became ripe in June and July. In this more mountainous region they probably collected wild cereals as well, carrying their harvest back to their home bases, and perhaps casually planting a few of the seeds. Between 8,500 and 8,000 B.P. the people of Ali Kosh were apparently cultivating wheat and barley more purposefully, clearing the land to plant cereal grains close to swamp margins. At the same time, they were also herding goats and sheep. As they continued to experiment, their economy became more specialized. After 8,000 B.P. there is a sharp decline in deposits of wheat and barley and an increase in the number of bones of domestic goats and sheep, suggesting that during this time Ali Kosh became primarily a herding village that relied on nearby farming villages for grain. (See Figure 7-1.)

Throughout the era of dry farming there is evidence of experimentation and general economic transition. Permanent villages became much more widespread, but temporary settlements were still common. At 8,000 B.P. the woodland valley area included sites that contrasted sharply. Jarmo, for example, was a village of about twenty-five permanent mud-walled houses with courtyards, storage pits, and ovens. Seeds of barley and emmer wheat found together with sickle blades and grindstones indicate the beginnings of cultivation and a fully sedentary lifestyle. In contrast, Tepe Sarab, a site of the same age at a slightly higher altitude, has no houses, grain, or grindstones. However, bones of domesticated goats and sheep have been found, and their ages suggest that the settlement was occupied in later winter or early spring. Possibly it served as a seasonal camp for herders who obtained their grain from farming villages such as Jarmo. Animal and grain deposits throughout the Near East continued to show a mixture of domesticated and wild characteristics, but the focus was clearly shifting toward food production. There were few areas without farming communities by this time.

By 7,500 B.P. a fairly intensive agricultural economy had developed throughout the Near East, fostered by an extensive network of regional interchange. More domesticates were added to the basic complex of wheat and barley, goats and sheep. New strains were developed—bread wheat and six-row barley—and the diet was supplemented by peas and lentils, domesticated cattle and pigs. In some regions, simple forms of soil and water control came into use. As technology became more sophisticated and the population grew, more and more people entered the arid lowland delta. With the development of irrigation around 7,000 B.P., crop productivity increased and larger numbers of people became concentrated on smaller areas of land. It was in this irrigated lowland area that urban life and state societies eventually emerged.

China and Southeast Asia China and Southeast Asia were among the first regions of the world to develop agriculture. Oddly enough, the first plants to be domesticated did not include rice, the crop that today provides the economic staple for millions of Asians. In China, the first domesticate was millet, a tall, coarse cereal grass that is still grown in North China, where it evolved. Bushels of foxtail millet seeds stored in pits, weeding knives, hoes, and spades have been unearthed at sites dating back to 6,000 B.P. In addition, dogs and pigs, and possibly cattle, goats, and sheep were domesticated (Chang, 1970). Some of these sites were rather large villages that covered several acres and included wattle and daub dwellings constructed partially underground with roofs supported by wooden pillars.

The origin of rice is still the biggest mystery in the development of Far Eastern agriculture. Domesticated varieties with a tough rachis and a large grain size date back to 5,000 B.P. in southern China and the Indus River valley. Archeologist K. C. Chang (1970) speculates that rice was first cultivated in Southeast Asia, where it originally grew as a weed in yam and taro gardens.

Mesoamerica At first glance, the differences between Old World and New World food production are striking. For one thing, in the New World, cultivation appeared at least 1,000 years later than in the Near East; and sedentary life, far from preceding the development of agriculture, was a relatively late development. In addition, New World food-producing economies were based on totally different resources. In Mesoamerica, few animals besides the dog and possibly the turkey were domesticated. Consequently, Mesoamerican farmers never practiced herding. Instead of wheat and barley, the agricultural base rested on corn, beans, squash, avocados, and a few other plants indigenous to the Americas. Starting from different resource bases, the two areas later developed different technologies. Wheat agriculture requires sickles for harvesting and threshing equipment as well. Corn, on the other hand, is picked and shelled by hand.

Despite these contrasts, the two areas share some basic similarities in their domestication processes. As in the Near East (with the exception of Israel), agriculture developed in several localities among seminomadic bands who moved seasonally from one resource area to another. Like the Near Easterners, Mesoamerican food collectors faced the problem of how to augment and stabilize their food supplies. Although we know very little about the details of early experiments with domestication, early cultivation in both areas probably began simply as an attempt to broaden the area in which useful plants grow. In contrast to the Near East, however, the pressure that triggered the initial stages of experimentation in Mexico did not come from population. In fact, prior to cultivation, population densities were quite low. Rather, domestication may have been more exclusively an effort to "even out" the extreme contrasts that occur in wild food supplies during wet and dry years. By enlarging the range of certain hardy and reliable weedy grasses, early cultivators may have been providing themselves with an extra margin of security (Flannery, 1973).

Between 10,000 and 7,000 years ago, populations living in the southern and central highlands of Mexico were exploiting literally hundreds of plant species and hunting small animals such as rabbit, deer, skunk, opossum, and ground squirrel. But the resources that were most heavily utilized were the century plant (maguey), various cactus fruits, tree legumes, white-tailed deer, cottontail rabbits, and a few wild grasses, including wild maize. The range of these focal resources crosscut several environments, and like all other foragers, Mesoamerican foragers were therefore not adapted to one particular environment. Instead, their adaptation was to a few plant and animal genera with a broad geographical range.

Some of these major resources were collected year-round, whereas others were available seasonally. In many instances, several resources were available at the same time, so that collectors had to decide which resources to exploit during a particular season, and how to exploit them. During the summer rainy season, great quantities of plants were available, and families often came together in large groups, or macrobands, to take advantage of this bounty. An intensive effort was needed to harvest the plants before they were eaten by birds and small animals or reduced to mush by the summer rains. During the dry season, however, edible resources were scarce and the group was fragmented and scattered. Under this economic system, a balance was maintained between human populations and wild resources. Why, then, did this highly efficient pattern change?

Beginning at about 7,000 B.P., plant foods became increasingly important at the expense of hunting. The diet had expanded to include squash, chiles, and avocados, foods that were later domesticated. Mortars, pestles, manos, and metates were used more intensively, and Flannery suggests that at this point, populations may have begun to take certain annual grasses out of their natural habitat. Under the selective pressures of cultivation, one of these grasses, wild maize, underwent many favorable genetic changes. As maize became more productive, the stable food-procurement system was upset. More and more time was spent planting and harvesting maize at the expense of collecting alternative resources. At this time, beans also changed in response to selective pressures, developing a limper pod and more permeable covering. They became increasingly important in the diet and provided an essential protein supplement to maize.

The transition to maize and bean cultivation was very gradual. By 7,000 B.P. populations in the Tehuacan Valley had begun to cultivate a variety of plants—maize, beans, squashes, amaranths, and chiles. But the corncobs found in the Coxcatlán rock shelter at Tehuacan were small and showed many wild characteristics. The Coxcatlán people were still basically foragers. Only about 10 percent of their diet was based on domesticates. By 5,000 B.P. maize had become fully domesticated. The corncobs found at Tehuacan during this period were much larger, and domesticates made up about 30 percent of the food supplies. Tehuacan was not the only center of domestication, however. In other areas of Mexico, people were experimenting with pumpkins, sunflowers, beans, and maize.

Sometime between 4,000 and 3,500 years ago, maize cultivation crossed a critical threshold: the productivity of corn became sufficient to make it worthwhile to clear away other plant resources in order to plant corn over large areas of the main river flood plains. Along with maize, the early agriculturalists also began planting beans and squash, sources of plant protein missing in maize. Together with avocados, a source of fats and oils, these domesticated resources provided a fully balanced diet.

Over the next few centuries, the highland populations became completely dependent on agriculture and full sedentism. MacNeish (1964) has found a larger number of macroband settlements on river terraces; some of these may have been occupied year-round. Agricultural production not only made sedentary village life *possible,* it may have made it *essential.* Increased planting and harvesting activities probably require macrobands to stay together for a longer period of each year (Flannery, 1968). By 3,000 B.P. permanent villages of wattle and daub houses were widespread on main river flood plains. Pottery came into use, and by 2,400 B.P. communal shrines and ceremonial centers were being built.

South America While food production was developing in Mexico, Peruvian populations 1,500 miles (2,500 km) to the south were experimenting independently with domestication. Groups in the Andean highlands were cultivating several varieties of beans by 7,500 B.P., well before the earliest beans appeared in Mesoamerica. But we know little about the nature of early plant cultivation in the Andes because the archeological record is so poorly preserved. Maize cultivation in particular remains a mystery. Was it domesticated locally or introduced from Mexico? Although the highlands lie within the natural habitat of ancestral corn, the earliest maize cobs in Peru date from 5,000 to 4,500 B.P., about 2,000 years after comparable specimens appeared in Mesoamerica. The Peruvian cobs belong to a race of corn that is closely related to a variety found in southern Mexico, suggesting that corn was in fact diffused from that region. Whatever the case, the new crop spread rapidly to the desert coast of Peru and to other parts of South America. During this period, other exchanges were taking place between the Amazon Basin and the tropical eastern slopes of the Andes, and the coastal area to the west of the Andes. Guava, manioc, peanuts, and lima beans were moved west and became firmly established on the coast.

We do not know why agriculture began in Peru. No significant increase in population occurred until 3,000 B.P. on the coast—much too late to have provided the initial stimulus for cultivation. Moreover, after domestication had begun, agriculture remained a secondary activity for a long period of time. On the coast, people continued to rely heavily on rich seafood resources, and followed a seasonal foraging pattern (Lanning, 1967). Agriculture did not begin to play a major role until at least 3,800 B.P., when more permanent settlements and ceremonial centers began to appear.

Diffusion: Northern Europe and the American Southwest

In the past, archeologists often assumed that once subsistence strategies based on domestication were developed, the new economies always proved successful and hence spread quickly to all corners of the earth. We now know that the spread of agriculture was not such a simple process and that diffusion, local innovation, and retention of old subsistence strategies often coexisted. Northern Europe and the southwestern United States are cases in point.

Europe After 9,000 B.P. we find evidence of all three situations in southeastern Europe. Domestication of pigs and cattle probably occurred earlier here than in the Near East, suggesting that these species were domesticated locally and independently. On the other hand, cereal cultivation was already fairly well established in the Near East at this point and had probably spread to Europe. While some populations in Greece and the Balkans were farming, making pottery, and building permanent houses from timber, and wattle and daub, others were maintaining a flourishing hunting culture. Based on rich river and forest resources, they were able to establish stable settlements that lasted many centuries.

By 7,000 B.P. food production had advanced up the Danube into the Hungarian plains. In addition to barley and wheat, the Danubians cultivated a number of crops, including flax, peas, beans, and lentils. They practiced a simple form of shifting agriculture that quickly exhausted the soil and forced them to resettle often. After they reached northwestern Europe, population growth forced some groups into areas with less fertile soils. Under these conditions, some cultivators began to experiment with new cereal crops, developing hybrid varieties of oats and rye better adapted to marginal conditions and the colder, damper northern climate (Butzer, 1971). Others, however, unable to grow sufficient food under these conditions, became more dependent on hunting and gathering.

The American Southwest The food-producing economies that developed in the American Southwest were based primarily on three plant domesticates: corn, beans, and squash — the same resources basic to Mesoamerican agriculture. Agriculture became important only after a long period of local experimentation involving the development of new hybrid varieties of corn, beans, and squash, and changes in population, technology, and social organization.

Corn was the first cultigen to reach the Southwest. The earliest traces of corn pollen appear at Bat Cave in central New Mexico and are between 4,000 and 5,000 years old. These early sites were simply seasonal camps where foragers may have sown seeds in the spring, returning to harvest the plants the following fall. There is no evidence that these crops were tended or that corn was an important part of the diet, and no cultivation technology had developed as yet.

By about 1,900 B.P. the amount and variety of domesticate resources had increased, and populations began to develop agricultural technologies. Cultivated beans and squash were added to the diet, and by 1,300 B.P. corn had spread widely throughout the Southwest. Although many groups had begun to rely more heavily on farming, agricultural products had not yet become the primary resources. Experimentation and a flexible economy involving both agriculture and foraging were the order of the day.

At the same time, some groups were settling down in more permanent villages composed of several dozen pit houses, dwellings that were dug into the ground and covered with a dome of timber and mud. More abundant resources and sedentism led to population growth and larger villages. However, the semiagricultural pit-house dwellers apparently were unable to develop the organizational structures necessary to maintain harmony and economic efficiency in a large community. Consequently, the large villages were abandoned. After 1,300 B.P. people began to live in smaller settlements, and for a time hunting and gathering were reemphasized. It was in the context of these smaller, dispersed villages that cultivation finally began to take hold.

Another transitional period began about 1,200 B.P. New varieties of corn, beans, and squash appeared. Some of these hybrid strains were apparently hardier and better adapted to conditions in marginal areas. Some strains also became more productive, developing a larger cob with more kernel rows. A new resource, cotton, became an important cultigen. Changes in technology and social organization, as well as direct evidence that domesticates were being used, indicate that agriculture played a basic part in the lives of the peoples of the Southwest. Larger villages were once again constructed where residents lived more sedentary lives, remaining close to their fields for most of the year. Grinding implements became more efficient, and pottery more abundant. At some sites we find substantial storage facilities associated with ceremonial structures, suggesting the development of some sort of communal or regional redistribution system. Gradually, as southwestern farmers became skilled in using limited water resources, they developed new planting techniques and soil and water control devices carefully adapted to desert conditions. Although farming patterns were modified somewhat over the centuries as population grew, and southwestern material culture and ceremonial life have since become more elaborate, many aspects of the early farming culture have continued relatively unchanged to modern times.

The Adoption Process

Northern Europe and the American Southwest provide clear examples of the important part that diffusion played in the adoption process. Extensive trade networks and casual exchanges contributed to the spread of agriculture in many areas. In Mexico, the Near East, and the Central Andes, the close juxtaposition of varied environmental zones encouraged exchange of products, and large-scale trade networks developed. Minerals and other exotic raw materials were traded by widely dispersed populations. Other resources such as seeds and animals were doubtless exchanged as well, along with the knowledge of new subsistence strategies. In the New World, cultivation probably spread via the trade network that linked Mexico to the American Southwest. In the Old World, extensive trade links among Mediterranean peoples enabled agriculture to diffuse rapidly from the Near East to southern Europe.

Diffusion, then, is one way to introduce a new resource, idea, or practice to a people, but it does not insure that any one of these will be adopted. For example, domestication may not prove particularly useful to a group living in an environment where wild food resources are more productive than cultigens, or in an environment unsuited to cultivating a particular domesticate. A certain plant may also fail to meet dietary requirements. Corn, for instance, is low in lysine, an essential amino acid and a building block of protein; consequently, it did not become a major staple until after beans, a rich source of lysine, and alkali-cooking technology, which enhanced the amount of protein available for digestion, were also present to fill the deficiency. Finally, social organization or technology may be unsuited to domestication. Where irrigation or terracing are needed to make the land usable, cultivation is impossible unless the population is sedentary and organized enough to coordinate a complex system of economic activity. Where agriculture *was* adopted, its adaptive value was the product of particular factors in the environment, technology, and social organization of the group in question, as well as the genetic nature and nutritional value of their domesticates.

In the final analysis, however, the transition

to food production in most areas probably began in response to an imbalance between population and resources — more people than the local food supply could support, or too few people to maintain a viable hunting and gathering economy. As a rule, hunting and gathering societies maintain themselves in equilibrium with their environment. They regulate the size of their population by infanticide, postpartum taboos, or forced or voluntary migration, keeping it below the point where they would begin to deplete their food supply. Most contemporary hunter-gatherers exploit a variety of local plants and animals and are able to adjust their habits according to the resources that are available and plentiful. Flannery (1973) and Binford (1968) suggest that an influx of colonists from some optimal areas of the Near East into more marginal areas may have disrupted the normal ecological balance in the less productive zones already inhabited by other seminomadic groups. In this "tension zone," population excess pressured food collectors to develop more effective means of food production. Experimentation with new subsistence strategies created a marked rise in the productivity of resources. The more food there is available, the more people can be supported. Thus, in the Near East, population levels rose after early cultivators had developed more productive strains of barley and wheat. In Mesoamerica, there was also a rise in population density after 7,000 B.P., shortly after maize had become more productive. In turn, the more people there are, the greater the need for more productive resources, a need that more intensive food production filled. It has been estimated that in southwestern Iran, for example, the number of people supported by the land increased 60-fold, "going from 0–1 persons per square kilometer in the late Paleolithic, to 1–2 persons per square kilometer under conditions of early dry farming, and up to 6 or more persons per square kilometer after irrigation appears in the archeological record" (Flannery, 1973:75).

The sedentary lifestyle that appeared at the end of the Pleistocene and during the early post-Pleistocene epoch may have contributed to this trend. First, it may have raised population levels. Spontaneous abortions, stillbirths, and infant mortality are generally somewhat higher among hunters and gatherers, and the problems of transporting infants discourage having many children. Where life is more settled, conditions are easier for infants and pregnant mothers, and more people survive. Archeological remains in both the New World and the Old World indicate that increased sedentism is associated with marked population growth (Binford, 1968).

Where sedentism preceded agriculture, as in the Near East, parts of Europe, and the American Southwest, the problems of managing a sedentary community may have created a need for new subsistence strategies. Once villages with permanent dwellings, storage facilities, wells, fish weirs, and similar fixed facilities have been built, and hereditary ownership has been established over a resource area, the residents must find some intensive strategy for obtaining resources without having to abandon their homes. If the population is of sufficient size, economic specialization is possible — some villagers might assume the foraging responsibilities, traveling to areas where needed resources are available, while other residents remain working at home. In this case, agriculture might be adopted as one means of producing more resources within a limited area.

Agricultural Technologies

As food production emerged and sedentism increased, new technological items were adopted to aid in managing this new subsistence strategy. Ground stone axes with a stronger working edge for clearing fields, sickles for harvesting grain, grinding implements for processing grain, and containers (or even buildings) for stockpiling surpluses were necessary. A few preagricultural societies made clay vessels, but the real development of pottery went hand in hand with the development of agriculture. Like the skin and gut pouches, the wooden containers, and the baskets of

Following the development of food production, clay containers became an important household asset. Because they kept out water and insects, they were more efficient than skin bags or baskets for the storage of agricultural surplus. In addition, the pottery made excellent cooking vessels; meat and vegetables could be boiled in them, a process that not only releases nutrients but also makes food more palatable. The vessels shown here are typical examples of this early handmade (as opposed to wheel-thrown) pottery. (American Museum of Natural History)

hunter-gatherers, pottery was portable. But it was more durable than the other items and kept food more secure from pests. Equally important, it could be used for cooking. Since boiling releases important nutrients in some foods and makes many vegetable products more edible, clay pots were an important adjunct to agricultural production. Metal, a more malleable raw material that can be used to mass-produce objects in a way that stone could not, was more and more frequently used.

The key change, however, was in the efforts of early agriculturalists to employ soil and water control devices. Just as they manipulated the plants and animals, so they also began manipulating the land and water supplies. In the beginning, farmers probably relied solely on rainfall, but in time more productive techniques were developed. Floodwater farming was one of the first. It involved planting crops where they would be watered by surface runoff—along the course of shallow rivers, in outwash fans, or in seasonally flooded bottom lands. Eventually farmers in both the Old and New Worlds developed elaborate water control methods, such as irrigation and terracing. Since they require a large investment of human labor, these innovations probably arose out of necessity, in response to scarcity. In the Near East, for instance, irrigation did not originate in fertile upland areas, where early dry farming produced high yields, but in the dry lowland steppe at a time when population was increasing and possibly straining food supplies (Flannery, 1969).

Many of these technologies are still practiced today. In some cases, they have substantially increased overall crop yields by simply increasing the area of cultivable land or by making it possible to use the land more intensively. Sometimes they have raised the productivity of the plants themselves. We have evidence from Turkey that the seeds of irrigated flax became perceptibly larger than the seeds of plants that were cultivated under dry farming (Flannery, 1969).

The increase in productivity is only the

most direct effect of this new technology, however. As we shall see in the following chapter, large-scale irrigation generated a variety of problems that led to more complex social institutions.

Trends in Sociocultural Organization

For the first two million years of human existence, people lived in temporary seasonal camps and apparently built no permanent settlements at all. Upper Paleolithic hunters in Europe may have taken the first steps toward a fully sedentary life, but it was several more millennia before settled communities became widespread—not until 10,000 B.P. in the Near East, about 6,000 B.P. in China and Europe, 4,500 B.P. in the Andes, and 3,500 B.P. in Mexico and the American Southwest. Such sedentary and food-producing communities faced a variety of problems that earlier groups had not had to deal with: defense of permanent homes and fields, allocation of agricultural land among different families, the scheduling of a complex array of activities involved in planting and tending crops, and the numerous problems in human interaction that must have arisen when people were living in *larger* groups with the *same* people throughout the year. In this context, band organization was replaced by a kind of organization that we refer to as the *tribe*. Like bands, tribes are egalitarian and leadership is informal. But the family, rather than the whole band, is the basic producing group, and its activities are coordinated with those of other families through associations defined on the basis of kinship, age, religion, and other criteria that unite people from a number of communities. Often membership in such associations is crosscutting: two individuals may be members of the same kin group (clan) but may belong to different military groups. Although leadership in the tribe is informal and often specific to particular activities, the leadership role here is more formally and strictly defined than it is in a band.

The ancient technique of pot irrigation is still used in many parts of the world today. In this Indian village, wells are located along the edges of the fields. Water drawn from them is dumped down shallow ditches that cut across the fields, watering the crops beside them. (Raghubir Singh/Woodfin Camp)

Compound Villages

A number of these characteristics are reflected in changes in Mesopotamian and Mesoamerican villages (Flannery, 1972). The first sedentary communities in the Near East were compounds or homesteads of small circular houses. These dwellings had stone foundations and room for only a few individuals. Central storage areas were probably used by the whole community. Between 11,000 and 8,500 B.P. villages of this type were widespread throughout the Near East. They reflected a social organization that was probably much like that of early Near Eastern foraging groups; that is, the organization of the villages was based on a sexual division of labor and communal sharing rather than on the nuclear family. The houses were built not for a husband and wife and their children, but for individuals; resources were the property of the whole community. There is evidence of social stratification, a few signs that some individuals were wealthier than others. Nothing comparable to the compound villages has been found in Mexico. During the early stages of domestication, Mesoamerican populations were still mobile. They probably occupied a variety of sites—temporary camps for planting, hunting, and gathering.

Villages of Rectangular Houses

Once agriculture became firmly established, a new settlement pattern became widespread in both areas: a community of rectangular houses built to accommodate nuclear families. Private courtyards or patios were walled off from neighboring houses. Variations in raw materials, luxury goods, and storage facilities from one household to another indicate that these villages were socially stratified. The settlement pattern reflects a form of social organization based on the individual household rather than an extended communal work group. This pattern has always been present among Mesoamerican populations, but it represented something new in the Near East. The transition occurred sometime between 9,000 and 7,500 B.P. But what caused it?

The new villages had several advantages over the old compound homestead. For one thing, they were larger and more compact and therefore more easily defended. Perhaps more important, social organization (as reflected in the architectural arrangements) was stronger. Stratification and political leadership enabled the village to grow. Unstratified compound settlements, lacking these organizational devices, were unable to coordinate activities and keep the peace once the community had grown beyond a limited size. Moreover, where the individual household is the basic economic unit and there is opportunity for personal gain, production generally intensifies. In the communal compound, on the other hand, there is no reward for intensive labor, and underproduction is the rule (Flannery, 1972). The chiefdoms and state societies that subsequently developed in the Near East and Mesoamerica were based on more concentrated populations, more intensive food production, and social stratification arising from inequalities in wealth and prestige. These developments were effectively promoted by the large, well-organized village societies that emerged late in this stage.

Trade

Much of this organizational change reflects the new problems resulting from a sedentary form of existence. During this period, trade networks also became increasingly important in bringing distant resources to now sedentary groups. One of the more elaborate trade networks we know of was developed by people of the Middle Woodland traditions (see Chapter 6) between 2,100 and 1,500 years ago. Archeologists Stuart Struever and Gail Houart (1972), who have excavated these Indian sites, call the network that stretched from New York to Kansas and from Michigan to Florida, the Hopewell Interaction Sphere. (See Figure 7–3.) Through this network circulated raw materials such as obsidian from the Rockies, copper from Lake Superior, stone from the lower Allegheny Mountains, and sea shells from the Gulf and south Atlantic coasts, as well as items manufactured from these materials, such as pipes, ear spools, and copper cutout figures. Exchanged among groups with distinctive regional variations in subsistence items, they served to unify different cultural traditions.

The name Hopewell comes from a site in south-central Ohio, one of about 12 large sites located 40 to 180 miles (64 to 288 km) apart on major rivers in the Midwest. Of these, Hopewell is the largest. It has the greatest number of mounds, unique kinds of burial constructions, and the widest variety of artifacts and raw materials. Hopewell was probably the

Figure 7–3. A wide variety of raw materials circulated within the Hopewell Interaction Sphere. This extensive trade network enabled sedentary peoples to obtain needed minerals and materials from places thousands of miles distant. By mapping the source areas and sites where raw materials have been found, archeologists have reconstructed the dimensions of this exchange system. (After S. Struever and G. Houart, 1972)

major receiving, manufacturing, and transaction center for the Ohio region, and perhaps beyond. Artisans and other specialists would have worked in this center. Since someone had to oversee the manufacturing and exchange processes, there is a good chance that some central coordinating authority was located here.

Increasing Stratification

Archeologists often use analyses of burial populations for studies of stratification, since the way in which people are buried closely reflects their status in life. When high-status groups exist in a community, they usually receive preferential treatment at burial. Archeologist Christopher Peebles (1971) has examined burial populations in the southeastern United States dating to around 1,000 B.P.

He discovered that signs of status were similar over a wide area, and that settlements were connected through an economic and political hierarchy in which the residents of larger sites dominated those of the smaller villages. These groups were also involved in a large trade network.

An increased tendency to accord certain individuals and groups of individuals preferential burial treatment is a characteristic limited primarily to later village farming communities. In this sense, we must regard egalitarian tribal organization, even though it still exists in some areas today, as a temporary and unstable form of organization. In the southwestern United States and northern Europe, in the Near East and Mesoamerica, tribal society was quickly replaced by new forms of organization based on the principle of stratification. In the next chapter, we turn our attention to the evolution of these new forms of social organization.

summary

A reliance on food raised on farms using a variety of technological aids in order to obtain the highest yields possible may seem eminently logical to us. But why would humans who for millions of years had flourished by food collection have abandoned such an enduring way of life for one based on food production? The domestication process was a complex series of events involving experimentation with various food crops, agricultural technologies, and forms of social organization.

First of all, there were changes in plants and animals themselves and in the ways humans treated these food sources. These two processes interacted to transform wild varieties into domesticates. As certain varieties proved more productive, humans relied more on them; this human intervention in turn exerted new selective pressures that nurtured variants more adapted to human needs. Most of the foods we know today have very different properties than their uncultivated ancestors.

Reliance on domesticates did not result from their greater nutritive value. If anything, poorer nutrition ensued with food production. But domestication resulted in a larger and more stable food base at a given level of output. In the Near East, for example, experimentation with food production probably began in the marginal areas, where populations could not depend on wild sources for survival. In Mesoamerica, food production began as a way of "evening out" the differences between wet and dry years.

Merely noting the lines of diffusion, however, does little to explain why this adoption took place. Many societies have known of domesticates and not assimilated them. Whether by local experimentation or by diffusion, the domestication process begins with an imbalance between population and resources that induces a search for more productive subsistence strategies. Food production provides this strategy. Because more people may then be sustained, population grows, leading to even greater reliance on food production. The process may be reinforced by sedentism, either because sedentary life contributes to marked population growth or because permanent settlements prompt people to find ways of increasing resources within a limited area.

Food production greatly accelerated developments that had already begun to occur among foraging populations and laid the basis for radically new developments in material culture and social life. Food producers began to make intensive use of tools and facilities that had been less important in the past—mortars, manos, and metates for grinding grain, storage pits or bins for banking harvest surpluses. They also developed entirely new productive techniques—tillage, irrigation, terracing, and other technologies for controlling soils and water.

Similar types of village organization proved adaptive to advanced agricultural societies in the Near East and Mesoamerica. Rectangular villages in the Near East evolved out of earlier preagricultural compound villages with communal social organization. In Mesoamerica, no such precursors are found, and agriculture developed for centuries without any permanent villages. But once agriculture became well established, both societies adopted the community of rectangular houses to accommodate nuclear families. These villages had rudimentary stratification systems, which promoted better coordination of activities and provided incentives for greater production.

Stratification can be seen in settlement patterns, in differential distribution of goods within a settlement, and especially in burial sites, where some corpses received preferential treatment. Often the signs of status were items obtained in trade over long distances. The Hopewell Interaction Sphere was one such network of trade and power relationships. It was hierarchically organized, with regional and local distribution centers forming focal points and status items unifying otherwise distinct cultural groups. This reflects a growing complexity in social organization that culminated in the creation of the state during the next stage of cultural evolution.

suggested readings

BRAIDWOOD, R. J., AND WILLEY, G. R.
    1962   *Courses Toward Urban Life*. Chicago: Aldine. Contains articles describing the developments leading to the emergence of food production in many areas of the world.

HEISER, C. B.
    1973   *Seed to Civilization*. San Francisco: W. H. Freeman. A discussion of the most important plant and animal domesticates and their origins.

STRUEVER, S., ED.
    1971   *Prehistoric Agriculture*. Garden City, N.Y.: Natural History Press. An anthology of the most important theories that archeologists have developed to account for the emergence of food production.

UCKO, P. J., AND DIMBLEBY, G. W., ED.
    1971   *The Domestication and Exploitation of Plants and Animals*. Chicago: Aldine. A collection of theoretical and substantive articles describing recent developments in the study of food production.

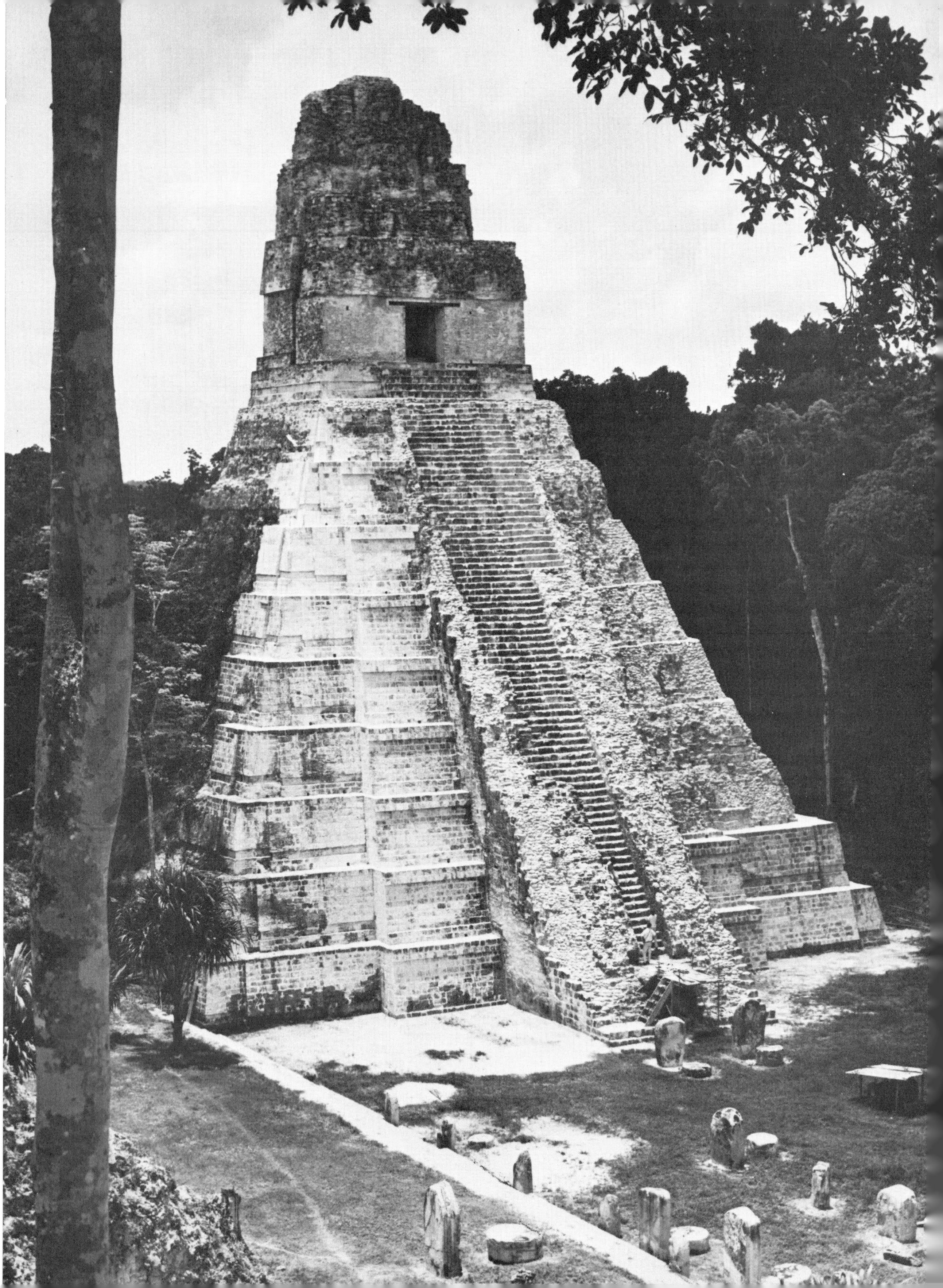

eight
The Emergence of the State and Urban Society

In many societies, people continued to live in small farming communities well into the nineteenth and twentieth centuries. In some areas, however, agricultural economies became more productive, diversified, and intensive. Within 2,000 to 3,000 years after the beginning of full-scale domestication in these societies, there was a remarkably swift transition to an entirely new kind of settlement pattern—the city—accompanied in many cases by an entirely new form of sociopolitical organization—the state. This change has been described as the second great revolution in human culture.

For many of these more complex societies, we no longer have to rely solely on imaginative reconstruction of the way of life from the debris of long-abandoned sites; ancient people begin to speak to us directly through written records. With these early documents, the prehistoric stage ends and history begins. (See the box on p. 158 for a discussion of the methods archeologists use to reconstruct prehistoric social organizations.)

Writing and notation are only signs of the more profound changes in society at this stage. Writing began as a device for managing the more complex organization of life that developed out of the simple villages of the early farmers. This complexity and its management are the essential feature of the comprehensive changes in this stage.

Civilization, City, and State

The development of complex societies has generally been associated with the appearance of civilization, urbanism, and the state. The terms have sometimes been used interchangeably; in fact, the word *civilization* comes from the Latin *civis,* meaning "citizen." Although the changes identified with each of the concepts do not always go hand in hand, each concept points to important changes that were occurring in many areas of the world between 5,000 and about 500 B.P.

Civilization

To most of us, civilization implies cultural refinement, the arts, and polite society. After a week in the woods, we might be inclined to equate civilization with television, hot showers, and all the moden conveniences made possible by advanced technology. But these rather vague notions apply to our own society and are not particularly helpful in identifying the fundamental dimensions and development of ancient civilizations. In one of the best-known attempts to define the concept, V. Gordon Childe (1952) has enumerated ten technological, social, and cultural criteria of civilization:

1. large population and settlement size (urbanism).
2. the accumulation of surplus capital as a result of intensive land use, increased productivity, and taxation; and the existence of some central authority to administer the capital.
3. public works and buildings on a monumental scale.
4. writing.

In the earliest states religion and "government" were one and the same, and the priest-officials lived in large ceremonial centers. The Mayan community of Tikal was one of the earliest and largest ceremonial centers in Mesoamerica. Numerous monumental religious structures, such as Temple I shown here, are the hallmark of these kinds of states. (George Holton/Photo Researchers)

5. the appearance of exact predictive sciences such as astronomy and mathematics.
6. proliferation of specialized nonagricultural occupations—craftsmen, merchants, priests, public officials, and so on.
7. division of society into different classes.
8. political organization based on social class and territorial residence rather than on kinship affiliation (the state).
9. long-distance trade networks involving the exchange of subsistence and luxury goods and services.
10. naturalistic or representational art reflecting sophisticated conceptualization and technique.

Thus, Childe's definition of civilization includes both urbanism and state organization, but also a great many more characteristics.

Although Childe's definition is very detailed, it presents several problems. Robert Adams (1966) has pointed out that, by giving all the variables of his definition equal weight, Childe fails to separate the more important attributes from the secondary ones, and the causes from the effects of civilization. Writing, art, and science, for example, are secondary features that may or may not follow more basic social and political transformations. The Inca, for one, developed a far-flung, stratified, and politically organized state society without ever developing a system of writing. Thus Childe's definition is weakened by its very comprehensiveness.

Despite such criticisms, however, archeologists have increasingly agreed that the emergence of a new form of settlement—the city—and a new form of organization—the state—are most critical.

Urbanism

Cities, to be sure, are larger than villages. But at what point does a town become a city? And is size the only difference? Archeologists William Sanders and Barbara Price (1968) have defined an urban area as a community with a large population concentrated in a compact area and characterized by a high level of social differentiation based on wealth, power, and economic specialization. After studying numerous ancient Mesoamerican sites, they found that all settlements with population densities of 5,000 persons or more per square mile had a high degree of social stratification. Thus their definition contains a density characteristic (5,000 people per square mile) and an organizational characteristic (class-stratified society). It also contains the implicit argument that once a settlement reaches a particular size, new organizational forms are needed to manage the affairs of its inhabitants, giving rise to the state.

The State

The emergence of the state marked a major change from earlier types of social organization.

However, as food-producing techniques became more efficient, a few societies reached a level of economic productivity and population density that encouraged, or perhaps required, more complex forms of social control and integration to handle the problems that normally arise in day-to-day human interactions. In these areas a hierarchical form of centralized leadership, or *chiefdom*, emerged. Many chiefdoms have arisen in areas where a sedentary population has been spread out over a wide range of ecological zones, and regional groups practice specialized local types of food production. The political leader, or chief, acts as a central agency to coordinate economic activity and to redistribute the specialized products of diversified zones to the whole population. Unlike tribal or band leaders, the chief is a full-time political administrator and occupies an office that is a permanent part of the social structure. His social power and prestige do not depend upon his personality or accomplishments but on his position as the ranking member of an elite family. He controls access to basic resources by hereditary right. But the chiefdom, like the band and the tribe, is still fundamentally a kin-based society. Social position and interaction are regulated through the rules of descent, marriage, age, and sex. And all members—from the lowest to the highest ranking—are always recognized as kinsmen.

Chiefdoms probably appeared as early as 7,500 B.P. in the Near East and 3,000 B.P. in Mesoamerica and the Andes. Although they are difficult to identify archeologically, chiefdoms usually comprise villages with large populations (sometimes running into the thousands) and some degree of craft specialization. Both of these characteristics are often detectable in the archeological record. Burials of infants of high status provide another clue. In the Near East, child burials with alabaster statues and turquoise and copper ornaments indicate that the social status was ascribed at birth, not achieved as a result of personal accomplishments, as in egalitarian band and tribal societies.

In some areas, a more complex *state* organization rapidly developed out of this ranked and centralized sociopolitical system. The state carried centralization and social differentiation still further. The privileges, power, and lifestyle of the elite were more clearly demarcated, and kinship bonds no longer served as a major basis of unification for individuals of different social statuses, as in a chiefdom. Although there are almost as many definitions of the state as there are social theorists, most anthropologists would agree on four essential characteristics: (1) society is divided into sharply differentiated social classes; (2) political organization is based on territorial residence; (3) a single individual along with an elite group monopolize social power; (4) political affairs are administered by a bureaucracy of officials.

In a state society, organization, management, and control of the social order are integrated more closely than in a band, tribe, or chiefdom. A state is administered by a ruling class headed by a leader; in the ancient states, this person was often an absolute monarch and a religious leader as well. The state has the power to levy taxes, draft soldiers, wage war, and exact tribute. A formal body of law may be administered by a judicial system that includes courts, judges, and other legal specialists. Members of the government bureaucracy collect taxes, manage the budget, and administer the day-to-day affairs of state, assuring that the whole system functions smoothly. Typically, priests comprise a nearly autonomous class that maintains a complex state religion. Peasants in the outlying areas produce food that supports the administrators, craftsmen, and other specialists who are integral parts of the state. Unlike a chiefdom, in which the leaders are required to redistribute many of the goods they receive to the population at large, the taxes and tribute collected by the state are normally used to support members of the elite and to build elaborate religious or governmental structures.

Few states have arisen without cities. The Maya, and possibly the Inca, were exceptions. Their populations were widely dispersed because of the subsistence strategies they employed, but these states were administered by a political and religious elite from recognized ceremonial centers such as the Mayan site of Tikal, which extended over 125 square miles (312 km^2) and consisted of some 2,000 structures, including a huge plaza, large pyramids, nearly 300 other religious-political buildings, and hundreds of small houses. More typically, however, states have full-fledged urban centers; and conversely, the emergence of cities seems to depend on the institution of the state as a political form. Clearly, there is an important connection between the two. But what other factors stimulated the development of the more complex forms of social organization we find at this stage?

Why Did the State Evolve?

It is simple to say, as we did earlier, that sedentism and agriculture produced the state. However, we must recognize that these two cultural developments involve many factors—technological, demographic, and economic ones. Archeologists have tried to determine how these factors interacted and which were most important. Was there a single factor that precipitated the development of the state? A number of archeologists think there was, but disagree about what this factor is.

Prime-Mover Theories

Wittfogel's Hydraulic Society Karl Wittfogel (1957) has proposed that state organization arose out of the need to construct and manage the large-scale irrigation systems necessary for intensive agriculture in arid regions. Since these elaborate hydraulic systems required the organization, coordination, and control of large numbers of people and of many resources, he argues that local control tended to pass to an increasingly centralized ruling class. Those who administered these projects were able to subordinate farmers in the area by denying water to anyone who resisted their authority. Because Wittfogel based his theory on ancient Chinese communities that practiced this kind of agriculture and exhibited this type of authority structure, he termed this kind of social order *oriental despotism.*

Circumscription and Warfare Robert Carneiro (1970) argues that throughout most of the world, warfare played a decisive role in the rise of the state: the state developed as a means of mobilizing armies to conquer competitive neighboring populations. Centralized military operations undoubtedly gave expanding states an advantage over less organized groups. But why did such competition and military conflict develop in the first place? Carneiro suggests that states arose where agricultural populations were circumscribed either environmentally by mountains, seas, or deserts, or socially by neighbors impinging from all sides. Within such regions, population pressure could not be handled by migration and social dispersal, since there was no place to go. Intense competition for scarce resources and arable land triggered warfare. State governments developed to mobilize and direct the armies, and eventually to control the conquered peoples, keep the peace, and allocate resources. As population increased and the state continued to push outward, the chain of events was repeated, and the state expanded still further.

Population Increase Traditionally, food surpluses from intensive agriculture have been regarded as an important stimulus to population growth (since more food feeds more mouths) and to increased leisure time for nonagricultural activities, which then leads to new forms of social organization. Recently, however, some anthropologists have questioned the direction of this chain of causation. They want to know why agriculture was improved to produce surpluses, and they find the answer in population growth that created pressure for increased productivity (Boserup, 1965). Food surpluses are not a direct product of agricultural improvements. Better technology does not automatically induce people to produce more than they can consume; farmers are more likely to produce enough for their needs and simply work less. What produces surpluses is pressure—population pressure backed by the demands of a powerful, centralized authority (Sahlins, 1972). Thus population density reinforces the formation of the state, which demands greater effort from those under its control.

Trade Some anthropologists have noted that states arose in areas that lacked essential raw materials and developed trade networks to obtain them. In southern Mesopotamia, building stone, wood, and metal were all imported; in Guatemala, salt, obsidian, and stone for grinding tools (Rathje, 1972). States were formed to control the traffic in desirable resources from one region to another. They may have arisen at vital points of supply and redistribution, or at the crossroads of established trade routes.

Multiple-Cause Theory

Most prime-mover theories of state formation are inadequate because they envision a single linear development initiated by a single force. The archeological record rarely evidences so simple a chain of events. Let us return to Wittfogel's argument as an example.

Archeological evidence suggests that irrigation was not the prime mechanism of change in all societies. Adams (1966) has pointed out two problems with Wittfogel's theory. First, some state societies developed in areas where irrigation was never terribly important. Second, early Mesopotamian and highland Mesoamerican city-states had emerged long before complex, large-scale irrigation appeared.

Although Wittfogel overemphasized the role of irrigation in the formation of early states, he deserves credit for stressing the importance of administrative and managerial factors in the evolution of bureaucratic political organization. The earliest hydraulic systems, described in Chapter 8, involved fairly simple forms of water control—for example, small-scale canal systems and pot irrigation—which could be managed by a small farming community or a few cooperating villages. But as irrigation systems increased in size, they demanded more elaborate administration. Moreover, the differential suitability of land for irrigation agriculture provided a basis for increasing inequalities of wealth between those with land that responded well to irrigation and those with land that did not. Thus, although irrigation was not a prime mover everywhere, the gradual growth of more complex hydraulic technology did contribute to the evolution of centralized bureaucratic state societies.

Because of such problems with prime-mover theories, many archeologists prefer to think of the development of the state in terms of the operation of multiple and interacting causes.

For Adams (1966), the important causes were irrigation agriculture, local resource variability, and increased warfare. The multiple effects of these developments were often mutually reinforcing, creating a positive feedback system. (See Figure 8–1.) Adams sees two effects as crucial—the creation of surpluses and the development of stratification—and is therefore concerned with two basic questions. First, since agricultural surplus was essential for the development of

Figure 8-1. Adams' model of the origin of the state is summarized in this diagram. Most of the models of state origins are at least as complex as this one when summarized. Adams' is the most comprehensive and insightful model developed to date.

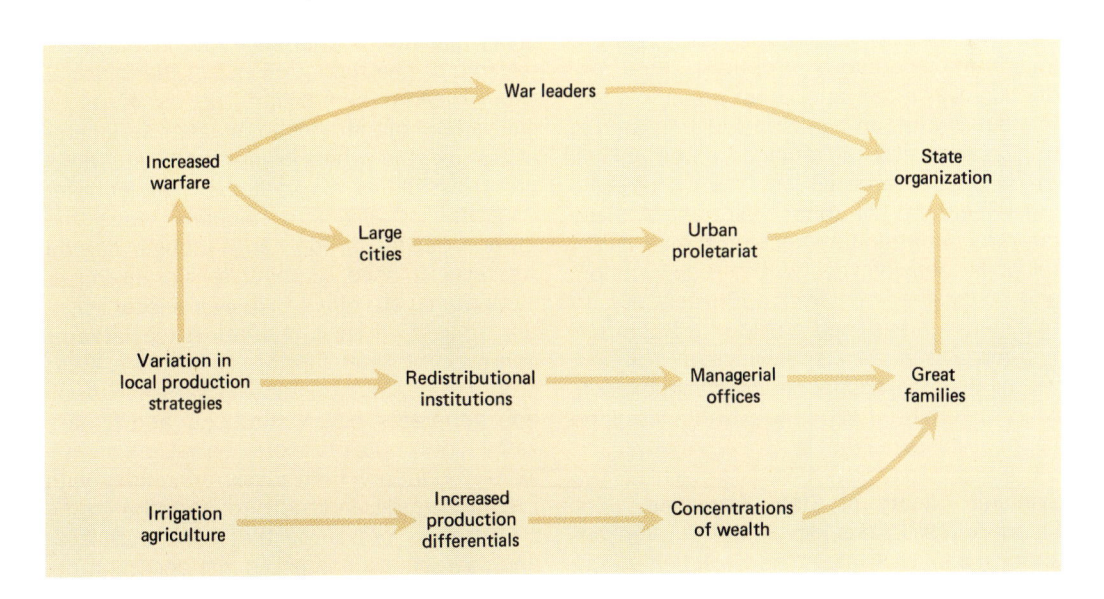

urban areas and the state, how did some farming communities come to produce food surpluses? Second, how did some members of society gain control of this economic capital? In other words, how did social stratification based on wealth and social power develop?

According to Adams, economic surpluses resulted initially from more efficient methods of food production—irrigation systems and more intensive and locally specialized agricultural economies—and from social changes—sedentism, higher population density, trade networks, and the establishment of redistribution centers. Later, as dominant groups began to develop, they were active in mobilizing these surpluses. Subsequently, such surpluses made it possible to support large numbers of people who did not produce their own food directly—craftsmen, traders, priests, political administrators, and the like.

Not all groups were equally successful in the transition, however. Adams argues that local resource variability, backed by armed might, made the difference. Certain residential groups and communities owned land in locations that proved more amenable to agricultural innovations such as irrigation, allowing these groups to produce more and to monopolize access to strategic resources. Eventually, these well-situated groups were able to manage and control agricultural production over larger and larger areas, to command resources and redistribute them, and to wage war on less advantaged communities. As outlying rural areas and the people who inhabited them fell under their control, these powerful communities became the center of religious activity, economic redistribution, and political administration. These early urban communities then provided a fertile setting for greater craft specialization, the arts, writing, science, and technological innovation, which in turn reinforced the advantages of the society over its neighbors.

Synthetic Theory of State Formation Kent Flannery (1972) has developed a more abstract model to explain the evolution of the state. He views human society as a series of subsystems arranged in a hierarchy. The most specific systems—such as herding or crop management—form the base; at the apex is governmental control or the decision-making institutions that determine social policy. Each institution is controlled by the systems above it. For example, in a band society, allocation of food is regulated by the system of ritual redistribution. Harvests, resources, obligations, and rights to land are ceremonially circulated among all members of society. The primary difference between states and simpler societies is not so much their technology per se, but the way in which economic and social activities are organized and controlled. In the state, there is an elaborate hierarchical system of management—a centralized bureaucracy that coordinates and maintains a complex division of labor and a complex segregation of institutions involving hundreds of thousands of individuals; and that allocates societal resources and rewards. Thus it is increasing segregation on the one hand and centralization on the other that we should seek to understand.

Flannery suggests that these processes are the result of two mechanisms: promotion and linearization. Promotion means just that; it occurs when an institution in the control hierarchy rises to a higher level—for instance, as the role of chieftain grew out of the informal tribal headman position, or as kingship evolved out of the priest-manager role. Linearization occurs when lower-order institutions are bypassed or eliminated by higher-order controls. Usually this happens when the lower-order institution can no longer control whatever it used to regulate. For example, state managers might take over a local irrigation project when it has grown too large or complex for local farmers to regulate. Both processes facilitate social change. Promotion generates new institutions, and linearization contributes to more centralized organization. Flannery then views difficulties with irrigation, trade, and such factors as the source of selective pressures that set centralizing and segregating processes into operation.

Adams and Flannery each provide us with a cogent model that can be used to help us understand the emergence of states. Let us now examine evidence for the emergence of this organizational form in two different areas of the world where our evidence is the best. It is important to remember that states were also emerging in the other areas of the world.

State Formation in the New and Old Worlds

More attention has been paid to the origins of agriculture and to the city-states at their peak than to the remains of the transitional phase. The problem is partly a physical one. The same site may have layer after layer of occupation (in the flat plains of Mesopotamia these sites rise as large mounds), and excavation of the upper layers is much easier. In addition, later occupants of the sites often used older material in their own buildings, destroying evidence of the earlier phases in the process. However, the problem is more complicated than that. State formation involves a change in social interaction rather than in subsistence or technology, which are far easier to deduce from the material remains. Once power is well consolidated, it becomes flamboyantly obvious in the form of monumental architecture or status goods, but archeologists find power devilishly difficult to trace in the early phases, especially before there is writing. In the discussions of Old and New World states, we will try to provide a glimpse of the kinds of evidence from which the rise of the state is adduced.

Later state societies were very different from early ones. In some cases, trends merely intensified: social stratification became more highly developed; craft specialization to serve the rulers became more differentiated; trade networks became larger and more complex. In other instances, new features appeared: writing, astronomy, mathematics. The early states were quite often coterminous with a city; the later states were often empires. One of the major trends in the development of states is the shift from a theocratic regime to a secular military one. At first, priests administered; politics, social control, and religion were integrated. As the territory of the state expanded, social cohesion became less a religious matter and more a military one. Gradually, politics became a separate sphere, and warriors reigned instead of priests. We will see this change recur in Mesoamerica and Mesopotamia.[1]

Mesoamerica

The change in the form of the state occurs in three stages in Mesoamerica. The first of these, which lasted from about 4,300 to 1,700 B.P., is called the *Formative* or *Preclassic* stage. In its earliest phase, it involved the appearance of permanent agricultural settlements and of pottery. In the middle phase, from about 3,500 to 2,500 B.P., ceremonial centers develop. It is also a time when we see the first signs of social stratification: certain individuals were supported by the labor of others. And very often these managerial people, who organized food production and distribution, were also religious leaders. At this stage, religion and the state were usually completely integrated. In the late Preclassic phase, temple pyramids appear, the calendar is employed to guide the ceremonial cycles, and writing is used for the first time.

The next stage lasted from roughly 1,700 to 1,100 B.P., and is called the *Classic*. During this time, there were great increases in population and in food production, and the urban centers themselves became much larger, 10 to 20 times larger than even the largest Preclassic settlements. Also during the Classic era, enormous ceremonial centers requiring a tremendous expenditure of labor were constructed; craftsmen and artists decorated these centers and created beautiful ritual objects for use in religious services. This full-

---

[1]These offer only a small sample of state societies. We could have used Egypt, the Indus Valley, the Greeks or Romans, any one of a number of African states, or the Incas of Peru.

Reconstructing Prehistoric Social Organization

Possibly as interesting as the social organizations of prehistoric societies are the ways in which archeologists go about reconstructing these ancient social organizations. Let us look at a few of the pioneering attempts at such reconstruction.

By studying prehistoric Pueblo architecture and artifacts and comparing his findings to modern Pueblo society, archeologist Jim Hill (1966, 1968) has been able to make several inferences about the residence patterns of a prehistoric Pueblo society in western United States. During his excavation of Broken K Pueblo in the Hay Hollow Valley of Arizona, Hill noticed differences in the size and structure of the rooms, which can be put into three categories. First, there were a number of large rooms with structural features such as firepits, mealing bins, and ventilators; Hill concluded that these were *habitation rooms*. The second type of room, on the other hand, was small, with few distinctive structural features; these were presumably *storage rooms*. Because there was an equal number of the small and large rooms, Hill inferred that each household occupied two rooms—a habitation room and a storage room. And because he could find no structural differences between individual rooms of each type, Hill hypothesized that each household unit was performing the same activities and therefore must have been self-contained and functionally independent. The third type of room Hill found had structural features indicating that it was the *kiva,* which in the prehistoric Southwest was a ceremonial room accessible only to men.

Ethnographic analysis of modern western Pueblo society supports Hill's inferences: modern pueblos do contain three types of rooms similar in size and structure to the types discovered at Broken K. Moreover, modern western Pueblo society is founded on a sexual division of labor in which separate tasks are carried out by the two different sexes in separate locations. And statistical analysis of male-associated and female-associated artifacts found in the different rooms of Broken K demonstrate that the sexual division of labor was also characteristic of that society.

Furthermore, by studying certain elements of design in different parts of the Pueblo, Hill was able to make a number of other conclusions regarding living patterns at Broken K. Statistical analysis of ceramics, and other artifacts demonstrated that there were five basic clusters of design elements used in five different parts of the Pueblo. Because the items he analyzed are ethnographically associated with female activities, because modern Pueblos pass down ceramic design elements from mother to daughter, and because modern Pueblos live in matrilocal residence units, Hill concluded that the five clusters of design elements represented five uxorilocal residence groups living in five different clusters of rooms within the Pueblo.

Other researchers have also been able to contribute to our knowledge of prehistoric social organization. For example, Robert Whallon's (1968) statistical tests on Owasco and Iroquois ceramic collections from New York State have enabled him to infer patterns of social autonomy and kinship over time. In this study, Whallon assumed that stylistic variation was a function of the rate of interaction between regional villages, and that if the items analyzed were manufactured by the members of one sex, then the variations would be a function of the rate of movement of the members of that sex between villages. Because there is ethnographic evidence that the Iroquois were matrilocal and that the Iroquois potters were women, Whallon hypothesized that matrilocality would be reflected by a high degree of stylistic homogeneity in ceramics. The styles would be homogeneous, because women remained in the villages where they were born throughout their lives, and would not be exposed to new stylistic influences. And the ceramic designs proved, in fact, to be largely homogeneous, thus bearing out the hypothesis. There were, however, changes in stylistic homogeneity through time, and Whallon argued that these changes reflected a decrease in the degree of matrilocality and of village autonomy.

In another study of various ceramic collections from the Hay Hollow Valley, Mark Leone (1968) has tested his hypothesis that increased dependence upon agriculture increases the social autonomy of neighboring villages. He reasoned that decreased communication between villages would be reflected in an increase in stylistic homogeneity, whereas increased communication would be reflected in an increase in stylistic heterogeneity. To measure the degree of stylistic homogeneity, Leone performed statistical tests on ceramic artifacts. His tests demonstrated a higher degree of stylistic homogeneity among sites most dependent upon agriculture, enabling him to conclude that the economic autonomy of agricultural communities resulted in increasing social autonomy and village endogamy.

The Emergence of the State and Urban Society

Thought to be the home of the Olmec civilization, Monte Alban was one of the first great temple-cities discovered in Mesoamerica. The city offers pyramids, a temple court, an observatory, and a stadium housing 120 rows of stone seats. (George Holton/Photo Researchers)

time nonagricultural craft specialization is a hallmark of the Classic stage. Two other important features were the further solidification of social stratification and the expansion of trade networks. This was the period during which Teotihuacan was occupied.

The third stage is referred to as the *Postclassic*. It lasted from 1,100 B.P. to the advent of Europeans in 430 B.P. This period was, by and large, one of unrest and more rigid social stratification. Militarism became much more important as states vied for territory. Within these states, military and religious leadership and organization were increasingly differentiated. Monarchs ruled, usually claiming divine power; and one became a member of the elite through inheritance.

What we see through these three stages is the transition from settlements that had a rather simple social organization to those with a fairly complex one; from small rural villages to much larger urban centers, even empires, that waged wars for goods, territory, and slaves; and from a culture in which virtually everyone took care of their own basic needs for food and shelter to one that allowed some people to continue to produce food while others provided goods and services.

The Olmec Civilization The Olmec, the first Mesoamerican civilization, flourished during the middle Preclassic phase and provide a more concrete picture of the developments during this stage (Coe, 1962; Culbert, 1974). These mysterious "rubber people," as their name is translated, inhabited the southern Gulf Coast from 3,500 to 2,500 B.P. and have left impressive ceremonial centers whose sophistication led earlier archeologists to place the dates for the sites far later than we now know them to be. The influence of the Olmecs extended far beyond their home area. There is evidence of trade and the spread of the Olmec style of art and religious ideology and practices, which were based on a jaguar god and a dual calendar system on a 52-year cycle. By the late Preclassic, large areas of Mesoamerica showed Olmec influence; Michael Coe concludes: "All later civilizations in Mesoamerica, whether Mexican or Maya, ultimately rest on an Olmec base" (1962:84).

The Mayan State According to T. P. Culbert (1974), the tropical lowlands of the Yucatan Peninsula, the foothills of Guatemala, and parts of Honduras and Chiapas, where the Mayan civilization was to develop, were occupied and the first sedentary societies developed by about 2,800 B.P. Three hundred years later, the population had increased and temple centers, the hallmark of Mayan civilization, began appearing throughout the forests. Excavation of the bottom strata of Tikal revealed an advanced culture even during the early Preclassic period. Small platforms dating from 2,260 B.P. were constructed of stone and elaborately decorated. Artifacts made of nonlocal resources such as jade and marine shells are evidence of trade. Burials indicate social stratification; the monumental scale of some of the religious architecture implies the existence of some central authority to direct the construction of buildings. Craft specialization is also in evidence—potters, sculptors, weavers, painters, stonemasons, and architects contributed to Mayan society in this early period. Thus by the late Preclassic, monumental architecture, trade, some occupational specialization, social stratification, and a central coordinating institution had arisen in the Mayan lowlands.

During the Classic period, all these developments came to fruition: society was more

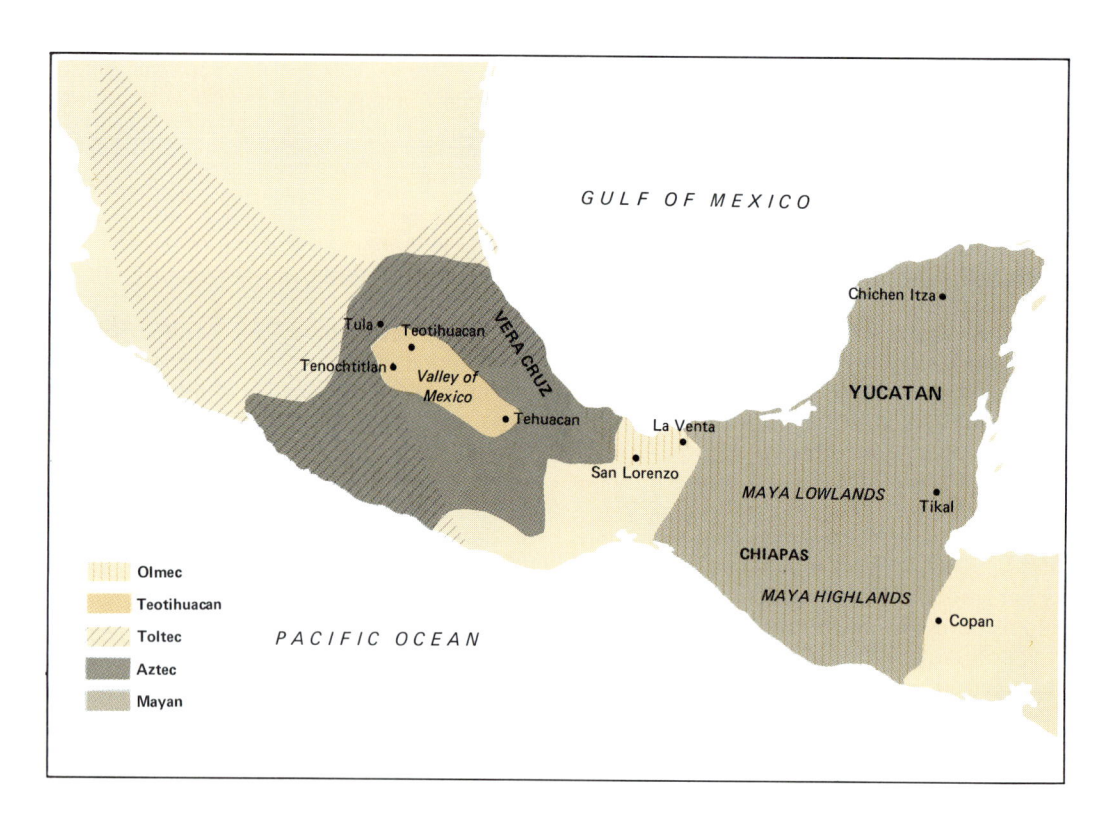

Figure 8-2. A complex mosaic of overlapping territories is formed when the different Mesoamerican states discussed in this chapter are shown on a single map.

stratified; the population grew larger; trade was growing; craftsmanship became highly developed; huge ceremonial centers were constructed; religion was extremely important, economically and politically as well as spiritually; and astronomy, writing, and mathematics, which developed in the late Preclassic, became more elaborate. The development of this elaborate civilization occurred in the complete absence of cities.

At first glance, the area inhabited by the Maya seems an unlikely spot for a major power to develop. In the rain forest, settlements were dispersed, transportation was difficult, and local resources were so uniform that villages had little incentive to trade with one another. However, three absolutely essential items were lacking in the area: stone to make the grinding tools necessary for maize, obsidian for sharp-edged cutting tools, and salt. These could be obtained from highland areas of Mexico if the society could reach a point where it was sufficiently organized to finance and mount long-distance trading parties. Households could not do this, so larger exchange networks had to be developed. As the lowland groups spread deeper into the rain forest, these networks became more and more important and required more powerful means of integration. The ceremonial centers became the site of economic as well as religious integration.

The evolution of the state in conjunction with the expansion of trade gave the Maya competitive advantages over groups inhabiting a similar environment but closer to the highlands and its necessary resources. The Maya could not export material resources different from those exploited by the groups in the buffer zone, but they had the advanced organization itself to offer. Thus according to Rathje, the knowledge of how to sustain complex organization was of prime economic value: "Such commodities were highly exportable" (1972:386).

It is quite clear that among the Mayan people a major state developed and was growing during the Classic period. During the late Classic (1,400 to 1,100 B.P.) and the Postclassic periods, Mayan civilization grew explosively. Population doubled, building increased, and the economy accelerated. At Tikal, for example, old temples were torn down and much larger ones—some over 150 feet high (45 m)—were erected in their place. Four acres (1.6 hectares) of plazas and palaces, involving millions of man-hours of labor, were constructed.

The social system also underwent change. Burials in temples and palaces indicate that entire families lived at the ceremonial centers, whereas previously only priests had lived in them. Funerary items reveal that these families were among the elite. Society had become more stratified and less mobile, with a few individuals controlling the wealth.

The palace began to assume more significance, indicating the separation of secular from religious authority and the rising importance of politico-military leaders. A bureaucracy ran the state, administering the daily affairs of the polity and overseeing construction of the ceremonial centers.

Militarism also increased. Late Classic art reveals scenes of military combat, some depicting large battles. The causes of this development are largely a matter of speculation. If Rathje's theory is accepted, the export of Mayan culture meant that the Maya were gradually losing the basis of their competitive advantage. As trade fell off, the integrating force was weakened and could be replaced only by increasing use of coercion. Circumscription may also have been at work, since the Maya lived on the Yucatan Peninsula where room for expansion was limited. Conflict with neighboring groups was inevitable. Finally, deterioration in agricultural productivity may have affected the health of the Maya. Some time around 1,060 B.P. the entire civilization suddenly and mysteriously collapsed.

The Valley of Mexico In the Valley of Mexico, the progression through the various stages of state formation and development is not so simple or continuous as in the lowlands, where only the Maya ruled. In the highlands, one group succeeded another, breaking the continuity of development. From about 4,100 to 3,800 B.P. the people in this region lived in small settlements and farmed the fertile soil of the valley, planting maize and other crops around the shores of Lake Texoco. From the lake they also obtained fish and waterfowl. Between 2,400 and 1,600 B.P. numerous settlements sprang up on the lakeshore, some like Cuicuilco with populations of 1,800 to 3,800 people. From this base, the first state developed.

In the Valley of Mexico, the state developed in an urban setting rather than from a strictly ceremonial complex. Around 2,200 B.P. the monumental city of Teotihuacan began its rise at the northeast end of the valley. The city remained the seat of power until around 1,150 B.P., when it was burned and sacked. The locus of power in the valley then shifted northeast to Tula, the monumental city of the Toltecs. According to legend, Tula fell about the twelfth century sacked by a ragtag coalition of colonists, who had initially moved to the frontier from the Valley of Mexico, of local farmers, and of hunter-gatherers retreating from drought conditions on the Mesoamerican frontier.

Following the fall of Tula, Tenochtitlan, the greatest city of all in Mesoamerica and the center of Aztec empire, was founded in 575 B.P. The city was at the height of its power when it was demolished by the Spanish in 430 B.P. Despite the shifting power in the area over the centuries, the same general progression of state forms from theocratic to conquest state is seen.

The evolution of the state in this area was facilitated by the growing productivity of agricultural techniques that provided an increasingly substantial subsistence base and required greater cooperative action (Flannery, 1967). Maize was the principal crop, supplemented by squash, beans, gourds, and other plants. Early farmers of the Preclassic stage used primitive wood and stone hoes and digging sticks to cultivate their small patches of land. The plow, which other societies developed depended on large beasts to pull it something Mesoamerican societies lacked throughout their history. As populations increased and settlements grew, more sophisticated techniques, such as canal and floodwater irrigation, terracing, and contour hoeing, were introduced. By far the most ingenious innovation was the *chinampa,* a swamp-reclamation technique developed during the Preclassic stage, perfected by the Aztec, and still practiced in certain parts of the valley today (Armillas, 1971). *Chinampas* are artificial islets of vegetation and mud that were constructed on Lake Texcoco and tended by farmers in canoes. By scooping up nutrient-rich mud from the bottom of the lake and placing it on the growing plants, manuring the soil with weeds and human wastes, and using seedbeds, the Aztecs transformed an otherwise useless marsh into a highly productive agricultural resource.

During the Preclassic stage, division of labor was rudimentary and society was relatively egalitarian. By the Classic period at Teotihuacan, as we have seen, society was differentiated and highly stratified. By the Postclassic period at Tenochtitlan, social organization had assumed a rigid, castelike quality. At Tenochtitlan, craftsmen were even organized into guilds. At the top of the Aztec social structure were the emperor and his court. Below this were the nobles; then came the professional warriors, merchants, and craftsmen. At the bottom of the social ladder were the serf bondsmen, the porters, and the slaves.

During the Preclassic and Classic periods, religious and political responsibilities were invested in a single individual. By the time of Teotihuacan, the evidence for a state is unmistakable. Teotihuacan was far larger than any earlier settlement in Mesoamerica and was far more elaborately laid out, which suggests a strong central administration. Because of the large number of temples and their elaborate decoration, Adams (1966) concludes that political and religious systems of authority were still combined. This does not mean that religion necessarily unified the vast areas under the control of the city. Adams believes that the people not only voluntarily contributed to the city and made pilgrimages there out of devotion but were also increasingly subjected to secular controls.

During the Postclassic era in Tenochtitlan, religious and political functions separated. Nowhere is this more evident than in the monumental architecture of the city. At the heart of Tenochtitlan, a city of 300,000 people at its peak, stood the twin pyramidal temple to the gods of war and rain. This monumental temple was 100 feet (29 m) high and measured 1,360 feet (400 m) on a side. Surrounding the temple were the royal palaces—that of the legendary Montezuma boasted 300 rooms capable of accommodating 3,000 persons. A number of civic buildings also were located in this vicinity. (In addition, the city contained about 60,000 houses.) From the temples, the Aztec priests conducted rituals and sacrifices, while from the palaces and civic buildings, the emperor ruled through a bureaucracy. Religious beliefs of course underpinned and legitimized the state, but the political authority was separate.

Militarism developed slowly in the valley. The Preclassic and Classic periods saw little military aggression, although Teotihuacan does have murals of warriors and evidence of conflict within the city well before its fall. With the Toltecs, however, the military spirit increased tremendously. The gods demanded human sacrifices, which were obtained through warfare. Toltec domination also included intensive trade through networks even more extensive and active than those of Teotihuacan. The same combination of intensive trade and military vigor was carried on by the Aztecs after the fall of the Toltecs. Huge military campaigns were launched to bring back victims for sacrifice; numerous expeditions resulted in the Aztec control of an area of 12,400 square miles (20,000 km²) that was inhabited by 5 or 6 million people. The Aztecs battled the peoples on their borders for control of territory, but this did not seem to harm their trade networks for long. They had a special class of long-distance trader-merchants, who traveled perhaps as far as the midwestern United States to buy and sell goods. In Tlatelolco, the sister city of Tenochtitlan,

The Aztec calendar is but one example of the civilization's scientific endeavors. The Aztec year is divided into 260 days, falling within a larger 52-year time cycle. A somewhat bloodthirsty civilization by modern standards, the Aztecs would sacrifice humans and offer their hearts to the gods—a practice accelerated at the end of each 52-year cycle to ensure the continuity of their world. (American Museum of Natural History)

there were marketplaces larger than any in Europe. Cacao beans and cotton cloaks were used for money to buy goods such as jewelry, gold, feathers, clothing, foods, pottery, chocolate, vanilla, copper tools, cigarettes, cigars, pipes, and slaves. In the Valley of Mexico, we can see a more highly developed form of the Postclassic phase than the abbreviated Mayan version. Cities were enormous and government was secularized. Empires, tied together by trade and military might, were ruled from the urban center.

Mesopotamia

Mesopotamian states went through similar steps of organization long before Mesoamerican peoples had even begun intensive cultivation of crops (Adams, 1966). In Mesopotamia, these stages are identified as the *Ubaid* (6,000 to 5,500 B.P.), *Protoliterate* (5,500 to 4,900 B.P.), and *Early Dynastic* (4,900 to 4,500 B.P.). The Ubaid period takes its name from al'Ubaid, an early settlement of Mesopotamia. The way of life to which it lent its name was centered around the temple and was regulated by priests serving as ritual, political, and economic leaders. The Protoliterate stage receives its name from the appearance of pictographs, an early form of writing that gave way to cuneiform later. The Early Dynastic refers to the rise of large and powerful Sumerian city-states in constant conflict with one another. As in the Valley of Mexico, city and state developed together, and hegemony passed from group to group over the course of time.

The evolution of the state in southern Mesopotamia occurred on the rich alluvial plain between the Tigris and Euphrates rivers sometime between 6,000 and 5,500 B.P. During this time, the first cities grew out of clusters of farming villages and hamlets, many of which had their own small ceremonial center, irrigation project, and clan-type central authority. The largest of these early communities, such as Eridu, consisted of mud-brick temples and two-story houses probably occupied by the elite, their retainers, and servants. Further from the urban center were the houses and workshops of craftsmen. Further still were the hovels of the peasants and farmers who provided the food that supported the urbanites. The population of an urban area of this period was probably about 5,000 persons. With the passage of time, this basic configuration remained, but the cities became more populated and the civic and ceremonial centers grew more numerous and monumental in scale. By 1,500 to 500 B.P. some cities had as many as 50,000 inhabitants, as well as imposing brick pyramids, walls, and somewhat later, other fortifications for defense.

As the society grew in size and complexity, the need for integrative institutions increased. Religious, political, and economic functions in the early Mesopotamian state were combined in a single individual, the priest. Thus priests oversaw large irrigation projects and redistributed food surpluses from the temples, which also served as food storage centers. They supported the crafts and innovated ways of managing. The priest was not the sole integrative institution in this increasingly complex society, however. The early state was embedded in a society of ancient corporate clan groups, who held land in common or practiced crafts. These groups also had civic duties — to provide labor for community projects such as irrigation systems or to furnish mili-

Cuneiform, one of the earliest forms of writing, evolved in the Near East from pictographs. "Cuneiform" is derived from the Latin word for "wedge," and refers to the wedge-shaped impressions of the symbols. The cuneiform tablet pictured here is Sumerian. (Courtesy, the University Museum, University of Pennsylvania)

tary manpower and leadership. Thus community organizations and leaders mediated between the state and the individual.

These corporate kin groups retarded the development of stratification by leveling the differences between members of the corporate group. These members were not all equals; there were the rich and the poor. But power, in the form of differential access to resources, was tempered by the need to preserve group esteem or by the sharing of resources. Thus bound by corporate ties, the rich could not rise too high or the poor fall too low.

The examination of burial sites confirms that status may have been relatively undifferentiated through the Protoliterate period. By as late as 4,900 B.P. (Adams, 1966) the degree to which social stratification had advanced is not clear. Not until around 4,400 B.P. does a fully stratified social organization appear. Many large houses and tombs containing considerable wealth point to the existence of a class of royalty and a wealthy upper class in the Early Dynastic period. Foundations of palaces excavated at Eridu and Kish measure 10,000 square feet (2,941 m^2) and reveal many private apartments. At Susa, some 950 people, not counting slaves, lived and worked in the palace. This development is largely a result of the concentration of land ownership that developed at this time. Although the great majority of the populace in the Early Dynastic period were still part of the corporate kin group rather than clients or serfs on a large estate, the rise of the great families represents the beginning change from clan-based divisions to class-based ones.

The increase in stratification swung the balance of power away from the priests. But as Adams (1966) notes, an increase in militarism in later Sumerian cities probably was primary in separating the role of the priest from that of the king. Traditionally, in times of crisis, a leader with extraordinary powers was chosen by the council of elders, an institution probably drawn from the corporate kin groups. An increase in the number of military expeditions and wars led to the selection of a permanent war lord to coordinate military activities. From this field marshal or five-star general arose the office of the monarchy, which in later times became hereditary. The king managed to displace not only the priests but the council as well. These did not disappear but became specialized institutions. The rise of the king is an excellent example of the processes of promotion and linearization at work, processes that transformed the society into a hierarchical and increasingly autocratic one.

Militarism arose as each state sought to protect and maintain its territories. The states became more defense-minded, erecting walls and other fortifications around their cities. Satellite villages, which had numbered close to 150 in 5,000 B.P., were consolidated because of the need for security, and only a few dozen remained by 4,400 B.P., the end of the Early Dynastic period (Hamblin, 1973). Armor, chariots, horses, and metal weapons became important, stimulating the economy in much the same way large military expenditures do in our own society. By about 4,800 B.P. several early city-states had formed defensive alliances, thus setting the stage for the rise of empires after about 4,400 B.P.

Trends in Evolution

The parallels between Mesopotamia and Mesoamerica are quite striking, even though the development of the state did not follow precisely the same path in the two areas. Three trends are especially important: the growth of population, economic complexity, and social complexity.

During the formation of these states, population grew steadily and became increasingly concentrated in cities. Like the cities of today, each had its own distinctive flavor. Compared to the earlier societies about which we have read, the settlements were massive. Clearly, this trend has not stopped. Today, large cities have populations in the millions. We are only beginning to understand the nature and degree of their destructive impact on the natural environment, and to worry about their negative effects on the quality of human life. Although we have begun to reassert our ability to regulate the growth of human numbers, here again we are really only beginning to consider ways of dealing with the numerous problems that result when humans are packed into massive cities.

The problems people encountered as they learned to use their new ability to produce food affected the way economic activities were organized. With agriculture came a greater variation in the productivity of land and a potential for greater surplus. Trade and craft specialization grew ever more important. Clearly, a more complex economic pattern emerged in these early states, and again, that complexity has steadily increased. Specialization then meant that an individual might spend his lifetime making pottery vessels; today, one can push a button that stamps designs on a plate or vase. And the modern problem of control of petroleum resources demonstrates only too well our continuing inability to manage the problems of trade among states.

Social institutions and social factors underwent changes as basic as those in demography and economics. Differences in wealth and occupation no longer reflected differences in production and craft specialization; instead, they became the definers of classes, which were themselves increasingly seen as parts of the natural order. Wealth became the justification for leadership control and wars. The philosophy that it is right for the many to be controlled by the few, which at first had a religious justification, became its own justification as political leaders and political ideology became more and more separated from the rest of society.

Social complexity did not, of course, leave the number of people and economic complexity unaffected. Rulers needed manpower; cities were convenient recruiting stations. Moreover, the increasing centralization of economic, religious, and political leadership in the cities drew people there. Similarly, the support given specialists and traders by the leaders caused economic complexity to increase further, justifying ever more social control. And so the pattern continued: as the state grew more powerful, it generated new problems that only further increased its powers.

This is a cycle in which we are still caught today. Of course, modern states are far bigger than those we have been discussing. The relations that affect the lives of an individual are increasingly relations between states, not relations between individuals. Differences in wealth and power have increased and are even more straightforwardly defined as the way things should be.

It is well to remember that the stage in human evolution we are now experiencing is only a few thousand years old, a very brief time in evolutionary terms; that of the many states that have existed, most no longer exist, due to wars and ecological disasters; and that the problems of the emergence of states and the problems that we read of every day are one and the same.

summary

Between 5,000 and 500 B.P. certain groups all over the world who had developed highly efficient and diversified food-producing techniques made a rapid transition to a new kind of settlement pattern—the *city,* an area characterized by a large, densely concentrated population and a high degree of social differentiation. Often this change was accompanied by a new form of sociopolitical organization—the *state,* characterized by sharply differentiated social classes, political organization based on residence rather than kinship, monopolization of social power by an elite, and bureaucratic administration. A state may be administered from a ceremonial center as well as from a city, so urbanism is not synonymous with state societies, but the emergence of cities seems to depend on the institution of the state as a political form.

The appearance of urbanism and the state have also generally been associated with the development of complex societies and *civilization*. V. Gordon Childe has listed ten technological, social, and cultural criteria for civilization, but has lumped the more important attributes in with the less important ones and has neglected to separate the causes from the effects of civilization.

The reasons for the evolution of the state are still being debated. Some theories see it as triggered by a single force such as irrigation, conflict between circumscribed populations, the pressure of population growth, or trade. Each of these is seen to demand centralized political management to deal with the problems it has created. But according to the multiple-cause theory of Robert Adams, all these forces—and more—interacted. The surpluses that became the underpinnings of a stratified system were a result of agricultural productivity and the development of social systems to mobilize them, while their concentration in the hands of dominant groups was a result of local resource variability, backed by armed might. The processes by which power became concentrated have been suggested by Kent Flannery's synthetic theory of state formation. Flannery sees human society as a series of subsystems arranged in a hierarchy, with the most specific systems at the base and with the decision-making institutions that determine social policy at the top. Each institution is controlled by the systems above it. Such an elaborate hierarchical system of management as the state evolves through promotion of lower-order institutions to positions of greater control, and through linearization by the takeover of lower-order institutional powers by higher-order institutions. Promotion creates new institutions, and linearization concentrates power in more centralized institutions. State societies are hardly static. One of the major trends is the shift from a regime dominated by priests to one dominated by a secular military ruler.

Perhaps the most useful way of viewing the developments of this stage is as a response to the problems created by sedentism and agriculture. These resulted in a growth in human numbers and density that demanded new institutions to solve the problems of conflict and coordination. Surpluses from agriculture permitted the development of craft specialization and encouraged trade, as did sedentism. The economic system became more complex. As certain groups gained control over resources and social institutions, social stratification became more pronounced and power more unequally distributed. Social complexity generated further complexity, and the rapid pace of social change, so unusual for most of human existence, became a predominant cultural feature.

suggested readings

ADAMS, R.
1966 *The Evolution of Urban Society: Early Mesopotamia and Prehispanic Mexico.* Chicago: Aldine. A major theoretical treatment of state-urban origins.

CULBERT, T. P.
1974 *The Lost Civilization: The Story of the Classic Maya.* New York: Harper & Row. A discussion of the organization of Mayan society during the Classic period.

DAVIS, K.
1973 *Cities: Their Origin, Growth and Human Impact.* San Francisco: W. H. Freeman. Articles from *Scientific American* describing prehistoric and modern cities and the particular problems of life in such settlements.

SANDERS, W. T., AND PRICE, B. J.
1968 *Mesoamerica: The Evolution of a Civilization.* New York: Random House. A discussion of the events and processes leading to the emergence of the state in Mesoamerica.

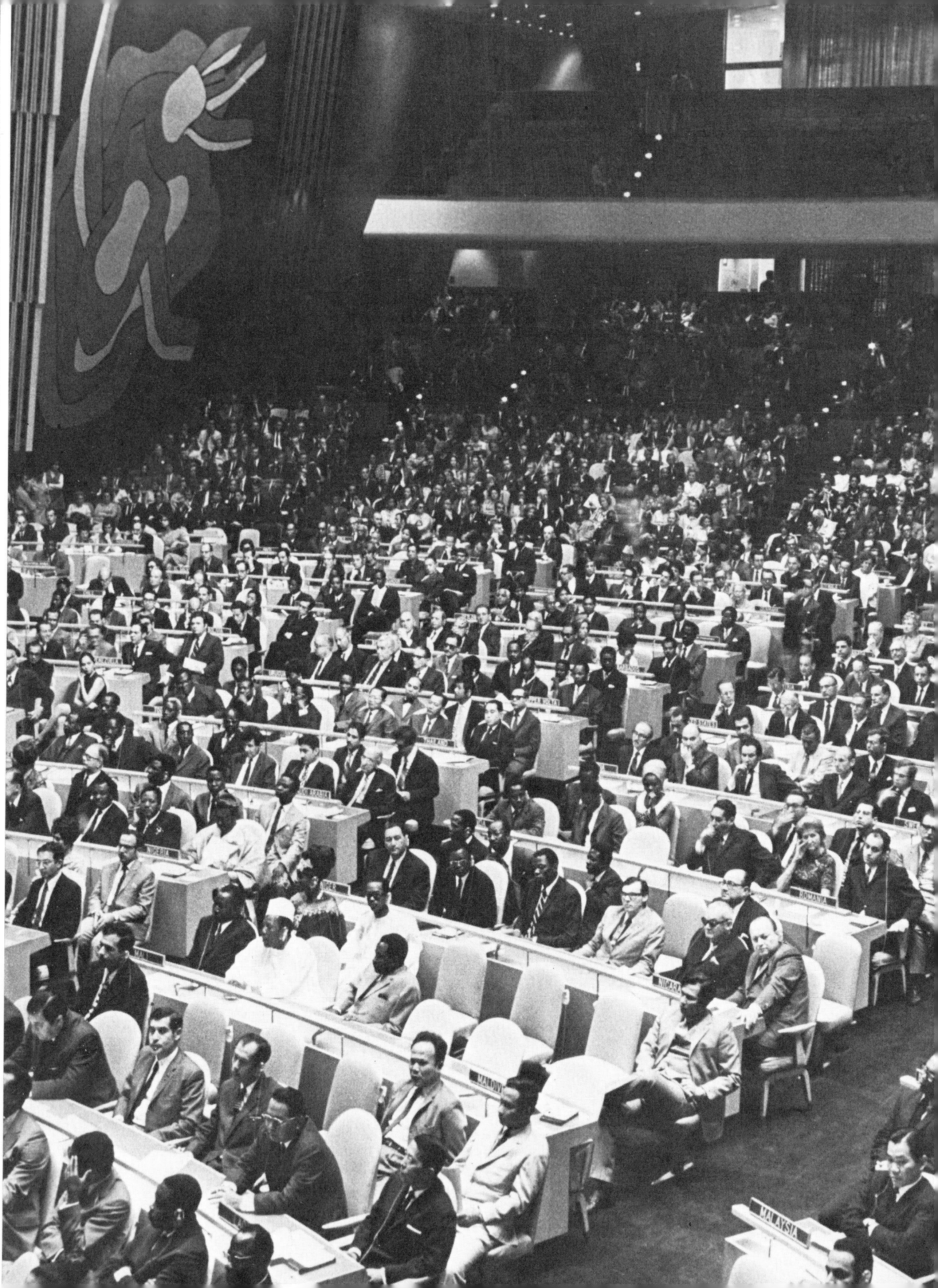
NIGERIA
ROMANIA
MALAYSIA

nine
Physical Variation in Modern Homo Sapiens

As we have seen, *Homo sapiens* has been geographically widespread since early in its history, and the range of the species has enlarged with each advance in technological control of the environment. Human populations have always lived in a wide variety of environments, been subject to different diseases, eaten different foods, and endured different climatic stresses. To this variety, cultural diversity has added yet another dimension.

In addition to having been widespread for most of its history, the human species has also been unevenly distributed. As bands of humans crossed the mountains and oceans, and as grasslands changed to deserts, and tundras to forests and back to tundras again, the gene pool of the human species has been repeatedly broken into smaller subunits semi-isolated from each other by barriers of geography or culture. These subpopulations have diverged and merged repeatedly as barriers to gene flow have come and gone.

As we discussed in Chapter 2, widespread and discontinuously distributed species inevitably become *polytypic*. Their populations diverge from one another as the evolutionary forces of selection, founder effect, and drift act upon their respective gene pools. The human species is no exception. All humans have in common certain genes which define their overall similarity as members of the species *Homo sapiens,* but there are other genes that differ in frequency among populations producing human variety. This variation is the subject of this chapter.

Interpreting Patterns of Human Variation

In attempting to interpret or explain the observed patterns of human variation, the anthropologist poses a series of questions.

1. How is this variation determined? How much is attributable to genotypic differences and how much to the direct action of the environment on the phenotype? These questions are extremely difficult to answer in many cases. Often, the only possible answer we can give is that both genotype and environment play a role in producing the variable character. Presuming that a genetic basis can be inferred for a character, we proceed to the next question.

2. Why are human populations polymorphic at this locus, or set of loci? As we saw in Chapter 2, polymorphisms may theoretically be balanced or transient, and genes may be neutral or subject to natural selection. To decide what factors are responsible for a particular polymorphism, anthropologists attempt to find evidence that selection is acting upon the polymorphism and to determine what the selective factors might be. This again can be a difficult problem. Selection theoretically can be detected by deviations of genotype frequencies from predicted ratios. But selection can also operate quite intensely without producing deviations sufficiently large to be distinguishable from those due to simple sampling error. So in practice we adopt a variety of tactics in our search for selective factors. Finally, we consider differences

The dimensions of human variation can be seen at international gatherings such as this session of the United Nations General Assembly. (Courtesy, United Nations)

among populations and ask the next question.
3. Why is the human species polytypic for this particular character? Why do some populations show a high frequency of a variant while others do not? Theoretically, populations may differ in gene frequency because of differential selection, accidents of gene flow, and genetic drift. To explain polytypy, we seek selective influences whose impact varies *among* populations within the species. If we fail to find selective factors, we may have to invoke genetic drift to explain polytypy. Drift, however, can only explain it in a statistical sense. As we saw, it cannot predict the outcome in particular populations.

The Nature of Genetically Controlled Variation

All variation is of a similar kind at the gene level. It consists of differences in the DNA base sequences, most of which code for polypeptide chains. But not all phenotypic variation can easily be related to variation at the gene or protein level. Much observable variation concerns characters that are determined by genetic and environmental interaction. Such variation raises problems of interpretation that are not encountered when we can examine proteins—the primary gene product. We shall therefore consider first a set of characters whose genetic basis is quite straightforward—the proteins of the blood.

Variation in Blood Proteins

By far the greatest number of genetic markers in humans involve blood proteins. We will concentrate upon variation in hemoglobin—the red, oxygen-carrying protein—and in two of the better-known blood group systems, which between them exemplify the search for selection in human populations.

Hemoglobin Polymorphism

Because hemoglobin is readily available, more is known about its structure, function, and genetically controlled variation than about any other protein. A large proportion of hemoglobin—about 97 percent of the total—consists of hemoglobin A. A smaller, minor component is hemoglobin A_2. The hemoglobins are produced by the interaction of the products of three distinct loci: alpha (α), beta (β), and delta (δ). Each locus codes for a different polypeptide chain. Variation in humans occurs at all three loci, but the best-known hemoglobin variants are all due to β chain alleles.

Sickle Cell Polymorphism The best-known hemoglobin polymorphism concerns HbS or sickle cell hemoglobin. We have already noted it as an example of balanced polymorphism—that is, one maintained by the action of natural selection. Sickled blood cells are brittle, and this leads both to anemia and to obstruction of the fine blood vessels. Sickle cell trait—the heterozygous condition—produces a mild anemia that normally has little effect on fitness. The symptoms are much graver in homozygotes. If untreated, the homozygous condition—sickle cell anemia—generally causes death in early adulthood.

The Relationship Between Malaria and HbS Distribution The major concentration of the Hb^s gene is found in tropical Africa, with a less extensive distribution in southern Europe and Asia (Figure 9–1). The distribution of Hb^s genes in human populations poses certain problems of interpretation. Why, especially in view of the low fitness of the homozygotes for this gene, do comparatively high frequencies of the gene occur in some populations? Why does it occur in some populations but not in others?

The answer to the first question seems to be that the sickle cell gene is maintained by selection in favor of heterozygotes in areas where the malaria parasite, *Plasmodium falciparum*, is prevalent. In some way that is not yet fully understood, the presence of HbS seems to reduce the severity of malarial infection, especially in children who are not yet immune to the disease. It may also protect the unborn children of heterozygous mothers from placental damage caused by malarial parasites.

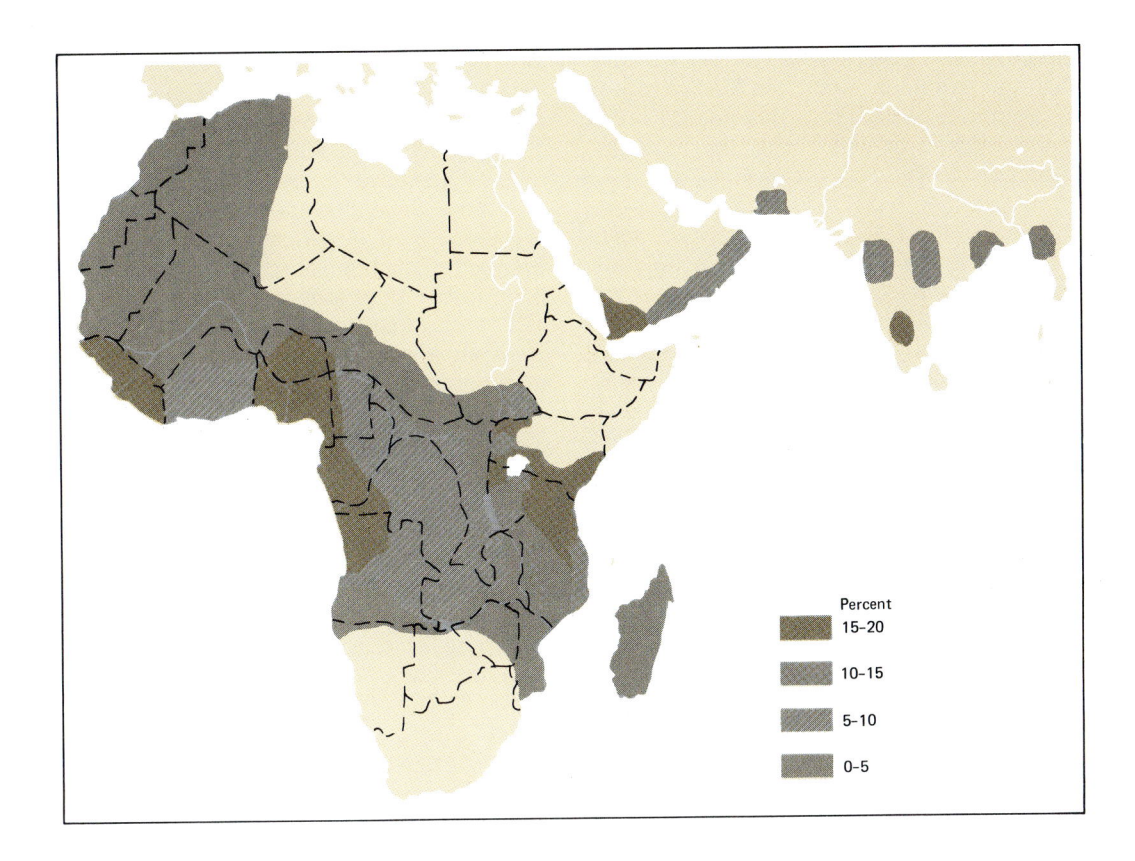

High frequencies of the sickle cell gene are concentrated in areas where falciparum malaria is common or has been until the recent initiation of control programs. The close correspondence between the distribution of the gene and that of malaria first gave geneticists the clue about this relationship and prompted clinical studies of the susceptibility of the different genotypes to malaria that finally elucidated the problem.

The Effects of Migration and Gene Flow on Hb^s Distribution

Although the malaria/sickle cell relationship partially explains the distribution of the Hb^s gene, it does not wholly account for the details

Figure 9-1. **The distribution and frequency of the sickle cell gene and the distribution of falciparum malaria in Africa, the Middle East, and Southern Asia. Note that, particularly in Africa, the distribution of the sickle cell gene agrees quite closely with that of malaria.** (After A. C. Allison, 1961)

of this distribution. For example, no Hb^s seems to occur in heavily malarial areas of Southeast Asia. Even in West Africa, the Hb^s gene is very unevenly distributed among ethnic and linguistic groups, all of whom live in a malarial environment. Similarly, there are people of African and Mediterranean ancestry who also carry the sickle cell gene in areas where falciparum malaria is totally absent, such as the northern United States.

These details are only explicable if we consider migration and gene flow as well as selection. The Hb^s gene probably arose as a mutation somewhere in Africa, the Mediterranean, or Southwest Asia. From this point, the Hb^s gene diffused or was carried by migration. According to this view, the absence of the Hb^s gene from Southeast Asia is due not to selection but to the fact that gene flow was never sufficient to carry it to the human populations in this part of the world.

Similarly, Livingstone (1958) has demonstrated that there are populations living in the malarial environment of the West African forest belt who have low frequencies of the sickle cell gene, and that such populations are likely to have abandoned hunting and gathering for subsistence agriculture relatively recently. The malaria-bearing mosquito, *Anopheles gambiae*, is rare in undisturbed forests but flourishes in the garden plots prepared by slash-and-burn agriculturalists. According to Livingstone, malaria and agriculture probably spread together into the West African forest, and those groups in this area with low frequencies of the Hb^s gene are still in the process of reaching equilibrium, having only comparatively recently acquired the gene, the disease, and the new subsistence pattern from invading agriculturists.

Finally, it is obvious that natural selection will not account for the presence of sickle cell genes in Newark, New Jersey, or Liverpool, England. Hb^s genes are not found in Newark because they are advantageous there or ever have been, but because they are found in West African populations, and many inhabitants of Newark have West African ancestry. Given enough time and selection against *SS* homozygotes, the absence of a compensating advantage for the *AS* heterozygote would lead the frequency of the gene to decline to very low values in such areas. But the rate of decline would become very slow as the frequency of the gene approached zero. Thus a residue of Hb^s genes would persist virtually indefinitely as part of the genetic load of these populations.

This illustrates an important consideration in the interpretation of human variability. The rate of human cultural and technological evolution, and the population movements and habitat modifications that these changes produce, have become so rapid that evolutionary changes in gene frequency mediated by natural selection have not been able to keep pace with them. Situations such as the occurrence of sickle cell in Americans reflect historical events, recent population shifts, and migrations rather than long-term evolutionary adjustment under the influence of selection. Such situations are undoubtedly very common in modern *Homo sapiens*.

Blood Groups

Perhaps the most familiar human variation that is under simple genetic control involves the blood groups. Two of the most well-known groups are the ABO blood system and the Rh, or rhesus, system. (Several other systems are shown in Table 9–1.) Each system is genetically distinct from the others and is determined by two or more alleles at a particular locus.

Almost everybody knows that he or she is "AB, rhesus positive," or "A, rhesus negative," and so on. Terms like these refer to the presence of proteins called *blood group antigens* on the surface of the red blood cell. Group A red cells carry the A antigen, for example. This is recognized by the fact that a test solution containing the antibody anti-A causes the red cells to clump together or agglutinate. AB cells are agglutinated by anti-A and anti-B antibodies, whereas O cells are agglutinated by neither.

A peculiarity of the ABO groups is that all people naturally carry in their plasma the antibodies to those factors absent from their red cells. This is not true of the other blood groups, where antibodies must be specially prepared. This feature of the ABO blood groups makes matching blood types crucial for blood transfusion, and this has insured that large numbers of people all over the world have been tested. In this way, we have obtained quite reliable estimates of the geographical distribution of the three major alleles of the ABO system.

Physical Variation in Modern *Homo sapiens*

Table 9–1. Some of the Better-known Blood Group Systems of *Homo sapiens*

System	Number of Recognizable Antigens	Notes
ABO	5+	Widespread polymorphism; highly polytypic. Many populations investigated.
MNSs	29	Widespread polymorphism; some antigens very rare.
P	3 (or more)	Widespread polymorphism, inter-populational differences.
Rhesus (Rh)	20	Polymorphic and polytypic. Some antigens very rare; most not widely investigated.
Lutheran	2	Polymorphic at least in some human populations.
Kell	6	Few populations yet examined.
Lewis	2	Part of synthetic pathing also involving ABO substances and genes.
Duffy	2	Polymorphic; inter-populational differences.
Kidd	2	Polymorphic; inter-populational differences.
Diego	2	Polymorphic in some populations; one antigen characteristic of East Asians and Amerindians.
Ye	2	Polymorphic in Western Europe; not widely tested.
I	2	Low-frequency variant.
Xg	1	The only X-linked human blood group system; polymorphic in many populations, with inter-populational differences.

The Distribution of Blood Groups As can be seen from Figure 9–2, there are very considerable differences between populations in blood group gene frequencies. Whereas O genes predominate throughout the world, some populations are highly polymorphic with high frequencies of A and/or B genes, and others seem totally to lack one or both of these alleles. The B gene exhibits a remarkable *cline* in frequency—a gradient of gradual change from a high frequency in central Asia to lower frequencies on the periphery of the Old World.

The genes of the rhesus system are also polymorphically distributed. Some genes are very common in some populations and virtually absent in others, whereas other genes are more evenly spread throughout the human species.

The Problem of Blood Group Polymorphisms Genetic drift should tend to eliminate variation within populations unless opposing forces are at work to maintain it. What forces, then, are responsible for maintaining the blood group polymorphisms in human populations? And why are some blood group genes common in some populations but rare or absent in others?

Some details of blood group distribution can best be explained by reference to the immediate ancestry of the populations concerned. The ABO frequencies of white, black, and Oriental Americans, for example, closely mirror those of the populations from which they were derived.

Founder effect has also been invoked to explain some peculiarities of blood group distribution. For instance, the allele for blood

Human Physical and Cultural Evolution

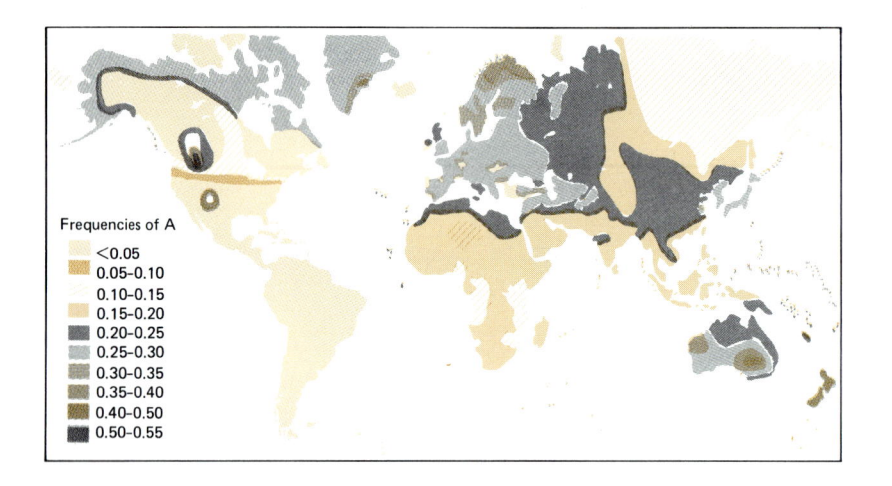

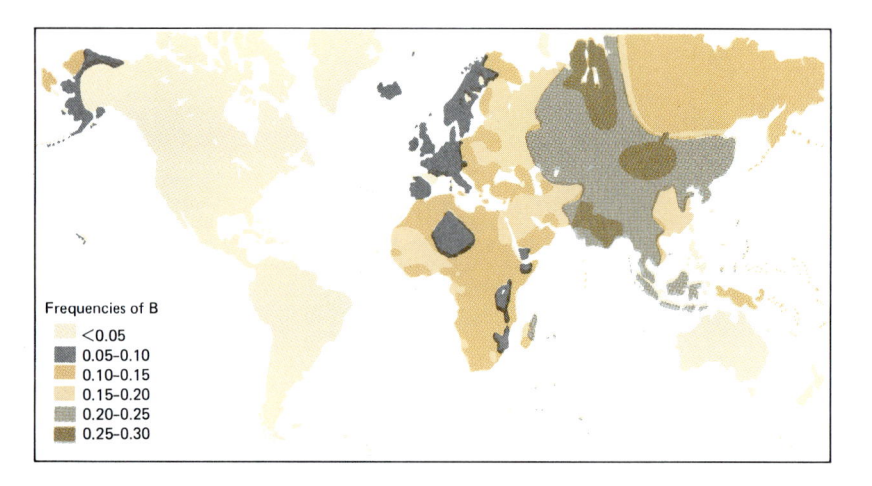

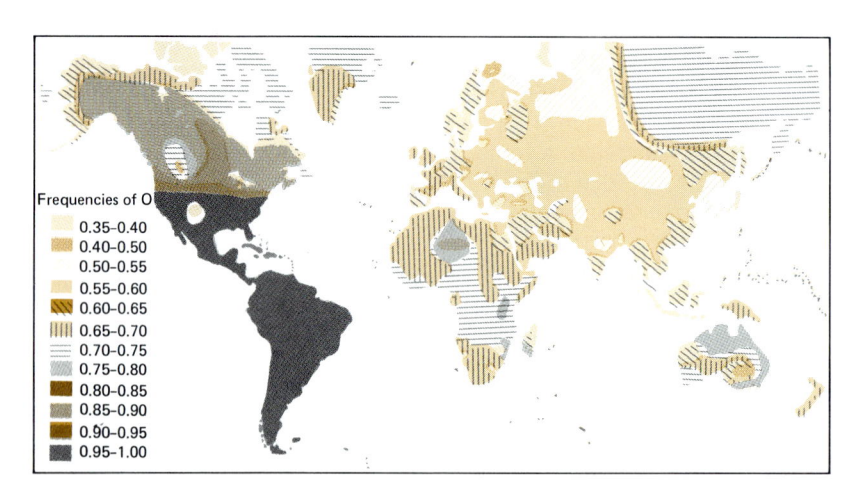

Figure 9–2. Distributions of genes I^A, I^B, I^O of the ABO system. In all three maps, the effects of population movements of the past 500 years have been eliminated as far as possible. Note the wide differences in frequency between populations, the cline in I^B from Central Asia, and the apparent absence of I^B from aboriginal populations of the New World. (After Mourant, et al., 1958)

group B probably was not present among American Indians before European contact, although the frequency of the B allele in populations in eastern Asia is rather high today. If the Americas were first peopled by small bands migrating across the Bering Straits land bridge, it is possible that purely by chance the B allele was never represented in their gene pool or that it was lost by drift while the original population was still small.

Theoretical explanations of distribution patterns in terms of random sampling error effects, such as drift, are very difficult either to prove or to disprove. Furthermore, since drift acts as a powerful force for divergence only in rather small populations, it is an unsatisfactory explanation for large-scale patterns of variation in gene frequency such as those observed in the blood groups. It also fails to account for the long-term persistence of polymorphisms.

Such phenomena call for explanation in terms of natural selection. Normative selection could act to maintain the different blood group alleles as balanced polymorphisms, whereas differential selection would account for geographical variation in gene frequencies. In their search for selectional factors acting upon human blood groups, biologists have adopted a number of different strategies.

ABO Blood Groups and Disease One approach is statistical—examining the incidence of various diseases in people of different blood groups. Some relationships have been confirmed by repeated investigations and seem to represent real associations rather than statistical artifacts. Certain apparent relationships between ABO blood types and disease are listed in Table 9–2. The second line of investigation is suggested by the presence of certain antigens that resemble blood group substances on the surface of pathogenic microorganisms such as viruses and bacteria. It has been suggested, for example, that similarities between specific blood group antigens and disease antigens would lead to differential mortality of A individuals to smallpox and of O individuals to bubonic plague. Bubonic plague probably originated in Southeast Asia and spread westward. Its appearance in Europe led to the Black Death of the mid-fourteenth century. It is interesting, therefore, that the lowest frequencies of group O gene, the phenotype thought to be most susceptible to bubonic plague, are to be found in Central Asia. Since such epidemics of plague and smallpox no longer decimate human populations, it is now difficult to investigate the incidence of the respective blood groups among their victims and thus to either confirm or disprove this hypothesis. The distribution of blood group frequencies suggests very strongly that some kind of selectional factors are at work. Human populations do not show the random distribution of allele frequencies that would be expected if genetic drift alone were responsible for the variation between them.

We should not conclude that all or even

Table 9–2. Blood Group Phenotypes That Have Been Statistically Associated with Specific Diseases in European and North American White Populations

Disease	ABO Phenotype More Susceptible
Duodenal Ulcer	O
Stomach Cancer	A
Pernicious Anemia	A

most selection is necessarily related to disease. The role of nutritional variation, for instance, is likely to be important in the evolution of enzyme systems involved in digestion. Yet we know almost nothing about genetic variation in such systems. In the following section, we examine two characters that offer a glimpse of the variation that exists in tissues and structures outside the blood.

Variations Apparently Related to Diet

PTC Tasting One of the more curious human polymorphisms involves the ability to taste PTC (phenylthiocarbamide). Most people taste PTC solutions, even at low concentrations, as intensely bitter. However, some people, especially among Europeans and other "whites," describe PTC as tasteless except in very strong solutions. The ability to taste PTC is determined by a pair of alleles, the "taster" gene (T) dominant to the "nontaster" (t). The frequency of t genes varies from a reported high of nearly 60 percent in an Asiatic Indian population to a low of about 10 percent seen in some South American Indians. It is known that PTC is chemically close to substances that inhibit thyroid function and that goiter, produced by thyroid malfunction, is disproportionately common among nontasters of PTC. Possibly PTC tasting confers a selective advantage upon tasters by causing them to perceive thyroid-suppressive substances as nasty and hence to avoid them in food. It is not known, however, why this selective pressure was apparently relaxed in some populations. PTC tasting is important because it is undoubtedly representative of a large array of biochemically mediated variations that produce selective effects by rendering the perception of particular stimuli either pleasurable or unpleasant.

Lactase Deficiency Another polymorphism related to diet is the ability to digest the sugar found in milk, called *lactose*. This ability depends upon having the enzyme lactase in the lining of the small intestine. All human infants, like the young of most mammals, produce lactase and can digest milk easily. So can the majority of adults in European and other "white" populations and in some African groups. Among other populations comprising a large majority of mankind, most people cannot digest lactose after the age of four years. Thereafter, no lactase is secreted, and drinking milk in any quantity leads to severe cramps and flatulence. Those who have studied the occurrence of lactase deficiency in families believe that it has a simple genetic basis. It seems to be determined by a pair of alleles—the gene for production being dominant to that for deficiency. Variations among populations in the frequency of the lactase deficiency gene correlate closely with the use of fresh milk by adults. In West Africa, populations of herders with low incidence of lactase deficiency live side by side with farmers who drink little milk and have a high frequency of the deficiency gene.

Since lactase deficiency in adults is normal not only for most humans, but also for other animals, the nondeficient gene probably represents a new mutation. Presumably the locus involved is one of those that regulates phenotypic development by switching genes at other loci on and off. In this case, the gene for lactase production in adults represents a mutation that prolongs the infantile condition. It has been hypothesized that the gene for lactase production probably arose by mutation sometime in the past 10,000 years and was strongly favored in populations that took up herding and dairying. In populations where milk was not drunk by adults, the primitive condition of so-called lactase deficiency was retained.

Once again, this system gives us a glimpse of a phenomenon that is undoubtedly widespread in the human species. Similar changes in enzyme activity probably accompanied all the major changes in diet associated with technological innovations in human history. One such change, early in hominid evolution, was from omnivorous vegetarianism to a diet including a regular intake of meat. A second, much later, was the adoption of diets including a high percentage of starchy foods with the development of food production.

The Significance of Human Polymorphism

We should end this brief examination of some simply inherited characteristics in *Homo sapiens* with a few general observations. One is that because of the difficulty of sampling, the genetically determined variation that we know about is undoubtedly only a tiny fraction of all such variation that actually exists in the species. Second, we should note the general prevalence of polymorphism in human populations. About 30 percent of the recognizable structural loci in humans seem to be polymorphic. The effect of this widespread polymorphism, as we saw, is that each human being is genotypically and phenotypically unique. Third, as we have pointed out, we have no idea of the evolutionary forces that establish or maintain the vast majority of these polymorphisms. We need to know much more about the selective effect of variant genotypes, and such effects when small are very hard to detect. In spite of the progress that has been made over the last few decades, genetic research has only barely started to unravel the evolutionary significance of the simply inherited traits of the human species.

More Complex Characters

Strictly speaking, the characters to be considered in this section are determined by the same kind of genetic factors as affect single-gene characters, but they raise different problems of understanding and interpretation. They are the result of the developmental process during which the gene products, the proteins, interact with one another and with the environment. Aside from the fact that many genes are known to be involved, the details of the developmental process are in most cases quite obscure.

Unlike the case of simple characters, variations in complex characters are generally distributed continuously rather than discontinuously within the population. The human ABO blood group phenotypes provide an example of discontinuous distribution. All normal humans can be assigned one of four common phenotypes: A, B, AB, or O. No refinement of technique will reveal intermediate phenotypes between A and AB. This pattern contrasts with the "continuous" distribution pattern of a characteristic such as stature, where no sharp boundaries exist, and the number of groups one makes is limited only by the precision of the measuring technique.

The continuously varying characters in natural populations commonly show a distribution that closely approximates the shape of

Figure 9–3. The distribution of stature among 91,163 army recruits, representing the young male population of England in 1939. The distribution of individual values plotted as a histogram closely matches a normal curve calculated from the data. M = **Mean value (67.5 inches).** (Martin, 1949)

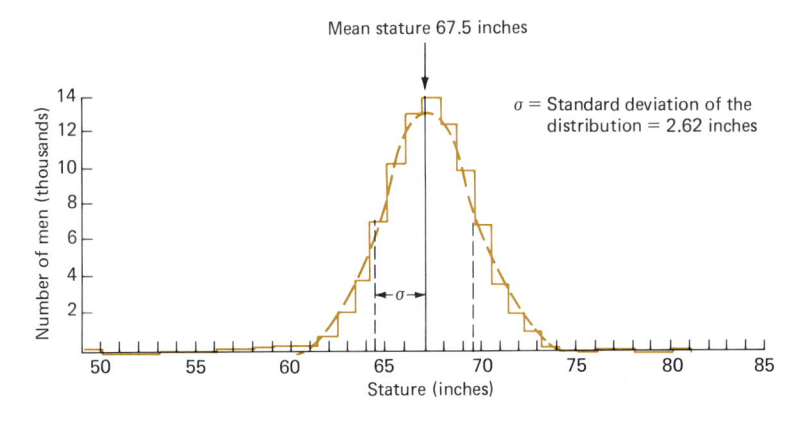

σ = Standard deviation of the distribution = 2.62 inches

the normal curve. Such a distribution can be described statistically in terms of its mean, or average, and its standard deviation from the mean—a measure of the scatter or dispersion of individual values around the average. (See Figure 9–3.)

Many traits of this kind are externally visible and obvious and have excited curiosity since the earliest recorded times. Some of them have formed the basis for defining the traditional "races" of mankind. Deciphering the way in which products of genes interact with each other and with the environment to produce these phenotypic characters is one of the most exacting challenges facing contemporary biology. We cannot consider here all the multifactorially inherited variations in the human species. We have therefore concentrated on one representative category that has attracted special interest and that illustrates general points about such variations.

Human Pigmentation

Human skin, hair, and the iris of the eye all vary in color. Of the three, the most anthropologically interesting is skin color, since variation in the color of the hair and iris in adults is virtually confined to populations of northern Europe and those derived from them.

The color of the human skin is determined by the concentration of various pigments in its layers and by the thickness of the layers themselves. The most important pigment in human skin is melanin. The greater the melanin concentration, the darker the color of the skin.

Modern experimenters measure the variations in skin color with an instrument called a reflectance spectrophotometer. Broadly speaking, the lower the concentration of melanin granules, the greater the reflectance of light from the skin. The color of the skin in human populations varies from very light, as in northwest Europe, to very dark, as in parts of tropical Africa, Asia, and Australasia, but even the darkest and lightest populations include many people who are darker and lighter than the average.

Skin color genes obviously do not segregate as a single pair of alleles at one locus, but beyond this the genetic basis of pigmentation is quite uncertain. Most work on the subject has assumed that the effects of skin color genes are additive in a simple manner and that there is no dominance or complex interaction between loci. With these assumptions, the distribution of skin color seen in real human populations is best explained by a model with about five loci, each with a single pair of alleles.

However, a biochemical approach to the problem suggests that the model based on simple additive effects of genes may not be realistic. Melanin is formed from the amino acid tyrosine via a metabolic pathway that is catalyzed by several distinct enzymes. A plausible (though speculative) hypothesis is that one or more of these enzymes is polymorphic, and that the variant forms of each enzyme have different activity rates. This enzymatic variation would in turn alter the rate of production and deposition of melanin in the skin. If this is the case, the observed variation in skin color could be due to multiple alleles, either of genes at several loci or perhaps at only a single locus.

The Distribution of Human Skin Color Why is the human species so strongly polytypic for skin pigmentation? The production of melanin by "tanning" is the usual response of human skin exposed to the ultraviolet components of sunlight. This is strong circumstantial evidence that ultraviolet light is one selective factor that determines the geographical variation in genetically determined skin color. Figure 9–4 shows the geographical distribution of human skin color (disregarding the colonization of the New World by people of Old World stock and of Australasia by Europeans over the past 500 years) as compared with the annual incidence of ultraviolet light. On the whole, deeply pigmented populations now live, or have lived until recently, in areas exposed to a relatively high incidence of ultraviolet radiation. There are many exceptions to this generalization, however. These include the comparatively light-skinned Indians of tropical South America and the dark-skinned aborigines of Tasmania, who live in a cool, misty climate not unlike that of northern California. As these exceptions indicate, no simple explanation in terms of selective factors will completely account for the modern distribution of human skin color. Population movements also have to be taken into account.

The geographical correspondence between deep pigmentation and the incidence of ultraviolet light does not explain *how* ultraviolet light might act as a selective agent. Several different selective effects of ultraviolet radiation have been suggested. In each case, the basis for the theory is the observation that melanin in the upper layers of the skin scatters and absorbs ultraviolet radiation, preventing its penetration into the deeper layers.

One of the most obvious and painful responses to excessive exposure to ultraviolet radiation is sunburn, which irritates and destroys the skin's outer layers, causing discomfort, blistering, and a risk of secondary infection. All of these could have been selective factors in primitive human populations. The melanin present in a "genetically" dark skin would protect against sunburn, but so would tanning. Only extreme genotypes are incapable of tanning to a point where sunburn is prevented. Sunburn could, however, pose a severe potential hazard to young infants if they were not protected.

Another potential selective agent that is influenced by exposure to ultraviolet light is skin cancer. Among "whites," tumors of the skin, especially of the exposed parts, are more frequent in sunny climates. Moreover, the "white" inhabitants of these regions have more skin tumors than their dark-skinned neighbors. However, these tumors apparently have little effect on fitness, since they are

Figure 9–4. **The distribution of human skin color, disregarding European and African population movements into the New World and the Pacific after 1400 A.D. Superimposed is the average distribution of ultraviolet light intensity in watt-seconds sq. cm.** (From B. J. Williams, 1973)

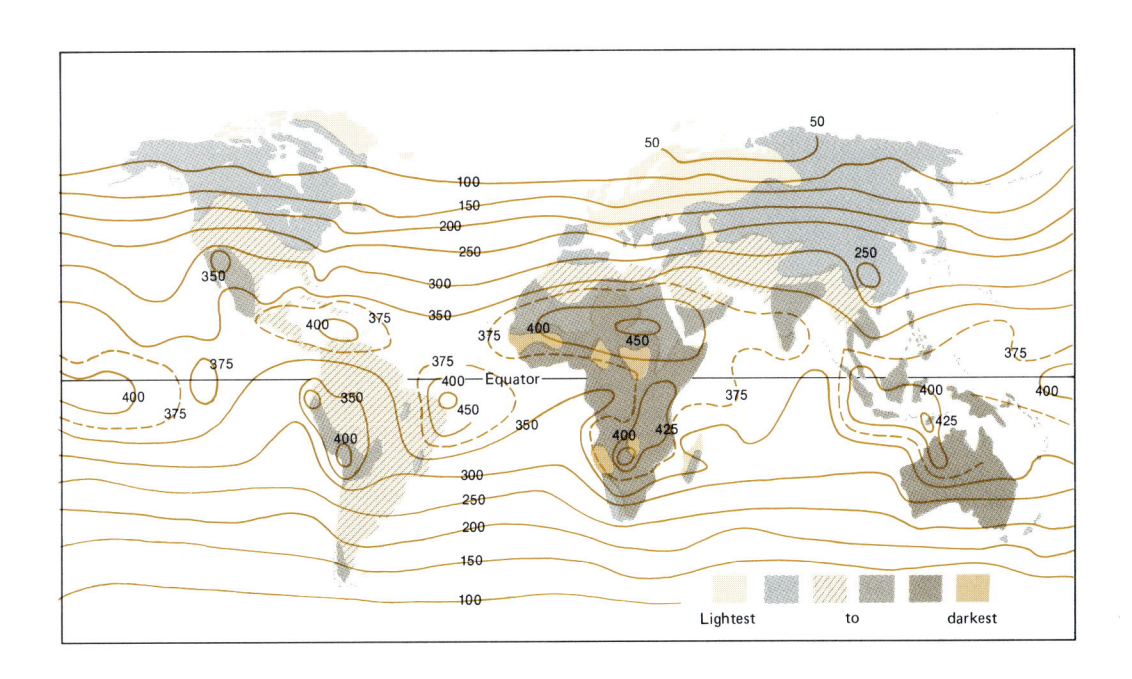

generally nonmalignant and usually occur after reproductive age.

A third possible selective agent involves an effect of ultraviolet radiation that is normally beneficial—stimulation of vitamin D production in the skin. Vitamin D is essential to the body's calcium metabolism, but too much is toxic. Possibly the melanin layer of dark-skinned peoples screens out excessive ultraviolet radiation and thus eliminates the danger of poisoning by excess vitamin D in sunny climates. We must admit, however, that there is no direct evidence that too much vitamin D is in fact a problem for light-skinned inhabitants of the tropics.

An alternative approach also hinged on vitamin D synthesis points to the selective advantage of *light* skin in a climate with a low incidence of ultraviolet radiation. A deficiency of vitamin D in the growing child can lead to skeletal deformities called rickets. There is some evidence that prior to the advent of regular dietary vitamin supplements, rickets occurred more frequently among black children than among white children of similar socioeconomic status living in cloudy Northern cities. The inference is that dark skins are less able to absorb sufficient ultraviolet radiation from weak sunlight to carry out synthesis of adequate amounts of vitamin D, especially in winter, when most of the body surface is covered. (Such selection would have ceased when vitamin D enriched milk became readily available.)

We need not assume that only one of these sunshine-related selective effects has contributed to the distribution of human skin color. All of them, as well as others still undefined, are probably implicated. And as with other variations, the distribution of skin color we see today is as much due to historical events as to differential selection.

Evolution of Human Skin Color—A Hypothetical Scenario Taking each of these various factors into account, we can suggest a tentative scenario of the evolution of human skin pigmentation and its distribution.

Judging by living African apes, the primitive condition for prehominids was probably a "white" skin with irregular pigmented blotches. Over most of the body surface, the skin was covered with a hairy coat. The naked parts of the face may or may not have been deeply pigmented; the palms and soles probably were not.

An early hominid species, presumably living somewhere in the tropics and probably in a nonforest habitat, lost its hairy coat. Selection then favored more intense skin pigmentation to protect against sunburn, and perhaps against overproduction of vitamin D.

As hominids colonized the more climatically seasonal higher latitudes of the Old World, "genetic pigmentation" was replaced by a fair skin capable of tanning. This condition permitted a more flexible response to the seasonal variation in the incidence of sunlight. It protected the individual against vitamin D deficiency during the winter and against sunburn in the summer.

Among "white" populations living in areas that remain cloudy even in summer (like Ireland), relaxed selection for the tanning response allowed the survival of mutant genotypes that tan poorly and respond to ultraviolet radiation by freckling or repeated sunburn.

During the Upper Pleistocene, America was peopled by "nontropical," light-skinned immigrants from eastern Asia, while Australia was colonized by "tropical," dark-skinned peoples from Southeast Asia.

The fact that in the 30,000 years or so since these movements occurred the populations of America and Australia have apparently diverged rather little in skin color from their relatives in eastern and Southeast Asia is itself interesting. It suggests that the selective factors that produced the original diversity in skin color have decreased in intensity, or that the process of adaptation is very slow, or perhaps both. This in turn would indicate that the evolution of adaptations to temperate zone climates was very ancient, perhaps much older than the species *Homo sapiens* itself.

The distribution of skin color variation was modified during the past 10,000 years by population movements spurred by technological innovations. In particular, the populations of the Near East, Europe, China, and central Africa, all of which adopted agriculture, burgeoned and expanded geographically at the expense of their hunting and gathering neighbors.

Several waves of light-skinned agricultural people moved into Southeast Asia from the north, largely displacing earlier dark-skinned populations. In Africa, it was dark-skinned herders and farmers who expanded, displacing and absorbing lighter-skinned hunter-gatherers whose remnants are represented by the modern Bushmen of the Kalahari.

In the past 500 years, the situation has been further complicated by colonization. While the invasion of the New World by people of diverse African, European, and Asian descent is the most obvious example of this process, other such movements should not be overlooked. The Chinese, for example, migrated into Malaysia, Indonesia, and Polynesia, and Asiatic Indians into Ceylon, Malaya, and Burma.

One point should be emphasized: If our scenario is correct, there would have been less juxtaposition of very different phenotypes before the movements of the early agriculturalists. In other words, human skin color was probably more *clinally* distributed at this time, exhibiting more continuous gradients of variation from region to region than at present. This point is worth emphasizing, since it directly opposes the commonly held view that population movements in recent times have tended to blur the boundaries between "races" that in earlier times were more "pure" and distinct.

Other Complex Characters

Skin color is representative of a large group of human variations whose mode of inheritance is obscure but which are believed to be determined by the interaction of many genes. These variants include the shape, size, and constitution of the whole body and of its parts—the head, face, and dentition—as well as physiological responses to heat, cold, and other environmental stresses. As with pigmentation, each of these variations poses problems of interpretation. There is still a great deal of work to be done to elucidate their genetic basis and mode of inheritance, to determine how far variation is due to genetic effects and how far to direct effects of the environment on the phenotype, and to relate them to selective influences.

Human Variation and the Concept of Race

Since the science of anthropology has on occasion been defined as "the study of race and culture," the reader has perhaps wondered how we have managed to describe and discuss a good part of human physical variation without using the first of these terms. We have done this by examining the distribution of variable traits as independent entities and by summarizing these distributions in terms of geographical, not "racial," units. Often, distributions of genes and phenotypes can be described in terms of geographical frequency gradients or clines, such as that for blood group B.

We, and perhaps the majority of contemporary physical anthropologists, regard this as the most productive way to tackle the interpretation of human variability. However, other anthropologists have objected that something is lost in examining variation only in terms of a single gene and gene complexes. Genes, they argue, do not float independently of each other. They belong to populations, groups of people with a common history, a boundary that separates each from its neighbors, and a common coadapted gene pool. According to this school of thought, comparing the overall constitution of the different populations, rather than describing the distribution of individual genes, provides a more useful approach. Traditionally, this aspect of human diversity has been approached by classifying mankind into races. First, we should look at some of the ways in which the term "race" has been used, for not all anthropologists have used it in the same way.

Races as Recombinants

Anthropologists of the late nineteenth and early twentieth centuries often sought to identify, in the existing heterogeneous population of Europe, individuals who "typified" a strain that supposedly had gone into its makeup. Each so-called race was identified by a series of characteristics, such as head form, hair color, and facial features. Races distinguished in this way included the "nordic—tall, blond, and long-headed," and the "alpine—shorter, brown- or red-haired, and round-headed." Sometimes authors would become quite lyrical about the personality traits they ascribed to the type.

A number of obviously weak assumptions are involved in this approach: (1) If traits like head form and hair color are genetically independent, segregation and recombination of the genes would give rise to round-headed blondes and long-headed brunettes, as well as typical alpines and nordics—and indeed it does. The more independent characters added to the list of diagnostic items, the more combinations will appear. The basis for selecting one or two "types" from the immense variety produced by recombination was never made very clear. (2) This approach also assumes the preexistence of strains or races that, if not totally invariant, were much less variable than modern populations—each of them including a high proportion of typical nordics, alpines, or whatever. There is no evidence to support the notion—nor is there any good theoretical reason for believing—that such "pure races" ever existed in Europe or elsewhere.

Linnaeus's classification of the genus Homo reflects the racist presumptions of eighteenth-century Europe. (Courtesy, The American Museum of Natural History)

Races as Subspecies

The "Major Stock" Concept The practice of selecting certain individuals from a variable population as racial archetypes has now virtually disappeared, partly because the development of evolutionary theory based upon population variability reveals its lack of biological and genetic foundation. However, the practice of grouping the populations of the human species into a few "major stocks" or "great races" dates back to Linnaeus's original classification of 1758, and a modified form of this practice is still followed by many physical anthropologists. Linnaeus's scheme used only a few diagnostic characters to distinguish his races, which were also defined geographically. His classificatory scheme was widely adopted, although it became customary to use terms such as "Negroid," "Caucasoid," and "Mongoloid" in place of his Latin names, and additional physical characteristics were added to his list of diagnostics.

Zoological Subspecies In zoological taxonomy, subspecies comprise groups of populations, usually geographically defined, that share obvious external characteristics. To avoid the problem of multiplication of subspecies, the zoologists have established an arbitrary threshold. If 75 percent of the individuals of a population can be unequivocally assigned to a subspecies on the basis of a particular diagnostic character, the population is sufficiently distinct to be designated as a subspecies.

Paradoxically, some anthropologists began to embrace the idea of subspecies just as zoologists were beginning seriously to question its worth. Zoologists found that as the extent of variation below the species level became better known, many characters were found to crosscut "subspecies" boundaries. The lively debate among zoologists on the utility of subspecies divisions still continues. However, there seems to be some agreement that the concept of subspecies can be a useful taxonomic category only under the following conditions:

1. If the major subdivisions of the species are strongly isolated geographically, with little gene flow between the subgroups to mitigate the effects of drift and disruptive selection, thus insuring that genes originating in one part of the species range cannot easily spread into other parts. Presumably such subspecies are often incipient new species; if their isolation were to continue, speciation would result. Under such circumstances, many characters and genes are likely to show concordant distribution — that is, all the characters would tend to vary in the same direction.
2. If the state of knowledge of the existing variation within the species is limited to one or two characters so that discordance in distribution is not a practical problem. Since the early nineteenth century this has not been the case with the human species.

It is clear that the living populations of *Homo sapiens* do not meet the first of these conditions. Human populations are in constant contact with each other, and barriers to gene flow invariably prove ephemeral. As expected, gene frequency distributions are often highly discordant. To take only two examples: the sickle cell gene has evidently spread between "white" Mediterraneans and "black" Africans or vice versa; and ABO frequencies vary enormously among so-called Mongoloid populations.

To sustain the subspecies idea, it must be postulated that major subdivisions of *Homo sapiens* were once more distinct, being separated in the past by sharper barriers to gene flow than exist at present. This hypothesis is widely accepted as fact even though it lacks support from the fossil record or from archeology. Indeed, as we have argued with regard to skin color, human variation in the past was probably *more* clinally distributed, with fewer sharp boundaries than it has today. There is no valid reason to consider that most patterns of human variation are the result of the prior differentiation of major subspecies and their subsequent hybridization.

Some genetically intermediate peoples obviously do result from hybridization. American blacks, for instance, exhibit many gene frequencies that are intermediate between those of American whites and West Africans, and this is clearly due to the dual African and European ancestry of black Americans. The point is that hybridization should not be assumed to be the cause of all physical intermediacy if historical evidence for it is lacking.

The use of such concepts as race or subspecies to organize our data can lead to other distortions in our perception of human variation. If one's preoccupation is with racial classification, then discordantly distributed traits are apt to be regarded as irrelevant, even if, like sickle cell, they are important keys to understanding the reasons for human variation.

In spite of these potential drawbacks, many physical anthropologists still refer to such categories as Mongoloid, Caucasoid, and Negroid, not necessarily to imply evolutionary hypotheses, but because they find them useful, descriptive categories. As we have mentioned, organizing available data on human variation population by population, as well as trait by trait, is certainly legitimate. The questions then arise: How far can such groups be defined without arbitrarily choosing particular characters as important or primary? Do the traditional racial groupings emerge as objectively defined entities from all our information on human physical variation?

Multivariate Analysis The capacity of modern electronic computers enables us to approach the analysis of variation in human populations through the use of multivariate statistics. We cannot here describe in detail the technicalities of multivariate methods. Suffice it to say that the methods utilize a series of dimensions describing an array of entities, such as a table that records the gene frequencies of a series of human populations. The difference between the entities (populations, in this case) is then expressed in terms of *generalized distance*—that is, distance based on all the variables taken together. Similarly, multivariate analysis can group populations pair by pair according to their overall resemblance. All variables are treated alike in this method; there is no weighting of variables because one or another is believed to be more fundamental or important in terms of human evolution.

Using these methods, Cavalli-Sforza and Edwards (1963) have produced a tree diagram, or *dendogram,* based on blood group gene frequencies (ABO, MNS, Rh, Diego, and Duffy) that depicts the degree of correspondence for these traits in fifteen human populations. The groupings produced by this technique agree quite well with the traditional ones, although there are some discrepancies. The Koreans, whom the traditional classifiers would call typical Mongoloids, fall with the Australian Aborigines.

One point should be emphasized here. A diagram such as this represents only resemblances and differences, not phylogeny or evolutionary history.

Our view of the concept of race, used as a means for globally classifying the populations of the human species, may be summarized thus: The concept of race conveys little or no information that could not be expressed in terms of populations and gene frequencies. It can lead to a mental set in which evolutionary schemes for which there is little justification are uncritically accepted. Although it is quite possible that there really are major divisions of mankind, distinguishable on the basis of unbiased estimates of generalized genetic distance between populations, the existence of such groupings has yet to be satisfactorily demonstrated. In general, subspecies classifications are useful only in special circumstances that do not seem to apply to modern *Homo sapiens,* and that may never have applied to the evolving human species.

Races as Ethnic Groups

If the term "race" is to be used at all, it can probably be most useful in a sense close to its normal everyday one—that is, to describe groups within a complex society that are basically defined sociologically, although such definitions may be based on certain physical traits and characteristics and may often designate Mendelian populations.

For example, the terms "white," "black," and "Indian" are used to define "races" in United States society. Such a usage of the term "race" has no pretensions to universality. Each society has its own definitions. In the United States, for instance, Asiatic Indians are regarded as white; in Britain they are part of an undifferentiated "colored" population that also includes Malaysians, Chinese, and West Indians of predominantly African extraction. In racially conscious South Africa, Asiatic Indians constitute a race apart from whites, Bantu, Khoisan (Bushmen and Hottentots), and "colored." This limited and unambitious sociological use of the word "race" fills a gap in our vocabulary, and fits everyday usage without implying scientific validity.

summary

For most of its history, the human species has been geographically widespread and unevenly distributed, resulting in its becoming highly *polytypic*. To study this variation, the physical anthropologist investigates easily recognizable, genetically determined variations, as well as those characteristics inherited in a less straightforward manner.

To interpret patterns of human variation, the anthropologist asks a series of questions: How is the variation determined? Why are human populations polymorphic at that locus or set of loci? Why is the human species polytypic for that particular character—what are the factors at work?

By far the greatest number of genetic markers in humans involve blood proteins. The search for selection in human populations is exemplifed by the study of variation in hemoglobin and two of the blood group systems. The best-known hemoglobin polymorphisms concern the beta variant hemoglobin HbS, or sickle cell hemoglobin, which produces sickle-shaped red cells that lead both to anemia and obstruction of blood vessels. These symptoms are much graver in homozygotes than in heterozygotes. The uneven distribution of the Hb^s gene appears to be partially accounted for by selection in favor of heterozygotes in areas where malaria is prevalent. Distribution is also affected by migration and gene flow. Through this distribution we can see that population movements and habitat modification have become so rapid that evolutionary changes in gene frequency mediated by natural selection have not been able to keep pace. Considerable differences also exist between populations in the frequency of genes in the ABO and Rh blood group systems. Explanations of distribution patterns based on random sampling error effects such as drift are not entirely satisfactory. Several studies have shown associations between blood groups and the incidence of various diseases.

Other variations such as the ability to taste PTC and the ability to digest lactose appear to be related to diet. PTC tasting is important because it represents a large array of biochemically mediated variations that produce selective effects by rendering the perception of particular stimuli either pleasant or unpleasant.

Whereas single-gene characters are distributed discontinuously, polygenic characters are generally distributed continuously in the population. Many traits of this kind are externally visible; human pigmentation is one example. Genetic studies suggest that several loci interact to determine variation in human skin color. It appears that ultraviolet light is one selective factor influencing variation in skin color among populations. On the whole, deeply pigmented populations have lived in areas with a high incidence of ultraviolet radiation, although there are many exceptions. Some of the selective agents possibly involved in skin-color variation are sunburn, cancers of the skin, and control of vitamin D production. Light-skinned people may have been at an advantage in climates with seasonal lack of sunshine.

A tentative scheme of the evolution of skin color and its distribution indicates that human skin color was more clinally distributed before the movements of the early agriculturists—a direct contradiction to the commonly held view that the boundaries between the "races" have only recently begun to be blurred.

The real issue over the use of "race" as a concept is whether or not it enhances our understanding of human variation. Early anthropologists often thought of races as types—groups of individuals who possess a particular series of characteristics. This concept is at variance with genetic theory. In the "major stock" concept of races, races are distinguished on the basis of certain physical characteristics and geographical location. This concept is vulnerable because many traits have distributions that crosscut traditional racial boundaries. Human variation has also been viewed in terms of the zoological category of subspecies. Yet living human populations do not meet the conditions necessary for the concept of subspecies to be useful. Through multivariate analysis, the differences among populations are expressed in terms of generalized distance based on a number of characteristics taken together. Eventually such methods may enable us to divide *Homo sapiens* objectively into major segments; as yet, its results are too incomplete to attempt this.

Our view is that the term "race" as a means of classifying human populations conveys little or no information that could not be expressed in terms of populations and gene frequencies, although the term may have a limited utility as a term for sociologically defined subgroups in a population.

suggested readings

COON, C. S., with E. HUNT
1965   *The Living Races of Man.* New York: Knopf. Includes a good review of human anatomical variation, and presents a coherent version of the view that human variation is best comprehended in terms of race.

HARRIS, H.
1959   *Human Biochemical Genetics.* New York: Cambridge University Press. The discoverer of many human biochemical polymorphisms considers their biological and evolutionary significance.

KATZ, S. H., ed.
1975   *Biological Anthropology.* San Francisco: W. H. Freeman. A collection of readings, including a number of useful articles on human adaptability and genetics.

RACE R. R., and SANGER, R.
1968   *Blood Groups in Man.* 5th ed. Philadelphia: F. A. Davis. Not only an authoritative work on a major set of human polymorphisms, but an enjoyable book for its own sake.

Having explored our physical and cultural evolution, we now turn to the study of contemporary peoples and their cultural patterns. It would be impossible to fully understand the field of cultural anthropology by looking only at what anthropologists have learned about cultural diversity among the world's populations. Of equal importance is a knowledge of how anthropologists approach and practice their own discipline—the theories that influence their thinking, the methods of data collection they use, the ethical standards they consider important. After all, anthropology is an ongoing science, an effort to compile information on human behavioral and cultural variation and to formulate explanations for it. In Part III, therefore, we will introduce the reader not only to cultural anthropology as a subject area, but also to cultural anthropology as an area of scientific inquiry.

No anthropologist—no scientist—approaches the tasks of gathering data and devising explanations with a totally unbiased perspective. We are influenced by the findings and insights of others who have gone before us. This is why we begin in Chapter 10 by surveying the history of anthropological theory. Our discussion is organized around three very broad questions that synthesize the many specific problems and questions with which anthropologists have been, and continue to be, concerned: Why do societies differ? How do they differ? What is the relationship between the individual and society? Within the general framework of these questions we will focus on the most important ideas and theoretical perspectives that have developed over the hundred years in which anthropology has existed as an academic discipline.

The theoretical perspectives anthropologists have developed are not based on secondhand accounts of the customs people in different societies practice. Anthropological theories are based on information that has been painstakingly and systematically collected by thousands of researchers traveling to every part of the world. Fieldwork—living among a population to compile firsthand information about their ways of life—is the principal means of data gathering in cultural anthropology. Of course, the specific methods of collecting data while in the field are as diverse as the topics researchers study. But regardless of the diversity of techniques available, the success of anthropological research is limited by the realities of the field situation. In Chapter 11, we will discuss four major aspects of anthropological fieldwork: how anthropologists prepare for the field, the data-gathering techniques they use while there, the actual experience of being in the field from the point of view of the anthropologist, and the methods researchers use to analyze and interpret data.

Whatever areas particular theoretical orientations may lead anthropologists to investigate, whatever techniques they may use in collecting and analyzing data, the course of their research is influenced as much by the impact a particular project will have on the people being studied as by the value of the information to be collected and the investigator's ability to obtain it. After all, anthropologists are studying people, not things, and the research they conduct may have far-reaching effects on the lives of those who are the subjects of investigation. In the final chapter of this part, therefore, we take up the important topic of ethics in anthropology. Specifically, we will consider the ethical standards that guide anthropologists in their selection of problems to study and methods of research to use, in their behavior in the field, and in the manner in which they choose to report their findings.

3
studying
contemporary peoples

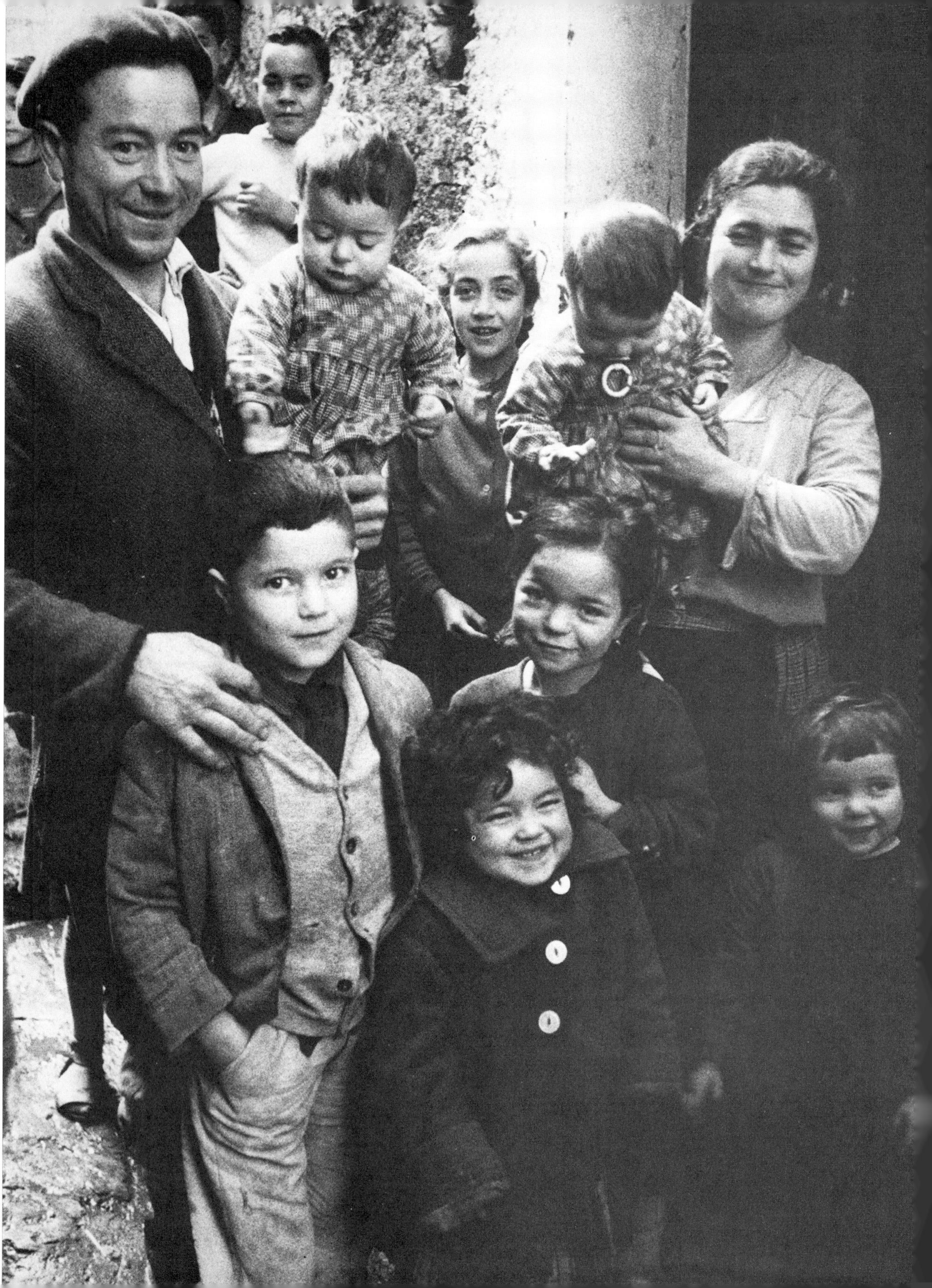

ten
History of Anthropological Theory

In everyday conversation we use the term *theory* to refer to unproven or unsubstantiated ideas. When someone makes a remark that we think is not at all based on "facts," we dismiss it by saying, "That's just a theory." Although ultimately scientific theories are unproven, they are more than guesses. For a scientist, a theory is a way of deciding what questions to ask and how to evaluate potential answers; a way of looking at and explaining phenomena. Scientists choose one theory over another because it provides more fruitful ways of framing questions about topics that are important to a discipline and because it suggests answers to those questions that account for more factual data in more likely ways.

At the end of Chapter 1 we discussed the theories that we find most basic and have used in organizing this book. In this chapter we trace the development of theories of culture over the hundred years that anthropology has existed as a discipline.

It is important to recognize that most of the anthropologists who have contributed to the growth of theory will not even be mentioned in the chapter. A history necessarily focuses on the most important ideas, works, and their authors. But many other anthropologists contributed in significant ways to the formulation of these ideas, and the figures that we will discuss had substantial effects on each others' work.

Moreover, the emphasis on individuals who contributed to the development of current theory should not cause us to forget that there were many ideas along the way that have now been rejected. Many anthropological works of the nineteenth century, totally ethnocentric by today's standards, expressed shock or condescension at, or presented titillating accounts of, the behavior of "savages." And much early anthropology was undertaken as a part of the European efforts to colonize, or exploit, vast areas of Asia and Africa. Even when early anthropologists were not working directly in such efforts, the theories they formulated were affected by these concerns, which were, after all, important concerns of the growing industrial societies of their time.

Of necessity, our comments about many of the early theories will be critical. In any vital, growing science, theories generated decades or centuries ago will have outlived their usefulness. But these early theories and the anthropologists who created them are of more than historical interest. They framed major questions that still concern us today: Why do societies differ? How do they differ? What is the relationship between the individual and society? And they made the initial suggestions as to how these questions might be answered. Moreover, although some of the early anthropologists' ideas seem to be truisms today, they were once the subjects of intense disagreement and debate.

Why Do Societies Differ?

The question of why cultural similarities and differences exist at all is one of the most difficult to answer. Early anthropologists attempted to explain cultural variation in terms of the then popular and daring theory of evolution—with little success, in the view of their younger, more skeptical colleagues. Theories of cultural evolution fell into disrepute, and anthropologists turned to studies of contacts between

Anthropologists have continually looked at the family—the basic social unit of every society—in their search to find answers to some of the most fundamental questions of their discipline. (© Hans W. Silvester, Rapho/Photo Researchers)

societies and questions about social structure and the relationship between culture and personality. However, in recent years studies of the interaction between people and their environment have revived interest in cultural evolution. Today, cultural change and adaptation are topics of central concern to anthropologists.

Tylor, Morgan, and Frazer: The Early Evolutionists

The weakness of many early theories of cultural evolution was summed up by Scottish classicist and anthropologist Sir James Frazer, author of *The Golden Bough* (1900), a monumental analysis of "primitive" religion and "savage" rites. When asked if he had ever seen any of the peoples about whom he wrote so eloquently, Frazer is said to have replied, "God forbid!" (Beattie, 1964:7). The early evolutionists were not interested in "primitive" culture per se—God forbid! Rather, they believed that in studying "savages," they might gradually uncover the origins of their own civilization and arrive at a general understanding of how human culture and behavior had evolved over the millennia.

Numerous theories of cultural and social evolution were advanced in the late nineteenth century. All rested on one basic premise: that human institutions everywhere evolve or progress along the same lines, through a series of stages leading to a common end—a pattern that we now refer to as *unilineal evolution*. The problem was to reconstruct the process of sociocultural evolution. To this end, the early evolutionists assumed that "surviving" primitive societies are living relics of the past, and provide a fairly accurate picture of what life had been like during various periods in man's history. For example, certain contemporary cultures, such as hunters and gatherers, were thought to resemble cultures that existed hundreds of thousands, even millions of years ago.[1] Others were viewed as typical of the earliest agricultural and pastoral societies, and still other groups as representative of the first state-organized societies. By analyzing institutions in a wide range of primitive[2] groups, the nineteenth-century evolutionists tried to establish a chronological sequence of development. Their model was the evolution of the species from the simple to the complex; and they assumed by analogy that the simpler the social institution, the older it must be.

Using this approach, the English scholar Edward B. Tylor examined data (mostly collected by government officials, missionaries, and European travelers) from several hundred societies. He then reconstructed possible sequences for a number of cultural institutions such as residence patterns and religion. He argued, for example, that the concept of the soul gave rise to belief in an afterlife. These doctrines in turn evolved into polytheistic religious systems based on a belief in many gods, and ultimately culminated in more enlightened and rational monotheistic religions, such as Judaism and Christianity. Tylor believed that the evolution of such cultural traits was part of a general scheme of progress whereby all societies developed in stages from savagery through barbarism to civilization.

Unlike many earlier social scientists who argued that people living in a state of savagery or barbarism were innately (biologically and/or psychologically) inferior, Tylor argued that all peoples had the same *capacity* for progress because they were equipped with the same mental abilities. Differences between cultures were due, he maintained, to differences in development rather than to inborn aptitudes. Through the 1870s, Tylor's prestige grew in academic circles, and in 1884 Oxford University awarded him the first professorship in anthropology. For the first

---

[1] In fact, they probably do to varying degrees, and this is one of the reasons we continue to study them.

[2] We are following nineteenth-century usage in using the word *primitive* without quotation marks. Anthropologists avoid using this term today, because it encourages ethnocentric assumptions of lower mental capacity or some other form of inferiority.

Table 10-1: Morgan's Stages of Cultural Evolution.

Level of Development	Identifying Features
Lower Savagery:	Invention of speech, subsistence on fruits and nuts
Middle Savagery:	Fishing and the use of fire
Upper Savagery:	Bow and arrow
Lower Barbarism:	Pottery
Middle Barbarism:	Domestication of animals in the Old World; cultivation of maize by irrigation, adobe and stone brick buildings in the New World
Upper Barbarism:	Iron smelting, use of iron tools
Civilization:	Phonetic alphabet and writing

Source: Morgan, 1963:12 (orig. 1877).

time, anthropology was recognized as a legitimate profession, or at least a respectable academic concern. Perhaps more important, Tylor inspired others to devote themselves to the study of cultural evolution—most notably Morgan and Frazer.

A lawyer by training, Lewis Henry Morgan became interested in anthropology as a young man, when he helped his Iroquois neighbors in rural New York to fight for their land. Morgan published his impressions of the Iroquois in 1850 and soon gave up the practice of law to follow his new avocation. Elaborating on Tylor's theories, Morgan's *Ancient Society* (1877) linked successive stages of cultural evolution to such technological developments as the invention of pottery and the domestication of plants and animals. Each technological level, he believed, was associated with specific cultural patterns or institutions—a particular kind of kinship structure or legal system, for example. In particular, Morgan focused on the evolution of the family. In the earliest stages of human development, he postulated, men and women mated indiscriminately; there was no family structure at all. Gradually a form of communal marriage evolved, groups of brothers marrying groups of sisters. In the next stage brother-sister unions were forbidden. People began to pair off, but continued to live in large groups. Gradually, as society continued to evolve, men established the right to their own households, with a wife or, more commonly, several wives. Only in the final stage of social evolution—Civilization—did men and women become partners in monogamous marriage.

In a similar vein, Frazer described an intellectual evolution from magic (the attempt to control nature), through religion (the admission of impotence in some matters), to science and secularism (the rational approach to life's mysteries) in *The Golden Bough*.

As these examples indicate, the early evolutionists were speculators whose theories rested on unsystematically collected and unverified information. In seeking the origins of human society, they necessarily went well beyond the facts. The notion that people once lived in unbridled promiscuity, for example, is historical fantasy. Nevertheless, they established the core notion that the variations we observe among contemporary societies are the result of different lines of evolution, not biological (so-called racial) differences. In speculating about developmental sequences, they inspired many archeologists to seek concrete data that would validate or refute their ideas. And they created an interest in formulating more precise comparative scales for measuring the relative *complexity* of different societies (as we shall see in the discussion of "neoevolutionists" Leslie White and Julian Steward).

Boas: Historical Particularism

The tendency of early evolutionists to let their speculations override their interest in data led to the downfall of their theories. One of the men who led the attack on the evolutionists was Franz Boas, a physicist turned cultural geographer. In *The Limitations of the Comparative Method of Anthropology* (1896), Boas argued that anthropologists knew far too little about preliterate peoples to construct valid and useful theories about the origins of social life. Perhaps one day it would be possible to explain the enormous variation in customs and practices travelers were discovering, but for the present, anthropologists should concentrate on gathering as much specific ethnographic information as they possibly could.

Boas chose to study the Kwakiutl Indians of the Northwest Coast. He learned their language and dedicated much of his career to recording their way of life in detail. While determined to refute speculative evolutionary theories about the origins of culture, Boas rigorously avoided constructing new theories to replace them. Rather, he contributed substantially to the growing sophistication of anthropological methods by instilling in his students an appreciation of the intricacy of

Reacting to the speculative nature of the anthropological theories of his time, Franz Boas insisted upon detailed, firsthand ethnographic accounts of non-Western peoples. Boas immersed himself in the life and culture of these Kwakiutl Indians, whose village on the coast of British Columbia is pictured here in a photo taken in the 1880s.
(Courtesy of the American Museum of Natural History)

non-Western culture and of the need for meticulous fieldwork. Because of his emphasis on collecting detailed facts concerning the cultures and histories of particular peoples, Boas's approach is usually referred to as *historical particularism* (Harris, 1968).

Boas had quite properly punctured the evolutionary balloon. In the first place, the evolutionists had carried speculation about sequences of events far beyond what their data could support. And second, they had fallen into a pattern of assuming that the differences observed among cultures in the present were a reflection solely of evolution, which they conceived of as an independent, self-generating, and inevitable process or force. The studies of Boas and his students (as well as those of other critics of the evolutionists) led to a far greater concern with interaction between contemporaneous societies, especially as evidenced by the diffusion of cultural traits from one group to another. In fact, one antievolutionist school of thought that had taken hold among scholars in Britain, Germany, and the United States is referred to as the *diffusionist* school.

The Diffusionists

Like the evolutionists, these anthropologists were also concerned with the question of how cultures had developed in various parts of the world. However, they proposed an entirely different answer: contact or interaction between societies, resulting in the diffusion of cultural traits. Taking issue with the evolutionist theory that social institutions and cultural traits arose independently in many different parts of the world and evolved along parallel lines, the diffusionists maintained that most aspects of culture originated only in one or a few places and gradually spread to peoples in other areas through diffusion or migration. Since individuals are basically uninventive—they reasoned—people are far more likely to borrow or imitate new elements from other cultures than to develop them for themselves.

The most extreme proponents of diffusionism—British anthropologists Elliot Smith, W. J. Perry, and W. H. R. Rivers—espoused the idea that all civilization in fact originated in Egypt where, they believed, the early invention of agriculture had stimulated the rapid development of literate society, the arts, and cities. After traveling in the Near East, Smith had been struck by the similarities between the Egyptian pyramids and stone monuments associated with sun worship and the English megaliths at Stonehenge. Investigating further, he found similar structures throughout the world—Mayan pyramids, Japanese pagodas, Balinese and Cambodian temples, and American Indian burial mounds. Consistent with colonialist attitudes of their time, the British diffusionists were certain that these "complex constructions" could not have been invented by these relatively late-blooming peoples, and concluded that the structures were simply imitations of Egyptian models. (In much the same way, ethnocentric social scientists assume that development in the Third World today must be an imitation of the American experience.) Smith and Perry extended their investigations to other aspects of culture and before long had marshaled a mass of evidence supporting their theory that most aspects of civilization—from pottery, weaving, and the wheel to art, law, government, and religion—had been invented in Egypt and introduced to the rest of the world by far-ranging Egyptian navigators.

Similar theories sponsored by Fritz Graebner and Wilhelm Schmidt gained a following in Germany and Austria. Unlike the British diffusionists, however, this school did not believe that all culture traits originated and diffused from a single center of invention. Rather, they proposed that language, toolmaking, and other basics of culture were invented by four or five primeval societies who, isolated in small bands, developed their own distinctive cultures. Descendants of these early peoples eventually migrated to all corners of the globe, forming distinctive culture circles or *Kulturkreise*. Accordingly, the German-Austrian diffusionists devoted their efforts to reconstructing these culture circles and to tracing worldwide sequences of diffusion. In contrast to the

British diffusionists, who were concerned with the spread of individual cultural items (from the pyramid to the loom to burial practices), Graebner and Schmidt concentrated on the diffusion of entire cultural complexes.

Clark Wissler and Alfred Kroeber (who made important contributions to almost every area of theory discussed in this chapter) were major diffusionist figures in this country. Wissler set out to classify American Indian populations according to their dominant traits and geographical locations. He noted, for example, that all of the many tribes from the Great Plains region depended largely on the buffalo for subsistence, lived in tipis, had men's societies, sweat lodges, scalp dances, and a well-developed tradition of leatherwork and geometrical art, but no agriculture, pottery, or basketry. Wissler believed it unlikely that this exact complex of traits had been invented independently by all the Great Plains groups; and since the complex appeared among peoples living in relative proximity, he explained the similarity in terms of diffusion. Altogether, Wissler isolated ten distinct culture areas (regions where several groups share similar cultural complexes) in North America, four in South America, and one in the Caribbean. He proposed that each area had a "culture center," the place where all the traits typically could be found. This, he maintained, must be where the complex originated, since the farther one moved from this location, the fewer traits appeared. Kroeber added an important dimension to Wissler's work by showing the relationship of the major cultural areas of North America to environmental variables like temperature and rainfall. This was an important beginning to the systematic study of how humans interact with their environment; it anticipated later investigations of the role of social institutions in cultural adaptation.

Although they amassed quantities of data, none of the diffusionists succeeded in proving the existence of any primary centers of invention. Modern anthropologists do not dispute the idea that institutions and artifacts must have begun somewhere, but the diffusionist method of investigation left many basic questions unanswered. For one, why did various traits develop in the first place? More important, where diffusion *is* a source of change, *how* does this process occur? There is little doubt that people borrow technology, ideas, and customs from neighboring peoples—*if* these items are useful. But by assuming that cultural borrowing is automatic, the diffusionists failed to explain why some groups might adopt certain items and reject others. Further, they failed to investigate the organized patterns of exchange and boundary maintenance that regulate the transmission of goods and ideas between groups.

Nevertheless, the diffusionists pointed out major lines of inquiry the evolutionists had ignored: differences in the patterns of contact and interaction between cultures, and differences in the way groups adapt to one another and to the natural environment. It is these areas that Leslie White, Julian Steward, and their students have chosen to investigate in a revival of evolutionary and ecological studies.

White and Steward: The Neoevolutionists

In the 1940s and 1950s, a number of anthropologists became interested in tracing broad regularities in cultural development and change. Reviving evolutionary issues that had been largely ignored since the early days of anthropology, they enlarged and refined the classical evolutionist approach on the basis of new information and ideas that anthropologists had acquired in the intervening years.

Although trained in the Boasian tradition, Leslie White greatly admired the work of nineteenth-century evolutionists Edward B. Tylor and Lewis Henry Morgan. Like them, he believed that culture evolved progressively. Instead of describing abstract notions of progress, however, White sought to pinpoint the cause of progress itself and to explain how it operates. His explanation was "energy." White reasoned that in order to provide themselves with the basic necessities of life, human beings must expend energy. During the early stages of human history, they used their own

Leslie White directed attention to variations in levels of energy use and the roles human groups play in different ecosystems. Today, anthropologists study the similarities and differences in food production and distribution to explain why, for example, in two societies practicing intensive agriculture, a large work group probably including most women in the village participates in a Javanese rice harvest (a), whereas it takes only three men to gather the hay on an Israeli kibbutz (b). (a © Georg Gerster, Rapho/Photo Researchers b Leon V. Kofod)

bodies as the major source of energy, but gradually they began to harness fire, water, wind, and other energy resources. People began to fashion increasingly efficient tools, to domesticate animals, to construct power-driven machines, and so on. And as technological efficiency increased and more and more energy was produced per capita, other aspects of culture evolved in response. White maintained that each level of technology—hunting and gathering, pastoralism, agriculture, metallurgy, militarism, and industrialism—produces a specific type of social organization (White, 1949). Because he believed that culture and development were rooted in material or technological factors, White has been labeled a *cultural materialist.* Because he argued that evolutionists should focus on human culture as a whole, without bothering about whether all or even the majority of groups pass through each stage, he has also been called a *universal evolutionist.*

White improved the concept of evolution by trying to develop observable indicators of change rather than vague notions of progress. He has been criticized for ignoring ideological aspects of adaptation and the complex interaction of technology, social organization, and environmental factors. Nevertheless, in substituting "energy produced per capita" for the largely subjective measures of development early anthropologists employed to distinguish lower from middle "savagery" and so on, White pointed to the need for more concrete and sophisticated scales of complexity in evolutionary studies.

As indicated above, White intentionally ignored particular events and patterns of change. His aim was to discover universal laws, not historical particulars. However, Julian Steward (1953) argued that like nineteenth-century classical evolutionism, White's general evolutionism fails precisely *because* it deals with culture in the abstract rather than with real cultures. Consequently, it does not shed much light on actual processes of development. Why, for instance, have certain societies become industrialized, while others have maintained an essentially Stone Age technology? Steward called for another approach, *multilineal* or *specific evolutionism*, that would focus on particular cultures and observable sequences of change in different areas of the world.

Steward maintained that by comparing sequences of change in different societies it was possible to discover certain cross-cultural regularities. For example, he noted that wherever complex state societies developed in the ancient world—in the Near East, Mexico, northern Peru, Egypt, and China—a parallel process occurred. In each case, people were using the same kind of technology to exploit a similar natural environment. They lived in arid or semi-arid regions, where crops could be grown relatively easily without iron tools but not without some rudimentary means of securing water, such as irrigation. Steward concluded that faced with similar adaptive problems, societies will come up with similar technological, political, and social solutions. Hence people living under roughly the same environmental conditions with similar technologies will develop along the same lines culturally.

Like White, Steward regarded technology as a basic and crucial aspect of culture. He pointed out, however, that tools and productive techniques always interact with the specific environment, and one cannot be considered apart from the other. In different environments, similar kinds of technology may not be equally productive and may entail different patterns of labor, economic management, and social organization. Hunters and gatherers who live in desert or arctic environments where conditions are harsh and resources relatively scarce tend to live in small, migratory bands with a relatively simple form of social organization and a meager material culture. Foragers who live in an environment that is rich in a variety of resources may develop a much more settled and elaborate sociocultural system.

Steward believed that in order to understand how cultures operate, how they are similar, and why they vary, anthropologists must investigate the relationships between populations, their technologies, their social organizations, and the external environment (including climate, terrain, natural resources, and other human populations). He called this approach *cultural ecology*.

Understanding Why Societies Differ

What did each of the theories we have discussed contribute to our understanding of why cultures differ? Breaking with conventional wisdom, the early evolutionists maintained that the diversity of the present is explained by evolution in the past—not by innate, "racial" differences. Historical particularists and diffusionists concentrated on the role past and present contacts between societies play in creating similarities and differences among cultures—something the early evolutionists had largely ignored. Some years later, White revived interest in the evolutionary approach by seeking the cause of cultural evolution; attempting to explain how it operates; and calling attention to the need for more exact measures of social complexity. In contrast to White's general or universal evolutionism, Steward advocated a multilineal approach. Called cultural ecology, it focuses on specific sequences of change in specific societies, and on the interaction between human populations, their technologies, social organizations, and social and natural environment. The approach we described in Chapter 1 incorporates still newer ideas as to how the interaction of individuals, societies, and their environments produces cultural diversity.

How Do Societies Differ?

The vast amounts of data collected by early avocational and professional anthropologists described the immense diversity of human cultures. Every conceivable topic was covered—from kinship, marriage, and sexual conduct to food, games, clothing, and types of houses. But how were these differences to be summarized? In the first place, the information that had been gathered was becoming so voluminous that a cross-cultural comparison of all known traits would be incomprehensible. But more importantly, anthropologists had begun to realize that there were more basic differences between cultures than simply differences between isolated culture traits. Culture, they had discovered, was organized. Thus anthropologists began to search for ways of defining the nature of this organization to focus the comparisons between societies and ultimately to shed light on our understanding of why cultural differences exist.

Malinowski: Functionalism and Institutions

One of the earliest contributors to our understanding of social institutions was Bronislaw Malinowski. Malinowski decided to become an anthropologist after he read Sir James Frazer's *The Golden Bough* while recuperating from an illness. Abandoning a planned career in physics and mathematics, Malinowski left Poland in 1910 and went to London to study with C. G. Seligmann. Five years later he embarked for the western Pacific, where, because of the outbreak of World War I, he was forced to spend three years on the Trobriand Islands, affording him an unprecedented opportunity to study the language, customs, and beliefs of the natives. When Hortense Powdermaker, a visiting anthropology student from America, met Malinowski at the London School of Economics in 1925, he was deeply engrossed in the process of analyzing the mass of data he had collected in the field. (His first volume, *Argonauts of the Pacific*, had been published in 1922.) She described him as a paradoxical man—belligerent with his peers, alternately kind and sarcastic with students—who delighted in shocking people he considered "bourgeois" and boasted about being able to swear in seven languages (1967: 35). But his enthusiasm for anthropology was infectious.

Malinowski's reflections on the material he had collected in the Trobriand Islands led him to the conclusion that every society has a basic set of recurrent activity patterns or *institutions*. These key elements of culture are *functional* in the sense of satisfying certain basic needs. He identified three types of needs that institutions satisfy: biological needs (such as food), instrumental needs (such as legal processes to resolve conflict), and integrative needs (such as a common "world view" to facilitate communication). This basic idea, that aspects of culture work to satisfy human needs, became the organizing principle in his studies of primitive kinship systems, magic, and law. He argued, for example, that the function of religion is to establish and reinforce "valuable mental attitudes such as reverence for tradition, harmony with environment, courage and confidence in the struggle with difficulties and at the prospect of death" (1954:89).

Radcliffe-Brown: Jural Norms and Structure

Alfred Reginald Radcliffe-Brown also lectured at the London School of Economics in 1925. Tall and distinguished-looking, surrounded by disciples, Radcliffe-Brown impressed Hortense Powdermaker as a polished performer. Compared to Malinowski, he seemed detached and aloof. Wherever he might be—in London or Sydney, Australia—he donned a cape and high hat for social occasions. But Radcliffe-Brown had also spent years in the field living with preliterate peoples.

While Malinowski stressed the institutional basis of society, Radcliffe-Brown stressed its structural base. In a 1922 revision of his original field report on the Andaman Islanders, Radcliffe-Brown acknowledged his intellectual debt to the French sociologist Émile Durkheim. In all of his writings, Durkheim had stressed the need to study society without reference to individual motives and psychology. He argued that society is more than the sum of its individual members—indeed, that social institutions have a coercive power over individuals. Following Durkheim, Radcliffe-Brown set out to develop a mode of analysis that was free from inferences about people's states of mind. He believed that anthropologists should focus on patterns of behavior, not individual actions.

In pursuit of these patterns, Radcliffe-Brown maintained that in spite of the varied range of behavior in any society, different classes of people act differently in given situations. For example, adults act one way at a ceremony, children quite another; similar differences can be seen between men and women, related and unrelated people, rich and poor, and so on. People act differently, for example, toward their friends than toward their parents or children. To be sure, every man does not behave in an identical manner toward his mother-in-law. But by observing a number of husbands in different situations with their mothers-in-law, a fieldworker can discern general rules or *jural norms* about what husbands in that society must and must not do in relations with their mothers-in-law.

Inferring the norms that govern relationships between different categories of individuals within a society is the starting point of structural analysis as Radcliffe-Brown defined it. Once these norms are identified, their function is also identified. Radcliffe-Brown's notion of function was more specific than Malinowski's, focusing on the maintenance of stability within a society. (Structuralists are often criticized for overemphasizing stability and underemphasizing conflict in social relations.) He liked to compare societies to organisms, whose different parts each perform functions that are vital to the whole.

Radcliffe-Brown believed that some degree of social solidarity is a "necessary condition of existence" if people are to live together successfully. Accordingly, he attempted to trace the ways in which different customs serve to establish such solidarity, to keep society running with a minimum of disruptive conflicts. From this perspective, for example, the function of rules prescribing avoidance relationships between a person and certain relatives by marriage—prohibiting them from entering the same room or speaking to one another—is to prevent conflicts by keeping the potential antagonists separated. The function of joking relationships between a person and certain in-laws is also to prevent conflict—this time by easing potential tension with laughter.

Radcliffe-Brown believed that once anthropologists had precisely described social structures and their functions for a wide range of cultures, they would be able to construct a taxonomy of societies. He also argued that anthropologists would ultimately discover laws of behavior that governed the relationships between different organizational forms.

While today we generally identify Radcliffe-Brown and Malinowski as the two leading figures in the development of structural-functional analysis, it is interesting to note that the two had violent disagreements; in fact, so heated was their controversy that Malinowski was prompted to throw Radcliffe-Brown out of the London School of Economics. One of the most basic differences was Malinowski's emphasis on institutions and behavior as contrasted with Radcliffe-Brown's more abstract and conceptual notion of jural norms. Subsequent developments in structural-functional analysis have come to emphasize the cognitive component of social structure even more.

Lévi-Strauss: Structure and Cognition

To Claude Lévi-Strauss (1963) and the French structuralists, the goal of anthropology is to uncover the common thought processes that underlie apparently dissimilar patterns of behavior and social organization. Although known as structuralism, their approach differs significantly from that of Radcliffe-Brown and the contemporary British and American structuralists. Whereas these theorists concentrate primarily on the structure of interpersonal relations in specific cultures, and secondarily try to derive major principles, rules, or abstract models of social behavior from empirical research, Lévi-Strauss tends to reverse the focus.

Drawing inspiration from modern linguistics, he begins by isolating abstract, inherent cognitive characteristics that pervade all aspects of culture. For a long time linguists assumed that children learned to talk by imitating adults. But children not only parrot what they hear, they invent sentences of their own—long before they have any conscious understanding of formal grammar. Linguists hypothesize that these rules are built into the human mind; that in a sense, children are preprogrammed for language. Similarly, Lévi-Strauss reasons that certain codes essential to social organization are built into the human mind. He argues that culture is shaped by these inner structures. For example, many of his studies are based on the premise that the mind is structured to think in opposites. This is one of the basic properties of human thought. People everywhere recognize distinctions between "self" and "others," "us" and "them," "animals" and "humans" or "nature" and "culture." The ability to make such distinctions marks the difference between human beings and other animals, makes symbolic communication and human sociocultural life possible, and gives form to our cultures.

The incest taboo provides a striking illustration of Lévi-Strauss's mode of analysis. Every culture has rules prohibiting sexual intercourse between certain categories of people. By specifying who is a kinsman and who is not, with whom it is legitimate to mate and marry and with whom it is not, such rules establish certain organized social relationships. According to Lévi-Strauss, incest taboos rest on the ability to think in terms of opposites (related and not marriageable versus nonrelated and potentially marriageable). This cognitive ability, he suggests, is one of the major differences between people and other animals, between the natural order and the world of culture. Such distinctions establish reciprocal relations and obligations among groups and are reflected in all kinship systems, myth, ritual, art, village layout, and the overall organization of societies everywhere, regardless of the particular forms they take.

As abstract and unverifiable as Lévi-Strauss's ideas may at first seem, recent research ("biogenetic structuralism") does suggest a potential biological basis for them in the opposition of the right (rational, instrumental) and left (artistic, expressive) hemispheres of the brain.

The Ethnoscientists

In many respects the goal of Lévi-Strauss and the French structuralists converges with that of a group of American anthropologists known as *ethnoscientists*. Both groups seek the logical mental structures on the basis of which a language, as well as an entire culture, is built; both use linguistic models to analyze culture. The methods of the two groups, however, are quite different. While the French structuralists try to understand the mental structures that underlie cultural traits intuitively, the ethnoscientists seek to discover underlying structures through a logical analysis of carefully collected ethnographic data. The major aims of ethnoscience are to discover how people in a particular society perceive and classify material and social phenomena in the world around them, and to find the rules which are used to generate appropriate conduct. Linguistic categories provide the key to such processes of classification. Consider, for example, color classifications. English has no words that correspond exactly to the color terms used by the Hanunóo of the Philippines. This is because they do not categorize colors in the same way as Westerners do. Whereas our classifications depend on hue, brightness, and saturation (we say fire-engine red, pale yellow, powder blue), the Hanunóo name colors in terms of moisture, surface texture, lightness, their association with plant life, and other attributes that we never consider (Conklin, 1955). Many other studies similarly demonstrate that art, food tastes, kinship relations, plant and animal classification, crime, supernatural entities, disease, and various other cultural categories are conceptualized by distinct criteria in different cultures.

The methods of the ethnoscientists have made an important contribution to anthropological thinking. Their approach is what is called an *emic* one—that is, they seek to understand a culture from the native's point of view and not from the point of view imposed by the anthropologist, the *etic* approach. [For example, natives might say that they observe their culture's incest taboo because they fear angering the gods or because they aren't attracted to their kinsmen (the emic explanation). Lévi-Strauss would say natives observe incest taboos in order to establish reciprocal relations and obligations among groups (the etic explanation).] Ethnoscientific research has made anthropologists increasingly aware of the confusion that arises when anthropologists do not make clear distinctions between a set of categories they invent to describe particular phenomena and the categories the members of a culture themselves use. Etic and emic categories are both useful, but for different purposes.

Understanding How Societies Are Organized

Our understanding of the ways in which individuals and groups organize their perceptions and experiences, relationships and activities, draws on all of these theories. Malinowski called attention to the fact that a society's recurrent activity patterns, or institutions, are adaptive: they satisfy basic biological, instrumental, and integrative needs. Radcliffe-Brown explored the structure of relationships in societies, focusing on rules or jural norms rather than behavior patterns themselves. He believed the primary function of norms is to create solidarity and maintain stability in a society (a static view many contemporary anthropologists question). Taking an entirely different tack, Lévi-Strauss argues that social organization is a projection of human cognitive structures: in a sense, we are all preprogrammed for culture. In particular, Lévi-Strauss emphasizes the point that people in all cultures create dichotomies, and that these serve to establish reciprocal rights and obligations among groups. Ethnoscientists in America provided a technique for uncovering cognitive structures: the systematic study of the varying ways in which people in different societies perceive and classify elements in the world around them. As we indicated in Chapter 1, studies of social organization today are focusing on the ways in which culture shapes decision making, and decision making produces organizational patterns.

What Is the Relationship Between the Individual and Society?

When the early anthropologists argued that the similarities and differences we find among cultures are not a product of racial (biological and psychological) differences, they led anthropology to the study of culture. In so doing, they created a serious dilemma. Anthropologists study culture by observing the behavior of individuals and the products of that behavior and then by drawing inferences about their culture. Yet the very concept of culture suggests that the differences among groups are not simply a summation of individual differences. What, then, is the relationship between the individual and culture?

Much of the early anthropological literature on this question focuses on the relationship between culture, personality (characteristic ways of thinking and behaving that distinguish individuals), and child-rearing. Through common child-rearing practices, it was believed, the relatively unformed personalities of infants were transformed into the dominant personality type of a particular society; the dominant personality type, in turn, influenced a wide diversity of cultural traits. Let us look at the historical development of these basic concepts and their interrelationships, beginning with their emergence in the 1920s and 1930s.

Early Culture and Personality Studies

Early researchers interested in the relationship between the individual and society attempted to study culture as it is expressed through the personalities of its members. For example, in her widely read book *Patterns of Culture* (1934), Ruth Benedict described through an analysis of basic personality traits the distinctly different cultural configurations represented by the Kwakiutl Indians of the Pacific Northwest Coast and the Zuni Indians of the American Southwest. The Kwakiutl, an aggressive people prone to excesses, sought supernatural insight through visions induced by elaborate self-tortures. The Zuni, in contrast, were peaceful and restrained; distrustful of excesses and disruptive experiences of any kind, they always kept to the middle road. Borrowing from the philosopher Nietzsche's studies of Greek tragedy, Benedict labeled these opposing configurations the Dionysian and the Apollonian. Although the factual basis of Benedict's portraits of these cultures is open to serious doubt, her pioneering work nevertheless sparked great interest in the problem of the relationship between personality and culture.

Influenced by the Freudian and neo-Freudian emphasis on the importance of early childhood experiences in shaping adult

Societies differ in the degree to which they emphasize such qualities as group cooperation and individual achievement. But how much do cultural variations in child-rearing practices affect personality development? The study of the relationship between culture and personality, launched by such anthropologists as Ruth Benedict and Margaret Mead in the 1920s and 1930s, continues today. (a © Audrey Topping, Rapho/Photo Researchers; b Ken Heyman)

personality, other anthropologists began to investigate how child-rearing practices vary from culture to culture and how these different patterns affect individual personality development. Margaret Mead was one of the earliest and most prolific contributors to this area of research. She and others drew heavily on the work of both psychologists and anthropologists. At Columbia University, Abram Kardiner, a practicing analyst, and Ralph Linton, an anthropologist, organized a number of interdisciplinary seminars that stimulated some basic ideas and approaches to psychological anthropology. While accepting Freud's thesis that the early years of life are critically important in personality formation and that interference with infantile drives leads to later character disorders and neuroses, Kardiner (1939) nevertheless rejected the Freudian view that these childhood experiences and emotional conflicts (such as the Oedipus complex) are necessarily the same in every society. Relaxing Freudian theory somewhat to allow for cultural differences, Kardiner subjected a number of field reports on child-rearing techniques in different cultures to intensive analysis. He concluded that most children in a given society experience the same kinds of frustration, beginning with weaning, toilet training, and other childhood disciplines. As a result, they grow up with the same "complexes" and have generally similar personalities and dispositions. Kardiner then suggested that religion, magic, taboos, myths, folk tales, and the like might be seen as projections of shared psychological conflicts. For example, the Judeo-Christian God can be seen as a projection of the stern, powerful Western father of a generation or two ago.

Kardiner's view that most members of a culture share a basic personality structure generated a great deal of research. In the East Indies Cora Dubois (1944) carried out a study of personality development among the people of Alor. She supplemented standard ethnographic observations with extensive descriptions of child-rearing practices and with detailed life histories. In addition, she collected dreams and children's drawings and administered a number of psychological tests. Upon returning from the field, she submitted this material to Kardiner and several other psychologists, who analyzed and interpreted it independently. Working separately and without any prior knowledge of Alorese culture, they arrived at roughly the same portrait. The average or *modal personality* of the Alorese was seen as emotionally shallow, insecure, apathetic, and suspicious—the result, Kardiner concluded, of sporadic feeding during infancy, severe shaming and humiliation, and parental indifference.

During World War II, a number of anthropologists applied the concept of modal personality to complex societies such as Japan, Russia, and the United States. These national-character studies were also based on the premise that similar childhood experiences produce a characteristic personality type, but the methods used in these studies were new. Because the war had sharply curtailed travel and made field research difficult, anthropologists began analyzing films, literature, propaganda, newspapers, and letters, conducting interviews with immigrants and collecting their life histories, and administering psychological tests. This approach, known as "the study of culture at a distance," produced some stimulating but speculative results. For example, Gorer and Rickman (1950) concluded that the manic-depressive mood changes supposedly typical of the Russian personality were rooted in the Soviet custom of swaddling infants, a practice that produced extreme frustration and impotent rage. Similarly, the obsessive personality structure allegedly typical of the Japanese was judged the result of harsh toilet training and disciplinary methods (Gorer, 1943; LaBarre, 1945).

The national character studies produced some lively descriptions but unfortunately very little hard evidence. Gorer and LaBarre's conclusions about the Japanese, for example, were not supported by later studies based on firsthand research and more representative data (see Norbeck and Norbeck, 1956; Lanham, 1956). And this is the main criticism of

Biology and Culture

When anthropology began to develop into a social science, it was widely believed that societies differed because races differed in their capacities for cultural achievement. White Europeans thought themselves to be a superior race that had consequently developed an advanced culture, whereas the black and brown, red, and yellow peoples of the world were capable of only primitive skills and superstitious ideas. The early evolutionists such as Morgan and Tylor rejected this rigid biological determinism, arguing that differential cultural evolution rather than biological inferiority accounted for differences in societies. Believing that all peoples had similar capacities for culture, they explained cultural differences by asserting that human societies were simply at different stages of cultural development. Although the evolutionary notions of these early anthropologists have been extensively modified since, culture rather than biology has remained the dominant concept in explaining variation in human behavior from society to society.

Over the years, some social scientists lost almost complete sight of humans as biological beings, focusing their attention instead on cultural and social factors exclusively. Our place in nature, our relationship to all other living creatures, was greatly neglected. The result has been called homocentrism, or human-centeredness—an inflated view of our uniqueness as a species. Because it was generally believed that only humans had culture, the study of culture became the all-important center of anthropological inquiry.

Recently, however, social scientists have started to rediscover the biological basis of human behavior. Today, anthropologists and sociologists again are beginning to look closely at the biological influences on the ways people think and act, although this time biology is not viewed as rigidly deterministic. One of the reasons why the social sciences originally lost interest in the biological basis of behavior was the racist and elitist slant of the doctrines of the early biological determinists. The issue of genetic make-up and racism is still very much alive today, as we see in the debate over race and intelligence. In the last several decades, certain scholars have argued that the average I.Q. of some races is lower than that of others. Most anthropologists reject this argument—first on the grounds that racial categories are far too crude to meaningfully measure human biological variation, and second on the grounds that almost all I.Q. tests are biased toward the members of the culture that created them.

But this is not to say that biology and genetic inheritance have no significant influence on human behavior, that culture and environment are the only really important factors accounting for human variation. Clearly, both biology and culture/environment play a role. In fact, some contemporary anthropologists argue that the very development of culture is grounded in psychobiological imperatives (d'Aquili, 1972). Human beings are cultural animals because of the interrelated influences of three biologically adaptive mechanisms—our basic drives for self-preservation, our urge to social living, which also has survival value, and our urge to cognitively order phenomena in the world around us. According to this view, these three biologically-based urges not only explain the genesis of culture but are also the keys to the common denominators of culture—the functionally similar elements that all cultures share such as marriage, sexual restrictions, the family, law, property rights, magic, religion, mythology, to name only a few. Because all human beings have the same biological imperatives, they have developed certain broad similarities in cultural patterns. But the exact forms these patterns take are extremely varied, for the cognitive process of creating culture is specific to the particular environmental situation. Thus, people can and do modify the expression of basic drives and the urge to social living in any number of ways.

From the belief that psychobiological imperatives provide the bases for the common denominators of culture, it is only a short step to the notion that the gene pools of different populations may also contribute in some way to cultural diversity. Genetic make-up, of course, is in no way a rigid determinant of culture as early observers once believed. Rather, biology may simply be one of many factors that influence a people's ultimate strategy for survival. Although there is currently little empirical evidence to substantiate this possibility, some anthropologists believe it is an area that should be more thoroughly explored.

the early culture and personality approach — that too much rests on the researcher's impressions and generalizations. Some anthropologists began to question not only the methods of these studies, but also the basic validity of the modal personality concept.

Cross-Cultural Studies of Personality

After World War II, in response to these criticisms, psychological anthropologists began turning their attention to more limited and verifiable questions. Whiting and Child (1953), for example, conducted a systematic cross-cultural study to find out whether there is a correlation between child-training practices and adult attitudes toward illness. They combined Freudian theories concerning child training with newer psychological theories emphasizing the importance of adolescent and adult experiences in personality development, and then tested these hypotheses statistically. Specifically, Whiting and Child suggested that differences in the ways children are trained to cope with their needs for expression of aggression, for dependency, and for oral, anal, and sexual gratification might be related to the attitudes they later develop toward illness. After systematically comparing ethnographic data on 75 cultures, Whiting and Child did indeed find some significant correlations. They concluded, for example, that children who were severely trained to cope with oral needs (nursed on a rigid schedule and weaned abruptly at an early age) developed a preoccupation with and a negative attitude toward oral gratification. As adults they tended to attribute illness to events associated with the oral system — drinking, eating, and so on.

Diversity Within Groups

To this point, anthropologists had more or less assumed that a core of homogeneous personality characteristics exists in all cultures. Anthony Wallace (1952) was among the first to test this assumption through rigorous statistical analysis. Wallace administered the Rorschach test to a carefully selected sample of Tuscarora Indians. After analyzing the results, he found that only 37 percent fit the supposed modal Tuscarora personality.

This study suggested that psychological anthropologists had been "barking up the wrong tree." Not only had they failed to make use of statistical techniques for analyzing psychological data, they had ignored the questions of how and why a single culture generates diverse personality traits. Wallace has devoted a major portion of his career to building a set of concepts and methods to resolve this problem. He and other anthropologists began looking for ways to conceptualize the interaction between individuals and culture that creates this diversity. "Belief systems," "models," "cognitive maps," and "mazeways" are some of the terms researchers have used to convey the idea that each individual internalizes his or her own distinct version of culture, that is, of the cognitive orientations his or her people employ in communicating and interacting with one another. The focus in this school of psychological anthropology is on the ways in which personality development reflects the individual and group adaptation to the social and natural environment. The Culture and Ecology Research Project is an example of the kind of research this new approach has generated.

Going beyond child-rearing practices and personality structure per se, Walter Goldschmidt, Robert Edgerton, and their colleagues launched the Culture and Ecology Research Project in 1961 to investigate whether general patterns of group behavior and perception — including attitudes, values, and personality — are influenced by environmental factors and economic strategies. To test this hypothesis, they located four East African tribes whose members were divided into separate farming and pastoral communities. If culture is the dominant factor in personality development, they reasoned, there would be little or no difference between farmers and pastoralists of the same tribe. However, if personality is an integral part of adaptation to the environment, as they believed, farmers and pastoralists of the same tribe would exhibit different personality traits (Edgerton, 1971).

Farmers are committed to their land; they live in relatively stable, fixed communities. As a result, their social survival depends on maintaining good relations with the people who will be their neighbors for life. Edgerton hypothesized that because of this, farmers would generally refrain from overt expressions of anger, but would harbor secret hostilities and engage in indirect, covert forms of aggression—for example, through magic. Pastoralists, in contrast, are highly mobile. If hostilities between individuals or groups build to the point where they can no longer live together, pastoralists can simply move. Because of this escape valve, Edgerton predicted, they would be much more open about expressing their feelings, good and bad. Farmers are at the mercy of the weather; when droughts come, there is little they can do except wait for rain. Pastoralists, again because they are mobile, are somewhat less vulnerable. They can move on to greener pastures and can fight the animal predators and raiders that threaten their stock. Edgerton predicted that farmers would be somewhat passive and fatalistic, whereas pastoralists would take the initiative more readily and would in general be more action-oriented and independent-minded. The pastoralists' livelihood depends on the ability to make quick decisions. In contrast, farming depends on hard, repetitive work; it is demanding but rarely dangerous. The observations of four ethnographers and batteries of psychological tests largely confirmed these expectations. Not all pastoralists were independent and open, and not all farmers were furtive and repressed. But while the most significant differences were between tribes, the differences between the two groups were statistically significant in all of the tribes studied.

Understanding the Relationship Between the Individual and Society

The emphasis in anthropological research today is on the dynamics of the acquisition and use of beliefs and belief systems by individuals. The theorists and schools we have described in this section all contributed to this position. Anthropologists of the culture and personality school took up the question of the relationship between the individual and society at a time when anthropology seemed to be losing interest in individuals. Abstract studies of culture and social organization had begun to obscure persons. Following their lead, Whiting, Child, and others launched cross-cultural studies of the transmission of personality traits from generation to generation via child-rearing practices, introducing statistical analysis to this area of research. Then, with a single study, Wallace raised a whole new series of questions relating to intra-cultural diversity. New research by Edgerton and others indicates that similarities and differences in personality traits are the result of individual and group adaptation to the environment.

summary

The many specific theories anthropologists have proposed involve three major questions: Why do cultures differ? How do they differ? and What is the relationship between the individual and society?

The most difficult question of the three is why cultures differ. In the late nineteenth century, numerous theories of cultural and social evolution were advanced, all of which assumed that human societies everywhere evolve along the same lines, and that this evolution leads to a common end. According to Edward Tylor, all societies progressed in stages from savagery through barbarism to civilization. Inspired by Tylor, Lewis Henry Morgan linked successive stages of cultural evolution to technological developments; each technological level was in turn associated with specific cultural patterns or institutions.

The predominantly speculative nature of early evolutionary theories led to their fall from favor, a demise largely prompted by Franz Boas, whose approach—now generally referred to as *historical particularism,* emphasized meticulous and detailed fieldwork. By the turn of the century a new group, the *diffusionists,* proposed a different explanation of cultural variation. According to the diffusionists, most aspects of culture originated in one of a few places and gradually spread to people in other areas. None of the diffusionist schools succeeded in proving the existence of primary centers of invention, but they did point to the major lines of inquiry that are needed to explain differences between cultures.

In the 1940s and 1950s the *neoevolutionists* enlarged and refined the classical evolutionist approach. One proponent, Leslie White, held that cultures evolve progressively and that this progress is rooted in material or technological factors. Another perspective is taken by Julian Steward, who calls for multilineal, or specific, evolutionism, which focuses on particular cultures and observable sequences of change in different areas of the world. According to Steward, societies will arrive at similar technological, political, and social solutions when faced with similar adaptive problems. Steward believes that in order to understand why cultures take the shape they do, one must investigate the relationship between populations and their technology, social organization, and environment. He called this approach *cultural ecology.*

One of the earliest contributors to our understanding of the second question, how societies differ, was Bronislaw Malinowski, who asserted that every society has a basic set of recurrent patterns of behavior, or *institutions*. Furthermore, he claimed, these institutions are *functional* in the sense of satisfying biological, instrumental, and integrative needs.

While Malinowski focused on the institutional basis of society, A. R. Radcliffe-Brown stressed its structural base. Radcliffe-Brown believed that anthropologists should focus on patterns of behavior—on general rules, or *jural norms,* not individual actions. Inferring the norms that govern relationships between different categories of individuals was the starting point of Radcliffe-Brown's structural analysis.

To Claude Lévi-Strauss and the French *structuralists,* the goal of anthropology is to uncover the common thought processes that underlie apparently dissimilar patterns of behavior and social organization. According to Lévi-Strauss, certain patterns of social organization and behavior are built into the human mind, and culture is a projection of these inner structures.

Like the French structuralists, the *ethnoscientists* seek to uncover the logical mental structures on which culture is built. However, while the French structuralists try to understand the mental structures that underlie cultural traits intuitively, the ethnoscientists seek to discover underlying structures through a logical analysis of ethnographic data. A major aim of ethnoscience is to discover how people in a particular society perceive and classify material and social phenomena. The ethnoscientific approach is *emic*—that is, it seeks to understand a culture from the native's point of view, not from that imposed by the anthropologist (the *etic* approach).

Three summary statements can be made about how anthropologists now approach the study of cultural variation: first, they recognize that the structure of a society, or of any behavior pattern, must be investigated; second, they generally try to understand the function or adaptive significance of particular patterns of behavior; and third, they focus on the ways in which individuals and groups of individuals use social concepts to structure particular situations and interactions.

The third question facing anthropologists is the relationship between the individual and society. Early culture and personality researchers, such as Ruth Benedict, attempted to study culture as it is expressed thorough its members' personalities (characteristic ways of thinking and behaving that distinguish individuals). Others, such as Abram Kardiner and Ralph Linton, began to study how child-rearing practices differ from society to society and how these differences affect individual personality development. According to Kardiner, most members of a culture share a basic personality structure, or *modal personality*.

When the modal personality approach was shown to rest too much on the researcher's impressions and generalizations, anthropologists began to turn to more limited and verifiable questions, using cross-cultural data. In more recent studies, researchers have begun to examine the diversity of personality traits within a single culture, viewing them as adaptive means, influenced by environmental factors and economic strategies.

Our understanding of cultural diversity is still growing. We are learning more about human interactions and about the ecological adaptations of societies as a whole, and we are undertaking more detailed studies of change through time.

suggested readings

HARRIS, M.
1968 *The Rise of Anthropological Theory*. New York: Crowell. The most comprehensive treatment of the history of anthropology available. The author is committed to an evolutionist-materialist perspective, and the emphasis of the book is on the development of this theoretical tradition within the discipline.

KAPLAN, D., AND MANNERS, R.
1972 *Culture Theory*. Englewood Cliffs, N.J.: Prentice-Hall. A survey of current anthropological theories and their origins, written at an introductory level.

MANNERS, R., AND KAPLAN, D., EDS.
1968 *Theory in Anthropology: A Source Book*. Chicago: Aldine. This edited volume contains essays on the many theoretical traditions that exist in the discipline, written by authors who have primary commitments to each of them.

STOCKING, G. W.
1968 *Race, Culture, and Evolution: Essays in the History of Anthropology*. New York: The Free Press. Emphasizes the historical viability of anthropology's major theoretical traditions.

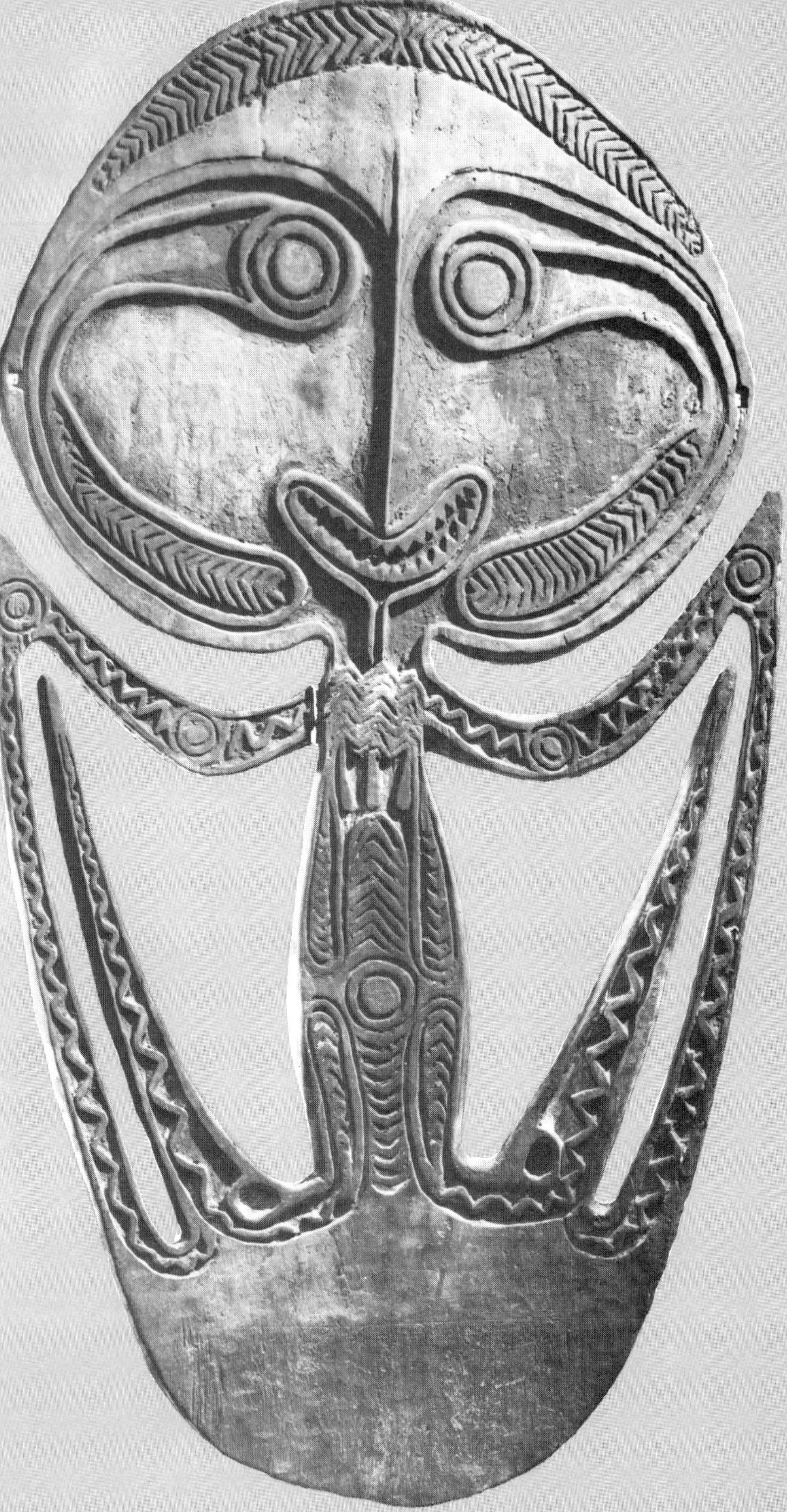

eleven
Methods of Cultural Anthropology

One of the distinctive characteristics of cultural anthropology is its reliance upon *fieldwork* as a means of gathering data and testing theories. The theories discussed in Chapter 10 were not developed by anthropologists in isolation, or through purely academic debates, nor were they verified or disproved through laboratory experiments. Rather, they evolved through continual testing among people whose behavior was under study.

The anthropologist gathers data in the field primarily through participant observation, living among the members of a group in an effort to understand the customary ways that people think and behave. The anthropologist spends extended periods of time observing the daily routines and interactions of people, asking questions and carefully recording their answers, and examining the products of their activities—their arts, literature, material possessions, and communities.

Anthropologists, of course, have not always gathered their data through firsthand observation in the field. Nineteenth-century anthropology was often a secondhand, armchair affair. Much of the data came from impressionistic travel journals and unsystematic historical records. But anthropology as we know it today is firmly rooted in field research. Just as the development of precision instruments in the natural sciences has allowed scientists to probe previously uncharted worlds, so improved techniques of field research have enabled anthropologists to explore the little-known cultures of non-Western peoples, opening up new dimensions of knowledge and producing a deeper level of understanding. Today, trained observation and questioning, systematic interpretation, and controlled comparison are the anthropologist's primary research tools.

We will focus on four major aspects of the anthropologist's work: preparing for the field, data collection in the field, adapting to the field, and analysis of field data.

Preparing for the Field

While fieldwork may seem like a vacation to the uninitiated, in reality anthropological research demands intense preparation. Today, virtually all anthropologists train at universities. Graduate programs are designed to give students an in-depth knowledge of the anthropological literature; to make them aware of the many theoretical disputes that motivate research; and to provide them with the intellectual tools needed to organize and interpret ethnographic data creatively, and to formulate realistic, significant research problems.

The most important activity in which an anthropologist engages before going into the field is the preparation of a research design—an overall plan as well as a justification for his proposed project. In the early part of this century, the primary goal of fieldwork was to describe a given culture as fully and completely as possible (given the researcher's energy and funds). Today, most research is problem-oriented: that is, the anthropologist focuses on an important theoretical issue that is being discussed or debated—for example, what the relationship is between child-rearing and adult personality structure, between food-getting techniques and residence patterns, or between economic innovation and social

Art is a valuable source of ethnographic data. This Papuan skull rack from New Guinea is of interest for its elegant design, but it also provides clues as to the belief system, world view, and social organization of the people who made and use it. (Charles Uht/Museum of Primitive Art)

change; or what strategies people use to further their position in society. There are two reasons for the problem-oriented approach. First, many anthropologists believe it is impossible for researchers to learn everything there is to know about a culture in a few months. If they focus on one area they are more likely to obtain accurate and full information than if they try to collect data on everything. Second, more and more anthropologists are studying peasant villages and heterogeneous urban communities, rather than the remote, small-scale, largely self-sufficient societies their predecessors studied. The heterogeneity of these communities makes data collection a trickier and more difficult undertaking. However, child-rearing, economic innovation, and so on do not take place in a vacuum, and problem-oriented fieldworkers must gather data on other aspects of the culture they are studying as a matter of course.

In formulating a research problem, anthropologists use particular theories about the topic or problem they are studying. These theoretical assumptions influence the kinds of questions they will ask, and therefore the kinds of information they will get. For example, a theory of politics that stresses social stability and integration will direct a researcher to one kind of data; a theory of politics that emphasizes conflict and competition will direct a researcher to quite another kind of data. Not that researchers see only what they are looking for and block out everything else, but observations are always selective and perceptions will inevitably be shaped by prior assumptions — by what the researchers expect or hope to find. Therefore, anthropologists spell out their theoretical orientations in their study designs, and then formulate one or more hypotheses based on their theoretical assumptions. Some anthropologists believe that such hypotheses are most easily derived from theories when those theories are formalized as "laws" of behavior and cultural processes. Similarly, viewing hypotheses as potential laws results in more tightly structured theories.

Hypotheses must be stated in such a way that they can be proved or disproved in the field. To this end, in the study design, the researcher first defines such concepts as politics or personality in concrete terms. (The process of translating abstract concepts into terms that can be observed and measured is called *operationalization*.) Next, the anthropologist specifies the sampling procedure that will be used in gathering information, as well as the techniques by which data will be collected — direct observation, formal or informal interviews, surveys, psychological tests, and so on. Finally, the anthropologist considers the procedures that will be used to analyze the data once they have been obtained in order to make sure that these are compatible with both the data and the data-collection techniques. Usually an anthropologist prepares a study design months in advance and may spend as much time on the design in the field. The last year or years of graduate training are spent in acquiring skills that are germane to an emerging research design.

Field Techniques

Methods of Gathering Data

The most important decisions an anthropologist makes concern the techniques of data collection to be used in the field. Because they investigate such a very wide range of problems, anthropologists must have an equally wide range of information-gathering techniques. We will begin with the two techniques that are basic to almost every piece of anthropological research.

Participant Observation The method most widely used by anthropologists to collect information in the field is called *participant observation*. Participant observation involves living in close contact for extended periods with the people whose culture is being studied, observing the ways they conduct their lives, learning to communicate with them, and trying to understand their culture as they themselves understand it. Thus participant observation begins the moment an

Margaret Kieffer, a doctoral candidate at the University of California, went to the village of Santiago Atitlan, Guatemala, to conduct research on variations in color perception and recognition. Like all anthropologists, she used a variety of techniques in the field—formal tests and questionnaires; informal, open-ended interviews; and participation. Here she is seen interviewing an embroiderer, talking with a dyer, and watching a weaver at work on a traditional Mayan back strap loom. (Yoram Kahana/Peter Arnold)

anthropologist enters the field and continues during the entire time the researcher is there. In practice, "participation" can range from commuting to a village or neighborhood to deep involvement in community life. But in general, participant observation means that to a greater or lesser degree researchers immerse themselves in the cultures being studied. Malinowski explains why it is essential for anthropologists to "participate" in the societies they investigate:

Soon after I had established myself in [Omarakana Trobriand Islands], I began to take part, in a way, in the village life, to look forward to the important or festive events, to take personal interest in the gossip and the developments of the village occurrences; to wake up every morning to a day presenting itself to me more or less as it does to the native. I would get out from under my mosquito net, to find around me the village life beginning to stir, or the people well advanced in their working day according to the hour and also the season, for they get up and begin their labors early or late, as work presses. As I went on my morning walk through the village, I could see intimate details of family life, of toilet, cooking, taking of meals; I could see the arrangements for the day's work, people starting on their errands, or groups of men and women busy at some manufacturing tasks. Quarrels, jokes, family scenes, events usually trivial, sometimes dramatic but always significant, formed the atmosphere of my daily life, as well as of theirs. . . .

Later on in the day, whatever happened was in easy reach, and there was no possibility of its escaping my notice. Alarms about the sorcerer's approach in the evening, one or two big, really important quarrels and the rifts within the community, cases of illness, attempted cures and deaths, magical rites which had to be performed, all these I had not to pursue, fearful of missing them, but they took place under my very eyes, at my own doorstep, so to speak. . . .

Also, over and over again, I committed breaches of etiquette, which the natives, familiar enough with me, were not slow in pointing out. I had to learn how to behave, and to a certain extent, I acquired "the feeling" for native good and bad manners. With this, and with the capacity of enjoying their company and sharing some of their games and amusements, I began to feel that I was indeed in touch with the natives, and this is certainly the preliminary condition of being able to carry on successful field work. (Malinowski, 1961:7–8)

Of course, fieldworkers must be more than just casual observers. They must learn to record what they have seen and heard accurately and in detail. Anthropologists Beatrice and John Whiting (1973) recommend that, in order to make observations as efficiently as possible, ethnographers make several schedules and maps so they will know where things are happening, at what time of day, and on what day of the week. The Whitings also suggest that fieldworkers systematize their observational techniques, focusing on one thing at a time instead of trying to take in everything at once. They should decide in advance whether to concentrate on activities, individuals, places, or the objects of group attention. For example, if the researcher chooses to study specific activities such as house-building or gardening, observations would center on the technological process, and this ethnologist would note what materials and tools are used, the sequence of activities, and the various roles involved; in observing how a marriage is arranged, the researcher would try to learn and describe the social calculations used in the formal transaction. Alternatively, the investigator might decide to concentrate on broader categories of activities: observing competitive or cooperative behavior, for example, in different kinds of situations—between children at play or men working in the fields. In studying a decision-making process such as a court session, an anthropologist might focus specifically on the center of the group's attention, observing the judge, prosecutor, defendant, and witnesses in turn. Sometimes the ethnographer might concentrate exclusively on interactions between pairs of people—for instance, on the relations between mothers-in-law and sons-in-law, noting how they behave toward each other, who initiates interaction, how the other responds, and so on. To learn how certain people behave—for example, men and women during a ritual or adolescent girls as opposed to married women—the researcher would study a number of individuals separately and note what they do. Finally, the investigator might focus on a setting—a marketplace, for example, or someone's living room—and observe who comes and goes, what they say and do. The chart below is one anthropologist's record of the morning activities of each member of a Mexican family.

Participant observation can mean a great deal more than being present and taking notes. Some anthropologists use very complex *code sheets* that list different attitudes and interactions as check lists in making observations. Recently, for example, observational techniques have been used to study the relationship between personality characteristics in children and various child-rearing practices (Whiting, 1963). Instead of measuring personality through the traditional method of psychological testing, the researchers decided to observe systematically and to rate personality characteristics in terms of how frequently they were expressed. First, they selected specific types of behavior judged as important indicators of personality—responsibility, nurturance, obedience, self-reliance, sociability, aggression, and several other similar categories. After many preliminary observations and assessments, they then worked out a coding system that investigators could use for simultaneously recording and evaluating different kinds of behavior. Thus, for example, ethnographers could observe a child during a five-minute period and give a score for nurturance based on the number of times he or she gave food to a younger child or provided help, emotional support, guidance, or information. Similarly, they could rate a child on aggression based on

Table 11-1. A Synchronic Record of the Activities of Each Member of a Tepoztecan Family.

Time	Father	Mother	Eldest Daughter	Second Daughter	Youngest Daughter
March 28 A.M.					
6:00-6:30	In bed	Rises, makes fire and coffee	In bed	In bed	In bed
6:30-7:00	Rises, feeds cattle, takes them to pasture	Goes to buy bread, sweeps patio	Rises, sweeps kitchen, prepares utensils	Rises, goes for milk	In bed
7:00-7:30	Drinks coffee	Serves husband and self coffee	Grinds corn, makes tortillas	Drinks coffee, cuts and stores dried fish	Rises, washes, combs hair
7:30-8:00	Hauls water, shells corn for mules	Resumes sweeping patio	Grinds corn, makes tortillas	Smooths and folds laundered clothes	Breakfasts
8:00-8:30	Breakfasts	Combs hair, breakfasts, serves others	Grinds corn, makes tortillas	Breakfasts	Goes to school
8:30-9:00	Talks with investigator	Cuts squash for animals, cooks squash, shells corn	Grinds corn, makes tortillas	Makes beds	At school
9:00-9:30	Goes to bed	Arranges squash in market basket	Breakfasts	Sweeps porch	At school
9:30-10:00	In bed	Arranges squash in market basket	Washes dishes	Washes arms and feet, combs hair	At school
10:00-10:30	In bed	Goes to market to sell corn and squash	Prepares corn for grinding	Accompanies mother to market to make purchases	At school
10:30-11:00	In bed	At market	Prepares and cooks stew	At market	At school
11:00-11:30	In bed	At market	Prepares and cooks stew	At market	At school
11:30-12:00	In bed	At market	Prepares and cooks stew	Returns home, polishes nails	At school

Source: Lewis, 1951:63.

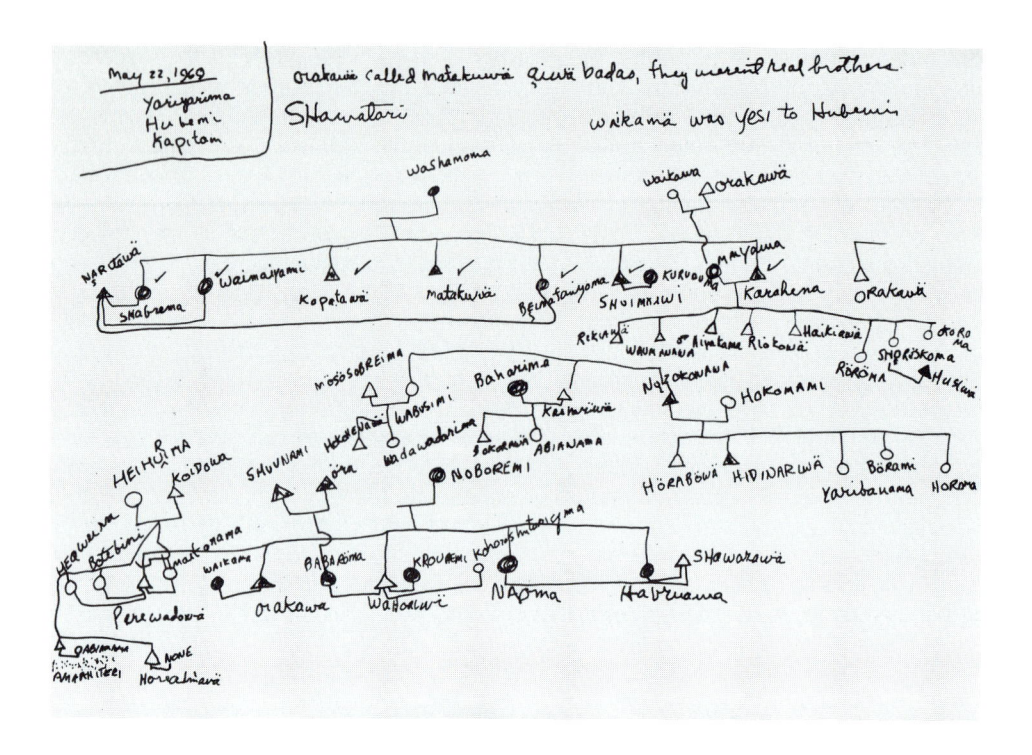

In order to remember complex kinship data given him by informants, ethnographer Napoleon Chagnon found it useful to make this detailed genealogy during his 1969 fieldwork among the Yanomamö. (Napoleon Chagnon)

how many times he or she hit, pushed, bossed, or verbally attacked others within a five-minute span. Altogether, 134 children in six societies were rated on nine different behavioral characteristics. On the basis of these observed ratings, researchers were able to formulate well-documented profiles of the personality characteristics of members of each culture.

The advantage of direct and systematic observation is that researchers are able to see — with their own eyes — things people do not consider worth mentioning or do not want to discuss. Being human, informants often do not remember relevant details accurately; they may also report what they think *should* happen or only what they want the researcher to know rather than the facts. On the other hand, direct observation alone is not enough. Coming from another culture, fieldworkers can easily misinterpret what they see, reading in meanings of their own that do not properly apply. For example, an ethnologist seeing a man beating his wife in public may assume that the husband is abusing her. But it may be that both women and men in that society believe flogging is the best way to drive away disease (Williams, 1967:24). In addition, direct observation does not tell a fieldworker about people's motives, how they perceive different forms of behavior, or what different activities and relationships mean to them. Interviews, questionnaire surveys, psychological tests, and other formal research methods fill in these gaps. But participant observation provides the investigator with the initial insights and clues and the preliminary data essential for developing these more specialized modes of analysis.

Interviews Interviewing provides much of the flesh-and-blood aspect of ethnographic research — it reveals what people think and feel, how they see events and the world around them. Interviews are used to check participant-observation data, to gather general information about a community, and to obtain very specific information about some particular aspect of belief or behavior. An interview may be formal (the fieldworker planning questions in advance, arranging a specific time, and adhering to a definite plan) or informal (a casual question-and-answer session that encourages the informant to follow his or her own train of thought wherever it might lead). The advantage of informal, open-ended interviews is that they tell a researcher what the local people themselves consider important because the anthropologist does not structure the discussion along preconceived lines. The informal method, however, makes it difficult to compare and evaluate answers given by various informants since they are not responding to a standardized question or situation. For example, a fieldworker investigating witchcraft beliefs might open a conversation by saying, "I have heard that some people practice witchcraft. What do you think of this?" However, if this same researcher phrases the question differently by asking a second informant, "Do you personally know any witches?" a completely different viewpoint may well be elicited. Do the different answers reflect real variations between the two informants' experiences with and opinions about witchcraft, or are the differences simply due to the way the anthropologist put the question? Since the questions are not uniform, it is often difficult to tell.

The formal approach avoids this problem because the researcher uses a standardized set of questions designed to elicit specific facts, attitudes, and opinions from informants (although it is clear that the very act of posing questions in so formal a manner affects the response in some way). Often the questions are carefully tested and screened in advance. To make sure that they are getting the kind of data that they want, the researchers may first try out a formal questionnaire on a few people and review the results. They may then eliminate questions that are confusing or sharpen those that bring ambiguous responses — changing vague questions, such as "How often do you visit other villages?" to more precise ones, such as "How many times did you visit Village X and Village Y last year?" They may also decide to add questions about new issues brought to light by the preliminary questionnaire, or to revise questions that seem to influence informants' answers. For example, social scientists have generally found that more people will answer no to a question that is phrased negatively ("You don't believe in witchcraft, do you?") than to one that is phrased positively or neutrally ("Do you believe in witchcraft?"). Once the final format has been worked out, a broader survey can be conducted. Because the questions are always presented in the same way to everyone and allow little room for personal discussion, the answers are more limited and clear-cut. Although this kind of information does not provide the same in-depth understanding of personal attitudes and opinions as extended informal responses, it has the advantage of being easier to compare and analyze statistically. Today, most fieldworkers combine informal methods of interviewing with more systematic and formal approaches that produce quantifiable information. They do this by conducting different kinds of interviews at different times and places, as well as by combining formal and informal questions in a single interview.

No fieldworker accepts information obtained through interviews at face value. Results must be checked against observations (Do people act as they say they do?), against information elicited from other people, and perhaps against reinterviews with the same person. In this way, Williams (1967) learned that although the Dusun boast about their sexual exploits, they are actually rather conservative in sexual matters. On the other hand, they shy away from talking about aggression but are highly aggressive in their behavior. As these examples suggest, discovering discrepancies between real and reported behavior and between reports from different people can be valuable in itself. Participant observation and interviewing are continuing aspects of every field experience. Other techniques are used for more specific purposes, and often for shorter periods of time.

Conducting a Census At some point during their fieldwork, most anthropologists conduct a census of their research population. This is often done early in the research project because the information to be gathered is quite basic. A census usually takes the form of a household survey based on observations and questionnaires. Basic demographic items—occupation and income; the number, age, educational level, and marital status of family members; and so on—are usually covered, along with a few standardized questions about opinions and attitudes. Some anthropologists conduct more extensive surveys to gather more comprehensive data.

Collecting Nonbehavioral Data In addition to investigating behavioral patterns—who marries whom and why; how people raise their children, carry out their daily routines, and conduct their rituals and formal transactions; what they believe; how they interact with one another generally—anthropologists are also concerned with the material aspects of culture and with a people's technology and physical environment. This kind of information is essential to understanding how and why people behave as they do.

Mapping is usually an early step in a fieldwork project. The ethnographer needs to learn the lay of the research setting—to establish the location of fields, forests, sources of water, homesteads, streets, paths, and so on. During the initial phases of fieldwork, when ethnographers may still be perfecting the language skills needed to conduct extensive interviews, a good deal can be learned simply by making inventories and describing material items. Detailed studies of tools, weapons, household utensils, buildings, vehicles, and the like are needed if a fieldworker is to explore the systematic relationship between a society and its physical environment. In addition, ethnographers need to investigate the kinds of resources used, the amount of time expended in procuring them, the quantity of food collected or produced, and the distribution of the research population per unit of land. In recent decades, anthropologists have been conducting more and more ecological studies of this kind, and some have produced radical new insights. For example, after carefully measuring time expenditures and food yields among the Kalahari Bushmen, Richard Lee (1968) has found that hunting and gathering often provides people with a much steadier, more abundant food supply and a more leisurely style of life than earlier impressionistic observations had suggested.

Additional Data-Gathering Tools Observation, conducting a census, interviewing, mapping, and compiling inventories do not exhaust the anthropologist's methods for collecting data. Official documents (statistical and historical records) often provide valuable information. Folk tales and myths often yield insights into a people's world view and system of values. Aerial photographs can reveal unsuspected data about land use. Photographs serve a number of purposes—from counting people on the streets more accurately than is possible with the naked eye, to eliciting stories from informants, to getting the anthropologist-photographer invited to ceremonies (see Collier, 1967). Films have become increasingly important as a research tool. They are used not simply to give the people back home an idea of what non-Western people and places look like, but as a way of studying social situations and interaction more intensively. Ethnographic films have been used to record and examine a wide variety of topics ranging from detailed investigations of socialization (how a mother holds, feeds, and bathes her infant; how siblings interact; how family members spend their days) to blow-by-blow accounts of ritual warfare and hunting expeditions. By watching such films carefully, much as athletes study films of games or of their own performances, ethnographers are often able to pick up significant details of behavior that might have eluded them.

The techniques a researcher uses depend on the problem being studied—on the setting (whether it is possible to interview, photograph, or test people), and on current theories about which data are relevant and how they should be collected. For a researcher concerned with population problems, the major instrument will be the census. Fieldworkers who study social relationships in societies that use kinship as a principle of organization collect extensive genealogies. Those who are interested in psychological characteristics and believe child-rearing practices shape personality will look for data about this. For these purposes a researcher might supplement careful observations of behavior and socialization techniques with detailed life histories and might use projective psychological tests such as the Rorschach and Thematic Apperception (TAT) tests to obtain quantifiable data. In the TAT, the subject is asked to tell a story about each of a series of pictures, while in the Rorschach, he is asked to describe what an ambiguously shaped ink blot represents. In both cases, people are actually projecting their own feelings into the story or the ink blot, and their responses therefore provide clues to their inner needs or motivations.

In most cases, fieldworkers use a combination of techniques to shed light on particular events or cultural phenomena. Using different techniques not only provides a wide range of data, but is also a way of checking and cross-checking both information and methods.

Sampling Methods

Within the single community, which is the most common focus of anthropological research, most anthropologists are only able to interact with a few of the people whose culture they are studying. Whether they administer formal surveys or conduct informal interviews with a few informants, anthropologists must somehow make certain that their findings, based on information gathered from a relatively small portion of the population, accurately reflect what is true or typical of most members of that culture and adequately represent the diversity of individual viewpoints and behavior. To this end, they must make sure that their sampling techniques are valid. Essentially, there are two kinds of samples: probability samples and judgment samples. In this section we will look at both these forms of sampling, discussing the particular techniques involved and the specific situations in which they are most applicable.

Learning how people make and use tools is an essential part of ethnography. Here a Bushman is preparing a poisoned arrow—a deadly weapon that improves the odds for Bushmen on a hunt, and inspires respect among their Bantu neighbors, who carefully avoid offending the Bushmen.
(Richard Lee/Anthro-Photo)

Probability Samples As anthropologists become increasingly interested in studying large, heterogeneous towns and complex urban populations, more and more fieldworkers are turning to the probability sampling and survey techniques developed by sociologists. For example, an ethnographer interested in alcohol use among particular ethnic groups living in an East African province of several thousand people obviously cannot interview every member of the population. Instead, a smaller segment or *sample* will be selected, and then a survey based on structured interviews or questionnaires will be conducted. If the study's findings are to describe accurately the distribution of attitudes among the residents as a whole, however, the researcher must make certain that the sample is representative—that it reflects in miniature the characteristics of the larger population.

To insure that their selected samples are truly representative, social scientists must follow careful procedures. First, they must delimit the population from which the sample is to be drawn. Usually the investigator can simply designate a particular community (for example, the people of San Pedro), but often the boundaries are not so clear-cut. For instance, in many parts of East Africa homesteads are dispersed in such a way that it is difficult to determine precisely where one community ends and another begins. The same is true of ethnic enclaves in large cities. Moreover, a single community is rarely representative of all communities in a region. Recently it has been suggested that, especially for large groups, samples from a number of communities may better represent both modal patterns and the existing diversity of cultural beliefs and practices.

To select the best possible ways of defining the research population, the investigators must first carry out some preliminary observation and interviewing. Once this process is completed, they can then select a representative segment from the population. They might decide to choose a *random sample*. This does not mean a haphazard selection, such as going into a room and arbitrarily interviewing ten people. The researcher might have an unconscious bias against short, fat people, or might forget about the people sitting on the fringes of the group, thereby distorting the sample. In a truly random sample, every individual must have an equal chance of being chosen: a researcher may place everyone's name in a hat and draw out a selected number or may use a table of random numbers for the same purpose. If the population contains important subgroups (social classes, ethnic groups, and so on) and the researcher wants to make sure that each is represented proportionately, a *stratified sample* can be selected by first dividing the population into a number of categories and then selecting a random sample separately from each group.

Sample surveys enable a researcher to assess the characteristics of a large group and to measure certain kinds of opinions and behavior with precision. However, sampling and survey research in the non-Western world can be extremely problematic (Speckmann, 1967). Official data may be highly inaccurate, making it impossible to know how large a population is or how a sample can be selected scientifically. Villages that appear on the map may or may not exist. Hiring assistant interviewers who understand the techniques of interviewing can also be a problem. Often local people assume that a stranger who asks a great many questions is a tax collector or worse, and refuse to cooperate. Finally, the results of any survey can be misleading. There is no way to make certain that the respondents take the questions seriously or that they are reporting accurately. Women may be reluctant to discuss certain topics if men are present, and vice versa; children may say only what they are supposed to say when adults are nearby. The social distance between the interviewer and informant is also a factor. Interviewing an illiterate person who is in awe of the researcher and perhaps anxious to please him or her is quite different from interviewing a member of the elite who regards the anthropologist an an equal or even a subordinate.

Judgment Samples Some anthropologists sample the population in a less highly structured way than the formal survey techniques we have been describing. *Judgment sampling* involves interviewing individuals on the basis of one or more criteria which the anthropologist has identified as critical to his research. This is often accomplished by collecting extensive information (usually through informal interviews) from a small number of key informants — carefully selected individuals who develop a close working relationship with the fieldworker and provide specialized, in-depth information about their personal experiences and the life of their community. Every anthropologist works with key informants in gaining an introduction to the customs of a society; some may go still further in choosing individuals who are experts in particular areas of native life. For example, key informants are crucial when an investigator is trying to recover information about the past. Much of our knowledge of American Indian culture, for example, is based on informants' recollected accounts of a way of life that no longer exists. Key informants are also essential for supplying details and background information about events that anthropologists witness themselves. By selecting the people who are most involved in a situation or who have specialized knowledge, investigators can cross-check and supplement their own observations.

Some researchers have collected and used the life histories of their informants in order to make abstract ethnographic descriptions more personal, concrete, and vivid. The major objections to life histories are that they cannot be checked against observations of real behavior, and that in recollecting past events, the informant often strays from the facts. However, if the anthropologist is mainly concerned with what people think or believe rather than with what actually happened, this consideration may not be terribly important. For example, the book *Cheyenne Memories* by John Stands-in-Timber and Margot Liberty (1967) includes a Cheyenne version of the famous Custer fight that differs significantly from other accounts. But as one anthropologist points out,

While it is of importance for historians and others to use this information as they attempt to piece together the story of what probably happened on that day in June, 1876, Stands-in-Timber's narrative is probably of greater anthropological significance as evidence concerning the beliefs and views of modern Cheyenne Indians, who are experiencing difficulties in adapting to life as a reservation enclave within American society. (Pelto, 1970; 99–100)

Key-informant interviewing and collecting life histories are important ways of gathering samples of data that can then be used to generalize about life in a community as a whole. But however fruitful these methods are, they are often used to best advantage when combined with more systematic research strategies designed to elicit information from a wider, more representative range of people.

Being in the Field

To this point, our discussion of fieldwork has painted a neat, orderly picture. Some of you may still wonder if fieldwork isn't just a vacation with a little work thrown in. Quite the opposite is true, however. In spite of the fact that anthropologists arrive in the field armed with an impressive array of research techniques, they usually find their new world full of immense difficulties from the very moment they set foot in it. In fact, the difficulties can begin even before they arrive. For reasons we will explore in the next chapter, some researchers have to spend considerable time and effort just to get permission to work in an area at all.

The first month or so in the field is usually spent making specific arrangements. The fieldworker has to find a place to live, as well as a way of obtaining food and supplies. Generally, anthropologists rent a house in the community they are studying, or live with a family. Some live in a tent or trailer, a house local people build, or a school; some commute from a nearby town. If the researchers are traveling to a remote village, they will have to purchase in advance everything they need to live. "My main trouble was that I had no idea of what I might need," Elenore Smith Bowen (1964) recalled.[1]

My own imagination carried me no further than a typewriter, paper, notebooks, and a miscellany for reading. . . . I had myself introduced to ex-traders and retired administrators. They all recommended a meat grinder to make goat meat edible and curry powder to make it palatable. . . . I was grateful, but I wanted to know more. . . . The best advice, in the long run, came from the ripe experience of two professors of anthropology. One said, "Always walk in cheap tennis shoes; the water runs out more quickly." The other said, "You'll need more tables than you think." (Bowen, 1964:3–4)

Food can also be a problem for anthropologists who work in remote towns and villages. Eating and drinking with local people may be an excellent way to establish rapport, but it can also present serious health and aesthetic difficulties. Bowen (1964) liked the roast yams and corn her African neighbors prepared, but could not swallow their mashes. To refuse a host's food was considered a serious insult. She solved the problem by taking a child along on her visits. People thought her extremely good-natured to give the food to a child. Napoleon Chagnon, who studied the Yanomamö of the Brazilian-Venezuelan border, primarily cooked for himself but found the task an ordeal:

It is appalling how complicated it can be to make oatmeal in the jungle. First, I had to make two trips to the river to haul the water. Next, I had to prime my kerosene stove with alcohol and get it burning. . . . Or, I would turn the kerosene on, hoping that the element was still hot enough to vaporize the fuel, and start a small fire in my palm-thatched hut. . . . Then I had to boil the oatmeal and pick the bugs out of it. . . . Eating three meals a day was out of the question. (Chagnon, 1968:6)

---

[1] Elenore Smith Bowen is the pen name Laura Bohannan used for her "anthropological novel" *Return to Laughter,* which is based on her experiences among the Tiv of northern Nigeria. She explains in a foreword that all of the characters except her are fictitious, but that the ethnographic details are accurate.

Of course, fieldwork today is not necessarily so arduous. Although the pioneer fieldworkers and many since them have ventured into remote communities beyond the amenities of civilization, more and more work is now being done in urban or modernized areas. As more rural communities acquire electricity and modern plumbing and transportation facilities, fieldwork has become less laborious and isolated (and perhaps also less romantic).

Fieldworkers as "Marginal Natives"

As soon as he settled in Sensuron, North Borneo, anthropologist Thomas Williams (1967) held a celebration for 60-odd neighbors, during which he learned that local parties last until the food runs out—in this case, two days later. The chief of the tribe Bowen studied arrived just hours after she did, his entire court in tow. She parroted the elaborate greetings she'd learned from a missionary and shook fists. They smoked, she smoked; they smiled, she smiled—and waited. She had not learned how to say goodbye (Bowen, 1964:7). Hortense Powdermaker (1967), newly arrived in Lesu, had an interpreter call villagers together for an assembly. She explained that her people knew nothing about Lesu, and that when she went home, she would put everything she had learned in a book. She passed around several monographs to illustrate. Thus, soon after arriving, all of these anthropologists in one way or another occupied themselves with an important concern—trying to establish friendly relations with the people they were about to study.

Some peoples see nothing odd about an outsider wanting to study their way of life; others, however, assume the researcher has hidden motives and remain suspicious. (Often anthropologists must dissociate themselves from local officials whom villagers have learned to distrust.) Paying people in money or gifts for their time is one way of overcoming resistance and suspicion. (Malinowski once said that local people see an anthropologist as a "necessary evil or nuisance, mitigated by donations of tobacco" (Malinowski, 1961:8.) But in the final analysis, one important element in the success of field research is the rapport the anthropologist establishes with informants.

As an uninvited guest, a fieldworker becomes at best a "marginal native"—a familiar face, perhaps even a friend and adopted relative, but an outsider nonetheless (Freilich, 1970). No matter how attached fieldworkers become to "their people," they rarely delude themselves into thinking local people consider them one of their own. And local people usually consider an outsider who tries to "go native" mildly ridiculous. The stranger role has certain advantages. Frequently people tell strangers things they would never reveal to their family, friends, or neighbors. In remaining unallied with a particular family or social group, a fieldworker (ideally) avoids antagonizing rival families and hostile groups.

But being a stranger leaves a fieldworker open to deception or exploitation (Hatfield, 1973). During his first week in Sensuron, Williams (1967) dutifully drank two large cups of potent rice wine as a toast to his mother-in-law in every house he visited, assuming this was the local custom. He was beginning to despair of ever being sober enough to get his work done when a local headman told him the villagers were playing a practical joke at his expense. Chagnon (1968) spent months learning names and collecting genealogies— only to discover that the Yanomamö have strict taboos against speaking the names of people who have died and only refer by name to the living to show lack of respect. His informants had made a game of inventing preposterous and obscene names. All his work was wasted. Making friends among the Yanomamö proved difficult. They considered Chagnon (and all other non-Yanomamö) subhuman and had no qualms about relieving him of food and equipment whenever they had a chance. Finally he retaliated. When some men chopped up a platform he'd had built to use the wood for paddles, he waded across the river, delivered a stern lecture to the culprits, and calmly cut their canoes loose to drift downstream. Thereafter his status rose dramatically among "the fierce people." But he had no way of knowing in advance how they were going to react.

One of a fieldworker's primary goals is to get "backstage," to see behind people's public images. But no matter how accepted an anthropologist is, there are certain kinds of information people do not want to reveal. The Africans considered Elenore Bowen (1964) a backward child in terms of their culture. No one discussed such serious matters as witchcraft in her presence. However, after one of the elders was found guilty of a serious crime and deserted by his family, he offered to tell her about magic. When she accepted the offer, virtually everyone else stopped talking to her. Bowen handled this crisis by "admitting" she was a witch and helping her neighbors scare away malevolent owls (with strips of metal such as her mother had used to keep birds out of the corn back home). As this example suggests, fieldwork requires extremely delicate public relations. An unwitting blunder can destroy the trust it took months to build.

Psychological Strains

The shock of finding oneself alone in a strange culture, the effort of maintaining friendly relations with everyone, conflicts between remaining an objective scientist and needing friends, and the knowledge that one's professional status depends upon what one accomplishes in the field can make anthropological research extremely trying.

Fieldwork is always a lonely undertaking. Often even anthropologists who work in teams spread out and work individually. Inability to communicate effectively and "culture shock" (the disorientation people feel when in a totally foreign social landscape) compound the fieldworker's sense of isolation. At some point during the first weeks, nearly every anthropologist wonders "What on earth am I doing here, all alone and at the edge of the world?" (Pow-

Anthropological fieldwork is not a vacation. It requires flexibility, ingenuity, and plain hard work to set up a kitchen and do laundry in the Kalahari Desert. Anthropologist Nancy DeVore doesn't seem to mind. (Anthro-Photo)

dermaker, 1967:51). Chagnon considered turning back the moment he saw the Yanomamö.

I am not ashamed to admit . . . that had there been a diplomatic way out, I would have ended my fieldwork there and then. I did not look forward to the next day when I would be left alone with the Indians: I did not speak a word of their language, and they were decidedly different from what I had imagined them to be. The whole situation was depressing, and I wondered why I ever decided to switch from civil engineering to anthropology in the first place. (Chagnon, 1968:5–6)

After a time, a researcher—particularly one living right in a village or with a family—may feel a strong desire to get away. In the field, anthropologists are always on stage. Particularly in the beginning, they are extremely anxious to be liked and willing to do almost anything to gain favor. Normal escapes, such as avoiding people you dislike, and spontaneous acts, such as getting angry, are "forbidden, leading to a build-up of tension which may be difficult to tolerate." Delmos Jones, who worked with the Lahu in northern Thailand, concluded that pretending to be impartial, unfeeling, and good-natured all of the time may be counterproductive; "the anthropologist should be more of himself in the field" (Jones, 1973:35).

At times a fieldworker may be unable to suppress feelings of disgust and revulsion toward local customs. Elenore Bowen was horrified to learn that her African neighbors thought telling a blind man there was a snake on the path and watching him stumble and fall trying to escape was a marvelous joke. "They were all savages. For the first time I applied the word to them in my own thinking. And it fit" (Bowen, 1964:230). Later Bowen began to understand their seeming callousness. A smallpox epidemic was threatening the village, and a chief's son who became infected was thrown out of the village to die alone. Bowen had been vaccinated against smallpox and could have at least taken him food and water, but it would have confirmed the villagers' suspicion that she was an evil-hearted witch. She chose not to. Deirdre Meintel (1973) argues that culture shock, which is usually explained in terms of a person's difficulty in adjusting to strange customs, more often results from difficulty in adjusting to uncomfortable things one learns about oneself in the field.

Added to these problems is the fact that fieldworkers often see their research as a do-or-die proposition. Their reputation and future employment depend on what they do in the field. Not infrequently, a carefully detailed research design simply does not fit the situation in the field. But there is no one to discuss this with. Modifying the original plan requires more self-confidence than many researchers—particularly novices—have.

Recognizing these problems, many anthropologists today are approaching fieldwork somewhat differently. First, they have come to realize that they must do more than simply collect reams of data. Instead of waiting until they are safely at home in their offices and living rooms thousands of miles away, many ethnographers are spending more time analyzing what they have collected while they are still in the field. By taking stock of what they have before leaving, fieldworkers are able to gather additional data to fill in gaps in the record, check questionable findings, and make any modifications that are needed before it is too late. Second, anthropologists have increasingly come to realize just how much there is to investigate in even the simplest societies and the smallest communities. We know too much about the richness and complexity of culture to think that one individual can collect adequate data on all aspects of culture. Consequently, more researchers are working together cooperatively as teams of specialists. On a team project, one researcher might concentrate on food-getting and technology, another on child-rearing practices, a third on religion. Or if the community includes distinct social classes and/or racial, ethnic, or religious groups, members of the research team might become individually involved with different social segments. By focusing on one relatively manageable research problem, each fieldworker is able to investigate a particular area in greater depth. And by pooling their efforts, the group can put together a more complete picture of the whole society under study. Teamwork also confers several other advantages. By comparing, debating, and discussing their findings with each other, members of the group are able to hammer out their ideas and gain fresh insights. In addition, teamwork helps to relieve the loneliness and sense of isolation that often besets solitary fieldworkers and sometimes clouds their objectivity.

Interpreting the Data

The process of analyzing data is as demanding as fieldwork itself. Fieldworkers' write-ups are not simply reports of what took place during their stays (although these write-ups may contain photographic records, verbatim transcripts of interviews, and blow-by-blow accounts of events). After leaving the field, most researchers spend a year or more sorting through their notes to see what is there, how the data can be organized, what patterns emerge. Have the original hypotheses been confirmed or refuted? Have new issues and problems arisen? How do the findings compare to related studies? What conclusions can be drawn about anthropological theory in general and this village or community in particular? Although much final analysis occurs after an anthropologist returns home, the analytic process actually began way back during the preparation of the research design, and it continued throughout the period in the field as the researcher struggled to make sense out of what he or she observed and heard. The Whitings (1973) suggest that fieldworkers analyze their data as they collect it, sifting and selecting out salient facts and findings.

Defining Patterns

But regardless of when interpretation of data occurs, anthropological analysis always has one ultimate goal: to uncover general cultural patterns. Unlike journalists or biographers, anthropologists are not interested in the unique or idiosyncratic aspects of people and events. Out of the welter of actions and interactions that they observe, ethnographers must determine the regularities of behavior or the general features that characterize the social life of a people. How do they accomplish this task?

Much of the interpretive work anthropologists have done consisted of attempts to summarize their observations simply by inferring major cultural patterns. While such impressionistic summaries are a vital component of anthropological research, many anthropologists have probably failed to be as careful as they should in distinguishing between what they observed and the inferences they have made based on those observations. For this reason, formal quantitative models are becoming more and more important as

Statistics and Mathematics in Anthropology

Over the last three decades, the use of statistical and mathematical techniques by anthropologists has increased markedly. In 1945 four of anthropology's leading journals published a total of two articles using such techniques, in 1957 there were twenty, and in 1965 as many as forty (Kay, 1971). What accounts for this trend? As the ranks of anthropologists grew into the thousands following World War II, and research data burgeoned, a need was felt for more efficient means of assessing the reliability of data-gathering procedures. Statistical and mathematical techniques met this need. But more importantly, they also permitted anthropologists to assess the implications of research findings and to rapidly identify patterns in large quantities of data that might not be obvious through visual inspection of field records alone. Let us look at one example of the important uses of mathematical models in anthropology.

In a later chapter, we will discuss age-set systems, a form of social organization in which people of roughly similar ages are organized into groups, each vested with certain privileges and responsibilities. Such a system exists among the Galla of Ethiopia (Murdock, 1959). The Galla have five age grades. A man enters the first grade forty years after his father. Obviously, this can lead to problems. If a father was very young when his son was born, the son may be very old before he enters the first age grade. This means that he must endure the humiliation of maintaining sexual abstinence and begging food from married women. By contrast, if many men enter the first grade at an early age, important political and religious offices associated with the higher grades may go unfilled because of an insufficient number of surviving senior citizens.

Using mathematical techniques, anthropologist Hans Hoffman (1971) has calculated the conditions under which the Galla age grade system could remain stable. One such set of conditions would be if the average age of initiation into the first grade remained the same from generation to generation, and if the average age of parenthood remained constant at approximately 40 years. But these conditions are unlikely.

Hoffman therefore approaches the problem from a more probablistic point of view. He asks: Is there a distribution of ages upon initiation into the first age grade that will result in stability from one generation to the next? He then proceeds to build a model in which males enter the system in one of three categories: s_1 composed of young men ages 13 to 19, s_2 composed of men 20 to 29, and s_3 of men 30 or over. Age distributions within these categories can be written as vectors. The vector (.25, .55, .20), for example, is read as follows: 25 percent of the population enter the age grade system at ages 13 to 19, 55 percent enter at ages 20 to 29, and 20 percent enter at 30 or older. This vector describes the distribution of entering ages for one generation. But what of succeeding generations?

With adequate demographic data, one could construct a transition matrix describing the probability that a father who entered the age grade system at a certain age would have a son who would enter at a certain age. Such data is not available for the Galla, but Hoffman has created the following hypothetical matrix:

$$\text{Fathers} \begin{pmatrix} & \text{Sons} & \\ & s_1 & s_2 & s_3 \\ s_1 & .15 & .38 & .46 \\ s_2 & .37 & .40 & .23 \\ s_3 & .20 & .60 & .20 \end{pmatrix}$$

Looking at the first line, we see that of all fathers who enter the age grade system at ages 13 to 19, 15 percent will have sons who enter at ages 13 to 19, 38 percent will have sons who enter at 20 to 29, and 46 percent will have sons who enter at 30 or over. The remaining two lines of the matrix are read in the same manner. Using matrix algebra, we can then multiply the vector by the transition matrix to determine the distribution of entering ages in the next generation. Hoffman is able to show that there is a distribution of ages in one generation which, when multiplied by the matrix, produces exactly the same distribution in the following generation. In other words, vector x matrix = vector. In this example, that vector is (.26, .45, .28).

Hoffman has not demonstrated that the Galla age grade system is stable, but he has shown that there are conditions under which it *could be* stable—a particular distribution of ages in the male population and particular patterns of birth and initiation. The model points the way for field studies to determine why and how stability is maintained in such systems. It also warns researchers that two systems that are in fact similar may appear quite different simply because they reflect different points in some larger pattern.

tools for determining cultural patterns and regularities. Statistical models are probably the most commonly used.

Quantitative Data and Statistical Analysis

Quantitative analysis often reveals relationships and patterns that might otherwise never come to light. For instance, Cancian's (1965) quantitative data on the *cargo* system (a system of religious offices) in Zinacantan, Mexico, revealed that, contrary to surface impressions, there is a definite system of social stratification among Zinacantecos. Although a seemingly egalitarian society, the quantitative reality uncovered by Cancian's statistical analysis showed that Zinacantecos tend to marry people from families of similar cargo rank and that sons generally achieve the same cargo status as their fathers.

Statistical analysis often is essential for establishing a clear-cut relationship between different kinds of social phenomena. For example, a social scientist who concludes that there is a close connection between drug use and income level or between witchcraft beliefs and certain marriage practices is on shaky grounds unless such a statement can be backed up by statistical conclusions that show a significant correlation between the two factors. Perhaps most important, quantitative measures are essential for making rigorous cross-cultural comparisons and for testing theoretical generalizations about human society. For this reason, anthropologists over the last two decades have dramatically increased their use of statistical tools.

Generating Models and Theories

Whether they use formal or informal, quantitative or nonquantitative techniques, anthropologists are ultimately interested in evaluating the theory with which the research began. The results of the field study may also form the basis of theorizing that will prompt another field effort, perhaps by a completely different anthropologist investigating a completely different culture. Alan Holmberg's (1969) study of the Siriono people of eastern and northern Bolivia illustrates this process. Holmberg began by collecting a wide range of information to present a complete picture of the Siriono way of life. In forming his summary description, he drew together a number of generalizations about the Siriono. He concluded that they generally have a difficult time collecting enough to eat and experience continual hunger and food insecurity or frustration. Based upon other observations, he also concluded that the Siriono are selfish and greedy about food and are generally uncooperative and suspicious of one another. From these generalizations, Holmberg proposed a list of general propositions about all societies that live under conditions of high food insecurity. He suggested, for example, that in such societies (1) aggression will be expressed primarily in terms of food; (2) individuals who are the most successful providers of food will occupy positions of authority; (3) those who cannot potentially contribute to the food quest (the ill, the aged, deformed infants) will often be abandoned, neglected, or killed. These relationships have not been tested cross-culturally, but Holmberg has stated his generalizations in such a way that other investigators can test these propositions in similar societies. If they hold true, anthropologists may develop a more abstract or higher-order theory about how food insecurity, environment and procurement systems, social institutions, and personality characteristics are related.

A theoretical model can never be established simply on the basis of data from a single society, because it is designed to organize knowledge about many different cases; it aims at a higher level of generalization. As more and more studies of particular societies have accumulated, anthropologists have paid more attention to developing techniques for testing theories by comparing different cultures.

Testing Theoretical Generalizations

One way of testing the general applicability of a theory is cross-cultural comparison. Once a general theory about human society has been developed, researchers may formally test it by means of a *holocultural study*—that is, a worldwide survey or a sample of all known cultures (Naroll, 1973). For example, an anthropologist might want to test the theory that as societies develop greater technological control over their environment (more complex, efficient tools and procurement systems), occupational specialization increases. The first step would be to select a representative sample of cultures at different levels of technological complexity. Then various statistical measures or tests would be applied to ascertain whether there is in fact a correlation between technological complexity and occupational specialization. If the relationship holds true in a significant number of cases—that is, in more cultures than chance or probability would indicate—then the researcher would conclude that there is indeed a positive correlation between these two factors.

Actually, the preceding theory has been verified by numerous holocultural studies. Other theories, however, have been disproved by the holocultural method. For example, in the past it was widely held that kinship systems tended to become less complex and less important as society became more complex. After testing this idea by analyzing worldwide correlations, anthropologists have found that this is not the situation. Cross-cultural statistical surveys suggest that there may be a curvilinear relationship: kinship groups tend to be small and relatively simple at both the highest and lowest levels of societal complexity; they tend to be large and elaborate at the middle level of societal complexity (Naroll, 1973:334–335).

To aid in such studies, a large number of anthropologists have worked strenuously over the past several decades to bring together all of the information that anthropologists have collected on the world's cultures. Written on a series of cards and xeroxed pages, the information is housed in a number of libraries in what are known as the Human Relations Area Files. By using the files' extensive indexing system, a researcher can find specific information on almost any feature of any culture that has been studied. The accessibility of such a wide range of cultural data greatly aids anthropologists in their statistical analyses and cross-cultural comparisons on a worldwide scale.

Holocultural studies do not tell us why a particular relationship exists—why, for example, kinship groups are most complex in middle-range societies. Nor do they establish cause and effect—whether occupational specialization is the consequence or the cause of technological complexity, for instance. However, they have enabled anthropologists to reach many firm conclusions about human behavior and social organization. In the future, this method will undoubtedly become more refined and more widely applied as our knowledge of human behavior broadens and social scientists develop more sophisticated methods of scientific analysis.

summary

Cultural anthropology is distinguished by its reliance on *fieldwork* as the primary means by which data is collected and theories are verified. The anthropologist enters into the culture in what has come to be known as *participant observation*—living in close contact for extended periods with the people being studied, observing them, communicating with them, and trying to understand their culture as they do. Fieldworkers must make detailed records of what they observe, and they should decide in advance whether they will concentrate on activities, individuals, places, or the object of group attention.

The advantage of direct and systematic observation is that the researcher is able to see things people may not consider mentioning or may not want to discuss. In interpreting what they observe, researchers must be careful to avoid cultural biases—both of their own and of their informants. Also, because direct observation cannot provide information on people's motives or on what different activities and relationships mean to them, it must be supplemented with other, more formal research methods.

Much of the flesh and blood of fieldwork is provided by *interviews*. In informal interviews, informants are encouraged to follow their own train of thought. The advantage to informal interviews is that they tell us what the people themselves consider important. But because the informants are not responding to standardized questions, it is difficult to compare the responses. This problem does not arise in formal interviews, which consist of a standardized set of questions designed to elicit specific facts, attitudes, and opinions. Because the two kinds of interviews provide different kinds of information, most researchers use both approaches, checking the results against actual observations of people's behavior.

Most researchers eventually conduct a *census* of their research population. The census usually takes the form of a household survey, covering such basic demographic items as occupation and income, and the number, age, educational level, and marital status of family members.

Anthropologists are also interested in collecting nonbehavioral data. Thus drawing a detailed map of the research setting is usually an early step in any fieldwork project. A good deal can also be learned simply by making inventories and describing material items. Additional means of gathering data include taking photographs (both from the air and on the ground), making films, studying official documents and folk tales, and using psychological tests. What specific techniques are used by researchers will depend on the problem they are studying. By using a number of different techniques, they will gather a wide range of data and also will be able to cross-check their information.

Because it is impossible for anthropologists to interact with every person in a culture, they select instead a *sample,* or smaller segment, of the population to study. It is especially important that the sample reflect the characteristics of the larger population. After the researchers have delineated the population from which the sample is to be drawn, they might decide to choose a *random sample*—a sample in which every individual has an equal chance of being chosen. Or if the population contains important subgroups, they may choose a *stratified sample,* which entails dividing the population into a number of categories, then selecting a random sample separately from each group.

In small, homogeneous societies, the anthropologist may use a judgment sample, obtained through key-informant interviewing. In this case, only a small number of informants are used. Because of the many possible biases in this kind of data, key-informant interviews should be supplemented with more systematic strategies.

One of the fieldworker's primary goals is to get behind people's public images. Doing so entails many problems. At best, a fieldworker becomes a "marginal native"—a familiar face and perhaps even a friend, but an outsider nonetheless. Because they are outsiders and sometimes have difficulty communicating, fieldworkers are open to deception and exploitation and often experience great loneliness and frustration. Also, because they are always on stage, they generally feel that they must continually be on their best behavior. This problem is exacerbated by the fact that they tend to see their research as being the deciding factor in their professional success or failure.

An especially difficult situation is when the researcher finds that the research design simply does not fit the field situation and there is no one to discuss this with. Recognizing this—and all of the other problems—anthropologists are beginning to spend more time analyzing their data while still in the field and are working increasingly in teams, with each member studying a particular question in depth.

Analyzing data always has one goal: to uncover general cultural patterns. Through statistical analysis, one can establish clear-cut relationships between different kinds of social phenomena, make rigorous cross-cultural comparisons, and test theoretical generalizations about human society. Often, the results so obtained form the basis of theorizing that will prompt another field effort. Once a general theory has been developed, researchers can test it by means of a *holocultural study,* or worldwide survey or sample of all known cultures. To do this, they select a representative sample of cultures, then apply various statistical measures or tests to determine whether the general theory does in fact hold up. Holocultural studies do not tell us why a relationship exists, nor do they establish cause and effect; but they have enabled anthropologists to reach many firm conclusions about human behavior and social organization.

suggested readings

BOWEN, E. S.
1964 *Return to Laughter: An Anthropological Novel.* New York: Doubleday/American Museum of Natural History. An extensive, amusing, and informative discussion of one anthropologist's experiences in the field, written in novelistic form.

FREILICH, M., ED.
1970 *Marginal Natives: Anthropologists at Work.* New York: Harper & Row. The essays in this volume are divided into two groups, one focusing on the problems of designing specific pieces of field research and the other covering field experiences.

KAY, P., ED.
1971 *Explorations in Mathematical Anthropology.* Cambridge, Mass.: M.I.T. Press. A collection of essays exploring the utility of mathematical models in the analysis of anthropological data.

NAROLL, R., AND COHEN, R., EDS.
1970 *A Handbook of Method in Cultural Anthropology.* New York: Natural History Press. Essays raising the important methodological issues that must be resolved in order to successfully carry out different kinds of fieldwork.

PELTO, P. J.
1970 *Anthropological Research: The Structure of Inquiry.* New York: Harper & Row. Emphasizes formal techniques of observation, data collection, and analysis.

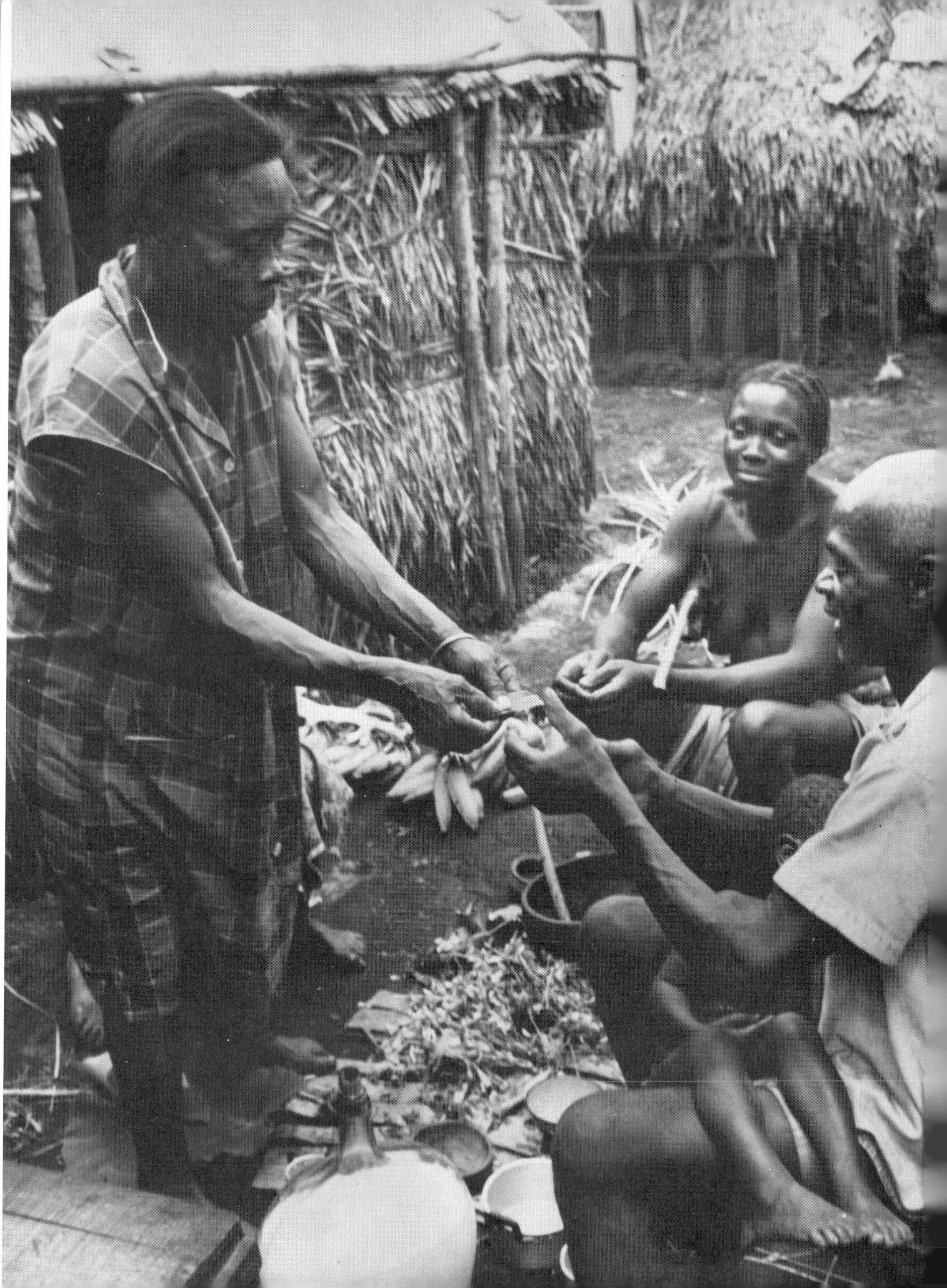

twelve
Ethics of Cultural Anthropology

In 1938, when Malinowski wrote, "Anthropology must become an applied science," he was thought quite revolutionary. But his challenge was difficult to ignore. He wondered if the fact that anthropologists had not taken an active role in the debate between those who thought natives should be kept in their place and those who felt they should have a place in the sun meant "that knowledge serves merely to blind us to the reality of human interests and vital issues" (Malinowski, 1938). As director of the International African Institute, Malinowski advocated "scientific control of colonial cooperation" and urged further research into native languages, legal systems, land tenure, and economics, and particularly into the effects of European influence on indigenous communities. In each case, Malinowski emphasized the practical need for and applications of such research. For example, how could natives be induced to work for Europeans?

The simplest experience teaches that to everybody work is prima facie unpleasant, but a study of primitive conditions shows that very efficient work can be obtained, and the Natives can be made to work with some degree of real satisfaction if propitious conditions are created for them. . . . In Melanesia I have seen this applied on some plantations. Use was made of such stimuli as competitive displays of the results, or special marks of distinction for industry, or again of rhythm and working songs. Again the arrangement of work in gangs corresponding to indigenous communal labour produced the desired effect, but all such things must never be improvised—an artificial arrangement will never get hold of native imagination. In every community I maintain there are such indigenous means of achieving more intensive labour and greater output, and it is only necessary to study the facts in order to be able to apply efficient incentives. (Malinowski, 1929:36)

This quotation underlines a major ethical problem: how—and to whose benefit—should anthropological research be used? Was Malinowski an agent of colonialism, betraying the peoples he studied to exploitation-minded officials? White settlers in Africa and Asia did not think so. On the contrary, they associated anthropologists with dangerously progressive views. Fieldworkers usually developed deep sympathy for "their people." Most opposed such practices as forced labor and approved such indulgences as indirect rule (ruling through indigenous institutions rather than outlawing and replacing them). In their writings, anthropologists made exotic customs seem reasonable and native traditions worthy of respect and appreciation. And many opposed the Europeanization of foreign peoples.

One might conclude from this that ethnographers in general were "pro-native." Certainly they considered themselves enlightened, and compared to many colonials, they were. But in subtle and often unintended ways, anthropologists have supported the status quo. The traditions that ethnographers sought to protect sometimes slowed the workings of European administrations, but in the long run they were less of a threat to colonialism than progressive natives who were gathering in cities and universities. In emphasizing the profound differences between native and Western world views and lifestyles, anthropologists inadvertently reinforced the social barriers between

A medicine man from the Libinza tribe of Zaïre, dressed in woman's garb, practices divination. Conflicts between traditional and modern medical practices are one source of the ethical dilemmas anthropologists face. (Jacques Jangoux)

them and even seemed to support their continued existence (Marquet, 1964). Some anthropologists, for instance, have separated non-Western populations from Western ones by describing them as "unacculturated" or "partially acculturated." However, other anthropologists, and a great many native peoples, argue instead that such groups *have* been acculturated—to an economically and culturally impoverished position within Western societies.

The question of exploitation also arises in the payment of fees to informants. It has been argued, for instance, that in paying for information, anthropologists are exploiting the needs of native people instead of training them so that they may become anthropologists themselves and ultimately replace foreign researchers. Because of numerous issues such as these, an increasing number of American Indian groups and Third World countries are unwilling to permit, much less support, anthropological work in their society.

As major factors determining the future shape of the discipline, the issues surrounding anthropological research deserve a closer look.

The Issues

The debate that began in Malinowski's time and continues into our own centers around two basic issues: objectivity and relevance. While these issues are most evident when anthropologists apply their knowledge in efforts to implement change, they are implicit in every piece of research an anthropologist undertakes.

Objectivity

A number of anthropologists argue that, as scientists, anthropologists have an obligation to strive for the "purity" associated with the physical sciences. This position is based on the belief that it is possible to suspend one's cultural and theoretical biases in the field and to observe and report what one sees with detached objectivity. An equal number of anthropologists believe this approach violates one of the most basic tenets of anthropology: that every individual is a product of his culture. Total objectivity is impossible. A researcher's cultural background, academic training, and personality influence what is perceived as well as what is reported. By pretending to objectivity, then—by leaving biases unstated instead of clearly identifying them—anthropologists may be deceptive, an approach that is ultimately unproductive.

Relevance

Equally controversial are questions about the topics anthropologists choose to study. Again, we find a number of "purists" who believe that the pursuit of knowledge is its own justification, and that researchers should address themselves to questions that will increase our understanding of human culture over the long run. Critics of this viewpoint argue that it is immoral to place the needs of the discipline ahead of human needs, and that anthropologists should address themselves to the pressing social problems of their day. They add that a discipline that focuses only on theoretical issues is destined to become involuted and obsolete.

Reduced to the bare bones, these issues may seem highly abstract. But to anthropologists—who very likely work alone in remote parts of foreign countries, who may be seen as agents of their government (whether they are or not), who may be called on to interpret unknown cultures to the world, and who will undoubtedly face challenges from their colleagues—these debates raise difficult questions that demand concrete answers.

Of particular importance in this regard are two specific questions: What are the obligations anthropologists have to the people they study? And what obligations do anthropologists have to their own government and that of their hosts? Let us look first at some of the problems concerning anthropologists' responsibilities to the people they study.

The Sánchez and Springdale Affairs: Responsibilities to Informants

In the early 1960s, Oscar Lewis published a life history of the Sánchez family (a pseudonym for an extremely poor Mexican family) as part of his continuing investigation of the "culture of poverty." Lewis allowed the members of the family to tell their own story, and transcribed their accounts verbatim—without censoring obscene language, political opinions, or the seamier aspects of their lives. He called *The Children of Sánchez* (1961) an autobiography. In keeping with the belief that scholars in host countries should see and have an opportunity to criticize foreign researchers' observations, Lewis arranged for a Spanish translation, which was issued in Mexico in early 1965.

The reaction in the Mexican newspapers was totally unexpected. Lewis was accused of both fabricating data and obtaining information with hidden recording devices; of characterizing Mexicans in general "as the most degraded, miserable and vile people in the whole world"; of stating that Mexicans were incapable of self-government; and (of course) of serving as an undercover agent for the FBI—all false accusations. Some of the Mexican reporters defended Lewis. In contrast to other foreign researchers, Lewis had maintained longstanding relations with Mexican scholars and employed a number of local assistants. He had been entirely open about his sponsorship and research goals; he had obtained the Sánchez family's permission to publish their story and taken every precaution to conceal their identity. Nevertheless, the attacks on Lewis continued, and in February the Mexican Geographical and Statistical Society filed suit against him for obscenity and slander against the Mexican people. The Attorney General ultimately rejected the suit. But suppose the case had gone to court. Would Lewis have been able to protect the identity of the Sánchez family, who had revealed embarrassing and potentially incriminating facts about themselves because he

Social Science and Ideology

The social sciences as well as the physical sciences are based not only on facts but also on a notion of how the world works. Scientists fit facts into a framework, or paradigm, that is seldom of their own making but reflects a prevailing point of view. Real changes in science involve the rejection of one paradigm and substitution of another that better fits the facts. Such changes do not come easily, however, for people do not quickly abandon a way of perceiving the world they have long viewed as true. For example, when Copernicus asserted that the facts of astronomy would make more sense using a model in which the earth revolved around the sun, the ensuing debate involved not only science but theology, the place of man in creation, and a host of other philosophical questions seemingly unrelated to celestial mechanics. Science, therefore, has an inherent ideological component.

One of the more important paradigms in sociology and anthropology has been the structural-functional approach, which essentially focuses on factors contributing to order and stability in a society. Critics of this approach contend that it easily becomes a celebration of the status quo, particularly in analyzing modern industrial societies like the United States. Take, for instance, a routine description of American organizations by a member of the functionalist school: ". . . once firmly established, an organization tends to assume an identity of its own which makes it independent of the people who have founded it or of those who constitute its membership." According to one critic, Alvin Gouldner, this seemingly neutral statement contains hidden values and assumptions. Gouldner points out that "aside from whether this is a 'fact' or a metaphysical assumption, it makes a difference whether one views such autonomy of social structures—their alienation from their own constituencies—as a normal condition to be accepted or as an endemic and recurrent disease to be opposed" (Gouldner, 1968).

Gouldner believes that the pattern of accepting as "normal" what he sees as the pathological conditions of a modern industrial society arises from the theoretical emphasis on stability of the structural-functional school of thought. While many social scientists would disagree with Gouldner's conclusions, all would probably concur that structural-functionalism, like any theoretical orientation, is in some respects ideological.

had guaranteed them anonymity? As it was, one newspaper assigned two reporters to locate them during the uproar. Had Lewis learned of this, he would have been powerless to stop them (Beals, 1969:11–15). And although he was exonerated, it is doubtful that Lewis would ever have been able to conduct research in Mexico again.

A similar incident involving possible violation of the right to privacy occurred some years earlier in America. In this case, it was the informants themselves—not the press or local scholars—who objected to public exposure. Arthur Vidich was one of a team of researchers who participated in a long-term study of "Springdale," a pseudonym for a small town in upstate New York, under the auspices of Cornell University's Department of Child Development and Family Relations. Cornell had obtained the townspeople's consent and cooperation by promising to disguise individual identity in all published reports. In collaboration with Joseph Bensman, Vidich wrote and published *Small Town in Mass Society* (1968), an unofficial account of the study. When this book appeared, the official report was still being written. Having given both the town and the individuals described fictitious names, Vidich believed he had fulfilled his pledge to the community.

The townspeople thought otherwise. They knew who he was talking about when he referred to the mayor or the school principal. (After all, it was a very small town.) And they were incensed by what they considered to be a Peyton Place-type book about their private lives.

Anthropologists invariably develop ties with the people they study, as Margaret Mead did in Bali. This makes guaranteeing the privacy of informants and protecting them from the misuse of data collected in the field that much harder. Anthropologists are not always able to return the confidence people extend to them. (Ken Heyman)

Vidich argued that no one would have accused him of violating the right to privacy if he had been writing about a small tribe in Brazil or a poor, minority community in the States. Anthropologists have always sought information on behind-the-scenes activities. In most cases, the populations they studied were either unaware that their lives would be exposed or powerless to object. Should anthropologists alter their approach when they are studying more articulate and influential groups? Vidich replied no to this question and also maintained that it is wrong for researchers to shape their reports to please informants.

There is in fact much debate among anthropologists about the extent of the researcher's responsibility to informants. Obtaining their consent and guaranteeing their anonymity may not be enough. The informants may not understand the full implications of having the details of their lives, their political opinions, and so on, examined and published, particularly if they have little or no education and are not familiar with the outside world. Indeed, anthropologists themselves may not anticipate the reaction to their findings. Once a study is published, they have no control over the uses to which it may be put by authorities. Physicians, psychiatrists, lawyers, and priests have the legal right to withhold from a court of law information that is given to them in confidence. Anthropologists do not. They may be required to submit their records or testify (or go to jail, as some reporters have). Thus living up to a felt responsibility toward the subjects of investigation may prove difficult or impossible. On the other hand, if a researcher explains these problems in full detail to informants, they may well choose not to cooperate, just as many governments have chosen not to cooperate with researchers who are receiving funds from the U.S. military and the CIA.

Just as anthropologists are attempting to more clearly define their responsibilities to individuals, so are they seeking to clarify their proper relationship with governments. Let us turn now to this other, equally important, area of concern.

The Anthropologist Between Two Governments

Given the common assumption that colonialism was beneficial in the long run, pre-World War II anthropologists who strove to enlighten the rulers and protect the ruled from the more brutal aspects of colonialism might consider themselves responsible and moral. Most of the populations they studied had no say in decisions regarding research; most could not read and therefore did not know if or how research might affect their lives. Today, the situation is far more complex. Little remains of the vast colonial empires of the early twentieth century. The government of modern Burma does not allow anthropological research; fieldworkers are barred from certain districts in Nepal and Afghanistan, from much of the Arabian peninsula, and from nonwhite districts in South Africa. Newly independent governments resent the fact that anthropologists are more interested in the "backward" sections of their countries than in the progress they've made. Some undoubtedly fear researchers will expose the lack of grass-roots support for the government and the failure to control corruption on the local level. Rightly or wrongly, many governments believe anthropologists are covert agents of American neocolonialism. Even within our own country, native American groups have accused anthropologists of exploiting them for self-gain and of failing to defend their interests in the face of corporate and governmental pressure.

Two generations ago, anthropologists might have dismissed such accusations outright. At that time, the common complaint among anthropologists was that the government neither funded their research nor listened to their advice. In the last decade, however, the U.S. government has become increasingly interested in the social sciences. More and more anthropologists receive funds directly or indirectly from AID, the National Institutes of Health, the National Science Foundation, the Defense Department, and the CIA—in some cases without the anthropologist's knowledge (Beals, 1969, Chapters 2, 4). Project Camelot is one example.

Project Camelot: The Question of Sponsorship

Project Camelot[1] was conceived by the Special Operations Research Organization (S.O.R.O.), a division of the Army that operated largely through American University in Washington, D.C. The goal of the project was to develop methods for analyzing political and social unrest in the underdeveloped world; identifying the conditions under which unrest develops into armed conflict; and devising effective measures for averting internal wars (called "insurgencies" in the military lingo). The Army budgeted approximately six million dollars for the project, to be spent over a period of three to four years, and set out to recruit established and respected social scientists—among them, Rex Hopper, a Latin America specialist who became the project's civilian director.

A number of social scientists objected to Project Camelot from the start. Norwegian sociologist John Galtung, for example, refused an invitation to a four-week planning conference (for a fee of $2,000) on the grounds that he would not take part in a study of counterinsurgency sponsored by the military. But many of the anthropologists who participated in the planning saw Project Camelot as a chance to make significant contributions to the field and to fulfill a lifelong ambition: a full-scale, amply funded study of conflict and conflict resolution. (Rarely, if ever, have anthropologists been offered financing on this scale. One participant is reported to have called Camelot the Manhattan Project[2] of the social sciences—an unfortunate choice of words.) Participants assumed they would have the intellectual freedom and authority researchers enjoyed at the RAND Corporation, the Air Force's legendary "think tank." A few believed the project would enable social scientists to "infiltrate," educate, and ultimately humanize the Army. And if all went well, the research might prevent the bloodshed and destruction that will inevitably accompany revolutions in the future.

These hopes were at best naïve. The Army did not attach nearly as much importance to Camelot as social scientists did. (Six million dollars is a relatively insignificant part of the Army's multi-billion-dollar annual budget.) Nor did they regard the social scientists as equals in the project. The Army had conceived Camelot and hired the staff (who became, in effect, "hired help"); it made no commitment to follow its employees' recommendations. (Had anthropologists initiated and designed the project, then gone to S.O.R.O. for funding, the relationship might have been different.)

In addition, the research design for Camelot was based on the assumption that a "breakdown of social order" (namely, revolution) is negative and should be avoided—by implication, at all costs. Researchers were not asked to investigate circumstances under which revolution would be preferable to the status quo. Nor were they asked to look into the role the United States plays in creating social unrest and suppressing opposition to incumbent governments. Moreover, as Galtung pointed out, the design was asymmetrical. The Army had not considered situations in which it might be beneficial for Latin American countries to intervene in U.S. internal affairs.

In July 1965, Project Camelot was abruptly canceled, due to a series of unanticipated events. Although Chile was not on the list of nations under consideration for study, an American anthropologist was given a small honorarium ($750) to conduct an informal survey while in Chile on other academic business. He was to discuss the project and the possibility of participating with Chilean scholars—nothing more. To this anthropologist's surprise, a meeting with a prominent Chilean

---

[1] Information for our discussion of this project was drawn from Horowitz, 1965; Sahlins, 1967; and Beals, 1969: 4–11.

[2] The code name for the group of scientists who developed the atomic bomb.

sociologist developed into a confrontation. The sociologist demanded to know the ultimate goals of this Army-sponsored research, and announced that he had turned a memo on Project Camelot over to the authorities and to the press. Chilean officials were understandably upset. They had not been contacted by American representatives about the project (the reason being, of course, that no research had been planned for Chile). Accustomed as Latin Americans are to U.S. meddling, government officials (spurred on by the press) naturally concluded that the U.S. Army was attempting to recruit Chilean academics as spies. Within a matter of days, the story filled the left-wing press. The American ambassador, caught completely off-guard, denied any knowledge of Project Camelot and fired an angry protest to the State Department. In Washington, Fulbright, Morse, and McCarthy scheduled hearings before the Senate Foreign Relations Committee for July 8. However, that morning the Army summarily terminated the project.

Thus, Project Camelot was canceled on political, not intellectual, grounds. Irving Horowitz considered this a blatant act of censorship: "Camelot was not canceled because of its faulty intellectual approaches. Instead, its cancellation came as an act of government censorship, and an expression of the contempt for social science so prevalent among those who need it most." In addition, the State Department used the Camelot "incident" to establish the right to screen all requests for government funds for research in foreign areas, and to veto those proposals it considers potentially or actually detrimental to U.S. interests, regardless of scientific merit.

Some anthropologists work as consultants to government and international agencies. Here an expert of the United Nations Food and Agricultural Organization from Australia advises a Libyan pastoralist on methods for improving the quality of his livestock. However, there is a fine line between assistance and interference or exploitation. An anthropologist has to determine whether a program is designed to benefit the people who need assistance or to further political interests. (United Nations)

Project Camelot was not unique. In March of 1967, The *New York Times* reported that no fewer than 157 anthropologists, engineers, and "ordnance specialists" were employed in Project Agile, a counterinsurgency study in northeast Thailand. The *Times* quoted one specialist who remarked, "The old formula for successful counterinsurgency used to be 10 troops for every guerrilla. Now the formula is 10 anthropologists for each guerrilla" (*New York Times,* March 20, 1967:11). In the early 1970s, the Defense Department attempted to recruit anthropologists for a study of the effects of defoliation in South Vietnam—over repeated objections by the American Anthropological Association (A.A.A. *Newsletter,* 1972:8–9). As a result of such projects and the well-known fact that the CIA has channeled funds through American universities and had its agents pose as researchers abroad, host countries have become increasingly cautious. In 1968, for example, India rescinded permission for the University of California's Himalayan Border Countries Project when it discovered the research was to be financed by the U.S. Defense Department. Six months earlier, India had requested withdrawal of the Asia Foundation, which had been receiving funds from the CIA (Berreman, 1969). Thus the government's new willingness to sponsor anthropological research turns out to be a mixed blessing.

A Code of Ethics

In response to years of soul-searching, discussion, and often heated debate (inflamed by the political controversies of the 1960s), the American Anthropological Association (A.A.A.) appointed a committee on ethics in 1968. The committee drafted a report for the April 1969 issue of the association's *Newsletter,* then presented a proposed code of ethics to the full meeting in November 1970. Their proposal was attacked from both the right (those who thought adoption of a code unnecessary) and the left (those who found the proposed code too bland). Eventually, however, the membership of the A.A.A. endorsed the code by an overwhelming majority (Berreman, 1973).

The Principles of Professional Responsibility, as the code was entitled, describes the anthropologists' responsibilities to the people studied, the public, the discipline, students, sponsors, and both home and host governments. The document states that the researcher's paramount responsibility is to the people under study. A thorough and honest explanation of the investigation, the right to remain anonymous, and fair compensation for all services are due to everyone involved. In addition, the researcher has a moral obligation to consider possible repercussions of the investigation and to communicate them to informants, making sure they understand.

The anthropologist's responsibilities to the public center around the commitment to disseminate results in a truthful and candid manner. No researcher should knowingly falsify or color any findings, or provide information to sponsors, authorities, or others that has been withheld from the public. In one of the more controversial sections, the code states that "anthropologists bear a positive responsibility to speak out publicly, both individually and collectively, on what they know and what they believe as a result of their professional expertise gained in the study of human beings." The researcher's obligations to the discipline include avoiding even the appearance of engaging in clandestine research, and conducting himself in a manner that will not jeopardize future research in a community.

As teachers, anthropologists are admonished to evaluate students solely on the basis of their intellectual abilities (not race, sex, or other criteria); to alert students to ethical problems; to realistically inform them as to what will be expected of them in graduate school and what their career opportunities will be; to acknowledge all student assistance in print; and to encourage and assist students in finding secure positions and legitimate sources of research funds.

In their dealings with sponsors, anthropologists should be honest about their qualifications and research goals, and should require that sponsors disclose the sources of funds and grant the researchers the right to make all ethical decisions.

Finally, the anthropologist's relationship with his own and host governments must be honest and candid. Under no circumstances should an anthropologist agree to secret research, reports, or debriefings of any kind. The report suggests that "where these conditions cannot be met, the anthropologist would be well-advised not to pursue the particular piece of research" (A.A.A. *Newsletter,* 1970:9).

Four Positions

Four distinct positions have emerged from the debates over the issues we have considered. A small but significant minority of conservative anthropologists believe values and politics have no place in social science. As Radcliffe-Brown wrote some years ago,

> the anthropologist is not [i.e., should not be] concerned, as an anthropologist, with whether such things as slavery and cannibalism, or the institutions of the United States or Russia, are or are not right, good, reasonable, or just. (1949:321)

As a private citizen, the anthropologist has the same social responsibilities as anyone else and the same rights to freedom of expression. As a scientist, however, the anthropologist has an obligation (and the ability) to remain objective and detached. According to the conservative view, moral judgments and social or political activism are incompatible with solid scientific investigation.

Liberal anthropologists are concerned about the ethics of research and the problems of the peoples among whom they work, but are wary of rendering judgments or interfering in other people's lives. What right have anthropologists to impose their values on others? liberals ask. This position is based on a deep commitment to cultural relativism, which many regard as anthropology's most significant contribution to humanist thinking. In essence, cultural relativism is the belief that no custom is right or wrong in and of itself, but each must be viewed in context. The liberal approach, grounded in cultural relativism, has dominated anthropology for the past thirty to forty years.

However, a growing number of "action anthropologists" are questioning the notions that a detached, objective stance is possible and that silence on social issues equals neutrality. According to these anthropologists, not speaking out and refusing to become involved is tantamount to supporting the status quo. These anthropologists see the fieldworker's role as making resources available to the people they are studying and helping them to understand possible alternatives and articulate their views. They support cultural relativism – so long as it does not become an excuse for inaction.

In contrast, "radical anthropologists" believe it is time anthropologists take a definite ideological or political stand. Kathleen Gough, a British anthropologist who has spent much of her career teaching in America, became the spokesperson for the radical view at association meetings in the late 1960s and in the pages of *Current Anthropology* (Gough, 1968). Anthropology, Gough states, is a child of Western imperialism. Analyzing the current situation, she concludes that

> much of the non-Western world is in a state of actual or potential revolution against [neocolonial] Western powers and against the kinds of native elites that are supported from the West. . . . The United States is the world's wealthiest and most powerful nation. It is dedicated to delaying or preventing social change throughout two thirds of the world, and anthropologists are either salaried employees of its state governments, or are funded by its federal government or by private segments of its power elite. (1973:163)

Gough believes anthropologists face a critical choice. They can serve neocolonial Western powers, or they can take sides with revolutionary forces and against capitalist ideology. She clearly favors the latter course (Gough, 1973).

Many anthropologists find the radical approach simplistic. Anthropologists have been on the side of right as well as might – in combating racist doctrines, for example. To categorically dismiss all anthropologists as puppets of Western imperialism is inaccurate.

And Ralph Beals, among others, sees no advantage in combating one ideology (capitalism) by surrendering wholly to another (radicalism), "with all its weary clichés." Beals argues that "when science succumbs to social pressures or comes to be regarded only as a means of satisfying immediate social demands, there is a loss of knowledge which is against the long-range interests of society itself" (Beals, 1968:408). Nevertheless, the A.R.P.A. (Anthropologists for Radical Political Action) has made itself "a force to be reckoned with."

There are no simple solutions for today's social scientist. Our consciousness of ethical issues has been raised; the need for each anthropologist to determine their relative merits is clear.

summary

When Malinowski called for anthropology to become an applied science in 1938, he began the debate over anthropological ethics that still continues, centering around two basic issues: *objectivity* and *relevance*. A number of anthropologists feel that they and their colleagues have an obligation to strive for the "purity"—meaning the objectivity—associated with the physical sciences. Another equally large group feels that total objectivity is impossible, and that it is therefore deceptive and ultimately unproductive for anthropologists to pretend to objectivity.

Equally controversial are the questions concerning the topics anthropologists choose to study. Some anthropologists feel that the pursuit of knowledge is its own justification. Others, however, argue that it is immoral for anthropologists to place the needs of the discipline ahead of human needs and that anthropologists should deal with social problems.

The difficulty of translating ethical principles into practice is visible in numerous examples. In Oscar Lewis's study of a Mexican family and Arthur Vidich's research in "Springdale," we see the conflict between the anthropologist's need to uncover as many aspects as possible of people's lives and the subject's right to privacy. Both of these studies raise the question of the extent to which the anthropologist is responsible for protecting the informants from embarrassment or other repercussions.

In the last decade, an increasing number of anthropologists have received funds for research directly or indirectly from the U.S. government. In Project Camelot, for instance, a number of researchers were funded by the Army to study political and social unrest in the underdeveloped world. Whereas some researchers saw the study as an opportunity to study conflict and conflict resolution on a large scale, others refused to take part in it on the grounds that it was a study of counterinsurgency sponsored by the military. Foremost among the issues here is how anthropological data is to be used: Is it ethical for anthropologists to study a culture under the sponsorship of an organization that may use the information against the better interests of the host country?

In response to heated debate over such issues, the American Anthropological Association's committee on ethics devised a code of ethics. The document concludes that anthropologists' paramount responsibility is to the people they study. It further asserts that researchers are obliged to disseminate their results in a truthful and candid manner, to avoid even the appearance of engaging in clandestine research, and to conduct themselves in such a way as to allow for future research in a community. As teachers, anthropologists are admonished to treat students fairly, to acknowledge their help, and to inform them of the issues and difficulties surrounding anthropology as a profession. Anthropologists also are asked to be honest with their sponsors about their qualifications and goals and to require that sponsors disclose their sources. Similar honesty and candidness should exist between the researchers and their own and host governments.

Four distinct positions have emerged from the discussions and debates of the last few years. A small but significant minority of conservative anthropologists hold that moral judgments and social or political activism are incompatible with solid scientific investigation. The second group, liberal anthropologists, are concerned about the ethics of research, but their deep commitment to cultural relativism—the belief that no custom is right or wrong in and of itself—makes them wary of rendering judgments or interfering in other people's lives. According to a growing number of "action anthropologists," refusal to become involved is tantamount to supporting the status quo; they support cultural relativism, but only so long as it does not become an excuse for inaction. In contrast, radical anthropologists believe it is time for anthropologists to take a definite ideological or political stand.

suggested readings

BECK, R., AND ORR, J., EDS.
1970   *Ethical Choice: A Case Study Approach.* New York: The Free Press. A collection of essays raising traditional ethical issues in the context of modern life.

HOROWITZ, I., ED.
1967   *The Rise and Fall of Project Camelot: Studies in the Relationship Between Social Science and Practical Politics.* Cambridge, Mass.: M.I.T. Press. A collection of articles exploring the history and implications of Project Camelot.

HYMES, D., ED.
1969   *Reinventing Anthropology.* New York: Random House. A number of essays in this volume focus on the changing status of anthropology in today's world.

KUHN, T.
1970   *The Structure of Scientific Revolutions.* Chicago: University of Chicago Press. Discusses how the theoretical traditions of the sciences are generated and the sociological factors that affect this process.

RUDNER, R.
1966   *Philosophy of Social Science.* Englewood Cliffs, N.J.: Prentice-Hall. Provides a major discussion of objectivity and subjectivity as they relate to the theories and methods of the social sciences.

The approach of anthropology is holistic—human societies are viewed as integrated wholes, not inventories of separate and distinct parts. Yet when one is introduced to what anthropologists have learned about cultural diversity, it would be bewildering to try to consider everything at once. Somehow the information anthropologists have acquired and the theories they have formulated must be organized into more manageable units. In this part of our text, we have chosen to divide our subject matter according to traditional topic areas in cultural anthropology—recognizing, of course, that these areas are closely interrelated. We will explore how and why various aspects of human behavior and culture differ from society to society. This approach emphasizes the different strategies peoples around the world develop in coping with similar problems.

We begin our discussion with language, a complex, symbolic form of communication which is the basis of human culture. Chapter 13 considers the nature of animal communication, the evolution of language, and the relationships between language and physiology and language and culture. Chapter 14 then turns to the topic of linguistic diversity, dealing with variations in language structure and classification, as well as how languages change and how they serve as adaptive mechanisms.

Before going on to discuss general patterns of human behavior, we pause in Chapter 15 to consider the individual. How do biological makeup, social learning, and particular situations give rise to the similarities and differences anthropologists observe in the ways people around the world think and act?

We then move to the resources essential to survival. Clearly, without first feeding and sheltering themselves, people could not create works of art, build monuments, or devise elaborate rituals. Chapter 16 discusses how different societies procure basic resources and adjust to variations in resource availability. Chapter 17 then focuses on the different ways human groups are organized to process, utilize, and distribute both resources and final goods and services.

In all societies, people interact in patterned, more or less predictable ways. Social behavior, in other words, is organized. Chapter 18 considers some of the principles—kinship, age, sex, and ethnicity—that structure human interaction and the formation of groups in almost every society. Then in Chapter 19 we explore the most basic of all human groups—the family.

Religion is a familiar topic to all of us. But what, actually, does religion involve? How has it evolved, and what psychological, social, and resource-management functions does it serve? These are some of the questions about religious belief and ritual we will be discussing in Chapter 20.

Then we turn to political behavior and organization. Chapter 21 examines how decisions affecting the life of the community are made in different societies, how authority and power are exercised, and how political relations between societies (both peaceful and violent) are conducted. Chapter 22 focuses on another aspect of political life, social control—the various methods people around the world use to resolve disputes and keep conflicts from getting out of hand.

In every chapter in Part IV we discuss the dynamics of day-to-day human interaction. But at what point do daily adjustments to particular problems and circumstances become major changes in customary ways of behaving? In Chapter 23 we attempt to synthesize our previous discussions of cultural change. In addition, we explore some of the ways that anthropologists try to influence the direction of change in today's world.

4
cultural diversity and adaptive strategies

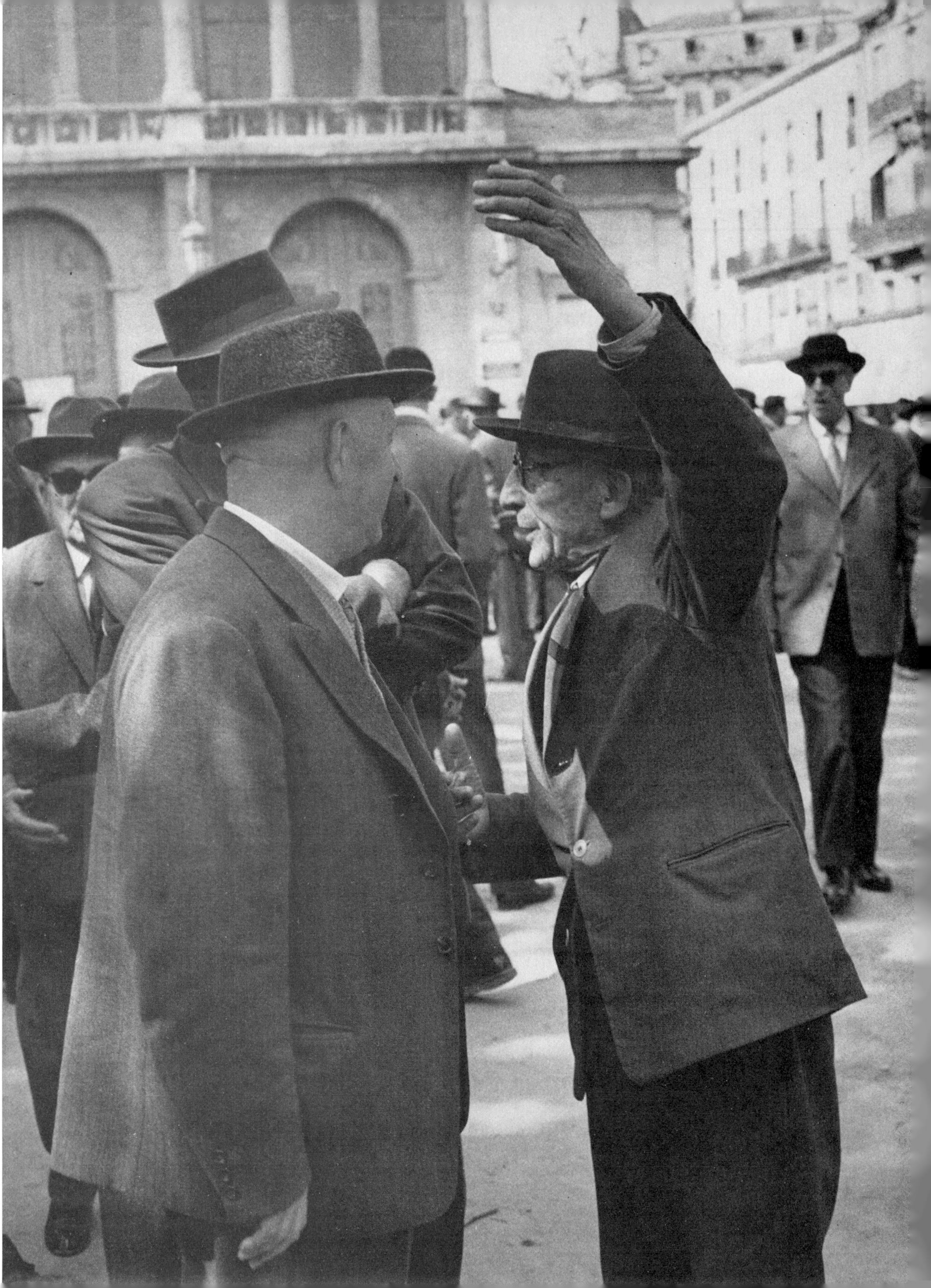

thirteen
Language and Communication

Communication is the keystone of human culture, and language is the primary means by which we communicate. Without language, culture as we know it would not be possible. Although this may seem an overstatement of the importance of language to human culture, it is difficult to conceive of a culture that has no language. Language makes possible the transmission of complex patterns of thought and feeling from one member of a society to another. In fact, some have claimed that language is the primary instrument of thought, without which thought would not be possible. Language also enables the members of a society to establish and enforce intricate codes of behavior and more subtle norms governing everyday activities. It is through language that one generation confers upon another a recounting of its failures and successes. And it is through language that the continuity of a culture is maintained and the sum of its rich and varied experiences, its expertise, its knowledge is stored. Without language we lose history.

Humans, of course, are not the only animals that communicate—that share information with other members of their species. But the ability to communicate through the creation and use of language is uniquely human. Human language is more than an elaborate, specialized form of animal communication; it involves dimensions and capabilities not used by any other creature. Only human beings have developed flexible, extensive systems of symbolic communication. Only humans, for example, have the ability to use language to talk about language itself (Farb, 1974:233–234). We use concepts to explore other concepts. In every human language—but not in any system of nonhuman communication—it is possible to say "How do you know that?" or "What does this mean?"

From questions like these, it is a relatively short step to the questions of existence and organization that are the basis of culture. With language it becomes possible to conceive of tomorrow and to plan for it; to imagine a tool and then to make it; to carry in our minds the lessons our ancestors learned, to use them ourselves, and then to pass them on to our children.

Animal Communication

While language is a distinctively human creation, a uniquely different type of communication from that used by other animals, it is nevertheless important to keep in mind that communication in some form is essential to the survival of all animal species. Without some means of communicating the threat of danger, the presence of food, or the readiness to mate, for example, not only individual animals but entire species would perish.

Even among what we consider the simplest of creatures, communication occurs. As ants of certain species travel across the ground near their nests, for example, they leave behind trails of pheromones, external secretions which may serve as a guide to other ants who later follow the same trail. Clearly there is some form of communication here. But the message can only be a simple "An ant has

We speak with our eyes and hands and bodies, as well as with words. Peoples in some parts of the world might find this French wine grower's animated delivery, punctuated with touches and extravagant gestures, comical or even rude. But in Southern Europe people tend to be strong in their opinions and demonstrative in expressing them. (Henri Cartier-Bresson/Magnum)

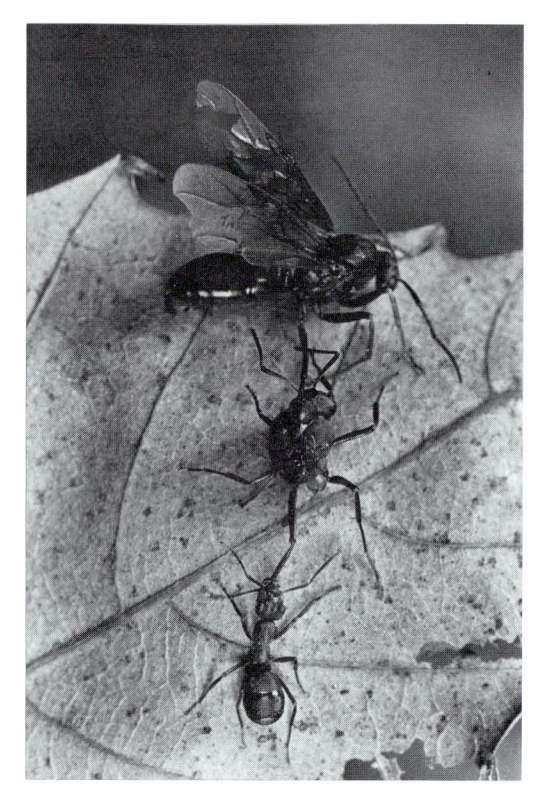

Worker ants let a large intruder (at the top of the photograph) know he is unwelcome. Ants, like all animals, inherit subtle but unambiguous means of communicating everything from danger to sexual receptivity. But human languages take communication into a new dimension. (© Stephen Dalton/Photo Researchers)

been here," and the ant leaving the trail does not do so intentionally.

At an even simpler level of animal organization, the slime mold *Dictyostelium* also seems to communicate. For most of the year each amoeba lives alone. But at certain times they swarm together in large aggregations and their behavior changes dramatically. The organisms could not suddenly begin coordinating their movements so precisely if they did not communicate with one another in some way. Apparently they transmit their "message" by releasing small amounts of carbon dioxide. This serves as a signal to other *Dictyostelium* to begin forming a colony.

These two examples of communication among so-called lower animals illustrate what a wide range of mechanisms evolution has devised to permit animals to communicate. While we tend to think of sound as the principal medium of communication, for most species this is simply not the case. Sight, touch, and smell are more widely used. Certain electric fishes seem to pick up and transmit electrical impulses through a specially modified muscle. Among insects, chemical communication is particularly important. Among the most specialized social insects—bees, termites, and ants—the social organization of the hive or colony depends entirely upon chemical communication (Maier and Maier, 1970, Chapter 10). Among honeybees, for example, almost all forms of social behavior—feeding the larvae, maintaining the caste system, and so forth—are regulated by hormones which are secreted by certain members of the hive and then passed from one individual to the next.

What we learn from these examples is that every animal, no matter how solitary it may seem throughout most of its life, must at some time come together with others of its kind, if for no other reason than to reproduce. At that time it is a social creature, and as a social creature it must have the ability to transmit and to receive information. The species we have mentioned so far, however, are only able to communicate in genetically patterned ways, and their messages can only be of the simplest sort. Theirs is a form of communication that is inherited, not learned. But what about the "higher" animals, those whose behavior is determined less by genetics and more by learning? Does their communication resemble human language any more closely?

Many of us are familiar with the ability of dogs to respond to commands in a way that seems "almost human." Dogs (probably the first of the animals to be domesticated) have been used for many thousands of years as hunting, tracking, herding, and draft animals. As rather intelligent mammals, most pet dogs can be trained to respond to human speech or gestures—to fetch, sit, stay, heel, and so forth. But while they can apparently understand human language to a limited extent, no dog has the ability to produce language. A hunting dog may point very well, but it cannot say, "There is a rabbit behind that bush." This is partly because the dog does not have the vocal equipment to produce human speech, but it is also a function of the dog's intelligence. It is not simply that the dog has *less* intelligence than a human, however; rather, evolution has not equipped the dog with the *kind* of intelligence that would permit it to learn, create, and use symbols.

Do any animals besides humans have this kind of intelligence? The search has focused primarily on our closest living relative, the chimpanzee. Although chimps have intelligence of a very high order—an intelligence surprisingly like our own—they do not have an extensive repertory of vocal expressions. Many attempts to teach human language to chimpanzees have been made during the past forty years. It soon became clear that chimps showed no tendency to use elaborate vocal signals. When they were raised in human households they made no attempt to imitate the vocabulary of the humans around them. In the 1940s, one family (Hayes and Hayes, 1953) did succeed in teaching their chimp Viki to pronounce crudely the English words "papa," "mama," "cup," and "up," but this required years of patient training.

Later researchers noted that chimpanzees in the wild often communicated with gestures, and they designed their research accordingly. Allen and Beatrice Gardner (1969) taught their chimpanzee Washoe to use the American Sign Language, the sign language used by the deaf in Canada and the United States. This experiment was more successful. Washoe learned and used some 150 signs, including those for "hurt," "hurry," "sorry," "please," and other relatively abstract concepts. Some of the symbols she had been taught she was able to use in novel situations. The Gardners concluded that Washoe had achieved a significant degree of two-way communication by using a genuine form of human language.

Ann and David Premack (1972:92) taught another chimpanzee, Sarah, to associate a large number of concepts with colored plastic shapes that could be arranged in different orders on a magnetic board. Through conditioning, Sarah built up associations for over 130 "terms," including such concepts as "different" and "same as." More importantly, she learned to use them in grammatical sentences. She was able to make relatively fine discriminations between different kinds of social interactions. And she was able to master the concept "name of"; that is, to a limited extent she could use symbols *as* symbols. For example, Sarah preferred bananas to raisins; when she was offered a choice, she would select the red square that stood for a banana rather than a real raisin. Recently, attention has turned to training very young chimps, and their capacity for acquiring these symbolic abilities seems even greater.

Interesting as these studies may be, they really tell us more about the differences be-

Although three to six months behind her human age-mates, Koko has a vocabulary of 170 words in American Sign Language and has invented a few new words of her own. In graduate student Penny Patterson's opinion, this four-year-old gorilla may prove to be even better at learning human language than the chimps previously studied. (Alan Capeland/The New York Times)

tween human and chimpanzee communication than about the similarities. Chimps in the wild do have an elaborate social and communication system, but it depends more on visual and tactile signs than on symbols of any sort. We have to conclude that chimps have no language in the human sense. They are able to learn to use language, but only in extremely artificial situations. In a natural setting, there would have been no need for these abilities, and they never would have developed.

Animal vs. Human Communication: Similarities and Differences

In comparing human language to other forms of animal communication, it is often easy to focus on the differences rather than on the similarities. After all, human language is unique; no other animal species has developed such an extensive form of symbolic communication as ours. The visual displays and tactile signs of other animals may seem to bear little resemblance to our own means of communication. But this is simply not the case. Although we tend to think of spoken language as the most basic form of human communication, human beings also have numerous modes of nonverbal communication that may replace, reinforce, and sometimes even contradict spoken messages.

Consider, for instance, some of the nonverbal messages you may have delivered upon leaving your house this morning. First, you may have pursed your lips together in a particular ritualized way and placed them on a relative's or a friend's face, in what we think of as a sign of affection. Then perhaps you raised your hand—probably the right one, palm facing outward—a bit higher than your shoulder, to indicate goodbye. At the same moment you may have parted your lips and bared your teeth in a gesture that is meant to convey good cheer. The fact is that human beings are constantly communicating in nonverbal ways. In this sense, human communication is similar to that of many other animal species.

Nonverbal Communication

Kinesics People are often completely unaware of the complex messages they are conveying simply with the position or motion of their bodies. The study of body movement as a means of communication is known as *kinesics*. We have only to observe a group of students listening to their instructor to gather enough kinesic data to keep us analyzing nonverbal messages for quite some time. One student stretches and keeps readjusting his legs. One nods eagerly every time the instructor makes a point. Another stares at the ceiling and then at the floor, avoiding eye contact with the lecturer. Even as listeners, these students are communicating complex messages that will in turn influence the communication of the speaker.

Nonverbal messages, however, are often intermingled with spoken ones. Much of current research in kinesics centers on such questions as how the flow of body motion changes in relation to speech. For example, there have been several in-depth analyses of parts of psychiatric interviews which record and interpret in great detail both the verbal and nonverbal communication that has taken place and the counterpoint they provide for each other. Indeed, Birdwhistell, who pioneered the study of kinesics, believes that the most successful research has evolved out of studies of the relationships between what he terms "visible and audible communication. . . . So intimate is this relationship that the trained linguist-kinesiologist has at times been able to describe many of the movements of a speaker from hearing a recording or listening to a telephone conversation. Further, we have found that an auditor may 'hear' intonational shifts that were not spoken but *moved* by the informant, and vice versa" (Birdwhistell, 1960:59).

Of course, unlike other animals, for whom visual messages are in part genetically determined, human beings have cultures which teach them to use certain movements to convey specific information. In fact, it is often surprising how many of the motor habits and

With nonverbal eloquence, two Buddhist monks perform a highly stylized cermony of greeting that is as different from our handshakes as Japanese is from English—and as different from the way Japanese friends would greet one another on the street as ballet dancing is from rock music. (René Burri/Magnum)

gestures frequently considered "instinctive" are in fact quite culturally limited. For example, although people everywhere have hands, not all point with their hands as we do—forefinger extended, the other fingers curled inward toward the palm. In many cultures, pointing is done with the eyes, nose, chin, or head. Nor are the Western head movements indicating negation and affirmation universal: a Malayan Negrito indicates "no" by casting eyes downward; thrusting the head forward is the way of gesturing "yes" among the Semang. Thus, for anthropologists, one of the most significant tasks of kinesic research will be to determine "the precise boundary line between instinctual movements, expressions, and acts *versus* the numerous culture-based kinesic codes that must be learned like any arbitrary, invented, symbolic system" (La Barre, 1964:194).

Proxemics Both humans and animals use certain gestures and behaviors to establish their private space. The spring song of the male bird, for instance, not only serves a courtship function but also is a warning to other males of the species to keep away from this male's mating terrain. In the animal world, the need to establish territoriality is closely linked to the reproductive instinct and ultimately to the survival of the species. The question of what space means to humans, however, is more complex, being influenced as it is by both biological and cultural factors.

The study of how people perceive and use space is called *proxemics*. Hall, who coined the term, defines proxemics as "the interrelated observations and theories of man's use of space as a specialized elaboration of culture" (Hall, 1966:1). Hall conceived of four different distance zones available for various interpersonal encounters—"intimate," "personal," "social," and "public"—and the distance at which communication takes place will depend on the nature of the communication as well as the cultures of the two communicators. Man's perception and use of space, however, involves much more than measurable distances between people; Hall has distinguished nineteen different proxemic scales, and these include not only body distance but body orientation, posture, and movement, and eye contact. Hall believes that different cultures, ethnic groups, and subcultures have different proxemic codes and that for the most part members of a particular group take their own code so much for granted that they rarely think of it. Yet the contrast between two proxemic codes can be unsettling. For example, consider the differences between the American view of public space and the Arab point of view:

> For the Arab, there is no such thing as an intrusion in public. Public means public. With this insight, a great range of Arab behavior that had been puzzling, annoying, and sometimes even frightening began to make sense. I learned, for example, that if *A* is standing on a street corner and *B* wants his spot, *B* is within his rights if he does what he can to make *A* uncomfortable enough to move. In Beirut only the hardy sit in the last row of a movie theater, because there are usually standees who want seats and who push and shove and make such a nuisance that most people give up and leave. (Hall, 1966:156)

Clearly, the Arab and the American live in very different proxemic worlds, and that is one of the central points of Hall's thesis: to some extent communication difficulties between people of different cultures begin—and perhaps ultimately some may be resolved—at the nonverbal level.

But proxemic codes do more than simply affect interpersonal communication. They also shape humanity's use of physical space at a more generalized, societal level. How we use room space; how we build houses, factories, and skyscrapers; how we organize settlements, towns, and cities; even how we come to view the world around us—all are influenced by proxemic codes.

Signs versus Symbols

The use of space, as well as the use of visual and tactile signs, are clearly nonverbal forms of communication that both humans and animals share. But when we enter the area of auditory communication, human language becomes unique when compared with the sound systems of other animal species. Most animals emit sounds—grunts, chirps, squeals, and calls—that carry information. These sounds, which may be referred to as *signs,* convey to other animals precise and important messages: hostility, sexual excitement, hunger, or warning of some approaching danger. Signs of this kind have great adaptive value, and many species have evolved sign systems that are quite elaborate.

Even so, such means of communication are limited in many important respects. First, the meaning conveyed by many animal signs is in large part genetically determined. For this reason, the message is generally precise and cannot usually be changed. Every herring gull that is threatened by an intruding predator invariably gives the same hoarse, rhythmic call: *hahaha! hahahaha.* In attacking a predator the gulls always utter a different call: a loud, staccato *keew* (Tinbergen, 1961:13–15). The "pant-hoot" call of the chimpanzee is used in many situations, but always for the same purpose—to establish or maintain contact between individuals or groups (Goodall, 1971:248–274).

A second limitation of animal sign systems is that such systems are *closed*—elements of one call cannot be combined with elements of another to produce a new utterance. This means that if an animal encounters food and danger at the same time, it can announce one or the other with an appropriate call (or it can remain silent), but it cannot blend the two calls to signal the presence of both.

Human language is infinitely more flexible than any other form of animal communication. This is because human language uses signs of a different sort, known as *symbols.* Two principal features distinguish linguistic symbols from the signs used by other animals. First, a symbol is *arbitrary*: it means whatever people have agreed it will mean. The word *perro,* for example, means "dog" in Spanish. In French the word for dog is *chien.*

In a third language it will be still another word. The meanings of human symbols are determined not genetically but culturally, by the users of the language.

Second, a symbol is *abstract*. By the use of symbols human beings are able to represent not merely single objects or events but categories of objects or events. For example, if two people discuss how a hammer might be made, they are talking not only about the hammer at hand but an entire class of hammers. And because the symbols of human language are abstract, humans can refer not only to what is part of their immediate environment but to objects, intentions, or relationships that are part of the distant past or that do not yet (and may never) exist. The hammers they themselves own, the hammers they once saw in a neighboring village, the hammers they plan to make—humans can refer to any or all of these. The sign-symbol distinction can also be made in reference to nonverbal phenomena. A smile, for example, is a sign, while a V made with the fingers is a symbol either of peace or of victory.

In addition to the use of symbols, human language differs from other systems of animal communication in another very significant way: while animal calls are closed systems of communication, human language is an *open system*. Humans are not confined to a limited number of stock phrases and sentences that can express only a certain set of ideas; we can blend and combine verbal symbols to express whatever ideas our minds construct. Through the manipulation of symbols, thoughts never before uttered can be conveyed.

The differences between language and animal sign systems, then, are very great. Human language is a far more flexible means of communication than that of any other species. How did these differences between human and animal communication develop? How did the proto-hominids of several million years ago, who probably had only a closed system of calls, eventually evolve into creatures capable of creating and using an open system of symbolic communication?

The Evolution of Language

Answers to the question "How did language evolve?" can only be speculative. Although we humans have always been curious about ourselves and have searched diligently in the earth for clues to our origin as a species, evidence of how language developed remains elusive. Ironically, language, which is most important in making us "human," leaves no fossils behind for a curious posterity. Nevertheless, there have always been theories to account for the rise of language.

A once favorite theory was that language was originally onomatopoetic; words were thought to mimic the sounds of the natural world. Certainly a few words in our language are onomatopoetic: *buzz, hiss, roar, drizzle.* But this theory doesn't tell us why a cat goes "purr" in English and "ron-ron" in French; apparently our perception of natural sounds depends to some degree on the language we speak. More importantly, this approach doesn't lead to an understanding of how language might have evolved from a collection of imitative sounds to an instrument for the free expression of thought and feeling. There are also a number of similar theories, many of which were taken very seriously at one time or another. One of these suggested that language arose from rhythmic grunts or chants that early humans would emit as they labored at a heavy task. Another held that involuntary exclamations—essentially laughs and cries—developed in the course of play and other interaction, and were later elaborated into language. Today these theories are taken seriously by few anthropologists. Recently, however, there have been more successful efforts, solidly based on modern evolutionary theory, to reconstruct the major features of language evolution.

Drawing from a large number of sources, Hockett and Ascher (1964) have put together a reasonable picture of how this may have occurred. The proto-hominids of several million years ago had no language, but they may have had a system of calls, something like the

A Theory of the First Language

What were the first languages ever spoken? How did they sound and how were they structured? Is it likely that there was once a single primordial language from which all others evolved? Questions like these may pique our curiosity, but most linguists consider them ultimately unanswerable. We have no records of languages spoken so many thousands upon thousands of years ago. And whatever clues about them were once contained in their daughter languages have probably long been eroded by the passage of millennia and cumulative language change. This is why Mary Lecron Foster's recent work (1970) is so unusual. She has set out to do nothing less than reconstruct the sound system and vocabulary of the first language ever spoken through a careful analysis of its descendants.

Foster was prompted to undertake this task when her research suggested that a single proto-language may have once existed. In attempting to reconstruct the ancestral form of American Indian languages, she discovered that many of the rules for sound change also applied to the development of Indo-European languages. (Indo-European is the large family of related languages to which English belongs.) The further she investigated, the more extraordinarily similar proto-Indo-European (the extinct language from which all others in the family evolved, and which has already been well reconstructed) and ancestral American Indian began to appear—far more similar than any of their present-day descendants might suggest. On the basis of this striking similarity, Foster hypothesized that the enormous number of very different languages spoken around the world today are all descended from a single ancestral proto-language. Furthermore, she suggested that by applying existing techniques for reconstructing languages no longer spoken and using the rules of sound change already discovered, we should be able to push these rules back several stages further and reconstruct at least a rough outline of the first language ever spoken.

Pursuing her goal, Foster compared nine languages from different speech families around the world. The results of her analysis of patterns of sound change pointed to 15 consonants and a single basic vowel as the likely component sounds of the original proto-language. The set of consonants, which correspond to six primary points of articulation from the front to the back of the mouth, form a logical basis for the more narrow distinctions between the basic sounds used in languages throughout the world today.

Foster's reconstruction does not end with the proposed sound, or phonemic, system of the original language, however; she goes on to reconstruct a basic vocabulary by looking at the various meanings attached to different reconstructed phonemic forms in her sample of nine present-day languages. The reconstructed phonemic form *er- (or *r-), for example, is related (by numerous regular sound changes) to modern words with such meanings as "cause, raise, flow, loose, split, male, shake, the nearer person or thing, rise, soon, early, originate, stimulus, early reach, start, and toward," to mention only a few. By semantically comparing these words and abstracting the general features of meaning that underlie many of the specific meanings, Foster postulates a general meaning of "move or be from or to close relationship, join, joined (rise, reach, start)." Similarly, *el- (or *l-) can be reduced to a general meaning of "move or be to or from separation, apartness (go, impel)"; *per- to a general meaning of "move or be outward to join"; and *pel- to a general meaning of "move or be outward to separate from."

Foster has reconstructed a total of sixty-two such forms with their abstract, almost impressionistic meanings. They suggest two important things about this possible primordial language. First, notice that these "words" are not names or labels for particular items in the speaker's world. Instead, each form is identified with several abstract features of meaning which can then be applied to things, actions, or ideas with equal effectiveness. Second, by comparing such forms as *er- and *per- or *el- and *pel-, we find that there is some overlap in the meanings attached to each of these pairs. Foster believes that each individual sound may have had a separate feature of meaning associated with it. Thus, the sound /*p/ may have represented the idea "outward from," the sound /*l/ "apart, separate," and the sound /*r/ "together, joined." The combination of these and other sounds with their associated meanings led to slightly different variations, blending, and expansion of the basic meaning, becoming the basis for more complex forms of communication.

Of course, Foster's reconstructed proto-language is only a theory. We have no way of empirically verifying her findings. Still, the possibility that she has offered some clue to the sound system and vocabulary of the first language is highly intriguing.

calls of modern gibbons, each of which could be used in a number of ways. Like all animal sign systems, however, this call system had several limitations, the most important of which was that it was *closed*.

As the proto-hominids left the trees for the open savanna, they faced new selective pressures, with resulting changes in behavior. They began to eat flesh as well as plant material. Presumably the meat was scavenged at first from the kills of the larger carnivores; later men did their own hunting. They began to move more often on the hind legs than on all four, perhaps at first for short bursts of speed; later this became the usual way of moving. (It is interesting to think that humans may have learned to run before they could walk.) As the erect, bipedal gait became widespread, the forelimbs were freed for carrying and manipulating food and other objects. In earlier species the mouth was used for grasping and carrying. Hockett and Ascher suggest that this development was of crucial importance:

It can quite safely be asserted that if primate and hominid evolution had not transferred from mouth to hand first the grasping and manipulating function and then the carrying function, human language as we know it would never have evolved. What were the hominids to do with their mouths, rendered thus relatively idle except when they were eating? The answer is: they chattered. (1964: 141)

Freeing the mouth from carrying made vocalization possible. But what led to the evolution of corresponding cognitive skills and the evolution of language? Occasionally, an individual confronted by both available food and an approaching predator might not have reacted in the normal way, but might have *blended* elements of the danger call with elements of the food call. If this happened often enough, the new, composite call, meaning "food and danger," would become established in the group. This in turn would have an effect on the original calls; the old food call, for example, would come to mean "food, no danger." The number of calls would increase, and more importantly, the creation and use of new calls could become a habit.

The authors admit that no direct evidence exists (or could exist) to prove that this is what happened. But they point out that all human languages are open systems, and that blending is the only logically possible way a closed system can be opened. It did not happen all at once, of course, but over hundreds of thousands of years. At the end of that time, a major revolution had occurred. Humans communicated through an open system, language, and language was transmitted culturally rather than genetically. Learning had begun to replace instinct, and from that time on human development would depend as much on culture as on relationship with the natural environment.

But what caused our evolution to take this unique direction? As people became hunters, cooperation between the members of a group was necessary to bring down large prey. Sharing food, and making the tools for its capture and storage, also called for cooperation. Given the advantages of cooperation, groups with only a slightly greater ability to communicate may have hunted more successfully, grown in numbers, and been imitated by other groups. Imagine, for example, trying to kill an elephant with nothing to go on but your own effort and imagination. If someone in the group has tried the same thing before, and can share his experience, everyone can benefit. And the more that is communicated about the behavior of the prey, the greater the probable success of the hunt. Thus there is strong selective pressure for the development of language and linguistic ability. The speech organs—and especially the parts of the brain which are the speech areas—became more efficient. Speech immediately enriched the culture, making it a more effective mechanism for adaptation.

It has been suggested (Alland, 1973) that humankind underwent its most rapid evolution at this point—when culture existed, but only in rudimentary form. At that time culture had not yet become so efficient as to buffer the human species against the demands of the natural environment. But culture, and especially language, was becoming this species' principal adaptation to that environment: language enhanced the human animal's ability to learn, to communicate, and to free itself from the constraints of the unspecialized, rather weak and slow human body.

In this way language has played a tremendous role in human evolution; in one sense it can be said that we did not invent language, but that language made us. We may be said to have become truly human when we acquired culture, and this acquisition became possible only with the ability to create and use language.

From the foregoing discussion it is clear that our evolution from proto-hominid to human being resulted from a complex interaction between language, culture, and physiology. In the remaining sections of this chapter, we will examine in greater detail the relationship between language and physiology on the one hand, and language and culture on the other.

Language and Physiology

Human language would not be possible if we were not physiologically equipped to use it. Basic to our ability to use language is the fact that the vocal organs—our lips, teeth, throat, lungs—are fashioned to produce language sounds. By taking air into our lungs and expelling it through either our mouth or nose (or a combination of the two), we generate sound. When a person speaks, the air coming from the lungs and through the trachea passes through the vocal cords, located in the larynx. These may be brought together, causing them to vibrate, or kept apart, so that no friction is produced as the air passes through. When the stream of air reaches the mouth area it is shaped by the position and action of the tongue, teeth, and lips into the different sounds which make up language.

Our brains, too, are equipped for the use of language. It seems paradoxical that the study of *aphasias,* the disorders of speech, has been the source of most of our knowledge about the physiology of language as it relates to the brain. From what we know today, it seems that three areas of the cerebral cortex, usually located in the left hemisphere, are responsible for the thought processes that allow humans to learn and to use language.

From the work of Broca, a nineteenth-century Frenchman, it was discovered that when a certain part of the left half of the brain (now called "Broca's area") was damaged, an individual's understanding of language was complete, but his or her speech was slow and labored. When a corresponding area in the right half of the brain was damaged, the person's ability to speak remained undisturbed. Broca's area adjoins the motor cortex, which controls the muscles of speech, determining how the vocal cords, soft palate, jaw, tongue, and lips move. In fact, Broca's area seems to be instrumental in coordinating these muscles while a person is speaking.

A second region of the brain crucial for language functions is Wernicke's area, which adjoins the region of the cortex that receives auditory stimuli. (Wernicke was another pioneer in the study of aphasia.) When people have brain damage in this area, it results in loss of comprehension. Their speech may sound fluent, but it is far from normal and lacks intelligible content. For example, such a person may substitute one term for another even though it has no bearing on what is being said, or may use the wrong sounds for part of a word so that it becomes incomprehensible.

Broca's area and Wernicke's area are connected by the *arcuate fasciculus,* a bundle of nerve fibers. A person who has damage in this area will have abnormal but fluent speech and will understand words but be unable to repeat them. Given what is known about the various aphasias, we must infer a model of brain organization in which all three of the areas discussed must function together if the formulation and production of language are to be normal (Geschwind, 1974).

As we have already mentioned, many theorists have questioned whether any animals other than man have the kind of intelligence that would enable them to learn, create, and use language. It is known, for example, that the cetaceans—whales, dolphins, and their kind—have cerebral cortexes nearly as large and convoluted as those of men (Kruger, 1966:232–239). Dolphins in particular have a great repertory of acoustic signals, including clicks, high-pitched whistles, and quacking and moaning sounds. An important function of these sounds is orientation; they are sometimes used as radar or the sonar of bats would be used. Some investigators (Lilly, 1967) believe that these sounds may be used as a communication system. Although this is a fascinating area of research, none of the work done thus far indicates that dolphins can be made to use language in anything like the human sense, or that they use any language system of their own in their natural environment (Maier and Maier, 1970:241n).

One reason that dolphins have attracted so much interest is that they have large brains. Many people have assumed that a large brain indicates high intelligence and the ability to speak, but studies of speech ability reveal that size is not the brain's most important characteristic. Other studies have tried to establish a relationship between speech ability on the one hand and the ratio of body size to brain weight on the other (Downs and Bleibtreu, 1972:168–171). The findings point to only one conclusion: humans of very different ages and sizes—endowed with complex cognitive and physiological equipment evolved over millions of years—can speak; other hominoids cannot.

Language and Culture

We are all aware that language is related not only to our physiology, but also to our culture. But the exact nature of the relationship between language and culture is not that easy to unravel. Is language simply a reflection of culture, a mirror on our customary ways of thinking and behaving? Or does language instead somehow serve to structure our ways of experiencing the world around us? Many people—among them George Orwell—have been intrigued by questions such as these; with the liberty allowed a writer of fiction, Orwell projected his own answer in the form of a nightmarish fantasy.

In *1984*, a novel of the future (written in 1949), Orwell writes about Newspeak, a language that makes it impossible to think certain thoughts. By constructing a new vocabulary and grammar, political leaders are able to mold citizens' thoughts into ideologically acceptable channels. Language becomes a tool for creating a new culture. Describing Newspeak, Orwell says:

Its vocabulary was so constructed as to give exact and often very subtle expression to every meaning that a Party member could properly wish to express, while excluding all other meanings. . . . To give a single example. The word *free* still existed in Newspeak, but it could only be used in such statements as 'This dog is free from lice' or 'This field is free from weeds.' It could not be used in its old sense of 'politically free' or 'intellectually free,' since political and intellectual freedom no longer existed as concepts, and were therefore of necessity nameless. . . . Countless other words such as *honor, justice, morality, internationalism, democracy, science,* and *religion* had simply ceased to exist. A few blanket words covered them, and, in covering them, abolished them. All words grouping themselves round the concepts of liberty and equality, for instance, were contained in the single word *crimethink,* while all words grouping themselves round the concepts of objectivity and rationalism were contained in the single word *oldthink*. (Orwell, 1949:246–251)

Orwell's fiction raises the question of how far the vocabulary and structure of a language can actually shape the way we perceive and experience the world. Since we are all born with eyes, ears, a nose, and about the same degree of intelligence, shouldn't we describe what we see, hear, and experience in the same way? Apparently not. Each language requires its speakers to report certain things and ignore others. For example, imagine two men returning from a fishing trip. One speaks English, the other speaks Kwakiutl. Asked where they made their catch, the English speaker answers, "I caught these fish near an island two miles north of here." The Kwakiutl, however, would consider such a description vague and perhaps meaningless. His language encourages him to pinpoint the time and place more precisely (Boas, 1964: 123). He would first clarify which fish—these visible fish near the speaker or those invisible fish behind the speaker?—and which island—that invisible island located downriver at the foot of a mountain or some other island? In case he had not seen the island himself, the Kwakiutl fisherman would have to specify whether he knows where the island is by hearsay or by other evidence, or whether he dreamed the location. Finally, he would indicate whether he caught the fish in the recent past, remote past, or mythological past. All of these specifications are denoted by adding the appropriate prefix or suffix to the verb stem. The Kwakiutl's answer does not take any longer to say than the white man's. But it would never occur to the white fisherman to make such distinctions simply because English does not require them and does not provide the convenient grammatical forms.

The Kwakiutl are a people whose survival depends on navigation, hunting, and gathering. So it is not surprising that the structure of their language enables them to designate place names with great precision. Locating and describing places has a clear practical benefit in navigation, hunting, and food-gathering. By adding a suffix to a verb stem, the Kwakiutl can pinpoint places where river fish, fruits, berries, shellfish, and other common foods can be found: "place having trout"; "place having sockeye salmon"; "place having herring spawn"; "place having salmonberry shoots"; "place where one tries to get grizzly bears." To describe what the Kwakiutl say in a simple suffix requires a long and cumbersome phrase in English. Our language makes it more difficult to talk so fluently about a specific place in terms of its description. Does this mean that we are less apt to perceive such places, or that we think about the world differently from the Kwakiutl? Does our language, in other words, prevent us from making certain observations and force us to think along other lines?

The Sapir-Whorf Hypothesis

Edward Sapir was one of the first linguists to argue that humans are in some respects prisoners of language. He felt that our view of "reality" is an abridged version of the world that has been edited by our language:

Human beings do not live in the objective world alone, nor alone in the world of social activity as ordinarily understood, but are very much at the mercy of the particular language which has become the medium of expression for their society. . . . The fact of the matter is that the real world is to a large extent unconsciously built up on the language habits of the group. No two languages are ever sufficiently similar to be considered as representing the same social reality. The worlds in which different societies live are distinct worlds, not merely the same world with different labels attached. (Sapir, 1929:209–214)

Drawing upon Sapir's ideas, Benjamin Lee Whorf made an intensive study of the Hopi language to determine whether radically different linguistic structures in fact produce contrasting views of the world. Concentrating on grammar rather than vocabulary, he found that Hopi does not categorize the world in the same way as English. For one thing, Hopi has no verb tenses comparable to our own. English forces us to specify *when* an event occurs and encourages us to think of time as divided into three distinct units: past, present, and future. The Hopi language does not share our concept of time. Instead of organizing the universe in terms of past, present, and future, Hopi organizes it in terms of objective and subjective—or "manifested" vs. "becoming manifested." The objective or manifested embraces all that is or has ever been physically accessible to the senses, with no distinction between past and present. The subjective or becoming manifested comprises all that is not physically accessible—what we call the future as well as all that we label mental such as thinking, wishing, or intending (Whorf,

1956). Thus the structures of their languages may encourage speakers of English and Hopi to view the same events differently. While an English speaker viewing a field of corn might comment, "That corn was planted in May, is now two feet tall, and will be ready for harvest in September," the Hopi speaker would view the same growing plants as being in the midst of a constant process of burgeoning, of advancing toward fruition with no concept of past, present, and future comparable to ours.

Whorf's observations convinced him that contrasting world views result from contrasting language structures. A few attempts have been made to test the Sapir-Whorf hypothesis experimentally. One such study was carried out with bilingual Japanese women who had married American servicemen and were living in San Francisco (Ervin-Tripp, 1964). Did these women actually think differently when speaking English and Japanese? According to the Sapir-Whorf hypothesis, they should. Each woman was visited twice by a bilingual Japanese interviewer. On the first visit, only Japanese was spoken. On the second visit, the same discussion was carried on in English. The results showed that each woman's attitudes differed drastically depending on which language she was speaking. For example, in completing the sentence "When my wishes conflict with my family's . . ." most women responded with ". . . it is a time of great unhappiness" in Japanese. But when speaking English, they answered, ". . . I do what I want."

Nevertheless, the Sapir-Whorf hypothesis raises many unanswered questions. First, it is extremely difficult to generalize about an entire culture's habits of thought and then to prove that they are *caused* by language. Perhaps the reverse is true: a people's belief system and cultural practices may determine the structure of their language. Hoijer (1954) has suggested a relationship between the Navajo language and Navajo religious beliefs and practices. Navajo world view and mythology emphasize the importance of preserving an established harmonious balance between man and nature. The Navajo believe that na-

To us, one reindeer looks about the same as the next. But the Lapps, who depend on reindeer for survival, have many words to describe the characteristics of reindeer and variations among them. (Dever/Black Star)

ture is more powerful than man. Consequently, in their religious ceremonies they never try to change anything or cause something to happen—to bring rain, for instance. They merely try to realign themselves in the dynamic scheme of events. These attitudes are also expressed in the structure of their language. When the Navajo say, *"Nińtí"* ("You have lain down"), they are literally saying, "One animate being (you) has moved to a position of rest (have lain down)." In the Navajo thought world, humans and other beings may not perform actions. They simply participate in ongoing universal processes. Every action—whether it is running, baking, weaving, or riding—is expressed in terms of a few universal processes. Grammatical categories clearly reflect the Navajo concept of a universe in orderly, continuous motion. But which came first? The language structure or the beliefs? Possibly the Navajo concern with dynamic events reflects their nomadic life, a cultural adaptation to their environment.

Perhaps the question can be answered by cross-cultural comparison. If language determines a people's thought world, then two groups who speak closely related languages should also share similar cultural beliefs and practices. In fact, this is not the case. The highly ritualized culture of the southwestern Navajo has little in common with the cultures of fellow Athapaskan-speaking tribes. It does not resemble the Hupa of northwestern California, a loosely organized hunting and gathering society; nor the highly competitive Apache of the Western plains; nor the simple fishing and hunting cultures of western Canada and Alaska (Sapir, 1921). But the Navajo do share many cultural patterns with other tribes who speak completely dissimilar languages. The same is true of other tribes who speak mutually unintelligible languages. The Hopi and the Tewa, for example, are both Pueblo peoples. Having lived in close association for centuries, they have borrowed freely from one another's cultures. Their languages, however, are quite divergent.

Finally, to test Whorf's own example, we can try to correlate different grammatical systems with methods of time-reckoning. We find that Americans and Europeans share similar methods of time-reckoning with the speakers of languages as different as Maya, Chinese, and Egyptian. On the other hand, the Hopi's lack of concern with time is shared by dozens of unrelated speech communities.Thus language has an important effect on the way people see their worlds. And the fact that similar concepts are expressed in different languages may be tied to the cultures of the groups in question.

Considering how much of culture is transmitted through language, it is easy to understand how language can shape our experience and channel our view of the world. But Whorf overemphasized one point: that language programs us to think only along certain prescribed lines and closes off alternative ways of looking at the world. Undoubtedly it is *easier* to express certain ideas in one language than in another, but it is rarely impossible. For example, it is admittedly difficult to translate the Biblical quotation "Get thee behind me, Satan," into the Quechua language of Peru simply because Quechua conceptualizes space and time relationships in a different way than Hebrew or English does. Quechua speakers regard the past as being "ahead of one" while the future is "behind oneself." They reason that an event which has already occurred can be seen in the mind and therefore must be in front of one's eyes. But events in the future cannot be "seen" and therefore must be behind one (Farb, 1974: 201). Still, the gist of the Biblical quotation can be expressed in Quechua if we allow for a certain amount of awkward phrasing. To take another example, "We left New Mexico two and a half months ago" is far easier to say in English than in Hopi, but it is certainly possible to express this idea in some form. It may also be true, as Whorf surmised, that the Hopi view of time and space is better suited to the concepts of modern physics than are European languages. Nevertheless, the theory of relativity was formulated by a person who spoke German.

Although the Sapir-Whorf hypothesis is far from proven, Whorf made a great contribution by stressing the interrelation of language and culture. In fact, many anthropologists today believe that a people's language provides a map of their culture. By studying how people classify and label colors, plants, diseases, relatives, and so on, they hope to discover what each culture considers important and trivial, how each regards the world.

Language and Cultural Focus

The human ear can distinguish several thousand different sounds; the human eye can distinguish some ten million colors. But it is humanly impossible to pay attention to all the colors, objects, and noises that besiege us daily. In order to deal with all this information, people simplify and organize these raw data by grouping them into verbal categories. The

English language reduces the millions of colors in the world to four thousand distinctly labeled colors at most. These words are normally grouped into still fewer categories—baby blue, sky blue, navy, and turquoise are lumped into the general category *blue;* grass green, lime, chartreuse, and emerald are all classified as *green.* Most European speech communities recognize and name six basic colors (in addition to black and white): red, orange, green, blue, yellow, and purple. These are the bands of colors we name when looking at a rainbow. Different languages, however, make different distinctions. The Shona of Rhodesia divide the spectrum into three basic color categories: *cicena* (yellow to yellow-green), *citema* (blue-green), and *cipsuka* (blue to purple and red to orange). The Jalé of New Guinea classify colors in terms of *ziza* and *hui* (light and dark) (Farb, 1974:172).

Everyone classifies objects in the physical and social environment. But categories that one speech community considers obvious may be completely ignored elsewhere. Often these categories reflect major cultural concerns. The Koya of South India do not have separate words to distinguish dew, fog, and snow. This is not terribly surprising, since they live in a tropical environment. On the other hand, they distinguish seven different kinds of bamboo. While English speakers have separate terms for rain, fog, sleet, ice, and snow, most of us do not make any further distinctions—unless we happen to be avid skiers. Then we may apply a more extensive classification system, distinguishing corn snow, powder, and deep powder, for example. The Eskimos carry snow classification slightly further with separate words for "snow on the ground," "falling snow," "drifting snow," and "a snowdrift" (Boas, 1940). But they have no general term meaning simply "snow." Similarly, the Garo of northeast India have at least a dozen words for different types of ants, but no generic name for the whole class that corresponds to the English word "ant." Living in an environment where ants are plentiful and varied, the Garo find it more useful to distinguish one variety from another than to distinguish ants, as a class, from other insects (Burling, 1970). Just as different speech communities consider contrasts between some sounds significant but ignore others, the vocabulary of a language makes distinctions that are culturally significant and ignores those that are not. By analyzing a people's system of verbal categories, anthropologists learn something more than how their language works: they also learn a good deal about this people's culture, thought, and world view.

The Evolution of Communications Media

A complex interaction between physiology and culture gave rise to language as we know it today. However much particular languages around the world may appear to vary, they are all similar in one very basic respect: they are all equally efficient and successful means of symbolic communication. Human language, then, is no longer evolving in the basic sense that it did millions of years ago. Although today's languages change in ways that have no particular adaptive significance—new words are added, language sounds shift, grammatical structures gradually alter—these changes do not constitute a revolution of the magnitude that led to language itself.

There are, however, areas in which language is changing in important ways. One example of adaptive evolution in contemporary human communication is the development and impact of mass media. Although languages have not increased in complexity for many thousands of years, systems of technology have, and with them the forms of communication available to mankind. With the recent advent of highly sophisticated technological systems, previously unimagined forms of electronic mass communication are at humanity's disposal. As a result, new questions are arising as to how human social organization may be influenced when humankind becomes, in Marshall McLuhan's words, one "global village."

McLuhan's controversial thesis is summed up by his now-familiar phrase "The medium is the message." In his view, each new medium (or technology) slowly creates a human environment that is completely new. The so-called message of that medium is not its content; the content or uses of any medium are diverse. The uniqueness and great influence of the medium lies rather in "the change of scale or pace or pattern that it introduces into human affairs" (McLuhan, 1964:8).

McLuhan interprets epochs of human history in terms of available media. As nomadic food-gatherers, human beings took on a great many tasks that were sedentary. As the media of writing and printing evolved, humans began to specialize. Knowledge and action were indeed separate roles, and the unique advantage of Westerners was a certain aloofness, an ability to act without involvement. Then in the age of mechanical industry, fragmentation and centralism (we have only to think of all that the assembly line implies) began to pattern relationships between human beings.

Now we are entering an age of electric technology and automation. Electricity makes it possible for information to be retrieved instantaneously; thus time and space are no longer significant variables in human affairs. In sum, this is the age of information—or, more literally, the age of illumination. For McLuhan the message of electric light and power is not only decentralized and radical but pervasive. Like the telegraph, radio, telephone, and television, electric light and power create intense involvement. And because of the speed with which social and political information is conveyed, people have a heightened awareness of their responsibilities:

Men are suddenly nomadic gatherers of knowledge, nomadic as never before, informed as never before, free from fragmentary specialism as never before—but also involved in the total social process as never before; since with electricity we extend our central nervous system globally, instantly interrelating every human experience. (McLuhan, 1964:358)

McLuhan also predicts that as electricity makes possible an increase in the speed with which we receive information, politics will ultimately involve the entire community in the process of decision making. In this view, the media of the electronic age have turned the world into a global village, so that in a sense we modern human beings have come back again to the values and perceptual modes of preliterate humans.

Although many theorists have challenged McLuhan's arguments and predictions, they do acknowledge that the mass media has put us in touch with a range of people, lifestyles, events, and options of which we were unaware. Yet the degree to which the means of mass communication can implement social change or even structure social organization is a question still to be answered in this age of electric technology.

summary

All living creatures need to communicate if they are going to survive. When responding to danger, the presence of food, or the desire to mate, all animals become social beings, needing the ability to transmit and receive information. Animals have evolved a wide and complex range of communication mechanisms depending primarily on sight, touch, and smell, rather than sound.

Although human beings may be considered the most sophisticated communicators, due to their unique use of language, we should not overemphasize the difference between animal and human communication. Like the lower animals, we communicate nonverbally. *Kinesics and proxemics* both deal with modes of nonverbal communication.

The information-carrying sounds animals emit are called *signs*. They convey precise and important messages to other animals and are of great adaptive value. But although efficient and even complex, such means of communication are limited in comparison to language. Not only is the meaning of a sign genetically determined, making it unvarying, but all animal sign systems are closed. Human language is superior in its greater flexibility. Rather than use signs, we employ *symbols,* which are both arbitrary and abstract. We determine what words will mean; our understanding of a term is not biologically determined. The abstractness of our symbols allows us to categorize objects and events, to refer to things that have existed in the past or will exist in the future. Furthermore, human language is an *open system.* We can manipulate symbols to express totally novel ideas. Our ability to conceptualize enables us to preserve our past, transmit our ideas, and ask the questions necessary for our survival.

Answering the question of how language evolved is not easy. Hockett and Ascher persuasively maintain that the closed system of calls used by the proto-hominids of several million years ago evolved into an open system when the grasping, manipulating, and carrying functions shifted from the mouth to the hands. Through the process of blending—in which various calls merged, while new ones were invented—language evolved over hundreds of thousands of years. By the end of the process, language was transmitted culturally rather than genetically, and learning had begun to replace instinct.

Undeniably, strong selective pressure existed for the development of linguistic ability. The human hunter was part of a complex social organization in which communication among members was imperative. Language and the culture that made it possible became *Homo sapiens'* chief environmental adaptations, compensating us for our body weakness.

Speculation as to the evolution of language underscores the interaction between language, physiology, and culture. The relationship between language and physiology is easy to elucidate. Language would not be possible if our vocal cords were incapable of producing sounds. And our brains—particularly three areas of the left hemisphere of the cerebral cortex—are also adapted for language use.

The precise nature of the relationship between language and culture is more difficult to ascertain. Is language a simple reflection of culture? Or does language in fact culturally condition our view of the world? Edward Sapir believed that we are to a certain extent prisoners of our language—that the language we speak determines our world view. Benjamin Lee Whorf, carrying this idea further in his study of the Hopi language, asserted that contrasting language structures result in contrasting world views. The problem with the Sapir-Whorf hypothesis is that it is difficult to generalize about a culture's habits and thought patterns and to say that they are caused by language. In fact, it has been shown that many highly divergent cultures speak culturally related languages. We might as readily state that what people believe, and their culture, determine the structure of their language. Nevertheless, Whorf made an important contribution by stressing the link between culture and language.

All languages have in common the fact that they are efficient and successful means of symbolic communication. Human language is not evolving as it once did; it has adapted to our needs. But the forms of communication are evolving in response to advanced technology. Marshall McLuhan speaks of the earth as a potential "global village." In his view, each new medium (or technology) creates a completely new human environment. The medium's content is less important than its effect on the "scale or pace or pattern of human affairs." Electric technology and automation involve us in the total social process as never before, and therefore decrease our sense of fragmentation and specialization. Although these views have been challenged, it must be acknowledged that the development of the mass media has put us in touch with an extraordinary range of stimuli, whose ability to foster social change or structure social organization is as yet little understood.

suggested readings

BURLING, R.
1970 *Man's Many Voices.* New York: Holt, Rinehart and Winston. A general introduction to linguistics that contains substantial coverage of ethnosemantics and comparisons of human and animal communication.

CARROLL, J. B., ED.
1956 *Language, Thought, and Reality: Selected Writings of Benjamin Lee Whorf.* Cambridge, Mass.: M.I.T. Press. A collection of Whorf's most important essays on the relationship between language and culture.

HALL, E. T.
1966 *The Hidden Dimension.* New York: Doubleday. A discussion of nonverbal communication and its role in human communication.

HAMMEL, E., ED.
1965 Formal Semantic Analysis. *American Anthropologist,* vol. 67, no. 5, part 2 (special issue). A collection of some of the most important early essays in ethnosemantics.

HOCKETT, C. F., ED.
1958 *A Course in Modern Linguistics.* New York: Macmillan. A general introduction to linguistics with considerable coverage of the origins of human language.

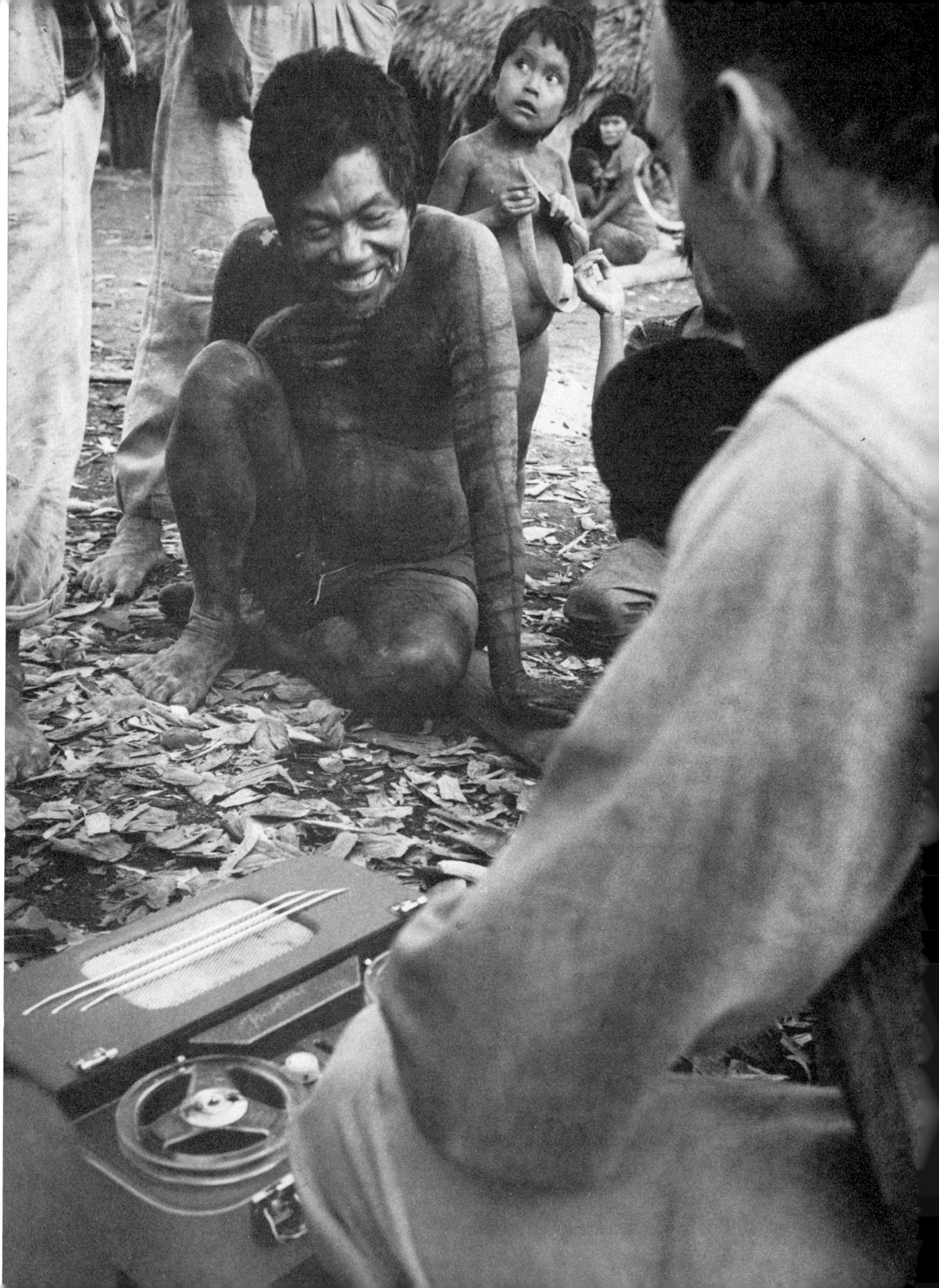

fourteen
Linguistic Variation

Some years ago, a journalist traveling through eastern Bolivia reported that he had discovered a group of Siriono Indians who had never developed any language. They communicated, he insisted, by whistling (Wegner, 1928). His claims were proven absurd by later ethnographers, who found that although the Siriono are sometimes uncommunicative, they share the same capacity for speech as all other human beings. Like the Chinese, the Germans, the ancient Greeks, and Americans, the Siriono speak a highly developed language complete with consonants and vowels, complex grammar, and a vocabulary to handle abstract concepts about time, space, and number (Holmberg, 1969).

After studying several thousand languages spoken by peoples living in isolated and marginal areas, linguists have yet to discover any group of people who speak a language so poorly developed that they are forced to rely on gestures, calls, or vague grunts. The misconception that "primitive" people speak "primitive" languages has persisted because few Westerners studied or even understood many of these languages until recently. Having communicated with native peoples through sign language or pidgin, they concluded that the natives were at best capable of only rudimentary, halting speech. Traveling in Tierra del Fuego in 1832, Charles Darwin reported that "the language of these people, according to our notions, scarcely deserves to be called articulate" (Darwin, 1962:206). However, a later study of the Yahgan, a people living at the tip of South America, revealed a vocabulary of some 30,000 words (Swadesh, 1971). A typical Yahgan probably uses about 10,000 of these in normal conversation. While an unabridged English dictionary contains approximately 260,000 words, a typical English speaker uses only 7,000 or so—a little less than a Yahgan and barely half the everyday vocabulary of an Eskimo (Ogburn, 1968).

Every language is capable of communicating the most complex thoughts, feelings, and observations of its speakers. Be the speaker Chinese, Zulu, or French, his language will express equally well what he needs to say. Yet, as any traveler has discovered, a language that is an effective system of communication in one part of the world is often found sorely wanting in another. When English speakers first hear Spanish or Italian, they are immediately aware that what they are listening to is quite different from what they have been used to hearing in the past. Differences in sounds are immediately apparent. The nasalized sound of ñ in Spanish, heard in such words as *mañana,* is unknown in English. And as we begin to learn a foreign language, we immediately realize that some words simply have no synonyms in our own language. We also become aware that the structures of languages vary. One cannot take an English sentence, translate all the words into Italian, and expect to have created a grammatical Italian statement; the rules for such things as proper word order differ significantly in the two languages.

Even the casual observer, then, is aware that there are many differences between languages—differences not only in language sounds, but also in vocabulary and grammar. It takes a trained linguist, however, to analyze these differences precisely. By ordering linguistic data into meaningful categories, the

Tape recorders are a valuable tool for all anthropologists, not only linguists. This researcher is taping an interview with an Amarakaeri Indian in a valley east of Cuzco in Peru. (Cornell Capa/Magnum)

linguist is able not only to understand the structure of a given language, but also to compare its structure to those of other languages. The way in which linguists analyze variations in language is the subject of the following section.

Variations in the Structure of Language

The sentence *mayavaaniaak' aza' mi* ("He will give it to you") is readily understood by all people who speak the Paiute language. However, to a linguist hearing the language for the first time, the phrase is just a meaningless set of sounds. While the Paiute speakers can easily distinguish different words and phrases, the linguist has no way to tell whether *aza' mi* is a complete word, part of a word, or three words. In order to make sense out of Paiute, he must learn the rules for organizing sounds into words and words into meaningful statements, rules that every native Paiute speaker conforms to unconsciously each time he speaks.

Phonetic Classification

Since linguists cannot simply ask a native speaker to tell them about the sound and structure of his or her language, they must discover these by systematically observing and recording what people say. First, a minimum vocabulary must be acquired. A possible beginning is to interview several informants, asking how to say various things: "What is your word for house?" "How do you say two houses?" The linguist then transcribes their responses. It should be kept in mind throughout this discussion that the linguist is dealing with the actual sounds of the spoken language, and is not concerned with the written language at all. This is for two reasons: first, there is no writing system for most of the world's languages. Second, if there is a writing system, the linguist cannot be sure that it represents the sounds in any consistent way. Take for example the various pronunciations of the *ou* sequence in English in such words as thr*ou*gh, r*ou*gh, b*ou*t, d*ou*gh, etc. To write down what they hear, linguists use a special system called the International Phonetic Alphabet (IPA), a notational system that provides a symbol for every sound that could occur in any language.[1] This provides a ready-made system for classifying raw data, the sounds or phones that can be heard. Once some rough notations have been made, the linguist continues to build and refine his or her transcription, asking people to repeat sounds and words. A complete description of the *phonology* or sound system is thus developed by trial and error.

A language, though, is not simply a collection of sounds or an assortment of phrases. It is also a set of rules for combining sounds into meaningful patterns, phrases, and sentences. Once the linguist has collected and phonetically classified the raw data, he or she begins to analyze the sounds more carefully to determine how they are used by this particular speech community, and to build a grammar of rules and patterns for the language as a whole.

Phonemics

The human voice is able to produce thousands of different sounds. Yet out of this full range, every language selects only a certain number of all the possible sounds. English speakers recognize about 45 distinct sound units, Italians 27, Hawaiians 13. Such units of sound, called *phonemes*, can be combined and recombined to form a huge number of words. (We will follow the linguistic convention here of enclosing sounds of the IPA in

---

[1] The compilers of the IPA originally intended to provide a distinct symbol for every sound that any language might use, but they finally gave up. There are enough symbols in the IPA so that linguists can indicate with distinct symbols any sounds they might wish to distinguish within a particular language; but the same symbol is sometimes used for similar but distinguishable sounds in different languages. Some of the symbols look like letters in the English alphabet, but they do not usually indicate the same sounds. For example, the symbol [i] stands for the vowel sound in *beet;* [I] stands for the vowel sound in *bit;* [e] stands for the sound in *bait;* and [a] stands for the vowel sound in *pot*.

brackets [ ], and phonemes in slashes / /.)

Probably no two languages use precisely the same set of sounds. The common Spanish trill in *burro* and *cigarro* does not exist in English. Both French and English lack the scrape-like throat sound written *ch* in German, as in the name of the composer Bach (in fact, we very often replace this sound with [k] and pronounce his name *Bahk*). And neither Spanish, English, nor German have adopted the click sounds used in the Bushman language. Each of these sound elements, ignored in one language, is significant in another. They are important not because they are considered particularly lilting, full-bodied, or pleasing to the ear; rather, they serve as contrasting elements in a language code. They enable a listener to clearly distinguish one sound from another, and thus allow a speaker to signal differences in meaning between two words that would otherwise sound identical. Thus phonemes may be further defined as the smallest *linguistically significant* units of sound in a particular language.

Every language has a unique system of sound contrasts. English speakers, for example, distinguish between sounds [v] and [b]. The contrast is crucial for differentiating numerous pairs of similar words such as *vest* and *best, vat* and *bat, very* and *berry*—what linguists call *minimal pairs*. The sentence "I want the vest" means something entirely different from "I want the best." Yet the two statements are kept distinct by a single phonetic variation. English speakers have learned to recognize and use the slight difference between [v] and [b]. But in Spanish the distinction between [v] and [b] is not significant. When two sounds of a language are distinct but are not used contrastively to distinguish meaning, they are called *allophones*. If a Spaniard pronounces the word *vaya* (meaning "go"), an English speaker would be unable to tell whether the word begins with a [v], a [b], or some blend of the two. A Spaniard would understand the meaning of *vaya* if an English speaker pronounced the initial sound as [v] or as [b]. Thus what we regard as separate phonemes, Spanish speakers do not; [v] and [b] are allophones and can be used interchangeably in Spanish without altering the meaning of a word, although the [v] variant of the phoneme is preferred between vowels.

In any language, however, the phonetic distinctions between one allophone and another are often indistinguishable to most speakers unless they make a special effort to perceive them. Most of us are probably unaware that the first sound in the word *pit* is not quite like the second sound in the word *spit* even though we regularly pronounce the two sounds differently. By holding your palm in front of your mouth while repeating both words, you will feel a slight puff of air in the case of *pit* but not in the case of *spit*. In phonetic terms, the first is aspirated (written phonetically as [p^h]), while the second is not (written [p]). In English, however, the two sounds are not classified as different phonemes because the meaning of a word is not changed by substituting [p^h] for [p]. The two sounds are simply allophones. In Hindi, in contrast, the distinction between [p^h] and [p] is crucial and is immediately heard. To substitute one for the other would be like substituting [p] for [b] in English. Thus one person's allophone is another person's phoneme.

The Range of Phonemic Systems Vowels and consonants are not the only kinds of phonemes. Stress, pitch, tone, and the linking and separation of syllables are just as important in distinguishing messages as the contrast between significant units of sound. For example, the words *desert, address,* and *present* may be either nouns or verbs, depending on which syllables are pronounced longer and louder. *DESert, ADdress,* and *PRESent* are nouns; *deSERT, adDRESS,* and *preSENT* are verbs. The vowels and consonants remain the same, but the difference in stress changes the meaning of each word.

Stress alone is often insufficient for distinguishing words. In the sentence "The tailor charged only thirty dollars per suit," there is a slight pause between *per* and *suit* that is not made in the sentence "The posse followed in hot pursuit." Such a pause, known as an *open*

Recreating the tonal inflections of his language on the drum, this man calls families scattered across the hills of Burundi to a tribal assembly. (Leon V. Kofod)

juncture, is also a common English phoneme. Without it, we could not distinguish between statements such as "We're waiting for Jack's son" and "We're waiting for Jackson." *Jack's son* is differentiated from *Jackson* by an open juncture plus a slight difference in stress.

Just as the total number of phonemes varies from one language to another, so do the types of phonemes used. In English, the phonemic system includes 24 consonants and 9 vowels. Some Arabic languages are based on 28 consonants and 6 vowels. In Lokele, a Congolese language, there are 19 consonants and 7 vowels. However, Lokele also includes two tonal phonemes that do not occur in English or Arabic. By changing pitch from syllable to syllable, the Lokele are able to distinguish otherwise identical words. For example, *liALA* (low-tone syllable followed by a high-tone syllable) means "fiancée"; *liala* (two low-tone syllables) means "rubbish dump." As one linguist found, this can create certain problems: "He who says *aSOoLAMBAboIli* instead of *aSOolaMBAboili* has stated that he is boiling his mother-in-law rather than watching the riverbank" (Carrington, 1971:90).

Many African and East Asian languages distinguish words on the basis of their tonal patterns. This feature makes it possible to communicate by drumming out tonal messages from one village to another. Sometimes gongs or wind instruments are used as substitutes for the human voice. The Chin of northern Burma communicate with xylophones; Fiji Islanders drum on canoes. In all these cases—unlike the Morse code or American Indian smoke signals—the tonal messages are extensions of the spoken languages. They adapt and pattern the tonal elements of the spoken language for long-distance transmission.

Grammar

Linguists are concerned with a different and considerably more complex sort of grammar than the kind most of us learn in school. They do not formulate rules about when to use *who* and *whom* or whether it is proper to say *shall* or *will*. They are concerned with describing how people actually speak, rather than how they ought to speak. The *grammar* of a language refers to its particular arrangement of linguistic elements: the way phonemes are combined to construct words (called *morphology*) and the way words are arranged to form phrases and sentences (called *syntax*).

Morphemes

When the phonemes /g/, /a/, and /d/ are strung together in English, they produce a meaningful unit of speech—the word *god,* or, if combined in reverse order, the word *dog.* Neither of these words can be split into smaller particles and still retain any meaning. Minimal units of speech that convey meaning are known as *morphemes*. Not all morphemes are complete words such as *god* or *dog*, however. In fact, most words can be further subdivided into several morphemes. The word *gods,* for example, can be split into two smaller meaningful units that recur in many different combinations: the root word *god* (which also occurs in *godlike* and *ungodly*), and the suffix *-s* (meaning "more than one," and recurring in *boys, dogs, books,* and so on). *Ungodly* can be split into three separate and meaningful elements: *god;* a prefix *un-* (meaning "not," as in *unhealthy, unwise*); and a suffix *-ly* (meaning "performed in the manner indicated by the root word," as in *calmly, slowly*). A word, then, may consist of two kinds of morphemes: those that can stand alone, such as *god*, called *free morphemes*; those that must be attached to other morphemes, such as *un-, -s,* and *-ly,* called *bound morphemes*.

Just as the phoneme /p/ includes different allophones—an aspirated [pʰ] and an unaspirated [p]—a morpheme may include a range of forms, or *allomorphs*. For example, the morpheme meaning "more than one item" includes three allomorphs: *-s* as in *hats; -s*, pronounced [z] as in *cars;* and *-es*, pronounced [əz] as in *courses*. The morpheme meaning "action that happened in the past" has two allomorphs: *-t* as in *built,* and *-ed* as in *cooked*.[2] These morphemes have no semantic meaning by themselves, but they do convey grammatical meaning (they indicate number or tense) when used in combination with other morphemes.

Morphology Any English speaker will immediately realize that the statement "Mary boil pot water" is not grammatical. It lacks certain morphemes needed to express relationships and concepts considered essential in English. There is no indication of tense, number, or the relationship between *pot* and *water*. To make this statement grammatical certain morphemes must be added: *-ed* or *is -ing,* for

---

[2]English includes many irregular forms where tense or number are indicated by changing an internal vowel, as when we change *hang* to *hung, think* to *thought,* or *man* to *men, mouse* to *mice*. The study of phonemic changes that occur when morphemes are combined is called *morphophonemics*.

Whistle and Drum Language

Among the Mazateco Indians of Oaxaca, Mexico, anything that can be said with words can also be said with whistles. One researcher observed an entire business transaction being carried out through whistling. A man, standing in front of his hut, whistled to another man carrying a bundle of corn leaves to market. After a good deal of whistled bargaining back and forth, the men agreed upon a price. The seller delivered his corn leaves to the buyer's hut, received his pay, and left. Throughout the conversation, neither of the two uttered a single word (Cowan, 1948).

How does such a language work? The Mazateco whistle language, like many languages that are hummed, pounded out on a drum, or played on some other musical instrument, is directly based on a tonal spoken language. The whistled pitches correspond to the patterns of tone in the spoken word. Unlike Morse Code, which uses symbols very different from the sounds they represent, many whistle and drum languages suggest the flow of sound in speech (Stern, 1957).

Of course, whistled or drummed messages can be ambiguous, for tonal languages have many words with identical tonal patterns. This problem is sometimes solved by limiting conversations to topics that are clear by the situational context. Another solution is to substitute phrases for words. In their drummed messages, the Lokele of Africa replace the words "moon" and "fowl," which have the same tonal pattern, with the easily differentiated phrases "the moon looks down at the earth" and "the fowl, the little one which says 'kiokio'" (Carrington, 1949:33). Naturally, this makes it more time-consuming to drum a message than to say it. Among the Duala of the Cameroons, it takes a man three syllables to tell his wife "I feel hungry" and 17 syllables to drum the same message to her from the fields (Nekes, 1912).

Why have people developed drum and whistle languages? The primary reason is to communicate over long distances or in other situations where the speakers are not face-to-face. The Mazateco frequently whistle messages when they are working in fields widely scattered over a mountainside, as do the Siriono of Bolivia when they are hunting in dense forest. But in some societies, whistle and drum languages have become routine means of daily communication, supplementing speech. The Mazateco sometimes switch back and forth between whistled and spoken language in a single conversation. And among the Duala, dogs are even taught to answer to their drummed names.

example, to make *boiled* or *is boiling; a, some, two,* or *three* to indicate the number of pots; and *of* to specify the relationship between *pot* and *water*. The statement "Mary is boiling a pot of water" is a perfectly grammatical sentence in English. In other languages, however, this statement may still require additional morphemes before it is considered complete. In Spanish or French, for instance, the gender of the noun *pot* must be specified. German requires special suffixes (called case endings) to indicate which words are the subject, predicate, and object of the sentence. A language such as Navajo might ignore number, gender, and case but require certain morphemes to specify the pot's shape and size and whether the object of "boil" is animate or inanimate. In Navajo, all of these modifications are expressed not by separate words but by particular bound morphemes that are added to the verb stem.

In many languages, complex statements can be expressed simply by combining morphemes to form a single word. In Aranda, for instance, the word *Erarijarijaka* means "full of longing for something that has been lost." One word consisting of several morphemes suffices to express what English speakers must say in a long phrase. In English, morphology never becomes extremely complex—*ungentlemanliness* with six morphemes is about as far as we go. In Fox, however, a language spoken by a Dakota Indian tribe, six is the average number of morphemes per word. Fox, Aranda, Turkish, Latin, and many other languages convey meaning largely through morphology—that is, by adding prefixes and suffixes, and by rearranging morphemes within a word. By contrast, English relies more heavily on arranging separate words in a sentence. What other languages do morphologically, we do through syntax.

Syntax It would never occur to a native English speaker to say, "Mike big three apples ate," rather than "Mike ate three big apples." Unconsciously, we all know the rules governing the order of subject, verb, adjectives, and adverbs. In Spanish, however, different rules apply. A Spanish speaker would say, "Miguel se comió tres manzanas grandes y rojas." Literally translated, this sentence reads "Mike himself ate three apples big and red." Every language has its own set of rules for constructing phrases and sentences. And all native speakers follow these rules intuitively and meticulously, whether or not they are capable of stating them explicitly.

Our understanding of grammatical constructions enables us to get the drift of a sentence even when the meaning of particular words may not be clear. Consider, for example, the following excerpt from the poem "Jabberwocky" in Lewis Carroll's *Through the Looking-Glass:*

> 'Twas brillig, and the slithy toves
> Did gyre and gimble in the wabe:
> All mimsy were the borogroves,
> And the mome raths outgrabe.

Although almost all the content words are meaningless, one is still left with the impression that somehow the poem "makes sense." Carroll achieves this effect by using enough grammatical connectives (such as *did* and *the*) and bound morphemes (such as *-s* and *-y*) to mark the poem as English. Because Carroll has preserved the form of English morphology and syntax, we are able to guess at the meaning of the fabricated words. *Brillig,* for example, must be a predicate adjective because it follows the contraction *'Twas,* and we surmise that it refers to something like the state of the weather or the condition of the sunlight. We know that *slithy* is an adjective because it ends in the familiar adjective suffix *-y,* meaning "full of" or "having the character of." Judging by its placement in the sentence, we guess that *slithy* is modifying the noun *toves*. A *tove,* we presume, is some sort of living creature. And although we are not exactly sure how to visualize the beast, we can tell by the plural suffix *-s* that more than one of them is present.

It is an easy matter to identify the parts of speech of the remaining nonsense words, as well as their functions in the sentence. From these grammatical cues, along with the impressions conveyed simply by the sounds of the words, we are somehow able to "understand" completely meaningless utterances. Yet if we did not intuitively grasp the rules for constructing English sentences, the poem would be totally incomprehensible.

If people learned a vast collection of specific sentences rather than learning the structural rules of their language, they would be unable to understand any statement unless they had already heard it and been told what it meant. But this is not the case; people readily understand statements they have never heard before. Moreover, all of us continually utter statements that no one has ever before spoken. We are not limited to a set of stock phrases and sentences learned over the years. Theoretically, every speaker can generate, or produce, an infinite number of utterances.

Transformational Grammar Part of a speaker's capacity to generate new sentences is based on his ability to say the same thing in various ways. We can say, "Harry painted the picture." By rearranging a few basic elements, we can convey exactly the same meaning by saying, "The picture was painted by Harry." In an effort to develop a grammar that explains how speakers make such transformations, Noam Chomsky (1957, 1965) distinguishes two levels of structure in every sentence: a surface structure and an underlying deep structure that is more abstract. The two sentences above have different surface structures but share the same deep structure. We intuitively know that they mean the same thing.

Conversely, we are able to say entirely different things using the same words in precisely the same order. On the surface, "I love Harry's painting" seems like a perfectly straightforward sentence. Actually it has several possible meanings. It can mean "I love a particular painting by Harry," "I love the fact that Harry paints," or "I love Harry's style of painting in general." In this case, a sentence with a very simple surface structure actually corresponds to several deep structures. Chomsky maintains that we are able to make sense out of such ambiguous statements because the context in which they are made enables us to see beneath the surface and recognize the deeper meaning implied. Without even thinking about it, we are able to make a series of complex transformations needed to translate the deep structure of "I love the fact that Harry paints" into its pronounceable surface form.

A speaker of Japanese or Eskimo will make such transformations just as easily as a native English speaker. From the time we are small children, our speech reveals an intuitive grasp of deep structure. On the strength of these observations, Chomsky argues that all human beings are born with a blueprint for language. Just as we are born adapted to bipedalism or a precision grip, we are adapted to rapid language learning. As children we can learn Navajo, Chinese, Hindi, or English with equal ease, depending solely on where we are raised. This fact suggests that all languages may share a common deep structure. Some linguists (Chomsky, for example) believe that the differences among the thousands of languages spoken on earth are simply adaptive surface variations of a deeper, universal grammar rooted in the human mind. But others (for example, Whorf) have suggested that linguistic differences are more fundamental, that each language structure molds our thought processes in particular ways.

Variations in Meaning and Linguistic Classification

The study of the meaning of language, called *semantics,* has developed a long way from efforts to provide precise "dictionary definitions" of a language's vocabulary. Contemporary researchers in semantics are primarily concerned not with single words and their definitions, but with whole categories of words and how their meanings relate to one another. Categories of semantically related terms—all the color terms of a language, for example, or all its kinship terms—are referred to as *semantic domains.* Semantic domains are important keys to a society's system of meaning;

they provide insight into the ways that members of that society view the world.

Of course, how people categorize phenomena in their universe varies from culture to culture and language to language. Every language is a system of symbols, with its own unique way of labeling and relating categories of experience, its own way of structuring the world its speakers perceive. This may at first seem surprising, for many of us take the order that our linguistic categories impose on natural and social phenomena completely for granted. We do not realize that other languages may order phenomena quite differently. The study of the ways in which different societies group experiences into domains, and the ways in which they use certain criteria to distinguish between the various terms in those domains, is known as *ethnosemantics*.

The approach of ethnosemantics is an *emic* one. Just as linguists distinguish between the phon*etic* system of a language (all the objectively heard sounds that an outside observer hears) and the phon*emic* system (the sounds that native speakers consider significant), so ethnosemantic analysis applies the same distinction to culture: there is an objective, or *etic*, viewpoint brought by an outside observer, and an *emic* viewpoint, the framework used by the people themselves. Anthropologists interested in ethnosemantics want to find out what items are grouped together in the minds of native speakers and attempt to avoid imposing their own categories. The way people categorize objects may provide important clues about their cultural beliefs and social practices. Asked to classify a couch, a chair, and a spear, an American will group the couch and the chair together in the category of "household furniture," and classify the spear as a "weapon." But an Ashanti would classify the chair and the spear together in the category of "symbols of authority."

The importance of the emic approach should not be underestimated. If a researcher imposes his own way of categorizing phenomena on speakers of another language, confusion or misunderstandings can result. Harold Conklin demonstrated this clearly in his study of color categories among the Hanunóo of the Philippines. When English speakers refer to an object's color, they are referring to a combination of hue, intensity, and brightness. Hanunóo "color" terms, however, refer not only to chromatic characteristics, but also to such qualities as wetness or succulence vs. dryness or desiccation, and unfading or indelible vs. faded or bleached. Had Conklin employed traditional testing methods—as, for example, the use of color chips—in his investigation, he would have entirely missed these other criteria for discriminating between different colors. It was only by taking the emic approach, by asking the Hanunóo about familiar objects in their everyday surroundings, that Conklin was able to discover the unique nature of the Hanunóo "color" classification system (Conklin, 1955).

The Nature of Linguistic Variation

When considering the diversity of human language, many people conclude that each culture has its own separate language or dialect which is quite distinct from the language or dialect spoken by any other culture. However widely held this notion may be, it simply does not reflect reality. Although language does vary, linguistic variation really involves gradual and slight changes as we move from one speech community to a neighboring one. The differences are seldom so overwhelming that we can justifiably label the various systems of communication separate and distinct languages. Linguistic variation can rarely be contained in such tidy packages; it is far more fluid and continuous in nature.

The continuous nature of linguistic variation can be seen among the Indians of the northwest Amazon. Here, the more than twenty-five tribes who inhabit sequential areas along the river are identified with different languages. The members of any given tribe, however, are multilingual; each individual speaks both his or her father's tongue (the language of the tribe into which he or she was born) and his or her mother's tongue (the language of a neighboring tribe), as well as being able to understand several other languages prevalent in the region. Because the geographical distribution of these languages is sequential, the prevalence of various languages changes as one moves up and down the river from one end of the multilingual area to the other. Thus from one community to the next, there is gradual variation in the inventories of languages available to individuals. Moreover, these gradual variations accumulate so that communities sufficiently far apart have entirely different inventories of languages. For example, the repertoire of languages known by a person from the center of the Papurí region is completely distinct from the repertoire known by a person from the center of the Pira-Paraná region miles away. Yet there are no abrupt boundaries where one language ceases to be understood and another one begins (Sorensen, 1970).

The difficulties involved in thinking about linguistic variation in terms of separate and

Many peoples have created written languages over the ages — none more elaborate than hieroglyphics, the stylized pictures ancient Egyptians used to represent words. This photograph shows a page in the epic of Ramses III, carved in stone at the Karnak Temple. (René Burri/Magnum)

distinct languages can also be seen when we consider a single society which presumably speaks exactly the same language. We all know, for example, that there are many regional variations in language throughout the United States. Consider the series of variations one encounters in traveling from Bangor, Maine, to Atlanta, Georgia. And frequently there are also variations in language between social classes or between men and women living in the very same community. A study of French speakers in Montreal, Canada, for instance, revealed that working-class people were far more likely than professional people to delete the sound of *l* when pronouncing such pronouns and articles as *elle, les,* and *la.*

In addition, a higher rate of dropping the /l/ sound was observed among men than among women (Sankoff, 1972).

The point of these examples is simply to show that attempting to differentiate between separate and distinct languages is problematical in much the same way that differentiating between separate and distinct races is problematical in the study of man's physical variation. Linguistic variation is better viewed in terms of gradual differences between speech communities as well as slight differences within the same community. This fluid and continuous nature of linguistic variation will become even more apparent as we explore the process of linguistic change.

Linguistic Variation and Change

In many East Coast communities, the *sound* of English is gradually being transformed as more and more speakers are pronouncing the postvocalic /r/, as in *car* or *farther*. Language itself, however, changes very slowly as many small variations in phonology, vocabulary, and grammar accumulate over a long period of time. While we do not speak exactly the same language our great-grandparents spoke, the basic structure of our language has not really changed over the past two hundred years. Although the phrasing sounds a bit archaic, we have little trouble understanding what Edgar Allan Poe meant when he wrote, in 1800, "Sleep came not near my couch—while the hours waned and waned away." But the farther back we go in time, the more differences we find. Reading the King James Version of the Bible, we appreciate the changes in words and structure that have taken place over the past three hundred years:

> Who hath measured the waters in the hollow of his hand, and meted out heaven with the span, and comprehended the dust of the earth in a measure, and weighed the mountains in scales, and the hills in a balance? (Isaiah 40:12)

And when we go back a full thousand years to the speech used by a tenth-century Englishman, the language becomes completely unintelligible: Se foresǣde dēma waes swīđe ārlēas crīstenra manna ēhtere and arod tō dēofles willan.* (Aelfric) This passage is Old English. But to a twentieth-century English speaker, it might as well be Icelandic. How did our language become what it is today? And why did these particular changes occur? To answer these questions, we will first look at some of the historical changes that have taken place in various languages of the world, attempting to trace them through time. Then we will examine some of the specific processes involved in the diversification and change of language. And finally we will look at how those processes as well as others are continuing to affect and alter our use of language today.

Historical Development of Languages

Since people talk more to those who live nearby or who belong to the same social class, geographical and social groups tend to share similar speech patterns. Peoples who are rarely in contact, on the other hand, will develop distinct usages or dialects. If social and geographical communities become separated and isolated, these dialects may become more and more divergent, eventually evolving into completely distinct languages. This is what happened when different geographical dialects of Latin drifted apart during the early stages of the Christian Era and developed into French, Spanish, and Italian. English and German evolved in the same way. Both are descended from an ancestral Proto-Germanic tongue spoken 1,500 years ago.

Tracing Developments: The Comparative Method How do we know that English and German or French and Spanish developed from the same ancestral language? First, we can look for regular sound correspondences between two languages. We find, for example, that many words that begin with a /t/ in English correspond to words beginning with a /z/

---

*The aforesaid judge was very merciless, a persecutor of Christian men and ready to do the devil's will.

in German—*to* and *zu, ten* and *zehn, tame* and *zahm*. Or an initial /d/ in English often corresponds to a /t/ in German, as in *daughter* and *tochter, day* and *tag*. Numerous other correspondences suggest that German and English are modern variants of an older Proto-Germanic tongue. Their vocabularies include many *cognates:* words descended from a single prototype form. Similar comparisons indicate that this same ancestral language gave rise to modern Swedish, Dutch, Icelandic, Flemish, and other northern European languages as well. We have no written records of Proto-Germanic and nothing to verify the development of different Proto-Germanic dialects into the distinct languages that are spoken today. But we can reconstruct the process by tracing certain regular patterns of sound change backward through time. And we can go back still further to reconstruct the development of Proto-Germanic itself from an even earlier language.

During the early nineteenth century, in the course of collecting fairy tales from various regions of the world, Jakob Grimm noted that regular phonemic changes took place from one language to another over the centuries. He found, for example, that the Sanskrit word *brăta* ("brother") became *phrăter* in Greek, *fräter* in Latin, *brōder* in Old English, and *bratŭ* in Slavonic. Similarly, Sanskrit *ád-mi* ("eat") became Greek *édomai,* Latin *edō,* Old English *etan,* and Slavonic *jadetŭ*. Numerous regularities such as these suggest that all these languages are related. Linguists classify them as members of the same language family, Indo-European. All are descended from a single original Proto-Indo-European tongue, a language probably much like Sanskrit.

By analyzing the vocabulary of various Indo-European languages, some anthropologists have tried to reconstruct a picture of this early speech community's culture. If several related languages share a number of terms in common, at one time they probably shared the customs or artifacts to which the terms refer. Cognate words for particular kinds of plants, weather, and animals will provide clues about the type of environment in which a language family originated. For example, cognates for *snow* appear in so many modern Indo-European languages that it was undoubtedly part of the original proto-vocabulary. It is probably safe to assume, then, that the Proto-Indo-European community did not originate in a snowless southern area such as India (Bloomfield, 1933). This hypothesis is supported by the numerous cognates for trees that grow in northern climates—*oak, spruce,* and *birch,* for example. In contrast, there are few cognates for trees that grow in southern climates (Thieme, 1964). Proto-Indo-European speakers probably also had domesticated cattle and used wagons, since cognates for *milk, yoke,* and *wheel* are fairly widespread. Finally, Bloomfield has suggested that among these early speakers it was customary for married couples to live with or near the husband's relatives. This he deduced from the fact that terms for a woman's relatives by marriage (people with whom she would be in constant contact) show widespread agreement, while those for a man's in-laws (people he would see only occasionally) do not.

By comparing languages and classifying them into language families, anthropologists have discovered a good deal about the movements and historical relationships of various cultural communities. We know, for example, that the Semitic languages—which include Hebrew, Arabic, and ancient Egyptian—originated in northern Africa. At some point the Semites probably migrated to Arabia from East Africa. Subsequently, they spread throughout the Middle East, developing local dialects and eventually distinct languages.

But when did these various developments occur? Without written records, is it possible to determine precisely when a single language community began to disperse and separate languages began to develop?

Dating Techniques: Glottochronology Working with unwritten American Indian languages, Morris Swadesh developed a technique for estimating the date when two languages began to diversify. This method, called *glottochronology* or *lexicostatistics,* is based on the assumption that certain items recur in the vocabulary of every language, regardless of culture or environment. This basic word list includes terms for numerals, body parts, and geographical features. Over time, however, some of these words will change. After much trial and error, Swadesh computed that, on the average, a language will retain 81 percent of its basic vocabulary after a period of 1,000 years. Two languages that diverged from a common parent 1,000 years ago will each retain 81 percent of the original vocabulary, and they will share 66 percent of their basic word lists. We know that English and German, for example, share 59 percent of their basic vocabulary. This means that they diverged about 1,500 years ago. Nootka and Kwakiutl, two languages spoken by tribes on Vancouver Island, have a 30 percent correspondence, indicating that they diverged about 2,800 years ago.

Glottochronology has increased the possibility of investigating historical developments in language and culture. But it is also open to criticism. First, it is difficult to establish a "basic vocabulary" for all languages. Researchers have tentatively narrowed the list to about one hundred words that recur in many (but not all) languages. Second, we cannot be sure that the rate of retention is the same for all languages. The forces of change may be stronger or weaker, depending on the cultural context. An isolated language such as Icelandic changes much more slowly than Melanesian Pidgin, a language open to many outside influences. One researcher has suggested that literacy may retard the rate of vocabulary change (Zenger, 1968). Finally, glottochronology cannot tell us why specific changes occurred—why Proto-Germanic, for example, developed into Flemish in one area and English in another. Glottochronology is still an experimental method that must be tested and refined further. But it has uncovered relationships between language groups that linguists had previously been unable to trace.

Do Languages Evolve? There is no question that languages change. But do they become more efficient or more complex? Were the proto-languages of the past any simpler than their modern descendants? Apparently not. Linguists have found no evidence to indicate that the sound systems, morphology, or grammar of ancestral tongues were necessarily either more or less complex than their daughter languages. Some languages may have manifested more complex structures, but many others seem to have developed in the opposite direction, becoming simpler over the years. English is a case in point. Modern English has lost many of the inflective tendencies of Old English. For example, today we distinguish between the singular word *fire* and the plural *fires*. The same two forms are used whether they are the subject of a sentence (The fire is raging), the object of a verb (He put out the fire), or the object of a preposition (He drove to the fire). But in Old English the word fire (*fȳr*) had six different case forms. A speaker would say *fȳr, fȳre, fȳres, fȳras, fȳrum,* or *fȳra,* depending on how the word was used in a sentence.

Processes of Linguistic Change

Although languages do not evolve, they most certainly change. But what causes these changes? Some of them, as we will see, are merely the results of the accumulation of very slight and random variations that occur in every language. Others are more adaptive in nature, being related to such processes as linguistic borrowing and accommodation to new social situations and needs.

Internal Changes Sometime between 1400 and 1600, during the Middle English period, speakers of English began to alter the sounds of their vowels. This phenomenon, known as the Great English Vowel Shift, was by no means a conscious one, but nevertheless, it eventually changed every vowel sound in our language. *Bot* and *stān* (rhyming with *cot* and *con*) became today's *boat* and *stone*. *Mūs* and *cū* (sounding like *moose* and *coo*) became *mouse* and *cow*. *Wīn* and *mīn* (pronounced like *wean* and *mean*) became *wine* and *mine*.

Similar regular and consistent changes occurred in every Middle English vowel sound.

Word meanings, grammatical structures, and word order have also changed somewhat. Linguists are not entirely sure why these changes occurred. They only know that they are the result of certain gradual, internal processes. Other changes, however, were brought about through contact with other speech communities. It is easier to pinpoint the source of such *borrowed* elements.

Culture Contact and Borrowing English vocabulary is a patchwork of words borrowed from other languages. Consider the menu for an American breakfast:

A typical meal might begin with juice or fruit—perhaps *grapefruit* (a compound of two French words first put together on American soil), *melon* (of Greek origin via French), or *cantaloupe* (named after a town in Italy). Or the meal might begin with *an orange,* derived from the Arabic *naranj.* . . . After juice or fruit, the American breakfast usually consists of *cereal* (derived from *Ceres,* the Roman goddess of agriculture) or *bacon* (French) and *eggs* (Old Norse), with *toast* (French), *butter* (Latin), and *marmalade* (Portuguese). The beverage might be *coffee* (Arabic), *tea* (Chinese via Malayan Dutch), or *cocoa* (Nahuatl via Mexican Spanish). (Farb, 1974:296–297)

Borrowed words are seldom adopted wholesale, however. Pronunciation is usually changed in accordance with the native sound system and patterns of stress, tone, and nasalization. But occasionally, entirely new sounds are also borrowed. The Norman Conquest brought to the English language many words *(vile, very, venom)* beginning with the phoneme /v/. Previously an allophone of the phoneme /f/, /v/ subsequently became an English phoneme in its own right. Similarly, the vowel sound in *boil* and *coin* was originally borrowed from the French and modified over the centuries. German and Yiddish also brought changes in the distribution of certain English sounds. The initial *sch* of *schnauzer, schnapps,* and *schlemiel* is an entirely new consonant cluster built out of already familiar sounds.

One element in language change is borrowing. While colonial French will not replace the native Arabic of these Algerian children, a borrowed word here and a borrowed phrase there will contribute to that kind of slow and subtle change languages are always undergoing. (© Georg Gerster, Rapho/Photo Researchers)

The Garo language provides an extreme example of linguistic borrowing (Burling, 1970). During the last century the Garos, once an isolated group in northeast India, were abruptly forced into contact with their Bengali neighbors, British administrators, and Christian missionaries. In order to discuss the new ideas and technology brought by Europeans and Indians, Garos incorporated many of the words used by the foreigners into their language. When Garos drink *oka* (the word for tea throughout most of Asia) or *kapi* (from *coffee*), they drink it in a *kap* (from *cup*), and flavor the beverage with *dut* (from the Bengali for milk) and *chini* (from the Bengali for sugar). The numbers on a clock, the names of the months and days of the week—all are derived from Bengali. A Garo reads by the light of a *kerosin lem* (from *kerosene lamp*), writes with a *pensil* or *pawnten* (from *fountain pen*), and studies from a *kitap* (Bengali for book). However, all of these borrowed words are arranged in Garo grammatical patterns. The basic structure of the language has remained essentially unchanged despite extensive modifications in vocabulary. In every language, grammar is much more resistant to borrowing than are either words or sounds.

The Garo example is but one of many that could be chosen to illustrate how variations in languages come about. Much of linguistic change is adaptive. People throughout the world use language to communicate; when communication is hindered by old forms or by the lack of important new elements, adaptations are made until the language is again an efficient means of expression.

The Ecology of Language

Every time a person asks for pie a la mode or says, "You will not go," instead of "Thou shalt not go," he or she is demonstrating that our language, like all others, is not a static set of rules, but a variable, ever-changing system of communication. As we have seen, speakers of a language will adapt their system of communication in response to new situations and new needs. If languages could not adapt, the ability of people to communicate would be severely restricted. In considering adaptations in language, it is important to recognize that such changes do not occur only as a result of contact between different language communities. People in every society are constantly adapting their patterns of speech to suit different social situations. As an example, we have only to consider the numerous terms people use to address one another, the choice of terms generally depending on the relative status of the individuals involved.

On different occasions the same man may be variously called *Professor Johnson, James,* *Jimmy, Father, Daddy, sir, darling,* or *buddy.* Not all these terms can be used interchangeably because each carries different social connotations. The man's wife would rarely say, "Good morning, *Professor Johnson.*" His son would never call him *darling.* And his students would probably not call him James; this term is reserved for colleagues, family (excluding children), and people of the same social standing. In casual conversation, male friends might simply call him *Johnson,* but female friends normally would not. His parents might use a term of endearment like *Jimmy* or *sonny.* What speakers say is limited not only by the strict definition of a word, by rules of grammar, or by the conceptual categories in their language, but also by social conventions and the setting. A person's choice of words will be influenced by the occasion, by notions of propriety, and by his or her relationship with or attitudes toward the listener; yet another factor is whether the speaker is addressing someone directly or merely talking about him or her.

In America there are two main patterns of address: title plus last name *(Professor Johnson, Ms. Jones),* and first name alone. This system tries to do two things at the same time: to signal both the degree of intimacy and the relative status between the speaker and the person being addressed. This can create problems. For example, if a younger colleague joins the faculty at Professor Johnson's college, she may have trouble finding an appropriate term at first. If she says *Professor Johnson* out of respect for their age difference, she is falsely indicating that Johnson has a higher social status. If she uses *James,* however, she is suggesting that they are closer friends than they have actually become.

An English speaker can usually get around such problems by avoiding any term of address at all. A Javanese, however, is absolutely obliged to indicate his or her social relationship to the listener every time he or she speaks. There are three social levels of speech in Javanese, and a person must decide which to use before speaking to someone. This is much more complicated than choosing a term of address or deciding whether to use the intimate or polite form of *you,* as in French *(vous, tu)* or German *(Sie, du).* Many common Javanese words such as *rice, house, now,* and *eat* have three entirely different forms. For "house," there is a plain form *(omah),* a fancy form *(grija),* and an elegant form *(dalem).* In this order, each term indicates an increasingly greater status distance between the speaker and listener. Two close friends of roughly equal rank would probably use the plain form. If they were not well acquainted, they might use the fancy form out of politeness. A government official will use the plain form in addressing a peasant. The peasant, however, must reply in the elegant form, in deference to the official's superior rank. To make matters more complicated, each dialect of Javanese is also ranked separately. Thus speakers convey status meaning not only by a choice of plain, fancy, or elegant word forms, but also by the dialect spoken as a whole (Geertz, 1960).

Speech Situations

Entering a speech community, then, involves more than simply learning the grammar and vocabulary of the language. Until a speaker understands the rules for adapting speech patterns to suit different situations, full communication will be impossible.

Often a speaker's choice of words is determined by the formality of the occasion. When casually introducing one friend to another, we might say, "Hey, Joe, meet my old college roommate, Judy." But if we were introducing Judy as an after-dinner speaker at a formal supper party, we might say something like "Ladies and gentlemen, it gives me great pleasure to introduce my close friend and esteemed colleague, Dr. Judith Spiel." Often our pronunciation changes in a more formal setting. A study made by John Fischer in a small New England town (1958) revealed that even children under the age of eleven respond to the formality of a situation by changing their pronunciation of the *-ing* and *-in* verb suffixes.

Fischer also found that girls used the *-ing* form twice as often as boys did. Apparently this pronunciation was regarded as more feminine. In English a few expressions like *goodness gracious* and *dear me,* and the intensifiers *so* and *such* ("It was *such* a delightful party!") are regarded as characteristically feminine. Similar "female" expressions have been noted in German, Danish, Russian, and French. Many languages make even sharper distinctions between male and female speech forms.

Usually, differences between male and

Computers not only enable us to count the number of words in Shakespeare's vocabulary or decipher ancient tongues and secret codes. They have generated a host of new words (print-outs, hardware, software, and flow diagrams among them) and even new "languages," such as FORTRAN and others technicians use to communicate with the machines. New technology is one of the things that forces languages to expand and change.
(Burt Glinn/Magnum)

female speech involve not just pronunciation or vocabulary, but ways of speaking. For example, among the Yakinankarate of Madagascar, males strive for diplomacy in speech. They are discreet, hide their feelings, and avoid open confrontations. This is the avowed ideal form of speech behavior. Female speech, however, does not live up to this ideal. Women are expected to express their emotions directly and bluntly. This has earned them the epithet "long tongues." Although they may not be aware of it, women actually have little choice in the matter. Whenever direct confrontations are unavoidable, the men incite females to handle the unpleasantness in their behalf; women are also expected to do the haggling in the marketplace and to reprimand children (Farb, 1974). In many cultures, however, the reverse is true. Women are expected to be quieter and more discreet than men. Among the Araucanian Indians of Chile, men are expected to be good conversationalists and orators. Since speaking is a sign of male intelligence and leadership, they are expected to speak often and well. Women, on the other hand, are supposed to be submissive and quiet. While men gather together to talk volubly, the women sit quietly, speaking to one another in whispers. A new wife is not permitted to speak at all. For the first few months of marriage, she sits quietly, facing the wall, avoiding direct eye contact with anyone (Hymes, 1972).

In general, male and female speech differences were apparently much sharper in the past than they are today. Possibly this is because more women are working outside the home, and the social lives of men and women are less separate than in the past. No one has found a definite answer as to why men and women speak differently in the first place, however. Studies of sex distinctions among English speakers have all come to the same conclusion: in comparison with men in the same social, educational, and age categories, women tend to use forms of speech considered more prestigious. But why? One researcher suggests that because the social status of women is less secure and apparent (they cannot be rated by their occupation or wealth as readily as men can), they signal their status by indirect means such as speech. Men, on the other hand, are less concerned with correct or refined form than with displaying "masculine" speech, typically associated with rougher, nonstandard forms (Trudgill, 1972).

The Prestige Factor

While Americans have borrowed some words from the languages spoken by European immigrants *(delicatessen, pizza, chile con carne),* for the most part these groups have incorporated a much larger number of English expressions into their own speech. In part this is because English is the dominant language of the country. But it is also true that people often imitate the speech of those whom they admire. In eastern Burma, tribal peoples are quite apt to learn Shan, a dialect of Thai spoken by members of a higher social class. But Shans rarely bother to learn any tribal languages. Sometimes both tribal peoples and Shans learn Burmese, the language spoken by the most politically influential group. Few Burmese, however, learn Shan, and fewer still learn the tribal languages (Leach, 1954). The lower-ranked groups, in other words, are adopting the speech of the social elite.

Social status, then, is another factor that determines speech habits. Until recently most New Yorkers, like other residents of major Eastern cities, did not pronounce /r/ when it preceded a consonant or fell at the end of a word. The word *bartender,* for example, would be pronounced something like *ba-tenda.* Since World War II, however, it has become more prestigious to pronounce the /r/, a mark of upper-class speech. To determine the correspondence between social class and /r/ pronunciation, William Labov (1972) made a study of three New York department stores patronized by people of different classes. He found that salespeople at Saks Fifth Avenue (upper-middle class) pronounced /r/ far more frequently than those at

Macy's (lower-middle class), and the clerks at Macy's more often than those at Klein's (lower class). In another study of speakers from Manhattan's Lower East Side, Labov (1964) found that the higher a person's social class, the more likely he was to pronounce /r/ in both casual and formal situations. But he found that the lower-middle class, the group most concerned with improving its social status, used /r/ more than any other group (including the upper-middle class) in formal situations when they were particularly conscious of their speech. In casual conversation with friends, however, they frequently dropped the /r/ form. Members of this class are also less consistent in pronouncing words like *tomato, vase,* and *aunt,* switching between the speech they learned as children and the upper-middle-class speech they aspire to. Asked to pronounce the word *vase,* one woman solved the problem neatly, telling the interviewer, "These little ones are my *vayses,* but these big ones are my *vahses.*"

Levine and Crockett (1967) found a similar pattern in a North Carolina town, where the most upwardly mobile members of the community pronounced postvocalic /r/ more often. Neither of these studies suggests why pronouncing /r/ has become a more prestigious speech pattern, but they do indicate that this form is becoming more widespread in America, and they suggest something about the way in which language adapts and changes.

summary

All human beings share the ability to use language. And all cultures, no matter how "primitive" they may seem, use languages capable of articulating and transmitting the most complex ideas and emotions. This shared potential does not, however, imply a uniformity of sounds, words, or structure among all languages, as anyone who has ever tried to speak a foreign language will realize. Through the analysis of particular categories of linguistic data, linguists seek not only to understand the structure of a given language, but also to compare it with others.

Languages may, first of all, be distinguished in terms of the set of sounds and sound contrasts that they use. Each language has its unique system of sound contrasts, called *phonemes,* which enable speakers to differentiate meaning in otherwise like-sounding words. When two sounds are phonetically distinct but are not used contrastively to distinguish meaning, they are known as *allophones*.

Language as a means of communication is, of course, concerned with more than sound systems. In further elucidating the structure of language, linguists concern themselves with the grammar of a language—how its phonemes are combined to construct words *(morphology)* and how words are arranged to form phrases and sentences *(syntax)*. When phonemes are combined in an appropriate way, they convey meaning. We use the term *morpheme* to speak of the smallest unit of speech conveying meaning. Morphemes may include a range of forms, or *allomorphs*.

Some languages are quite complex morphologically, and one word may be sufficient to express a complicated meaning. But English in its grammar relies more heavily on syntax, the rules governing the order of subject, verb, object, adjectives, and adverbs in a sentence. Every language has its own rules determining how these elements are ordered. Each person who speaks a language responds intuitively to these rules, even if he or she could not consciously articulate them. This intuitive grasp enables us to generate new sentences and to understand words and ideas that we have never heard before.

Linked to this ability to say new things is an ability to say the same things in different ways.

Conversely, we may express a diverse range of meanings while using the same words in the same order. In an attempt to understand these transformational aspects of language, Noam Chomsky has posited two levels of structure in every sentence: a surface structure and an underlying, more abstract deep structure. The observation that humans are capable of discerning the underlying meaning of even ambiguous statements has led Chomsky to the belief that we carry within us a blueprint for language. Some linguists have gone so far as to suggest that all languages share a common deep structure.

Researchers are concerned primarily not with single words and their definitions, but with whole categories of words and how their meanings relate to one another. These categories of semantically related terms, called *semantic domains,* yield important insights into the way particular societies view their world. *Ethnosemantics* attempts to study, from the emic point of view, how different societies group experiences into domains and how they employ different criteria to distinguish between the various terms in these domains.

The question of linguistic variation has proved to be problematical. Evidently, differences between languages in neighboring communities are not so distinct as we once thought. Variations exist, but they are gradual rather than absolute. On the other hand, individual languages are not so homogeneous as was once asserted. Regional differences abound, as do variations between the language of different social classes or that of men and women. The basic structure of a language actually changes very slowly; nevertheless, over time, languages have manifested extensive changes. If we apply the comparative method and watch for correspondences between the vocabularies of two languages, we may find that they share many cognates, indicating a common ancestral tongue. By tracing certain regular patterns of sound change backward through time, we can reconstruct the process whereby the dialects of a language evolved into distinct languages.

The recognition that languages are related has been useful to anthropologists in attempting to reconstruct the culture of early speech communities. They have also, through comparison of languages and their classification into language families, discovered much about the movements and historical relationships of various cultural communities. Recently, Morris Swadesh has developed a statistical method of estimating the date at which two languages began to diversify. This technique, called *glottochronology* or *lexicostatistics,* has increased the possibility of investigating historical developments in language and culture.

Gradual changes in language that do occur may then be understood as arising from a complex of factors. Some are due to poorly understood internal processes, others to contact with foreign cultures and the subsequent borrowing of terms. Adaptive changes also occur to maintain a language as an efficient and effective means of communication.

Because it is a flexible means of communication, language is responsive to the particular social situation in which it is being used. This extends even to the pronunciation of words. It has been observed, for example, that women tend to use more formal speech expressions than men do. Many languages, in fact, make sharp distinctions not only between male and female pronunciation, but also between male and female vocabulary. A final element in adaptive change is the prestige factor—the fact that the language used by the social elites in a culture tends to filter down to the classes below. Our social status, too, has a close connection with our speech habits.

suggested readings

CHOMSKY, N.
1969 *Aspects of the Theory of Syntax.* Cambridge, Mass.: M.I.T. Press. Presents the principles of transformational grammar particularly as they apply to syntax.

GIGLIONI, P. P., ED.
1972 *Language and Social Context.* London: Nicholls. An especially able treatment of the relationship between linguistic behavior and particular sociocultural variables.

GUMPERZ, J., AND HYMES, D., EDS.
1965 The Ethnography of Communication. *American Anthropologist,* vol. 67, no. 6, part 2 (special issue). Essays in this volume describe language behavior in specific communicative contexts.

HYMES, D., ED.
1964 *Language in Culture and Society.* New York: Harper & Row. A general survey of linguistics, containing some especially important articles on sociolinguistics.

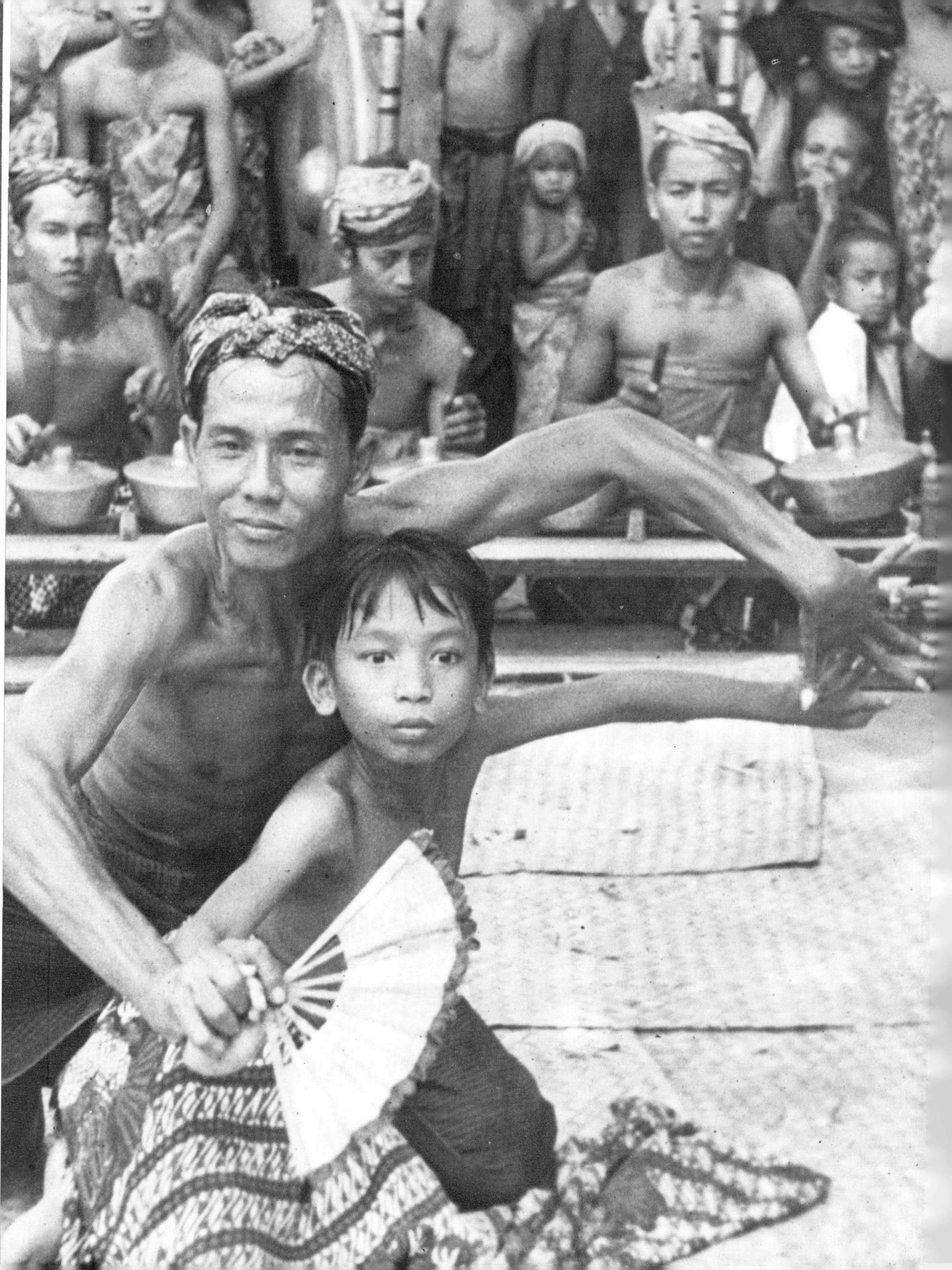

fifteen
Culture and the Individual

Quite obviously, no two people are exactly alike. Looks, mannerisms, public and private motives, talents, hang-ups, lifestyles, experiences remembered and forgotten all contribute to the sense of individuality we have about ourselves and others. To an outsider, however, the similarities between us and our family members, fellow students, fellow city dwellers, or countrymen might outweigh the differences. People all over the world speak of "crazy Americans" with knowing looks. Although their meaning might elude us, we can usually recognize a compatriot abroad, just as we can readily distinguish between an English person and a Spaniard. Yet the differences between members of different societies can be overstated. With a little patient translation, we can almost always establish some common ground with a German, a Watusi, a Samoan, or a Japanese — after all, we are all human.

Every person may be thought of as being, in certain respects, like no one else; in other respects, like some other people; and in still other respects, like all other people (Kluckhohn and Murray, 1953). For the most part, anthropologists are concerned with the ways in which people are like some other people (the traits of a given culture) and like all other people (the universals of human behavior). We study social aggregates and are not directly concerned with the unique aspects of each and every human being. But a careful balance between similarity and diversity of individual behavior is necessary for survival in all societies. In this chapter, therefore, we will consider how biology, social learning, and the ability to think, decide, and act create similarities and differences among people.

The Influence of Biology on Human Behavior

Although all animals have the capacity to learn, much of the behavior of certain animal species is significantly influenced by instinct. Even in dogs, animals with considerable capacity for altering their behavior through learning, we find instinct at work. For instance, dogs living in high-rise city apartments will circle around and around before settling onto the living-room carpet—an action originally used to chase away snakes. Generations of controlled breeding and pampering have not erased this instinct. Instinctive behavior in less "social" species has been well documented. In the period immediately following birth, goslings will attach themselves to anyone or anything who produces the proper quacks—including naturalist Konrad Lorenz, who became an unnatural "Mother Goose" for a small brood. Lorenz and others have shown time and again that animals raised in isolation from their kind will perform exceedingly complex behavior patterns they have had no opportunity to learn. They are genetically programmed to respond in a certain way to a certain stimulus. Is this also true for humans? Is our behavior, too, motivated by inherited biological imperatives?

The process by which new members of a society are taught the attitudes, values, behaviors, and skills upon which that society is based is called socialization or enculturation. It is a lifelong and culturally variable process, beginning at birth and continuing until the death of the individual. Here, through both modeling and explicit instruction, a Balinese dancer trains a pupil in one of his culture's most expressive arts. (Gregory Bateson and Margaret Mead, *Balinese Character,* New York Academy of Sciences, 1942)

On a very basic level, the answer is yes. All human beings are born with certain fundamental biological drives. We cannot survive for very long without food and water, rest and sleep, and our body chemistry pressures us to fill these needs. We get hunger pains when our blood sugar is low; there are times when no amount of effort will keep our eyes open. Hormones stimulate our sexual desires; how we express and satisfy these desires, whether we do, and whether our satisfactions result in offspring are variable. Nature has not locked us into a single, unchanging mating dance, as it has other species. But we are biologically endowed with preprogrammed survival mechanisms, and these contribute to the success of our species.

Basic drives are not our only biological adaptive mechanisms. The need for social contact is as basic to humans as the needs for food, rest, and sexual satisfaction. Children require attention from other human beings in order to develop normally.[1] Institutionalized infants are slow to learn how to sit up, grasp objects, and walk, and are often undersized, even though they receive adequate nutrition. Totally dependent on others for an extended period, human infants usually become extremely attached to the person who cares for them (not necessarily their mother). In our society, at least, they go through a stage when separation from this caretaker makes them intensely anxious. The infant's joy in being handled and fussed over lays the foundation for a widening circle of attachments in the coming years (Bowlby, 1969). Although a small number of adults choose to remove themselves from human society in varying degrees, isolation causes most people acute psychological stress. We seem impelled to live in social groups—a fact that improves our chances of survival.

To these two biological imperatives—basic drives and the need for social contact—we might add a third, what Eugene d'Aquili (1972) calls the "cognitive imperative." According to d'Aquili, cognition is the "supreme adaptive specialization" characteristic of our species. Our brains have evolved in such a way as to permit problem solving, conceptualization, and complex communication through language. The ability of people everywhere to impose order on their observations is not simply a cultural phenomenon. It reflects the biologically rooted cognitive imperative, the unique structure of our brains which allows us to construct this order. As humans, we become acutely anxious if we cannot impose order—at least in our minds—upon the bewildering array of stimuli that reach us from the outside. Thus, we have invented magic, religion, science, and political philosophy; we have become cultural animals.

All people, then, share certain biological traits that in part account for the broad similarities in human behavior. But biological makeup also accounts for behavioral differences. On the individual level, a person's build, health, and stamina affect his or her ability to perform certain kinds of activities. For example, malnutrition during the first years of life prevents full development of the brain, and in extreme cases may cause mental retardation. And even if people eat well, some are simply not strong enough to work as stevedores or professional athletes, just as some lack the manual dexterity to assemble minute transistors or perform intricate passages on the piano. Biology sets outside limits on individual capabilities that exercise and practice cannot always overcome.

We are beginning to learn more about the biological correlates of certain kinds of behavior. Some of this knowledge has been acquired through the study of behavior disorders. It has been discovered, for example, that when people are severely depressed, their nerve cells do not fire as quickly as they normally do, so their general level of activity is repressed. It has also been found that deficiencies of the vitamin B complex can have significant effects on the nervous system, causing confused thought processes, severe

---

[1] This is also true of our nearest relatives in the animal kingdom, the apes and monkeys.

anxiety, and exhaustion. Massive doses of nicotinic acid, a component of the B complex, are now being used in the treatment of schizophrenia. In addition, many kinds of psychological disturbances have been traced to biochemical imbalances in the brain. An absence of lithium in the brain chemistry, for instance, can cause psychotic symptoms, and lithium is now widely prescribed to control manic episodes. Even the amount of sugar in our blood can affect behavior. It has been shown that blood sugar level is an important factor underlying certain kinds of aggression. In short, biological factors affect individual behavior in ways that most of us are only superficially aware of.

The Extent of Biological Influences on Behavior

Although there is no doubt that biology affects behavior, it can be extremely difficult to establish the exact extent of its influence when we look at real events in human life. Often, behavior patterns that we attribute largely to cultural or other causes turn out to have very important biological dimensions, as Foulks (1972) discovered in his investigation of arctic hysteria.

Arctic Hysteria Interestingly, "madness" takes distinctive twists and turns in different parts of the world. The term "arctic hysteria" refers to fits of frenzied, uncontrolled activity and incoherent speech that sometimes overtake Eskimos in remote northern villages. Researchers have usually considered this a psychological phenomenon. It is easy for an outsider to imagine "going crazy" from sensory deprivation in this silent, barren land, with its unbroken horizon and its months of darkness. Moreover, in small, close-knit villages the slightest deviation from normal behavior is subject to high-pitched ridicule—the kind of repressive social environment we associate with psychological problems. Foulks found, however, that biological factors may play a significant role in arctic hysteria.

Exposure to the ultraviolet component of sunlight stimulates the skin to produce vitamin D, which is essential to calcium metabolism. But Eskimos cover everything but their faces with thick clothing that shuts out light. Over prolonged periods, and especially during the dark winter, the low calcium level in the blood produces dysfunctions in the central nervous system. In addition, the coal stoves Eskimos use to heat the wood shacks they have lived in ever since they came in contact with Europeans create a dry atmosphere that makes them highly susceptible to respiratory infections and fevers. These disorders also affect the nervous system, in extreme cases causing retardation, hyperactivity, inability to control emotions, hypersensitivity to drugs, and epileptic-type seizures—symptoms associated with arctic hysteria.

As the example of arctic hysteria illustrates, it is often easy to overlook certain of the complex of factors that contribute to particular behavior patterns. And it is as easy to overlook or misunderstand cultural influences as biological ones. The issue of sex roles provides an excellent example. Just as researchers for many years ignored the biological aspects of arctic hysteria, so too have many people long ignored the social and cultural dimensions of sex roles and "sex-linked" personality traits.

Sex-linked Traits Americans, like people in most societies, have traditionally held very stereotyped notions about the "innate" abilities and personality characteristics of men and women. Men have been viewed as aggressive, tough, logical, and independent; women as passive, sensitive, intuitive, and supportive. On the basis of these assumptions we have traditionally justified a parallel set of appropriate roles for the members of each sex—homemaker, nurse, receptionist for women; truckdriver, doctor, business executive for men.

Although many people imagine that the biological differences between men and women are very clear-cut, this is really not the case. Males and females do have distinct sex chromosomes (XX for females, XY for males), but for the first eight weeks after conception the fetus is undifferentiated, and although it is basically femalelike, it has the rudiments of both male and female sex organs. Sex hormones determine how the fetus develops—testosterone and androgens produce males; estrogen and progesterone, females. With the onset of puberty, males and females both produce all of these hormones, including those associated with the opposite sex, in varying degrees. The key point is variation. Sex is multidimensional: it involves genes, hormones, and anatomy, in various levels and combinations. Thus there is great variation within the sexes, as well as between them. Generalizations based on a simple male/female dichotomy overlook this fact.

In addition, there is abundant evidence that femininity and masculinity (the personality traits we associate with females and males) have little to do with biology. Over forty years ago, Margaret Mead discovered a tribe in New Guinea where both men and women were emotional, gentle, and nurturant—characteristics we consider "feminine." Even more interesting was a neighboring tribe where the women were practical and aggressive (in sexual as well as other matters); their men, sensitive, submissive, and exceedingly vain—the exact opposite of the traits attributed to men and women in our own society. Mead concluded that masculinity and femininity reflect the manner in which children are taught to think of their sex. They are cultural constructs, not biological givens (Mead, 1935). John Money's studies of hermaphrodites and children who were assigned the wrong sex at birth because of anatomical abnormalities further support this conclusion. In all the cases, the children accepted the sexual identity that had been assigned to them, regardless of their genes, hormones, and anatomy (Money et al., 1967).

Why, then, do most societies teach girls to be docile, boys to be independent? Why do societies assign women to household chores and positions behind the throne; men to business, political, and religious leadership, and other dominant roles? One often cited reason is that it is women who bear and nurse children. This restricts women's mobility to some extent, making it convenient for them to orient their lives around the home. Some biologists and anthropologists suggest that this pattern increases a woman's reproductive success: by gearing her life around the time-consuming tasks of child care, she can increase her children's chances for survival.

Another reason posited for the traditional distribution of roles has been the greater physical strength of men in warfare. According to anthropologist Marvin Harris, "We are still living with the remnants of male supremacy because we have not yet emerged from the phase of human evolution in which the physical strength of males was necessary for cultural survival" (Harris in Tavris, 1975:66).

The reduced importance for survival of these biological factors illustrates that, at present, learning plays a far more significant role than biology in the majority of the behavioral differences that we associate with the sexes. The stereotypes of the passive female and the assertive or aggressive male are very much alive, however, not only in our own culture but in most others as well. Once such patterns become established, they are difficult to perceive and even more difficult to challenge or change. Children learn who and what they are in a social context; the dictates of their culture soon become, in a very real sense, "second nature."

The Influence of Culture and Social Learning on Behavior

A few years ago, a researcher by the name of James Tenzel, who was investigating attitudes toward disease in a Guatemalan village, found himself in a rather awkward position. With perfectly straight faces, villager after villager told him about an illness that causes spines to grow on a person's head. Try as he might, Tenzel was unable to see the spines when informants pointed out afflicted individuals. Were the villagers pulling his leg? (Examples of local people amusing themselves at an anthropologist's expense are legion.) Tenzel concluded they were not: these Mayan people *saw* spines (Tenzel, 1970). There is little doubt that if he had explained the germ theory of disease to the villagers, insisting that tiny organisms invisible to the naked eye cause illness, they would have been equally incredulous.

The fact is, people from different cultures learn to view the world quite differently. Surprisingly, even visual perception, which most people assume to be a strictly physiological process, is in fact greatly influenced by social learning. Research confirms this. A. C. Mundy-Castle (1966), for example, showed four simple line drawings, like the ones in Figure 15–1, to a group of Ghanaian youngsters. Any Western child of seven or eight looking at these pictures would perceive that the elephant is some distance beyond the man and the deer in all four drawings. But the Ghanaian children saw nothing of the sort. To them it was obvious that the man in Card 1, for example, could not see the deer because the hill blocked his line of vision. The fact that the elephant was small in proportion to the other figures did not evoke the impression of distance in their minds. Mundy-Castle associates this two-dimensional perception with a lack of experience with picture books, drawing materials, and the like. Perceiving depth in a drawing on a flat surface is an acquired skill. What the Ghanaian children lacked was familiarity with a certain symbolic technique, a particular, culturally learned way of constructing reality. Although this technique may be perfectly common to Europeans, it is by no means a cultural universal (D'Andrade, 1973).

It is evident that we do not see the world around us directly. The way we see reality is shaped by the way our society teaches us to structure that reality. The logical next question is, Does social learning also shape the way we think?

A number of anthropologists have given close attention to the crucial relationship between culture and thinking. In 1910 the French sociologist/anthropologist Lucien Levy-Bruhl formulated a theory of "primitive" thinking. According to him, "primitive mentality," as found among the peoples of tribal Africa, is incapable of distinguishing between

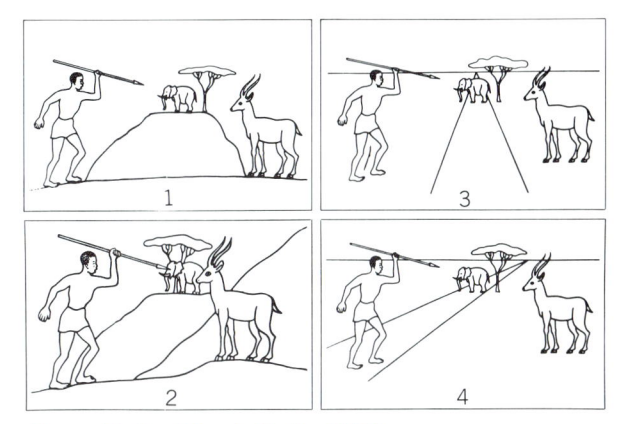

Figure 15–1. (Mundy-Castle, 1966)

the subjective and the objective components of the real world. Levy-Bruhl concluded that this *prelogical* mode of thinking, as he called it, explained why primitive societies so often accounted for illness or misfortune in terms of magic and witchcraft; they simply had not yet developed the intellectual sophistication of the civilized Westerner.

At about the same time that Levy-Bruhl began publishing, the American anthropologist Franz Boas was coming to virtually the opposite conclusion. Boas acknowledged that any mind would be shaped in part by the process of social learning: even the existence of what we call mind was "unthinkable" in the absence of culture. Nevertheless, Boas rejected the idea that the traditions and customs of a culture can tell us about the thought processes of individuals. He concluded, rather, that there is no significant difference in function between the mind of an African or Amerindian and that of a European or American. If ethnologists believed they had found such a difference, it was the result of poor observation or, quite likely, prejudice.

In our society this debate is very much alive, especially among educators. Clear differences have been observed between well-to-do white Americans on the one hand and so-called culturally disadvantaged groups on the other, in terms of educational achievement and measured I.Q. According to the "social pathology" theorists, such minority groups as

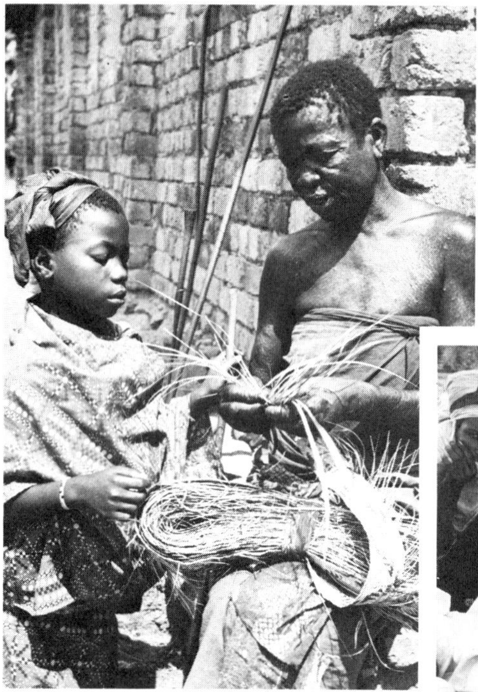

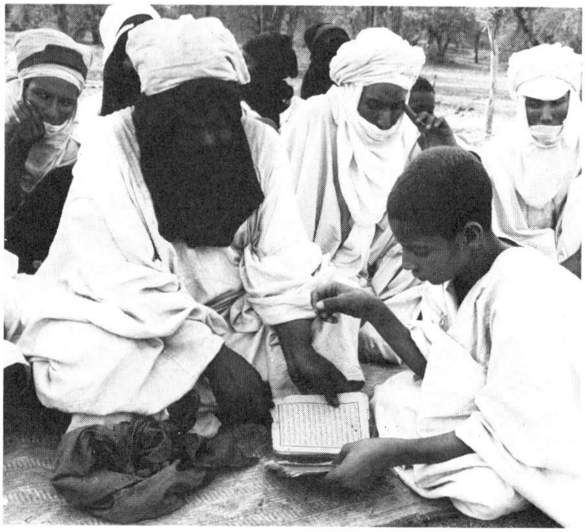

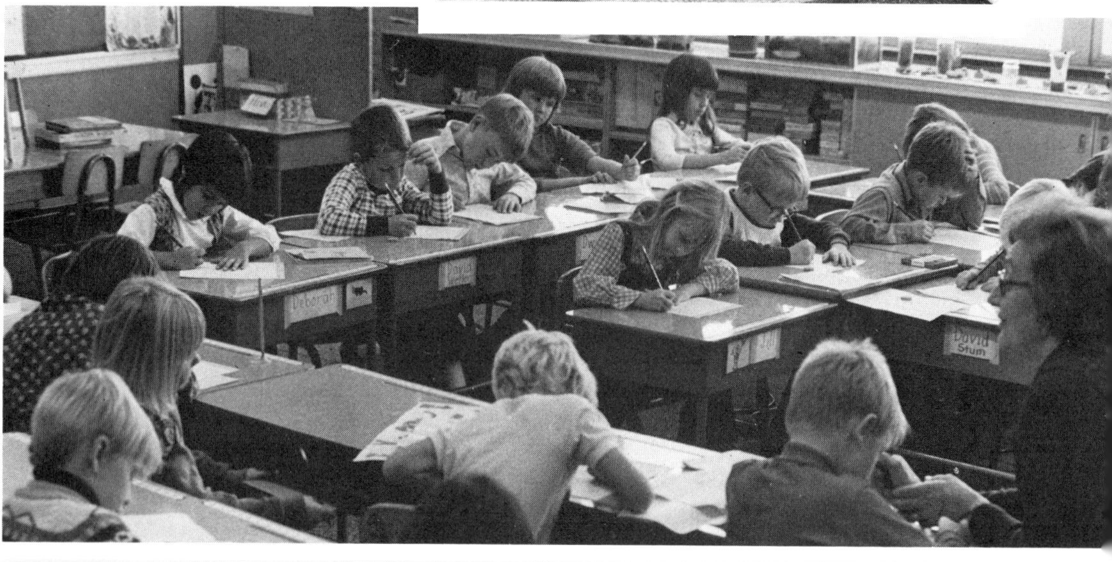
Deborah
David
Stum

blacks, Indians, and Latin Americans suffer from stunted cognitive development: their cultural background will not prepare them to concentrate patiently on intellectual tasks, and they do not learn to use language as a tool of thought (see Jensen, 1969; Deutsch, 1969).

To this argument Cole et al. (1971) respond with the suggestion, similar to Boas's rebuttal of Levy-Bruhl, that there is no clear evidence that *any* cultural group has abilities that are missing from others. Rather, the testing situation itself may reflect an unintentional cultural bias, so that the minority children make a poor showing not because they lack cognitive abilities but because they are unfamiliar with the categories or presentation of the test.

Thus at the moment it is not possible to present a more definite answer to our initial question. Individuals from different cultures obviously do think differently, but there is no way to show clearly that their thought processes themselves are different. What is clear is that every culture is unique in what it does teach its children and in how they are taught. This process of imparting the group's culture to each generation of children is referred to as *socialization* or *enculturation*.

The Process of Socialization

Socialization is the process whereby a person acquires the technical skills of his or her society, the knowledge of the kinds of behavior people in that society understand and find acceptable, and the attitudes and values that make going to school or work and abiding by social rules personally meaningful, even gratifying. It involves both explicit instruction and unconscious, sometimes unwitting, modeling by the family and by society as a whole. Although the particular manner of socialization varies around the world, its effect is everywhere much the same: a helpless, ill-mannered, uninformed infant is transformed into a knowledgeable and more or less cooperative and productive member of society. Thus socialization is the process whereby a society reproduces itself in a new generation.

It would be a mistake, however, to view human infants as complete blank slates. As we noted earlier, many social scientists today argue that humans are biologically endowed with a cognitive imperative, a predisposition to classify and organize phenomena in the world around them. In this regard, Swiss psychologist Jean Piaget (1958) has suggested that for children in all societies cognitive development follows a basically similar set of stages. From birth to two years of age, children acquire a basic understanding of their physical selves and their surroundings, learning to modify behavior in response to a relatively gross perception of the environment. Then, during ages two to seven, children learn to classify phenomena, but at this stage they have only a limited notion of what the bases for classification are. Over the next four years of maturation, ages seven to eleven, children begin to classify with a clear understanding of the criteria used to define categories. And finally, beyond age eleven, they are able to grasp abstract concepts, principles, and theories and to manipulate them in solving complex problems. Thus the kinds of things children are capable of learning depend in part on their level of maturity.

Within these basic stages of cognitive development, however, there is a wide diversity in both what children learn and how they are taught it. Such diversity exists not only between different societies but to some extent for every individual in the same society. In our

---

Education is not just the teaching of the technical skills necessary for survival — it is part of the socialization process itself. This process may be informal or formal, as is illustrated by these three photographs. Socialization by observation and imitation is an informal and often unconscious method common to all societies. The Congolese girl learns to weave straw matting by watching her grandmother. In a slightly more formal way, the Tuareg nomad boy learns to read the Koran in Arabic from his father and the village elders. In western societies, much social learning takes place in the formal framework of a classroom. (Leon V. Kofod; Marc and Evelyne Bernheim/Woodfin Camp; David Strickler/Monkmeyer)

own culture, for example, some children are brought up strictly. Parents tell them what to do and bribe, threaten, even beat them into conformity. Other parents are affectionate and more patient with their children's failures, allowing them to learn gradually. Children are also influenced by their other relatives, as well as by friends, neighbors, and the entire community in which they are raised. Variations in the methods of socialization used by people of different ethnic groups, regions, or economic standings can produce variations in how the children of these groups think and act. But despite such intergroup differences, there are broad similarities in how and what Americans are taught about their culture— enough similarities that a wealthy city dweller from the East might well share many values and traits with a middle-class farmer from the West. These similarities strike us most forcefully when we are abroad, where regional or class differences within a country often seem insignificant compared to the nationwide similarities we perceive.

It is important to remember that the process of socialization involves more than simply the training of young children. In every society the task of learning one's culture commences at birth and continues throughout childhood, involving more and more of the community until the individual is ready to assume the responsibilities of adult life. But the process does not stop there; throughout our lives we are constantly being educated and reeducated into new roles and statuses. Yet although there are certain broad similarities in the kinds of socialization people around the world receive, no two cultures use exactly the same methods or teach the same ideas.

Child-Rearing Practices Those responsible for raising children (usually the parents) teach and train them, turning the basic drives and instincts of infancy into socially acceptable behaviors. Children must be weaned; they must learn the general customs associated with elimination, sex, and the expression of aggression; and finally, they must learn a certain degree of independence from their parents and family. The most obvious way in which this training varies from culture to culture is in its harshness or severity. Are children permitted to simply grow out of their infant behaviors, or are they compelled in one way or another to drop them? Variations in the degree of severity are enormous. Among the Kwoma of New Guinea, for example, children are not toilet-trained until they are old enough to simply be told how to go about it, usually age five or six. The Dahomeans, on the other hand, will beat children of four who wet their beds. Sometimes the differences are truly startling. The Marquesan Islanders of Polynesia wean their children at six months; the American middle class, at about eight months; the Chenchu tribe of India, at six years; and among the Lepcha of India, it is not unknown to nurse until the age of puberty (Whiting and Child, 1953).

Some societies are generally more severe or indulgent in all things, but for the most part, a culture will indulge children in one respect and be severe in another. Anal training might be harsh and abrupt while the same society will allow children to grow out of dependence gradually. The Marquesans, for example, one of the most severe cultures in weaning practices, are indulgent in sexual training, encouraging early sex play and masturbating children to quiet them. On the other hand, the Kurtatchi of New Guinea are severe in sexual training and indulgent in weaning. Our own culture is relatively strict in both. In fact, there is little predictability that severity or indulgence in any aspect of child rearing will lead to severity or indulgence in any other aspect.

Education Child-rearing practices involve training and teaching, but the education of any individual extends well beyond the channeling of basic drives. Education involves "the transmission of the knowledge, understanding, attitudes, sentiments, and ways of doing things that characterize a particular society" (Goldschmidt, 1971). From parents, neighbors, and friends, and from religious and civic ceremonies, a child learns what he can expect in life and what is expected of him or her. He or she begins to learn particular ways of behaving and acting, as well as new skills and capabilities.

Education takes many forms. In our culture, for example, we learn informally, even unconsciously, from our parents and others. They may instruct us or simply provide an example of a behavior which we emulate. But our culture also utilizes a formal system of education. Until age sixteen, everyone is expected to attend school. Instruction is provided by teachers, specialists whose primary role is to teach us skills—reading, physics, medicine, and so on. At the same time, schools teach proper behavior, such as waiting in line or sitting quietly while a teacher is speaking, as well as attitudes and values, such as hard work and obedience to authority.

Most societies have no formal schools or educational specialists; nearly anyone may adopt the role of teacher. Skills as well as attitudes are learned "on the job" or through observation. Yurok women, for example, are skilled basket makers. Young girls watch their elders and without being told or prodded often begin to imitate them. In time, they receive more direct help, but they develop their expertise without formal education or training (O'Neale, 1932).

A considerable amount of cultural information is in fact learned through observation and imitation. The way people walk or talk will, for example, correspond to the way others of their region or economic status walk and talk. A Scot cannot be mistaken for a Londoner after he has spoken, and perhaps even before he has spoken. Other cultural traits are also thought to be acquired in the same manner. Thus a Crow Indian learns to be exceptionally generous, a Yurok comparably stingy (Kluckhohn, 1949).

Rites of Passage One of the most effective means of socialization is the participation of people in ceremonies that mark their induction into a new role. Such *rites of passage* give the person a sense of identification with his or her new status, a notion that privileges and obligations are not merely abstractions but are to be translated into action.

Particular rites of passage vary from society to society, just as other methods of enculturation do. They may be marked with very little ceremony or other fanfare, or they may involve elaborate ritual, even feats of endurance intended to prove that the initiates have the personal qualities needed to assume their new roles.

In our own culture, there are many rites of passage, although in most cases we do not see them that way. A Scout initiation, for example, marks the passage from very young childhood into an age category to which greater responsibilities toward the community are attached. Graduation from school is probably the most common of our rites—one that many people experience at three or more different times during their lives. Each graduation represents a new level of culturally sanctioned achievement. Perhaps religious rites of passage are the most enduring and at times the most difficult in our society. They can take the form of simple ceremonies such as confirmations or baptisms, or more complex ones such as weddings; they may even involve operations, such as circumcision. Religious rites may designate a change in responsibility, or may even involve a lifetime commitment to religious life.

Like people in many non-Western societies, the Hopi Indians undergo rites of passage to mark the transition from childhood to young adulthood. In these ceremonies, a child receives another set of parents—a spiritual family—and another name, also spiritual (Thompson and Joseph, 1947). By expanding familial ties, such a ceremony expands the young person's ties to the community as a whole. Boys are also expected to join secret societies, again increasing their community participation; girls, on the other hand, leave their natural homes for those of their spiritual families. The ceremonies themselves, which are often physically severe, serve another important function. The activities and trials in which the youths participate reinforce in a very concrete way some of the values and

Cultural Diversity and Adaptive Strategies

A major method of socialization is the rite of passage, a ceremony marking the "passing through" of an individual or an age-group from one social role to another. A very common form of this ritual is the puberty rite, during which a person passes from childhood to adulthood. The Masai Eunoto ceremony, depicted here, marks the end of a boy's childhood and the beginning of his role as a junior elder in the community. Similarly, the Jewish Bar Mitzvah signals the close of childhood and the initiation into the privileges and obligations of manhood. (Mohamid Amin/Nancy Palmer; Monkmeyer)

ideals they have heard about from birth (Goldschmidt, 1971).

The Limits of Socialization Any discussion of socialization requires a word of caution. It would be easy to conclude from what we have said that the members of any society are essentially the same in behavior and attitudes, shaped to a uniform pattern by the process of socialization. Nothing could be farther from the truth, as we can tell simply by looking at the people around us. American children, for example, are taught to express aggression in certain socially acceptable ways, but some people are simply more aggressive than others. Similarly, Chinese children were traditionally taught reverence for their ancestors, but some were more respectful than others. Socialization, then, is far from a perfectly efficient system of molding a child's emerging personality.

The reasons lie in two broad areas. First, the agents of socialization—parents, teachers, priests, and so on—are a varied lot. Even if they all (for some reason) tried to transmit exactly the same knowledge, rules, and values in precisely the same way, their own idiosyncrasies would make this impossible. Some of them would be strongly traditional, others more tolerant of deviance or change; some would deliver the cultural message with conviction and authority, while others would not be so effective.

Even more fundamental, the individual is an active participant in the socialization process, and no two people participate in quite the same way. All people vary in their reactions to the world and to what they are taught about it. Two children might be exposed to an almost identical pattern of socialization and yet turn out quite differently, perhaps because of a slight difference in metabolism or body chemistry, perhaps because of an inherent difference in disposition. And as people are exposed to different situations for different periods of time during their lives, individual differences increase further. The result is that each of us remains unique in some important ways, and we each retain a unique understanding of our culture and our place in it. As we go into more detail in the following sections, it is important to remember that socialization describes a great part, but not all, of the relation between the individual and his or her culture.

The Results of Socialization

Though it is by no means the only influence on our lives, culture does play an important part in shaping human thought and behavior. Americans are different from French people; Eskimos are different from Bushmen. Members of each group act in certain ways, talk in certain ways, and think certain thoughts. But what exactly is it that an individual acquires from his or her culture? Anthropologists have employed a number of concepts in their attempts to answer this question. In the following sections, we will discuss four of these—personality, roles, values and beliefs, and models of and for behavior. Although these concepts in some ways overlap, they are distinct enough to be treated as different answers to the same question: What are the results of socialization?

Personality Generally, people think of personality as an individual characteristic. Someone has a "pleasant personality"; another, a rather nasty one. One may even be said to have "a lot of personality," while another person simply fades into the scenery. These judgments are actually about a person's behavior, his or her habitual ways of acting and modes of expression. To the social scientist, however, personality is not so much the outward expression, but rather the underlying cause. It is "a more or less enduring organization of fairly consistent attitudes, values, and modes of perception which account in part for the individual's consistency of behavior" (Barnouw, 1973). Naturally, there will be differences in personality from one individual to the next. But in studying personality in various societies, anthropologists have found cultural regularities suggesting that there are certain personality traits that tend to be shared by members of a particular society.

Margaret Mead's studies in New Guinea are among the earliest and most famous attempts to characterize common personality traits in various cultures. She found, for example, that the Mundugumor were fierce and aggressive, mistrustful and violent. In fact, people in that society seemed to be fighting constantly. Sons battled fathers, and brothers fought or publicly abused each other. The neighboring Arapesh, in sharp contrast, were mild and cooperative people. Warfare was virtually unknown, and they tended to help each other rather than battle. Not surprisingly, Mead noted differences in the two societies' processes of socialization: their child-rearing practices were noticeably different. For example, the Arapesh were noted for their gradual dependence training. An Arapesh woman would offer a frightened child her breast even if the child was past weaning age. The Mundugumor woman, on the other hand, certainly would not. In fact, weaning was especially severe among the Mundugumor. Children were yelled at or beaten if they did not comply with adult demands (Mead, 1935).

There has been criticism of Mead's work, however. Some have regarded it more as literature than scientific research, especially since she did not use psychological tests to probe deeply into people's thoughts and motivations. She was an outside observer, and some have suggested that what she reported was only the surface of the society. Her strict cultural determinism—regarding culture as the primary or only influence on personality traits—has also met with some skepticism. Nevertheless, Mead did pioneer in the effort to understand how individual personality is related to culture—how the process of socialization, particularly in early child-rearing practices, serves to shape a people's habitual ways of thinking and acting.

Roles and Role Models Some anthropologists prefer to discuss the results of socialization in terms of the roles that individuals learn to play. Every society classifies its members in a system of statuses or social positions, according to age, sex, family background, wealth, occupation, achievements, and the like. The role a person is expected to play in daily life depends on his or her status. In our society, children are not expected to support themselves, but adults are (either by working or marrying someone who works); the pressures on women to respond sympathetically to children are greater than the pressures on men; executives have different obligations and privileges than janitors. This is not to say that roles are rigidly prescribed behavior patterns; to be sure, each individual interprets his or her roles somewhat differently. But our culture does provide us with some notion of what is expected of a person in a particular social position. Teaching people to play their proper roles—to behave in ways appropriate to their sex, age, status, and so on—is part of socialization.

Sex-role training occurs in nearly all societies. (As indicated earlier, femininity and masculinity do not develop spontaneously.) Parents everywhere begin to indoctrinate their children at a very early age into the roles considered appropriate to their sex. The Hopi, like many other peoples, give a little girl dolls to reward good behavior; when she is especially well-behaved they say glowingly that she will grow up to be a fine cook. Boys are rewarded with arrows and praised with hints that they are destined to become swift runners (Thompson and Joseph, 1947).

Culture and the Individual

All societies classify their members into a system of age statuses, each of which is accompanied by a more or less defined set of privileges and obligations. However, in the United States the role of the elderly is not at all clear — they seem to have no explicit duties or rights at all. The value of people in American society declines with the approach of old age, as this view of a senior citizens' home clearly illustrates. (Irene Bayer/Monkmeyer)

A person's sex remains the same for life. Therefore, the individual's sex role is learned once and does not change greatly afterward. (This may be one of the reasons why the aim of the women's liberation movement to change adult sex roles is so difficult.) Socialization also teaches us age roles, however, and since we are constantly getting older, at each stage of our lives we have to learn the types of behavior — the privileges and obligations — appropriate to our years. Our own culture makes rather vague discriminations between infants, children, adolescents, and young, middle-aged, or elderly adults. In a general way, we expect a certain degree of self-reliance, responsibility, or wisdom from an individual, a degree appropriate to his or her age. But we are not very surprised if a person behaves or dresses in ways more typical of someone considerably younger or older. In most cultures studied by anthropologists, such relative indifference to age roles would be unthinkable.

Many African societies in particular have developed rather elaborate age-class systems. Among the Galla of Ethiopia every male is a member, along with the other males of his generation, of an *age class* whose membership remains rigidly fixed throughout life. At any moment each class occupies one of five clearly defined *age grades*. The class occupies that grade—and a well-defined set of social roles that goes with it—for a period of eight years, and is then initiated into the next higher grade. With each advancement comes increased status and responsibility. The group occupying the fourth and final age grade, for example, referred to as *Luba*, is expected to exercise major military and governmental responsibility within Galla society (Prins, 1953). Thus at each stage in the life cycle, society instructs its members in their appropriate roles, and people learn to anticipate future changes in their roles and in those of their contemporaries.

Values and Beliefs In addition to personality and roles, the results of socialization have also been described as the values and beliefs people come to hold. In this view, socialization teaches us, sometimes overtly and sometimes without our being fully aware of the process, to accept as our own the basic assumptions of our society. A useful distinction can be made between the assumptions we generally refer to as *cultural values* and those special values we define as part of our system of *ethics* (Goldschmidt, 1971). In either case, socialization teaches us social values in such a way that they become part of both our behavior and our character.

Values are emotionally charged ideas or beliefs about what is right and wrong, appropriate and inappropriate, desirable and repugnant, important and trivial, sacred and profane. The Japanese, for example, place a great deal of emphasis on duty, respect, and above all, filial piety. In contrast, Americans value individualism, consider adolescent rebellion normal, and admire the self-made man or woman. The Hindus seek balance and harmony much as we seek excitement.

One interesting attempt to determine the primary values that people hold in different societies has been conducted by Florence R. Kluckhohn and Fred L. Strodtbeck (1961).

These researchers began with the idea that there are a limited number of solutions to certain universal human problems, and that people in a given society tend to prefer some solutions to others. They see five basic problems, each of which has three possible solutions:

1. What is the innate nature of people? (evil, good-and-evil, or good)
2. What is the relation of people to nature? (subjugated to, in harmony with, or dominating nature)
3. What is the nature of time orientation? (past, present, or future)
4. What is the modality of human activity? (being, being-in-becoming, or doing)
5. What is the modality of human relationships? (lineal, collateral, or individualistic)[2]

Using this framework, Kluckhohn and Strodtbeck presented twenty to twenty-five adult members of both sexes from five different communities in the American Southwest (the Spanish-American, Texan, Mormon, Navajo, and Zuñi) with a series of problems and possible solutions. Each was asked to rank the solutions in order of preference. A problem might state, for example, that a man's crop has failed or he has lost his sheep or cattle, and he and his family will not be able to survive the winter without help. Possible solutions given were: (a) to ask his brothers, sisters and other relatives to help as much as they can (a collateral solution); (b) to try to raise the money on his own, from outsiders (an individualistic solution); or (c) to appeal to his boss or the head of his family (a lineal solution).

Some of the responses were surprising. Texans seemed to be oriented not toward the future, as the researchers had expected, but toward the present; Mormons had absorbed

---

[2] By lineal, Kluckhohn and Strodtbeck mean an essentially hierarchical orientation based on respect for and reliance on elders or other authority figures; by collateral, orientation based on respect for and reliance on the family as a whole, age mates, or some other group.

more of the feeling of dominance over nature from mainstream American culture than anticipated. More significant, however, people from the same community tended to make the same choices, and there were marked differences between members of different communities. This strongly suggests that the culture in which a person is raised has a decisive impact on his or her beliefs and values. In other words, a person's beliefs and values are in part the result of social learning.

There are a number of ways of conceptualizing the system of values that we acquire from our culture. Scholars have described it as a "world view," or "ethos," consisting of cultural "themes" or "postulates." Essentially, these terms all represent the same idea. Our system of values is a set of commonly held attitudes toward the world, a prevalent sentiment, the basic ideas that add up to a deeply entrenched, fundamental "conception of the structure of things" (Barnouw, 1973).

Models of and for Behavior Specifically how and to what extent the process of socialization molds our attitudes and shapes our roles and behavior are matters of some dispute. At one extreme, there is a strongly deterministic view that most of the content of our lives is the result of socialization. But some scholars have put forth a more rationalistic approach, suggesting that mostly what we get from our culture is a structure, some rules and general models that serve as a basis of behavior. (Wallace [1970] has referred to such models as "mazeways.") These behavior or decision models allow people a certain amount of room for manipulating their culture, because while the principles of the culture are strong, the specific content can be altered to suit different situations (Leaf, 1972).

The most obvious behavior models are practical ones. Yurok girls learn basket weaving by observing the work of their elders; Hopi children learn to farm by watching their parents in the field. Of course, all such activities allow for creativity, manipulation, and improvisation, but behind them may well lie a cultural belief or idea. That belief is the primary model for behavior because it represents a view of reality. For example, a farmer might experiment considerably in raising crops because his culture's view of reality holds that one can only know nature by observing it and altering behavior accordingly.

Cultural models may exist and underlie activity in all aspects of our lives. Most are open to wide manipulation because, although models are regarded as truth within the culture, they provide little specific information. For example, our own culture's model of reality holds that all men are created equal, and yet we can quite comfortably live with great divergence from this ideal, for models never tell us exactly how our ideals should be put into practice. Thus societies can often give up cultural content easily while models of and for behavior may never change at all.

Personality, roles, values and beliefs, and behavior models are all different ways of conceptualizing essentially the same thing—what it is that people acquire from their culture as a result of socialization. Yet in spite of these different notions for defining the end product of social learning, there is growing agreement among anthropologists about the way in which cultural knowledge is actually used by human beings. The information we acquire from our culture, however we define it, is not in the form of inflexible rules to which all our thoughts and actions must conform. Instead, we use our cultural knowledge creatively to make decisions in adapting to particular situations. Human life, after all, is not a predictable script, but a series of ever-changing events and situations with which people, armed with their biological and cultural inheritance, must somehow cope.

The Influence of Situations on Human Behavior

Each individual has experiences that are influential in shaping his or her life. The nature of these experiences varies greatly: a child might be traumatized by a dog and grow up in fear of dogs, while someone with positive experiences with animals may have pets all his life. People who face a life of moving from city to city or country to country undoubtedly have a different perspective on some things than people who live in one place. Any and every situation may affect us, and as we each have our own experiences, this is a part of what makes us unique.

While the effect of situations in shaping or changing individuals is quite clear, an entire society can also encounter situations that influence the attitudes of all its members. One obvious example is war which, if long and devastating, might make a people more wary and suspicious, more prone to aggression in their daily lives. Other less catastrophic events can have equally far-reaching consequences. On Great Abaco Island in the Out Islands of the Bahamas, for instance, change in some of the inhabitants' economic situation had an enormous effect on their system of values. At one time there were two communities on the island—Crossing Rocks and Murphy Town—that shared similar ways of life and cultural values. Both had little contact with the outside world, and the people lived by subsistence farming and fishing. Sharing was a trait highly valued in both communities, and in both, the family was largely the center of life, with family members generally cooperating for their mutual benefit. Then Murphy Town was destroyed by a hurricane, and the people were forced to move to a town that boasted an airport, hotel, and so on, and was completely oriented to a money economy. Very rapidly, as the Murphy Towners entered this new economic system, their sense of mutual dependence and their family ties began to break down. Their values changed. They thought in terms of getting ahead, and considered success and responsibility more important than agreeableness and friendliness. These latter traits, characteristic of the old Murphy Town, were still dominant in Crossing Rocks, which had not been faced with change and could adhere to traditional values. Although the people of both communities had been socialized into the same type of value system, the people of Murphy Town changed as a direct result of their altered situation (Rodgers and Gardner, 1969).

Culture versus the Situation

In much of this chapter, we have noted that culture has more impact on personality development, behavior, attitudes, and values than most people would care to acknowledge. We have suggested that to a surprising degree, culture influences who we are, what we are, what we believe, what we do, even what we perceive. But it is also clear that human behavior is influenced by the individual's setting, the particular situation in which a person or a group of people find themselves. The question remains, therefore, To what extent does each of these factors actually contribute to shaping human behavior? Does culture have a greater effect than the situation, essentially dominating diverse aspects of our lives? Or is the reverse the case; is the situation the primary determinant of how we think and act? Or does the truth perhaps lie somewhere in between?

One way to help unravel these different threads of influence is to look at a specific example. Take the question of alcoholism, for instance. The cultural determinist's position would hold that society creates the conditions and the personality traits that lead people to drink excessively. Stereotyped views of drinking problems among some Native American groups follow this line of reasoning. Presumably, the Native Americans drink because there is something in their own culture that frustrates abstinence and drives people to excess.

Theodore D. Graves, however, drew the opposite conclusion from a study of drinking problems among Navajo migrants to Denver. Compared to other urban groups (including other minorities), Indians do have a high rate of arrests for drunkenness and alcohol-related offenses—twenty times the rate for Anglos, and eight times the rate for Spanish-Americans in Denver. But rather than seeking explanations in Navajo culture, Graves looked for answers in individual situations—situations characteristic of non-Indian as well as Indian drinkers. Intensive interviews with over 250 Denver Navajos revealed a high correlation between lack of parental models for wage labor, inadequate training for successful urban employment, the absence of family ties in the city, unrealistically high expectations about what their new urban way of life would hold, peer pressures, and problem drinking. Navajos who were single (to pick one variable) were arrested more often than Navajos who were not, and more Navajo immigrants to Denver were single than either Spanish-Americans or Anglos in a comparable economic bracket. Graves concluded that the situation in which Navajo find themselves in urban centers, not Navajo culture, explains high rates of alcoholism. He maintained that "generally speaking, recourse to a group's 'culture' for explaining their behavior simply serves to conceal our ignorance of the underlying processes in operation" (Graves, 1970).

Graves's view, however, probably underestimates, at least to some extent, the importance of culture in influencing certain behavior patterns. In singling out the situation as the dominant influence, he tends to overlook the fact that culture and the situation constantly interact in shaping human behavior. A more "interactional" approach to the problems of alcoholism is expressed by James Spradley (1973) in a study of chronic alcoholics on Seattle's skid row. Spradley acknowledges that the reasons why these people became alcoholics in the first place were situational. Once they became a part of the skid row and "drunk tank" jail life, however, they suddenly found themselves in a subculture with its own identity apart from the larger culture encompassing it. The drunk subculture actually served to perpetuate drinking habits, and once a person became a part of it, it was increasingly difficult to get out and stop drinking. Giving up alcohol meant giving up a way of life that involved certain expectations and ways of relating to the rest of society. In effect, the people in the study were in a kind of loop: situational

Defining Basic Personality Type
A New Approach

Early students of culture and personality took the concept of basic personality type (the idea that people in a society are psychologically similar) more or less for granted. Later researchers were more wary of overgeneralization. Cora DuBois (1944), for example, in her study of the people of Alor, an Indonesian island, introduced projective psychological tests to obtain quantifiable data. She described her findings in terms of "modal personality," by which she meant the central psychological tendencies in a population. Yet attempts to statistically identify exactly how alike people in the same society are have raised certain questions. Anthony Wallace (1952) administered Rorschach tests to a sample of Tuscarora Indians and found that less than 40 percent fit the modal psychological traits. Is such variation compatible with the concept of basic personality type? And if so, how can it be explained?

Borrowing the concepts of genotype and phenotype from evolutionary theory, Robert A. LeVine (1973) has suggested some answers. In genetics, an organism's genotype is its inherited potential for a certain trait, while its phenotype refers to the observable characteristics that are the product of interaction between genotype and environment. LeVine describes an individual's internal personality makeup—one's genetic endowment, drives, self-image, disposition, and the emotional residue of childhood experiences—as analogous to the individual's biological genotype. The personality genotype is a complex set of potentials and limitations. It may be suppressed or disguised either consciously or unconsciously, but it cannot be eliminated. Continuing with this analogy, LeVine calls the way a person behaves—his or her observable characteristics—the personality phenotype. Like its biological counterpart, the personality phenotype is the result of interaction between the personality genotype and the environment.

LeVine assumes random variation in personality genotype in all populations. Children are born with different capacities and dispositions; they have different experiences in their early, formative years and as adults. But the fact that individuals with varying personality genotypes strive to adapt to the same sociocultural environment produces similarities in personality phenotype in a society. The process of adaptation to social demands is highly selective, however; people do not blindly conform to all the social norms that impinge on them. Rather, phenotypic behavior represents each individual person's "compromise" between genotypic dispositions and environmental pressures.

factors led them into behavior patterns which in turn were reinforced by cultural factors.

As we can see, culture and the individual situation are not neatly separated factors. Culture and the situation, as well as biological factors, all interact to influence human behavior. Yet people can also manipulate both culture and the situation, at least to some extent. This ability is one of the things that distinguishes us as human beings.

The End Product: People as Decision Makers and Manipulators

Those who hold that culture largely determines people's behavior view human beings in a rather passive role, absorbing the values of the past and by and large upholding them. This is also true for those who maintain that the situation is the dominant influence on our lives, that people in a sense are buffeted by one set of external circumstances after another. These positions, when rigidly applied, ignore the fact that both cultures and situations are themselves the creations of humans, and people are always shaping and modifying them in different ways. A more meaningful way of viewing the relationship between culture and the individual, therefore, is to see culture more as a guide for solving human problems. Culture is simply our society's accumulated notions about what constitutes proper behavior, notions that we are constantly putting to use in making decisions about what we should and should not do in particular situations.

But cultural guidelines are *general,* and people act in *specific* situations. Consequently, there is always need for individual interpretation and choice. In attempting to apply the norms of their culture, people must improvise from time to time; they must be creative and imaginative. But creation often takes a person outside the rules of propriety. In any society, then, there is room not only for "proper," culturally approved behavior, but also for "smart" behavior (Freilich, 1971). Smart behavior might be explicitly improper, but it may nonetheless be admired for its ingenuity and ability to solve a problem. In many societies, for example, people boast about managing to escape a particularly unpleasant obligation or getting around an especially burdensome rule. In fact, who obeys all the rules all the time? No one really, and many of those violations are not simply omissions, but willful acts that are considered better than the norm in a given situation. We all manipulate norms to suit our particular needs; a person does not have to be a nonconformist to practice smart behavior. It is in fact the freedom to manipulate and step beyond cultural norms that serves to redefine those norms and renew their vitality.

Freilich has suggested that we are all scientists of a sort, constantly gathering data to apply to decisions. We make decisions on the basis of expert authority, use experience to predict the consequences of an act, or sometimes base a decision purely on theory. Much of the data we use is part of the content of our culture, but some is acquired through experience, group interaction, or our own powers of reasoning.

That human beings possess the freedom to act beyond the limits of their cultural norms does not mean, however, that they necessarily will. Norms do have the force of public opinion on their side, and society often employs social, psychological, and even physical sanctions against those who violate the rules. Even when the smart behavior of the individual is generally approved, that person stands alone when he acts. Evading the tax collector may mean a heavy fine or imprisonment; different sexual mores may mean social ostracism. Though there is room for individual initiative, it is often easier to conform.

In a study of the Gwembe Tonga of Zambia, E. Colson and her associates (1973) discovered this to be the case. It was learned that people were more alarmed by uncertainty than by calamity. When, for example, there was a drought, the farmers repeatedly sought the advice of the elders, who could try to divine the proper course of action by communicating with the dead. The farmers were very worried, more worried than they were later on when crops were decimated by floods. In that case, they knew what they had to do. The situation was clear-cut. Faced with many alternatives, on the other hand, they experienced anxiety.

To avoid making decisions people develop social mechanisms to make decisions *for* them. The diviners of the Gwembe Tonga proved to be a way of isolating choices, and as the dead made the decisions, the living were relieved of any culpability or feelings of incompetence. Thus culture simultaneously provides individuals with models used in making decisions and models used to avoid making them.

summary

Despite the emphasis of anthropology on social aggregates, the question of why individuals behave as they do underlies all anthropological theorizing and research.

In addition to the two biological imperatives—basic drives and the need for social contact—Eugene d'Aquili has posited a third, the *cognitive imperative,* the need to impose order on the world by classifying, categorizing, and seeking explanations for the array of phenomena we perceive. The creation of culture—magic, science, history, religion—results from the expression of this need. Biology also affects us on the individual level. It sets outside limits on us—in terms of our health, stamina, and body build, for example—which cannot be overcome.

It is difficult to pin down the precise relations among biological, psychological, and cultural factors in determining human behavior. We have undoubtedly ignored the biological determinant of many types of behavior—as in the case of arctic hysteria—but we have often sought biological correlations for behavior that may be better explained as socially or culturally determined. Thus there is a stereotypical view of the very great biological differences between men and women, which has been used to justify a definitive set of social roles for each sex. Yet recent studies have shown that our notions of femininity and masculinity are socially conditioned. The pervasiveness of such sex roles may best be understood by the fact that once behavior patterns are established, they tend to be perceived as natural and are therefore difficult to challenge or change.

Anthropologists have become increasingly interested in how, if at all, social learning influences the way we think. However, although we know that individuals from different cultures think differently, no way has been found to prove conclusively that their thought processes are different.

Social learning occurs primarily through *socialization,* the process whereby the social group and the family, through formal teaching and unconscious modeling, pass on skills, knowledge, values, attitudes, and behavior to the next generation. Each culture socializes its children in its own way, but the purpose is always the same: to transform the young into purposeful, productive members of society. One of the most effective means of socialization is the *rite of passage,* which marks the induction of a person into a newer, more responsible role. One of the most common rites of passage in all societies is that which marks the transition from childhood to young adulthood.

It should not be assumed that the socialization process imposes uniform behavior patterns on all individuals. On the contrary, we each interpret in our own way what we are taught and observe, and so develop into unique individuals. Nevertheless, members of a society tend to share similar personalities, attitudes, behaviors, and values. In her work of the 1930s, Margaret Mead found a direct correlation between the child-rearing practices of a society and its dominant personality type. Although there has since been criticism of Mead's work, she is credited with pioneering in the effort to understand how individual personality is related to culture.

Socialization affects not only sex roles, but also age roles. Perhaps most importantly, socialization teaches us cultural values and a system of ethics. As unspoken assumptions about the nature of life, values and ethics are very difficult to study, although a good attempt has been made by Kluckhohn and Strodtbeck. Starting from the thesis that there are certain universal human problems and that these can be solved or reconciled in a limited number of ways, they devised a test to discover the primary values held by people in varying societies. They found that people from the same community tend to share the same value system, while those from different communities have different value systems. Thus a person's beliefs and values are at least in part a result of social learning.

Many scholars today suggest that while some patterns of behavior are culturally imposed, what our culture primarily does is give us a structure that serves as a basis for our behavior. Since we are never told exactly how to realize our ideals, we have a certain amount of leeway in our conduct.

Not only are human beings affected by biology and socialization, but also, on both an individual and cultural level, by situations. Situation and culture interact in determining human behavior: cultural guidelines are general, and people act in specific situations. Therefore culture does not lock us into a passive role of merely learning the values of the past and repeating them. In coping with the situations we find ourselves in, we are given the opportunity to improvise solutions to our problems, to make choices, and to interpret information on an individual level. In the process, we may find ourselves practicing what Morris Freilich has called "smart behavior," behavior that is explicitly improper but nonetheless efficient and ingenious. This freedom to manipulate and bypass culturally imposed rules has the effect of continually redefining culture and renewing its vitality.

suggested readings

BARNOUW, V.
1973 *Culture and Personality*. Rev. ed. Homewood, Ill.: Dorsey Press. Surveys at an introductory level the ideas developed by the anthropologists working with psychological phenomena and the relationship between culture and the individual. Barnouw emphasizes the culture and personality approach.

EDGERTON, R. B.
1971 *The Individual in Cultural Adaptation*. Berkeley and Los Angeles: University of California Press. A study of the relationship between personality and values and ecological and cultural factors.

LEVINE, R.
1973 *Culture, Behavior and Personality*. Chicago: Aldine. An attempt to refocus and rebuild some of the more traditional concepts of psychological studies. LeVine seeks to develop a genetic approach to the study of individual phenomena.

WHITING, B. B., AND WHITING, J. W.
1974 *Children of Six Cultures: A Psycho-Cultural Analysis*. Cambridge, Mass.: Harvard University Press. Summarizes the results of the comparative studies of socialization that the Whitings have directed over the last decades.

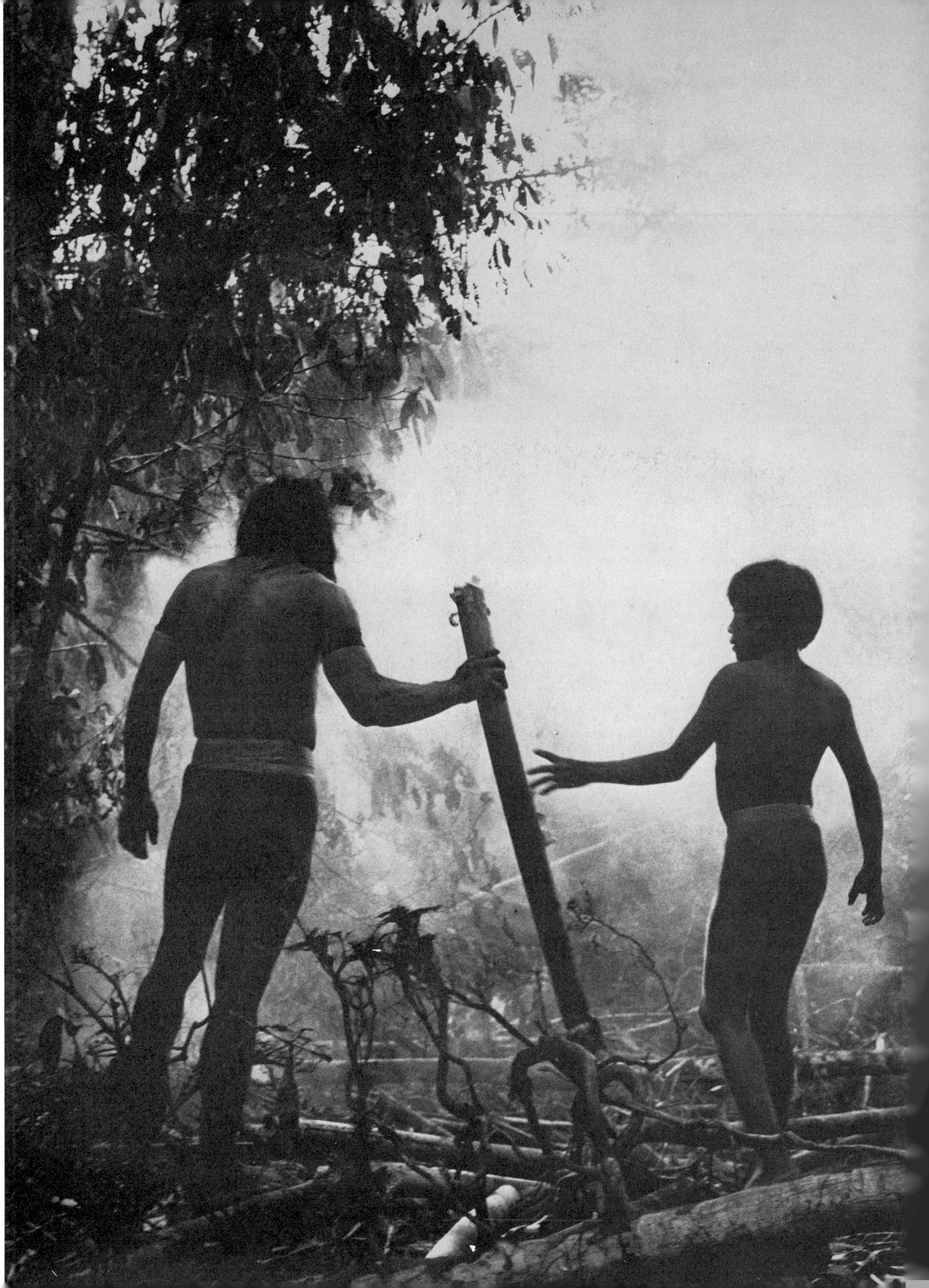

sixteen
Resources, Environment, and Procurement Strategies

Humans have evolved unique attributes that allow for survival in a wider variety of environments than any other animal. First, we are omnivorous: we eat almost any sort of animal food large enough to be worth the trouble and also a great variety of plant foods, especially seeds, fruits, and starchy roots. Consequently, we can find food in most of the diverse natural environments on the earth. Second, our brains and muscles enable us to devise a wide number of techniques for harnessing energy. With tools and machines, we are able to use many external sources of energy without passing them through our metabolic system. The extent to which we have developed this ability is unique in the animal kingdom. In order for most animals to use the energy stored in a tree, for instance, they must drink its sap or eat its leaves and branches. Humans, however, can cut the tree down and use its energy in the form of fire to warm their homes or cook their food. Or we can use the energy stored in the muscles of other animals by riding the animals or by harnessing them to a plow. We supplement our own strength by using tools and machines, extracting from the earth the metals to make them and the fossil fuel to run them.

Early humans had one all-purpose tool, the hand axe, which they used for everything from skinning and butchering animals to digging edible roots. Over the millennia an enormous range of tools and techniques were devised for exploiting the environment to satisfy our basic biological needs for nutrition, shelter, and defense against the elements and other animals. As a result of this adaptation to a variety of environmental situations, we are the most widely dispersed species on the planet, ranging all the way from the barren arctic regions to equatorial rain forests. In this and later chapters we will examine how people with distinctly different technologies manage to acquire and use the basic resources essential to human survival. In particular, we will focus on major variations in procurement strategies and how they relate to processes of cultural adaptation.

Obtaining Resources: Variations in Procurement Systems

The resources required to support human life do not simply fall into people's hands. In every society, no matter how bountiful the natural environment, people must apply their accumulated wisdom and skills to the task of obtaining those things needed for survival. They fashion tools to make their efforts more efficient, employ special knowledge to utilize and manage resources successfully, and organize their labor to extract a living from the world around them. Tools, knowledge, and organization are the central components of every society's system for procuring resources.

Tools

Our ability to procure resources is directly tied to our ability to create and use tools. In a

Burning the overgrowth, planting crops for a few years, then abandoning the garden and moving to a new site, as these Ecuadorians do, may seem irrational and wasteful. However, research on tropical ecosystems indicates it is a highly adaptive strategy. Tropical soils are low in nutrients and can only support domesticated plants for a limited period. Rather than using fertilizers or other additives, these agriculturalists allow nature to regenerate itself. The land becomes reusable after eight to ten years' rest. (Cornell Capa/Magnum)

sense, tools are simply extensions of the body, extra appendages that can be removed, exchanged, and specifically tailored to perform tasks far more efficiently than could the human body alone. It is much easier and quicker, for example, to cut open and clean a fish with a knife than with your fingers or teeth, or to carry a bushel of grain in a basket than in your arms.

Human beings, however, are not the only animals to use tools; in fact, chimpanzees actually *make* rudimentary tools. Jane Goodall (1971) has observed chimpanzees chewing wads of leaves which they then use as sponges to absorb water from shallow depressions that cannot be reached by the lips. Occasionally they will strip leaves from twigs and use these tools to extract honey from bees' nests. But no other animal makes as many or as complex tools as do human beings, nor does any other animal use tools nearly as much or as inventively as we do; by the same token, no other animal approaches *Homo sapiens* in dependence on tools and technology.

In terms of the kinds, number, and complexity of tools they use, societies differ widely. In cultures where people make their living by hunting and gathering wild foods, tools are relatively simple and require little specialization in their manufacture and use. They are quickly improvised from appropriate local materials and often tossed away after they have served their function. Most are used directly either for procuring or storing food or for defense. Hunters around the world have devised many implements for catching wild

Although the Eskimos are not the only hunters to use harpoons, their other equipment—warm and water-resistant clothing and sturdy but flexible boats that do not crack on contact with ice floes—are vital parts of their adaptation to the Arctic environment. (© Georg Gerster, Rapho/Photo Researchers)

animals, birds, and fish—chiefly clubs, traps, and piercing weapons such as spears or bows and arrows. They have also developed tools for gathering plant resources. The most essential are digging sticks for prying up edible roots, tools for cutting and binding, and lightweight containers for transport and storage.

Technology is generally more elaborate in societies where people cultivate plant foods and lead more sedentary lives. All food-producing peoples use specialized implements for ground clearing, planting, weeding, harvesting, storing, and transporting crops. The kind and quality of tools used for these purposes, however, varies enormously from one farming society to another. For example, some peoples rely primarily on wooden digging sticks for poking holes in the soil to plant seeds. Others have a more complex set of tools, including metal hoes with a separate blade and handle that can turn up the soil far more quickly and effectively than a digging stick. Most societies that practice agriculture on a large scale have a still more advanced technology based on the plow and draft animals. In modern industrial societies the plow has been replaced by the tractor and combine. Food producers also require special tools for storing foods. Again, the range of storing devices is quite broad—from baskets to carefully fired ceramic vessels to plastic bags and hermetically sealed tin cans. Those who raise grain crops must have processing tools. In many parts of the world, farmers still grind their grain by hand, using simple stone tools developed thousands of years ago. By contrast, in industrial societies grain is ground in hydroelectric mills.

A full catalog of all the technological devices used to procure resources would probably require several books. Since the nineteenth century, when mechanization began to intensify rapidly, the inventory has expanded enormously, and today tools whose sole purpose is to make other tools greatly outnumber those used directly to acquire resources. But whether people rely on many complex tools or just a few simple ones, their survival and prosperity are directly related to their ability to harness and regulate energy through technology.

Knowledge

Using and managing resources requires—in addition to tools—specialized knowledge: which plants are edible and provide the most reliable food resources, where the best pastures and water holes can be found at different seasons of the year, how soil and water conditions will affect the growth of crops, how procurement activities should be carried out to make the most of available resources. Without this kind of detailed understanding, no population can survive.

Peoples who employ a simple technology are sometimes dismissed as having a poor understanding of basic ecological relationships, an inability to plan and manage their resources. We might ask why, for example, the Bushmen of the Kalahari Desert don't stockpile more food or learn to plant so that they will have a more stable food supply; or why tropical farmers continue to practice a shifting form of cultivation that exhausts the soil quickly and limits production. In fact, however, anthropologists have found that such peoples often have a far more realistic understanding of environmental limitations and advantages than we do. Most tropical farmers are well aware of the problems associated with soil erosion, exposure of tropical soil to sun, and overcultivation, and often take preventive measures. Fields are purposely allowed to lie fallow for long periods to build up the mineral content of the soil, and surface layers are protected by a covering of cut vegetation.

Similarly, the Pueblo peoples, who live primarily on the Colorado Plateau of the American Southwest, have devised a number of planting strategies that take into account all the complex ecological factors associated with their arid and variable environment. Living in an area where precipitation, temperature, wind, and soil conditions often vary radically from year to year and from one location to another, the Pueblo nonetheless have managed to make a go of agriculture. In the eastern portion of the Pueblo heartland, the environment has been improved for cultivation through irrigation. But to construct and maintain these devices for soil and water control, the Pueblo have to assess and cope with a number of problems created by water conditions, soil, and slope. For example, rainfall tends to be a boom-or-bust phenomenon in the American Southwest. A stream that is normally no more than a trickle may become a raging torrent after a storm. This pattern creates a serious problem in constructing dams to divert water from a stream into an irrigation ditch. The Pueblo have solved the problem by taking water from the smallest and most permanent streams, where the danger of flooding is somewhat reduced but the water supply does not usually disappear completely in dry periods.

As difficult as environmental conditions are in the eastern portion of the Pueblo lands, they are not as severe as those in the western portion. Here precipitation and soil conditions make irrigation almost impossible. Consequently, the Western Pueblo have devised strategies for raising crops that would not have been possible without a detailed understanding of ecological variables. Since wind, drought, or temperature problems may affect any given growing season, the Western Pueblo plant separate varieties of wind-resistant, drought-resistant, and temperature-resistant strains of corn. Moreover, their corn is adapted to deep planting. Since the soil is both warmer and moister at greater depths, the Pueblo are able to deal with two problems at once. To make maximum use of the limited amounts of water available, they plant their fields in a variety of locations—on slopes exposed to the northeast where they catch large quantities of snow, near springs, and in stream beds. To circumvent the boom-and-bust water cycle, they plant at different points along the stream channel; if water is scarce, upper-elevation fields receive water; if the channel is in flood, upper fields may be washed away, but the lower ones will receive water. Thus for each of the variables—water, temperature, soil, and wind—the Pueblo, like other peoples with relatively simply technologies, have devised numerous alternative agricultural strategies based upon a complex interplay of ecological factors (Plog, n.d.). Every society possesses similar knowledge of its environment, and that knowledge is an essential part of its procurement strategy. The basic objective of many of these strategies is not simply to increase productivity, but also to insure the reliability of production—that is, to minimize risk.

Organization

Whatever their physical environment, tools, and knowledge, people must put their own efforts into the task of securing resources. This demands cooperation and division of labor, for even with the simplest technologies no one is able to do everything for himself or herself. The organization of work—allocating human energy and systematizing various phases of productive activities—varies from

Weaving may be women's work and fishing a job for men in Western societies. But among the Kpelle of Liberia the roles are reversed: it is the men who work the looms, and the women who catch the fish that add a steady contribution of animal protein to their diet. (Jacques Jangoux)

society to society. In part it is determined by the tools that are used and the type of work to be done. Some types of hunting are handled more efficiently by a solitary hunter. This is the case with the Eskimo hunter when he sits noiselessly for hours beside a hole in the ice waiting for a seal to surface. A different form of work organization is required to capture animals that range widely in herds. In such cases, groups of hunters often cooperate to set up huge deadfalls or barricades and then to drive the herds into the trap. In agricultural societies, the change of weather or seasons may make it urgent for farmers to pool their efforts at planting or harvest time. Other productive activities can be divided into a number of tasks performed by separate individuals.

Division of Labor by Age and Sex In all societies, from the simplest to the most complex, certain tasks are allocated on the basis of age and sex. Young and middle-aged people generally form the nucleus of the work force, with children and older people performing peripheral functions or tasks that are less strenuous physically. This is particularly true in hunting societies, where economic activities require a good deal of strength and stamina. In industrial societies, by contrast, the young are given a long period of "off-the-job" training in preparation for highly skilled work, and the old are frequently regarded as obsolete. In our own society, the law states that anyone under the age of sixteen is not supposed to be formally employed, and retirement from the work force is usually mandatory at age sixty-five. In agricultural societies, however, the young and the old are more readily integrated into the work force. Both groups can assume various responsibilities around the home or in the fields and often perform simple tasks that involve little physical strength. In some of these societies, jobs are assigned formally and quite specifically on the basis of age. Among the Yoruba of Nigeria, males traditionally have been classified according to five age grades, each of which has designated tasks.

Sex is also an important basis for work organization almost everywhere. Well before adolescence, children are encouraged to begin practicing the skills defined as appropriate to their sex. In most societies, "women's work" has traditionally been tied to the family and household—caring for children; gathering plant food, water, and firewood; cooking; and cleaning. Work that involves relatively long periods spent some distance from home is usually performed by men. To them generally fall such jobs as hunting, herding large animals, or plowing. There are many variations on this basic pattern, however. In hunting societies, although men are usually responsible for hunting and women for gathering, women often participate in communal hunts, helping to drive game into the hunters' traps by beating the bushes. Moreover, work involving considerable physical strength is not as consistently allocated to men as we might expect. In agricultural societies women often perform fairly strenuous tasks alongside their husbands in the fields. And in every society some jobs appear to be assigned to the sexes quite arbitrarily. Milking is women's work among the Fulani and Nuer of the Sudan, but among the Swazi and the Xhosa of southern Africa, it is exclusively men's work. In most European societies, weaving and sewing are considered female jobs. Among the Pueblo and in many parts of West Africa, however, only men were allowed to weave cloth and sew it into garments.

Division of labor on the basis of sex is beginning to break down in many industrial societies as more and more women step into jobs previously reserved for men. Heavy physical labor is performed by machine rather than by muscle power; and because families are smaller, and child care can be purchased like any other service, women can more easily free themselves for work outside their traditional roles in the home. Conversely, more men are entering professions such as teaching and social work, once considered the province of women. But although many people in our society are currently challenging the assumption that women are better suited to such service occupations as nurse, teacher, or secretary, arbitrary sex-role distinctions persist. Although division of labor by sex is a universal cultural feature, anthropologists are just beginning to investigate its evolution and adaptive significance.

Specialization As technology and production activities become more elaborate, as they call for many different kinds of tasks, the division of labor becomes more specialized. People develop special skills and concentrate on providing a particular service or producing a certain product or even part of a product. Specialization, an extreme division of labor, may be carried out on a full- or part-time basis. In horticultural societies, people will often spend part of their time on subsistence activities and part in a specialized occupation. Among the Kpelle of Liberia, as in most preindustrial societies, families produce most things for themselves: chairs, rice spoons, clay pots, winnowing trays, hammocks, twine, and fishnets are all handcrafted by individuals for their own use (Gibbs, 1965). Some tasks, however, are performed by part-time specialists. Men have traditionally acted as part-time medicine men and blacksmiths. More recently they have taken up other part-time occupations such as tailoring, shopkeeping, carpentry, and sandal making. Kpelle women may augment their subsistence activities by working as midwives or caring for the sick.

In societies where the production process and technology have become extremely complex, full-time specialization becomes essential. The jobs of computer programmer, brain surgeon, and aeronautical engineer are specialized economic positions unique to industrial societies. Specialization reaches its most extreme form in the assembly line, where workers are stationed before steadily moving conveyor devices and spend their days performing a highly specific, repetitive task such as tightening the same five nuts on the left rear wheel of a car, or feeding candy bars into a machine that wraps and seals them. Here each worker is part of a highly organized industrial operation where everyone from the upper-echelon executives on down has a limited and specifically defined function.

Motivation The success of any system for procuring resources depends upon people's willingness and ability to work and produce. Therefore, in addition to asking who does what, we must find out how the task force is motivated. Why do people work? Why do they get up when the sun rises or the alarm clock rings, venture out into freezing weather to hunt seals, spend long hot days weeding in the fields, or stay cooped up in an office day after day? The obvious answer is that people work out of necessity—they have to eat. But survival is only part of the story. When sociologists asked a large number of American workers whether they would continue to work even if they inherited enough money to live comfortably for the rest of their lives, eight out of ten said they would (Tausky, 1970). People work for a variety of reasons—because they do not know what else to do; because they find work stimulating; because work brings important personal and social rewards, including a sense of accomplishment, an opportunity to be with friends, prestige, and a feeling of being useful. These personal and social rewards are important in all societies, because work is socially valued everywhere. But they are perhaps especially significant in preindustrial societies where people work not as part of a factory but as a member of a family or kin group, not for a business corporation but as part of a community or as a friend.

People in most hunting, farming, and herding societies work in close-knit groups that share many social ties and functions, one of which happens to be procuring basic resources. The cultural system not only governs

In Amish communities such as this one in Lancaster, Pennsylvania, a barn raising is an occasion for kin, neighbors, and friends to join hands. Communal construction was very common before societies began to become technically specialized, but in technologically advanced societies construction is a full-time business, employing a hierarchy of specialists. (David Strickler/Monkmeyer)

the organization of the work force, but also structures the framework of rewards and options within which the individual functions. For example, Thai rice farmers obtain the labor they need at harvest time through a complex exchange system based on different kinds of rewards. Among relatives or close friends help is given freely and informally and without regard to any specific return. The reward is fellowship. In other cases, two households may formally agree to cooperate on a specific task. Here the reward is the exchange of equal amounts of labor. Exchange of this type creates reciprocal obligations and means that a family in need can count on the support of another household. Commerce enters the picture only between distant kinsmen or when a Thai farmer must hire additional help from outside his village. In such cases, wages are paid either in rice or cash. Since worker and farmer are not bound by close friendship or kinship ties, fellowship and exchange are supplanted by economic rewards (Moerman, 1968). Economic and social incentives bind individuals to their common task of making a living and assure the continued success and organization of a procurement system. Although the direct social rewards of work may not be so great in an industrialized society such as our own, they are nevertheless present.

Organizational Decision Making Of course, people do not mindlessly respond to work incentives, pitching in their labor on any task that comes along. Individuals and societies are far more selective than that. In most societies there are usually more tasks to be done than there are people to do them. As a result, people, both alone and in groups, must choose among the alternatives. At the group or societal level, such decisions are referred to as *scheduling decisions* (Flannery, 1968). These are especially important among groups living in areas where seasonal and annual resource fluctuations are substantial. But decisions about what tasks to perform and when to perform them are not always made by large groups; individuals must make at least some of these decisions on their own.

People's ability to make such decisions depends on the knowledge they have. We saw how complex this knowledge can be in the case of the Pueblo—to insure a successful yield, individuals plant crops in a variety of locations. The Kapauku of New Guinea make similar decisions about what mix of crops to plant and where to plant them. White (1973) shows that their choices follow an optimization strategy: they attempt to obtain the greatest output consistent with the least possible risk. He also notes that individuals can and do decide to follow strategies different from those of the group under certain circumstances. Selection operating on variability of just this sort is an important part of the evolutionary process.

Procurement Systems, Resources, and Human Numbers

Human beings, then, are constantly creating, combining, modifying, and recombining the tools, knowledge, and organizational strategies needed to secure essential resources. But given a people's procurement system and the resources they can acquire through it, there still remains the problem of keeping human numbers in balance with the available food supply. This is a crucial adaptive problem in every society, for a human population cannot grow beyond its means of obtaining food without serious consequences. Exactly how is this critical balance maintained?

Central to the relationships between procurement strategies, resources, and human numbers are the concepts of *natality* (birth rate), *mortality* (death rate), and *life span*. Assuming one controls for migrations, changes in human numbers and rates of population growth or decline can be studied in terms of the factors influencing how many people are born per unit of population, how many die, and how long individuals can be expected to live. The factors affecting these variables include such things as the quantity and quality of the food supply, as well as overall conditions of "risk." A nomadic lifestyle, for example, may have more inherent risks to birth and life than does a sedentary existence. Consequently, most hunting and gathering groups have a greater number of spontaneous abortions and stillbirths, a higher infant mortality rate, and a generally shorter life span than do most cultivators.

Birth and death rates are also related to specific cultural practices. "Family planning" is hardly a new phenomenon. Since prehistoric times, humans have practiced deliberate forms of population control. Self-induced abortion, abstention from sexual intercourse, and prolonged nursing—conception being less likely to occur when a woman is lactating—are perhaps the most traditional and widely practiced forms of birth control. In some societies, when families cannot afford the burden of feeding a number of small children, the solution is commonly infanticide. While this seems like a shocking practice to us, people in other societies would think it shocking to allow children to live who were certain to face starvation.

Many other cultural practices not deliberately designed to control the birth rate may have the net effect of limiting or enhancing fertility. For example, marriage customs—the age at which women marry, for example, or traditions concerned with remarriage after widowhood or divorce—can influence reproductive behavior. In reality, any religious, economic, or social practice that affects natality, mortality, or life span may be directly related to maintaining a viable relationship between the size of a human population and the resources on which it depends.

This is not to say that every society manages the size of its population in a totally rational and effective manner. The cultural and natural mechanisms that regulate the interaction between resources and human numbers are complex and not yet fully understood. Still, we know that the environment is a key factor influencing the ultimate size of any human group. Societies are continually adapting to their environments, in part by regulating human numbers, but primarily by adjusting their procurement strategies to suit environmental conditions. In the following section, we will explore some of the ways in which such adjustments are made.

Procurement Systems and Adaptation to Environmental Conditions

People have devised a great diversity of procurement systems—a wide assortment of tools, technologies, and organizational strategies all created with the ultimate goal of securing the resources needed for survival. Each of these systems reflects the present-day adaptation of a particular group to its environment, as well as the accumulated adaptive successes and failures of its ancestors in that same environment. It is therefore easy to state the relationship between environment and procurement strategies in general terms. But specifically what do we mean by environment, and exactly how does it affect the ways in which resources are obtained?

All of us are aware that the world is made up of a variety of environmental zones (or *biomes*), each with a characteristic climate,

Even the best efforts to manage resources may fail. The drought and famine that hit the northern edge of black Africa in the 1970s was the result of climatic changes. It is said, the Sahara moved. (UPI)

soil composition, typography, and plant and animal life. Grasslands, deserts, the arctic and subarctic, tropical forests, and temperate forests are the five major environmental zones on our planet. Table 16-1 shows that the distribution of the earth's human population bears some relationship to these broad environmental types. Arctic and subarctic areas, for example, have only one-sixteenth the human population one would predict simply on the basis of the land mass they cover. Temperate forests, on the other hand, are inhabited by 2½ times as many people as their extent would seem to justify. This distribution reflects the fact that temperate forests offer a more hospitable environment to human beings than do polar tundras. Nevertheless, human beings can adapt and have adapted to virtually every kind of environmental region.

It is clear that the resources of each major environmental zone can be better exploited with some procurement strategies than with others. Arctic regions, for example, are not well suited to growing crops of any kind; and agriculture faces other limitations and restrictions in deserts, due to lack of water, and in tropical forest regions, due to certain soil deficiencies. These broad environmental limitations on procurement systems, however, do not explain why a particular strategy will be practiced in a particular region, why people in generally similar regions will practice different strategies, and why strategies change when broad environmental zones do not.

Anthropologists have found that the designs of individual procurement systems are not so much responses to broad environmental characteristics as to patterns of environmental variation in local areas. Such local environmental variations include differences in the quantity and quality of available resources, differences in seasonal and yearly resource fluctuations, and differences in the number of other human groups competing for the same resources. In the following sections, we will look at each of these topics, investigating some of the ways that different peoples, each with a different technology, adapt to varying environmental conditions.

Adapting to the Quantity and Quality of Available Resources

Every environment has a rather specific potential for supporting human life. Anthropologists estimate this potential, referred to as the *carrying capacity* of the environment, by computing the minimum amount of vegetable and animal matter available on a regular basis for human consumption. In the Kalahari Desert, for example, it has been estimated that the ecosystem can indefinitely support 41 individuals per 100 square miles (Lee, 1968). Here a major *limiting factor* (a key fac-

Table 16-1: Distribution of Human Population

Major Environmental Zone	Percent of Earth's Land Mass	Percent of Human Population
Grasslands	26	12
Deserts	18	6
Arctic and subarctic	16	less than ½ of 1%
Tropical forests	10	28
Temperate forests	17	43

Note: Figures do not add up to 100 percent because smaller environmental zones—such as mountain regions or scrub forests—have been omitted here. (James, 1966:22-23)

tor in short supply) is water. An average water hole can support approximately thirty people during years when rainfall is normal, and fewer individuals during periods of drought. Thus Kalahari residents of necessity live in small groups broadly scattered over a large territory. Compared to many other environments, the Kalahari is sparsely populated. In areas where food and water supplies are more abundant, population levels rise accordingly.

The carrying capacity of an area is affected not only by the total amount of food available, but also by the short supply of any essential dietary item such as protein, vitamins, and minerals. The nutritional quality of resources is as critical as their quantity. To avoid malnutrition, human populations must somehow adjust to the variations in nutritional value among available foods. The preparation of corn in many societies is an example of this adjustment process. In a recent survey of corn preparation in fifty-one North and South American societies, Katz, Hediger, and Valleroy (1974) found that unless processed with alkali (obtained from lime, wood ash, or lye) before it is eaten, corn is deficient in several essential amino acids and in niacin, a member of the B vitamin complex. Any population that relied primarily on corn without alkali processing would suffer malnutrition. The researchers therefore predicted that wherever corn was used as a dietary staple, people would be found to make the necessary cooking adjustment. Their results confirmed this hypothesis. In Mesoamerica, shelled corn is boiled in a limewater solution before grinding. In some areas of North America where lime is not available, corn users obtain the necessary alkali from wood ashes or lye. Without this cultural adaptation to available food resources, societies could not depend on corn as a dietary staple.

The carrying capacity of an area is therefore not an environmental given. It varies with the nature of the procurement systems practiced in the region, with the exchanges of resources one group carries on with others, and with climatic factors. But when a population continually exceeds the carrying capacity of its environment, the result is often malnutrition, and in extreme cases, famine.

Adapting to Resource Fluctuations

In addition to the quantity and quality of food supplies and raw materials, populations must also adjust to seasonal and yearly fluctuations. For example, because of extreme variations in rainfall, the Shoshone Indians of the Great Basin were never able to predict with any certainty from one year to the next where or how much plant and animal food would be available. A locality highly productive one year might offer little food the following season. In order to adjust to these environmental uncertainties, families relied on a broad variety of resources and maintained a mobile lifestyle, changing their location and residence patterns according to the kind and quantity of resources available. During most of the year a Shoshone family traveled alone or with one or two related families, gathering roots and seeds and hunting small animals. Periodically, however, when rabbits or antelope became unusually plentiful, a number of families might band together temporarily for a collective hunt. And when isolated families heard reports that a resource such as pine nuts seemed promising in a particular locality, they would plan to arrive in time for the harvest and would separate again after the resources had been collected (Steward, 1953). Most peoples who live by foraging wild foods make such seasonal adjustments.

People who cultivate crops or keep animals for subsistence generally have a more consistent and localized food supply than those who depend on wild resources alone. But these groups too are affected by seasonal and yearly fluctuations. The Karimojong of northeastern Uganda are primarily a cattle-keeping people. However, occasional droughts and epidemics of livestock disease can decimate herds. Moreover, they have no means of storing perishable milk and blood (their dietary mainstays) or meat as a hedge against future shortages. To help insure a continuous food supply, the Karimojong collect wild fruits and berries and hunt wild game from time to time; they also raise a few cereal crops. But agriculture too is perilous, and cattle continue to provide the most reliable food resource. To maintain their herds, the Karimojong must move the animals periodically according to the seasonal availability of water and good grazing land. Over a two-year period, a group of herdsmen might range across a 500-square-mile area with their livestock (Dyson-Hudson, 1969).

In our own society, consumers do not see seasonal and yearly fluctuations affecting their food supply quite so drastically (although we do see fluctuations in food prices, which are often responses to variations in quantity). Most of us are able to buy all kinds of meats, fruits, grains, vegetables, and dairy products throughout the year. This is because we have developed a highly sophisticated technology that enables producers to preserve and transport foods efficiently and gives them the means to control environmental factors within broad limits. When a cattle rancher's pasture lands go dry, he need not move his animals; he simply brings forage and water to the cattle. Similarly, a farmer can bring water to his crops through irrigation; he keeps insect pests away by using chemical sprays; when his fields become depleted he can add nutrients to the soil with artificial fertilizers; he can even grow crops in the dead of winter by constructing hothouses. These, of course, are highly sophisticated devices for controlling and minimizing periodic ecological changes. But regardless of the exact ways in which they accomplish it, all societies, within the limits imposed by their technologies, make similar adjustments.

We should not make the mistake of assuming, however, that industrialized societies are somehow more effective at this adjustment process than technologically simpler ones. Perhaps the greatest paradox of recent human adaptation is that responses made to minimize the threat of uncertainty in food production often have far-reaching consequences and may themselves pose a new threat to the stability of the procurement system. For example, a community may increase its dependence on irrigation agriculture in order to diminish the threat of drought or rainfall irregularity and then may later be faced with the more serious problem of irreversible soil damage due to an excessive build-up of salt content in the soil. Even advanced technologies, therefore, although they may impress us with numerous instances of dramatic environmental engineering, are really engaged in a complex juggling act that depends on a series of environmentally correct responses made at the appropriate times. All human societies, regardless of their technological levels, may well be ultimately judged in terms of how well they maintain the ecological systems of which they are a part.

Adapting to Other Groups

The type and distribution of basic resources comprise only one aspect of an environment—the natural setting. But human populations make up another and no less basic aspect; every society must adjust to the presence and activities of neighboring peoples just as surely as it must adapt to the quality and distribution of food supplies and raw materials.

Humans engage in a great deal of exchange with people outside their own group. They also engage in competition with one another for access to resources. If we step back from the study of cultures or groups as individual entities, we are often struck by a social panorama resembling a giant and ever-changing mosaic with each local population occupying its place in the larger picture. This broader perspective is in many ways similar to the one used by ecologists when studying interdependence and competition among different animal populations in the same area. Each animal population, usually a separate species, is said to occupy a special place or *niche* in the greater scheme.

E. P. Odum (1963), an ecologist, has described an animal's niche as its profession. Much like distinctive human professions, a niche is defined by the unique techniques of food procurement and strategies for survival that an animal uses. The profession or niche of every animal is usually different from those of others in its local community. One can say that in nature, diversity is favored; each animal tends to specialize in or improve upon those activities that it can do more efficiently than its potential competitors. With humans it has been much the same story, but with one major difference: within the genus *Homo* there has been no recent genetic specialization in the form of new but closely related species; instead, we have developed great diversity in professions or niches *within* our species. Not only are we the most far-ranging of all large animals, we are also distinguished by the most widely different local patterns of behavior. As we shall see, this diversity among human groups is by no means random; it represents different responses or solutions to universal biological problems as they occur in different environments.

Frederick Barth (1956), in his study of three populations in the Swat province of Pakistan, gives a clear example of both the concept of niche as applied to humans and some of the dynamics of human adaptation. Three ethnically distinct populations—the Kohistanis, the Pathans, and the Gujars—co-inhabit one mountainous area, where each has selected a distinctive set of techniques and resources as its adaptive strategy. Barth suggests that what may at first seem like arbitrary, even senseless, ethnic boundaries may instead be part of the evolutionary adaptive process, much like specialization and speciation among other animals.

According to local history, the Kohistanis were the original inhabitants of the Swat province. They were driven progressively farther north by the Pathan invaders, who established domain over the fertile alluvial plains. Today, however, the boundaries between the two groups are stable and they manage to coexist fairly peacefully because each has become adapted to a different econiche, or segment of the total environment. The Pathans are primarily farmers and are therefore restricted to the warmer, low-lying valley regions, where conditions are suitable for raising wheat, corn, and rice. The Kohistanis, on the other hand, have a broader-based economy that enables them to survive in the colder mountainous regions. They practice herding: sheep, goats, cattle, and water buffalo provide them with wool, meat, and milk. They also raise corn and millet, crops that can be grown where the climate is severe and the growing season relatively short. The Kohistanis have been able to maintain their independence because they are able to wrest a living from areas that the Pathans consider uninhabitable.

A third ethnic group, the Gujars, have adapted to both regions. As a free-floating population of full-time herders, they occupy marginal mountainous areas left vacant because they are unsuitable for the Kohistani mixed herding and farming economy. The Gujars also occupy a place in Pathan society, forming a specialized caste of herders. While maintaining different lifestyles, the two groups have become economically interdependent. The Gujars contribute milk products, meat, and manure to the Pathan villagers and care for their water buffalo and draft oxen. They also rent pasture land from the Pathans and serve as agricultural laborers during seasons of peak activity. Although militarily inferior to both the Kohistanis and the Pathans, the Gujars are able to coexist with both groups because they exploit a distinct set of resources and do not compete with either population directly (Barth, 1956).

When several different societies occupy different niches in the same environment, various kinds of adaptations are possible. One group may be taken over or driven out by a larger, more aggressive, or technologically more advanced population. This is what occurred when European and American settlers moved into regions occupied by American Indian groups. It is also the situation today in parts of highland New Guinea, where intertribal wars are frequently fought to gain more agricultural land (Rappaport, 1967). In other cases, neighboring populations may simply divide up the environment, either remaining economically self-sufficient and socially dis-

People's Effect on the Environment

Every time people cut down trees and clear land to plant crops, build dams to store irrigation water and generate electricity, kill off predators that attack domesticated animals, or otherwise modify the environment to suit their own immediate needs, they upset the ecological balance, setting off a chain reaction in nature. For example, predators control the sizes of animal populations and prevent disease from spreading by killing off the weak and sick. When humans decimate populations of predators to save their own livestock, they deprive other animals of natural methods of population control which in turn may have disastrous long-range consequences for the entire ecosystem.

People's potentially harmful effect on the environment is not a new phenomenon. Prehistoric peoples created environmental crises of their own. For example, by learning to cultivate crops, early societies enabled their population to grow too large to be supported by hunting and gathering, but over time some of these groups also depleted vital nutrients in the soil. They literally "sowed the seeds of their own destruction," and in the process effectively cut off any chance of turning back to a hunting-gathering way of life.

Today, human beings are interfering with the environment on a far greater scale. The cause is our unprecedented rate of population growth and the industrial technology supporting the nearly 4 billion people currently alive. To supply the needs of this enormous world population, we have exploited the resources of virtually every area of the earth, and many of our methods have had ruinous effects on the environment. Due to ignorance of ecological relationships or simple lack of foresight, we are progressively limiting our own chances for survival.

The building of the Aswan Dam is a dramatic example of the magnitude and complexity of the problem. (See Collier et al, 1973) The dam was constructed to provide Egypt with abundant electricity for industrialization and, perhaps more important, enough fresh water to turn millions of square miles of desert into productive farmland capable of feeding the nation's burgeoning population. But Aswan designers failed to take into account many ecological relationships in the Nile Valley. For thousands of years, despite continual cultivation, this region has maintained its fertility through the natural process of flood irrigation. During the rainy season from August to November, the river overflows its banks, covering the bordering land. These flood waters are beneficial in that they wash away salts that have accumulated in the soil, and add a deposit of silt which serves as a fertilizer.

But the construction of the Aswan and its network of irrigation canals has changed all this in the valley below the dam. Here, soil salinity is increasing so rapidly that many areas will soon be unfarmable if authorities do not take costly remedial action. In addition, most of the river's rich organic silt has been deposited in the bottom of Lake Nasser behind the dam. Without artificial fertilizers as a substitute, many farmers have found their crop yields dropping yearly. As if this were not enough, the dam has also helped to spread serious diseases such as bilharzia (a debilitating illness caused by parasitic blood flukes), malaria, and trachoma (an eye disease), all of which are carried by aquatic invertebrates that thrive in irrigation canals. Thus, the very technology that was meant to keep millions of people from going hungry may actually be destroying them.

The Aswan Dam is far from the only example of harmful human intervention in the environment. We live daily with the despoiled landscapes, the air and water pollution, the toxic chemicals and pesticides that are part of our industrial way of life. But today, survival involves more than somehow managing to live with our environmental mistakes, or simply trying to correct them after we have realized the extent of the damage. Modern technology is capable of such an enormous impact on the environment that the results can be far-reaching, even world-wide, before they are fully recognized. Moreover, experience has shown that many of today's remedies may only become tomorrow's problems. Survival, therefore, requires a thorough knowledge of basic ecological relationships, as well as a desire to put that knowledge to use. Ecologists have suggested that natural selection favors species that contribute to the stability of their ecosystems. A species that continually disrupts the ecosystem in which it participates is itself seriously threatened.

tant, or trading the resources of the areas they occupy. The Pathans and Kohistanis are an example of two groups that have maintained economic and social separation. Many other neighboring populations, however, have instead developed important exchange networks. The Tewa Indians of the American Southwest, for instance, established a variety of trade contacts with fellow Pueblo peoples. Itinerant traders visited various communities exchanging their own village specialties for local craft products. Furthermore, the Tewa exchanged many resources with neighboring Plains Indian groups who inhabited an environment very different from their own. With the nomadic Comanche, the Tewa traded their own corn meal, wheat flour, bread, melons, and other agricultural goods for such things as antelope hides, horses, and buffalo meat (Ford, 1970). The exchange of resources or goods between groups occupying different environments, or different niches within the same environment, is extremely widespread.

When we view human populations as occupying different niches in the same environment, however, we should keep in mind that they do so in a different way than other animals in that environment. Each human niche or profession is filled by members of a single species, and every human group is capable of changing its basic adaptive strategy in a short period of time. A situation of noncompetitive, specialized land use, for example, might change suddenly, with one group adopting the techniques of the other and thereby becoming its competitor. Adaptation to other human groups, then, is a dynamic process, as is adaptation to any environmental condition.

Major Procurement Patterns

So far we have been focusing largely on variation, not only in environmental conditions, but also in the tools, knowledge, and labor human beings combine in an effort to obtain the resources they need. But despite such differences, the ways in which humans procure resources are not unlimited. Essentially, there are five major procurement patterns practiced in the world today: hunting and gathering, extensive or shifting agriculture, intensive agriculture, pastoralism, and industrialism. It is important to remember that this is a simplified typology, one which in reality encompasses wide diversity. Every human society has its own distinct subsistence system, and to label a group a "hunting and gathering society" does not reveal anything very specific about those people. It does, however, indicate some basic facts about their adaptive patterns. In later chapters we discuss each procurement pattern in detail, noting the similarities and differences among societies in each category. At this point, however, we will merely present a brief overview.

Hunting and Gathering

People who practice a hunting and gathering subsistence strategy simply rely on whatever food is available in their local habitat, for the most part collecting various plant foods, hunting wild game, and fishing (where the environment permits). They *collect* but do not *produce* any food—crops are not cultivated and animals are not kept for meat or milk. Today, only about 30,000 people make their living in this fashion. Technologically more advanced peoples have pushed most hunters and gatherers out of the areas where plant food and game is abundant into the more marginal areas of the earth—the barren arctic, arid deserts, and dense tropical rain forests.

Extensive Agriculture

Extensive agriculturalists practice a simple form of cultivation, working small plots of land without draft animals, irrigation, or plows. Planting, clearing, and weeding are carried out with simple hand-held tools: digging sticks, hoes, and spades. Today horticultural societies are still found in the tropical forests of Southeast Asia, in sub-Saharan Africa, on certain islands in the Pacific, and in the remote interior of the Amazon Basin. Most of these groups practice shifting cultivation based on some form of slash-and-burn technology. First, they clear a field by chopping down and burning the trees and bushes. The burned vegetation is left in place to shield the soil against the hardening effect of the sun; it also helps to return nutrients to soil which has been leached by heavy rains and to protect growing crops against insect pests. After several years of constant use, the land must be allowed to regenerate for ten to twenty years, and new fields must be cleared meanwhile. But not all horticulturalists engage in shifting cultivation. Where they have settled on rich alluvial flood plains, for example, they are able to farm the same piece of land for decades. Elsewhere, root and tree crops can be cultivated continuously, since they do not exhaust the soil so quickly. Often a horticultural people will practice shifting cultivation for some crops and continuous cultivation for others.

Intensive Agriculture

Intensive agriculture is a more efficient form of food production characterized by the use of the plow, draft animals, and improved soil and water control techniques such as fertilization and irrigation. The plow is a far more efficient tool for loosening the soil than are hoes, digging sticks, or spades. It also reduces the problems of weeds and soil infertility. By turning the soil deeply, the plow buries weeds, builds up the humus content, and lifts nutrients to the surface. Feasible only in land free of stumps and boulders, plowing requires farmers to clear their fields thoroughly and demands more initial labor than slash-and-burn cultivation. However, it also makes it unnecessary for farmers to shift every few years from one area to another. Instead, they may continue to grow crops on the same acreage for generations.

Pastoralism

Pastoralism, a form of subsistence based on herd animals, is practiced by some groups as a special adaptation to particular environmental conditions that make farming impractical or impossible. While it is usually difficult to raise crops on hilly or mountainous terrain, or in steppes, semideserts, and subarctic regions, the native vegetation will often support animals if they are allowed to range over a wide area. Milk, curds, whey, butterfat, and blood are important in the diets of most pastoral peoples, but very often the main food item is bread. Flour and grain are frequently obtained through trade with neighboring agriculturalists. While some pastoralists also rely on meat for sustenance, others only butcher animals on ceremonial occasions.

Industrialism

Industrialism is an adaptive strategy based on machines, which are run by fossil fuels. Planting and harvesting, breeding chickens and hogs and cattle, collecting eggs and milking cows, slaughtering and butchering, and indeed almost all subsistence activities have been mechanized. Clothing, homes, furniture, tools and gadgets, means of transportation, and most artifacts that people depend on daily are all mass-produced by machines. Mechanization has raised productivity levels dramatically and freed large numbers of people from primary subsistence activities—agriculture, herding, and fishing. Today less than one percent of Americans are farmers, yet they are able to feed slightly over 200 million Americans and about 160 million others around the world.

Mixed Technology

When we refer to an industrial people, hunters and gatherers, horticulturalists, agriculturalists, and pastoralists, we are simply pointing up a cultural *emphasis* on particular subsistence methods. In reality, many cultures use several different methods to obtain food. For instance, horticulturalists often supplement their food supply by hunting and collecting wild foods. In some societies, plow farming is practiced along with slash-and-burn cultivation. In Tepoztlán, Mexico, families practice hoe cultivation in steep and rocky areas where plowing is impossible. Here they are able to produce a limited amount of corn for their own subsistence. The flatter valley areas are cultivated more intensively and on a larger scale by private landowners to produce a marketable surplus (Lewis, 1960). Pastoralism is also frequently found in conjunction with other procurement strategies. While the pastoral Turkana of northern Kenya supplement their economy by hunting and collecting wild foods, the Karimojong of northeastern Uganda combine pastoralism and cultivation. Many agriculturalists keep animals for transportation and as a source of protein, wool, and hides. However, they work chiefly toward producing marketable surpluses of crops.

The Evolution of Procurement Patterns

How did these major procurement patterns — hunting and gathering, extensive and intensive agriculture, pastoralism, and industrialism — evolve? In the beginning, man was a scavenger, living off the natural foods of the savannas and what predators left behind. About 2.5 million years ago, he began to gather in a more systematic way and to hunt. Gradually over the next 2 million years people learned to make spears and became increasingly efficient hunters. The invention of spear-throwers and of the bow and arrow added enormously to man's accuracy as a hunter and to the range of animals he could kill. By 40,000 B.P. different populations had begun to specialize in certain kinds of game.

From specialized hunting and intensive gathering, with frequent dependence on and manipulation of particular plant and animal species, it is a relatively short step to systematic planting and herding. Although we do not know precisely how or why, we do know that about 12,000 years ago men in various parts of the world began experimenting with plant and animal domestication. However, another three or four thousand years passed between the first appearance of agriculture and its widespread use. Not until 5,000 B.P. do we find signs of irrigation and the beginnings of intensive agriculture in the Near East. (In this period, too, specialized pastoralism probably became important.) Over the next two thousand years agricultural practices became more efficient and productive in some areas. Large-scale irrigation works were built in Mesopotamia and Egypt, making it possible to support larger and larger populations in limited areas.

The mechanization of farming and other subsistence activities brought about the Industrial Revolution in the nineteenth century. In industrialized societies, the family farm was replaced by agribusiness and cottage industry by the factory system. Improved fertilizers and pesticides and new high-yield grains have resulted in the Green Revolution of our times. And today automation is leading us into the postindustrial era.

A World Ecosystem

From an evolutionary perspective, what is more important than the simple fact that certain procurement patterns have developed and persisted is the increasingly global organization of procurement systems. Today, long-distance trade integrates local economies in a larger network of mutual interdependence. The factory worker in Japan finds his job dependent in part on the decisions of oil producers in the Middle East, the delivery of iron ore from Nevada, the worldwide demand for his firm's product, and so on. This process of global economic integration can be viewed in terms of evolutionary ecology: the human ecosystem is becoming simpler.

But how can our ecosystem be growing simpler when we have repeatedly referred to the evolution of increasingly complex forms of technology and social organization? The reason for this apparent contradiction lies in the fact that our ecosystem, like any system, can be described not only in terms of its different components, but also in terms of how these components are related to one another. For the first several million years of hominid adaptation, local populations pursued procurement strategies that were essentially self-sufficient. Specialization was relatively rare, and most societies followed very diversified strategies of production with many "fail-safe" devices to insure a continuous food supply. From this point of view, the world was a complex place indeed; human beings had developed hundreds of thousands of more or less independent and highly diversified local production systems.

Today, however, with the advent of industrial production, agribusiness, widespread international trade, and rapid global communication, once local and diversified production systems have become specialized components in a larger system. Farmers all over the world rely on the same international market system to sell one or two crops, using the money they receive to acquire food and a wide range of technological items. Whole communities become specialized in this same way, and consequently most economies are highly vulnerable to disturbances in the global system of supply. This is what we mean when we say that the world ecosystem has become simpler even though technology has become far more complex.

summary

Two attributes unique to humans—being omnivorous and having the ability to utilize external energy sources—have enabled us to inhabit a wider variety of environments than any other animal. Survival in any environment demands that people develop means of obtaining and using resources efficiently. Tools, knowledge, and organization are vital in every society's system of resource procurement.

Populations employing a simple technology have been criticized for a poor understanding of basic ecological relationships and an inability to plan and manage resources. However, anthropologists have discovered that these societies do show sophisticated understanding of their environment and have devised efficient strategies for dealing with local conditions.

Once a society develops its procurement strategy, some division of labor will be used in carrying it out. All societies divide labor to some extent on the basis of age and sex. Usually the young and middle-aged do the majority of the work, while the children and elderly are involved with less strenuous, peripheral activities. Traditionally, women have been assigned tasks connected with the home; men have been assigned work (such as hunting) requiring long periods spent away from home. Nevertheless, women in many societies do work requiring considerable physical strength. Despite the pervasiveness of the sexual division of labor, anthropologists are just beginning to investigate its adaptive significance.

Equally important for the success of a procurement strategy are the means of motivating people to work and produce. On one level we work in order to survive, but on another we do so because of the personal and social rewards that accrue. This is especially true in preindustrial societies where people work as much for prestige, fellowship, and security as for food or economic gain.

The elaboration of a successful procurement strategy and the combination of knowledge and organization to carry it out do not guarantee human survival. There remains the crucial adaptive problem of maintaining human numbers in balance with the food supply. *Natality* (birth rate), *mortality* (death rate), and *life span* are affected by the quality and quantity of the food supply and the overall conditions of "risk" within each society.

The procurement strategy developed by a society is a reflection of its adaptation to the environment. The distribution of the human population is related in turn to the five major environmental zones—grasslands, deserts, the arctic and subarctic, temperate forests, and tropical forests. Anthropologists have discovered that procurement systems vary less in response to broad environmental characteristics than to local patterns of environmental variation.

Every environment has a specific *carrying capacity,* or potential for supporting life, that is computed by establishing the minimum amount of vegetable and animal matter, as well as its nutritional value, regularly available for human consumption. To avoid malnutrition, human populations must adjust to variations not only in the quantity and quality of their resources but also to seasonal and yearly fluctuations. Thus an area's carrying capacity is not an environmental given. Rather it is variable, depending on the nature of a particular procurement system, the efficiency of resource exchange among groups, and climatic factors.

Each society must also adapt to the presence and activities of neighboring populations. Human groups compete for available resources and are at the same time mutually dependent within the larger environmental framework. Thus we find human beings exhibiting the most varied local patterns of behavior of any animal. Often populations inhabiting the same local environment are able to peacefully coexist because they adapt to different econiches—or segments of the total environment—by exploiting a distinct set of resources within that environment. But other forms of adaptation are possible, as when groups become socially and economically interdependent and do not compete directly. Or conversely, one group may be taken over or driven out by a more aggressive or technologically more advanced population. No form of environmental adaptation is static, however; every human group can change its adaptive strategy when conditions warrant it.

There are five major procurement patterns practiced in the world today: hunting and gathering; extensive or shifting agriculture; intensive agriculture; pastoralism; and industrialism. These procurement patterns have an evolutionary history, dating from 2.5 million years ago when human beings began to systematically gather and hunt for food. Today automation is leading us into a postindustrial era, whose parameters we are not yet sure of. From an evolutionary perspective what is most important is that procurement strategies are increasingly being organized on a global scale.

suggested readings

BOUGHEY, A. S.
1973 *The Ecology of Populations.* 2d ed. New York: Macmillan. An introduction to ecology, providing definitions of many of the ecological concepts anthropologists have found useful in their studies of resource acquisition and demography.

STEWARD, J. H.
1972 *Theory of Culture Change: The Methodology of Multilinear Evolution.* Urbana: University of Illinois Press. A collection of Steward's theoretical and substantive essays. These works provided the initial impetus for the development of an ecological tradition within anthropology.

SWEDLUND, A.
1975 Population Studies in Archaeology and Biological Anthropology. *Memoirs of the Society for American Anthropology.* No. 30. An anthology containing essays by some of the physical anthropologists, archeologists, and sociocultural anthropologists currently considering the importance of demographic variables to human society and their effects upon us.

VAYDA, A. P., ED.
1969 *Environment and Cultural Behavior: Ecological Studies in Cultural Anthropology.* This anthology contains a broad spectrum of theoretical and substantive articles, indicating the manner in which ecological studies are carried out in anthropology and the results of such studies.

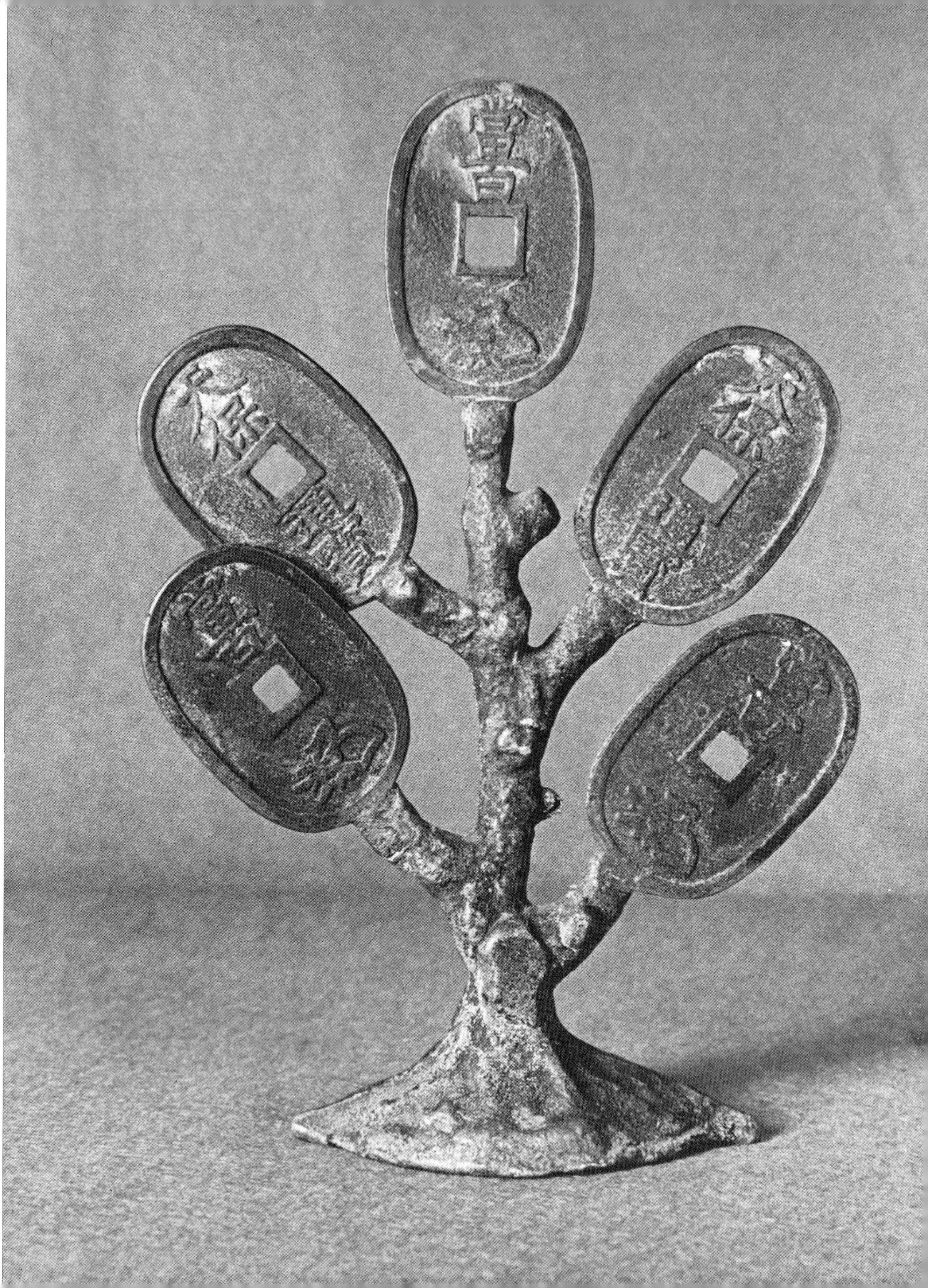

seventeen
Economics: Ownership, Production, Distribution, and Exchange

The Shilluk of the Sudan are enthusiastic stock breeders. But although a man may keep hundreds of cattle, he chooses to hunt wild game rather than to slaughter his cattle for meat. His cows yield very little milk, and he rarely uses his oxen for any purpose at all. To many of us who are accustomed to putting our capital resources to work, this may sound like the grossest kind of resource mismanagement. Similarly, we might view the Moala or Mandari chief who gives away most of his accumulated surplus food at a lavish feast and winds up poorer than his subjects as foolish and improvident. What about the profit motive, or saving? Why do some Melanesians pile yams in the chief's house, leaving them to rot? How do we explain economic systems that operate along principles seemingly so different from our own?

To answer these questions, we must first understand what we mean by an economic system. In Chapter 16, we examined some of the different ways in which people obtain resources. But resources are seldom used in exactly the same state as they are found in nature. Every society processes its resources for ultimate consumption and use; and every society also distributes both its resources and the goods and services it produces. These two activities—production and distribution—are the basic tasks of all economies. But the ways in which these tasks are accomplished vary greatly from culture to culture. To understand how different peoples process, distribute, and use their resources, how they balance what is available against needs and wants, we must broaden our own notions of production, distribution, and consumption and frame general questions about the functions of economic systems and how they are carried out. First, who controls resources and how is access to their use regulated? Second, what is the nature of the production process? How are natural resources combined with tools, technology, and human labor to produce final products, and what are these final products? Third, how is the final distribution of goods and services achieved? Who ends up getting what? And finally, through what mechanisms are exchanges of resources and goods and services accomplished? The various solutions that different societies have come up with for these universal problems are the subject of this chapter.

Regulating Access to Resources

A group's strategy for securing natural resources is generally based on some assurance of continued access to an area of land on which resources are located. This can be accomplished by establishing a territory and giving community members the right to use the land, water, wild plants and animals, and various raw materials within that defined region. But societies vary in terms of how rigidly they establish and maintain territorial boundaries. The United States, like most agricultural and industrial societies, maintains clear-cut boundaries defining the area within which our

Market exchange is the basis of the American economy. But in many nonindustrial societies, reciprocity and/or redistribution are the predominant forms of exchange. This was true in the nineteenth-century Orient when money was only infrequently used. Pictured here is a money "tree" of the period, cast in bronze and/or brass. The money was broken off and used whenever a good or service could not be secured by more traditional means of exchange. (William R. Devine, courtesy, The Chase Manhattan Bank)

The Yörük of Turkey are a pastoral group whose economic base is sheepherding. Like many other pastoralists, they must make seasonal migrations based upon the availability of water and fodder for their herds. Seasonal nomadism requires fairly free access to resources, and so the territorial boundaries of pastoral groups are much more flexible than those of sedentary agricultural and industrial societies. (Daniel G. Bates)

citizens are free to travel, settle, and make a living. Although normally these borders are not actively patrolled, they are respected tacitly and by international agreement; Canadians or Mexicans cannot simply move to the United States and start a farm or factory. In other societies, however, boundaries are more flexible and open. The Eskimo, for example, have no concept of trespass; although distinct groups are associated with particular regions by tradition, people move freely from one area to another, often joining other bands to hunt and fish. A hunting and gathering way of life such as that of the Eskimo requires that people move according to the seasonal availability of resources. Restricted to its own limited territory and unable to range in search of fresh water sources, stands of plants, or herds of game, a hunting and gathering band would probably starve when a climatic fluctuation depleted the local water supply or altered the distribution of wild animals and plants. Typically, the more uncertain or mobile the food supply, the greater the need for flexible boundaries and resource sharing.

Property Rights to Resources

But maintaining a territory is only a first step in allocating rights to resources. Human societies have also developed principles concerning who may use which resources and under what circumstances. In capitalistic industrial societies, control of resources is based on the concept of private property. Americans tend to regard land, water, minerals, machinery, and all types of productive resources as things that someone can own more or less exclusively. Owners, whether individuals or corporations, decide who has access to their resources and when. They have a free hand in determining how those resources will be exploited. Their rights include the right to sell their property or to rent it for any period of time. Of course, even the most capitalistic economies recognize that the concept of private property has certain limitations. Transportation systems and the equipment for generating and distributing fuel and electricity are often considered "public utilities" and are heavily regulated, sometimes even owned outright by local or state governments. Zoning laws further limit the actual use one may make of private property. Nevertheless, our basic definition of resource ownership emphasizes individual control for individual benefit. The idea that productive resources can be owned exclusively by certain individuals, however, is alien to many peoples. In many societies, a whole host of people—kinsmen or community members—have broad rights of access to land and natural resources, as well as to tools and other productive implements.

Land-Holding Systems: Ownership versus Use
In the case of land and other natural resources, some societies vest ownership in the community or kin group at large. Individual members or households may have the right to use these resources for limited periods, but users do not own them—they can neither buy nor sell the land they farm, for example. The community holds collective *proprietary rights,* while individuals have *rights of use*. Thus while people in most Western societies acquire land and other natural resources through purchase or rental, people in the majority of hunting-gathering, horticultural, and pastoral societies establish their rights to land resources through membership in a social group. As a member of a band, a Bushman automatically acquires the right to hunt and collect wild foods within the territory belonging to his or her group. If a woman marries and joins her husband's band, she acquires additional foraging rights in that band's

This Pennsylvania farm is a symbol of the concept of private property—ownership is in the hands of an individual farmer, who has exclusive rights to both the land and everything on it. Only he or his family can make decisions regarding the renting or selling of the farm and determine how and to what extent its resources will be exploited. (Grant Heilman)

territory. The Bushmen say it does not matter who owns the land itself, since one cannot eat the ground. Rather, each band collectively holds rights to exploit specific water resources and patches of wild plant foods (Marshall, 1966). With few exceptions, pastoral peoples, like hunter-gatherers, do not subdivide their territories or allocate portions to specific families or individuals. Grazing lands are generally treated as a communal asset, open to all members of the tribe, or at least to all members of the large and cooperating kin groups which typically migrate and settle together.

Cultivators, on the other hand, are generally concerned with allocating rights to use specific plots. In most horticultural societies, people acquire land by virtue of their social position and retain title to certain plots by actively using them. Among the Tiv of Nigeria, for example, the head of a household is allowed to cultivate and settle on any unused piece of land within the territory belonging to his lineage — a group of 200 to 300 people, all of whom are descended from a common ancestor. He may lay claim to as much land as his household can handle. So long as he actively works these fields and keeps them clear, he is entitled to exclusive use. When fields revert to fallow, however, these rights lapse and the land becomes part of the public domain, to be claimed by other families in the lineage. Nevertheless, a Tiv man always retains a right to some land — if not to one particular field, then to another — simply because he is a member of a particular kin group (Bohannan, 1960). Other cultivators usually have similar systems for establishing rights to land use. These rights, however, may not be determined by membership in a kin group, but rather through residence in a village or through the performance of some social obligation.

Under the impact of commercialization and Western influence, private property has replaced traditional land-use systems in many parts of the world. As a result, the economic system has become more impersonal and less tied to the general system of social relationships. For example, Buganda chiefs traditionally allotted portions of their estates to tenant farmers. These grants could be revoked at any time. The British colonial administration, however, passed a law enabling tenants to do as they liked with their land grants — even pass them on to their heirs without permission from the chief. The aim was to protect tenant farmers from exploitation, and in the process to bring them more thoroughly under colonial control through land registration and systematic taxation. As a result, Buganda land is now individually owned (Southwold, 1966). In some societies this process has been carried out without the direct intervention of the state. In the Swiss canton of Valais, farmlands once kept within the family now circulate freely on the open market. Originally, land changed hands only when passed from one generation to the next within the same family. But as more and more people became wage laborers, attitudes toward the land changed. Farming became a secondary means of production, and community members were able to buy what land they needed with money obtained by working or selling surplus goods outside their villages. Today, farming has become even less important, and land is regarded primarily as an investment. No longer farmed, it is merely kept as security for possible future needs or for its resale value (Berthoud, 1972). This same process has affected a very large number of societies.

The Control of Capital Goods In addition to a system for allocating land, all peoples must have some way of establishing and coordinating rights to tools, storage equipment, means of transportation, and other capital goods. In our own society, most capital goods such as factories, machinery, tools, trucks, or warehouses are privately owned. In most tribal societies, however, few tools and other man-made productive resources are held unconditionally and exclusively by single individuals.

Among hunters and gatherers, a person may be said to own a weapon or a tool, but that seldom implies exclusive rights to them. A hunter who makes a spear thrower or a bear trap owns the implement only in the sense that he has first right of use; when he is not using the tool, others may lay claim to it. Since hunters work together closely and survival depends on sharing, tools and weapons are lent and exchanged freely. Proprietary rights usually become more fixed and formalized where productive goods are more complex and difficult to make or acquire.

Manufacturing is largely a specialized activity in most agricultural societies, and it becomes even more specialized as industrialization develops. In agricultural societies, the specialist who makes plows or pottery is owner and master of the production implements — the forge, potter's wheel, kiln, or whatever materials and instruments he or she uses. The maker sees the product through from start to finish and owns it until it is sold. In a capitalistic industrial society, however, the relationship between workers, their tools, and their products is far less intimate. The factory workers who make tractors and combines will probably never use any of the farming machinery they produce. They are involved only in a specific and limited portion of the production process, and they own neither the product (unless they choose to buy it from the company) nor the factory and manufacturing equipment. They are simply selling their labor to a business firm at a rate set by the workings of the market system. Labor, then, becomes a commodity like any other. Alienation — the fragmentation of relations between individuals, their work, and ownership of products and capital resources — is one consequence of industrial specialization and private enterprise.

Production

Assigning rights of access to resources is only a starting point in the actual use of those resources. Very few of the resources people use are used exactly as they come from nature. Animals must be butchered and are usually cooked; plant foods are pounded, ground, sliced, and also frequently cooked; stone and wood are transformed in a variety of ways before they ultimately become our tools and houses. Producing usable goods, then, is as important a part of survival as acquiring resources.

The Organization of Production

How is production organized? How are the resources found in nature processed to fulfill human needs and wants? The organization of production takes many different forms in different societies. In our own society, the basic producing unit is the business firm, be it an individually owned gas station or a giant oil corporation. The work of the firm is carried out by a group of trained specialists — sales representatives, marketing managers, accountants, typists, technicians — each hired to accomplish a designated task in the total production process. Firms engage in an enormous number of different productive activities, from converting raw materials into other usable resources — as, for example, processing iron into steel — to producing our extraordinary array of final goods and services — industrial machinery, office equipment, cars, appliances, clothing, frozen foods, insurance, and health care, to name just a few. It has been aptly said that the business of American society is business. This is to say that production in our society is not directly geared to social ends. Instead, the well-being of our economy is gauged by rates of production, regardless of the ends to which production is directed. Should production levels falter, as they do cyclically, unemployment is an accepted consequence despite there being areas in which the idle labor force might be usefully employed.

In most nonindustrial societies, in contrast, the business firm as we know it may not exist. Instead, the basic producing unit is often the household or domestic group. When technology is relatively simple, all the skills needed for production can be found in a single household. In most horticultural societies, for instance, the members of a household will have the knowledge and abilities required to plant and tend their gardens, to fashion hoes,

Among the Kpelle of Africa the household is the basic producing unit. All the skills and techniques required for production—such as the pounding of manioc to an edible foodstuff with wooden mortar and pestle, which is pictured here—are performed by its members. As in most nonindustrial societies, production strategies are geared to the needs of the household. Virtually everything produced is consumed by it; there is little interest in creating a surplus to sell in the marketplace. (Jacques Jangoux)

spades, digging sticks, and other cultivating tools, and to make clothing and ornaments, as well as pots, baskets, and other cooking or storing utensils. If a certain task is too large to be handled efficiently by a single household, the additional effort will simply be supplied by kinspeople or friends, who jointly participate in many different activities—political, religious, and social, as well as economic. The construction of a canoe is a village event for the Trobriand Islanders; relatively large groups of friends and kin cooperate in this large-scale project, which is also marked by ritual and feasting (Malinowski, 1922). Sometimes, too, factors of risk suggest that a particular task is better handled jointly than individually. Among the Jie of East Africa, a man herds some of his kinsmen's cattle along with his own animals. This system minimizes the risk that a person's entire stock will be destroyed if disease strikes a particular herd (Gulliver, 1955).

The kind of domestic production we have been discussing has declined somewhat with the spread of Western industrialism. However, it is still useful to compare such a system, organized around close-knit groups of friends and relatives, with our own. In the United States, although a person may occasionally work in the same company as a relative and may make friends through work, business firms are only rarely organized around a group of friends or kinspeople. Moreover, our business firms are directed almost exclusively toward production, with profitability being the final measure of their success. In technologically simpler societies, on the other hand, productive activities are usually embedded in an organization that directly serves many functions we would term "noneconomic." This does not mean that social organization is unrelated to the organization of production in industrial societies such as our own. On the contrary, the basic fabric of our social order is formed by the allocation of different productive roles to different people in a systematic way. But it does mean that producing units in our society are concerned almost entirely with economic ends.

Strategies of Production

Like resource acquisition, production requires special knowledge of economic relationships and carefully devised strategies based on that knowledge. In our own society, the knowledge and strategies relevant to the operation of a firm are the domain of specialists—economists and business managers. In societies based on the domestic mode of production, however, such knowledge is held by all people to a far greater degree. Individuals, as well as the domestic and larger groups of which they are members, routinely use knowledge of economic variables to formulate production strategies.

But regardless of *who* is formulating production strategies, in all societies people are attempting to *economize* — that is, to get the most they can (in either a quantitative or a qualitative sense) out of the scarce resources available to them. But societies differ in how they define and what strategies they use to solve this basic economic problem. In our own society, at least in the private sector, production strategies are formulated primarily around the goal of maximizing profits. Business firms attempt to increase their profitability by minimizing some cost of production, be it the cost of natural resources, capital equipment, or labor. Our economic philosophy is based on the assumption that out of the many profit-motivated production decisions made by business firms in response to consumer preferences, the "right" production strategies from the point of view of society will ultimately be formulated; specific goods and services will be produced in quantities consistent with people's willingness and ability to purchase them. Production strategies in our society are also formulated around the goal of growth. Most business firms aim ultimately to increase their volume of output. Such growth is possible because firms are producing not for a small group of people but rather for a large market that frequently spans an entire nation, or even many nations.

In societies where the household is the basic producing unit, in contrast, production strategies are based on a different set of considerations. People are devising means of producing goods to fulfill their own needs, and these needs are often defined in a way that limits the production of a surplus.[1] A household's needs are perceived within a social environment that places little value on or may even ridicule the acquisition of material goods. Consequently, a household that produces a surplus converts this "excess" output into social prestige by giving it away; it does not reinvest the surplus in order to increase its own capital holdings. Thus the central production question in such societies is not how can goods be produced and sold to earn the greatest financial profit, but rather how can enough goods be produced to meet this household's material or social requirements?

Since people in preindustrial societies are working not for themselves alone but as part of a domestic group, the answer to this question is heavily influenced by the number of productive individuals in a particular household as well as by the energy and skills of those individuals. Marshall Sahlins has stated this relationship more precisely in what is known as Chayanov's rule: intensity of labor in a system of domestic production for domestic use varies inversely with the relative working capacity of the producing unit (Sahlins, 1972: 91). This simply means that people in a given household must work harder when there are many mouths to feed relative to the number of people capable of performing basic subsistence tasks. For example, if a household is composed primarily of very young and very old people, the small proportion of adults in their prime productive years will have to work quite intensively to supply the group's needs. Conversely, if a household has many productive members and few dependent ones, its producers will find themselves in the enviable position of having much time to devote to leisure.

But exactly how do households in preindustrial societies vary the intensity of their labor so as to provide for their own needs? The answer is by modifying one of several factors, all of which are governed to some extent by cultural norms. First, there is the speed and efficiency with which a person works, how much he or she accomplishes in a given period of time. This is often referred to as output per man-hour or level of productivity. The

---

[1] Our discussion is based on the traditional pattern of the household as a self-sustaining unit. However, it should be noted that as more and more societies begin to participate in the world economy, production, even at the household level, becomes more oriented to surpluses for sale in the marketplace.

Production Decisions Among the Kapauku

How are production decisions made and how do they relate to ecological factors? To help answer these questions, let us consider the case of the Kapauku of New Guinea, already discussed in Chapter 16, and how they utilized land located at the bottom of mountain valleys (Buchler and Kozelka, n.d.; White, 1973).

The accompanying table shows the factors relevant to the decision-making process. The choice of crops includes root crops, sugar cane, and sweet potatoes. The second column shows the various crop yields in terms of kilograms per peka (a unit of land). The third column indicates the nutritional value (measured in terms of calories per kilogram) of each of the crops; the fourth column, the yield of a peka of land in terms of thousands of calories; and the last column, the hours of labor needed to cultivate a peka of each crop. We will assume that there are 30 pekas of valley bottom land available for cultivation and 10,556 hours of labor.

If the Kapauku tried to make their decision based on caloric yield alone, they would choose to plant all 30 pekas in sugar cane. However, this would require 12,030 hours of labor (30 pekas × 401 hours per peka), more labor than is available. Similarly, if they tried to make their decision based solely on labor, cultivating all 30 acres in root crops would minimize the labor expenditure (30 pekas × 210 hours per peka = 6300 hours), but it would also yield a minimum number of kilocalories (30 pekas × 1200 kilocalories per peka = 36,000 kilocalories).

Solving a set of equations, it is possible to determine that the Kapauku can obtain a maximum of 44,160 kilocalories by planting 4.5 pekas in root crops, none in sugar cane, and 25.5 in sweet potatoes. How closely do the Kapauku approximate this optimal yield? Pospisil (1963) reports that they use 5.8 pekas for root crops, 9.6 for sugar cane, and 14.6 for sweet potatoes. This strategy yields 44,127 kilocalories, very close to the optimal. Apparently, the Kapauku wish to grow sugar cane in the valley bottoms, and given that they do, their balance among the three crops is an optimal one in terms of kilocalorie yield.

This is not to say that the Kapauku actually go through the kinds of calculations we have just made in determining how much of each crop to plant. We do not know to what extent the ratio between the three crops is a result of explicit decision making at a single point in time or of trial and error over decades. But we must suspect that both these processes were and continue to be important.

Crop	Yield in Kilograms Per Peka		Caloric Value Per Kilogram		Yield in Kilocalories Per Peka	Hours of Labor Required Per Peka
Root crops (shifting cultivation of taro and sweet potatoes)	1200	×	1,000	=	1200	210
Sugar cane	5200	×	300	=	1560	401
Sweet potatoes (intensive cultivation)	1520	×	1,000	=	1520	376

members of every society have a general notion of what the average person's productivity should be for a particular task. Productivity is of course greatly influenced by the types of tools people have at their disposal. A person with a tractor can obviously furrow a field more quickly than a person with an ox and simple wooden plow. But even using similar equipment, people in different societies define the acceptable level of productivity in different ways.

A second factor influencing intensity of labor is the concept of productive life span, the culturally established ages at which a person should ideally enter and retire from the work force. The Bushong of Africa, for instance, define the productive years as ages twenty to sixty; the neighboring Lele regard ages thirty to fifty as one's appropriate working life (Douglas, 1962). Clearly the average Lele household will have more nonproducers than the average Bushong household; consequently, most Lele will have to work more intensively during their productive years than will most Bushong.

Finally, there is the concept of workday or workweek, the proper number of hours each day and days each week that people believe they should spend working. Members of many hunting and gathering bands consider it normal to work three to five hours a day; and in most other preindustrial societies, underproduction—that is, working fewer hours a day than *could* be worked—is also the rule. This does not mean that people in such societies are lazy. It simply means that they attach a good deal of value to leisure and to the fulfillment of social obligations, and relatively little value to consumption and the acquisition of goods for their own sake.

The concepts of productivity, life span, and workday, although culturally defined, are often redefined by individuals and households in making adjustments to their own particular circumstances. We know in our own society, for instance, that some people will ignore cultural guidelines regarding the normal length of a workday and take on two eight-hour jobs, one in the daytime and one at night. Their reason is usually to make ends meet or to accumulate a large savings account rapidly. The same is true in preindustrial societies. For example, a Lele household that found itself particularly short of members in the culturally defined productive years might well be forced to assign tasks to those under thirty or over fifty. If we were to survey a sample of Lele households, we would find significant variation in the ages of the youngest and oldest working members of each domestic group. Such variation reflects adjustment to individual circumstances. Every household is engaged in the process of varying the intensity of its labor to the level needed to produce an appropriate amount of goods. Households can and do adjust both working age and working hours, as well as output per man-hour, to meet their particular requirements.

As we mentioned earlier, however, intensity of labor is also affected by factors other than need. Sahlins found, for instance, that among the Kapauku of New Guinea some households produced more than would be expected on the basis of their numbers alone, while others produced far less than their sizes seemed to warrant. Why was this so? The Kapauku have a form of political organization with well-established leaders known as "big men." These leaders and their families tend to be overproducers, while their followers and their followers' families tend to be underproducers. The big men maintain their authority primarily through conspicuous and carefully calculated generosity toward their followers. In the end, all receive enough to fulfill their individual needs. Among the Kapauku, therefore, political and economic decisions are very closely related.

Production, Investment, and Saving

In every society, no matter how technologically simple or complex, production cannot be carried out in the absence of some form of investment. Investment can be defined simply as the acquisition of capital goods or equipment, items that are not consumed but rather used to produce other goods and services. In our own society, business firms invest whenever they buy new machinery, build a new factory or warehouse, or acquire a new fleet of trucks, for example. All these purchases are investments in capital goods which in turn will be used to produce other goods and ultimately bring in revenue. Investment is not possible without saving, for investment must somehow be financed. Again, in our own society, businesses save a portion of their own profits to be used for investment purposes, or they borrow some of the accumulated savings of households and individuals through bank loans or through the sale of bonds. For us, then, consumption, saving, and investment are relatively distinct activities.

In many parts of the world, however, the boundaries between consumption, saving, and investment are much less clear. Harold Schneider has pointed out that in many African societies, cattle are capital goods, savings, and consumer goods all in one. They are capital goods in the sense that they produce milk and manure; savings in the sense that, like money in our own society, they are a means of storing wealth; and consumer goods in that they are butchered for meat and their hides used for leather. Here, it is very difficult to separate an act of saving from an act of investment, or the acquisition of a consumer good from the acquisition of a capital good. As with many aspects of life in preindustrial societies, our own distinctions and categories do not neatly apply; many areas and activities that we consider separate and distinct are instead highly overlapping.

Economic Equality and Inequality: The Final Distribution of Products

Whatever the organization and strategies for producing goods and services, in the end those products will be distributed to members of society along systematic lines. But while there is a set of mechanisms governing distribution in every society, those mechanisms vary from culture to culture. In some societies everyone receives roughly the same material benefits; in others, economic holdings are markedly unequal. How are these distribution patterns organized and maintained? And how did they develop in the first place?

Egalitarian Distribution Patterns

Economic disparities might easily develop in any society. Within every population there are certain individuals who are more skillful, smarter, or stronger, or who work harder. What is to prevent such people from acquiring an extra piece of pie? In some societies, such as our own, this is roughly what does occur—a factory foreman who works overtime receives more pay; a skillful lawyer is likely to get more clients and command higher fees than one who has less ability; a person who runs a very profitable corporation will probably be more successful financially than one whose firm is just struggling along. Moreover, the distribution of material rewards in our society is related to the place one occupies in the productive system. Even the hardest-working foreman cannot expect to earn anywhere near the salary of a corporation president. Thus our economic system generally rewards both occupational status and personal accomplishments with material benefits.

In many societies, however, this is not the case. For instance, among the Bushmen, as in most hunter-gatherer societies, the capable hunter receives a certain amount of respect and social esteem, but his prowess does not bring him wealth in the sense of an unusually large store of food. Like all hunters he is obligated to share his game equally with other members of the band. The Bushmen regard any sort of material inequality—whether in the form of food or nonperishable items such as tools and weapons—as a source of jealousy and conflict that may cause the band to disintegrate (Marshall, 1966). Hoarding or simply refusing to share brings severe social disapproval. Prestige goes to the person who is open-handed and generous. Inevitably, the successful hunter or the skilled toolmaker will end up providing a larger than average share of the total pool of goods. But he is motivated to do so because in return for his economic contribution, he gains personal status in the eyes of his fellow band members. Thus the system has a built-in *leveling mechanism* that prevents certain individuals from accumulating a disproportionate amount of economic goods.

The situation is somewhat more complicated in societies where the procurement system enables people to produce economic surpluses more readily, and a sedentary lifestyle permits them to acquire a relatively large number of material possessions. Moreover, in many horticultural and agricultural societies, individuals are unequally ranked in an elaborate status hierarchy that confers certain social advantages and ceremonial prerogatives on those at the top. Such a social system — referred to as a *rank society*—would seem to promote disparities in wealth. In fact, however, economic equality is the norm. Here again, powerful leveling mechanisms serve to keep economic distribution patterns relatively egalitarian.

For example, many rank societies are headed by a chief. He may have achieved this position through his own personal accomplishments or inherited the title as the senior member in a line of descent. In either case, it is incumbent on the chief to manage the community's economic resources and to redistribute them for the general well-being. As chief, he collects surplus food and material goods from his followers. Although he usually keeps a certain amount for his own personal use, the greater portion is given away in payment for special social services (military defense, road building, irrigation construction, and so forth), as economic assistance for those in need, or in the form of ceremonial feasts and gifts. In fact, the chief cannot maintain his position of authority unless he fulfills these economic obligations. As among the Bushmen, material wealth is given up in exchange for social prestige.

The Kwakiutl Indians of British Columbia are one of the few recent hunting and gathering peoples with a sedentary lifestyle and a rank society. They developed a particularly competitive leveling mechanism — the potlatch, an elaborate ceremonial event where vast quantities of food were consumed and the guests were lavished with gifts. Kwakiutl society was divided into *numayms,* kin-based groups headed by chiefs, the members of which worked together to hunt, fish, and gather wild plant foods. Each numaym had access to roughly equivalent sets of economic resources. Owing to yearly fluctuations, however, a group might prosper one year and then find itself short of food the next season. The potlatch provided a way to equalize the distribution of resources by preventing one group from amassing large surpluses while another numaym went hungry or lost its material goods. For example, if one numaym suffered severe food shortages, it could always sell some of its blankets, totem poles, canoes, and the like for food. As a result, however, the group's economic stores would be severely depleted while another numaym became the richer. The potlatch enabled the first group to recover its loss. With the material goods received, the second numaym could hold more potlatches and bestow more gifts. Their prestige was thereby enhanced. As guests, the members of the first numaym would receive large numbers of presents — perhaps even more goods than they had sold in the first place. Thus they were able to regain their wealth in return for granting more prestige to their hosts (Piddocke, 1965). Although leveling mechanisms are not always as intensely competitive as the Kwakiutl potlatch, rank societies have all devised one means or another to ensure a relatively even economic distribution.

Stratified Distribution Patterns

In most complex agricultural and industrial societies, economic resources are not allocated in such an equal fashion. Although Americans pride themselves on being relatively open and egalitarian, there are wide socioeconomic differences between various segments of our society. There is in fact a discrepancy between the ideal ("America is a classless society in which all men are equal") and the economic reality (the wealthiest fifth of our population makes at least six and one-half times more than the poorest fifth). Our society is divided into *social classes* — categories of people who share roughly the same economic status, the same degree of access to economic resources, and similar lifestyles. Nevertheless, all Americans, we believe, have a chance of bettering themselves economically, of acquiring material wealth and moving up the class ladder. When we compare ourselves to societies in which the population is divided into *social castes* — categories of people whose economic and social position is permanently ascribed at birth — our own gap between rich and poor may seem relatively smaller and less absolute. But this is not necessarily the case. Actually, there may be a far greater difference between the economic standing of an American factory owner and factory worker than between upper- and lower-caste individuals in a society where economic inequality is openly avowed and accepted.

India provides a case in point. There are about 3,000 unequally ranked castes in India. Many of these are associated with particular occupations — Brahmans with the priesthood and scholarship, Chamars with leatherworking, Katis with carpentry, Lohars with blacksmithing, and so on. In many Indian villages, the various caste groups are tied together in an exchange network known as the *jajmani system.* Usually there is a dominant caste that not only outranks the others but also owns most of the land in the community. Each upper-caste family is served by a particular blacksmith, carpenter, washerman, barber, and so on. The relationship between a client *(jajman)* and a servicing family *(kamin)* is hereditary and bound by tradition. For example, the washerman must continue to provide his jajman with regular weekly service in exchange for a fixed annual fee; he cannot demand a raise or suddenly change to a more lucrative occupation; if he becomes ill or leaves town, he must provide his clients with a substitute. For his part, the client cannot change his washerman even if he is dissatisfied with his services; at harvest time the jajman must provide each of the families who have served him with the customary amount of grain, regardless of his economic circumstances. When the harvest is good, he usually manages to make a substantial profit. But during bad years, after distributing their grain an upper-caste family may have less to show for their efforts than members of the lower castes. Kamins also benefit in other ways from this system — usually they receive a small amount of land, free fodder, timber, and credit facilities from their jajman. Thus a good deal of economic equality may prevail even where the social system is explicitly based on the premise of inequality (Epstein, 1967).

The Development of Economic Inequalities

Before the development of agriculture roughly 10,000 years ago, economic equality was probably universal. People lived in nomadic bands and tribes, sharing their resources much as modern hunting and gathering populations do today. With farming and the domestication of animals, however, production became more specialized and complex, and a structure of authority emerged to direct and coordinate activities. Although early agricultural societies established systems of social ranking in which chiefs had the authority to control resources and production, economic differences between individuals remained relatively small. Leveling mechanisms probably operated then, as now, to maintain a relatively egalitarian distribution pattern. The first evidence of significant inequalities in wealth dates from the development of large-scale cities and states. As societies became larger, positions and roles more specialized, and political control more concentrated in centralized bureaucratic organizations, certain families and professions acquired enormous power over resources and economic activities. Rulers exacted tributes and taxes from the less powerful, accumulated vast stores of food and valued articles, and lived in a manner altogether different from peasants and artisans. These differences were solidified in the form

Most complex agricultural and industrial societies are divided into social castes or classes, each with differential access to economic resources. As a result, goods and services are unequally distributed among the population. In American society, for example, there is a wide discrepancy between the economic holdings of the upper-class elite and those of the New York City slum dwellers pictured here.
(Bruce Davidson/Magnum)

of rigid social classes or castes, which have been passed down from generation to generation. Although today more people enjoy a moderate standard of living than ever before, in some societies the gap between the poorest and the wealthiest segments is greater than ancient kings or priest-rulers could ever have imagined.

Colonialism and the spread of capitalism in the modern world have contributed heavily to the development of economic inequities between individuals, communities, and nations. When Europeans established colonies in Asia, Africa, and the Americas, they extracted a great deal of wealth in the form of tropical and semitropical plantation crops (sugar, cotton, coffee, tobacco) and raw materials (gold, silver, lumber, oil). Instead of investing their profits to develop the regions where these items were grown and produced, most of the wealth was used for the development of the colonizing nations. Heavy taxes, one-sided trade arrangements that forced colonists to sell only to the mother country and to buy commodities at excessive prices, and laws forbidding the operation of local industries or

Sisal Agriculture in Northeastern Brazil

People throughout history have tried to increase their chances of securing a better and more dependable living from their environment. But as is the case with most human endeavors, not all of our efforts succeed or bring about the results we had intended. A clear example of such unmet expectations was recently reported by Daniel Gross and Barbara Underwood (1971), who investigated the impact of a new crop on the people of the arid *sertão* region of northeastern Brazil.

Traditionally, the *sertão* inhabitants raised cattle and engaged in subsistence farming. In years of adequate rainfall, many families were able to be self-sufficient, but in years of low rainfall or drought (which occurred approximately once every 11 years), families were forced either to leave the area or depend on the more influential members of the community, who would petition for and sponsor Federal aid programs.

In the mid-1900s, many people thought they could see the end to the subsistence farmers' cycle of dependency and uncertainty. At that time, a drought-resistant plant known as sisal was beginning to be harvested on a relatively large scale as an export crop. Sisal, which takes four years to reach maturity, contains a tough, fibrous material that is used as twine. Extracting this fiber from the leaves, or *decorticating,* is long and arduous work requiring heavy machinery.

The first sisal plantations were owned by large local landholders. Later, small landholders were to give up subsistence farming in hopes of profiting from the rapidly escalating—although fluctuating—sisal profits. While waiting for their crops to mature, they would work for cash on the large plantations. Unfortunately, the small farmers often found that by the time their plants were ready to be harvested, the market price of sisal had drastically fallen, leaving their potential profits marginal at best. Even in cases where profits might have been high, they often would be greatly reduced by the owners of decorticating machines, who would charge excessive rates for equipment rental. Thus, many of the ex-subsistence farmers discovered that, in order to make a living, they had no choice but to remain as laborers on the larger sisal farms. (Because sisal is virtually impossible to eradicate once planted, their chances of using the land for subsistence farming again were very small.)

By comparing the number of calories sisal workers expend in their work with the energy available in the amount of food they can afford to buy, Gross and Underwood have shown the degree to which the sisal workers have suffered. In many instances, the researchers found that sisal workers simply cannot afford to buy enough food to both meet their own high energy needs and feed their families. The result of this inadequacy is indicated by the fact that a full 45 percent of the children of sisal workers are significantly underweight.

In contrast to what was originally anticipated, then, the introduction of sisal as an export crop has *decreased* the standard of living for the majority of *sertão* inhabitants rather than increased it. Furthermore, the laborers are now almost completely dependent on the minority that owns the farms and controls the machinery.

businesses that might compete with those "at home" often prevented colonial dependencies from accumulating capital of their own. In short, traditional economies were harnessed to the development of the colonial powers.

Colonial entrepreneurs managed to minimize production costs by keeping labor costs down. In some areas, the initial solution was slavery. Eventually, however, after slavery was outlawed by most Western nations and the cost of maintaining a large slave population had become prohibitive, the *corvée* system was adopted as an alternative. The corvée, especially prevalent in colonial Africa, requires that members of each native household pay an annual tax or work on European-owned farms and public projects for a certain period of the year. In other regions, particularly in Latin America and Asia, Europeans expropriated fertile agricultural areas and established landed estates worked through the *tenancy* system. In exchange for a few acres of land, the tenant farmer is compelled to turn over a large portion of his harvest to the owner. In some cases, tenants are bound to the land directly by law, but typically, the landlord maintains control over his tenants by keeping them in perpetual debt. Forced to buy machinery, seeds, fertilizers, household articles, and other basic necessities from the landlord on credit or to meet their cash needs by borrowing money at exorbitant interest rates, the tenants rarely manage to free themselves financially. Since they cannot leave the land until they have paid their debts and each year they must buy or borrow more, the farmers are effectively locked into the system. Like the corvée, tenancy guarantees landowners a cheap source of manpower.

Today, even after many former colonies have gained their independence, a lopsided distribution of wealth persists. In most areas of Latin America, where debt bondage has been abolished and many peasant communities have regained legal title to the land, their holdings are often so small or marginal that they cannot grow enough to meet subsistence requirements. As a result, many are obliged to work for low wages on cash-crop plantations. In effect, they still remain under the control of a dominant landowning class. In terms of per capita income and general economic prosperity, most Third World countries lag far behind the industrialized West. To overcome their lack of capital and to stimulate economic development, many have encouraged foreign investment. Often, however, industries are developed in terms of what foreign companies find profitable, rather than what the underdeveloped nation as a whole needs. The result is to stimulate profits for investors and a few local industrialists, landowners, and politicians, with little benefit to the rural and industrial workers. With basic manufacturing and subsistence needs frequently ignored, underdeveloped countries are forced to import large quantities of goods, leaving them with severe trade deficits. Moreover, many find that they are losing more capital than they are gaining as foreign corporations continue to extract high profits and interest payments on loans without reinvesting a commensurate amount. All this adds up to persistent, and in some cases growing, economic inequality both within and between nations.

Exchanging Resources and Products

Exchange is basic to any economic system. In fact, some anthropologists have argued that regardless of *what* is exchanged, the very act of exchange is the primary bond that holds societies together. In the processes of production and distribution, resources and goods continually change hands, and in every society there are mechanisms governing how each type of exchange should be carried out. In our own society, the *market* mechanism or commercial exchange predominates. Most people receive wages or salaries in exchange for their labor, which they then use to purchase goods and services—food, a house, shoes, dental treatment, a refrigerator, a car, entertainment. To a lesser degree, exchange also takes place through noncommercial channels. At weddings, holidays, and birthdays, relatives and friends exchange gifts.

Neighbors often exchange favors *reciprocally,* running to the grocery store for a friend who is ill, or lending the proverbial cup of sugar. Family members do not itemize how much each has contributed in terms of financial support, services, or affection; the exchange is part of the reciprocal give-and-take of domestic life. In a different sort of exchange transaction, a portion of everyone's income goes to the state and federal government to be *redistributed* to the taxpayers in the form of schools, police and military protection, Social Security payments, and other public services.

Exchange Mechanisms

These three forms of exchange—the market, reciprocity, and redistribution—are all found in our own society. But societies differ in how many and what kinds of transactions are carried out through each mechanism. In capitalistic industrialized societies, the majority of economic exchanges are conducted through the marketplace. In other economies, however, the market is only peripheral, and reciprocity and redistribution predominate. And in still other parts of the world, the market mechanism may be absent entirely, with exchange conducted by reciprocity alone or by a combination of reciprocity and redistribution. In the following sections we will discuss the various types of exchange mechanisms people have developed, pointing out the different ways they are utilized in different societies.

Reciprocity Reciprocal exchange involves mutual giving and taking between people who are bound by certain social ties and obligations. Money does not enter the picture. Although people in Western society often exchange presents and help one another informally, reciprocity plays a much more major role in preindustrial societies. Gifts are given more often, in greater quantity, and to more people; there is a stronger obligation to reciprocate; and most important, reciprocity plays a fundamental part in the actual production process (Dalton, 1962).

Depending on the closeness of the social relationships involved, reciprocity may take various forms. Family members or close friends usually engage in *generalized reciprocity*—informal gift-giving where no "accounts" are kept and no immediate or specific return is expected (Sahlins, 1965). However, it operates with the implicit understanding that goods and services exchanged usually balance out in the long run. This system of cooperative exchange is central to the survival of many hunting and gathering peoples. Among the Kalahari Bushmen, who have no means of preserving perishable meat, a hunter will immediately distribute his kill among his hunting companions, who will share their portions of the animal with specific kinsmen, who in turn will share with other kinsmen. The end result of all this sharing is an intricate web of mutual obligations that sustains the whole group through the years (Marshall, 1966).

Gift-giving that clearly carries the obligation of an eventual and roughly equal return usually occurs among more distantly related individuals who are on roughly equal terms socially, or between formal trading partners. This sort of *balanced reciprocity* is characteristic of the labor exchange systems in many horticultural and agricultural societies. At planting and harvest time, neighboring households or kin groups often take turns working on one another's farms. A person who does not repay such assistance within an appropriate time and with the same measure of labor or an equivalent gift will meet with severe social disapproval and hard feelings.

Exchanges between enemies and strangers are generally impersonal transactions, with each side trying to get the better end of the bargain. *Negative reciprocity* involves an effort to get something for nothing. It can range from unfriendly haggling to outright theft. The Mbuti Pygmies, for example, find it expedient to exchange forest products and their own labor for crops and metal with their horticultural neighbors. But these exchanges are marked by a good deal of mutual antagonism. The villagers use threats and bribes in an effort to get as much from the Mbuti as they can, while the Pygmies try to work as little as possible and only when it pleases them (Turnbull, 1966). In negative reciprocity, the "reciprocation" is contingent upon one party being more clever or stealthy in one dealing, and the other party in the next.

Redistribution Redistribution involves obligatory payments of goods, currency, or services to some central agency (a king, a chief, or the state) which subsequently reallocates some of these resources in the form of community services, emergency help, or special rewards. In our own society, this is the intended function of the federal income tax. In nonmonetary societies, the chief typically redistributes unused land, hunting sites, and food surpluses to members of his tribe. This system has several functions. While it may guarantee adequate subsistence to all members of a society, it also enhances a chief's prestige and authority. Among the Bantu, the chief reserves some of the goods received as tribute to maintain his own private stores; but most goes into providing for members of his tribe. If a man's crops fail, the chief is obligated to provide his family with food; he keeps large herds of cattle to repay warriors for their services and to provide milk for poorer families; whenever his subjects come to visit, he entertains and feeds them. In contrast to reciprocity, where exchanges are usually carried out between social equals, redistribution systems are most prominent in societies with political and social hierarchies (Sahlins, 1965).

Market Exchange Unlike reciprocity and redistribution, market exchange is a purely impersonal commercial transaction. Goods and services may be bartered directly, but are usually bought and sold at a conventional location and time, and using a standard medium of exchange—money. Beyond the requirement to pay the agreed amount for goods purchased, there is no social obligation between the parties—no ties based on kinship, friendship, or political affiliation. Instead, transactions are usually based on purely economic considerations—the producer can sell the product to whoever will give the best return; the buyer can shop around for the best bargain.

To some extent, market exchange occurs in almost all contemporary cultures; but it remains peripheral in some traditional societies. A West African farmer, for example, may well meet most of his family's subsistence needs through his own productive activities. If there happens to be a small surplus, his wife may sell some of the extra crops in the marketplace and use the profit to buy a few modest manufactured items or to pay taxes. But the range of consumer goods sold in peripheral market systems is usually quite limited. Land, labor, and capital resources are not sold

In most nonindustrial societies, each household produces virtually all of the goods and services required for its survival. Exchange, when it occurs, is usually either reciprocal or redistributive. Yet nowadays even people who produce all of their own necessities have become tied into the larger market structure, as this photo of a typical Javanese marketplace illustrates. (Nancy Palmer)

on the market at all; these change hands only through reciprocity and redistribution. By contrast, the economies of most industrial nations are largely based on market exchange. A vast commercial network, linking millions of individuals and business firms, allocates not only an enormous array of consumer products, but land, labor, and capital resources as well.

The Organization of Exchange

Usually all three forms of exchange—reciprocity, redistribution, and market exchange—operate to some degree in a society, but there are always rules governing which mode of exchange applies to particular goods or situations. Anthropologists say that societies have different *spheres of exchange*. Among the Siane of New Guinea, for example, luxury goods—tobacco, salt, nuts, oil—circulate in a free market setting; subsistence items, on the other hand, are distributed through reciprocity (Nash, 1966). In the Trobriands, treasured ceremonial objects are exchanged according to the principle of reciprocity; subsistence items, through purchase and sale. The islanders keep these two spheres of exchange entirely separate. One can never sell a ceremonial armband for yams or a canoe, for instance. There are, however, occasions and strategies for *conversion* between spheres. Among the Tiv of Nigeria it is acceptable to use brass rods (a local valuable used as a trading item in its own sphere of exchange) to obtain food, but not to exchange food for brass rods (Bohannan, 1959).

Just as there are rules governing which modes of exchange are appropriate in particular spheres, so too are there rules governing the terms on which a given exchange is transacted. Supply and demand, of course, are inevitable factors in setting a price, but other factors are also involved. Among the Kapauku of New Guinea, for example, the relationship between the traders and their relative statuses can affect the terms of the deal (Pospisil, 1963). And in our own society, although we are fond of saying that business is business and a person always sells to the highest bidder, black families could not buy houses in many areas of our country only a few years ago.

Economic Experimentation and Change

Like all aspects of a society, an economic system is never static. By experimenting with new approaches or by being forced to deviate from traditional ones, people inevitably hit on new methods that may eventually alter their economic organization. Today most underdeveloped nations are undergoing a period of economic change and social ferment that may gradually lead to overall reorganization of production. Many of these changes are coming not from broad, nationally conceived policies directed by government officials and social planners, but from the piecemeal responses of many individuals to the new conditions of industrial capitalism. In Java, for instance, commercial activity in many small towns is being altered by a group of Islamic traders who are attempting to transform their businesses from unstructured, individualistic trading operations regulated by centuries-old trade customs to more systematic enterprises dedicated to long-term economic ends. In place of the old quick turnover bazaar system where traders made only small capital investments and conducted most of their business on a one-deal-at-a-time basis, many Javanese merchants are establishing small factories and retail stores with permanent locations, fixed prices, regular hours and employees, systematic bookkeeping and planning, and new inventories more geared to urban tastes. In short, through their own initiative these *entrepreneurs* are introducing a more modern commercial organization that will probably have a profound effect on village economies throughout Java (Geertz, 1963). Whether or not the efforts of entrepreneurs reflect a conscious strategy, a number of important trends underlie their emergence. First, entrepreneurs are most commonly found engaged in activities that take them over the boundary between traditional and modern economic organization. Second, while an entrepreneurial effort may originate with an individual, it rarely succeeds unless a group is formed around the new enterprise (Barth, 1963). And finally, while entrepreneurial activities often have a highly specific focus at the outset, they typically launch fundamental changes in the systems of production and distribution.

It is important to remember, though, that economic innovations, no matter how they are introduced, are not always successful. People may experiment a good deal before coming up with an idea, technique, or product that proves more effective or socially beneficial than the old method. Moreover, changes may be relatively easy to effect in one situation, but not in another. For example, in exploring Indian villagers' willingness to accept new production methods, Epstein (1967) found that the farmers in one rural community were completely opposed to trying a new and more productive form of rice planting but were eager to take up sugar-cane cultivation. Although the farmers had no doubt that the new wet-rice technique would increase their yields, they objected because the method would have upset the traditional jajmani system and caused more social disruption than it was worth. Sugar-cane cultivation, however, was another matter. As an entirely new venture, it was not tied to the customary system of work and fixed rewards. Consequently, farmers felt free to experiment with it. Epstein also found that in another village where the jajmani system did not operate, farmers eagerly and successfully branched out into both wet-rice farming and sugar-cane cultivation.

Similarly, in our own society, we are often willing to adopt economic changes in some areas but not in others. A more mechanized system of agriculture that reduced production costs and the burden of labor for the individual farmer has been readily accepted, but not a communal method of farming that would achieve the same result. Although the first innovation has had a profound impact on agricultural production and rural American society, the second would have required us to reorganize our family structure in culturally unacceptable ways. What these examples illustrate is that in every society many aspects of the economy are strongly tied to the overall system of social organization. One aspect cannot simply be changed without far-reaching changes in the others.

summary

In order to understand how different societies cope with the basic tasks of production and distribution, we must answer four questions: 1) Who controls resources and how is access to their use regulated? 2) What is the nature of the production process? 3) How is the final distribution of goods and services accomplished? and 4) How are resources, goods, and services exchanged?

Strategies for securing natural resources are linked to access to resource-rich land. Agricultural and industrial societies generally maintain clear-cut territorial boundaries, which restrict use of land to certain groups. Hunting and gathering ways of life, however, require greater territorial flexibility to account for seasonal variation in availability of resources. Typically, the more precarious or mobile the food supply, the greater the need for flexible boundaries and resource sharing.

In capitalistic industrial societies, control of resources goes beyond maintaining a territory, involving the concept of private property and emphasizing individual control for individual benefit. Yet the idea of individual ownership of productive resources is alien to many societies, where the entire community has broad rights to land, natural resources, and tools, and rights to land resources are established through membership in a social group. In such societies, the community holds *proprietary rights,* while individuals have *rights to use.* Many societies, however, have been affected by the Western ethos, and private property is replacing traditional land-use systems; economic systems are becoming more impersonal and less tied to the general system of social relationships.

Once resources have been acquired, usable goods must be produced from them, and production must be organized in some coherent way. In Western societies the production unit is the business firm, staffed by specialists trained to accomplish a designated task in the production process. Production is not directly geared to social ends, but rather to increased rates of production without regard to the ends of that production. On the other hand, in nonindustrial societies the basic production unit is often the household or domestic group. Labor is not very specialized—if a task is too large or dangerous to be handled well within a single household, it will be accomplished as a group effort, additional labor being supplied by kinsmen or friends. In these societies, productive activities are actively linked to many more "noneconomic" functions than in our own.

Production in all societies requires carefully elaborated strategies based on specific knowledge of economic relationships. All these strategies attempt to *economize*—that is, to make the most efficient qualitative and quantitative use of available resources. Western societies seek to accomplish this through the maximization of profits and the minimization of production costs. Furthermore, production strategies in these societies are formulated around the idea of growth and that of increasing volume of output. In contrast, in societies where the household is the basic procurement unit, production is geared simply toward fulfilling the material and social needs of the domestic unit; this usually precludes the production of a surplus.

Anthropologists also seek to understand how distribution patterns are organized and maintained and how they developed. In our own society, personal accomplishments and occupational status are awarded with material benefits. In many others, however, built-in *leveling mechanisms* exist to avoid just this kind of disproportionate accumulation of economic goods.

Before the development of agriculture, economic equality was probably universal. As societies became larger, however, positions and roles became more specialized, political control became centralized, and certain families and professions acquired enormous power over resources and economic activities. Colonialism and the spread of capitalism also have contributed heavily to the development of economic inequities. In general, colonialism entailed harnessing traditional economies for the development of the colonial powers. Even today, after many former colonies have gained their independence, a lopsided distribution of wealth persists.

In all societies, products and resources are continually changing hands. In every society in almost every age, three forms of exchange can be found: reciprocity, redistribution, and market exchange. *Reciprocal exchange,* which plays a much greater role in preindustrial societies than industrial ones, involves giving and taking between people who are bound by certain social ties and obligations. *Generalized reciprocity* is informal gift-giving where no "accounts" are kept and no immediate or specific return is expected. This system is basic to the survival of many hunting and gathering peoples. *Balanced reciprocity* is gift-giving that clearly carries the obligations of an eventual and roughly equal return; it is characteristic of the labor exchange systems in many horticultural and agricultural societies. *Negative reciprocity* entails generally impersonal transactions between enemies and strangers, with each side trying to get the better end of the bargain. *Redistribution* involves obligatory payments of goods, currency, or services to some central social figure who then reallocates some portion of them. *Market exchange* is a purely impersonal, commercial transaction. Goods and services may be bartered, but they are usually bought and sold through a standard medium of exchange. In most traditional societies, purchase and sale are peripheral to the economy, but the economics of most industrial nations are completely based on marketing exchange. Usually, all three forms of exchange operate to some degree in a society; conversely, certain economic transactions often crosscut all three types of exchange.

As a member of society, every person must conform to certain rules and practices for producing, acquiring, and distributing products and resources. People do not always follow the rules precisely, however, and there are always choices to be made. In fact, a degree of economic experimentation and variation is usually necessary for survival. In examining examples of economic innovation, we see in every society that many aspects of the economy are deeply embedded in the overall social organization.

suggested readings

DALTON, G., ED.
1967 *Tribal and Peasant Economies: Readings in Economic Anthropology.* New York: Natural History Press. A collection of articles focusing on the economic institutions of a variety of different cultures and emphasizing the more important theories and concepts that anthropologists use in studying economic institutions.

1971 *Economic Development and Social Change: The Modernization of Village Communities.* New York: Natural History Press. A series of articles that describe the theories and results of studies on changing economic patterns in nonindustrial societies and the social concomitants of these changes.

LE CLAIR E. E., JR., AND SCHNEIDER, H. J.
1968 *Economic Anthropology: Readings in Theory and Analysis.* New York: Holt, Rinehart and Winston. Focusing principally on economic behavior and economizing in different societies, these articles provide a detailed examination of some of the issues that have arisen in the dialogue between anthropological economists who focus on economic institutions and those who focus on economic behavior.

SAHLINS, M.
1972 *Stone Age Economics.* Chicago: Aldine. An especially thorough study of the social importance of economic exchange and of the factors affecting production at the household level.

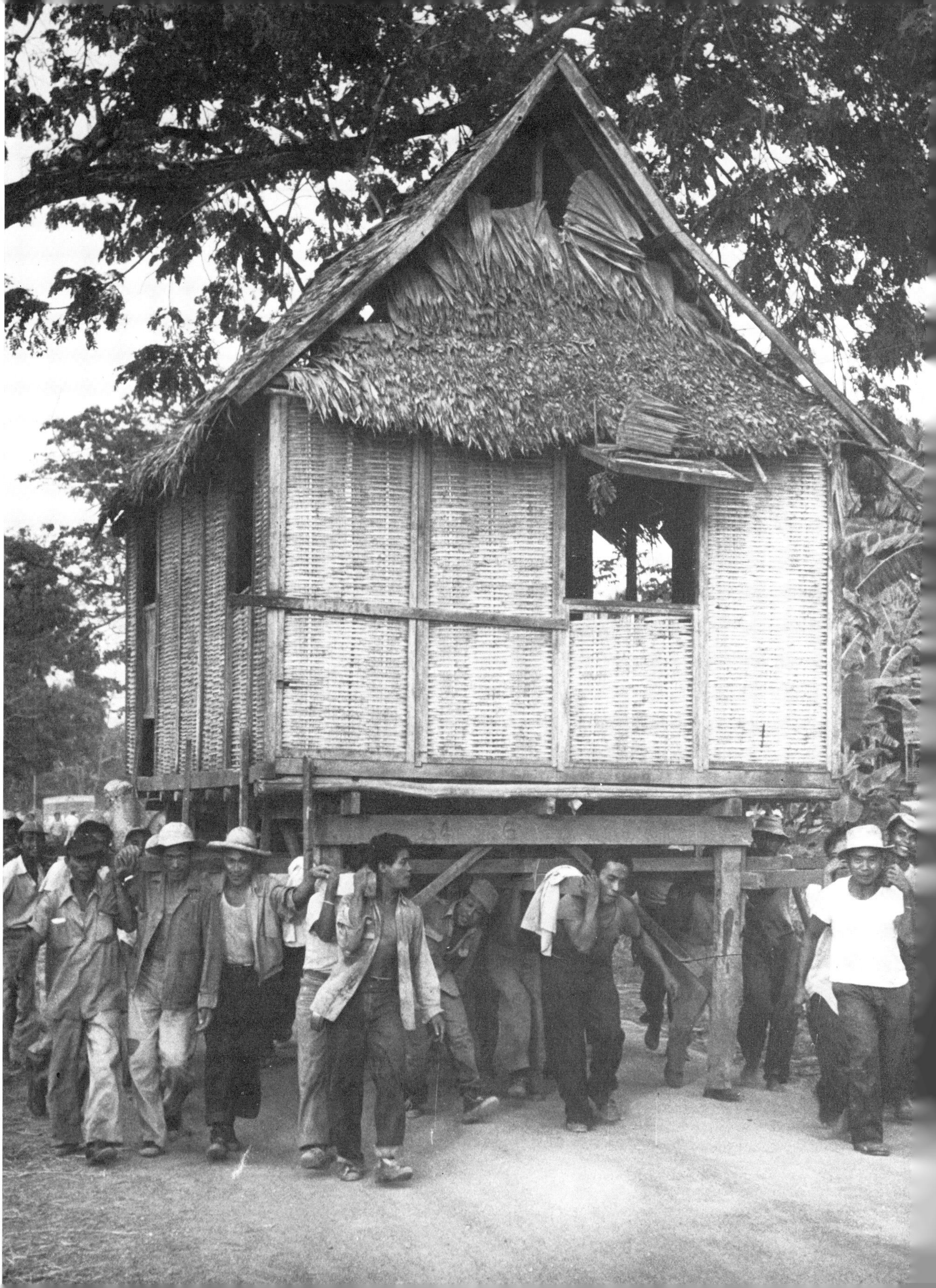

eighteen
Social Structure and Social Behavior

The ways in which a society is structured are by no means immediately obvious to the outside observer. In fact, it has been said that an ethnographer who has just begun to study a totally unfamiliar society is in a similar position to a blind person whose sight has just been restored and who is viewing the world for the first time (Durkheim and Mauss, 1963). As the former blind person must learn to structure visual data in order to see the world as others see it, the ethnographer must learn to structure a confusing welter of impressions in order to "see" the complex relationships that make up the society, and which its members take for granted. He or she must discover the patterns of social organization and social structure which exist in every society—the recurring networks of social relations that link people together, the groups formed in the process of social interaction, the social categories that people everywhere establish, and the kinds of behavior expected of their members. These are some of the topics we will be exploring in this chapter. Throughout, we will emphasize that the patterned relations among the members of any society are many and complex. Although much of the anthropological literature on social organization focuses on simplified analytical models, one should realize that any actual system encompasses a wide range of individual variation. Yet these abstract principles of social organization are important because they are used in structuring activities in all areas of life—political, economic, and religious as well as social.

Networks, Groups, and Social Categories

In every society people are bound together by various kinds of relationships—relationships that give rise to the kinfolk, friends, business or political associates, clients and patrons that make up the individual's social universe. In this section we will briefly survey some of the concepts social scientists have found useful in classifying and analyzing the web of relationships that make up a society. First, we will look at patterned relationships through the study of what social scientists call *networks*. Second, we will discuss some of the different kinds of *groups* that emerge in the process of human interaction and the varying characteristics of such groups. And finally, we will examine what can best be called *social categories*—classifications of people based on some shared attribute or set of attributes.

Networks

From the individual's customary vantage point, he or she is at the center of a network of social relationships, an intricate set of links, both direct and indirect, between oneself and others. Although many of these links are perceived by the person at the hub of the network, certain indirect links may only become apparent when an outside observer studies the patterns of social interaction involved. But in any event, it is clear that a person's network of contacts serves many vital functions. One can obtain help from his or her network in accomplishing a particular task or in solving a

A house-moving is a reason for men to join forces in a Philippine village. Those who have helped out can be sure of receiving assistance when they need it. (George Rodger/Magnum)

certain problem. Intermediaries may be used as contacts to obtain information or to send messages. Furthermore, a person's network offers an important measure of psychological support. "[I]t provides him with a surrounding field of friends and relatives who help give his life meaning, establish and maintain the norms by which he regulates his behavior, and protect him from the impersonal world beyond (Bott, 1957:200 ff.). A network, then, is an *ego-centered*[1] set of relationships—a web of social ties of various kinds which emanates from a particular individual.

Individual networks vary in important ways. One way is simply the number of contacts a person has. One might assume that a person with many contacts can obtain help or communicate more quickly than one with fewer. But this is not necessarily the case, for the efficacy of a person's network also depends on *who* one's contacts are. The person whose contacts include several very influential people will often find his network more effective than the networks of those with more but less powerful contacts.

Another way in which networks vary is the number of interests served by individual relationships. One man may be another's lawyer and his brother-in-law at the same time. Generally speaking, the more interests served by a relationship, the stronger the tie will be. The lawyer is more likely to go out of his way for the client who also happens to be his brother-in-law than he is for the client with whom he has no other ties.

Finally, a network may be closely or loosely knit. If an individual's contacts are also linked to one another through other ties, the network is said to have a high *density*. This is the case in many small homogeneous populations where everyone is known to everyone else, and all interact on a regular basis. In complex societies such as our own, in contrast, many of the contacts in a person's network are unknown to one another, being linked only indirectly through their individual relationships with ego.

Groups

Network analysis is primarily a way of looking at patterns of social relationships from the individual's point of view, a way of determining which people interact with which others and in what sorts of ways. As we have pointed out, certain clusters of relationships in a network may have high density—that is, the people involved are linked to one another in more ways than simply through their individual connections with ego. Such a situation may indicate the existence of a group, an association of individuals who interact on a fairly regular basis and whose members have a sense of collective identity. A family, a street gang, a work party, a club, and a political caucus are all groups of one kind or another. The analysis of groups, how they are formed and what functions they serve, is extremely important to the study of social organization.

Groups may vary in a number of ways, one being their degree of formal organization—the extent to which they have officially designated positions and roles, are guided by formal rules and regulations, and are bureaucratically structured. Groups may also vary according to permanence. Certain groups may be created to perform a specific task, and when the task is completed, they dissolve. Other groups, however, far outlive any particular collection of individual members.

Corporateness is another characteristic of certain groups. *Corporateness* refers to the extent to which membership in the group entitles one to a specifically defined set of collective rights—as, for example, rights in group property. A village may be a group with a high degree of corporateness if membership automatically brings with it the right to share in land and other resources. It is important to recognize, however, that in actual practice it is often difficult to measure a quality such as

---

[1] In the analysis of social organization, the term *ego* refers to the hypothetical individual whose relationships with others are being studied.

Work groups around the world are usually informal and last only as long as the job to be done. Unions, however, form a major exception to this rule. Their strict internal organization and their permanence are factors in assuring bargaining rights for workers vis-à-vis the powerful management class of highly industrialized societies. These Kentucky miners on their way into the mine illustrate another feature of many work groups all over the world — their arbitrary division along sexual lines. (Earl Dotter/Magnum)

degree of corporateness. This is particularly true because the rights and privileges bestowed by group membership are usually achieved by negotiation and social and political maneuvering on the part of the individual.

Social Categories

Studying how people in a particular society categorize the individuals that make up their social universe is another part of understanding how that society is organized. A social category is composed of all people who share certain culturally identified characteristics. Analyzing the ways in which people in a given society categorize one another is important to understanding patterns of social interaction, because very often how we classify people heavily influences how we behave toward them and how we expect them to behave.

Social categories are neither networks nor groups, but they can and do influence the composition of networks and supply the basis for the formation of groups. For example, in the United States, people classify others on the basis of certain perceived social and physical differences which together are used to define race. Such classifications in turn influence which people we are likely to interact with and in what ways. In other words, racial categories often establish boundaries to our personal networks. In a recent experiment, Charles Korté and Stanley Milgram (1970) revealed just how impenetrable such boundaries can be. They asked white volunteers in Los Angeles to send messages to eighteen "target" individuals in New York, nine white and nine black. The targets were not known personally to the senders, so the messages had to be passed through intermediaries, each of whom was requested to either pass the message to the target or relay it to someone else who might be able to do so. Five hundred and forty messages were sent from Los Angeles. Thirty-three percent of those aimed at white targets reached their destinations, while of those aimed at black targets, only 13 percent were delivered. Moreover, it was found that those messages successfully reaching blacks did not cross the color line until they were only one or two links short of their targets. In most cases, the people responsible for relaying the message across the color line were individuals, either black or white, whose relations with their black contacts tended to be impersonal ones. This study thus identifies racial categories as important factors in establishing network boundaries.

Because people in a particular social category are somehow "set apart" from others on the basis of certain shared characteristics, it is not surprising that those same shared traits can also serve as the basis for the formation of groups — associations of interacting individuals who have a sense of collective identity. Thus, although all Italian-Americans comprise a social category, not a group, we also find groups formed largely on the basis of shared Italian identity — the Sons of Italy, for example. This is not to say that groups *necessarily* emerge out of all social categories. It is simply to say that some of the people who are socially classified together on the basis of certain shared characteristics may also be active groups.

The concepts of networks, groups, and social categories will be used throughout this chapter. We have selected four major topic areas — kinship, age, sex, and ethnicity — each of which to varying degrees is an important dimension of social organization in many societies. In discussing each area, we will be focusing on the relevant social categories people establish, on the ways in which these categories structure patterns of social behavior, and on how social categories influence the composition of networks and groups.

Kinship and Kin-Based Groups

"Kinship is the heart of primitive social structure," asserts Napoleon Chagnon (1968) in his study of the Yanomamö Indians of South America. Such a statement may be somewhat surprising to those of us who live in a highly industrialized society where most of our relatives — our grandparents, aunts, uncles, cousins, and in-laws, for example — have a rather limited effect on our day-to-day decisions. But anthropology's heavy emphasis on the study of kinship cannot be written off simply as a peculiar obsession. The fact is that in societies such as the Yanomamö's, a knowledge of the kinship system is essential to understanding their social structure and organization.

The Yanomamö inhabit over a hundred widely scattered villages in the dense jungle of southern Venezuela and northern Brazil. Each village is composed of two or more distinct groups of kinsmen. Membership in a kin group is inherited through the male line; both males and females belong to the kin group of their father. The kin group to which a person belongs is particularly important when it comes to marriage, for men and women are required to find a spouse outside their own group. This prescription usually leads to sister exchange between young men of different kin groups. A man from kin group A will typically marry the sister of a man in kin group B, who in turn will marry the sister of the first man. When exchanges of women between the same two kin groups continue for generations, strong bonds of alliance between them are created.

Interestingly, the terms the Yanomamö use to refer to many of their relatives reflect the requirement that one marry outside one's own kin group as well as the expectation of sister exchange between brothers of different groups. Within a particular generation, all the members of a kin group refer to one another as "brother" and "sister," reflecting the prohibition of marriage between them. But a man's father's sister's daughter and his mother's brother's daughter, for example, *are* potential spouses because they belong to "outside" kin groups. Therefore, a man refers to all his marriageable female relatives in other kin groups as "wife" — regardless of whether or not he in fact marries them. Similarly, that same man refers to the brothers of all of his "wives" as "brother-in-law," indicating their close potential ties through marriage. In Yanomamö society, men customarily find important allies among the people they call "brother-in-law."

We have described only a part of the Yanomamö's system of kinship terminology. But it is enough to indicate that the culturally defined categories into which different types of relatives are classified is critical in establishing patterns of social interaction. In fact, many aspects of a person's role in particular social situations can be described with a simple kin term. Chagnon describes the case of an orphaned adolescent boy who came to live in the village where Chagnon was conducting his fieldwork. The boy had no real relatives in the village, but he managed to define his own "place in society" by calling the headman of one of the kin groups "father." This tactic immediately established the boy's relationship to others in the village.

Our discussion of kinship and kin groups among the Yanomamö has not been intended to suggest that kinship is the *only* organizing principle in their society—that *all* Yanomamö social relations are based on kin ties. But clearly kinship is extremely important in structuring their patterns of social interaction. We have seen how groups are formed on the basis of kin bonds, how the kinship system defines one's relationship to other people in society, and how it also serves to structure interpersonal behavior. Obviously, kinship is a far more important principle of social organization among the Yanomamö than among Americans. One should not assume, however, that kinship, by comparison, is quite insignificant in industrialized societies such as our own. Kinship is an organizing principle of every human group; it is simply more important in some than in others. In the following sections, we will explore some of the different types of kinship classification systems societies utilize, the different kinds of groups they form on the basis of kinship, and the different ways that kinship serves to structure human behavior.

Kinship Classification

Like the Yanomamö, people in every society have a host of relatives. First, there are those who are related to us by birth—our *consanguineal* kin. A person's mother and father, his brothers and sisters, his grandparents, all his grandparents' children, and their childrens' children are some, although far from all of his consanguineal kin. We are also related to other people by marriage. Our own husband or wife, our in-laws, the spouses of our parents' brothers and sisters are some of our *affinal* relatives—that is, our relatives by a marriage. The list does not stop here, however. In many societies, including our own, families may adopt unrelated individuals, who thereby acquire the rights and obligations of kinship and are socially recognized as members of the family. In addition, people create fictive relations using consanguinity as a model—old family friends children call aunt and uncle, godparents, *compadres,* or "blood brothers," to name but a few.

In no society do people refer to each and every one of their many relatives by a separate term. Instead, we group certain relatives into a single category and refer to them all by one kin term: brother, sister, aunt, uncle, grandmother, grandfather, for example.[2] This is to say that all systems of kinship terminology are to some extent classificatory in nature. Why are anthropologists interested in how people in different societies classify their relatives? Although the study of kinship terminology may at first glance seem irrelevant to the study of human behavior, in fact there is a strong relationship between how people classify others and how they act toward them. We behave quite differently toward those we call "brother" or "sister" than toward those we call "cousin." In general, people in every society classify together those relatives who they view as being quite similar and toward whom they are expected to behave in a similar man-

---

[2]In collecting information about kinship terminology systems, anthropologists are interested in *terms of reference*—those used to refer to a relative when speaking about him or her to a third person—rather than *terms of address*—those used to address a relative directly. Terms of address, however, are significant because they are part of the linguistic behavior characteristic of a given relationship.

ner. Conversely, they distinguish between relatives who they perceive as dissimilar and toward whom they are expected to behave somewhat differently.

Societies use various bases for classifying kin. Most distinguish between relatives on the basis of *sex,* using different terms for male and female kin. For example, we refer to our female parent as "mother," our male parent as "father," distinguish between brothers and sisters, aunts and uncles, and so on. Some societies also distinguish between the mother's and father's side of the family. Such a basis of classification, called *bifurcation,* is used by the Yanomamö, as by many other peoples. Societies that employ bifurcate terminology use separate terms for mother's brother and father's brother, for example. In our society, in contrast, both these relatives are called "uncle." Many people also use different kin terms to distinguish between *generations.* We have separate terms for grandmother, mother, daughter, and granddaughter, for example. In addition, we separate *lineal* relatives (direct ascendants and descendants) from *collateral* relatives (people to whom we are related through a connecting person). An example of a collateral relative is an uncle, who is related to his nephew through one of that boy's parents. Not all groups make this distinction, as we shall see. And a number of those that do emphasize the sex of the connecting relative by using one word for a mother's sister and another for a father's sister; one word for *cross-cousins* (a mother's brothers' children and a father's sisters' children), another for *parallel cousins* (a mother's sisters' children and a father's brothers' children).

In the following pages we will be focusing on the ways that consanguineal kin are classified. It is important to emphasize at the outset that consanguineal kin terms refer to culturally, not biologically, defined categories. Although all consanguineal relationships are biologically based, the manner in which these relationships are linguistically classified is a cultural creation. For this reason, systems for classifying kin can and do vary considerably from one society to another. In the case of the Yanomamö, for example, the terms "brother" and "sister" refer not only to one's siblings but to other kinds of kin as well. The Yanomamö also include relatives that we do not under the terms "mother" and "father." Very few Yanomamö have only one "mother" and one "father." The norm is to have at least two or three of each and a very large number of "brothers" and "sisters." This is because the Yanomamö, like many other peoples, use a single term to refer to one's biological mother and her sisters, and a single term to refer to one's biological father and his brothers. The children of all these "mothers" and "fathers" are referred to as "brothers" and "sisters," many of which relatives we would call "cousin." Thus systems for classifying consanguineal kin are culturally determined; they are not the biological givens that many people mistakenly assume.

Although particular societies may have their own variations, kin classification systems fall into six general types—Sudanese, Eskimo, Hawaiian, Iroquois, Omaha, and Crow—which derive their names from peoples that exemplify the types or from areas in which such peoples live.

Sudanese Kin Terminology The kin terminology system known as Sudanese is named not after a particular people, but after the area of the world in which such a system is most prevalent. Sudanese kin terminology is highly descriptive. (See Figure 18–1.) There is one term for father and another for mother; one term for brother and another for sister. Furthermore, in ego's parent's generation, father's brothers, mother's sisters, father's sisters, and mother's brothers are referred to by four separate terms (relatives we lump under two terms—aunt and uncle). Similarly, the male and female children of each of these different relatives in ego's parents' generation are called by separate terms. This yields eight different "cousin" classifications in ego's own generation. Thus, in the Sudanese system, there are a total of sixteen different kin terms in ego's and ego's parents' generations. As numbered in **Figure 18–1** they are:

Social Structure and Social Behavior 357

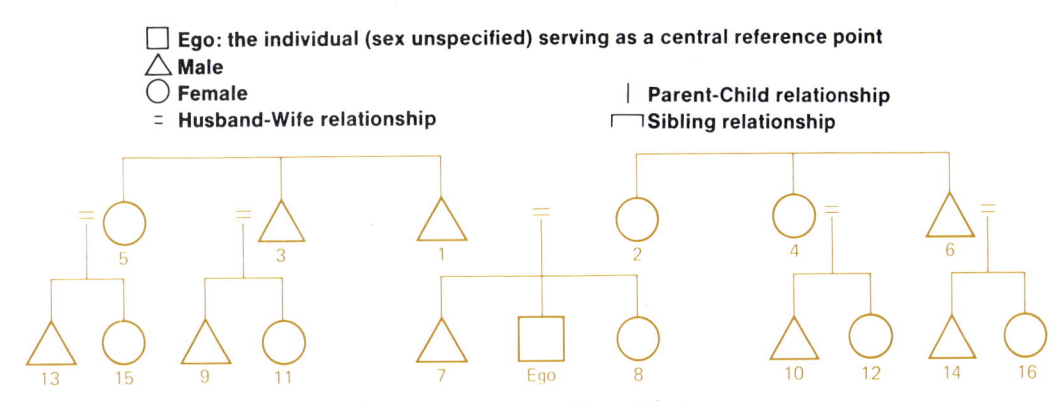

- ☐ Ego: the individual (sex unspecified) serving as a central reference point
- △ Male
- ○ Female
- = Husband-Wife relationship
- | Parent-Child relationship
- ⊓ Sibling relationship

Figure 18.1 Sudanese Kin Terminology

1. father
2. mother
3. father's brothers
4. mother's sisters
5. father's sisters
6. mother's brothers
7. brothers
8. sisters
9. father's brothers' sons
10. mother's sisters' sons
11. father's brothers' daughters
12. mother's sisters' daughters
13. father's sisters' sons
14. mother's brothers' sons
15. father's sisters' daughters
16. mother's brothers' daughters

Eskimo Kin Terminology People in our own society, as in many others, use the system of kin terminology known as Eskimo. (See Figure 18–2.) In some respects, the Eskimo system is highly exclusive in the application of kin terms. It draws a sharp distinction between lineal and collateral kin, using separate terms for mother and father, sisters and brothers that do not extend to relatives beyond the immediate family. In other respects, however, the Eskimo system employs terms that are quite inclusive. No distinction is made between relatives on the paternal and maternal sides of ego's family. For example, the same terms—aunt and uncle—are used to refer to the brothers and sisters of both ego's mother and ego's father (as well as their spouses, thus making no distinction in this case between consanguineal and affinal relations). Moreover, the Eskimo term "cousin" refers to all the children of ego's aunts and uncles regardless of whether they are related to him through his mother or his father. This term is also used to refer to the children of both ego's parents' cousins and to still more distant relatives. Indeed, the word "cousin" in English once meant any kinsman or even a friend whom ego treated as a kinsman.

To summarize, the Eskimo kin terminology

Figure 18.2 Eskimo Kin Terminology

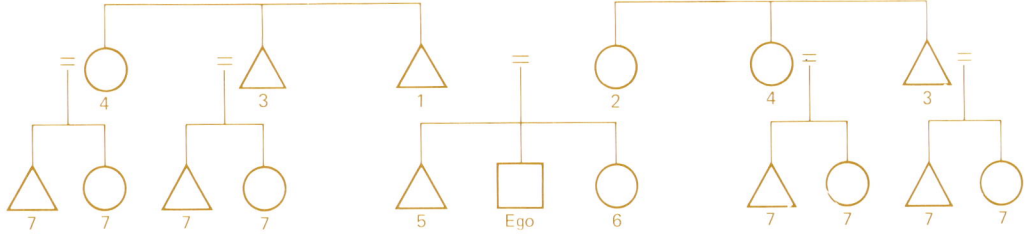

system includes a strange mix of one-person and "catch-all" categories:

1. father
2. mother
3. uncle (all our parents' brothers and parents' sisters' husbands)
4. aunt (all our parents' sisters and parents' brothers' wives)
5. brother
6. sister
7. cousin (the children of mother's brothers and sisters and father's brothers and sisters, plus more distant relatives)

The emphasis on the nuclear family (parents and children) is the most distinctive feature of Eskimo kin terminology. In singling out the immediate family, it creates a small, rather private niche in the kinship system that does not exist in other people's terminology or practices.

Hawaiian Kin Terminology Hawaiian kin terminology employs a relatively small number of different categories. (See Figure 18-3.) It lumps together under the same kin term all of the people of the same sex and generation who are related to ego in any way. There is a single term for mother and mother's and father's sisters; a single term for father and father's and mother's brothers; a single term for sisters and all female cousins; and a single term for brothers and all male cousins. Thus in the Hawaiian system, kin are grouped as follows:

1. all males of the ascending (parental) generation
2. all females of the ascending generation
3. all males of ego's generation
4. all females of ego's generation

In contrast to the Eskimo system, Hawaiian kinship terminology does not distinguish between lineal and collateral relatives (mother and aunt, sister and female cousin, and so on). Instead, members of the nuclear family are lumped with other consanguineal kin. This approach to classifying kin is generally associated with societies where the nuclear family is submerged within larger kin groupings that are important in the life of the individual. Nor does the Hawaiian system distinguish between the maternal and paternal sides of the family. Such a system is frequently found in societies where the individual is affiliated with a number of different kin groups through ties on both his mother's *and* his father's side of the family.

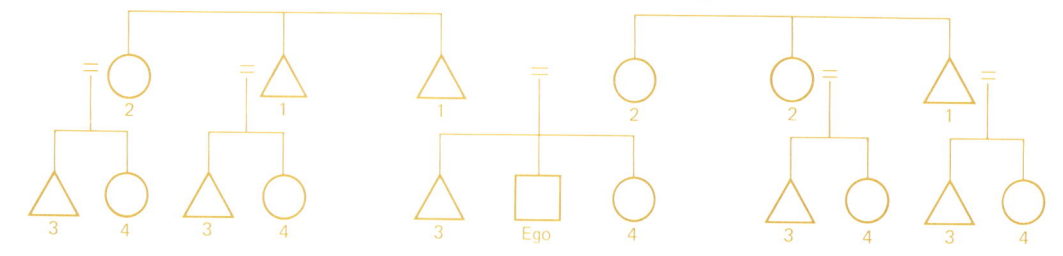

Iroquois Kin Terminology Found in every part of the world, Iroquois is perhaps the most common system of kin terminology. (See Figure 18-4.) An important feature of the Iroquois system is that it distinguishes between *parallel* cousins and *cross*-cousins. Parallel cousins are children of ego's parents' siblings of the same sex. Cross-cousins are children of ego's parents' siblings of the opposite sex. Thus ego's parallel cousins are his father's brothers' sons and daughters, and his mother's sisters' sons and daughters. In Iroquois kin terminology these relatives are called by the same terms as ego's own brothers and sisters. Ego's cross-cousins are the children of his father's sisters and his mother's brothers.

Figure 18.3 Hawaiian Kin Terminology

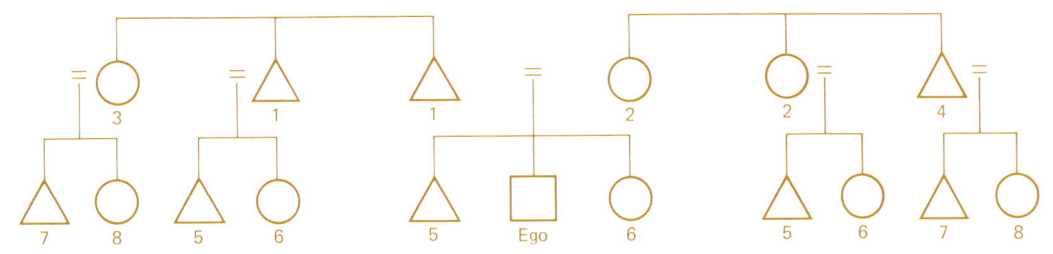

Figure 18.4 Iroquois Kin Terminology

The fact that they are not lumped together with ego's own sisters and brothers shows that they are thought of as being at a greater relational distance from ego.

Since parallel cousins are classified with ego's brothers and sisters, it would seem logical for the parents of parallel cousins to be classified with ego's parents. In fact, this is the case. In the Iroquois system, ego uses the same term to refer to his father and his father's brothers, and the same term for his mother and his mother's sisters. Father's sister and mother's brother are referred to by different terms.

Thus in the Iroquois system, as in the Hawaiian, members of the nuclear family (mother, father, brother, sister) are classified with collateral relatives. However, the Iroquois system does not go as far in lumping as does the Hawaiian, but makes distinctions between collateral relatives on the basis of sex in ego's parents' generation, and the sex of the connecting link in ego's own generation. The Iroquois kinship classification system can be summarized as follows:

1. father and father's brothers
2. mother and mother's sisters
3. father's sisters
4. mother's brothers
5. brothers, father's brothers' sons, and mothers' sisters' sons
6. sisters, father's brothers' daughters, and mother's sisters' daughters
7. father's sisters' sons and mother's brothers' sons
8. father's sisters' daughters and mother's brothers' daughters

Omaha Kin Terminology From our point of view, it may seem strange to use the term "mother" not only to refer to one's biological mother, but one's mother's sisters as well. It may seem even stranger, however, to use the term "mother" to refer to tiny female infants. Yet this is a feature of the Omaha kin terminology system: mother, mother's sister, and mother's brothers' daughter are all lumped under the same term. Similarly, mother's brothers and mother's brothers' son are referred to by a single term. (See Figure 18–5.) These classifications, moreover, do not occur on ego's father's side of the family. What can explain such a system?

Figure 18.5 Omaha Kin Terminology

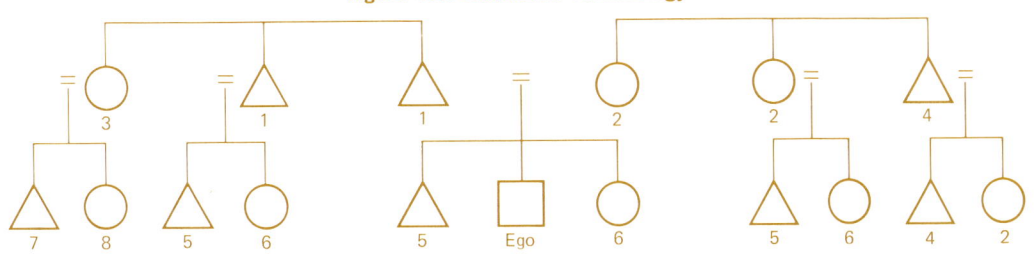

Most societies employing Omaha terminology are divided into kin-based groups, membership in which is determined through the paternal line (patrilineal). On ego's father's side of the family—the side from which he inherits kin group affiliation—we find the father and father's brothers are referred to by a single term. This "lumping" serves two purposes. First, it symbolizes the great importance of paternal uncles who, like ego's biological father, are senior male members of ego's own kin group and therefore have the same claim to his respect and loyalty and the same obligations toward him as a biological father. Second, placing ego's father and father's brothers in the same category serves to distinguish them from ego's mother's brothers, who are *not* members of ego's kin group and do not share the same rights and responsibilities.

By somewhat the same logic, societies with an Omaha system use a single term to refer to mother, mother's sisters, and mother's brothers' daughters. This lumping across generations reflects the similar strong ties between ego and all of these female consanguineal relatives, women who are members of the same kin group. Such ties are all the more likely to be established because these women are *not* members of ego's own kin group and are therefore removed from the kinds of political considerations that might tend to restrain close attachments. Moreover, this classification emphasizes the fact that the kin group to which ego's mother's sisters and mother's brothers' daughters belong is ego's mother's group, a group into which ego may well marry and thus form important alliances. By the same token, ego's mother's brothers and their sons are all referred to by a single term. These men are all male members of ego's mother's kin group, and ego's relationship to them is heavily influenced by this fact.

Like Iroquois, the Omaha kinship terminology system lumps brothers and male parallel cousins (father's brothers' sons and mother's sisters' sons) under one term; sisters and female parallel cousins (father's brothers' daughters and mother's sisters' daughters) under another term. The rationale for this is the same as in the Iroquois system. Societies using the Omaha system consider all children of men and women they call "father" and "mother" brothers and sisters.

To summarize, the Omaha and many other peoples who trace descent through the paternal line classify consanguineal relatives as follows:

1. father and father's brothers
2. mother, mother's sisters, and mother's brothers' daughters
3. father's sisters
4. mother's brothers and mother's brothers' sons
5. brothers, father's brothers' sons, and mother's sisters' sons
6. sisters, father's brothers' daughters, and mother's sisters' daughters
7. father's sisters' sons
8. father's sisters' daughters

Crow Kin Terminology Crow kin terminology is associated with societies that establish membership in kin-based groups through the maternal line (matrilineal). As one can see by comparing Figures 18–5 and 18–6, the Crow

Figure 18.6 Crow Kin Terminology

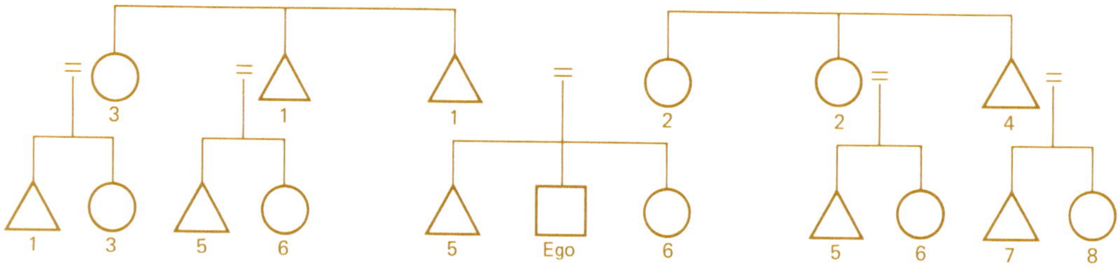

system is the mirror image of the Omaha. People in societies using Crow kin terminology lump ego's mother and her sisters under one term; ego's father, his brothers, and his sisters' sons under another term; ego's father's sisters and their daughters under still another. They equate male parallel cousins with brothers, female parallel cousins with sisters. This produces the following kin classifications:

1. father, father's brothers, and father's sisters' sons
2. mother and mother's sisters
3. father's sisters and father's sisters' daughters
4. mother's brothers
5. brothers, mother's sisters' sons, and father's brothers' sons
6. sisters, mother's sisters' daughters, and father's brothers' daughters
7. mother's brothers' sons
8. mother's brothers' daughters

Thus Crow terminology lumps female members of ego's own kin group in the ascending generation under a single term (mother and mother's sisters), male members of ego's father's kin group regardless of generation under a single term (father, father's brothers, and father's brothers' sons), and female members of ego's father's kin group regardless of generation under another term (father's sisters and father's sisters' daughters).

Kinship Terms and Social Behavior In every society, some of the rules of appropriate behavior governing interaction between different types of relatives are symbolized by the kinship terms people use. Particularly in situations in which a person has more than one possible kinship link with another person—cousin *and* brother-in-law, for example—kinship terms can be manipulated to stress different relative statuses and different reciprocal obligations. Or one can use a kinship term that has absolutely no genealogical justification in order to invoke a desirable role relationship—referring to an unrelated person as "brother," for instance. Lévi-Strauss has reported on a population of Brazilian Indians that included members of two tribes not even speaking the same language. The men of the two merged groups called each other "brother-in-law," a term they had previously applied only to the brothers of all eligible brides in their own separate groups. This manipulation of kinship terminology helped to promote peaceful relations in a situation of potential conflict (Lévi-Strauss, 1943).

Kinship terminology can also be manipulated by members of the same group in adapting to different events or situations. Robin Fox (1967) has observed the inhabitants of Cochiti Pueblo using different kin terms as terms of address under different circumstances. The decision as to whether or not to use kin terms at all, and if so which term to employ, is influenced by whether or not the meeting between the two speakers is casual or formal, the nature of a formal occasion, whether or not one of the speakers is seeking help, and the relative statuses of the two. For example, the Cochiti kinship terminology system can generally be described as Iroquois-like. But on formal occasions, such as a wedding, healing, or naming ceremony, the terminological system people use can best be described as Crow-like. This is because Crow kin terms, which are commonly found in societies with strong kin group organization, are particularly well suited for use in ceremonies in which kin group bonds are being emphasized.

The opportunities for manipulating kinship terminology may increase when one society is in contact with another and knows the other's system of kin terms. Edward Bruner studied such a situation among the Mandan-Hidatsa Indians living on the Fort Berthold Reservation in North Dakota. These people traditionally had a Crow system of kinship terminology, and despite over half a century of white domination, the majority of the villagers still used Crow-type terms most of the time. Not infrequently, however, they would attempt to manipulate a situation by suddenly switching to English terms. By the same token, those villagers who had completely adopted English

Kinship Classification Systems as Ideal Types

In the preceding pages, we have discussed the major types of kinship classification systems anthropologists have identified. It is important to understand, however, that these are idealized types. Although most societies have kinship systems that are more or less like one of these models, only a few conform to the model exactly. Nevertheless, the idealized types are useful for discussing kinship terminologies at a general level.

In a study of forty-one societies identified as having Iroquois kinship terminology systems, Buchler and Selby (1968) show that very few of the groups actually have all the traits associated with this system of classification. Using a technique called *scalogram* analysis, the researchers followed three steps: (1) they identified the traits that define the Iroquois kinship terminology system; (2) they ordered the societies in their sample in terms of how closely they fit this model from those with the fewest of the defining traits to those with the most; and (3) they ordered the traits in terms of frequency of occurrence from those that occur in the greatest number of societies to those that occur in the least. The table below is an abridged version of the analysis Buchler and Selby performed. The traits are listed across the top of the table. Eight of them correspond to our earlier discussion of the Iroquois kinship system: single terms are used to refer to father's sister's son and mother's brother's son; father's sister's daughter and mother's brother's daughter; father's brother's son and brother; father's brother's daughter and sister; mother's sister's son and brother; mother's sister's daughter and sister; father and father's brother; mother and mother's sister. The last two traits involve merging lineal relatives of the generation that we refer to as grandparents and great-aunts and -uncles with those of ego's parents' generation, and merging lineal relatives of the generation that we refer to as grandchildren and grandnieces and -nephews with ego's children's generation. (Certain other mergings associated with the Iroquois are not shown in this table.)

Almost all societies labeled Iroquois have the first four traits, and most have some of the other identifying characteristics as well. But only a minority have every single trait. Surprisingly, even the Iroquois, for whom the system is named, do not have all of the traits. Thus we see that the systems of kinship classification that anthropologists identify are ideal constructs which only roughly approximate the particular terminological systems of different societies. And if we were to analyze in a similar fashion societies with Crow, Omaha, Hawaiian, and Eskimo kinship systems, we would find that these, too, are characterized by variation, and that there is a great deal more overlap among them than ideal-type definitions would imply. This is particularly important when we begin to consider how and why changes in kinship terminology systems occur. If the differences between systems are relative rather than absolute, it is easier to understand how changes can come about over relatively short periods of time, and apparently have neither major causes nor major consequences.

CULTURE	Kapauku	Maria Gond	Havasupai	Lau	Vedda	Iroquois	Navajo
FZS = MBS	+	+	+	+	+	+	+
FZD = MBD	+	+	+	+	+	+	+
FBS = B	+	+	+	+	+	+	+
FBD = S	+	−	+	+	+	+	+
MZS = B	−	+	+	+	+	+	+
MZD = Z	−	−	+	+	+	+	+
F = FB	−	−	−	−	+	+	+
M = MZ	−	−	−	−	+	+	+
Ascending Lineals	−	−	−	−	+	+	+
Descending Lineals	−	−	−	+	+	−	+

terms in daily usage would surprise their neighbors by adopting traditional terms when they wanted to gain control of a situation. At a political meeting, for example, Bruner observed a man who ordinarily used English terminology completely disarm an outspoken member of the opposition by using Crow-type terminology and calling him "father"—knowing full well the older man would not attack his "son" in public. Similarly, a woman who needed a ride into town one day approached one of the wealthier villagers with her problem, addressing him with the traditional term for "older brother." Acquiescing to the woman's skill in manipulating kin terminology, the man turned to Bruner on the way to the car and whispered, "The only time she ever calls me 'brother' is when she wants something" (Bruner, 1955).

These examples of the manipulation of kin terminology reinforce the point we made at the beginning of this section: kinship categories are cultural constructs people use to order their lives. As such, they can be readily changed to adapt to new problems and situations.

Descent Ideologies and Descent Groups

So far we have been focusing on how people in different societies classify their relatives. Clearly, kinship categories have an important influence on structuring human interaction and are therefore crucial to an investigation of social organization. Kin relationships are perceived differently in societies with different kin terminology systems, and people shape their roles in accordance with those perceptions. But as we saw in the case of the Yanomamö, kinship systems are more than ways of establishing social categories. They are also the basis for the formation of important social groups—collections of people with a sense of common identity. The most significant of such groups are referred to by anthropologists as *descent groups*. In many societies, including the Yanomamö, certain consanguineal relatives are set apart from others on the basis of a concept of descent from a common ancestor.

In the following sections, we will explore the various kinds of *descent ideologies* that different societies utilize and the characteristics of the groups formed on the basis of these ideologies. We refer to concepts of descent as "ideologies" because they are just that—sets of beliefs, myths, and symbols that underlie a group's sense of collective identity. Descent ideologies, like political ideologies of any kind, are a rationale for group formation. To anthropologists, therefore, concepts of descent are more than simply notions of ancestry. They are the basis for determining membership in groups that are extremely significant in the social order. The ideological basis of descent groups is perhaps most obvious in societies with what are called "unilineal" concepts of descent. It is to such societies that we now turn.

Unilineal Descent Ideologies and Descent Groups Descent ideologies can be said to fall into one of two general categories—*unilineal* or *nonunilineal*.[3] Unilineal ideologies are those in which membership in a descent group is traced through one line only, whether the maternal or the paternal line. If membership is established through the maternal line, the ideology is called *matrilineal,* if through the paternal line, *patrilineal*.

Matrilineal Descent   Under a matrilineal concept of descent, membership in a kin group is determined by virtue of ties in the maternal line only. Sons as well as daughters are de-

---

[3]What is called *double descent* could be considered a third type of unilineal descent ideology. It involves the simultaneous existence of two separate unilineal principles, a matrilineal and a patrilineal. An individual affiliates with his or her father's patrilineal descent group for some purposes and his or her mother's matrilineal descent group for others. In other words, all people in the society belong to both a matrilineal and a patrilineal group. Such a system, however, is quite rare, and we will not consider it in any detail in this chapter.

fined as members of their *mother's* descent group. (See Figure 18–7.) This is not to say that a child in a society with a matrilineal descent ideology has no feeling of attachment to his or her father. A father is simply not a member of the same descent group as his children.

One should not assume, however, that women in societies with matrilineal ideologies are vested with authority in their kin groups, for this is not always the case. Although membership is inherited through the female line, leadership within a matrilineal descent group is often bestowed on the male members. For this reason, men in societies with matrilineal ideologies rarely move far from their natal homes after marriage; a man usually remains in or near the village in which he was born, enabling him to assume a directing role in kin group affairs.

Patrilineal Descent Under a patrilineal descent ideology, which is very widespread, membership in a kin group is determined by virtue of ties in the paternal line only. Daughters as well as sons are defined as members of their *father's* descent group. (See Figure 18–8.) As with matrilineal descent, a patrilineal ideology does not mean that children have little attachment to their mothers. A mother is simply not a member of the same descent group as her children.

A patrilineal descent ideology means that female members of a kin group cannot bear new lineage members for the succeeding generation; the children a woman bears will be members of her husband's lineage, not her own. What this means for the role of women in societies with patrilineal ideologies varies. Among the Yanomamö women play an extremely subordinate role. "As members of local descent groups, girls have almost no voice in the decisions reached by their agnates [fathers and brothers] concerning their marriage. . . . In many cases the girl has been promised to a man long before she reaches puberty, and in some cases her husband actually raises her for part of her childhood. In short, they do not participate as equals in the political affairs of the corporate kinship group and seem to inherit most of the duties without enjoying many of the privileges" (Chagnon, 1968:81). In contrast, the Tallensi, who also have a patrilineal descent

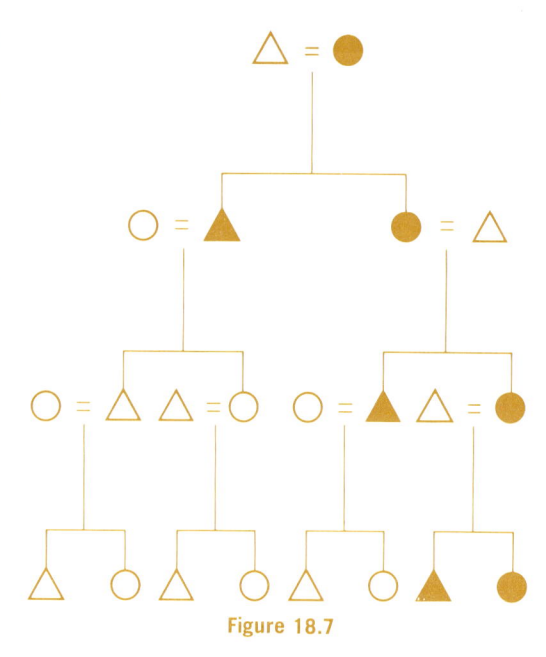

Figure 18.7

Figure 18.8

Social Structure and Social Behavior 365

This Yörük family, which lives together in one household, consists of a man and his wife, their married son with his wife and child, and their unmarried children. Along with several other families, they comprise an important political unit in this society—the lineage, whose membership is determined by patrilineal descent. Even after marriage, the sons will remain close to their father, and together with the father's brothers and their sons, will form a closely interacting group.
(Daniel G. Bates)

ideology, assign women important roles in their kin groups (Fox, 1967).

Types of Unilineal Descent Groups What are the kin groups formed on the basis of unilineal descent ideologies like? How are they structured and what functions do they serve? Unilineal descent groups follow certain basic patterns whether the ideology involved happens to be matrilineal or patrilineal. Generally speaking, anthropologists categorize such groups according to how inclusive they are.

A *lineage* is a unilineal descent group composed of males and females who are able to trace their genealogies through specified links to a common ancestor. Lineages can be either matrilineages or patrilineages depending upon whether descent is traced through the maternal or paternal line. Some societies have hierarchies of lineages, with individuals belonging to smaller minor lineages, as well as more inclusive major lineages.

Kin groups, however, may extend beyond the limits of known ancestry. In some societies, people believe themselves to be descended from a common ancestor and therefore have a sense of collective identity, even though they are unable to reconstruct exact genealogical connections. Anthropologists generally refer to such groups as *clans* (from the Gaelic word *clann,* meaning descendants). In many societies, a matriclan or patriclan will be named after a plant or animal, called a *totem* (from the Ojibwa Indian word *ototeman,* meaning "relative"). A totem usually holds some special meaning for the members of a clan, perhaps being implicated in the group's mythical ancestry. If little else, such symbols help to make a clan's sense of collective identity and unity more concrete. Undoubtedly, many clans derive from matrilineages and patrilineages that became too large or too dispersed to keep track of their genealogies. Others may be the result of two or more lineages that joined forces, perhaps after a famine or invasion reduced their populations, and invented a common ancestor to cement their union. The details of clan formation can only be guessed from the myths that commonly surround them.

A number of clans may unite in a *phratry,* extending the rights of kinship to one another yet retaining distinct identities for some purposes. On occasion, an entire society is organized into two large descent groups, such as the Land and Water *nena* of the Miwok American Indians. The anthropological term for such groups is *moieties* (from the French word *moitié,* meaning "half"). Or a society may be organized into several phratries, which are divided into a series of clans and subclans, which in turn are divided into lineages and sublineages.

The Evolution of Unilineal Descent Groups It is important to understand that kin groups in any society are not formed simply because people perceive themselves to be related to one another through descent. For a group to exist at all, its members must recognize some shared set of interests which gives them reason for joining forces and viewing themselves as a collective entity. As anthropologist E. R. Leach has explained:

Kin groups do not exist as things in themselves without regard to the rights and interests which center in them. Membership of such a group is not established by genealogy alone. Properly speaking, two individuals can only be said to be of the same kinship group when they share some common interest — economic, legal, political, religious as the case may be — and justify that sharing by reference to a kinship nexus. The anthropological problems that then arise are: What are these common interests? What individuals share them? (1961:66)

Some anthropologists have argued that the common interests that give rise to unilineal descent groups are economic ones: such groups evolve when there is some permanent resource, such as land, that requires allocation (Barth, 1966). Thus among hunting and gathering bands, whose ecological adaptation requires mobility and dispersal across wide-ranging territories, we seldom find lineages and clans. With the development of cultivation, however, and the changes that accompany it — a sedentary way of life, increased population pressure, and exclusive ties to specific territories — we find unilineal descent groups proliferating. These economic-related conditions, coupled perhaps with an external political threat such as warfare, can give rise to a need for solidarity and unambiguous group identification which are the hallmarks of unilinear descent systems. But these events can of course be reversed. For instance, if population drops significantly, and pressure on the land is alleviated, unilineal descent groups may begin to break up.

While many possible explanations for the evolution of unilineal descent groups have been proposed, it is our impression that they all fail to take into account the great diversity that is now recognized to exist among societies with unilineal descent groups. Once this diversity has been described and analyzed in more detail, anthropologists will be in a better position to formulate explanations of the rise of unilineal descent groups.

But whatever the common sets of interests are that initially prompt the development of unilineal descent groups, it is clear that such groups organize many important activities for their members. The regulation of marriage is one such activity, as we saw in our discussion of the Yanomamö. In societies with unilineal descent ideologies, lineages and clans, and very often phratries as well, are usually *exogamous* — that is, marriage within one's own descent group is strictly forbidden. Rules of exogamy are effective means of reducing competition for spouses and sexual favors *within* kin groups. Furthermore, they create ties of alliance and cooperation *between* kin groups.

Unilineal descent groups also provide mutual aid and support for their members. Those belonging to the same descent group are bound together by a network of reciprocal rights and obligations. The strength of these bonds, however, often varies depending upon the closeness of the kinship ties involved. The mutual obligations between the members of the same lineage, for example, are usually quite strongly felt; those between members of the same clan somewhat less so; and the members of the same phratry are so distantly related and often so widely dispersed that they feel virtually no reciprocal duties at all toward one another.

The mutual aid and support provided by unilineal descent groups cover both political and economic activities. In some unilineal societies, the entire lineage is held accountable for the actions of individual members if they infringe on the rights of members of other lineages. If a person murders a man from another lineage, for example, vengeance may justifiably be inflicted on any of the slayer's kinsmen. By the same token, an individual can depend on his kin to help him exact justice for a wrong committed by a member of another descent group. In some societies people also have the right to expect food from other members of their descent group when their own crops fail. Under such circumstances, unilineal descent groups can be seen as functioning to redistribute wealth in the absence of such things as welfare systems and unemployment insurance.

Nonunilineal Descent Ideologies and Descent Groups Many of the first societies that anthropologists encountered had strongly unilineal descent ideologies. Most African and American Indian societies, for example, are either patrilineal or matrilineal, and early studies done among these peoples led anthropologists to expect that most other societies in the world follow a unilineal ideology. There was one large and obvious exception to the unilineal rule, and that was society in America and Europe, in which corporate descent groups do not really exist. This fact, however, was explained away as the result of modern conditions. In a complex society, individuals can obtain help from many different sources: employers, friends, government agencies, clinics, and so on. Therefore, they did not have to align themselves with a strictly defined kin group.

But this assumption proved to be false. Anthropologists encountered nonindustrialized societies where descent ideology existed, but it was less strongly enforced, more ambiguous, or used less extensively as the basis of group formation than in unilineal societies. Surprisingly, many of these societies were small groups of hunters-gatherers with very simple technologies. This discovery laid to rest forever the assumption that nonunilineal concepts of descent were found only in complex societies. Anthropologists have classified nonunilineal descent ideologies into two basic types: *ambilineal* and *bilateral*.

Ambilineal Descent In societies with an ambilineal descent ideology, a person affiliates with kin groups on the basis of ties traced through either the paternal line *or* the maternal line. In some ambilineal societies, a person is expected to choose between the various kin groups to which he or she is in some way lineally related. In many such societies, the functions served by descent groups are quite similar to those in unilineal societies: collective ownership of land and other productive resources, regulation of marriage through rules of exogamy, provision of mutual aid and support. In other ambilineal societies, however, a person is free to move from one descent group to another, as long as he or she affiliates with only one group at a time. And in still others, a person can affiliate with as many groups as he or she has ties, for whatever different purposes.

Ambilineal descent systems, then, have more built-in flexibility than unilineal ones: they leave more room for individual choice concerning kin group affiliation. On the Gilbert Islands, for example, membership in a landholding ambilineal descent group, called an *ooi*, is open to all individuals who can trace their descent to the person who originally owned the *ooi*'s land. Some of these members may not have actually inherited shares of land belonging to that particular *ooi,* but they are entitled to do so if the current shareholders die without heirs. As a result, the distribution of people on the various *ooi* is invariably guided by population pressure. If one *ooi* becomes overcrowded, people will affiliate themselves with another *ooi* that is short of heirs (Goodenough, 1955). Such flexibility, however, is purchased at the cost of clear-cut loyalties, as in the case of most ambilineal societies.

Bilateral Descent A second nonunilineal concept of descent is bilateral descent. This is the concept that we use in our own society. With bilateral descent, individuals define themselves as being at the center of a group of kin composed more or less equally of their mothers' and fathers' relatives of all kinds — up to a point, that is; usually we must draw the line at second cousins, or our kindreds (as bilateral kin groups are generally called) would become impossibly complex.

It is important to recognize that a bilateral concept of descent does not create descent groups like those we have been discussing so far. In fact, a kindred is not necessarily a *group* in the true sense of the word, for most of its members do not perceive themselves as having a collective identity. Instead, a kindred is usually a network with ego as the focal point. Consequently, everyone in a bilateral system has a different kindred than everyone else (except siblings). And each individual also belongs to a large number of their own relatives' kindreds, the memberships of which all overlap. A child's kindred, for example, is not the same as his parents' kindreds, since his own combines relatives from both of theirs; yet he is included in the kindreds of his parents, and they in his. This is why anthropologists say a kindred is ego-oriented rather than ancestor-oriented. While descent groups consist of people who have a real or fictive ancestor in common, kindreds consist of people who have a relative (ego) in common.

Kin in societies with bilateral concepts of descent may form ad hoc associations. For example, when an Iban decides to organize a headhunting or trading party, he calls upon members of his kindred, who call upon members of their kindreds, who in turn call upon members of theirs. In this way, a large group is assembled in an astonishingly short time (Freeman, 1961). In our own society, one's kindred is commonly assembled for weddings, christenings, funerals, and other important ceremonial events, and we have general cultural guidelines governing who will be included in such groups and who will not. This kind of loosely organized system of kindred is particularly suited to societies such as our own which place a premium on personal independence and mobility.

In some societies with bilateral concepts of descent, groups are more clearly structured and lend themselves to corporate enterprises. Among the nomadic, reindeer-herding Lapps of northern Sweden, Finland, and Norway, for example, residential kin groups are formed on the basis of bilateral descent, with sibling ties forming the core of such groupings (Pehrson, 1954). Usually a group of brothers with their wives and children will band together, with other consanguineal kin attaching themselves to the sibling core. Although an individual may belong to several bands during his lifetime, each affiliation will be based on bilaterally reckoned genealogical links.

Descent, Kinship, and Social Behavior In considering descent principles and the groups formed on their basis, it is a mistake to assume that all societies with the same descent ideology have almost identical systems of social behavior with regard to kinship. Human beings are resourceful creatures who readily adapt to the wide variety of circumstances they encounter in daily life. Consequently, patterns of social behavior from culture to culture are characterized by great diversity — far greater diversity than many discussions of kinship imply.

Perhaps a clearer picture of this diversity can be seen by comparing four societies with patrilineal descent ideologies: the Tiv and Tallensi of Africa and the Chimbu and Mae Enga of New Guinea (Buchler and Selby, 1968). As we might expect, all four have patrilineal descent groups. In each case, the patrilineage is a localized, landholding group, the members of which are strictly forbidden to intermarry. And in all four, a wide variety of other behavioral norms are stated in terms of descent ideology.

Yet in spite of these broad similarities in how kin groups are formed and the basic functions they serve, there are also important differences in how people in these four kinship systems actually behave. Among the Tiv and Tallensi, for example, membership in a lineage is rather strictly defined on the basis of patrilineal descent, as the model of such a system would predict. The Chimbu and Mae Enga, however, behave somewhat differently: although their descent ideologies define kin group membership in patrilineal terms, these groups quite often extend the full rights and privileges of lineage membership to people related through maternal ties or through marriage. And even among the Tiv and Tallensi, who seem to have less flexible rules of group membership, descent groups are sometimes redefined to fit changing political, economic, and demographic realities. If there are no sons in a particular generation, for example, a lineage must somehow bend its rules of group membership or face extinction. Being practical-minded like most peoples, the Tiv and Tallensi see the wisdom of abandoning proper behavior for smart behavior under certain circumstances.

A similar diversity of behavior can be seen when we consider land ownership in these four societies. Again, as we might expect, land in all four is said to be held collectively by the lineages, with lineage members and their families having rights to its use. But as we have seen, social behavior seldom corresponds exactly with descent ideology. Consequently, among the Tiv and Tallensi, people who have no patrilineal ties to a descent group can nevertheless borrow land from that group, and among the Chimbu, more than half of all landholdings cannot be defined on strictly patrilineal grounds.

At first glance, evidence such as this might lead us to conclude that people in these societies do not understand their own descent systems. Why isn't kin group membership consistently ascribed according to patrilineal descent ideology? Why isn't lineage land consistently worked by lineage members? The problem, however, lies not with the peoples involved, but rather with the Western observers who expect a kind of rigid consistency that they would never expect of their own society. A more realistic way of understanding kinship systems would be to view behavior and the reasons for it from the individual's point of view: what factors do people consider in arriving at decisions about what they will and will not do? To be sure, social rules and ideological principles are among these considerations, but so are individual circumstances and events. Principles of descent, like any ideologies, are not rigid laws but rather guides for social behavior, the interpretation of which can be readily manipulated depending upon a wide variety of special circumstances.

An instance of how descent ideology may be reinterpreted to fit the contingencies of ecological conditions can be seen in the example of the Bedouins of Cyrenaica (Emrys-Peters, 1959). All Bedouin trace their descent patrilineally to a common ancestor, while each of the different tribes claims to be the descendants of one of this ancestor's nine grandsons. These links provide a kin group structure that regulates not only the ties between individuals but also the relationship between individuals and land. But under the pressure of limited water availability, large groups are continually splitting into smaller ones, while smaller, less successful groups often collapse. These rearrangements would soon make the structure of the patrilineal kin groups hopelessly complex if it were not that the Bedouin are less interested in keeping meticulous records of their relationships than they are in maintaining order in their society. Thus by foreshortening and telescoping genealogies and by fusing names, they are able to change their descent structure to correspond to the actual distribution of local groups, thereby contributing to long-run political, social, economic, and ecological stability.

As we have suggested throughout this book, people everywhere are involved in a kind of social calculus, always weighing the costs and benefits of many different courses of action before coming to a final decision. Social rules alone, including rules of descent and kinship, can only partially predict how a person will act in a given situation; they are simply one among many important factors a person will consider.

One example of how this kind of social calculus operates can be seen among the Kwaio of the Solomon Islands. Here, people are obligated to contribute to a close kinsman's bride price (the payment he makes to his bride's family when that man marries). Many factors are considered in determining whether a person is close enough to the groom to be expected to make a contribution, and if so, what size payment their relationship warrants. The degree of "closeness," and thus the size of a bride-price contribution, is calculated as follows:

1. Co-members of a descent group are more closely related than nonmembers at similar genealogical distance.
2. Persons who lived together in childhood . . . are more closely related than persons at similar genealogical distance who did not.
3. Persons habitually living in the same settlement or proximate settlements in adulthood are more closely related than persons at similar genealogical distance who are living apart. . . .
4. Agnates [patrilineal kinsmen] are more closely related than nonagnates at similar genealogical distance. (Keesing, 1967, as summarized by Buchler and Selby, 1968:95–96)

In addition, a number of other considerations enter into a calculation of who is obligated to make a contribution and what the size of each contribution should be. A person's age, sex, his reciprocal obligation based on the groom's contribution to *his* bride price, his opposition to the marriage (if any), past quarrels he may have had with the groom, past failures on the groom's part to meet kinship obligations, a closer relationship with the bride than with the groom, and simple financial insolvency are all weighed and evaluated. If calculations such as these sound somewhat familiar, it is because we too go through similar mental calculations when deciding, for example, whether or not to send a wedding gift to a second cousin, and if so, how expensive a gift it should be. Social behavior, then, can seldom be based on simple rules or notions of what is proper. This would be impossible, for rules are *general* principles and behavior occurs in *specific* situations. Social rules must always be weighed and interpreted in light of particular circumstances.

As they actually exist in functioning societies, systems of descent and kinship can never be rigid constructs. We can see this most clearly when people in a society are faced with a choice between survival and preserving a traditional code of behavior: it would be foolish indeed to choose to perish rather than change. Systems of descent and kinship are basically adaptive mechanisms. They are a means by which a society relates to its environment and to the conditions of life. In fact, it is this very adaptability that has given rise to the enormous diversity of kinship and descent systems to be found throughout the world.

We should not leave our discussion of kinship, however, with the impression that in many societies kinship is virtually the only organizing principle. In some societies, including our own, kinship is a less important principle of social organization than, say, among the Yanomamö. But even in societies that rely heavily on kinship as a means of structuring human interaction, other organizing principles are also important. Social categories and formal groups based on age, sex, or ethnicity, for example, crosscut kin categories and kin-based groups, creating additional ties and loyalties, and additional sets of expectations regarding interpersonal behavior. Although these three principles of social organization are by no means the only ones that societies utilize in patterning human relationships, the first two are significant to varying degrees in every population, and the last is extremely important in most complex societies. Consequently, we have chosen to focus on age, sex, and ethnicity in the final sections of this chapter.

Age and Age-Based Groups

In every society age is a commonly used criterion for socially categorizing people. Our own culture labels people according to several rather loosely defined age categories: infants, children, adolescents, young adults, the middle-aged, the elderly. All societies identify social categories on the basis of age, but the particular categories established and the expected roles associated with each one vary greatly from one culture to another. Among the Masai of East Africa, for example, young men in their late teens and twenties made up the warrior class. They were expected to live in special camps, from which they launched their military campaigns against neighboring tribes. When a man entered his thirties, he was considered to have passed his prime as a warrior and was forced to retire, marry, and settle down. In our own society, in contrast, many people in their late teens and twenties are expected to be completing their educations, selecting occupations, and only beginning to establish themselves in careers. Far from being a category of "retirees," those in their early thirties are viewed as not yet having reached the peak of their productive years.

Age categories also serve to structure human interaction. In every society, a person's network of social relationships is composed of many people approximately his or her own age; this is to say that people tend to interact extensively with their peers. Moreover, how we behave toward others and how we expect others to behave toward us is influenced to some extent by relative age classifications. A young adult will behave quite differently toward a child than toward an elderly person. A child, on the other hand, will behave differently toward another child or toward an elderly

Kin Ties, Ambiguity, and Choice

We have discussed the Kwaio wedding at which one of the guests was related to both the bride and the groom and therefore had to resolve the conflicting roles he was assigned on the basis of each relationship. Such ambiguity concerning kin ties is by no means uncommon. The extent to which this problem can occur in a society is made clear by a computer analysis of marriage among the Hawaashleh Bedouin of the Negev Desert in Israel, a population of some 350 people, all claiming patrilineal descent from a common ancestor (Randolph and Coult, 1968). The subtribe Randolph and Coult chose for analysis was corporate in nature, having a common name, territory, camel brand, and leader.

Unlike most peoples with a patrilineal descent ideology, the Bedouin prefer marriages *within* their own lineage—that is, between patrilateral parallel cousins. Randolph and Coult obtained data on 150 marriages. Of these, 61 were between spouses belonging to the same lineage, while 89 were between spouses belonging to different lineages (19 out of the 89, however, were between consanguineal relatives of some sort). This may seem simple enough, but when examined closely the kin ties between spouses were enormously complex. The researchers observed that "41 of the 61 cases in which a Hawaashleh man married a patrilateral cousin, he could trace at least one other consanguineal tie to that spouse. Many could trace more; one man had 21 distinct consanguineal kin-types vis-à-vis his spouse" (p. 91). (Randolph and Coult go on to show that degree of distance and number of consanguineal ties are both important in calculating which of a number of different parallel cousins to marry.)

Clearly, if the kin ties between husband and wife are this complex, the ties between each spouse's other consanguineal relatives are equally or even more complex. Thus in small societies such as that of the Hawaashleh Bedouin, a marriage rule or any kind of rule stated in terms of kin relations is likely to be ambiguous and open to conflicting interpretations.

adult. Thus the age categories into which people are placed structure their behavior in social interaction.

In addition to influencing social roles and structuring personal interaction, social categories based on age also supply the basis for the formation of groups. In our own society, some examples of primarily age-based groups are the grades of a school, a Cub Scout den, a singles' club, a senior citizens' organization. Generally, we do not consider such groups crucial influences on our lives. In certain other societies, however, age-based groups are of far greater significance in the life of the individual. Among the Karimojong, a cattle-herding people of northern Uganda, every boy is assigned at birth to an age set, a group of peers with whom he maintains close ties throughout the rest of his life. Age sets, in turn, are the building blocks for larger groups known as generation sets that organize the social, economic, and political life of the Karimojong (Dyson-Hudson, 1966).

In spite of the strong ties between Karimojong men of the same age set, the members of such a set do not actually live together in separate age-graded communities. Among the Nyakyusa of the Great Rift Valley of Africa, however, permanent villages are formed by young male contemporaries. As described by Monica Wilson (1949), a group of boys age ten or eleven will build huts at the edge of their father's village, sleeping there and returning home only for meals. Mothers take turns feeding groups of boys until they are old enough to marry. The boys' village grows as the original founders are joined by other boys of similar age from nearby men's villages. Each boys' village closes membership after about five years, and the next group of boys age ten or eleven must start a new village.

But there is more to the Nyakyusa age system than separate villages for peer groups. The entire society is divided into three generation sets, each with certain rights and duties: the elders, who are retired from active political life but whose leaders perform certain ritual functions; the ruling generation, which exercises administrative and military leadership; and the young, who have no authority but can be called upon for military defense when needed. Thus, the Nyakyusa, like certain other peoples, use the concept of age as a basis for forming a variety of different kinds of groups.

Sex and Sex-Based Groups

All societies identify social categories on the basis of sex. In most cases, of course, this involves a duality—male and female. But there are cultures in which an intermediate role is recognized, as, for example, the Crow berdache or the Cheyenne "half-man, half woman." In most societies, social categories based on sex are associated with culturally defined male and female roles. As we have seen in earlier chapters, there are significant regularities around the world in the kinds of work people consider appropriate for men and women. Although there are many cross-cultural variations in the assignment of specific tasks, women in most societies have traditionally been expected to orient their lives around the home and children, while men are usually expected to engage in work outside the home—hunting for game, working in the fields, holding down a factory or office job. By the same token, many societies, including our own, have held somewhat similar notions about the proper personality traits that males and females should exhibit. In general terms, women have traditionally been expected to be relatively dependent, emotional, and nurturant, while men have frequently been expected to be relatively independent, practical, and aggressive. There are, however, many important exceptions to these broad patterns. In her study of male and female roles in New Guinea, Margaret Mead (1935) found that the Tchambuli, for example, virtually reversed the sex-role stereotypes prevalent in many other societies. Males are expected to be "catty" and gossipy, highly concerned with their status and physical appearance, while females are expected to be hard-working and cooperative, and are responsible for carrying out the work of the village.

As with social categories based on age, cat-

Social Structure and Social Behavior 373

Because of the supposedly polluting influence of menstruation, husbands and wives of some societies live separately. This has been a common practice in the New Guinea Highlands, where this men's house is located, but is gradually changing through contact with other cultures. (Robert Glasse)

egories based on sex serve to structure personal interaction. In many societies, a person's network of friends is largely composed of people of his or her own sex. Moreover, how one individual behaves toward another is often influenced to a large extent by their respective sexes. In our own society, in spite of recently changing sex roles and attitudes toward them, certain kinds of behavior are expected in a man's interaction with a woman that are not expected in his interaction with another man, and vice versa.

Social categories based on sex can also supply part of the foundation for the organization of groups. In our own society, certain formal groups are based, at least to some extent, on sex classifications: fraternities, sororities, men's lodges, and veterans' organizations all limit membership on the basis of sex. Like age-based groups, however, groups restricted to members of a single sex seldom play a central role in our lives. Yet in other societies groups with membership criteria based on sex are highly significant in structuring social interaction. Among the Plains Indians, for example, military associations, open exclusively to men, were important social institutions. These groups, based on the experience of their members as warriors, were devoted to the glorification of war. Club leaders, who were also the principal war chiefs of the tribe, carried the honor of their clubs into battle. Yet the various associations did not participate in battle as separate regiments; rather, their functions more closely resembled those of our own American Legion or V.F.W. Essentially, the Plains military societies were groups of comrades-in-arms who reinforced their bonds through conversation, song, dancing, and ritual celebration (Hoebel, 1960).

The men's associations in many Melanesian societies are well known for their strict sexual segregation. Among the Siuai, a group of pig herders and cultivators in the Solomon Islands, the men's clubhouses have resident demons who are said to kill any female who ventures too near (Oliver, 1955). Among the Mae Enga of New Guinea, all males except the youngest boys live in men's houses and are permitted to visit their wives only under certain strictly regulated conditions. In this society, rules of exogamy mean that men are often forced to find wives in enemy groups, thus causing more or less constant hostility and distrust among spouses. Unmarried Mae Enga men belong to their own organization which conducts purification rituals called *sanggai,* during which the bachelors go into complete seclusion and even the glimpse of a female footprint is contaminating. These bachelor retreats serve not only to reinforce masculine identification but also to display the fighting strength of a village (Meggitt, 1964).

Ethnicity and Ethnic Groups

Particularly in industrialized societies, ethnicity is an important criterion for establishing social categories. Ethnic classifications are usually based on social perceptions of shared national origin, language, religion, and/or certain physical characteristics. In our own society, native Americans, Chicanos, Blacks, Jews, Puerto Ricans, Chinese- and Japanese-Americans, Italian-Americans, and Polish-Americans are some of our most significant ethnic categories. The diversity of ethnic classifications in the United States stems from the fact that our society is made up of generations of immigrants, many of whom have entered the cultural mainstream, although others still remain segregated in ethnic communities, either through their own choice or because the opportunity for assimilation into the dominant society has been denied them.

It is important to point out that ethnic classifications are cultural constructs which can and do vary from society to society. In our own country, for example, Asiatic Indians are usually classified as "white ethnics" while in England they are lumped together with Malaysians, Chinese, and West Indians in a broad, undifferentiated "colored" category. A third ethnic classification scheme can be seen in South Africa. Here, Asiatic Indians are categorized as distinct from both "whites" and "colored."

Because ethnic categories are culturally defined, they can be readily manipulated and changed. A striking example of ethnic transformation associated with economic change can be seen in the case of the Fur of the Sudan, a hoe-agriculture people, some of whom are abandoning their separate identity to become part of the nomadic, cattle-herding society of the Arabs. Oddly enough, this process depends not on people being pushed off the land and into a nomadic group but rather on the accumulation of wealth which has no outlet in the traditional Fur society. But the Fur cannot simply leave the land and take up cattle herding without giving up an important part of their ethnic identity. As Barth explains, "a man has access to the critical means of production by virtue of practising a certain subsistence; this entails a whole style of life, and all these characteristics are subsumed under the ethnic labels Fur and Baggara" (Barth, 1969:26). A Fur who herds cattle, therefore, becomes a Baggara.

In many instances, ethnic classifications will largely define social roles. For example, members of ethnic minorities are often traders, sometimes to the exclusion of the native majority. We can think of the Chinese in Southeast Asia, and the Asians in East Africa as two prominent examples. Brian Foster (1974) has examined the same phenomenon in Thailand, where the Mons are the traders. Originally from Burma, this group is similar to the Thai people in most ways except language. Mons are most likely to be traders, and those Mons who are traders are least likely to be assimilated into the larger society. Why has this pattern persisted? Foster hypothesizes that ethnic distinctions serve important functions. "Ethnic difference sets off commercial people from the society around them in such a way as to (1) minimize the stress inherent in market transactions, and (2) free the merchants from the social constraints of an anti-commercial peasant society that would otherwise strangle commercial enterprises" (Foster, 1974:5). Traditional Thai society stressed generosity, lack of profit in dealing with others, and extreme civility to avoid conflict and competition. So long as villages were self-sufficient, these values proved viable. But as the possibilities for more outside trade developed, Thais faced the choice of forgoing trade or breaking social expectations. This was a serious conflict. But an outsider to such a society may violate social rules without endangering the society, since the conflict then becomes interethnic and the means of dealing with it are different and less threatening to the social fabric. Being alien is actually an advantage. Thus under certain circumstances ethnic minorities are likely to succeed in trade, especially if they preserve their alien identity. Of course, ethnic minorities are not always assigned the role of trader. Quite obviously in our own society, many ethnic minorities—blacks and native Americans, for example—have traditionally been excluded from participating in commerce. The factors that select for an ethnic minority assuming a particular role in society are many and complex. Neither is it the case that ethnic differences generally promote harmonious relations. Frequently, dealings between members of different ethnic categories are characterized by a great amount of conflict, even warfare.

Early in this chapter we discussed how ethnic categories can impose boundaries on individual networks. By the same token, ethnic

Some ethnic groups that have migrated to cities manage to retain aspects of their old way of life. In this middle-class housing complex in Abidjan, Ivory Coast, the courtyard provides a social meeting place and playground as well as an area for work groups, such as these women pounding yams. (Marc & Evelyne Bernheim/Woodfin Camp)

classifications also tend to structure human interaction. This can be seen most clearly when members of the dominant group in a society discriminate against those classified as ethnic minorities. In this country, for example, until quite recently, blacks and members of many other ethnic categories were refused housing in "white" neighborhoods, enrollment in "white" schools, and access to many hotels, restaurants, and other public accommodations.

Finally, ethnic distinctions, like social distinctions based on age and sex, may give rise to the formation of groups. We have seen this over and over again in the United States. Members of ethnic minorities have organized a large number of formal organizations aimed at enhancing their ethnic pride and combating discrimination by the dominant society.

The same process of ethnic group formation can be seen in other societies as well. The Ibo of Nigeria, for example, who have migrated from the tribal territory to the cities have formed tribal associations to assist newcomers, sponsor events where Ibo culture is preserved, use their income to start businesses and educate the children, and serve as political pressure groups.

In this chapter we have surveyed some of the most important social categories people in different societies establish. In particular, we have focused on the ways in which these categories structure patterns of behavior, and how they influence the composition of networks and groups. In the following chapter, we will look at some of the most important groups in every society—families and domestic groups.

summary

In every society people are bound together by various kinds of patterned relationships that collectively make up their system of social organization. Social scientists have found several concepts useful in analyzing the complex relationships that exist in all societies: *networks,* sets of social relationships viewed from the perspectives of the individuals at their focal points; *groups,* associations of individuals who interact on a fairly regular basis and whose members have a sense of collective identity; and *social categories,* classifications of people all of whom share certain culturally-identified characteristics.

Kinship is an important dimension of social organization in every society, although it is more important in some than in others. All societies classify people on the basis of kinship. First, peoples around the world distinguish between *consanguineal* kin (relatives by birth) and *affinal* kin (relatives by marriage). In addition, a number of other criteria are used for classifying kin, including sex, bifurcation (maternal or paternal side of the family), generation, and lineality (direct descent relationships) vs. collaterality (relationships traced through a connecting person). The study of kin classification is important because how we classify others strongly influences how we act toward them. Although particular societies may have their own variations, kin classification systems fall into six general categories—Sudanese, Eskimo, Hawaiian, Iroquois, Omaha, and Crow.

Because they are cultural creations, not biological givens, kin terms can be manipulated to stress different relative statuses and different reciprocal obligations. Thus, kin terminology systems can be readily changed by the member of a particular society in order to adapt to new problems and new situations.

Kinship is also the basis for the formation of important social groups, the most important of which are what anthropologists call *descent groups.* In many societies, certain consanguineal relatives are assigned membership in a particular kin group on the basis of a descent ideology. Such ideologies can be said to fall into one of two general categories—*unilineal* or *nonunilineal.* Unilineal ideologies are those in which membership in a descent group is traced through one line only, whether the maternal (*matrilineal* descent) or the paternal (*patrilineal* descent).

The kin groups formed on the basis of unilineal descent ideologies are generally defined according to how inclusive they are and whether or not the members can actually specify their geneological links to a common ancestor. It is important to remember, however, that kin groups are not formed simply because people perceive themselves to be related to one another through descent. For a group to exist, its members must recognize some shared set of interests which gives them reason for joining forces. Regardless of what these common sets of interests are, it is clear that unilineal descent groups serve many important functions for their members. Two important functions are the regulation of marriage and the provision of mutual aid and support.

Anthropologists have classified nonunilineal descent ideologies into two basic types— *ambilineal* and *bilateral.* In societies with an ambilineal descent ideology, a person affiliates with kin groups on the basis of ties traced through either the paternal line *or* the maternal line. With bilateral descent, individuals define themselves as being at the center of a group of kin composed more or less equally of their mother's and father's relatives of all kinds. A bilateral kindred is really a network with ego as the focal point.

It is a mistake to assume that all societies with the same descent ideology have almost identical systems of social behavior with regard to kinship. Patterns of social behavior vary greatly from society to society. Principles of descent, like any ideologies, are not rigid laws but rather guides for social behavior, the interpretation of which can be readily manipulated depending upon the particular circumstances.

Even in societies that rely heavily on kinship as a means of structuring human interaction, other organizing principles are also important. Social categories and formal groups based on age, sex, and ethnicity, for example, cross-cut kin categories and kin-based groups, creating additional ties and loyalties, and additional sets of expectations regarding interpersonal behavior. Although these three principles of social organization are by no means the only ones that societies use in patterning human relationships, age and sex are significant to varying degrees in every population, and ethnicity is extremely important in most complex societies.

suggested readings

BENNETT, J. W.
    1975   *The New Ethnicity: Perspectives from Ethnology,* New York: West Publishing. Readings dealing with the use of traditional ethnic symbols in the development of social identity and cohesiveness in the modern state.

BOISSEVAIN, J., AND MITCHELL, J., EDS.
    1973   *Network Analysis: Studies in Human Interaction,* The Hague: Mouton. A collection of essays that provide a general background to the anthropological uses of network analysis; it is especially important for a discussion of alliance and symmetrical and asymmetrical exchange.

FOX, R.
    1967   *Kinship and Marriage,* Baltimore, Md.: Penguin Books. An excellent review of the theoretical issues relevant to the study of social groups, as organized according to principles of kinship.

GOODENOUGH, W. H.
    1970   *Description and Comparison in Cultural Anthropology,* Chicago: Aldine. Examines the broad theoretical and methodological issues involved in the anthropological study of social structure.

GRABURN, N. H., ED.
    1971   *Readings in Kinship and Social Structure,* New York: Harper & Row. An extensive collection of essays representing the major theoretical positions in the study of social organization.

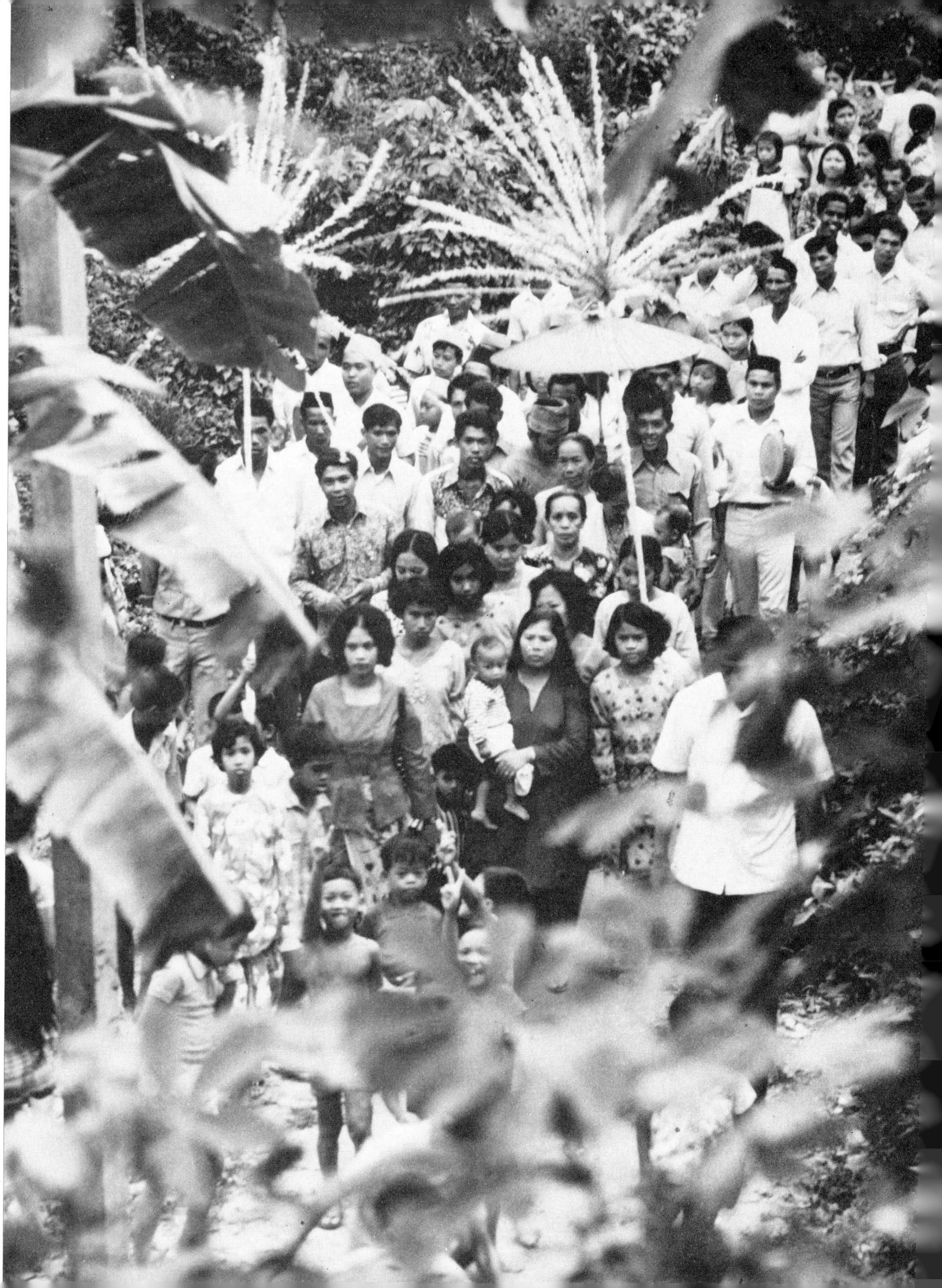

nineteen
Marriage, Families, and the Organization of Domestic Groups

In every human society there are families, but families are not everywhere the same. While the typical American would define the family as being composed of a husband and wife and their young children, a nineteenth-century Mormon would have found this definition somewhat deficient. The Mormons at that time considered it proper for a man to have more than one wife, so they would have defined a family as a husband, his several co-wives, and all of their immature offspring. And in many parts of the world our own notion of the family as a single set of spouses and their children would be an anomaly. Instead, the family is thought of as extending over several generations. Among the Hopi, for example, the family would be defined as a woman and her husband, their unmarried sons, their adult daughters and *their* husbands, and all their daughters' children. The family, therefore, is a cultural construct, not a biological given.

In spite of their diverse compositions, however, families around the world have certain characteristics in common: they are the minimal kinship groups that to varying degrees cooperate economically, are entrusted with the care and socialization of children by older members, and exchange offspring, through marriage, with other family units. Although many conceivable groups could perform these basic functions, people identify the family as performing them in an ideal way. In a sense, the family is an idealized domestic unit. Consequently, many people in every society conform to the family model in organizing their domestic lives.

And yet when we stop to observe a particular society, we realize immediately that not all domestic groups are families, and not all families are domestic groups. Human beings often find it convenient to behave in ways other than the ideal prescribes, and how they organize themselves into domestic groups is no exception. Thus in our own society we find some 65 million domestic groups or households, all composed of different assortments of sometimes related, sometimes unrelated individuals. Of course, many households are indeed made up of families composed of a mother, a father, and their young children; but others are composed of what we call "broken" families, one parent living with his or her children; still other households include additional relatives (a widowed grandparent or an unmarried aunt, for example), while yet others are made up of people who are not kin at all — namely, roommates or lovers. A household, then, is a minimal residential unit, the members of which share the same roof, be it a buffalo-hide tipi or a high-rise apartment; cooperate in performing various domestic tasks, such as obtaining and preparing food; and typically share economic abundance or scarcity as the circumstances — availability of wild game, success of crops, or state of the job market — dictate.

The family as the ideal domestic group is clearly only one thing that people consider in choosing among alternative living arrangements. Although cultural ideals certainly affect our thinking and behavior, numerous other practical and subjective considerations

Marriage customs show a wide range of cultural variation. Americans, for example, usually have parades to celebrate national holidays, such as Memorial Day or the Fourth of July. Yet this parade is a Malayan wedding procession — an integral part of the wedding ceremony. (Charles Moore/Black Star)

also influence the ways we ultimately act. Groups are the products of decisions individuals make based on self-interest, and may or may not conform to the ideal social structure. In this chapter we will examine the different ways people choose spouses, establish families, and organize themselves into households. Throughout, we will emphasize the variations within as well as among societies, attempting to show how factors in addition to socially prescribed rules influence *marriage,* the formation of *families,* and the organization of *domestic groups.* The topic of marriage is a logical starting point for our discussion, for in almost every society it is through marriage that the domestic unit—the family—has its beginnings.

Marriage

Throughout the world marriage is the means by which new families are created or existing families are expanded. In our own society, weddings celebrate the beginnings of entirely new families. A man and woman vow to live as one until death (or divorce) do them part. Marriage is a license for living together, having sex, and conceiving children. (Desertion, failure to consummate a marriage, and adultery are grounds for divorce; children born out of wedlock are considered illegitimate.) Marriage also involves reciprocal economic obligations. Traditionally, wives were expected to provide domestic services; husbands, financial support. This of course is changing, but the courts still hold a man responsible for his wife's support, sometimes even after the marriage has ended. Unless otherwise arranged, a couple's private wealth and future earnings become joint property upon marriage. In addition, a husband and wife are jointly responsible for supporting and raising the children they have together, whether or not they remain married. Thus marriage in our society involves a public commitment to a more or less permanent and exclusive heterosexual relationship, a set of well-defined economic rights and obligations, a means of legitimizing children, and certain responsibilities of parenthood.

Is marriage as we define it found throughout the world? The answer is no. Simply in the matter of intended permanence, marriage customs vary widely from culture to culture. The Navajo, like certain other peoples, do not marry with the expectation of remaining together for life. Most Navajo men and women divorce and remarry four or five times during their lives. In Iran, prior to a recent reform of the marriage law, members of the Shia faith could stipulate how long their marriage contracts were to last. And among the Kipsigis, when a wealthy man has a son old enough to manage his farm, he marries again, moves to his new bride's home, and begins the family cycle again, maintaining what amounts to visiting relationships with his older wives.

Our concept of exclusive sexual rights is also alien to many cultures. In many societies a man is permitted more than one wife at a time, and in a few others a woman is permitted more than one husband at a time. The Copper Eskimo practice "sexual hospitality" (they lend and borrow wives); and the people of Lesu consider adultery proper—if a wife's lover presents her with gifts to be turned over to her husband. Marriage does not prohibit a Nayar woman from having sexual relationships with any suitor of an appropriate caste status; her "ritual husband" had no more claim to her sexual favors than any other appropriate mate.

The economic rights and obligations that accompany marriage also vary. A Trobriand husband is expected to help support his sisters and is only partially responsible for the support of his wife and children. A Nayar husband is not expected to provide any financial support for his ritual wife and her children at all. In fact, he may never even see his wife again after their wedding (Gough, 1959).

Marriage is not a prerequisite for the legitimacy of children in all societies. Without marrying her, a Nuer male can legitimize the child of an unwed mother by making a specified payment. Nor are parents everywhere responsible for the care and teaching of their children. Samoan youngsters wander freely from one group of relatives to another. Trobriander boys move to their maternal uncles' village when they approach adolescence. On Israeli kibbutzim, children live apart from their parents in nurseries and dormitories. Although parents have a special relationship with their own children, the entire community assumes responsibility for their upbringing.

Generations of anthropologists have tried to write a definition of marriage that covers all these variations, but the effort is ultimately futile. The most we can say is that almost all societies have some form of marriage involving a sexual and economic union between two or more people that legitimizes their offspring, and that establishes reciprocal rights and obligations between husbands, wives, and their children.

The Functions of Marriage

Why is marriage nearly universal in human societies? What makes it so important? One answer is that marriage is a way of binding family to family, kin group to kin group. When a man or woman marries, he or she acquires not only a spouse, but also a new set of parents, brothers- and sisters-in-law, and other affinal relatives. Thus one way to look at marriage is as the union of two families, via the newly wed couple. To the ancient tribes of Israel such unions were extremely important: "Then will we give our daughters unto you, and we will take your daughters unto us, and we will dwell with you, and we will become one people" (Genesis 34:16). The family alliances created through marriage can be highly adaptive.

Marriage as Exchange Exchange is the most basic way of establishing a bond between individuals and groups. Quite apart from *what* is exchanged, the *act* of exchange itself creates social solidarity. In many societies, marriage is the most important form of exchange. Usually it is daughters who are "given away" to their new husbands, and to the families of those husbands.

In some societies interfamily alliances are created by exchanging daughters directly. A Tiv man may exchange one of his sisters for the sister of another man, mutually binding their families together. But direct exchange of women is relatively rare. More commonly, a man pays the family from whom he takes a daughter in marriage or works for them; this payment helps them to replace the daughter with a wife for one of their sons. Indirect exchange of women, via the *bride price* or *bride service,* is found throughout the world. This is not to say that women are bought and sold, or that they suffer the social status of chattel. Quite the contrary, it means that people place a high value on a woman's labor and her reproductive capacity: they do not give daughters away.

Bride prices range from token gifts to massive payments, sometimes taking years to pay in full. The currencies used in paying a bride price also vary. The Plateau Tonga give their future in-laws cows; the Ifugao, pigs; the Hopi, food; the Kurtatchi, shell money.[1] Sometimes a new husband will be required to work for his wife's family for a certain period of time. Such bride service may involve small chores or full-time labor for anywhere from a few weeks to several years. Among the Chukchee and Muria, a man has a choice between making bride payment or doing bride service.

The reverse custom, paying a groom's family a dowry to take a daughter "off one's hands," was common in medieval Europe, but exists only in remote parts of eastern Europe and India today. However, in a number of societies, the families of the bride and groom exchange payments. For example, a Cheyenne suitor asks an older woman in his family to lead a prize horse laden with gifts to his intended's camp. If her family accepts his proposal, they take the horse and spend the next

---

[1]This discussion is based on Stephens, *The Family in Cross-Cultural Perspective* (1963).

Marriage among the Fore people of Okapa, a subdistrict in the eastern highlands of New Guinea, is preceded by the payment of a bride price—goods presented by the groom's family to that of his intended. Here we see a formal presentation of the price, which includes pigs, bananas, and sugar cane; the bride's male relatives are examining the goods to ascertain their worth. (Robert Glasse)

several days collecting presents for his family. Great care is taken to return gifts of equal value.

Bride payment and service are most common in societies where a woman leaves her family to live with her husband's kin and the children she bears will become members of *his* patrilineal kin group. In effect, the husband is compensating his wife's family for the loss of her economic services and reproductive capacity. (When the couple remains in the vicinity of both kin groups and the husband's and wife's families have equal rights to the couple's and their children's assistance, reciprocal gift exchange is more common.) Bride payments and gift exchange help to insure that neither the couple nor their families will take the marriage lightly. Perhaps more important is the fact that when potentially hostile groups exchange women over a number of generations, they establish a lasting bond. Each group has vested interests in the other, in terms of both the past and the present.

The *levirate* and *sororate* exemplify the widely held conception of marriage as an exchange between kin groups. These customs extend the marriage contract *beyond* the death of a spouse. Under the levirate, a man has both the right to marry his dead brother's widow (or to demand bride payment from another husband she chooses) and the obligation to provide for her. Under the sororate, a widower has the right to claim one of his dead wife's sisters, and her kin have the obligation to provide him with a new wife. Even in our own society, where marrying one's deceased spouse's brother or sister might be considered somewhat questionable, individuals assume at least some continuing responsibility toward the family into which they marry.

Marriage and Economic Cooperation It has been suggested by many anthropologists that marriage is so widespread partly because of its economic advantages. Marriage unites two economically complementary people, a man and a woman. Because of their strength, men can perform certain physical tasks more easily than women. Because they are not encumbered with the physical limitations pregnancy and nursing place on women, men can travel greater distances from home for longer periods of time—to hunt or trade, for example. But pregnancy, nursing, and lesser muscular development do not prevent women from doing other kinds of work, work men cannot do if they are away tracking game or trading. The division of labor by sex is of course by no means inevitable and today is rapidly changing, but in the past it has proved workable in societies around the world, in all sorts of environments. And even if a couple do not allocate tasks along traditional sexual lines, they can still share the burden of work in some way, thus reaping the benefits of division of labor. Marriage is a convenient way to institutionalize such economic cooperation, although there is no necessary relationship between sexual division of labor and marriage.

Marriage and the Responsibilities of Parenthood As often as not, marriage hinges on a wife's ability to bear children. Samoans do not consider a girl marriageable until she has proven her fertility by conceiving a child. Among the Thongai, a man has the right to exchange a barren wife for one of her sisters. In Dahomey, a childless woman may raise the bride price for a second wife and remain in her husband's household as a "maiden aunt." By and large, a preference for childless marriages is a late-twentieth-century Western phenomenon.

Marriage helps to define the obligations of parents toward their children. Like Americans, most peoples consider a child's biological parents responsible for his support and upbringing. But there are exceptions to this rule, particularly with regard to the father's role. The Nayar of India are an extreme example. A Nayar woman customarily has sexual relations with a number of men throughout her life. When she becomes pregnant, one of these men (any one of them, in fact) acknowledges "probable paternity" by paying for a midwife to deliver the child. This is the end of the "probable father's" responsibilities; the mother and her sisters and brothers raise the child. Among the Marquesans, too, it is perfectly acceptable for a woman to have several lovers or husbands, but her first husband is considered to be the father of all her children, regardless of by whom they were conceived. Thus the roles of "genitor" (biological father) and "pater" (socially recognized father) do not necessarily coincide. And even when a man is socially recognized as the father of the children he conceives, his role in their care and training may be limited and to a large extent entrusted to others. On the Trobriand Islands, for example, a boy nearing adolescence goes to live with or near his maternal uncle, who assumes responsibility for his education and initiation into adulthood. In essence, the uncle becomes the boy's "pater" at this point. And in Samoan villages or Israeli kibbutzim, the entire community assumes responsibility for rearing children. Parents may have a special relationship with their offspring, but the parent/child bond is not as exclusive as it is in our society.

Marriage Rules

Given the importance of marriage in creating bonds between kin groups, promoting economic cooperation, and providing for the care and education of children, the institution is not taken lightly in any society. In fact, all societies have both explicit rules and implicit norms defining who is an appropriate spouse, how many people one should marry, and where a newly married couple should settle. These rules, backed by social pressure, make it easier for individuals to live in a socially accepted family unit than not. They also serve to strengthen the alliance bonds between groups. Perhaps the most significant marriage rules, at least in terms of the possible range of choices open to an individual, are those prescribing whom a person should and should not marry.

Who Should One Marry? In every society there are rules that set limits on who is considered an acceptable mate. Many of these rules are based on kinship ties. In the vast majority of societies, marriage within the nuclear family is not permissible; almost every human culture has strict rules prohibiting sexual relations, and hence marriage, between brothers and sisters, parents and children as incestuous. Beyond these incest rules, individuals in most societies are also pressured to marry outside particular groups with which they are identified. Such rules of exogamy (*ex-* meaning out, *-gamy* meaning marriage) may apply to members of villages, so that men must seek wives, and women husbands, in other communities. More commonly, however, they apply to some or all of a person's kin.

The Incest Taboo

In virtually every society, sexual relations (and by extension, marriage) between parents and children, brothers and sisters are taboo. The exceptions are few. For religious and political reasons, the ancient Egyptians, the Incas, and the aboriginal Hawaiians permitted brothers and sisters of royal families to marry, but they did not extend this privilege to other members of society. Why this universal taboo on incest?

One possible explanation, popular at the turn of the century, is that people have no desire to mate with members of their immediate family. Today, the idea that human beings have an instinctive aversion toward copulating with their parents, siblings, and children is completely rejected. Psychoanalysts devote much of their careers to untangling incestuous wishes. Besides, if most people find incest repulsive, why should they bother to create rules prohibiting it?

Others have argued that the kind of familiarity that exists in homes breeds sexual indifference, that eroticism thrives (and perhaps depends) on mystery. There appears to be some truth to this. Marriages between people born and raised together on the same Israeli kibbutz are extremely rare—despite the fact that parents strongly encourage such unions. When asked why, young adults claimed that familiarity breeds disinterest (Talmon, 1964). Still the question remains, why prohibit sexual and marital unions if people don't want them?

A second school of thought regarding intrafamily taboos centers on the social consequences of incest. Among the negative consequences, it has been argued that allowing parents and children, brothers and sisters to mate would create unmanageable jealousies, ultimately destroying the family unit. This is highly questionable, however. First, prohibiting sex is not the only way to minimize competition and friction within the family. For example, a man might establish an orderly schedule of spending one night a week with his wife, one with each daughter. This is how men in many polygynous societies handle relationships with their several wives. Second, there are many ethnographic examples of sisters sharing a husband, brothers sharing a wife, and men taking their first wife's niece as a second wife, without disastrous consequences. Finally, bringing an outsider into the household as a bride or groom can be as "disruptive" as sex within the family.

On the opposite side of the coin are the positive consequences of "marrying out." By forcing individuals to seek mates in families other than their own, the incest taboo functions to create interfamily alliances and enhance social cohesion. This may be true, but there are numerous other ways to create interfamily bonds. Moreover, describing the consequences of incest taboos does not explain why they came to be.

The answer to the universality of the incest taboo may be that people began mating outside their families at some distant point in human history because they had no choice. If our inferences are correct, early man had a very short life span (about thirty years), and many of his offspring died in infancy, so that children were widely spaced. Thus when a boy reached sexual maturity, his mother was too old and his unmarried sisters too young to be suitable mates. He had to look elsewhere. (The same would have been true for girls.) According to this theory, what began as necessity persisted as tradition: people developed the habit of marrying outside their families, and continued to do so as the adaptive advantages of outside ties became clear, or as groups with interfamily alliances grew at the expense of others without them. We have no way of proving or disproving this theory.

We do know, however, that inbreeding has negative biological consequences, particularly in species like ours that have few offspring. Animals avoid excessive inbreeding in two ways. Some are promiscuous, copulating with any member of their species during the mating season. Some inbreeding occurs, but not enough to cause serious problems. Alternatively, members of species that form stable heterosexual bonds and families usually expel offspring when they reach sexual maturity, at least during the mating season, so that they are forced to find sex elsewhere (Aberle et al., 1963). But this is not possible among humans, for the simple reason that young people are still dependent on adults when they reach sexual maturity. Thus the only way for humans to live in families *and* avoid inbreeding is to prohibit mating within the family.

We are not suggesting that early man knew about genetics and consciously avoided inbreeding. This would be absurd. The more likely conclusion is that people who mated outside their family—because they had to, because they weren't attracted to family members, because there was too much jealousy within the family, because they found alliances formed with other families through the exchange of offspring to be advantageous, or because of reasons we haven't guessed—stumbled onto a complex of biological and social benefits that improved their chances of survival. People maintained the incest taboo because it proved adaptive.

Rules of Exogamy Because cultures classify kin in different ways, rules of exogamy take many forms. In societies that have nonunilineal concepts of descent, such as our own, rules of exogamy generally apply to most of a person's blood relatives. Americans frown on a person marrying a first, and to a lesser degree a second, cousin. Such unions are not illegal and do not inspire the same kind of disgust that incestuous mating does, but neither are they socially applauded. Traditionally, the Chinese carried bilateral exogamy to the extreme, forbidding marriage between individuals who had the same last name on the theory that they *might* be related, however distantly.

In societies with unilineal concepts of descent, rules of exogamy generally apply to all members of an individual's lineage. Thus in a patrilineal society, individuals may be permitted to marry first cousins on their mother's side of the family but not on their father's. Usually, the prohibition against marriage forbids unions with all the people one calls "brother" or "sister." In many societies, rules of exogamy declare all members of a person's clan or even phratry unmarriageable.

Rules of exogamy have two main adaptive advantages. First, they create alliances between families and lineages. On the simplest level, a man is less likely to attack or cheat the family or village from which his mother or wife comes or the one into which his sister has married than he is unrelated groups. Second, exogamy brings "new blood" and perhaps new ideas into the family, fostering cultural innovation. These advantages were pointed out by Talmon (1964) in her studies of Israeli kibbutzim. Kibbutz exogamy creates links between communities and various communal movements; brings new members into the kibbutz, members who through marriage to a person raised there are committed to the community; and checks the emergence of powerful kin groups within the kibbutz. Village exogamy has the added benefit to some peoples of removing a new spouse from his or her kin group. Traditional Chinese preferred village exogamy because it was easier to control a daughter-in-law who could not run to her family every time she felt abused (Wolf, 1970).

Rules of Endogamy The choice of a mate may also be limited by rules prescribing that a person marry *within* a group with which he or she is identified, or rules of endogamy (*en-* meaning in, *-gamy* meaning marriage). The most obvious example of this is the Indian caste system, which is based on an essentially racist conception of the biological, intellectual, and moral differences between culturally defined groups. Marriage between castes was nearly always forbidden in traditional India. Gough (1959) reports that the Nayar approved of unions between well-born Nayar women and the higher-caste Brahmans. But whereas the Nayar considered this marriage, the royal Brahmans considered it concubinage. A Nayar woman who had sexual relations with a man from a *lower* caste was expelled from her lineage, or in some cases put to death. Although castes and caste endogamy have been outlawed in modern India, the custom of endogamy persists.

The Kurds and many other Near Eastern peoples practice endogamy within a very narrowly defined kin group. First-cousin marriages of all sorts are common, with some societies strongly preferring daughters to marry their fathers' brothers' sons (patrilineal parallel cousin marriage). Such a marriage, of course, means that both the husband and wife belong to the same descent group, and usually grew up with one another as children. Indeed, in some Near Eastern groups a man has a recognized right to his father's brother's daughter, and must be consulted and compensated amply if she marries another man (Barth, 1954).

Although we may not always think of it as such, endogamy is practiced in our own society. Marriages across socioeconomic, religious, national origin, and racial lines are rare. Why? In part because our society is structured in such a way that we do not have frequent social contacts with people from different backgrounds; in part because parents and

The Yörük of Turkey are an endogamous group; cousin marriages are common. The three Yörük brides pictured here are all from the same lineage as their husbands and are themselves closely related. Two are brides in the same household, married to two brothers. Thus, the lines of kinship are complex—the brides are cousins and their husbands are their cousins as well. (Daniel G. Bates)

others pressure young adults to marry "their own kind." In complex societies such as our own, the outer limits to an acceptable marriage are often set by ethnicity.

The chief advantages of endogamy are, first, that it allows a person to marry and live among people he or she knows and trusts, and second, that it enables a group to consolidate its strength to resist incursions. By incursions, we mean both physical and cultural invasions. Endogamy is strongest in this country among groups who fear "Americanization," such as the Amish or Orthodox Jews.

Cousin Marriages Although many societies such as our own prohibit first-cousin marriages, people in many other parts of the world *prefer* to marry certain selected cousins. The reasons are not altogether clear. Let us begin by looking at a typical example. Suppose a young man belongs to an exogamous patrilineage. It is likely that he cannot marry any cousin on his father's side of the family; that would be considered incest if the kinship terminology, as it often does, labels members of ego's descent group in his own generation "brother" and "sister." Nor could he marry any of his parallel cousins on his mother's side of the family; he probably refers to these females as "sister" as well. But he *can* marry cross-cousins from his mother's side of the family because he does not consider them relatives. Moreover, marrying his mother's brother's daughter may have certain advantages. It would allow him to formalize affectionate ties he has developed with his mother's family, and enable him to marry into a family he knows and trusts, without violating rules of exogamy. (His wife is his cousin; his father-in-law, his mother's brother.) And it would reinforce interfamily ties established in the preceding generation by his mother and father. In matrilineal societies, marrying one's father's sister's daughter serves the same purposes. Thus anthropologists generally believe that exchange and alliance are the most

Elopement and Bride Theft Among the Yörük

People do not always want to do what is expected of them. Departures from social norms often occur in the relatively minor decisions we make in the course of our everyday routines, but they may also affect major life decisions, such as marriage. A clear example of a discrepancy between "real" and "ideal" behavior is provided by Daniel Bates in his study of marriage practices among the Yörük of Turkey (1974).

The population in question is a patrilineal, nomadic group that concentrates kin ties by strongly emphasizing first cousin marriage, especially of father's brother's daughter (son). The Yörük consider marriage a serious affair, and the heads of households take great care in arranging appropriate matches for their children.

Given this stress on arranged marriages, Bates was surprised to discover the number of marriages that were the result of elopement and bride theft, or *kacirma*. (In bride theft, the prospective husband kidnaps a woman and rapes her, an act which, in a society that places a premium on virginity, greatly diminishes her other prospects for marriage and increases the chances that she will stay with her abductor.) The Yörük frown intensely on both of these procedures—when they occur, the result is extreme shame and outrage. Yet together they account for over 23 percent of all Yörük marriages. What accounts for this high proportion?

In addressing himself to this question, Bates concludes that, in part, *kacirma* provides a means for the expression of individual choice in an otherwise highly structured system. (That a boy and girl may love each other, for instance, plays little or no role in the arrangement of a marriage.) Furthermore, because it is through marriage that one gains adult status, *kacirma* allows young men to hasten their entry into mature society by bypassing the proper procedure of marrying in order of birth and only after the substantially high bride price has been raised (which can take several years).

Although most *kacirma* marriages do result in the payment of the average bride price, a large majority of the cases involving a nominal payment or none at all occurred among the least wealthy members of the community. Once the act has been committed, there is little the girl's family can do to collect if the boy's family has little money. In this way, *kacirma* can also be seen as equalizing the burden of high bride prices for people of differing wealth.

On a structural level, it is striking to note that, unlike normative marriages, a significant number of *kacirma* unions involve nonconsanguineal kin outside of the lineage. Thus, *kacirma* serves to extend kin ties outside of the restricted lines expressed in preferred marriages. The significance of these new ties is most apparent in the summer and winter, when camp groups are redefined in the negotiations for seasonal grazing rights. The ties created by *kacirma* marriages provide families with greater flexibility in choosing members for their group.

Kacirma, then, although vigorously disavowed and discouraged as deviant behavior, plays a significant—and in some cases even predictable—role in Yörük social interactions.

important functions served by cousin marriages and the cultural preferences that structure them.

How Many Should One Marry? Just as societies have rules regulating who an individual may or may not marry, so they also have rules regulating how many spouses an individual may have. Our own rule of *monogamy* (marriage between only one man and one woman at a time) is not preferred by most societies of the world. (Monogamy is, however, statistically the most common form of marriage simply because there is usually an approximately equal number of men as women in a population.) Most human societies prefer some form of *polygamy* (plural marriage). In addition, many groups that prescribe monogamy consider it acceptable for a man to maintain one or more mistresses and their children in separate households, if he is reasonably discreet. In our own society, "serial monogamy" (divorcing and remarrying, perhaps many times) is becoming an acceptable alternative to lifelong marriage with one partner.

Accustomed as we are to thinking of marriage as an exclusive relationship, it is difficult for us to imagine a husband or wife accepting a "rival" into their home. How does polygamy work? Essentially, it works different ways in different societies, depending upon the type of polygamy involved. There are actually two basic forms polygamy can take—*polygyny*, marriage between one man and two or more women at the same time, and *polyandry*, marriage between one woman and two or more men at the same time.

Polygyny   Polygyny was the preferred form of marriage among the ancient Hebrews, in premodern China, and traditional India, and remains the preferred form in much of South America, Africa, the Middle East (the Koran permits a man four wives), and Asia. In most polygynous societies, only a few wealthy and powerful older men actually accumulate wives. But it is something most men strive for.

There are several reasons for this preference. First, women are an economic asset. Women not only perform a significant amount of work themselves, they also bear sons to support a man in his political struggles and daughters who will someday be exchanged for bride payments. The Siwai of Melanasia are quite explicit about this: the more wives a man has to tend his gardens, the more food for pigs; the more pigs he has, the more feasts he can give; the more feasts he gives, the more people become obligated to assist him when he calls on them (Oliver, 1955). Thus multiple wives are a source of wealth, power, and social status. Polygyny also makes life easier for a man in societies where sex is strictly prohibited during ceremonial periods, during menstruation, and after the birth of a child. (Post-partum taboos may last two, even three years.) And it is a distinct advantage in societies where women outnumber men.

However, in some societies and under certain circumstances, polygyny has its drawbacks. Unless the husband is an accomplished diplomat, the household may dissolve into bitter competition for his attention, sexual favors, and economic considerations. Gussi wives, for example, nearly always blame a miscarriage or a child's death on a co-wife's witchcraft, and seek to retaliate (LeVine, R., and LeVine, B., 1963). To minimize friction, polygynous husbands usually provide a separate dwelling for each wife and her offspring. The one exception is with sororal polygyny (the marriage of one man and two or more sisters). Perhaps because they have learned to resolve jealousy over their parents' attention, sisters seem to have fewer problems about sharing a dwelling as well as a husband (Murdock, 1949). However, most polygynous families are organized as composite families: a group of separate mother/child households linked by a common husband/father.

Conflict among co-wives is often regulated through an established pecking order. In polygynous families the senior wife nearly always enjoys superior status and authority over younger wives. She, not the husband, assigns women's work. Often wives encourage and even assist their husband in obtaining new wives. As a Tiv senior wife told an anthropologist, "Never . . . let your husband rest with one wife. Men are lazy. If they have one woman to cook for them, they are content. If you leave it to your husband, you'll never get another wife to help you carry firewood and the water and to look after you when you are ill" (Bowen, 1964:120).

Polyandry Although much rarer than polygyny, polyandry is the preferred form of marriage in a number of societies. The Toda of India and the Tibetans, for example, allowed a woman to marry a set of brothers (fraternal polyandry), who shared her bed and the responsibility for rearing her children. Marquesan men thought it advantageous to marry a woman who had several unrelated lovers and make them subsidiary husbands. Why? Because co-husbands were allies. Although the senior husband had first rights to the wife's attention, he made sure the others did not feel deprived. And with her first husband's consent, a Lesu woman might marry a second husband, for a bride price paid to the first (Stephens, 1963).

Under certain conditions, polyandry is clearly advantageous for all concerned. It reduces the number of offspring a group of men will produce and keeps the ratio of working adults to dependent children high. This is clearly adaptive when resources are scarce, as fields are in Tibet, for instance. If brothers marry one woman and have only one set of

This man with his two wives and children form a typical family unit among the Joti Indians of Venezuela. Multiple wives are both an economic and political asset to a man; each wife not only provides more goods and services for household consumption and exchange but also more children for future economic and political support. For the elder wife, the co-wives not only lighten her daily work load, but also ally with her whenever their husband engages in unacceptable behavior—for example, excessive drinking, gambling, or wife beating. (Jacques Jangoux)

children, and the sons continue to practice polyandry, the land (not large enough to support several families) passes intact from generation to generation. Polyandry is useful when men go away from home for extended periods. One of a woman's several husbands can remain to protect the household. Polyandry also eliminates the problem of unmarried men in societies where men outnumber women. Indeed, this is the only firm explanation G. Berreman (1962) could find for polyandry being practiced in one group of Pahari-speaking Hindus, but not in a single neighboring group whose culture and subsistence practices were essentially the same. Anthropologists suspect that the shortage of women in some polyandrous societies is the result of female infanticide.

Residence Rules

Rules regarding marital behavior do not stop after a couple has been socially sanctioned as husband and wife. Societies also have norms governing where newly married couples will live. Our own norm concerning marital residence—that a married couple establish their own household apart from either the husband's or the wife's kin (called *neolocal* residence, the preface *neo-* meaning "new")—is comparatively rare. In Samoa, for example, it is customary for a bride to move into her husband's household.

[T]he young couple live in the main household, simply receiving a bamboo pillow, a mosquito net and a pile of mats for their bed. . . . The wife works with all the women of the household and waits upon all the men. The husband shares the enterprises of the other men and boys. Neither in personal service given or received are the two marked off as a unit. . . . For even in the care of the young children and in the decisions as to their future, the uncles and aunts and grandparents participate as fully as the parents. (Mead, 1928:88)

Like Samoans, married couples in many societies move in with one or the other spouse's kin, joining an established household.

Patrilocal residence—a couple living with or near the man's kin—is the preferred arrangement in most of the world's societies. The couple may build their own dwelling in the compound or village of the husband's father or of another senior male of his kin group, rather than moving into the husband's father's house. But in all cases, they are absorbed into the husband's kin group and are subject to its authority.

Matrilocal residence—a couple living with or near the woman's kin—is also quite common. Matrilocal residence is usually found in matrilineal societies where marriage to someone from the same village is preferred (village endogamy), and most male members of the matrilineage remain in the neighborhood.

However, in some matrilineal societies sons move to their mother's brother's community and set up households there. This pattern of residence—a couple living with or near the husband's mother's brother, who is a senior member of his matrilineage—is known as *avunculocal* residence.

A fifth pattern of residence, called *bilocal* residence, involves a couple living with or near either the wife's *or* the husband's kin, depending on circumstances and preference.

Can we explain different patterns of marital residence? Neolocal residence seems to be limited to societies with high mobility and/or commercial economies that permit a couple to earn their own living, without depending on kin. Bilocal residence is almost always associated with a sudden decline in population or loss of economic stability, which forces people to abandon customs and regroup ad hoc, to meet the emergency (Nimkoff and Middleton, 1960).

The preference for patrilocal over matrilocal residence (or vice versa) is the subject of much debate. For some time, anthropologists have associated patrilocal residence with hunting, herding large animals, and complex agriculture—all of which require cooperative male labor. Matrilocal residence was thought to be adaptive for horticultural societies, where subsistence depends largely on female labor. However, cross-cultural data do not support this view. Although most matrilocal societies practice horticulture, more than half of all patrilocal societies are also horticultural.

In a recent paper, Ember and Ember (1971) suggested that residence rules reflect military rather than economic activities. When feuding between lineage segments or villages (internal warfare) is common, it is advantageous for the males who will fight together to also live together. Otherwise, they might be forced to choose between attacking their father's or their wife and children's homes. When internal warfare is rare but fights with outlying societies common, male members of a family needn't live together. Moreover, external warfare often requires all able-bodied men to leave home for long periods, so that women become responsible for subsistence activities at least some of the time. Under these circumstances, matrilocal residence, which promotes female solidarity, becomes adaptive. The available data seem to bear out the Embers' hypothesis.

Families

Through marriage families are formed, so it is not surprising that differences in marriage customs affect the composition of families. Of course, other factors also affect how the family is defined in a particular society. Essentially we can say that definitions of the family vary from society to society according to how people conceptualize the three relationships that develop in the family. First, there is the *conjugal relationship,* that between husband and wife. In most but not all societies, the conjugal bond is considered basic to the family structure. In terms of numbers of husbands and wives involved, the conjugal relationship may be defined as monogamous, polygynous, or polyandrous. Then there are the *maternal* and *paternal relationships,* those between mother and child and father and child. Both these relationships can be broadened to encompass more than a single generation, in which case we find what is known as an *extended family.* The maternal relationship, no matter how it is conceptualized, is always part of the definition of the family; the paternal relationship, in contrast, may not be, although such cases are relatively rare.[2] Thus numerous definitions of the family are possible, depending upon what relationships are included in the definition and how they are conceptualized.

Independent versus Extended Families

Because the extended family is such a widespread phenomenon in all parts of the world, it is useful to discuss the composition of such family units in greater detail and to explore some of the reasons for its popularity. The alternative to the extended family, of course, is the independent family—a single family unit (be the marriage relationship monogamous, polygynous, or polyandrous) residing by itself apart from relatives of other generations.

Over 80 percent of the world's hunters and gatherers are organized into independent families. In the Kalahari Desert, which harbors some of the last hunters and gatherers, resources are too sparse to support large groups or permanent settlements. Either would quickly exhaust food and water supplies. To survive, the Bushmen who inhabit the region disperse into small, mobile, self-sufficient family groups for much of the year. The independent family is highly adaptive for such groups (Nimkoff and Middleton, 1960).

Independent families are also frequently found in industrial societies, where individuals require much the same kind of mobility. "The hunter is mobile because he pursues the game: the industrial worker, the job" (Nimkoff

---

[2] The Nayar are an example of a society where the definition of the family excludes both the conjugal bond and the father-child relationship. Nayar women have no husbands in the usual sense of the word. A girl takes a ritual husband at an early age, but she does not live with that man, nor need she ever have sexual relations with him if she does not wish to; in fact, she may never see him again after their wedding. The paternal bond is also absent in the Nayar family. Children are conceived by one of their mother's lovers, but these men play no role whatsoever in the children's care and upbringing. The Nayar definition of the family, then, is based solely on the maternal bond; this is called a matrifocal family. Moreover, the Nayar family is viewed as spanning several generations; it is a matrifocal extended family (Gough, 1959).

The young American couple pictured here are an independent family; the large family of Brazilian peasants represent an extended family of several generations of relatives. Each type of family has advantages and disadvantages. The American couple, for example, have a great deal of privacy, mobility, and independence; in general, they are not "dominated" by elder relatives. But the family unit is unstable and easily disrupted by death or divorce, and economic pressures fall upon them alone. By contrast, the extended family is more stable because economic expenses and productive activities are shared by all of its members. (Charles Moore/Black Star; Daniel R. Gross)

and Middleton, 1960:283). The fact that industrial laborers usually work for nonfamily organizations, are hired for their skills rather than for their family connections, and are paid in wages rather than in shares of the things they produce reduces the individual's dependence on kin.

The chief benefits of this small domestic unit are mobility, privacy, and independence. But the costs of independence may be high. The independent family is temporary (lasting only from marriage to the departure of the last child, perhaps twenty to twenty-five years later), and it is rather prone to instability (divorce or death destroys it). Moreover, the spouses have to "make it," as breadwinners and parents, on their own.

In contrast, the extended family, which unites several generations, may continue indefinitely. The advantages of extended families include economy (sharing expenses), security (illness or death do not leave individuals stranded), and companionship. And extended families are flexible: the men and women of the family can divide into teams to perform different kinds of work simultaneously, sharing what they produce with the entire group. The disadvantages of extended families? Lack of individual initiative; friction between parent and child, sibling and sibling; domination by elders (leadership based on age, not ability); and lack of privacy (Nimkoff and Middleton, 1960).

Extended families usually center around either the paternal or maternal relationship. A *patrilineal extended family* consists of a man and his wife or wives, his unmarried daughters, his sons, and their wives and children. In the village of Keteira on the Fiji Island of Moala, for example, sons bring their wives to their father's homestead. Each couple has a separate dwelling, but they share a common hearth and eat together. The father has more or less absolute authority over all the family, and responsibility for daily work assignments. Everything individual members grow or make or earn through trade belongs to the family as a whole (Sahlins, 1957). A *matrilineal extended family* consists of a woman and her husband or husbands, their unmarried sons, their daughters, and their daughters' husbands and children. Traditionally, within the Iroquois matrilineal extended family, great emphasis was placed on the mother-daughter bond. The oldest woman ruled, and husbands, as well as sons to some extent, occupied only peripheral positions in the household.

Extended families are most often found in agricultural societies, where owning land is a source of power and prestige as well as subsistence. Inheritors are reluctant to divide the land into small individual farms, because to do so would mean losing some of the power and prestige they possess as a group (Nimkoff and Middleton, 1960). Marshall Sahlins's (1957) research on the island of Moala illustrates the relationship between land tenure and family form. Despite much exposure to Western customs and the Western ideal of the independent family, the people of the village of Keteira continued to prefer patrilineal extended families. The advantages of this family structure were clear. The fields immediately surrounding the village would not support the population, so Keteirans also tilled ancestral fields miles away. This meant some of the male labor force had to leave home for weeks, even months at a time, but some had to remain behind to work the fields at home. One man and woman could not have managed both, but the extended family was well suited to these people's needs. In the village of Naroi, across the island, in contrast, extended family life had virtually been abandoned, and most couples lived in separate households, working separate fields. Why? They could make a good living from the fields surrounding their village and no longer needed to work in cooperative teams. This example illustrates not only that land use and family form are related, but that domestic arrangements can and do change.

One should not conclude from this discussion, however, that the independent family occurs only in hunting and gathering and industrial societies, while the extended family is unique to agricultural societies. The extended family, for example, can be found in many urban settings and is not entirely rare in industrialized parts of the world. In India, extended families are legal, corporate entities which play an important role in the organization of trade and industry. Often such families reside in a single corporately owned apartment building, with individual domestic groups occupying the separate flats. In Lebanon, too, extended families are common among middle-class urbanites and are influential in politics and commerce, with brothers or cousins each pursuing different but complementary professions (Farsoun, 1970). Thus, although the extended family is most frequently found in agricultural societies, it can be advantageous under other circumstances as well.

Domestic Groups

If people always followed their rules of marriage and residence, domestic groups would always conform to a society's definition of a family. This, however, is not the case. Anthropologists always find more forms of domestic groups than the idealized definition of the family and the rules of marriage and residence would suggest. There are a number of reasons why people do not live up to their own ideal of the family.

First, it may not be possible to follow the rules. As suggested earlier, in most societies that practice polygyny it is not possible for every man to have more than one wife. Even if women marry at a much earlier age than men, there are simply not two or more marriageable women for every marriageable man. Monogamy, then, must be the statistical norm, even though it is not the cultural ideal. In other words, many people follow the rules in principle, as best they can, but circumstances prevent them from following the rules to the letter.

Second, cultural rules may be ambiguous or even contradictory, particularly in small societies. For example, in Tikopia, an island in the South Pacific, the kinsmen of the groom are supposed to give food and valuables to the bride's kinsmen at a wedding. However, at one of the weddings Raymond Firth (1957) attended while doing fieldwork on Tikopia, he noted that one of the bride's relatives did not receive any gifts. Rather, he was helping to prepare the food, which is the responsibility of the groom's kinsmen. This struck Firth as highly peculiar. Cooking is a long and tiring job. Why was this man working instead of exercising his right to receive gifts? Firth learned that the man was also a kinsman of the groom. The Tikopia had no established rule for resolving this type of conflict, which rarely occurred. The man therefore had to decide whether to play the role of the bride's or groom's kinsman. The necessity for making individual decisions creates a far more dynamic situation than a simple reading of marriage and residence rules would suggest. Individuals making decisions in different ways generate variations in behavior. Decisions and behavior concerning the organization of domestic groups are no exceptions.

In many societies, marriage and residence rules take the form of guidelines for making decisions rather than explicit directives. This came to light when Ward Goodenough discovered that he and John Fischer had drawn strikingly different conclusions from their studies of residence patterns in a community on the island of Truk. For example, Goodenough (1955) had classified a household consisting of a man, his second wife, his sons by his first wife, and one of his sons' wives as patrilocal—logically enough. Reopening the case, he later found that the family was living in the hamlet belonging to the first wife's matrilineage. The sons, who had the right to live there, had invited their father, who had no such right, to stay. Pursuing the issue, Goodenough concluded that the Trukese recognize six viable residence alternatives: living with the wife's extended family (her matrilineage), living with the husband's extended family (his matrilineage), living with the extended family of the wife's father's or husband's father's lineage, living with some specific lineal kinsmen, or living independently. Trukese prefer living with the husband's or wife's lineage to living with either of their father's lineages, living with a localized landholding lineage to a nonlocalized one, and living with a lineage on the wife's side to living with a lineage on the husband's. Thus the Trukese live with the wife's lineage if it is localized, with the husband's if it is localized and the wife's is not, or with the wife's or husband's father's lineage if neither of the first two choices are localized (Quinn 1975:23). The result is a great deal of diversity in the actual place of residence of married couples. Such decision-making models fairly accurately reflect how many decisions concerning marriage and the organization of domestic groups are actually made — how the various alternatives are weighed, evaluated, and ultimately selected among.

Seasonal changes, changes in the "age" of a domestic group, and changes in the society as a whole also produce still other variations in the composition of domestic groups. Among the pastoral Fulani of Africa, for example, a domestic group's survival depends upon having enough members to manage the cattle it owns. A newly married couple cannot handle this task on their own, and therefore live with the husband's father. However, the birth of children and/or additional marriages may make it possible for a man to set out on his own, establishing a new domestic group with his wife or wives and his children. During the dry season, a Fulani domestic group may divide into a number of smaller units to take the cattle to different grazing areas (none of which would support the whole herd at one time). The wife may collect some of her younger, unmarried female kin to help with her tasks; the husband may do the same with some of his young, unmarried male kin. In addition, when Fulani men and women become too old to care for a herd by themselves, they join a son or daughter's domestic group. Thus the Fulani participate in a large variety of household groupings as a part of normal adaptation to their environment (Stenning, 1965). While specific patterns of domestic cycles vary from society to society, the result of such cycles — variation in household composition — is evident in all societies.

Factors such as age and economic circumstances are not the only ones that influence decisions regarding marriage and the formation of domestic groups. For example, people in the highlands of the island of Martinique engage in three very different patterns during their lifetimes. In late adolescence and early adulthood, men prefer mating ties that do not involve cohabitation. However, as they approach middle age and increase their land holdings, men begin to consider living with the mothers of their children more attractive. Why? In large part because they no longer have the time to market their produce, and find living in a consensual union with a woman who can perform this task convenient. The final shift occurs when men pass the age of forty. At this point, men usually want to legalize their marriages in order to make their children legitimate and insure the orderly transmission of their property to their children at death (Horowitz, 1971).

We should not conclude, however, that cultural norms play only a fairly minor role in shaping individual behavior concerning the organization of domestic groups. In many instances, social pressure convinces people that it is better, or at least easier, to follow the rules. Societies of course vary in the degrees to which they enforce different rules of all kinds, including marriage and residence rules. Barth (1954), for example, found that nomadic Kurds reacted strongly when a woman married someone other than her father's brother's son, without obtaining his consent. However, Kurds who had settled in permanent villages and become farmers no longer enforced the rule of parallel cousin marriage. The reason was simple lack of necessity. Nomadic Kurds depend on family ties for political bonds: the only way for a man to secure the allegiance of young male relatives is to make them his sons-in-law. Settled Kurds had developed a feudal political structure, and no longer depended so heavily on kin. Village (rather than lineage) endogamy had became the preferred form of marriage.

Thus marriage rules and the organization of

the family are important aspects of a group's total adaptation to its environment. A society's rules and ideals define alternative patterns available to members of that society, and perhaps suggest which of these patterns has proven most adaptive for most people in the past. A shared notion of what marriages and families should be like facilitates individual decision making and communication regarding these decisions. But people do not obey the rules mechanically. The processes involved in defining the family and forming domestic groups represent a major ongoing source of change in every human society.

summary

As cultural constructs, the idea of the family varies considerably from society to society. Nevertheless, all may be said to share the characteristics of economic cooperation, care and socialization of children, and exchange of offspring through marriage. Not all domestic groups, however, are families—as the ideal domestic unit the family is not always possible to realize.

Universally, marriage is the way in which new families are begun. In our society, marriage involves a commitment to a permanent heterosexual relationship, reciprocal economic obligations, and the responsibilities of parenthood. But marriage is culturally variable in terms of number of possible spouses, sexual rights, and economic rights and obligations. Also, legitimacy of children is not dependent on marriage in all societies.

Marriage is important because it binds families and kin groups together. The act of exchange inherent in marriage creates social solidarity. In some societies interfamily alliances are created by direct exchange of daughters. Usually, however, women are exchanged for a *bride price* or a *bride service,* which is paid or rendered by the prospective husband to the kin of his wife. This custom is most common in patrilineal societies, where women leave their families to live with their husband's kin. A lasting bond is thus formed between the groups, which tends to alleviate any potential conflict.

As an economic unit marriage provides a workable division of labor, institutionalizing economic cooperation whether labor is divided along traditional sexual lines or not.

Marriage very often is dependent on the ability of a woman to bear children and serves to define the obligations of parents toward their children. Biological parents are usually responsible for their children, but the roles of *genitor* (the biological father) and *pater* (the socially recognized father) do not necessarily coincide.

Almost all societies maintain incest taboos prohibiting sexual relations—and, therefore, marriage—between brothers and sisters or parents and children. Most also enforce rules of *exogamy* that require people to marry outside their social group. These rules take various forms depending on the method of kin classification operant within the culture. Exogamy functions adaptively to create alliances between families and lineages and fosters cultural diffusion by bringing new people into the family group. In other societies rules of *endogamy* apply. Thus, a person is required to marry within a usually narrowly defined kin group, for example, a caste. The advantages of this form of marriage are its guarantee that one marries and lives among people one is familiar with and, more importantly, that it enables a group to consolidate against both cultural and physical invasions.

Societies also enforce rules governing how many people one may marry. Although our society prohibits marriage with more than one person at a time, most societies practice (at least ideally) some form of *polygamy*. The two basic forms of plural marriage are *polygyny,* marriage between one man and two or more women, and *polyandry,* marriage between one woman and two or more men.

Rules also apply to where a married couple must establish residence. Our society requires a newly married couple to establish *neolocal* residence, apart from both the husband's and the wife's kin. But as with our preference for monogamy, this is a rare pattern. Most other societies prefer *patrilocal* residence, in which the married couple live with or near the husband's kin. Other alternatives are *matrilocal, avuncular,* or *bilocal* residence. It has recently been suggested that residence rules reflect military rather than economic considerations.

Differences in marriage customs affect how the family will be composed. In most cultures the conjugal bond, whether monogamous, polygynous, or polyandrous, is considered basic to the family structure. But families may further be characterized as either *extended,* composed of several generations, or as *independent,* composed of a single family unit residing apart from relatives of other generations. Extended families provide the benefits of economy through shared expenses, security, and companionship, but are marked also by lack of individual initiative, friction between parents and children and between siblings, domination by elders, and lack of privacy. The independent family, in its turn, provides mobility, privacy, and independence, but is liable to be unstable and temporary and puts great pressure on husband and wife to succeed on their own. We generally speak of extended families as characteristic of agricultural societies where land is a source of wealth. Independent families are usually found in hunting and gathering societies and in industrialized societies that prize mobility.

Anthropologists have found more forms of domestic groups than the idealized definition of the family and the rules would suggest. Monogamy turns out to be the statistical norm, rather than some preferred form of plural marriage, because there are not enough women of marriageable age in most populations. Sometimes, too, rules are ambiguous or act only as guidelines to appropriate conduct, allowing for different applications to particular situations.

In sum, it may be said that marriage rules and the organization of the family are important indicators of a group's adaptation to its environment. The rules and ideals of a society define a society's expectations of its members and show what has worked best in the past. But necessity and personal inclination contribute to an ongoing process of change in which the family and domestic groups are continually redefined.

suggested readings

BOHANNAN, P., AND MIDDLETON, J., EDS.
1968 *Marriage, Family, and Residence.* New York: Natural History Press. A collection of articles on marriage and family organization, with special emphasis on cross-cultural problems and comparison.

BUCHLER, I. R., AND SELBY, H.
1968 *Kinship and Social Organization: An Introduction to Theory and Method.* New York: Macmillan. A review of the theoretical and methodological issues pertinent to the study of social structure; includes an important discussion of alliance theory.

GOODY, J. R., ED.
1971 *The Developmental Cycle in Domestic Groups.* Cambridge: At the University Press. Essays examining the changing structure of the family group and its role in the organization of social systems.

MURDOCK, G. P.
1949 *Social Structure.* New York: Macmillan. A classic of cross-cultural research that explores the possible determinants of cultural variation in family organization, residence patterns, and the regulation of sex.

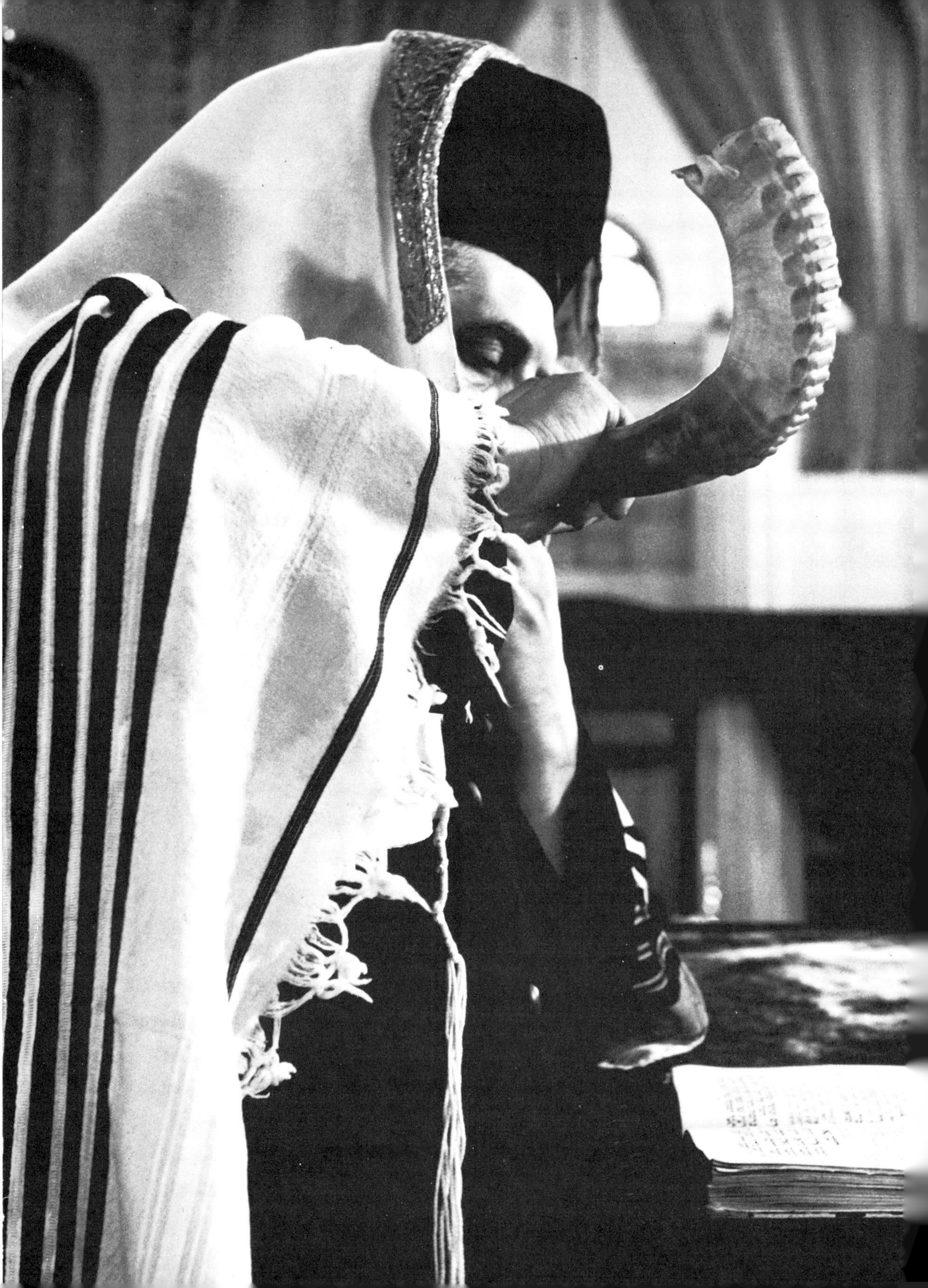

twenty
Religious Belief and Ritual

When the Mbuti Pygmies of the Ituri Forest are plagued by sickness or poor hunting and every practical remedy has failed, a festival known as the *molimo* is held in order to "awaken" the forest to their plight and restore balance and harmony to their world. For about a month, all the adult men gather nightly to sing and "rejoice" the forest. No specific invocations are made asking for better hunting or an end to sickness. Their purpose is simply to express, through song, their trust in the forest as the benevolent provider of all good things. Having done this, the Mbuti say that whatever happens must be the will of the forest, and therefore good.

When a person dies, members of the band express grief at a personal loss, but there is no formal expression of mourning. A death *molimo* is held to honor the memory of the deceased, to emphasize that nothing evil or unnatural has happened, and to restore continuity and normalcy to the lives of the bereaved. The Mbuti achieve these objectives through relatively informal ritual acts that stress the need for unity and cooperation among members of the hunting band and emphasize their ties to their forest home. They close all paths leading out of the forest to the villages of their Bantu neighbors; eat forest foods in preference to village foods; clothe themselves with leaves, flowers, feathers, and vines; and sing songs of praise to the forest with greater fervor than usual. On such occasions the *molimo* singers use a wooden trumpet to broadcast their songs as widely as possible. The *molimo* trumpet is also brought into direct contact with basic forest elements—earth, water, air, and fire—symbolizing the sanctity and power of these physical surroundings. The death *molimo* serves to reinforce identification with the forest as the giver of life, a feeling that is clearly expressed in the Mbuti creed: "The Forest is Mother and Father, because it gives us all the things we need ... food, clothing, shelter, warmth ... and affection. We are the children of the forest. When it dies, we die" (Turnbull, 1965:312).

Defining Religion

Intuitively we sense that what the Pygmies believe in and the ceremonies they perform fall under the general category of religion. But why? How can we identify certain beliefs and behaviors as religious and others not? One conclusion we come to in looking at the example of the Pygmies is that the specific content of religious beliefs and practices does not provide an adequate answer. The ceremonies of the Mbuti involve no priests or religious leaders as many ceremonies in the Judeo-Christian tradition do; and their beliefs do not incorporate the idea of a god in the Western sense of the word. Yet the Mbuti beliefs and practices are no less religious than our own. How, then, can we define religion in order to encompass variations from culture to culture?

The use of symbols to express beliefs about the world is a basic feature of religion. Those of the Jewish religion, for example, reflect a constant ethical concern—both the tallis, or prayer shawl, and the Talmud, or Book of Laws, emphasize a system of moral responsibilities that is an integral part of the Jewish world view. The use of traditional symbols serves also to preserve the cultural continuity of religion. For people of the Jewish faith, the blowing of the shofar, or ram's horn, is the traditional way of ushering in—and marking the end of—the High Holy Days. (Louis Goldman, Rapho/Photo Researchers)

Religion as Belief in the Supernatural

Sociologist Emile Durkheim (1961) argued that the essence of religion is not a specific set of beliefs, attitudes, or practices, but a broader, more universal phenomenon: the expression of a community's moral values and collective beliefs, whatever these might be. He maintained that each society distinguishes between the *sacred*—the sphere of extraordinary phenomena associated with awesome supernatural forces—and the *profane*—the sphere of the ordinary and routine, the natural everyday world. Religious beliefs express what a society considers sacred. These values may be represented symbolically by a cross, a statue, a rock, an animal, a tree, or anything that society selects; and they become the focus of collective ceremonies—communion, dances, feasts, and so on—that serve to unite believers into a single moral community. In this sense, the annual ceremonies of the Australian aborigines that center around a sacred totem are no less religious than the celebration of Easter or Yom Kippur.

Critics have pointed out, however, that few societies make such a clear-cut distinction between the sacred and profane or the natural and supernatural. For the Mbuti, the forest is not an awesome and mysterious entity that exists on a different level of reality. It is an ever-present factor that shapes every aspect of their lives and must be dealt with and mastered in concrete, practical terms. Thus the categories sacred and profane or natural and supernatural do not always reflect what people themselves actually believe, and we must take care that we are not forcing stronger distinctions than the people themselves make. However, it is accurate to say that a supernatural dimension of one sort or another is common to all religions.

Religion as Ideology

Recently some anthropologists have defined religion broadly as any system of beliefs, symbols, and rituals that makes life meaningful and intelligible. Clifford Geertz (1966) maintains that religion is essentially an ideology, or system of symbols, that has a powerful emotional appeal and can provide a rationale for human existence. Religious symbols serve both as models *of* reality by expressing cultural conceptions about the way the world is actually organized, and as models *for* reality by representing how the world should be organized ideally and how people should behave to bring about this goal. Thus the use of symbols in expressing deep-seated beliefs about the world—in particular, supernatural symbols—is the basic feature of religion. But the specific systems of belief and systems of action which we associate with religion vary considerably from one society to another.

Variations in Religious Belief Systems

The nineteenth-century anthropologist Edward B. Tylor (1871) was one of the first to make a sustained and systematic effort to understand and explain the phenomenon of religion. Tylor asserted that the foundation of all religion is the idea of a soul, a spiritual essence that differs from the tangible, physical body. Tylor speculated that the concept of a soul developed from primitive people's curiosity and concern about the difference between living and dying, waking and dreaming. He called this belief in a soul or a personal supernatural force *animism,* arguing that primitive peoples applied the idea of a soul not only to humans, but also to animals and plants.

Marett, one of Tylor's contemporaries, maintained that the concept of a soul was too sophisticated to have supplied the foundation of religion. He argued instead that animism was preceded historically by *animatism,* a belief in an impersonal supernatural force (Marett, 1909). An example of animatism can be seen among the people of Melanesia, who attribute extraordinary events, unusual prowess, and both good luck and misfortune to *mana. Mana* may reside in people, places, or things, and affects anyone who comes in contact with it. (Somewhat like electricity, it is an invisible force transmitted by touch and may be harnessed for good or evil.) An unusually shaped stone found in an unusually productive garden, an exceptionally swift boat, a particularly skillful leader might all be said to possess *mana*. Similarly, the Fox Indians believed that *manitu* came to warriors in visions, endowing them with temporary supernatural power. Many in the Near East believe a person may acquire *baraka*, or holiness, by touching the clothes a holy man wore or the ground on which he walked, or by visiting Mecca. Roman Catholics in many parts of the world attribute healing powers to saints' relics, holy water, and places where miracles occurred, such as Lourdes. Thus the belief that supernatural forces may reside in both people and inanimate objects is widespread.

A belief in supernatural beings is also common, although these beings are conceived in many different ways. Some have human origins. The Tonga of northern Rhodesia, for example, believe that the souls of all who have died live on as *zelo*, or ghosts; those of people who have attained some prominence become *mizimu* (something more than ghosts). *Mizimu* maintain a lively interest in the kin they leave behind—in part because they cease to exist if no one calls their name or brings them beer and other offerings. The Tonga see *mizimu* as their protectors. When one of the living violates tradition, *mizimu* may inflict an illness on the person, on their own initiative or because they hear the elders grumbling. But in general, *mizimu* act in their kin groups' best interests (Colson, 1954). In contrast, the Ifaluk of Micronesia believe that malevolent people become malevolent spirits *(alusengau)*, who delight in stirring up immoral behavior and making the living sick and unlucky. The Ifaluk spend much of their time worrying and complaining about *alusengau* (a fact that gives the living an enemy in common and helps to defuse quarrels among them) (Spiro, 1952).

In addition to supernatural forces and ghosts, religion in many parts of the world also centers around one or more gods of extrahuman origin. Such a pattern of belief is called *theism*. Dahomeans, for example, worshiped a pantheon of Great Gods, each involved in Creation, each responsible for some part of nature, each endowed with a human or animal form and a strong personality. Like humans, Dahomean Great Gods occupied themselves with sex, war, economic endeavors, and mischief. Although ultimately concerned about human beings, their attitude toward and intervention in life on earth was largely unpredictable (Wallace, 1966:93–94). In many respects, then, Dahomean Great Gods resembled the deities of ancient Greece and Rome. Similar forms of *polytheism* (belief in many gods) flourished in the Inca, Mayan, and Aztec cultures and East Asian kingdoms, as well as the central African kingdoms, Greece, and Rome.

Judaism, Christianity, and Islam, in contrast, all of which took root in the Middle East, recognize only one supreme God who created the universe and all that is in it, watches over human affairs, occasionally sends messengers to earth, and works "in mysterious ways." *Monotheism* (belief in one god), however, is relative. All three of these religions deify their saints and prophets to some extent, and all have made room for other supernatural beings such as angels, demons, and witches at various points in their histories. Hindus, who see all life as part of a divine Oneness (the ultimate monotheism), also worship the Great Gods Shiva, Krishna, Rama, Vishnu, and Lakshmi, thus combining mono- and polytheism.

Symbols and Beliefs As we have seen, the supernatural entities that are part of a people's religious belief system can take many forms, but in all of the cases we have discussed the beliefs about the supernatural are embodied in symbols. These symbols promote understanding by translating the abstract and unknown into the concrete and familiar. The Biblical description of Judeo-Christian cosmology is filled with symbolism. The book of Genesis, for example, describes the creation of the world and man's place in it in simple symbolic terms, thus making intrinsically complex and abstract notions more concrete and understandable.

Lévi-Strauss and many anthropologists following him have argued that the symbolic expressions embodied in myths—descriptions of the origins, interests, and powers of supernatural entities and people's relationship to them—are arranged in a common pattern. The typical structure of myths and legends juxtaposes three sets of symbolic elements: those that define a value, desirable object, or course of action; those that define its antithesis; and a third, mediating set that resolves the conflict between the first two. Thus myth may be a symbolic formula for resolving the value conflicts and the resulting moral quandaries which arise from the structural contradictions of societies. According to Lévi-Strauss, myths have an internal logic of their own which is in no sense "about" the real world. Instead, myths are highly abstract models, open to a variety of interpretations, permitting people a certain amount of leeway in defining a position in the real world (Lévi-Strauss, 1955).

Variation in Religious Ritual

It is difficult to talk about religious beliefs and symbols as distinct from religious behavior. In all societies, basic beliefs are embodied in how symbolic objects are used, set up, and manipulated in religious observance, or *ritual*. In the modern Maya community of Chamula, for instance, ritual display of religious symbols reinforces fundamental beliefs and values. Symbolizing the first light, the first heat, the first maize, and the beginnings of order in the universe, the sun represents all that is good and desirable to the people of Chamula. The symbol of the sun is actively manipulated in the ritual procession of saints' images from the eastern side (where the sun rises) to the western side of the church, and in the ritual arrangement of candles—the largest, whitest, longest burning, and most expensive are lined up closest to the east, while the "inferior" candles are placed to the west (Gossen, 1972). Thus beliefs, symbols, and ritual are very closely interconnected.

But the manipulation of symbols is not the only element of religious ritual. In all societies there are particular behaviors associated with the practice of religions, although these vary considerably from one society to another. Anthony Wallace (1966) has suggested certain broad categories of behavior that are associated with religion in different parts of the world. These include prayer, music, physical exertion, pleading, reciting codes, taboos, feasts, sacrifice, congregation, inspiration, as well as manufacturing and using symbolic objects. The items of behavior encompassed by these categories are in turn organized into more complex and stereotyped ceremonial events known as rituals.

In general terms, the explicit goal of much ritual is to help effect some sort of transformation in people or nature from one state to another. Anthropologists have usefully identified two major categories of ritual that occur in every culture— *rites of passage* and *rites of intensification*. Although not all rituals fit neatly into one or the other of these, the two categories do encompass much of ritual behavior. We will briefly explore each of them in turn.

Rituals that mark a person's transition from one set of socially identified circumstances to another are known as rites of passage. Birth, puberty, marriage, parenthood, and death are all occasions for such ceremonies. According to Arnold Van Gennep (1960), rites of passage normally include three separate phases: rites of separation, rites of segregation, and rites of integration. For instance, in many societies the transition from childhood to adult status is marked by an extended ritual that involves first a symbolic end to childhood status; then a period of physical separation from normal community life; and finally, ceremonial reintegration into society as an adult. Among the Ndembu (Turner, 1967), this transformation ritual from boyhood to manhood, known as *mukanda,* lasts four months. After a night of feasting, singing, and sexual license, the initiates receive a last meal from their mothers (rites of separation). Then they are marched to another camp known as the "place of dying," where they remain in seclusion under the supervision of a group of male guardians.

The Logic of Myth and Ritual

Largely as a result of the work of Claude Lévi-Strauss, anthropologists have devoted a great deal of attention to analyzing the logic of the elements comprising collections of myths and rituals. A single myth or ritual cannot be fully understood apart from the group of myths or rituals to which it is related, for each separate element is only a portion of the total information being communicated. The manner in which the total message is conveyed is somewhat like the way in which information shouted over a long distance is understood (Leach, 1970). Each time the sender shouts, the receiver understands some part of the total message, but not always the same part. For example, if there are five elements to the message and the sender makes four attempts at communication, the exchange might proceed as follows:

```
             elements understood
attempt I:   1  2     4
attempt II:     2  3  4
attempt III: 1        4
attempt IV:  1  2        5
             ─────────────
             1  2  3  4  5
```

In no single attempt at communication is the entire set of elements understood. The total message is only conveyed when the four attempts are combined.

According to Lévi-Strauss, the same is true of understanding myths. It is the way in which the elements of a set of myths are combined—the logic underlying their arrangement—that he attempts to explain. The best known example of Lévi-Strauss' approach is his treatment of the Greek Oedipus myths (1955). He focuses on eleven elements in this set of myths, assigning each of the elements to one of four categories. Juxtaposed to one another, the categories of elements point out two important conflicts in the Greek system of values and beliefs. The elements in category I (Kadmos sees his sister Europa ravished by Zeus; Oedipus marries his mother; Antigone buries her brother in spite of a prohibition) are all incidents in which kin relationships are overvalued, whereas the elements in category II (the Spartoi kill one another; Oedipus kills his father Laios; Eteocles kills his brother) are all incidents in which kin ties are undervalued. Similarly, the elements of category III (Kadmos kills the dragon; Oedipus kills the sphinx) are the converse of those in category IV (Oedipus, his father, and his father's father are three men who are all somehow deformed and have difficulty in walking): category III deals with the knowledge of biological reproduction, because human beings cannot live and reproduce until the monster is killed; category IV deals with the belief in the autochthonous origin of humans, that they are born of the earth, from which they emerge stumbling. Thus, considered as an interrelated set, the myths state, although they do not resolve, these two significant conflicts (Leach, 1970).

Like the logic of collections of myths, the logic of sets of related rituals can be subjected to similar analysis. For example, Metzger and Williams (1963) have analyzed marriage ceremonies in the highlands of Chiapas, Mexico, and have found that five ceremonial elements are potentially involved. But not all of these are performed in the case of every marriage; under certain circumstances some will be eliminated. When either the bride or the groom is dying, only one of the five ceremonies is performed. And if the bride has run away with the groom, or if she has already lived with another spouse, only three of the five are performed.

But although Metzger and Williams have observed only these two exceptions to the five-part set of marriage rituals, we have no way of knowing whether there are other circumstances under which other ceremonial combinations would be used. Certainly there are many other ways in which several of the five elements could theoretically be combined. Consequently, the Metzger and Williams analysis may well be incomplete (Hoffman, n.d.). Lévi-Straussian analyses of the logic of myths have been criticized for much the same reason. Since there are many ways in which the elements in a set of myths might be logically arranged for purposes of analysis, one has no way of knowing whether the chosen arrangement is the correct one.

On the island of Tanna, in the New Hebrides, male puberty is celebrated by a rite of passage. The circumcision ceremony marks the separation phase of the rite and signifies the severing of the boys from their childhood status. Here we see them in the segregation phase, standing in straw cubicles, waiting for their wound to heal. They are kept apart from the others and are not allowed to see anyone or to do anything. After a subsequent washing ceremony and a feast, they will return to their village as men and be reintegrated into the community. (Kal Muller/Woodfin Camp)

Here they are circumcised, hazed, harangued, and lectured on the rules of manhood (rites of segregation). Finally, daubed in the white clay that signifies rebirth, the initiates are taken back to their families. At first their mothers greet them with songs of mourning, but as each realizes that her son is safe, these turn to songs of jubilation. After the novices are washed and given new clothes, each performs the dance of war to signify his new status as a man (rites of integration). The function of these rites is not merely to celebrate the changes in the life of an individual, but to give public recognition to a new set of roles and relationships within the community.

Unlike rites of passage, which are directed toward individual transitions, rites of intensification are usually directed either toward nature or toward society as a whole. Their avowed intent is to reinforce or bolster some natural process essential to survival, or to reaffirm the commitment of a community to a particular set of values and beliefs.

In many agricultural societies, for example, rites of intensification are performed in relation to the coming of spring and the renewal of fertility. Among the Iroquois, as among many peoples, part of the annual calendar of ritual celebration is tied to important events in the agricultural cycle of the seasons: the rising of the sap in the maple trees, the ripening of the strawberries, the maturing of the corn, the harvest.

Just as some rites of intensification are aimed at insuring the continuation of natural processes, others are aimed at insuring the continuation of commitment to a particular set of beliefs. In our own society, weekly church services are such rites of intensification; they are intended to reinforce the commitment of the believers. Similarly, the *molimo* festival of the Pygmies, described at the beginning of this chapter, is a social rite of intensification, its purpose being to strengthen the trust of the community in the will of the forest.

The Organization of Religion

In any society, ritual behavior does not occur on a random basis. Religion, in other words, is organized. In the United States, for example, the weekly church service rite of intensification is usually presided over by a religious leader. The Pygmies, on the other hand, have no such leader in their *molimo* celebration. The two societies differ, therefore, in how they organize religious activity. In this section, we will investigate the various ways that religion is organized in different societies.

In some societies, many religious rituals are organized in a highly individualistic way. For example, a Crow Indian who wanted to excel in hunting or war, to find a cure, or perhaps to revenge the death of a relative would go off alone for four days (four being the Crow's mystic number) to fast, pray, and seek visions. Interestingly, this individual-oriented seeking usually produced revelations that fitted neatly into Crow traditions. Spirits nearly always appeared on the fourth day of the supplicant's ordeal, bringing him a sacred song, telling him special ways to dress and what medicines to use, imposing certain taboos (Lowie, 1954:157–161). In individualistic rites the worshiper must rely on himself to draw on the powers of the supernatural.

This is the Jain temple in Sanganer, a village near Jaipur, India. Jainism is a highly developed religion with elaborately evolved belief systems and a full-time priesthood. Yet the solitary figure praying at the altar demonstrates that individual ritual behavior is common even within highly organized religions. (Jacques Jangoux)

But in no society do people perform all religious rituals completely on their own behalf. Rather, they seek help from intermediaries who are specialists in the art of reaching the spirits and gods. One such religious specialist is the *shaman,* a medium of the supernatural in many nonindustrialized societies. Shamans assume their religious status through birth (sometimes all the men of a particular family will become shamans), through visions, through contact with some form of supernatural force, or through what amounts to simple vocational training. They are able to transport themselves to the world of the supernatural (however it is conceived) and to act as mouthpieces for spirits. For example, each year an Eskimo shaman would undertake a dangerous spiritual voyage to the bottom of the sea to seek out the goddess Sedna, stroke her hair, and listen to her complaints against humans. When the shaman returned, he or she would exhort the living to confess their sins so that Sedna would release the game for another year, enabling success in the hunt (Rasmussen, 1929:123–129). On other occasions, shamans might be called upon to reveal a witch or thief, to cure illness, or to help people make decisions. In all cases, the rituals involved would be organized around the role of the shaman. Shamans performed their services when asked, for a fee. The mainstay of religion in many Eskimo, American Indian, and other hunting and gathering societies, shamans of one sort or another are found throughout the world. Our own astrologers, mediums, and fortunetellers are essentially shamans, and a number of anthropological studies have suggested that the techniques employed by the shaman are not terribly different from those of the psychiatrist in our own society.

Religious rituals may also be organized communally, with everyone in a particular group or society participating. Although special roles may be assigned, the people performing these roles are not imbued with unusual powers or vested with full-time religious duties. They simply adopt a particular role—dancer, speechmaker, prayer leader, for ex-

Every year in the Sierra Madre mountains of Mexico, the Tateineira ceremony is held, thanking the gods for sufficient rainfall to ensure a mature corn harvest. The children of the community, symbolized by the young ears of corn, are introduced to the gods by being taken by a shaman on an imaginary pilgrimage to the god, Peyote. Here we see the shaman lifting a young ear of corn and singing of the pilgrimage, in a rite similar to the Christian sacred communion. (Kal Muller/Woodfin Camp)

ample—just for the occasion. Communally organized rituals are found throughout the world. In our own society, ceremonies associated with our "political cult"—such as the Fourth of July celebration—are organized as communal rituals, with particular roles being assigned to different community members, groups, and associations.

In our own and many other industrialized societies, however, "true religion" is administered by a full-time, professionalized clergy. Priests, like shamans, are religious specialists who act as intermediaries between the community and the supernatural. Also like shamans, priests are considered qualified to perform sacred rituals individuals cannot perform for themselves because of the priests' specialized training and initiation into the profession. But priests are also different from shamans in many important respects. Whereas shamans are called in to resolve immediate crises and usually work in the context of the family group, priests more often perform rites for the community as a whole, in a public forum, on a regular, calendrical basis. Whereas shamans are individual entrepreneurs whose influence in a group depends on their ability to perform or "deliver" cures and the like, priests are part of an established, bureaucratically organized church. Priests, however, vary in the extent of their own specialization. In many societies, religious and political authority overlap: the head of the church is also the head of the state. Elsewhere, political and religious organizations are more separate.

The existence of a professional, bureaucratically organized clergy which administers religious rites individuals cannot perform for themselves tends to emphasize the distinction between the sacred and profane. Religion is somewhat removed from everyday life. This split is characteristic of stratified societies that depend on food production and a highly specialized division of labor; it is rarely found in small-scale hunting and gathering societies. Of course, established churches and priesthoods do not preclude individualistic worship, belief in shamans, or communal observances. Religious diversity exists *within* as well as *among* societies. But despite the fact that people in complex societies may in practice find individualistic or communal rituals rewarding, the importance of the established and bureaucratized religion for maintaining social and economic stratification cannot be ignored.

Evolution of Religious Practices

The origin and evolution of religious beliefs and practices is a very difficult topic to study because pertinent evidence is rarely preserved in the archeological record. Nevertheless, some generalizations can be made. The earliest evidence of ritual behavior dates to over 50,000 years ago. Neandertal populations in Europe and Southwest Asia engaged in a variety of ritual practices in burying their dead. Neandertal skeletons have been found buried in graves dug in the floors of caves, the positions of the skeletons indicating that the bodies were carefully laid out. In addition, grave goods such as tools or parts of animals were deposited with some of the dead. Such evidence seems to indicate that neandertal people had practices that can probably be labeled religious in nature. But because so much of what constitutes a religious system is lost without written records, we can say very little about the origins and early evolution of religion. Nevertheless, some generalizations about the development of religion can be made on the basis of data collected from various types of contemporary societies.

Guy Swanson (1960) has conducted the most extensive study to date on the relationship between religion and social organization. The highlights of Swanson's findings can be summarized as follows:

1. Supernatural sanctions for morality are significantly related to economic and social complexity, measured by such factors as the private ownership of important resources, the prevalence of debt relationships, the cultivation of grain crops, and most importantly, the existence of social classes with considerable inequalities in wealth among groups. Swanson suggests that the elites in such societies invoke the authority of high gods to preserve their privileges and to prevent or at least to control rebellion in the lower classes. (This is what Marx meant when he called religion "the opiate of the masses.")
2. Monotheism is strongly associated with a high degree of social complexity and is very common among societies with three or more politically important groups.
3. Polytheism is associated with the existence of social classes and occupational specialization. Societies with a polytheistic belief system, however, are intermediate rather than extreme in social complexity.
4. Belief in ancestral spirits is related to a system of social organization in which the extended family is politically important.
5. Animism is associated with a number of social conditions found in less complex societies, among them the absence of sovereign kin groups larger then the nuclear family; only one or two politically important groups in society; and organization into small hamlets or hunting and gathering bands.

In short, where social organization is highly stratified, so is the conception of the supernatural; where social organization is egalitarian, the same is true of the conception of the supernatural. Religious belief systems seem to reflect basic characteristics of the social order in which they appear. This leads to the conclusion that as social structure has evolved in complexity, the nature of religious beliefs has also changed.

Robert Bellah (1964) has proposed an evolutionary sequence that parallels Swanson's ideas, but is based on notions of a dialectical pattern in religious evolution rather than a completely linear sequence. Bellah's stages include Primitive, Archaic, Historic, Early Modern, and Modern religions. Primitive, Archaic, and Modern religions deemphasize formal religious organizations which are important to Historic and Early Modern religions. The distinction between the supernatural and real worlds is subject to varying interpretations as well. In Primitive religions, the supernatural is *in* the real world (as seen in the *molimo,* for example). In Archaic religions, the supernatural world is more objectified and not totally part of the real world. Historic religions (Catholicism, for example) emphasize the duality of the real and the supernatural and suggest that the superior life of the supernatural world is obtained through the rejection of the natural world. Early Modern religions (such as Protestantism) maintain the natural/supernatural duality but suggest that salvation is achieved through action in the natural world. In Modern religions, the natural/supernatural dichotomy is removed, with the emphasis placed on ethical action in the real world. Finally, Bellah sees dialectical patterning in the emphases placed on participation as opposed to worship or sacrifice. Primitive religious rituals focus entirely on participation; worship and sacrifice are completely absent. In Archaic and Historic religions, worship and sacrifice are key elements, while in Early Modern and Modern religions, participation again becomes primary.

In somewhat different ways both Swanson and Bellah are suggesting that there are definite patterns of religious beliefs and practices which are related to the social context of religion. If this is so, it strongly suggests that religion must be another of people's adaptive strategies. In the following section we will explore in what ways this is so.

Adaptive Aspects of Religious Belief and Ritual

Because religion is so universal a phenomenon, anthropologists have long been concerned with discovering precisely what needs religious beliefs and practices fill and how they do so. What, in other words, does religion do for people, and what do people do with religion? The adaptive aspects of religion can generally be viewed according to three categories, although clearly there is overlap among them: psychological, social, and ecological. We will examine each of these in turn.

Psychological Functions: Reducing Anxiety

Religion reduces individual anxiety by supplying some answers to the imponderables of human experience—especially illness, death, and other inevitable processes of nature. In addition, religion helps people find answers to more mundane questions, such as why we have the particular parents we do or why we are members of a particular society. As we mentioned earlier, nineteenth-century theorists believed that religion developed as an antidote to ignorance by providing acceptable cognitive explanations to events that cannot be otherwise explained. It satisfied the need to know. But religion is not merely an intellectual response to philosophical puzzles about life, death, and the universe; it also provides people with a means of emotional support and comfort in times of personal stress. "Religion," Malinowski observed, "is not born out of speculation and reflection, still less out of illusion or misapprehension, but rather out of the real tragedies of human life, out of the conflict between human plans and realities" (1931:99).

In addition to supplying a system of meaning, a way of thinking about human existence, religion also reduces anxiety by prescribing clear-cut institutionalized ways of dealing with the often frightening uncertainties of life. Though highly skilled navigators and fishermen, the Trobriand Islanders perform a number of magico-religious rituals before embarking on long ocean voyages. The Trobrianders do not bother with such rituals when going on everyday fishing expeditions, since their own expertise and knowledge provide adequate insurance against danger. A long voyage on the open seas in a fragile canoe, however, is far more dangerous, and ritual helps to relieve some of their anxiety. Similarly, when people with little knowledge of medicine are stricken with illnesses they cannot cure, religion may provide both an explanation and a course of action that relieves the sense of helplessness and frustration.

It would be incorrect, however, to assume that reduced anxiety simply means a more peaceful state of mind and nothing more. We know that in the case of many diseases a patient's attitude is as important to his or her recovery as medical treatment; reducing anxiety therefore may also strengthen the commitment to recover and tip the balance toward a return to health. In the same way, ask yourself who is more likely to complete a successful canoe voyage on the open seas, a crew paralyzed by fear or one confident of being protected by providence and able to concentrate on the voyage? The commitment to action and the ability to act with the confidence that what is being done is "right" underlie the adaptive significance of the psychological effects of religion.

Social Functions

Religious beliefs and rituals provide more than ways of dealing with tensions and anxiety; they also contribute to integrating society and maintaining social stability. They help to socialize individuals, express and reinforce social solidarity, and offer a means of dealing with events or conflicts that threaten to disrupt the social fabric.

Socialization One important social function of religion is the socialization of the individual into belief and commitment to a particular social universe. No society would survive if people did not accept some things they cannot prove. It is not simply a matter of taking on faith what earlier generations have verified for themselves, but rather of accepting abstract principles about what is ultimately unknowable. This ability is important in diverse activities with an ideological base, from politics to aesthetics, and in its absence societies could not function. Religion is a means by which people are led to accept propositions about activities and events remote from any experience or sensation. Through symbols and their manipulation, people are taught not only how to accept certain beliefs but also how to demonstrate those beliefs in socially effective ways.

Social Solidarity Following the lead of Emile Durkheim, Radcliffe-Brown (1939) argued that the main function of religion was to establish, codify, reaffirm, and help enforce fundamental social values. In this way, religion contributes to social solidarity. There are many ways, of course, that religion can help to promote social unity and stability. Here we will consider four: by providing models of and for behavior; by supplying a set of shared values; by reducing conflict; and by promoting social control.

Providing Models of and for Behavior Religion often contributes to social solidarity when religious symbols are arranged in ways that reflect and support the social order. Consider, for example, societies that practice *totemism.* In these cultures, people are organized into lineages or clans, and each descent group is identified by its own particular emblem or totem — an animal, an insect, a plant, or sometimes a natural phenomenon such as fire or rain. Through this symbolic association with a particular species or some aspect of nature, each descent group relates itself to the natural order. Moreover, the natural world also serves as a model of the social world of people. For instance, a tribe might be divided into two separate clans — the bear and the raven. The members of this tribe might say that just as the bear is unlike the raven, by analogy the members of the bear clan are unrelated to members of the raven clan. On another level, however, the bear and the raven are united because they are both part of the natural world, and so the two clans are ultimately united as members of the same tribe. Nature, in other words, is made to reflect or symbolically imitate the organization of society, and as such provides a model of and for behavior. The fundamental principles of the social order itself — the diversity of subgroups and the solidarity of society as a whole — are preserved through the totemic system of belief.

Reinforcing Shared Values The role of religion in promoting social solidarity need not be discussed in such an abstract way. Individuals and groups are constantly using religious values to explain and justify often very different courses of action. In this way, religion supplies an area of fundamental agreement in human social relations. Murray Leaf (1972) had described the case of two political factions in an Indian village. In political campaigns, court contests, and a variety of day-to-day events the members of these factions justify the rightness of their own position and the fallacy of their opponents' by claiming that theirs is the only one consistent with the tenets of the Sikh religion of the area. Thus religion serves to structure their points of disagreement and provides a common ground which all of the participants accept as valid for the entire community. This role of religion is possible because religious ideologies are sufficiently general and ambiguous to support many different patterns of action. Whichever course of action is chosen, it can be validated by appeal to commonly held beliefs, creating a sense of rightness in the community.

Reducing Conflict In every society there is tension and strife built into social roles and relationships — between kinfolk, spouses, men and women, or rulers and subjects, for example. Ritual is frequently used as a way of channeling and controlling conflicts that arise when a person is caught between incompatible social obligations or when the moral norms of the social order as a whole run counter to the self-interest of particular groups.

Rites of conflict, for example, publicly express both the bonds of social unity and the tensions inherent in these bonds. Among the Shilluk of the Sudan, the coronation ritual is a rite of conflict which dramatizes the surface struggles between rival settlements of kin groups. At a deeper level, it also represents the conflict that arises because a single prince who comes from a particular kin group and settlement is supposed to represent all of Shilluk unity. Before the new king is able to take office, competing groups stage a mock battle. One army carries the effigy of Nyikang, the medium between God and men and the symbol of Shilluk unity; the other army includes the king-select. The two meet in a ritual confrontation in which the army of the effigy captures the king from his clansmen and takes him to the capital. Here he is placed upon the throne and the spirit of Nyikang is said to enter his body. Physically and symbolically separated from his relatives and followers, the new king is placed above sectional loyalties. Only then is he qualified to represent the Shilluk nation as a whole and to receive homage from all chiefs. The coronation ritual effectively integrates Shilluk society by giving expression to the conflicts that mark the social order and by reconciling these conflicts through symbolic actions that reaffirm basic loyalties. By bringing the sources of these tensions out into the open and appearing to deal with them, such rituals make life more bearable and help to promote cooperation and committed action.

Promoting Social Control But religion does more to promote social stability than simply defusing conflict through ritual. Every religion is a system of ethics that defines right and wrong ways to behave. By investing a community's moral standards of conduct with supernatural authority, these values and prescriptions are made more compelling. The Bible, for instance, describes in graphic detail how those who broke God's Ten Commandments would be severely punished, if not in this world then inevitably in the next. In other belief systems, misdeeds are thought to provoke the wrath of ancestral spirits. The ancestors may bring misfortune to the person who fails to perform obligations to the spirits themselves—the offerings and sacrifices required on specified occasions during the year, for instance. Or they are said to penalize a person who does not live up to his social obligations, or who ignores his rights and duties toward his lineage elders or toward those who are dependent on him (Gluckman, 1965). In such cases, religion is used as a powerful sanction against antisocial behavior among close kin.

Ritual often functions as a means of reducing tensions and conflicts in social relationships. Sometimes, however, it serves to ameliorate some relationships at the expense of others. Among the Karaja Indians of Brazil, for example, masked male dancers act out a ritualized sexual antagonism, which temporarily relieves friction among the men—who as a group express their antagonism toward the women—but exacerbates tension between the sexes. (Christopher Taverner)

Revitalization At times strain and tension within a society become so great that religion can no longer patch up conflict and instability. As Anthony Wallace has explained: "Societies are not, after all, forever stable; political revolutions and civil wars tear them apart, culture changes turn them over, invasion and acculturation undermine them. Reformative religious movements often occur in disorganized societies; these new religions, far from being conservative, are often radically destructive of existing institutions" (Wallace, 1966:30). The primary goal of such revitalization movements is to resolve conflict and promote stability by reorganizing society. They are often important in the adaptation of a society to external forces that threaten to overwhelm it.

Anthropologists have been particularly concerned with those revitalization movements that have arisen as a result of social disorganization caused by contact with Europeans. This topic has been of such interest in part because anthropologists have often been eyewitnesses to (and sometimes even agents of) the drastic impact of Western culture on other societies. Consequently, there is a substantial anthropological literature on revitalization or nativistic movements involving the use of religious symbols in forming groups to promote a new social order.

There are many examples of revitalization movements. In the late 1800s the "Ghost Dance" appeared among the Indians of the western United States. The Ghost Dance ideology focused on the belief that dead Indian forebears were soon to return riding trains to take possession of the technology of the whites and simultaneously exterminate them. In Melanesia, there have been periodic "cargo cults" whose adherents believed that ships or airplanes were soon to arrive bringing white technology and wealth to the area. In some instances, these belief systems call for passive behavior, while others call for rebellion. In all instances, however, an unstable and conflict-ridden society uses a combination of old and new symbols to define a new view of the world and their place in it in light of changing circumstances. This can be the basis for successful political and cultural resistance to external threats and hostility.

The nature of such movements has been analyzed most clearly in Anthony Wallace's (1966) study of the Handsome Lake Movement among the Iroquois during the late eighteenth to early nineteenth centuries. In the decade preceding the appearance of this movement, the Iroquois had increasingly suffered from disease, poverty, death, and confinement to reservations as the result of policies pursued by colonial Americans. The prophet Handsome Lake claimed to have received word of a means of resolving these problems in a series of visions. His first visions emphasized the need to return to traditional Iroquois practices. Moreover, the symbols he used in conveying his ideas and the parallel of his behavior to the legendary founder of the Iroquois confederacy Daganawidah emphasized traditional religion. A second set of visions revealed proscriptions—against drinking and witchcraft, for example. A third set prescribed radical departures from traditional Iroquois practices. White farming patterns were to be employed; and men, not women, should do the labor. Couples should live in neolocal, not matrilocal extended households. The husband-wife relationship rather than the mother-child was held to be the most important. Thus what had at the outset seemed like a very conservative movement ultimately embodied radical suggestions for change. While not all revitalization movements lead to exactly the same end, they all involve similar manipulations and recombinations of new and traditional symbols to define a new world view and/or a new set of behavioral rules. Again, it is precisely because of the richness and ambiguity of religious symbols that they can be used to justify what is or what should be, even if this differs markedly from currently accepted social practices.

Significance of Religious Practices and Beliefs for Regulating Resources

From the examples we have discussed, we can see that religious beliefs and rituals are important means of promoting stability and facilitating orderly interaction between individuals and groups. But religion may also be used in regulating the relationship between a people and their environment. In many societies religious beliefs include important environmental information, and ritual observances frequently trigger events that are critical to the success of economic production and distribution. Let us look at some examples.

Religious Beliefs and Resource Management
To the Waswanipi Cree, hunting success is believed to depend upon acting in a responsible manner toward the animals that nourish them. An animal, they say, will not give himself to a hunter unless the man fulfills certain moral obligations: not to kill too many animals and to use all of what he takes; to show respect for the bodies and souls of the animals by following certain established procedures for hunting, butchering, and consuming the game. Failure to live up to these responsibilities will anger the animals and bring a hunter "bad luck." According to Harvey Feit (1973), these beliefs and practices are a critical factor in determining how the Waswanipi use their environmental resources. Living in a subarctic ecosystem where productivity is low, they must manage their resources carefully. Waswanipi hunters regulate the harvests of moose and beaver and control the distribution and population levels of these species by using alternative resources such as fish during certain years and by occupying a different hunting territory each season. These practices allow the animal populations to expand for several years after each periodic harvest. In effect, Waswanipi religious beliefs and practices actually incorporate a basic ecological principle: the concept that people and animals will survive as long as they remain in balance.

The ecological significance of religious beliefs and practices need not be recognized so explicitly in order to be effective. Among the Naskapi of Labrador, hunting strategies are sometimes regulated by divination. When food supplies get low and Naskapi hunters are

Religion may help maintain the equilibrium between a society and its environment. These Trobriand Island youths are performing a ceremony at their yam harvest festival. The decorated storage huts in the background contain the yams, a Trobriand staple. The festival, which includes dancing, feasting, and religious acts of thanksgiving, not only relieves the anxiety of the village about next season's yam crop but helps to redistribute the food to all of its members. (Photo Trends)

uncertain about where to find game, they usually consult an oracle, who tells them what direction the hunt should take. He decides the question by holding the scraped shoulder blade of a caribou over hot coals and "reading" the cracks and burnt spots that appear in the bone. Thus, instead of continually returning to certain places where they had particular success in the past, hunters select their routes on a random basis—wherever the spots and cracks indicate. As a result, the game supply is not depleted in particular places and the chances of a successful hunt are increased since the hunters follow no habitual routes which animals can learn to avoid. Thus, in addition to reducing anxiety in a precarious subsistence situation and providing people with a specified course of action, shoulder-blade divination has direct, if unintentional, survival value (Moore, 1957).

The ecological advantages of many religious beliefs and practices, such as those of the Naskapi, may not be immediately apparent, but they certainly do not strike us as necessarily disadvantageous to the groups that observe them. In other cases, however, the religious beliefs and customs of non-Western peoples may seem positively maladaptive to the Western eye. For instance, the Hindu doctrine of *ahimsa,* or nonviolence—especially its prohibition against the killing or eating of cattle—strikes us as totally illogical in a land where starvation is so prevalent. If they would just give up this practice and eat meat like anybody else, the reasoning goes, fewer people would starve.

But a closer look at the role of cattle in the Indian economy shows that to relinquish this taboo might bring disaster to the Indian subcontinent (Harris, 1966). First of all, were beef to become a staple, as in the American diet, more cattle would be necessary and cattle would begin to compete with humans for food. And since it takes about ten calories of grain to produce one calorie of meat, calories are actually being lost when grain is converted into meat.

But why not eat the cattle that already roam India? Cattle produce two essential products: dung, used for cooking fuel and for fertilizer, and oxen (the adult castrated males), used to plow the fields. (They also produce some milk, hides, and even beef for the outcastes, who obtain badly needed protein from it.) The dung is virtually free, since cattle survive by browsing on stubble in the fields and vegetation on nonarable land. Any substitute, either for fuel or fertilizer, would be far more expensive. Second, preserving cattle for breeding is absolutely essential, since without oxen, fields would remain fallow. In times of famine, the temptation to eat the cattle is nearly irresistible, but to do so would be rather like an unemployed worker selling the car he uses to go to work. In the short run, the car money (or the beef) would come in handy, but in the long run the means of livelihood would have been eliminated. Hence the taboo against killing cattle is particularly adaptive in an area where hunger and starvation are chronic.

Ritual and Resource Management Like religious beliefs, ritual cycles are also important in regulating the relationship between a people and their resource environment. The Pueblo Indian groups of the Southwest, for instance, celebrate most major occasions in the life of an individual and all major religious festivals with an exchange of food. On certain saints' days, feasts may be held by particular people or food may be thrown from the rooftops. One observance involved the collection of three to five wagonloads of food and clothing for the principal participants (Ford, 1972). The result of this method of celebration is to redistribute food within the community, a necessity given the environment and social setting.

In the area of the Southwest where these groups live, there is a great deal of variation in productivity from acre to acre not only because of the quality of the land but because of unpredictable factors like the amount of rainfall and irrigation water available at critical times or the extent of damage by frost, wind, insects, and animals. One farm can harvest a bumper crop, while on neighboring land, the crops fail. The next year the reverse may occur. Since the land is farmed by individual households, one family may be living in abundance while another faces lean times. But in many pueblos, food is given to relatives at critical times such as births, marriages, or sickness, when rites are performed in exchange for food. Since any individual is included in a number of these rituals during a year, he or she is assured of receiving food from time to time. The most important mechanism of redistribution, however, is not the randomly occurring rituals but the time-dependent ones. (Our holidays, which fall at the same time each year, are examples of time-dependent observances.) These rituals occur throughout the year in the pueblos but are most frequent in late winter when families with lean harvests are likely to be out of food. Thus Pueblo groups have built a welfare system into their ritual celebrations.

Richard Ford, whose theory of Pueblo rituals we have been discussing, suggests that this system depends on surplus within the total society and that in the face of real famine, the society would have to turn to other mechanisms, ones that were nonperiodic and involved feedback from the environment. The best example of such a regulatory ritual system can be found among the Maring of highland New Guinea. Roy Rappaport (1967) has demonstrated how the ritual slaughter of pigs functions as a mechanism for redistributing pig surpluses, providing local populations with a supply of animal protein at critical times, and ultimately for regulating the distribution of Maring territorial groups.

The Maring are inveterate fighters. Neighboring groups often fight sporadically for weeks until one group is driven from its ancestral territory. The victors then perform a ritual called "planting the *rumbim*." Every man places his hand on the ritual *rumbim* plant and the ancestors are addressed as follows:

> We thank you for helping us in the fight and permitting us to remain on our territory. We place our souls in this *rumbim* as we plant it on our ground. We ask you to care for this *rumbim*. We will kill pigs for you now, but they are few. In the future, when we have many pigs, we shall again give you pork and uproot the *rumbim* and stage a *kaiko* (pig festival). But until there are sufficient pigs to repay you the *rumbim* will remain in the ground. (Rappaport, 1967:23–24)

This ceremony is accompanied by the ritual slaughter of all adult and adolescent pigs. These animals are dedicated to the ancestors and their meat is distributed among the group's allies in repayment for military assistance. A period of truce follows. Until the *rumbim* is uprooted and the *kaiko* staged, the group is not allowed to engage in hostilities. The Maring believe that until these rituals are completed, they have not fully repaid their debts to their ancestors and allies and therefore will not be given further military aid. Rappaport maintains that by limiting warfare, this taboo on fighting insures that regional population levels do not become dangerously low.

The dynamics of this system are evident at the local level. Before the *rumbim* can be uprooted, a tribe must raise a sufficient number of pigs. If a place is "good," the Maring say that this requires only about five years. If a place is "bad," however, it sometimes takes ten to twenty years. A "bad" place is one where there are frequent misfortunes that require people to kill large numbers of pigs. For example, ritual demands that whenever a member of the group is injured or falls ill, he and his family must be given pork to eat. This practice effectively insures that the afflicted person receives enough high-quality protein at a time when he needs it most. But it also serves to slow the growth of local pig herds. Sooner or later, however, the number of pigs will increase. And as the herds become larger, they become more burdensome. The animals require more and more food, and Maring women are forced to expend more energy in caring for them. In addition, the pigs begin to invade gardens and cause trouble between neighbors. When this situation becomes intolerable and pigs are actually competing with humans for food, the community normally decides that it is time to hold a *kaiko*. The ceremony begins with the uprooting of the *rumbim* and generally lasts for most of a year. During this period, allies are invited to feast and dance. Goods are traded, marriages arranged, and future military support enlisted. The *kaiko* concludes with a major pig sacrifice and pork is distributed to tribes throughout the region. Once a group has completed this ritual cycle, it is free to begin fighting again and to lay claim to any territory that has been vacated in the meantime by groups that were unsuccessful in war. By this time, members of the defeated, landless groups will have dispersed and joined other local settlements.

In sum, then, the Maring ritual cycle helps to redistribute the regional population and adjust the ratio between local groups, food resources, and available land.

summary

A functional definition of religion must encompass the wide variety of religious beliefs and practices that we find in human society. Sociologist Emile Durkheim posited that religion is each community's way of expressing its moral values and collective beliefs. He suggested that each society distinguishes between two levels of reality: the *sacred,* the world of supernatural forces; and the *profane,* the everyday, natural world. Religious beliefs, according to Durkheim, embody the sacred. Although most societies do not make clear-cut distinctions between the sacred and the profane, the supernatural dimension in one form or another is common to all religions.

The nineteenth-century anthropologist Edward Tylor believed that religion is based on the idea of a soul or a personal supernatural force that is distinct from the physical body. He called the belief in the soul *animism* and postulated that it originated in early people's perception of the differences between states of being, such as living and dying, waking and dreaming. A soul was assigned to all living things. Tylor's contemporary, Marett, believed that a less sophisticated notion preceded animism historically; he called it *animatism.* Animatism is the belief in an impersonal supernatural force which bestows prowess and holiness on animate and inanimate objects alike.

In addition to the belief in the supernatural, many religions are characterized by *theism,* or the belief in gods. Gods are extra-human in origin but are often portrayed as having human emotions and preoccupations, as, for example, the gods of the classical Greek pantheon. *Polytheism* is the belief in many gods; *monotheism,* in one supreme god. In many monotheistic religions, however, many lesser figures, both supernatural and human, are deified.

Currently, some anthropologists have defined religion more broadly as a system of beliefs, symbols, and rituals that make existence meaningful and intelligible. *Symbols* translate the abstract and unknown into the concrete and familiar. Within the system, they function in two important ways. First, religious symbols embody people's perception of the real world; second, they exemplify an idealization of the world and of human behavior. Symbols have great psychological value because, in serving these functions, they provide strong emotional support.

Religious practices vary as widely as religious beliefs. All people systematize and celebrate their religions in more or less complex, ceremonial events called *rituals.* Evidence of ritual behavior dates back more than 50,000 years. The two major categories of ritual identified by anthropologists are *rites of passage* and *rites of intensification.* By celebrating events such as birth, puberty, or marriage, rites of passage note an individual's transition from one social circumstance to another. Rites of intensification are practiced to express appreciation of a life-giving natural process or to emphasize the community's commitment to a set of values or beliefs.

Many societies practice rituals by means of an individual or group possessing special abilities to mediate between the community and the supernatural. In many nonindustrialized societies, a *shaman* performs ritual services, usually for a family in a crisis situation, for a fee. In industrial societies, there is a professional, bureaucratized *clergy* that performs religious functions full-time, on a calendrical basis. Its services are not limited to the family group, but are provided for the entire community.

Guy Swanson, in his extensive study of the relationship between religious practices and social organization, has found that beliefs reflect the basic characteristics of the social order: highly stratified societies have stratified conceptions of the supernatural; egalitarian societies have egalitarian religious concepts. He also noted that monotheism is characteristic of societies with complex political structures; polytheism is associated with class-structured and economically specialized social orders. Animism, according to Swanson, is associated with less complex societies, such as hunting and gathering bands. Belief in ancestral spirits is characteristic of communities that are organized politically around the extended family.

Bellah proposed stages of religious evolution that developed dialectically rather than lineally based on the premise that religions approach the duality of natural/supernatural worlds differently. The stages of religion he outlined include Primitive, Archaic, Historic, Early Modern, and Modern. The duality is also reflected in the emphasis in different religions on participation as opposed to worship and sacrifice. Bellah found that those religions that deemphasize the duality between the natural and supernatural worlds—the Primitive, Early Modern, and Modern—are the most participatory. Archaic and Historic religions, which emphasize that duality, are structured upon the practices of sacrifice and worship.

Swanson's and Bellah's findings suggest that religions serve *adaptive functions* in society. These functions are classified as psychological, social, and ecological. The psychological functions of religion are to relieve personal anxiety by supplying a system of meaning, and to promote confidence in action by providing an institutionalized way of dealing with uncertainties. The social functions of religion are primarily to socialize individuals, express and reinforce social solidarity, and provide the means, through ritual, of dealing with the conflicts inherent in social roles and relationships. Religion invests the community's moral standards of conduct with supernatural authority, thereby providing a powerful sanction against antisocial behavior. In addition, religion often revitalizes a disorganized social system by incorporating new goals and symbols into its own structure.

Religion also functions to maintain a balance between people and the environment. The practice of many religious customs regulates society's participation in various ecological systems, especially those that provide it with food and shelter.

suggested readings

BANTON, M., ED.
    1966   *Anthropological Approaches to the Study of Religion.* London: Tavistock. A collection of essays that is of primary interest for its examination of the symbolic and communicative aspects of ritual and belief.

LESSA, W. A., AND VOGT, E. Z.
    1972   *Reader in Comparative Religion: An Anthropological Approach.* 3d ed. New York: Harper & Row. A comprehensive anthology, including both ethnographic studies and theoretical discussions of all aspects of ritual and belief.

LÉVI-STRAUSS, C.
    1963   *Structural Anthropology.* New York: Basic Books. An important outline of the methods of structural analysis; part three deals with the logical development and structure of myth.

SWANSON, G. E.
    1960   *The Birth of the Gods: The Origin of Primitive Beliefs.* Ann Arbor: University of Michigan Press. An analysis of the possible determinants of the social organization of religion.

WALLACE, A. F. C.
    1972   *The Death and Rebirth of the Seneca Nation.* New York: Vintage Books. A case study that provides a historical perspective on the role of religious revitalization in the adjustment of a society to disruptive culture contact.

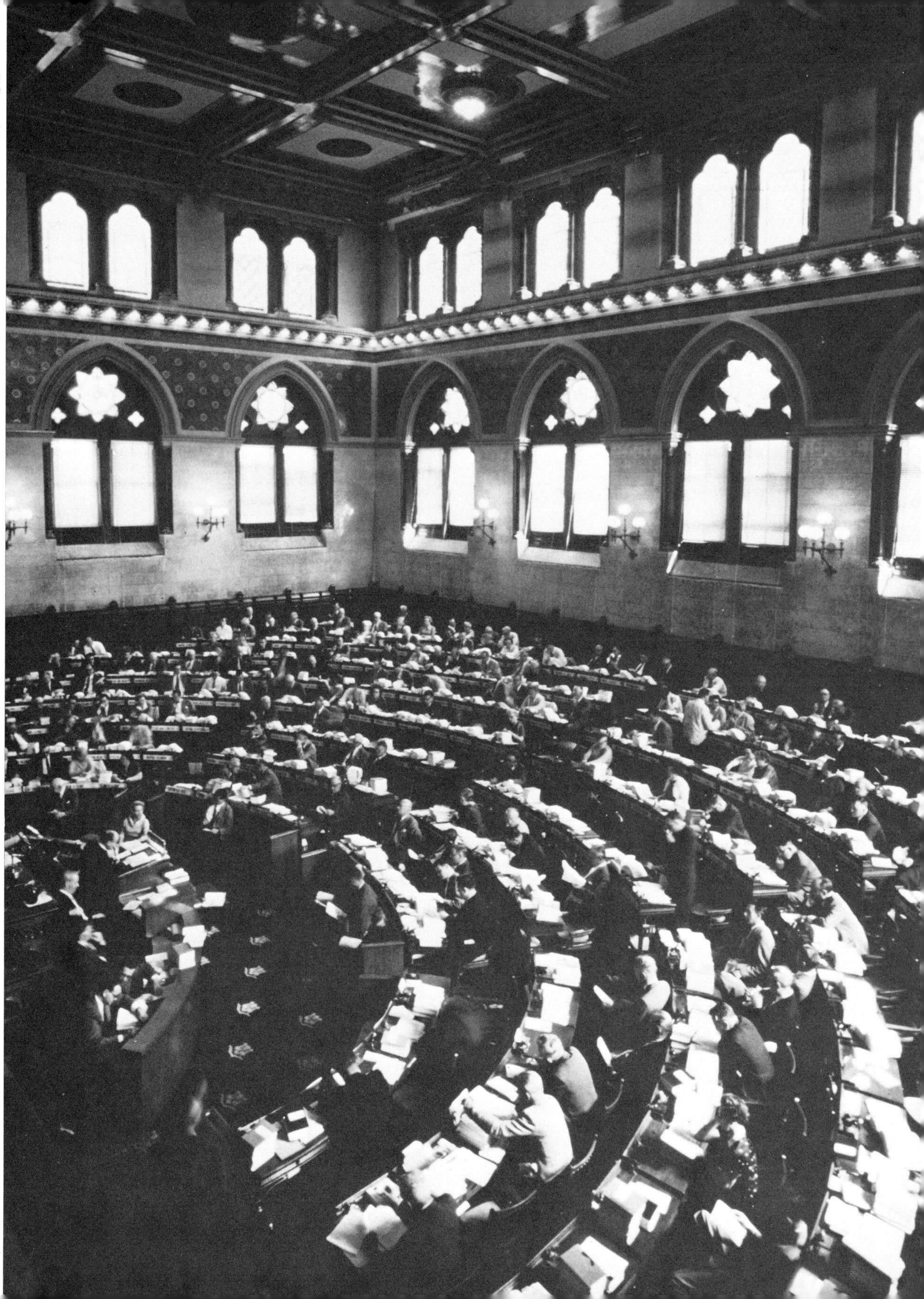

twenty-one
Politics: Power, Authority, and Conflict

During the colonial era, British officials attempted to organize and politically consolidate the Tiv of northern Nigeria in order to facilitate colonial administration. Their initial attempts failed, however, in part because they did not understand the nature of the Tiv political system. Applying their own standards and notions of government, the British tried to create a local administrative hierarchy of chiefs, judges, and police officers by appointing particular individuals to fixed political positions. What they did not understand was that the Tiv have no formal or centralized positions of authority, no permanent offices or officeholders, no "chiefs" who can command the society as a whole. While there are men who are influential in settling disputes within their own community, compound heads with the authority to make decisions concerning their extended family, and men who may gain prestige as traders in the marketplace or as ritual specialists, authority is not vested in particular individuals, and political activities are not institutionalized. Rather, political organization is based on shifting alliances among small, semiautonomous lineage groups roughly equal in status. When the British tried to create political functionaries by concentrating power in the hands of a few individuals and creating a more permanently centralized form of political organization, they were violating basic principles of Tiv society.

Despite the absence of rulers, centralized decision-making bodies, written legal codes, and law enforcement agencies similar to those found in state societies, the Tiv clearly do not live in a state of anarchy or lawlessness. Many societies lack the elements we consider basic to government, but this does not mean they have no political system. If we look beyond specific governmental structures and institutions, we find that in one way or another every society engages in political activity. In every society there are scarce rewards for which people compete, norms regulating the conduct of this competition, and both formal and informal procedures for acquiring roles of influence in decisions affecting the community. In this sense, all societies are political (Bohannan, 1965).

When defined very generally, political activity can be said to occur even within very small groups such as families or households, with each individual pursuing a strategy that optimizes his or her immediate self-interest. People who coordinate their economic lives can rarely do so with all parties consistently benefiting in an equal fashion. Thus politics is a universal aspect of all human relations. In this chapter, however, we will not be concerned with politics as it occurs in such small groups. Instead, we will focus on political processes at the societal level—how decisions affecting the life of a community are made, how authority and power are exercised. In addition, we will explore political relations, both peaceful and violent, between societies.

The Nature of Political Processes

Politics has been rather succinctly defined as the process of "who gets what, when, and how" (Lasswell, 1936). Although this definition was formulated to characterize the political process in our own and other state systems, it is broad enough to apply to societies through-

The Connecticut Senate has the highly specialized task of creating laws that will later be interpreted, implemented, and enforced by other branches of government. (Fred Maroon/Photo Researchers)

out the world. In all societies, politics is concerned with the distribution of rewards, whatever those rewards may be. Political competition is always waged over specific objectives, and in the end, one side will almost always benefit more than others. The study of politics is fundamentally concerned with who benefits. How equally or unequally are rewards allocated? One way to help answer this question is to look first at who has access to the political process, and second at how leadership within it is determined. Finally, in order to understand the workings of the political process, we must also look at the "rules of the game" of politics. What are the limits of political competition? How are these limits imposed and how effectively are they maintained? These are some of the questions we will be exploring in the following sections.

Political Decision Making and the Distribution of Rewards

Behind all political competition lies disagreement—conflicting ideas about how issues affecting community life should be decided. The specific issues involved can be almost anything society considers important, something that is worth competing for. In all cases, however, the decisions that are eventually reached benefit some people more than others, in spite of any lofty rhetoric to the contrary. There is, however, wide variation from society to society in the kinds of decisions people are attempting to influence, in how intensively they compete for that influence, and in what the rewards will be.

In hunting and gathering societies, for example, political competition might arise over disagreements about where to search for game, when to move camp, where a new camp should be located, or any other matter relating to the entire group. The resolution of these disagreements is politics, even though the process does not involve the use of force and may seem highly uncompetitive by our own standards. A decision affecting the community is made, and often one individual's desires or needs prevail over those of others. The personal rewards accruing to those who dominate the decision-making process are generally increased status and prestige, but at times they may also include increased wealth.

As the level of social complexity increases, so do the number and scope of political objectives, as well as the use of force in achieving political ends. In our own society, political competition is waged over such issues as what portion of public revenues should be spent on defense and what portion on health care, where a new jetport or nuclear power plant should be built, or what kind of trade agreement should be reached with a foreign nation. Parties to the competition typically mobilize impressive support to bolster their positions and apply pressure of all sorts, both legal and illegal, in an effort to turn the decision in their favor. The outcomes of such contests affect the lives of millions of people, and the personal rewards for those who prevail are similarly far-reaching.

Access to the Political Process

Because politics is the means by which rewards are allocated to members of society, an important question is, Who is allowed to participate in political decision making? Who has access to this important process? In every society access to political competition is restricted through both formal and informal means. All societies impose certain formal qualifications for participation in different areas of politics. Group membership is the most basic of these formal qualifications. Age and sex restrictions are also common, with children and often women being excluded from political decision making.

But formal exclusion from the decision-making process does not necessarily mean lack of political influence. As anyone familiar with the American political system knows, formal offices and positions of authority do not tell the whole story about who actually holds power. Frequently, informal channels of

Politics: Power, Authority, and Conflict

Among the Bakhtiari of Iran, access to political decision making is formally restricted to male adult tribal members. As there are no institutionalized leaders among them, the political process may be carried on by any of the tribesmen. Here we see the men holding a council during one of their biannual migrations.
(Tony Howarth/Woodfin Camp)

access to decision making are open to those who cannot or simply do not hold recognized positions of authority. Women, for example, may exercise great power in societies that formally restrict their access to political office. This is accomplished by the informal influence women can exert on their husbands, brothers, and sons. Among the Iroquois, for example, men held the dominant political positions, but women selected the officeholders. Thus we must not confuse norms defining formal participation in the political process with the actual exercise of influence and power. The two may be quite different.

The number of criteria restricting access to political roles increases as societies become more complex. In state societies, although group membership, age, and sex are still factors, political participation is also affected by ethnicity, religion, caste, wealth, education, and many other criteria. These criteria can be embedded in formal rules as well as informal practices. Although sex, ethnicity, and wealth are no longer formal restrictions to political access in our own society, women, members of ethnic minorities, and the poor still are disproportionately represented among officeholders and political influentials. This is because societies such as our own are hierarchically organized in terms of political access. Although all minority groups may have finally achieved access at one level of participation—the right to vote—they have not achieved access to the higher levels—membership in the ruling elite. Thus members of minority groups clearly participate less in the exercise of power and in the system of leadership than do members of the dominant groups.

Political Leadership: Authority versus Power

Given that all societies impose both formal and informal restrictions on access to political influence, how, within these restrictions, is leadership determined? Who will prevail over others in the decision-making process and how? Certain criteria for leadership may be highly idiosyncratic. A person might be able to influence others because he possesses charisma or a magnetic personality, because he has persistently demonstrated courage or good fortune, or perhaps because he has superior strength or wisdom. On the other hand, leadership can also be established not so much by virtue of personal characteristics but by success in mobilizing organizational support. The prince rules because he has the strongest army; the candidate is elected to office because he has won the most votes; the bureaucrat gains support for his programs because he has the most allies. Often these two kinds of leadership criteria work together. In Melanesia, for example, status and prestige are accorded to certain individuals known as "big men." A big man has typically demonstrated certain personal qualities such as bravery or speech-making ability which make him worthy of admiration. But these qualities alone will never accord him the status of big man. To become a big man he must have a following, and a following can only be acquired through exceptional, habitual, and calculated generosity. Such generosity, in turn, is largely based on the skillful manipulation of trade relations with others (Sahlins, 1968).

In discussing political leadership, it is useful to distinguish between *power,* the ability to exert influence because one's directives are backed by negative sanctions of one sort or another (the ultimate sanction being the use of physical coercion), and *authority,* the ability to exert influence simply because of one's personal prestige or the status of one's office (Fried, 1967). Among the !Kung Bushmen, for example, certain individuals may acquire authority, but not power. They can affect the behavior of others because their opinions for one reason or another are respected, but they cannot effectively impose threats or sanctions of any kind. In Melanesia, a big man has a somewhat more clearly defined political position, but again his authority rests largely on his persuasive abilities. In state societies, in contrast, officials can force citizens to behave in certain ways through the use of sanctions— ultimately the threat of coercion. They exercise both power and authority. Power, of course, need not always be accompanied by authority. But as a result of evolutionary processes, we find that as population densities increase with the development of more effec-

The dignified bearing and assurance of this Kpelle clan chief leave no doubt as to his role within the community. However, in reality the power and authority of the chief are not absolute—he can resolve conflicts, but his political clout is dependent on the support of other clan members. (Jacques Jangoux)

tive food-production strategies, positions of authority become increasingly formalized and power is centralized in them.

The Rules of Political Competition and Mechanisms of Control

Political leadership and the exercise of authority or power imply that decisions will be made, obstacles overcome, and opposing forces reckoned with. But political competition, as heated as it may become in some societies, is rarely a free-for-all; there are always norms governing how people can and cannot compete. In any political process, then, there are rules of conduct—rules that allow some types of political activity and prohibit others. Yet as we well know, rules are not necessarily followed; people may find it more advantageous to pursue strategies that carry them outside the culturally defined limits of acceptable behavior. Conflict is fundamental to all political processes, and when conflict becomes intense enough it will almost always erupt into violence or rebellion. If this is so, what is to prevent the political process from dissolving into chaos? Part of the answer lies in the existence of certain mechanisms present in all societies that serve to restrain violence and disruption in the resolution of conflicting interests.

One such mechanism, which is built into the social order, is simply the fact that there are many competing demands for an individual's or group's loyalty, that individuals and groups are interrelated in complex ways. This means that opponents in one area may well be allies in another, or they may be united by a mutual interest outside the political sphere. Such crosscutting ties tend to discourage wholehearted enmity and reduce the potential for violence.

But crosscutting ties may also limit the possibility for unity when important matters requiring solidarity arise. Consequently, although they are a deterrent to violence, they may also be a source of instability. An Arab proverb runs: "I against my brother; my brother and I against my cousin; I, my brother,

Politics, Religion, and Economics in an Indian Village

In the last several chapters, we have been discussing economics, religion, and politics as separate topics. That these aspects of culture are not so easily separated in ongoing behavior is indicated by a study carried out by Murray Leaf (1973) in a Sikh village in the state of Punjab India. Leaf's analysis focuses on two political factions in the village, one allied with a statewide political leader, Master Tara Singh, and the other with his counterpart, Sant Fateh Singh. The faction of Master Tara Singh is said to be "allied" with the Congress party and that of Sant Fateh Singh with the Communist party.

At the village level, the ideology of both these factions is substantially that of the Sikh religion. Both claim that their policies and positions taken on particular issues are the only ones that are consistent with Sikh religious tenets: "that the community be defended, that the material welfare of its members be cared for, and that its doctrines be made continually known" (Leaf, 1973:43). By the same token, local religious rituals that are dominated by one or the other faction are occasions for making a political "cause" for that faction.

Not all households are clearly identified with either faction. But when a household is allied with one faction, all of its adult members are so allied. Kin ties are crosscut by these alliances, but not household ties. It is said that forming a new household is the only way to resolve factional conflict within a household.

Finally, there are clear economic differences between the two factions. The households allied with the Master Tara Singh faction have 172 percent more land per capita than members of the Sant Fateh Singh faction. And a higher percentage of the latter's land is held by mortgage rather than ownership. Leaf suggests that the two factions ultimately reflect the tails of an economic curve within the village—those who are land-rich but lack the labor to work that land at one end of the curve, and those who are labor-rich but lack the land on which that labor can be used at the other end of the curve. Most households in the village arrive at a more even balance of land and labor. But the land/labor issue can ultimately be described in religious and political as well as strictly economic terms.

and my cousin against the next village; all of us against the foreigners" (quoted in Service, 1966). What this saying describes is the idealized tribal political structure in which ties of descent override all others as a principle of mobilizing people for action. What it does not express is the fact that such unity may be very difficult to achieve. In reality, the local descent group is composed of individuals who are related in numerous other ways and are involved in continually shifting alliances. Thus even if unity, say for warfare, is achieved, it is frequently short-lived. The result is a very dynamic political system in which violence is limited but long-term stability is highly elusive.

Mechanisms designed to keep political competition within reasonable bounds are also built into the formal structures of most political systems. In most societies, there are recognized positions of authority that help to regulate the political process. When a case concerning a possible breach of the rules occurs, these individuals are called in to mediate the issues between the contending political factions or to decide which one is in the right. In some instances, these "referees" have the power to enforce their rulings, as does the United States Supreme Court. But in other instances, they can only arbitrate, using their own status or the status of their office to persuade.

In the next chapter we will take up in greater detail the topic of how societies go about the problems of resolving disputes and settling conflicts that might otherwise disrupt the social order. In the following section of this chapter, we will focus on decision making and leadership—how authority or power are gained and exercised in different political systems.

Variations in Political Organization

Political activity, although it often involves innovative strategies, does not occur on a random basis. In every society, procedures for making decisions and defining authority follow certain patterns which are used recurrently in different situations. Essentially, political organization varies broadly along four separate dimensions. The first is the degree to which political roles and institutions are specialized or differentiated from other roles and institutions. For example, does a society have political offices such as king, chief, judge, or legislator, and to what extent are these roles vested with power and authority? The second dimension concerns the degree to which power or authority is divided among the members of a society. Do certain individuals or elite groups have the power to control others? Or does everyone have an equal chance to influence decision making? Third, what are the criteria for obtaining political authority? Is it ascribed, achieved, or based on ancestry, military success, or some other factor? And finally, what is the degree of formal organization and centralization? Is there a hierarchy of decision making and administration or are political activities loosely and informally organized?

Individual political systems vary, of course, even where close similarities exist among them. But four patterns of political organization have been usefully identified. Ranging from the simplest and least formal to the most complex and highly structured, they are bands, tribes, chiefdoms, and states. In considering these four organizational patterns, however, one should be careful not to assume that a certain population has a certain type of political system which is somehow fixed and inflexible. A highly centralized state system, for example, can "decompose" into competing tribal or ethnic factions; and by the same token, decentralized tribal systems can, almost overnight, form more complex polities when faced with some particular problem or goal. Change in political organization, then, is a constant process.

Bands

The band is the least complex and probably the oldest form of political organization. A band is essentially a small group of individuals who belong to a larger population, but that larger population is integrated only by virtue of a shared language and a sense of common identity. There is no overarching set of explicitly political institutions uniting various bands into a larger polity. Moreover, bands are extremely fluid in composition, with people shifting residence frequently. In general, though, bands remain small, their exact numbers varying from perhaps thirty to a hundred people, depending upon the carrying capacity of their territory.

Today, nomadic hunter-gatherers are characteristically organized as bands, although this type of political organization is not a necessary outcome of a hunting and gathering procurement strategy. Hunters and gatherers in areas of rich food supplies may well be similar in political organization to sedentary agricultural communities. Thus the relative abundance of the food supply has an important effect on population size and density, which in turn have an important effect on political organization.

In a band society, political life is simply one dimension of social life; it is part of the fabric of all social relations. There are no specialized political roles—no official leaders with designated authority. Matters in which some degree of competition for influence arise concern day-to-day problems such as the strategy of the hunt. These are settled in give-and-take discussions involving all members of the group. Although there are positions of "headmen" within !Kung bands, a headman has no power and only limited authority. He is essentially a symbol of the group, and as such, he is given certain ceremonial prerogatives, such as walking at the head of the line when the band moves. But the position carries no rewards of power or riches, and the headman hunts, works, and shares his food like all others in the band (Marshall, 1960).

Age and sex are generally factors in determining who will exert influence within a band. Leadership among the Bushmen is strongly male-dominated, as it is in most band societies. And frequently age also bestows some degree of influence. In some Eskimo groups, for example, old people, both men and women, are given great respect; when they offer opinions, younger people listen (Weyer, 1932). However, they are given this deferential treatment not because it is mandatory, but rather because the elderly are considered to have great experience and are therefore likely to give sound advice.

Although access to political influence is broadly circumscribed on the basis of age and sex, within these limits band societies are

The Kalahari Bushmen of southern Africa are nomadic hunters and gatherers, organized into bands in which there are neither formal positions of leadership nor political offices. All male adult Bushmen may participate in the decision-making process. Through personal prestige, a few men may acquire "headman" status—because of their reputation, their ideas carry more weight among the group than those of other members. But this respect is voluntarily accorded them by the group and may be withdrawn at any time; the status provides no rewards or power to command.
(Marvin E. Newman/Woodfin Camp)

politically as well as economically egalitarian. Given that prestige is awarded primarily on the basis of superior skill, intelligence, or fortune, anyone with one or more of these attributes will achieve social status. In fact, there are always as many positions of status in band societies as there are people capable of filling them. This does not mean that all members of a band will necessarily be accorded prestige and influence. At any one time there will inevitably be some people who are particularly clever and skillful and others who are much less so. What it means is that the number of status positions will be fluid from generation to generation: in one generation a band may have a large number of bright and able individuals who will gain prestige, while in the next, very few.

Yet all positions of prestige and influence in band societies are ephemeral, existing solely because others accept a person's superior judgment, experience, skill, or simple luck in a particular endeavor. A leader has no coercive authority whatsoever, and if his advice proves unreliable, the group will simply follow someone else. Among the Eskimo of Coronation Gulf, for example, "a man acquires influence by his force of character, his energy and success in hunting, or his skill in magic. As long as these last him, age but increases his influence, but when they fail, his prestige and authority vanish" (Jenness, 1922:33). Thus a position of influence may dissolve or be created in an instant.

In band societies an influential person, no matter how much status he may have acquired in the eyes of his fellows, never has the power to command beyond the charismatic power to persuade. Others are always at liberty to accept or not accept his advice, depending upon how sound it seems. For the most part, vital decisions affecting the entire group are made by consensus. Never is a decision concerning the community simply decreed by one person, or even a group of people. A band is a society of equals which is led by one of its members only because the other members think it wise for a given situation.

Tribes

The term "tribe" is used in many ways in anthropological literature, and often these uses are contradictory — or at best confusing. The most general meaning of the term "tribe" is a culturally distinct population that uses various principles of kinship and descent to distinguish its political boundaries. But "tribe" can also be used in a more specific, restricted sense to describe a particular form of political organization. This is how we will use it here.

In many respects, the political organization of the tribe is similar to that of the band. Tribal societies have no specialized political roles, no authoritative leaders, no centers of administration, no formal mechanisms of coercion. Also like the band, the tribe is egalitarian, with access to status or prestige equally available to everyone within certain age and sex categories. The political organization of the tribe, however, differs in one important respect from that of the band: there are mechanisms for pantribal solidarity which integrate all the various local segments of the tribe. Without these mechanisms there can be no concept of a tribe.

Pantribal sodalities unite the local segments of a tribe for different reasons: to participate in common religious ceremonies, to help settle disputes, or to cooperate in work projects, for example. The main purpose of pantribal sodalities, however, is to create a unified force to deal with threats and attacks from neighbors. Tribal societies are more threatened by outside groups than band societies because the land they occupy is generally more vulnerable. Why is this? Agriculture, the most common means of supporting the larger populations associated with tribal societies, involves an investment in time and energy which "pays off" only in the course of several seasons. Crops must be harvested, seeds dried, and fields prepared for another planting. All these are involved processes, the disruption of which can have serious results. Consequently, organized defense and a common front are necessary to protect resources that are vital to the tribes' survival.

Tribes, of course, can be united through a number of different mechanisms. Chief among these are kinship networks, age-grade systems, and certain pantribal organizations such as military associations or secret societies. Here we will consider kinship networks in some detail in order to understand how pantribal sodalities function.

Lineal descent reckoning often provides the framework for tribal organization. Clans are one type of pantribal sodality. A clan name and other symbols of clanship are an easy method for creating a sense of unity or common purpose among various local groups. With these symbols, they become a group of cousins with ties of blood and history. The functions of pantribal clans may vary, but they almost always include political dealings with outside groups. As in the band, where older members often assume roles of influence, it is usually the clan elders who act for the clan as a whole in disputes with others. Elders may also mediate disputes between kinsmen and arrange communal work parties, but they still lack the power to compel others to follow their advice.

Segmentary lineage systems are another mechanism of pantribal unity based on kinship, although a less common one than a system of clans. The Tiv of Nigeria, for example, are organized into segmentary lineages, with minimal lineages being encompassed as segments of minor lineages, minor lineages as segments of major lineages, and so on with the result that all of the 800,000 Tiv are related in a single genealogical hierarchy (Bohannan, 1965). Segmentary lineage systems often develop under conditions of tribal expansion into territory already occupied by another group (Sahlins, 1961). They enable a particular lineage segment to progressively enlist the aid of a larger and larger group of related segments if faced with external border threats. Of course, the entire tribe hardly ever functions as a completely integrated whole. But the system does provide the basis for broad military alliances that will endure as long as they are needed to ward off attack or defend newly acquired territory. Moreover, the segmentary lineage system also serves to regulate the relations between the various lineage segments. In conflicts between minimal segments, for example, other minimal segments will take the side of the party to whom they are most closely related. One segment joins another until minor and even higher order segments are pitted against each other.

Chiefdoms

A chiefdom is distinguished from a tribe by the presence of a permanent central agency to coordinate certain economic, social, and religious activities. Although this agency may be composed of a number of people, at its core is the office of chief. Chiefdoms, like tribes, predominantly practice agriculture and/or herding, but in many significant ways they differ economically from tribes. Production in chiefdoms is generally far more specialized. One segment of the society may raise a particular crop while another may fish or raise a complementary foodstuff. It is believed that such specialization often arises when different segments of a population occupy different adjacent ecological zones. With such specialization, a society can usually support a larger population by means of intragroup exchange and the redistribution of surplus goods from one area to another.

The office of chief is a specialized political position with well-defined areas of authority. Hawaiian chiefs, for example, were considered the "owners" of their people's resources and had the right to call upon their labor and collect a portion of their crops. These chiefs accumulated great storehouses filled with goods of all sorts—food, cloth, clothing, and so on. Redistribution of this wealth, largely among the chief's own people, was all part of the chief's carefully calculated generosity. He would use the surplus to support lavish community feasts or to subsidize such large-scale

This ruler of a Ghanaian chiefdom holds a specialized political position in a society where commoners wear either traditional or modern dress. The chief's assumption of traditional costume is deliberate—it is a symbol of his high rank and political power. Other symbols of his status are the ceremonial umbrella, the intricately carved scepters, and the attentive dignity of his retinue. (Jacques Jangoux)

construction projects as the building of irrigation works, all of which would enhance both his status and his potential for accumulating ever-larger chiefly funds (Sahlins, 1963).

An important distinction between the chief's role in these activities and the role of tribal leaders in the economic and social life of the tribe is that the chief can deploy labor, give commands, and ask others to do things that he himself might never do. The authority of a chief is backed by sanctions of one kind or another. In most Polynesian chiefdoms, for instance, the chief's religious status was probably his most compelling tool of persuasion. The chief was believed to be richly infused with a supernatural force known as *mana*, which sanctified his right to office and otherwise protected his chiefly person. When a chief is considered to have this kind of strong spiritual power, he is able to back up his authority by threats of curses or other spiritual sanctions.

Chiefdoms are ranked societies in that positions of status and authority are not open to everyone, but this does not mean that they are necessarily stratified as well. Unequal distribution of status does not affect access of all members of the population to the resources needed for survival. Those of high rank, however, are accorded special honors or are permitted symbols of status and prestige—a certain form of dress, an insignia, or even a particular vocabulary. Etiquette is also a very common means of differentiating those of status from the rest of the population. Deferential manners—bowing, kissing the hand—or titles of address are some typical examples. In Polynesia, those of rank were separated from the common people by elaborate sets of taboos. Commoners, for instance, could not eat with people of higher rank, and on some islands could not even watch a person of higher rank eating.

In chiefdoms, a person acquires rank through heredity—being the eldest son of a chief or his sister's eldest son is the route to a chiefly title. In many such societies, however, kinship ties may be complex and overlapping, enabling more than one person to lay claim to the position of chief. Violent conflict may often result. In fact, political assassinations appear to have been frequent events in many chiefdoms.

In chiefdoms kinship and ancestry are often the basis of many status positions other than that of chief. Often the chief's closest kin are somewhat like a noble lineage. In many cases, a hierarchy develops in which those closest to the chief have a higher status than more distant relations. On Tahiti, for example, the population was divided into basically three grades of people, although there were levels of rank within each of these three major grades: the immediate families of the paramount chiefs; those of a lesser, intermediate lineage; and the commoners. But although the "nobility" of a chiefdom may exercise various levels of authority and possess prestige and influence, they are nevertheless more of a hierarchy among kin than a government like that which exists in state societies.

States

The most complex and centralized of political systems are states. A state is essentially a complex of institutions by means of which power is organized on a supra-kinship basis. This does not mean that all power in such societies is preempted by the state. Kinship networks possessing limited authority usually coexist. In the Nupe state of central Nigeria, for example, civil offenses came under the jurisdiction of the village and kinship groups, while criminal offenses were the province of the state exclusively (Nadel, 1935). In fact, localized kinship systems (which serve the function of relating local populations to the central government) may be the only polities that some people in state societies actually participate in. But even so, it is the state that holds ultimate power, because the state alone has the right to the legitimate application of pure force. Thus the state holds a monopoly over the use of physical coercion. All acts of violence not legitimized by the state are punishable by law.

To maintain order internally and to regulate relations with other populations, the state maintains the mechanisms of coercive control: a police force, militia, army, arsenal of weapons, and so on. Coercive power is essential to state control, but the state continues to exercise its power not only by force, but also through ideology. There is in any state system some philosophic basis of legitimacy which establishes in people's minds the right of the state to govern. The ideology of the state may be purely rational—such as a social contract theory whereby members presumably give the state its authority, voluntarily—or the ideology may be essentially religious, as with the divine right of kings. But no matter what the nature of the state ideology, no state society has ever existed without one. On the basis of such an ideology, obedience to the state is justified, regardless of how popular or unpopular particular state policies may be.

Political roles in state societies are highly specialized. Lawmakers create laws, judges interpret them, agencies implement them, and armies and police forces attempt to insure that no one violates them. Such specialization can lead to competing centers of power within state governments. Any one agency of government, though powerful, may be itself greatly restricted by others.

State-level political organization is associated with large, dense populations, substantial segments of which live in towns and cities. The complex of communities that comprises a state is supported by intensive agriculture, highly developed technology, and extensive

A corollary of the trend in state societies for power and authority to become increasingly centralized is the extent to which the modern state is personified by its leader. Mao Zedung, the chairman of the Chinese Communist Party, is so politically powerful that throughout the world he is viewed virtually as the physical incarnation of the Chinese state—as this 100-foot statue of Mao in Sian, China, makes clear. (© Marc Riboud/Magnum)

economic specialization. Although specialization allows for the production of large surpluses, these are not equally distributed among the population. State societies are stratified. Access to factors of production—such as land or capital—is restricted in many cases to elites who control others through their monopoly on strategic resources. Thus wealth and political power are closely related in state societies, and very often the relationship is self-perpetuating. If political power is based at all on wealth, those in power might choose to prohibit others from gaining wealth, thus denying them power as well. The fact is that unequal access to both wealth and power are primary characteristics of state society. Maintenance of the system of social stratification is one of the primary functions of the state.

The vast extent of social, economic, and political control in a state requires a centralized system of administration. At the hub of the system will be those with the greatest power— a king, his ministers, a president, legislators, governors. This group will create laws and formulate the overall political strategy of the government. A bureaucracy is then established to carry out laws. Even when there is a single ruler with absolute power, a hierarchically organized bureaucracy is needed to implement policies down to the smallest details. In fact, the leaders are dependent to a large extent on information given them by the lowest levels of the state bureaucracy. In order for the system to work, they must gather data about the citizenry throughout the state.

In the Inca state system, a census was taken regularly, and it was actually illegal for people to confuse the census count by moving from town to town. The Incas' main reasons for keeping such close track of the peasants had to do with the army and labor pools. As in most states, people in Inca society were conscripted into the military, but the Incas also required that everyone work part time for the state as a form of taxation (Murra, 1958). While forced labor is not a common method of taxation in present-day states, all have taxation in some form. A large fund of public revenue is vital to the maintenance of a complex, highly centralized structure like a state.

The Evolution of Political Organization

From the beginnings of human society until about ten thousand years ago, it is generally believed that all groups were organized as bands. Today, such societies exist only in some of the more isolated and inhospitable places on earth; in the rest of the world, more complex forms of political organization prevail. Over these thousands of years, political society has moved toward greater specialization of roles and institutions. Access to positions of influence, authority, or power has generally decreased even as governments have incorporated more and more people into their hierarchies. And administration in most societies continues to grow more centralized as bureaucracies become involved in more and more aspects of people's lives.

These are the general trends in political evolution. Although there are forms of organization today that have not changed significantly for hundreds, even thousands, of years, the broad trend toward more specialized, stratified, and centralized forms of political organization is clear. Over the course of human history, Paleolithic bands formed into tribes, tribes became chiefdoms, and out of tribes or chiefdoms, states that had no prior models developed in such diverse places as Mexico, China, and Mesopotamia. What accounts for the evolution of political organization that has brought us from the band to what we know today? And why have some societies developed stratification and institutions for hierarchical decision making while others have not?

The development of political centralization is actually fairly recent. It probably began long after the Neolithic revolution in food production — the changeover from hunting and gathering wild food sources to the domestication of plants and animals. This is not to say that a shift from food collection to cultivation caused bands to form into tribes. But the effects of the Neolithic revolution on the way people lived eventually selected for greater political and social integration. With food production, human populations became larger and denser, and resources relatively scarcer. Vital resources had to be protected from external threats and competition. In conflicts between groups, the one that is best organized and best consolidated will usually prevail. Pantribal sodalities are a means of achieving intergroup unity and a common front in warfare. It is fair to say that without threats from external groups, mechanisms of pantribal integration would probably not develop (Service, 1971).

External threats or competition among tribes may also be a factor in the rise of chiefdoms, as there are obvious benefits to having warfare planned, organized, and directed by a central authority (Service, 1971). Or, as one anthropologist has suggested recently, chiefdoms may be the result of the effects of states on tribal society (Fried, 1975). It is likely, however, that certain economic factors are most important in the chain of causation leading to the creation of a chiefdom. Warfare does not generally need a permanent agency of coordination, but an increasingly specialized economy does. Once that agency exists in the economic realm, extension of its planning capabilities into other areas such as warfare would be logical and would undoubtedly prove advantageous.

There are a number of theories of the origin of the state, each one focusing on a different factor that is believed to have initiated state development. Population pressure, for example, may have contributed to the emergence of stratification. As the size of a population increased, economic resources may have become relatively scarcer and competition more intense, with the result that differential access to resources eventually developed (Fried, 1967). Such competition for resources would ordinarily arise in areas where agricultural populations were circumscribed either environmentally by mountains, seas, or deserts, or socially by neighbors impinging from all sides. Robert Carneiro (1970) has argued that intense competition for resources in circumscribed areas triggered warfare, and state governments developed to mobilize and direct the armies and eventually to control the conquered peoples and allocate resources. Another theory of the emergence of the state centers on the organization needed to construct and manage large-scale irrigation systems for intensive agriculture in arid areas. Karl Wittfogel (1957) has suggested that such extensive coordination and control tended to pass into the hands of an increasingly centralized ruling class and thus the beginnings of a bureaucratic political organization were born. The need for control over trade in essential resources may also have been a factor in the rise of the state, according to some anthropologists (Rathje, 1972). Centralized political organizations may have developed at vital points of supply and redistribution, or at the crossroads of established trade routes.

Although these various theories are insightful, it is doubtful that any single factor was solely responsible for the emergence of state society in different parts of the world. Far more likely, a complex of interrelated factors contributed to state evolution. Robert Adams (1966) has suggested a comprehensive, multicause theory of the state. Initially, more efficient methods of food production (such as irrigation or greater specialization) coupled with social changes (a more sedentary way of life; higher population density; the development of trade networks and centers of redistribution) provided important stimuli to the production of economic surpluses. These surpluses could be used to support large numbers of people not directly engaged in food production. Dominant groups important in mobilizing the surpluses began to develop. Of course, this chain of events did not proceed with equal effectiveness in all communities. Those communities that controlled land highly suitable for agricultural innovation were able to produce more and monopolize access to strategic resources. Eventually, they came to control food production over large areas, becoming important centers of redistribution and waging war on less advanced groups. As outlying groups fell under their control, these powerful communities gradually became the centers of economic, political, and religious life, and fertile settings for technological, artistic, and scientific innovations. These developments in turn would reinforce the advantages of the dominant societies over their neighbors. Thus the foundations of a highly centralized form of political organization — the state — were established.

Various economic and social pressures, then, are central to political evolution. But the presence of these pressures will not always lead a society to a greater level of integration or complexity. Faced with pressures, external or internal, some societies might revert to less integrated forms. Chiefdoms threatened by outside armies, for instance, might at first unite, only to break apart and return to a tribal way of life should the external force be too strong. And considering our own society, it is possible to envision conditions that would cause the state system to fragment, just as established states have so often done in the past.

Political Relations Between Societies

In most societies, people live in close proximity to human groups other than their own. Even in band societies, which are generally widely dispersed across large regions, there are always other bands occupying neighboring territories. Strategies and methods for dealing with outside groups are important aspects of every culture's political system. Many of these strategies, of course, are peaceful; intergroup laws, mediation, and diplomacy are common ways of regulating relations and resolving conflicts and disputes between societies in a nonviolent manner. But inevitably some conflicts will be more difficult to settle peacefully than others, and many of these will ultimately reach the point of armed force and counterforce. In this final section we will be looking at some of the ways, both peaceful and violent, in which political relations between societies are conducted. In particular, we will attempt to understand some of the circumstances that tend to promote armed conflict.

Peaceful Mechanisms for Mediating Intergroup Relations

Since other populations are often the most critical part of a group's environment — sometimes its most important resource — it is not surprising that societies have evolved peaceful mechanisms for regulating intergroup exchange. While we cannot explore all of these mechanisms here, a few examples will indicate some of the forms they can take.

Among certain New Guinea tribes, for instance, ritual feasts are commonly held to appease the ghosts of ancestors. These events are used as occasions to entertain neighboring groups and thereby establish what are hopefully more lasting alliances. Thus religion functions as a mechanism of intergroup communication and exchange. Often, the relationships strengthened at these ritual feasts are further cemented through marriages between the groups (Rappaport, 1968). In North Africa and the Near East, where intergroup conflict was common in tribal areas, religion also served as a means of mediating disputes. Here, certain tribes came to be recognized as "holy tribes." Removed from the threat of attack because of their presumed sanctity (injuring a member of a holy tribe was a serious religious offense), these tribes were free to play an important role in mediating disputes among warring groups. Among the Turkman of northeast Iran, such holy tribes, thought to be descended from early figures in Islam, actually occupy land between competing tribes.

Among Bedouin tribes of the Arabian Peninsula, elaborate rules regulating hospitality to members of other groups and protection of travelers all facilitate intergroup communication. Such communication is particularly important among nomadic pastoralists living in a harsh and often unpredictable environment. Knowledge of rainfall and conditions of pasturage in different areas are critical to survival. Bedouin etiquette requires a person to give three days of hospitality—a place to sleep, food, entertainment—to anyone who enters his tent. If the visitor happens to be an enemy, the rule still holds, and in addition the guest must be given a head start out of camp when he leaves. The Bedouin also have rules protecting travelers from attack. As long as travelers are accompanied by the proper guides, it is considered wrong to harm them. Traveling merchants are also protected under tribal rules. If a raid on a tribal section occurs while a merchant is camped there, the raiders are required to make restitution to him. The result of these rules regulating intergroup relations is a constant flow of information between groups despite conflict among them.

One interesting kind of intergroup political relationship is that between rural communities and the government of a state-organized society. Frequently, a "culture broker," or person who essentially straddles both cultures, is involved in such exchanges. Because he is able to acquire some of the attributes of membership in each group, the culture broker is in a unique position to reconcile conflicting values between cultures. In situations of culture change, he is often pivotal in making a transition to "modern" ways more palatable to the local population.

Irwin Press's study of political change in a small peasant community in Yucatan centers on the role of the culture broker in effecting that transformation. In a relatively short period of time, the village of Hach Pech, which had been known for its backwardness, was turned into an involved, forward-looking community largely by one person—Cetina, a man of traditional *mestizo* upbringing who had obtained a formal education outside Hach Pech and had returned to become the village teacher. Cetina managed to form a variety of citizen committees, secure state funds for a new school, and convince the courts that Hach Pech did not have to give the state the sizeable revenue it raised each year during its fiesta. Cetina effectively created a new government with a new treasury. Press suggests that if a teacher brought in from the outside had attempted such dramatic innovations, people would have regarded his activities with grave suspicion. Cetina's freedom and power derived from the ambiguity of his position as half insider, half outsider. He never overstepped the lines of acceptable behavior because there was no precedent for his case.

Armed Conflict

Not all political relations between societies are peaceful. Anthropologists have found that armed conflict occurs in all types of societies, regardless of their level of political organization. In less complex societies, such conflicts are typically tied to specific perceived transgressions, while wars of the state are often justified by broad political and religious ideologies. Nevertheless, the frequency of warfare, when defined simply as combat between separate territorial groups, is apparently no greater among states than among bands (Otterbein, 1970). This is not to say that all band societies make war against neighboring groups. But the majority of bands do engage in some form of armed conflict that can generally be classified as warfare. We can surmise, therefore, that warfare has existed for many thousands of years — probably long before the Neolithic and the development of political organizations more complex than the band.

Evidence seems to indicate that the relative casualty rate in warfare is no higher among states than among societies with less centralized forms of political organization. This appears to be true even though state societies clearly have more highly specialized and complex military establishments and more sophisticated weapons. In band societies, for example, people usually fight with spears, clubs, or bows and arrows, and often both sides to a conflict will withdraw if they incur any serious injuries. But because the total populations of bands are so small, only a few deaths due to warfare can result in a significant overall casualty rate. Among the Murgin of Australia, 28 percent of all male deaths have been attributed to combat. Among Western nations during this century, in contrast, less than 1 percent of all male deaths have occurred because of warfare (Livingstone, 1968). In absolute numbers, of course, our own combat losses have been enormous, and those of the Murgin infinitesimally small.

Since armed combat clearly involves serious risks to life and property, we might well ask why people engage in warfare. What is to be gained by violent relations with other political communities? One answer is that warfare serves certain psychological functions: it enables people to release pent-up aggressions against other groups. In this way, warfare is a kind of "safety-valve institution" for society (Murphy, 1957). Another answer various anthropologists have proposed is that warfare is a particularly effective means of promoting social solidarity; it allows a people to forget their internal differences and conflicts and channel all of their energies toward a common goal. But warfare is not the only way that aggression can be released or social cohesion achieved. And given the highly destructive consequences of warfare, it would appear that these two functions are insufficient to explain why people wage war.

Warfare, Population, and Land Resources
More compelling reasons for warfare can often be found in a society's ecological circumstances. Studying warfare among extensive agriculturalists, Andrew Vayda (1961) has argued that such conflict is frequently precipitated by population pressures on scarce land resources. The Maori of New Zealand provide one model of how this relationship can work. Traditionally, the Maori were divided into descent-based tribes, or *iwi,* which in turn were divided into subtribes, or *hapu.* By the eighteenth century, the Maori had expanded from a very small population to a total of as many as 300,000 people, with corresponding proliferation in the number of tribes and subtribes. In the course of this population growth, warfare would periodically erupt between more distantly related Maori groups. Given this simultaneous occurrence of population growth and warfare, what, if anything, was the relationship between the two?

Vayda hypothesizes that Maori groups at some time must have reached the point where they needed more land for cultivation. Initially they may have been able to obtain this land by expanding into adjoining virgin rain forest. But eventually, with successive waves of expansion, there must have been certain groups whose territories no longer bordered on any stretch of unoccupied land. These people essentially had two choices: they could expand into virgin land some distance away, separated from their "home" territory by potentially hostile groups, or they could take land from neighboring communities, by force if necessary. The first of these two strategies would have had several drawbacks. The people who "colonized" the outlying land would be in an extremely insecure position. Cut off from close kin, they would have no help in clearing the forest—a task that often required over forty men, since the Maori at the time had only stone and wooden tools. Moreover, the "colonizers" would have no allies for defense; their newly cleared land would be a valuable prize and they would be left quite vulnerable to attack.

By contrast, the second strategy—taking land from neighboring groups by force—may have been appealing for several reasons. In attacking a neighboring village, a group would be able to muster the support of all close relatives in the area, thus greatly enhancing their chances of success. In addition, taking already cleared land would dispense with the long and arduous task of clearing virgin forest. Consequently, warfare may well have appeared the best possible solution to the problem of population pressure in spite of the risks to life involved.

Although there is no firm evidence that this is what actually did happen among the Maori, we know that armed conflict resulting in the displacement of groups from their territories did occur in Maori history, and the factors outlined here may very well have been those underlying the decision to fight. In any case, Maori warfare resulted in a redistribution of populations on the land. It may have happened that as each group was displaced by one neighbor, it in turn attacked another neighbor, until finally some group expanded into virgin territory and the chain reaction ceased. Or alternatively, vanquished populations could have been so reduced in size that the territory left to them would be sufficient for their needs, at least for the present generation. Either way, warfare would have provided a mechanism for establishing a balance between available resources and human population.

Raiding, Ecology, and Animal Populations
Land, of course, is not the only resource over which armed conflict can arise. Among certain Bedouin tribes of northern Arabia, camels are the object of armed raids and counter-raids. The camel is a strategic resource for the Bedouin—in fact, the foundation of their culture. First, camels are a reasonably stable source of food, providing milk, a dietary mainstay among the Bedouin, and occasionally meat. Second, the camel is an effective means of transportation in a desert environment. Using camels, the Bedouin can reach areas inaccessible to sheep or goat herders, they can migrate long distances, and they can rapidly launch mounted raids against other tribes. Finally, camels are valuable commodities for trading. Male camels and old or barren females can be exchanged in oasis town markets for such valuable items as grain, cloth, domestic utensils, or weapons. Because the camel is so central to the Bedouin way of life, there is constant pressure on tribal sections to increase the sizes of their herds. This is particularly necessary in order to insure a stable food supply, for a single female camel yields only a small amount of milk a day. Thus, relatively large numbers of animals must be kept simply to meet subsistence needs.

But it is impossible to increase the size of a herd quickly through breeding, since camels reproduce and mature at very slow rates. Consequently, raiding has proved to be an efficient way of replenishing a herd that has declined because of drought, disease, accident, or theft, or of increasing the size of an adequate herd just as a safeguard against future losses. Elaborate rules govern raids between Bedouin tribes, all of whom are thought to be related to one another, however distantly. These rules insure that no group that is the target of a raid will be completely routed; only camels (particularly adult females) are taken, and enough camels will always be left for the victims to later reach their nearest kinsmen for aid. In this way, camel raiding serves as a mechanism for distributing a valuable and scarce resource between different groups spread out over a large area (Sweet, 1965).

Warfare, Resources, and the State What does the study of warfare in tribal societies such as the Maori or the Bedouin reveal about warfare among modern state societies? This is a difficult question to answer. Most anthropologists believe that warfare must have played some role in the evolution of state-level political organization, and that this warfare was related to the control of strategic resources. In modern states, the relationship between warfare and economic factors is a familiar one. Some social scientists have argued that to survive, a large and highly industrialized state society such as our own needs to protect its economic interests abroad—the markets for its industrial goods, and more importantly, the raw materials required to produce those goods and keep its vast economic system running. Consequently, it will protect those interests through military force if necessary. Thus, although many of the wars between modern states have been ostensibly tied to competing political or religious ideologies, some underlying economic factors have been identified in most of them.

summary

The study of politics is concerned with who benefits in any struggle for power and rewards. It also tries to determine the particular "rules of the game" in a given society: Who has access to the political process? How is leadership determined? What are the limits to competition? and How are these limits imposed and maintained?

In all societies access to political power is limited by both formal and informal means, with the number of such restrictions increasing as societies become more complex. Political leadership may be established either through a person's idiosyncratic qualities or through his or her ability at mobilizing organizational support. In discussing political leadership one should distinguish between *power,* the ability to exert influence because one's directives are backed by such negative sanctions as the use of force, and *authority,* the ability to exert influence because of one's personal prestige or the status of one's office.

Although variations between individual political systems exist, four general organizational patterns have been identified: bands, tribes, chiefdoms, and states. Of these, the band is the least complex and the oldest form of political organization; it may be defined as a small group of individuals with a fluid membership. There are no overriding political institutions to unite several bands into a larger polity, and there are no specialized political roles. In effect, political life is an integral part of all social relations.

The tribe is similar to the band in that it is egalitarian, has no specialized political roles, no authoritative leaders, no centralized administration, and no formalized mechanism of coercion. However, the tribe possesses mechanisms for pantribal solidarity, capable of integrating all of its local segments. These bring people together for such activities as participation in religious ceremonies or settlement of disputes. However, their major role is to create a unified force capable of dealing with outside threats of violence. The unity necessary to organize the defense of crucial agricultural resources is accomplished through kinship networks, age-grade systems, and such pantribal organizations as military associations and secret societies.

The chiefdom is distinguished from the tribe by the existence of a central agency, headed by the chief, that coordinates economic, religious, and social activities, and also by a greater specialization of the means of production. This specialization allows for support of a larger population and for the production of surpluses. The office of chief is a specialized political position, with well-defined areas of authority. He is in charge of redistributing wealth, and since his authority is backed by various sanctions, he can coerce his people.

The state is the most complex and centralized of political systems. It may be defined as a complex of institutions that organize power on a suprakinship basis. Although the state does not hold absolute power, it is the only polity with the right to exercise force and coerce the population to its will. In order to maintain internal order and to regulate relations with outside populations, the state maintains such mechanisms of coercive control as a police force and an army. But the state exercises its authority through ideology as well as force. This ideology legitimizes the state's right to rule. No state has yet existed that did not possess a validating philosophy.

State-level political organization is associated with densely populated, largely urban units, which are supported by intensive agriculture, sophisticated technology, and extensive economic specialization. The surpluses created are not equally distributed. In many cases, only the elites have access to the factors of production; through this monopoly of resources, they control the rest of the population. There is thus an alliance of wealth and political power in a state society.

Until about 11,000 B.P. all human groups were organized as bands. Generally speaking, there has been an evolution from Paleolithic bands, to tribes, chiefdoms, and, finally, the state. Political society is, in effect, moving toward greater role specialization and centralization of the locus of authority and of the bureaucracy, and it is becoming ever more stratified.

All societies must deal with outside groups. Different mechanisms have been developed to regulate intergroup exchange and to minimize conflict. The most obvious of these are intergroup laws, mediation, and diplomacy, but other more subtle mechanisms are also operative. Among these are 1) religion: for example, in some cultures land in disputed territories is set aside as sacred and, therefore, off limits to armed conflict; 2) etiquette and hospitality, which protect certain groups and provide for exchange of information despite conflict; and 3) the *culture broker,* who is a person capable of reconciling value conflicts between traditional and modern cultures because he or she shares membership in both.

Despite these mechanisms, warfare is a universal phenomenon. The reasons for war are manifold. Its outbreak is related to the ecological status of a population, in that population pressures or scant resources will often precipitate conflict. War, then, acts as a mechanism for establishing a balance between available resources and population or, in other words, to redistribute resources. There is usually an economic reason for all wars, even those in state-based societies.

suggested readings

DYSON-HUDSON, N.
1966   *Karimojong Politics.* London: Clarendon Press. Case study of the structure of a decentralized society, organized by age-sets rather than by lineage segmentation.

FRIED, M.
1968   *The Evolution of Political Society: An Essay in Political Anthropology.* New York: Random House. A valuable introduction to political anthropology, which develops the concept of evolutionary levels of political organization.

FRIED, M., HARRIS, M., AND MURPHY, R.
1968   *War: The Anthropology of Armed Conflict and Aggression.* New York: Natural History Press. A collection of essays that is particularly valuable for an understanding of the role of organized violence and warfare in the origin and maintenance of the state.

SWARTZ, M., ED.
1968   *Local Level Politics: Social and Cultural Perspectives.* Chicago: Aldine. Readings on the political organization of those societies in which face-to-face relations dominate political life.

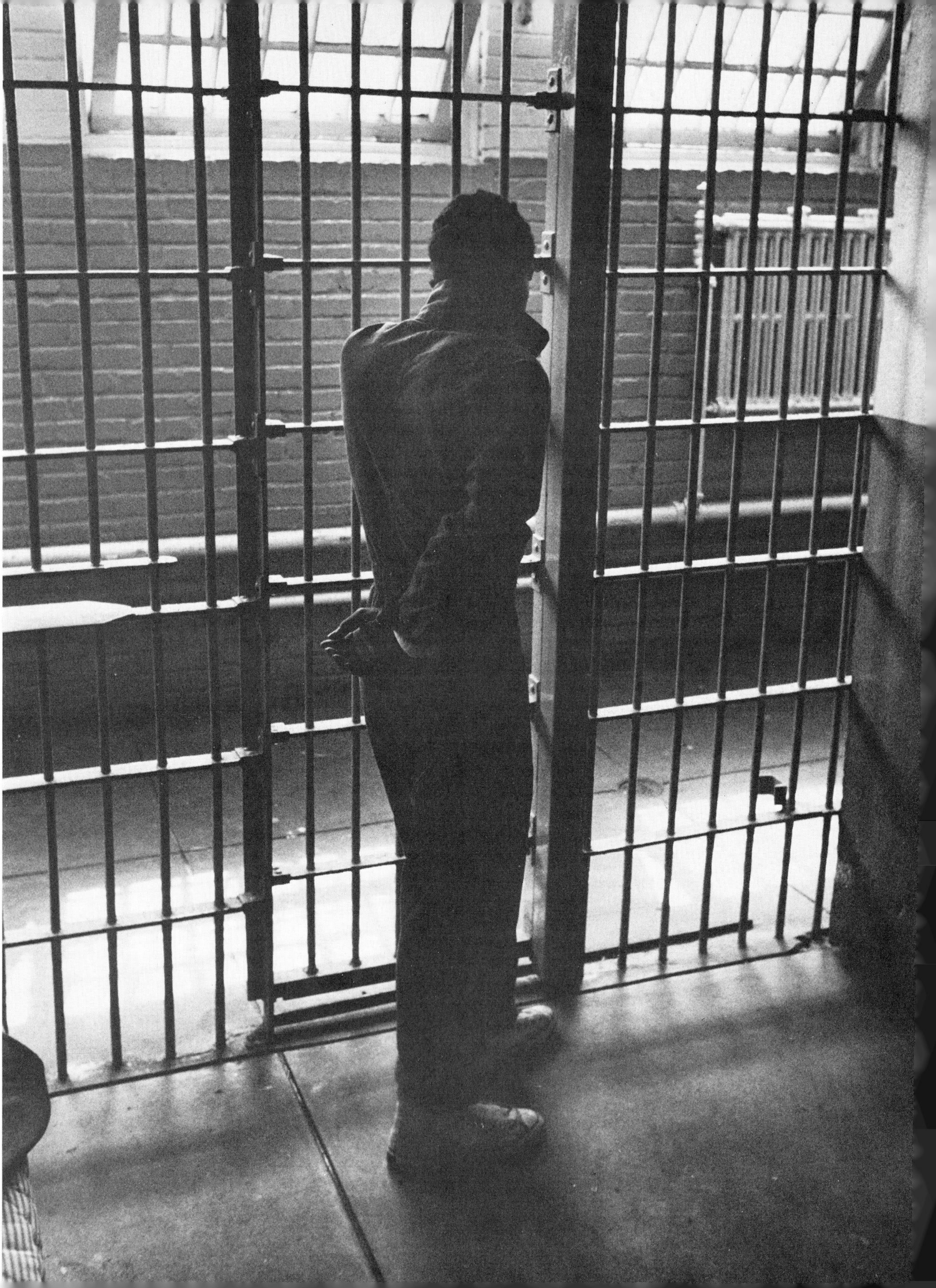

twenty-two
Social Conflict and Social Control

The Nuer have been described as a turbulent people, easily roused to violence (Evans-Pritchard, 1940). When disputes develop over a cow or rights to water or pastures, when a man discovers adultery, when someone "borrows" ornaments or other personal property without asking first, a Nuer will challenge the person who has wronged him to a fight and usually such a challenge will be accepted. For either party to the dispute to react in any other way would be to invite abuse. From the time they are very small, Nuer boys are encouraged to settle all conflicts by fighting. By the time they are adults, most Nuer bear many scars.

But this does not mean that the Nuer have no way of preventing a violent resolution to every dispute, no way of assuring that a challenge, once issued, will not end in the death of one or both combatants. In Nuerland it is customary for a man who is convinced he has been cheated to simply confiscate one of the offender's cows or to take some other compensatory action. If the alleged offender knows that he is wrong and his kinspeople will not support him, he allows the man to take the animal If the alleged offender disagrees, he issues a challenge. But when fights develop between neighbors, third parties nearly always intervene before the two seriously injure one another. The fighters protest vigorously but ultimately quiet down, and peaceful relations are restored.

Homicide presents special problems, for it is incumbent upon the Nuer to avenge the death of a kinsperson. If a man kills someone, by accident or intent, he immediately seeks sanctuary in the home of a leopard-skin chief. A leopard-skin chief holds no formal political power; he is simply a man whom people respect and would not directly challenge or attack. His home is inviolate. In homicide cases, the leopard-skin chief acts as an intermediary between the murderer and the victim's kin, trying to persuade the latter to accept compensation (perhaps forty or fifty head of cattle) in lieu of blood vengeance. He has no way of *forcing* the injured parties to accept a settlement, but in most cases they do. The leopard-skin chief is successful because he enables both sides to avoid a blood feud neither really wants without losing face. Typically, the kin of the dead person refuse to accept payment for several months, but eventually concede—not because they forgive the murderer, but "out of respect for the chief." The chief's intervention gives them an excuse not to fight.

In short, although their system of justice is very different from our own, the Nuer, like all peoples, have shared ideas about correct and incorrect behavior as well as formal and informal procedures for resolving conflicts and settling disputes. Both rules governing behavior and means of enforcing them exist in every human society. The different mechanisms societies use to maintain social control are the topic of this chapter.

Rules, Deviance, and Social Control

Rules governing proper behavior vary greatly around the world. Among the Walbiri of north-

---

Incarceration is the common punishment for disobeying the law in our society. In societies where this is impractical or undesirable, other forms of punishment, such as fines, seizures of property, or banishment, may be imposed. (Paul Conklin/Monkmeyer)

central Australia, for example, hunters are always expected to share their kill with other members of the band. An individual who violated this prescription of sharing would be ostracized or perhaps beaten for his selfishness (Meggitt, 1962). People in our society, in contrast, have little inclination to share their paychecks with their neighbors, and there is no social expectation that they should do so. We do, however, expect that a person should repay a debt on time, and we have fairly clear-cut guidelines for collecting payments that are long overdue—we go to the courts and sue. An Ifugao, in contrast, will muster numerous kinsmen and the group will descend on the debtor's household, eating their way through his or her store of food and otherwise forcing his or her hospitality until the "bill" has been paid (Barton, 1919).

But however different social rules and expectations may be from culture to culture, all societies have prescriptions regulating individual behavior. The need for social rules of some kind is clear. Rules allow us to predict with relative accuracy what other people will do in a given situation and how they will respond to our behavior. We act on the faith that most people will live up to our expectations most of the time. The Walbiri hunter, for example, is willing to share his kill because he knows that when other hunters are successful they in turn will share their food with him. Coherent social life would not be possible if the relationships between people were not, for the most part, orderly and predictable.

But this is not to say that people always abide by the rules nor that social prescriptions tell us exactly what to do in every conceivable situation. The right and proper course of action is seldom that clear-cut; there is almost always room for individual interpretation and choice. The prescription "Thou shall not kill," for example, may at first sound quite unambiguous. But under certain circumstances, this rule may be waived: thou shall not kill except during wars, in self-defense, when acting on behalf of the state, and so on. Social rules, then, set broad guidelines for much of our behavior, but it is people who do the acting. Individual decision making is inevitably involved, and with it comes variation in how the rules are actually followed or not followed.

The complexity of actual patterns of behavior and the ways in which individuals use and manipulate the formal rules of their society have encouraged many anthropologists to attempt to analyze behavior in terms of "generative models." These models are much like grammars formulated to describe actual language usages; "rules" are devised to account for the conditions under which certain types of behavior will occur. But regardless of whether or not anthropologists can ultimately construct accurate "grammars" of behavior capable of predicting how a person will behave under certain circumstances, we do know that social prescriptions and expectations usually set some limits on the extent to which societies will permit individual behavior to vary—that is, the extent to which people are allowed to *deviate.*

Deviance from social rules is part of the fabric of daily life. In the United States, the concertgoer who talks too loudly during the performance, the occasional illegal drug user, the prostitute, the thief are all breaking some social prescription, and they will be tolerated or censured depending upon how serious society considers their infractions. In every society, certain minor acts of deviance will be overlooked by nearly everyone most of the time. But there are other deviant acts—theft, incest, murder, for example—that are seldom tolerated. When an infraction is considered serious enough, and such major offenses occur in every culture, society's response can be extremely severe.

Definitions of what is deviant, however, are in no way universal. What is considered deviant in one society is not necessarily considered deviant in another. The American host who invites an overnight guest to sleep with his wife would certainly be deviating from expected behavior, but many Eskimo husbands would be breaking a social norm if they did *not* make this gesture of hospitality. And even within a single society, definitions of what is deviant vary with the particular situation. During events called wars, for example, men are expected to kill the enemy; not only is killing considered permissible and proper behavior, but anyone who refuses to take part in it may be punished. Similarly, during such carnivals as Mardi gras, large groups of people are allowed to sing and dance in the streets, drink excessively, and dress up in costumes, often as members of the opposite sex. When the war or carnival is over, however, the license to deviate is revoked, and people are expected to observe the rules once again. Thus many deviant acts, like the rules they break, are culturally defined.

When we consider the variability of human behavior, it is not surprising that people deviate from social expectations; where there are individuals, there are bound to be differences in the ways that people think, feel, and act. Instead, we might well ask why people do not deviate more often than they do. How are people induced to follow the rules even when their own self-interest may lead them to do otherwise? The answer lies in *social control*. In a sense, social control restructures individual self-interest by providing a framework of rewards and sanctions that channel behavior.

Just as every society has its own ways of defining deviant behavior, so every society has its own means of dealing with deviance. These means of course vary. Some involve the dealing out of punishment; others the prospect of reward if the wrongdoer mends his ways. But whatever the particular technique for handling deviance that may be used, in every case society has evolved mechanisms to control the behavior of its members. This is not to say that society always responds in some fashion to every deviant act. When deviance is not damaging to anyone, it is often tolerated and may eventually even become part of acceptable behavior. In fact, a society would not survive without a certain amount of deviance. The point is that culture not only defines what behaviors are considered deviant, it also defines what the proper response to a particular act of deviance is.

Informal Means of Social Control

The most obvious means of social control are often the formal or institutionalized ones. In our own society, police forces, courts, reformatories, and prisons are ever-present reminders of what may happen to those who step too far out of line. The full force of these formal agencies of social control, however, is seldom exerted on the average citizen. It does not need to be. For most people, society's informal means of control are sufficient to insure a reasonable amount of conformity to the rules. In the following sections we will discuss two informal mechanisms of social control — the process of socialization and various forms of social pressure.

Socialization

Socialization is a highly effective means of social control. In the process of learning their culture, children are not only instructed in the rules and values honored by society, they are also taught to accept these rules and values as intrinsically good and proper. The intrinsic "rightness" of social rules, moreover, is reinforced throughout adult life in a variety of ways and in many different settings. People refrain from breaking society's rules because they have come to believe that there is really no other acceptable way of acting. In other words, they have *internalized* the rules of their society, made them part of themselves. Some rules are so deeply internalized that the very thought of transgression is offensive, even repugnant, to most people. The horror many societies attach to breaking the incest taboo is a case in point. Among the Ashanti, for example, sexual intercourse between members of the same matriclan — known as *mogyadie* or "eating up of one's own blood" — is a heinous offense, punishable by death for both parties. The Ashanti believe the world would literally be plunged into chaos should *mogyadie* go unpunished (Rattray, 1929).

In all societies, many other rules, although they do not evoke horror at the thought of violation, are nevertheless very effectively inter-

Obedience, Responsibility, and Social Control

We are all agents of social control. Whether we realize it or not, we all attempt in various ways to make the behavior of others conform to social expectations. But to what extent are we willing to go in helping to establish conformity to social rules? Would we obey a request to impose conformity even if we did not agree with the values being imposed? What if the request came from a religious or political authority?

Questions such as these are not easy to answer. Although most of us think there is a reasonable limit beyond which we would not go in obeying authority, our actual limits may be much less "reasonable" than we imagine. In a startling series of experiments, social psychologist Stanley Milgram (1964) revealed that the majority of people are likely to be far more obedient to authority and far more willing to punish others for trivial transgressions than they would like to believe.

Over 1,000 people from diverse social, economic, and educational backgrounds took part in Milgram's experiments. Each subject was told that he or she was participating in an effort to evaluate the effects of punishment on learning. The "learner" was usually a jovial, middle-aged man attempting to solve relatively simple word-association problems. The punishment, delivered by the subject, was an electric shock. Seated before the "shock equipment," the subject was shown 30 switches numbered from 15 to 450 volts, and labeled: slight shock; moderate shock; strong shock; very strong shock; intense shock; extreme intensity shock; danger: severe shock; and XXX. The subject was told that the learner was connected to the machine (this in fact was *not* true) and was instructed to deliver shocks of increasing intensity whenever the learner made an error. The learner, who was actually a confederate in the experiment, pretended to feel the pain of the shocks. He responded first with grunts and groans at low voltages, then with requests to stop the experiment at higher voltages, and finally with hysterical pleas for help at intense voltages. When the subject questioned the advisability of continuing the experiment, the psychologist in charge (an authoritative figure usually dressed in a white laboratory coat) responded with polite but firm commands such as "Please go on" or "You have no other choice; you must go on." Some of the subjects were so emotionally overcome by the sounds of the anguished victim that they actually began to cry—while they obediently continued to increase the voltage.

While the maximum shock the participants were willing to deliver to the learner varied, the average was generally in the "intense shock" or "extreme intensity shock" ranges. Fully 62 percent of the subjects delivered the potentially lethal 450 volts. Why? What could possibly account for the willingness of so many people to inflict such severe punishment on an innocent person simply because they were told to do so? Perhaps after millennia of urban life, our bureaucratic institutions have habituated us to overlook the wider implications of our actions, and to perform with few questions the specific tasks we are assigned. In any case, the excuse "I was only obeying orders" is clearly not limited only to morally weak or neurotic individuals. As Milgram observes:

> . . . ordinary people, simply doing their jobs and without any particular hostility on their part, can become agents in a terrible destructive process. Moreover, even when the destructive effects of their work become patently clear, and they are asked to carry out actions incompatible with fundamental standards of morality, relatively few people have the resources needed to resist authority. (1974:6)

In a highly stratified state society such as our own, where a large percentage of our efforts to shape the behavior of others are undertaken at the implicit or explicit direction of political and religious authorities, Milgram's findings are particularly significant.

nalized. Social rules prescribing proper table manners, subjects for polite conversation, or which parts of the body should be clothed in public are usually accepted and followed with very little deviation. Most people would feel some degree of private shame or embarrassment to do otherwise. In effect, socialization turns individuals into their own policemen.

Social Pressure

When people venture over the boundaries of the rules of their society, social pressure is often exerted to bring them back into line. Such pressure can be very subtle or equally blunt, but regardless of the particular form it takes, social pressure can be a highly successful means of social control. An icy stare or a biting remark is often sufficient to convince a person that it is preferable to follow the rules.

Among the Kapauku Papuans of New Guinea, the public reprimand is a rather blunt but nonetheless quite effective instrument of social pressure. A reprimand sometimes lasts for days at a time, with different members of the community intermittently hurling angry

Among the Huli of Papua, New Guinea, the public reprimand is the punishment for adultery. The adulterous wife here is shown being forced to the ground while her husband's kinspeople scream insults and point at her. The reprimand lasts for several hours and may include, in addition to beatings, other forms of physical punishment.
(Robert Glasse)

Several subtle functions of social control are served by the privately owned coffee house in the Jordanian village of Kufr al Ma. For one, disputes can be settled here informally before they escalate. In addition, obligations are tacitly acknowledged, since those who accept the hospitality of the host — already an important figure by virtue of his having a coffee house — agree to support him in a general sense. Finally, status in the village is made overt through the ritual of the meal: everyone refuses to eat at first, until the host goes around and literally drags people up to serve themselves — in the order of the "biggest" first, on down to the least powerful men in the village. (Richard T. Antoun)

reproaches at the hapless offender. For the person being reprimanded, it is a humiliating ordeal; the shame he experiences is so deep that the Kapauku consider the public reprimand a worse punishment than anything else but death (Pospisil, 1958).

Satire and Gossip The Kapauku, like people everywhere, dislike being publicly ridiculed or having their misdeeds broadcast to others. This is why satire and gossip are such powerful social pressures in many societies. In the Arab village of Kufr al Ma in Jordan, for example, satire has been honed to a sharp edge in an elaborate system of nicknaming (Antoun, 1968). The system is organized in such a way as to indicate the degree of dissatisfaction caused by the violation of social expectations. The hierarchy of terms begins with neutral occupational names, proceeds to slightly ironic names based on personal habits, and culminates in distinctly pejorative names based on physical defects and illegitimate status. Because no one in the village is exempt from this form of satire, the system serves to reassert the fact that all members of the community are equally subject to social control and evaluation.

The behavior the villagers most often criticize through nicknaming is slander and backbiting, behaviors that are also expressly condemned in the Koranic verses and traditions. The satirical use of such epithets as "gossipper" or "busybody," then, serves to humiliate a person who has violated an important social rule. As with most of the nicknames, however, the term meaning "gossipper" is actually ambiguous and can be taken to mean a diversity of other things. As a result of this ambiguity, the system takes on an increased sophistication, with villagers being able to soften or intensify their dissatisfaction to fit the type and extent of the offense.

Gossip can be a similarly sophisticated and potent device for deterring inappropriate behavior. Indeed, among the Makah Indians of the Pacific Northwest, gossip is an important part of everyday life. The Makah are a small group of approximately four hundred people intent on maintaining their uniqueness within a larger, surrounding white culture. In line with this goal, people focus a good deal of attention on achieving status within the society, on gaining recognition as a "true" Makah. The importance of this goal is clearly reflected in the Makahs' fondness for gossiping about one another's social status, or lack thereof. Thus, when a person behaves in a manner that in any way conflicts with the society's values, he runs the risk of being derided in gossip that challenges his claims to status (Gluckman, 1963).

Shunning and Ostracism Social pressure can also take the form of shunning and ostracism. Being ignored is generally a painful experience, and the threat of it can often be a very effective means of social control. The Mzab of southern Algeria have long been aware of the potential uses of shunning and ostracism. Female religious leaders among the Mzab have the authority to impose a period of complete isolation known as *tebreya* on women who have violated community rules. The sanction is particularly strong against women who have violated rules related to sexual conduct and religious duties. In such instances, the offender is excluded from public ceremonies and is denied customary religious rituals if she dies before being released from *tebreya*. Furthermore, other women are forbidden to speak with the offender or associate with her in any way throughout the period of isolation, which can last as long as two years. When the *tebreya* is ended, a formal ceremony is required to reinstate the offender in her social roles and relationships. Among the Mzab the isolation imposed through the *tebreya* is supplemented by other informal mechanisms of social control such as gossip and scandal (Farrag, 1971).

Examples of shunning and ostracism in our own society can be seen in the practices of lobstermen along the Maine coast. To go lobstering in this area, one must first be accepted by the established lobstermen; until that time, newcomers must expect to be met with hostility and harassment. A newcomer will encounter particular difficulties if he happens to set traps in an established lobsterman's territory: he will not only have to deal with being ignored, but he may well discover one morning that his fishing gear has been destroyed (Acheson, 1972).

Vengeance In those instances where the informal controls of satire and ostracism either do not apply or do not succeed, pressure can be brought to bear in the form of threatened vengeance. The Tonga of northern Rhodesia, for example, have no formal political institutions directly involved in social control. Instead, order is maintained by organized "vengeance groups" whose members join together to uphold their common rights and obligations and to avenge injuries to one another. Membership in a vengeance group is determined by descent from a common ancestress. The members within a group are also bound in a complex network of additional loyalties, however; individuals are responsible to the members of their paternal clan, to both the paternal and the maternal clans of their marriage partners, to the individuals who are herding their cattle or for whom they are herding cattle, and finally to their fellow villagers. Each of these ties cuts across the others, so that individuals attempting to apply vengeance are faced with counterclaims by other groups. Opponents in one set of relationships, in other words, are allies in another. The existence of crosscutting loyalties exerts strong social pressure on vengeance groups to seek fair settlements and avoid the social disruption resulting from the use of force (Colson, 1957).

But at times, violent settlements of disputes do erupt. This is the case of the blood feud, which usually pits kin groups or families against each other with revenge the principal motive. A typical blood feud starts when a member of one family is murdered. The victim's relatives then seek to avenge the crime, attempting to kill the murderer or one of his close relatives. Blood feuds are common among the Jivaro Indians of South America. When a person is killed, it is not simply a matter that the family wants justice; obtaining an eye for an eye is a religious obligation. But those seeking revenge must take only one life. To do more creates general indignation and transfers the blood guilt (Karsten, 1923).

The threat of vengeance can also come from supernatural forces. For example, Lugbara mythology teaches that when a person brings shame on his house (by acting disrespectfully towards kinsmen, for example), the ghosts of his ancestors will hear the village elders grumbling and bring sickness to him (Middleton, 1960). Similarly, the Bible and the Koran define rules for behavior in light of man's relationship to God, and provide vivid illustrations of the rewards for following and penalties for breaking thses rules. In giving social rules a supernatural dimension, religion translates conformity into righteousness, nonconformity into sin. It is one thing to fear ridicule or ostracism; another, to fear divine retribution.

Formal Means of Social Control

Few societies can function with only informal means of social control. Sooner or later in the course of daily life, conflicts and disputes between individuals will erupt, or acts will be committed that are viewed as threatening to the entire community. Such events are the inevitable result of human beings living together. Of course, the extent of conflict varies. Among the Zuni, for example, controversy of any sort is so strongly disapproved of by society that conflicts and disputes come to the surface only rarely. But the Zuni are by far the exception. In most societies, conflicts and disputes are a normal part of everyday existence. And when such problems arise, most societies have established some kind of formalized action that can be taken either to resolve the dispute before it becomes too heated or to deter the offender before he disrupts the fabric of social life.

Law and the Legal Process

Without some formal means of social control, disputes or retaliation for wrongs committed could get out of hand. The Andaman Islanders, for example, appear to have virtually no formal means of resolving conflicts, no established mechanism for deterring a person who violates some important social norm. When disputes do arise, as they frequently do, considerable violence may result. A person who feels aggrieved because a wrong or injury has been inflicted on him will take whatever retaliatory action he thinks is appropriate. He may physically assault the alleged offender or destroy his property. In fact, if he is sufficiently enraged, he may destroy not only the property of his adversary, but whoever else's property that unfortunately happens to get in the way.

The Andaman Islanders have no conventional procedures for intervening in such incidents and resolving the dispute, no formal methods of punishing the wrongdoers or of compensating any injured parties, nor even any systematic way of making sure that the whole affair will not simply flair up again. In this sense, the Andamanese can be said to have no procedures comparable to what we call a legal process (Redfield, 1964).

In our own and other industrialized societies, in contrast, the legal process is highly developed and ever present. The rules of our society are recorded in scores of legal texts, and their interpretation is handed over to specialists. When disputes between individ-

State apparatus rather than local mechanisms may exert social control even in rural communities spatially and culturally remote from the central bureaucracy. The armed policemen present at this peasant wedding in Turkey symbolize the integration of peasant communities into the larger political system. (Daniel G. Bates)

uals arise, the parties will quite routinely seek settlement and redress in a court of law. Similarly, when an act is committed that is considered threatening to society itself, our legal machinery moves into action to find the wrongdoer and punish him for his crime.

Between these two extremes lies a broad range of formal procedures for settling disputes and righting wrongs that can justifiably be called "legal" mechanisms. The legal mechanisms of technologically simpler societies are of course quite different from our own. In our own society, for example, many laws are codified, while in simpler societies the legal tradition is largely oral. Our own society, too, has judges, formal officeholders who are vested with the authority to make legal rulings and impose sentences; many simpler societies, in contrast, have no such authoritative positions, no person capable of forcing a settlement. Yet despite these and many other obvious differences, the underlying processes involved in formally settling disputes or righting serious offenses can be seen as nearly universal. Almost all societies have the basic ingredients—rules, procedures of inquiry, methods of mediation or adjudication, and modes of redress—which are in essence what is meant by "law" (Epstein, 1967). In this sense, almost every human society has some kind of legal process.

Rules Conflicts and disputes can arise for any number of reasons, but underlying all such incidents is a sense of grievance—a feeling that one's rights have been violated and an injury or injustice inflicted. Such a sense of grievance of course necessitates the existence of a set of fairly well-accepted rules on which expectations of behavior are based. Rules—assumptions about what is right, good, and proper—are found in every human society and are the conceptual basis for what is known as law.

Rules, however, do not establish who is right and who is wrong in a particular case. Statements of norms are somewhat vague: they are not so much explicit regulations concerning what people should and should not do, as implicit notions about what constitutes proper behavior. Determining how a particular rule applies to a given situation is therefore difficult. And to compound this difficulty, conflicting rules will frequently apply to the same case. Thus disputants can use and manipulate different norms to argue their respective cases and attempt to prove that each is in the right.

A dispute that arose among the Ndendeuli of southern Tanzania involving a claim for additional bridewealth illustrates how different rules can be manipulated to support both sides of a case. Rajabu, a young man from the village of Ligomba, returned home after having been gone for more than a year as a migrant worker. Upon his arrival, he presented his father-in-law, Sedi, with a blanket and a length of inexpensive cloth. Sedi commended Rajabu on the gifts, but several days later demanded that Rajabu also make an additional bridewealth payment with the money he had earned while abroad. In the legal proceedings that followed, Rajabu argued that Sedi was proving himself to be a bad father-in-law by making additional demands for bridewealth. He claimed that Sedi had previously acknowledged that all bridewealth payments had been completed and was breaking his word by making new demands at this time. Moreover, he, Rajabu, needed the money to repay a loan from his cousin so that the cousin would be able to pay his own bridewealth; this was the obligation of a good kinsman. Sedi countered these arguments by denying that he had ever acknowledged completion of bridewealth. He maintained that as a father-in-law he had a right to a larger gift from Rajabu than he had received so far and that Rajabu had an obligation not only to his cousin but also to his wife's family (Gulliver, 1969).

Arguments and counterarguments such as these do not sound unfamiliar; they are part of the legal process in our own society, as in nearly all others. In this case, the primary question was one of defining obligation: what kinds of obligations existed, to whom were they owed, and what were their limits? Each party to the dispute appealed to various social rules requiring different obligations, and each manipulated rules to show that they required some other obligation than his adversary claimed.

The manipulation of norms has interesting consequences for a legal system, for it is through such manipulation that rules are clarified and redefined, and that change in the law may eventually occur. The way in which manipulation of rules can lead to a change in law is well illustrated by the case of Awiitigaaj, a village headman of the Kapauku Papuans.

Awiitigaaj, a clever man well-versed in the rules of his society, had fallen in love and eloped with his third paternal parallel cousin, an act specifically tabooed and punishable by death. The couple fled to the forest to avoid the punishment destined to be inflicted by their kinsmen. Awiitigaaj, however, guessed that if they could hold out long enough, the relatives would eventually give up the search and the girl's father would agree to accept a very large bride price, an act that would automatically validate the marriage. Awiitigaaj's guess was correct—the search was eventually given up, and the girl's father offered to accept the bride price. The young groom was not yet through, however, for he had concocted a way to avoid paying the bride price. Awiitigaaj knew that according to Kapauku law his wife's relatives could collect compensation either in money or in blood, but not both. Therefore he informed his own kinsmen that he had no money with which to pay the bride price and that it was therefore up to them to do so. As he knew would happen, his relatives refused to pay, which prompted the girl's relatives to attack them—just as Awiitigaaj had hoped they would. Because the attack absolved Awiitigaaj's relatives from their obligation to pay the bride price, the incestuous union was automatically validated. Then, to further legitimize his act, Awiitigaaj took one more step. Having already impressed the villagers with his cleverness and apparent legal expertise, he introduced a new ruling making it legal for cousins to marry as long as they were at least third cousins. After some debate, the law was agreed upon, and Awiitigaaj had the pleasure of seeing it extend to other members of the tribe (Pospisil, 1969).

Procedures of Inquiry When a grievance arises and it is felt that an injury or injustice has been inflicted, the first step is to establish who did what to whom. Perhaps one of the oldest means of determining guilt is the taking of an *oath*. Among the Comanche Indians of the nineteenth century, for instance, responsibility and guilt in cases concering adultery were determined in a ceremony known as "sun-killing." In this ceremony, the suspicious husband would address the sun with his accusations and the wife in turn would take an oath that she was innocent. The couple would then wait for the verdict to be handed down by the powers invoked. If the wife was innocent, nothing would happen; if she was guilty, death or disease was believed bound to result (Hoebel, 1940).

Another procedure of inquiry is the *ordeal*. Generally, ordeals entail having the accused, or a representative of the accused, undergo some form of physical stress, with innocence being determined by the degree of damage or pain suffered. Among the Ifugao, for instance, a person accused of a crime is required to retrieve a pebble from the bottom of a potful of rapidly boiling water, then replace it. People who are innocent can presumably perform this act much more slowly and with less pain than those who are guilty (Barton, 1967). A similar ordeal was prevalent in medieval Europe. In this case, however, after the accused party had pulled the pebble from the boiling water, his hand was wrapped in a cloth. When the cloth was removed after three days, a verdict was given on the basis of the damage done to the hand (Tewksbury, 1967).

Divination is a third procedure of inquiry largely dependent on some form of supernatural assistance. Usually diviners attempt to explain occurrences or determine guilt entirely through relevations. But among certain peoples, diviners make use of both mystical and nonmystical elements. Among the Ndembu of Zambia, for instance, a diviner's inquiries into such things as misfortune and death include both the interpretation of symbolic objects and the formal interrogation of the appropriate people (Turner, 1957).

Trials are more rationalistic approaches for inquiring into guilt. Here, the participants are clearly identified, evidence is submitted and evaluated, and witnesses brought forth to testify. It is interesting to note, however, that even in our own society, where court proceedings and the rules of evidence are highly regulated and oriented toward eliciting "the facts," a witness must first swear to God that he or she will tell the truth—presumably having to suffer both supernatural and legal consequences if he or she lies.

Methods of Adjudication In our own society, the trial is not only a procedure of inquiry but also a method of adjudicating or deciding a case. It involves a contest over the interpretation and application of laws in particular situations. Some method for deciding a case, comparable in aim if not in form to our own trial system, is found in nearly every society. Typically, such methods involve some sort of hearing conducted according to well-known procedures. The final settlement can be arrived at in any one of several ways. Disputants may, for instance, seek a solution through negotiation, a process that may or may not be mediated by an impartial third party. Or they may state their case in the presence of an adjudicator, someone whose job it is to "hand down" a decision. There are numerous variations on these basic themes both within and among societies, variations that in a very general sense can be seen as falling under the categories of "informal" and "formal."

The process of informal adjudication is seen among the Ndendeuli of southern Tan-

The king's palace serves as the court of law for the Akure of western Nigeria. Here the king, after consultation with his palace advisors and court elders, renders judgment as to the guilt or innocence of the defendant. (Marc & Evelyne Bernheim/Woodfin Camp)

zania, who have neither courts nor judges and arbitrators. Each party to a dispute relies instead on an ad hoc group of neighbors and kinsmen. The function of these groups is to advise the parties, speak on their behalf, and assist them in the complex process of negotiating a settlement satisfactory to all concerned. Generally, the disputes are heard in someone's home, perhaps on the verandah, and anyone present is allowed to speak. In those instances in which a mediator is present, his role is minimal. The settlements are invariably compromises based not only on the relevant social rules, but on the bargaining strengths of principals and supporters and the effect a settlement would have on the day-to-day relationships in the community. Because the adjudication process is an integral part of the larger social order, the discussion often rambles far from the specific grievances at hand to encompass the broadest possible base for settlement (Gulliver, 1969).

The Lozi tribe of northern Rhodesia, by contrast, have a highly formal court system that also serves as an administrative body through its power to enforce decisions. In the formal proceedings, the plaintiff states his case in full detail, followed by the defendant and by witnesses for both parties. Because there are no lawyers, the "judges" then cross-examine aggressively (much as our own counsels do), arrive at a decision based on the evidence, and deliver an exposition of the Lozi law in support of their decision. Because members of a Lozi community are interrelated in a number of different ways, the judges frequently go beyond the narrow issues raised in the case and focus instead on the complete history of the relations between the litigants. In so doing, they increase their chances of arriving at a solution that considers all the relevant rules and expectations and will promote rather than hinder reconciliation (Gluckman, 1967).

Some societies, such as the Kpelle of central Liberia, have both formal and informal proceedings, which tend to be appropriate for different kinds of cases. Formal adjudication takes place in a court where procedures are basically coercive and authoritarian. Because of its somewhat "harsh" tone, the court seems better suited for disputes in which reconciliation is not of primary importance. When reconciliation is important, however, the informal meetings, or "moots," are better suited. These proceedings take place in a home, where the complainants sit among a group of kinsmen and interested neighbors and before a mediator. Unlike the rigid structure of the courtroom, the structure of the moot is relatively loose, with people mixing freely and both sides being able to fully state their case and question each other and anyone else present. After all of the evidence has been given, the group as a whole determines who is in the right. The proceedings then close with the "guilty" party making a public apology and giving token gifts to the wronged party and the "winner" reciprocating with small gifts of acceptance (Gibbs, 1967).

Modes of Redress Once it has been determined that a person's or group's rights have been impinged upon and responsibility for the deed has been determined — through whatever procedures of inquiry and adjudication — the final step in the judicial process is to redress the breach. As with all of the other elements of law, modes of redress, of "righting a wrong," vary from society to society as well as within a single society. Indeed, few are the societies in which the remedy for a particular offense is precisely established in advance. In our own society, for example, the courts respond to public drunkenness in a variety of ways, depending on the person and situation involved. People who are often arrested for drunkenness are aware of this flexibility and manipulate the facts of the case whenever they can to avoid being put in jail. Such people know, for instance, that if they can prove they have a job or an offer of one, they will generally receive less severe treatment. Similarly, they know that it is possible to beat the charge if they can "justify" their behavior by pointing to extenuating circumstances or can prove that family ties would be endangered if they were put in jail (Spradley, 1974).

Regardless of the particular issues involved in a case, modes of redress generally fall into one of three categories—restitution, punishment, or counseling. Restitution typically occurs when it is agreed that a person has been wrongfully deprived of something he owns or is entitled to. In our own society, for example, the damages awarded in, say, an auto accident is a case of redress by restitution—the injured party is compensated for the losses he has and will incur. Restitution, of course, need not involve large sums of money, as Nader observed in a courtroom in the Mexican town of Ralu'a. The case was quite simple: a truck, while passing through a crowded marketplace, had collided with a basket of chiles, bruising some of its contents; the merchant accused the truckdriver of negligence, while the truckdriver claimed that the merchant had been careless in placing the basket too close to the roadway. The municipal president ruled that the driver was essentially at fault and must pay the merchant for all the chiles that had been damaged. The basket was brought to the courtroom, its contents emptied on the floor, and the damaged chiles separated and weighed. Their value came to precisely three pesos, which the driver agreed to pay. The merchant, satisfied with the restitution, left the courtroom with the damaged merchandise still strewn on the floor (Nader, 1969).

Punishment of the wrongdoer is another mode of redress which can take many forms. In our own society, incarceration is a common means of punishment, but many simpler societies, lacking prisons and jailers, find incarceration impractical. Such societies may inflict other forms of punishment instead. Frequent means of punishment, for example, are fines or the seizure of property. Among the Ifugao, seizure of property is considered the appropriate punishment for such crimes as theft, malicious killing of animals, or arson when the offender refuses to voluntarily pay the assessed fine (Barton, 1919). Corporal punishments are also common. Among the Kapauku, beatings with sticks are administered for a wide range of offenses from theft to refusal to pay a debt; incest, murder, sorcery, and violation of a taboo are punishable by death (Pospisil, 1958). Banishment is another form of punishment that in some societies is tantamount to execution. In ancient Bali, a couple found guilty of incest were banished from their village forever and forced to fend for themselves in the dangerous jungle (Belo, 1936).

Counseling is a third mode of redress, particularly applicable in disputes where reconciliation is important, such as domestic quarrels or conflicts among kinsmen. Among the Kpelle, for example, reconciliation and counseling are the primary goals of the moot, as Gibbs clearly demonstrates in describing a case concerning an ousted co-wife. Wama Nya, the husband in the case, had inherited his dead brother's widow, Yokpo. When Yokpo moved into Wama Nya's house, violent conflict had ensued, particularly between Yokpo and Wama Nya's first wife, Yua. Wama Nya became increasingly angry with Yokpo and began accusing her of various misdeeds: harvesting rice without his knowledge, staying out late at night, and having lovers. After one incident in which Wama Nya and Yokpo became engaged in a physical struggle, the husband took a basin of water and "washed his hands of her." Yokpo, of course, denied her husband's allegations of wrongdoing, charging that Wama Nya had physically assaulted her and thrown her out of the house at the jealous instigation of Yua, her co-wife.

The parties to the dispute were at an impasse when the moot began, but as the proceedings unfolded, and each had a chance to air his or her feelings in the presence of concerned relatives and friends, all were gradually reeducated in their social obligations. Yua, for instance, discovered that her neighbors did not think her jealousy of Yokpo was justified, and she came to realize that the way in which she had treated her co-wife had contributed greatly to the family strife. Wama Nya, too, with the help of his neighbors, came to accept the fact that his suspicions of Yokpo were false and were not conducive to harmonious marital relations. Thus, by the end of the moot, all parties had been effectively counseled in their proper roles and marital obligations, and all were willing to forget their past differences and try to live together peacefully.

Although a society's formal means of social control are often the most overt, they are not the only procedures for reducing conflicts and settling disputes. Every society has a range of both formal and informal mechanisms of social control. As we said earlier, the norms that underlie social control mechanisms are often ambiguous; moreover, such mechanisms are never completely effective. Mechanisms of social control do serve to reduce deviance, but they do not eradicate it.

Nor would the elimination of deviance be a socially desirable thing. A certain amount of deviance is as essential to the survival of a society as are rules and expectations. It is also important to realize that social rules are not necessarily agreed upon by all members of a society, nor do mechanisms of social control affect all people equally. Particularly in highly stratified societies, social control mechanisms may be devices used by the rich and powerful to control the lower classes. This charge has been brought against our own mechanisms of social control—both our laws and our legal procedures are said to work to the advantage of the rich and the disadvantage of the poor.

summary

Standards for proper behavior vary widely among cultures, but every society has rules governing behavior and means of enforcing its rules. Rules provide order and a certain amount of predictability in social relationships, essential to the functioning of society. Social rules establish broad guidelines for behavior, but individual interpretation and decision-making bring variation in how the rules are actually followed, or not followed.

Social prescriptions limit the extent to which individual behavior can vary or *deviate*. The concept of deviance varies among societies. Even within a society, the definition of deviance may change according to the situation. Thus, both acts of deviance and the rules they defy are in part culturally defined.

Deviance is unavoidable, given the variation in human behavior; in fact, a certain amount is essential to the survival of society. Deviant behavior and the exclusive pursuit of self-interest are modified by a social system that channels behavior. It also defines deviant behavior and the proper responses to acts of deviance, helping to maintain *social control*. Every society has evolved mechanisms for dealing with deviance. These mechanisms of social control vary but have been broadly classified as formal and informal.

The process of *socialization* is one highly effective informal mechanism of social control. In the process of learning their culture, children learn acceptance and respect for society's rules. They *internalize* these rules and avoid breaking them because the rules exemplify what they believe are the only acceptable behaviors. Thus socialization provides for self-regulatory behavior.

Social pressures—including satire, gossip, and ostracism—are applied when infractions of the rules do occur. When these mechanisms are not applicable or do not succeed, vengeance or threatened vengeance may take place. The threat of vengeance may come not only from human but also from supernatural sources. Social rules assume stronger meanings when they have a supernatural dimension; conformity becomes equated with righteousness, nonconformity with sin.

Few societies can function with only informal mechanisms of control. The conflicts that are an inevitable part of social life often need to be resolved through formal, institutionalized channels. Formal mechanisms resolve disputes before they become violent, or deter an offender before the fabric of social life is threatened.

Law is an almost universal formal mechanism of control. The elements of the legal process—rules, procedures of inquiry, methods of adjudication, and modes of redress—are nearly universal, though they vary widely from one society to another. In our own and other industrialized societies, the legal process is highly developed. Laws are codified, or systematically recorded and preserved. There are specialists who interpret and explain the laws, and elected judges with the authority to make rulings and impose sentences. In technologically simpler societies, the legal tradition is largely oral, and there are no persons with the authority to enforce settlements in disputes.

Rules, or assumptions about what is right or proper, are the universal conceptual basis of law. Rules themselves do not determine who is right or wrong if one person has a grievance against another; because they imply proper behavior, instead of explicitly regulating it, legal rules are often vague. Use and manipulation of the rules or norms is beneficial because it clarifies, redefines, and sometimes changes the laws.

Procedures of inquiry are the first steps in legal action; they establish the grievances of the parties, and hopefully, the guilt. The taking of an *oath* is one of the oldest means of determining guilt. The *ordeal* is another procedure of inquiry, in which the accused suffers some form of physical stress, with innocence or guilt being determined by the degree of pain suffered. *Divination* is largely dependent on supernatural assistance. A diviner determines guilt through revelations, although this procedure can also involve nonmystical elements.

Trials are more rationalistic procedures of inquiry in which witnesses give testimony, and evidence is submitted. The trial is also a *method of adjudication,* or a decision in a dispute. It is a contest over the interpretation and application of laws in a particular situation. In general, a hearing is conducted according to well-known procedures. Settlement is achieved through negotiation, or an adjudicator makes a decision. Methods of adjudication are found in every society; they may be "formal" or "informal." An informal procedure involves mediation between parties and usually reaches compromise decisions. Formal procedures often take place in an established court that has the power to enforce decisions. Each party states its case, and witnesses speak on its behalf.

The final step in the judicial process involves *modes of redress* or actions taken as a result of the decision in a case. Like the other legal processes, modes of redress vary among societies, and within individual societies. Modes of redress fall into three categories—restitution, punishment, and counseling. Restitution involves compensating a wronged party for his losses, not necessarily with large sums of money. Punishment of a wrongdoer can involve incarceration; imposition of a fine; seizure of property; corporal punishment; or banishment. Counseling is applicable especially in situations where reconciliation is important.

Both the formal and informal mechanisms of social control are never entirely effective: they reduce, but do not eradicate, deviance. Further, social rules and mechanisms of social control are not always applied in an egalitarian manner. Especially in highly stratified societies, these mechanisms are often used by one group to control and even to oppress another.

suggested readings

BOHANNAN, P., ED.
1967 *Law and Warfare.* New York: Natural History Press. A collection of essays that provides a broad ethnographic basis for an understanding of the regulation of social conflict.

COHEN, A. K.
1966 *Deviance and Control.* Englewood Cliffs, N.J.: Prentice-Hall. A concise review of the general theories of deviance, including a discussion of the process by which social control and deviance interact and evolve.

COLSON, E.
1974 *Tradition and Contract: The Problem of Order.* Chicago: Aldine. This valuable survey considers the social devices for organizing and regulating affairs in small communities.

MILGRAM, S.
1974 *Obedience to Authority: An Experimental View.* New York: Harper & Row. A controversial experimental study that examines the willingness of individuals to accept control through the simple assertion of authority.

NADER, L., ED.
1965 *The Ethnography of Law. American Anthropologist, Special Publication.* Vol. 67, No. 6, Part 2. Containing papers delivered at a conference on the anthropological study of law, this anthology includes general statements of theory and method, as well as specific case studies.

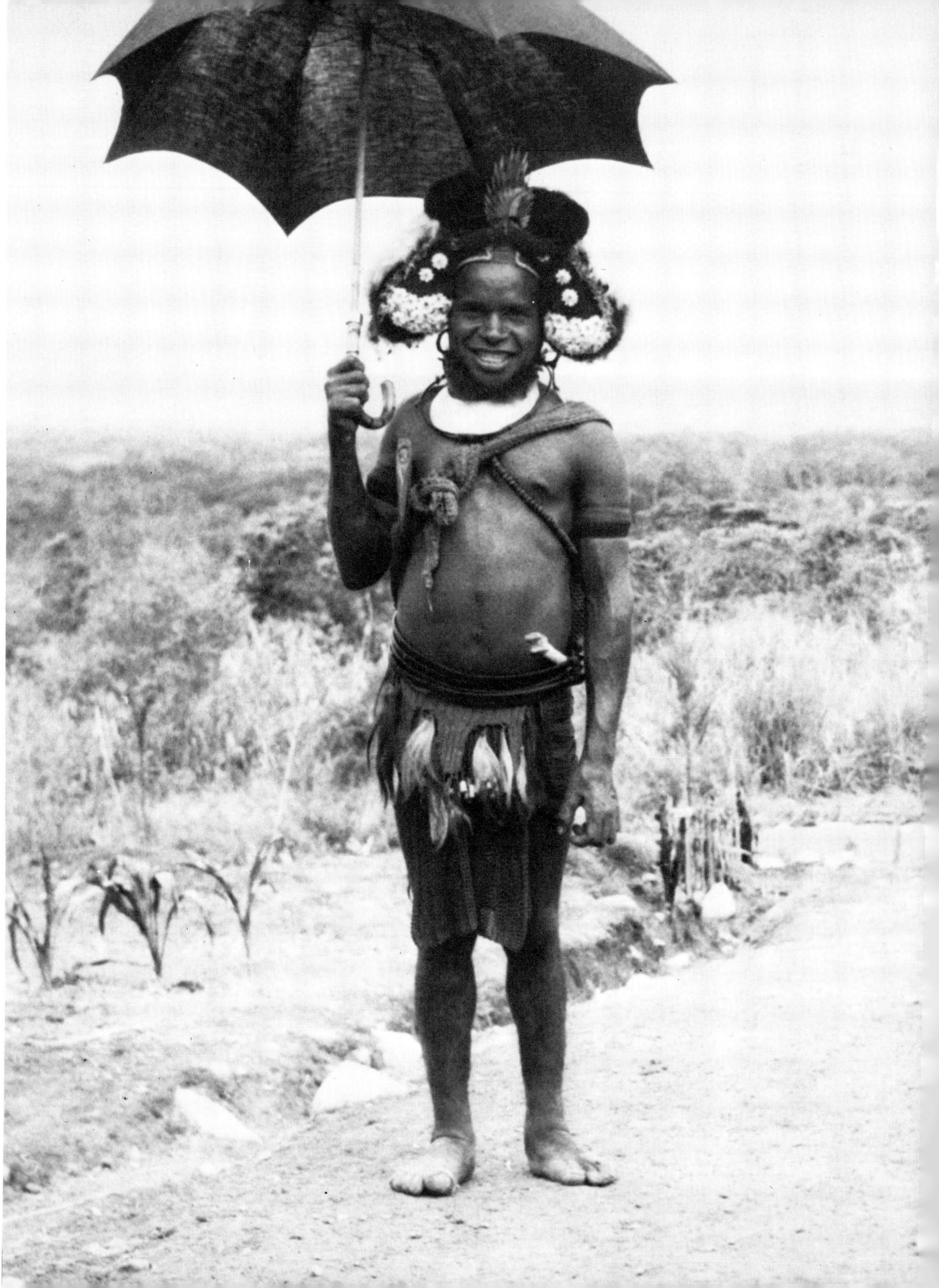

twenty-three
Culture Change and Applied Anthropology

If we could visit North America as it was 1,000 or so years ago, we would find a situation very different from today's. While there would be many millions of native Americans across the continent, their way of life would be quite unlike that of modern Americans. Most people would be living in hunting-gathering bands or agricultural tribes, with occasional populations organized as chiefdoms. Although there would be several large, thriving settlements such as Cahokia near what is now St. Louis and the towns of Chaco Canyon in New Mexico, none would even approach the size of today's cities. And although we would find exchange networks in which resources moved over tens of thousands of square miles, the quantity and diversity of resources would be extremely limited compared to the present.

What has become of these native Americans? Most of the land that once belonged to them has been taken by European immigrants. Some now live on reservations, others in cities or rural communities where they form disadvantaged minorities. Today's native Americans suffer the worst health, dietary, and economic conditions in the country. How and why these drastic changes came about is of interest to all of us. But anthropologists, in attempting to understand the fundamental processes underlying such events, generally focus on more specific problems. They might ask, for example, what happens when people with different technologies compete for land? Or, why might a single native American population become divided into two or more distinct groups as a result of contact with other societies? Cultural evolution, the process by which customary patterns of behavior originate and change in relation to particular environmental conditions, is the body of theory underlying all such questions, and is one of the central focuses of this chapter. We will be examining both *general evolution* — the broad patterns of change that have characterized the development of human "culture," using the term in a very general sense — and *specific evolution* — the patterns of adjustment that people in particular societies make to specific situations and that in turn produce the overall cultural evolutionary patterns we observe. We will discuss this important distinction in greater detail later in this chapter. But first let us examine how anthropologists conceptualize change, and what methods they use to study it.

What Is Change?

Exactly what do anthropologists mean by the term "change"? Initially, the answer to this question may seem easy — change is simply variability in culture and behavior over time. But when one looks at a particular society, it is often difficult to determine whether or not change has occurred. Part of the problem lies in differences in the scope of one's perspective. For example, E. R. Leach (1965) found that political organization among Kachin populations in highland Burma fluctuated between a hierarchically ranked system and an essentially egalitarian one structured around lineages more or less equal in status. Although from a more narrow perspective, variability or change is occurring in this case, from a broader perspective, both patterns of

No society has been unaffected by the spread of Western technology. But the product of mass-production this New Guinea man holds so nonchalantly still strikes a jarring note in a landscape far removed from highly industrialized society. (Robert Glasse)

organization are persistent aspects of Kachin political life. Thus we find that cultural patterns that appear variable from one vantage point may appear quite stable from another, more inclusive one.

The distinction between short-term variability and long-term trends lies at the heart of this seeming paradox. From the first perspective, all societies are changing all of the time as people experiment with new solutions to the daily problems they encounter. Some societies, however, are changing in a direction that over the long run will lead to the point where they began—that is, their short-term changes are cyclical. The political organization of the Kachin is such a case. Other societies, in contrast, are changing in directions that will eventually lead to their being very different than they are at present. While using one level of analysis we may wish to refer to the former condition as stability, it is important to recognize that it is actually no more than another form of change.

One should not conclude from this discussion, however, that people always perceive their cultural traditions to be in a state of flux. Sometimes, particularly in the past, the rate of change has been so slow that people themselves are hardly aware that it is occurring. Nor should we conclude that people have a natural proclivity toward change. In fact, anthropologists have found quite the opposite to be true: there is a marked tendency for human populations to maintain the status quo in their customary patterns of behavior. People do not usually seek and accept change easily, for change always involves inherent risks. But how could this be when we have just said that change is a constant phenomenon in every society? Aren't these two trends inherently contradictory? Most anthropologists think not. Although all societies are changing all of the time in the sense that people are employing different ways of coping with changing circumstances, people everywhere also try to maintain some ties with the past—ties that will help to integrate the old and the new and thus contribute to a kind of social equilibrium. In this sense, there is a tendency toward maintaining stability in all human groups regardless of the constant occurrence of change (Bee, 1974).

Studying Culture Change

As used by anthropologists, the term "culture change" generally refers not to the short-term dynamics of particular cultures but to large-scale alterations in the organization and operation of a society. As we have pointed out, such major changes are likely to be the accumulated product of much smaller changes occurring over a period of years, the final results of which would have been extremely difficult to predict. This creates a basic problem for anthropologists studying change—it is difficult to know where the changes observed on a day-to-day basis are leading unless the time frame of a study is particularly long. For this reason, most anthropological studies of change are retrospective—that is, they attempt to reconstruct the patterns and processes of change after they have occurred. Let us examine some of the methods anthropologists use to collect data on change—their strengths and weaknesses.

Informants, Documents, and "Historicism"

One obvious way to learn about change is to ask informants what life was like in the past, and how and why their world has changed. Some of the best accounts of traditional native American culture are based on long, intensive interviews with old-timers. On occasion, anthropologists also use historical documents for studies of culture change. Of course, journalists and record-keepers can be as selective as storytellers. But by uncovering and comparing numerous sources, a researcher can arrive at a reasonably close approximation of the chronology of change in a population and the reasons for it. For example, Anthony Wallace's (1956) study of revitalization movements, such as the Handsome Lake movement which we discussed in Chapter 20, draws on manuscript journals and diaries as well as published accounts and official

Culture Change and Applied Anthropology 459

statistics. In many instances, however, written records simply do not exist.

Restudies

A second way to investigate change is for an anthropologist to return to the site of a field study some years later, or for another anthropologist to do so. Margaret Mead, for example, went back to the South Pacific Island of Manus twenty-five years after her original study of this isolated, nonliterate, kin-based society. In the interim, Americans had used the island for a military base, bringing with them a whole new set of perceptions, desires, and norms (Mead, 1956). In 1943, Oscar Lewis went to the Mexican village of Tepoztlan, which Robert Redfield had studied seventeen years earlier, and found not the well-integrated, harmonious community Redfield had described, but a violent people, consumed by envy and fear (Redfield, 1955). As we shall see in a moment, however, there are problems with interpreting different findings from original and subsequent studies as an indication of change.

Comparative Studies

A third approach to the study of culture change is based on the systematic comparison of various societies. This general method encompasses several different specific techniques. For instance, some anthropologists have attempted to infer patterns of change

The transition to Western clothing that struck Margaret Mead when she returned to Manus after a 25-year absence no more than hinted at the dramatic and fundamental changes that had taken place in this once-remote island, largely as a result of World War II. Exchanges of shell money and dogs' teeth had given way to participation in a modern money economy; relationships between spouses, in-laws, and age-mates, once burdened with taboos and enforced hostility, had become freer, more egalitarian, and open to expressions of love and affection. (Margaret Mead, *New Lives for Old*, William Morrow, 1956)

from scaled cross-cultural data. First, a selected set of culture traits is arranged in a scale from those that occur most frequently in the sample of societies to those that occur least frequently. In addition, the societies are arranged on a scale from those possessing the fewest of the selected traits to those possessing the most. An evolutionary sequence is then deduced from the scaled data. The traits that occur most frequently are assumed to be the oldest; those that occur least frequently, the most recent. Similarly, a society with many of the given set of traits is believed to be further along some evolutionary trajectory than one with only a few.

Archeology

Archeologists are in an ideal position to study long-term cultural change. Recovering evidence of prehistoric societies and making inferences about cultural evolution based on artifacts and ecological remains is central to their profession. Since the evidence archeologists recover pertains to well over 99 percent of humankind's existence, these data are extremely important to our understanding of change.

Problems in Studying Change

All of these approaches add to our understanding of culture change. None, however, can be relied upon exclusively because each has certain problems that make it less than a completely accurate source. In interviewing informants about the past, for example, it is necessary to remember that memory is a selective process. Over time, most individuals come to believe conventionalized accounts even of events to which they were eyewitnesses, if only because bending the facts makes a better story. Historical documents and accounts do not completely overcome this problem. The story of Columbus discovering America, for instance, is a gross oversimplification of history—yet we still teach this to our children. The American Revolution was not the broadly based, populist uprising described in grammar school texts. A great many settlers resisted or ignored the battle as best they could. But what would we tell an inquisitive, probing outsider about the birth of this nation? In both their verbal and written accounts, people everywhere tend to shape the past to justify the present.

The primary difficulty with restudies as a method of assessing change is that they tend to create the impression that groups move steadily in one direction or another. For example, suppose a researcher returns to a group of people who had depended largely on hunting and gathering ten or fifteen years earlier and finds most have settled down to farming. The fieldworker might assume, logically enough, that dependence on agriculture had increased steadily over the years. But a straight line (steady increase) is only one of many routes from one point to another. It is quite possible that these people tried and abandoned farming several times over the years. If the anthropologist had returned two years earlier, or perhaps two years later, he might have found most people hunting and gathering and assumed their subsistence practices had not changed—again, a logical assumption. Moreover, when different anthropologists conduct the initial and follow-up studies, another problem arises. It is difficult to know whether the apparent differences in their findings reflect cultural changes or simply differences in their theoretical orientations and methods. This problem was probably the primary reason for Lewis's and Redfield's different characterizations of Tepoztlan.

There are also several difficulties with comparative techniques as a method of reconstructing culture change. For instance, making inferences from scaled cross-cultural data, the method we discussed earlier, is based on two questionable assumptions: first, that societies can be described simply on the basis of some cluster of selected traits, and second, that societies acquire but do not lose traits. Moreover, the evolutionary sequence arrived at by such a method is usually just one of many that could explain the patterns of change observed. Societies, in other words, do not always follow exactly the same line of development.

The amount of information we can derive from archeological studies is limited by what can be reconstructed from material remains. Such aspects of past cultures as social organization or symbolic phenomena are difficult (some would say impossible) to infer from the analysis of artifacts and ecological remains. Moreover, archeological studies, like all the methods of studying change we have been discussing, tend to conceptualize change as a series of stages which differ from each other as measured by one or more variables. But this way of viewing change ultimately focuses on stability—the stages or broadly defined periods—and restricts change to the boundaries between these stages. Change becomes not a process but a residual—the difference between stage A and stage B.

Thus, because of the various problems with all of the commonly used methods of studying change, most research incorporates a number of different methods. In the long run, however, anthropologists must find more sophisticated ways of obtaining data on the continual change that characterizes all sorts of cultural phenomena through time. Conceiving of change as a periodic interruption of stability is no longer justifiable given our growing understanding of the dynamics underlying the operation of every society. Anthropologists cannot continue to be satisfied with simply attempting to reconstruct patterns of culture change. Instead, they must try to find ways of conducting studies of change that stretch over many years, yielding precise records of what has transpired over the long run. One interesting development in this area is the information available from satellite scans. Earth satellites are currently gathering data about every part of our world, including data on such aspects of human culture as demographic, settlement, and agricultural patterns. In years to come, these records may prove invaluable to anthropologists studying change. A continuous record of culture change as it is occurring will allow anthropologists to discuss the *processes of change* that lead to major culture *changes*.

Patterns of General Evolution

What have we learned from studies of culture change? In 1970 Raoul Naroll summarized the major patterns of evolution as suggested by cross-cultural studies. We believe that with some additions, these general evolutionary patterns are supported by alternative data bases, especially the archeological record. Various theories about the causes of these patterns and their interrelatedness have been discussed in Chapters 17 through 22. Here we simply want to review the overall trends themselves.

1. *Low to High Energy Capture.* In a general sense White's arguments concerning the relationship between evolution of sociocultural forms and energy capture has received increasing support. As we shall see in Chapters 24 through 29, earlier societies, such as hunting and gathering bands, were able to obtain less energy from a unit of land or labor than can more complex, recent societies.

2. *Generalists to Specialists.* If we focus on the evolution of procurement systems, we find a general pattern of increased diversification. Whether we are discussing the resources themselves or the tools and methods of organization used to exploit them, earlier societies are less diverse than later ones. Moreover, individuals in more recent societies are likely to be involved in a very limited range of the entire set of activities that make up the production process. In other words, they are likely to be specialists rather than generalists.

3. *Wealth Sharing to Wealth Hoarding.* In Chapter 17, we defined egalitarian, ranked, and stratified societies. In general, earlier societies were more egalitarian, while in later societies a smaller and smaller percentage of the population has held a higher and higher percentage of the wealth. In other words, there has been a trend toward greater inequality in access to resources.

4. *Consensual Leadership to Authoritative Leadership.* In Chapter 21 we saw how leadership in band societies is ephemeral, while in state societies, leadership is in the hands of a clearly defined, legally and militarily established elite. Tribes and chiefdoms have patterns of leadership intermediate between these two. Thus there is an evolutionary trend from consensual to authoritative leadership.
5. *Responsible Elites to Exploitative Elites.* This pattern is a joint product of the two we have just discussed. As elites have become increasingly the wealth hoarders in a society and have acquired greater legal and military backing, their need to be responsive to the other members of society has decreased.
6. *Nomadic to Urban.* In every part of the world evolutionary patterns 3, 4, and 5 are associated with the appearance of large population centers or cities. Cities are virtually an exclusive characteristic of state-organized societies and are dominated by a wealthy elite.
7. *Vengeance War to Political War.* In Chapter 21 we discussed the various forms that intersocietal conflict may take. In general, warfare in earlier societies seems to have been undertaken to revenge some wrong committed by another group. In chiefdoms, but especially in states, warfare simply to acquire territory or resources becomes more prevalent.

Anthropologists have attempted to synthesize many of these separate trends by focusing on the increasing *complexity*[1] of societies through the course of evolution. Contrasting "complex" with "simple" societies need not be pejorative if the terms in question are carefully defined. Generally speaking, complexity refers to the number of parts composing a system or a society. Thus the number of individuals in a society is one scale that has been used to measure complexity. The more members in a society, the smaller the proportion of people a given individual will know. Moreover, individuals will know less about many of the people with whom they interact, and they will interact with many people about whom they know nothing at all. Consequently, in societies with many members, there are likely to be fundamental problems with the flow of information, and complex social institutions must compensate for the factors impeding information flow. In talking about complexity, therefore, anthropologists tend to focus on the social institutions themselves. Naroll, for example, has suggested that complexity can be measured by the number of "teams" or "activity groups" in a society—whether religious, social, political, or economic. This measure is based on the assumption that the more activity groups there are in a society, the greater the diversity of situations with which an individual must cope, the greater the need for specific societal mechanisms to integrate these groups.

But regardless of what index we use to measure complexity, it is clear that societies have generally become more complex over the course of human existence. Why, then, has complexity increased? Some anthropologists suggest that complex societies are more adaptable to changing circumstances. Because the diversity of specialized solutions to any problem increases with cultural complexity, so does the probability that a group of people will have at least one solution that works. For example, a pastoral society, highly dependent for its survival on a single species of domesticated animal, would face disaster if its herds should be decimated by disease or drought. In contrast, an industrial society, which employs a greater variety of

---

[1] In using the term "complexity," a cautionary note should be emphasized. Anthropologists have created scales of complexity to provide a relatively firm basis for comparing societies. In other words, societies can be said to differ in complexity according to where they measure on the scale. It is true that at the general evolutionary level, considering as a whole all societies over the course of human existence, cultural evolution has followed the direction of the scale—that is, from simple to complex. But it is a mistake to believe that all societies pass smoothly or uniformly along the scale. And it is also a mistake to equate increasing complexity with "progress" or with improved adaptation.

subsistence strategies, is less likely to be seriously imperiled if one crop fails or if one species of domesticated animal is stricken with disease. Increased complexity, therefore, and the diversification associated with it seem to have survival value. Margalef (1968) has argued that complexity plays a similar role in the evolution of nonhuman animals. It should be pointed out, however, that other anthropologists would argue that because there are more parts composing complex societies, such societies also have more areas where potential problems might arise.

Are There Laws of Evolution?

Given the general evolutionary patterns we have been discussing so far, is it possible to drive general rules or laws that have governed the course of evolution? Some anthropologists think so. David Kaplan has proposed the Law of Cultural Dominance:

That cultural system which more effectively exploits the energy resources of a given environment will tend to spread in that environment at the expense of less effective systems. (In Sahlins and Service, 1960:75)

This is because the more effective system will tend to grow in human numbers, and controlling more resources, it will be better able to compete with other groups in its environment.

Kaplan uses the Law of Cultural Dominance to explain, for example, the spread of agriculture. There have of course been societies, such as certain indigenous populations in the American West, for which hunting and gathering rather than farming was the more effective and preferred subsistence strategy. Nevertheless, in the American West, some of these hunting-gathering groups did adopt agriculture after Europeans arrived. Kaplan suggests this was because the Spanish and others forced their ways on local populations (and that force accounts for most exceptions to the Law of Cultural Dominance).

Coombs's and Plog's (1974) research on the Chumash suggests otherwise. The missionaries in the Santa Barbara area of California were not on particularly good terms with the Spanish military establishment, and themselves lacked the power to force the Chumash to change from hunting and gathering to agriculture. There is no indication that they employed coercion of any kind. Why, then, did the Chumash take up farming? Although they had achieved an effective adaptation to the environment through hunting and gathering, the Chumash had not eliminated seasonal and annual shortages, and in most years some people went hungry. The missionaries arrived with abundant supplies and were able to feed a few converts quite well. While the number of resident converts remained small, the mission system of agriculture seemed more effective than the indigenous system of hunting and gathering. But this proved to be an illusion. In attracting productive adults away from their communities, the priests caused villages to decline. More and more people became dependent on the missions, and as a result, the effectiveness of the missions also declined. Thus hunting and gathering was replaced by agriculture in this case not because the latter was more effective in an absolute sense, nor because of the Spanish military force. When the Spanish agriculturalists interacted with the native hunting-gathering groups, the effectiveness of both procurement systems declined, but that of the agriculturalists less so.

Thus, as long as we read the Law of Cultural Dominance as pertaining to relative rather than absolute effectiveness, and as long as we take into account the interaction between societies and their mutual effects on one another, the law may provide valuable insights. In the Spanish-Chumash case, the system that had become relatively more effective did tend to grow, although both systems were becoming less effective in absolute terms. The Law of Cultural Dominance, therefore, does not indicate that a more effective subsistence pattern will replace a less effective one in every setting.

Carried to an extreme, the specialization that normally underlies effective exploitation of an environment can also be considered a mixed blessing. The more highly specialized

Processes of Change: Baptism of the Chumash Indians

The difference between "change" and "changing" is a subtle but important one. A focus on "changing"—that is, on the *process* of change rather than a more static, before-versus-after view—is likely to yield much more information about the phenomenon under study. Coombs's and Plog's study of the baptism of the Chumash Indians of Southern California in the late eighteenth and early nineteenth centuries is an example. Virtually all of the Chumash were baptized between 1782 and 1804. It is tempting to view this event quite simply—the non-Christian Chumash hunter-gatherers became Christian agriculturalists—and to search for fairly straightforward causes such as Spanish military might or the attractiveness of agriculture, a seemingly more effective subsistence strategy. But such an approach overlooks a great deal of what actually occurred.

Using data on the baptism of the Chumash and agricultural yields at the mission, Coombs and Plog are able to identify three separate patterns of change. First, there is the pattern in the overall rate of baptism, which may be represented as a sigmoid or S-shaped curve. At first the rate was slow; then it increased rapidly for a period of time, after which it slowed again. Such a pattern is typical when an innovation is adopted in a finite group. In this instance, the pattern was reinforced by the Spanish practice of baptizing the most productive Chumash age groups first. This led to a collapse of the native villages and a rapid increase in the baptism rate, followed by a lower rate when few Chumash remained unbaptized.

But within this overall pattern in the rate of baptism there is another pattern having to do with yearly fluctuations. Substantial year-to-year variations in the number of baptisms correlate significantly with the size of the harvest at the mission. The better the harvest, the greater the number of Chumash the mission could support, the more Indians were baptized.

Finally, there are two seasonal patterns closely related to the ability of the mission fathers to predict the success of the coming harvest, to what those predictions were, and also to variations in the size of the local Chumash food supply. In years when the fathers expected a good harvest, the rate of baptism began to increase during the winter months, reached a peak during the early summer, and then declined. This seasonal pattern, beginning with the winter increase in baptisms, was largely due to the fact that winter is the rainy season in southern California and the first point in the agricultural cycle when predictions about the future harvest can be made. In addition, winter was also the time of year when the Chumash local food supply was likely to be substantially depleted or entirely gone, so during winter the Indians were more willing to come to the mission to be baptized. In contrast, during years when the winter conditions indicated a poor harvest the following fall, there was no seasonal increase in the baptism rate.

Thus, by focusing on processes of change, we find that much more was involved in the baptism of the Chumash than the simple effort to convert them to Christianity. While the goal of the Spanish was to convert the Chumash, the fathers at the mission employed a complex calculus involving the relation between human numbers and food supply in making decisions about when and how many Indians to baptize. Although we may deplore much of the behavior of European colonizers (the Chumash, for example, were eventually exterminated), at least in this one area of interaction they showed concern for the welfare of the indigenous peoples.

an organism is, the more effectively it exploits the environment, the greater its chances of survival and growth—as long as the environment remains stable. But a finely adapted animal is committed to a particular way of life, entrenched in a specific ecological groove, and hence more vulnerable than other, less specialized animals to environmental change. The same is true of societies. We can see this in what happened in the Near East several thousand years ago. Once people had made the transition to agriculture and earlier food resources were no longer available, once populations had grown to a certain level and new forms of government based on dominance and inequality had taken over, turning back would have been extremely difficult because many former options had been eliminated. Past responses to a particular set of circumstances tend to structure what future responses to changing circumstances will be. The more specialized the solution a group finds to a given problem, the less flexibility it will have in coping with problems in the future, and the more likely that the solutions it does come up with will not be major evolutionary breakthroughs.

Elman Service (1971) calls this the Law of Evolutionary Potential: the more specialized an organism or society is, the less likely that it will be the source of important evolutionary changes. Thus "an advanced form does not normally beget the next stage of advance; . . . the next stage begins in a different line" (p. 34). There are numerous examples. The Egyptians, who had invented a complex system of hieroglyphics, did not create the phonetic alphabet; Mediterranean peoples who lacked such a formal system of writing did. England, which launched the Industrial Revolution, did not become the most efficient mass producer; countries that were relatively "primitive" when England was industrializing —Germany, America, and later Japan—did.

It is this awareness of the paradoxes of evolution that distinguishes contemporary research on cultural change from many early evolutionary theories that assumed cultural evolution is linear and cumulative. Although many anthropologists disagree that the Law of Cultural Dominance and the Law of Evolutionary Potential are laws at all, the effort to find such evolutionary patterns is an important thrust in most contemporary studies of culture change. However, other anthropologists argue that regularities in patterns of change should not be sought at the *general* evolutionary level of very broad cultural trends but rather in the *specific* adjustments of groups to their natural and social environments, adjustments that long-term trends retrospectively summarize. In the following section, therefore, we will turn to the topic of specific evolution.

Specific Evolution

In the preceding pages, we have scanned tens of thousands of years of human existence, focusing on the broad patterns of culture change that emerge. To do so, we had to ignore the hesitations and retreats, the sudden burst of creativity, the humdrum daily activities of millions of people who had no notion that they were involved in anything so momentous as the transition from hunting and gathering to agriculture, for example. In this section we attempt to rectify this omission by narrowing in on the specifics of cultural change. Research into specific evolution (the evolution of specific cultures) suggests that the patterns we observe in general evolution are the result of myriad short-term adaptations to changing environments, contacts between people of different cultures, and individual creativity and opportunism. Some of these innovations proved successful: the people who practiced them grew in numbers and/or the innovations were copied by other groups. In this sense, general evolutionary studies are summaries of what worked in solving particular problems. Why certain innovations worked can only be understood at the specific evolutionary level. We will consider the nature and source of innovations and the environmental factors, both natural and social, that affect them.

Innovation

In Chapter 22 we discussed the case of Awiitigaaj, the Kapauku headman who eloped with a member of his clan and thereby began a major reform in his society's definition of exogamy. Why did Awiitigaaj risk death to marry a relative? Publicly, he proclaimed the virtues of free choice in marriage (except between parallel first cousins on the male side of the family). Privately he confided, quite simply, "I liked her; she was beautiful." Pospisil suggests other reasons why Awiitigaaj "got away with" incest. Whether he realized it or not, he had come up with a solution to serious political problems. Awiitigaaj's clan, the Ijaaj, was surrounded by hostile groups who considered them upstarts (they were relatively recent immigrants) and resented their prosperity. Although they had formed confederacies and exchanged women with these groups, relations remained tenuous. On numerous occasions Ijaaj fathers had not been able to collect full bride prices for their daughters; non-Ijaaj wives had betrayed their husbands; no fewer than eleven wars had been fought over divorces in recent memory. Marrying within the clan, as Awiitigaaj did, solved these problems (Pospisil, 1958).

This example is indicative of the conditions surrounding most innovations. It would be inaccurate to attribute to Awiitigaaj a completely conscious and rational role in the innovation or its success. To some extent he was acting out of personal self-interest. But consciously or unconsciously the existing political problems influenced his willingness to take the risk.

In previous chapters we have mentioned the importance to the survival of all societies of achieving a balance between social rules and deviance. It is in the area of innovation that deviance is essential. When certain members of a society violate a social rule and their actions prove successful in resolving some problem they are called entrepreneurs or inventors rather than deviants. Thus most innovations are not solely a matter of cool, careful calculation, but also of serendipity.

Nevertheless, considerable attention has been given to the social and psychological characteristics of innovators. For example, Everett Rogers (1969), studying patterns of innovation in rural villages in Colombia, attempted to discover the characteristics of the more innovative members of these communities. Rogers found that innovators were more literate, listened to the radio and read newspapers more, and made more trips to the city. They were also less fatalistic than noninnovators—less prone to believe that people have no control over their lives—and more empathetic—able to project themselves into new and different roles. Innovators, too, tended to be larger landowners, perhaps because wealth permits experimentation, perhaps because experimentation leads to wealth.

While Rogers was able to identify several of the personal characteristics innovators had in common, it was much more difficult for him to use this data to explain why change occurred. He had more success explaining why traditional villages remained traditional than why some villages were modernizing. This was because the success of innovation depends not simply on its occurrence but on its acceptance, and acceptance is very much a matter of the surrounding situation. As Table 23-1 indicates, our historic records show that many important innovations have been introduced simultaneously in different places. (How many times these same innovations were made but were not recorded because they had no immediate utility is impossible to estimate.) This leads to the conclusion that the introduction and acceptance of innovations is not a random process. Consequently, the current trend in studies of cultural innovation is away from a focus on the psychological characteristics of innovators and toward a focus on the conditions under which innovations are adopted and then become routine. All people innovate to some degree, and all populations include at least a handful of highly inventive individuals. Change occurs when these people and their ideas are accepted as legitimate alternatives, not rejected as deviant.

As we pointed out in Chapter 21's discussion of the role of the culture broker in bringing about culture change, acceptance of innovation is often associated with ambiguity concerning what constitutes proper behavior. Fredrik Barth's study (1963) of fishing villages in northern Norway reveals certain conditions of ambiguity that can prompt acceptance of innovation. Isolated geographically and culturally (most were Lapps), the villagers occupied a marginal position in the modern nation of Norway. Many wanted the goods industrialization has to offer, but lacked the means to obtain them. Fishing for export and farming for home consumption made for only a precarious existence. The price they obtained for fish depended on a world market they did not understand. They did not have the capital to invest in large boats or processing factories, or the know-how to obtain loans from the state through bureaucratic channels. Isolated but economically dependent, anxious to become part of the modern world but unable to make connections, the villagers were "neither here nor there."

Such conditions create a niche for what Barth calls entrepreneurs: individuals who are more single-minded in their concentration on making a profit than most people; who are not committed to existing business practices or bureaucratic structures; and who are willing to take risks, "delighting in gambler's odds." Barth suggests that in marginal communities the entrepreneur acts as an agent of change by playing the role of mediator between local communities and outside institutions. "This is the niche where he can find most clients: persons who need and desire goods, services and leadership, who are unable by traditional means and skills available to them to obtain what they wish. It is also the niche where he most readily can raise the capital needed for enterprises: the loans, subsidies and technical assistance which the Welfare State offers to ameliorate and remedy conditions in the area" (Barth, 1963:16). The success of the entrepreneur's innovations depends on his ability, or the ability of others, to bring together a relatively self-conscious group of people who see the utility of change. He is able to do this because he makes opportunistic use of existing possibilities in ways neither local people nor state bureaucrats perceive or plan. Under other conditions, the entrepreneur might be considered deviant or even criminal. Here he fills a need.

Regardless of the exact conditions under which innovations will be accepted, variation in customary ways of acting is essential to adaptation and is the source of changes in a people's way of life. Individual decision making—efforts to find "smart" solutions to di-

Table 23–1: Some Simultaneous Discoveries and Inventions.

Telescope: Jansen, Lippershey, Metius, 1608
Sunspots: Fabricius, Galileo, Harriott, Scheiner, 1611
Logarithms: Napier, 1614; Bürgi, 1620
Calculus: Newton, 1671, publ. 1687; Leibnitz, 1676, publ. 1684
Nitrogen: Rutherford, 1772; Scheele, 1773
Oxygen: Priestley, Scheele, 1774
Water is H_2O: Cavendish, Watt, 1781; Lavoisier, 1783
Steamboat: Jouffroy, 1783; Rumsey, 1787; Fitch, 1788; Symington, 1788
Theory of Planetary Disturbances: Lagrange, Laplace, 1808
Telegraph: Henry, Morse, Steinheil, Wheatstone and Cooke, about 1837
Photography: Daguerre and Niepce, Talbot, 1839
Surgical anaesthesia by ether: Long, 1842, results disregarded; Jackson, Liston, Morton, Robinson, 1846
Sunspot variations correlated with disturbances on earth: Gauthier, Sabine, Wolfe, 1852
Natural selection: Darwin, Wallace, 1858
Telephone: Bell, Gray, 1876
Phonograph: Cros, Edison, 1877
Rediscovery of Mendel's Laws: De Vries, Correns, Tschermak, 1900
Flight orientation of bats due to hearing reflections of uttered sounds: Griffin and Galambos, U.S.A., 1941–42; Dijkgraat, Holland, 1943—during total severance of communications in war years

Source: Abridged from A. L. Kroeber, *Anthropology*, New York: Harcourt, Brace, & World, Inc., 1923 (1948 revision), p. 342.

verse problems—occurs in every society, and such decision making gives rise to behavioral variation. There are enough conflicting versions of proper behavior in every society to create some ambiguity and thus allow for the introduction and acceptance of innovation, although ambiguity is clearly greater in situations such as those we have been discussing. Moreover, the general tolerance of different societies for innovation varies, depending upon surrounding circumstances. But in any case, the point to remember is that some degree of innovation occurs in every human population, and consequently all societies are in the process of continual adaptation and change.

Culture Change and Adaptation

Whatever the internal processes that affect the acceptance of innovations, the long-term survival of those innovations depends on their adaptiveness—whether or not they are useful in a people's efforts to deal with particular aspects of their environment. Innovations may be accepted on a permanent basis because they help a group to cope with day-to-day changes in its social and natural environment. Or an innovation may remain relatively insignificant until major environmental changes make it an important part of a population's adaptive mechanisms.

Adaptation to the Social Environment

In Chapter 16 we discussed the meaning of adaptation to the natural environment very specifically, pointing out the many different problems with which any group must deal in order to obtain essential resources. At the same time, we mentioned that major changes in aspects of the natural environment that are beyond the control of a given group can and do occur. While we also talked about adaptation to the social environment in this chapter, our discussion of adaptation in a social context has really been spread throughout Chapters 13 to 22, and it is useful to try to bring many of these studies together here.

Perhaps the best way to begin a discussion of adaptation to changes in the social environment is to examine a case in which very similar populations responded quite differently to contact with new groups. Take, for example, the case of the Pima and Papago of southern Arizona (Hackenberg, 1962). While these two native American groups are similar in language, material culture, and physical appearance, they are also different in a number of critical ways. In the recent past, the Pima derived roughly 60 percent of their subsistence from agriculture and 40 percent from hunting and gathering. They lived in approximately a dozen permanent villages along the Gila River, where they practiced irrigation agriculture. The Papago, on the other hand, had a semimigratory lifestyle. They lived in "field villages" adjacent to locations used for floodwater farming, and also in "well villages," hunting and gathering base camps where permanent water was available during the dry season. Along with these differences in subsistence and settlement patterns between the Pima and Papago, the Pima also had more powerful headmen with greater authority, greater inequalities in the distribution of wealth, and more formal mechanisms of intervillage interaction.

Thus we find two groups inhabiting a similar area, each with some cultural and linguistic similarities to the other but also with significant differences in subsistence strategies, settlement patterns, and social organization. How did this situation come about? Both ethnohistoric and archeological data suggest that the major differences between the groups are of relatively recent origin. Between 2000 B.P. and about 400 years ago, the area seems to have been inhabited by populations whose subsistence strategies ranged from almost 100 percent hunting and gathering to a heavy reliance on irrigation agriculture with some hunting and gathering during the winter months. But instead of two easily distinguishable cultural traditions there was a continuum of subsistence and settlement patterns, with populations varying their strategies in response to changing climatic conditions.

During the 1500s, however, the Spanish and the Apache came to Arizona, and both groups had an impact on the ways of life of native peoples. The Spanish introduced winter wheat, which proved a successful crop in the irrigated fields of small villages along the river. Because winter was the traditional hunting-gathering season, dependence on hunting and gathering decreased in these villages. But winter wheat did not prove successful in the floodwater fields of the more migratory groups, and their reliance on hunting and gathering did not decline. The Apache, too, had a significant effect on indigenous ways of life. A predatory group, the Apache frequently raided agricultural populations in the area. Consolidation and a stronger political organization centered around defense helped enable local people in the more sedentary villages to protect themselves against the Apache. Another means available to less sedentary groups was increased mobility, allowing them to stay out of the way of the invaders. Thus the effect of the joint arrival of the Spanish and Apache seems to have resulted in two very distinct patterns of subsistence, settlement, and social organization in an area where a continuum of patterns had previously existed.

Why did this outcome occur? Ecological factors seem to have played a central role. Slight differences in subsistence strategies and economic behavior among the original native populations had a critical influence on how people responded to contact with the Spanish and Apache. Those in one set of ecological circumstances were led to react in one direction, while those in a second set of circumstances reacted in an entirely different direction. The result was the development of two distinct groups with very different cultural patterns.

Anthropologists are interested in understanding the range of factors affecting the outcome of contact between societies. Studies of *acculturation*—cultural changes that occur from extended, firsthand contact between two or more previously autonomous groups—offer important insights. It has been found, for example, that one factor influencing the outcome of direct and prolonged culture contact is the characteristics of the societies in question, particularly the permeability of their boundaries and the flexibility of their internal structures. When a society's boundaries are very rigid, for instance, marriage with members of another group may not be permitted. The interactions of the Spanish and the British with native American groups was quite different in this respect. The Spanish intermarried, while the British did not. This is one of the reasons why the population of modern Mexico is substantially a blend of New World and Old World peoples, while in North America, the population is largely of European extraction with a distinct native American minority. In general, the more permeable the boundaries of a given society and the more flexible its internal structure, the more open it is to acculturative change (Broom et al, 1954).

Second, the representatives of the two societies who actually come in contact, and the kinds of links they establish, have an important effect on the outcome of prolonged interaction between previously autonomous groups. Ultimately, societies as a whole do not come into contact with each other; only the individual members of those societies do. And frequently, these individuals do not represent a broad cross-section of their societies. The native peoples of Southeast Asia have had culture contact with a number of different societies: Hindu, Buddhist, Chinese, Islamic, and European. Not only were these societies different, but so were their individual representatives. The Hindus were soldiers and administrators; the Buddhists, priests and teachers; the Chinese, traders; the Europeans, soldiers and businessmen. Only in the case of the Moslems was a broadly representative group present. Needless to say, the effects of each group on the indigenous society were quite different (Bekker, 1951).

A third factor influencing the effects of culture contact is the relative political and military strength of the two groups. When one group is more powerful than another, a differ-

This British officer is unmistakable as he sits high above his Indian bearers during a procession in the late eighteenth century. Anthropologists and others have come to question more and more whose interests the colonial powers had in mind when making policy decisions regarding colonized peoples. (Victoria and Albert Museum)

ent pattern of change may well emerge than if the two populations are of approximately equal power. This is because the society of greater strength is often capable of forcing its domination over the weaker society. This is precisely what happened in the encounters between European colonizers and indigenous peoples. Acculturative change among native groups was largely accomplished through the threat of coercive force. It is important to recognize, however, that cultural domination does not necessarily occur simply because one society is larger than another. There are many instances on record of numerically smaller groups having a dominant influence over larger ones. Chinese military colonizers in Imperial times, to take only one example, were frequently outnumbered by so-called national minority peoples, but nevertheless they did not lose their cultural identity. In fact, in many instances the cultural influence worked in the other direction—the numerically superior people became more Chinese.

Thus the results of extended contact between previously autonomous groups can be quite different under different situations. At one extreme we have instances in which one society is virtually "taken over" by another, replacing most of its own cultural traditions with those of the dominant society. This is what happened when the Dutch arrived on the out islands of Indonesia. Here a number of native groups were drastically transformed from self-sufficient slash-and-burn cultivators to populations economically centered around export for a world market, with significant inequalities in the distribution of wealth, a new individualism, and even a type of Protestant work ethic—in essence, an entirely different culture core.

At the other extreme, we find populations that respond to contact with other societies by attempting either to avoid or expel the newly arrived group. In the case of the Pima and Papago, for example, some groups attempted to avoid the Apache by adopting a more migratory lifestyle. Similarly, revitalization movements (such as those described in Chapter 20) or armed rebellions are efforts to ward off or reverse the influence of intruding societies.

And finally, somewhere in between these two extremes, are situations in which certain new traits are successfully incorporated into the cultural practices of the recipient society, but without a pervasive loss of traditional customs. Most groups adopt traits from other societies only selectively, and they modify what they borrow to blend with their own beliefs and practices. On Haiti, for example, people combined elements of West African and Catholic myths and rituals into a new magico-religious system, voodoo, which is quite different from either of the "donor" religions.

In concluding our discussion of accultura-tion, it is interesting to return to the question raised at the beginning of this chapter: what has happened to native Americans since white contact? Some anthropologists would say that they are becoming *assimilated*—that is, integrated into white culture. But Joseph Jorgenson disagrees that native Americans are still in the process of assimilation. In a study of native Americans in California, he found them to be the most disadvantaged minority group on the basis of every social, economic, and health criterion. Native Americans, for example, have lower-paying jobs, lower-status occupations, higher unemployment, lower incomes, and shorter life spans. Jorgenson asks if these facts indicate that native Americans have not yet been fully assimi-

Though anthropologists disagree about the ultimate impact of missionaries, they agree that missionaries have been important in bringing literacy to people all over the world. Here some of the first members of the central Tanzanian Barabaik tribe to get an education return to share their new knowledge. (Leon V. Kofod)

lated into white society. His answer is no. It is precisely the manner in which native Americans *were* assimilated—as an exploited class—that has created their current situation. Jorgenson concludes that "the modern American Indians are the progeny of the super-exploited Indians of the nineteenth century who were forced to relinquish their territory, their self-governance, and their self-esteem so that the metropolis could grow. . . . The modern Indian, too, is super-exploited" (1971:110). Thus assimilation, like many of the terms social scientists use to describe acculturative change, can unfortunately create the impression of ongoing, essentially beneficial change when none is occurring.

Problems Caused by Change in Today's World

In the last few generations, Western man has developed a peculiar sense of omnipotence—as if there were no problem that is not capable of scientific solution. Nothing could be farther from the truth. A few examples suggest how difficult and complex the problems facing today's world are, and how many of them are the result of rapid and far-reaching changes that have occurred during the twentieth century. Although anthropologists may not be directly involved in finding solutions to these broad problems, they are certainly concerned about them, and often their work deals with specific aspects of the general dilemmas.

Despite an enormous increase in food production in the last century (due largely to the development of high-yield grains, improved fertilizers and pesticides, and so forth), millions of people are starving.[2] Approximately one-third of the world's population (50 to 60 percent of the populations of developing nations) is undernourished. Somewhere between ten and twenty million deaths a year (including most infant deaths) are the direct or indirect result of slow starvation.

In principle, we could eliminate starvation by distributing food more equitably. Today there is probably enough food for all the people in the world. But this would only be a stopgap solution. Much sooner than most people realize, there will not be enough food to go around. An unprecedented rate of population growth is literally eating up whatever gains we make in food production, particularly in the Third World. At current rates of population growth, food production, and food consumption, we will reach a crisis point in the year 2000. If, through the "miracles of technology," we are able to quadruple food production, we will only delay this crisis another fifty years. At that point, there will not be enough food to prevent mass starvation, even if we have committed ourselves to an equitable system of food distribution.

The most obvious way to prevent such a crisis would be to increase the number of acres under cultivation (we are using only half the potentially fertile land on the globe) and at the same time to increase the productivity of each acre. But could we live in a world in which almost all of the land surface had been turned into agricultural fields? Ecologists point out that noncultivated areas are critical to our global ecosystem. Moreover, greatly increasing the number of cultivated acres would require massive expenditures. It costs an average of $1,150 to develop each hectare of new land. And to raise productivity a mere 34 percent, farmers spent an additional 64 percent for tractors, 146 percent for fertilizers, and 300 percent for pesticides between 1951 and 1966. The capital needed to fund a massive agricultural program depends on industrial development, which in turn depends on nonrenewable fuels and metals, resources that are rapidly running out. Moreover, if we consume resources at an even higher rate than we do today, we are coming closer to exceeding the earth's capacity to absorb pollutants.

Like food shortages, rapid population growth, and the depletion of natural re-

---

[2] The following discussion of food production, resource depletion, and pollution is based on Meadows et al., 1972.

sources, pollution is a very difficult problem to solve. The facts about the extent of pollution are often startling. To mention just a few examples, we know that on a world-wide basis we are using 100,000 tons of DDT annually and that people all around the globe (from Alaska to New Delhi) are accumulating DDT in their body tissues; we know that we are releasing 200 billion tons of carbon dioxide into the atmosphere every year, and that the level of lead in the ice in Greenland, far removed from industrial centers, has risen 300 percent since 1940. If by the year 2000 the world's projected 7 billion inhabitants are consuming as much energy as Americans do today, the pollution load on the environment will be ten times the current level. Whether such a world would be livable is difficult to say. And what makes the situation even more alarming is that it takes years to erase the negative consequences of pollution. Even if we began to reduce world-wide usage of DDT today, the levels of this poison in fish would not return to 1970 levels until 1995.

But food production, resource depletion, and pollution are not the only problems related to the rapid changes of the twentieth century. We know very little about the limits of people's capacity to adapt to change. Economist Kenneth Boulding once commented that as much had happened since he was born as had happened in all of history before (in Toffler, 1971). Never have so many people adopted transience as a way of life. We are becoming accustomed to planned obsolescence — in our automobiles, our jobs, even our friendships and marriages. Temporary task forces are replacing organizational charts in government and industry; serial monogamy is replacing stable family life in some urban populations. The deluge of information is equally bewildering. Today some 1,000 new books are released every day, and the scientific and technical literature is growing at the rate of 60,000,000 pages a year. This growing body of knowledge requires more and more specialization, and the rate of growth makes it necessary for people to adapt to new specializations

Necessary as change is to the survival of societies, extreme technological advances may become unwitting agents of destruction. These dead fish illustrate what can happen when thermal pollution from a nuclear power plant disrupts the ecosystem of a river. (Gordon Alexander/FPG)

as the old ones become obsolete. It has also contributed to social disorganization, as people feel that they must rely on professionals to solve every problem, and relate less meaningfully to one another.

Have the rate of change and the pace of life outstripped man's ability to adapt? Social critic Alvin Toffler thinks they may have. He coined the term "future shock" to describe the disorientation and anxiety people experience when they are cut adrift from traditions and certainties, forced to invent and reinvent their lives without the benefit of authoritative cultural guidelines or knowledge of the future.

The overwhelming problems facing today's world have prompted many to ask if we are not doomed to extinction. Most people think not yet. There is still time to choose between controlling births and mass starvation, between a reduced standard of living and fatal levels of pollution, between setting limits on growth and waiting for natural limits to stop growth and perhaps life as we know it. The problems we face are beyond technical solution (that is, beyond solutions that depend solely on new scientific techniques, and do not require changes in human values). How we adapt, who or what the future selects, depends largely on social choices, on whether by examining evolutionary processes in the past we can learn to manage technology, food resources, and human interaction. One encouraging development is our growing effort to face these problems more consciously and explicitly. In anthropology, this area of study is called *applied anthropology*.

Applied Anthropology

According to George Foster (1969:54), applied anthropology is the activity of professional anthropologists "in programs that have as primary goals changes in human behavior believed to ameliorate contemporary social, economic, and technological problems." Anthropologists have, for example, undertaken specific efforts to solve nutritional, medical, educational, and a variety of other pressing human problems in particular environmental contexts. It is perhaps more accurate to describe such efforts as applications of anthropology rather than as applied anthropology. But in any case, alleviating some of the pressing problems facing societies today through the implementation of change is part of the domain of anthropology. In recent years, too, applied anthropologists have been concerned not only with when and how to implement change, but also with understanding the many negative consequences that change can have on societies. In this section, we will consider both these aspects of applied work.

The Anthropological Approach

Of course, social scientists in many other disciplines are involved in activities that fit the definition of applied anthropology. What is distinctive about the anthropologist's approach, however, is the use of the holistic perspective discussed in Chapter 1. Anthropologists emphasize the cultural complexity of even the smallest and most piecemeal innovation, the values, attitudes, and social relations that are likely to affect its success or failure. As Foster has explained:

It is axiomatic to anthropologists that each culture is a functional, integrated, internally consistent system, and not just a haphazard assemblage of customs and habits. . . . *No change can occur in isolation*. . . . The basic technique of the applied anthropologist is to attempt to determine the relationships between the institutions or elements central to a proposed change, and the total cultural pattern. (1971:75–76)

Such an undertaking is, of course, complex and may involve a variety of different considerations. The ultimate outcome of any applied anthropology project can be influenced by many factors. Some of the most important of these are environmental and ecological factors, traditional values and beliefs, social ties, and the agents of change.

1. *Environmental and Ecological Factors.* In Chapter 17 we discussed the increase in human diseases that resulted from the construction of the Aswan Dam. This is an instance where a major technological change has clear-cut negative consequences. But the impact of technological change on the total environment can be even more subtle. For example, several years ago a new strain of rice was introduced in Nepal which produced yields up to 200 percent greater than that of native crops. But because the rice grew on short, tough stalks producing little fodder for cattle and requiring threshing machinery that was not available locally, the innovation

was not successful (Foster, 1971:6). Thus sensitivity to the impact of a proposed innovation on economic-ecological relations is an important part of the applied anthropologist's work.

2. *Traditional Values and Beliefs.* Innovations may also have drastic effects on traditional beliefs and values. In Ethiopia, for example, the introduction of formal schooling and professional teachers severely threatened the father's traditional role (Foster, 1971:87). And in Mexico, local people expelled government economists sent to launch a village development program because they were unwilling to believe that something would not be demanded of them in return (Foster, 1971:103). Such problems can even arise in strictly symbolic areas. A Dutch effort to resettle rural agriculturalists ran into difficulty over a poster in which women were in the foreground and men in the background. The farmers concluded from the relative size of the figures that although the project might be fine for females, it would certainly stunt the growth of males (Foster, 1971:11).

3. *Social Ties.* Many innovations have unintended consequences for social relations as well. In many parts of the world, attempts to introduce improved clothes-washing facilities have run into resistance. Women often refuse to use the more private, modern facilities because by doing so they would lose the opportunity to meet and gossip with their neighbors in a community washing place. Of course, an innovation may have an even more significant impact on traditional social ties, as when a traditionally subordinate group is placed in an economically competitive position with a traditional elite. It is this kind of development that underlies revolution in many Third World countries today.

4. *The Change Agents.* The attitudes, beliefs, and values of change agents also have an important effect on the outcome of a project. Rural villagers may be hostile toward representatives of a distant urban government. Or the change agents, coming from an elite class, may be totally condescending toward rural farmers. Even the inability to speak local languages or the violation of proxemic rules may have substantial negative consequences. Applied anthropologists must investigate factors such as these when evaluating the merits of a proposed plan or when attempting to insure the success of an ongoing project.

A Case Study of Applied Work: The Vicos Project

An unprecedented example of concerted involvement by anthropologists in applied work is a project carried out by Cornell University at Vicos, Peru, 250 miles north of Lima. Like many other Latin American *haciendas,* Vicos was a public manor, owned by a charitable society. When the project began in the 1950s, the owners rented the land to the highest bidder for periods of five to ten years. Traditionally, the renter or *patrón* reserved the fertile bottomlands for his own use, and sublet the less profitable highlands to the Indians (who had lived there for perhaps four hundred years). Each tenant family paid for a one-half- to five-acre plot by sending one adult to work the land of the *patrones* for three days a week, free of charge. The peasant community was also expected to provide cooks, grooms, servants, watchmen, and the like free of charge. In addition, each family paid a land tax. Usually, the *patrón* did not live on the *hacienda,* but hired a Mestizo (person with mixed Spanish and Indian blood) administrator and foreman (always outsiders). These overseers in turn appointed local *mayorales* or straw bosses to mobilize the Indian peasants in their area. The *patrón* or his agents settled all disputes relating to the operation of the manor; all other problems were left to councils of village elders. For the most part illiterate subsistence farmers who lacked modern skills, modern health care, and any form of social respect or hope of participating in decisions affecting their lives, the Vicos tenant farmers were extremely fatalistic. (Records showed that their few attempts at protest had been suppressed by a coalition of landlords, clergy, and police.) "The peon was subservient to the overlord; the child, to the parents; and both were beaten into submission. Even the supernatural forces were punishing, and the burdens one bore were suffered as naturally ordained powers beyond one's control" (Holmberg, 1965). In 1951, the potato crop failed, and Indians resigned themselves to starving.

However, Vicos was up for rent that year. In a revolutionary move and after much consultation with the Peruvian government, Cornell University bid for the *hacienda* and was granted a five-year lease. In January 1952, the university became the *patrón*. The goals of the Vicos project were, first and foremost, to give Vicosinos the right to self-determination by gradual diffusion of power; to raise the standard of living by increasing productivity and sharing of wealth; to introduce modern agricultural techniques and medical care; to use schooling and other media to bring Indians into the modern world; and to raise their status among their neighbors.

Cornell anthropologists proceeded on the following assumptions: "First, innovations are most likely to be accepted in those aspects of culture in which people themselves feel the greatest deprivations; and second, an integrated or contextual approach to value-institutional development is usually more lasting and less conflict-producing than a piecemeal one" (Holmberg, 1965). They began by paying Vicosinos back wages (a symbolic gesture, for the pay amounted to three cents a week) and hiring volunteers to perform services Indians had long been forced to provide for free. In the first year, the new *patrones* introduced modern seeds, fertilizers, and agricultural techniques, producing a cash crop and plowing the profits back into the *hacienda*. Between 1952 and 1957, productivity rose from $100 to $400–600 per acre. All residents shared in the profits from the bottomlands and all were taught modern techniques for farming their own land. They built a school with a capacity for 400 students (the old school accommodated 10 to 15 students) and a health clinic.

Initially, Cornell administrators did not attempt to alter the traditional system of *mayorales* or straw bosses. However, they used the weekly meetings previous *patrones* had established to hand out work assignments to explain innovations, discuss goals and plans, draw Vicosinos into the decision-making process, and to give residents news of the outside world. By 1957, a council of ten elected delegates had taken over management of community affairs. Younger men, who were committed to improvement rather than to traditions, had largely replaced the elders in positions of village authority.

In addition, Cornell sought to regularize relations with local authorities (ending abuses of draft laws, for example) and to create numerous occasions on which Vicosinos could meet neighboring Mestizos on an equal footing. By 1957, Mestizos were coming to the *peones* they had once regarded as unworthy of the slightest respect for advice on agricultural techniques. And despite strong resistance from the local elite, the Indians were able to purchase Vicos—and their independence—in July 1962. Since then, the Peruvian government has initiated five similar programs on other *haciendas,* in some cases with Vicosinos acting as advisers (Holmberg, 1958, 1965). In almost all respects, then, the project was a success. Cornell took power (something anthropologists have rarely had the opportunity and/or inclination to do) in order to restore power to the Indians, with the deliberate intention of changing their way of life.

The Pros and Cons of Applied Anthropology

Despite its success, Project Vicos was criticized by those who believe that science and social action are incompatible. Alan Holmberg, who participated in the Vicos project, admits that at first he felt extremely uncomfortable in the role of *patrón.* In time, however, he came to consider Vicos a model for a research and development approach to anthropology. The project was a "natural experiment" in the sense that he and his colleagues were able to test numerous hypotheses empirically—for example, the idea that the conservatism and fatalism often found in peasant communities in Latin America is the product of centuries of exploitation, and that attitudes will change rapidly if Indians are given the right to self-determination. In Holmberg's view, direct intervention is the ideal method for testing such hypotheses.

Others, however, object to this point of view, believing it is unethical for anthropologists to interfere in other peoples' lives. Certainly there *are* moral questions about anthropologists working for political agencies. Few dispute the fact that U.S. foreign aid and development programs are operated in the national self-interest. (And both locally and internationally funded programs often serve the indigenous elite, not the people for whom help is intended.) But this was not the case with Vicos. To the contrary, it was one of the first opportunities anthropologists have had to act as policy makers, not just advisers and go-betweens (Manners, 1956). Thus some people respond to the charge that direct intervention in another society is unethical by asking if it is ethical for anthropologists *not* to put their expertise to practical use.

No matter what stand one takes, ethical issues are a major concern in applied anthropological work—from the time the anthropologist is making his initial decision as to whether he should work for a given agency, to later decisions about what innovations should be introduced and how, and on through final evaluations of the project's effects. Taking simple right or wrong positions on these issues is easy. Some people claim that to work for any government agency is to become a tool of capitalist imperialism. But thoughtful and creative approaches to solving ethical problems are more difficult. Moreover, as we pointed out in Chapter 12, while ethical issues may be more sharply focused in applied work, they are present in all kinds of anthropological research. Whenever people are the subjects of scientific investigation, almost inevitably ethical considerations arise.

Applied Anthropology: Analyzing the Effects of the Sahelian Drought

In doing applied work, anthropologists must go beyond the immediate and obvious causes of a problem and view events in their cultural context, often considering their development over a long period of time. This is what Jeremy Swift did in his study of the effects of the Sahelian drought on the Kel Adrar Tuareg of Mali. The Sahel is a hot, dry belt of savannah stretching 4,000 miles across Africa just south of the Sahara Desert. Between 1969 and 1973, changes in patterns of atmospheric circulation caused the summer monsoon rains to fail, and the pastoral Kel Adrar along with other populations inhabiting the area suffered severe starvation. Yet drought is not a new problem in the Sahel. Pastoral nomads like the Tuareg have successfully adapted to such conditions for centuries, even millennia. Why, then, was this drought so catastrophic? Swift argues that various political developments of the recent past prevented pastoral groups from responding with their traditional strategies for survival.

Important changes in traditional cultural patterns began with the French colonial occupation during the first half of the nineteenth century. The peace imposed by French troops ended the dominance of pastoral peoples over neighboring agriculturalists from whom the pastoralists had traditionally obtained grain, a dietary mainstay. It also put an end to raiding between nomadic groups, allowing them to spread their camps more widely across tribal territories. Consequently, much less pasturage was left in reserve, and land that was in use was grazed more intensively.

Political independence for Mali in 1958 brought further changes in traditional ways of life. Borders with neighboring states were closed completely or transport taxes were imposed, thus denying nomadic groups access to the full range of their former territories. The government, dominated by agricultural groups, taxed the nomad's livestock very heavily, and by establishing trading centers, it gradually drove the pastoralists to participate more and more in a market economy. Because the nomadic way of life was considered a "problem" by the new government, little was done to increase its viability.

The subsequent disastrous drought must be viewed in the light of these important political developments. Many of the traditional responses were no longer possible. The problem, then, was as much political as climatic. Swift suggests that similar disasters can be prevented only if governments recognize the effectiveness of traditional nomadic practices and ask what can be done to improve, not to replace, the pastoral subsistence strategy.

Applied Anthropology in Our Own Society: Impact Assessment

In recent years anthropologists have started to become heavily involved in a new area of applied work that has developed in our own society. As a result of problems such as pollution and urban sprawl, a variety of state and national environmental protection acts have been passed. These require that we first evaluate the effects on biological, geological, social, historical, and cultural resources of projects supported by government funds. The agency proposing to undertake a potentially harmful project must prepare an environment impact statement that identifies any adverse consequences, direct or indirect, the project will have. These impacts must be taken into account in planning the project at the earliest feasible stage. If the impacts are judged to be damaging, *mitigation* procedures must be proposed either by changing the project design or providing for the protection of the resource.

Archeological anthropologists who call themselves conservation archeologists or cultural resource managers have become involved in preparing statements describing the impact of resource exploitation on historic and prehistoric sites. They argue that without such actions most historic and prehistoric remains in this society would be destroyed. The environmental protection laws also require assessing the impact of government-funded projects on the life of existing communities, and sociocultural anthropologists are becoming involved in this area of research as well. In both instances, anthropologists are working to help resolve conflicts between our society's growth and development and the preservation of our cultural heritage and current traditions.

summary

The methods anthropologists use to collect data on change include obtaining accounts of the past from informants and historical documents, doing a field study at one point in time and then conducting a follow-up study some years later, looking at contemporary "primitive" societies as to some extent indicative of cultures in the past, and digging up remains of past societies and then reconstructing processes of change on the basis of this evidence. Although all of these methods add to our understanding of culture change, none can be relied upon exclusively because each has certain problems. Consequently, most research on change incorporates a number of different methods.

The broad patterns of change that have characterized the history of human culture—that is, patterns of general evolution—can be summarized as follows: low to high energy capture; generalists to specialists; wealth sharing to wealth hoarding; consensual to authoritative leadership; responsible elites to exploitative elites; nomadic to urban; vengeance war to political war. Anthropologists have attempted to synthesize many of these separate evolutionary trends by focusing on the increasing complexity of societies through time.

Several anthropologists have suggested overall rules or laws that govern the course of general evolution. One is the Law of Cultural Dominance: that the system which more effectively exploits the energy resources in a given environment will dominate in that environment. Another is the Law of Evolutionary Potential: the less specialized an organism or society is, the better able it is to adapt successfully to changing conditions. Although many anthropologists would deny that these patterns constitute real laws, the effort to find general evolutionary rules is an important thrust in contemporary studies of culture change.

Research into specific evolution suggests that general evolutionary patterns are a summary of myriad short-term adaptations to changing environmental conditions. Innovation, or deviance from customary patterns of behavior, is essential to social change and is an ongoing process in all societies. Current studies of cultural innovation often focus on the conditions under which innovations are adopted and then become routine.

When people of different societies come into contact with one another, several different outcomes can result, depending upon various factors, including the characteristics of the two societies, the representatives of each who interact, and the relative size of the two groups. Thus, depending on the situation, the results of culture contact can be an incorporation of some new traits with little or no modification of traditional cultural patterns; a drastic replacement of traditional customs and practices with those of the alien culture; or a mix of old and new customs to create some entirely new pattern.

The problems facing today's world—such as food shortages, rapid population growth, resource depletion, pollution, and the difficulty of adapting to continuous change—are many and complex. The area of anthropology concerned with changing human behavior in an effort to alleviate current social, economic, and technological problems is called applied anthropology. The ultimate outcome of any applied project can be influenced by many factors, among them environmental and ecological conditions, traditional values and beliefs, social ties, and the agents of change.

Ethical issues, a major consideration in all aspects of applied work, are difficult to resolve. But ethical questions are raised in all kinds of anthropological research.

In recent years a new area of applied work has developed in our own society with the enactment of environmental protection laws requiring evaluation of the effects on biological, geological, social, historical, and cultural resources of any government-supported project. Anthropologists are becoming heavily involved in this area, referred to as impact assessment.

suggested readings

BEE, R. L.
1974 *Patterns and Processes: An Introduction to Anthropological Strategies for the Study of Sociocultural Change.* New York: Free Press. An excellent review of the various approaches to the study of cultural change from the perspective of pattern and process.

FOSTER, G. M.
1969 *Applied Anthropology.* Boston: Little, Brown. Explores the relationship between theoretical findings and the practical application of these to contemporary problems of social change.

STEWARD, J. H.
1972 *Theory of Culture Change: The Methodology of Multilinear Evolution.* Urbana: University of Illinois Press. An important work, which develops a general method for determining the evolutionary stages that recur in the specific adaptations of particular societies.

WADDELL, J. O., AND WATSON, O. M., EDS.
1971 *The American Indian in Urban Society.* Boston: Little, Brown. Essays on the influence of urbanization on the American Indian and its impact on both the Indians in the cities and those who remain on rural reservations.

WHITE, L.
1959 *The Evolution of Culture: The Development of Civilization to the Fall of Rome.* New York: McGraw-Hill. A classic presentation of the theory of universal cultural evolution.

In Part V we explore the adaptive patterns of different societies, using case studies to illustrate important problems of adaptation faced by all human populations. For each of five major subsistence patterns we ask: How do people extract a living from their environment? How productive are their subsistence strategies? How efficient? What kind of social organization is characteristic? What problems do people solve by their procurement patterns? What new problems do they create?

We begin in Chapter 24 with hunting and gathering, the oldest of human subsistence patterns. Although a hunting and gathering technology may not be highly productive, it is efficient in that people need to invest relatively little time and effort to obtain an adequate diet. Moreover, hunters and gatherers usually interfere with their environments to a rather limited extent, and their social organization is highly flexible and egalitarian.

In Chapter 25 with horticulture we begin to see an intensification of production. Horticulturalists extract more resources from a given area of land than do hunters and gatherers, with a consequent rise in population density. Horticulturalists also have a greater effect on their environments than do hunters and gatherers. Their societies are generally organized around groups based on kinship and descent. Intergroup exchange, including trade, is quite common, as is organized warfare.

Pastoralism, discussed in Chapter 26, is a subsistence strategy that is not completely independent of farming. It usually involves a complex interaction on a regional basis between groups specializing in herding and those specializing in farming. Like horticulture, pastoralism is more productive than hunting and gathering, but it is not a particularly efficient way of converting resources into food for human consumption. Nevertheless, pastoralists are able to adapt to marginal environments where farming would be extremely risky or totally impossible.

The adaptive pattern of intensive agriculture is dealt with in Chapter 27. With intensive agriculture comes high productivity. Farmlands are made to yield large harvests, and the surpluses are used to support people not directly engaged in agriculture. Economic specialization, social stratification, and political centralization are characteristic of such societies. Clearly the technology of intensive cultivation can solve certain problems. Irrigation, for example, can compensate for low or unpredictable rainfall. But intensive agriculturalists also pay a price in widespread environmental interference and the difficult problems it raises.

In Chapter 28 we discuss industrialism. Modern industrial technology, with its diverse means of harnessing energy, has raised production levels enormously, with a consequent explosion in population and an ever-increasing degree of economic specialization and social complexity. Industrialism is also marked by its world-wide organization, the vast web of systems that make up our global economy. Our focus, therefore, is on global economic developments and their consequences.

The general sequence we present in this part—from hunting and gathering to agriculture to industrialism—is an evolutionary one. Ten thousand years ago, all human populations made their livings by hunting and foraging. Today only a few thousand hunters and gatherers remain in relatively remote corners of the earth. Industrialization has tied most of the world into a single intricately interconnected economic system. Chapter 29, the final chapter in this part, views the human species from an evolutionary perspective, exploring some of the major problems of human adaptation.

5
adaptive patterns

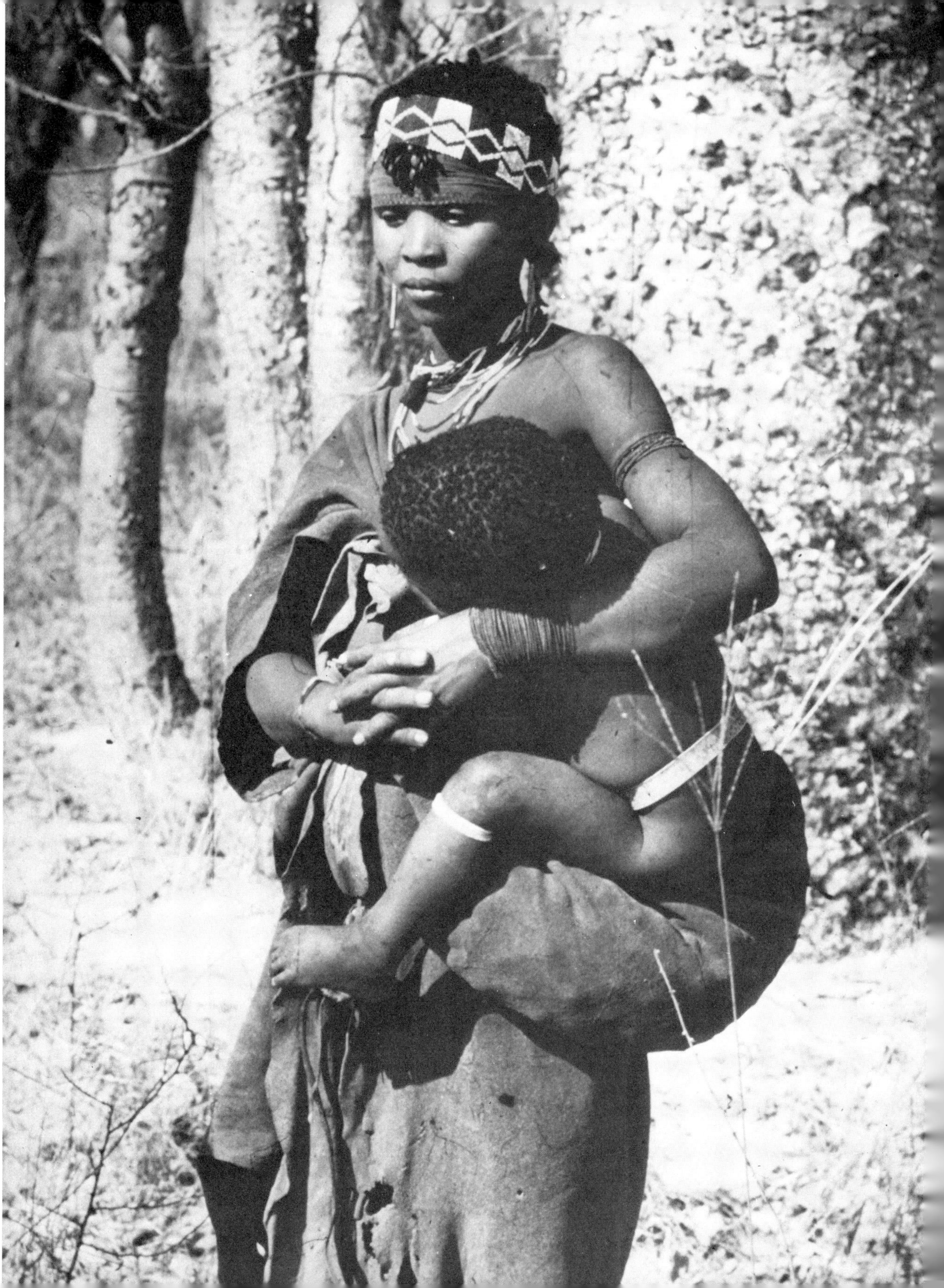

twenty-four
Hunters and Gatherers

In this chapter we compare three different groups of people who live in very different environments—the !Kung Bushmen of Botswana, the Eskimo of southern Baffin Island, and the Miskito of eastern Nicaragua. Richard Lee counted 466 !Kung living in a semi-arid corner of Botswana—466 people who support themselves with a few simple tools they make mainly from raw materials collected in the bush, and use to gather wild nuts, vegetables, and fruits and hunt wild animals. The Eskimo William Kemp studied sell skins and carvings to outsiders and occasionally work for wages to buy fuel for their snowmobiles and motorboats, ammunition for their rifles, and food to supplement what they acquire by hunting seals. Their production is largely by and for the household, although they now have the technology to produce more goods for the commercial market. In contrast to the Baffin Island Eskimo, the Miskito Indians, studied by Bernard Nietschmann, are allocating more and more time to hunting, and selling for a profit, the turtles they used to share with each other. Despite obvious differences, however, all of these groups depend on the skills they have developed to exploit wild animals and plants. With the exception of the Miskito, they do not produce food; they forage.

The Hunting and Gathering Adaptation

Hunters and gatherers exercise little or no control over the plants and animals on which they depend. They have to accommodate themselves to seasonal and annual fluctuations in resources that are spread over wide areas. This involves distinctive technological and social adaptations.

The technology that foragers employ is limited in terms of the amount of energy harnessed, but it is often ingenious in concept and construction. Until quite recently, the only sources of power the Eskimo used were seal oil for light and heat, sled dogs, and their own muscles. They didn't have metal or clay or fibers for ropes and baskets, and during the long arctic winters lived miles from the nearest trees. Yet they devised clothing, housing, weapons, boats, and sledges that enabled them to survive—even prosper—for thousands of years in an environment in which no other group could operate until the nineteenth century.

Social Organization

Foragers have devised equally ingenious social solutions to the problems of living on scattered and variable resources. For example, groups of Australian hunters and gatherers have evolved elaborate kinship systems. The tribe as a whole may be divided into as many as eight sections, bound together by complex ritual relations and strict marriage rules. These facilitate the establishment of marriage ties with distant bands. As a result, each person has ties with individuals and groups throughout the tribal area, to whom they can appeal when resources around their home base run dry. Thus the kinship system accommodates the dispersion or concentration of

A Bushman woman balances a child on her hip on a cape fold filled with mongongo nuts. These nuts and the other vegetable foods the women gather make up the main part of the Bushman diet. (Laurence K. Marshall)

Demography and Marriage among Australian Hunters and Gatherers

Some years ago, physical anthropologist J. B. Birdsell demonstrated a close correlation between annual rainfall and population density among aboriginal Australians, hunters and gatherers who live primarily on wild vegetable food. For example, population density among the coastal Kariera is approximately one person per 5 square miles; among the Walbiri who live in the central desert, approximately one person per 35 square miles.

Going a step farther, Aram A. Yengoyan showed that an important feature of the social organization of Australian tribes is directly related to population density and thus indirectly to rainfall. Where rain and therefore food are plentiful and the population density relatively high, tribes are generally small groups (200 to 500), organized as a single social unit or divided into moieties. However, in the central arid regions, where rain and therefore food is scarce and the population scattered over wide distances, tribes consist of large groups of 1,000 or more, organized into four sections or eight subsections, in the most desolate areas.

Yengoyan describes the section system as "a shorthand index for combining kin relations into categories for multiple purposes, be it possible marriage mates, ritual, or economic activity" (1968:188). Classing large numbers of people into sections or subsections is one way to extend kinship terminology to people who may or may not be actual relatives, and thus to create and define reciprocal rights and obligations. In fertile areas where tribes are small, sections would be a nuisance. If a hypothetical tribe of 100 is divided into two exogamous moieties, most people will find marriage partners. However, if the same tribe is divided into four subsections with populations of 25 or so and a man is supposed to marry a woman from only one of these sections, the chances of finding a suitable mate are greatly reduced. However, in a hypothetical tribe of 1,000, sectioning does not create this problem. Indeed, in arid regions it is highly adaptive. The section system integrates large numbers of widely dispersed people who are not in frequent contact into meaningful marital, ceremonial, and, economic units, and protects local bands by guaranteeing them access to more favorable environments in hard times.

the population, according to the availability of resources. (See the box on page 484.)

Typically, hunters and gatherers live in small, seminomadic bands that expand and contract according to the seasons and the members' dispositions. They have home ranges and migrate on seasonal rounds, finely adjusted to the availability of resources in different places at different times. People are constantly coming and going—separating for a season to exploit scattered resources, then regrouping later to share a water hole or organize collective hunts; visiting or entertaining kinspeople; moving away from a band in which they do not get along; moving into a band that is short of people and/or long on resources and fellowship. The resulting bands have neither permanent structure, exclusive rights to territory or resources, nor formal leadership. "Law and order" are maintained on a day-to-day ad hoc basis rather than by the threat or use of formal punishments.

The Eskimo, for example, have what are called "dueling songs" to resolve all disputes but murder (Hoebel, 1954). The two disputants, with their families serving as choruses, prepare songs to express their side of the story and to vent their anger, and the winner is chosen by the applause of those attending the song duel. No decision is made as to who is right or wrong in terms of a body of law. What is most important is that the parties feel the complaint has been raised and laid to rest, and that this is sufficient to allow them to resume normal social relations.

Individuals who repeatedly violate rules and social expectations may be ostracized. But in most cases hostile parties simply move apart.

Typically, men hunt and women gather singly or in small groups, but all share some or all of what they obtain with other members of the band. As a result, few go hungry if others have adequate food, and no one has to work all day, every day. Tools, ornaments and other material possessions pass from hand to hand in endless rounds of informal but expected gift giving and taking, so that inequalities are minimal. Thus flexibility and sharing are important.

Low Energy Budget

Hunters and gatherers are unusual because they are able to sustain themselves on an extremely low energy budget. Humans, like all animals, require fuel in the form of food energy or calories. And humans, like all animals, expend energy to acquire food. Hunters and gatherers invest relatively little energy in the quest for food. They rely almost exclusively on their own muscle power—and even so, devote many fewer hours and much less energy to making a living than does the average farmer or factory worker in industrial societies. This is a point which we build on in later chapters.

Hunters and gatherers have limited *energy extractive* mechanisms, and thus we might say they are less efficient than farmers, since farmers extract many more calories of food energy from a given amount of land. However, this is only one aspect of energy efficiency. In terms of the uses of energy, the hunting and gathering population must be regarded as very efficient. Very little of the energy extracted goes into the infrastructure; it is mostly put toward supporting people. The amount of energy used to support a unit of population in the industrial world, on the other hand, is many times what it is for the hunters and gatherers, and thus could be called inefficient.

Nor do hunters and gatherers interfere with their environments to the degree that groups employing other subsistence strategies do. They use many species of plants and animals; their place in the ecosystem is that of "top predator" and other animals clearly have to adapt to their presence. However, they do not reshape it to the degree that agriculture does.

Foragers are not immune from the problems of exploiting the environment, of course. The Miskito—who are decimating the turtle population for cash payments—are every bit as typical of hunters and gatherers as the !Kung Bushmen and Baffin Island Eskimos, who exercise more caution. Indeed, the archeological record gives evidence of hunting populations who apparently drove the game on which they lived to extinction and were forced to make substantial changes in their adaptive strategies as a result. Of course, one product of such changes is the development of agriculture itself. But compared to our own indulgences in overkill, the indulgences and mistakes hunters and gatherers have made seem minor.

What we see in the case studies that follow is the delicate balance between people and food resources hunters and gatherers must achieve if they are to maintain their way of life, and the degree to which social controls affect this balance.

The !Kung Bushmen

The !Kung are one of five physically and culturally related groups of Africans who are known collectively as Bushmen. The Bushmen are something of an historical mystery. An educated guess would be that they once controlled most of southern Africa, but could not resist successive waves of Bantu and European invaders. Today, most of the estimated 45,000 Bushmen are being absorbed into surrounding farming and pastoralist communities.

The 466 !Kung Bushmen who live in an area known as Dobe on the northern edge of the Kalahari Desert in Botswana are an exception.[1] Although the Dobe !Kung have been in contact with Bantu and Europeans since the 1920s, share their water holes with Bantu pastoralists, and sometimes work for them, the majority (over 70 percent) remain almost wholly self-sufficient hunters and gatherers. When Richard B. Lee lived with them in the mid-1960s, they had no interest in agriculture, domesticated animals (beyond their hunting dogs), or firearms. They neither paid taxes to nor received services from the government of Botswana (except for smallpox vaccinations). They traded with neighboring Bantu pastoralists, but rarely worked for them as day laborers. Thus although the Dobe

---

[1] This number—466—includes 379 permanent residents and 87 seasonal visitors (Lee, 1968:30).

!Kung are not isolated, they are largely independent—mostly because they occupy territory no one else wants.

By almost any measure, the Dobe area is an inhospitable environment for humans—a fact that has protected the !Kung from invasion and assimilation. Dobe is a sandy plain, crossed by fixed dunes and dry riverbeds, stretching from the Aha Mountains in the west to the Okavango swamps in the east. The temperature ranges from below freezing on winter nights (May through August) to 100°F (37°C) in the shade during the summer (August through October). Sandy soil and alternation between too much and too little rain make the area unsuitable for agriculture. The open woodland and scattered shrubs and grasses that grow naturally do not attract large herds of migratory animals.

Nevertheless, the !Kung live comfortably in this environment. They collect raw materials (including scraps of metal from the Botswana Veterinary Station fences for arrowheads) and easily make everything they need. It takes a woman two or three hours to construct a shelter with bent wood and grass. Ostrich eggshells, which are readily available, make ideal water containers. A wooden digging stick, whittled in an hour, lasts several months; a bow, arrows, and quiver, which take several days to manufacture, last years. They also make ostrich eggshell necklaces, thumb pianos, intricately carved pipes, and children's toys from materials lying around. In general they keep their possessions to a minimum. In a matter of minutes a !Kung can pack everything he or she owns, except the house, into a pair of leather carrying sacks.

The Dobe also provides the !Kung with a variety of foods. They gather wild nuts (chiefly from mongongo trees), berries, melons, and

Although it is not a dietary staple, the ant bear, or great anteater, is frequently hunted as a source of food by the !Kung Bushmen. Here two men try to trap an animal within the burrow it has made in its search for ants and termites. (Richard Lee/Anthro-Photo)

Table 24-1: The Bushman Annual Round. Bushmen move regularly throughout the year, largely as the availability of water dictates. The availability of water also strongly conditions the size of the local groups and the activities of men and women. (After Lee and DeVore, 1968)

	Jan. Feb. Mar.	April May	June July Aug.	Sept. Oct.	Nov. Dec.
SEASON	SUMMER RAINS	AUTUMN DRY	WINTER DRY	SPRING DRY	FIRST RAINS
Availability of Water	Temporary summer pools everywhere	Large summer pools	Fewest water points (permanent waterholes only in dry years)		Summer pools developing
Group Moves	Widely dispersed at summer pools	At large summer pools	All population restricted to few points (permanent waterholes in dry years)		Moving out to summer pools
Men's Subsistence Activities	Hunting with bow, arrows, and dogs (year-round) Running down immature animals Some gathering (year-round)		Trapping small game in snares		Running down newborn animals
Women's Subsistence Activities	Gathering of mongongo nuts (year-round) Gathering fruits, berries, melons		Gathering roots, bulbs, resins		Gathering roots, leafy greens
Ritual Activities	Dancing, trance performances, and ritual curing (year-round) Boys' initiation*				†
Relative Subsistence Hardship	Water-food distance minimal		Increasing distance from water to food	Distance maximal	Water-food distance minimal

*Held once every five years.
† New Year's: Bushmen join the celebrations of their missionized Bantu neighbors.

other fruits; dig for roots and tubers; and hunt everything from wart hogs and kudu (two favorites) to springhare, guinea fowl, and rock pythons. According to Lee, the !Kung consider 85 plant and 54 animal species edible. Although they definitely prefer some of these to others, they are rarely at a loss for food. The main problem is the water supply, and the rains in large part determine Bushman migrations.

In May, the beginning of the dry season, Dobe !Kung congregate near the permanent water holes in camps of 35 or more. (The largest concentration Lee observed was at the Lailai water hole, which 147 !Kung, living in seven different camps, shared with 67 Bantu pastoralists and their herds (Lee, 1972:333–334). During the dry season, the Dobe !Kung rely primarily on roots and tubers within a day's walk of their camps, or about a six-mile radius. The clear, cool weather makes for good tracking and hunting; small groups periodically hike to the mongongo forests to collect nuts. By August, however, many local foods have been eaten up, and rising temperatures make either hunting or long treks hard, uncomfortable work. Out of necessity, the !Kung turn to less desirable foods—the bitter roots and melons, acacia gum, and palm hearts they passed up a month or two earlier. October storms begin to fill hollow trees and standing pools in the up-country. In November, the !Kung break camp and spread out over the land. Small groups move to different locations in the nut forests, taking advantage of the variety of fruits, melons, berries, and leafy greens and the influx of birds and animals that follow the rains. This is the season of plenty. The !Kung usually remain up-country through April, when the pools of water begin to dry up. In May these wandering groups converge on the permanent water holes, set up new camps, and the cycle begins again (Lee, n.d.).

At first glance this would seem to be a precarious, hand-to-mouth existence. After all, the chances of bringing down an animal with a bow and arrow are slim, particularly in an area where game is scarce, and the Dobe !Kung rarely have more than a day or two's supply of vegetables on hand. They have no storage facilities and make no attempt to spend extra hours gathering or hunting in anticipation of a possibly poor season. However, Lee's careful study of the Dobe !Kung proved that their lives are not a "constant struggle for survival," as had been assumed (Lee and DeVore, 1968:5).

From July 6 through August 2, 1964, Lee kept a diary of subsistence activities at an average-sized dry-season camp. Each day he recorded the number of people in camp, how many went out to hunt or gather (on a given day, only some adult !Kung work), and the hours each spent acquiring food. He weighed all of the animals the hunters brought back to camp during this period and the bags of nuts and other foods women acquired in a day's foraging. He even counted the number of mongongo nuts the !Kung crack and consume in an hour. By dividing the population of the camp in a given week into the total number of hours worked by different individuals and into the total amount of meat and vegetable foods acquired, Lee was able to calculate the !Kung workweek and daily consumption of food. The Dobe !Kung share the food they acquire with all members of the band, so averages are accurate representations of how much individuals work and how much they eat (Lee, 1969:62–74). Lee's results were surprising.

Lee found that the vegetable foods the women gather account for 60 to 80 percent of the !Kung diet by weight; the meat men bring in, only 20 to 25 percent. Thus meat is a delicacy for the !Kung, not a staple. The reason for this is obvious. A man who spends four days hunting *may* kill one animal (this is the average). In contrast, a woman who goes out to gather vegetables and fruits *always* finds something for her family to eat. Lee estimates that gathering is 2.4 times as productive as hunting in the Dobe area. One man-hour of hunting brings in approximately 800 calories; one woman-hour of gathering, approximately 2,000 calories. This not only means that vegetables and fruits are a more reliable source of food, but also that women are the chief "breadwinners" in !Kung society.

How nutritious are the foods Dobe !Kung acquire through hunting and gathering? Drought-resistant mongongo nuts are the !Kung staple, making up 50 percent of their vegetable diet. The average daily consumption (about 300 nuts) provides individuals with 1,260 calories and 56 grams of protein—the equivalent of 2½ pounds of rice or 9 ounces of lean meat. In addition, everyone in the camp Lee studied ate about 9 ounces of meat per day. Together, mongongo nuts and meat gave each person 2,140 calories and 92.1 grams of protein per day—well over the U.S. Recommended Daily Allowance for small, active people like the !Kung Bushmen (1,975 calories and 60 grams of protein).

Lee destroyed the myth that the !Kung are chronically malnourished. In addition, by counting the numbers of hours each person devoted to acquiring food during the 28-day period, he discovered that the !Kung do not work very hard by Western standards. Typically, a man will spend five or six days hunting, then take a week or two off to rest, visit, and arrange the all-night dances !Kung hold two or three times a week. It is not at all unusual for a man to decide his luck has run out temporarily and take a month's vacation. In one day, a woman collects enough food to feed her family for three days. Household chores take between one and three hours. So women, too, have plenty of free time to rest, visit, entertain, and embroider. Lee calculated that the average Dobe !Kung adult spends only 6 hours a day, 2½ days a week acquiring food—a total of 12 to 18 hours *per week*.

These figures are all the more surprising when one considers !Kung demography. It was once thought that few people in such societies lived beyond what we would consider

Table 24-2:	A Typical Week in July of a Young Bushman Mother of Two.
First day	To the mongongo forests with mother-in-law and sister-in-law; collect enough nuts for three days.
Second day	In camp: rethatch hut in morning, sleep in afternoon.
Third day	Visit a married sister at a neighboring camp; stop at Tswana cattle post in the afternoon to ask for tobacco. Return home at dusk.
Fourth day	In camp: youngest child has a cold; visitors arrive in the afternoon bringing the news that a curing dance is to be held at their camp the following night.
Fifth day	To the dance with husband, children, and husband's brother and his wife; stop to collect baobab fruit along the way; dance begins after dark and continues all night.
Sixth day	Sleep until early afternoon, return home by evening.
Seventh day	In camp: eat wart hog killed by father-in-law the previous day.

(After Bicchieri, 1972)

middle age. This, too, proved false. Lee found that 10 percent of the Dobe !Kung were over 60 years old. Neither the elderly members nor the young, who constitute another 30 percent of the population, directly participate in subsistence activities. (!Kung Bushmen do not expect young people to work regularly until they marry, which is usually between ages 15 and 20 for females, ages 20 and 25 for males.) Thus 40 percent of the population is made up of dependents, who live on the food young and middle-aged adults gather and hunt. Such a proportion of nonproducers is surprisingly high, and resembles that in agricultural communities.

This is not to say, however, that hunting and gathering in the Dobe area support a large number of people. Every society has to maintain a balance between its population and the food it gathers or produces. One way to achieve this balance is to limit the population. The !Kung Bushmen are particularly interesting in this regard, for their fertility rates are unusually low. !Kung women generally do not become pregnant again for three to five years after the birth of each child. The advantages of birth spacing are clear. Bushman women nurse their babies for at least two years, primarily because the food they eat is too tough for a small child to digest. And they carry children under the age of four wherever they go. Carrying two children plus water and supplies on a long visit, or two children plus 15 to 33 pounds of vegetables home from a foraging trip would be extremely tiring. Why Bushman women become pregnant so infrequently remains unclear. They do not have a long post-partum taboo or mechanical birth control devices, but the long lactation period and the lack of soft foods may have an inhibiting effect on fertility. Lorna Marshall, who studied the neighboring Nyae Nyae Bushmen in the 1950s, reported (1960) that they practiced infanticide, but Lee (1972) found no evidence of this. Whatever the explanation, the low fertility rate among !Kung Bushmen clearly contributes to their success in the Dobe area. Were their population to increase significantly, they would very quickly deplete their food resources.

The !Kung have a saying "Only lions eat alone," by which they mean that one of the characteristics that distinguishes human beings from most other animals is sharing and exchange. This is in fact the case. No other animal regularly shares the bulk of its food (except with infants). To !Kung Bushmen, this self-centered, hand-to-mouth existence is inconceivable — inhuman.

Exchange is one of the primary reasons why the !Kung are able to lead such leisurely lives and support so many dependents. Everyone in the camp gets a share of the food acquired during the day, whether or not they or a member of their family participated in the hunting or gathering. The sharing of meat is more formally organized than the sharing of vegetable foods, and appropriate distribution of food is one of the few common causes of conflict within groups. Each morning a number of adults leave the camp in different directions to search for food. Working individually or in pairs, they are able to cover a wide range and have a better chance of acquiring desirable foods than if they worked together. The rare big kill is a major social occasion. The owner (the person who owns the fatal arrow,

A kill having been made, these !Kung Bushmen cut up the meat, preparatory to dividing it among the members of their band. This extensive sharing of food assures an adequate portion for everyone. (Sherwood Washburn/Anthro-Photo)

whether or not he actually killed the animal) divides the meat into five or six portions, all of which he gives to other hunters. The recipients cut up their shares and distribute them among their relatives and friends, who in turn give pieces to their relatives, and so on until everyone has eaten.

The size and distribution of shares of meat are a matter of individual discretion, but Bushmen take care to meet their family's needs and repay past generosity. Smaller animals and vegetables are distributed informally. A family may invite someone standing nearby to sit at their fire, send children to neighbors with gifts of raw or cooked vegetables, or carry bits of meat and nuts on a visit. Thus each family's dinner is a combination of the food its members collected and the food they are given. The next morning, a different group of adults leaves camp to search for game and vegetables, returning in the evening to distribute food to those who stayed in the camp. Once again, everyone eats, producers and nonproducers alike.

The various artifacts used or enjoyed in daily life circulate in a similar manner. When a person receives arrows or a dance rattle as a gift, he keeps the present for a few months, then passes it on to someone else—with the expectation of receiving a gift of more or less equal value in the future. As with food, there is no immediate return for the giver; no systematic way to calculate the relative worth of gifts or to guarantee that the other person will reciprocate in kind. The !Kung consider bargaining and direct exchange undignified, and although they sometimes trade with the Bantu, they never trade among themselves (Marshall, 1961:242). Food sharing and gift-giving are based on norms of reciprocity which are understood and accepted by all Bushmen.

The principle of circulation in Bushman society extends to people as well. When a Bushman couple marries, the husband moves to the wife's camp for an indefinite period of bride service—perhaps bringing his parents or a sibling with him. Ideally, he stays with his wife's people until the birth of their third child (about ten years). At this point he may return to the camp where he was born and raised (perhaps taking some of his wife's kin along), stay where he is, move to a camp where one of his brothers is doing bride service, or more to one where his wife's siblings have settled. In addition, the Bushmen recognize an affinity with all individuals who bear the same name as they do, and address all of that person's relatives with kinship terms. Because the number of names Bushmen give their children is limited, a person is quite likely to find a "name-mate" in camps where he has no relatives and to be welcomed there too. Thus there is considerable freedom of choice with regard to residence and Bushmen take advantage of that freedom.

Lee (1968) estimates that every year, about a third of the population makes a shift in long-term group affiliation. Added to this is the fact that Dobe Bushmen are gregarious people and spend about a third of their time visiting other camps, a third entertaining guests. The size of the camp Lee studied varied from 23 to 40 persons in a single month. The openness of Bushman groups enables them to adjust the population of camps to the available resources. Further, this open mobility prevents quarrels from turning into serious fights, which are carefully avoided. The Bushmen are keenly aware of the fact that all of them possess deadly poisoned arrows and in the past fights have led to killing. Instead, when individuals cannot get along, one or both move. Thus social control, like economic exchange, is achieved by custom rather than by formal institutions.

The final key to the Dobe !Kung's adaptation is knowledge of the environment. Both Marshall (1961) and Lee describe the constant babble of voices at night in !Kung camps, when residents and visitors exchange notes on rainfall and water holes, ripening vegetables and fruits, and animal tracks, as what amounts to a "debriefing." In this way all individuals are kept informed about what the environment has to offer each week. In effect, the !Kung use the environment itself as a storehouse, and their collective knowledge of that environment as a tool. To live otherwise— to hoard food and accumulate goods or to attempt to garden or keep animals—would probably overload the limited capacity of the environment to provide for them. Indeed, in times of shortage, Bantu pastoralists fare worse than the !Kung, and Bantu women turn to foraging with the !Kung to feed their families. Although the !Kung Bushmen may not be "the original affluent society," as Sahlins has called early hunters and gatherers, neither do they live on the brink of starvation.

The Eskimo

Until quite recently, the Eskimo peoples who lived on the vast, treeless plains (or tundra) and along the changing coastlines of the arctic were isolated from the rest of the world by their formidable environment. In summer, temperatures in the arctic rise above freezing and daylight lasts as long as 22 hours. Lichens, mosses, shrubs, and tufted grasses appear, attracting a variety of wildlife—herds of caribou, musk oxen, polar bears, foxes, rabbits, and migratory birds. Seals and walruses bask in the sun; whales may appear; large schools of salmon run downriver to the sea in July or thereabouts, returning to inland lakes in August. However, the arctic summer is a short six to twelve weeks. The sea begins to freeze in late September. With the exception of seals and walruses, the arctic animals either migrate south or go into hibernation. By midwinter, the ice is 6 to 7 feet thick. Temperatures during long, 18-hour arctic nights may drop from a mean 30° below F to 50° below F (16°C to −27°C). Forty-mile-per-hour winds with gusts to 70 miles per hour are common. In the Hudson Strait area, 45-foot tides build walls of broken ice along the coast, making navigation extremely hazardous. Most years, the freeze continues into late July.

Traditionally, the Eskimo move inland during the summer (in groups of 20 to 30 individuals belonging to one or more extended families) to take advantage of fish runs and caribou migrations. For example, each August the Netsilik Eskimo carry their belongings up the waterways to the stone weirs (circular dams) built to trap schools of salmon. Once in the weir, salmon (whose instincts prevent them from turning back) become easy prey for the waiting Eskimos. The Netsilik eat some of the fish raw, on the spot, drying the surplus for the next winter. Toward the end of the month the group pack up once again, moving farther inland to await the predictable herds of caribou. Depending on the terrain, the Netsilik construct knife-lined pits in the caribous' path, stalk them with bows and arrows, or, howling in imitation of wolves, stampede them into narrow valleys where hunters lie concealed or into rivers where hunters wait in kayaks. Caribou provide not only meat but highly valued skins for clothing. Balikci estimated that a family of four needs about 30 skins for each winter (1970:47). In October and November, the Netsilik live primarily on food stored during the caribou hunts, supplemented by occasional fresh fish and musk oxen. The most important activity in this period is making winter clothing (one of the Eskimo women's vital contributions).

By December they are ready to return to winter camps along the bays and straits, where 50, 60, or as many as 100 people may join forces for seal hunts. Although some seals migrate south for the winter, others remain in the arctic, digging breathing holes up through the sea ice. (Seals need air every 15 or 20 minutes and construct several holes.) Hunting seals in midwinter involves hours of silent, motionless waiting at the breathing holes, harpoon in hand. For much of the winter, seals plus an occasional fox are the only sources of fresh food. In May or June, when the ice begins to melt, the Netsilik move to tents on solid ground. Hunting seals is easier and more productive in these months, for the sea mammals often come out of the water. But in July the ice starts to crack, making sealing dangerous, and Netsilik camps divide into smaller groups for their annual inland treks (Balikci, 1970, Chapter 2).

Thus hunting and gathering in the arctic is quite different from living off wild foods in the Dobe area. Eskimos depend almost entirely on hunting and fishing, and to a lesser extent on trapping and gathering duck eggs, clams, and the like. Except for the summer berries, there are no vegetables, edible roots, or fruits in the arctic; the long, dark winters, incessant winds, poor soil, and short growing season discourage plant life. Whereas the availability of water largely determines Bushman migra-

Having harpooned his seal, this Baffin Eskimo drags it home across the ice. Today, however, most Eskimos have turned to the use of high-powered rifles—they kill more animals but, ironically, lose more, because the unharpooned animals often sink through the ice or fall too far away for the hunter to reach them. (NFB, 5/58)

tions, the availability of animals and fish — and the cold — structure Eskimo patterns of movement.

Low temperatures enable the Eskimo to take advantage of seasons of plenty to stockpile food for periods of shortage (something !Kung Bushmen cannot do). The Eskimo have always collected as much food as they could when fish were running and game was abundant, storing the surplus in stone or ice caches. The cold also means that Eskimos have to invest more time, energy, and raw materials in building shelters (traditionally, igloos in the winter, skin tents in the summer), making clothing (multilayered garments, boots, and mittens), and heating their homes (in the past, with soapstone lamps that burned seal oil). In addition, the Eskimo cannot always simply walk from their camps to food sources. Dog sleds and kayaks (or, today, snowmobiles and motorboats) are essential for crossing the sea ice and using the bays, rivers, and lakes. And the Eskimo need a variety of specialized tools to construct this equipment. All in all, they have many more possessions than the !Kung Bushmen do.

From what we can gather from early explorer's and ethnographers' accounts, this lifestyle did not enable the Eskimo to support sizable numbers of dependents, as the !Kung Bushmen can. Old and sick individuals who could not keep up with the group were often left behind to manage for themselves (Balikci, 1970). Women did not enjoy the independence and equality of !Kung women, perhaps because of their more limited role in food production. Indeed, the unequal sex ratio in some Eskimo groups at the turn of the century suggests that they practiced female infanticide (see Freeman, 1971; Balikci, 1970). Infanticide (and particularly female infanticide) is one possible response to the need to keep population levels in harmony with the amount of food available. The threat of hunger is a recurring theme in Eskimo conversation — even in communities on southern Baffin Island, where official records and elderly informants' recollections suggest that hunting accidents have caused many more deaths over the years than hunger (Kemp, 1971).

Both !Kung Bushmen and Eskimos must adapt to outsiders pressing at their borders. Sealskin coats and soapstone statues in shops around the world, and the roar of snowmobiles and crack of rifles in the Far North, testify to the fact that arctic peoples have entered the world market. Today, Eskimos live by hunting, buying, and selling. "Money [has become] an important component in the relation between the Eskimo hunter and the natural environment," as William B. Kemp documented in fieldwork in one of the last all-Eskimo communities on Baffin Island (Kemp, 1971).

The village Kemp studied consists of four households whose total population varied from 26 to 29 over the period of the study. Three of the families live in *quagmaqs* (wood-frame tents covered with skins and old mailbags sewn together, insulated with a layer of dry shrubs and heated by traditional seal-oil lamps); the fourth, in a prefabricated wood house supplied by the government and heated by a kerosene stove. Among them, the villagers own two snowmobiles, a large, motorized whaling boat, and a 22-foot freight canoe with an outboard motor, as well as several large sledges and 34 sled dogs. Hunting remains their most important subsistence activity, but they hunt with rifles as well as harpoons. The younger men divide their time between hunting and mining and carving soapstone. And some leave the village periodically to work for wages at government construction sites. In one year, village members earned $3,500 for carvings, $1,360 for animal skins, $1,225 in wages, and received $670 in government subsidies, which enable them to purchase fuel, ammunition, and processed foods.

Kemp's analysis of energy flow in this small community is similar to Lee's study of the !Kung Bushmen's subsistence practices and standard of living. But Kemp had to take into account the use of fuel as well as muscle power, the hours spent working for wages as well as hunting and gathering, and the acquisition of store-bought as well as wild foods. To calculate the energy flow, he reduced both the number of hours individuals spent at various activities, and the different foods they acquired and consumed, to the common denominator of kilocalories (thousands of calories). This enabled him to analyze in considerable detail the sources of energy, the routes along which it flows, and the uses to which it is put. Kemp calculated that over the 54 weeks during which he kept records of village activities (February 14, 1967, through March 1, 1968) the Eskimo expended some 12.8 million kilocalories of human energy hunting, mining and carving, working for wages, taking care of household chores, traveling, and visiting. In addition, they used 885 gallons of gasoline, 615 gallons of kerosene, and 10,900 rounds of ammunition. During the same period, they acquired 12.8 million kilocalories in wild food for human consumption (plus 7.5 million kilocalories in food for their dogs) and 7.5 million kilocalories in store-bought food.

How well do the Baffin Island Eskimo eat? Game is their staple. The common seal and smaller amounts of bearded seal, beluga whale, caribou, arctic char, eider ducks, and duck eggs account for 85 percent of their diet. The villagers show no strong desire for non-Eskimo foods, and rarely buy canned meat and vegetables. However, they do purchase quantities of flour and lard for *bannock* (a pan-baked bread), sugar, and powdered milk; small amounts of such delicacies as jam, peanut butter, and honey; and tea and tobacco, which they prize. Kemp estimates that this combination of wild and store-bought food provides each adult with 3,000 calories per day. Approximately 44 percent of these calories is in the form of protein, 33 percent in carbohydrates, and 23 percent in fat—a diet unusually high in protein. Here it should be noted that the caloric needs of Eskimos are almost certainly greater than those of the Bushmen. Not only is the weather extremely cold, requiring greater food intake, but until the snowmobile became available they probably spent more energy in the hunt. In terms of nutrition, the Baffin Island Eskimo, like the !Kung Bushmen, live well. But Kemp noted that when the men in one household abandoned hunting for a month to work for wages and the family ate only store-bought food, 62 percent of their diet consisted of carbohydrates and only 9 percent of protein—according to Kemp's analysis, an unhealthy balance.

How have motorized equipment and cash affected the Eskimo lifestyle and interaction with the environment? The most obvious change is that these Baffin Islanders have become sedentary. The snowmobiles and boats enable hunters to travel to their hunting grounds in a relatively short time. Thus it is not necessary for the whole village to pack up and move, as in the past. In addition, store-bought food provides the insurance against hunger that moving seasonally to exploit a wide variety of game resources did in the past. Today, the only time the whole village moves is in August, when they camp near the trading post to await supply ships. In the words of one old man, "as my son always gets animals, we are no longer hungry."

The villagers express some ambivalence about their new high-powered equipment. Hunters complain that the mutual trust between humans and animals has broken down. Seals are wary of the rumbling motors and rifle reports; only young animals can be coaxed within shooting range. Moreover, the Eskimo point out that rifles are not necessarily better than their old weapons. In the spring, for example, seals fast, losing their winter layer of fat, and melting snow reduces the salinity of the water. As a result, the animals are less buoyant. Unless a hunter immediately secures an animal he has killed by rifle with a harpoon, it will sink—a fact that renders the long range of these weapons useless. Kemp notes that in one session of 30 hours of continuous hunting, the Eskimo killed thirteen seals, but retrieved only five. These reservations may in part explain why it is important that the Baffin Islanders exercise restraint in their game harvests.

Elsewhere, the introduction of modern technology into the arctic ecosystem has spelled disaster. In the area west of Hudson Bay, for example, hunters have virtually exterminated

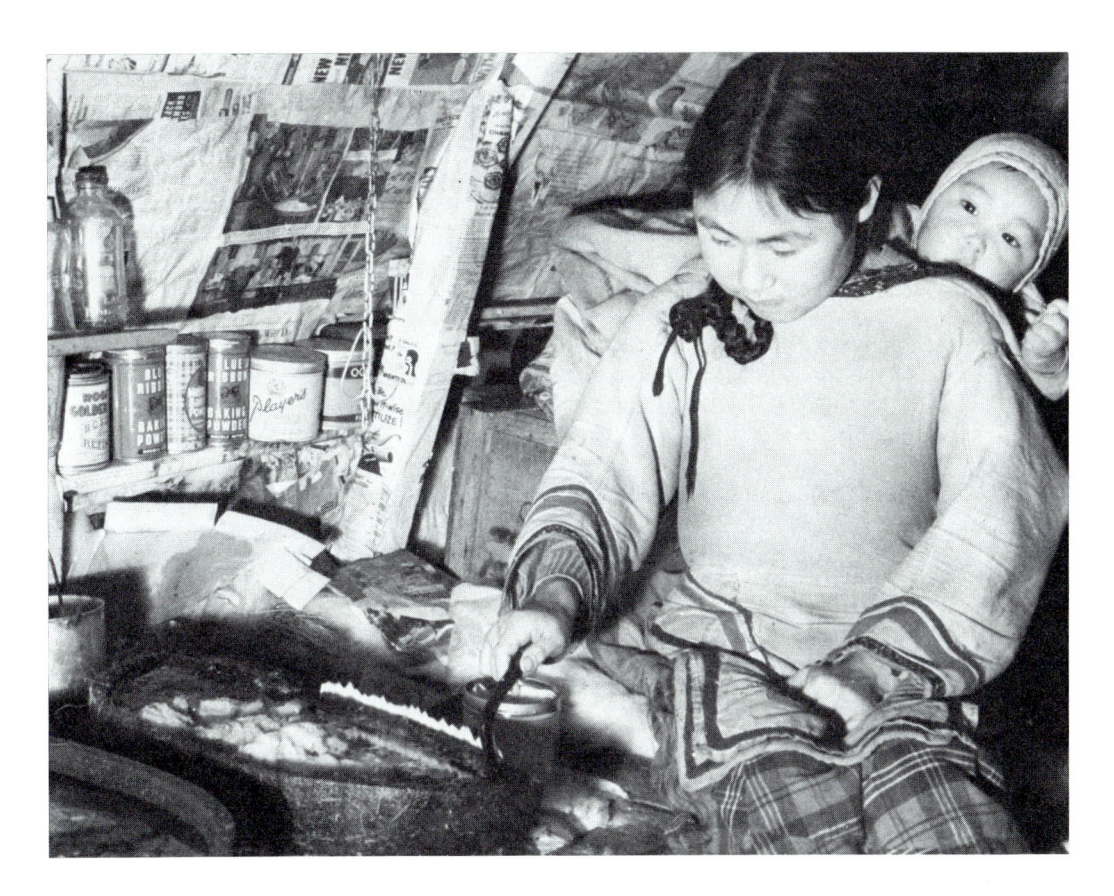

The lifestyle of the Eskimos has changed considerably as they have become part of the global market system. This Eskimo woman is tending a seal oil lamp, a traditional heat source. But the presence in her home of English tobacco and foodstuffs is proof of the increasing influence of the outside world. (NFB, 1954)

the once-large herds of caribou with rifles. Apparently, this is not happening in the area Kemp studied, however. Because the fall hunt has provided enough food to last through the winter that year, villagers spent more time visiting than hunting in February, March, and April. They might have used this time to collect extra skins for trading and perhaps dangerously reduced the seal population, but they chose to travel instead. The reason why any population, or for that matter any person, decides to do something is always hard to explain. But here the effects of the decision to increase rates of social visits among households has an important conservationist function. It may be that the people are conscious of the need to preserve the supply of wild game. It may be, too, that the returns on hunting are simply less than those gained from the equivalent time spent on soapstone carving, or even the rewards of visiting friends and relatives. The custom of taking Sundays off, adopted from non-Eskimos, has much the same effect of averting overkill. Whether the villagers are conscious of the need to maintain a balance between their needs and available resources is debatable. But they do it nonetheless.

The Baffin Island Eskimo also maintain balance in the distribution of resources among themselves. Although the snowmobiles are individually owned, all of the hunters contribute money to pay for gasoline to run them. Although the men hunt individually, for themselves and their families, they store food collectively. And when a hunter brings in a big kill, there is a community feast. Everyone eats until they are full, and the leftovers are distributed equally among the four families. Thus no one goes hungry in the village.

The point of these examples is that adaptation is not simply a matter of the direct interplay between technology and the environment. The Eskimo ethic of sharing reduces the incentive to slaughter large numbers of animals for cash. The need to earn money through carving takes young men away from the hunt. And the same snowmobiles that enable them to kill more sea mammals give them the opportunity to visit distant kinsmen. In this community, then, *social controls* "put the brakes" on new techniques for exploiting animal resources. This is not always the case, however.

The Miskito

The village of Tasbapauni, on the eastern coast of Nicaragua, lies on a narrow strip of beach separating the Pearl Lagoon from the Caribbean. The Miskito Indians who live there practice slash-and-burn agriculture, but depend on hunting and fishing for protein, which is why we include them here. And although they have access to a wide variety of fauna — in the sea, in the lagoon, and in the surrounding rain forests, palm swamps, and gallery forest — the Miskito harvest only a few of the available species. Of the 160 men that worked during 1968 and 1969, 80 did nothing but hunt turtles, 26 combined hunting with turtling, and 18 hunted exclusively, concentrating on peccary (a small, piglike mammal) and deer (Nietschmann, 1972).

There are several reasons for this selectivity. First, the Miskito do not consider certain readily available games "real" meat. They only eat these animals when they have nothing else. Second, although the yield from hunting is about the same as the yield from turtling, turtlemen are successful on over 70 percent of their trips, hunters on less than 55 percent of theirs. In addition, equipment (canoes, guns, harpoons, and nets) is expensive, and few individuals can afford two sets (one for hunting, one for turtling). Thus the initial in-

Table 24-3: Time and Yield Data for Hunting and Turtling for One Year (1968–1969). A comparison of the hunting strategies employed by Miskito men shows that turtling involves fewer hours of work per return, especially in terms of protein captured. Turtle hunting is increasing, primarily because of the demands of the market economy. (After Nietschmann, 1972)

	Pounds of meat (share)	Total hours	Hours traveling	Hours hunting and turtling
Hunter	875	533	305	228
Turtleman	812	455	241	214

	Pounds of meat:hour	Calories	Protein (grams)	Fat (grams)
Hunter	1.64:1	677,044	73,317	41,496
Turtleman	1.78:1	437,500	78,750	7,875

	Calories per hour	Grams of protein per hour	Grams of fat per hour
Hunter	1270	138	78
Turtleman	962	173	17

	Number of trips	Number of successful trips	Percentage of successful trips
Hunter	26	14	54
Turtleman	15	11	73

Major changes in Miskito society have resulted from the commercialization of turtle fishing. Some Miskito have made so much money from the sale of sea turtles that they have been able to build expensive new homes of foreign design. (Bernard Nietschmann)

vestment locks a turtleman or a hunter into one strategy.

Traditionally, the Miskito harvested only what the community needed. The fact that fields had to be cleared and planted during the season when turtles were most abundant acted as a check on overkill. The Miskito sold some of the turtles they caught to buy and maintain equipment—but only after they had fulfilled their obligation to share with kin. All this changed when two turtle-packing companies set up factories in nearby towns in 1960 and 1970.

With a guaranteed return of $8 to $13 per turtle, the Miskito began to concentrate even more heavily on this species. In the first six months of 1971, the number of green turtles killed rose 228 percent; the number of hawksbill turtles (which the Miskito seldom eat), 400 percent. During the same period, consumption of turtles within the village declined by 14 percent. It had become more profitable to sell the turtles and buy other food than to eat what they caught. However, the food the Miskito bought was usually high in carbohydrates and low in protein. Thus the quality of nutrition dropped. Men neglected their gardens (which had provided 74 percent of their food) to hunt turtles. Many stopped honoring their obligations to kin, upsetting the system of distribution within the community. Perhaps most damaging in the long run is the fact that the green turtle (which supplied 70 percent of their meat) is becoming an endangered species. The Miskito are mortaging their future for short-term profits.

When people hunt for subsistence only, the population limits their exploitation of resources. When people hunt for monetary gains and social controls break down, it is as if the population suddenly multiplied. In fact, this is exactly what has happened. Now the Miskito are simply one segment of a larger population to which they are linked by the market system. The Miskito are hunting for an unlimited number of people (represented by the export companies). What we see here is the breakdown of a social system based on reciprocity, and the transformation of an economy of underproductive to one oriented toward market demands. The Miskito are certainly not alone in the problems they are experiencing as they adjust to pressures from the outside world.

summary

In this chapter we examined the hunter-gatherer adaptive pattern, using as examples the !Kung Bushmen of Botswana, the Baffin Island Eskimo, and the Nicaraguan Miskito. It is easy, from the perspective of our society, to view such groups as anachronistic; however, these groups inhabit environments that provide a variety of subsistence resources, and they have developed fully adequate, although disparate, means of exploiting them and surviving.

Hunter-gatherer societies, unlike those that cultivate their food resources, tend to be more vulnerable to seasonal and annual fluctuations in their environment. Consequently, survival necessitates an adaptive pattern that delicately balances the environment, the group's technology, and its social organization. Nonetheless, the hunter-gatherer subsistence pattern has been dominant for much of human existence. One reason for its past and present success is its low energy budget. In contrast to groups with other adaptive patterns, hunter-gatherer groups invest relatively little energy in the quest for food resources and obtain substantial returns. Imperative for the success of the hunter-gatherer adaptive pattern are minimal interference with the environment, minimum energy outlay, and minimum exploitation of resources.

Social organization is an important part of their adaptation. Typically, groups are organized into flexible bands that can disperse and convene as the available resources permit. Their kinship system creates ties over large areas that maximize individual and group access to food sources especially in times of shortage.

The !Kung Bushmen inhabit the sparse Dobe area of the Kalahari Desert, where they exploit local food sources in seasonal migrations. To early observers, the Bushmen seemed nutritionally impoverished. However, the Bushman diet is varied and nutritionally sound. Although meat, hunted by men, is a prized and important resource, vegetables and fruits, gathered by women, are the staple of the Bushman diet. The communal sharing of foods is customary, as is the circulation of goods in gift-giving. Fluid band composition, kinship relations, and name-mates in other bands provide individuals with mobility and sources of sustenance during hard times, and also help to reduce friction among band members.

Traditionally, the Eskimo quest for food is seasonal; and animals are the primary source of food, clothing, tools, and fuel. However, the contact with a world market has caused changes in aspects of Eskimo life. When men shifted to wage labor, giving up hunting, the normally balanced diet was abandoned for one relying on store-bought items that do not provide adequate protein. Seasonal migrations are no longer necessary, since the Eskimo can travel long distances by snowmobile. Long-range weapons are effective, but the rate of retrieval of killed animals is low and overkill sometimes threatens their existence. But unlike other Eskimo groups, the Baffin Islanders seem to be aware, even if unconsciously, of the dangers these new tools present: they have maintained values of sharing which may prevent overkill, and have chosen means other than animal exploitation to achieve additional cash income.

The Miskito of Nicaragua have entered a world market at the expense of their traditional subsistence activities (hunting and slash-and-burn agriculture) and social system. The hunting of turtles has a higher success rate than the hunting of any other animal and is the preferred way to obtain protein. Traditionally, horticultural responsibilities and sharing with kin acted as a check on turtle overkill, but the introduction of turtle-packing companies offering lucrative cash returns has disturbed this pattern. As a result, consumption of turtles by the Miskito has declined, although the killing of them for sale has increased. The Miskito diet has declined in quality, and kin obligations have been neglected in favor of personal cash incomes. Most important, however, is the threatened extinction of the cash source itself—the turtles. The greatly increased demand has put strain on the ecosystem, which cannot support the stress.

suggested readings

BICCHIERI, M. G.
1972 *Hunters and Gatherers Today: A Socioeconomic Study of Eleven Such Cultures in the Twentieth Century.* New York: Holt, Rinehart & Winston. Presents original material on hunting and gathering societies using historical reconstructions as well as ethnographies based on participant observation to provide a general perspective on the adaptations of food collectors.

COON, C. S.
1971 *The Hunting Peoples.* Boston: Little, Brown. Lively and readable survey of the general outlines of hunting and societies.

DAMAS, D., ED.
1969 *Contributions to Anthropology: Band Societies* (National Museums of Canada, Bulletin 228). Ottawa: National Museums of Canada. Collection focusing on the forms of social and political organization typical of hunters and gatherers.

SERVICE, E.
1966 *The Hunters.* Englewood Cliffs, N.J.: Prentice-Hall. General introduction to hunting and gathering cultural patterns, including short sketches of a variety of foraging societies.

TURNBULL, C.
1961 *The Forest People.* New York: Simon and Schuster. Intimate view of the Mbuti Pygmies of equatorial Africa which explores the relationships of the people to the forest and to their horticultural neighbors.

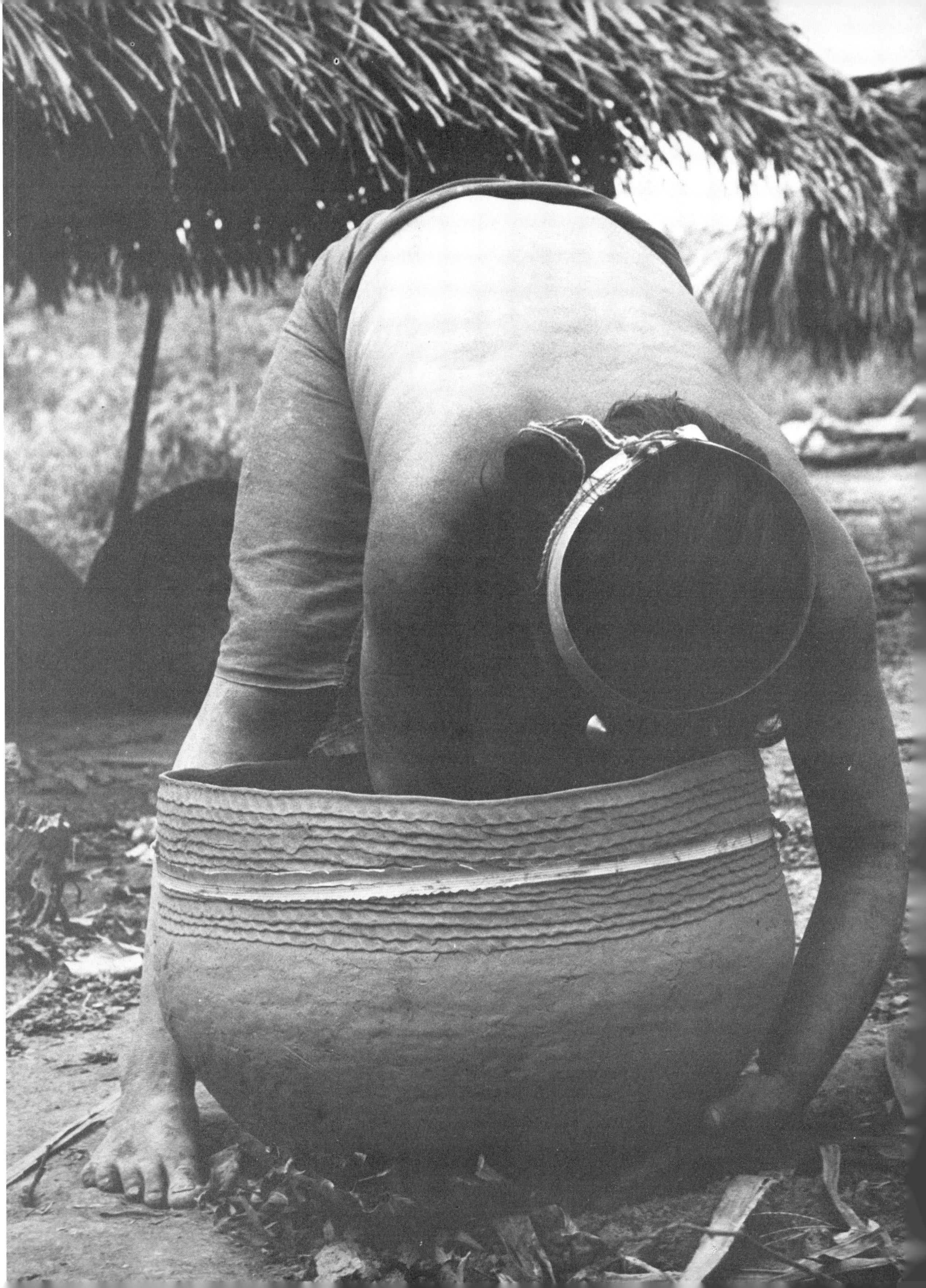

twenty-five
Horticulturalists

Horticulturalists rely on domesticated plants for the bulk of their diet. They may hunt, fish, and gather, as well; but unlike the peoples in the previous chapter, the tribes described here count on their gardens as their mainstay for food. This adaptive strategy results in many other differences between the two types of societies.

Horticulturalists are farmers, but not all farmers are horticulturalists. The particular societies we shall study depend on human labor and a few simple tools to make a living. Often such agricultural practices are termed "extensive" because of the low yields per acre. The amount of energy they extract from the environment through crops is enough to sustain themselves, but they do not produce consistently large surpluses for others' consumption. In fact, the absence of market demands is what limits pressures to intensify productivity and thereby produce exportable surpluses. Each household is usually capable of raising all it needs. The diversified and limited nature of production is why horticulturalists are called "subsistence farmers."

Horticultural Adaptations

Horticultural adaptations take many forms, with their common denominator being the high degree of self-sufficiency of local populations, the relatively low yields achieved per acre of land, and the generally simple technology associated with such farming. These characteristics, for example, are shared by the Yanomamö, Tsembaga, and Pueblo, even though their agricultural practices differ substantially in detail.

Slash-and-Burn Agriculture

Today, however, one form of horticulture is more common than others, in part because it occurs in areas where intensification is not feasible or where market pressures have not encouraged it. This agricultural system is called "slash and burn" or "swidden." Fields are used for only a year or two, then allowed to lie fallow a number of years to rebuild the forest cover and restore the fertility of the plot, then set aflame to clear the vegetation and lay down a bed of ash, full of organic nutrients for the crops. Thus horticulturalists need land for the plots under cultivation, and five to six times that amount lying fallow at the same time.

Swidden increases the flow of energy to humans not so much by changing the ecosystem as by creating what Clifford Geertz calls "a canny imitation" of it (1969:6). A tropical ecosystem contains a remarkable diversity of living things packed into a small area—that is, the ecosystem is *generalized* rather than *specialized*. Although tropical soil is often thin, it can support this dense variety because the nutrients are rapidly recycled in the humid, teeming jungle vegetation rather than being locked up in deep, rich soil. And it is a vertical world, where the closed canopy of trees prevents the thin layer of rich organic floor from being washed away by rains and baked hard by sun. Similarly, swidden plots contain a jumble of crops, from roots and tubers to fruit trees and palms, flourishing primarily on a bed of ash. The trees form a cover that pro-

A woman of the Amahuaca tribe of Peru fashions a coiled pot from clay she has collected. (Cornell Capa/Magnum)

tects the soil from erosion or parching and reduces the encroachment of luxuriant tropical undergrowth. "The swidden plot is not a 'field' at all in the proper sense but a miniaturized tropical forest composed mainly of food producing and other cultivates" (Geertz, 1969:14). Properly managed, each plot can be rotated from field to forest indefinitely.

As with other strategies, however, the environment can be degraded. If people use a piece of land for too long, crops will fail, the soil may bake hard or erode away, and the only plant that may grow there is *imperata* (also known as savanna, razor, or elephant grass). This is a particularly hardy plant that can survive in depleted soils; once it appears, for all intents and purposes the land is ruined.

Productivity and Population

Obviously, then, there are limits to the intensification of production, despite the lack of external pressure to do so. Not only is the soil vulnerable to depletion, but seasonal variations also limit the time during which land can be prepared for growing. Burning a field during the rainy season, for example, is difficult. Despite the limits, the horticulturalists do wring more resources from a given area than do hunter-gatherers, though far less than more intensive cultivators. They modify the environment more than hunter-gatherers but have far less impact than more advanced agriculturalists.

Planting and harvesting crops is not necessarily easier than hunting and gathering. Some agriculturalists work as many hours as the Bushmen do, for about the same returns in food calories. (See the box on p. 512.) Thus domesticated plants are not a "labor-saving device," as one might expect. Rather, they produce more food from a given input of land, permitting more people to be supported. Adopting agriculture permits somewhat greater population densities.

However, there are limits to population density among subsistence farmers, not simply because of the vulnerability of the ecosystem and seasonal limits but because of the limited availability of sources of high-quality protein. In the tropics, most cultigens are low in protein, so most protein comes from what can be brought home by hunters or raised in domesticated animals. This places limits on the amount of protein available. Actually the complete degradation of the environment and the specter of starvation are seldom limits in and of themselves. Rather, environmental limits select for cultural mechanisms that control population. A subsistence population may control its population growth (and demand for protein) by such means as infanticide or warfare. (This is by no means fail-safe — whole areas of Southeast Asia became a "green desert" of imperata because of overcropping and collapse of the forest ecosystem.)

The Importance of the Domestic Unit Actually, horticulturalists make the fullest possible use of neither land nor labor, according to the evidence assembled by Marshall Sahlins in his *Stone Age Economics* (1972). The basis of such societies is the domestic unit or household rather than the band, and its goal is to produce a livelihood for its members. Producing for subsistence takes far less work than the people are capable of, so many of the able-bodied, such as adolescents, may not have to work at all, and those who work do so intermittently. In fact, "productive intensity is inversely related to productive capacity" (Sahlins, 1972:91). This means that households can be highly independent of one another and populations highly dispersed, which explains why land may be less heavily utilized than its potential would allow.

In horticultural societies, higher-level social institutions — primarily wider kinship ties and political organization — are the force which unites these domestic units. Certainly the kinship network is usually larger and more elaborate and the domestic group more clearly delineated in agricultural than in hunting and gathering societies. The fact that agriculturalists invest time and labor in the land probably selects for more precise means of regulating and limiting access to it. Indeed, these societies are organized around groups defined by kinship and descent, which are often (but not invariably) the basis for recognizing individual rights to the use of land. Kinship carries with it obligations that extend beyond the immediate household, and that place more demands on the household to increase productivity. Political leadership arises out of kinship in these societies; the tribal headman, too, represents obligations beyond the domestic unit. Political power stimulates productivity in part by spurring the headman to create surpluses to maintain the show of generosity that is a sign of power in such societies.

Intergroup Relations

Exchange As population density and social complexity increase, intergroup exchange—including trade—becomes more important. All of the groups we will be describing engage in some trade. The Yanomamö of the South American jungle and Tsembaga of New Guinea acquire metal tools from neighbors, government officials, and missionaries. The Pueblo Indians of the American Southwest at one time obtained buffalo meat and hides from their nomadic neighbors, the Navajo and Apache. But for the most part, exchange in these societies involved gift-giving, not direct trade. A Yanomamö gives a man in another village a dog; some months later that man gives him a bow. Neither party necessarily depends on what the other gives: both can acquire dogs in their own village and make their own bows. What they need is each other's support either in warfare or in obtaining a wife. Gifts are given in the hope of creating and cementing alliances; exchange is as much a social as an economic transaction. The exchange of women is the ultimate expression of solidarity among the Yanomamö and many other tribal agriculturalists.

Conflict Such intergroup cooperation is only part of the story, for horticultural societies are not entirely peaceable. The Yanomamö engage in endless rounds of threats, duels, kidnappings, and raids; the Tsembaga spend as long as a year mobilizing allies with pig feasts when they are considering testing their neighbors' hold on territory; and the Pueblo Indians maintained war societies and organized war parties to overthrow the Spanish and fight the same nomadic tribes with whom they traded. More often than not, war consists of what Andrew Vayda (1974) has called "nothing fights": chest-pounding duels, club fights with definite rules, prearranged encounters with bows, arrows, and shields across wide spaces so that no one is mortally wounded. Some of these exercises are closer to our contact sports than to our wars. However, intervillage conflict can and does escalate to raids and attempts to rout a group from its territory. Even if antagonists who kill one or two people in the enemy camp are satisfied with the result of the skirmish and retire home, casualties can mount significantly if raids are frequent. In most of these societies, religious beliefs and rituals limit or regulate the slaughter. Even so, the existence of premeditated, organized, intergroup armed combat contrasts sharply with the near absence of war parties, raids, and the like among contemporary hunters and gatherers. (We should note, however, that paleo-hunter-gatherers living in higher densities in richer habitats were most probably more warlike; and that contemporary hunters and gatherers are pacified by neighbors and national governments, while horticulturalists are, in comparison, fairly autonomous.)

The Yanomamö

Napoleon Chagnon, who has lived among the Yanomamö on and off for nearly ten years, believes them to be one of the largest unacculturated tribes in the modern world. When Chagnon arrived in 1964, missionaries had established posts in two villages, but most of the Yanomamö knew of the world outside only indirectly, from metal axes and pots obtained through trade.[1]

The Yanomamö, who number 10,000 or more, live in villages of 40 to 250 inhabitants

---

[1] See Chagnon, 1974, Chapter 1, for a description of his attempts to reach a village whose inhabitants had never seen a non-Yanomamö.

distributed through the tropical jungle in southern Venezuela and Brazil. For the most part, the land is low and flat, with occasional rolling hills and mountain ridges and sluggish, muddy rivers that become rushing torrents in the rainy season. Palms and hardwoods rise above a tangle of vines and shrubs on the ground, creating a dense canopy. There is a downpour of rain two or three times almost every day, rainfall reaching a peak between May and August. The humidity rarely drops below 80 percent, intensifying year-round temperatures of 80° to 90° F (26°C to 32°C).

This habitat provides the Yanomamö with a variety of wild foods. They collect palm fruits, nuts, and seed pods in season; consider wild honey a gourmet dessert; snack on grubs, a variety of caterpillars, and roasted spiders. In addition, they hunt monkeys, wild turkeys, feral pigs, armadillos, anteaters, and other species with bows and poisoned arrows. They eat alligators and occasionally fish that they collect by damming a stream, pouring a drug in the water, and gathering the stunned fish in baskets. But these wild foods could not support the average Yanomamö settlement of 70 to 80 people. The fruits are seasonal; the animals are small, many are nocturnal, and except for monkeys and peccaries, they live singly, which makes them difficult to hunt. Chagnon notes that although on one occasion he and a group of Yanomamö hunters killed enough game to feed an entire village for one day, on another occasion five days of searching did not yield enough meat to feed the hunters (1968:33). Moreover, Yanomamö technology does not allow them to exploit the rivers as they might. (Their bark canoes are too awkward to navigate upstream, and so fragile they are generally abandoned after one trip downstream.)

Thus the Yanamamö depend on the food they grow: plantains and bananas (which make up 52 percent of their diet), manioc (used to make flour for cassava bread), taro, sweet potatoes, and less frequently maize, avocados, squash, cashew trees, and papaya. They also cultivate sugar cane for arrow shafts, cotton for hammocks and garments, hallucinogenic drugs, and tobacco.

Like other Indians of the South American jungles, the Yanomamö practice slash-and-burn agriculture. To clear land for a garden, they first cut away the undergrowth and small trees with steel axes they get from the neighboring Makiritare or from missionaries—or from anthropologists. They let this dry in the sun, then burn it off on a day when there is enough breeze to fan a fire but not enough to cause problems. This done, the Yanomamö set about felling the large trees, which they leave in the fields to mark boundaries between plots and to chop for firewood when the need arises. The most important part of planting a new garden involves carrying cuttings from plantain trees in the old garden to the new site—an arduous job, for a single cutting can weigh up to 10 pounds (4½ Kg). Planting other crops involves little more than making a hole with a digging stick and depositing seeds or small cuttings. Gardens are individually owned, and each man plants a variety of crops on his land. Once the garden matures (in two to three years), overlapping plant cycles produce a constant supply of food (Chagnon, 1968:33–39; Meggers, 1971:19–20).

Yanomamö do most of the heavy work during the rainy season, when swamps and swollen rivers make it impossible to engage in visiting and feasting, or raiding and fighting with other villages. Once established, a garden takes only a few hours a day to maintain. Accompanied by their wives and children, men leave for their plots at dawn and return to the village around 10:30 (if they have not decided to hunt that day). The men work in the gardens while the women help with weeding or gather firewood and the children play nearby. No one works during the heat of midday. Some may return to the gardens around four and work until sundown. However, most spend the afternoon in their villages, resting or taking drugs, while the women go out to collect firewood and haul water.

Cleared land in a tropical forest will not support crops indefinitely, however. After a time

A woman braids vines that have been stained with red pigment to form a basket. Making large baskets for carrying firewood and other materials is one of the tasks women perform in Yanomamö society. (Napoleon A. Chagnon/Anthro-Photo)

(perhaps six to eight years), the garden becomes "an old woman"—that is, barren—and a new site must be cleared. Left fallow, the land recovers its natural tropical growth and productivity in ten years or so and might be recleared for planting—but the Yanomamö rarely return to an old site.

Yanomamö live near their gardens in circular villages they call *shabono*. Each man builds a shelter of poles and vines for himself, his wife or wives, and his children. These homes are arranged around a central courtyard, and the spaces between them thatched over to form a continuous roof with an open space over the courtyard. For safety, the Yanomamö also construct a high pole fence around the circumference with a single opening that can be barricaded at night.

These villages usually include members of two exogamous patrilineages whose members have intermarried over several generations. Yanomamö lineages are not corporate in the sense of joint ownership of property or religious rites. Each man builds his own section of the *shabono,* clears and tills his own garden, prays when and where he chooses. The eldest member of a lineage does not have authority over younger members. The only headmen in Yanomamö villages are individuals who have proved their superiority in combat, diplomacy, hunting, or some other skill. (And these individuals have no right to order others around; they lead only to the extent that people respect and/or fear them.) Sons do not necessarily remain in their fathers' villages or live with their brothers. Indeed, it is not at all uncommon for brothers to line up on opposite sides of bloody intervillage feuds.

The really important ties are not with the man's brothers but with the lineage from which a wife can be drawn. The Yanomamö have a single term for all of the males of their generation and lineage, another for all the males of their generation from the lineage or lineages with which they intermarry, and one for all the eligible women. Those members of a lineage who are living in a village take an active interest in who acquires their lineage-mates' daughters and sisters in marriage. This is the one responsiblility or prerogative male members of a local patrilineage share.

Neither the composition nor the location of Yanomamö villages is permanent in any sense. Villages commonly break apart and regroup because of internal disputes. Even when this does not happen, villages move every few years. Some moves take place when new gardens have to be cleared. But as a rule, the villages are widely separated, and there is plenty of land to clear for crops in the immediate vicinity. Most often, Yanomamö move because hostilities with other villages have reached the point where the only way for them to survive is to flee. Intervillage duels, raids, ambushes, kidnappings, and other forms of treachery are a constant feature of Yanomamö life. They are always fighting with someone. The reason? Women — at least, that is the reason Yanomamö usually give (Chagnon, 1968:124).

The only form of population control the Yanomamö practice is infanticide. If a woman becomes pregnant while she is nursing a child of two or three, she will kill the baby rather than deprive the first child of vital nutrition. A woman will also commit infanticide if her first baby is a girl, for this is sure to displease her husband, and displeased Yanomamö husbands can be brutal, even murderous. As a result, there are more boys than girls in all of the villages — as many as 30 percent more (Chagnon, 1967:139). The fact that older, powerful men take second and third wives makes the shortage of females even more severe.

This unbalanced sex ratio creates conflicts within and between villages. Competition for a limited number of women eligible for marriage under the rules of exogamy turns real and classificatory brothers into potential enemies. Suppose, for example, there are ten young men in a lineage, only seven young women eligible for them to marry, and older men take two of these girls as brides. The men grow up knowing that only five of them will be able to marry within the village. Somehow they must outshine or disgrace the competition, and this tends to undermine whatever solidarity might develop among them as brothers. In addition, the shortage of women increases the temptation to commit adultery — particularly for the five "losers" in the marriage race. If one succeeds in seducing another man's wife and is caught, the husband will retaliate with all the ferocity he can muster. Repeated incidents may cause a village to divide into two hostile camps. If a member of one of the new villages falls sick of unknown causes, suspects his garden has been burglarized, or the like, he will probably blame it on members of the other village and organize vindictive raids.

A young Yanomamö may seek a bride in another village, but most are reluctant to do so because this means years of bride service. One popular alternative is to ambush a party from another village and kidnap some of their women. Of course the wronged husbands seek revenge, setting off a round of raids and counterraids. The fact that members of a village that is chased off its land must seek refuge in another village until they have planted new gardens exacerbates the problem. The hosts are almost certain to take advantage of their guests' weakened position to demand temporary or permanent access to their women.

All of this locks the Yanomamö into a vicious cycle. The more they fight for women, the more anxious they are to have sons who will help in the fighting, the more female infants they kill, the more they fight. Moreover, they raise their sons to be suspicious, hot-tempered, and quick to take violent action

Table 25-1: Causes of Death Among 240 Adult Ancestors of Three Related Groups. Note the effects of warfare on mortality, especially among males. (From Chagnon, 1967)

Stated Cause of Death[1]	Males	Females	Total	Percentage
Malaria and epidemics	58	72	130	54.2
Dysentery, diarrhea	16	5	21	8.8
Warfare	31	6	37	15.4
Club fights	2	0	2	0.8
Snakebite	2	3	5	2.1
Sorcery[2]	15	10	25	10.4
Tigers	1	0	1	0.4
Chest infections	3	1	4	1.7
Hayaheri[3]	1	2	3	1.2
"Old age"	4	0	4	1.7
Pains in groin	3	0	3	1.2
Childbirth	0	3	3	1.2
Other	2	0	2	0.8
Totals:	138	102	240	99.9

[1] These diagnoses were made by the Yanomamö.
[2] These deaths were probably due to such pathological causes as malaria. When malaria first reached epidemic proportions in some of the Yanomamö villages in the middle 1950s most of the deaths were attributed to the practice of harmful magic on the part of enemies.
[3] This is a peculiar sickness associated with intense pains in the upper abdominal region; the pains may last several days. In most cases the Indians recover.

against the slightest offense. In raising sons this way, they perpetuate inflammable conditions in the effort to defend against them.

Given this hostile social environment, the Yanomamö devote considerable time and resources to cultivating friendly neighbors. Alliances begin cautiously, with parties of visitors bearing gifts. The gifts are not free, however; the takers are obliged to reciprocate at some point in the future with gifts of equal or greater value. If visiting goes well, one village may rather suddenly "forget" how to make pots, the other how to manufacture arrow points, so that they become dependent on one another. These shortages are an expression of growing trust rather than need; all Yanomamö have the resources and skills to make everything they require.

The next step toward alliance is for one village to throw a feast for the other. This involves harvesting and cooking great quantities of food, amassing goods for exchange, and preparing elaborate costumes and dances. Because giving and attending feasts implies a higher level of commitment, the occasion must be handled with caution and diplomacy. The dances and songs are essentially displays of strength. Each side tries to impress the other with the fact that it does not really need allies and probably never will. Usually, disputes break out, and the men challenge one another to chest-pounding, side-slapping, and if they become very angry, clubbing contests. This brinksmanship can easily escalate into full-scale violence. Sometimes an attack on the guests or hosts is premeditated; other times it simply develops out of Yanomamö versions of the game of "chicken." If all goes well, however, the guests depart peacefully, the hosts can expect to be invited to a return feast, and both groups assume they can count on one another for refuge and food in times of trouble.

The final step would be for the two groups to exchange women. This does not occur unless the villages are convinced of one another's good intentions, or one is so weak it has no choice. Exchanging women usually means that the villages can expect support in their raids and skirmishes with other Yanomamö. However, even alliances based on marriage ties are tenuous—no village honors a commitment when there is some advantage in breaking it. As a consequence, the Yanomamö live in a world of chronic suspicion and warfare. Warfare accounts for at least 24 percent of all

The wrestling match of these Yanomamö men rapidly escalated into a side-slapping duel and beating contest. (Napoleon A. Chagnon/Anthro-Photo)

male deaths (Chagnon, 1967:140), a figure that is startling but not that remarkable when compared with New Guinea tribes or other Amerindian societies that are regularly fueding (Livingstone, 1968:8–9).

Chagnon suggests that the Yanomamö's militant, male-centered ideology is an adaptation to a hostile social environment. Marvin Harris (1974:276–79) and Daniel Gross (1975) believe the hostile social environment is related to the shortage of game and other sources of protein. Although the Yanomamö grow more than enough to fill their stomachs and have miles of virgin forest to clear for new gardens, the foods they cultivate do not provide large amounts of protein. For this they must hunt or fish. Harris suggests that at some point the Yanomamö began to intensify their agricultural activities, causing the human population to grow. As the population grew, they began killing increasingly larger numbers of wild animals—in effect, destroying their future sources of game. Thus they are hostile because they are fighting (albeit unknowingly) for hunting territory. Gross, on the other hand, looks at a variety of features besides warfare as adaptive to low protein availability: small settlements that minimize impact on the environment, dispersion, maintenance of a no man's land between settlements, frequent movements of settlements to avoid overexploitation of an area, and low population growth resulting from practices such as female infanticide and long post-partum taboos. Although the hypothesis of warfare being related to protein limitations is difficult to test, warfare among the Yanomamö is intimately bound up with many features of social organization.

The Tsembaga

The Tsembaga of highland New Guinea, who also practice slash-and-burn agriculture in a tropical environment, differ from the Yanomamö in two important respects. First, they do not depend on nature for animal protein. Like many other New Guinea peoples, they raise pigs. Moreover, although they do hunt, taboos that prohibit certain categories of Tsembaga from eating certain species limit the slaughter of wild animals. (For example, men are not allowed to trap marsupials between the planting of a sacred tree at the end of a war and its ritual uprooting ten to twelve years later.) Second, although the Tsembaga, too, believe in settling differences by fighting, they also observe long truces between wars, so that both sides have a chance to recuperate.

The approximately 200 Tsembaga (one of several Maring-speaking tribes) live in small clusters of houses scattered across 3.2 square miles (5.1 sq. Km) of tropical forest. The land rises sharply, from the Simba River, which is 2,200 feet (676 m) above sea level, to mountain ridges 7,200 feet (2,215 m) above sea level—all in less than 3 miles (4.8 m). Temperatures are in the seventies year round. Rain falls virtually every day, for an annual total of 154 inches. From August to November, the ground is permanently wet, and clouds regularly descend to levels of 4,000 feet (1,215 m) above sea level. Roy Rappaport, who studied the Tsembaga in the early sixties, identified three ecological zones in this territory: a band of secondary forest (the vines, shrubs, and young trees that appear when cleared land is left fallow) between 2,000 and 5,000 feet (615 and 1,538 m); between 5,000 and 6,000 feet (1,538 and 1,846 m) a strip of virgin forest (with mature trees growing as high as 125 feet or 38 m) that is marginally suitable for agriculture; and above this, a moss forest blanketed in clouds for most of the year and unsuitable for agriculture (1968: 32–37). Although the Tsembaga do not use

Building a fence to keep out both wild and domestic pigs is one of the major tasks in preparing a garden. (Roy Rappaport)

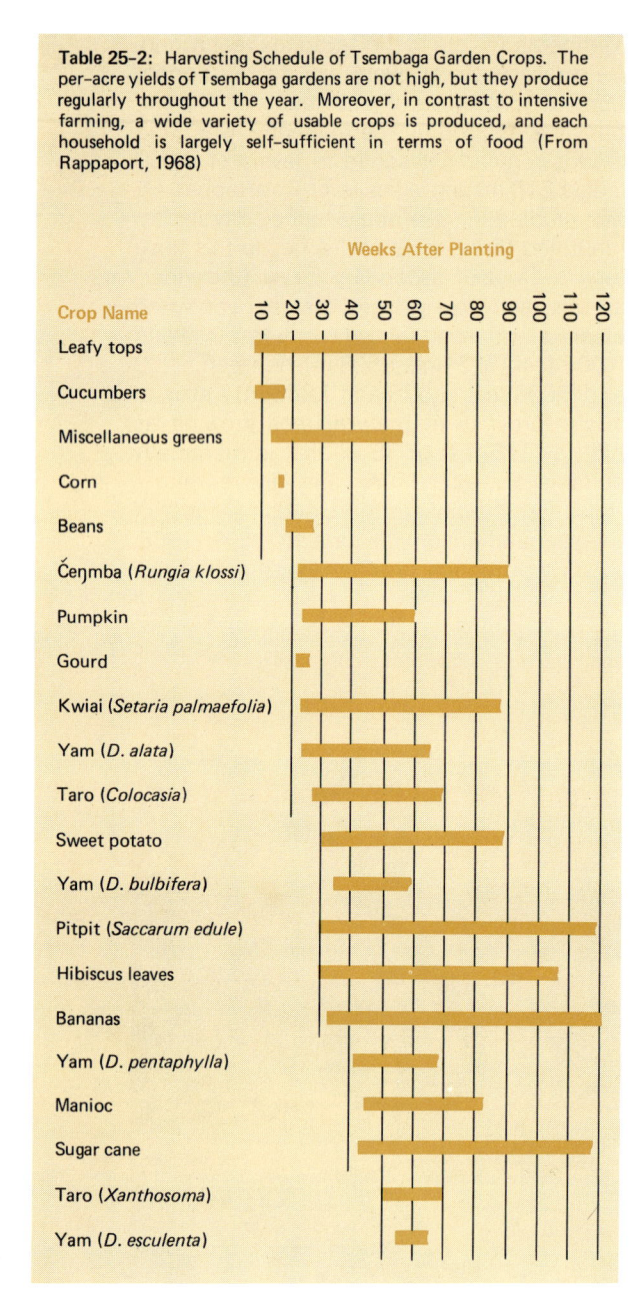

Table 25-2: Harvesting Schedule of Tsembaga Garden Crops. The per-acre yields of Tsembaga gardens are not high, but they produce regularly throughout the year. Moreover, in contrast to intensive farming, a wide variety of usable crops is produced, and each household is largely self-sufficient in terms of food (From Rappaport, 1968)

Crop Name	Weeks After Planting
Leafy tops	10–60
Cucumbers	10–15
Miscellaneous greens	15–55
Corn	20
Beans	20–25
Ćeŋmba (*Rungia klossi*)	25–90
Pumpkin	25–70
Gourd	25
Kwiai (*Setaria palmaefolia*)	30–70
Yam (*D. alata*)	35–65
Taro (*Colocasia*)	35–80
Sweet potato	35–95
Yam (*D. bulbifera*)	40–65
Pitpit (*Saccarum edule*)	40–90
Hibiscus leaves	40–90
Bananas	40–120
Yam (*D. pentaphylla*)	45–80
Manioc	50–90
Sugar cane	50–95
Taro (*Xanthosoma*)	55–85
Yam (*D. esculenta*)	60–65

the upper reaches of this territory for farming, they depend on the wildlife there for hunting and for raw materials for their houses and artifacts.

Whatever grows naturally in the area belongs to all Tsembaga. Individuals are free to hunt and gather where they please. However, gardens provide 99 percent of their food, and each local patriclan[2] (groups ranging from 20 to 70) owns and jealously guards the area where it gardens. Men and women work together to clear the land with machetes they acquire through trade; arrange felled trees to separate gardens and prevent the soil from washing downhill; build fences to keep pigs out; and plant with digging sticks. Although each domestic group has its own garden, Tsembaga often help their parents, siblings, or in-laws complete these tasks.

The arrangement of Tsembaga gardens resembles the tropical growth around them. This intermixing protects the soil from overexposure and leaching, and prevents diseases from spreading as quickly as they might if all specimens of a given crop were located in one place. Once planted, a garden can be expected to produce for between 14 and 24 months. The Tsembaga do not plant in the same location twice in a row. Indeed, they protect young trees that sprout among their crops — knowing that these sprouts are the first step toward reforestation, which will replenish the soil and allow them to use the land again 10 or 15 years hence.

Tsembaga also keeps pigs, as noted above. Pigs perform several useful jobs for their owners. They act as "sanitation men," cleaning up garbage and waste around Tsembaga homes, and as "plows," rooting up the last tubers and turning over the soil in abandoned gardens, thus hastening the reforestation process. Oddly, the Tsembaga do not slaugh-

---

[2]The Tsembaga are divided into three small and two large exogamous patriclans. Each of the small clans has its own territory; the other two are divided into smaller subclans with distinct territories, so the population is widely dispersed.

ter and eat their pigs on any regular basis. Since a grown pig consumes as much food as a human being and people often have to start a second garden just to feed the pigs, this seems an enormous waste. However, Rappaport's careful analysis of the occasions on which the animals are slaughtered reveals that pig husbandry is a vital aspect of the Tsembaga's adaptation to their environment. It also illustrates the importance of ideologies and ritual behavior to human adaptation.

The Tsembaga kill pigs only in a ritual context, when a person is sick or injured, when someone dies, or when a group is preparing to go to war. As Rappaport suggests, all of these occasions are emergencies. The consumption of pork provides the sick and injured people with protein that aids in their recovery. Relatives who are worried or in mourning and warriors also eat pork. This is important. Psychological stress increases a person's rate of protein use, and an individual whose protein intake is marginal (as the Tsembaga's usually is) may suffer a variety of painful symptoms.

In short, the Tsembaga eat pork when they need it most. Pigs are a "device" to convert starchy foods into high-quality protein and store this for emergencies (Rappaport, 1967: 89).

The *kaipu,* the pig feast Tsembaga hold in preparation for war, is particularly interesting in this regard. The Tsembaga believe that in order to win their ancestors' support, they must stage an extravagant series of pig feasts. (During the *kaipu* Rappaport observed, 105 pigs, weighing a total of about 8,500 pounds [3,864 Kg] were killed and distributed.) Each man in the group invites his kinsmen and allies, they invite theirs, and so on until a large war party has assembled. The feasting, which may continue intermittently for a year, serves a number of functions. Most obviously, it assures the protagonists that they have enough

Tsembaga men and boys practice for the kaipu. They are not wearing the elaborate regalia they would at the actual event. (Roy Rappaport)

A Food-Energy Formula

Lee's study of the !Kung Bushmen and Kemp's analysis of the flow of energy through an Eskimo community reflect a growing trend among anthropologists to replace subjective evaluations of a group's standard of living with objective measures—the number of people engaged in food collection or production, the amount of time and energy they devote to subsistence activities, the energy (food calories) they acquire. Marvin Harris (1975:233–255) has devised a simple formula for calculating the productivity and efficiency of different methods for acquiring food:

$$E = m \times t \times r \times e$$

where,

E stands for the food calories a group acquires annually (a measure of productivity);

m, for the number of people engaged in subsistence activities;

t, for the average time each of these individuals spends collecting or producing food annually;

r, for the calories each expends per hour (an estimate based on the rate of work an average person can maintain without becoming overheated or running out of breath); and

e, for the number of food calories acquired for every calorie expended.

The latter is particularly significant. If a person acquires only one calorie for every calorie he expends getting food, he will have no energy left over for other activities. Thus e is a measure of what Harris calls "technoenvironmental efficiency": the more surplus calories a group acquires, the more energy is available for other activities and for individuals not directly involved in food acquisition.

Using Lee's records, Harris calculates the technoenvironmental efficiency of the Bushmen as follows:

$$E \qquad = m \times t \times r \times e$$
$$23{,}000{,}000 \quad 20 \quad 805 \quad 150 \quad 9.6$$

How does hunting and gathering compare to other ways of making a living?

The Tsembaga of highland New Guinea, who plant taro, yams, sweet potatoes, and other crops in fields they clear in the tropical forest by slashing and burning, do not work as many hours as the Bushmen and produce more food calories for every calorie expended in gardening.

$$E \qquad = m \times t \times r \times e$$
$$150{,}000{,}000 \quad 146 \quad 380 \quad 150 \quad 18$$

However, the Tsembaga also keep pigs, and pigs have to be herded, penned, and fed. A. R. Rappaport's (1968:62) estimates of the amount of time 66 women spent tending a large herd of 160 pigs that ultimately yield 5,252,000 food calories suggest this is not a very efficient means of acquiring energy.

$$E \qquad = m \times t \times r \times e$$
$$5{,}252{,}000 \quad 66 \quad 758 \quad 150 \quad 0.7$$

The Tsembaga thus spend more time and energy feeding their pigs (which weigh as much and eat as much as humans do) than they do feeding themselves. However, pigs are a necessary source of protein, and, as we discuss in the chapter, the Tsembaga balance the need for pigs with the cost of raising them.

Irrigation increases the level of productivity and technoenvironmental efficiency dramatically, as Fei Hsiao-t'ung and Chang Chih-i's (1947) data on the Luts'un villagers of pre-Communist China demonstrate. The Luts'un villagers cultivated rice and small amounts of soybeans, corn, manioc, and potatoes on irrigated terraces, with the following results:

$$E \qquad = m \times t \times r \times e$$
$$3{,}788{,}000{,}000 \quad 418 \quad 1{,}129 \quad 150 \quad 53.5$$

Assuming the 700 residents of Luts'un consumed about 2,500 calories per day, irrigated agriculture enabled them to produce a surplus of 638 million calories—enough to feed over a million people not directly engaged in farming. The villagers converted their surplus into money (via markets) to pay rent and taxes and to purchase nonfarm goods and services.

With the mechanization of agriculture, productivity takes a quantum jump. In 1964, for example, 5 million U.S. farmers produced approximately 260 trillion food calories—enough to provide themselves and 250 million other people with 3,000 calories per day. However, it is difficult to calculate the technoenvironmental efficiency of mechanized agriculture. For every farmer, there are at least two additional workers who produce fertilizer and pesticides, manufacture and repair farm equipment, work in canning factories, and the like. We do not have accurate figures on the amount of time and energy these workers invest in food production. Given an average salary of $3.42 an hour for blue-collar work and an average food bill of $600 per person per year (in 1970), we can estimate that an American works about 180 hours a year for his or her food. However, the same average worker puts in another 1,820 hours a year working to supply other needs and desires—a 40-hour workweek Bushmen would undoubtedly find intolerable. Thus despite an abundance of "labor-saving" devices, people in industrialized societies have considerably less leisure time than people in nontechnological societies.

allies to risk war; builds morale among those who will fight and those who will wait for them; and allows warriors to build up their strength by consuming large amounts of meat. A *kaipu* is also an opportunity for trade and for young, marriageable men and women to look one another over.

The *kaipu* ends with the distribution of salted pork to the warriors.[3] This signals the beginning of hostilities. The war—sporadic skirmishes with bows and arrows, spears, axes, and wooden shields—usually continues for several weeks. Frequently both sides grow weary and arrange a truce, but occasionally one side is able to drive the other off its land, forcing them to take refuge with kinsmen in other areas. The victors burn their houses, destroy their gardens, and kill their pigs—but they do not occupy the land. They fear the losers' ancestors. Instead, both groups retreat to the borders of the disputed territory. All remaining adult and adolescent pigs are slaughtered and distributed to the allies. Then each group plants a sacred tree, called the *rumbim*, and vows to its ancestors that it will not attack the other until the tree has grown and it has enough pigs to thank them properly with a *kaipu*. As a rule, this takes about ten years.

Tsembaga wars and the rituals surrounding them have two important consequences. First, war redistributes the population and insures that a piece of land will lie fallow for an extended period. The territory is not reoccupied until the *rumbim*—and presumably the trees in the empty land—have grown. Secondly, the feasts before and after a war all but eliminate large herds of pigs that had begun to compete with humans for food. The Tsembaga give many reasons for going to war—kidnapping women, rape, shooting a pig, stealing food, witchcraft, and so on. However, in Rappaport's view the real reason is population pressure. As the pigs mature and multiply, the number of incidents involving pigs invading gardens, breaking fences, and the like increases. Tensions build; quarrels become more and more frequent. Women, who are responsible for the herds and beginning to feel overworked, egg the men on. The more people there are in an area, the more pigs there are, the more incidents. Thus pigs "sound the alarm" when people become overcrowded.

The Pueblo Indians

The Pueblo Indian tribes stand in marked contrast to the two societies just discussed in the environment they inhabit, the agricultural techniques they employ, and the way their societies are organized. Furthermore, they have been beset for several centuries by competing populations—Spaniards, other Indian tribes, and Anglo settlers.

The Pueblo Indians are the cultural and biological descendants of hunters and gatherers who migrated to the American Southwest over 10,000 years ago. The ancestors of today's Pueblos became skilled basket makers, weavers, potters, and above all, architects. Their pueblos (or villages) rose three and four stories above the ground in honeycombs of interconnected rooms opening onto a protected inner courtyard and the kivas (round, semiundergound ceremonial chambers). This one compact "apartment building" housed an entire village of as many as 2,000 people. The outside wall was often blank, so the only way to enter the pueblo was by ladders that could be easily pulled up during an attack (Dozier, 1970). There is marked diversity in the size and surrounding environment of pueblo settlements, as the prehistoric Classic period was a time for experimentation with different strategies for survival and different social organizations. However, selective pressures (climatic changes and raiding, for example) reduced this diversity, and the less adaptive strategies disappeared. Essentially two patterns survived. The most common pattern of

---

[3]This in itself is interesting. Tsembaga warriors always eat salted pork before engaging the enemy; they also observe a taboo against taking any liquid while they are fighting. As a result, many battles break off because the men on both sides are thirsty.

prehistoric times survived only in the Rio Grande and a few other areas; it is referred to as the "eastern Pueblo" adaptation. The other pattern, found in eastern Arizona and western New Mexico is called the "western Pueblo" adaptation.

The semi-arid mesas and canyons of the western part of Pueblo territory seems an unlikely choice for farmers. The growing season is short; the frosts begin in mid-September and persist through mid-May, though they may occur unpredictably through early summer. There are few permanent streams, and rainfall (usually in the form of sudden torrents) rarely exceeds 15 inches (38 cm) a year. In this extreme environment wild plants abound, including cacti, yucca, grasses, and occasional junipers and piñons.

The ancestors of the western Pueblo learned to exploit the water-holding sands, alluvial fans, and flood plains through an agricultural technique known as flood farming. Some years July storms filled the arroyos (or gullies) to overflowing, providing natural irrigation for adjacent fields. Other years the rains came too late or were so violent that crops were uprooted and a season's labor washed away. But in those years flat sandy areas at the bottoms of the mesas would hold enough water for domesticated plants and sandstorms might not destroy maize planted in deep holes in the dunes as they did other years. By planting their staple crops of maize, beans, and squash (plus cotton and tobacco) in three or four locations, these farmers discovered they could meet all contingencies: one crop would succeed when another failed. Indeed, working with very simple technology (digging sticks, wooden shovels, and stone axes), they were able to stockpile large quantities of food as insurance against drought, enough food from a normal growing season to last through at least the next one and often the next two. For variety and nutrition, they also kept turkeys, hunted, gathered small amounts of wild food, harvested some wild plants which were allowed to grow in the fields, and traded for buffalo meat and skins with neighboring hunters and gatherers.

Two of the Pueblo's artistic achievements — architecture and pottery — are visible here in this austere landscape of the Rio Grande Pueblo. (Bureau of Indian Affairs)

In the area inhabited by the eastern Pueblo, irrigation is possible because rainfall is far more predictable (as is frost). By diverting the river and its tributaries into irrigation ditches, the eastern Pueblos were able to control the supply of water for their crops. This involved substantial investments of labor. There were dams to build; ditches to maintain; land to clear, level, and grade in descending terraces so that water would flow down into the fields. And it required coordination along with some means of resolving the conflicts over water control.

Because of differences in environment and technology, the eastern Pueblo were not dependent on the vagaries of nature as were the western Pueblo. The social structure of the two groups reflected this difference in subsistence practices. Flood farming is a family affair, requiring ingenuity and patience but a relatively small input of labor. Each western Pueblo household provided for itself. The women and girls tended the group's vegetables, prepared its food, hauled water, made the baskets, pottery and clothing, and cared for children. The men and boys farmed and hunted for the group, collected fuel for fires, spun and wove cotton, and tanned leather for their clothes. As a result of economic independence, western Pueblo domestic groups were relatively autonomous.

These groups were organized into lineages and clans. The western Pueblo traced descent through the female line. The women of the clan owned the houses, fields, seeds, stored food, and rituals associated with the group. Daughters usually stayed in their mothers' households for life, and although sons moved to the brides' households, they continued to regard their mothers' houses as home. Each matriclan recognized one household as its religious center and the eldest woman of the clan as its ceremonial head. However, in practice her brother was in charge of the clan's ritual objects and was responsible for performing ceremonies. (Indeed, women were excluded from some rituals.) And although these cults belonged to the clan, membership was drawn from the community at large, regardless of clan affiliation. Initiates chose to join in the curing or bear or hunting society because they felt a calling; except for the clan head, participation was voluntary. Nearly all members of a pueblo were related, through either clan affiliation or membership in overlapping religious societies (Thompson, 1950:66–70). The religious societies crosscut boundaries, preventing western Pueblo from dividing along clan lines under normal conditions.

Although the western Pueblo invested considerable time, energy, and faith in religion, cult leaders did not exercise control over other aspects of people's lives. They were religious men, not chiefs, and although the heads of the societies met periodically, they confined their deliberations to ceremonial matters. The western Pueblo had no formal political structures, no formal means of social control (laws, judges, trials, and so on). Gossip and ridicule—institutionalized in the so-called clown cult, which mocked deviants—kept most people in line.

The weakness of large-scale political integration combined with the strength of the clans was probably a response to a highly variable and unpredictable resource base. Villages were likely to break up when times grew hard. A clan provided the core of a new village because government, religion, subsistence, and community affairs were already organized around the clan.[4]

For the eastern Pueblo the problems were

---

[4] There were other facets of the society besides the ease of village fission that can be seen as adaptive, of course; in the chapter on religion, for example, we saw how rituals served to redistribute food, especially at times of the year when people whose harvests had been lean were facing a shortage of food.

different—and so were the ways in which the society was organized. The eastern Pueblo were beginning to experiment with intensive agriculture. Irrigation and terracing controlled water supplies, thereby increasing yields. Building and maintaining irrigation works requires the coordinated efforts of a relatively large labor force. Domestic groups working independently would not be efficient and might even be in conflict. Moreover, the eastern Pueblo were not as vulnerable to changes in the weather as their western counterparts; their livelihood was more certain.

In the western Pueblo the katchina cult, into which all children were initiated, was most important. Katchina ceremonies involved masked dancers representing supernatural beings who were thought to control the rains and thereby the general well-being of the people (Dozier, 1970:140). Although the katchina cult existed in the east, it was weak compared to the medicine and war societies. In theory these societies were religious associations, like the katchina cult, but, in practice they were a good deal more. When cult leaders of the eastern Pueblo met, it was not only to arrange religious activities, but also to organize war ceremonies (which served as boot camp for young Pueblo) and to coordinate communal hunts, planting and harvesting, work on the irrigation system, and maintenance of the kivas. Membership in eastern Pueblo cults was voluntary, but cooperation and obedience to cult leaders were not. Medicine men, backed by war chiefs, exercised considerable influence over all the eastern Pueblo—and in some cases, despotic power. A family that could not discipline one of its members turned to these big men. Not infrequently, an individual or group that disagreed with the medicine men's arch-conservative views was expelled from the pueblo and its holdings confiscated.

Power over individual activities was centralized in highly structured, powerful societies, not diffused among independent households as it was in western pueblos. In fact, the village was the basic unit of eastern Pueblo society. Anthropologist Edward Dozier (a Tewa Indian) traces the replacement of independent kin groups with quasi-religious political organizations and centralized authority directly to the need to coordinate work on the irrigation systems among the eastern Pueblo (1970:131-133).

When the Spanish invaded and subdued the American Southwest, these contrasts between western and eastern Pueblo intensified rather than disappeared under the pressures of colonization. The western Pueblo were protected by their harsh environment from the full onslaught of the Spanish. The eastern Pueblo areas were much more attractive, not only because of the environment but because of the greater similarity of eastern Pueblo farming practices to those of the Spanish.

In a relatively short time the eastern Pueblo were obeying commands for tribute and labor to avoid brutal punishment by the Spaniards. In "return," the Spanish introduced wheat, melons, tomatoes, chilies, fruit trees, and domesticated animals. The Pueblo also learned how to herd, work metal and wood, and weave wool. They began to use Spanish as a lingua franca to bridge language barriers between different groups of Pueblos. Some individuals even moved into Spanish communities. But although the Pueblos accommodated themselves to Spanish demands, most never accepted the Spanish way of life. As demanded, each pueblo appointed a governor and civic and religious police, but in most pueblos these individuals were merely figureheads appointed by the medicine men and war chiefs, who, unknown to the Spanish, actually ruled the pueblos. As demanded, they attended mass, but continued to perform traditional ceremonies in secret. Thus they went through the motions of accepting Spanish culture, compartmentalizing the alien ideology and institutions while exploiting the material culture.

Even today the contrast between eastern Pueblo cultivators and western Pueblo horticulturalists is marked, a contrast having its roots in the differing environments but also affected by adaptations to differing social environments. We have already seen the importance of external relations among the Yanomamö: villages move not only to avoid exhausting the land but also to avoid the threat of being overwhelmed by their neighbors. At the center of Yanomamö territory, where villages are densest, moving is most difficult and conflict is most intense; at the periphery the reverse is true (Chagnon, 1973).

There are other points of comparison among the three very different tribes we have been examining. First of all, horticulturalists know an enormous amount about their environment: they can distinguish many varieties of soil, cultivate an enormous range of plants, and arrange gardens quite productively. Swidden itself requires a sense of when to move, how to burn, and when a plot has lain fallow long enough to be reoccupied. Likewise, the western Pueblo must plant complementary areas in order to insure a good harvest, which demands sensitivity to the topography and microclimate.

Next, we have seen that reliance on domesticates has many consequences for social organization. It is generally associated with higher population densities, requiring greater complexity. As Robert MacC. Netting observed, "agriculture impinges directly on social organization because it is people in groups who do the work, share in the consumption of food, and have the rights to the resources necessary for subsistence. In many farming groups the household is almost self-sufficient . . ." (1971:22). Pantribal political organization may be weak, often with the community or even a clan within the community being the effective unit of decision making.

Finally, we have seen that horticultural societies are neither utopias based on sharing and trust, nor atomized groups of armed and hostile camps. Like their adjustment to the physical environment, their response to the social environment is sensitive and flexible. Even the Yanomamö have fine gradations of escalation in their warfare, as well as escalations in cementing alliances (Vayda, 1974: 186).

What we see in these societies is something more complex than bands, involving slightly denser populations wringing somewhat more energy from comparable land areas. Whether cooperative or agonistic, contacts between groups are more routinized, through exchange customs and warfare. The changes from hunting and gathering to horticulture (or pastoralism), while profound, are fully realized only with the arrival of intensive agriculture. The basic trends were seen in the contrast between the eastern and western Pueblo, but will be taken up in greater detail in Chapter 27. Nevertheless, horticultural tribes are distinguished from band organization by far greater political integration of defined subtribal groupings. Also, in contrast with most intensive farmers, local populations are politically autonomous, as are all of the groups we have discussed in this chapter. Most peasants or intensive farmers live in communities within complex state systems, and these local communities have very limited political functions; they are actually dependent satellites.

summary

Horticultural societies are based on subsistence farming. Human labor and simple tools are the primary means of working the land, and horticulturalists do not produce consistently large surpluses for others' consumption. They are generally not part of a market economy; what is planted and harvested is consumed by the local group.

The most common method of horticulture is "slash-and-burn" or "swidden" agriculture. Trees and undergrowth are burned to form a layer of fertilizing ash. Several varieties of plants are cultivated for several years, after which the area is left fallow and new land is cleared. A swidden field resembles the overgrown jungle—a jumble of crops, from roots and tubers to fruit trees, intermingle in the same plot of land. The tropical environment, however, is fragile, and overuse of an area can lead to complete soil degradation.

Horticulture can support more people per unit of land area than hunting and gathering, but intensification is limited by several factors: long fallow periods, limited technology, and, most important, a lack of political or social pressures on local producers to produce a surplus.

The household is the basic unit in horticultural societies. Kin obligations frequently extend beyond the local group, and trade and exchange relationships establish ties both near and far. Although surpluses are not used for market purposes, they are a means of achieving status. Political leadership is based on kinship and carries with it very limited coercive rights. Rather, a headman has the skills and the goods that attract others to him. His influence does not extend beyond his own group.

The Yanomamö, Tsembaga, and eastern and western Pueblo are horticultural peoples, but since each inhabits a different environment, their adaptations have taken different forms.

The Yanomamö hunt and gather in addition to practicing swidden agriculture. Villages are not permanent due to inter- (and sometimes intra-) village hostilities. Frequent agonistic behavior can be traced to a shortage of women due to female infanticide and the polygyny of the older men, which instigates competition for women and creates conflict between villages; but Harris and Gross suggest that the real basis of this behavior is a shortage of game and other sources of protein. Nonetheless, the Yanomamö have evolved methods of creating friendly contacts and maintaining alliances.

The Tsembaga rely on slash-and-burn agriculture but supplement their diet with pork from their carefully tended pigs. Warfare is not an unusual occurrence, and the slaughter of pigs for feasts with allies plays an important role in preparing both nutritionally and psychologically for fighting. War among the Tsembaga redistributes the population and permits some areas of land to lie fallow. Similarly, the slaughter of pigs at the *kaipu* ceremony reduces an animal population that potentially competes for the same food as the human population.

The western and eastern Pueblo were groups that did *not* use swidden agriculture: the western Pueblo used flood farming, and the eastern groups used irrigation farming. Different subsistence techniques led to different social organizations. Flood farming is associated with family work groups, matrilineal lineages and clans, and religious cults that are ceremonial in purpose; the irrigation and terracing of the eastern Pueblo led to intensive agriculture, large, organized labor groups that centralized political control of community descent, and some shift toward patrilineal descent. The Spaniards had more of an effect on the eastern Pueblo because they could more readily adopt the crops introduced by the colonizers. Increased contact also led the eastern Pueblo to superficially assimilate aspects of Spanish life and language.

suggested readings

BASCOM, W.
1969 *The Yoruba of Southwestern Nigeria.* New York: Holt, Rinehart & Winston. Examination of the elaborate social and political organizations of a complex kingdom based on shifting cultivation.

COHEN, Y.A., ed.
1974 *Man in Adaptation: The Cultural Present.* 2d ed. Chicago: Aldine. Section on cultivating in stateless societies offers a number of selections which examine the role of the horticultural adaptation in the process of cultural evolution.

HARNER, M. J.
1973 *The Jíbaro: People of the Sacred*

KELLY, R. C.
1976   *Waterfall*. Garden City, N.Y.: Anchor Books. General ethnography of an Amazonian horticultural people, particularly interesting for its discussion of the interplay between religious beliefs and warfare.

Etoro Social Structure: A Study in Structural Contradiction. Ann Arbor, Mich.: University of Michigan Press. A general ethnography of a horticultural people with a strong emphasis on concepts of social structure and their relationship to actual behavior.

SAHLINS, M.
1968   *Tribesmen.* Englewood Cliffs, N.J.: Prentice-Hall. Excellent survey of the economic arrangements, social structure, and ideology typical of horticultural societies.

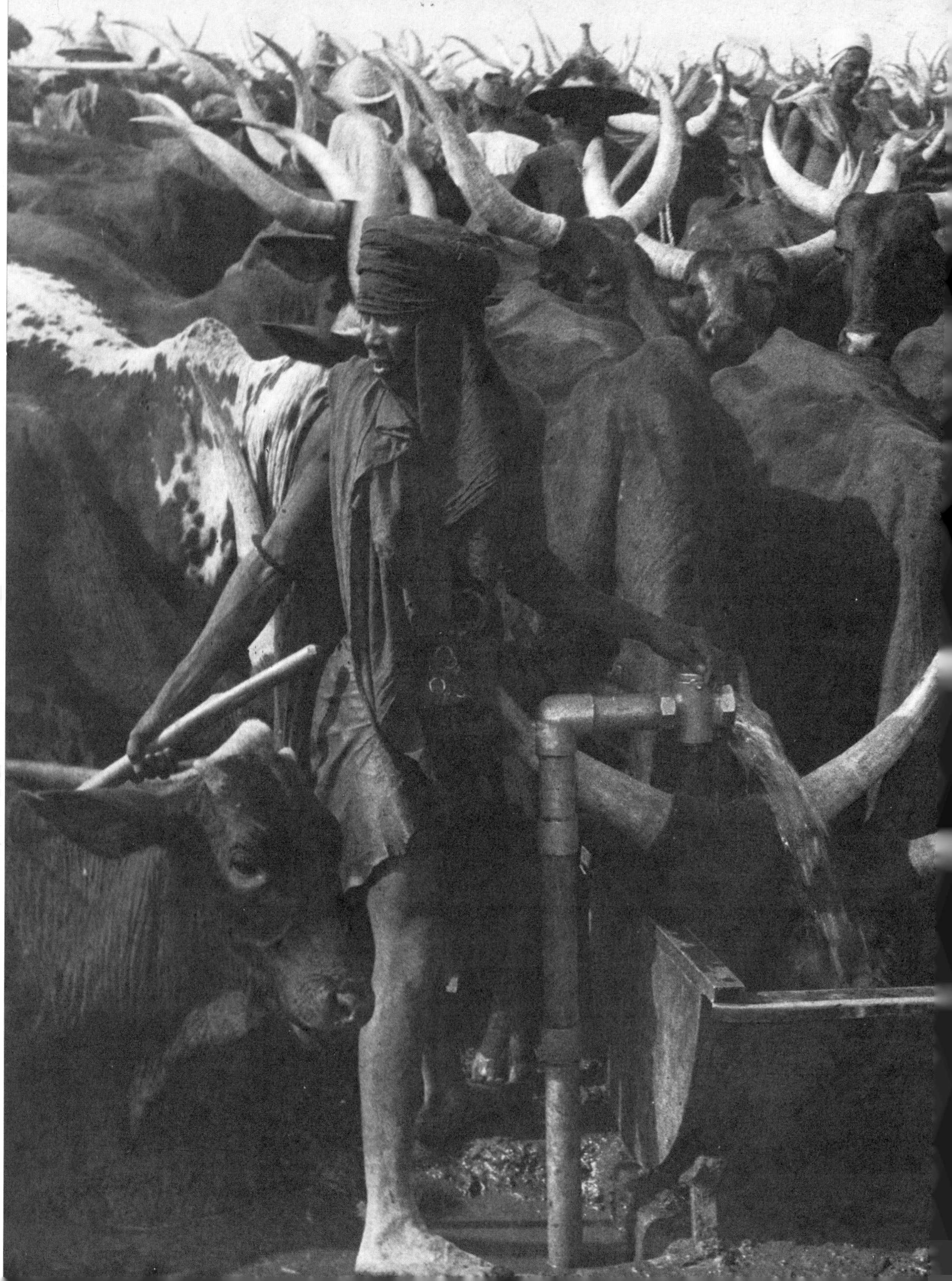

twenty-six
Pastoralists

Pastoralists differ from horticulturalists not simply because one raises animals while the other raises plants. Actually, many groups raise some domesticated animals. We have seen how much energy and time the Tsembaga devote to their pigs, yet these tribes are not pastoralists, but horticulturalists who engage in some *animal husbandry,* or the keeping of domesticated animals. *Pastoralism* is a specialized form of animal husbandry based on herds of grazing animals such as sheep, goats, cattle, yaks, or camels. In a preindustrial economy, most pastoralists are nomadic, moving among pastures on a regular schedule within a well-defined territory. The narrowness of specialization (that is, the extent to which they rely on animal husbandry) and the amount of mobility vary from group to group and can change, depending on conditions encountered by a group.

Few populations rely directly and exclusively on their herds for subsistence. One common adaptation is a generalized subsistence strategy based on a combination of farming and herding (Salzman, 1971; Conant, 1966). The Karimojong of East Africa, for instance, are part of a group of African tribes for whom cattle are central to cultural identity. The meat produced by their cattle is not a staple in the diet, but meat, along with dairy products and animal blood, is a hedge against crop failure, a necessary alternative source of food in a harsh and unpredictable environment. This generalized strategy is aimed at subsistence production; little is exported. On the other hand, one group among the Yörük of Turkey concentrate exclusively on their herds, which they raise to sell to other groups. They move on a tight schedule to get adequate pasturage and do not have permanent settlements as the Karimojong do. They do not raise crops, preferring to use the income from selling their stock to buy grain and other foodstuffs from the agriculturalists of their region. The changes in market prices for their products, for food, and for grazing land have altered their way of life in recent years. The Navajo are the third group we will consider. They are family ranchers within a larger agro-industrial system. With the Navajo, as with other pastoralists, individual strategies and the resultant groups vary, depending on local conditions.

The Pastoralist Adaptation
The Organization of Energy

Like horticulture, pastoralism is more productive than hunting and gathering. Hunters merely "harvest" animals; they do not invest labor to increase the productivity of the herds. Pastoralists increase the reproductive and survival rates of their animals by investing time in caring for them. In fact, a successful herder can increase his holdings at a pace generally faster than is possible with farming.[1]

This is not to say that pastoralism is more efficient than farming. In areas where cultivation is possible, humans can produce approxi-

---

[1] Of course, this is offset by the precarious nature of herding in most areas: animals are susceptible to disease, drought, and theft, all of which can reduce a rich household to poverty overnight.

Pastoralists of the Sahel have come increasingly to rely on driven wells such as this one for water for their flocks, and recent droughts have caused considerable hardship. (F.A.O. Photo)

mately ten times as much food by farming rather than by relying on animals to convert vegetation into meat and dairy products. Specialized pastoralism is most common in regions where agriculture is very risky or completely impossible.

The inefficiency of energy exchange and the marginality of the environment mean that societies relying solely on their herds for survival necessarily have low population densities. The more common adaptations are ones already mentioned—herding integrated in agricultural cycles, as among the Karimojong, or raising animals for exchange in a market system, as among the Yörük. Animals are a convenient way of storing energy and building up protein reserves, as we saw with the Tsembagas' pigs. Pastoralists can concentrate the energy of their environment into a form that can be advantageously traded for agricultural foods, clothing, or other items they cannot otherwise obtain. Thus, pastoralism is an alternative to agriculture, but one not independent of it.

The Importance of Mobility

In preindustrial societies, sedentary pastoralism or ranching is relatively rare. Land that is rich enough to support herds indefinitely will yield far more output if given over to crops. However, using the mobility of herd animals, pastoralists can adapt to marginal areas by moving as conditions dictate. This is why pastoralists are also often nomads.

Generally we think of pastoralist migrations as simply a means of securing adequate grazing on a year-round basis. However, this is not the whole story. William Irons (1975) has pointed out that the Turkoman pastoralists of northern Iran moved more than was necessary if all they sought were grasslands. They also moved to maintain their political autonomy. In the past, they frequently raided non-Turkoman sedentary populations and caravans, often enslaving their victims. If pursued by a more powerful force, they would simply disperse with their animals into inaccessible areas. Although "pacified" by the Iranian government in the early twentieth century, they still managed to largely control their own affairs until recently. They did so by the one thing they could do more effectively than anyone else: moving. In this way, mobility often allows nomadic pastoralists the opportunity to maintain political autonomy even within the boundaries of highly organized state bureaucratic systems.

Also, through the use of large riding animals—horses or camels—some populations have developed a very effective means of raiding. The history of the Middle East, to name only one region, is filled with instances of nomadic warriors mobilized to raid villages, even to threaten and sometimes to overthrow state bureaucracies. The Mongols of central Asia, a horse- and sheep-herding people, conquered China again and again, and toppled the great Middle Eastern empires.

What is ironic is that often the stimulus for predation on sedentary communities comes from the very dependence of specialized pastoralists on agricultural products. A shift in the relative values of, say, wheat and sheep may drastically alter the number of animals needed to provide an income for a household. If the terms of trade are unfavorable enough, the herders may change from trading to increased reliance on raiding.

We should be wary of simple characterizations of pastoralists, however. Nomadic pastoralism is only one rather specialized form of animal husbandry, and those who pursue it are not typically engaged in the pillaging of villages or the raiding of caravans.

Pastoralism and Farming

Farming using a combination of domesticated plants and animals preceded specialized pastoralism. Mixed farming was a multifaceted strategy that was a hedge against droughts, crop failures, diseases, and other natural calamities. If the herds died of an epidemic, the crops were there; if the crops failed, the animals could provide food to tide people over. In other words, diversification offered the reserves necessary to face fluctuations of food

Pastoralism on the Great Plains

The Plains Indians are different from the other pastoralists described in this chapter because the herds they depended on were wild. These tribes hunted buffalo on horseback, following the movements of the herds as they dispersed over the range during most of the year and congregated in vast numbers during the late summer breeding season. Despite their common subsistence strategy, there were marked differences in social organization among the tribes, differences that Symmes C. Oliver (1962), a Texas anthropologist, ascribes to the time when the various tribes were not buffalo hunters but rather subsistence farmers or foragers. The Plains Indians, therefore, provide a glimpse of the ways in which people have responded to their habitats and some of the processes of cultural evolution.

The adaptation to the Plains was relatively recent for all the tribes, because it depended on the horse, an animal not found in North America until the arrival of the Spaniards. As these diverse groups began using horses to hunt buffalo and gave up earlier subsistence practices, they were exposed to similar selective pressures: "the crucial reliance on the buffalo, the mobility given by the horse and the nature of the treeless terrain, the competition with other tribes for horses, guns, land and survival itself" (Oliver, 1962:310).

The movements of the buffalo, the constant raiding, and the necessity for mobility both in hunting and raiding created a unique way of life. Like the buffalo, or rather because of the buffalo, the tribes tended to be dispersed in small bands for most of the year and to congregate as tribes only in the late summer for the communal hunt. Social organization in the bands was relatively flexible and informal; in the summer months, however, other levels of organization were necessary to integrate the bands and coordinate them in tribal ceremonies and in the communal hunt. Tribal societies provided necessary integration and coordinated many important common activities. All Plains tribes had "police societies" that regulated the communal hunt in the summer. The societies were military ones glorifying the warrior, whose skills were essential for the survival of the group. In such a world, prestige and status were less a matter of heredity than of military prowess. Horses (the essential means of hunting, the means of raiding, and the object of raids) were the principal status symbols. A man with many horses was obviously a successful warrior and probably a good hunter, since the quality of horse made a great difference in the hunting of buffalo. His horses were also a form of wealth, conveniently portable. In short, all the Plains Indian groups evolved similar flexibility in social organization, developed tribal societies to provide unity, and based status on military skills.

In other dimensions of social organization, the tribes were less similar. Oliver identified two variable features in particular: the presence of clans and the degree of formal leadership. Both clans and formal positions of authority were associated with tribes who had come to the plains from horticultural backgrounds. Tribes that had been hunters and gatherers did not have clans and had relatively less formal tribal authorities. Clans were adaptive for sedentary farmers, but the nomadic life on the Plains was hardly compatible with groups organized around corporate land rights and hereditary leadership. Although the clans survived in some former horticultural tribes, in others they were abandoned entirely. In all tribes, the primary form of social organization was the band-tribal encampment described earlier. The regular annual shift between highly dispersed segments and their later concentration in encampments demanded a new form of leadership, one different from that practiced by either horticultural or hunter-gatherer systems. The tribes that had been solely band organized as hunter-gatherers tended to evolve some sort of chieftancy. Tribes that had been horticulturalists retained formal leaders in the summer and evolved informal systems during the time the tribe was split into bands.

So, although the tribes of contrasting origins still differed, these differences blurred under the unique requirements of Plains life. What we see on the Plains are instances of convergent evolution, in which greatly contrasting societies developed similar patterns in the face of similar challenges.

supply in a single area. Such a strategy is still common in many parts of Africa, as well as in Europe and the Middle East, particularly among mountain villages. With the Karimojong we shall see how households diversify production, hedging against possible agricultural losses with the time-consuming maintenance of costly herds of cattle. If such a diversified strategy has so many advantages, why did some groups begin to specialize in animal husbandry?

One suggestion is that changes in agricultural practices, especially the development of canal irrigation, created the preconditions for specialized pastoralism. As with so many changes, these practices eliminated certain risks and created others; and they also may have selected for a more specialized system of land use and division of labor (Lees and Bates, 1974). Canal irrigation probably increased productivity, which made possible population growth and expansion of settlements, with a consequent decrease in the land available for animals. As more land was exclusively employed in farming, grazing areas were pushed farther from the settlement region into areas where grazing was not as lush. To get adequate food and water for their herds, animal owners would have had to expend more labor and travel greater and greater distances. Away from the settlement, the animals would have been more vulnerable to predators, especially raiders. To protect and herd the animals took energies away from agricultural pursuits at the same time that agriculture was becoming more time-consuming: canals had to be cleared, kept in repair, and tended in addition to the attention the fields required.

The increased demand of each of these strategies could well have led certain households to specialize in increasingly intensive agriculture while others chose pastoralism. Canal irrigation, although capable of creating an agricultural surplus, has its drawbacks and limitations. Extended irrigation systems may reach a point where they are no longer effective. Water tables may drop or soil salinity may result in decreased productivity. These factors might therefore further select for some farmers shifting their attention to a more specialized reliance on animals. Eventually each segment might organize itself into more clearly differentiated groups.

In this view, pastoralism may have developed hand in hand with intensive agriculture. Whatever the reasons for its development, pastoralism is a strategy predicated on agricultural surplus and the interaction on a regional basis between those specializing in herding and those specializing in farming.

Interaction Between Groups

As we have noted in our chapter on horticultural societies, regular transactions between groups increase in importance with the emergence of food production. Pastoralists are not only involved in regular interactions, but in some cases are completely dependent on them. For example, as we have said, most pastoralists have grain rather than animal products as their main food staple; and while some households engage in limited agriculture to produce as much of this staple as possible, others depend on exchange. In fact, the more specialized the groups, the more dependent on others they are.

For example, the Yörük of Turkey are dependent entirely on marketing animals and other products of their flocks to buy the food they eat. Since their income, even the survival of this group's distinct way of life, depends on this exchange, relatively small fluctuations in market prices can bankrupt some households and make them seek another way of earning their livelihood.

In contrast with most hunters and gatherers or extensive farmers, highly specialized pastoralists often faced threats from two sides: they have to maintain their herds physically, and then successfully convert them into the food they eat, the clothes they wear, and the tools they do not produce themselves, all by means of exchange. Given this, it is not too surprising that where the habitat permits, most populations depending on animals also raise at least some crops.

Variability Within Pastoral Populations

Variations in individual household economic and social strategies are sketched very clearly in the ever-changing composition of the camp group and in individual patterns of migration. Some individuals—as among the Navajo and the Karimojong, for example—may move frequently one year and be largely sedentary the next. Often there are systematic regulations underlying this variability. Households with many animals—as, for example, among the Yörük of Turkey—may move early in the spring to pastures in the mountains, risking cold weather to get the first spring grasses. Others with smaller flocks may feel they cannot afford the risk. They move later in the season. One household may herd alone, using the labor of the immediate or extended family; one, perhaps because of the opportunity to share the labor, might herd temporarily with another.

Often in looking at a pastoral society, we see families giving up pastoralism for other pursuits altogether. Commonly in the Near East, families do this either when they have accumulated enough wealth to invest in a more secure form of capital—land or shops—or when they have "gone broke" because their herds have declined to the point where they cannot support the household. Conversely, agricultural households may shift to herding if they feel it is advantageous to do so. Here again we see the extent to which most pastoralists are segments in a larger economic system. This sets the pastoralists apart from earlier groups we have discussed.

The Karimojong

The Karimojong, an East African tribe, are relatively self-sufficient. They live in a semi-arid region of northern Uganda, a territory that consists of three distinctly different areas: eastern highlands, a riverine and fertile central sector, and western plains. Each is exploited by the Karimojong. The fertile areas are farmed during the rainy season; the other areas are more suitable for herding.

The caloric bulk of their diet is from agricultural products, and raising crops takes substantial amounts of time and energy. The work begins toward the end of the dry season when the fields are cleared and fences repaired. Sorghum, the principal grain crop, is planted in March but may be replanted if it fails to grow. In later months, crops such as millet, peanuts, tobacco, and vegetables may be planted. By the end of July, the sorghum harvest begins and continues for several weeks. The millet crop also begins to ripen during this period. The last tasks of the agricultural cycle are drying and threshing the grains and harvesting some of the other crops.

Despite the importance of agriculture to their economy, the Karimojong view themselves primarily as pastoralists. Cattle are the principal animal herded, although goats and other animals are raised. The cattle herds, which are owned by individual households, range in size from 50 to 150 head.

The Karimojong have a subsistence economy and have relatively little interaction with other tribes. They sell and trade only a small portion of what they produce, keeping or consuming the rest. They achieve this degree of self-sufficiency through a balanced, diverse mode of production.

The Cattle Complex

A number of years ago, anthropologist Melville Herskovits called the particular region of which the Karimojong are a part "The East African Cattle Area." This designation was not simply a matter of geography, nor was it based on the fact that cattle are extensively herded. What distinguishes the people of the cattle area is the importance of cattle in their social life. In this system, dubbed the "cattle complex," cattle were employed as indicators of prestige and status as well as wealth. In Karimojong society, cattle are part of all important rituals from birth to death (the name for a public ritual of any importance can be translated "a cattle gathering"). Men develop strong personal associations with particular animals: they compose poems and songs about their cattle, decorate them and train their horns in special patterns, and adopt a favorite ox whose qualities are incorporated into a man's most formal title, his ox name. Social ties — be they kinship or friendship — depend on mutual obligations and rights concerning cattle. In fact, those recognized as closely related are called "cattle kin." Neville Dyson-Hudson describes this central role of cattle in a man's life:

> This manifold interest is apparent in the life of any individual Karimojong. When born, a child has a father because of the passage of cattle; he is linked to siblings by common interest in cattle allocated to his mother's compound, to half-siblings by common interest in a single herd which will be their shared inheritance; he has a descent group and a clan which are symbolized by a common cattle brand. His most distinctive name is drawn from cattle, he is initiated into adulthood through cattle, he marries by cattle, founds and feeds a family of his own with cattle. His adult life centers on defending the cattle he has and fighting to acquire more. When he dies, he is wrapped in cattle hide and laid in a grave beneath his cattle corral. In short, to Karimojong, as individuals and as a society, nothing is more important than cattle. For them, herding is more than a mode of livelihood, it is a way of life. (1966: 102–103)

Early anthropologists were convinced that the noneconomic uses of cattle were the main rationale for keeping them in the first place. On the surface, it appeared that the Karimojong were expending considerable time and labor in inefficient, if not irrational, ways. Cattle were not being used to their potential. They were not employed as beasts of burden, and meat was eaten only at ceremonies or when animals died. Most of their food appeared to be cultigens, with milk the only regularly consumed animal product. Furthermore, the herds were too large and were overgrazing pasture lands in some places.

Part of the reason that anthropologists downplayed the economic importance of cattle among the Karimojong (and other "cattle complex" societies) was that the Karimojong themselves stress the social rather than economic aspects of cattle ownership. Actually, the Karimojong make more use of animal foods than initially was apparent. At the cattle camps, for example, men eat primarily, if not exclusively, fresh and curdled milk, and blood taken from the cattle by shooting a small dart into an animal's jugular vein. It is true that the major proportion of the caloric intake of their diet is from agriculture, but milk, blood, and a small amount of meat represent most of their protein consumption.

Cattle herding is sound strategy for the Karimojong. In their territory, arable land is limited and much of it can only support grasses suitable for grazing. Water is scarce and rainfall extremely unpredictable. It can fluctuate enormously in the course of several years. As a result, periodic crop failure is all but certain, and chronic failures are quite possible. Cattle, who can be moved hundreds of miles to follow the rainfall, are what might be called "famine insurance." When crops fail, cattle provide a backup supply of food.

The desire for large herds, although they may indeed overgraze, is also logical. The cattle of the Karimojong are not very productive. Their cows, for example, give only about 5 percent as much milk as cows in the United States, and many die from disease and malnutrition, so a large herd is necessary to maintain a significant reserve of food.

Herding is a solution to a problem faced by many populations — that of lessening the effect of environmental unpredictability. Given the harsh conditions of Karamoja (the area where the Karimojong live), the cattle complex is more than simply an ideological peculiarity.

Variability Among the Karimojong

Settlement Patterns Though they move their cattle with some regularity, the Karimojong have permanent settlements located near their agricultural fields. These settlements, near sources of water, consist of groups of huts and corrals for the herds. Fields may be close to the homestead, although they may also be a few miles away. Settlements are, for the most part, year-long residences of the women, children, and old men. Adult men live there for at least several months of the

This Karimojong settlement is a permanent home for women, children, and old men. Adult men leave the settlement for pasture lands during the dry season, generally from September to March. During the rest of the year, they may live in the settlement for a varying length of time. (N. and R. Dyson-Hudson)

year, although the length of time can vary greatly. Generally, though, they are there during the rainy season (March to September), because there is enough nearby water and forage for the animals and the men are needed in the fields. From September to March, however, it is considerably drier, and the men move away from the settlements to pasture lands in the east and west. During this period, they live in rough camps, moving as far and as often as the cattle owners think best.

The basic unit of society is not a vastly extended kinship network. Karimojong have terms for three generations of descent, and as we have seen, maintain ties more through interest in cattle than formal kinship relations. This domestic unit expands and contracts as conditions allow, and each one is relatively independent of other units in the society.

Herd Movements Such independent choice results in a wide range of agricultural and herding practices. Herding is men's work, and gardening is ostensibly women's. But a family that has few women able to work will employ men in the fields to a greater extent. Similarly, a family with few cattle may have to invest more in its crops and may raise a greater variety and have men spend more time in the fields (R. Dyson-Hudson, 1972). Even more variable are the deployment of herds. Some of the owners, for example, keep their herd separate, while others herd with relatives or friends. Moreover, cattle are not necessarily kept in a single herd; on occasion, the owner divides his animals into two groups, one of which stays permanently in the settlement while the other remains in cattle camps throughout the year. Nor are cattle moved at the same time each year nor for the same length of time. One man, for example, kept his herd in the settlement for 15 consecutive months and then never moved them more than 13 miles away. At the other extreme, another man had a camp herd that never came *closer* than 13 miles and was as far away as 57 miles from the settlement.

Decisions about herding are shaped by the particular environmental conditions at the time (rainfall, condition of the vegetation, diseases, and so on), by the composition of the herd and the labor force, and by individual skills, temperament, and industriousness. The harshness and variability of the climate are important determinants. Years of plentiful rainfall might persuade one owner to keep his herd at the settlement longer. Another might choose to move in any case, but will avoid the western plains region because it can become too muddy and risky for the livestock.

Herding practices are also determined by the herd itself. Milk cows are for the most part kept at the settlement, with only a few allocated to the cattle camps to provide milk for immediate nutritional needs. Furthermore, while cattle belong in theory to the head of the family, some are considered to be the property of the wife (or wives) and others are the favorites or pets of younger boys. These cattle are kept at the permanent settlement as long as possible. This may mean that despite a general practice of herd movement, a significant portion of a household's animals may be entirely sedentary.

Equally important in the development of individual deployment of herds is the labor force immediately available to the herder. This labor force is a man's family. A man with several healthy grown sons has an advantage over those who have few or none because cattle herding is almost exclusively man's work. Herd owners who do not have enough sons have to arrange to keep their cattle in cooperation with other men in similar straits.

Finally, a herder's choice is affected by his own personality. One rather elderly man, for example, was particularly fond of a flock of goats which he tended himself. As a result, he lived most of the time at the permanent settlement and kept his cattle close to the settlement, even though he had grown sons who

Karimojong boys may begin early to help tend the cattle that will play such a central role in their lives. Cattle figure in all the important rituals, from birth to death, and movements of a man's herd determine his own movements between the permanent settlement and the rougher cattle camps. (N. and R. Dyson-Hudson)

could have taken the herds out to the cattle camps. Of course, his advanced age affected his strategy, but his interest in his goats was important, too.

Social Organization What we see in Karamoja is a social landscape of temporary groups, coalescing and dissolving as expediency dictates. The permanent settlements have their own organization based on territory and kin; but in the nomadic world of the cattle herders, groups meet, join forces at times, then go their own ways. These groups may well be from vastly distant settlements and have no kinship ties to cement their relationship. How, then, do these groups of diverse origin combine and operate?

Neville Dyson-Hudson (1963) argues that the Karimojong system of age and generation sets serves as the social cement. Authority resides in the elders, while obedience is expected of the junior set and the uninitiated. As soon as two Karimojong groups meet, the elders in one group can recognize elders in the other by their distinctive decorations and can confer on matters of mutual interest. The younger men can be expected to defer to men in more senior age sets and to obey the elders.

If a man is a Karimojong and an adult, both of which are definable by specific criteria, then he can be grouped and ranked by age no matter what the company or circumstances in which he finds himself. Thus, any aggregate of Karimojong in any place at any time can be easily structured to take common action if their general interest requires it. (Dyson-Hudson, 1963:399)

The Karimojong, like any group that adapts successfully, are opportunistic, committing their attention to where the greatest yields compatible with security are to be found. Thus within their generalized adaptation to farming and herding, individual practices and group organization vary widely. This variability is a fitting emblem of pastoralism itself, since this subsistence strategy admits of many other approaches besides the generalized one of the Karimojong. In the next section, we shall see some contrasting approaches to herding.

The Yörük of Southeastern Turkey

The Yörük are a Turkish-speaking people who migrate between two distinct regions of the Republic of Turkey. Winter pastures are located on low plains areas in southeastern Turkey on what is geographically part of the Syrian steppe. In the spring, the Yörük move their animals inland along a route of some 100 kilometers to summer pasture lands. These pastures, several thousand feet above sea level, are alpine in climate and topography.

These nomadic pastoralists raise sheep for the most part. These animals, unlike the cattle of the Karimojong, are seen almost exclusively as capital. Camels are also kept, and they are maintained to transport household possessions during migration. The Yörük do not have a subsistence economy, and little of what is raised is used for food. The animal products eaten regularly are sheep's milk, butter, cheese, and yogurt. Meat is seldom consumed except on important religious or social occasions. The Yörük regularly market both animals and animal products. Wool, of course, is a major source of income, and milk, cheese, and male lambs also are sold. Female animals are kept for the obvious reason that they provide milk and lambs to increase the flock's capital potential.

The Market Economy

Because the Yörük live, purchase foodstuffs, and manage their flock in the context of a market economy, the demands and rewards of the market system shape many of the options or productive strategies pursued by herd owners. All transactions are made on the basis of established market values even when barter exchange is used. For example, if a Yörük trades wool for tocacco, the exchange will be made according to the relative market values of each item. The supply and demand within a particular area will alter the values, of course, but this is only a restructuring of market prices to fit local conditions. The vast majority of transactions are in cash. Fluctuations in the prices of animal products, of the

A large cauldron used for washing clothes goes on top as a Yörük family loads its household possessions on camels during fall migration. (Daniel G. Bates)

foods they buy, or of the land they rent become serious problems to which they must continually respond.

Probably the most significant feature of Yörük interactions with other groups is their reliance on them for pasture land. The Yörük do not own or even have traditional claims to the pasture lands they use. Instead, they must rent them and sometimes pay for access to lands along the migration route as well. Thus although the outer limits of their migration schedule is established largely by climate and topography, political and social factors also affect the actual migratory schedule. Yörük herd owners cannot move strictly on the basis of when it is best for the animals to move, because they must also take into account the wishes of the people who own the land along the migration route. This land they must cross is predominantly agricultural, which further complicates matters. Animals would almost certainly stay longer in the lowland plains were it not that moving too late in the season could cause extensive crop damage. Before coming down for summer pastures, they must wait again until the harvest is in. Still, disputes frequently develop between nomads and agriculturalists over crop damages, although there would probably be many more serious disputes if the government did not intervene to see that all crop damage claims are satisfied. Actually, certain agricultural lands would most likely have to be abandoned were it not for the government, because damages would be too regular and too expensive. Each animal migration then is itself a complicated strategy determined by the availability of grass, village planting or harvest schedules, and the restrictions set by the government.

Flexible Social Organization

The need for pasturage affects social organization. As tent dwellers, the Yörük pastoralists live in camp groups whose composition changes regularly. As many as twenty and as few as two households may make a camp together, with larger clusters generally gathering in the summer pasture areas. Although in some pastoral societies, labor for herding is pooled among members of a camp group, the Yörük household is in effect a self-sufficient producing unit. It relies almost exclusively on its own labor, and cooperative pooling of herds and labor is very limited.

But the camp group still serves a number of important functions. It is the main means by which the Yörük acquire access to grazing. Members of a camp group rent pastures from villagers, as the tribe has no exclusive territory of its own. Often the people who reside together and who jointly rent pastures are members of the same patrilineage. Even though the society strongly stresses patrilineal relationships, a tent will often camp with families more closely related to the wife than to the husband. Sometimes this is simply because the woman of the tent wants to be with her sisters or brothers for a season or two. Sometimes it is a way for families to secure better grazing than could be had by cooperating with the husband's close agnates (relatives in the male line). Although most groups have a largely agnatic makeup, economic strategy, sentiment, and conflict with other households make such communities of camps highly flexible. They have to be. The amount of grazing available in any single location changes from season to season and from year to year, and they must be able to respond to these changes.

Changes in Strategies

In recent years, the Yörük have been facing the problem of inflation. The rising cost of pasture rental, which has been much greater than the rise in the selling price of animal products, has affected households differently and has resulted in a significant transformation of Yörük society.

The Yörük households of today actually practice two rather different adaptive strategies: nomadic pastoralism and sedentary agriculture or trade. The former group, as we have seen, is very specialized, engaging in animal husbandry and trading in animals and animal products. At the same time, there are now entire villages of settled Yörük engaging in agriculture as well as shopkeeping and artisan trades. While the nomadic and sedentary populations are economically distinct, there is no difference in cultural identity nor is there any antipathy between the two. The two strategies are actually interrelated: households move from one economy to the other as circumstances warrant, although the general tendency now is for pastoralists to settle. In fact, the settled Yörük shopkeepers and merchants often depend on the nomadic households for their trade and extend them the credit necessary for these households to survive in a volatile market economy. The determinant of whether a household herds or settles down is wealth.

At the lower portion of the spectrum are those with just enough animals to continue, though shifts in market conditions may bankrupt them at any time. They are often faced with debts and a shortage of ready cash with which to rent pasture. This forces them to shear their sheep at the beginning of spring to pay debts accumulated during the winter. Shearing, however, leaves them at a disadvantage in the migration. First, they must wait longer before leaving, as it can snow or be extremely cold, and shorn sheep would be vulnerable to disease. When they finally do leave, however, they must travel over lands already grazed by sheep belonging to wealthier herd owners, who could forgo an early shearing. The poor grazing leaves the last flocks tired and hungry by the time they reach summer pasture. It is likely that more sheep will die during migration in the flocks belonging to poorer herd owners.

But even with the sale of spring wool, many Yörük herders do not usually have the cash necessary for rental of summer pasture. For this they need an additional source of income or credit, and in recent years they have found it by selling milk to mobile dairy tents that follow the flocks from the plains to the alpine pastures.

Most of these dairies are owned by other Yörük. Many, in fact, are owned by the wealthier herders. Just as there is a lower limit below which a flock is not economically viable, there is an upper limit as well. Huge numbers of animals require large deployments of labor, so there is an incentive for the wealthy not to enlarge their herds but instead to diversify. They have bought land or stores, or they have established dairy businesses.

The dairies are rather sizable enterprises which benefit poorer herders and provide high profit margins to the dairymen at the same time. These men have a ready supply of capital which allows them not only to buy the milk but to buy it in advance. These milk futures are purchased at a relatively low price, but they give the poorer herders the money they need for pasture rental. Once they have the milk, the dairymen process it into cheese and sell it for a substantial profit in urban markets.

It is easy to see that this system would have the effect of limiting economic mobility while making the dairy owners increasingly wealthy, and indeed, economic stratification has been occurring. Because animals are in themselves such a highly volatile form of capital, economic stratification was not possible in the past. Traditionally, a wealthy herder faced periods of high attrition from disease or predation while poorer herders had the opportunity to build up their herds. In the course of a lifetime, a family could reasonably expect to go from rich to poor several times.

That is rapidly changing. Despite the Yörük egalitarian ideology, the realities of present-day economic life are leading to entrenched economic differences among the Yörük. This has all been very recent, the result of social, economic, and political changes of the past ten or so years.

The adaptation of the Yörük, then, is not simply a matter of accommodating to the physical environment, but of being part of a larger social system. Thus simply seeing the distribution of pasturage in the region is useless in understanding their economy unless we also take into account who *owns* that vegetation. Likewise, discussing the specialization of nomadic pastoralism among the Yörük without reference to the other specializations

In Yörük dairy tents such as this one, sheep's milk is processed into cheese, which is then canned and sold in urban markets. The dairies, which follow the herds at spring milking time, are important as a means for families to get the cash they need to rent pasture lands. (Daniel G. Bates)

within the larger society upon whom the Yörük depend to buy their products and sell them necessities is equally impossible. As we have said, ecology has a political and social dimension as well as a physical and biological one. As we shall see in the final example of the Navajo, social organization is continually adjusted to environmental conditions, even in the context of ranching in the United States.

The Navajo

The largest Indian tribe in the United States, the Navajo, live primarily on a semi-arid reservation area that covers parts of three states, although the bulk of it is in northeastern Arizona. While they work at a variety of wage-labor enterprises, traditionally and culturally the Navajo are pastoralists. A Navajo who lives on or near the reservation usually has some interest in one or more flocks of sheep and possibly cattle and horses as well. There is agriculture on the reservation, though the fields are usually small and there is much less interest in them, due in part to the lack of rainfall. Although the Navajo maintain a strong sense of tribal identity, they are ranchers in

This Navajo shepherdess tending her flock is the rule and not the exception in Navajo society, where women usually own the flocks, tend them, shear the sheep, card the wool, spin it, and weave it into rugs. (Santa Fe Railway Photograph)

an industrial economy. Let us look at how social organization is related to their economic strategy.

A matrilineal society, the basic social unit of the Navajo is the extended family, with daughters typically settling with their mothers. A family group might include a mother, her daughters, sisters, and their respective sons and brothers. Other kin may be important and called on in certain situations, but they usually do not figure in the day-to-day life of the family group. These units, called "outfits," do not live together in the same residence but share a homestead site and live in separate dwellings called "hogans." Outfits will herd and keep their livestock together, although animals may be considered to belong to different individuals.

The Navajo do not migrate regularly with their animals as do the Karimojong or the

Yörük. Frequently, however, outfits will take their animals to winter quarters in places considered traditional use areas of the group. While the land generally provides enough forage, winters can be quite cold, and outfits wish to be near adequate supplies of fuel. Snow can prevent them from going elsewhere to bring in supplies, so the move becomes desirable.

Though fuel is a factor in strategies, water is more so because it is the commodity that is most difficult to find in abundance with any regularity. Ordinarily, there is only an adequate supply taken from windmill pump wells, springs, water holes, streams, and so on. But water being so crucial, the sudden acquisition of a major water source or the elimination of one can cause changes in herding practices, can precipitate unscheduled movement, and can even alter the social relationships of the people involved.

"The Social Consequences of a Dry Well"

One Navajo outfit provides an example of the social effects of a water surplus and a subsequent drought (Downs, 1965). The group, the "Broken Foot outfit," was an extended family composed of an elderly woman, her two middle-aged daughters, and their children and grandchildren, for a total of about fifty adults and children. This number was abnormally large. Usually outfits will fragment after they reach a certain number, approximately thirty.

The Broken Foot outfit stayed together, however, because a dam had been built on their land, which provided a regular supply of water for years. As a result of the dam, the members of the outfit were constructing a relatively permanent homestead near it, and they lived there except for relatively brief migrations to pastures during the coldest part of the winter. The dam was also making their herding much easier than it had been when they had had to search for water. Despite the outfit's size, tasks were handled cooperatively, and the members of the outfit themselves said that the dam was a major reason for their closeness.

The dam affected their relations with their neighbors as well. Because the outfit used the dam exclusively, they were never in competition with others, and there was little interoutfit tension. In fact, the outfit was a distributor of water for anyone who wanted to use it. They considered themselves the owners of the water, but it was always available. Users were only expected to ask, and members of Broken Foot would merely grumble privately when anyone failed to do so.

Then the situation of the Broken Foot outfit was suddenly altered by several years of serious drought. As the water level of the dam began to fall, the outfit began to restrict usage, creating some tense confrontations with neighbors, until it was finally forbidden to outsiders. Soon it was not even adequate for their own use, and they had to look elsewhere. From being a major distributor of a valuable commodity, they once again had to compete with other groups. Their herding practices were changed. To see that their animals were properly watered, members of the outfit had to be out all day with their herds. Finally, the outfit had to make an agreement with an affinal relative, and they moved their flocks temporarily to his lands.

Meanwhile, tensions within the outfit were beginning to reach an intolerable level. As the main reason for staying together had been the dam, the outfit broke into two separate units, with the two elder sisters as family heads. Still, there were periods—such as the move to the affinal relative's land—when the outfit could get back together and work constructively, and some ties were maintained throughout. But essentially they had become two separate outfits. The homestead was dispersed, and the people began pursuing different strategies.

The experience of the Broken Foot outfit illustrates several important points. It shows, for example, how groups can organize themselves and stay together for extended periods when there are definite advantages to that strategy. On the other hand, they will work separately when that approach is more viable. Although we often speak of such things as group cohesiveness, corporateness, and economic stratification as characteristics of the society, we should not lose sight of their ultimate origins in individual motivation and behavior.

Another point to be drawn from the Broken Foot example is that a group can be more or less nomadic depending on conditions. The Broken Foot group was practically sedentary for five years because it had a surplus of water. As that commodity became more scarce, they incorporated an increasing amount of movement into their strategy. The view of pastoralists as people who are by nature reluctant to settle is clearly contradicted in this instance. Anthropologist James Downs notes that "a pastoralist is no more anxious to move than is a farmer if he can maintain his herds while remaining in the same place" (1965). Nomadism is a strategy, a means of making specialized animal husbandry work.

summary

Pastoralism is a specialized form of animal husbandry based on herds of grazing animals such as sheep, goats, cattle, yaks, or camels. Pastoralists are often nomadic, moving from place to place as conditions dictate, but the amount of mobility is highly variable. The mobility may not simply be a matter of seeking sufficient grazing land; it may also be a means of maintaining political autonomy, and can even be part of a pattern of raiding settled groups.

Some groups combine herding with agriculture and are relatively self-sufficient; others concentrate exclusively on their herds. These highly specialized pastoralists must rely on regular transactions with other groups to supply all their needs. Because there are advantages to combining farming and herding, specialized pastoralism is usually adaptive only in areas where agriculture is risky or impossible.

Specialized pastoralism may have developed out of a farming/herding pattern. With the use of canal irrigation, grazing lands may have been pushed farther away from settlement areas. Animal owners would therefore have to expend more labor to get adequate food, water, and protection for their animals. At the same time, irrigation agriculture became more time-consuming. The increased demands of each of these strategies may have led some households to specialize in agriculture and others to choose herding exclusively.

Pastoral populations are highly variable. Households may move frequently one year and be largely sedentary the next. The households may differ in the time of the season in which they migrate. Some households act alone while others cooperate; some also shift between agriculture and herding.

The Karimojong of East Africa exploit arable land during the rainy season and use the more arid areas for herding. A balanced and diversified strategy makes them relatively self-sufficient. Although agriculture is important, the Karimojong consider themselves pastoralists. They are part of an East African "cattle complex," in which cattle play a significant role in social ties, obligations, and rituals. Importantly, the cattle also serve as a reserve food supply in the event of crop failures.

The Karimojong have permanent settlements mainly occupied by women, children, and old men. The adult males camp in pasture lands during the dry season and tend the crops near the settlements in the wet season. The domestic unit expands and contracts as conditions warrant, and each unit can function independently of the others. The independence and variability of domestic units permit herding strategies to be responsive to environmental conditions, the composition of the herd and labor force, and individual initiative. The Karimojong are opportunistic, committing their population where the greatest yields are found.

The Yörük of southeastern Turkey are nomadic pastoralists who move their sheep between winter and summer pastures. Their sheep are considered capital with which they participate in a market economy. The price of products which they must buy or sell fluctuates considerably, according to supply and demand, and presents problems to which the Yörük must continually respond. Because the Yörük rent pasturage, political and social factors affect their migratory schedule as much as climate and topography do.

Yörük social organization is flexible, with each household an independent producing unit. Households may unite to share pasturage or labor. In recent years, inflation has had significant effects on Yörük society. Changes in market conditions have caused a large number of Yörük to become farmers or shopkeepers, and have increased differences between poor and rich herders.

The Navajo of northeastern Arizona keep flocks of sheep and some cattle and horses. Agriculture is not important to them because they have so little rain. The basic social unit of their matrilineal kin system is the extended family. The family unit, an *outfit,* shares a homestead site and herds its livestock together. The Navajo do not migrate regularly with their animals, but water shortages may force a migration. Our example of the Broken Foot outfit shows how a group can remain together and cooperate if it has a regular water supply. However, a prolonged drought disrupted the large outfit. It had to break up, with various units moving in an attempt to once again find adequate water for their animals.

suggested readings

BARTH, F.
1961 *The Nomads of South Persia: The Basseri Tribe of the Kamseh Confederacy.* New York: Humanities Press. Analysis of the relationship between subsistence practices and political organization, with particular emphasis on the interaction of groups.

IRONS, W., AND N. DYSON-HUDSON, EDS.
1972 *Perspectives on Nomadism* (Symposium on Nomadic Studies, New Orleans, 1969). Leiden: E. J. Brill, Collection which presents a reappraisal of traditional approaches to pastoralism, concentrating on recent field reports from a wide range of pastoral societies.

LATTIMORE, O.
1962 *Inner Asian Frontiers of China.* Boston: Beacon Press. Classic study of the nomadic peoples of Inner Mongolia and Chinese Turkestan, using the historical and geographical context of ancient China to develop an understanding of nomadic origins.

LEEDS, A., AND A. P. VAYDA, EDS.
1965 *Man, Culture, and Animals: The Role of Animals in Human Ecological Adjustments.* Washington: American Association for the Advancement of Science. Contains a number of selections which describe widely varied pastoral groups, stressing the effects of keeping animals on cultural patterns.

SALZMAN, P. C., ED.
1971 *Comparative Studies of Nomadism and Pastoralism.* Anthropological Quarterly, Special Issue, Vol. 44 no. 3. Collection of comparative essays which provide a general background to the social and economic organization of pastoralists.

SPENCER, P.
1973 *Nomads in Alliance: Symbiosis and Growth Among the Rendville and Samburu of Kenya.* New York: Oxford University Press. Study of the economic interdependence of two tribes,

one depending primarily on camel herding, the other on cattle, who are linked by a strong traditional political alliance.

SPOONER, B.
1973 *The Cultural Ecology of Pastoral Nomads*. Reading, Mass.: Addison-Wesley. A general account of aspects of social organization and culture for selected nomadic pastoralists.

STENNING, D. J.
1959 *Savannah Nomads: A Study of the Wodaabe Pastoral Fulani of Western Bornu Province, Northern Region, Nigeria*. London: Oxford University Press. Ethnographic and documentary sources are used to provide a historical perspective on the changing material and political conditions affecting the society.

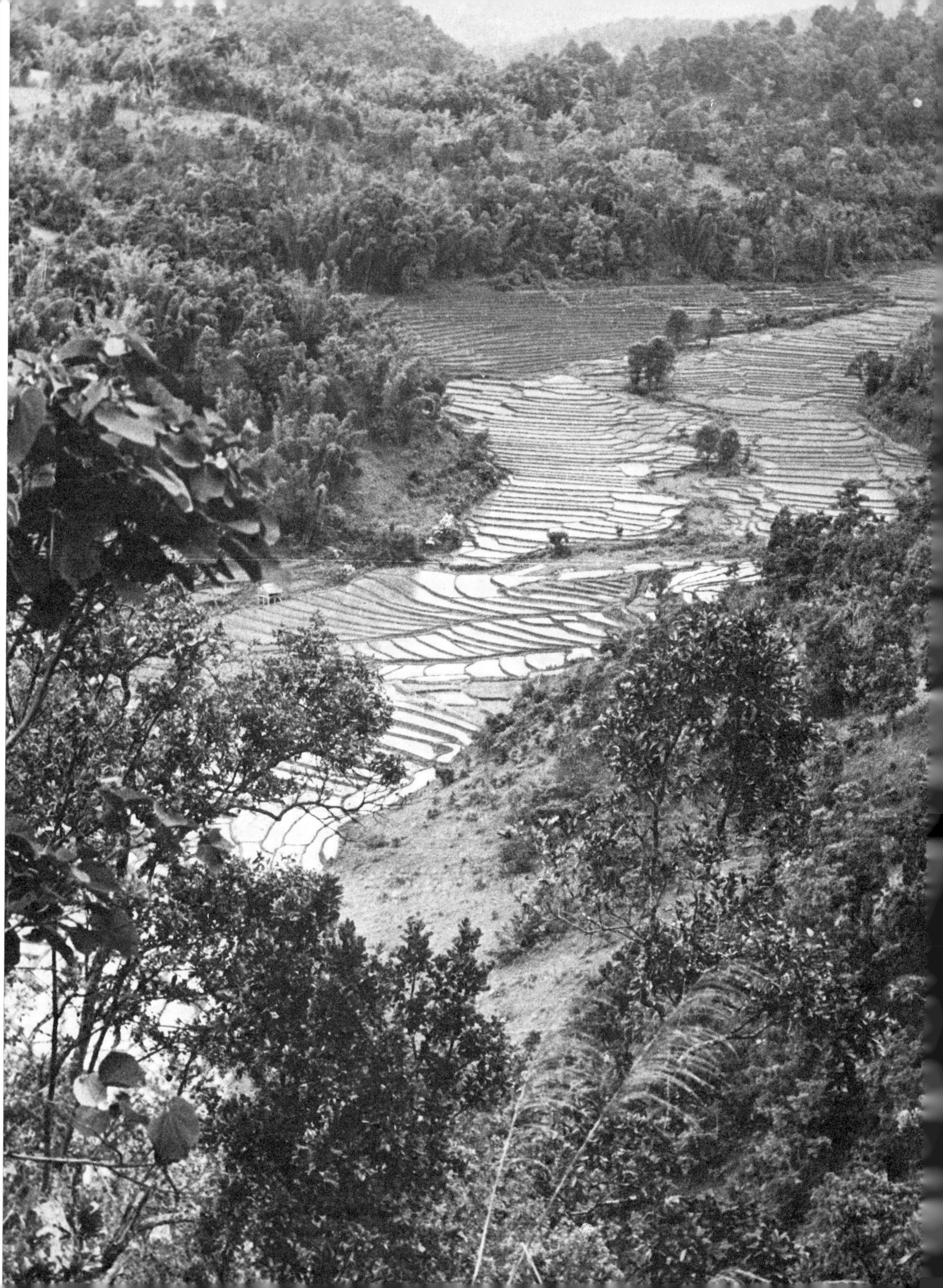

twenty-seven
Intensive Agriculturalists

In terms of size, the island of Java is a relatively insignificant part of Indonesia—about 9 percent of the total land area. But two-thirds of the population of Indonesia live on Java. And 63 percent of Indonesia's rice, 60 percent of her sweet potatoes, 70 percent of her casava, 74 percent of her maize, 86 percent of her peanuts, and 90 percent of her soybeans are produced on Java (Geertz, 1963).

The technological reason is agricultural intensification. The majority of cultivators on Java practice wet rice farming, whereas most outer islanders rely on slash-and-burn agriculture. By cleaning and terracing the land, building irrigation canals and drainage systems, and carefully controlling the flow of water through the paddies, Javanese cultivators are able to continually reuse the same land and produce far more food per unit of land than is possible with slash-and-burn technology. The water replaces nutrients drawn by rice plants from the soil, so the continuous cultivation does not degrade the soil. The warmth of the water encourages an abundance of blue-green algae which fix nitrogen in it, a characteristic particular to the kind of irrigation used in rice paddies. And the harder the Javanese work—the more care they put into planting, regulating the water supply, and weeding—the more food they produce.

Agricultural Intensification

Anthropologists and archeologists are interested in the development of irrigation systems because they so often accompanied the rise of centralized political organization in early civilization. Still, irrigation is but one of many ways to intensify agricultural production. Animal traction (a nonhuman source of energy); terracing and otherwise changing the landscape of the soil; various natural fertilizers; crop rotation; and selective breeding of crops and livestock are all preindustrial forms of intensification. These techniques, especially the increased investment of energy per unit of land they represent, cause the level of productivity to rise greatly. Through intensification, cultivators can grow much more food on the same plot. According to one estimate based on data on Veracruz, Mexico, 100 families practicing the slash-and-burn method of growing corn would require 2,964 cultivable acres (1,200 ha) to feed themselves; 100 families using canal irrigation and crop rotation, only 212 acres (85.8 ha) (Palerm in Wolf, 1966: 29). Intensified agriculture decreases the necessary fallow period, permitting continuous cultivation in some areas with some crops, double- and triple-cropping elsewhere. Although intensification usually means more work—Tsembaga horticulturalists work an average of 380 hours per year; Luts'un wet rice cultivators 1,129 hours a year—the proportion of productivity is higher. Most important perhaps is that intensive agriculture enables cultivators to produce a surplus.

Environmental Consequences of Intensification

What are the consequences of intensified agriculture? Most obviously, all of the techniques mentioned above involve substantial reshaping of the environment. We know horti-

Terraced paddy fields in Burma show the degree to which extensive agriculture can dramatically reshape the environment. (F.A.O. Photo)

culturalists interfere with natural growth for a brief period of time, after which they allow the land to return to its natural state. The Yanomamö's and Tsembaga's multicrop, multilayered gardens resemble the tropical forest around them. In contrast, a rice paddy is an artificial pond, created and maintained by human beings for the purpose of growing a single crop.

Intensification is an attempt to solve certain problems. For example, a population is able to compensate for irregular rainfall and droughts by using irrigation. Irrigation may also allow them to plant crops that would not otherwise grow in the region. They may intensify for political reasons—to pay taxes, for example. In the beginning, this strategy pays off in greater productivity, either for the local population or the larger society of which it is a part.

However, certain problems may arise. Irrigation may leave mineral deposits in the soil and in time raise the level of salinity.[1] As a result, productivity may level off and even decline. The common response to this problem is to further intensify production by expanding the area under irrigation, building larger dams, digging deeper wells, and the like. These efforts may work at first, but in the long run they may create as many problems as they solve. If, for example, the water table is not being replenished at a comparable rate, tapping greater and greater amounts of this vital resource is only a stopgap, emergency measure. In a relatively short time, the water table in the area sometimes begins to drop. Wells and ditches run dry; cultivators have to work harder and harder just to keep up the same level of productivity.

Clearly, cultivators do not free themselves from environmental constraints. On the contrary, they may generate new, complex problems that become increasingly difficult to solve. The more humans alter their ecosystems, the more labor and organizational effort—even often external sources of energy—are required to maintain their source of production. Hunters and gatherers do little to maintain their sources of food except to avoid overutilization. Horticulturalists are more committed to a regime of regular labor to maintain their productive system. Intensive agriculturalists—for example, those relying on grain—are vulnerable in many respects. Should disease kill the animals used in plowing, or should the canals in an irrigation system be allowed to silt up, production drops precipitously. Even disease probably increases in the severity with which it strikes and disrupts local communities as populations increase in density and frequency of contact. Intensification opens up new possibilities for things to go wrong and magnifies the costs of mistakes.

Social Consequences of Intensification

In general, intensification is associated with higher population densities (as in Java), the rise of urban centers, specialization in craft production and trade, the emergence of hierarchical religious organizations, economic stratification, political centralization, and the development of territorial states. As this occurs, previously autonomous groups become gradually interdependent. Traditional systems of social control and exchange may continue to be effective on the community level, but more centralized forms of social organization develop to regulate intercommunity relations.

The Cultivators Called "Peasants" Cultivators are drawn into these large political systems and into market systems over which they have little or no control. Indeed, frequently the means of production—the land itself as well as access to resources and capital to

---

[1] Rice paddies, which are unusually stable and capable of sustaining high yields over long periods, appear to be the main exception (Geertz, 1963), partly due to the nitrogen-fixing action of the algae. However, the degree of soil damage does vary depending upon local conditions and hydrology.

maintain intensified levels of production—are even taken out of their hands. Defined as a class or caste because of their involvement in food production, which is generally devalued, once autonomous cultivators become "peasants." The surplus food they produce is transferred to a dominant group of rulers that uses the surpluses both to maintain its own standard of living and to distribute to other groups within the society that provide nonagricultural goods and services (Wolf, 1966:2, 4).

The growth of states affects cultivators when political centralization significantly alters the local context in which the cultivators work. For instance, peasants practicing preindustrial intensified agriculture are more like hunters and gatherers, horticulturalists, and pastoralists than like farmers in highly industrialized countries. Such farmers regard planting and harvesting primarily as a business, and should agricultural production cease to bring adequate rewards, they may invest their capital elsewhere. Peasants, however, farm for the primary purpose of supporting their households, within extremely localized community standards. They rarely control much capital, and though they may grow cash crops in addition to supplying their own needs, their decisions are more often based on private needs than merely on potential profits.

Like the groups studied in preceding chapters, peasants devote a substantial proportion of what they produce to religious and social activities—feasts, rituals, marriages, birth rites, funerals, and so on. Eric Wolf (1966:7) calls this the "ceremonial fund." One function of expensive celebrations, he suggests, is "to explain, to justify, and to regulate" social relationships. In addition, the ceremonies may serve to redistribute wealth, to spread the risks of living in a particular environment, and to limit exploitation of resources in that environment. We have seen this before.

However, peasants differ from the other groups we've discussed in their relationship to the large, complex political and economic systems that exercise control over their lives. Other groups have much more direct control over their means of production. They "own" their land (so long as they can defend it). In the same sense, they own their livestock, their tools and their labor. Peasants, however, have to pay in some form for access to land, and this factor alone robs them of some of their autonomy. This may entail paying rent in cash, delivering a percentage of the harvest, or working a specified number of weeks for a landowner; or it may take the form of tribute paid to a superior power or taxes to a national government. However it is levied, peasants must devote some part of what they produce to what Wolf calls the "rent fund." This is something we have not seen in the other groups—and something which forces peasants to work that much harder than those in other groups.

Finally, intensive agriculturalists require a relatively large "replacement fund"—that is, funds to buy seeds and equipment, and to maintain such necessities as tools and irrigation works. To buy these things, peasants participate in market economies. Today this means that the value of what they produce and the cost of what they need is determined by the forces of the global market—forces far removed from them. Together, the ceremonial, rent, and replacement funds induce peasants to produce food or other crops in excess of strictly local requirements, but at the same time prevent their accumulating wealth. (See box on p. 549.) Moreover their participation in complex political economic systems poses a new set of problems to which the local community has to continually respond.

What all this comes down to is that centralization, like intensification, has built-in liabilities. When local populations begin to orient themselves toward the outside world, toward national (and increasingly world) markets and political systems, traditional methods of maintaining environmental and social equilibrium may be inadequate. Unless the state is sensitive to local environmental conditions and local problems, the local producing systems may weaken and ultimately disintegrate. Furthermore, should enough surplus-producing local communities be disrupted, there are likely to be adverse consequences for the larger political system, which depends on the regular production of food surplus and local revenues.

The next two sections of this chapter focus on peasants. The first study is a comparative analysis of two externally similar but internally quite different Taiwanese villages. The second uses survey data to illustrate the ways in which a number of peasant communities in Oaxaca Valley in Mexico cope with the dynamics of intensified agriculture and political centralization.

The last section deals with the transformation of social organization associated with the rise of agrarian states and empires. The case described is the early Islamic state. From both a functional and historical viewpoint it examines the rise of a kin-based system of relationship; and how that system altered under the impact of events which led to the local development and spread of the centralized politico-religious state in the seventh century A.D.

Two Chinese Villages

In many respects, Tatieh and Chungshe on the island of Taiwan are twin villages. Tatieh lies 15 miles (25 km) south of the city of Pintung, on a narrow plain between the mountains and the sea. Founded in the early nineteenth century by Hakka immigrants from the Chinese mainland, it is today a compact village of 1,602, surrounded by rice paddies and fields of sugar cane, sweet potatoes, and other marketable crops. Small shrines mark the four entrances to the residential center, with its brightly lit paved roads, well-kept brick houses, and small shops at the crossroads. Temperatures are generally warm, and although rainfall is highly erratic, irrigation works enable Tatieh villagers to prevent floods during heavy rains and water their fields during dry spells. Nearly all of Tatieh's 265 households depend on agriculture.

Chungshe, settled about 200 years ago by Hokkien immigrants, is 18 miles (30 km) northeast of Tainan City and about 30 miles (50 km) north of Tatieh. The land around Chungshe is not as fertile as that around Tatieh; the water supplied through irrigation is more limited; and the village's dirt roads and mud-brick and bamboo houses appear somewhat shabby. But the two villages are alike in size, physical layout, access to urban centers, and technology. The population of Chungshe is 1,115, divided among 194 households of about 6 members each (the same as the average household in Tatieh). Houses are clustered together as in Tatieh. Nearby highways and train stations provide easy access to urban centers, which are beginning to attract young people from both Chungshe and Tatieh. But as in Tatieh, the vast majority of households depend on agriculture, not wage labor. With irrigation, they are able to feed themselves and also produce a surplus to be marketed commercially. In 1957, the average household income in Chungshe was $7,163, compared to $7,596 in Tatieh (Pasternak, 1972:58). But here, as Pasternak's study shows, the similarity between the villages ends.

In Chungshe, the descendants of one of the original settlers, Lai Yuan, have always dominated local political and economic affairs. In the old days, this lineage owned much of the land surrounding Chungshe, and because so many villagers were their tenants (and hence their loyalty), effectively owned local political offices as well. The nine sublineages (or "fangs") that recognize Lai Yuan as their founding father control a total of 50.2 acres (20.3 ha)—far more than any other descent group in Chungshe or Tatieh controls. They are markedly better off than the average villagers, and consider themselves socially superior. Entrenched in adjoining compounds in the "head" of the village, Lai Yuan's descendants spurn those who live in the village "tail" as ignorant and lazy. Though reforms begun by the national government in 1949 have weakened their hold on the poorer villagers, once their control of political offices slipped, the offices themselves began to decline in importance. When disputes arise or villagers need loans, it is not the elected headman and neighborhood chiefs who settle matters but the "big men," who are invariably members of old and wealthy lineages.

Powerful corporate lineages have not developed in Tatieh. Residents do maintain ceremonial ties with branches of their descent groups in other communities, but downplay kin ties within the village. The largest descent groups—the Liu, Hsü, and Ch'en, who together account for 46 percent of all households—are scattered all over the village. They are no better or worse off than their neighbors. The three lineages that maintain corporate estates control a grand total of less than 4 acres (about 1.5 ha). Two other descent groups have set up modest trust funds for their members. Otherwise, kinship has virtually no effect on Tatieh villagers' access to land, water, or labor (three critical resources).

In fact, villagers prefer to keep family and business matters separate—to avoid the embarrassing situation of having to accuse relatives of faulting on contracts. While planting and harvesting require more hands than any one household can supply, Tatieh farmers call on friends and neighbors, whom they pay in wages or in kind (equivalent amounts of labor), whereas Chungshe farmers expect relatives to assist them. Each household head in Tatieh belongs to the *hsiao-tsu* or "small group" in charge of the irrigation system that waters his land. Because most households own land in two or more areas, most villagers belong to several irrigation associations whose memberships overlap. Many villagers invest in grain associations, which function more or less as banks loaning money when capital is needed for new equipment, ceremonies, and so on. Father-mother associations are organized to help defray the cost and labor involved in funerals. And most households in Tatieh own shares in the Make Prosperous Corporation—a public corporation that manages 42 acres (17 ha) of public land.

These organizations cut across kin lines, uniting Tatieh villagers in overlapping networks of rights and obligations and preventing the development of sharp inequalities. There are no "big men" operating outside the official political system, as there are in Chungshe. The people of Tatieh take elections seriously, vote without regard to kinship, appeal to their headman when disputes arise, and generally abide by his judgments. Important decisions regarding the community are made in town council meetings, convened every two months or so and attended by a male representative from every household in the village. In contrast, the village council of Chungshe rarely meets unless an outside government official calls household heads together for announcements. In general, Chungshe has no strongly developed sense of civic pride.

The contrast between the self-important lineages of Chungshe and the civic-minded households of Tatieh shows clearly in their different approaches to marriage and other ceremonies. One way to insure the integrity and exclusivity of patrilineages is to acquire brides from other, preferably distant, villages. This takes the bride away from her kin, reduces their influence on the new couple, and places her under the authority of her husband's kin. This is the preferred form of marriage in Chungshe. The villagers say that marrying someone from the same community is asking for trouble, and that in-laws get along much better if they see each other only infrequently. Less than 21 percent of all marriages contracted in Chungshe between 1959 and 1964 were intravillage marriages. In contrast, 48 percent of the marriages contracted in Tatieh during this period took place between residents of the village. The people of Tatieh consider marriage an opportunity to acquire new friends and allies within the village, and prefer their children to marry people they have watched grow up. In-laws in Tatieh are frequent visitors, exchange labor and financial aid as well as gifts, attend one another's celebrations, and often maintain ties over two or more generations. Tatieh wedding ceremonies symbolize this reciprocity. The bride and groom honor one another's ancestor in turn. Many friends and relatives of both sides of the family are invited to help prepare and share in the feasts. In Chungshe, the marriage ceremony centers around the groom honoring his

Two ways of celebrating a festival point up the contrast between two Taiwanese villages. (a) The villagers take part in the celebration of the birth of village sons in Tatieh. Each household that produced a son during the year provides cakes, which are distributed from the temple throughout the village. (b) A priest brought in from the outside officiates at a village festival in Chungshe, where ritual labor is more often hired than exchanged. (Burton Pasternak)

ancestors, but not the bride's. Only a few of the bride's kin are invited to the wedding feast. If the groom's family needs outside assistance, it hires professional caterers rather than calling on friends and neighbors as parents do in Tatieh.

As this example suggests, the people of Chungshe treat ceremonies as private family or lineage affairs, whereas Tatieh villagers celebrate with friends, neighbors, and consanguine and affinal kin. The elegant temple in Tatieh, carefully maintained and improved by succeeding generations, is a source of pride to all villagers. Old people gather there each morning; there is a nursery for village children and a dormitory for lay devotees; bimonthly and annual festivals draw individuals from all over the village. The comparatively drab, square concrete building that doubles as a temple and meeting hall in Chungshe is locked most of the time. On feast days in Tatieh, people honor their ancestors at home, then gather at the temple to honor their ancestors at home, then gather at the temple to honor the village gods. These celebrations involve numbers of unrelated households in cooperative labor, joint expenditures, and communal worship. On feast days in Chungshe, families borrow symbols of the gods and celebrate in their own homes—a custom that reinforces privacy and underlines class differences.

All other things being equal (size, physical layout, access to urban centers, and technology), why have these villages evolved such different modes of social organization? Burton Pasternak (1972), who made comparative case studies of the two villages, traces both the elaboration of patrilineages in Chungshe and the deemphasis of kinship in Tatieh to historical and ecological conditions. The land around Tatieh, long under irrigation, is highly productive and therefore highly desirable. From the beginning, Hakka immigrants had to defend themselves against attacks by predatory Taiwan aborigines and the Hokkien groups that arrived well before they did. Competition for scarce land and water encouraged them to band together in fortified multisurname* settlements and to establish ties with other villages through extended kinship. Moreover, the irrigation system—six main canals, each of which supplies water to a large number of fields—forced cooperation among unrelated neighbors.

Lack of sufficient rain and poor soils made the Chianan Plain less desirable. Pioneer families could claim large tracts of virgin land and live in relative isolation, without fear of incursions by competitors. Large descent groups that had been able to accumulate land and wealth had little incentive to form ties with other descent groups or villages. The first irrigation works in the area were not built until the 1920s, when the Japanese constructed a massive system to water the entire Chianan Plain. This system requires professional management by outside officials who make decisions and deliver orders regarding maintenance of local canals and water distribution. Prior to the construction of the present system, the people of Chungshe depended almost entirely on the yearly rainfall for irrigation, so there was not the need to organize the local irrigation groups which in Tatieh fostered early cooperation across lineage lines. Chungshe villagers still fight over access to water, diverting it illegally whenever necessary and possible for their needs, and siding with neighboring kinsmen whenever disputes arise. Land and political reforms have done relatively little to change the kin-centeredness of Chungshe.

Problems relating to water supply occur in Tatieh, too, but alignments among farmers take place according to field position rather than kinship, since the owners of most adjoining fields are unrelated to one another and obtain their water from the next higher field instead of directly from the canal. The need for cooperation has lessened as pumps now provide regular amounts of water to the lower fields. Nevertheless, watchmen keep close supervision of water distribution, especially in times of drought, while limits on usage help prevent increased salinization of the soil.

In the next chapter we will see how even such an equal distribution process can reverse itself if there are not adequate limits placed on the number of taps into water reserves, and if pumps are allowed to be operat-

---

*That is, people tracing their ancestry through different lineages and clans.

ed and wells dug without reference to the effects of overexploitation of the water table.

Oaxaca Valley

Cultivators in the Valley of Oaxaca in southern Mexico have been building stone dams to control floodwaters from the mountains and diverting streams into earthen irrigation canals for over 2,000 years. On the valley floor, some peasants still irrigate by hand, using buckets to draw water from 10- to 12-foot-deep wells (that is, 3 to 3.5 m) as their ancestors did millennia ago. Lately, however, these wells have begun to run dry after 2 to 4 hours' use. Why? As a direct result of agricultural intensification and urbanization, water has become more scarce, and the use of diesel pumps increases the speed of its use.

Oaxaca City is growing, and with it the demands for water for domestic and industrial use. Water once available to cultivators is now being diverted to the city. In an effort to intensify agricultural production in the valley, the government of Mexico has subsidized the construction of concrete canals and dams and the installation of high-powered diesel pumps. This equipment enables Oaxacans to grow alfalfa, which is far more profitable than the once major cash crops of wheat or sugar cane, or traditional subsistence crops like corn, beans, or squash. Alfalfa is profitable because dairy farmers use it for feed, and dairy products are in demand in Mexican cities. But it requires a great deal of water and puts a serious drain on this critical resource.

Fossilized canals, the ruins of large stone dams, and abandoned reservoirs indicate this is not the first attempt to raise levels of productivity in the valley. Nor is it the first time Oaxacan cultivators have become involved in a centralized political state and a broad market economy. Excavations at Monte Albán suggest that a complex, stratified, urban civilization developed in the valley between 2,300 B.P. and 1,200 B.P., alongside other Mesoamerican states. When the Spanish arrived in the sixteenth century, they found a broad class of peasants and a small elite of professional governors or nobles, who regulated intercommunity relations and maintained order within villages. The Spanish eventually replaced the upper levels of the Indian nobility but by and large left local Oaxacan communities to their own devices, thus stimulating a gradual process of decentralization which culminated in the Mexican Revolution. The postrevolutionary governments abolished the *hacienda* system, removing authority from the class of wealthy landlords who had dominated political and economic affairs in the valley (though not life within the villages). Peasant villages in Oaxaca Valley were soon on their own (Lees, 1973:9–10; 1974:167).

In a survey of 24 villages conducted between 1967 and 1970, Susan H. Lees focused on the management of irrigation systems. Were it not for irrigation, most of the land would not support crops so reliably or productively. Rainfall is highly variable, averaging between 20 and 30 inches a year, most of which falls between June and July. Except for those cultivators who own land on the wet valley floor, most piedmont Oaxacans depend on dams and canals. Who is in charge of water control in the villages? How is water distributed? When and how often do individuals irrigate their fields? Who is responsible for maintaining dams and canals? Given the importance of water, the answer to these questions should reveal a great deal about political structure in Oaxacan villages and about the relationship between irrigation and forms of social organization. When viewed as a dynamic system, certain unexpected regularities did emerge between irrigation systems and social and political structure. The people were engaged in increasing production of cash crops through intensifying their use of water resources. This is strongly related to a decrease in local control over resources and general centralization of the production system. But the actual responses of the different villages to the problem of water control are extremely varied.

In one village, Tlaliztac, the municipal *presidente* decided who received water, when, and for how long. He had complete control over

A farmer in Oaxaca Valley irrigates his flowers, which will be sold in Mexico City, by the time-consuming method of hand-watering the rows. Today most irrigation is through larger-scale canal systems, often set up by the government. (United Nations)

the irrigation system. However, the *presidente* of San Juan del Estado left the matter of water control to five low-ranking officials, each of whom supervised one of the main canals. As Lees's survey progressed, the variations multiplied. In another community, villagers elected a full-time water commissioner. In the twenty-second and twenty-third villages Lees visited, each household made private arrangements with an upstream village that could shut off the water that flowed into their irrigation ditches. No one was in charge. Nine villages required household heads to pay for water, according to the amount of land they were farming or the length of time they used the water. In others, payment was indirect. The more money an individual gave to the church, or the more labor he contributed to building and maintaining the village school, the more water he got. In short, Lees found wide variations in the way Oaxacan villages handled the problem of distributing water. The survey revealed that there are nearly as many ways to organize access to irrigation works as there are villages. But what Lees was interested in determining was what sorts of systemic regularities characterized the entire region's agriculture (Lees, 1973).

All the villages Lees studied were essentially egalitarian, democratic communities. In general, the standard of living in the valley was low. Most families produced just enough to get by. Inequalities existed: every village included poor and not-so-poor households. But no matter how much land a man owned, there was always a chance his crops would fail—if not this year, the next—and he would have to borrow to feed his family. Oaxacan villagers shared their risks in two ways: through *guelaguetza* and fiestas.

Guelaguetza is the delayed exchange of equivalent goods and services. When it was time to plant or harvest, men formed teams and moved from the field of one to the field of the next until all of their work was done. When a child was born or a couple married, friends and relatives donated a few pesos, candles, bread, chocolates, or coffee (whatever they could spare)—with the expectation of receiving equivalent goods in the future. A man who had had a good year lent to one who had not (Lees, 1973:13–14).

Guelaguetza was essential to celebrations of major saints' days. Every man was expected to sponsor at least one such fiesta in his lifetime, perhaps more if he were relatively well-off. Fiestas were the major social event in Oaxacan villages, and a source of great pride and prestige for the sponsor. There was considerable competition among individuals to provide lavish amounts of food and liquor and spectacular fireworks and music. As a result, staging a celebration involved large expenditures. A man might plan and save for four or five years—and even then few individuals could bear the total cost alone. The solution was *guelaguetza.* The sponsor borrowed money and goods, mortaging future surpluses for a day's celebrity.

This constant lending and borrowing distributed the risks of uncertain harvest across the community. Virtually everyone had made loans to some villagers and owes food or money to others. If a man's crops dried up or washed away in floods, he could collect old debts and borrow from friends, relatives, and neighbors. There was no shame in borrowing. The household that had food to spare this year knew it might run short in the future. Thus there was a continual circulation of small surpluses in Oaxacan villages. Extra food and money found their way to the people who needed assistance, to feed their families or to sponsor celebrations.

At the same time, *guelaguetza* and fiestas encouraged underproduction. If a man worked extra hard and produced a surplus, he could expect debtors and would-be borrowers to line up at his door. All his extra work would be siphoned off. As a result, most household heads consciously aimed to produce just a little more than they themselves would need. If the spring rains were light and farmers anticipated a poor season, they planted a little more than usual; if the rains were heavy, they planted a little less. Given low levels of production and large expenditures for ceremonies, cultivators had very little left over to invest in new equipment, fertilizers, or other improvements. But then they had little incentive to intensify their efforts. On the one hand, this meant that Oaxacans had a relatively low standard of living. On the other, it meant that they maintained a balance with the environment and did not overuse critical resources, in particular water. Thus *guelaguetza* and fiestas performed homeostatic functions.

Lees found similar social controls on private ambitions in village politics. In general, Oaxacans considered holding public office a necessary evil, not a route to self-aggrandizement. In most villages each household contributed to a communal fund used to build and maintain the church, school, roads and so on (through direct or indirect taxation), and every able-bodied man was required to devote a specified number of days a year to public works. In addition, all men were expected to fill increasingly responsible political offices, beginning as young men with the job of *topil* (a combination night watchman/messenger boy). Higher officials were elected or appointed by elected officials; most officials were not paid. Social pressure, public scrutiny, and limited terms of office prevented individuals from using public office for personal gain. Indeed, to be eligible for election to higher offices, a man first had to sponsor a fiesta out of his own pocket. Thus there was little to gain from serving as *presidente,* school commissioner, or judge. But failure to accept election or appointment was considered a crime, punishable by fines or jail terms in some villages.

All this is changing, however. The government of Mexico, which is struggling to make ends meet in the world market and cannot afford underproduction, is pressuring Oaxacans to modernize. As indicated above, new irriga-

A boy takes a drink of water from an irrigation pipe on an experimental irrigation project in Oaxaca Valley. (United Nations)

Custom, Incentive, and Productivity

Planners and government officials around the world tend to be baffled by the economic behavior of people in traditional market or nonmarket societies. They label it "backward" or "irrational" when people in these societies prove reluctant to adopt new, more productive techniques. For example, the Indian Agricultural Department introduced the Japanese method of rice cultivation, which could increase crop yields significantly, only to be rebuffed by farmers in a rural South Indian village. Even their attempts to persuade farmers to use a cheaper, more efficient tool for weeding rice failed in this village. How are we to interpret such responses? S. Epstein (1967) has shown that their refusals were not simply stubborn conservatism but were backed by strong economic incentives arising from the traditional social arrangements of Indian society.

Indian agricultural villages are composed not of self-sufficient households but of specialized units whose division of labor is buttressed by the beliefs and practices of the caste system. Members of landowning castes usually have clients from dependent castes who perform particular services for them. The landowning castes are obligated to pay a fixed amount of their produce annually to their client castes. The one caste is bound to provide services, the other is bound to distribute set quantities of produce. These economic relationships were reinforced by political and social conventions, giving Indian society great stability. The incentives in the system functioned to preserve the status quo. A client who produced more still received the same fixed amount that he had before. A landowner who tried to extract more met resistance from clients not only because their pay would not increase but because the customary rhythm of life and work would be disrupted. If farmers adopted labor-saving devices, they were still obligated to pay their clients. Thus, hereditary labor relations inhibited "progress."

Why, then, did these relationships persist? For the client, the system made a great deal of sense, since it ensured a minimum amount of food even during bad harvests. In fact, the fixed payments were not some arbitrary amount but instead closely corresponded to the amount each member of the village would receive if the total agricultural output were divided equally during a lean year. To the farmer, the arrangement also made sense, since during a good harvest, he would have a handsome surplus if the fixed payments were based on bad harvest output levels. The surplus could be invested in throwing feasts and other means of gaining status, contributing to further economic differentiation. Moreover, the farmer had an assured supply of labor. Since neither group could tell what the next harvest would bring, they both had hopes of "winning." The system was perpetuated by the hope of profit for the farmers and the guarantee against lean times for their clients.

But Indian villagers were also capable of seizing upon opportunities for increasing production. Besides the hereditary, rigidly prescribed labor relationships, there were more contractual relationships between landowners and artisan castes whose services were irregularly used. Moreover, with entirely new crops unregulated by hereditary relationships, farmers did not institute prescribed relationships but behaved like classical capitalist entrepreneurs. Workers were paid in cash according to the value of their output, and farmers used every means to increase output and productivity. One village that Epstein examined had begun raising a new crop and had shifted from the old ways; its average yield of rice per acre was about 30% higher than the more traditional village, even though its wet lands were fewer and its fields more distant from the village, factors that detract from productivity.

Thus we see that economic exchange occurs in a social context and is often regulated by values we would regard as non-economic. The potential for different responses to economic opportunity is crucial today, when traditional societies are being pushed to modernize. Epstein suggests the response depends on whether or not traditional incentives govern the situation. "Planners would be well advised to bear in mind that it may be easier to improve productive efficiency by introducing entirely new crops or products rather than by attempting to change the traditional methods and techniques of production" (1967: 248).

tion works, the growth of Oaxaca City, and the demand for alfalfa have put a serious strain on the water supply in the valley. Hand irrigation is becoming all but impossible. The introduction of new equipment has helped farmers to adjust to this, and indeed helped to create something of an economic boom in the valley. But the rewards of intensification may prove short-lived.

Young men welcome innovations as an opportunity to improve their families' standard of living and status. They are anxious to make more money and get ahead, and consider sponsoring fiestas old-fashioned. This means that social controls within the villages are breaking down. There is no limit on the incentive to produce as much as one can and less social pressure to share through loans and celebrations.

In addition, cultivators are having to dig deeper and deeper wells, to invest more and more in equipment, just to *maintain* current levels of production. Why? Intensive use causes the water tables to recede very quickly. Oaxacan villagers have neither the funds nor the skills on their own to purchase and maintain diesel pumps and concrete irrigation systems. By necessity, they are becoming increasingly dependent on the federal government and its experts.

If history repeats itself, the process of agricultural intensification, intertwined with political centralization, will continue—continue until the environment is overloaded, crops fail, and farming no longer pays off. At that point, many cultivators will have to seek alternative ways of making a living. This has happened many times in the Near East (Adams in Lees, 1974). Small-scale irrigation laid the foundation for Mesopotamian states by producing a surplus to feed urbanites and religious and political specialists. At first farmers prospered. But in time the dams silted up, salt deposits from irrigation water degraded the soil, and they had to work harder and harder to maintain the *status quo*. The government stepped in, building more elaborate irrigation systems which it controlled, making the cultivators its dependents. This response often led to short-term gains. Ultimately, however, the scale tipped in the other direction. Intensification exacerbated the problems it was designed to solve. Farmers found they were working longer hours for diminishing returns, and began turning to nomadic pastoralism. No longer tied to specific parcels of land, they broke away from their former rulers, regaining their former autonomy. The process of decentralization continued with the environment recovered, new cultivators appeared, and new states built on the ruins of the old. Thus the "organizational response to short-term degradation of environmental resources is centralization while long-term degradation elicits responses of decentralization" (Lees, 1974: 160). Perhaps this is part of the reason why states expand and contract in cycles.

Whether Oaxacan cultivators, who do not have the option of nomadic pastoralism, will turn to factory jobs, slash-and-burn agriculture, or some other alternative when they reach the point of diminishing returns is difficult to say. What is clear is that intensifying agricultural production does not solve the problem of supplying growing populations and states once and for all. To the contrary, it creates a dynamic situation that is both politically and ecologically unstable.

The Rise of Islam

Large, complex political states emerged in connection with the agricultural revolution, and the social transformations that take place within these states also affect populations hundreds of miles from the centers of power. The world has been a very different place indeed since the rise of early states in the Old and New World. No local population in contact with such powerful political systems can help but be itself affected. Eric Wolf's and Barbara C. Aswad's studies of the rise of Islam on the periphery of the Byzantine, Persian, and Abyssinian empires show this clearly (Wolf, 1951; Aswad, 1970).

In the first and second centuries A.D., the Koreish, like other Bedouins, were nomadic pastoralists who lived in small, fluctuating camp groups whose loose unity comprised the tribe. These groups cooperated in matters relating to access to water and grazing lands and defense. Some paid tribute to satellite states of the great agrarian empires around them. But by and large Bedouin bands were independent. The Koreish, like many others, were a relatively poor and insignificant people who lived by herding camels and raiding the caravans that periodically crossed the Arabian peninsula.

But in the third century, the number of traders using overland routes increased—in part because fighting within and between the Persian and Byzantine empires made travel by sea precarious. Taking advantage of this, the Koreish began selling protection to caravans passing through their territory. By the end of the century they had established themselves as respected middlemen—trading grain, oil, wine, and luxury items extorted from the caravans to desert nomads for leather, precious metals, incense, and other goods, and skimming a large profit off the top. In the early fourth century, the Koreish settled at Mecca, a small oasis strategically located on the trade routes.

At first the Koreish maintained their desert customs. Chiefs surrounded themselves with their family, kin who chose to live with them, and clients ("protected strangers" who were given the honorary status of kin). In time, however, the more prosperous chiefs abandoned the custom of distributing wealth among their dependents. Those merchants who amassed great fortunes began to attract larger and larger numbers of clients, some of whom joined the group voluntarily, others because they were unable to repay debts. These clients received protection but did not share in their patron's wealth. In effect, they were vassals. The population of some "kin groups" multiplied through the fiction of blood brotherhood that tied patron to client. On the one hand, this gave a small group of patrons great power and gave many freed slaves, refugees, and other displaced persons a kin group to provide support. On the other hand, it involved chiefs in rounds of "blood feuds." According to the customary law of the area, men are obliged to assist real or fictive kinsmen in avenging raids, murders, insults, and the like.

At the same time, Koreish merchants attempted to protect their financial interests by maintaining Mecca as a religious center. Again, according to the customary law of the area, no blood may be shed in a sacred place. The Koreish expanded the main shrine of the local cult, the Ka'ba, to house a large market where food, milk, wine, camels, slaves, and precious metals were traded, and where men invested in caravans, hired laborers, and camels. For insurance, the Koreish ringed the Ka'ba with idols and religious relics from the many groups that traded there, including Christian icons. Peace reigned within. People from far and wide began to pay homage to Allah, the guardian of patron/client relations, as well as to their tribal and ancestral gods. The Koreish made treaties with neighboring tribes (who became "kin") to protect pilgrim-traders on their way to and from Mecca.

Thus Mecca became a large, cosmopolitan religious and trading center. But the desert custom of organizing social relations around real and fictive kin ties masked the emergence of a complex, stratified oasis society and in large part thwarted centralization. The clique of Koreish merchants who dominated Mecca lacked the formal political authority and monopoly over the use of force of a true state government. It was a city without a political center: it lacked a centralized hierarchy of decision makers.

The situation in Medina, another oasis, was quite different. The people of Medina regularly traded for leather, dairy products, and other goods with nomadic herders who had aligned themselves with the Persians or Byzantines. The empires protected them from unaligned, marauding tribes. Medina was one of the larger oases on the Arabian Peninsula, with abundant water for crops. It was a potentially self-sufficient agricultural settlement.

Jewish cultivators, who brought new crops, new agricultural techniques, and iron tools to Medina, established a foothold there in the

This thirteenth-century miniature shows Arabs making a pilgrimage to Mecca. Following the rise of Islam, Mecca became an important pilgrimage site and trade center for Muslims all over the world. (Bibliothèque Nationale, Paris)

latter part of the first century. Kin groups and their clients scattered among the palm groves, living in and around private fortresses. Under the protection of the great empires they grew wheat, barley, and clover, and they flourished. However, when the empires began to fall apart in the third century, there was nothing to stop pastoralists from invading Medina. The lush oasis drew raiders like a magnet. Bedouins also began to farm.

When Mohammed arrived in Medina, he found a society torn by fights between cultivators and pastoralists and by feuds among rival Bedouin settlers. But Meccans did not take kindly to Mohammed's criticism of powerful merchant-chiefs or his monotheistic teaching. Mohammed preached that Allah was the Patron of all men, and that his clients on earth had a sacred obligation not only to protect but to provide for their less fortunate neighbors—a doctrine Meccans feared would alienate polytheistic traders. Moreover, he attempted to recruit from among all of the clans. In short, Mohammed was a troublemaker. With little ado, the great Koreish clans banished him and his followers, and returned to their trading.

Mohammed and the Emigrants (as those who left Mecca with him came to be known) found welcome in Medina, where one of the many warring factions took them in as clients and allies. However, in a short time the Emigrants broke away and established themselves as an independent "tribe," based on ideological commitment rather than real and fictive kin ties. Mohammed proved highly successful at organizing and leading raids on caravans bound for Mecca. Like a traditional desert chieftain, Mohammed collected one-fifth of the booty from raiders for redistribution among his followers. Even so, the profits were sufficient to attract the powerful Kharaj and Aus tribes, who became his Ansars, or "helpers." The critical difference between Mohammed and the usual Bedouin practice was that in return for participation in his alliance of tribes, each had to submit to his authority as collector of tribute and arbitrator. Word of the success of Muslim raiders spread rapidly.

Mohammed accomplished in Medina what he failed to bring about in Mecca—the creation of a political-religious community or *umma*—largely because Medina was in a state of upheaval even before he arrived. The oasis was divided and the clans that first protected and later followed Mohammed were eager to recruit his support. Mohammed tipped the balance and provided the leadership. Meccans were, of course, enraged by attacks on their caravans and eventually laid siege to Medina. But unpracticed Meccan soldiers were no match for the accomplished Muslim raiders, even though they greatly outnumbered them. The Meccans were poorly organized and poorly motivated. The merchants of Mecca were more concerned about their private financial empires than about defeating Mohammed. Indeed, so many wealthy Koreish merchants had joined Mohammed by 630 A.D., he didn't have to use force to conquer Mecca. It was a relatively bloodless coup.

Mohammed reentered Mecca as the undisputed leader of the dominant faction in the Arabian Peninsula. He was the head of a large confederation of tribes, a desert chieftain—with some important differences. First, many of Mohammed's client tribes did not convert to Islam. They viewed him as they would any powerful chief from whom they sought protection, not as the Prophet. But the inner circle, the dominant "clan" of Islam, was united by religious beliefs and practices, not by kinship. This was unprecedented in Arabia. Second, Mohammed took over many of the functions that were performed locally in traditional Bedouin tribes. Voluntary alms for the poor became fixed taxes, collected by the Emigrants and Ansars who fanned out across the peninsula. The fifth of all booty reserved for redistribution went to Mohammed. This meant first, that a central authority handled the redistribution of wealth, and second, that the Emigrants and Ansars were becoming full-time administrators, the beginning of a multi-level state bureaucracy. While still in Medina, Mohammed had urged quarreling tribes and lineages to settle differences by paying "blood money" rather than by conducting blood feuds. Once in Mecca, he declared blood feuds illegal. The use of force became the prerogative of Muslim authorities—one more step toward statehood. Finally, Mohammed insisted that loyalty to Islam—to the state—supercede kinship ties. The Emigrants were honored for having "fled their homes and spent their substance for the cause of God" (*Koran* 8, 73:381; in Wolf, 1951:346). "God has put an end to the pride in noble ancestry, you are all descended from Adam and Adam from dust, the noblest among you is the man who is most pious," Mohammed declared (Wakidi, 1882:338; in Wolf, 1951:344).

Thus the system of kin ties that had hitherto been the only formal basis for social organization in Mecca became simply one level in a political system. Meccan society had been organized around commercial or contractual economic relationships arising from trade for more than a century, despite the fiction of kinship. Mohammed provided an ideological rationale for organizational changes that had already taken place. He replaced the confused tangle of overlapping patron-client relationships with a centralized authority, better capable of managing this complex a society.

All this would not have happened if agriculturally based empires had not begun using the Arabian Peninsula for long-distance trade, irrevocably changing the lives of Bedouin pastoralists. It would not have happened if Medina had not reflected the disorder in these empires and welcomed a leader preaching a new way of life. And it would not have happened if Mecca hadn't developed to the point where kin-based social organization became "overloaded" and ultimately dysfunctional.

summary

Attempts to intensify agricultural production have led to the use of irrigation systems, nonhuman energy sources (such as animal traction), terracing and the changing of the landscape, natural fertilizers, crop rotation, and the selective breeding of crops and livestock. These techniques increase the investment of energy per unit of land and cause the level of productivity to rise greatly. Through intensification, much more food can be grown on the same plot of land while the necessary fallow period can be decreased. Although more work is required for intensive agriculture, the proportion of productivity to work-hours is considerably higher than that of horticulture. Moreover, intensification allows cultivators to produce a substantial surplus.

There are, however, important environmental and social consequences of intensification. As with every adaptation, there are environmental constraints. In their attempts to overcome a problem, such as insufficient rainfall, by utilizing irrigation, cultivators may instigate new, complex problems that become increasingly difficult to solve. The more humans alter their environment, the more labor, organizational effort, and energy are necessary to maintain their source of production. Socially, agricultural intensification is associated with higher population densities, specializations in craft production and trade, economic stratification and centralization, hierarchical religious organizations, the development of territorial states, and the growing interdependence of previously autonomous groups. Under these circumstances the autonomous cultivator in preindustrial societies is categorized as a peasant, one who farms primarily for the purpose of supporting a household. But peasants also allot a substantial portion of what they produce to what can be called ceremonial, rent, and replacement funds, as well as to the political institutions that exercise control over their lives. As a result, peasants are forced to produce food or other crops in excess of strictly local needs while they do not accumulate personal wealth.

The intensive agricultural villages of Tatieh and Chungshe resemble each other in size, physical layout, access to urban centers, and technology. However, they have evolved very different modes of social organization: in Tatieh, kinship has virtually no effect on villagers' access to the critical resources of land, water, and labor; in Chungshe, the descendants of one of the original settlers dominate village politics and economics, and they control access to critical resources. The reason for this is that social organization, the elaboration of patrilineages in Chungshe and the deemphasis of kinship in Tatieh, is a result of the historical and ecological conditions surrounding the formation of these villages.

Studies of water control and social organization in numerous villages in the Oaxaca Valley of Mexico demonstrate that there are nearly as many ways to organize access to irrigation as there are villages. However, despite this variety, there were systematic regularities: *guela-*

guetza, the delayed exchange of equivalent goods and services, and fiestas serve to distribute the risks of uncertain harvest across the community. They also encourage underproduction and thereby maintain a balance with the environment that prevents the overuse of critical resources. However, recent government policy encouraging agricultural intensification has disrupted the water supply as well as these social controls, and this may lead, as it has historically, to a diminishing of returns making cultivation unprofitable.

The loss of social control in the Arabian Peninsula by the great agricultural empires provided an environment for a more efficient social organization. Mohammed created a politico-religious community and provided sorely needed leadership in an area racked by belligerence. He superseded the functions that were performed by local Bedouin tribes—he collected taxes and booty and thereby created a central authority administered by his followers that redistributed wealth. By finally superseding kinship ties with politico-religious affinities, Mohammed created a centralized authority.

suggested readings

DALTON, G., ED.
- 1967 *Tribal and Peasant Economies: Readings in Economic Anthropology.* Garden City, N. Y.: Natural History Press. Collection of studies including a worldwide survey of the economic integration of peasant communities.

GAMST, F. C.
- 1974 *Peasants in Complex Society.* New York: Holt, Rinehart & Winston. Valuable introduction to the anthropological study of the peasant community and its relations with the larger society.

LOCKWOOD, W. G.
- 1975 *European Moslems: Economy and Ethnicity in Western Bosnia.* New York: Academic Press. Case study of a Balkan Moslem community which explores the mechanisms of ethnic boundary maintenance and the role of the peasant market as a vehicle for interethnic transfer of cultural patterns.

POTTER, J. M., M. N. DIAZ, AND G. M. FOSTER, EDS.
- 1967 *Peasant Society: A Reader.* Boston: Little, Brown. Collection of major essays on peasant cultivators, focusing on local community organization and its relationships to complex market and state systems.

WOLF, E. R.
- 1959 *Sons of the Shaking Earth.* Chicago: University of Chicago Press. Classic study of agrarian development in Mexico and Guatemala, from its prehistoric beginnings, through the period of colonial expansion, and in the modern national state.

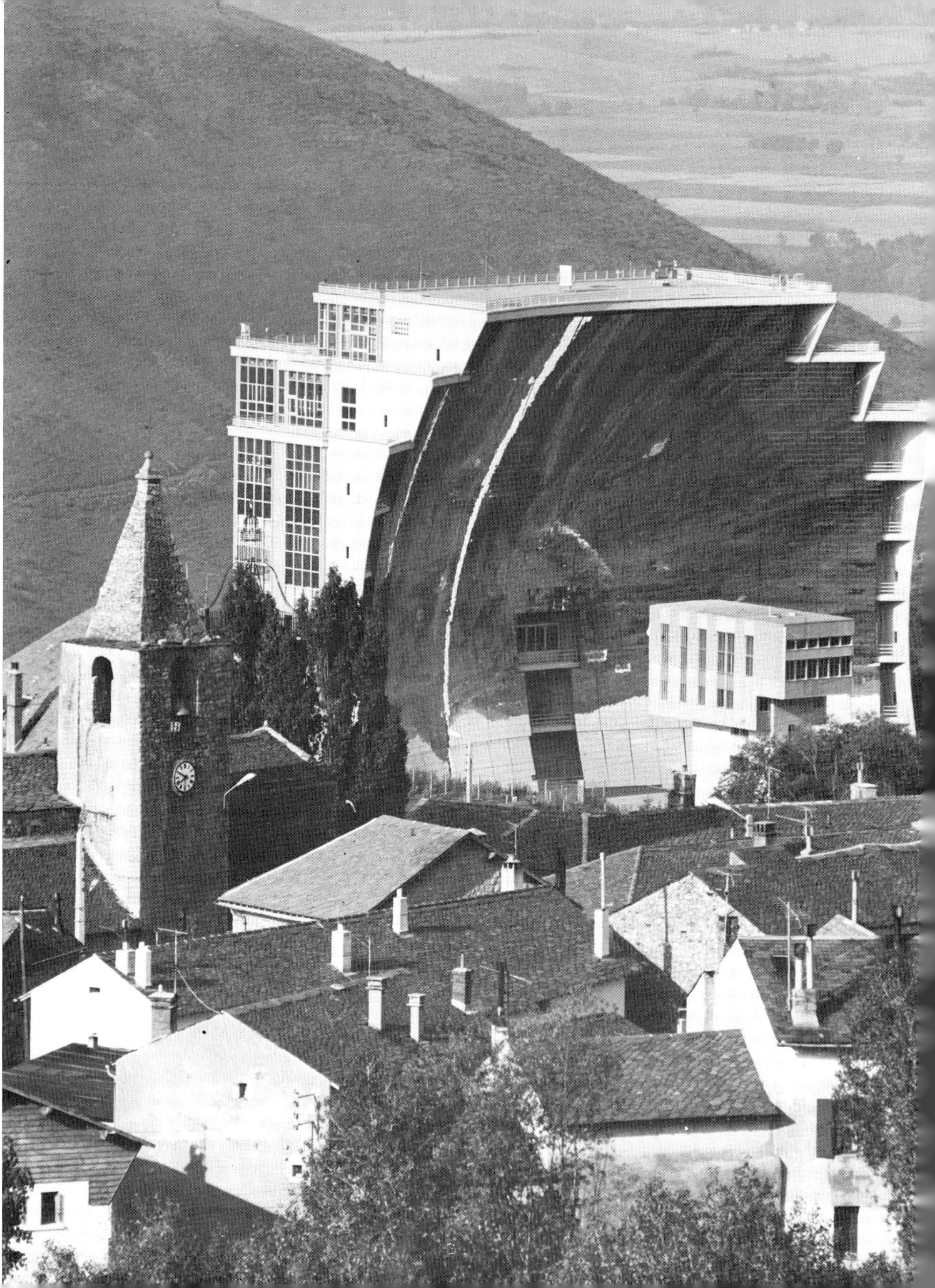

twenty-eight
Industrialism in a Global Society

All of us are aware of the accomplishments of the industrial era. Most of us can cite personal instances of accident or illness that might have been tragic without the availability of modern health care. All of us have probably enjoyed the friendship or support of people unrelated by kinship whom we would not have met were we not participating in a global society organized around fast, efficient systems of communication and transportation. We regularly eat foods out of season or consume items not produced at all on our continent. All of us, too, have had our lives touched in ways that are not so pleasant, again for reasons arising from the transformation of the world by industrialism. We may have had relatives die in foreign wars or political uprisings; or we may have seen a lake we once enjoyed swimming in grow polluted; or we may simply have suffered the ignominy of a bad credit rating disseminated by a distant and errant computer.

These examples indicate that industrialism involves more than just new machines. Mechanization is certainly part of industrial society but by no means the most essential part. Industrialization refers to the development of specialized productive units, utilizing concentrated forms of solar energy—fossil fuel—through highly mechanized procedures. These specialized units include not only the familiar ones—the factories, warehouses, and showrooms—but also the mechanized fields of agro-industry and the intricate social and economic structure that interconnects the specialized subsystems forming today's global economy. No region of the world, no population, however remote, is unaffected by our contemporary advanced industrial economy. Thus industrialized society is organized quite differently from the groups we have studied in the preceding chapters of this part. It is this organizational aspect as well as the technology that interests anthropologists who study industrialized or industrializing societies.

The development of mechanized procedures for harnessing new forms of energy—first coal, then oil and gas—is closely related to the evolution of specialized production units. We know that many human populations had learned to extract the solar energy stored in plants more efficiently by domesticating them; harnessed animals to plows; on occasion used wind or water to power mills; traveled over the seas on boats powered by sail; and waged war with explosives. But the exploitation of energy sources outside the human body was relatively limited. It was only with the invention of the steam and later the diesel and internal combustion engines that populations were able to harness the concentrated solar energy stored in the fossil remains of organic matter (namely, coal, oil, and gas). With these new sources of energy, industrialized populations have vastly increased the scale of mechanization, specialization, mass production, and so on. And this is what sets the Industrial Age—what Leslie White calls the Fuel Age—apart. (See White, 1949, Chapters 13 and 14). Modern industrial techniques harness more energy per capita than ever before in history.

Industrialized societies may employ more energy than other groups, but this is not to say

The medieval bell tower at the left took sheer human energy to build, but since the Industrial Revolution, our energy output has been enormously amplified by the use of fossil fuels. Now, aware of the finite supply of such fuels, people are looking to the sun as a direct source of energy. In Odeillo, high in the French Pyrenees, this solar furnace uses a collection of mirrors to concentrate enough of the sun's heat to furnish energy for industrial uses. (© Georg Gerster, Rapho/Photo Researchers)

that they use energy more efficiently. To the contrary, farmers in industrial societies often invest more energy in fertilizer and gasoline for their tractors than they harvest in calories of food energy, even with high-yield grains. Moreover, large quantities of energy are diverted to non-food-producing activities. Thus industrialization significantly *decreases* efficiency in the sense that more energy is needed to support a unit of population than in any other type of society. Nevertheless, new sources of energy and the technology to harness them laid the groundwork for expansion of production on a scale never witnessed before, and dramatic, if costly, change.

Changes in Population

The Industrial Age ushered in a whole host of social changes. First, and perhaps most obviously, population increased much more rapidly than before. In Europe, where the Industrial Revolution began, the population grew from 100 to 187 million between 1650 and 1800, then leaped to 400 million in the nineteenth-century Coal Age—an increase of 260 percent (White, 1949:384). World-wide population doubled between 1650 and 1800; today, the world population is doubling every 35 years (Ehrlich and Ehrlich, 1972:450). However, much of the increase is now taking place in underdeveloped areas. Birth rates are significantly higher in the Third World than in industrial nations today, while death rates are declining. The result? Explosive population growth. In the industrialized nations the rate of population growth has leveled off—a phenomenon associated with advanced industrialism.

The reasons for the rapid explosion followed by declining rates of population growth are exceedingly complex. One important selective pressure in the initial stages is the devaluation of labor, particularly agricultural labor, on the world market. More and more families come to depend on the sale of labor to meet their needs, and very often the income they derive in this way is less in terms of the food it buys than if they produced the food directly. Mechanization and commercialization of agriculture precludes that option for most. Rural people who have migrated to the cities simply do **not** earn enough to get by unless their children work as well. The more children they have, the more likely they are to survive. Children can help in the fields, work in the factories, peddle produce or crafts, scavenge, and otherwise bring in needed income. Given high rates of infant and childhood mortality, the more children a couple has, the more likely some will survive to take care of them when they are too old to support themselves. In countries where there are no publicly supported health or welfare programs, these are vital considerations.

The process of devaluing agricultural products and labor relative to other commodities, along with the mechanization of agriculture, serves to push people off the land and set up population movements, both within and between nations. The influx of Europeans to America reached a peak at the turn of the century. By and large, the immigrants were displaced from farming by mechanization, monoculture, and other changes. They came to America believing that U.S. factories offered opportunities for wage labor. Today, all over the world, country people are pouring into cities for similar reasons. Others have adapted to changing patterns of food production by becoming migrant farm laborers. (Of course, migration is not limited to peasants. The true nomads of industrial society are middle-class, white-collar workers who move from job to job or from city to city in the same job.)

Specialization and Segmentation

Secondly, industrialization has accelerated the trend toward specialization and segmentation[1] in production. On the simplest level, an industrial society needs miners and drillers to

---

[1]Breaking production of a single item down into a series of small tasks performed by different individuals and groups, as on an assembly line.

extract fuel; truckers to deliver it to plants; engineers to design plants and machines; machinists to build and maintain the machines; laborers to work them; administrators to coordinate all these activities. All of these people have to be housed, clothed, and fed, which generates more specialized jobs—and so on.

Specialization has a very direct effect on people's lives. Take food producers, on whom we have focused throughout these chapters: Industrialization tends to turn farmers into businessmen, in the sense that they concentrate on producing cash crops while buying food to eat, rather than concentrating on provisioning their households and selling only the surplus. Farmers may choose to shift to cash crops because it seems more profitable. Or they may be forced to do so by landowners, colonial administrators, government planners, or others. In either case, to the extent that farmers make the transition from domestic to commercial production, they are at the mercy of world markets. The price of wheat or rice or sisal may plummet in the space of a day. There is little farmers who have committed their resources to one or another crop can do except tighten their belts or go into debt. Even slight changes in relative prices have a profound impact on small farmers or agricultural laborers.

The nature of social relations changes as the organization of work changes. When agriculture becomes agribusiness, it is increasingly removed from the networks of familial and social relations we have seen in the groups described in preceding chapters. The same is true of other areas of production. In general, work groups tend to become more important than kin groups in a variety of contexts. Workers spend their days with people whose only relationship to one another is that they do the same or related jobs. They live in neighborhoods composed of people who do similar kinds of work. While kinship ties may be socially and economically important, they are only a limited aspect of overall social organization. Class, ethnicity, work affiliation, union membership, political clubs, and so on all take over functions formerly associated with kinship.

Concentration of Wealth

Thirdly, economic differences tend to increase with industrialization. Wealth is concentrated in the hands of a few individuals and families, a few nations. The silent majorities—not to mention the poor—do not enjoy equal economic rewards or equal access to political processes. Nor do underdeveloped nations. This is not to say that preindustrial ruling classes did not engage in conspicuous consumption, nor is it to say that industrialism necessarily leads to greater economic inequalities. But the gaps between classes often widen in industrial systems.

Decreasing Cultural Diversity and Increasing Interdependence

Although wealth may be more concentrated, causing differentiation *between* classes to increase, cultural and ethnic diversity has decreased, resulting in greater world-wide similarity *within* class lines. Industrialism draws people all over the world into one global system. Products are manufactured from raw materials grown or extracted on one continent, assembled on another continent, and sold on still another. The decisions an Iowa corn farmer makes affect wine growers in Chile, politicians in Russia, manufacturers in Turkey, shopkeepers in Hong Kong and Kinshasa, street vendors in Brussels. We are all interconnected. As a result, when studying industrialized societies, anthropologists must focus on larger units than simply a village or a tribe. All of the trends—population growth, mass migrations, specialization and segmentation in work, changes in social relations, greater social stratification along with greater interdependence—demands this comprehensive view.

Therefore, the organization of this chapter is somewhat different from the preceding ones in this section. Examining all the complex manifestations of industrialization is beyond the scope of this chapter. Rather, we have chosen to narrow in on changes in food production and adaptations to these changes in the first part, then take a sweeping look at global corporations, which seem to be emerging as a way of organizing world trade and production and to be taking on policy functions that are usually associated with governments. These two trends are interrelated, of course. The people displaced from the agricultural sector by its industrialization form a low-wage force that attracts multinational plants, and multinational corporations are increasingly becoming involved in agro-industry.

Even limiting the chapter to two developments, our coverage must be brief. We have focused on some of the problems created by agro-industry and multinational corporations. This problem-oriented approach should not blind us to the contributions industrialization has made, but the reason for emphasizing the problems is that they raise issues that are in public debate right now and will continue to be debated throughout this decade and probably longer. They affect the lives of all of us.

Agro-Industry: The Second Agricultural Revolution

Imagine a driverless tractor, moving up and down a field with absolute precision, turning over the soil. Perhaps some birds circle overhead, but there are no human beings for miles. Science fiction? Not at all. Driverless tractors are on the drawing boards and could be in production in a few years (Cohen, 1974). Farmers will be able to work hundreds of acres by remote control. It is a relatively short step from driverless tractors to a glass and steel building in Chicago where "farmers" operate tractors and combines all over the Midwest by pushing buttons on a computer console. Many U.S. farms have already become factories. "More and more food is being planted, tended, harvested, packaged, and sold without being touched by human hands until it reaches the dining table" (Cohen, 1974:520). How has the mechanization of agriculture affected both industrial and preindustrial societies?

The Urbanized Rural Society

In the early 1940s, Walter Goldschmidt (1947) undertook a case study of Wasco, California—a town of 7,000 to 8,000 people, most of whom were involved in varying aspects of industrialized commercial agriculture. After living in the town, participating in local organizations, conducting interviews, and examining official records and historical documents, Goldschmidt concluded:

From industrialized sowing of the soil is reaped an urbanized rural society. . . . Industrialization has changed farming enterprise from a livelihood to a means of achieving wealth. Diversification [varied crops and livestock], the drudgery of the farm yard, self-sufficiency are gone and in their stead is the single cash crop grown at high cost in the ever-present expectation of large profits. This means on the one hand the need for large groups of farm laborers and on the other hand the interest of large commercial enterprises in the farming community. These are the elements which make for the breakdown of the old community and for the development of urbanized social relationships. (pp. vii–ix)

Goldschmidt explains the present by examining the past. Years ago, the land now being farmed was desert, and the only industry in the area was sheepherding. Wasco itself consisted of one store, one hotel, and a handful of saloons frequented by cowhands and an occasional homesteader.

In 1907 a developer convinced the corporation that owned the entire Wasco area to sell part of its holdings, and began advertising for homesteaders, promising to provide the necessary irrigation. The sales pitch worked (the land was bought up quickly), but the irrigation system did not. In all probability, the farmers would have abandoned Wasco to the sheep if a major utilities company had not brought in a power line, enabling settlers to install electric pumps. This was the beginning of the industrialization of Wasco.

For a small farmer, as most of the original settlers were, an electric pump is a major investment. In order to recoup that investment, farmers turned to cash crops—specializing in potatoes or cotton, sugar beets, melons, or grapes. Profits were such that the settlement grew steadily. Indeed, some years the payoff for commercial farming was spectacular. In 1936, for example, one farmer was rumored to have made a million and a quarter dollars from his potato crop. Such booms encouraged Wasco farmers to expand. Some rented land to grow profitable but soil-depleting crops for a year or two, after which the landowner could plant alfalfa to revitalize the soil, then rent again. This strategy required the planter to hire large numbers of workers and to make substantial investments in tractors and other motorized equipment. Other Wasco farmers used their profits to build— say, a packing shed. Having made this investment, a farmer would then look for ways to maintain a steady flow of produce through the shed. He might buy the fruits of another landowner's trees and hire his own laborers to pick them—or, better still, purchase more land. In this way, the average size of landholdings increased through consolidation from 20 acres in the beginning to 100 acres at the time of the study.

In no time, Wasco was attracting outside corporations—first the utilities companies, then a national bank, salesmen from farm-equipment manufacturers, oil companies, chain supermarkets and the like. These developments changed the social landscape. The representatives of state and national corporations, whose loyalties lay outside Wasco, tended to become leaders within the town, Wasco's elite. Even farmers with relatively small holdings began to see themselves as entrepreneurs rather than tillers of the soil. One informant told Goldschmidt, "There is one thing I want you to put in your book. Farming in this country is *a business, it's not a way of life*" (p. 22). City newspapers, the radio, and the movies reinforced this orientation—creating urban desires and setting urban standards of behavior. Wasco was definitely not a peasant community, like those described in the preceding chapter.

At the same time, Wasco began to attract large numbers of unskilled laborers who could find work in the town and dream of buying a place of their own one day. First Mexicans, then (after World War I) blacks, and in the 1930s refugees from Oklahoma, Arkansas, and other drought-stricken states poured into the town. Between 1930 and 1939 alone, 2,500 people immigrated to Wasco—two-thirds of them from the dust-bowl states. Most of these people worked only seasonally. They were markedly poorer than the farmers, who did not consider them racial, cultural, or social equals. The farmers hired them impersonally, by the group, sometimes using a member of one of these communities as a recruiter. They did not consider themselves responsible in any way for the laborers' well-being once a harvest was completed. (This is what Goldschmidt meant by "urbanized social relationships.") At the time of the study, the Mexicans, blacks, and to a lesser extent the "Okies" lived in their own separate communities, with their own stores, churches, and so on. They were outsiders in every sense, which is just what Wasco's commercial farmers needed—"a large number of laborers unused to achieving the social values of the dominant group, and satisfied with [a] few of the luxuries of modern society" (p. 62). And the laborers needed the jobs.

The Displaced

As often as not, the unskilled laborers who settle in towns like Wasco, migrate from harvest to harvest, or try their luck in big cities are people who were forced off their land by farmers undertaking large-scale industrialized agriculture. In the next two sections we follow different migrants to the work camps and the city.

Migrant Laborers Most of us are aware of migrant workers in the United States thanks to the grape and lettuce boycotts of the United Farm Workers, but migrant labor is common all over the world, from copra plantations in the Pacific that recruit workers from a

Industrialized agriculture has brought with it the impersonalization of relations between landowner and land worker. Migrant farm workers are becoming increasingly unionized in an attempt to secure adequate wages and working conditions.
(Joffre Clarke/Black Star)

thousand miles away, to Turkish, Greek, Yugoslavian, and Spanish laborers in Europe, or mine workers in the gold fields of South Africa. The organization of this mobile labor force varies considerably, as does the extent to which migrants can raise their standards of living. For example, nearly one million Turks working as "guest laborers" (*Gastarbeiter,* as the Germans call them) in the factories of Western Europe receive the same wages as native workers and are able to return to Turkey with considerable savings. Our own domestic migrant workers, on the other hand, are seldom able to earn an adequate living or to save enough to allow them to upgrade their salable skills. It is this latter group that we will describe in more detail.

In the summers of 1966, 1967, and 1968, sixteen Cornell University students joined the stream of migrant laborers that starts in Florida and travels by bus and car to farms in the Northeast every summer (Friedland and Nelkin, 1971). On one of the many mornings when the migrants awoke to find there would be no work that day, an informant explained how it all began. In the old days,

"There were no people like us traveling up and down the road to pick beans or corn. Everybody had their own gardens. Life was good then; you would have your own pig, you would kill it and smoke it, and you would have the food from your own garden. You could make a good life that was much better than the type of life we are living now." She went on to explain how somebody got the idea about making money, so they started growing beans and corn in large plots. Then they needed people to pick it. Once they got people like us to do the picking, they could sell food at prices cheaper than we could grow it ourselves. "So then what happened was that we decided it would be better to go to work and earn money so we would have more time. So, we would go out and work a little while to earn money to buy the beans and corn that we no longer planted." But then, she said, "They pulled a dirty trick. Once they got us out there working a little bit, then they had us working for other, bigger things. We started working longer hours so we could get more and more things. Pretty soon, we didn't have any garden at all. Pretty soon, we didn't have a little pig, and they just got people working and buying. Now we got the same things we had before, only we must work longer and we don't have as much and we don't enjoy it as much. That's how the gardens became farms and how we began working the season." (pp. 174–175)

Recruitment for migrant labor is extremely casual. A crew leader who has connections with farmers up north, vehicles, and enough money to make the trip lets his regulars know when he's leaving, advertises, and stops by local hangouts in the South announcing he has work. Many people hear about jobs, pack, and leave the same day. Why do they go? A few are taken in by the promise of steady work and good wages. Others have nothing better to do and decide to see what things are like in the North. A number become migrants because a jail record or alcholism prevents their getting and holding a regular, steady job. Most simply have no alternative: there is no work for farm laborers in Florida in the summer.

Conditions in the migrant camps vary from bad to worse. Housing may consist of rows of anonymous, cinder-block, motel-type structures, old trailers, or wooden shacks. Migrants usually live two or three or in many cases seven or eight to a room (the latter called "bull pens"), often sharing beds with total strangers. There is virtually no privacy. Even in those camps that meet housing standards, the migrants have to share meager cooking and sanitation facilities. As bad as this seems, the impossibility of keeping the environment or oneself clean is only a small part of the personal degradation.

Migrant camps are virtually always isolated from surrounding towns, both physically and socially. It may be a four- or five-mile walk to the nearest store. As a result, migrants depend on the crew leader, who usually has the only cars, for transportation and supplies. Frequently crew leaders charge workers for a trip to town—and overcharge them for the food, tobacco, and alcohol they buy and resell in the camp. Migrants may have no choice but to join a meal plan run by the crew leader's wife, at whatever price she and her husband decide to charge. Just as often, however, they prefer paying high prices in the camp to going to towns, which they regard with fear and suspicion. As one of the students pointed out, the migrants (most of whom were black) tend to hold the same stereotypes about whites as the townspeople (most of whom are white) hold about migrants. Whites are violent, promiscuous, stupid, and lazy, and will cheat you any time they have the chance. Migrants avoid them.

The work itself is highly irregular and often disorganized. The crew leader makes all the arrangements. Often migrants do not know from day to day where they will be working, what they'll be picking, or even when and how much they will be paid. If the necessary equipment is not available, the migrants, who are almost always paid for piecework (that is, by the bucket), bear the cost of delays and confusion. Wages are totally unpredictable from week to week.

Usually the crew leader acts as a personal loan service to cover gaps between paydays and days when there is no work because of bad weather or poor planning. Being the only person in a position to make regular loans, these men are able to keep the laborers in an indebted, dependent position. (Most migrants cannot eat regularly without borrowing, much less leave the camp to seek work in a nearby city or to return home.)

Given poor living and working conditions and the fact that they are cramped together twenty-four hours a day, social relations among migrants are generally mistrustful. All in all, the mood in migrant camps is one of apathy, tempered by the escapism of games of chance and alcohol. As migrants see it, individuals have little or no control over what happens to them.

The Urban Poor This resignation was part of a complex of attitudes that Oscar Lewis found among the urban poor in Mexico City, whose daily lives he describes in *Five Families* (1959). The Gomezes, on whom we will focus, are one of the millions of families that migrated to Mexico City during what appeared statistically to be a boom period in that nation's history. Between 1940 and 1957 (the time of Lewis's study), the population of Mexico grew from 10 to 30 million. With 4 million residents, Mexico City had more than tripled its population to become the third or fourth largest city on the American continent. During this period, Mexico had irrigated some one and a half million new hectares, increasing the land under cultivation by 70 percent. The number of tractors in the country leaped from 4,600 to 55,000. Despite this, 89 percent of Mexican families still earned less than $69

Rural migrants often seem ill-equipped for urban life. However, most of the time they have little alternative but to move to the city. Most large cities—such as Rio de Janeiro, pictured here—have huge slum growths around them. (Mann/Monkmeyer)

a month, and over 60 percent of the population was ill-housed, ill-clothed, and ill-fed (Lewis, 1959:20, 22). National prosperity had widened, not narrowed, the gap between the poor and well-off in Mexico. Mechanization, the change from small- to large-scale intensive agriculture, the shift from subsistence farming to the production of commercial crops, and the risks of monocropping forced millions off the land into the shantytowns and slums of big cities.

Like migrant workers, the urban poor are by and large unskilled, unspecialized, and underemployed laborers, equally exploited by their employers. Agustín, the head of the Gomez family, has worked as a bus driver for seventeen years. Agustín is paid by the number of circuits he drives. If the bus breaks down and he cannot make his usual number of rounds, he loses money. During the seventeen years he has held this job, he has not received one raise or promotion. Compounding his problems are the debts the family has piled up from buying on credit, a necessity if the family is to have clothing and furnishings.

Like migrants, the urban poor occupy crowded, substandard housing. Gomez and his family live in a single, windowless room that is barely big enough for the cot he shares with his wife, a bed for their daughter and two sons (a third son having moved out), a wardrobe, and a dresser. A new American stove and dinette set in the corridor that serves as the kitchen make it impossible to move around without bumping into people or furniture. Rosa Gomez doesn't mind the fact that the faucet only works an hour or two each day. There were no sinks or faucets in the village where she and Agustín were raised. But the indoor toilet, separated from the kitchen by a plastic curtain, still embarrasses her. (At

The Memphis Garbage Strike of 1968

Migrants are not always content to remain downtrodden. The strike of garbage workers in Memphis fundamentally changed the relationships not only between these recent urban immigrants and the white establishment of this Southern city, but also among the blacks themselves, according to anthropologist Thomas Collins. Traditionally, Memphis had been the first stop for rural Southern blacks on their way to Chicago or other cities of the North. Most of the migrants came from places like Fayette County, Tennessee, where 68 percent of the blacks were unemployed, 44 percent of all county residents had incomes below $3,800 a year, and the median educational level was 8.6 years. People used to such deprivation were willing to accept any job in Memphis, whatever the wages or working conditions. Those who grew dissatisfied moved North rather than fighting to improve conditions. Blacks, rather than demanding better wages, job conditions, and treatment, relied on informal mutual aid networks for support in the alien city environment.

The jobs available were menial service ones, since Memphis was a commercial and marketing center rather than an industrial town. Garbage collecting was one job open to blacks. The pay was abysmal—$1.30 an hour at the beginning of the 1960s—and job security was nil. The main benefits offered to garbage workers were the privilege of retrieving useable items from the trash, and a holiday tip from people on their route. For such compensation, men were expected not only to collect trash from cans but also to pick up yards, cut and haul away trees, cart off construction debris, and, in general, uphold the honor of the "Nation's Cleanest City," an award Memphis won repeatedly in the 1950s.

By 1963 union organizing had begun, but Memphis had a long history of crushing municipal workers' unions, and local 1733 of the American Federation of State, County, and Municipal Employees took five years to become powerful enough to sustain a strike. In those five years, cutbacks on pay and on equipment maintenance created more reasons for dissatisfaction. Moreover, the black middle class had become frustrated with the slow pace of desegregation, especially when a hard-line white mayor was elected in 1967. Thus, when the sanitation workers walked off the job over a blatant incident of racial discrimination in February 1968, they had a militant union and a unified black community behind them. Intimidation, scab labor, and outright force did not budge the workers. They resolved to put pressure on the white community by a boycott. It worked, and when national attention was focused on the strike by the assassination of Dr. Martin Luther King, Jr., the city really had no choice but to capitulate.

Since then black garbage workers have been somewhat more emphatic in their approach to the power structure, although the old passive ways die hard. The men are less willing to sit back and take either vindictiveness or paternalism. They have greater job security and can afford to use the grievance procedures won in their contracts. Unionism is expanding in Memphis, giving the sanitation workers more allies if they ever strike again. Younger blacks are more militant, because they no longer feel that they can improve their lot by moving North; instead they are making demands and pressing the union to bargain for more in Memphis.

Several general points can be drawn from this case study. First, recent migrants are outsiders and therefore potential objects of discrimination and exploitation, especially when they are of a different race or ethnic background. Second, they may adapt to this vulnerability by maintaining close ties with sources of support in their own communities or by organizing groups to press their interests. Third, the degree of militance is at least partially determined by migration patterns. The North once provided an escape valve for discontented Memphis blacks. As fewer blacks felt drawn North, there was more reason to make changes in the bad conditions in Memphis. Finally, their success depended on the assistance of other sectors of the black community, especially the black middle class.

home, people walked to the far edges of the fields in modesty.) This home is one of hundreds of identical row houses lining the plazas of a giant, one-story, walled tenement, or *vecindad*.

Casa Grande, as this settlement is called, is a small, self-contained world, with its own shops and market, its own social life. Many of the tenants know practically nothing about the rest of Mexico City. Like migrants, they regard the police, government officials, social workers, and even priests with fear and suspicion, and avoid the institutions these people represent.

Lewis associated economic marginality, lack of privacy, loss of traditional social supports, and fear of larger institutions with certain behavior patterns. In particular, he called attention to the high incidence of alcoholism, violence, and family disorganization among the urban poor. Lewis believes that resignation and escapism are not reactions to poverty per se, but to poverty in a developed or developing country that seems to promise upward mobility and thus makes being poor feel like a personal failure. Hector, the son who moved out and the one member of the Gomez family given to social climbing, illustrates this. Hector tried desperately to convince the family that by working together they could move out of the *vecindad* into an apartment, which to him is an important step out of poverty and away from the stigma of the slums. When all his arguments failed, Hector gave up dreams of moving up in life and began spending all his money on women, clothes, evenings at expensive cafés, on immediate gratification.

Lewis went on to suggest that the "culture of poverty"—the whole complex of feelings of resignation, escapism, lack of impulse control, family instability, and so on—is self-perpetuating. Perhaps without meaning to, Lewis thus implied that to some extent the urban poor are responsible for their marginality.

Lewis and others consider splurging on immediate pleasures, buying on credit, drinking heavily, and failing to live up to the ideal of stable, monogamous marriage as pathological, self-destructive behavior that handicaps the poor. But this kind of behavior is as characteristic of the middle and upper-middle classes as it is of the poor. If succeeding generations of husbands in Mexican and other slums desert their wives, it may be because they run into the same obstacles that their fathers did, not because they were raised or enculturated to be irresponsible. In reality, there *is* little or nothing the Gomezes and others like them can do to improve their standard of living. Resignation and snatching whatever pleasures are available is a more realistic and possibly "healthier" adaptation to the trap of poverty than constantly fighting against impossible odds.

Lewis recognized the importance of social cohesion in finding a way out of the trap the Gomez family was in. He suggested that joining movements—labor unions, political causes—offered hope to the urban poor. The problem—as organizers of the poor such as César Chavez well know—is to convince the poor to make common cause with one another to press for change. The box on page 565 shows some of the pressures that bring about such organizations.

Beyond Industrialism

Today many of the urban poor and migrants—as well as the more affluent—work not for a local employer but rather for a huge international conglomerate. That most large U.S. companies have plants and outlets abroad is common knowledge. But the degree to which international corporations have taken over functions once performed by governments and succeeded where governments have failed in creating "a global organization for administering the planet" is difficult to comprehend, for the sheer size and scale of their operations.[2]

Michael Fribourg owns an empire with international sales estimated at almost $3 billion per year. He

---

[2] This section is based on R. Barnet and R. Müller, 1974a and 1974b. All quotations otherwise unattributed are from these articles.

heads a corporation which includes: vast real estate holdings in Switzerland, Long Island, France, and Morocco; 50,000 head of cattle grazing in Argentina; hybrid grain seed in Latin America; ski resorts in Spain; a nail manufacturing plant in the United States; Oroweat Bread, Polofood Frozen Dinners, and Hilburn Chickens; Wayne Feed, Full-o'-Pep Animal Food; the worldwide Continental Grain Company; Overseas Shipholding Group Incorporated; and—believe it or not—even more. (Miller, 1973: 705)

There are today about five hundred giant multinational corporations whose operating budgets exceed those of most nation-states. The gross national product for Switzerland—hardly an underdeveloped nation—was 26 billion dollars in 1971. In the last two decades, global corporations have been growing to two to three times the growth rate of the United States and other advanced industrial nations. This fiscal expansion is based on "global reach," for today's major corporations know no boundaries. About 30 percent of corporate profits in America are derived directly or indirectly from foreign operations. And more than 25 percent of the employees of the largest international corporations based in the United States live and work outside the country. No wonder we read in the newspapers that major U.S. corporations have been implicated in foreign politics; that heads of the oil companies and others deal with foreign heads of state as if they themselves were political leaders.

Through expansion and diversification, global enterprises have insulated themselves from political and market pressures, creating what amounts to a privately run world economy. In addition, the world corporation frequently controls everything from raw materials to distribution centers for its products. It avoids taxes by trading with itself. For example, a corporation may import goods manufactured by one of its own divisions in South America or elsewhere at less than the real cost, to avoid U.S. tariffs. (Because it is buying from and selling to itself, this may well produce a savings.) Or it may sell goods to its foreign divisions at inflated prices to transfer income out of this country, where taxes are comparatively high. Or a corporation may ship parts manufactured in this country to its assembly plants in Hong Kong—a logical decision, for laborers there work for as little as 30¢ an hour, compared to wages of $3.00 to $4.00 an hour in this country. It is extremely difficult for any government to identify (much less prosecute) price-fixing within a corporation or violation of labor laws across national boundaries. (Indeed, there are no international labor laws.)

Dependency on large-scale coordination characterizes not only multinational corporations but also the agricultural advances that comprise the "green revolution," a promise of sufficient food for all the earth's people. The success of new high-yielding varieties of wheat, like that shown here in India, involves educators, plant breeders, agronomists, entomologists, pathologists, agricultural engineers, and economists. Production relying so heavily on so many diverse specialists is unfortunately also more vulnerable to environmental problems. (The Rockefeller Foundation)

The very fact that a corporation operates on a global scale places it beyond the reach of national governments. Regulatory agencies lack the information and in many cases the jurisdiction to investigate global enterprises. IBM divisions relay data from around the world to central headquarters on a daily basis. An executive there need only push a button to find out what is going on in Ecuador or Indonesia—and another button to deliver instructions to divisions in these and other countries. Sophisticated communications and tight organization give global enterprise a competitive edge in confrontations with governments: "corporations plan centrally and act globally, and nation-states do not" (p. 109).

As a result, world corporations play a dominant role in shaping the present and future. "By making ordinary business decisions, the managers of firms like G.M., IBM, General Electric, and Exxon now have more power than most sovereign governments to determine where people will live; what work they will do, if any; what they will eat, drink, and wear; what sorts of knowledge schools and universities will encourage; and what kind of society their children will inherit" (p. 53).

Sources of Power

The power of global corporations derives from their control of finance, technology, the labor market, and communications. It takes capital to buy land and equipment, build factories, and invest in research and development that insures technological superiority. With the power to pick and choose among locations, multinationals can go where labor is cheapest. And with their power over communications, these corporations can create a taste for their products that is nearly irresistible.

Capital Banks manage much of the liquid capital in this and other countries. In 1971 this nation's banks had assets totalling some $3 trillion—including large blocks of stock in such vital industries as airlines and railroads, power companies, and telephone companies. Banks have financed and even supplied key personnel for corporate mergers, fostering the process of global centralization. Financial institutions that appear on paper to be separate may in fact be interconnected. The Rockefeller-Morgan empire—which controls Chase Manhattan, First National City Bank, Manufacturers Hanover Trust, Chemical Bank of New York, Morgan Guarantee Trust, and Bankers Trust—is a case in point. Banks, like corporations, are expanding geographically. The Orion Banking group, which links Chase Manhattan to National Westminster of the United Kingdom, the Royal Bank of Canada, and Westdeutsche Landesban Girozentrale, is one of many international banking syndicates. Moreover, the management of international banks and corporations often overlaps: the individuals who sit on the boards of directors of the banks hold similar positions in global corporations.

"Global corporations can borrow almost anywhere." It makes more financial sense for a bank to lend money to ITT or Renault than to lend to smaller local businesses. By the same logic, it makes sense for businessmen and -women in politically and economically unstable nations to deposit their assets in foreign banks that are unlikely to fold (Swiss banks being the obvious example). Thus a relatively small number of interlocking banks control enormous amounts of capital, which they invest in a relatively small number of business enterprises.

New Technology Giant corporations have far more to invest in the development of new technology than do smaller businesses—or, for that matter, than do most governments. Multinational corporations have the added advantage of being able to manipulate foreign economies via the amount and quality of the technology they export. "A country can have rivers of gold and thousands of potential workers to mine it and yet be on the brink of starvation if it lacks the [technical] knowledge to exploit its natural resources." Underdeveloped nations need technical assistance; global firms provide it. However, a corporation may build a plant in a foreign city, teach local people how to operate the machinery, but withhold knowledge about how to make and repair the machines.

Labor Global corporations exercise the same kind of power over the world labor market. General Motors or Volkswagen can afford to shut down a plant and walk away. This gives them considerable bargaining power with even the strongest unions. More significant, however, is the fact that any one of these companies can decide to transfer operations to Taiwan or another location where labor is extremely cheap and the political structure such that government leaders can promise to prevent strikes. Indeed, many corporations have. Despite the international rhetoric of many leftist unions in Europe and elsewhere, labor has not even begun to organize on a global scale.

Communications Finally, global corporations dominate the communications industry and thereby influence the tastes, values, and goals of people the world over. For example, CBS distributes major news stories throughout the "free world" via satellite. The company estimates that 95 percent of the people who watch the news on TV in these countries are watching reports from CBS. Such shows as "I Love Lucy," "Perry Mason," and "Mary Tyler Moore" are broadcast in 100 countries. (It is much cheaper for foreign telecasters to buy old programs from U.S. companies than to produce their own.) And Madison Avenue now operates on an international scale. In 1970, one-third of the ad campaigns created in the top thirty American agencies were designed for foreign audiences. Over 50 percent of J. Walter Thompson's and Interpublic's (the two largest agencies) profits came from overseas that year.

With vast facilities and experience in com-

Similarity in social behavior of similar economic classes the world over is one result of an increasingly global economy. This Taiwanese wedding scene, complete with European wedding costume and taxi in background, could be replicated in almost every country of the world. (Burton Pasternak)

munications at their command, multinational corporations "are successfully marketing the same dreams [to underdeveloped nations] they have been selling in the industrial world." The middle and upper classes in these countries are living imported lives (for example, buying locally made serapes only after they become chic in New York). Even the poorest families can afford an occasional Coke or Twinkies (manufactured by Continental Baking Company, a division of ITT).

Global Enterprise and the Third World

Just as agro-industry creates a class of exploited people, the internationalization of industry takes advantage of Third World nations. Many are rich in natural and human resources (that is, large potential labor forces and markets). But their wealth is being siphoned off in royalties, dividends, and technical fees.

Global corporations defend intervention in foreign economies (and surreptitiously in foreign politics) on the grounds that they are investing in countries that badly need capital; introducing new and vital technology; providing jobs; and helping to modernize backward segments of the population through the media. Each of these assertions is open to question.

First, global corporations do not as a rule make major investments in Third World countries. Rather, they finance operations by borrowing from local banks (who consider General Motors a better risk than the local shoe factory) and reinvesting their earnings. According to studies conducted in the late 1950s and 1960s, American-based corporations financed about 17 percent of their activities in Latin America with U.S. dollars; the remainder, with local capital—effectively taking money away from local businesses.

Second, these companies frequently use the Third World as a dumping ground for obsolete goods and equipment, overcharging for outdated technology. Even more significant, the technology they export is designed for already industrialized societies whose economies are based on the high levels of individual consumption that have made labor expensive. As a result, much of our technology is designed to save labor. But is labor-saving machinery beneficial to nations where labor is cheap because the cost of living and rates of individual consumption are not so high? "Typically, these countries abound in human resources, yet the sort of technology that global corporations offer them is capital intensive and labor-saving. . . . Instead of making efficient use of the manpower of third world countries, such transferred technology tends to convert their human resources, which are their biggest asset, into social liabilities."

There is no denying that foreign investors employ large numbers of people in the Third World. However, in clearing land for commercial crops and introducing labor-saving technology, they destroy as many jobs as they create—perhaps more. Although somewhat difficult to interpret, statistics suggest that corporate efforts to develop the Third World are causing unemployment rates to rise, not fall (at home as well as abroad).

Finally, there is considerable evidence that the expansion of mass media and the advertising that supports it are having an adverse effect on Third World populations. Madison Avenue has put years of research into techniques for convincing people "you are what you buy." The result is that many poor people go without things they need to buy such status symbols as radios and TVs.

The Third World nations are torn between the short-run need for capital, technology, and jobs, and the long-run desire to receive the full benefits of the investments rather than coming under the sway of global corporations. One way to achieve some independence is to use raw resources, upon which these global empires depend, as a lever in bargaining. In part, Third World nations are able to bargain today because the rich, industrial nations no longer constitute a solid bloc. The club is falling apart: American, Japanese, Western and Eastern European–based corporations are in direct competition. But whether countries that are struggling to achieve a sense of nationalism at home will be able to organize on an international level remains to be seen. And the irony is that even if these organizations succeed, global corporations can adapt simply by passing on increased costs to their customers—as they have done with oil and gasoline prices.

Global Enterprise and Global Disaster

Barnet and Müller, on whose research this section is based, conclude:

> The vision of a world without borders dominated by a few hundred corporations is a seriously flawed vision, because it violates three fundamental human notions—those of social balance, ecological balance, and psychological balance. As owner, producer, and distributor of an ever-increasing share of the world's goods, the global corporation appears to be an instrument for accelerating the concentration of wealth, and, in so doing, it is aggravating social imbalance. For the majority of the world's population, living in squalor, and particularly for the hundreds of millions who subsist on the edge of starvation, the corporation's development offers no hope....
>
> Driven by the ideology of infinite growth, the corporations act as if they must expand or die, and in multiplying they have made thrift into a liability and waste into a virtue. Their growth depends on converting ever-greater portions of the earth into throwaway societies. As central planners, hoarders of information, and creators of sophisticated hierarchies, the corporate managers are seeking to legitimize new organizational loyalties to rival family, town, church, and state, and in so doing they are accelerating the process of alienation which aggravates psychological distress....
>
> Obviously, the corporations are not responsible for the world-wide onslaught on the possibilities for human freedom, but their approach to the world as a huge management problem to be solved in boardrooms is a final playing out of the late-twentieth-century Orwellian nightmare....If the rise of the global corporation does threaten social, ecological, and psychological balance, how can it survive? Is the earth—or, for that matter, the corporation—so lacking in self-correcting mechanisms that we are doomed to be diverted with upbeat balance sheets while we and our descendants wait for the air to give out? (1974:140)

Put another way, the selective pressure on global corporations is to maximize profits for a few, not to solve the world's problems.

The Post-Industrial Society

A more subtle problem, which underlies Barnet and Müller's analysis, is the instability that interdependence creates. Once famines were local. The crops failed, some societies starved, but elsewhere life went on. Today, people all over the world depend on distant places for their sources of food or other vital resources. What happens in Nebraska at harvest time may affect people in the U.S.S.R., in India, in Sahelian Africa. In one sense, trade evens out the surpluses and makes life better for all. But it also puts people who were once able to survive on their own at the mercy of events in very distant places. Interdependence and vulnerability are two sides of the same development.

summary

Industrialization refers to the development of specialized productive units utilizing concentrated forms of solar energy—fossil fuels—through highly mechanized procedures. Industrial societies are able to extract more energy from the environment, though there is considerable loss in the efficiency by which this energy is used to support people. Nonetheless, industrial populations have vastly increased the scale of social organization. Today, the entire world is becoming organized into a single economy, presided over by vast multinational corporations, state-run international trading concerns, and special-interest cartels.

This situation is only the last in a series of profound changes wrought by industrialization. First, like any population entering a new niche, human population has grown rapidly with the advent of industrialization. Massive migrations both between and within nations have occurred, as groups have left the land for the city and the hope of jobs in the factory. Specialization and socioeconomic segmentation have increased, resulting in new kinds of social relations and organization. Differentiation between peoples based on economic role and status has increased, while differentiation based on cultural and ethnic distinctions has declined. In the section on agro-industry we focused on how industrialization has transformed food production and rural society. In the section on global enterprises we explored some of the mechanisms that organize much of the world's production and trade.

The example of Wasco, California, showed how mechanization brought about the transformation from farming for livelihood to farming for profit, the change in social reference from the local community to the wider world, and the breakdown in social relations from close personal ties to urbanized, relatively impersonal ones. Large-scale farming creates a class of landless workers who either follow the harvest or migrate to the cities. The economic marginality and isolation from traditional social support or from institutions in the larger society induce an array of disorders that Oscar Lewis calls "the culture of poverty." Characterized by resignation, escapism, family instability, and impulsiveness, the culture of poverty is self-perpetuating, according to Lewis. This conclusion has been challenged because it places the problem in the adaptation of the poor to their situation rather than in the society that cannot furnish a decent standard of living to its members.

In order to see industrialized society in its most fully developed form, we cannot study a single industry—or even a single nation. Today, for example, the entire globe is commercially integrated by multinational conglomerates and large international trading houses that seem to be beyond the effective regulation of any single country. Their power rests in their access to vast amounts of capital, their control of advanced technology, their ability to locate where costs (especially labor costs) are lowest, and their grasp of communications and marketing techniques. They are rapidly introducing industrialization to Third World nations, but the beneficiaries of this development do not seem to be the poverty-stricken masses, according to Barnet and Müller, upon whose studies we relied in this part of the chapter. They argue that multinationals compete with local businesses for indigenous capital rather than investing outside funds, sometimes use the Third World as a dumping ground for obsolete technology, introduce labor-saving systems to places where labor surpluses are already severe, and, through advertising, persuade people of the Third World to waste their meager incomes on empty status symbols. Barnet and Müller conclude that the international corporate search for profit endangers social and ecological well-being by increasing the gaps between haves and have-nots, by turning ever-increasing amounts of the world's resources to wastes, and by alienating people's allegiance to family, community, and even nation.

Daniel Bell feels that our society is no longer in an industrial phase but instead is coping with the problems of transition to a post-industrial, information-powered society. The major problems will arise from contradictions between the social structure, which is increasingly bureaucratic; the political structure, which is ideologically democratic; and the cultural dimension, which stresses individual fulfillment.

These conflicts are ultimately concerned with who shall have the power, and therefore the goods, in the future. This problem will be international as well as national. But perhaps the greatest difficulties will arise from the economic interdependence of all peoples. Such interdependence makes people more vulnerable in some ways, because a crisis in one area of the world sets up repercussions throughout the system.

suggested readings

BANTOM, M. ED.
1966 *The Social Anthropology of Complex Societies* (A.S.A. Monographs, 4). London: Tavistock. Collection of essays which examine theoretical and methodological problems in the anthropological study of industrial society.

GANS, H. J.
1962 *The Urban Villagers: Groups and Class in the Life of Italian-Americans.* New York: Free Press. Case study which considers concepts of class, ethnicity, and subculture in a description of a Boston working-class community.

LEACOCK, E. B. ED.
1971 *The Culture of Poverty: A Critique.* New York: Simon and Schuster. Critical reviews of the concept of the culture of poverty, including valuable discussions of class-linked norms and values in complex society.

LEWIS, O.
1966 *La Vida: A Puerto Rican Family in the Culture of Poverty—San Juan and New York.* New York: Random House. Controversial study of Puerto Rican family life.

MANGIN, W. ED.
1970 *Peasants in Cities: Readings in the Anthropology of Urbanization.* Boston: Houghton Mifflin. Selections that consider the adaptation of peasants to urban, industrial society.

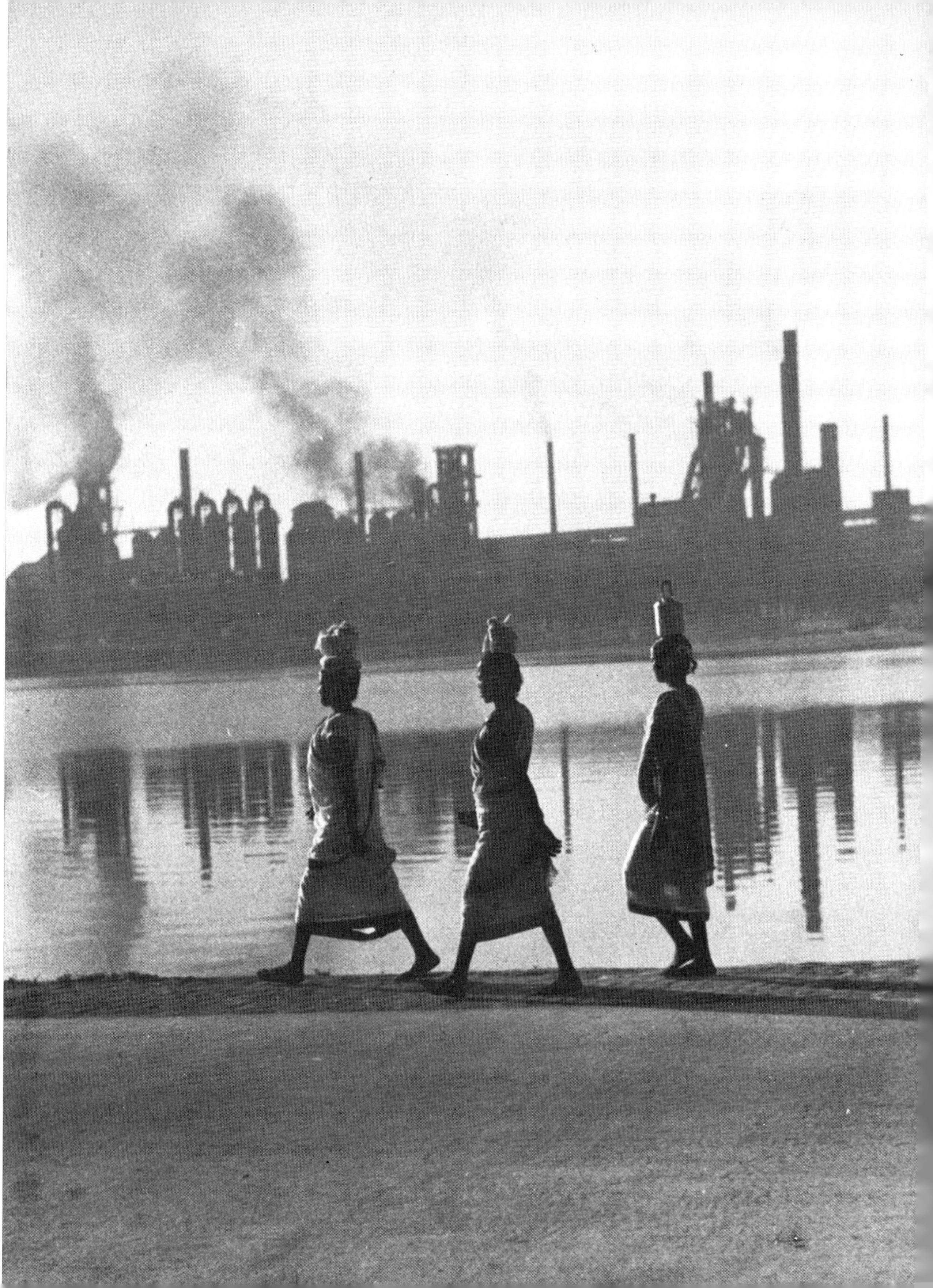

twenty-nine
Humans in Evolutionary Perspective

Humans are relative newcomers on earth. It has been calculated that if the entire history of earth were compressed into a single year, the appearance of human life would occur at 8:00 P.M. on New Year's Eve (Baur, 1975: 29). Despite our recent appearance, we often seem to view ourselves as something separate from the natural world. True, *Homo sapiens* has been an extraordinarily successful species in an evolutionary sense. However, many anthropologists (along with other scientists) are beginning to think that we may yet turn out to be merely one of the more spectacular of evolution's many mistakes.

As we have observed, whether humankind persists as a species will depend entirely on our responses to the problems presented by the environment. We have defined evolution as the process by which life forms originate and change in relation to particular environmental conditions, very often conditions established by the previous activities of the organisms. Thus we are continually adapting to an environment shaped in great measure by ourselves. Natural selection, the mechanism of evolution, has determined human physical attributes: upright posture, sensitive hands, large cranial capacity. Many social scientists view culture as something apart from biological evolution, something in a class by itself. But it is important to bear in mind that culture is simply a complex pattern of learned behavior associated with humans, and that humans are ultimately subject to the same laws of natural selection that apply to any other organism. Accordingly, culture can also be viewed and studied in just the same way as any other aspect of human adaptation. In this book, we have emphasized the adaptive significance of culture and behavior, from procurement systems to kinship systems to political and religious life. In this chapter, we will take this discussion a bit further by examining adaptive and evolutionary problems and processes in greater detail.

The New Synthesis

In the past, the study of evolution concentrated primarily on genetically defined, biological processes rather than on behavioral responses whose genetic basis is difficult, at best, to describe. For this reason, anthropologists who wished to discuss human culture in evolutionary terms, often confined themselves to the "parallel" or "analogous" model. Cultural evolution was "like" biological evolution. No serious attempt was made to show how cultural patterns were the result of such biological evolutionary forces as natural selection. Today, however, many anthropologists who seek to explain human behavior in evolutionary terms have turned, at least in part, to biological models as a means of analysis. By relating the study of human behavior to biological models, these anthropologists are attempting to view humans within a holistic framework, to describe the connections between human societies and the larger web of life. They also seek to understand the connections between behavior and the evolutionary success of the organism.

It is interesting that while anthropologists have been turning to biology for a more com-

The future of the human species is uncertain. Survival will depend upon our ability to sustain ourselves in the face of vast and complicated environmental problems. (Banoun/Caracciolo, W.F.P./F.A.O. Photo)

prehensive perspective, biologists have been turning to the social sciences in an attempt to place the study of living things in a holistic framework as well. The resulting synthesis is called *sociobiology*. It is an attempt to explain behavior — including the complex, learned behavior which we call culture — in terms of the same model that would account for biological variability. Looking at human beings in this way, sociobiologists hope to interpret much of human behavior according to its genetic basis and adaptive value according to the laws of natural selection. Edward W. Wilson (1975), the leading spokesman for sociobiology, has taken such an approach to explain the behavioral trait of altruism.

For example, altruistic actions such as sharing and self-sacrifice are often cited as particularly human attributes. They are not. (In a number of chapters we have discussed the nature and importance of such sharing for human society.) Altruistic behavior occurs in rudimentary form among chimpanzees and a few other Old World monkeys and apes. Among social insects such as bees, ants, and termites, it is carried on with great intensity. The sociobiologist looks upon all examples of altruism, human and otherwise, as something to be explained in evolutionary terms. How does altruistic behavior benefit the individual? How does it become established as an outstanding trait in some species? Clearly, this is a vital issue because all complex social organization depends on individuals delaying or sacrificing their immediate self-interest. The question is the extent to which such behavior has an impact on genetic or reproductive success in humans.

It would seem that, if the tendency to act altruistically is genetically controlled, altruism should be a rapidly disappearing trait. An organism which acts for the benefit of another organism diminishes its own chances of reproducing and thus passing on its own genetic material. Altruistic genes should quickly be bred out of existence, while selfish genes gain greater representation. But such is not the case. Organisms which act altruistically can benefit other organisms which share their own genetic material. Children of most organisms that reproduce sexually contain precisely half of the genes of each parent. Thus altruistic behavior may not benefit the individual directly, but it does benefit others who are genetically related to him and thus be selected for (Wilson, 1975:119). Apart from explaining particular behavioral events in such terms, anthropologists have found other biological concepts useful in direct rather than analogous ways.

The Concept of the Ecosystem

In order to better study the interaction of human populations with their environment, many anthropologists have adopted the biological concept of the ecosystem. The ecosystemic approach is a way of describing the flow of energy and materials among particular populations of plants and animals. The energy available to an ecosystem comes ultimately from the sun. This energy, in the form of light rays, falls on the leaves of chlorophyll-bearing plants and is used by them to convert water and minerals into carbohydrates through the process of photosynthesis. Because they are the primary source of usable nutrients, plants are known as producers. Plants serve as food for herbivores, who in turn are preyed upon and eaten by carnivores. Herbivores are also known as primary consumers, while carnivores are described as secondary consumers. In some ecosystems, there may be carnivores which feed upon other carnivores. These would be called tertiary consumers.

There is one other group of organisms which play an important role in all ecosystems, and these are the decomposers. Decomposers are bacteria and fungi which break down nonliving organic matter, using some for their own purposes and converting the rest to a mineral form. Decomposers return dead organic matter to the soil, where it becomes available once more to the producers — that is, the plants. The decomposed matter is then used by them to produce more carbohydrates in the process of photosynthesis.

It is apparent that there are two separate flows in any given ecosystem. There is the flow of energy which is unidirectional and noncyclical. Energy is derived only from the sun. Without solar energy, an ecosystem would soon break down, and its living components would expire. Energy is not returned to the system in any way. For this reason, we say that an ecosystem is an open system. The other kind of flow in an ecosystem is the flow of biochemical nutrients. As we have seen, the flow of nutrients *is* cyclical. Producers, consumers, and decomposers process the same nutrient material over and over again.

How do humans fit into the concept of an ecosystem? Basically, the same principles apply to humans as to any other population of organisms. The numbers of humans relative to other populations is set by the relative amount of energy available to them; humans acquire this food energy through the same "web of life" as do all other animals, that is, by feeding on other species. Thus, like any life form, the most important environmental features for humans are the other life forms on which we feed—or, if need be, escape from. Like all populations, our survival depends on maintaining a mutually viable relationship with these other species. That means we have to "regulate" our consumption of energy and the use of biochemical nutrients so as to ensure their continued availability. In this sense, human behavior can be analyzed ecosystemically like that of any other species. We are faced with the same problems and interact with other species of animals and plants as simply one part of a web of life. Culture is part of the solutions we find, but it does not release us from our place in the world ecosystem or from our dependence on appropriate flows of energy and availability of biochemical nutrients.

Humans are unique, however, in that they produce certain types of ecosystems which are not found under natural conditions. These human ecosystems are of two basic kinds: (1) productive systems devoted to the creation of a single resource; and (2) urban systems in which very high human population densities are maintained by greatly increasing the inflow and outflow of energy and materials. These specialized (or simplified) ecosystems entail certain problems not found in natural systems. The productive system known as a farm, for example, is a deliberately simplified ecosystem devoted to a single species of high-yield plant. Other organisms, such as weeds and insect pests, which try to gain a foothold in such a system are systematically eliminated. This results in a greater amount of human nourishment, but it also causes the productive ecosystem to be an unstable one, highly subject to different types of ecosystemic breakdown, which are known in ordinary language as crop failure. Urban ecosystems also have special problems. Cities exert a tremendous drain on surrounding ecosystems in terms of food, water, and other resources. They also produce large quantities of waste products which the surrounding ecosystems must absorb. When urban ecosystems become excessively large or excessively numerous, the balance between them and other kinds of ecosystems on which they depend tends to break down.

How can the concept of ecosystems be used in the study of human beings? Obviously, it is more difficult to describe the place of a human population within an ecosystem because human behavior is so much more complex and varied than the behavior of any other animal-consumer. Even among very primitive people, the task becomes quite formidable. Nevertheless, an ecosystemic approach has been used by many anthropologists, often with highly rewarding results.

To cite an example we have used in the text before, Roy Rappaport has shown how the large-scale ritual pig feasts practiced by the Tsembaga of New Guinea help to maintain the complex ecosystem of which the Tsembaga are a part. The Tsembaga raise taro, yams, sweet potatoes, and other vegetable crops in gardens which they cultivate by the slash-and-burn method. These foods consist mostly of carbohydrates, however, so the Tsembaga must look elsewhere for a source of protein. They find this source in the domesticated pigs which they occasionally slaughter and eat. The pigs derive their nourishment partially from foraging in the bush, but also by sharing the produce of the Tsembaga's gardens. When the pig herd becomes very large, the drain on the vegetable food supply becomes detrimental to the well-being of the people. It is at this point that the Tsembaga organize a giant pig slaughter and feast. The pig herd is reduced to manageable size, preventing the degradation of the ecosystem.

Periodic pig feasts are one of the mechanisms by which the Tsembaga have adjusted to food conditions in their particular ecosystem. It must be remembered, however, that this explanation is a systemic one, and that this approach is merely a useful way of pointing out the relationships among important variables in a particular situation. It tells us little about how that situation came into being. The analysis tells us how the system works, not why some solutions, as opposed to others, were arrived at.

Individuals and Populations in Ecosystems

Rappaport uses the biological concept of populations as a device to delimit the group of humans under consideration. A population is a group of organisms belonging to one species and occupying a particular space at a particular time. Populations, whether human like the Tsembaga or not, participate in biological systems characterized by certain variables: physiological, structural, environmental, and behavioral. Culture, then, can be seen as an elaborate set of behavioral mechanisms, but one which can best be explained in terms of the same processes that structure the behavior of nonhuman organisms and which maintain their populations. Although these processes are best studied as a system, it is important to remember that this concept is really no more than a descriptive tool.

An example we have described earlier will help to clarify this point. In the chapter on pastoralism, we noted how the Yörük of Turkey have become more stratified as a result of increases in pasture rental fees. It is possible to describe this change in systemic terms. In the case of the Yörük, we could say that the organization of social and economic relationships has become more centralized. While formerly, Yörük society was characterized by economic egalitarianism, in which both wealth and poverty were temporary conditions, today economic power is increasingly concentrated in the hands of a wealthy minority. The rest of the Yörük have become dependent on these few, creating a very different economic pattern from that which obtained in the past. This centralization of economic power is part of the means by which the Yörük pastoral population is maintained: the richer individuals supply the credit needed to operate in a cash-based market economy.

Although the systemic approach is essential for understanding the ways in which the different processes of adaptation are interrelated, but it does not in itself explain the mechanism by which change has actually been brought about and established in a population. The increased stratification of the Yörük, for example, came about when specific Yörük individuals began accumulating greater wealth and diversifying their activities in such a way that economic inequalities were frozen into permanence. This is not to say that these wealthy Yörük were necessarily innovators, men who by virtue of superior insight saw their opportunity and seized it. For the purposes of understanding the sources of behavioral variability and change, these people are the units on which the forces of environmental change exerted their influence. The environmental forces were those of the marketplace. Whether the change we are interested in is cultural, biological or both, we must keep in mind that it is the behavior of *individuals* we are describing, and that it is individuals who respond in various ways to specific problems.

Success in Evolution

We have said that the forces of natural selection operate through the individual, that we must look at individual behavior in order to see the mechanisms of change, whether cultural or biological. Interestingly, it is true that a significant degree of regularity is to be found among populations faced with similar problems. For example, the Yörük are not unique; egalitarian societies around the world have become stratified when drawn into volatile market systems where even relatively small changes in the price of commodities affect some people more than others.

At the same time, we can see certain regularities characteristic of successful species. Populations that succeed at the game of evolution have certain characteristics in common. Such patterns are the result of a very special kind of competition, and organisms which give a good account of themselves are apt to be ones that acquire and pass on special qualities which insure their success. But before we can describe these qualities, we must first understand more about the nature of evolution itself. Only then can we take up the question, what constitutes success in evolution?

Adaptation: A Hierarchy of Responses

As we have seen, evolution is a process by which organisms adapt to changes in their environment. Adaptation, however, usually proceeds on several different levels, involving responses which range from conservative and relatively reversible to extreme and virtually irreversible. At one level is adaptation through genetic response. This type of response is perhaps the most familiar to us, since it is visible in the great proliferation of different species throughout the world. In terms of adaptive responses, however, genetic change is often really a last resort.

An example of genetic adaptation is the development of the sickle cell trait among certain populations of humans. Humans who possess the genetically controlled variation in the hemoglobin cells which produces the condition known as sickle cell anemia also possess a high resistance to malaria. Apparently the sickle cell trait evolved as a response to the prevalence of malaria in swampy areas created by certain farming practices. A greater proportion of those possessing the sickle cell trait (in heterozygous form) were able to survive to maturity and produce offspring. This resulted in an eventual shift in the makeup of the population. These individuals obtained immunity to malaria, but at the expense of enduring the deleterious effects of the sickle cell trait itself. Moreover, the sickling trait is hard to get rid of once malaria is eradicated. An unfortunately large number of black Americans continue to be afflicted by the disease which no longer has any selective advantage whatsoever.

But this is not the only way an organism may adapt. Genetic change is a long-term solution to environmental challenges. There are also ways of adapting on a short-term basis. Adaptation may be physiological in nature. People, like other animals faced with the problem of surviving a sudden drop in temperature, will exhibit a series of responses beginning with simple shivering—a muscular response designed to increase body heat—and proceeding to other responses of a respiratory, metabolic, and cardiological nature. In many cases, organisms undergo physiological transformations of a relatively extensive nature in response to environmental conditions. For example, Indians living at extremely high altitudes in the Andes Mountains of South America develop as they grow to adulthood increased lung capacity in response to the rarefied atmosphere. The problem of nutritional deficiency in the case of arctic hysteria that we discussed in an earlier chapter is a problem resolved not genetically but by ingesting large quantities of animal fats which relieves the mineral deficiency. These physiological dimensions of the process of adaptation may be seen as alternative strategies for solving environmental problems. That is, as long as an organism is able to meet the challenges of its environment by adapting in the short-term sense, it will have no need for long-term genetic commitments as measured by changes in gene frequencies in the population.

Culture As Learned Behavior

Genetic and physiological change are ways in which organisms respond to changes in their environment, but they are by no means the only way. A separate but related dimension of response is through a change in behavior. Behavior may be instinctual, or it may be learned. Instinctual behavior seems to be far more common among other species than it is among human beings. Humans, however, are not entirely devoid of instincts. Research shows that the interpretation facial expressions which accompany the basic emotions are universal among all human populations and are probably instinctual. Learned behavior is found in greatest profusion in human beings, but it is not a uniquely human attribute. Many animals besides humans exhibit learned behavior. One particular troop of macaques in Japan, for example, was observed washing sweet potatoes before eating them. In this case, there was no doubt that the behavior was learned because a primatologist introduced the sweet potato as a new food and a particular female macaque "genius" was seen to have introduced the innovation, which was then taken up by the others. Another group of this same species of monkeys were found to exhibit another learned behavior pattern: ocean swimming. Initially observers rarely saw the macaques swim. However, one animal introduced the innovation, and soon after it was a common activity (Frisch, 1968).

But despite these and other examples of learned behavior among other species, human beings use learned behavior as a means of responding to problems presented by the environment more than any other organisms. The sum total of human learned behavior patterns is known as culture. Many anthropologists have assumed that the acquisition of culture puts man in a class by himself. It is easy to see how such a conclusion could be reached. Human beings have evolved such obviously complex ways of interacting with each other and with their environments that anthropologists have been led to put an inordinate amount of emphasis on these patterns. Thus, in the eyes of many anthropologists, culture has become the only thing about humans worth studying. It is undeniable that human culture in its various aspects—technological, political, economic, linguistic, aesthetic—is extremely impressive. Yet one should not allow the array of humankind's achievements to blind one to the fact that, as we have tried to show throughout the book, culture is essentially an adaptive device. Learned patterns in all areas of human life are applied by individuals to particular environmental conditions as they attempt to cope with them.

Grouping and Ungrouping

Looking at evolution through the responses of individuals can also be used to explain the formation—and destruction—of human social groups as part of adaptation. Earlier in the book we described the behavior of Navajo Indians in response to the changing availability of water. As you may recall, the Navajo pastoralists tend to group themselves into matrilineal extended families called "outfits." The average size of an outfit is about thirty, but environmental conditions, particularly the availability of water, are the determining factor in deciding just how big or how small a particular outfit is to be. J. F. Downs (1965), who studied one particular Navajo outfit whose land contained an abundant supply of water, found that the response of the group to these conditions was to increase in size. Later, when drought caused the water supply to diminish, this same group would fragment. This shift toward smaller family size and social fragmentation is as much an example of adaptive behavior in response to specific problems, as is the earlier formation of more cohesive groups.

It should be pointed out that while in the humanistic sense we may deplore the fact that harsh conditions caused the Navajo to sever family ties, from the scientific point of view, family structure, kinship, and group formation are simply examples of learned behavior used by human populations for their adaptive value. When changing conditions make such behavior detrimental to the genetic success of individuals, it soon ceases to be practiced.

The above principle holds true in the case of "cultural loss." Sometimes conditions make it necessary for individuals to entirely abandon the culture of which they had been a part and allow themselves to be absorbed by some other culture (Vayda and McCay, 1975). Again, from a humanistic point of view, such an action may be lamentable if accompanied by suffering and a sense of personal loss. From a scientific viewpoint, however, it is merely an example of individuals discarding a set of learned behavior patterns which have lost their adaptive value. In such a case, we may say that the act of giving up participation in a particular culture may in itself constitute a successful adaptation. It is wrong to equate "cultural extinction" with "biological extinction."

For example, the Bushmen of Africa live under conditions so harsh that at the best of times they are just barely able to sustain themselves. For this reason, portions of the Bushmen population continually break off from the tribe and join the neighboring groups of Bantus. They give up their participation in the Bushmen culture, and in effect become Bantus. From one point of view, it may seem that the Bushmen are becoming extinct, since their way of life is dying out. But while Bushmen culture may be dying, individual Bushmen are not failing in an evolutionary sense. They are successfully adapting to environmental problems. Their adaptation happens to involve the abandonment of their culture and absorption into a neighboring one.

The process of adaptation, in its various dimensions, is the means by which a species becomes related to its environment—responds to the problems which must be solved. However, judging from the fact that some species have flourished while others have been driven to extinction, we can conclude that the adaptations of some species have been more successful than those of others. How can we measure the success of adaptations? Given the ways in which we have drastically altered our environment, the question is even more difficult to answer. Whether our object is to save the whooping crane or eliminate the anopheles mosquito, the problem ultimately comes down to one of organisms adapting or failing to adapt to environmental problems. Moreover, man's manipulation of the environment has a profound effect on his own welfare. Developing a standard for measuring adaptive success is critical in understanding where we ourselves stand on the endangered species list.

Persistence As Success

A criterion often used to measure the short-term evolutionary success is "fitness," or reproductive success over a short period of time. Since we know that different individuals (or genotypes) are rewarded by different reproductive rates, it should follow that the most successful animals are the most numerous. But this is not strictly true. A large population may act as a safety factor in the survival of a species, but there is no reason to assume that the opposite is true—that an organism which is extremely rare is necessarily in danger of extinction. Of course, all animals which have vanished from the earth have gone through a stage immediately preceding extinction in which they were very rare indeed. But on the other hand, many animals have persisted over very long periods of time at very low population levels. We should not allow this fact to inure us to the plight of organisms which truly are in danger of extinction, such as the whale, for example.

"Fitness" and Its Limitations

There is still another reason why high reproductive rates do not necessarily mean that an organism is well adapted to its environment. An organism may evolve a new technique for extracting energy from the environment. If the organism then translates this ability into increased population size, it may find that it has committed itself to an energy-extractive system whose very efficiency eventually destroys the resource on which it was based. A horse population, for example, may develop longer teeth which allow the horses to eat larger amounts of grass. The greater energy which results from this increase in food intake would then allow the long-toothed horses to reproduce faster. The resulting population increase would increasingly be "long toothed." But what if the horses' habitat was a small, enclosed valley which could not recover from such close-cropping? Obviously the long-toothed horses would increase relative to short-toothed horses through natural selection. But when they outrun food supply, there would be a sudden crash in population.

A fate similar to that of our hypothetical horses looms prominently in the future of earth's most numerous large mammal: man. As we pointed out in our chapter on industrial society, humans have developed an energy-extractive system immeasurably more efficient than that of any other animal. The energy gains of that system have been used to support a human population far greater than that of any other species and growing at an ever-increasing rate. The drain placed by humans on the environment in terms of energy demand and polluting by-products is fast approaching a critical level. Thus, while our "success" is considerable, in the sense that population is growing by leaps and bounds, we are actually very vulnerable. For unless something is done to reverse these trends, humans will surely suffer the same fate as any other organism which uses energy-extractive ability to purchase population growth within a limited environment. We will literally eat ourselves out of house and home.

The Evolutionary Poker Game

One constructive suggestion for measuring adaptive success has been made by L. B. Slobodkin (1969). His answer involves a view of evolution which is somewhat different from those usually proposed. Slobodkin metaphorically describes evolution as a game of "existential poker," whose object is not to win a large amount of chips, but simply to stay in the game. In the game of existential poker, to leave the table is to become extinct. The chips which the player wins represent the total population size of that particular species. Thus there is a certain advantage to having a large pile of chips on the table, since a player with many chips has a longer way to go before being forced out of the game than a player with few. Large numbers of chips, however, do not necessarily ensure success, nor does a small stake necessarily lead to failure.

Since the objective of the existential poker game is simply to stay in it, nothing counts but strategies which increase the ability of the organism to respond to possible challenges. Another way of stating this is to say that the optimal strategy in the game of evolution is to maximize homeostatic ability. Homeostasis is the maintenance of an equilibrium state by means of self-regulating mechanisms. Slobodkin's metaphorical poker game implies that the organism which is best able to maintain homeostasis will have the highest degree of adaptive success.

If the maximization of homeostatic ability is the key to evolutionary success, then the best advice for aspiring organisms would be identical to the Boy Scout motto: "Be prepared." Organisms do not have the advantages of Boy Scouts, however. It is extremely unlikely that an organism's response to any given situation will be the ideal one. An organism never quite catches up to the demands which the environment puts upon it. Each adaptation—each trait—is the result of an historical process involving varying periods of time. Each trait has its own evolutionary history, its own series of transformations committing the organism to a greater or lesser degree of dependence on that adaptation. But since the environment is continually changing in ways that are never perfectly predictable, there must always be a lag between these adaptations and the ideal solution.

The historically determined traits to which each species is committed further limit its response to new environmental problems.

Organisms must respond to challenges using whatever traits are available to them at that particular time. Another way of stating this is to say that evolution is always opportunistic.

The opportunistic aspect of adaptation becomes clearer when we think about it in terms of solutions to problems in our own society. Around the beginning of the twentieth century, industrial societies began using oil as a fuel. This adaptation solved the problem of furnishing an effective, cheap fuel to power modern machinery, but the use of oil was far from the perfect solution to the problem. Its use was opportunistic in the sense that it was there to be found, and our technology happened to have developed to a point that allowed us to make use of it. In adapting to oil power, we made considerable commitments which have altered the structure of our society. In recent years the environment has changed in ways that were unexpected—namely, oil deposits are being depleted at the same time energy needs have increased, prices are going up, and economic power is shifting in favor of those nations who control the most abundant remaining resources. But while we may bemoan the fact that we committed ourselves so deeply to oil in the first place, it is unrealistic to assert that we should have known better. It is normal for cultures and organisms to respond in ways which later fail to keep up with changing environmental conditions. Moreover, it is certain that whatever power source we seize upon next, it will also be a less than perfect solution and will itself generate a host of new and unforeseen problems.

Given these limitations under which organisms or cultures must respond to environmental challenges, what is the best strategy for maximizing homeostatic ability? As we said earlier in this chapter, there are a number of dimensions to the process of adaptation, a hierarchy of responses ranging from superficial changes to profound and permanent genetic changes. Slobodkin suggests that the organisms that succeed at the game of existential poker are those which are able to solve environmental problems with the cheapest possible response. A response is considered cheap if it involves the least possible loss of future adaptive ability. An inappropriate response would be one that is too costly for the problem to be solved. Thus the organism with the best chance of success is the one which maintains its ability to respond in a wide variety of ways, but which does not necessarily remain in simple equilibrium.

An instance of too costly response to an environmental problem may be seen in the example, already cited, of the adaptation of the sickle cell trait as a solution to the problem of endemic malaria. The genetic mutation which causes the sickle cell trait does indeed solve the problem, but at too great a loss of future adaptive ability. Individuals who move to areas where malaria is not present cannot discard the adaptation. They must endure the symptoms of sickle cell anemia and risk passing it on to their descendants.

Behavioral and cultural responses to environmental problems may also be too costly. Suppose, for example, that there is a persistent traffic problem in a large, modern city. The immediate, low-level response of the authorities is to hire more police to direct traffic in the afflicted areas and restore normal flow. If this does not work, the city may send even more policemen. So far, the response to the problem is a relatively cheap one, since it does not seriously impair the city's ability to respond to future problems. The response is reversible: the extra policemen can always be fired if necessary, and the money which was used to pay their salaries employed for some other purpose.

If the addition of extra policemen is insufficient, however, the city will be forced to go on to the next level of response. It may, for example, decide to construct a traffic bypass. This is a much more expensive solution to the problem than merely adding more police. It involves considerable commitment of labor and materials. Once constructed, the bypass will radically change the patterns of traffic flow in the city, possibly bringing on new problems which could not have been predicted prior to its being built. The bypass cannot easily be unbuilt. It cannot be traded back for the cost of its construction. If it does the job which it was designed to do, its value to the city may be enormous. If it does not, it may become a liability, seriously imperiling the city's future health and survival.

Although there are many cases of human overreaction to environmental problems, in general we see that human behavioral strategies seem to be designed to fulfill the goal of flexibility of response, the ability to absorb change without drastic overhaul. This is not to suggest that human behavior is universally characterized by the capacity to take into account all future contingencies. Obviously this is not the case. However, there is a conservative tendency among most human populations. People are by no means wildly innovative in facing new problems. As one anthropologist, Marshal Sahlins (1972), puts it, people usually "change enough to stay the same." This trait is in itself a response to environmental pressures, since any cultural response in excess of what is needed carries a potential penalty.

Resilience and Stability

Persisting through "staying the same," however, does not mean maintaining a steady state. Turning our attention now from species to the ecosystems in which they live, we find that natural ecosystems are highly persistent entities. This is not surprising, since those ecosystems comprised of species which were unduly delicate have been eliminated through natural selection. Ecologists have tried to isolate the properties which allow ecosystems to adjust to changes and thus persist through time. One ecologist, C. S. Holling (1973), has identified two related but separate concepts: *resilience* and *stability*.

Resilience is a measure of the degree of change which a system can undergo while still maintaining its basic elements or relationships. *Stability* is a measure of the ease and rapidity with which a system returns to equilibrium after absorbing disturbances. Systems with high resilience and low stability may undergo continual and profound changes but still continue to exist as a system: for instance, component populations may regularly decline only to bounce back. Systems with high stability and low resilience may show very little initial change in response to disturbances but collapse suddenly. Eventually, however, all potentially have limits to resilience, at which they collapse as a system. The concepts of stability and resilience have considerable significance for the study of ecosystems. We often assume that viable or healthy ecosystems tend toward the steady state of simple equilibrium, that a system is healthy if it is in a condition of perfect balance. It now seems that dynamic change may enter into the functioning of systems, provided that change remains within certain limits.

However, even this capacity for dynamic change has to be thought of as limited. This is important, for we often feel that we are having no impact on particular populations of animals or ecosystems simply because we see little evidence of immediate changes. For example, the seas around us seem little changed by the dumping of nuclear and other wastes, and we are thus encouraged to continue such practices. However, each such disturbance caused by dumping requires the organisms and microorganisms of the sea to respond in some way, and there are finite limits to their capacities to continue to do so. In many cases, the resilience of a natural system reaches its breaking point as a direct consequence of humans entering the picture.

G. E. Hutchinson's study of a small crater lake in Italy makes this fact clear. Using paleontological evidence, Hutchinson was able to reconstruct ecological changes in the lake from about 4,000 B.P. to the present. He found that up until Roman times, the lake persisted over centuries, in spite of dramatic changes in the character of the surrounding flora. At a certain point, however, this equilibrium was disturbed. The clear water quite suddenly became choked with organic matter. The change coincided with the construction of a Roman road, the Via Cassia, about 2,121 B.P. Obviously, the influx of human beings, and with them, the introduction of new land-use patterns in the surrounding area had a drastic effect on the lake's ecosystem which finally drove it beyond the limits of its resilience (in Holling, 1973:7).

In the more than 2,000 years since this ecological disaster occurred, man has been instrumental in overtaxing the resilience of many an ecosystem, and in recent years the frequency of such events has increased many times over. In an article comparing the problems of ecology and social planning, C. S. Holling and M. A. Goldberg (1971) discuss some of the steps by which the resilience of ecosystems is destroyed. For example, during the 1960s, the World Health Organization initiated massive mosquito eradication programs in Borneo in an attempt to check the spread of malaria. The DDT that was used to accomplish this proved highly effective, but in some cases it led to unexpected results. When DDT was sprayed in the large communal houses of the inland Dayak people, for example, it was picked up by the cockroaches. The poison then became concentrated in the bodies of the lizards which preyed upon these insects, then finally entered the bodies of the cats who preyed on the lizards. By this time, the DDT had reached very high concentrations, high enough to cause the deaths of the entire cat population. With the cats gone, the houses soon became infested with rats, and the fleas, lice, and other parasites which entered with them created another health hazard by introducing sylvatic plague. The DDT also destroyed the predators and parasites which kept a certain thatch-eating caterpillar under control. Relieved of their natural enemies, the caterpillars increased dramatically, with a corresponding increase in the destruction of thatch. As a result, the roofs of the houses fell down.

Ecologically speaking, the application of DDT caused a reduction in the complexity and diversity of the ecosystem, which in turn brought about a tremendous loss in resilience. With a large proportion of its components eliminated, the system lost its ability to bounce back (Holling and Goldberg, 1971: 222–223).

Based on this and other cases, Holling and Goldberg draw several conclusions about the relevance of ecology to social planning. They find that any attempt to alter the behavior of one component of an ecosystem causes the rest of the system to respond in unexpected ways. Programs that concentrate on narrow goals—such as eliminating mosquitos or slums or traffic congestion—without regard for the rest of the system are certain to have disastrous effects. The authors present a number of guidelines which, if followed, should prevent similar occurrences in which the solution is worse than the problem. They recommend, first, that planners avoid paying the penalties of overresponse by limiting the scope of their solutions. Solutions should also be as diverse as possible in order to preserve the natural complexity of systems. "Scatter your shots" is the watchword. Second, they feel that complex systems have the capacity to solve their own problems and should be encouraged to do so. In practical terms, this might mean giving the residents of a slum the chance to direct improvements on their own rather than having "experts" overhaul their environment. The final recommendation is that planners take as their goal not the elimination of problems but the minimization of disastrous consequences. Substituting these modest aims for more grandiose and dangerous ones should help eliminate some of the ecological disasters that appall twentieth-century man, and also give the human species a decided edge in the existential poker game (Holling and Goldberg, 1971: 229).

summary

Homo sapiens can in some ways be considered an enormously successful species. However, there is some doubt about whether or not the species will continue to be successful. Like all living things, humans must adapt to a changing environment, even when the changes are of our own making. Ultimately, we are subject to the same laws that apply to all living organisms, and the complex patterns of human culture should be understood as adaptive mechanisms.

Increasingly, anthropologists have been using biological models to explain behavior in evolutionary terms. Likewise, biologists have created a discipline, *sociobiology,* that seeks to analyze behavior in genetic terms and according to the laws of natural selection.

Anthropologists have adopted the biological concept of the *ecosystem* to better study the interaction of human populations with their environment. Culture is developed as a response to the need to acquire and regulate our consumption of energy and biochemical nutrients so that their continued availability will be assured. Humans have created two unique forms of ecosystem: the productive system, in which a single resource is created; and the urban system, which is characterized by high human population density and which is maintained by increasing the cross-flow of materials and energy.

The concept of the ecosystem may also be applied to the study of human behavior. The systemic approach does not really explain why a particular solution was chosen, but it does describe the relationships among variables in a given situation.

In analyzing both biological and cultural change, one must remember that it is individuals who respond to specific problems. And the individual's response, which is variable, must be seen in relation to the particular biological system, which is itself variable in terms of physiology, structure, environment, and behavior. Nevertheless, there is a significant regularity in the solutions to similar problems found by different populations. Similarly, successful species have certain characteristics in common.

Evolution, the adaptation of organisms to their environment, takes place on several levels, ranging from conservative and relatively reversible responses to such extreme, and virtually irreversible, responses as genetic change. In addition to genetic and physiological changes, organisms adapt through changes in behavior. Humans use learned behavior more often than other living creatures; the total of these human learned behavior patterns is known as culture. Culture is essentially an adaptive device to cope with environmental challenges.

Of course, not all adaptations are equally successful. A criterion often used to measure such success is the reproductive rate of a given population. However, a high reproductive rate, or "fitness," does not necessarily mean that an organism is well adapted to its environment. Human beings are undeniably fit, but our success at developing an efficient energy-extractive system, the modern industrial society, and its use to support an ever-growing population carry their own dangers—we may become so efficient that we will consume all of our resources.

L. B. Slobodkin understands evolution as a game of "existential poker," where the object is merely to stay in the game. Viewed in this way, strategies that increase an organism's ability to respond to challenges become of paramount importance. The optimal strategy is thus to maximize *homeostatic ability*—that is, to maintain equilibrium through self-regulating mechanisms. However, organisms strive for this goal under certain limitations. Traits are historically determined and develop over time, but the environment is in constant flux. It is therefore unlikely that any particular adaptation will yield an ideal solution. Furthermore, evolution is *opportunistic,* in that the organism responds with whatever traits are available at the time. This can become problematical when an adaptation that initially proved successful fails to keep up with environmental conditions.

Given these limitations, it follows that the most successful organisms are those that respond to problems in the cheapest way. A response is considered cheap if it represents the least possible loss of future adaptive ability. An organism that can maintain its ability to respond in a wide variety of ways, without remaining in simple equilibrium, will be most successful. The conservative tendency among human populations has, in general, guaranteed that our behavioral strategies be flexibly designed. Humans then "change enough to remain the same," which is not to imply stasis.

C. S. Holling has identified two related concepts that permit ecosystems to adjust to change and therefore persist: *resilience,* a measure of the change a system can undergo and still maintain its basic elements; and *stability,* a measure of the ease and speed with which a system returns to equilibrium after disturbances have been absorbed. Dynamic change, then, is necessary to the health of an ecosystem, but this must be within limits or the system will collapse.

Often a natural system's resilience will reach its breaking point as a direct consequence of the introduction of humans into the system. In order to avoid this, it has been suggested that attempts to alter the behavior of one component of an ecosystem take the rest of the system into account. The solutions of social planners should therefore be limited in scope; be diverse in order to preserve the natural complexity of systems; and be oriented toward the minimalizing of dangerous consequences, rather than problem solving.

suggested readings

COHEN, Y. A., ED.
1974   *Man in Adaptation: The Cultural Present.* 2d ed. Chicago: Aldine. Collection of case studies which provides an overview of the diversity of human adaptations.

FARVAR, M. T., AND MILTON, J. P., EDS.
1972   *The Careless Technology: Ecology and International Development—The Record.* Garden City, N.Y.: Natural History Press. Collection of studies which examine the ecological consequences of the rapid spread of technology in the modern world.

ODUM, H. T.
1970   *Environment, Power, and Society.* New York: Wiley-Interscience. Valuable introduction to human ecology that considers the organization of society in terms of systems of energy flow.

SUTTON, D. B., AND HARMON, N. P.
1973   *Ecology: Selected Concepts.* New York: J. Wiley and Sons. Excellent introduction, in the form of a self-teaching guide, which provides a clear understanding of the basic concepts of ecology and its implication for human society.

VAYDA, A. P., ED.
1969   *Environment and Cultural Behavior: Ecological Studies in Cultural Anthropology.* Garden City, N.Y.: Natural History Press. Selections which consider the interaction between social systems and the environment.

(continued from page iv)

modified from C. V. Haynes, Jr., "Elephant Hunting in North America," *Scientific American* (June 1966). Permission granted by W. H. Freeman and Company, Publishers; and J. D. Jennings, *Prehistory of North America,* 2/e, McGraw-Hill Book Co., 1974. Reprinted by permission. P. 135: Figure, after K. V. Flannery, "Ecology of Early Food Production," *Science* 147 (March 1965). Permission granted by the author. P. 147: Figure, from S. Struever and G. Houart, "Hopewell Interaction Sphere Analysis," in *Social Exchange and Interaction* (University of Michigan Museum of Anthropology Papers, no. 46, 1972). Reprinted by permission. P. 171: Figure, from A. C. Allison, "Abnormal Haemoglobin and Erythrocyte Enzyme-Deficiency Traits," in *Genetical Variation in Human Populations,* G. A. Harrison, ed., Pergamon Press, Ltd. Reprinted by permission. P. 175: Figure, from A. E. Mourant et al, *The Blood Groups,* Blackwell Scientific Publications, Ltd. Reprinted by permission. P. 177: Figure, from W. J. Martin, *Physique of Young Adult Males,* H.M.S.O., 1947. Permission granted by Her Majesty's Stationary Office. P. 179: Figure, from B. J. Williams, *Evolution and Human Origins: An Introduction to Physical Anthropology.* Copyright © B. J. Williams. Reprinted by permission of Harper and Row, Publishers, Inc. P. 215: Table, "A Synchronic Record of the Activities of Each Member of a Tepoztecan Family," from O. Lewis, *Life in a Mexican Village.* © 1951 by the Board of Trustees of the University of Illinois. Reprinted by permission of the University of Illinois Press. P. 240: From P. Braestrup, "Researchers Aid in Thai Rebel Fight," *The New York Times,* March 20, 1967. © 1975 by The New York Times Company. Reprinted by permission. P. 336: Table, from D. R. White, "Mathematical Anthropology," in *Handbook of Social and Cultural Anthropology,* ed. J. J. Honigmann. Copyright © 1973, Rand McNally College Publishing. Reprinted by permission. P. 362: Table, abridged from I. R. Buchler and H. A. Selby, *Kinship and Social Organization: An Introduction to Theory and Method.* Copyright © 1968 by I. R. Buchler and H. A. Selby. Reprinted by permission of Macmillan Publishing Co., Inc. P. 467: Table, "Some Simultaneous Discoveries and Inventions," from A. L. Kroeber, *Anthropology,* Revised Edition. Copyright 1923, 1948 by Harcourt Brace Jovanovich, Inc., abridged and reprinted with their permission. P. 487: Table, "The Bushman Annual Round," from R. B. Lee and I. De Vore, eds., *Man the Hunter* (Chicago: Aldine Publishing Co.). Copyright © 1968 by Wenner-Gren Foundation for Anthropological Research, Inc. Reprinted by permission. P. 489: Table, "A Typical Week in July of a Young Bushman Mother of Two," adapted from M. Bicchieri, *Hunters and Gatherers Today.* Copyright © 1972 by Holt, Rinehart and Winston, Inc. Reprinted by permission. P. 496: Table, "Time and Yield Data for Hunting and Turtling for One Year (1968–1969)," from B. Nietschmann, Hunting and Fishing Focus Among the Miskito Indians, Eastern Nicaragua, *Human Ecology* 1 (1972). Reprinted by permission of Plenum Publishing Corp. P. 507: Table, "Causes of Death Among 240 Adult Ancestors of Three Related Groups," from N. Chagnon, The Effects of War on Social Structure, in *War: The Anthropology of Armed Conflict and Aggression,* eds. M. Fried, M. Harris, and R. F. Murphy. Copyright © 1960 by Doubleday & Company, Inc. Copyright © 1967 by The American Museum of Natural History. Reprinted by permission of Doubleday & Company. P. 510: Table, "Harvesting Schedule of Tsembaga Garden Crops," from R. A. Rappaport, *Pigs for the Ancestors: Ritual in the Ecology of a New Guinea Peoples.* Copyright © 1968 by R. A. Rappaport. Reprinted by permission of the Yale University Press.

Glossary

acculturation the results of extended contact between two or more previously autonomous cultures.

acetabulum the socket in the hipbone for the head of the femur (thigh bone).

Acheulean tradition or industry a Middle Pleistocene tool tradition utilizing the direct-percussion softhammer technique; it characteristically produced the hand axe and the cleaver.

adaptation the response of organisms to changes in their environment.

adaptive character a characteristic that is advantageous to its bearers in a particular environment.

adaptive patterns ways in which different populations discriminately select and secure resources from their environment.

adaptive radiation an array of related species, resulting from repeated speciation from a single stock, of which many of the new branches survive. Typically, the species comprising the radiation occupy a wide spectrum of econiches.

affinal relations relatives by marriage; in-laws.

age-grade systems a means of pantribal solidarity; a tribal member will fulfill a distinct and different political role, according to the age-grade he has attained.

age-set a group of individuals of the same sex and similar age, who maintain close ties throughout their lives and pass together through age-related roles and statuses. See generation set.

agonistic behavior social interaction, often of an aggressive nature, that involves a power relationship among the actors.

allele one of a set of genes with the same locus on a particular chromosome.

allomorphs the range of forms included within a single morpheme.

allophones sounds of a language that are phonetically distinct but are not used to distinguish meaning.

Alouatta the howler monkeys, members of the Cebidae and arboreal leaf eaters.

ambilineal descent descent reckoned through either the male or female line, depending on circumstances and choice.

analogy a resemblance between animals that is due to parallelism or convergence, rather than common ancestry.

angiosperms flowering plants, including flowering grasses, herbs, shrubs, and trees.

animatism according to Robert Marett, the belief in an impersonal supernatural force.

animism the belief that all objects, animate and inanimate, share a spiritual as well as a visible essence. According to Edward B. Tylor, who coined the term, it is characteristic of the most "primitive" forms of religion.

Anthropoidea a suborder of the Primates, whose living members are the higher primates—the monkeys, apes, and humans. They have large rounded brain cases with close-set eyes that face directly forward from above the nose, immobile rounded ears set close to the side of the head, and mobile expressive faces.

anthropological linguist anthropologist who specializes in the study of language.

antibody one of a class of proteins that "recognize" and combine with substances foreign to the body. The production of antibodies is stimulated in the body when such a foreign substance, or antigen, is introduced into it.

antigen a substance, usually a protein, capable of stimulating antibody production. Blood group substances are one kind of antigen.

aphasia an inability to understand or use language, caused by injury to the left hemisphere of the brain.

applied anthropology a specialization that has as its primary aim changes in human behavior believed to ameliorate social, economic, and technological problems of contemporary societies.

Archaic a New World cultural stage that began about 10,000 B.P. in the Southwest and about 8,000 B.P. in the Midwest and East, overlapping with and eventually succeeding the Upper Paleolithic big-game hunting traditions; characterized by the intensive seasonal foraging of localized resources and the establishment of regularized long-distance trade. Its Old World counterpart is the Mesolithic cultural stage.

Archaic *Homo sapiens* early *Homo sapiens* fossils whose brain size was at least as large as that of modern humans; differentiated from modern *Homo sapiens* by their larger teeth, heavy brow ridges, and smaller frontal lobes. Skeletal remains have been dated at between 120,000 and 35,000 years B.P. and associated with Mousterian tools.

archeologist anthropologist whose subjects are extinct human societies and ecosystems.

archeology derived from the Greek word *archaios,* meaning ancient;

the study of the culture of prehistoric social groups through the analysis of their products of behavior (i.e., artifacts, food remains).

artifacts things made by human hands, such as tools and shelters.

assimilation the integration of a minority group into the larger society, resulting in the loss of its distinctive cultural characteristics.

Ateles the spider monkey, a highly arboreal, mainly fruit-eating member of the Cebidae.

atlatl a spear thrower consisting of a hooked rod with a groove into which the upper spear shaft fits, thereby increasing the range and force behind the thrust of the spear; first found in Upper Paleolithic contexts.

Aurignacian one of the two earliest Upper Paleolithic cultural traditions in Europe, dated at between 35,000 and 20,000 B.P. The earliest sites are to be found in southeast Europe and the Near East; all are characterized by bone tools, especially those with split bases, and the faunal remains of herd animals.

Australopithecus a bipedal, small-brained, and heavy-jawed hominid genus that flourished until about 1 million B.P. and is found in fossil faunas dating from 5½ million years ago.

Australopithecus africanus a habitual biped, the size of a small chimpanzee, that was the most primitive of the three recognized australopith species; thought to most closely resemble the ancestral hominid.

Australopithecus boisei the most evolved australopith species; it was about the size of a human being.

avuncular residence a pattern of residence characteristic of certain matrilineal societies, in which a newly married couple lives near or with the brother of the husband's mother. (This uncle is a senior member of his matrilineage.)

balanced reciprocity a type of exchange relationship in which an equal return is expected for any gift given; prevalent in horticultural and agricultural societies, this exchange occurs between distantly related persons who are social equals or formal trading partners.

band a type of egalitarian social organization involving informal leadership, small social groups, and a lack of a separate political life distinct from other aspects of social life; prevalent among nomadic hunter-gatherers.

base camp the main, although temporary or semisedentary, settlement of a social group, from which work groups set out to collect food sources. Food is divided among group members upon the return of the groups to the base.

Bering Plain (Beringia) a land mass stretching across the Bering Straits from northeastern Siberia to northwestern Alaska; it was exposed before 80,000—35,000 B.P. and several times thereafter, the last exposure occurring about 11,000 B.P. During the last glacial maximum (the Würm) in about 20,000 B.P., the plain was about 1,300 miles wide.

bifacially worked a tool that has been produced by removing flakes from both of its sides.

bilateral descent reckoning of kinship through equal affiliation with the relatives of one's father and one's mother.

bilocal residence a flexible pattern of residence in which a couple establishes a household with or near the kinsmen of either the husband or the wife, depending on preference and circumstances.

biological species a group of interbreeding populations that are reproductively isolated from other such groups. It is the most inclusive Mendelian population.

biome any of the major environmental zones, which impose biological and physical limits upon the organisms living within them.

bipedal animal an animal that walks on two hind feet.

blade a thin, parallel-sided flake whose length is usually more than twice its width. In blade manufacture, the core was first percussion flaked into a pyramid or cylinder; the blade, whose basic shape had already been formed on the core, was then struck off by either the direct or indirect (punch flaking) percussion technique.

blood group substances a class of proteins that are associated with the surface of the membrane that encloses the red cell contents. There are several blood group systems, including the ABO system and the Rh or rhesus system.

borrowing the adoption of words into a language as a result of contact with a culture speaking another language; pronunciation is generally changed to accord with the existing sound system, but occasionally new sounds are borrowed as well.

bound morpheme a morpheme, such as *-ly,* that carries meaning but can only occur in combination with other morphemes.

B.P. an abbreviation for the phrase "before present." By convention, the "present" for all B.P. calculations is the year 1950. Dates are calculated from that base year.

brachiation a type of arboreal locomotion in which an animal swings beneath the branches, supporting its weight by its hands and arms alone.

bride price payment in goods or money, prior to marriage, by a prospective husband and/or his kinsmen to the kinsmen of his bride; also known as *bride wealth.*

bride service labor or other work performed by a husband for his wife's kinsmen, either before the marriage or after. It may take the place of, or supplement, the *bride price.*

browsing feeding upon the leaves of trees and bushes. Most deer are browsers.

bureaucracy an elaborate hierarchical system of management characteristic of state organizations.

Callitrichidae a highly arboreal family of the infraorder Platyrrhini, whose members are the genera of marmosets; includes the smallest extant monkeys.

canal irrigation a type of irrigation system in which channels or canals are dug connecting the fields with streams or rivers; the water thus diverted nourishes the fields.

canines the cone-shaped teeth, situated in the jaw immediately behind the incisors, that are used to seize food and in fighting and display.

cargo system from the Spanish *cargo,* meaning "charge" or burden; used to describe a system of obligations that establishes religious, political, and social hierarchies within certain Latin American highland communities.

carpus the wrist; its skeleton consists of a number of carpal bones.

carrying capacity the potential of an environment to support human life.

caste a hereditary social category in which economic and social position and often occupation are ascribed at birth.

Catarrhini an anthropoid infraorder including the superfamilies Hominoidea (apes and humans) and Cercopithecoidea (Old World monkeys); a characteristic readily distinguishing the catarrhines from the platyrrhines is the presence of two rather than three premolars in each jaw.

cattle complex an area culture pattern of East Africa in which cattle are important indicators of prestige, status, and wealth.

Cebidae a family of the infraorder Platyrrhini, whose members are highly arboreal monkeys found in South and Central America.

Cenozoic translated as "recent life"; the last of the three major eras on the geological time scale, in which the dominant terrestrial animals were birds and mammals.

central camp a base camp.

Cercopithecidae the only family of the superfamily Cercopithecoidea, including the monkeys of Asia and Africa. The various genera live in many habitats, from tropical rain forests to treeless savannas. The Cercopithecidae are divided into two subfamilies, the Colobinae and Cercopithecinae.

Cercopithecoidea an anthropoid superfamily whose members are the Old World monkeys.

Cercopithecus aethiops the vervet monkey; inhabits savanna woodland, where it often forages on the ground.

cerebral cortex the part of the brain whose functions include memory, storage of information, comparison of new experiences with those of the past, and integration of information and memories from different sensory channels; also controls the primary motor and sensory areas.

Cheirogaleus the dwarf lemur of Madagascar; a member of the lemuroid family Cheirogaleidae, which is composed of small, nocturnal, mainly insectivorous lemurs. It is believed to be postcranially close to the primitive primate form.

chiefdom a type of sociopolitical organization consisting of a pyramidal hierarchy of statuses. The chief, who rules by hereditary right and is the full-time political leader of the community, acts as a central agency to coordinate economic, religious, and social activities and the redistribution of goods.

chinampa artificial islands of mud and vegetation constructed on lakes and tended by farmers in boats. Mud from the lake bottom is shoveled onto plants growing on top of the lake and fertilized. Seeds are then planted, resulting in a crop growing on the lake surface.

chopper-chopping tradition a tool tradition associated with *Homo erectus* sites in Asia; consists of crude core choppers and flake tools.

choppers crude, heavy unifacial and bifacial tools that functioned as general-purpose chopping and cutting implements.

chopper-scraper complex a prehistoric assemblage of heavy, crude choppers and scrapers found in the New World. Because its tools are similar to those found in Early and Middle Paleolithic Eurasian sites, it is thought to be over 12,000 years old; has also been called the preprojectile point horizon.

chromosomes long strands of DNA located in the nucleus of the cell. At cell division, they are visible as microscopic rod-shaped structures.

city an urban area; a community with a large population concentrated in a compact area (i.e., a density of at least 5,000 people per square mile) characterized by a high degree of social stratification.

civilization derived from the Latin word *civis,* meaning city; a cultural stage characterized by the city type of settlement and the state form of organization.

clan the most common form of tribal lineal descent reckoning, in which "blood" cousins unite around a name and/or other symbols of clanship, providing a framework for tribal organization. Elders usually represent the clan as a whole in political disputes with outside groups.

class a social category composed of individuals who share similar economic and social status, access to economic resources, and lifestyles.

Classic a Mesoamerican cultural stage that lasted from 1,700 to 1,100 B.P.; characterized by greatly increased populations, enormous urban areas and ceremonial centers, expanded trade networks, increased social stratification, and full-time craft specialization.

clavicle the collar bone.

cline a geographic gradient of gradual change in morphology or the frequency of a character.

closed system a system of communication limited in that each message is autonomous and unchangeable; elements of one sign cannot be combined with elements of another to form a new sign. Animal sign systems are spoken of as closed.

Clovis tradition the earliest Paleo-Indian fluted-point tradition in the New World. Also called the Llano tradition, it dates from 11,500 to 9,500 B.P. and is found throughout North America. Its diagnostic tool is the Clovis fluted point, which was used in the hunting of mammoth, upon which the Clovis economy was apparently based.

coccyx the vestigial "tail" of hominoid primates; a series of bony nubbins at the base of the vertebral column or backbone.

cognates words in related languages that are descended from a single prototype form.

cognitive imperative according to Eugene D'Aquili, the biological need of human beings to order their world through the use of their cognitive abilities.

collateral relative a person who is related to another through a third connecting person.

Colobinae a generally arboreal subfamily of the family Cercopithecidae (Old World monkeys), whose members have a specialized stomach for digesting mature tree leaves; they include the colobus monkey, the langurs, and the proboscis monkey.

Colobus the only African genus of the subfamily Colobinae; highly arboreal, leaf-eating monkeys, many species of which exhibit striking fur patterns.

consanguineal relations relatives by birth.

continuous distribution a distribution pattern of a characteristic where no sharp boundaries exist between values, and the number of classes or "types" one makes is limited only by the precision of the measuring instruments. An example of such a distribution is the weight of members of a population.

convergence the phenomenon wherein dissimilar unrelated lineages evolve superficially similar forms.

corvée in feudal Europe and especially in colonial Africa, an obligation imposed on the inhabitants of a region to pay a landowner taxes or to render him periodic services without remuneration.

cranial capacity the volume of the inside of the cranium or skull.

cranium the skull.

Cretaceous the Age of Reptiles; the last period of the Mesozoic era, which lasted from 135 to 70 million B.P. During the last Cretaceous, mammals and birds began to play important roles in the ecosystem.

cross-cousins the offspring of siblings of the opposite sex; for example, the children of a mother's brother.

cross-cutting mutual alliance among political opponents outside the political sphere; discourages absolute enmity and allows for unity during emergencies, such as wartime.

crossing-over the process whereby homologous chromosomes exchange parts of their length before being drawn into different gametic cells. This is a potent cause of variation among gametes.

cultural ecology a theoretical approach formulated by Julian Steward emphasizing the interaction of technology and environment in the development of a culture; asserts the need for the anthropologist to investigate the relationship between a population and its technology, social organization, and external environment.

cultural materialism term used to identify the theory developed by the anthropologist Julian White, which asserts that culture and development are dependent on material or technological factors.

cultural relativism seeing foreign cultures in relation to one's own; being receptive to cultural diversity and to cultures with which one is not familiar.

cultural values according to Walter Goldschmidt, the unspoken beliefs shared by each particular community regarding right and wrong, the moral and immoral, and good and bad.

culture broker a person who is able to mediate between and reconcile the value conflicts of a traditional (usually rural) and a modern (usually state-organized) culture, because he or she shares membership in both groups.

Darwinian evolution the evolutionary theory based upon the idea that changes within species are directed largely by the demands of selection.

dendogram a tree diagram that depicts the degree of resemblance or evolutionary relationship between populations or other groups.

Dendropithecus **(formerly *Limnopithecus*)** an extinct hominoid, about the size of a gibbon, whose fossil remains have been found in Africa; has been dated to the early Miocene. It was adapted to arboreal, quadrupedal locomotion, with a limb structure suggestive of initial adaptation to brachiation. That, and some of its facial and dental traits, indicate to some authorities a close relationship to the modern gibbons.

density the degree of relatedness of the contacts within one's network; the higher the density, the more *lateral links* exist among an individual's contacts, which is suggestive of overlapping affiliations and loyalties.

derived characters (habitus characters) traits acquired by a lineage in the course of its evolution, as opposed to those inherited from an earlier, ancestral form.

descent affiliation with one or both parents that establishes a person as a member of a specific consanguineal kin group.

deviance departure by an individual from societal norms. The definition of deviant behavior is variable and dependent on the situation and culture involved.

diploid number the double set of chromosomes normally found in the

Glossary 593

nucleus of somatic cells.
directional selection a type of natural selection that produces change in the gene frequencies of a population.
direct-percussion flaking a toolmaking technique in which a stone is used as a hammer to chip off flakes on one or two sides of another stone or core until a tool is formed.
discontinuous distribution a distribution pattern in which phenotypes can be grouped in discrete classes, and there are no intermediate phenotypes between these types. An example of such a distribution is provided by ABO blood groups.
divergence a pattern of evolution in which, after speciation, the daughter species become progressively more different.
divination a means of judicial inquiry through appeal to the supernatural.
DNA deoxyribonucleic acid. DNA has a double-strand structure, stretches of which (believed to correspond to genes) carry information necessary to make a particular protein or part of a protein. Genetic material (genes and chromosomes) consists of DNA.
domestication the process leading to plant and animal food production.
dominance a gene is said to be dominant to its allele(s) if its phenotypic expression in heterozygotes is indistinguishable from its expression in homozygotes.
double descent a rare type of unilineal descent, in which descent is reckoned through both the maternal and paternal lines. One affiliates with one's patrilineal descent group for some purposes and with one's matrilineal descent group for others.
dry farming farming in areas where irrigation is not necessary.
Dryopithecus a genus of apes known from Early and Middle Miocene fossils discovered in Europe, Asia, and Africa. Most authorities believe the genus contains the common ancestor of hominids and modern pongids; several species are known.

Early Dynastic a Mesopotamian cultural stage dating from 4,900 to 4,500 B.P.; characterized by the rise of large Sumerian city-states, which were in constant conflict.
Early Woodland a cultural period in the eastern United States dating from about 3,000 to 2,200 B.P.; characterized by small groups of seasonally nomadic, egalitarian hunters and gatherers.
ecological strategy the distinctive survival techniques used by a species in its interaction with other species and its nonliving environment.
econiche the position of a species within the ecosystem of which it is a part. It is defined by the species' relationships with its nonliving environment and with other species—what it eats, what eats it, the diseases and parasites that afflict it, and so on.
economizing the necessary attempt of societies to develop production strategies that will make most efficient use of available resources, in a qualitative as well as a quantitative sense.
ecosystem a system formed by the interaction of populations within an environment.
egalitarian society a social group in which all families have the same degree of wealth, political power, and prestige. No institutionalized political leaders, ruling classes, or elected officials exist; decisions are made by a group of elders or by a man respected for his personal accomplishments.
ego in the analysis of kinship terms, the person serving as the central reference point of a study.
embryo the organism during its earliest development stages.
emic approach attempting to understand a culture from the native's point of view, without imposing one's cultural viewpoint on the analysis. Contrasted to the etic approach.
endocranial cast a plaster or plastic cast of the internal surface of the brain cavity.
endogamy a cultural rule requiring marriage within one's social group.
enzymes proteins that act as biological catalysts, producing and controlling chemical reactions in the cells, such as breaking down compounds taken in as food and using them as sources of energy.
Eocene the second epoch of the Cenozoic era, dating from ca. 58 to 34 million years ago, during which the radiation of primitive mammals continued. Among the primates, families appear showing traits that typify living members of the order.
equability climatic uniformity, with little annual variation in mean temperatures and precipitation to promote seasonal contrasts.
ethics according to Walter Goldschmidt, the values of a society as formulated into an integrated system of ideas; a culture's moral philosophy.
ethnocentricity cultural self-centeredness; viewing other cultures from one's particular cultural vantage point.
ethnosemantics the study of the ways in which societies categorize their experiences into domains of semantically related terms; also deals with the criteria societies use to determine the ordering of these terms within domains.
etic approach an analysis of a culture through the use of categories invented by the anthropologist, which reflect his or her point of view. Contrasted to the emic approach.
evolution a process by which organisms adapt to changes in their environment.
evolution, cultural the process by which customary patterns of behavior originate and change in relation to particular environmental conditions.
evolution, general the broad patterns of change that have characterized the development of human

culture, exhibiting a general trend moving from simple to complex.

evolution, specific the particular patterns of adjustment that people in specific societies make to their natural and social environments.

exogamy a cultural rule requiring marriage outside one's kin group or community.

extended family a social group composed of a monogamous, polygynous, or polyandrous conjugal unit, plus offspring, and containing at least three generations of blood relations.

extensive agriculture See horticulturalists.

faculative biped an animal that can walk well on two feet, but does so only occasionally.

family a cultural term assigned to the minimal domestic groups that cooperate economically, are entrusted with the care and socialization of children by older members, and exchange offspring through marriage with other family units; the ideal domestic group.

feeding system the functional system concerned with the behavior and structures related to eating habits, such as the lips, tongue, cheeks, teeth, jaws, jaw muscles, stomach, and intestines.

femur (pl., **femora**) the thigh bone.

fictive relation a person, such as a godparent or a "blood brother," who is informally regarded as a relative, although not one's blood or affinal kin.

fitness the reproductive success of a particular subclass within a population compared to that of other subclasses. Fitness is usually partitioned into components of fertility and viability.

fixation an allele that reaches 100 percent frequency in a population is said to have become "fixed" in that population.

floodwater farming a type of food production that involves planting crops where they will be watered by surface runoff, either along the course of shallow rivers, on outwash fans, or in seasonally flooded bottomlands.

fluted point a distinctive blade tool flaked from the base along the center in order to form a groove or flute for hafting the point to a shaft.

Folsom tradition the second Paleo-Indian fluted-point tradition in the New World, overlapping with and eventually succeeding the Clovis tradition; dates from 11,000 to 9,000 B.P. and is limited to western North America. Its diagnostic tool is the Folsom fluted point, which was mainly used for hunting the extinct long-horned bison.

Formative a Mesoamerican cultural stage lasting from 4,250 to 1,700 B.P.; characterized by permanent agricultural settlements and the first pottery, ceremonial centers, signs of stratification, calendrics, and writing. It is also known as the Preclassic.

fossils the remains of plants and animals that have been preserved and mineralized through geological accident.

founder effect the loss of genetic variation within a population when a new population is established by a few colonists or survivors of a catastrophe. Because the founders constitute a small sample of the population from which they are derived, they carry only a small fraction of its gene pool. Consequently, their gene frequencies will probably differ from those of the parent population, and certain alleles may be totally absent.

fraternal polyandry marriage of one woman with two or more brothers.

free morpheme a morpheme, such as *god*, that can convey meaning on its own.

frontal lobes the part of the cerebral cortex located in the forehead area. In humans their function seems to be related to the ability to direct sustained attention to a long-term task or goal, to screen out distracting stimuli, and to inhibit conflicting impulses.

gene flow the process whereby genes are carried from one population to another, either by migration or interbreeding.

gene frequency the abundance of a particular gene in a population relative to that of its alleles.

gene pool the combined genes of a Mendelian population from which the genotype of each individual and each new generation is drawn.

generalized distance in multivariate analyses, the distance between entities based on all the variables taken together.

generalized reciprocity a system of cooperative sharing and exchange in which there is no expectation of immediate return; central in the life style of many hunting and gathering societies.

generation set a group composed of related age-sets, which performs a particular societal role during a specified time span. Within a given society, all members will be assigned to a generation set, each of which has its own rights and duties.

genes the individual units of heredity, which are carried on the chromosomes.

genetic drift a mechanism by which gene frequencies of a population may change. The changes are due to sampling error and are random in direction, unlike those produced by natural selection.

genetic marker an easily recognizable, genetically determined variation.

genitor a person's biological father.

genotype the genetic makeup of an organism.

geological time scale a scale dividing the earth's history into different eras, periods, and epochs, each of which is characterized by particular geological and faunal events.

gibbon See Hylobatidae.

Glacial pertaining to a period during which much of the land was covered by large masses of ice and snow.

glottochronology (or **lexicostatistics**) a statistical method, developed by Morris Swadesh, to determine the approximate date when two languages began to diversify; useful for disclosing relationships between language groups.

glumes hard cases or husks that enclose the seed-bearing portion of many plants, especially those of the wild ancestors of many domesticates, such as domesticated wheat, barley, and corn.

Gorilla gorilla one of the great apes (Pongidae) and the largest living primate; its distribution is confined to the tropical rain forests of Africa.

grammar the particular and systematic way in which the formal elements of a language are organized —sounds, morphemes, words, and phrases.

Gravettian an Upper Paleolithic cultural tradition contemporary with the Solutrean and late Aurignacian and Perigordian traditions. It dates from 27,000 to 17,000 B.P. and is found mainly in eastern Europe; characterized by backed blades, developed bone- and ivory-working technologies, and mammoth hunting.

grazing feeding upon grasses and other rough herbage. Horses are specialized grazers.

grinding tools tools such as mortars, pestles, manos, metates, and mullers, used for processing plant foods; they did not attain importance until Mesolithic-Archaic times.

groups the overlapping social units structuring society; they tend to exhibit *corporateness,* that is, an autonomous existence independent of the individuals who compose them.

gymnosperms nonflowering plants, such as mosses, cycads, and conifers.

habitat the area where a species lives; its surroundings.

Hadropithecus an extinct Malagasy lemur that exhibited baboonlike features.

hallux the big toe; the first digit of the foot, which is freely mobile and used for grasping by most nonhuman primates.

hand axe a large pear-shaped core tool with a cutting edge and a picklike end probably used for cutting, piercing, and chopping; characteristic of the Acheulean tradition.

hedonic behavior a social relationship that involves relaxed friendliness and mutual enjoyment among the actors.

hemoglobin the red, oxygen-carrying protein that makes up 95 percent of the contents of red blood cells.

heritage characters (ancestral characters) traits inherited from an ancestral form by a species or group of species.

heterozygote (adj., **heterozygous**) an individual carrying two different alleles at a certain locus.

holistic perspective an anthropological approach seeking to integrate varying and diverse perspectives in order to arrive at the most complete understanding of human culture.

holocultural study a worldwide survey of all known cultures, used by anthropologists to test general theories of human society.

hominid a member of the family Hominidae.

Hominidae a family of open-country, bipedal animals belonging to the superfamily Hominoidea; probably arose sometime during the Miocene period from an African member of the genus *Dryopithecus*. It includes the genera *Australopithecus, Homo,* and perhaps *Ramapithecus.*

Hominoidea an anthropoid superfamily that includes extinct and living apes and hominids. It includes three related families, Hominidae, Pongidae, and Hylobatidae.

Homo a hominid genus that first appears in the fossil record about 2.7 million years ago during the late Pliocene; probably includes only a single lineage, of which modern *Homo sapiens* is the living representative.

Homo erectus an early human, evolving after *Homo habilis,* who apparently thrived during the Middle Pleistocene from 250,000 to over a million years ago. Remains have been associated with both the developed Oldowan and the Acheulean traditions.

Homo habilis the earliest fossil hominid in the direct human line; has an East African provenance and dates back almost three million years; was most probably the founder of the Oldowan tool tradition.

homology a resemblance between animals due to inheritance from a common ancestor.

Homo sapiens the only living species of the human family.

homozygote (adj., **homozygous**) an individual carrying two indistinguishable alleles at a particular locus.

horticulturalists self-sufficient, subsistence, low yield per acre farming societies, which use human labor and simple tools and are organized around higher-level social institutions (involving wider kinship ties and political organization).

household the minimal residential unit, whose members cooperate economically and in everyday domestic activities to ensure survival.

human as used in this book, refers to a member of one of the species of the genus *Homo.*

human biology the branch of biology dealing with the description and explanation of human evolution and physical variation.

human ecology the culturally conditioned relationships between individuals, between human populations, and between human populations and their environments.

hunters and gatherers seminomadic foraging societies that are based on the collecting of wild foods using a few simple tools; incorporate no formal leadership, structure, or territory and resource ownership.

Hylobatidae a family of the superfamily Hominoidea, whose living members are the several species of gibbons. These small apes are confined to the temperate and tropical rain forests of southeast Asia. Their most striking characteristic is their elongated arms.

ilium one of the three bones that fuse to form the innominate or hipbone; forms the upper part of the hip. Its broad upper rim is called the iliac crest.

incisors the front teeth; generally used for seizing food and preparing it for chewing.

independent family a single family unit—whose marriage relationship may be monogamous, polygynous, or polyandrous—plus their offspring, residing apart from relatives of other generations; highly adaptive in hunting and gathering and in industrial societies.

industrialization the development of specialized productive units, utilizing concentrated forms of solar energy—fossil fuel—through highly mechanized procedures.

institutions a term coined by Bronislaw Malinowski to denote the set of recurrent behavior patterns that function to satisfy the basic needs of a society.

intensive agriculturalists societies based upon cultivation with a high labor investment, including the use of landscaping, irrigation, nonhuman energy sources (such as animal traction), natural fertilizers, crop rotation, and the selective breeding of crops and livestock, thereby increasing the investment of energy per unit of land and causing productivity to rise greatly.

intensive agriculture a form of cultivation characterized by improved techniques of soil and water control, such as fertilization and irrigation, and the use of the plow and draft animals.

interglacial between glaciations; a period during which the glaciers receded, and the climate became warmer and moister.

internalization the process by which members of a society, through socialization, adopt that society's values and mores as their own.

ischium that part of the pelvis projecting behind and below the hip joint; one of the three bones that fuse to form the innominate or hipbone (the other two being the ilium and the pubis).

jajmani **system** an exchange network operative in India among caste groups, in which an upper-caste family (the *jajman,* client) provides lower-caste families (the *kamin*) with grain in return for such services as washing and carpentry. The system is hereditary, traditional, and mandatory and serves to bind the castes together in a relationship of mutual obligation.

jump a group hunting method used by Upper Paleolithic groups, in which large herds of animals were stampeded toward cliffs, where they would jump to their deaths.

jural norms according to Alfred R. Radcliffe-Brown, the general rules governing relationships among different categories of individuals within a society.

killsite an area where game has been killed and butchered.

kindred a bilateral kin group, which is ego-oriented rather than ancestor-oriented.

kinesics the study of body movement as a means of communication; also deals with analysis of the relationship and counterpoint between nonverbal and verbal communication.

knapping the manufacture of stone tools by chipping or flaking.

lactase the enzyme found in the lining of the small intestine that acts upon lactose, making it possible for the individual to digest milk.

lactose the sugar found in milk.

language a complex communication system, largely symbolic, that is shared only by humans.

larynx the voicebox; muscle and cartilaginous tissue at the top of the windpipe that enclose the vocal cords.

Lemuriformes an infraorder of the order Prosimii, whose members are the lorises and bush babies of Africa and Asia and the lemurs of Madagascar; characterized by a rhinarium, well-developed organs of smell, "cat's whiskers," a special kind of placental membrane, and a claw on the second toe of the foot and a comblike structure formed by the lower front teeth, both for grooming the fur.

Lemuroidea a superfamily of the infraorder Lemuriformes, confined to Madagascar. It includes the families Lemuridae and Indriidae (lemurs) and Daubentoniidae (aye-aye).

Levallois technique a method of tool manufacture in which a core was percussion flaked to a desired shape, so that a large flake with a predetermined form and a very sharp cutting edge could be struck off; such a flake could function as a special-purpose tool without being retouched.

leveling mechanism in egalitarian and rank societies, the built-in social process that prevents individuals from accumulating a disproportionate amount of economic goods and wealth.

levirate the custom whereby a man may marry his deceased brother's widow (or demand a bride price from any other man she marries) and has an obligation to provide for her.

lineage a unilineal descent group (either matrilineal or patrilineal) whose members can trace their genealogies, through known links, back to a common ancestor.

lineal relative a direct descendent; one who is in a direct line of descent from ego.

linearization a process in which lower-order sociopolitical institutions are bypassed or eliminated by higher-order institutions because the former have lost regulatory control. Linearization promotes increasing centralization.

linguistics the study of language.

living floor a site preserving traces of the human activities carried on there.

locomotor system the functional system dealing with the behavior and structures concerned with posture and body movement; it includes the bones, joints, and muscles of the limbs and trunk.

locus (pl., **loci**) the place of a particular gene within the set of chromosomes.

Lorisoidea a superfamily of the infraorder Lemuriformes, containing the families Lorisidae and Cheirogaleidae. Lorisoids are small nocturnal animals with an omnivorous diet of fruit, tree gum, and insects.

lumbar vertebrae the bones composing the part of the spinal column lying in the lower back, between the pelvis and the ribs.

Macaca a cercopithecine genus (including several species) found throughout tropical and subtropical Asia and North Africa; adaptable, successful monkeys able to forage on the ground and in trees.

macroband a population composed of several microbands.

Magdalenian an Upper Paleolithic European cultural tradition following the Solutrean and Gravettian traditions; dates from 17,000 to 10,000 B.P., the end of the glacial period. It is characterized by bone and antler harpoons, atlatls, the first microliths, and reindeer hunting. Paleolithic cave art reached its apex during the Magdalenian.

magic a means of directing and controlling supernatural forces through a particular combination of ritual actions or mechanical verbal formulas; seen as an alternative to religion, yet not always clearly distinguished from it.

maize Indian corn.

mana among the people of Melanesia, an impersonal supernatural force, residing in animate or inanimate objects, which is responsible for good and evil.

mandibles the lower jaws.

market exchange an impersonal commercial transaction in which goods and services are purchased and sold through a standard medium of exchange, money. This exchange relies on the law of supply and demand, rather than on social obligations between individuals or groups. Most of the industrialized nations are distinguished by a market economy.

marriage a socially approved sexual and economic union between two or more individuals, which serves to legitimize their offspring and establish reciprocal rights and obligations between husbands and wives.

masseter muscle one of the muscles of mastication (chewing), running from the zygomatic arch (cheekbone) to the mandible (lower jaw).

masticatory muscles used for chewing and biting; they run from the cranium to the mandible.

matrilineal descent ancestory traced solely through the maternal (female) line; defines children as members of their mother's descent group.

matrilineal extended family composed of a woman and her husband or husbands, their unmarried sons, their daughters, and their daughters' husbands and children.

Maya a Mesoamerican theocratic civilization that flourished in Guatemala, the lowlands of the Yucatan Peninsula, and parts of Honduras and Chiapas from 2,265 to 1,060 B.P.; it was based upon swidden agriculture.

meiosis a special form of cell division during which sex cells are produced. The fundamental process in meiosis is reduction of the number of chromosomes in each cell from the double set to the single set. In this way, the fusion of two sex cells (e.g. the sperm and ovum) will create a zygote with the normal diploid number of chromosomes characteristic of its parents' species.

melanin a granular organic substance that appears dark brown in its oxidized form. It is the most important pigment in human skin and is found mainly in its basal layers.

Mendelian population a group of organisms in which each member is more likely to mate with another member than with an outsider. It is thus a group within which a body of genetic material is usually transmitted.

Mesolithic an Old World cultural stage that began about 10,000 B.P., after the termination of the Pleistocene epoch and the Upper Paleolithic cultural stage. It is characterized by the extensive use of microlithic and ground stone tools, the intensive seasonal foraging of localized resources, and the establishment of regularized long-distance trade. Its New World counterpart is the Archaic stage.

Mesozoic translated as "middle life"; the second of the three major eras of the geological time scale, during which the reptiles were the dominant land vertebrates.

metacarpals the bones of the palm.

microliths small bladelets, an inch or less in length, used alone or with handles; manufactured by being struck off a prepared miniature cylindrical or pyramidal core or by snapping a blade into several pieces of stone. They first occur in Late Upper Paleolithic (Magdalenian) contexts but do not become abundant until Mesolithic times.

Middle Woodland a cultural period in the eastern United States dating from about 2,200 B.P.; characterized by intensive harvesting economies and social groups that were more sedentary, of larger size, and more complex in sociopolitical structures than those of the preceding Early Woodland period.

millet a tall, coarse cereal grass that grows wild in Asia; first domesticated in North China.

minimal pair term used by descriptive linguists to designate similar words, such as "pin" and "bin," that are distinct in meaning due to a single phonological variation.

Miocene the fourth epoch of the Cenozoic era, occurring between 22½ and 5 million years ago; many modern families of mammals originated at this time.

modal personality according to Abram Kardiner, the basic personality structure shared by most members of a particular culture.

moiety from the French *moitié*, "half"; one of the two unilineal descent groups into which a given society is divided.

molars the large teeth at the back of the jaw, which erupt behind the milk teeth in growing mammals; used for chewing, grinding, and shearing of food in preparation for swallowing.

molimo among the Mbuti pygmies, a festival held during periods of sickness and poor hunting in affirmation of their trust in the forest as a beneficent provider; alternately, a ritual act performed on the death of a band member that serves to restore continuity and emphasize ties with their forest home.

monkey an anthropoid having a tail and a trunk, which is long and narrow from side to side but deep from front to back; belongs variously to the catarrhine family Cercopithecidae and the platyrrhine families Cebidae and Callitrichidae.

monogamy marriage with only one person at a time.

monotheism worship of one god as the creator and omnipotent ruler of the universe; practised by the religions of Judaism, Christianity, and Islam.

morphemes minimal units of speech that convey meaning.

morphology the study of the way morphemes are combined to construct words.

morphophonemics the study of the phonemic changes that occur when morphemes are combined.

Mousterian or Acheulean tradition a Mousterian cultural tradition characterized by the presence of hand axes and such flake tools as scrapers, borers, burins, notched flakes, points, and backed knives.

multilineal or specific evolutionism an approach to cultural development, associated with Julian Steward, which holds that evolutionary processes are specific and, therefore, focuses on observable sequences of change in different societies.

multituberculates a group of mammals with rodentlike teeth suggestive of a vegetarian diet; prominent during the Late Mesozoic and Early Cenozoic, they are not closely related to any living mammal.

musoli (tree) a religious symbol among the Ndembu of Zambia used to bring success to hunters and children to barren women; through the *musoli* the unknown is identified with a concrete symbolic object.

mutation a random change in a stretch of DNA. Mutations are the source of new genetic variation in genes.

natural selection the mechanism of evolutionary change; when one or more genotypes in a population are regularly less successful than other genotypes in transmitting their genes to the next generation.

neandertals short, stocky, barrel-chested Archaic *Homo sapiens* with heavy bones and musculature, especially in the facial region. Fossils have been found in areas of Europe and the Near East; associated with Mousterian tools.

negative reciprocity gift exchange between enemies or strangers, usually undertaken for reasons of expediency; sometimes acts to mitigate social friction but most often involves mistrust between parties and attempts to take advantage of a situation.

neolocal residence establishment by a newly married couple of a household completely apart from the kinsmen of both husband and wife.

network the pattern of interlocking and overlapping social relations that each individual, as a social being, manipulates to obtain, for example, support and information and that ties him or her to others in the larger society.

non-Darwinian evolution changes in the gene frequencies of populations that are caused by random processes, such as genetic drift and the founder effect.

normative selection a type of natural selection in which the process acts as an agent of stability, maintaining more or less constant, optimal gene frequencies within a population so long as the latter's environment remains stable.

Notharctus an Eocene lemuriform genus, manifesting typical prosimian characteristics, such as mobile, elongated digits tipped with nails rather than claws, long hind limbs, and powerful, mobile big toes; one of the most completely known Eocene genera.

nuclear family a social group consisting of a man, his wife, and their children.

nuclear zones environmental zones to which the wild ancestors of today's domesticates were indigenous. In the Near East they were located in the foothills of the Zagros and Taurus mountains.

oath a method of determining guilt, utilized in many societies, in which the accused solemnly testifies his or her innocence before a god or some other authority.

Oldowan technology a toolmaking tradition in which pebbles are crudely percussion flaked to form an irregular cutting edge along one of their sides. The slightly modified pebble is then used as an all-purpose chopping and cutting tool.

olfactory pertaining to the sense of smell.

Oligocene the third epoch of the Cenozoic era, dating from ca. 33 to 23 million years ago, during which the platyrrhines and catarrhines made their first appearance (in South America and North Africa respectively).

Olmec the first Mesoamerican civilization, which flourished along the Gulf Coast during the Preclassic, from 3,500 to 2,500 B.P. The earliest Mesoamerican ceremonial centers are Olmec.

open-air site a site in an open area, rather than a cave or rock shelter.

open juncture a pause occurring between words or clauses that acts as a phoneme to determine meaning.

open system a flexible system of communication in which it is possible to combine verbal symbols in continually different ways and thereby express an infinite number of new ideas; characteristic of human language.

operationalization the process of translating abstract concepts, such as "politics" or "personality," into concrete terms that can be measured and observed; used by anthropologists in the development of their study design.

orangutan (*Pongo pygmaeus*) one of the living members of the Pongidae, a highly arboreal ape confined to the forests of Sumatra and Borneo.

ordeal a method of judicial inquiry in which the accused, or a representative of the accused, undergoes a physical trial—innocence being decided by the degree of pain or injury suffered.

Oreopithecus a fossil apelike primate, skeletal remains of which have been found in Italy and dated to the Middle Miocene. Its structure suggests that it was an accomplished brachiator and perhaps occasionally biped.

Oriental despotism according to Karl Wittfogel, a state organization that arose out of the need for the construction and management of large-scale irrigation systems. The systems were controlled by an increasingly centralized ruling class, who established social control by denying water to resisting farmers. So-named because the ancient Chinese communities studied by Wittfogel seemed to manifest this form of social order.

ostracism (or **shunning**) an informal form of social control in which a person judged guilty of deviance is isolated from other members of the community.

overkill theory the theory that the numerous animal extinctions in the New World were due to the advent of human groups into regions where animals were not adapted to human depredations and, therefore, were easy prey for hunters.

palate the roof of the mouth.

paleoanthropologists scientists who study fossil remains and their context in order to discern the lifeways of extinct hominids.

Paleocene the first epoch of the Cenozoic era, dating from ca. 69 to 59 million years ago; it saw the earliest extensive radiation of primitive mammals.

Paleo-Indian traditions Upper Paleolithic cultures of the New World, which date from between 12,000 and 8,000 B.P. They are individually named (from the oldest to the youngest): Llano or Clovis, Folsom, and Plano; characterized by lanceolate points and big-game hunting economies.

paleontology the study of plant and animal fossil remains.

Paleopropithecus an extinct Malagasy lemur, whose skeletal structure indicates that it was a brachiator.

Paleozoic literally translated as "ancient life"; the earliest of the three major eras on the geological time scale, during which the ancient fish, amphibia, and primitive reptiles dominated the earth.

Pan troglodytes the common chimpanzee; one of the great apes, a member of the Pongidae, found in the tropical rain forests and savanna woodlands of west and central Africa.

Papio the common baboons, members of the subfamily Cercopithecinae. Widespread and successful monkeys, they live in a wide variety of habitats; distinguished by projecting muzzles and large canines.

parallel cousins the offspring of siblings of the same sex, as, for example, the children of a mother's sister.

parallelism a phenomenon that occurs when related species of similar general adaptation independently take up similar ways of life, and so come to resemble each other in special adaptations more than either resembles the ancestral form.

parietal association area the part of the cerebral cortex located beneath the parietal bones of the skull, whose function seems to be the integration of information already internalized by the primary association areas.

pastoralism a specialized form of animal husbandry based on large herds of grazing animals such as sheep, goats, cattle, or camels. It is a strategy predicated on agricultural surplus and the interaction on a regional basis between those specializing in herding and farming.

pater a person's socially recognized father, who is not necessarily his or her *genitor*.

patrilineal descent ancestry traced solely through the paternal (male) line; defines children as members of their father's descent group.

patrilineal extended family composed of a man and his wife or wives, his unmarried daughters, his sons, and their wives and children; the father exercises primary authority within this extended family unit.

peasants intensive agriculturalists who are part of complex state societies and market systems over which they have little or no control.

pelvis the pelvic girdle. The ring of bones (including the hipbones) forming the base of the trunk of the body in Primates; the uppermost part attaches to the vertebral column (backbone), while the lowermost portion attaches to the femur or thighbone.

Perigordian one of the two oldest cultural traditions of the Upper Paleolithic in Europe. Found mainly in Spain and France, it dates from 35,000 to 20,000 B.P. and is characterized by the Chatelperronian knife and big-game fauna.

phalanges the bones of the fingers and toes.

phenetic distance the overall resemblance among species, found by comparing their morphological and physiological characters and counting up the similarities and differences.

phenotype the manifest physical characteristics of an individual, which are determined by a combination of both genetic makeup and environmental effects.

phonemes the smallest linguistically significant units of sound that function in a language to indicate differences in meaning.

phonemic system the sounds in a language that native speakers consider significant.

phonetic system the sounds of a language that are heard by an objective outside observer.

phonology the study of speech sounds.

phratry a unilineal descent group in which several clans are joined and share certain kinship rights, while maintaining distinct identities for some purposes.

phyletic relationship a relationship between species based upon descent from a common ancestor.

phyletic tree a branching diagram representing the phyletic relationships of a group of species.

phylogeny the evolutionary history of a taxon.

pit houses semisubterranean dwellings whose floors were dug a few feet into the ground; the superstructure was dome-shaped and made of timber and mud.

Plano tradition the late Paleo-Indian cultural tradition in the New World, which overlapped with and eventually succeeded the Clovis and Folsom traditions. Dating from 10,000 to 7,000 B.P. and found throughout North America and Mexico, the tradition is characterized by Plano points; long, narrow unfluted points with a fine patterning of parallel pressure-flaked scars. The earliest houses in the New World, small circular structures, date to this cultural period.

plant-processing station a type of site where grasses and plants were gathered and prepared for consumption.

plasma the clear yellowish fluid in which the red blood cells are suspended.

plates large blocks of material making up the earth's upper crust that "float," in constant motion, on a weak substratum some 40 miles beneath the surface.

plate tectonics the study of the continuous restructuring of the earth's surface that takes place through the relative motions of the continental plates. Current theory maintains that most geological phenomena can be related ultimately to plate tectonics.

Platyrrhini an anthropoid infraorder that includes the monkeys of South and Central America (Cebidae and Callitrichidae). A characteristic readily distinguishing them from the catarrhines is the presence of three rather than two premolars in each jaw.

Pleistocene a geological epoch lasting from 2½ million years ago to about 9,000 B.P., during which large-scale glaciations covered most of the Northern Hemisphere. The Lower, Middle, and Upper Paleolithic cultural stages belong to this period.

Plesiadapis a squirrel-like Paleocene primate genus having claws and rodentlike incisors.

Pliopithecus a Miocene anthropoid whose limb structure indicates that it was arboreal and a beginning brachiator. This, plus certain facial and dental features, indicates to some authorities ancestry to the modern gibbon.

polyandry marriage between one woman and two or more men at the same time.

polygamy plural marriage.

polygyny marriage between one man and two or more women at the same time.

polymorphic population a population in which more than one genetically determined physical type is found, and the frequency of the least common type is greater than can be accounted for by mutation alone.

polypeptide a chain of amino acids linked end to end. Polypeptide chains are the basis of protein molecules.

polytheism belief in many gods; characteristic of ancient Greece and Rome, the central African and East Asian kingdoms, and the Inca, Mayan, and Aztec cultures.

polytypic species a species whose constituent populations differ in their gene frequencies and phenotypic characters.

Pongidae a family of the superfamily Hominoidea, its members include both extinct and living apes; those extant include the gorilla, chimpanzee, and orangutan.

population a group of organisms be-

population genetics that branch of genetics that develops mathematical models of the behavior of genes in theoretical populations and seeks to test these models against actual living populations.

Postclassic a Mesoamerican cultural stage lasting from 1,100 to 437 B.P.; characterized by rigid social stratification, social unrest and warfare, and increasing secularization within the state organization.

postcranial skeletal material all of the skeleton below the skull.

potassium-argon dating (K-A dating) a radiometric method of absolute dating based upon the constant rate of decay of a radioactive isotope of potassium. It can be used to date many volcanic rocks more than 500,000 years old.

pot irrigation a simple type of irrigation system that involves digging wells right in the fields; water is drawn from the wells in several-gallon pots, and individual plants are watered by hand.

potlatch among the Kwakiutl Indians of British Colombia, an elaborate festival held by the members of an economically successful *numaym* (a kin-based group), during which gifts and food were given away in exchange for social prestige.

power grip a simple grasp in which the fingers and thumb press the object to be held against the palm.

preadaptation a characteristic that is acquired as an adaptation to a specialized or narrow econiche, but which turns out to be generally advantageous in a new set of circumstances. Thus, the lung of the crossopterygian fish was a specialization for life in fetid swamps, but was preadaptive for life on dry land, and thus formed the basis of the radiations of land vertebrates.

precision grip a grasp in which the object to be held is clasped between the thumb and index finger, permitting finer manipulation of the object; characteristic of monkeys, apes, and man.

Preclassic the Formative stage.

prehensile tail a tail with the ability to grasp objects; acts as a fifth hand and is used mainly to support the animal as it hangs to feed in the canopy; possessed by some New World or platyrrhine monkeys.

prelogical mode a term used by the nineteenth-century sociologist/anthropologist Lucien Levy-Bruhl to denote (in his terms) "the primitive mentality," which was incapable of distinguishing between the subjective and objective components of reality.

premolars the series of cheek teeth immediately behind the canines, used in chewing, grinding, and shearing of food for swallowing; in primates, as in other placental mammals, they replace the jaw's "milk molars."

pressure flaking a toolmaking technique in which the knapper finished off a tool by placing the tip of a bone, antler, or wooden punch near the edge of the tool, pressed forward and down, and removed flakes; created a very smooth, flat tool surface and a well-chipped, sharp edge. It was first used during Upper Paleolithic times.

primate a member of the mammalian order Primates.

Primates an order of mammals whose members have flexible hands and feet; divided into the suborders of Anthropoidea (humans, apes, monkeys) and Prosimii (lemurs, tarsiers).

primatology the study of members of the Primate order.

prime-mover theories theories envisioning a single linear development from a single causal force.

primitive in evolutionary studies, means "resembling the ancestral form."

promotion a sociopolitical process whereby an institution in the control hierarchy rises to a higher level of social control; generates the evolution of new institutions.

proprietary rights in nonindustrialized societies, the collective ownership of land and/or resources by the community or kin group.

Prosimii a suborder of the order Primates, whose members are the lower primates, the tarsiers, lemurs, lorises, and bush babies. They have brain cases that are smaller and flatter than those of the Anthropoidea and a pointed muzzle that usually projects from between the eyes.

Protoliterate a Mesopotamian cultural stage dating from 5,500 to 4,900 B.P.; characterized by theocracies and the earliest form of writing in the Near East.

proxemics the study of how people perceive and use space; defined by Edward T. Hall as "the interrelated observations and theories of man's use of space as a specialized elaboration of culture."

PTC phenylthiocarbamide, a bitter-tasting substance that is chemically close to substances that inhibit thyroid function. Most people can taste PTC, but some persons cannot; significantly, thyroid malfunctions are common among the latter.

punch flaking an indirect-percussion technique, first used during the Upper Paleolithic, in which the knapper places an intermediate tool, the punch, between the hammer and the prepared core; increases knapping precision, enabling the toolmaker to produce thin, evenly chipped tools.

quadrupedalism walking or running on all fours.

quarry workshops sites where lithic materials were gathered and manufactured into blanks or finished tools.

rachis the portion of the stalk of a plant that bears the seed pods.

radiocarbon dating a radiometric

method of dating organic materials based upon the constant decay of the radioactive carbon isotope C^{14}; can be used to date organic materials up to about 70,000 years of age.

radius one of the two bones of the forearm.

raids organized forays by one society against another, usually for limited purposes such as stealing cattle or kidnapping women; casualties are minimal.

Ramapithecus a Miocene hominoid that possessed characteristics of the jaw and teeth suggesting it may be an early member of the family Hominidae.

random sample a process of selection used by anthropologists that ideally guarantees every individual in a population an equal probability of being chosen.

rank society a social system, characteristic of many agricultural and horticultural societies, wherein people are ranked in a complex graded hierarchy of unequal statuses.

recessive gene a gene that is "dominated" by its allele and so is not expressed in the phenotype of heterozygotes.

reciprocity involves the mutual exchange of gifts between individuals who are linked by social ties and obligations. *See* balanced reciprocity; generalized reciprocity; and negative reciprocity.

redistribution compulsory payment of goods, money, or services to a central figure, such as a king, chief, or government, who redistributes them to the community; acts to increase a leader's prestige, while simultaneously providing for his subjects. It is the major exchange mode in chiefdoms and in other societies possessing social and political hierarchies.

redistribution center a place where economic goods, produced in various environmental zones, were brought to be distributed among all areas of the community, especially among those to which the products were not indigenous.

reflectance spectrophotometer an instrument used to measure skin color. It projects a beam of light of known wave length onto the patch of skin to be assayed and measures the proportion of the light that is reflected from it. The greater the reflectance, the lower the concentration of melanin granules.

religion may be broadly defined as any system of beliefs, symbols, and rituals that serves to make life meaningful and intelligible; provides a culture with an integrated world view, ethical system, and concept of reality. Involving some belief in the supernatural, it is an expression of what a society considers sacred.

resilience a measure of the degree of change that a system can undergo while still maintaining its basic elements or relationships.

rhinarium a wet, naked patch of skin, like a dog's nose, tipping the muzzle of an animal. Among living primates, rhinaria are found in Lemuriformes (lemurs and lorises).

rights of use in nonindustrialized societies, the rights of an individual to use the land or resources that are held in common by the community at large.

rites of passage culturally defined ceremonies, marking the transition from one life stage and status to another.

ritual a ceremonial event, making use of religious symbols, that reinforces the fundamental values and beliefs of a society.

sacrum a triangular bone composed of fused vertebrae, articulating firmly with the two innominate bones to form the bony pelvis.

sample a segment of a population chosen by the anthropologist to represent the population at large.

Sapir-Whorf hypothesis the theory first developed by Edward Sapir and then amplified by Benjamin Lee Whorf, maintaining that our vision of reality is conditioned and limited by the particular language that we speak. Carrying this further, Whorf asserts that contrasting world views actually result from contrasting language structures.

savanna in subtropical or tropical regions, a grassland area scattered with trees.

seasonal nomadism a settlement pattern in which the social group continually moves between certain locations within their territory, in order to collect seasonally available resources indigenous to these areas, which are the basis of the group's economy.

seasonal transhumance a pattern of habitation among certain pastoral peoples in which they move seasonally from fixed settlements to established areas in highland pastures and back again.

secularization the separation of religion and political power.

sedentism a settlement pattern in which the social group lives in permanent, year-round villages or towns.

segmentary lineages one of the mechanisms for tribal organization based on linear descent and kinship. The maximal, major, minor, and minimal lineages consolidate temporarily during periods of military conflict.

selection pressure for the adoption of characteristics most favorable to certain environmental and/or social situations.

semantic domains refers to categories of semantically related terms, as, for example, the color terms of a language.

semantics the study of the meaning of language.

sex ratio the ratio of male to female members in a population.

shaman a man or woman who acts as an intermediary between the gods and spirits and humanity; especially important in Eskimo, Amerindian, and other hunting and gathering societies, they exist worldwide.

signs the genetically determined sounds animals use to communicate danger, sexual arousal, hunger, and hostility. Some sign systems have evolved to a very complex state, but all are closed systems and limited when compared to human language.

slash-and-burn agriculture a technique in which natural vegetation is burned off, fields are used for a year or two, and then are allowed to lie fallow for a number of years to rebuild the forest cover and restore the fertility of the plot.

social control the formal and informal means by which a society enforces its norms of behavior and ensures that its members do not deviate too far from legitimate modes of behavior.

socialization (or **enculturation**) the process whereby a group, through implicit teaching and unconscious modeling, passes on its culture (skills, knowledge, values, attitudes, and behavior) to the next generation.

social organization the pattern of interaction between individuals or societies (groups of individuals).

social stratification the division of the members of a social group into different social statuses (or classes) based upon their wealth, political power, and economic specialization.

Solutrean a short-lived Upper Paleolithic cultural tradition limited to southwestern France and Spain. It dates from 21,000 to 17,000 B.P. and is distinguished by the laurel-leaf blade, eyed bone needle, and reindeer faunal remains.

sororal polygyny marriage of one man with two or more sisters.

sororate the custom whereby a man is entitled to marry any of his deceased wife's sisters, and her kin are obligated to provide him with another wife.

speciation the process by which the gene pool of a species splits permanently and irreversibly, producing "daughter" species separate from the "parent." The parent and daughter species can then follow different evolutionary paths; their gene pools are independent of each other and gene flow no longer occurs between them.

spheres of exchange refer to the considered application in many societies of different modes of exchange depending on the item being exchanged and its use. Although goods are organized into specific categories, occasions and strategies exist for *conversion,* or crossing between spheres.

stability a measure of the ease and rapidity with which a system returns to equilibrium after absorbing disturbances.

standard deviation a measure of the scatter or dispersion of individual values around the mean or average value of a distribution.

stasis a state of equilibrium, of stability. In evolution, it is a period during which little or no evolutionary change is occurring, and the species is occupying a stable adaptive plateau.

state a type of sociopolitical organization in which: (1) society is divided into sharply defined social classes instead of a hierarchical series of statuses; (2) political organization is based upon territorial residence rather than kinship; (3) a single individual and/or an elite group monopolize social power; and (4) political affairs are administered by a bureaucracy of officials.

stratified sample a segment of a population chosen by first dividing the population into categories and then selecting a random sample separately from each category; ensures the proportional representation of important subgroups that might otherwise be overlooked.

surround kill a group hunting method used by upper Paleolithic groups, in which a large herd of animals was stampeded into a box canyon, arroyo, or specially constructed corral, and then was surrounded by hunters and killed.

swidden agriculture See slash-and-burn agriculture.

symbols arbitrary, culturally determined, and abstract linguistic signs, the use of which distinguishes the human communication system of language; through their flexible manipulation totally new ideas can be expressed.

sympatric occupying overlapping geographic ranges.

syntax the study of the patterns formed by the combination of morphemes and words into phrases and sentences.

taphonomy derived from the Greek word *taphos,* meaning tomb; the study of "death assemblages," groups of fossils that have been buried together. The taphonomist attempts to reconstruct the processes that brought each fossil to its burial place.

Tarsiiformes an infraorder of the order Prosimii, whose only surviving member is the tarsier, a rat-size animal indigenous to Borneo and the Philippines; distinguished by enormously enlarged eyes and extremely elongated hind limbs.

tarsus the ankle; in man and other primates consists of seven tarsal bones.

technology the raw materials for tool manufacture, their techniques of manufacture, and the tools themselves used by a group.

temporal muscles muscles involved in mastication (chewing) that run from the side walls of the cranium to the mandible (lower jaw). In many primates, including some primitive hominids, they meet in the middle of the skull, forming a sagittal crest.

tenancy a system of exploitation in which, in exchange for a few acres of land, a tenant farmer is obligated to surrender a large portion of his harvest to the landowner. Forced to purchase all necessities at exorbitant prices or on credit, farmers are locked into perpetual debt bondage, thus providing a continual source of cheap labor.

Tenochtitlan a city-state that ruled

the valley of Mexico from 575 B.P. until the arrival of the Spanish; the center of the Aztec empire.

tension zone the zone created when population migrations from an optimal food resource area to an adjacent marginal resource area disrupt the ecological balance and produce pressures for more effective means of food production.

terracing a technique used when surface slopes made irrigation impractical. It involves building terraces and using rock fences to hold in the soil and water.

territorial pair a type of primate social organization in which a single male and a single female live together in a small territory that they defend against other pairs.

theocracy a state organization in which the ruling elite are members of the priesthood, and political power and government are inseparable from religion.

Theria the group of mammals including both marsupial (pouched) and placental mammals. Common in the late Cretaceous, early members were small, opossumlike omnivores.

Theropithecus a genus of open country baboons, members of the subfamily Cercopithecinae. The only living species, *T. gelada*, inhabits treeless uplands, where it spends most of its time foraging for grass stems and roots.

tool kit the assemblage of artifacts used to perform the various activities undertaken at a site.

totem from the Ojibwa Indian word *ototeman*, meaning "relative"; a natural object, animate being, or natural phenomenon that is emblematic of a clan or descent group. Group members conceive of themselves as descended from their totem and usually observe a taboo on killing or eating it. The totem serves to relate the group to the natural order and to concretize a clan's sense of collective identity and unity.

transporters proteins that carry nutrients from the site where they are taken into the body to the tissues where they are to be used.

tribe an egalitarian social group similar to the band in its informal leadership; it differs from the band in that mechanisms for pantribal solidarity exist, which integrate all the local tribal segments.

troop a social group among primates. Many primate species live in multimale troops that include several mature males, as well as females and immature animals.

tropical rain forest a vegetation zone, most characteristic between latitudes 5°N and 5°S, of continuously hot and humid climate with little seasonal variation. Most primary food sources are found within the continuously closed canopy formed by its large evergreen trees. Rain forest floras and faunas are typically rich in species diversity.

tropical savanna a vegetation zone flanking the tropical forests whose seasonal variations in rainfall affect the growth of tree and ground cover. For at least part of the year, sunlight reaches the ground, permitting the growth of a vigorous herbage. Tree growth is less vigorous than in the forest, and trees may be scattered or even absent.

tropical woodlands a vegetation zone flanking the tropical rain forest whose seasonal variations in rainfall restrict tree growth. Because most trees are deciduous, for at least part of the year the woodland floor is exposed to sunlight, permitting the growth of vigorous ground cover.

Tula a city-state that ruled the valley of Mexico from 1,150 to 750 B.P.; the center of the Toltec empire.

tundra extensive, nearly level treeless plains characteristic of arctic and subarctic regions.

Ubaid a Mesopotamian cultural stage dating from 6,000 to 5,500 B.P.; the earliest theocracies in Mesopotamia and the Near East appeared at this time.

ulna one of the two bones of the forearm.

unifacially worked a tool produced by the removal of flakes from one of its sides.

unilineal descent descent reckoned through one line only, either the maternal or the paternal.

unilineal evolutionism the nineteenth-century, classical theory maintaining that all human societies pass through certain set stages of cultural evolution.

Upper Paleolithic a cultural stage associated with the remains of modern man, which in Europe extended from about 40,000 to 10,000 B.P. It is characterized by the blade tradition, pressure flaking, specialized big-game hunting economies, cave art, and supraband social organization.

uxorilocal residence a residence pattern in which a newly married couple lives near or with the kinsmen of the wife; common in matrilineal societies.

vendetta an intersocietal conflict between members of a kin group or between families, with revenge as the principal motive.

vengeance an informal means of exerting social pressure through the infliction of violence (or some other injury) on a person or a group of persons in order to exact justice, avenge an injury, and/or uphold rights and obligations that have been compromised.

virilocal residence the establishment of residence by a newly married couple near or with the kinsmen of the husband; the couple becomes part of the husband's kin group and is subject to its authority.

warfare extended conflict between and within societies, engaged in according to specific rules. Reasons for war are frequently stated in ideological and moral terms and often concern the way of life and survival of the participants; war serves variously to balance populations and economic systems, resolve psychological frustrations and anxieties within a society or community, punish abuses of power, and exploit resources and people.

Würm glaciation a series of rapid glacial advances and retreats that began during the late Pleistocene, about 80,000 B.P., and continued until the Recent epoch, the end of glacial times.

ziggurat a stepped pyramid.
zygomatic arches the cheek bones.
zygote a fertilized egg; the single cell produced by the fusion of two cells—a female's ovum and a male's sperm. Also, by extension, the individual that develops from such a cell.

References

ABERLE, D. F., et al.
　The Incest Taboo and the Mating Patterns of Animals. *American Anthropologist* 65 (1963): 253–265.

ACHESON, J. M.
　Territories of the Lobster Men. *Natural History* 81 (1972): 60–69.

ADAMS, R. M.
　1972　The Mesopotamian Social Landscape: A View from the Frontier. Unpublished paper presented at the Cambridge Archeology Seminar Colloquium.

―――.
　1966　*The Evolution of Urban Society: Early Mespotamia and Prehispanic Mexico.* Chicago: Aldine.

ALLAND, A., JR.
　1973　*Human Diversity.* Garden City, N.Y.: Anchor Books.

―――, and MCCAY, B.
　1973　The Concept of Adaptation in Biological and Cultural Evolution. In *Handbook of Social and Cultural Anthropology,* ed. J. J. Honigmann. Chicago: Rand McNally.

AL-WAKIDI, M. I. U.
　1882　*Muhammed in Medina.* Translated and abbreviated by J. Wellhausen. Berlin: Reimer.

AMERICAN ANTHROPOLOGICAL ASSOCIATION
　Appendix A, American Anthropological Association, Principles of Professional Responsibility. *Newsletter of the American Anthropological Association*, special ed., 69th Annual Meeting (1970): 9–10.

ANTOUN, R. T.
　On the Significance of Names in an Arab Village. *Ethnology* 7 (1968): 158–170.

ARMILLAS, P.
　Gardens on Swamps. *Science* 174 (1971): 653–661.

ASWAD, B. C.
　1970　Social and Ecological Aspects in the Formation of Islam. In *Peoples and Cultures of the Middle East,* ed. L. Sweet. Vol. 1. Garden City, N.Y.: Natural History Press.

BAILEY, F. G.
　1969　*Stratagems and Spoils: A Social Anthropology of Politics.* New York: Schocken Books.

BALIKCI, A.
　1970　*The Netsilik Eskimo.* Garden City, N.Y.: Natural History Press.

BARNES, J. A.
　Social Networks. *An Addison-Wesley Module in Anthropology,* module 26 (1972): 1–29.

BARNET, R., and MÜLLER, R.
　Multinational Corporations I. *The New Yorker,* December 2, 1974, 52–128.

―――.
　Multinational Corporations II. *The New Yorker,* December 9, 1974, 100–159.

BARNOUW, V.
　1973　*Culture and Personality.* Rev. ed. Homewood, Ill.: Dorsey Press.

BARRY, H., III, CHILD, I. L., and BACON, M. K.
　Relation of Child Training to Subsistence Economy. *American Anthropologist* 61 (1959): 51–63.

BARTH, F.
　The Problem of Comparison. *Royal Anthropological Institute,* occasional paper no. 23 (1966): 22–33.

―――.
　1963　*The Role of the Entrepreneur in Social Change in Northern Norway.* Bergen: Norwegian Universities Press.

―――.
　Ecologic Relationships of Ethnic Groups in Swat, North Pakistan. *American Anthropologist* 58 (1956): 1079–1089.

―――.
　Father's Brother's Daughter Marriage in Kurdistan. *Southwestern Journal of Anthropology* 10 (1954): 164–171.

―――, ed.
　1969　*Ethnic Groups and Boundaries: The Social Organization of Cultural Difference.* Boston: Little, Brown.

BARTON, R. F.
　Ifugao Law. *University of California Publications in American Archaeology and Ethnology* 15 (1919): 1–186.

BASSO, K. H.
　Semantic Aspects of Linguistic Acculturation. *American Anthropologist* 69 (1967): 471–477.

BATES, D.
　Normative and Alternative Systems of Marriage Among the Yörük of Southeastern Turkey. *Anthropological Quarterly* 47 (1974): 270–287.

BAUR, S.
　Kneedeep in the Cosmic Overwhelm with Carl Sagen. *New York Magazine,* September 1, 1975, 26–32.

BEALS, R.
　1969　*Politics of Social Research.* Chicago: Aldine.

BEALS, R.
Comments. *Current Anthropology* 9 (1968): 407–408.
BEATTIE, J.
1964 *Other Cultures.* New York: The Free Press.
BEKKER, K.
Historical Patterns of Culture Contact in Southern Asia. *Far Eastern Quarterly* 11 (1951): 3–15.
BELLAH, R. N.
Religious Evolution. *American Sociological Review* 29 (1964): 358–374.
BELO, J.
A Study of a Balinese Family. *American Anthropologist* 38 (1936): 12–31.
BENEDICT, R.
1959 *Patterns of Culture.* New York: New American Library (orig. 1934).
BERNARD, H. R., and SIBLEY, W. E.
1975 *Anthropology and Jobs: A Guide for Undergraduates.* Washington, D.C.: American Anthropological Association.
BERREMAN, G. D.
1973 The Social Responsibility of the Anthropologist. In *To See Ourselves: Anthropology and Modern Social Issues,* ed. T. Weaver. Glenview, Ill.: Scott, Foresman.
———.
Pahari Polyandry. *American Anthropologist* 64 (1962): 60–75.
BERTHOUD, G.
From Peasantry to Capitalism: The Meaning of Ownership in the Swiss Alps. *Anthropological Quarterly* 45 (1972): 177–195.
BICCHIERI, M.
1972 *Hunters and Gatherers Today.* New York: Holt, Rinehart and Winston.
BINFORD, L. R.
1968 Post-Pleistocene Adaptations. In *New Perspectives in Archeology,* eds. S. R. Binford and L. R. Binford. Chicago: Aldine.

BIRDSELL, J. B.
Some Environmental and Cultural Factors Influencing the Structuring of Australian Aboriginal Populations. *American Naturalist* 87: 171–207.
BIRDWHISTELL, R. L.
1960 Kinesics and Communication. In *Explorations in Communication,* eds. E. Carpenter and M. McLuhan. Boston: Beacon Press.
BLOOMFIELD, L.
1965 *Language.* Edited by H. Hoijer. New York: Holt, Rinehart and Winston.
BOAS, F.
1966 *The Limitations of the Comparative Method of Anthropology.* New York: The Free Press (orig. 1896).
———.
1964 On Grammatical Categories. In *Language in Culture and Society,* ed. D. Hymes. New York: Harper & Row.
———.
1940 *Race, Language and Culture.* New York: Macmillan.
BOHANNAN, P.
1965 The Tiv of Nigeria. In *Peoples of Africa,* ed. J. L. Gibbs, Jr. New York: Holt, Rinehart and Winston.
———.
Africa's Land. *The Centennial Review* 4 (1960): 439–449.
———.
The Impact of Money on an African Subsistence Economy. *Journal of Economic History* 19 (1959): 491–503.
BOISSEVAIN, J.
The Place of Non-Groups in the Social Sciences. *Man,* new series 3 (1968): 542–553.
BORDES, F.
1968 *The Old Stone Age.* New York: McGraw-Hill.
BOSERUP, E.
1965 *The Conditions of Agricultural Growth.* Chicago: Aldine.

BOTT, E.
1957 *Family and Social Networks.* London: Tavistock.
BOWEN, E. S.
1964 *Return to Laughter: An Anthropological Novel.* Garden City, N.Y.: Doubleday/American Museum of Natural History.
BOWLBY, J.
1969 *Attachment.* Attachment and Loss Series, vol. 1. New York: Basic Books.
BRAESTRUP, P.
Researchers Aid Thai Rebel Fight. *The New York Times,* March 20, 1967.
BRAIDWOOD, R. J.
1967 *Prehistoric Men.* 7th ed. Glenview, Ill.: Scott, Foresman.
BRIUER, F. L.
1970 Causes of Late Pleistocene Megafaunal Extinction: Some Hypotheses and Tests. Master's thesis, University of California at Los Angeles.
BROOM, L., et al.
Acculturation: An Exploratory Formulation. *American Anthropologist* 56 (1954): 973–1000.
BRUNER, E.
Two Processes of Change in Mandan-Hidatsa Kinship Terminology. *American Anthropologist* 57 (1955): 840–849.
BUCHLER, I., and SELBY, H. A.
1968 *Kinship and Social Organization: An Introduction to Theory and Method.* New York: Macmillan.
BUCHLER, M., and KOZELKA, D.
Mathematical Thinking in Cultural Anthropology. Unpublished paper, n.d.
BUNZEL, R.
Zuni Katcinas. *47th Annual Report of the Bureau of American Ethnology* (1932): 837–1086.
BURLING, R.
1970 *Man's Many Voices: Language in Its Cultural Context.*

New York: Holt, Rinehart and Winston.

BUTZER, K. W.
1971 *Environment and Archeology: An Ecological Approach to Prehistory.* 2d ed. Chicago: Aldine.

CANCIAN, F.
1965 *Economics and Prestige in a Maya Community: The Religious Cargo System in Zinacantan.* Stanford, Calif.: Stanford University Press.

CARNEIRO, R. L.
A Theory of the Origin of the State. *Science* 169 (1970): 733–738.

CARRINGTON, J. F.
The Talking Drums of Africa. *Scientific American* 255 (1971): 90–94.

———.
1949 *Talking Drums of Africa.* London: Carey Kingsgate Press.

CAVALLI-SFORZA, L. L., and EDWARDS, A. W. F.
1963 Analysis of Human Evolution. In *Genetics Today,* ed. S. J. Geertz. Vol. 3. Elmsford, N.Y.: Pergamon Press.

CHAGNON, N. A.
1974 *Studying the Yanomamö.* New York: Holt, Rinehart and Winston.

———.
1973 The Culture-Ecology of Shifting (Pioneering) Cultivation Among Yanomamö Indians. In *Peoples and Cultures and Nature of South America,* ed. D. Gross. Garden City, N.Y.: Natural History Press.

———.
1968 *Yanomamö: The Fierce People.* New York: Holt, Rinehart and Winston.

———.
1967 The Effects of War on Social Structure. In *War: The Anthropology of Armed Conflict and Aggression,* eds. M. Fried, M. Harris, and R. Murphy. Garden City, N.Y.: Natural History Press.

———.
1967 Yanomamö Social Organization and Warfare. In *War: The Anthropology of Armed Conflict and Aggression,* eds. M. Fried, M. Harris, and R. Murphy. Garden City, N.Y.: Natural History Press.

CHANCE, M. R. A., and JOLLY, C.
1970 *Social Groups of Monkeys, Apes, and Men.* London: Jonathan Cape.

CHANG, K. C.
The Beginnings of Agriculture in the Far East. *Antiquity* 44 (1970): 175–185.

CHILDE, V. G.
1952 *Man Makes Himself.* New York: New American Library.

———.
1952 *New Light on the Most Ancient East.* London: Routledge & Kegan Paul.

CHOMSKY, N.
1965 *Aspects of the Theory of Syntax.* Cambridge, Mass.: M.I.T. Press.

———.
1957 *Syntactic Structures.* The Hague: Mouton.

COE, M. D.
1962 *Mexico.* Mexico City: Ediciones Lara.

COHEN, Y.
1974 *Man in Adaptation: The Cultural Present.* 2d ed. Chicago: Aldine.

COLE, M., HAY, J., GLICK, J. and HARP, D. W.
1971 *The Cultural Context of Learning and Thinking: An Exploration in Experimental Anthropology.* New York: Basic Books.

COLIER, B., COX, G., JOHNSON, A., and MILLER, P.
1973 *Dynamic Ecology.* Englewood Cliffs, N.J.: Prentice-Hall.

COLLIER, J., JR.
1967 *Visual Anthropology: Photography as a Research Method.* New York: Holt, Rinehart and Winston.

COLLINS, W. T.
An Analysis of the Memphis Garbage Strike of 1968. *Public Affairs Forum* (Memphis State University) 3 (1974): 1–6.

COLSON, E.
1973 Tranquility for the Decision-Maker. In *Cultural Illness and Health: Essays in Human Adaptation,* eds. L. Nader and T. W. Maretski. Washington, D.C.: American Anthropological Association.

———.
1967 The Intensive Study of Small Sample Communities. In *The Craft of Social Anthropology,* ed. A. L. Epstein. London: Tavistock.

———.
Ancestral Spirits and Social Structure Among the Plateau Tonga. *International Archives of Ethnography,* pt. 1, 47 (1954): 21–68.

———.
Social Control and Vengeance in Plateau Tonga Society. *Africa* 23 (1953): 199–211.

CONKLIN, H. C.
Hanunóo Color Categories. *Southwestern Journal of Anthropology* 11 (1955): 339–344.

———.
An Ethnoecological Approach to Shifting Cultivation. *Transactions of the New York Academy of Sciences,* 2d. series, 17 (1954): 133–142.

COOMBS, G., and PLOG, F.
1974 Chumash Baptism: An Ecological Perspective. In *Antap: California Indian Political and Economic Organization,* eds. L. Bean and T. King. Ramona, Calif.: Ballena Press.

COWAN, G. M.
Mazateco Whistle Speech. *Language* 24 (1948): 280–286.

CULBERT, T. P.
1974 *The Lost Civilization: The Story of the Classic Maya*. New York: Harper & Row.

DALTON, G.
Primitive Money. *American Anthropologist* 67 (1965): 44–65.

———.
Traditional Production in Primitive African Economies. *The Quarterly Journal of Economics* 76 (1962): 360–378.

D'ANDRADE, R. G.
1973 Cultural Constructions of Reality. In *Cultural Illness and Health: Essays in Human Adaptation*, eds. L. Nader and T. W. Maretski. Washington, D.C.: American Anthropological Association.

D'AQUILI, E.
1972 *The Biopsychological Determinants of Culture*. McCaleb Module in Anthropology. Reading, Mass.: Addison-Wesley.

DAVID, N.
1973 On Upper Paleolithic Society, Ecology and Technological Change: The Noaillian Case. In *The Explanation of Culture Change: Models in Prehistory*, ed. C. Renfrew. London: Duckworth.

DEUTSCH, M.
Happenings on the Way Back to the Forum. *Harvard Educational Review* 39 (1969): 523–557.

DINEEN, F. P.
1967 *An Introduction to General Linguistics*. New York: Holt, Rinehart and Winston.

DOSIER, E. P.
1970 *The Pueblo Indians of North America*. New York: Holt, Rinehart and Winston.

DOUGLAS, M.
1962 The Lele—Resistance to Change. In *Economic Anthropology: Readings in Theory and Analysis*, eds. E. E. LeClair, Jr. and H. K. Schneider. New York: Holt, Rinehart and Winston.

DOWNS, J. F.
The Social Consequences of a Dry Well. *American Anthropologist* 67 (1965): 1387–1417.

———, and BLEIBTREU, H. K.
1972 *Human Variation*. Beverly Hills, Calif.: Glencoe Press.

DUBOIS, C.
1944 *The People of Alor: A Social Psychological Study of an East Indian Island*. Minneapolis: University of Minnesota Press.

DURKHEIM, E.
1961 *The Elementary Forms of the Religious Life*. New York: Collier (orig. 1912).

———, and MAUSS, M.
1963 *Primitive Classification*. Chicago: University of Chicago Press.

DYSON-HUDSON, N.
1966 *Karimojong Politics*. New York: Oxford University Press.

———.
The Karimojong Age System. *Ethnology* 2 (1963): 353–401.

DYSON-HUDSON, R.
1972 Pastoralism: Self Image and Behavioral Reality. In *Perspectives on Nomadism*, eds. W. G. Lions and N. Dyson-Hudson. Long Island City, N.Y.: E. J. Brill.

———, and DYSON-HUDSON, N.
Subsistence Herding in Uganda. *Scientific American* 220 (1969): 76–89.

EDGERTON, R. B.
1971 *The Individual in Cultural Adaptation: A Study of Four East African Peoples*. Berkeley and Los Angeles: University of California Press.

EHRLICH, P., and EHRLICH, A. H.
1972 *Population, Resources, Environment*. San Francisco: W. H. Freeman.

EISENSTADT, S. N.
African Age Groups. *Africa* 5 (1954): 102.

EMBER, M., and EMBER, C. R.
The Conditions Favoring Matrilocal Versus Patrilocal Residence. *American Anthropologist* 73 (1971): 571–594.

EPSTEIN, A. L.
1967 The Case Method in the Field of Law. In *The Craft of Social Anthropology*, ed. A. L. Epstein. London: Tavistock.

———.
The Network and Urban Social Organization. *Human Problems in British Central Africa* 29 (1961): 28–62.

———.
Linguistic Innovation on the Copperbelt, Northern Rhodesia. *Southwestern Journal of Anthropology* 15 (1959): 235–253.

EPSTEIN, S.
1967 Productive Efficiency and Customary Systems of Rewards in Rural South India. In *Themes in Economic Anthropology*, ed. R. Firth. London: Tavistock.

ERVIN-TRIPP, S.
Interaction of Language, Topic and Listener. *American Anthropologist* 66 (1964): 86–102.

EVANS-PRITCHARD, E. E.
1940 *The Nuer: A Description of the Modes of Livelihood and Political Institutions of a Nilotic People*. Oxford: Clarendon Press.

EWERS, J. C.
1958 *The Blackfeet*. Norman: University of Oklahoma Press.

FARB, P.
1974 *Word Play: What Happens When People Talk*. New York: Alfred A. Knopf.

FARRAG, A.
Social Control Amongst the Mzabite Women of Beni-Isguen. *Middle Eastern Studies* 7 (1971): 317–327.

FARSOUN, S.
1970 Family Structure and Society in Modern Lebanon. In *Peo-

ples and Cultures of the Middle East, ed. L. Sweet. Vol. 2. Garden City, N.Y.: Natural History Press.

FEIT, H. A.
1973 The Ethno-Ecology of the Waswanipi Cree; or How Hunters Can Manage Their Resources. In *Cultural Ecology: Readings on the Canadian Native Peoples,* ed. B. Cox. Toronto: McClelland & Stewart.

FIRTH, R.
1957 *We, The Tikopia: A Sociological Study of Kinship in Primitive Polynesia.* Boston: Beacon Press.

———
1951 *Elements of Social Organization.* London: Watts.

FISCHER, J. L.
Social Influences on the Choice of a Linguistic Variant. *Word* 14 (1958): 47–56.

FLANNERY, K. V.
The Origins of Agriculture. *Annual Review of Anthropology* 2 (1973): 271–310.

———.
The Cultural Evolution of Civilizations. *Annual Review of Ecology and Systematics* 3 (1972): 399–426.

———
1972 The Origins of the Village as a Settlement Type in Mesoamerica and the Near East. In *Man, Settlement and Urbanism,* eds. P. J. Ucko, R. Tringham, and G. W. Dimbleby. Cambridge, Mass.: Schenckman.

———.
1969 The Ecology of Early Food Production in Mesopotamia. In *Environment and Cultural Behavior,* ed. A. P. Vayda. Garden City, N.Y.: Natural History Press.

———.
1969 Origins and Ecological Effects of Early Domestication in Iran and the Near East. In *The Domestication and Exploitation of Plants and Animals,* eds. J. Ucko and G. W. Dimbleby. Chicago: Aldine.

———.
1968 Archeological Systems Theory and Early Mesoamerica. In *Anthropological Archeology in the Americas,* ed. B. J. Meggers. Washington, D.C.: Anthropological Society of Washington.

———.
Ecology of Early Food Production in Mesopotamia. *Science* 147 (1965): 1247–1256.

———, KIRKBY, A. V. T., KIRKBY, M. J., and WILLIAMS, A., JR.
Farming Systems and Political Growth in Ancient Oaxaca. *Science* 158 (1967): 445–454.

FORD, R. I.
1972 An Ecological Perspective on the Eastern Pueblos. In *New Perspectives on the Pueblos,* ed. A. Ortiz. Albuquerque: University of New Mexico Press.

FORDE, D.
1964 *Yako Studies.* London: Oxford University Press for International African Institute.

FOSTER, B.
Ethnicity and Commerce. *American Ethnologist* 1 (1974): 437–448.

FOSTER, M. L.
1970 A Theory of the First Language. Unpublished paper, Hayward State University.

FOULKS, W.
1972 *The Arctic Hysterias of the North Alaskan Eskimo.* Washington, D.C., American Anthropological Association.

FOX, R.
1967 *Kinship and Marriage: An Anthropological Perspective.* Baltimore, Md. Penguin Books.

FRAZER, J. G.
1900 *The Golden Bough: A Study of Magic and Religion.* 3d ed. 2 vols. London: Macmillan.

FREEMAN, J. D.
On the Concept of the Kindred. *Journal of the Royal Anthropological Institute* 91 (1961): 192–220.

FREEMAN, M. M. R.
A Social and Ecological Analysis of Systematic Female Infanticide Among the Netsilik Eskimo. *American Anthropologist* 73 (1971): 1011–1019.

FREILICH, M.
1971 *Meaning of Culture: A Reader in Cultural Anthropology.* Lexington, Ma.: Xerox College.

———, ed.
1970 *Marginal Natives: Anthropologists at Work.* New York: Harper & Row.

FRIED, M. H.
1967 *The Evolution of Political Society: An Essay in Political Anthropology.* New York: Random House.

FRIEDLAND, W. H., and NELKIN, D.
1971 *Migrant: Agricultural Workers in America's Northeast.* New York: Holt, Rinehart and Winston.

FRISCH, J. E.
1968 Individual Behavior and Intertroop Variability in Japanese Macaques. In *Primates: Studies in Adaptation and Variability,* ed. P. C. Jay. New York: Holt, Rinehart and Winston.

GARDNER, R., and GARDNER, B.
Teaching Sign Language to a Chimpanzee. *Science* 165 (1969): 664–672.

GEERTZ, C.
1969 Two Types of Ecosystems. In *Environment and Cultural Behavior,* ed. A. P. Vayda. Garden City, N.Y.: Natural History Press.

———
1966 Religion as a Cultural System. In *Anthropological Approaches to the Study of Religion,* ed. M. Banton. New York: Praeger.

GEERTZ, C.
- 1963 *Agricultural Involution.* Berkeley and Los Angeles: University of California Press.
- 1963 *Peddlers and Princes.* Chicago: University of Chicago Press.
- 1960 *The Religion of Java.* Glencoe, Ill.: The Free Press.

GESCHWIND, N.
- 1974 *Selected Papers on Language and the Brain.* Boston, Mass.: Reidel.
- Language and the Brain. *Scientific American* 226 (1972): 76–83.

GIBBS, J. L., JR.
- 1965 The Kpelle of Liberia. In *Peoples of Africa*, ed. J. L. Gibbs, Jr. New York: Holt, Rinehart and Winston.
- The Kpelle Moot. *Africa* 33 (1963): 1–10.
- ———, ed.
- 1965 *Peoples of Africa.* New York: Holt, Rinehart and Winston.

GLADWIN, T., and SARASON, S.
- 1953 *Truk: Man in Paradise.* New York: Johnson Reprint.

GLUCKMAN, M.
- 1965 *Politics, Law and Ritual in Tribal Society.* Chicago: Aldine.
- Gossip and Scandal. *Current Anthropology* 4 (1963): 307–315.
- 1963 *The Judicial Process Among the Barotse of Northern Rhodesia.* Manchester, Eng.: Manchester University Press.

GOLDSCHMIDT, W.
- 1971 *Exploring the Ways of Mankind.* New York: Holt, Rinehart and Winston.
- 1947 *As You Saw.* New York: Harcourt, Brace.

GOODALL, J. VAN L.
- 1971 *In the Shadow of Man.* Boston: Houghton Mifflin.

GOODENOUGH, W. H.
- A Problem in Malayo-Polynesian Social Organization. *American Anthropologist* 57 (1955): 71–83.

GORER, G.
- Themes in Japanese Culture. *Transactions of the New York Academy of Sciences*, 2d series, 5 (1943): 106–124.
- ———, and RICKMAN, J.
- 1950 *The People of Great Russia: A Psychological Study.* New York: Chanticleer.

GOSSEN, G. H.
- 1972 Temporal and Spatial Equivalents in Chamula Ritual Symbolism. In *Reader in Comparative Religion: An Anthropological Approach*, eds. W. A. Lessa and E. S. Vogt. New York: Harper & Row.

GOUGH, E. K.
- New Proposals for Anthropologists. *Current Anthropology* 9 (1968): 403–407.
- 1968 World Revolution and the Science of Man. In *The Dissenting Academy*, ed. T. Roszak. New York: Random House.
- The Nayars and the Definition of Marriage. *Journal of the Royal Anthropological Institute* 89 (1959): 23–34.

GOULDNER, A. W.
- Disorder and Social Theory. Review of *American Sociology*, ed. T. Parsons. *Science* 162 (1968): 247–249.

GRAVES, T. D.
- The Personal Adjustment of Navajo Indian Migrants to Denver, Colorado. *American Anthropologist* 72 (1970): 35–54.

GREENBERG, J. H.
- 1957 *Essays in Linguistics.* Chicago: University of Chicago Press.

GROSS, D. R.
- Protein Capture and Cultural Development in the Amazon Basin. *American Anthropologist* 77 (1975): 526–549.
- ———, and UNDERWOOD, B.
- Technological Change and Caloric Costs: Sisal Agriculture in Northeastern Brazil. *American Anthropologist* 73 (1971): 725–740.

GULLIVER, P. H.
- 1969 Dispute Settlement Without Courts: The Ndendeuli of Southern Tanzania. In *Law in Culture and Society*, ed. L. Nader. Chicago: Aldine.
- 1955 *Family Herds: A Study of Two Pastoral Tribes in East Africa, the Jie and Turkana.* Westport, Conn.: Negro Universities Press.

HALL, E. T.
- 1966 *The Hidden Dimension.* New York: Doubleday.

HAMBLIN, D. H., and EDITORS OF TIME-LIFE BOOKS.
- 1973 *The First Cities.* New York: Time-Life.

HARRIS, M.
- 1975 *Culture, People, Nature: An Introduction to General Anthropology.* 2d ed. New York: Crowell.
- 1968 *The Rise of Anthropological Theory: A History of Theories of Culture.* New York: Crowell.
- The Cultural Ecology of India's Sacred Cattle. *Current Anthropology* 7 (1966): 51–66.

HATFIELD, C. R., JR.
- Fieldwork: Toward a Model of Mutual Exploitation. *American Quarterly* 46 (1973): 15–29.

HAYES, K. J., and HAYES, C.
- Picture Perception in a Home-Raised Chimpanzee.

Journal of Comparative and Physiological Psychology 46 (1953): 470–474.

HILL, J. N.
1968 Broken K. Pueblo: Patterns of Form and Function. In *New Perspectives in Archaeology,* eds. S. R. Binford and L. R. Binford. Chicago: Aldine.

———. A Prehistoric Community in Eastern Arizona. *Southwestern Journal of Anthropology* 22 (1966): 9–30.

HOCKETT, C. F.
Implications of Bloomfield's Algonquian Studies. *Language* 24 (1948): 117–131.

———, and ASCHER, R.
The Human Revolution. *Current Anthropology* 5 (1964): 135–168.

HOEBEL, E. A.
1960 *The Cheyennes: Indians of the Great Plains.* New York: Holt, Rinehart and Winston.

———.
1954 *The Law of Primitive Man.* Cambridge, Mass.: Harvard University Press.

———.
The Political Organization and Law-Ways of the Comanche Indians. *Memoirs of the American Anthropological Association,* no. 54 (1940).

HOFFMAN, H.
N-Cubes in Anthropological Theory. Unpublished paper, State University of New York, n.d.

———.
1971 Markov Chains in Ethiopia. In *Explorations in Mathematical Anthropology,* ed. P. Kay. Cambridge, Mass.: M.I.T. Press.

HOIJER, H.
1954 The Sapir-Whorf Hypothesis. In *Language in Culture,* ed. H. Hoijer. No. 79. Washington, D.C.: American Anthropological Association.

HOLE, F., FLANNERY, K. V., and NEELY, J. A.
1969 *The Prehistory and Human Ecology of the Deh Luran Plain.* Memoir no. 1. Ann Arbor: University of Michigan, Museum of Anthropology.

HOLLING, C. S.
Resilience and Stability of Ecological Systems. *Annual Review of Ecology and Systematics* 4 (1973): 1–23.

———, and GOLDBERG, M. A.
Ecology and Planning. *Journal of the American Institute of Planners* 37 (1971): 221–230.

HOLLOWAY, R. L.
1972 Australopithecine Endocasts, Brain Evolution in the Hominoidea, and a Model of Hominid Evolution. In *The Functional and Evolutionary Biology of Primates,* ed. R. Tuttle. Chicago: Aldine.

HOLMBERG, A.
1969 *Nomads of the Long Bow: The Siriono of Eastern Bolivia.* Garden City, N.Y.: Natural History Press.

HOROWITZ, I. L.
The Life and Death of Project Camelot. *Trans-action* (December 1965).

HOROWITZ, M.
1971 A Decision Model of Conjugal Patterns in Martinique. In *Peoples and Cultures of the Caribbean,* ed. M. Horowitz. Garden City, N.Y.: Natural History Press.

HOWELL, F. C., and CLARK, J. D.
Acheulian Hunter-Gatherers of Sub-Saharan Africa. *Viking Fund Publications in Anthropology,* no. 36 (1963).

HYMES, D.
1972 Models of the Interaction of Language and Social Life. In *Directions in Sociolinguistics,* eds. J. J. Gumperz and D. Hymes. New York: Holt, Rinehart and Winston.

IRONS, W.
1975 *The Yomut Turkmen: A Study of Social Organization Among a Central Asian Turcicspeaking Population.* Anthropological Papers, no. 58. Ann Arbor: University of Michigan, Museum of Anthropology.

IRWIN-WILLIAMS, C.
Archaeological Evidence on Early Man in Mexico. *Contributions in Anthropology* (Eastern New Mexico University) 1 (1968): 39–41.

ISAAC, G. L.
1972 Chronology and the Tempo of Cultural Change During the Pleistocene. In *Calibration of Hominid Evolution,* eds. W. W. Bishop, J. A. Miller, and S. Cole. Toronto: University of Toronto/Scottish Academic Press.

JAMES, P.
1966 *The Geography of Man.* 3d ed. Waltham, Mass.: Blaisdell.

JANSON, H. W.
1969 *History of Art.* Englewood Cliffs, N.J.: Prentice-Hall, and New York: Abrams.

JENNESS, D.
1922 *Life of the Copper Eskimos.* Report of the Canadian Arctic Expedition, 1913–1918, vol. 12.

JENSEN, A.
How Much Can We Boost I.Q. and Scholastic Achievement? *Harvard Educational Review* 39 (1969): 1–123.

JONES, D. J.
Culture Fatigue: The Results of Role-Playing in Anthropological Research. *American Quarterly* 46 (1973): 30–37.

KARDINER, A., ed.
1939 *The Individual and His Society.* New York: Columbia University Press.

KARSTEN, R.
1923 *Blood Revenge, War, and Victory Feasts Among the*

Jibaro Indians of Eastern Ecuador. Bureau of American Ethnology, bulletin 79. Washington, D.C.: Smithsonian Institution.

KATZ, S. H., HEDIGER, M. L., and VALLEROY, L. A.
Traditional Maize Processing in the New World. *Science* 17 (1974): 765–773.

KAY, P., ed.
1971 *Explorations in Mathematical Anthropology.* Cambridge, Mass.: M.I.T. Press.

KEMP, W. B.
The Flow of Energy in a Hunting Society. *Scientific American* 225 (1971): 104–115.

KLUCKHOHN, C.
1949 *Mirror for Man.* New York: McGraw-Hill.

———, and MURRAY, H. A.
1953 Personality Formation: The Determinants. In *Personality in Nature, Society, and Culture,* eds. C. Kluckhohn and H. A. Murray. Rev. ed. New York: Alfred A. Knopf.

KLUCKHOHN, F., and STRODTBECK, F. L.
1961 *Variations in Value Orientations.* Evanston, Ill.: Row, Peterson.

KORTÉ, C., and MILGRAM, S.
Acquaintance Networks Between Racial Groups: Application of the Small World Method. *Journal of Personality and Social Psychology* 15 (1970): 101–108.

KRETCHMER, N.
Lactose and Lactase. *Scientific American* 227 (1972): 70–78.

KROEBER, A. L.
1948 *Anthropology.* Rev. ed. New York: Harcourt, Brace and World.

———.
Classificatory Systems of Relationship. *Journal of the Royal Anthropological Institute of Great Britain and Ireland* 39 (1909): 77–84.

———, and KLUCKHOHN, C.
1952 *Culture: A Critical Review of Concepts and Definitions.* New York: Alfred A. Knopf.

KRUGER, L.
1966 Specialized Features of the Cetacean Brain. In *Whales, Dolphins, and Porpoises,* ed. K. S. Norris. Berkeley and Los Angeles: University of California Press.

KUPER, H.
1965 The Swazi of Swaziland. In *Peoples of Africa,* ed. J. L. Gibbs, Jr. New York: Holt, Rinehart and Winston.

———.
1963 *The Swazi: A South African Kingdom.* New York: Holt, Rinehart and Winston.

LA BARRE, W.
1964 Paralinguistics, Kinesics, and Cultural Anthropology. In *Approaches to Semiotics.* Transactions of the Indiana University Conference on Paralinguistics and Kinesics, eds. T. A. Sebeok, A. S. Hayes, and M. C. Bateson. The Hague: Mouton.

———.
Some Observations on Character Structure in the Orient: The Japanese. *Psychiatry* 8 (1945): 326–342.

LABOV, W.
1972 *Sociolinguistic Patterns.* Philadelphia: University of Pennsylvania Press.

———.
Phonological Correlates of Social Stratification. *American Anthropologist,* special issue, 66, part 2 (1964): 164–176.

LANHAM, B.
1956 Aspects of Child Care in Japan: A Preliminary Report. In *Personal Character and Cultural Milieu,* ed. D. Haring. Syracuse, N.Y.: Syracuse University Press.

LANNING, E. P.
1967 *Peru Before the Incas.* Englewood Cliffs, N.J.: Prentice-Hall.

LASWELL, H.
1936 *Politics: Who Gets What, When, and How.* New York: McGraw-Hill.

LEACH, E. R.
1970 *Claude Lévi-Strauss.* New York: Viking.

———.
1961 *Pul Eliya: A Village in Ceylon.* Cambridge: Cambridge University Press.

———.
1954 *Political Systems of Highland Burma.* New York: Humanities Press.

LEAF, M. J.
1972 *Information and Behavior in a Sikh Village: Social Organization Reconsidered.* Berkeley and Los Angeles: University of California Press.

LEE, R. B.
1972 The !Kung Bushmen of Botswana. In *Hunters and Gatherers Today,* ed. M. Bicchieri. New York: Holt, Rinehart and Winston.

———.
1972 Population Growth and the Beginnings of Sedentary Life Among the !Kung Bushmen. In *Population Growth: Anthropological Implications,* ed. B. Spooner. Cambridge, Mass.: M.I.T. Press.

———.
1969 !Kung Bushmen Subsistence: An Input-Output Analysis. In *Environment and Cultural Behavior,* ed. A. P. Vayda. Garden City, N.Y.: Natural History Press.

———.
1968 What Hunters Do for a Living, or, How to Make Out on Scarce Resources. In *Man the Hunter,* eds. R. B. Lee and I. DeVore. Chicago: Aldine.

———, and DEVORE, I., eds.
1968 *Man the Hunter.* Chicago: Aldine.

LEES, S. H.
Oaxaca's Spiraling Race for

Water. *Natural History* 84 (1975): 30–39.

———. Hydraulic Development as a Process of Response. *Human Ecology* 2 (1974): 159–175.

———. The State's Use of Irrigation in Changing Peasant Society. *Anthropological Papers of the University of Arizona*, no. 25 (1974).

——— 1973 Sociopolitical Aspects of Canal Irrigation in the Valley of Oaxaca. Memoir no. 6. Ann Arbor: University of Michigan, Museum of Anthropology.

———, and BATES, D. G. The Origins of Specialized Nomadic Pastoralism: A Systemic Model. *American Antiquity* 39 (1974): 187–193.

LEHMANN, E. J. Keeping Current: The View from 1703. *Newsletter of the American Anthropological Association* 13 (1972): 8–9.

LEONE, M. P. Neolithic Economic Autonomy and Social Distance. *Science* 162 (1968): 1150–1151.

LEROI-GOURHAN, A. The Evolution of Paleolithic Art. *Scientific American* 218 (1968): 59–70.

LESSA, W. A., and VOGT, E. S., eds.
1972 *Reader in Comparative Religion: An Anthropological Approach.* New York: Harper & Row.

LEVINE, L., and CROCKETT, H. J., JR. Speech Variation in a Piedmont Community: Postvocalic r. *International Journal of American Linguistics: Explorations in Sociolinguistics* 33 (1967): 76–98.

LEVINE, R. A.
1973 *Culture, Behavior and Personality.* Chicago: Aldine.

———, and LEVINE, B.
1966 Nysansongo: A Gusii Community in Kenya. New York: Wiley.

——— 1963 Culture and Personality Development in a Gusii Community. In *Child Rearing in Six Societies,* ed. B. B. Whiting. New York: Wiley.

LÉVI-STRAUSS, C.
1963 *Structural Anthropology.* New York: Basic Books.

———. The Structural Study of Myth. *Journal of American Folklore* 67 (1955): 428–444.

———. The Social Use of Kinship Terms Among Brazilian Indians. *American Anthropologist* 45 (1943): 398–409.

LEWIS, O.
1961 *The Children of Sánchez.* New York: Random House.

——— 1960 *Tepoztlán, Village in Mexico.* New York: Holt, Rinehart and Winston.

——— 1959 *Five Families.* New York: Basic Books.

——— 1951 *Life in a Mexican Village.* Urbana: University of Illinois Press.

LILLY, J. C.
1967 *The Mind of the Dolphin.* New York: Avon.

LIVINGSTONE, F. B.
1968 The Effects of Warfare on the Biology of the Human Species. In *War: The Anthropology of Armed Conflict and Aggression,* eds. M. Fried, M. Harris, and R. Murphy. Garden City, N.Y.: Natural History Press.

———. Anthropological Implications of Sickle Cell Gene Distribution in West Africa. *American Anthropologist* 60 (1958): 533–562.

LLOYD, P. C.
1965 The Yoruba of Nigeria. In *Peoples of Africa,* ed. J. L. Gibbs, Jr. New York: Holt, Rinehart and Winston.

LONGACRE, R. E., and MILLON, R. Proto-Mixtecan and Proto-Amuzgo-Mixtecan Vocabularies. *Antropoligical Linguistics* (April 1961): 1–44.

LOWIE, R. H.
1954 *Indians of the Plains.* New York: McGraw-Hill.

MCLUHAN, M.
1964 *Understanding Media: The Extensions of Man.* New York: McGraw-Hill.

MCMANAMON, F.
1974 Analyzing Post-Pleistocene Adaptations. Unpublished paper, State University of New York at Binghamton.

MACNEISH, R. S.
1973 Early Man in the Andes. In *Early Man in America,* ed. R. S. MacNeish. San Francisco: W. H. Freeman.

———. Ancient Mesoamerican Civilization. *Science* 143 (1964): 531–537.

MAIER, R. A., and MAIER, B. M.
1970 *Comparative Animal Behavior.* Belmont, Calif.: Brooks/Cole.

MALINOWSKI, B.
1961 *Argonauts of the Western Pacific.* New York: Dutton (orig. 1922).

——— 1954 *Magic, Science and Religion and Other Essays.* New York: Anchor Books.

——— 1938 *Methods of Study of Culture Contact.* Memorandum 15, International African Institute. London: Oxford University Press.

——— 1931 Culture. In *Encyclopedia of the Social Sciences.* Vol. 4. New York: Macmillan.

———. Practical Anthropology. *Africa* 2 (1929): 23–38.

MANGELSDORF, P. C., MACNEISH, R. S., and GALINAT, W. C.

Domestication of Corn. *Science* 143 (1964): 538–545.

MAQUET, J.
Objectivity in Anthropology. *Current Anthropology* 5 (1964): 47–55.

———.
Le Problème de la Domination Tutsi. *Zaïre, revue congolaise* 6 (1952): 1011–1016.

MARETT, R. R.
1909 *The Threshold of Religion.* London: Methuen.

MARGALEF, R.
1968 *Perspectives in Ecological Theory.* Chicago: University of Chicago Press.

MARSHACK, A.
Lunar Notation on Upper Paleolithic Remains. *Science* 146 (1964): 743–745.

MARSHALL, L.
1965 The !Kung Bushman of the Kalahari Desert. In *Peoples of Africa,* ed. J. L. Gibbs, Jr. New York: Holt, Rinehart and Winston.

———.
Sharing, Talking, and Giving: Relief of Social Tensions Among !Kung Bushmen. *Africa* 31 (1961): 233–249.

———.
!Kung Bushman Bands. *Africa* 30 (1960): 325–354.

MARTIN, W. J.
1949 Physique of Young Adult Males. *Medical Research Council* (Her Majesty's Stationary Office), no. 20.

MAYER, A.
1966 The Significance of Quasi-Groups in the Study of Complex Societies. In *The Social Anthropology of Complex Societies,* ed. M. Banton. London: Tavistock.

MEAD, M.
1935 *Sex and Temperament in Three Primitive Societies.* New York: Morrow.

———.
1928 *Coming of Age in Samoa.* New York: Morrow.

MEGGARS, B. J.
1971 *Amazonia: Man and Culture in a Counterfeit Paradise.* Chicago: Aldine.

MEGGITT, M. J.
Male-Female Relationships in the Highlands of Australian New Guinea. *American Anthropologist,* special issue, 66, part 2 (1964): 204–224.

———.
1962 *Desert People.* Chicago: University of Chicago Press.

MEINTEL, D.
Strangers, Homecomers and Ordinary Men. *American Quarterly* 46 (1973): 47–58.

MELLARS, P. A.
1973 The Character of the Middle-Upper Paleolithic in Southwestern France. In *The Explanation of Culture Change,* ed. C. Renfrew. London: Duckworth.

METZGER, D., and WILLIAMS, G. E.
Formal Ethnographic Analysis of Tenejapa Ladino Weddings. *American Anthropologist* 65 (1963): 1076–1101.

MIDDLETON, J.
1960 *Lugbara Religion: Ritual and Authority Among an East African People.* London: Oxford University Press.

MILGRAM, S.
1974 *Obedience to Authority.* New York: Harper & Row.

———.
Group Pressure and Action Against a Person. *Journal of Abnormal and Social Psychology* 69 (1964): 137–143.

MILLER, R. L.
1973 *Economics Today.* San Francisco: Canfield Press.

MOERMAN, M.
1968 *Agricultural Change and Peasant Choice in a Thai Village.* Berkeley and Los Angeles: University of California Press.

MONEY, J., HAMPSON, J., and HAMPSON, J.
Imprinting and the Establishment of Gender Role. *Archives of Neurology and Psychiatry* 77 (1967): 633–636.

MOORE, O. K.
Divination—A New Perspective. *American Anthropologist* 59 (1957): 69–74.

MORGAN, L. H.
1963 *Ancient Society: Researches in the Lines of Human Progress from Savagery through Barbarism to Civilization.* Cleveland: World (orig. 1877).

MUNDY-CASTLE, A. C.
Pictorial Depth Perception in Ghanaian Children. *International Journal of Psychology* 1 (1966): 290–300.

MURDOCK, G. P.
1967 *The Ethnographic Atlas.* Pittsburgh: University of Pittsburgh Press.

———.
1959 *Africa.* New York: McGraw-Hill.

———.
1949 *Social Structure.* New York: Macmillan.

———., ed.
1963 *An Outline of World Cultures.* New Haven, Conn.: Human Relations Area Files.

MURPHY, R. F.
Outergroup Hostility and Social Cohesion. *American Anthropologist* 59 (1957): 1018–1035.

MURRA, J. V.
1958 On Inca Political Structure. In *Systems of Political Control and Bureaucracy in Human Societies, Proceedings of the 1958 Annual Spring Meeting of the American Ethnological Society.*

NADEL, S. F.
Nupe State and Community. *Africa* 8 (1935): 257–303.

NADER, L.
1969 Styles of Court Procedure: To Make the Balance. In *Law in Culture and Society,* ed. L. Nader. Chicago: Aldine.

NAROLL, R.
1973 Holocultural Theory Tests. In

Main Currents in Cultural Anthropology, eds. R. Naroll and F. Naroll. New York: Appleton-Century-Crofts.

NASH, M.
1966 *Primitive and Peasant Economic Systems.* San Francisco: Chandler.

NEKES, H.
Trommelsprache und Fernruf bei den Jaunde und Duala in Südkamerun. *Mitteilungen des Seminar für orientalische Sprachen* 15 (1912): 69–83.

NETTING, R.
The Ecological Approach in Cultural Study. Addison-Wesley Modules in Anthropology (1971): 1–30.

NIETSCHMANN, B.
Hunting and Fishing Focus Among the Miskito Indians, Eastern Nicaragua. *Human Ecology* 1 (1972): 41–67.

NIMKOFF, M. F., and MIDDLETON, R.
Types of Family and Types of Economy. *American Journal of Sociology* 66 (1960): 215–225.

NORBECK, E., and NORBECK, M.
1956 Child Training in a Japanese Fishing Community. In *Personal Character and Cultural Milieu,* ed. D. Haring. Syracuse, N.Y.: Syracuse University Press.

ODUM, E. P.
1963 *Ecology.* Modern Biology Series. New York: Holt, Rinehart and Winston.

ODUM, H. T.
1971 *Environment, Power, and Society.* New York: Wiley-Interscience.

OGBURN, C. K.
1968 *Basic English: International Second Language.* New York: Harcourt, Brace and World.

OLIVER, D. L.
1955 *A Solomon Island Society: Kinship and Leadership Among the Siuai of Bougainville.* Cambridge, Mass.: Harvard University Press.

OLIVER, S. C.
1973 Ecology and Cultural Continuity as Contributing Factors in the Social Organization of the Plains Indians. In *Man in Adaptation: The Cultural Present,* ed. Y. Cohen. Chicago: Aldine.

O'NEALE, L. M.
1932 *Yurok-Karok: Basket Weavers.* Berkeley and Los Angeles: University of California Press.

ORWELL, G.
1949 *1984.* New York: New American Library, Signet Classics.

OTTERBEIN, K. F.
1970 *The Evolution of War: A Cross-Cultural Study.* New Haven, Conn.: Human Relations Area Files.

——.
The Evolution of Zulu Warfare. *Kansas Journal of Sociology* 1 (1964): 27–35.

PALERM, A.
1955 The Agricultural Bases of Urban Civilization in Mesoamerica. In *Irrigation Civilizations: A Comparative Study,* ed. J. H. Steward. Social Science Monographs 1, Social Science Section, Department of Cultural Affairs. Washington, D.C.: Pan American Union.

PASTERNAK, B.
1972 *Kinship and Community in Two Chinese Villages.* Stanford, Calif.: Stanford University Press.

PEEBLES, C. S.
Moundville and Surrounding Site: Some Structural Considerations of Mortuary Practice 2. *American Antiquity* 36 (1971): 68–91.

PELTO, P. J.
1970 *Anthropological Research: The Structure of Inquiry.* New York: Harper & Row.

PIAGET, J.
1954 *The Construction of Reality in the Child.* New York: Basic Books.

PIDDOCKE, S.
The Potlatch System of the Southern Kwakiutl: A New Perspective. *Southeastern Journal of Anthropology* 21 (1965): 244–264.

PLOG, F.
Knowing the Pueblo Environment. State University of New York at Binghamton, n.d.

POLANYI, K.
1944 *The Great Transformation.* Toronto: Farrar and Oxford.

POSPISIL, L. J.
1969 Structural Change and Primitive Law: Consequences of a Papuan Legal Case. In *Law in Culture and Society,* ed. L. Nader. Chicago: Aldine.

——.
1963 *The Kapauku Papuans of West New Guinea.* New York: Holt, Rinehart and Winston.

——.
1958 *Kapauku Papuans and Their Law.* New Haven, Conn.: Yale University Publications in Anthropology.

POWDERMAKER, H.
1966 *Stranger and Friend: The Way of an Anthropologist.* New York: Norton.

PREMACK, A. J., and PREMACK, D.
Teaching Language to an Ape. *Scientific American* 227 (1972): 93–101.

PRINS, A. H. J.
1953 *East African Age-Class Systems.* Westport, Conn.: Negro Universities Press.

QUINN, N.
Decision Models of Social Structure. *American Ethnologist* 2 (1975): 19–45.

RADCLIFFE-BROWN, A. R.
1964 *The Andaman Islanders.* New York: The Free Press (orig. 1922).

——.
Functionalism: A Protest. *American Anthropologist* 5 (1949): 320–323.

RADCLIFFE-BROWN, A. R.
- 1939 *Taboo* ("The Frazer Lecture," 1939). Cambridge: Cambridge University Press.

RANDOLPH, R., and COULT, A.
- A Computer Analysis of Bedouin Marriage. *Southwestern Journal of Anthropology* 24: 83–99.

RAPPAPORT, R. A.
- The Flow of Energy in an Agricultural Society. *Scientific American* 224 (1971): 116–132.

- 1968 *Pigs for the Ancestors: Ritual in the Ecology of a New Guinea People.* New Haven: Yale University Press.

- Ritual Regulation of Environmental Relations Among a New Guinea People. *Ethnology* 6 (1967): 17–30.

RASMUSSEN, K.
- 1929 *Report of the Fifth Thule Expedition, 1921–1924*, vol. 7, no. 1, *Intellectual Culture of the Iglulik Eskimos.* Copenhagen: Gyldendalske Boghandel, Nordisk Forlag.

RATHJE, W. L.
- 1972 Praise the Gods and Pass the Metates: A Hypothesis of the Development of Lowland and Rainforest Civilizations in Mesoamerica. In *Contemporary Archeology: A Guide to Theory and Contributions*, ed. M. P. Leone. Carbondale: Southern Illinois University Press.

RATTRAY, R. S.
- 1929 *Ashanti: Law and Constitution.* London: Oxford University Press.

REDFIELD, R.
- Primitive Law. *University of Cincinnati Law Review* 33 (1964): 1–22.

RODGERS, W. B., and GARDNER, R. E.
- Linked Changes in Values and Behavior in the Out Island Bahamas. *American Anthropologist* 71 (1969): 21–35.

SAHLINS, M. D.
- 1972 *Stone Age Economics.* Chicago: Aldine.

- 1968 *Tribesmen.* Englewood Cliffs, N.J.: Prentice-Hall.

- 1967 The Established Order: Do Not Fold, Spindle, or Mutilate. In *The Rise and Fall of Project Camelot: Studies in the Relationship Between Social Science and Practical Politics*, ed. J. L. Horowitz. Cambridge, Mass.: M.I.T. Press.

- 1965 On the Sociology of Primitive Exchange. In *The Relevance of Models for Social Anthropology.* Association of Social Anthropologists, monograph no. 1. New York: Praeger.

- Poor Man, Rich Man, Big Man, Chief: Political Types in Melanesia and Polynesia. *Comparative Studies in Society and History* 5 (1963): 285–303.

- The Segmentary Lineage: An Organization of Predatory Expansion. *American Anthropologist* 63 (1961): 332–345.

- Land Use and the Extended Family in Moala, Fiji. *American Anthropologist* 59 (1957): 449–462.

SANDERS, W. T., and PRICE, B. J.
- 1968 *Mesoamerica: The Evolution of a Civilization.* New York: Random House.

SANKOFF, G.
- 1972 A Quantitative Paradigm for the Study of Communicative Competence. Paper prepared for the Conference on the Ethnography of Speaking, Austin, Texas, April 20–23.

SAPIR, E.
- The Status of Linguistics as a Science. *Language* 5 (1929): 207–214.

- 1921 *Language: An Introduction to the Study of Speech.* New York: Harcourt Brace.

SERVICE, E. R.
- 1971 *Primitive Social Organization: An Evolutionary Perspective.* 2d ed. New York: Random House.

- 1966 *The Hunters.* Englewood Cliffs, N.J.: Prentice-Hall.

SLOBODKIN, L. B.
- 1968 Toward a Predictive Theory of Evolution. In *Population Biology and Evolution*, ed. R. C. Lewontin. Syracuse, N.Y.: Syracuse University Press.

SORENSEN, A. P., JR.
- 1970 Multilingualism in the Northwest Amazon: Papurí and Pira-Paraná Regions. Paper presented at the Thirty-ninth International Congress of Americanists, held at Lima, Peru, August 2–9.

SOUTHWOLD, M.
- 1965 The Ganda of Uganda. In *Peoples of Africa*, ed. J. L. Gibbs, Jr. New York: Holt, Rinehart and Winston.

SPECKMANN, J. D.
- 1967 Social Surveys in the Non-Western World. In *Anthropologists in the Field*, eds. D. G. Jongmans and P. C. W. Gutkind. Netherlands: Van Gorcum.

SPIRO, M. E.
- Ghosts, Ifaluk and Teleological Functionalism. *American Anthropologist* 54 (1952): 495–503.

SPRADLEY, J. P.
- 1974 Beating the Drunk Charge. In *Conformity and Conflict: Readings in Cultural Anthropology*, eds. J. P. Spradley and D. W. McCurdy. 2d ed. Boston: Little, Brown.

―――
1973 The Ethnography of Crime in America. In *Cultural Illness and Health: Essays in Human Adaptation,* eds. L. Nader and T. W. Maretski. Washington, D.C.: American Anthropological Association.

STANDS-IN-TIMBER, J., and LIBERTY, M.
1967 *Cheyenne Memories.* New Haven, Conn.: Yale University Press.

STENNING, D. J.
1965 The Pastoral Fulani of Northern Nigeria. In *Peoples of Africa,* ed. J. L. Gibbs, Jr. New York: Holt, Rinehart and Winston.

STEPHENS, W. N.
1963 *The Family in Cross-Cultural Perspective.* New York: Holt, Rinehart and Winston.

STERN, T.
Drum and Whistle "Languages": An Analysis of Speech Surrogates. *American Anthropologist* 59 (1957): 487–506.

STEWARD, J. H.
1972 *The Theory of Culture Change: The Methodology of Multilinear Evolution.* Urbana: University of Illinois Press.

STOCKING, G. W.
From Physics to Ethnology: Franz Boas' Arctic Expedition as a Problem in the Historiography of the Behavioral Sciences. *Journal of the History of the Behavioral Sciences* 1 (1965): 53–66.

STRUEVER, S.
1968 Woodland Subsistence-Settlement Systems in the Lower Illinois Valley. In *New Perspectives in Archeology,* eds. S. R. Binford and L. R. Binford. Chicago: Aldine.

―――, and HOUART, G. L.
1972 Hopewell Interaction Sphere Analysis. In *Social Exchange and Interaction,* ed. E. N. Wilmsen. Anthropological Papers, no. 46. Ann Arbor: University of Michigan, Museum of Anthropology.

SWADESH, M.
1971 *The Origin and Diversification of Language,* ed. J. Sherzer. Chicago: Aldine-Atherton.

SWANSON, G. E.
1960 *The Birth of the Gods: The Origin of Primitive Beliefs.* Ann Arbor: University of Michigan Press.

SWEET, L. E.
1965 Camel Pastoralism in North Arabia and the Minimal Camping Unit. In *Man, Culture, and Animals: The Role of Animals in Human Ecological Adjustment,* eds. A. Leeds and A. P. Vayda. Publication no. 78. Washington, D.C.: American Association for the Advancement of Science.

SWIFT, J.
1974 The Future of Twareg Pastoral Nomadism in the Malian Sahel. Paper presented at the SSRC Symposium on the Future of Traditional Societies, December.

TALMON, Y.
Mate Selection in Collective Settlements. *American Sociological Review* 29 (1964): 491–508.

TAUSKY, C.
1970 *Work Organizations: Major Theoretical Perspectives.* Itasca, Ill.: Peacock Publishers.

TAVRIS, C.
Male Supremacy Is on the Way Out. *Psychology Today* 8 (1975): 61–69.

TENZEL, J.
Shamanism and Concepts of Disease in a Mayan Community. *Psychiatry* 33 (1970): 372–380.

TEWKSBURY, W. J.
1967 The Ordeal as a Vehicle for Divine Intervention in Medieval Europe. In *Law and Warfare: Studies in the Anthropology of Conflict,* ed. P. Bohannan. Garden City, N.Y.: Natural History Press.

THIEME, P.
1964 The Comparative Method for Reconstruction in Linguistics. In *Language in Culture and Society: A Reader in Linguistics and Anthropology,* ed. D. Hymes. New York: Harper & Row.

THOMPSON, L.
1950 *Culture in Crisis: A Study of the Hopi Indians.* New York: Harper & Row.

―――, and JOSEPH, A.
1947 *The Hopi Way.* Chicago: University of Chicago Press.

TINBERGEN, N.
1961 *The Herring Gull's World.* New York: Basic Books.

TRUDGILL, P.
Sex, Covert Prestige and Linguistic Change in the Urban British English of Norwich. *Language in Society* 1 (1972): 179–195.

TURNBULL, C.
1965 The Mbuti Pygmies of the Congo. In *Peoples of Africa,* ed. J. L. Gibbs, Jr. New York: Holt, Rinehart and Winston.

TURNER, V. W.
1967 *The Forest of Symbols: Aspects of Ndembu Ritual.* Ithaca, N.Y.: Cornell University Press.

―――
1957 *Schism and Continuity in an African Society.* Manchester: Manchester University Press.

TUTTLE, R.
1972 *The Functional and Evolutionary Biology of Primates.* Chicago: Aldine.

TYLOR, E. B.
1931 Animism. In *The Making of Man: An Outline of Anthropology,* ed. V. F. Calverton. New York: The Modern Library.

―――
1871 *Primitive Culture: Researches into the Develop-*

ment of Mythology, Philosophy, Religion, Language, Art, and Custom. 2d. ed. 2 vols. London: John Murray.

UCKO, P. J., and ROSENFELD, A.
1967 *Paleolithic Cave Art.* New York: McGraw-Hill.

VAN GENNEP, A.
1960 *The Rites of Passage.* Chicago: University of Chicago Press.

VAYDA, A. P.
Warfare in an Ecological Perspective. *Annual Review of Ecology and Systematics* 5 (1974): 183–193.

———.
Expansion and Warfare Among Swidden Agriculturalists. *American Anthropologist* 63 (1961): 346–358.

———, and MCCAY, B. J.
New Directions in Ecology and Ecological Anthropology. *Annual Review of Anthropology* 4 (1975): 293–306.

VIDICH, A., and BENSMAN, J.
1968 *Small Town in Mass Society.* Rev. ed. Princeton, N.J.: Princeton University Press.

———.
Freedom and Responsibility in Research: Comments. *Human Organization* 17 (1958–1959): 2–5.

WALLACE, A. F. C.
1970 *The Death and Rebirth of the Seneca.* New York: Alfred A. Knopf.

———.
1966 *Religion: An Anthropological View.* New York: Random House.

———.
1952 *The Modal Personality Structure of the Tuscarora Indians as Revealed by the Rorschach Test.* Bulletin 150. Washington, D.C.: Bureau of American Ethnology.

WEGNER, R.
Die Quruñqu'a, ein neuentdecker Stamm primitivster Kulture ohne artikulierte und grammatische sprache in Ostbolivien. *Phoenix, Zeitschrift Deutsche Geistesarbeit für Südamerika* 14 (1928): 369–384.

WEYER, E. M.
1932 *The Eskimos: Their Environment and Folkways.* New Haven, Conn.: Yale University Press.

WHALLON, R.
1968 Investigations of Late Prehistoric Social Organization in New York State. In *New Perspectives in Archaeology,* eds. S. R. Binford and L. R. Binford. Chicago: Aldine.

WHEAT, J. B.
1973 A Paleo-Indian Bison Kill. In *Early Man in America,* ed. R. S. MacNeish. San Francisco: W. H. Freeman.

WHITE, D. R.
1973 Mathematical Anthropology. In *Handbook of Social and Cultural Anthropology,* ed. J. J. Honigmann. Chicago: Rand McNally.

WHITE, L. A.
1949 *The Science of Culture.* New York: Farrar, Straus and Cudahy.

WHITING, B. B., ed.
1963 *Six Cultures: Studies of Child Bearing.* New York: Wiley.

WHITING, B. B., and WHITING, J. W. M.
1974 *Children of Six Cultures: A Psycho-Cultural Analysis.* Cambridge, Mass.: Harvard University Press.

———.
1973 Methods for Observing and Recording Behavior. In *A Handbook of Method in Cultural Anthropology,* eds. R. Naroll and R. Cohen. New York: Columbia University Press.

WHITING, J. W. M.
1964 Effects of Climate on Certain Cultural Practices. In *Explorations in Cultural Anthropology: Essays in Honor of George Peter Murdock,* ed. W. H. Goodenough. New York: McGraw-Hill.

———, and CHILD, I.
1953 *Child Training and Personality: A Cross-Cultural Study.* New Haven: Yale University Press.

WHYTE, W. F.
Freedom and Responsibility in Research: The 'Springdale' Case. *Human Organization* 17 (1958): 1–2.

WILLIAMS, T. R.
1967 *Field Methods in the Study of Culture.* New York: Holt, Rinehart and Winston.

WILMSEN, E. N.
1972 Introduction to the Study of Exchange as Social Interaction. In *Social Exchange and Interaction,* ed. E. N. Wilmsen. Anthropological Papers, no. 46. Ann Arbor: University of Michgan, Museum of Anthropology.

———.
1968 Paleo-Indian Site Utilization. In *Anthropological Archeology in the Americas,* ed. B. J. Meggers. Washington, D.C.: Anthropological Society of Washington.

WILSON, E. O.
1975 *Sociobiology: The New Synthesis.* Cambridge, Mass.: The Belknap Press.

WILSON, M.
Nyakyusa Age-Villages. *Journal of the Royal Anthropological Institute* 79 (1949): 21–25.

WINTERS, H. D.
1968 Value Systems and Trade Cycles of the Late Archaic in the Midwest. In *New Perspectives in Archeology,* eds. S. R. Binford and L. R. Binford. Chicago: Aldine.

WITTFOGEL, K.
1957 *Oriental Despotism: A Comparative Study of Total Power.*

New Haven: Yale University Press.

WOBST, H. M.
Boundary Conditions for Paleolithic Social Systems: A Simulation Approach. *American Antiquity* 39 (1974): 147–178.

WOLF, A. P.
Adopt a Daughter-in-Law, Marry a Sister: A Chinese Solution to the Problem of the Incest Taboo. *American Anthropologist* 70 (1970): 864–874.

WOLF, E. R.
1966 *Peasants*. Englewood Cliffs, N.J.: Prentice-Hall.

———. The Social Organization of Mecca and the Origins of Islam. *Southwestern Journal of Anthropology* 7 (1951): 329–356.

YENGOYAN, A. A.
1968 Demographic and Ecological Influence in Aboriginal Australian Marriage Sections. In *Man the Hunter,* eds. R. B. Lee and I. DeVore. Chicago: Aldine.

ZENGEL, M.
Literacy as a Factor in Language Change. *American Anthropologist* 64 (1962): 132–139.

Index

aborigines (Australian), 92, 127, 484
acculturation, 468–472
Acheulean tradition: and contemporary peoples, 94–95; housing, 96; killsite, 97; stone tool culture, 82, 83, 94, 95–96; tools, 82, 83, 94, 95–96
Adams, Robert, 152, 155–156, 157, 162, 165, 432
adaptation, 13, 29; australopith pattern, 75–76; bipedalism, 49–51, 79–81; continuing, 317–321, 323, 575–587; cultural, 468–472; genetic, 579; language, 280–282; primates, 39–64; primate teeth and jaws, 51; *Ramapithecus*, 73–74; of religion, 408–416; social organization, 145; subsistence, 15, 311–312, 317–321, 323–326. *See also* human adaptations
adoption of agriculture, 134–143
age, as a social category, 371, 372
age-set systems, 226–227
agonistic behavior, 56–57, 61
agribusiness, 559, 560–561
agriculture: adaptive values, 142; adoption of, 134–143; and animal traction, 539; crop rotation, 539; intensive, subsistence strategy, 324, 539–555; and irrigation, 138, 142, 143, 144–145, 155, 156, 162, 539, 540; in Java, 539; and malaria, 172; mechanization and communalization of, 558, 560–561; Mesoamerica, 130, 133, 139–140; Near East, 133, 134–135, 138; nuclear zone, 128, 134; origins, 128–130; and the peasantry, 540–550; and pottery, 143–144, 157; and sedentism, 122, 141–143, 145–146, 153, 156; selective breeding of crops and livestock, 539; sisal, in northeastern Brazil, 342; and social organization, 540; and state formation, 155–156, 541, 550–554; swidden, 326, 501–502, 517; technology of, 142, 143–146, 325–326. *See also* domestication; horiculturalists
alcoholism, 302–303, 304
alienation, in industrial societies, 333

Ali Kosh, agricultural innovation, 135, 138
Alland, Alexander, 14
allele, 21, 23, 24; neutral, 25
Alorese culture, 204
American Anthropological Association, 240; Principles of Professional Responsibility, 240–241
American Indian, 196, 471–472. *See also specific tribes*
American Southwest, 143, 148; diet, diffusion of domestication, 141–142; housing, 141; Pueblo, social organization, 158; villages, 141–142. *See also* Paleo-Indians
amino acid, 142, 178
anatomy, evolutionary change, 27–28
Ancient Society (Morgan), 193
Andaman Islanders, 199, 447
animal husbandry, 521, 522, 524
animals: changes, in domestication, 130–131; communication, 55, 247–250, 252; domesticated in China and Southeast Asia, 138; domesticated in Europe, 141; wild vs. domesticated, 131
animatism. *See* animism and animatism
animism and animatism, 400, 408
Anthropoidea, 46
anthropoids, transition, 71–85
anthropological linguistics, 10, 11–12, 12–13, 201. *See also* descriptive linguistics; language
anthropology, 5–17; applied (*see* applied anthropology); cultural (*see* cultural anthropology); physical (*see* physical anthropology); scope and definition, 5–17; statistics and mathematics in, 226–227
Anthropology (Kroeber), 467n
antigens, blood group, 172
Apache Indians, 469, 471
apes. *See* chimpanzee; gorilla; primates
applied anthropology: and culture change, 474–478; methodology, 458–461
Arapesh, 298

archeology, 10, 11; and physical anthropology in action, 12; and tracing human prehistory, 87, 89–90, 109, 132, 158, 460, 461
Archaic *Homo sapiens*, 101, 102–103
Archaic stage. *See* Mesolithic-Archaic stage
archeomagnetism, 117
architecture: Aztec, 162–163; Egyptian, 195; Mayan, 195; Mesoamerican, 157; Pueblo, 158
Arctic hysteria, 289
Argonauts of the Pacific (Malinowski), 199
art: Aurignacian, 110; Magdalenian, 111; Paleolithic, 111–113
artifacts, 87, 95, 97; in estimating population, 132; vs. geofacts, 89–90
Ascher, R., 253, 255
Ashanti, 274, 441
Aswad, Barbara C., 550
Ateles, 49
atlatl (spear thrower), 108, 111
Australopithecus, 74–85, 88, 91; adaptation pattern, 74–76; *africanus*, 76–83, 94; back tooth dominance in, 77, 78, 82; *boisei*, 76, 82, 83; brain, 76–77; evolved forms, 82; extinction, 82–83, 94; feeding adaptations, 77; gracile vs. robust, 75–76; hominid status, 75; pattern, 75–76; *robustus*, 76, 82, 83; upper dentition, 78
authority vs. power. *See* power vs. authority
avocado cultivation, 139, 140
Ayacucho, Peru, 116
Aztec: architecture, 162–163; calendar, 163; social organization, 162–163; state formation, 161–163; trade network, 163

baboon (*Papio*): Awash project, 58–59; feeding habits, 51, 52, 53, 81; hand, 53; hedonic and agonistic interaction, 57; multimale group, 60; one-male group 60
back tooth dominance, *Australopithecus*, 77, 78, 82
Balikci, A., 492, 493

band: aborigines (Australian), 92; Kalahari Bushmen, 92; Mesoamerica, 139, 140; as political organization, 424–426
banks, 568
Bantu, 345, 399, 485, 490, 491, 581
barley cultivation, 133, 138, 141, 143
Barnet, R., 566n
barter system. *See* reciprocal exchange systems
Barth, Fredrik, 321, 374, 395, 467
Bat Cave, New Mexico, 141
Beals, Ralph, 242
bean cultivation, 139, 140, 141, 142, 162
Bedouins, 369–370, 433, 435–436
begettors vs. nurterers, 56
behavior, 55; agonistic, 56–57; biological basis of, 287–290; specialized, emergence of, 99–102; studies of, 58–59. *See also* social behavior
Bellah, Robert, 408
Benedict, Ruth, 203
Bensman, Joseph, 236
Beringia land bridge, 114–115, 175
Berreman, G., 390
Bible, 276, 411; Genesis, 401
Binford, Lewis R. and Sally R., 100, 101, 143
biology: and behavior, 287–290; and culture, 205
biomass, 40
biomes, 317–318
bipedalism, 49–51; adaptive value, 49–51, 79–81; in *Homo sapiens*, 49–50; and toolmaking, 81–82
Birdsell, J. B., 484
Birdwhistell, Roy L., 250
birth control and culture, 316–317
blood group: ABO, and disease, 172, 175–176; human systems, 172
Bloomfield, Leonard, 277
Boas, Franz, 194–195, 291, 293
Bohannan, Laura. *See* Bowen, Elenore Smith
Bordes, Francis, 100, 101
Boulding, Kenneth, 473
Bowen, Elenore Smith, 222 and n, 223, 224
brachiating, 43, 47, 49, 72, 73
brachiators, locomotion, 47, 49
Braidwood, Robert J., 128
brain: *Australopithecus,* 76–77; *Cebus,* 54; chimpanzee, 54; Eocene primates, 71; *Homo erectus,* 98; *Homo sapiens,* 54, 102; *Microcebus,* 54; neandertal, 102; primates, 53–54
Brett, Frederick L., 58
bride price, 370, 381–382, 448, 449
bride service. *See* bride price
bride theft, 387
Broca, Paul, 256
Broken K Pueblo, 158
Bruner, Edward, 361, 363
Buchler, M., 362
Buganda, 332
burial: date, in estimating population, 132; Mesolithic-Archaic, 121; ritualized, 102; and stratification, 147, 153
Bushong, 337
business firms, in industrialized societies, 333, 334

Calico Hills, California, 116
Cancian, Frank, 227
Canis familiaris, 34
Canis lupus, 34
Carneiro, Robert, 154, 431
Cartmill, Matt, 42
catarrhine monkey, 43, 46, 53, 55
Catarrhini, Fayum, 72
Catholicism, 408
Cauble, Ronald, 58
Cavalli-Sforza, L. L., 184
cave painting, 111
Cebus, brain of, 54
census taking, 218, 219
Central Intelligence Agency (CIA), 237, 240
ceramics. *See* pottery
Cercopithecidae, 43, 72
Cercopithecoidea, 43, 72
Chagnon, Napoleon, 222, 223, 224, 354, 355, 503, 504, 508
Chance, M. R. A., 57
Chang, K. C., 138
Chang Chig-i's, 512
Chavez, César, 566
Chayanov's rule, 335
Cheyenne, 372, 381–382
Cheyenne Memories (Stands-in-Timber and Liberty), 221
chiefdom, 152–153, 431; as political organization, 427–429
Child, Irvin L., 206

Childe, V. Gordon, 128, 151–152
child-rearing practices, 204–207, 294, 298; toilet training, 294
children, cognitive development, 293–294
Children of Sánchez, The (Lewis), 235
Chimbu, 369
chimpanzee (*Pan troglodytes*): biological classification, 34; brain, 54; communication, 249–250; vs. dryopith, 73; hand, 52; implement use, 52, 73, 310; locomotion, 49; meat-eating, 61; pelvis, 80; skeleton, 50; social behavior, 61; social organization, 60–61; upper dentition, 78
China, 127; *Homo erectus* finds, 97, 98; housing, 138; and Southeast Asia, agricultural innovation, 138–139
chinampa, 162
chipped stone technology, 95–96, 99–100, 110, 111
Chomsky, Noam, 273
chopper, Oldowan, 88–91, 96
chopper-chopping tool tradition, 95, 97
Choukoutien, 98; emergence of division of labor, 97; subsistence in, 97
chromosomes, 21–23
Chumash, 463, 464
Chungshe, 542–546
circumscription and state organization, 154, 156, 157, 159, 161, 163, 165
cities: ancient, 165–166; Aztec, 162–163; beginnings, 151–152, 153; Eridu, 164; Olmec, 159; Sumerian, 164, 165; Tenochtitlan, 162, 163; Teotihuacan, 159, 162, 163; Toltec, 162, 163. *See also* urbanism
civilization, emergence of, 151–167; Mesoamerican, 159–163; Mesopotamian, 163–165
clan (kin groups), 145, 365–366; pan-tribal, 427
Clark, J. G. D., 97
Classic stage, Mesoamerican civilization, 157, 159, 160, 161, 162, 163
classification: biological, 34–35; primates, 34
cline, 173, 181
Coe, Michael, 160
cognitive development of children, 293–294
cognitive imperative, 288, 293

cognitive maps, 206
Cole, Michael, 293
Collins, Thomas, 565
colonialism: and anthropologists, 233–234, 237; and economic exploitation, 341, 343
Colson, E., 304
Comanche Indians, 323, 449
communication: animal, 55, 247–250, 252; animal vs. human, 250, 252–253; chemical, 248; chimpanzee, 249–250; dogs, 248–249; dolphins, 257; insects, 247–248; nonverbal, 250–252
Conklin, Harold, 274
convergence and parallelism, 31–32, 35
Coombs, G., 463
corn, 142; cultivation, 139, 141, 142; domestication changes, 129–130
Cornell University, Department of Child Development and Family Relations, 236
corporations, global, 568–570
corvée system, 343
Coult, A. D., 371
cousin marriages, 386, 388
Coxcatlán, 140
Crockett, H. J., Jr., 283
cross-cultural studies, 228–229
crossopterygians, adaptive radiation, 31
Crow Indians, 372, 405; kin terminology, 360–361
Cuicuilco, 162
cultural anthropology, 10, 13; ethics of, 233–234, 476–477; fieldwork, methodology of, 211–231; research in, 191–209, 211–231, 458–461
cultural diversity, 15, 107–125, 198–202, 206, 317–326, 559
cultural evolution, 14–15, 87–105; and acculturation, 468–472; and applied anthropology, 457–479; contemporary problems, 472–474; general vs. specific, 457; and innovation, 465–468, 475–476; Law of Cultural Dominance, 463, 465; Law of Evolutionary Potential, 465; multilineal theory, 198; patterns of, 461–463; study of, 194–209, 211–213, 458–461; and subsistence, 128, 143, 325–326; unilineal theory, 192

cultural relativism, 6–7, 241
cultural values vs. ethics, 300
culture, 8–10, 90, 94; Acheulean, 94–97; adaptation, 468–472; and biology, 205; and birth control, 316–317; change, and applied anthropology, 457–479; and ecology, 13, 14–15, 128–131, 196, 198, 435–436, 472–474; emic vs. etic viewpoint, 202, 274; evolution of (see cultural evolution); and the individual, 287–305; and labor, 313–316; and language, 257–261, 267–285; marriage, families, domestic groups and, 379–397; and personality, 202–204, 206–209, 297–298; and political organization, 418–437; and religion, 399–417; simple vs. complex, 462–463; and social behavior, 439–455; and social organization, 351–377; structural-functionalist theory, 200; structuralist theory, 200; study of, 194–209, 211–231, 458–461; and technology, 197, 198; transmission of 9, 12
Culture and Ecology Project, 206
culture center, 196
culture change. See applied anthropology; cultural evolution
culture shock, 223, 224
Current Anthropology (periodical), 241
Cuthbert, T. P., 160

Dahomeans, 401
d'Aquili, Eugene, 288
Dart, Raymond, 81
Darwin, Charles, 13, 267
Darwin, Erasmus, 13
data analysis and interpretation, 225–229; generating theoretical models, 227–229; quantitative, 227
data collection, techniques, 212–221
dating techniques, 90, 117, 184
death assemblages, fossils, 67
decision making, 316; criteria for participation in, 420–422
Defense, Department of, U.S., 237, 240
dendogram, blood group gene frequencies, 184
dendrochronology, 117
dendroclimatology, 109
Dendropithecus, 72
dentition: hominid, 78–79; and masti-

catory muscles, primates, 51, 77; Old World monkeys, 43; primates, 51–52, 78. See also teeth
deoxyribonucleic acid. See DNA
descent groups: evolution of, 366; matrilineal, 363–364; patrilineal, 364–365; segmentary, 427. See also kinship
descent ideologies: ambilineal, and descent groups, 367–368; kinship, and social behavior, 368–371; nonunilineal, and descent groups, 367; unilineal, and descent groups, 363–367
descriptive linguistics, 12. See also anthropological linguistics; language
dialects: comparative study of, 276–277; glottochronology, 277–278
Dictyostelium, 248
diet, 133; American Southwest, 141; Mesoamerican, 139–140; Mesolithic-Archaic, 121; Near East, 138; pastoral peoples, 326; polymorphisms related to, 176–177; Upper Paleolithic vs. Mesolithic-Archaic, 119, 121
Dietis level, 98
diffusionist school of anthropology, 195–198
directional selection, 24, 25
distribution: blood groups, 173, 175, 177; skin color, 178–180
distribution of goods, in industrial vs. nonindustrial societies: class vs. caste systems, 339–340; and colonialism, 341, 343; exchange systems, 343–347
diversification, 29; and specialization, 107, 114; and speciation, 29–31, 58
diversity: cultural, 15, 107–125, 198–202, 206, 317–326, 559; and environment, 321; Eocene primates, 71; and founder effect, 113; hominids, 74; of primate social organization, 57–60; primates, 39, 43–47; regional, in subsistence and settlement, 101–102, 122–123; and specialization, 99–101, 107, 110–111, 114; Upper Paleolithic, 107, 110–111
divination as a social control, 449–450
division of labor, 87, 92, 94, 97, 146,

158, 162; by age and sex, 313–314, 382–383; Pueblo, 158
DNA (deoxyribonucleic acid), 21–22, 23
domestication, 127, 128–131, 133, 193; and bone size of animals, 131; and changes in animals, 130–131; diffusion in Old and New World, 134–142; and phenotypic changes, 128–130, 133, 140; reconstruction of, 130. See also agriculture
domestic groups, 394–396. See also family, marriage
Downs, J. R., 580
Downs, James F., 535
Dozier, Edward, 517
dry farming, 135, 138, 143, 144
Dryopithecus, 72–73, 77; upper dentition, 73, 78; vs. chimpanzee, 73
Duala language, 271
Dubois, Cora, 204, 303
Durkheim, Emile, 199–200, 400, 410
dwarf lemur, locomotion, 48–49
Dyson-Hudson, Neville, 526, 529

Early Dynastic, Mesopotamian state formation stage, 164
Early Woodland groups, 121
East Africa, *Australopithecus* in, 76, 78, 82, 83
East Rudolf, 88, 94
ecological strategy, social organization as, 55, 60
ecology: and culture, 13, 14–15, 128–131, 196, 198, 435–436, 472–474; human, 5–6, 13, 14–15, 317–323, 575–587; and origins of agriculture, 128–131, 133; primates, 40, 42, 61; and religion, 413–416
econiche, 14–15, 27, 29, 31, 128, 320–321; primates, 40, 42, 61
economic organization: control of capital goods, 332–333; distribution of goods, 338—347; division of labor, 313–314; private vs. community property, 330–333; procurement strategies, 323–325; production, 333–335, 337; productivity, 335, 337; seasonality, 319–320; specialization, 314–315; technology, 311; and warfare, 433–436
ecosystem, 576–578; resilience vs. stability, 584

Edgerton, Robert, 206
education, 294–295
Edwards, A. W. F., 184
elephant, evolutionary changes in, 27–28
Ember, M. and C. R., 391
enclosure situation in studying primate behavior, 58–59
enculturation. See acculturation; socialization
endogamy, 385–386
entrepreneurial system, 346–347
environment: Aswan Dam's effects on, 322; carrying capacity of, 132, 318–319; and culture, 196; in estimating past populations, 132; and evolutionary change, 28, 472–474; and genotype, 22; hominids, 91–92; and human diversity, 321; human impact on, 322, 472–474; and human survival, 575–587; past, 109, 132; and phenotype, 22, 128–131, 133; and pollution, 473–474; protection of, 478
Epstein, S., 347, 549
equability and extinctions, 119–120
Equus caballus, 34
Eridu, 164
Eskimo, 127, 267, 289, 330, 380, 406, 425, 426, 440, 483, 484, 485, 491–496, 512; kin terminology, 357–358
ethics: of cultural anthropologists, 233–243; and cultural values, 300
ethnicity, as a social category, 374–376
ethnocentrism, 6
ethnography, 11
ethnoscience, 201–202
ethnosemantics, 274
Europe, 143; advanced hunters, 108, 111; diffusion of domestication in, 141; settlements, 141; Upper Paleolithic developments, 108
evolution: biological, 21–37; change rates, 27–31; continuing human, 575–587; cultural, 14–15, 87–105, 457–479; Darwinian, opportunism of, 28; diversification and speciation, 29–31, 58; of evolutionary theory, 13–15; of gene complexes, 25; *Homo,* 85–105; irreversibility of, 28–29; of language, 253, 255–256; Mesoamerica vs. Mesopotamia, 145–

146; Mesolithic-Archaic trends, 122–124; Middle Pleistocene, 96, 98; non-Darwinian, and gene frequency, 25–26; of political organization, 430–432; primates, 65–85; processes and patterns, 21–37; of religion, 408; skin color, 180–181; specialization and generalization, 29; time charts, 67, 69; trends, 82–83, 103–104
ex-brachiator, locomotion, 49
excavation and surveys, archeological, 89–90
exchange systems, 503; market exchange, 345, 346; reciprocal exchange, 344–345; redistribution, 345; spheres of exchange, 346
exogamy, 61, 97, 385
expansion vs. migration, New World, 115–116
exploitation of natives, problem of, 234
extended family, 392–394
extensive or shifting agriculture, subsistence strategy, 323–324
extinction, 31, 32
extinctions, Pleistocene epoch, 119–120

family, 193; extended, 392–394; vs. household, 379; independent, 391–392; matrifocal, 391n; residence rules, 390–391. See also domestic groups, marriage
Family in Cross-Cultural Perspective, The (Stephens), 381n
fauna. See flora and fauna
Fayum, Oligocene primates, 72
feeding and bipedalism, 50–51
Fei Hsiao-t'ung, 512
Feit, Harvey, 413
femininity vs. masculinity, 289–290
field research, 58–59; adapting to, 221–225; data analysis and interpretation, 225–229; data collection, techniques of, 212–221; ethical problems, 233–243; preparation of research design, 211–212, 224
Fischer, John, 281–282, 394
Five Families (Lewis), 563
flake tools, 88–91, 95
Flannery, Kent, 128, 134, 139, 143; state formation model, 156–157
flex cultivator, 141, 144

flora and fauna: Cretaceous, 69; early Miocene, 72; hominid, 91
Folsom tradition, 118; hunting, 118
food-energy formula, 512
Ford, Richard, 415
Foreign Relations, Committee on, Senate, U.S., 239
fossils, 12; *Australopithecus,* 76; context, *Ramapithecus,* 69; hominid, 92; identifying, 66–67; phyletic relationships, 67; taphonomy, 67; unevenness of record, 66
Foster, Brian, 374
Foster, George, 474
Foster, Mary Lecron, 254
Foulks, W., 289
founder effect, 25; and blood group polymorphism, 173, 175; and diversity, 113
Fox, Robin, 361
Fox Indians, 401
Frazer, James, 192, 193, 199
Freilich, Morris, 304
Freud, Sigmund, 203, 204
Fribourg, Michael, 566–567
fruit-eating adaptations, 51–52
Fulani, 395
Fulbright, J. William, 239
funding for anthropologists, 237
Fur (Sudan), 374

Galla, 226–227, 299–300
Galtung, John, 238
gametes, 21; formation and meiosis, 22–23; genotype, 22–23; variation, 23
Gardner, Allen and Beatrice, 249
Garo language, 279–280
gatherers. See hunting and gathering
gathering, 127; Europe, 141; Paleo-Indians, 119. See also hunting and gathering
Geertz, Clifford, 400, 501
gelada (*Theropithecus*): hand, 53; small-object feeding, 51, 53
gene(s): in families, 22; fixation, 24, 25; and genotypes, 21, 22, 23; and locus, 21, 22; particulate nature, 22; in populations, 23; and proteins, 21–22
gene flow, 23–24, 27, 29; and gene frequency, 24; and migration, effect on sickle cell anemia, 171–172, 183; and mutation, 24
gene frequency, 23; factors affecting, 23–26; and gene flow, 24; and genetic drift, 25, 26; and non-Darwinian evolution, 25–26
gene pool(s), 23, 24, 26, 29; and populations, 23
generalization and specialization, 29
generalized distance, 184
generalized reciprocity system, 344
generation sets, 372
genetic drift, 25, 26, 27, 29; and gene frequency, 25, fig. 26
genetic information, 21, 22, 23
genetic markers, 58; in human blood, 170
genetic variation and mutation, 24
genetics, 11; controlled variation, 170; and domestication, 128; Mendelian, 23–25
genotype: in ABO blood group system, 172; and environment, 22, 28; and genes, 21, 22, 23; natural selection, 24, 28; zygote, 21
geofacts vs. artifacts, 89–90
geographical variation, *Homo erectus,* 98
geological processes, 66–67
geological time scale, 67, 69
Ghost Dance ideology, 412
gibbon, locomotion, 48, 49
Gibbs, J. L., Jr., 452
glaciation, and plant communities, 115, 116, 128
glacier, 66; Pleistocene, 114–116
glottochronology (lexicostatistics), 277–278
Goethe, Johann Wolfgang von, 13
Goldberg, M. A., 585
Golden Bough, The (Frazer), 192, 193, 199
Goldschmidt, Walter, 206, 560, 561
Goodall, Jane van L., 310
Goodenough, Ward, 394
Gorer, Geoffrey, 204
gorilla (*Gorilla gorilla*), 52; biological classification, 34; precision grip, 52
Gough, E., Kathleen, 241, 385
Gouldner, Alvin, 235
government sponsorship of anthropological research, 237–240
Graebner, Fritz, 195, 196
grain collection, early, 134–135, 138
grammar, 270; transformational, 273–274
grass-eating adaptations, 52
Graves, Theodore D., 302–303
Great English Vowel Shift, 278
Grimm, Jakob, 277
Gross, Daniel, 342, 508
ground tools, 123, 143
group: multimale, 60; one-male, 57; Woodland, 120–122
groups. See social groups
Gujars, 321
Gussi, 388
Gwembe Tonga, 304–305

habitat(s): *Australopithecus,* 76; and realms, primates, 39, 41
Hall, E. T., 251–252
hamadryas, 60, 61
hammer, soft, 95, fig. 96, 96
Handsome Lake Movement, 412, 458
Hanunóo language, 274
harem, primate, 60, 61
Harris, Marvin, 290, 508, 512
Hawaashleh Bedouin, 371
Hawaiians, 427; kin terminology, 358
Hay Hollow Valley, 158
Hediger, M. L., 319
hedonic relationships, 56–57, 61
hemogloblin, 24, 170; polymorphism, 170–172
herding, 133; cattle, 525–529; origins, in Near East, 135, 138; sheep, 529–533
heritage characters, 28, 34
Herskovits, Melville, 525
heterozygous, 21, 22
Hill, Jim, 158
Himalayan Border Countries Project, 240
Hindus, 390, 401, 414
historical particularism, 195
Hockett, Charles F., 253, 255
Hoffman, Hans, 226–227
Hoijer, Harry, 259
holism, in anthropology, 5–6, 474, 575
Hollings, C. S., 584, 585
Holloway, R. L., 76
Holmberg, Alan, 227–228, 476–477
holocultural studies, 228–229
hominid: *Australopithecus,* 92; environments, 91–92; fossils, 92; Mio-

cene, 72–73; phylogeny, 74–75; Plio-Pleistocene, 93; upper dentition, 78–79
Hominidae, 34, 43, 74; lineage, 74
Hominoidea, 43
Homo, 75, 82, 83, 92, 98; early sites, 91–92; lineage, 93; Linnaeus classification, 34; origins, 74
Homo erectus, 88, 97–98; brain, 98; jaw, 98; skeleton, 98; skull, 92, 98; teeth, 98
Homo habilis, 98; Oldowan, 83, 88, 92, 93; skull, 92; teeth and jaws, 94
Homo sapiens, 5, 10, 27, 49, 74, 75, 82, 88, 93, 97, 98; archaic, 101, 102–103; bipedalism, 49–50; brain, 54, 102; pelvis, 80; skeleton, 50; skull, 92–93, 102–103; upper dentition, 78. *See also* humans
homozygous, 21, 25
Hopewell Interaction Sphere, 122, 146–148
Hopi, 298; language, 258–259; rites of passage, 295
Hopper, Rex, 238
horticulturalists: and conflict, 503; and the domestic unit, 502–503; food-energy formula, 512; Pueblo, 158, 311–312, 323, 361, 414–415, 501, 503; Tsembaga, 501, 503, 508–511, 513; Yanomamö, 222, 223, 224, 354–355, 356, 363, 364, 366, 370, 501, 503–508, 517. *See also* agriculture; pastoralists
Houart, Gail, 146
household vs. family, 379
housing, 127; Acheulean, 96; and agriculture, 138, 140, 141, 145, 146; American Southwest, 141; China and Southeast Asia, 138; in estimating populations, 132; Europe, 141; European advanced hunter, 114; Near East, 138, 145; Plano tradition, 118
Howell, F. Clark, 97
human adaptations, 93–95, 133; *Homo erectus,* 98; *Homo habilis,* 98; *Homo sapiens,* 98. *See also* adaptation
Human Relations Area Files, 228–229
humans: behavior, 202–204, 206–209, 287–290 (*see also* social behavior); biological classification, 43; blood group systems, 172; cognitive development, 293–294; cognitive imperative, 288, 293; complex characters, 177–181; diet and health, 133; distinguishing characteristics, 61, 87–88, 98, 201, 247; diversity, 321; division of labor, 87, 92, 94, 97, 146, 158, 162, 313–314, 382–383; domestication of plants and animals, 131, 133; ecology, 5–6, 13, 14–15, 317–323; genetic markers in blood proteins, 170; impact on environment, 322, 472–474; locomotion, 49–50; marriage (*see* marriage); masticatory apparatus, 52; Mendelian population, 23; need for social contact, 288; pigmentation, 178–181; polymorphisms, significance of, 177; socialization, 8–9, 290–291, 293–295, 297–305, 441, 443; social organization (*see* social organization); subsistence strategies, 128; survival, and ecology, 575–587; variation patterns, 173. *See also* evolution; *Homo sapiens*
hunters, advanced: of Europe, 108, 111; of New World, 118–119
hunting, 127; Europe, 141; Folsom tradition, 118; jump technique, 108, 118; Mesoamerica, 139; Near East, 134; Paleo-Indians, 118–119; Plano Indians, 118; surround kill technique, 108, 118
hunting and gathering subsistence strategy, 323; Australian aborigines, 92, 127, 484; Eskimo, 127, 267, 289, 380, 406, 425, 426, 440, 483, 485, 491–496, 512; Kalahari Bushmen, 6, 92, 127, 181, 218, 219, 311, 318–319, 331–332, 338–339, 391, 422, 425, 483, 485–491, 492, 493, 494, 502, 512, 581; Miskito, 483, 485, 496–497. *See also* gathering; hunting
Hutchinson, G. E., 584
hydration, obsidian, 117
hydraulic society, Wittfogel's, 154
Hylobates, 43, 48, 49

Ibo, 376
Ifaluk, 401
Ifugao, 440, 449, 452
Illinois River Valley, 120–121
implements, chimpanzee use of, 52, 73, 310
Inca, 152, 153, 430
incest taboo, 202, 210, 383, 384, 441
independent family, 391–392, 393
India, caste system in, 340, 385
Indian Knoll sites, 122
individual and culture: socialization, 8–9, 290–291, 293–295, 297–305. *See also* social behavior
industrialism, subsistence strategy, 324, 556–573; and cultural diversity, 559; and economic inequality, 559; and energy consumption, 557–558; and mechanization, 557; and multinational corporations, 566–571; and social change, 558–559; and unskilled labor, 558, 561–563; and the urban poor, 563–566
insect-eating adaptations, 51
instability, specialization, and diversity, 113–114
instinct and behavior, 287
intensive agriculture, subsistence strategy, 324, 539–555
intergroup competition and subsistence, 320–321, 323
intergroup relations, 432–436
International African Institute, 233
International Phonetic Alphabet (IPA), 268
interpersonal relations. *See* social controls
interviewing techniques, 217–218
inventory compilation, in field research, 218
investment and production, 337–338
Irons, William, 522
Iroquois, 158, 372, 404, 412, 421; kin terminology, 358–359, 362
irrigation, 142, 143, 144–145, 156, 162, 539, 540; canal, 155, 524; development, 138; pot, 145, 155, 546; and state formation, 154, 155
Isaac, G. L., 97, 103
Islam, origin and rise of, 550–554
isotype, half-life of, 68
Ituri Forest, pygmies of, 127

jajmani system, in India, 340, 347
Jarmo site, 138
Java, 98, 539

jaws: *Australopithecus*, 77–78; *Homo erectus*, 98; *Homo habilis*, 94; and teeth, primates, 51
Jie Indians, 334
Jivaro Indians, 446
Jolly, Clifford J., 58
Jones, Delmos, 224
Jorgenson, Joseph, 471–472
judicial processes: method of adjudication, 450–451; modes of redress, 451–453; procedures of inquiry, 449–450; rules, 448–449. *See also* social controls
jural norms, 202, 220

K-A. *See* potassium-argon (K-A) dating
Kachin, 457–458
Kalahari Bushmen, 6, 92, 127, 181, 218, 219, 311, 318–319, 331–332, 338–339, 391, 422, 425, 483, 485–491, 492, 493, 494, 502, 512, 581
Kalambo Falls, 97
Kapauku, 316, 346, 443–444, 449, 466; production decisions, 336, 337
Kaplan, David, 463
Kardiner, Abram, 204
Kariera, 484
Karimojong, 319–320, 325, 372, 521, 522, 533; herd movements, 527–529; settlement patterns, 526–527; social organization, 529
Katz, S. H., 319
Kel Adrar Touareg, 477
Kemp, William B., 483, 493–494, 512
Kibbutz (Israel), 381, 384, 385
kinesics, 250–251
King, Martin Luther, Jr., 565
kin group (clan), 145
kinship: affinal, 355; bonds, 97, 355, 371, 381, 383; classification systems, 356–361, 362; consanguineal, 355; descent, and social behavior, 368–371; nonunilineal, 367–368; terminology, 355–356, 361, 363; unilineal, 363–367. *See also* descent groups
Kipsigi, 380
Kish, 165
Kluckhohn, Florence Rockwood, 300
knapping, 99, 110
knuckle walker, locomotion, 49. *See also* quadrupedal locomotion

Kohistanis, 321, 323
Kpelle, 314, 334, 451, 452–453
Kroeber, Alfred, 196, 467n
Kufr al Ma, 444–445
Kummer, Hans, 58, 59
!Kung Bushmen. *See* Kalahari Bushmen
Kurds, 385, 395
Kwaio, 370, 371
Kwakiutl, 194, 203, 339; language, 257–258, 278

LaBarre, Weston, 204
labor: and culture, 313–316; division of (*see* division of labor); migrant, and industrialism, 558, 561–563, 565; motivation, 315–316; scheduling decisions, 316; specialization, 314–315, 333
labor, division of. *See* division of labor
Labov, William, 282–283
lactase deficiency polymorphism, 176–177
Lahu, 224
land ownership and use, 323, 332, 369
language, 9, 12–13, 97, 103, 104, 195, 252–265; adaptation, 280–282; change, 276–283; and culture, 257–261, 267–285; culture contact and borrowing, 279–280; dialects, 276–278; evolution of, 253, 255–256; Hopi, 258–259; Indo-European, 277; International Phonetic Alphabet (IPA), 268; Kwakiutl, 257–258, 278; male vs. female usage, 281–282; and mass media, 261–262; Navajo, 259–260, 272; and physiology, 256–257; primordial, theory of, 254; Proto-Germanic, 276, 277, 278; semantics, 273–274; and social status, 282–283; structure, 268–273; syntax, transformational grammar, 273–274; variation, 267–285; whistle and drum, 271. *See also* anthropological linguistics; descriptive linguistics
Lantian, *Homo erectus*, find, 98
Lapps, 368
Law of Cultural Dominance, 463, 465
Law of Evolutionary Potential, 465
Leach, E. R., 366, 457
Leaf, Murray, 410, 423
Lee, Richard B., 218, 483, 485, 487, 488, 489, 491, 493, 512

Lees, Susan H., 546, 547, 548
Lele, 337
lemur, 46, 47; locomotion, 48–49; Madagascars, 46, 48–49
Leone, Mark, 158
Leroi-Gourhan, Andre, 113
Lesu, 380, 389
Levallois technique, 99, 100
leveling mechanism, in distribution of goods, 339
Levine, L., 283
LeVine, Robert A., 303
levirate and sororate, 382
Lévi-Strauss, Claude, 200–201, 202, 361, 402, 403
Levy-Bruhl, Lucien, 291, 293
Lewis, Oscar, 235, 236, 459, 460, 563, 566
lexicostatistics (glottochronology), 277–278
Liberty, Margot, 221
Limitations of the Comparative Method of Anthropology (Boas), 194
Limnopithecus. See Dendropithecus
lineage, 27, 28; of descent groups, 365; *Homo*, 93; segmentary, 427
linearization, in state formation, 156
linguistics, anthropological. *See* anthropological linguistics
Linnaeus, Carolus, 34; classification of genus *Homo*, 34, 182–183
Linne, Karl von. *See* Linnaeus, Carolus
Linton, Ralph, 204
lithic technology, 123
Livingstone, R. B., 172
lobe-fins, adaptive radiation, 31
locomotion: bipedal, 49–51, 79–81; and natural selection, 47–48; and posture, *Australopithecus*, 78–82; primates, 47, 48–51; quadrupedal, 49; repertoires and profiles, primates, 47, 48–50
locus and gene, 21, 22; linked, 22
Lokele language, 270, 271
Lorenz, Konrad, 287
loris, 43, 46, 47
Lozi, 451
Lugbara, 446
Luts'un, 512, 539
lysine, 142

McCarthy, Eugene J., 238
McCay, Bonnie, 14

McLuhan, Marshall, 261–262
macaque (*Macaca*), 580; multimale troop, 60
Mae Enga, 369, 374
maize cultivation, 130, 139, 140, 162
Makah Indians, 445
malaria: and agriculture, 172; and sickle cell anemia, 24, 170–171, 579, 583
Malinowski, Bronislaw, 199, 200, 202, 214, 222–223, 233, 234, 409
mammals: Mesozoic, 67–70; multituberculate, 69
mammoths: Gravettian, 114; hunting, 111
Mandan-Hidatsa Indians, 361, 363
manufacturing in agricultural and industrial societies, 333
Maori, 434–435
mapping, 218
Marett, R. R., 400
Margalef, R., 463
Maring, 415–416
market exchange system, 345–346
marriage, 61; and culture, 379–397; and economic cooperation, 382–383; as exchange, 381–382; exogamy, 61, 97, 385; monogamy, 8; and parental responsibility, 383; polyandry, 389–390; polygamy vs. monogamy, 388; polygyny, 8, 388–389; rules, 383, 385–391. See also domestic groups; family
Marshack, Alexander, 113
Marshall, Lorna, 489, 491
marsupials, adaptive radiation, 31
Marx, Karl, 408
Masai, 371
masculinity vs. femininity, 289–290
mathematics and statistics in anthropology, 226–227
matrilocality, 158, 390–391
Maya, 153; religion, 161; state, 160–161; Tikal, 160, 161; trade network, 161
Mazateco language, 271
mazeways, 206
Mbuti Pygmies, 344–345, 399, 400, 405
Mead, Margaret, 204, 236, 290, 298, 372, 459
Meadows, D. H., 472n
mechanization and industrialism, 557–566

Meintel, Deirdre, 224
melanin, 178, 179, 180
Mendel, Gregor, 14
Mesoamerica, 143, 155, 157; agricultural innovation, 130, 133, 139–140; chiefdoms, emergence of, 153; diet, 139–140; hunting, 139; vs. Mesopotamia, 145–146; settlements, 140; sites and materials, 140, 152; state formation, 157, 159–163
Mesolithic-Archaic stage, 109, 120–123; burial, 121; diet, 121; subsistence and settlement, 120–122; technology, 123; trade and social organization, 122
Mesopotamia, 155, 157; vs. Mesoamerica, 145–146; state formation, 163–165
Metzger, D., 403
Mexico, 127, 142, 146; agricultural innovation, 139, 140; Valley of, state formation, 161–163
Mexico City (Mexico), 563–564, 566
Microcebus, brain of, 54
microlith, 111, 123
Middle Woodland groups, 121, 122, 146
migrant labor and industrialism, 558, 561–563, 565
migration, 122; vs. expansion, New World, 115–116; and gene flow, effect on sickle cell anemia, 171–172, 183; of laborers (see migrant labor and industrialism)
Milgram, Stanley, 353–354, 442
militarism, and state formation, 154, 156, 157, 159, 161, 163, 165
Miskito Indians, 483, 485, 496–497
Miwok American Indians, 366
Moala, 392, 393
modal personality, 204, 206, 303
Mohammed, 552–554
moieties, 366
Money, John, 290
Mongols, 522
monkey: Miocene, 72; New World, 43; Old World, 43, 46
monogamy, 8; vs. polygamy, 388
monotheism, 401, 408
Mons, 374
Monte Alban site, 159, 546
Montezuma, 163
Morgan, Lewis Henry, 193, 205

morphemes, 270–271, 272
morphology: comparative, 12; domesticated plants, 130; in linguistics, 270, 271, 272
Morse, Wayne, 239
Morse Code, 271
Mousterian tradition: chipped stone technology, 99–100; ritual and religion, 99, 102; subsistence and social organization, 99, 101; variety of, 100–102
Müller, R., 566n
multinational corporations, 566–571; capital, 569; communications, 569–570; labor, 569; new technology, 568–569
multituberculates, 69–70
Mundugumor, 298
Mundy-Castle, A. C., 291
Murgin, 434
mutation, 23, 27; and gene flow, 24; and gene frequency, 23; neutral, establishment of, 25
myths and legends, 402, 403
Mzab, 445–446

Nader, L., 452
Nagel, Veli, 58
Naroll, Raoul, 132, 461, 462
Naskapi, 413–414
national character, studies of, 204, 206
natural selection, 24–25, 27; and evolutionary change, 27–31; and gene frequency, 24; genotypes in, 24, 28; and locomotion, 47–48; and non-Darwinian evolution, 25–26; and social behavior, 55
Navajo, 521, 525, 533–535, 580; and alcoholism, 302–303; language, 259–260, 272; marriage and divorce, 380
Nayar, 380, 383, 385, 391n
Ndembu, 402, 404, 449–450
Ndendeuli, 448, 450–451
neandertals, 102–103, 406
Near East, 127, 128, 142, 143; agricultural innovation, 133, 134–135, 138; chiefdoms, emergence of, 153; diet, 138; herding, 135, 138; housing, 138; hunting, 134; sites and materials, 138; villages in, 138
negative reciprocity system, 344
Neolithic stage, 109

neolocal residence, 390
Netting, Robert MacC., 517
networks. *See* social networks; trade networks
New World: advanced hunters, 118–119; monkeys, 43; route to, 115–116
Nietschmann, Bernard, 483
Nietzsche, Friedrich Wilhelm, 203
1984 (Orwell), 257
nomadic pastoralism, 522, 529–533
nonbehavioral data collection, 218
nonunilineal descent groups: ambilineal, 367–368; bilateral, 368
nonverbal communication, 250–252
Nootka language, 278
norms and rules of political behavior, 423–424
North America: Archaic stage, 120–121; Paleo-Indian traditions, 118–119; in Paleolithic times, 116, 118
Notharctus skeleton, 70, 71
Nuer, 439
Nupe (Nigeria), 429
nurturers vs. begettors, 56
Nyae Nyae Bushmen. *See* Kalahari Bushmen
Nyakyusa, 372

oath taking as a social control, 449
Oaxaca Valley, 546–548, 550
objectivity, in anthropological research, 234, 241
obsidian, hydration technique, 117
Odum, E. P., 320–321
Oedipus myths, 403
Oldowan tradition: human adaptations, 93–95; people, 91–93; sites and material, 91–92, 96; technology, 88–91; tools, 88–91, 94, 96
Olduvai Gorge, 88; australopith findings, 82
Old World: Miocene primates, 72; monkeys, 43, 46
Oliver, Symmes C., 523
Olmec, 90, 159–160
Olsen-Chubbuck site, 119
Omaha kin terminology, 359–360
Omo Valley, 88
open juncture in phonemic systems, 269–270
operant conditioning, 14
operationalization, 212

opossum, 27, 32; primitive characteristics, 70
ordeals as a social control, 449
oriental despotism, 154
Origin of Species, The (Darwin), 13
Orwell, George, 257
Owasco social organization, 158

Paleo-Indians: and extinctions, 119; gathering, 119; hunting, 118; 119; settlement patterns and social organization, 119; tools, 118
paleontology, 67
palynology, 109
pantribal sodalities, 426–427, 431
Pan troglodytes. *See* chimpanzee
Papago, 468–469, 471
participant observation, 212–216
Pasternak, Burton, 542, 545
pastoralism, subsistence strategy, 324, 325; Karimojong, 319, 320, 325, 372, 521, 522, 524, 525–529, 533; Navajo, 259–260, 272, 302–303, 380, 521, 525, 533–535, 580; nomadic, 522, 529–533; Yörük, 365, 387, 521, 522, 524, 525, 529–533, 578
patas monkey (*Erythrocebus patas*), one-male group, 57, 60
Pathans, 321, 323
patrilocality, 390–391
patterns of cultural evolution, 461–463
Patterns of Culture (Benedict), 203
peasantry, 540–550
Peebles, Christopher, 147
pelvis: adaptation to bipedalism, 79–81; *Australopithecus*, 78–79, 80
peoples: Acheulean and contemporary, 94–95; in Oldowan tradition, 91–93
percussion flaking, 88, 91, 108
Perry, W. J., 195
personality: and child-rearing practices, 204–207, 294, 298; and culture, 202–204, 206–209, 297–298; defining basic, 303; modal, 204, 206; and sex, 289–290
Peru, 127; origin of agriculture in, 140
Petralona, 98
phenetic distance, 32, 34
phenotypes, 23; change in domestication, 128–131, 133; and environment, 22; and natural selection, 28

phonemes and phonemic systems, 268–271
photography in field research, 218–219
phratry, 366
phyletic relationship, 32, 33, 35; of fossils, 67
phyletic tree, 32; primates, 43, 44–45
phylogeny: hominid, 74–75; reconstructing, 33, 67, 70–73
physical anthropology, 10, 11, 12; and archeology in action, 12
physiology and language, 256–257
Piaget, Jean, 293
pigmentation, human, 178–181
Pima, 468–469, 471
Pithecanthropus erectus, 98
Plains Indians, 373, 523
Plainview site, Texas, 118
plants: changes, in domestication, 129–130; communities, and glaciation, 115
Plasmodium falciparum, 170
platyrrhine monkey, 43–46, 53; brain, 53
Pleistocene epoch, 114–120
Pleistocene primates, 74–85
Plesiadapis, 70
Pliopithecus, 72
Plio-Pleistocene finds, 93
Plog, Fred, 463
political organization: in band societies, 424–426; in chiefdoms, 427–429; and culture, 418–437; evolution, 430–432; and intergroup relations, 432–436; and interpersonal relations, 439–455; leadership criteria, 422; norms and rules, 423–424; participation in decision making, 420–422; and the peasantry, 541; power vs. authority, 422, 424–430; in state societies, 422–423, 429–430; in tribal societies, 426–427
polyandry, 389–390
polygamy vs. monogamy, 388
polygyny, 8, 388–389
polymorphism: balanced, 24–25, 170, 175; blood group, 173, 175; hemoglobin, 170–172; related to diet, 176–177; significance of, 177; transient, 24
polytheism, 401, 408
polytypy, 26
Pongidae, 43, 53

population: and food shortage, 472–474; and gene pools, 23; genes in, 23; growth, and industrialism, 558; inbreeding, 23; interbreeding, 23; Mendelian, 23; Mesolithic-Archaic, 120, 121, 122; Pleistocene, 114; polymorphic, 24–25; prehistoric, estimating, 132; regulation, hunters-gatherers, 143; size, and food supply, 316–317; size, and survival, 581–582; and state formation, 152, 154, 156; and subsistence strategies, 142–143; and territoriality, 122, 329; warfare, and land resources, 434–436
Pospisil, Leopold J., 336, 466
Postclassic stage, Mesoamerican civilization, 159, 161, 162
potassium-argon (K-A) dating, 66, 68–69, 90
pot irrigation, 145, 155, 546
potlatch, 339
potsherds, 95
pottery, 140, 141, 193; and agriculture, 143–144, 157; seriation in dating, 117; Southwest, 143–144
Powdermaker, Hortense, 199, 222, 224
power vs. authority, 422; in band societies, 424–426; in chiefdoms, 427–429; in state societies, 429–430; in tribal societies, 426–427
Preclassic stage, Mesoamerican civilization, 157, 159, 160, 161, 162, 163
prehistory tracing, 87, 89–90, 109, 132, 158, 460, 461
Premack, Ann and David, 249
Press, Irwin, 433
pressure flaking, 110
Price, Barbara J., 152
priests vs. shamans, 406–407
primates, 29; adaptation themes, 39–64; agonistic and hedonic social bonds, 56–57, 61; behavior studies, 58–59; brain, 53–54; classification, 34; dentition and masticatory muscles, 42, 51; diversity, 39, 43–47; econiches, 40, 42, 61; Eocene, 71; evolution, 65–85; Fayum, 72; feeding habits, 50–52; hand, 42, 52–53; information systems, 55; locomotor repertoires and profiles, 47, 48–50; Miocene, 72–73; multimale group, 57–60; Oligocene, 71–72; one-male group, 57; origins, 69–73; Paleocene, 70–71; phyletic tree and classification, 34, 43, fig. 44–45; Pleistocene, 74–85; Pliocene, 74; primitive form, 42–43; radiation, 43–46, 47, 71; realms and habitats, 39–42; reproductive strategy, 42–43; senses, 42, 53; social organization, 54–61; teeth, 51
primitive characteristics, 32; primates, 42–43
primordial language, theory of, 254
Principles of Professional Responsibility (American Anthropological Association), 240–241
private vs. community property ownership, 330–333
probability samples: representative, 220; stratified, 220
procurement strategies, in industrial vs. nonindustrial societies, 323–325
production of goods, in industrial vs. nonindustrial societies: and investment, 337–338; specialization of, in industrial societies, 557, 558–559; surplus, 335, 339
productivity: Chayanov's rule, 335; custom, incentive and, 549; and life span, 337; and tools, 337; and work periods, 337
Project Agile, 240
Project Camelot, 238–239
prosimians, 46–47, 55; beginnings, 71; brain, 53–54
proteins, 142; and genes, 21–22; as indicators of evolutionary relationship, 26; structure and function, 26
Protestantism, 408
proxemics, 251–252
PTC tasting polymorphism, 176
Puebla, Mexico, 116
Pueblo, 323, 361, 501, 503, 513–517; architecture, 158; Katchina cult, 516; religious ritual, 414–415; social organization, 158; subsistence strategy, 311–312
punch flaking, 108, 110
pyramids, 157; Aztec, 163; Egyptian, 195; Mayan, 195; Mesoamerican, 157

quadrupedal locomotion, 49. See also kunckle walker, locomotion

race(s), 11, 178, 181–182; and human variation, 183, 184; as subspecies, 183–184; as types, 182–183
Radcliffe-Brown, Alfred Reginald, 199, 202, 241, 410
radiation, 32; adaptive, 31; primates, 43–46, 47, 71
radiocarbon dating, 68, 90
radiometric dating, 67, 68–69
rain forests, tropical, as primate habitat, 40–41
Ramapithecus, 73–74, 77; K-A dating, 69
Randolph, R. R., 371
rank societies, 339
Rappaport, Roy, 415, 509, 511, 513, 577, 578
Rathje, William, 161
reciprocal exchange systems, 344–345
Redfield, Robert, 459, 460
redistribution (economic), 345, 415
reflectance spectrophotometer, 178
religion: as adaptive strategy, 408–416; Aztec, 162–163; and culture, 399–417; definition, 399–401; evolution of, 408; Hindu, 401; in intergroup relations, 433; Mayan, 161, 402; monotheism and polytheism, 401, 408; myths and legends, 402–403; natural/supernatural dichotomy, 408; psychological effects of, 409; and resource management, 413–414; and ritual (see ritual and religion); and ritual, Mousterian, 99, 101–102; sacred vs. profane, 400; shamans vs. priests, 406–407; and socialization, 409–412; and social organization, 407–408; symbols and beliefs, 401–402, 404–409; theism, 401
reproduction, process, 21–26
reproductive strategy: primates, 42–43, 55–57; social organization as, 55–56
research design, preparation of, 211–212
resource depletion, 472–474
Return to Laughter (Bowen), 222n
rhinarium, 46, 47
"Rhodesian man," skull of, 93
rice cultivation, 138, 319
rites of intensification, 402, 404–405
rites of passage, 295, 297, 402

ritual and religion, 402–407; Crow Indians, 405; Maring, 415–416; Mayan, 161, 402; Mbuti Pygmies, 399, 400, 405; Mousterian, 99, 102; Ndembu, 402, 404; neandertal, 407; Pueblo, 414–415; resource management, 414–416
Rogers, Everett, 466
roles and role models, in socialization, 298–300
Rorschach test, 219

Sahlins, Marshall, 335, 337, 393, 491, 502, 584
sampling techniques: judgement samples, 221; probability samples, 220
Sánchez affair, 235, 236
Sanders, William, 152
Sapir, Edward, 258
Sapir-Whorf hypothesis, 258–260
savanna as primate habitat, 41–42
Schmidt, Wilhelm, 195, 196
Schneider, Harold, 338
seasonality, subsistence, and settlement, 121, 319–320
seasonal nomadism, 319–320, 324, 325
sedentism, 99, 127; and agriculture, 122, 141–143, 145–146, 153, 156; Mesolithic-Archaic, 121–122; and population, 122; and resource distribution, 122; specialization, diversity, and, 99, 101, 113–116
Selby, H. A., 362
selection: directional, 25; natural, 24–25, 27–31; and society, 55
Seligmann, C. G., 199
semantic domains, 273–274
semantics, 273–274
seriation, 117
Service, Elman, 465
settlement: American Southwest, 141–142; Europe, 141; Mesoamerica, 140; Mesolithic-Archaic, 120–122; and social organization, Paleo-Indians, 119; South America, 141; Upper Paleolithic, 111
sex: and language usage, 281–282; and personality, 289–290; and social behavior, 289–290; as a social category, 372–374
Shanidar cave, 102
shelter. See housing
Shilluk, 410–411

Shoshone Indians, 319
Siane, 346
sickle cell anemia: and malaria, 24, 170–171, 579, 583; migration, gene flow and, 171–172, 183; and natural selection, 24; and polymorphism, 24, 170
Sikhs, 410, 423
single species hypothesis, 83
Siriono, 228; language, 267, 271
sites and materials: Acheulean, 96–97; China and Southeast Asia, 138; in estimating population, 132; Mesoamerican, 140; Mousterian, 101–102; Near East, 138; Oldowan, 91–92, 96
Siuai, 374
skeleton: chimpanzee, 50; *Homo erectus*, 98; *Homo habilis*, 94; *Homo sapiens*, 50; *Notharctus*, 70, 71; *Plesiadapis*, 70
skin cancer, 179–180
skin color: distribution, 178–180; evolution, 180–181; and vitamin D, 180
Skinner, B. F., 14
skull(s): *Homo erectus*, 92, 98; *Homo habilis*, fig. 93; *Homo sapiens*, 92–93, 102–103; neandertal, 102; New World monkeys, 43; Oldowan, 92–93
slash-and-burn agriculture. See swidden agriculture
Slobodkin, L. B., 582, 583
small-object feeding adaptations, 51, 52–53
Small Town in Mass Society (Vidich), 236
Smith, Eliot, 195
social behavior: altruism, 576; chimpanzee, 60–61; controlling (see social controls); descent, kinship and, 368–371; and education, 294–295; interpersonal relations, 439–455; intragroup relations, 432–436; and kinship terms, 361, 363; models of and for, 301; and natural selection, 55; roles and role models, 298–300; and sex, 289–290; situational influence on, 301–303, 304; values and beliefs, 300–301. See also behavior; humans, behavior; individual and culture
social bonds, agonistic vs. hedonic, 56–57, 61

social categories: age, 371, 372; definition, 353; ethnicity, 374–376; sex, 372–374
social classes vs. social castes, 340–341, 408
social controls: and authority, 442; legal mechanisms, 446–453; pressures toward conformity, 443–446; rules, 439–441, 448–449; satire and gossip, 444–445; shunning and ostracism, 445–446; socialization, 89, 290–291, 293, 297–305, 441, 443; vengeance, 446. See also judicial processes
social function of religion, 409–411; revitalization, 411–412; social solidarity, 410–411, 433
social groups: age-based, 372; clans, 145, 365–366; corporateness, 352–353; definition, 352; descent groups, 363–369; ethnic-based, 376; moieties, 366; phratry, 366; sex-based, 373
socialization, 8–9, 290–291, 293, 297–305, 441, 443; child-rearing practices, 204–207, 294, 298; education, 294–295; rites of passage, 295, 297; roles and role models, 298–300; values and beliefs, 300–301
social networks: analysis of, 352; definition, 352; in tribal societies, 427
social organization: aborigines (Australian), 92; Acheulean, 97; adaptation, 145; age-set systems, 226–227; and agriculture, 540; Aztec, 162–163; band, 92; categories (see social categories); chimpanzee, 60–61; city, 152–153; and cultural change, 473–474; diversity, 57, 60–61; as ecological strategy, 55, 60; groups (see social groups); and intensification of agriculture, 540; Iroquois, 158; Kalahari Bushmen, 92; Karimojong, 529; and kinship, 354–363; Kwakiutl, 339; and linguistics, 201; matrilocality, 158; Mesoamerica, 139, 140, 146; Mesoamerican vs. Mesopotamian, 145–146; Mousterian, 99, 101; and natural selection, 55; networks (see social networks); Oldowan tradition, 97; and organization of production, 334; Owasco, 158; patrilocality, 390–391; pri-

mates, 54–61; Pueblo, 158; and religion, 407–408; as reproductive strategy, 55–57; reconstructing, 158; and settlement patterns, Paleo-Indians, 119; state, 152–153; and trade, Mesolithic-Archaic, 122; tribal, 145–148; United States of America, 339–340

society, 15; hydraulic, 154; and politics, 418–437; reconstruction, 87, 89–90, 109, 132, 158, 460, 461; and selection, 55; simple vs. complex, 462–463

sociobiology, 576

sociocultural organization and food production, 151–153

Solutré, France, 108

sororate and levirate, 382

South America, 142; agricultural innovation, 140–141; chiefdoms, emergence of, 153

Southeast Asia: and China, agricultural innovation, 138–139; housing in China, 130

specialization, 29, 31, 32, 431; in chiefdoms, 427; and diversity, 99–101, 107, 110–111, 114; and generalization, 29; in industrial and nonindustrial societies, 314–315

Special Operations Research Organization (S.O.R.O.), 238

speciation and diversifications, 29–31, 58

species: biological, 23; displacement of, 31; polytypic, 26, 29; sympatric, 29

speech. *See* language

Spencer, Herbert, 13

spheres of exchange, 346

spider monkeys: brachiation, 49; locomotion, 49

Spradley, James, 303

Springdale affair, 235, 236–237

squash cultivation, 139, 141, 142, 162

Stands-in-Timber, John, 221

"starvation food," 130

state: and agriculture, 155–156, 541, 550–554; Aztec, 161–163; and circumscription, 154, 156, 157, 159, 161, 163, 165; evolution of, 151, 152–153, 157, 159, 431; Maya, 160–161; multiple-cause theory, 155; and politics, 422–423; prime-mover theories, 154–155; synthetic theory of formation, 156–157

State, Department of, U.S., 239

statistics and mathematics in anthropology, 226–227

stature variations, 177–178

Steinheim, 98, 102

Stephens, William N., 381n

Sterkfontein, 80

Steward, Julian, 193, 196, 197–198

Stone Age Economics (Sahlins), 502

Stonehenge, 195

stratification, social, 152–153, 155–156, 157, 159, 160, 161, 165, 431; and agriculture, 127, 146, 147–148; cargo system, 227; in state societies, 430

stratigraphy, 66, 90

Strodtbeck, Fred L., 300

Structural-functionalism, 200, 235

Struever, Stuart, 146

subsistence: Acheulian, 96–97; adaptation strategies, 15, 311–312, 317–321, 323–326; and change, 128; and cultural evolution, 128, 143, 325–326; intergroup competition, 320–321, 323; Mesolithic-Archaic, 120–122; Mousterian, 99, 101; Oldowan tradition, 96–97; and seasonal variation, 319–320; and social organization, 91, 97; strategies and population, 142–143; Upper Paleolithic, 108, 122

Sudanese kin terminology, 356–358

Supreme Court, U.S., 424

surveys and excavations, archaeological, 89–90

Susa, 90, 165

Swadesh, Morris, 277–278

Swanscombe, 98, 102

Swanson, Guy, 407–408

swidden agriculture, 326, 501–502, 517

Swift, Jeremy, 477

symbols, 252–253; and beliefs, 401–402, 404–409

syntax, 272–273

taboos: incest, 201, 202, 383, 384, 441; post-partum, 388

Taiwan, 542–546

Tallensi, 364–365, 369

Talmon, Yonina, 385

tarsier, 43, 46, 47

Tatieh, 542–546

taxon, 34

Tchambuli, 372

technology: Acheulian, 82, 83, 94, 95–96; adaptation, 311–312; agricultural, 142, 143–146, 325–326; in agricultural vs. industrial societies, 311; chipped stone, 95–96, 99–100, 110; and culture, 197, 198; hydraulic, 154, 155; Mesolithic-Archaic, 123; Mousterian, 99–100; Oldowan, 88–91, 94, 96; slash-and-burn, 324; Upper Paleolithic, 108, 110. *See also* toolmaking; tools

teeth: *Australopithecus*, 77–78; *Dryopithecus*, 73; Fayum primates, 72; *Homo erectus*, 98; *Homo habilis*, 94; New World monkeys, 43; Old World monkeys, 43; primates, 51; *Ramapithecus*, 73; *Theria*, 69–70. *See also* dentition

Tehuacán Valley: agricultural innovation, 140; corn development in, 129, 130

tenancy system, 343

Tenochtitlan, 162, 163

Tenzel, James, 290–291

teosinte, 130

Teotihuacan, 159, 162, 163

Tepe Sarab site, 138

Terra Amata, 96

terrace farming, 142, 144, 162

territoriality, 251; and population, 122, 329

Tewa, 323

Thai, 374–375

Thailand, 127

Thematic Apperception Test (TAT), 219

theocracy, 157

theoretical models, establishment of, 227–229

Theria, 69–70

Tikal, 160, 161

tipis, 196

Tiv, 222n, 332, 346, 369, 389, 419, 427

Tlatelolco, 163

Toda, 389

Toffler, Alvin, 473

Toltec, 163

Tonga, 401, 446

toolmaking, 195; Acheulean, 82, 83, 94, 95–96; and bipedalism, 81–82; Mesolithic-Archaic, 123; Oldowan,

82, 88–91, 94; traditions, 88–91, 95–96, 99–100, 108, 110–111. *See also* technology; tools
tools: Acheulean, 82, 83, 94, 95–96; bifacially vs. unifacially worked, 88; chipped stone technology, 95–96, 99–100, 110, 111; earliest, 88; hand axe, 95, 97; Mesolithic-Archaic, 123; Oldowan, 88–91, 94, 96; Paleo-Indians, 118; and productivity, 337; specificity of function, 309–311; Upper Paleolithic, 107, 108, 110. *See also* technology; toolmaking
Torralba, 97
totem and totemism, 365–366, 410
trade: Aztec, 163; Hopewell Interaction Sphere, 146–148; Mayan, 161; networks, 142, 146, 148, 154, 156, 157, 159, 163; and social organization, Mesolithic-Archaic, 122; and state formation, 154
tradition, 90; Acheulean, 94–97; Aurignacian, 110, 111; chopper-chopping tool, 95, 97; Clovis, 118; Fauresmith, 99; Folsom, 118; Gravettian, 111; Llano, 118; Magdalenian, 111; Mousterian, 98–102; Oldowan, 88–94; Paleo-Indian, 118–119; Perigordian, 110, 111; Plano, 118; Sangoan, 99; Solutrean, 111; toolmaking, 88–91, 95–96, 99–100, 108, 110–111; Upper Paleolithic, 110–111
tree shrew (*Philocercus*), 70; locomotion, 48
tribe, 145–148, 431; as political organization, 426–427
Trinil, *Homo erectus* excavations, 98
Trobriand Islanders, 199, 214, 409
troop, multimale, 57–60
Trukese, 394–395

Tsembaga, 501, 503, 508–511, 513, 521, 522, 539, 540, 577–578
Tula, 162
Turkey, 144
Turkman, 433, 522
Tuscarora Indians, 206
Tylor, Edward B., 192, 193, 205, 400
typology, 95

Ubaid, Mesopotamian state formation stage, 164
Underwood, Barbara, 342
unilineal descent groups: evolution of, 366; matrilineal, 363–364; patrilineal, 364–365
United Farm Workers, 561
Upper Paleolithic, 103: art, 111–113; diversity, 107, 110–111; technology, 108, 110; tools, 107, 108, 110; traditions, 110–111
urbanism, 151–152, 558; and poverty, 563–566. *See also* cities

Valleroy, L. A., 319
values and beliefs, 300–301
Van Gennep, Arnold, 402
Vayda, Andrew, 434, 503
Vicos, Peru, 475–476
Vidich, Arthur, 236–237
village(s), 127; American Southwest, 141–142; Mesoamerica, 140, 145; Near East, 138, 145
von Linne, Karl. *See* Linneaus, Carolus

Walbiri, 439–440, 484
Wallace, Anthony, 206, 300, 402, 412, 458
warfare, 433–435; and animal populations, 435–436; Aztec, 163; and economic interests, 436; population, and land resources, 434–435; and

state formation, 154, 156, 157, 161, 163, 165
Wasco, California, 560–561
Waswanipi Cree, 413
Wernicke, Carl, 256
Whallon, Robert, 158
wheat cultivation, 133, 135, 138, 141, 143
White, Leslie, 193, 196, 197, 198, 557
Whiting, Beatrice and John, 214, 225
Whiting, John W., 206
Whorf, Benjamin Lee, 258–259, 260, 273
Williams, G. E., 403
Williams, Thomas, 217, 222, 223
Wilson, Edward W., 576
Wilson, Monica, 372
Wissler, Clark, 196
Wittfogel, Karl, 154, 155, 431
Wobst, Martin, 116
Wolf, Eric R., 541, 550
woodland, tropical, as primate habitat, 41–42
woodland groups, subsistence and settlement, 120–122
writing and notation, beginnings of, 151, 157; cuneiform, 164; early Mesopotamian form, 164
Würm glaciation, 108

Yanomamö, 222, 223, 224, 354–355, 356, 363, 364, 366, 370, 501, 503–508, 517, 540
Yengoyan, Aram A., 484
Yörük, 365, 387, 521, 522, 524, 525, 529–533, 578

Zinacantan, Mexico, 227
Zuni, 203, 446
zygote, 21, 22; genotypes, 21

FRED PLOG was born in New Jersey in 1944, and raised in the Southwest. He received his B.A. from Northwestern University in 1966, and his Ph.D. from the University of Chicago in 1969. Before coming to Arizona State University, he taught at S.U.N.Y. at Binghamton and at U.C.L.A. He is the author of *The Study of Prehistoric Change,* co-author with Paul S. Martin of *Arizona Archaeology,* and co-editor with Paul J. Bohannan of *Beyond The Frontier.* He has contributed numerous articles to a variety of journals and edited collections. At present he is conducting research on adaptive strategies of modern and prehistoric patterns in northeastern Arizona.

CLIFFORD J. JOLLY was born in 1939, and raised in Leigh-on-Sea in Essex, England. He received both his B.A. with a First Class Honors Degree in 1960, and his Ph.D. in 1964 from University College, London. He began teaching at University College in 1963 and came to the United States in 1967 to teach at New York University, where he is now an Associate Professor. Dr. Jolly has published with Michael R. Chance a book entitled *Social Groups of Monkeys, Apes, and Man.* He has also edited *Early African Hominids.* His articles have been published in edited collections and in journals such as *Nature, Man, Proceedings of the Royal Society,* and *Folia Primatologica.*

DANIEL G. BATES was born in Long Beach, California. He studied at Robert College in Istanbul, Turkey, and the University of Freiburg in Germany and received both his B.A. in 1964 and his Ph.D. in 1971 from the University of Michigan. An Assistant Professor of Anthropology at Hunter College of the City University of New York since 1971, he is also a member of the Doctoral Faculty in Anthropology at the Graduate Center of the City University. Dr. Bates has done extensive fieldwork in Southeastern Turkey and among the Göklan Turkmen of Northeastern Iran. He is the author of a monograph, *Nomads and Farmers: The Yörük of Southeastern Turkey* and has published articles in edited collections and in such journals as *Journal of Asian and African Studies, Journal of American Antiquity,* and *Anthropological Quarterly.*

The text was set on the linofilm in Trade Gothic Light. This type face, a lineale type with short ascenders and descenders, was originally designed for the Mergenthaler linotype, 1948-60, by Jackson Burke.

This book was composed by The Clarinda Company, Clarinda, Iowa. Printed and bound by Von Hoffmann Press, Inc., St. Louis, Mo., on Mead Publishers matte paper provided by Allan & Gray Corp., New York.